GUNS
ILLUSTRATED®
2007 39th Annual Edition

Edited by
Ken Ramage

© 2006
by Gun Digest Books

Published by

Gun Digest Books
An imprint of F+W Publications
700 East State Street • Iola, WI 54990-0001
715-445-2214 • 888-457-2873
www.gunlistonline.com

Our toll-free number to place an order or obtain
a free catalog is (800) 258-0929.

Manuscripts, contributions and inquiries, including first class return postage, should be sent to the
GUNS ILLUSTRATED Editorial Offices, KP Books, 700 E. State Street, Iola, WI 54990-0001. All materials
recieved will receive reasonable care, but we will not be responsible for their safe return. Material
accepted is subject to our requirements for editing and revisions. Author payment covers all rights and
title to the accepted material, including photos, drawings and other illustrations. Payment is at our
current rates.

CAUTION: Technical data presented here, particularly technical data on handloading and on firearms
adjustment and alteration, inevitably reflects individual experience with particular equipment and
components under specific circumstances the reader cannot duplicate exactly. Such data presentations
therefore should be used for guidance only and with caution. KP Books accepts no responsibility for
results obtained using these data.

Library of Congress Catalog Number: 0072-9078

ISBN 13-digit:978-0-89689-426-6
ISBN 10-digit:0-89689-426-6

Designed by Patsy Howell & Tom Nelsen

Edited by Ken Ramage

Printed in the United States of America

Guns Illustrated Staff

EDITOR
Ken Ramage

CONTRIBUTING EDITORS

Holt Bodinson – Ammunition, Ballistics & Components
J. W. "Doc" Carlson – Blackpowder Review
John Haviland – Shotgun Review
John Malloy – Handguns Today: Autoloaders

Layne Simpson – Rifle Review
Larry S. Sterett – Handloading Update
John Taffin – Handguns Today: Six-guns & Others

About The Covers

THE FRONT COVER:

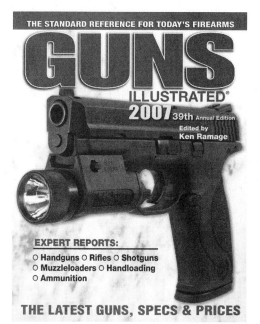

THE BACK COVER:

The M&P pistol is the latest big news from Smith & Wesson. In early 2006, Smith & Wesson entered the law enforcement and military arena in a big way. I refer to the M&P line, consisting initially of an autoloading pistol with a reinforced polymer frame offered in three chamberings. More recently, the pistols have been joined by several variations of an AR-style rifle, the M&P15.

At present, the new M&P pistol comes in 9mm, 357 SIG and 40 S&W. Major features of the M&P pistol include a reinforced polymer chassis, superior ergonomics, ambidextrous controls and proven safety features. Additional features include a three-piece grip insert set that allows the shooter to customize the grip size to fit his hand, an accessory rail forward of the trigger guard and ambidextrous controls. Our test pistol, shown with light attached to the universal accessory rail, shot to point of aim, functioned flawlessly and was exceptional for the consistency of the DA trigger pull, an aspect appreciated by all who used the gun. For more details: www.smith-wesson.com

The Stag-15 Rifle...another AR-15 clone? Well, yes and no. This particular (right-hand) specimen is made by the relative newcomer Stag Arms and is chambered for the 5.56mm NATO (223) cartridge. New for 2006, Stag Arms has the distinction of offering the only southpaw AR-15 rifle or carbine, in several versions and in two chamberings: 5.56mm NATO and the new 6.8mm. Designations of the various models begin with Stag-15 or Stag-6.8. The left-hand models are logically identified as the Stag-15L and the Stag-6.8L

Stag Arms LLC was founded in early 2003, and is located in New Britain, Conn. Actually, this new armsmaker sprang from a sister company with 30 years' experience manufacturing aerospace and rifle components. According to the manufacturer, all components are made in-house, none are imported. The sample we had was well made and functioned flawlessly. For more details: www.stagarms.com

CONTENTS

PAGE 47

CATALOG OF ARMS AND ACCESSORIES

PAGE 6

PAGE 22

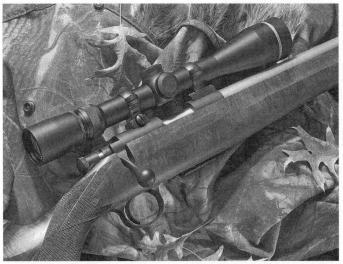

PAGE 35

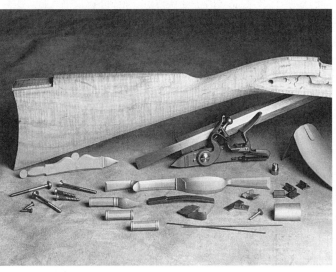

PAGE 50

Kimber Pro Carry II with night
sights and X200 weapon light.

Photo courtesy of Kimber.

AUTOLOADING PISTOLS

by John Malloy

The world of autoloading handguns is an exciting world, one in which traditional ideas and new concepts share the spotlight together.

What could be more traditional than the Colt/Browning 1911 design, which is now nudging its way toward a century of service? Just within the last few years, companies such as Smith & Wesson, SIG-Sauer and Taurus introduced new 1911-type pistols, and have become new players in the 1911 market. Established companies such as Colt, and somewhat more recent entries such as Auto-Ordnance, Kimber, Para-Ordnance, High Standard and others have kept the 1911 design in continuous production since, well … 1911. Other, generally smaller, companies offer 1911s, often made by other overseas manufacturers. A number of American companies make what have been called "production custom" pistols, and the design used is almost exclusively the 1911. There seems to be no concern the 1911 may not make it to its 100th birthday a few years from now.

At the same time, the semiautomatic pistol market is changing to more modern designs. Several decades ago, a category of full-size large-capacity 9mm autoloading pistols gained popularity for service and self-protection use. They were commonly dubbed the "wondernines." Although polymer-frame pistols were being made, most of the new big nines had steel frames, sometimes stainless steel. Then came the "Assault Weapons Ban" of 1994, which limited pistol magazines to a capacity of 10 rounds. Ten rounds of 9mm didn't have as much appeal in a large heavy pistol, one that was designed to hold many more than that. So a decade ago, in the aftermath of the magazine ban, we saw the beginning of a new category of pistol. Small polymer-frame 10-shot pistols for personal defense became popular. Concealed-carry legislation had been growing across the country and there was a demand for affordable pistols of small size. Then, in 2004, the ban sunset, and large-capacity magazines came back.

Now, we have seen a new category arise. The magazine ban is gone, but there is no move back to the big heavy full-size pistols of the wondernine days. Instead, large-capacity pistols are being introduced with light polymer frames. The Glock design showed that such pistols could find a large market. So, within the last few years—with some introductions just this year, on these pages—new full-size light polymer-frame pistols have come on the market. This year's Smith & Wesson M&P and Kimber KPD join a list of recent pistols that include the new Beretta Px4 Storm, the Springfield XD, The Taurus 24/7 and the Walther P99.

It is obvious that what happens in the political arena influences what happens in the world of autoloading handguns. More so perhaps than any other type of firearm in wide use, semiautomatic pistols are related to the world of politics.

So, perhaps it is worthwhile to take a brief look at the political highpoints of the past year or so, just to keep our frame of reference current.

In March 2005, John Bolton became ambassador to the United Nations. Bolton has strongly stated that we will not accept any UN firearms regulations that go against United States citizens' right to keep and bear arms.

In April, Governor Jeb Bush of Florida signed into law an extension of the "Castle Doctrine" that allows citizens to legally defend themselves in places they have a right to be, without retreating. Other states are considering similar legislation.

Starting on July 10, 2005, a series of four devastating hurricanes hit the Gulf Coast. On August 29, Hurricane Katrina hit the upper coast and subsequently flooded the city of New Orleans. Looting began, and many people armed themselves for protection. Local officials announced that only police would be allowed to have guns, and began illegally confiscating firearms from law-abiding residents. People protested, and gun rights organizations filed a lawsuit. By September 23, a court in Louisiana had banned further confiscation and ordered the return of guns taken.

On October 26, President George Bush signed the "Lawful Commerce in Firearms Act," which gives protection to firearms makers when their legal products are used illegally by criminals.

However, on November 9, 2005, a proposition passed in San Francisco that made it illegal to buy, sell or transfer firearms or ammunition in the city. In some ways, this has been interpreted as showing how desperate the antigunners are. For, a similar law was passed before, in 1982, and was struck down in the courts. Another court challenge is sure, but at the time of this writing, no resolution has been made in this situation.

The antigun forces, realizing that "gun control" is not a winning issue in most areas, have tried to cloud the issue by changing the name. The very same objectives of restricting firearms are now presented as "gun safety." We must guard against their getting away with it.

On January 31, 2006, Samuel Alito joined the Supreme Court of the United States. Alito has gone on record in favor of the right to keep and bear arms. He was sworn in by the new Chief Justice, John Roberts, who took his position late in 2005. Roberts is also believed to be a strict constitutionalist.

Antigun forces never rest. In early 2006, a move began to apply New York City restrictions in other cities throughout the country. Antigunners know that if they can win just one battle, they can deprive us of some of our rights, whereas we must win every battle to retain our rights.

However, concealed carry legislation continues to grow across the country. By early 2006, 38 states reportedly had in effect "shall issue" laws. This type of law requires officials to issue licenses to people who met the qualifications. A number of other states have concealed carry licenses, but they may be issued at the whim of issuing officials.

For the time being, things look positive. Nationally, the Bush administration is generally pro-gun rights. The Supreme Court may now be more inclined to interpret the Constitution as it was written. Local governments in many places have supported concealed carry, and other efforts have been made to allow legal armed access to businesses…and their parking lots.

The sunset of the so-called "Assault Weapons Ban" in 2004 has caused manufacturers to supply larger-capacity pistols to meet increased demand. Along with autoloading pistols, the shooting public seems to like pistol-caliber carbines, often with extended-capacity magazines. Because such carbines are generally not covered in the reports of common hunting and target rifles, they will again be covered here.

With all this in mind, let's take a look at what the companies are doing.

AMT

Since AMT came back into existence, pistols reportedly began shipping in February 2006. The double-action-only AMT Back-Up pistols are now available in 380 and 45 ACP calibers. Other calibers will follow later.

The AutoMag II, in the 6-inch barrel version, is in production. Chamberings are 22 Winchester Magnum Rimfire (22WMR) which was the original caliber, and a new variant, the 17 Hornady Magnum Rimfire (HMR).

ArmaLite

ArmaLite, essentially a rifle manufacturer since the start of the company in the mid-1950s, makes AR-15- and AR-10-type rifles in 223 and 308, and other rifles in larger calibers. Although the company has never offered a pistol before, the ArmaLite name has been associated with pistols in the past. In the 1980s, when Charter Arms was making the ArmaLite-designed AR-7 Explorer 22-caliber survival rifle, that company brought out a pistol version, the Explorer II. Serious readers of these pages may also remember that in the 1998 edition, it was reported that ArmaLite was considering marketing a 45-caliber 1911-style pistol. However, the ArmaLite 45 never materialized.

But now, the company will definitely be in the pistol business. ArmaLite and the Turkish firm of Sarsilmaz announced an agreement on February 11, 2006. Sarsilmaz will produce ArmaLite rifles under license for the Turkish armed forces, and ArmaLite will be their link to the United States handgun market.

The ArmaLite pistols will be based on the Sarsilmaz 9mm "Kilinc" (sword) pistol, which is the standard sidearm of the Turkish military. It is essentially a modified CZ75 design, with a cam-operated tilting-barrel locking system and conventional double-action trigger mechanism. ArmaLite is making modifications, so that the pistols will reflect the tradition of the company.

Three pistol variants will be offered by ArmaLite.

The AR-24 will be all-steel, with forged and machined parts. The large-capacity double-action pistols will be offered in full-size and compact models, and in 9mm and 40 S&W.

The AR-25 will have similar variants, but with lightweight polymer frames replacing the steel frames.

Introduction of the new AR-24 and AR-25 pistols was scheduled for the 3rd quarter of 2006.

In addition, the AR-26, a full-size steel-frame 45 ACP pistol, is in the works.

Beretta

Beretta has three new pistol developments, and some modifications to its Storm pistol-caliber carbine.

The Storm Px4 pistol, introduced on these pages last year, is now in production. Recall that the new polymer-frame sidearm was designed in what Beretta calls a "modular concept." Three interchangeable grip backstraps, reversible controls and a convertible trigger mechanism can customize a gun to meet the specifications of just about any shooter or any organization. It is available in 9mm and 40 S&W. As to the question posed last year about a 45-caliber version? Beretta is "exploring the options."

The M9A1 is a variation of the military M9 pistol with modifications for the U. S. Marine Corps. The new A1 variant has a frame accessory rail and other features. There is checkering on the front and rear frame straps, a chromed-lined bore, and a new sand-resistant magazine.

A new variant, called the 90-TWO (interesting play on words, as it is a modified "92" pistol) has a lightweight aluminum frame with a choice of sizes of a composite one-piece wraparound grip. The 90-TWO uses the same internal parts as the 92/96 series pistols, but the dimensions of the slides and frames are slightly different, and they will not interchange. The new pistol has an integral accessory rail on the frame, but a detachable cover is also provided to smooth out the profile if the rail is not used. Many manufacturers are putting frame rails on their pistols, figuring that users will want to hang things on the guns. However, some shooters hold that the purpose of a rail seems to be to keep one from ever being able to put the pistol in his waistband. Beretta's rail cover should pacify them somewhat.

The Cx4 Storm carbine is now offered with the options of using Px4 or 92/96 series pistol magazines. A kit is also available to adopt the carbine to use Beretta Cougar magazines. The ability to use the same magazines in a pistol and carbine carried together is an obvious advantage.

Browning

Several new variants of Browning's 22-caliber Buck Mark pistol line have been introduced.

The Buck Mark Lite Splash is light in weight, and has gold "splash" anodizing over matte blue. The lightness comes from a sleeved alloy barrel. Barrel lengths are 5.5 and 7.25 inches. This variant has the Ultragrip (a soft nitrile grip with ambidextrous finger grooves) and a fiber-optic front sight.

The Buck Mark Contour has a specially contoured barrel, with a scope base and target sights. It also has the Ultragrip and offers a choice of 5 1/2- or 7 1/4-inch barrels.

The Buck Mark Bullseye Target Stainless has a fluted 7 1/4-inch barrel and adjustable sights. Grips are laminated rosewood.

In addition, a limited number of special John M. Browning presentation pistols will be made, with a portion of the price paid for each pistol to go to the John M. Browning Endowment, to benefit the National Rifle Association (NRA) Shooting Sports Camp Program. The Grade I pistol will be stainless, with Black DymondWood grips and special engraving. Two thousand, five hundred will be made. The High Grade pistol will be engraved, with gold and copper accents. Two barrels and checkered walnut grips come with each High Grade pistol, of which only 1001 will be produced.

All new Buck Mark pistols have gripping flanges (ears, to some) at the rear of the slide now. Earlier versions were criticized for a lack of a positive gripping surface, and retracting the slide when the pistol was uncocked could be difficult.

Bushmaster

Recall that two years ago, Bushmaster acquired Professional Ordnance, and continued the lightweight 223-caliber Carbon 15 pistols and carbines. Carbon 15 variants have receivers made of carbon fiber composite.

In February 2006, Bushmaster added to the Carbon 15 offerings a new 9mm pistol and a 9mm carbine. The new pistol and carbine have the same "AR-15" appearance and controls of the other Bushmaster products. However, in place of the rotating bolt and direct-gas-impingement opening system, the 9mm firearms use the simpler blowback system of operation.

The pistol has a 7 1/2-inch barrel, and an overall length of about 22 inches. Weight is 4.6 pounds. The 9mm carbine has a 16-inch barrel, which gives it an overall length of 34-1/2 inches, and a weight of 5.7 pounds. Both the pistol and the carbine come with 30-round magazines.

Century

The Philippine-made S.A.M. (Shooters Arms Manufacturing) 45-caliber pistols that were discontinued last year by Century International Arms have been partially reinstated.

Two variants of the 1911-style pistols have returned to Century's handgun lineup. The Military pistol is essentially a modernized recreation of the WWII-era service pistol. The Elite model has a number of the embellishments many shooters favor, such as beavertail grip safety, skeletonized trigger and hammer, and slam pad on the magazine. Both have 5-inch barrels, and, of course, are in 45 ACP. These are nice pistols, and it is good to see them back.

Another new offering is the Romanian Carpati Model 95, a double-action compact in 380

Top: *Browning's Bullseye Target Stainless pistol has a fluted barrel and rosewood grips.*
Below Top: *The Buck Mark Lite Splash is also made with a 7 1/4-inch barrel.*
Above Bottom: *The Browning Buck Mark Lite Splash is a lightweight pistol with gold "splash" decoration. This is the 5 1/2-inch version.*
Bottom: *The Browning Buck Mark Contour has a specially contoured barrel, with a scope base and target sights.*

ACP. For those who like a bonus, the 380 Carpati comes with a cleaning rod, spare magazine and a shoulder holster.

Charles Daly

With the sunset of the "Assault Weapons Ban" in 2004, larger capacity pistols now have advantages for some competition and personal-protection situations. Charles Daly has introduced a new steel frame high-capacity 45 based on the Colt/Browning 1911 design. Most higher-capacity 45 frames are now made of polymer material, but many shooters still prefer a steel frame.

CZ

Since 1998, when CZ-USA was established to import Czech firearms to the United States, the offerings to American shooters have grown. New in the CZ lineup as of February 2006 were a number of autoloading pistols, most modifications of the basic 9mm CZ75.

The CZ75B Stainless is the first stainless-steel firearm to carry the CZ name. Except for rubber grips and an ambidextrous manual safety, the stainless-steel version is functionally the same as the blue-steel CZ75B.

Two new SP-01 models have been introduced. The SP-01 Tactical pistol is a full-size version with a 4.7-inch barrel, a larger version of the standard SP-01 Service Pistol introduced recently. It has a beavertail tang, rubber grips and a full-length frame with an accessory rail.

The SP-01 Shadow is a competition version with adjustable rear sight, fiber-optic front sight and walnut grips. It has a lighter recoil spring and mainspring to handle "minor" power factor 9mm loads. The magazine capacity, as with the other SP-01 pistols, is 19 rounds.

The CZ75 Tactical Sport pistol was built for IPSC competition. It features high sights, a single-action trigger of special configuration, and a full-length frame with beveled magazine well. Available in 9mm (20+1) and 40 S&W (16+1) variants, the Tactical Sport has a nickeled frame with blued slide.

The compact CZ2075 RAMI pistol, introduced recently, is an aluminum-frame subcompact based on the SZ75 mechanism. The little pistol has found a following, and this year, a polymer-frame version with a lightened slide is available. It is offered in 40 S&W (8+1) or 9mm (10+1). An extended 14-round 9mm magazine is also available.

On January 25, 2005, CZ USA purchased the assets and trademark of Dan Wesson. Within the CZ framework, the Dan Wesson group continues a separate product line of revolvers and 1911-type semiautomatic pistol and are now included in the CZ catalog. (See Dan Wesson)

Dan Wesson

The alphabet being arranged as it is, this is certainly a convenient place to report on the Dan Wesson handguns being offered, following the acquisition of the company by CZ-USA.

Some revolvers and three automatic pistols appeared in the 2006 CZ catalog. The autoloaders are of interest to us here.

The Pointman 7 (PM7) is a 1911-style match-grade pistol with a 5-inch barrel. Enhancements such as adjustable sights, beavertail grip safety, extended thumb safety and extended magazine release are standard.

The Commander Classic Bobtail has many of the same features, but has a 4.25-inch barrel and fixed night sights. The lower rear edge of the grip frame and mainspring housing area has been beveled off ("bobbed") to make the gun easier to conceal as a carry pistol.

The Razorback is a new 1911-style pistol chambered only for the 10mm Auto cartridge. A 5-inch barrel and fixed sights are standard. While the other Dan Wesson pistols are basically 45s, they may be ordered in 10mm chambering. The Razorback is made as a 10mm only.

Detonics

Detonics USA reports that the short-frame CombatMaster with 3

1/2-inch barrel and the short frame StreetMaster with 5-inch barrel are now in good production, and other models are coming on line. A Detonics Combat Master pistol was used in the motion picture *Mr. and Mrs. Smith,* allowing some recognition outside normal shooting circles.

A new variant, listed as a medium-sized CombatMaster, is now in the catalog. In heritage, it is related to the original 4 1/4-inch

Top: *The CZ75B Stainless 9mm is the company's first stainless-steel pistol.*
Bottom: *The CZ75 SP-01 Tactical pistol is a larger version of the SP-01 service pistol.*

ServiceMaster, and in appearance is the ServiceMaster with a short grip, giving a 6+1 capacity.

How do the new Detonics pistols hold up? Pretty well, if a recent 3-day endurance test is any indication. In those three days, 31,000 rounds were fired through a single full-size 5-inch Model 9-11-01 pistol. Students of firearms history will recall that the original Colt 1911 was subjected in that year to a 6000-round test—the longest recorded shooting test of any pistol to that time. Now, Detonics has put over five times that many rounds through one of their pistols. Oh, yes, for good measure, they also shot the pistol out of a mortar before running accuracy tests. The gun functioned well and gave good accuracy.

Because Jerry Ahern, president of Detonics, and pistolmaker L. W. Seecamp have had a long relationship, 100 cased sets of two pistols—a Detonics 45 and a Seecamp 32—are being made up. Both pistols in each set have identical serial numbers, with the prefix DETLWS.

DSA

At the February 2006 SHOT Show, DSA displayed a prototype long-range 308-caliber pistol with an 11-inch barrel. The pistol is a modification of the company's 11-inch "entry rifle" made without a stock. The thinking is that other chamberings—243 Winchester, 260 Remington—may come into the line after production begins.

EAA

European American Armory has introduced the Witness "Elite Match" pistol. Decked out for competition, the new Witness is available in 9mm, 10mm, 40S&W and 45 ACP. Witness pistols are a modified CZ75 design.

EAA is also offering high-end carry guns from their custom shop. Designated "Match Special," the pistols are available in compact and subcompact sizes.

Ed Brown

Ed Brown Products offers a line of high-grade 1911-style pistols. New for 2006 was the Executive Target model, an enhanced 5-inch-barrel pistol. It has many of the features favored by a lot of shooters today, such as adjustable sights, beavertail grip safety, checkered front and back grip straps, and ambidextrous manual safety. It is offered in blue, stainless steel or a blue/stainless two-tone combination.

New also is the Special Forces 5-inch "Government" style pistol. The fixed sights are 3-dot Novak. Front and rear grip straps have a chainlink pattern to provide a gripping surface. The finish is a hard dark coating over forged carbon steel.

Firestorm

Not all that long ago, it seemed as if the 32 ACP cartridge was a dead duck.
Because of the perceived superiority of the 380 ACP, no company that made pistols suitable for either cartridge made a 32. Then things changed. Perhaps because of the appearance of 25-sized 32s, or perhaps because of the ballistically-improved ammunition available, the 32 ACP chambering experienced a resurrection. Now, a number of manufacturers make 32s again.

The latest purveyor of 32 ACP pistols is FireStorm. For some years offering compact pocket pistols in 380 ACP, the line now includes a 32 ACP chambering in its MiniFireStorm series. Magazine capacity of the new 32 is 10 rounds, three more than the similar 380. With a 3 1/2-inch barrel, the pistol weighs 23 ounces.

Made in Argentina, the new 32 and other FireStorm pistols are imported by SGS Importers in New Jersey.

The large-frame FireStorm 45-caliber pistols were previously manufactured by Llama in Spain. With the demise of Llama, these pistols are no longer available. (See Llama)

FNH USA

FNH USA is the American company that handles Belgian Fabrique Nationale (FN)-designed firearms. The firm continues to modify their pistol line, and has introduced a carbine that is sure to generate interest.

The FNP 9 and FNP 40 pistols are available in black finish or black with a silver (stainless-steel) slide. New double-action-only variants are also available, and a double decocker version has been introduced.

The Five-seveN pistol, chambered for the interesting 5.7x28mm cartridge has a new variant. Although most makers are putting magazine disconnectors in all their pistols in an attempt to make their products universally salable and ward off lawsuits, most law-enforcement officers and others who carry a pistol regularly seem not to prefer them. The pistol has been available in an Individual Officers Model without the disconnect.

Recall that the Five-seveN is a light, mostly-polymer pistol with what is called a delayed-blowback mechanism. Although not locked together, the barrel recoils a short distance with the slide before the slide continues rearward.

The most attention-getting new FNH offering is the new P90 semiautomatic carbine based on the firm's M90 submachine gun. Chambered for the 5.7x28mm cartridge, the new carbine has a 16-inch barrel and can fire single shots only, in autoloading fashion. The magazine, like that of the submachine gun, lies on the top of the gun, and the cartridges in the magazine lie crosswise to the long axis of the gun until they are fed into the feed mechanism. The innovative design allows magazines of different

The new Ed Brown Special Forces Pistol has Novak sights and a chain-link pattern on the grip straps.

capacities without increasing the size of the firearm. 10-, 30- and 50-round magazines are reported to be available. The appearance is unconventional (to say the least), and the P90 is sure to attract attention.

Heckler & Koch

As of January 2006, Heckler & Koch (HK) has experienced some changes in organization structure. Merkel (shotguns and rifles) is now part of HK, and Anschutz guns are now imported by Merkel. HK itself has been split into two entities—sporting arms will be handled from Trussville, AL, and military and defense items will be handled from Sterling, VA.

High Standard

High Standard has introduced its "Mil-Spec" series of pistols––and carbines. The pistols are 1911-type 45s, and are of, in High Standard's words, "original design, with a few improvements." The Parkerized 45 shares the spotlight with the company's new line of 223-caliber AR-15-style rifles and carbines, dubbed HSA-15. The pistol carries

the model number TX1911.

Other 45-caliber 1911-type pistols are new in the line. The "Camp Perry" National Match pistol is tuned for competition, but avoids some of the exotic accessories some like to add on. As were the original military National Match pistols, they will be offered with either fixed or adjustable sights. A "Supermatic" 45 will be offered with a 6-inch barrel. A "Crusader Compact" with a 3 1/2-inch barrel is in the offing. It will be all-steel, with Novak-style sights.

In the world of 22 pistols, High Standard will offer the "Bob Shea" series of specially-constructed pistols. Shea began working for High Standard in 1942, and is still active in repairing and accurizing various models of the 22 pistols. When asked about retirement, Shea replied that he seems to be spending "less time fishing and more time making guns." High Standard has returned to production a limited edition of the old Supermatic Tournament—the early target pistol with the sight on the slide instead of on a bridge. The company will also return the fixed-sight Sport King to production.

Although it is not pertinent to

this report, the High Standard team seems to enjoy bringing back old names. The group is forming a company to manufacture ammunition. The name they have acquired may be familiar to many old-timers—U. S. Cartridge Company.

Hi-Point

Hi-Point Firearms now has an association with Charter Arms, and both brands will be distributed by MKS Supply. This relationship should work well. Both brands are American-made, and Hi-Point autoloading pistols and Charter revolvers will complement each other, offering more handgun choices. As a sign the Hi-Point niche is really expanding, note that a line of reproductions of historic lever-action rifles has also been added.

Hi-Point carbines are probably the most popular single brand of pistol-caliber carbine being used today. The popular 9mm and 40-caliber carbines were scheduled to be joined by a long-awaited 45-caliber version in the Spring of 2006.

With the sunset of the "Assault Weapons Ban," Hi-Point has been working on extended magazines for its carbines, but at the time of this writing, has not marketed any. Charles Brown, president, said that they have not yet been satisfied with the reliability of the prototype extended magazines. Hi-Point products have a reputation for working right, and the company wants the new magazines to continue that reputation.

Iver Johnson

The Iver Johnson 45-caliber 1911-type pistol, introduced on these pages in the last edition, is not yet in production, but was getting close in early 2006. The 45 pistols have steel frames, but an aluminum-frame 22-caliber version is also planned. Twenty-two-caliber kits are under development, and the company is also testing pistols and kits for the 17 Mach 2 cartridge.

Kahr

Kahr has a number of new products in both its traditional Kahr line and in its Auto-Ordnance/

The Heckler & Koch P30 9mmx19 with adjustable 3-dot sights, 10-shot magazine, M3 tactical light and left and right hand conversions.

Thompson line. In the Kahr line, the new CW series (think "concealed weapon") are designed, not for the armed professional, but for the average citizen who carries a concealed pistol for his or her own personal protection. The CW pistols use some simpler manufacturing processes, and sell at a lower price. The CW pistols have conventional rifling rather than polygonal. The front sight is fixed on the slide instead of fitting in a dovetail. The slide stop, instead of being machined, is an MIM (metal injection molded) part. Such changes allow offering the same basic pistol at a substantially lower price. CW pistols are double-action-only, have polymer frames and matte stainless-steel slides. They are available in 9mm and 40, and have 3 1/2-inch barrels.

The P45 is a new 45 ACP polymer variant, with a blackened stainless-steel slide. The barrel is 3.54 inches long and has polygonal rifling. With a capacity of 6+1, the new 45 weighs just a bit over 20 ounces with its magazine. Like all Kahr pistols, the P45 does not have a magazine disconnector. Many consider this an advantage.

The Auto-Ordnance/Thompson Custom line of 1911-style 45 automatics has two new 4 1/4-inch variants. One is all stainless steel, and the other has a stainless-steel slide and an aluminum frame. The pistols have a number of the enhancements favored by today's shooters.

Thompson long guns may be considered the modern offspring of the original pistol-caliber carbine— the Thompson submachine gun. The several variants of the modern Thompson semiautomatic carbine have been upgraded with more authentic features. Fifty- and 100-round drums are now available (and, interestingly, 10-round drums for those who want the Thompson look, but live in capacity-limited states or localities).

Now, I have walked into a trap by including pistol-caliber carbines in this report. Auto-Ordnance also offers a reproduction of the U. S. M-1 30-caliber carbine. Is the 30 Carbine cartridge really a pistol cartridge? Certainly pistols have

been made for it. At any rate, the company is making M-1 carbines.

Kel-Tec

Kel-Tec has introduced a number of new pistols and modifications to its existing pistol models.

The most eye-catching is the PLR-16, a long-range pistol in 223. The big new pistol is a modification of the company's SU-16 rifle design. It has a 9.2-inch barrel and weighs 3.2 pounds. The PLR-16 uses the turning-bolt locking system of the military M-16. The muzzle is threaded for standard attachments.

The company's fortunes were built on the excellent 14-ounce P-11 pistol of 1995, a 10+1 polymer-frame 9mm. For 2006, the basic mechanism was put into an even more compact package—the new PF-9. A single-column magazine offers 7+1 capacity and allows a slimmer, lighter 12.7-ounce pistol. A new simpler extractor has been introduced with the PF-9.

The new extractor design is now also being used by the company's P-32 (32 ACP) and P-3AT (380 ACP) guns. Those two little pocket pistols also have new sights—very low sights with a broad square notch and a broad blade front. The sights are made as part of the slide and are not adjustable.

Kimber

Kimber, one of the largest manufacturers of 1911-type pistols, announced a departure for 2006. The new Kimber Pro Defense (KPD) is a polymer-frame 40-caliber designed for both service and personal defense use. At 25 ounces, the double-action-only pistol has a 4-inch barrel and has 12+1 capacity. Three interchangeable backstraps allow fitting the gun to a specific hand. The stainless-steel slide is covered with a black "Kim Pro II" finish. As most new introductions seem to have, the KPD has an accessory rail on the front of the frame. Introduced in 40 S&W chambering, a 9mm is planned for the near future.

Introduced back in May 2005 (and not yet included on these pages), the Kimber Desert Warrior is an interesting 1911 pistol with an accessory rail––and of all things––a

lanyard loop at the butt. Earth tones (sand tones) for the metal finish and grips reflect the desert theme and give the pistol distinctive appearance.

From the Kimber Custom Shop, the Grand Raptor II features scaled serrations, polished flats of the stainless-steel frame, and a matte slide. A full-size 45, the two-tone pistol is loaded with Custom Shop features.

Les Baer

Les Baer Custom builds 1911-style pistols for service, defense and competition use. The company celebrated its 25th anniversary last year. This year, a book, *Les Baer, Sr.– A Legend in His Own Time,* by Charles K. Stroud, Jr., was published. Baer is one of a number of gunmakers who began making guns on a custom basis, then realized many customers wanted similar guns. The result is what many call "production custom" pistols.

Llama

The grand old name of Llama is gone. It was introduced by the Spanish firm of Gabilondo over a century ago, in 1904. A variety of pistols and revolvers have been made under the Llama name. In 1931, the company began making centerfire pistols based on (but not exact copies of) the Colt/Browning 1911 design, and such guns were used during the Spanish Civil War. Stoeger was the long-term importer of Llama pistols into the United States after World War II. In the 1990s, the firm had financial problems, but in 2000, manufacture was continued by a cooperative of Gabilondo employees. Import Sports became the importer.

Now it looks as if Llama is gone for good. The cooperative went out of business in early April 2005. For those who want to keep their Llamas shooting, Eagle Imports of New Jersey has acquired the last supply of Llama parts and magazines. A listing of Llama parts can be seen at www.yourgunparts.com.

Magnum Research

Magnum Research has introduced a line of lightweight rimfire semiautomatic rifles. In limited production (only one production run was planned for 2006) is a pistol version, called the "PiCuda."

The unusual name seems to stem from the fact that it is the "pistol" version, with what the company calls the "barracuda" stock. Based on the Ruger rimfire rifle action, the receiver and sight rail are machined as one piece, and the barrel is a steel tube in a graphite carbon fiber sleeve. The barracuda stock is a design of unusual-shape that does not contact the barrel. It is laminated in a pattern of browns and greens that the company calls "forest camo." The PiCuda has a 10-shot magazine, and is available in 22 Long Rifle or 17 Mach 2.

Majestic Arms

We have not considered Majestic Arms in this report previously, but now that we are covering pistol-caliber carbines, it is worth paying some attention to this company's products. Their autoloading model MA 4 is based on what they call the Majestic Arms Rimfire Rifle System (MARRS). Using a new action patterned after the AR-7 survival rifle action, the company makes interchangeable-barrel carbines that can use 22 Long Rifle (22LR), 17 Mach 2, 22 Winchester Magnum Rimfire (22WMR) and 17 Hornady Magnum Rimfire (17HMR).

Mitchell

Mitchell Manufacturing has brought out a new rimfire semi-auto pistol and carbine duo.

Regular readers of these pages may have noted that similar guns were introduced in the 2005 edition. At that time, they had just been introduced by Excel Arms. In the interim, Mitchell acquired the rights to these interesting guns, and is offering them under the Mitchell name. The pistol is named the White Lightning, and the carbine is marketed as the Black Lightning. Either version is available as one of four rimfire calibers—22LR, 17 Mach 2, 22WMR or 17 HMR. A nine-round magazine works with either the pistol or carbine. A bolt handle on the right of the slide (even on the pistol) aids in operation.

The pistol has an 8 1/2-inch barrel, is equipped with adjustable open sights and has a top rail for mounting optical or electronic sights. The carbine has an 18-inch barrel and a full-length top rail that can mount a variety of scopes and other sights. Scope rings come standard with the carbine.

Nighthawk

A new name has entered the arena of high-end "production custom" semiautomatic pistols based on the 1911 Colt/Browning design. Nighthawk Custom was formed in 2004, but the first large-scale public display of the pistols was made at the February 2006 SHOT Show, in Las Vegas, NV.

One of their offerings had been called the Global Response Pistol (GRP), a 5-inch 45 suited to extreme conditions. Their newest pistol was a similar gun, but with a 4 1/4-inch barrel. The new arrival has been dubbed the GRP II.

Olympic

Olympic Arms has introduced a series of pistol-caliber carbines based on the AR-15. The code is not hard to break, for the model numbers are K9, K10, K40 and K45. With 16-inch barrels, they are offered in 9mm, 10mm, 40 S&W and 45 ACP. The 9mm uses a 32-round converted Sten magazine. The other calibers use 10-round converted UZI magazines. There are two additional models—models K9-GL and K40-GL. These carbines, in 9mm and 40 calibers, use standard factory Glock magazines of varying capacities. Although the controls are the same, the locked-breech mechanism of the AR-15 is not needed with the pistol calibers, so the new guns are blowback-operated. Pistol-caliber kits (uppers) are also available to convert an existing AR-type rifle to a pistol-caliber 16-inch carbine.

The Whitney Wolverine reincarnation has been in production long enough now that Olympic has a line of accessories available. Adjustable sights are planned as an option. Checkered wood grips, a suitable nylon holster and extra magazines may be had now. The magazines offered will also fit the original Whitneys of the

The Para Tac-Five is a 9mm with the LDA trigger system.

1950s—a good situation for those who need a magazine for an old Whitney.

Para-Ordnance

Para-Ordnance has brought out a number of new pistols, all variants of the 1911 Colt/Browning design. Most of them can be found in the 2006 Para catalog, but at least one was too new to make it in. Let's look at them:

The "Hog" series has some new members. The Stainless Warthog is the 3.5-inch 10+1 Warthog, made in stainless steel. The Slim Hawg, introduced last year, is now a production item. It is a single-column version of the Warthog, with

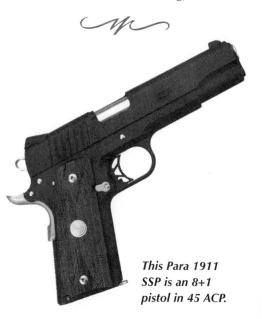

This Para 1911 SSP is an 8+1 pistol in 45 ACP.

6+1 capacity. The Lite Hawg 9 is a modification of the 9mm-chambered Hawg 9 of last year. The "lite" in the new model's name doesn't mean that it is lighter than the original, but that it has a rail on the frame to hold a light. The 12+1 9mm is also joined by a 10+1 Lite Hawg 45.

The Tac-Five has Para's LDA (light double action) trigger mechanism, and is available as an 18+1 9mm. New calibers of Nite-Tac full-size LDA pistols have light rails. They are offered as a 9mm (18+1) or as a 40 S&W (16+1).

The 1911 SSP model is a single-column full-size pistol made in 45 ACP (8+1) and—in 38 Super, with a 9+1 capacity.

Todd Jarrett uses Para pistols in competition, and the company has brought out special pistols to attest to that fact. Todd Jarrett USPSA Limited Edition pistols are available in two versions. A 45 version is a single-column pistol with an 8+1 capacity, and a 40-caliber version has a double-column magazine and holds 16+1 rounds. For every one of these pistols purchased, a portion of the price will go to the United States Practical Shooting Association (USPSA).

A new caliber for Para is 45 G.A.P. A compact single-column Carry model is offered in the 45 G.A.P. chambering, although the new addition did not make it into the catalog.

Rock Island

"Rock Island Arsenal" is the name used on the 1911-style semiautomatic pistols produced for American sales by the Philippine manufacturer Armscor. Along with the standard service model, a new target model with adjustable sights is now available.

Rock River

Rock River Arms makes high-grade 1911-style pistols and AR-15 type rifles and carbines.

New for 2006 were LAR-15 pistols, large AR-type pistols in 223 and 9mm calibers. Either version comes with barrel choices of 7 or 10-1/2 inches. Other choices are AR-15 style sights, or no sights, but with front and rear rails for sight mounting. 223 pistols are locked breech, and 9mm

pistols are blow-back operated.

Tooled up for the 9mm AR-style pistol, it is logical to reason that Rock River would also offer 9mm carbines based on the AR design. The company does indeed offer two 9mm blow-back carbines. The CAR A2 has a 16-inch Wilson barrel, and has AR-style front and rear sights. The CAR A4 is similar, but has a front sight and receiver rail that allows different types of rear sight mounting.

Both 9mm carbines and the 9mm pistols use modified 25-round UZI magazines. For those in areas where magazine freedom has not reached, 10-shot magazines are also available.

In their 1911 line, Rock River Arms offers new variants. The Basic Carry is a "dehorned" full-size 45, with edges smoothed out for easier carry. The Tactical Pistol adds a light rail on the forward part of the frame. Two new 9mm Police Competition pistols are offered now, for use in Limited and Unlimited events. The Limited version has a 5-inch barrel, while the Unlimited pistol has a 6-inch barrel.

Rohrbaugh

The lightweight all-metal 9mm Rohrbaugh pistols are now available in three cosmetic variants—black, silver, or black-and-silver (the original version). New variations in grips, and choices of sights (Model R9S) or no sights (Model R9) are offered.

New for 2006 were presentation models. Production has gone well past 1000 pistols, and the landmark serial number R1000 is up for auction. Rohrbaugh pistols have been used in *Mr. and Mrs. Smith* and the *Miami Vice* movie, so they are acquiring recognition outside the shooting world.

RTI

Recoilless Technologies, Inc. is developing recoilless and multi-caliber pistols. Avid readers of these pages may recognize that the company was first reported in the 1997 edition as Ultima Technologies. By the 1998 edition, it had become Recoilless Technologies, to better reflect the operating characteristics of the pistol under development.

The design is of some interest. A collar around the rear portion of the barrel can be removed from the front of the frame. With the collar off, the frame can be opened as if it were a clamshell, hinged at the rear. With the frame open, the barrel can be simply lifted out, allowing easy interchange of barrels. The geometry of the internal parts minimizes recoil. The rearward moving breechblock is linked to an internal mechanism that moves down against spring pressure as the action operates. Inertia of this motion acts against the upward rise from recoil, and diminished felt recoil comes back at near a straight line.

The late 1990s pistol was a 9mm, and it was claimed that loadings to produce very high velocities could be handled safely. At the February 2006 SHOT Show, three different variants were shown, handling 9mm (9x19, 9x21, 9x23), 9mm Winchester Magnum (with reported velocities of 1980 fps) and a special 50 caliber, made by shortening a 300 Winchester Short Magnum (300WSM) case.

Ruger

All right, the big news from Sturm, Ruger & Co. was the 50th Anniversary model of their 44 Magnum revolver. That said, the company did bring out some new variants of autoloading pistols.

Last year, Ruger brought out the stainless-steel Mark III Hunter 22-caliber pistol, with a 6 7/8-inch fluted barrel. This year, the firm is giving the same treatment to the 22/45 pistol line. The new 22/45 Mark III Hunter has the polymer frame, introduced in 1992, which has the same grip angle as the 1911 45-caliber pistol. The polymer frame was slimmed down recently, and the new pistol has this thinner grip frame. The new Hunter version has the long fluted stainless barrel, and an adjustable rear sight with a HiViz front sight. The stainless-steel receiver is drilled and tapped for a scope base adapter, which is included with the gun. Also included are a gun lock and a storage case in, of course, Hunter Green color.

Also new in February 2006 was Model P95 9mm pistol with an integral frame light/accessory rail.

The polymer frame has new textured grip areas to provide a better hold, and the trigger guard has been modified to a smoother, more rounded shape. Offered with a manual safety or as a decock-only version, the new P95 pistols have 3.9-inch barrels, weigh 27 ounces and have 15+1 capacity.

Sarsilmaz

The Turkish firm of Sarsilmaz has become a big player in the international handgun field. A few years ago, the reappearance of the Italian Bernardelli pistol line was due largely to association with Sarsilmaz. This year, an agreement with ArmaLite will provide a new line of Sarsilmaz-produced pistols under the ArmaLite name. (see ARMALITE.)

Under the Sarsilmaz name, the Turkish firm offers a line of shotguns and 9mm pistols that are based on the CZ 75 operating mechanism. The pistols they produce run the gamut from full size to compact, from steel-frame to alloy-frame to polymer-frame variants, and from service pistols to competition guns. A version of their steel-frame full-size pistol is the official pistol of Turkish armed forces.

Other companies that base their pistol line on the CZ 75 design often offer variants in 40 S&W as well as the original 9mm. Sarsilmaz, for whatever reason, has chosen not to do this. The firm seemed satisfied with the 9mm chambering. Thus, it was a surprise to see a 45 ACP pistol displayed at the Sarsilmaz booth at the February 2006 SHOT Show. Little could be learned about the company's plans for the Sarsilmaz 45, and it is not mentioned in their catalog.

SIGARMS

After the successful introduction of the SIG-Sauer 1911 a couple years back, it seems safe to say that SIGARMS has embraced the 1911 design. The 2006 catalog lists no fewer than 15 different versions! Called the Granite Series Revolution (GSR) upon its introduction, "Revolution" seems to have won out as the identifier, and all the SIG 1911s are now various Revolution models.

SIGARMS has a number of new entries in its traditional pistols lines. Model P220, P226 and P229 pistols in various calibers now can be had with factory-installed Crimson Trace Lasergrips. Rails and night sights (and the extra set of original factory grips, in case you want to change back) come standard with these pistols.

From the SIGARMS custom shop, a series of "SAS" variants is available for Models P220, P226, P229 and P239. These are good-looking carry pistols that feature a bright slide, dark frame and strikingly attractive laminated wood grips. The metal has been "dehorned" to give smooth edges. All models wear a Siglite front sight.

Smith & Wesson

Smith & Wesson must have held its corporate breath when it introduced the Chiefs Special automatic pistols a few years ago. The Chiefs Special 38 revolver had been a mainstay in the S&W line for half a century. Would the shooting world accept an autoloader also named Chiefs Special? Apparently it did. Now, S&W has reapplied the Military & Police (M&P) name—a designation applied to a revolver in production since 1899—to a modern semiautomatic pistol. And, not just to a pistol, but to the company's new AR-style 223 rifle!

The rifle is interesting, too, but the pistol is what we will consider here. The new M&P pistol is a full-size gun with a light Zytel polymer frame with a hardened, Melonite-coated stainless-steel slide. It is a locked-breech mechanism with a 6.5-pound trigger that operates a striker-fire ignition system. The M&P has three interchangeable backstrap grip inserts to fit a particular pistol to a particular hand. Slide stop is ambidextrous, and the magazine release is reversible. Barrel length is 4-1/4 inches, and weight is about 24 ounces. The frame has an accessory rail. The M&P pistol was introduced in early 2006 in 40 S&W caliber. 9mm and 347 SIG also were scheduled for introduction shortly thereafter. Compact versions are also in the works.

The M&P was the star of the show for S&W's auto pistols, but the 1911 line has received plenty of attention. No less than 14 different variants appear in the 2006 catalog. Newly introduced in 2006 are the SW1911 Tactical Rail pistols, which have an accessory rail at the front of the frame. Two versions are offered—a stainless steel pistol, and one with a black scandium frame and stainless slide with black Melonite finish.

The Model 1911PD "Gunsite" pistol has a 4 1/4-inch barrel. The frame is scandium, with a carbon steel slide; both finishes in matte black. Sights are Novak, with a brass bead front sight.

From the performance shop, a new Model 952 Long Slide is available. The pistol is a 9mm version of the old Model 52 target pistol, now with a 6-inch barrel and long slide to match. The single-action pistol is fitted with a Wilson Micro adjustable rear sight.

Top: *1911 Gunsite L The scandium-frame "Gunsite" pistol from S&W has special grips and a 4 1/4-inch barrel.*
Bottom: *S&W Tactical Rail pistol in stainless steel, left view.*

Springfield

Springfield continues to make lots of 1911-type pistols, but their big news is the new 45-caliber version of their polymer-frame XD pistol. Introduced at the February 2006 SHOT Show, the new XD is chambered for 45 ACP, and has 13+1 capacity.

The company had brought out a 45 G.A.P. version of the XD last year, but the longer 45 ACP cartridge required some redesign. Now the pistols are here, in two variants. The 4-inch barrel XD 45 weighs 30 ounces, and is 7 inches long. The variant with the 5-inch barrel weighs 32 ounces, and has an overall length of 8 inches. Dovetailed 3-dot sights are standard, with Tritium sights as an option.

Steyr

The uncertainty expressed here last year is over. Import arrangements for Steyr firearms have been established, and Steyr pistols (and rifles too) have a new importer, Steyr Arms of Cummins, GA.

Steyr and Mannlicher-branded rifles are being imported, but the Steyr M-A1 pistol is the gun that fits this report. The ergonomic polymer-frame pistol has a 4-inch barrel and is available in 9mm, 40 S&W and 357 SIG. An accessory rail is located at the front of the frame.

Because we are including pistol-caliber carbines here, it is of interest to note that the Steyr AUG—a gun of unusual appearance, and one that antigun forces love to hate—is now available as a 9mm carbine with a 16-inch barrel.

Taurus

In January 2005, Taurus introduced their version of the 45-caliber 1911 Colt/Browning design, the PT-1911. At that time, there were only two specimens in the United States. As of February 2006, the new guns were still not in full production, but Taurus had already brought out four new models.

A full-size 5-inch model in 38 Super is now offered, available in blue or stainless. A second full-size pistol is offered in 40 S&W caliber, also with

a choice of blue or stainless, and also with or without a frame accessory rail. The third full-size offering is a 9mm, also blue or stainless. The fourth is a compact 45, with a 4 1/4-inch barrel. Actually, there could be any number of variations, adding up to a very large number of 1911 choices. It seems safe to say that Taurus is definitely in the 1911 business.

Taurus seems to have wanted to provide something for everyone with their new 2006 offerings. How about a full-size PT59 in 380 ACP, with 15+1 capacity? Or the 9mm PT917, with a 20-round magazine, giving a full 21 shots? The PT 745 polymer compact 45 has two new variants, one a long-slide version with a longer 4 1/4-inch barrel. The other is a version in 45 G.A.P.

The compact Millennium pistol is available in a titanium variant that provides 13+1 rounds of 9mm capacity. The polymer-frame 24/7 service pistol is now available with a titanium slide, as a long-slide version with a 5-inch barrel, or as a short-slide/short grip model with a 3.3-inch barrel. Or, as the short slide/long grip model. You probably get the idea—Taurus offers a lot of variations in its line of autoloading pistols.

Uselton

Uselton's pistol line of "totally customized out of the box" 1911-type pistols had a new addition for 2006. The Officers Damascus variant has a damascus slide, a titanium frame—and grips made from genuine ray skin. The ray skin grips feel as if they would provide a non-slip hold under almost any circumstances.

U. S. Firearms

United States Firearms Manufacturing Co., a company that made its reputation by manufacturing replicas of historic Colt revolvers, surprised a lot of people last year by bring out their first autoloading pistols. The guns were Colt 1911-type pistols, but looked even earlier, as they were fitted with grips that recalled the wide flat grips of the Colt 1905 pistol.

USFA liked the look, and this year they have brought out two new 1911-

Top: *Springfield's XD pistol is now available in 45 ACP chambering. This is the 4-inch barrel version.*
Bottom: *Springfield XD 45 ACP pistol, angled*

style handguns with those grips. One is in the 38 Super chambering, with the slide marked "USFA Super 38 Automatic." The second is a recreation of the old Colt Ace 22 pistol, and is marked "USFA ACE .22 Long Rifle." Two appropriate magazines are furnished with each pistol.

Volquartsen

New from Volquartsen is the Predator pistol, a long-range rimfire handgun. Introduced in stainless steel, the company also plans to offer a version with an aluminum receiver and a lightweight sleeved barrel. The Predator comes with a fiberglass stock, and calibers are 22 Winchester Magnum Rimfire (22WMR) and 17 Hornady Magnum Rimfire (17HMR).

Walther

According to Walther records, the Walther PPK pistol was introduced in 1931. Thus, 2006 marked the little pistol's 75th anniversary. Such a milestone obviously called for a special commemorative pistol.

The commemorative pistol will be of carbon steel, with a highly-polished blue finish, accented with engraving on the slide and frame, and the Walther logo in gold. "75th Anniversary" will be engraved on the slide. Serial numbers will be in a separate group, starting with 0000PPK.

The 75th year PPK is close to the original, which was one of the first commercially-made pistols to introduce the double-action trigger mechanism to autoloading handguns. The current version is in 380 ACP and has a 3.3-inch barrel, is six inches long and weighs 20.8 ounces. The original had a very short tang, which could result in "hammer bite" to the web of the shooter's hand; the current production pistol has a longer tang to prevent this. The Anniversary PPK will wear wood grips for the occasion, instead of the plastic grips of the original.

Wildey

Recall that back in the 2004 edition, it was reported that Wildey had reintroduced the 44 AutoMag cartridge as a current chambering in a production pistol. In February 2006, Wildey brought out the 357 AutoMag as a regular chambering. Wildey plans to provide ammunition, reloading dies and brass for the 357, as they do for all their calibers. Owners of original Automag pistols in the 357 and 44 calibers can also benefit from having a reliable source for these items.

The JAWS Viper pistol, which was developed as a joint venture between Wildey and the country of Jordan, is ready to go into production. Readers may remember that the pistol can be converted to several different calibers by quick replacement of just a few parts. A Wildey representative said that it was hoped that the pistol would be in full production by the end of 2006.

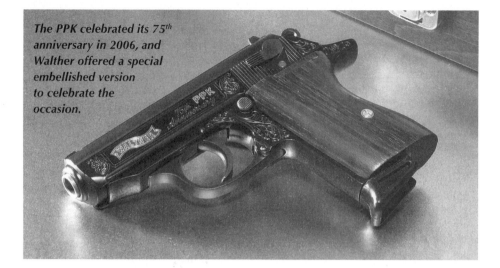

The PPK celebrated its 75th anniversary in 2006, and Walther offered a special embellished version to celebrate the occasion.

Wilson

Wilson, long known for the company's line of "production custom" pistols based on the 45-caliber 1911 Colt/Browning system, has introduced a new pistol that is a departure for the company. The new gun, called the ADP (Advanced Design Pistol) is a 9mm compact pistol with a polymer frame and a gas-retarded operating mechanism.

Readers of these pages will recall that the Heritage Stealth pistol was introduced about a decade ago. The design went out of production a few years later, but the mechanism, based of the concepts of South African designer Alex Du Plessis, was of interest. The pistol had a unique gas-retarded system, in which a port in front of the chamber allowed gas from a fired round to operate against a piston underneath the barrel that was attached to the slide. As the slide and piston recoiled rearward, the gas pressure tried to push the assembly forward, thus effectively retarding the initial opening of the mechanism, and softening the felt recoil.

This is the system used on the new Wilson pistol. Alex Du Plessis has worked with Wilson and an improved version of the original pistol has been introduced as the Wilson 9mm ADP. In Wilson literature, the ADP notation signifies Advanced Design Pistol. Note that this designation just happens to also be the initials of the designer.

The Wilson ADP has a number of improvements over the original. A squared-off slide with good grasping serrations allow purchase for retracting the slide. The polymer frame has an ergonomically-shaped rear grip strap and finger-groove front strap that provide a good grip, and the gun offers good control during shooting. The 10+1 pistol weighs just 19 ounces.

Wilson has not ignored developments in its 1911 line. A polymer-frame 9mm, the new KZ is offered in two styles—a full-size 17-round pistol weighing 32 ounces, and a compact 15-rounder that weighs 30 ounces.

The Carry Comp is a compact carry pistol with a 4 1/2-inch barrel, fitted with the company's ACCU-COMP. Wilson states the compensator reduces recoil and muzzle rise, while adding only minimal bulk.

The Sentinel is a 45-caliber compact carry pistol with 3 5/8-inch cone barrel. With a shortened grip frame that allows 6+1 capacity, Wilson feels this pistol reaches the maximum degree of compactness for complete reliability.

Postscript

Those of us who enjoy autoloading handguns should remember that some people just do not like our guns, and will do everything they can to deprive us of them. We have to win *every* political and legislative battle to retain our rights. The antigun forces need only to win once in a while to cause us to gradually lose our rights. Enjoy shooting, but stay informed and stay active.

SIXGUNS & OTHERS

by John Taffin

It was 50 years ago I fired a 44 Magnum for the first time. Fifty years is a long time even in light of the old cliché, "I wonder where all the time went?" However, it is something I'll never forget. We were teenagers, we shot together and we thought we had a lot of experience as we all had 1911s, 45 Colts and 357 Magnums—none of which prepared us for the 44 Magnum. Shell's Gun & Archery Farm had one of the earliest 4-inch Smith & Wesson 44s and, instead of selling it, Shell rented it out to all those who were brave enough to try it. We all did and we all lied about how bad it wasn't.

It took a while for the first 44 Magnums to show up on dealer shelves; the first one I saw for sale was not a Smith & Wesson but a Ruger Blackhawk. With its grip frame identical to the size and shape of the Colt Single Action Army (noted for rolling up in recoil), I figured the Blackhawk would kick less than the Smith & Wesson. I was wrong! I touched off that first round of those original 1450 fps+ factory loads and that Blackhawk rotated all right; it rolled backwards and didn't stop it until the hammer dug into my hand between thumb and forefinger, cutting out a good-sized hole. Obviously it would take

some time to learn to handle the recoil; it not only took time but experience and custom grips as well, but I eventually conquered both the Ruger and Smith & Wesson 44 Magnums.

Now both Ruger and Smith & Wesson are celebrating the 50th year of their original 44 Magnums by offering anniversary models. The original 44

Magnum Blackhawk, now known to collectors as the Flat-Top, disappeared from Ruger's catalog in 1963 and Smith & Wesson's 44 Magnum, which became the Model 29 in 1957 and then went through a long list of 'dash' models (29-1, 29-2, etc.), was pulled from production in 1999; in the latter case the Model 29 had varied

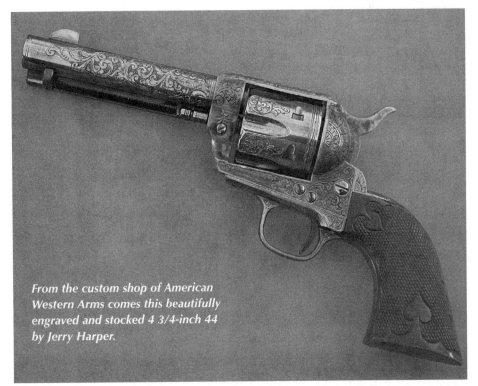

From the custom shop of American Western Arms comes this beautifully engraved and stocked 4 3/4-inch 44 by Jerry Harper.

considerably from the original by being round-butted and heavy underlug barreled before it was finally dropped.

Both Anniversary Models follow the same general configuration as their original 44 Magnum parents but are built to 21st century standards. In addition to these two Anniversary Models, we have a new cartridge from Freedom Arms; several new offerings from both Smith & Wesson and Taurus; Hi-Point and CZ-USA are now part of the six-gun scene; more 19th-century replicas have been added to the lines of several companies; six-guns announced last year are now starting to show up in quantity, and we have two examples of Mare's Legs built on rifle actions. So with that, let's begin our yearly trip —traveling alphabetically —through a long list of manufacturers and importers.

Consecutively numbered to the AWA 10 1/2-inch Ultimate is this 7 1/2-inch version, also with an octagon barrel and two cylinders in 44 Special and 44-40.

American Western Arms (AWA)

As with most inventions and discoveries the Internet can be used for good or ill. In the case of American Western Arms, the Internet was used in the worst possible way with someone posting erroneous information two years ago stating American Western Arms was going out of business. They definitely were not, however the damage was done and the posting almost became a self-fulfilling prophecy by causing many to cancel orders. The truth then and now is AWA is alive and well and producing first-class six-guns —plus a new surprise.

AWA's standard offering is The Ultimate, a beautifully blued single-action six-gun with a case-colored frame and hammer, one-piece walnut stocks and a coil mainspring. The Ultimate is offered in all the standard single-action chamberings such as, but not limited to, 45 Colt, 44-40, 44 Special and 38-40, with all the standard barrel lengths of 4-3/4, 5-1/2, and 7-1/2 inches. In addition the custom shop takes The Ultimate even further by offering custom stocks, engraving, octagon barrels, and dual cylinder versions. Octagon-barreled versions pictured have cylinders for both the 44 Special and 44-40 as well as custom mesquite stocks by Jim Martin. Martin has specially designed his version of single-action stocks to be a trifle longer to facilitate both point shooting and hip shooting by making the single action point even more naturally. AWA has a reputation for smooth actions and beautiful finishes; both are evident in standard production models as well as custom models. The finish on both of these custom 44s cannot be captured in a picture; brilliant case colors and deep blue.

The surprise this year from AWA is the Lightning Bolt, which is the handgun version of their Lightning slide- or pump-action rifle. The idea of the Lightning Bolt comes from the old TV series *Wanted Dead or Alive* in which Steve McQueen used a cut-down lever-action rifle. AWA has applied the idea to their pump rifle, and a slick little "handgun" it is. Yes, it is classified as a handgun by ATF, holds six rounds, has a blued finish with walnut buttstock and forearm, and a saddle ring on the right side that mates with a hook on a special holster. The saddle ring goes over the hook while the barrel snaps into a spring clip at the bottom of the holster —a fun gun to be sure.

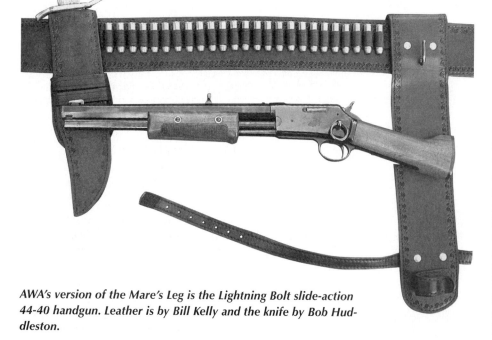

AWA's version of the Mare's Leg is the Lightning Bolt slide-action 44-40 handgun. Leather is by Bill Kelly and the knife by Bob Huddleston.

Beretta/Uberti

I predicted we would see some new offerings from Uberti when they were purchased by Beretta. The first of the new Ubertis to arrive a couple years ago under the Beretta banner was the Single Action Army-styled Stampede, complete with a very smooth action mated with a transfer bar safety, and a beautiful blue/case-colored finish. The very first guns had some problems with broken transfer bars, however that has been solved and the Stampede has proven to be both rugged and reliable. Our test version of the Beretta Stampede is a 45 Colt with a 7 1/2-inch barrel, blued with a case-colored frame. The deep bluing is carried out on a nicely polished barrel, cylinder, grip frame and ejector rod housing, while the mainframe is finished with brilliant case colors.

Sights are the traditional single-action style with a rear square notch mated with a nicely shaped front sight, again of the traditional style. The smooth trigger is wider than the traditional single-action style; although the action has a trigger-actuated transfer bar the trigger does not set as far forward in the trigger guard as one might expect. Metal-to-metal fit is excellent and the checkered black plastic grips are also well fitted to the grip frame. The grips also have a very good shape and feel to them. Although the Stampede has a transfer bar safety allowing it to be carried safely with six rounds, it also operates traditionally in that the loading gate is opened and the hammer placed on half-cock for loading and unloading. In fact, everything works so smoothly it feels like a traditional single-action six-gun. In addition to the Single Action Army version of the Stampede, Beretta is also offering the Bisley Model, complete with wide trigger and hammer and Bisley target-style grip frame.

The newest Beretta/Uberti six-gun is the Smith & Wesson Model #3-styled 45 Colt Laramie, a beautifully blued top-break, automatic-ejecting single-action revolver with a 6 1/2-inch barrel. The six-gun itself is blued, however the hammer, trigger guard and operating latch are all case-colored, and a nickel version is also available. To load or unload, the hammer is placed in the

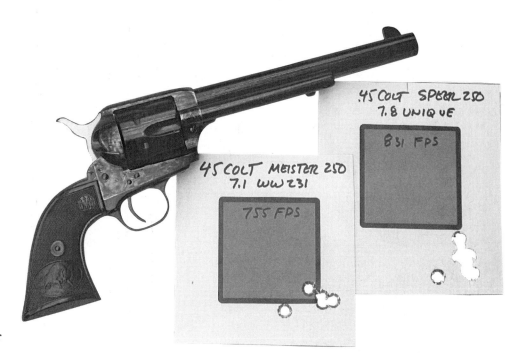

Beretta's 45 Colt Stampede not only looks and feels good, it also shoots very well.

first notch, the combination rear sight/top latch is lifted, allowing the barrel, top strap and cylinder to rotate 90 degrees downwards to automatically eject the cartridge cases. The cylinder is then reloaded, the barrel grasped and rotated upwards 90 degrees and the latch is carefully locked in place.

The Beretta/Uberti Laramie has a rebounding hammer and is safely carried with six rounds. The stocks found on the Laramie are highly functional and feel good, though a trifle thick for my hand; they are near duplicates of the original New Model #3 stocks. When the Schofield Model, the first replica of Smith & Wesson single-action six-guns, arrived nearly 15 years ago, I hoped for a New Model #3; with the arrival of the Model #3 Russian, my hopes went even higher. Now finally we have a version of the New Model #3 —if they would only chamber it in 44 Russian.

CZ/Dan Wesson

In the early days of long-range silhouetting, Dan Wesson revolvers were extremely popular for several reasons. They were offered with long barrels, interchangeable front sights, were incredibly accurate, and the manufacturer listened to the needs of shooters. First came the 357 Magnum DW revolver with a 10-inch heavy

barrel version; it was followed by the 44 Magnum and the 357 SuperMag. Dan Wesson himself started the company, and then his family lost it, got it back, and finally closed the doors. Dan Wesson Firearms was then purchased by Bob Serva, moved to New York, and, using all new machinery, Wesson Firearms began producing probably the best Dan Wesson revolvers ever.

Now Wesson Firearms is part of CZ-USA and, after concentrating on 1911s the past few years, Wesson is once again building revolvers, beginning with the 445 SuperMag. The 445 is basically a 44 Magnum case stretched to 1.6 inches. Muzzle velocities are substantially higher than the 44 Magnum and the 445 is at its best with 300-grain bullets. In addition to the long-barrel versions of the 445, CZ/Dan Wesson is also offering the Alaskan Guide Special with a barrel length of 4 inches, plus an integral muzzle brake.

Freedom Arms

In this report two years ago I showed three "mystery" cartridges. One of those was a belted 50-caliber six-gun round. The shroud of mystery has now been lifted and the 500 Wyoming Express can be announced. This latest six-gun cartridge was designed by Bob Baker and crew at Freedom Arms and is chambered in their Model 83

The Freedom Arms Model 83 chambered in 500 Wyoming Express carries easily in a Freedom Arms cross-draw holster.

This 7 1/2-inch Model 83 50AE from Freedom Arms has been fitted with a second cylinder chambered in 500 Wyoming Express. Scope is a LER Leupold on an SSK T'SOB base.

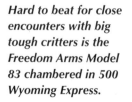

Hard to beat for close encounters with big tough critters is the Freedom Arms Model 83 chambered in 500 Wyoming Express.

five-shot stainless-steel revolver. The Freedom Arms revolver arrived in 1983 chambered in the now legendary 454 Casull, then came the 44 Magnum, 357 Magnum, 41 Magnum, 50 AE and even the 22 Long Rifle. Several years ago the 475 Linebaugh was chambered in a Freedom Arms revolver, and once this project was off and running well, Baker began taking a serious look at the 500 Linebaugh. To chamber such a cartridge in the Freedom Arms cylinder would necessitate cutting into the ratchet at the back of the cylinder as well as significantly reducing the rim diameter to fit the cylinder. To make a 500 work in the Model 83, Freedom Arms' cartridge headspaces on a belt rather than the cartridge rim.

Factory-chambered 500 WE revolvers are now available in three barrel lengths: 4 3/4-, 6- and 7 1/2-inch versions. For testing purposes, two revolvers were obtained from Freedom Arms (actually one new revolver and one retrofitted with a 500 WE cylinder). The brand-new Model 83 is my favorite 4 3/4-inch Perfect Packin' Pistol version. I returned my older 7 1/2-inch Model 83 chambered in 50 Action Express to have a new 500 Wyoming Express cylinder fitted. Both the 500 Wyoming Express and the 50 Action Express use the same 0.500-inch diameter bullets, not the 0.511-inch diameter of the original 500 Linebaugh.

The 500 Wyoming Express revolver is capable of major horsepower: 370-grain bullets at 1600 fps; 400-grain bullets at 1550 fps and 440-grain bullets at 1450 fps —through relatively light-weight revolvers. The 4 3/4-inch Model 83 chambered in 500 WE weighs less than three pounds, while the 7 1/2-inch version —even with scope, base and rings —comes in around four pounds. I soon found my upper limit of comfort to be 1200 fps with a 440-grain bullet in the 7 1/2-inch version. With the lighter 4 3/4-inch Model 83 I find 370-grain bullets at the same muzzle velocity about all I want to handle. If you can use it, the horsepower is definitely there; for everyday use, I prefer loads that are more enjoyable. A 440-grain bullet even at 900-1000 fps will handle most six-gunning chores quite well, reserving the really heavy loads for hunting big tough game.

Freedom Arms has a reputation

for producing the finest factory made single-action revolvers ever offered to six-gunners. They continue to offer the Model 83, in either Premier Grade or Field Grade, in all calibers mentioned except the 50 Action Express; they also offer the mid-sized Model 97 (Premier Grade only) in 22 LR/22 Magnum, 32 Magnum/32-20, 357 Magnum, 41 Magnum, 44 Special, and 45 Colt/45 ACP. They have the precision and strength of the proverbial Swiss bank vault.

Gary Reeder Custom Guns

Gary Reeder has long been known for performing custom conversions on single-action and double-action revolvers, as well as Thompson/Center Contenders, thus creating some of the most powerful handguns available. In addition, Reeder also belongs to that select group of connoisseurs who really appreciate the century-old 44 Special. Until the arrival of the 44 Magnum, the handloaded 44 Special was the most powerful revolver round to be had. The 44 Magnum almost pushed the 44 Special into oblivion —almost, but not quite. It took awhile, but shooters discovered the extra weight and power of a 44 Magnum was not always needed and that the 44 Special really was special, after all.

Reeder is offering three single-action packages made for the 44 Special. The Arizona Classic is built on Reeder's own frame, which he characterizes as "sort of a half breed between the 1st Generation Colt and the early 1st Generation Ruger Three-Screw. Its a small frame, not meant for the big magnums. Internal parts are early Three-Screw Ruger for strength, with coil springs and such." The Arizona Classic has a transfer bar safety and Reeder has made the necessary arrangements with Ruger to use the safety conversion Ruger retrofits in their early Three Screw Blackhawks. The Arizona Classic operates with the standard half-cock position to rotate the cylinder combined with this transfer bar safety. In addition to 44 Special, it is also available in 45 Colt and 357 Magnum.

A second offering from Reeder is the El Diablo, which is built on

Gary Reeder's rendition of the Elmer Keith #5SAA is this stainless-steel, octagon-barreled 44 Special with woolly mammoth stocks.

Gary Reeder's Border Special turns a Schofield Model into an easy-handling 3 1/2-inch six-gun, complete with engraving and ivory stocks.

an Old Model Ruger Blackhawk. Instead of Reeder rechambering the original cylinder, a new 44 Special cylinder is installed and fitted to a 3 1/2-inch premium barrel with a deep dish muzzle crown and special throating. The steel grip frame is the Reeder Gunfighter design, the barrel/cylinder gap is set tightly, an interchangeable gold bead front sight on a ramp is matched with a V-notch rear sight, and the entire package is finished in Black Chromex. Reeder also offers gold or silver bands on the barrel and cylinder, scroll engraving on mainframe and cylinder, with the barrel marked "El Diablo" and the frame "44 Special" —both in script. Grips are Corian ivory and the owner's name is added at no extra charge, resulting in a very attractive and easy-packing 44 Special. The same

basic six-gun with a standard barrel length is known as the Wichita Classic and is also available in 41 Special.

It was my good fortune two years ago to test the prototype #5 Improved, one of the most beautiful six-guns ever offered by Gary Reeder, based upon Elmer Keith's #5SAA from the 1920s. This Deluxe Grade all-steel six-gun is of high-polish stainless steel highlighted by bright blue screws, engraved, a deep-crowned octagonal barrel, chambered in 44 Special and stocked with elephant ivory. There is one major change of the Reeder #5 compared to the Keith #5. When Bill Grover built his Texas Longhorn Arms #5 he duplicated Keith's #5 grip frame; however, Keith had very small hands, which is evident in his grip frame. Reeder maintained the same basic grip frame and made it more useable by adding 3/8-inch to the length.

The prototype #5 Improved had to be sent back, and I fully intended to order a #5 44 Special later. Before I could act, my wife, Diamond Dot, got together with Gary Reeder and ordered a very special #5 Improved and I now have one of the first production #5 Improved 44 Specials. Barrel length is 5-1/2 inches, stocks are certificated 20,000-year old wooly mammoth ivory out of Russia with a heart-stopping creamy smooth texture; the high-polish stainless is set off with scroll engraving and blue screws, and the serial number —MPM66—was specially ordered as it has special significance to me; a very special Special to be passed on in my family for many generations.

Hi-Point/Charter Arms

Four decades ago Charter Arms had a better idea; an idea based on the old British Bulldog 44, but carried out in a much better fashion. The result was the 5-shot, double-action 44 Special Bulldog revolver. The Bulldog was available in both blue and stainless steel versions, and they have a very special part in my heart. Three times in my life I have had to rely on a six-gun in a serious situation. Fortunately the presence of the big-bore revolver was all that was needed and two of those times the six-gun I had with me was the Charter Arms 44 Bulldog.

Charter Arms is now owned by Hi-Point Firearms, which means we'll be seeing more production and added models. The original 44 Special Bulldog was replaced by the Bulldog Pug several years ago and is available in blue or stainless with a 2 1/2-inch barrel and rubber finger-groove grips. It has now been joined by the Mag Pug, a 2 inch-barreled 357 Magnum also in blue or stainless. Two 38 Specials are offered: the Undercover which was the first Charter Arms revolver ever offered, in a 2-inch blued version and available either with or without a hammer; and the Off Duty, the ultralight version of the Undercover.

Those who shoot 22s are not forgotten. Hi-Point/Charter Arms offers the Pathfinder, a 2-inch stainless steel six-shot revolver available in 22 or 22 Magnum; and the newest revolver from the purchase of Charter Arms by Hi-Point is the Dixie Derringer, a five-shot stainless steel mini-gun also offered in 22 or 22 Magnum. Once all the necessary arrangements are made when one company purchases another, we can expect Charter Arms revolvers to be much easier to locate.

JB Custom

The Mare's Leg is back. Two years ago JB Custom offered a limited number of Mare's Legs on Winchester Model 94 actions; they all sold out immediately. The Model 92 action is slightly smaller, much stronger and naturally much smoother in operation than the Model 94. It was the Model 92 that was used by Steve McQueen (Josh Randall) in the TV series *Wanted Dead or Alive*. The natural choice to produce the Mare's Legs was Rossi, a longtime producer of 1892 lever-action replicas dating back to the days when they were known as The Puma. Rossi is definitely a quality producer of lever-action rifles and has now become the only manufacturer of lever-action pistols featuring brand-new actions from their South American plant.

The Mare's Leg, as expected from Rossi, is a quality "handgun" beautifully finished and fitted with a nicely grained walnut forearm and abbreviated buttstock with the wood-to-metal fit in the 'excellent' category. Sights are the traditional elevation-adjustable buckhorn mated with a brass bead front sight in a dovetail, allowing for windage adjustment. It is currently offered in 45 Colt, 44-40, 44 Magnum and 357 Magnum; a replica of Josh Randall's belt and holster is also available in black or brown. The Mare's Leg holds six rounds of 45 Colt and can be safely carried with one in the chamber as it does have the top-mounted Rossi safety.

North American Arms (NAA)

NAA offers the world's smallest single-action revolvers, five-shooters, with the tiniest being chambered for 22 Short, and the same basic revolver with correspondingly longer cylinders in 22 Long Rifle, 22 Magnum, and also a 22 Magnum with an auxiliary cylinder chambered in 22 Long Rifle. When the 17 HMR was introduced several years ago, North American Arms added this tiny little cartridge as well as an even smaller version, the 17 Mach 2. In addition to cartridge-firing Mini-Revolvers, NAA also offers 22-caliber blackpowder versions requiring powder, round ball and percussion cap.

NAA has just recently introduced two new versions of their Mini-Revolvers, much easier to hold onto and shoot them quite accurately. The new guns are known as Boot Guns and are simply the basic Mini-Revolvers fitted with

Even with the Boot Grip, the NAA 22 Mini-Gun is still concealable.

a longer grip —a boot grip. As the name implies, they fit nicely into the top of the boot. NAA also offers ankle holsters, clip-on belt holsters, and even a flap holster for their Boot Guns.

Three versions of Boot Gun are offered: the standard 22 Long Rifle, 22 Magnum, and the 22 Magnum/ 22LR dual-cylinder model —all can be had with 1 1/8- or 1 5/8-inch barrels. The longer boot grip makes the NAA Mini-Revolver slightly harder to conceal but decidedly easier to shoot well, and the boot grip can also be fitted to the other Mini-Revolvers from NAA.   Although they are five-shot revolvers and most single actions are only safe when carried with the hammer down on an empty, these little Mini-Revolvers have a slot between chambers so they can be safely carried with five rounds when the hammer is resting in one of these little slots.

To load or unload the Mini-Revolver it is necessary to remove the cylinder. This is easy because the cylinder base pin is spring-loaded and, when pushed in at the front, the base pin is unlocked and can be removed, and the cylinder with it. Use the base pin to poke out the empty cases, reload the cylinder and replace. With CCI's MiniMax HP+V, the 22 Magnum version clocked out at 1094 fps while with the 22 LR Mini-Revolver, CCI's Mini-Mag +Vs registered 932 fps.

Smith & Wesson

To celebrate fifty years of the 44 Magnum S&W originally introduced, we now have the 50th Anniversary Model of the Smith & Wesson 44 Magnum. The Bright Blue finish almost rivals that of 50 years ago. The sights are a white outline rear and a red ramp front as on the original, and the barrel length is the original 6-1/2 inches —not the 6-inch length found on 29s and 629s since 1979. The hammer and trigger are the original checkered and serrated style; however, the hammer has a decidedly different look and has the best-looking profile I've ever seen on a Smith & Wesson six-gun.

The stocks are the same color, though a lighter shade, as the

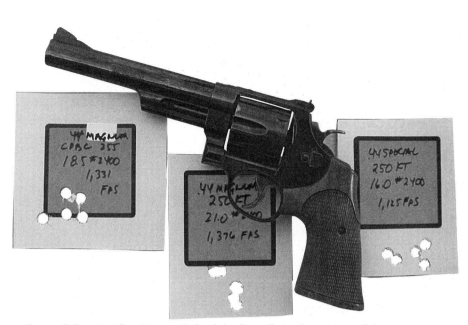

The Model 29 Smith & Wesson is back as the 50th Anniversary Model 44 Magnum.

Smith & Wesson's 50th Anniversary Model 29, here equipped with Herrett's Trooper Stocks from the 1950s, shoots well.

originals and also have the diamond around the grip screw holes; they also feel much better to me than the originals, being slightly thinner and tapered to the top of the grip frame. The 50th Anniversary Model 44 Magnum also has something we had not seen for quite a while: a square-butt grip frame identical in size and shape to that found on the original 44 Magnum, and original grips will fit. I replaced the factory stocks with a pair of Herrett's Troopers that are almost as old as the original S&W 44 Magnum.

The Anniversary Model comes in a lockable, padded plastic case. The sides of the barrel are marked as the original were, though in reverse. The left side of the barrel is marked "44 MAGNUM", while the right side carries "SMITH & WESSON". Since this is a 50th Anniversary Model, there is a gold

seal on the right side of the frame announcing "50th ANNIVERSARY, SMITH & WESSON" above the S&W logo with "1956-2006, 44 MAGNUM" found below the gold logo.

Last year Smith & Wesson brought back a revolver that had not been seen for nearly 40 years, a 4-inch, fixed-sight, six-shot, blue steel, big-bore six-gun. That was the Model 21-4 Thunder Ranch Special chambered in 44 Special, complete with an enclosed ejector rod. Except for the round butt and 21st century manufacturing requirements it is a dead-ringer for the 44 Special Model 1926 and the 38/44 Heavy Duty of 1930. Now new for this year we have the next version following along the same lines, the Model 22-4 chambered in 45 ACP/45 Auto Rim and as an even further improvement: it has a square butt just like the great guns of the first three-quarters of the 20th century.

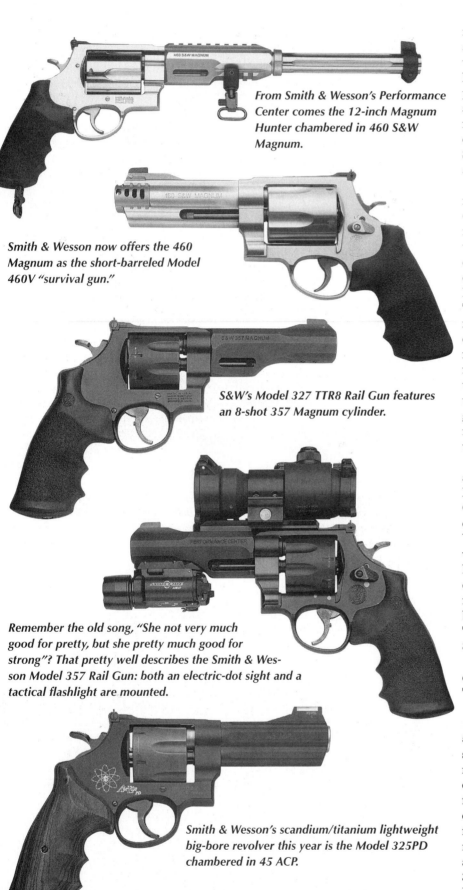

From Smith & Wesson's Performance Center comes the 12-inch Magnum Hunter chambered in 460 S&W Magnum.

Smith & Wesson now offers the 460 Magnum as the short-barreled Model 460V "survival gun."

S&W's Model 327 TTR8 Rail Gun features an 8-shot 357 Magnum cylinder.

Remember the old song, "She not very much good for pretty, but she pretty much good for strong"? That pretty well describes the Smith & Wesson Model 357 Rail Gun: both an electric-dot sight and a tactical flashlight are mounted.

Smith & Wesson's scandium/titanium lightweight big-bore revolver this year is the Model 325PD chambered in 45 ACP.

The fixed sights on both of these new big-bore six-guns consist of a square notch rear sight cut into the top of the frame in front of the hammer, matched with a half-moon pinned-in front sight. The 44 Special and 45 ACP/Auto Rim also have frame-mounted firing pins, instead of the hammer-mounted firing pin Smith & Wesson used in their double-action revolvers for about 100 years.

Last year Smith & Wesson introduced the Model 460XVR (Xtreme Velocity Revolver) chambered in 460 S&W Magnum, and just as they did with their 500 S&W Magnum chambered Model 500, they now offer a shorter-barreled version the Model 460V with a 5-inch barrel. This version has an interchangeable muzzle compensator, and as on the original Model 460, Sorbothane finger-groove rubber grips, and a five-shot cylinder capable of handling the 460 S&W, the 454 Casull and the 45 Colt. All Model 460s feature gain-twist rifling, which means the rate of twist becomes faster towards the muzzle end of the barrel.

Two other versions of the 460XVR are offered by the Smith & Wesson Performance Center. The 10 1/2-inch Compensated Hunter has a 360-degree muzzle brake, an integral Weaver scope base and sling swivels, while the 12-inch Magnum Hunter has integral Picatinny-style bases on both the top and bottom of the fluted barrel, sling swivels and a bipod adapter at the end of the barrel. These two special Model 460s weigh 82-1/2 and 80 ounces, respectively.

Also from the Performance Center comes the Model 327 TRR8 Rail Gun. This 8-shot 357 Magnum features a scandium frame, steel cylinder, rubber finger groove grips and a 5-inch shrouded steel barrel. It is set up for full-moon clips and has removable Picatinny-style rails both on the top and bottom of the barrel for the installation of a full range of optical or laser sights, and tactical flashlights. With both a red-dot scope mounted on the top of the barrel and a tactical flashlight below, the Model 327 TRR8 is not the prettiest revolver I've ever seen —but it would look awfully good in a serious situation.

Three years ago Smith & Wesson

The slim-barreled stainless-steel Mountain Gun from S&W this year is the Model 625 chambered in 45 Colt.

For the handgun hunter S&W offers the 5-inch Model 629CT 44 Magnum fitted with Crimson Trace Lasergrips.

To celebrate the 50th Anniversary of the 44 Magnum, Ruger offers the 6 1/2-inch "Flat-Top."

introduced the 4-inch Model 329PD, a scandium-framed, titanium-cylindered, 26-ounce, 6-shot 44 Magnum. Recoil with full-house loads is brutal, but it packs oh, so easy. Now the same basic revolver is offered as the Model 325PD, and as anyone with working knowledge of Smith & Wesson revolvers will know, the model number says 45-caliber; in this case 45 ACP, which means it also accepts 45 Auto Rim loads. This gives the six-gunner a very easy-to-carry, lightweight, big-bore revolver without excess recoil. With so many excellent 45 ACP offerings available for defensive use, this revolver would be an excellent choice for the hiker, outdoorsman or fisherman —and an excellent choice for either open carry or CCW use.

Smith & Wesson also offers a second 45 revolver this year: the stainless steel Model 625 Mountain Gun now chambered in 45 Colt. The Mountain Gun concept consists of a 4-inch tapered barrel as found on such old favorites as the original 357 Magnum, the Highway Patrolman and the 1950 Target. Both the 325PD and 625 Mountain Guns are built on the Smith & Wesson

N-frame, with adjustable sights and a round-butt grip frame.

Smith & Wesson has offered several models with Crimson Trace Lasergrips for defensive use, and has now expanded this concept to the hunting field with the Model 629CT. The stainless steel 6-shot N-frame

Taffin shooting the Smith & Wesson 50th Anniversary Model 29.

44 Magnum has a heavy-underlug 5-inch barrel with the standard sights consisting of an adjustable rear sight and a red-ramp front sight. Sometimes hunting requires very fast target acquisition, so the Model 629CT comes complete with a Crimson Trace Lasergrip. Anyone who has ever hunted dangerous game up close —such as wild pigs —knows how fast the action can be and a red dot projected on the shoulder of a big mean hog can be very comforting.

SSK Industries: J.D.

Jones as SSK has been offering custom-barreled T/C Contenders for three decades. Two of his very early designs are still the number-one sellers as custom barrels for the Contender. One is the 6.5 JDJ on the 225 Winchester case, and the other the 375 JDJ on a necked-down 444 Marlin. The 375 JDJ uses a 220-grain bullet for deer-sized game and a 270/300-grain bullet for the big stuff; while the 6.5 JDJ will take care of everything and anything in-between. The 375 is now a standard chambering by Thompson/Center, and factory ammunition is also available. In addition to the 6.5 JDJ, there are others: the 226, 270 and 7mm JDJs, as well as the 309,

8mm, 338 #2 and 416 —JDJs all, plus the 375 JDJ on the 444 Marlin. Currently SSK chambers over 200 cartridges in Contender barrels.

By going to the Thompson/Center Encore, SSK is able to offer more powerful cartridges such the 454 Casull, 500 S&W, 460 S&W, 300 Winchester Magnum, 338 Winchester Magnum, and 375 H&H as well as the 280, 30, 338, 35, 375 and 416 JDJs on the 30-06 case. Currently SSK has more than 300 reamers in stock for custom Encore barrels.

SSK also offers the best available muzzlebrake, the Arrestor Muzzle Brake, and for any heavy-recoiling handgun there is simply no better scope mount base than his T'SOB. This is the only scope mount base I will recommend for really hard-kicking handguns. When installed properly and used with three or four scope rings, the scope will stay in place.

Sturm, Ruger

Ruger's first centerfire single action, the 357 Magnum Blackhawk, now known to collectors as the Flat-Top, arrived in 1955 and only lasted until it was "improved" into what is now known as the Old Model Blackhawk. Last year Ruger offered the 50th Anniversary Model of the original, and per the original —and unlike current Ruger Blackhawks —the Anniversary Model had a true Flat-Top frame the same size as the original with no protective ears around the rear sight, plus the original grip frame size, shape, and black rubber grips complete with the black eagle medallion. The grips are shaped perfectly for my hand and feel exceptionally good. As on the original, the barrel length is 4-5/8 inches and the rear sight is Micro-style. Unlike the original, the grip frame is steel and the action is the standard Ruger New Model style, complete with transfer bar safety.

The Anniversary Model feels very good in the hand, has the balance of the original, and shoots as well as — in many cases better than —the 1950s 357 Flat-Top. It is a beautiful well-made six-gun and I have asked Ruger to not only keep it in the line as a standard offering, but also to chamber it in the 44 Special and 357 Magnum.

This year is the 50th anniversary of Ruger's first 44 Magnum and that original Ruger 44 Magnum, the Flat-Top Blackhawk, is now offered as this year's Anniversary Model. The 44 Magnum Blackhawk was slightly larger than the 357 Magnum Blackhawk that preceded it which was a mite small in cylinder and frame —both were enlarged to house the 44 Magnum in 1956.

Just as with the 50th anniversary 357, this 44 Magnum is in the original barrel length (6-1/2 inches), carries a Micro rear sight on a flat-top frame, plus a ramp front sight and is built on the New Model action. The top of the barrel as on the 357 version has gold-filled lettering identifying this as a special anniversary model. The grip frame is steel and the grips, instead of the walnut found on most of the Flat-Top Blackhawks, is the checkered black rubber with black eagle insert found on the very first run of the 44 Blackhawks. Just before Skeeter Skelton died in 1988, Ruger was working on a custom 44 Blackhawk for him using the New Model action. We can consider that the prototype of the 50th Anniversary Model. I hope Ruger keeps the Anniversary Model 44 Magnum in the line after the anniversary run is over.

Ruger has not announced any other new handguns this year but rather continues to concentrate on providing a large lineup chambered in everything from 17 HMR to 454 Casull and 480 Ruger. The latter chamberings are found in the Super Redhawk Alaskan, which was designed to be an easy-to-pack survival six-gun. On the Super Redhawk Alaskan, the end of the barrel is flush with the frame, with a deep inverted muzzle crown, and a serrated sloping-forward ramp front sight has been added to the flat-topped frame matched with a standard white outline rear sight adjustable for windage and elevation. To handle the heavy loads used in such a short-barreled six-gun, the Alaskan comes with Hogue's rubber cushioned, finger-grooved Tamer Monogrip. As one might expect, recoil is quite heavy. However, thanks to the Hogue Tamer grips, it does not reach the uncontrollable level.

Last year Ruger also introduced the New Vaquero, replacing the standard Vaquero. The new version is basically the same size as the Colt

Ruger's big-bore survival gun is the Super Redhawk Alaskan chambered in 480 Ruger and, as shown, 454 Casull.

Single Action Army and has already become quite popular with both cowboy action shooters and anyone else desiring a sturdy and reliable single-action six-gun. The New Vaquero is offered in both blue and stainless, 357 Magnum and 45 Colt, and in barrel lengths of 4-5/8 and 5-1/2 inches for both calibers, as well as 7-1/2 inches for the 45 Colt. For years several reloading manuals had a special 45 Colt section with heavy loads marked for Ruger Blackhawk only. The same loads could be used in the original Vaquero which was built on the same frame size as the 45 Colt Blackhawk. These loads are NOT to be used in the 45 Colt New Vaquero because it has a smaller cylinder and frame than the Blackhawk.

Ruger continues to offer four of the most popular hunting six-guns: the Super Blackhawk, the Hunter Model, and the Redhawk in 44 Magnum as well as the Super Redhawk chambered in 44 Magnum, 454 Casull and 480 Ruger.

Taurus

As usual Taurus has a large lineup of revolvers for this year. The single-action Gaucho is now readily available in several versions. Four finishes are offered: blue steel, blue steel with a case-hardened frame, polished stainless steel and matte stainless steel. Calibers are 45 Colt, 357 Magnum and now 44-40. The first three traditional standard barrel lengths: 4-3/4, 5-1/2 and 7-1/2 inches, have been joined by a 12-inch "Buntline Special." The Gaucho is basically the same size as the Colt Single Action Army, and replicas thereof. It has a transfer bar safety, making it safe to carry fully loaded with six rounds.

It did not take long for Taurus to chamber their revolvers in both 500 and 460 S&W Magnums. This year they have gone both directions, offering a 10-inch and a 2 1/2-inch version in both calibers. All wear the soft rubber finger-groove grip that goes a long way to tame felt recoil. These are serious six-guns for serious purposes.

Another offering from Taurus with both a serious and a fun purpose is the five-shot .410/45 Colt. The cylinder is long enough to accept both .410

The Taurus Gaucho is now available as a 7 1/2-inch stainless-steel version, shown here in 44-40.

Now this one looks like fun! A Taurus 3-inch barreled .410/45 Colt.

shotshell loads and 45 Colt cartridges. This Model 4410 is offered with both 3- and 6-inch barrels. It looks like a fun six-gun for clay pigeons or tin cans, and could also serve for dispatching snakes and varmints up close.

Taurus's medium-frame Tracker models are very popular in several calibers and this year's version is a five-shot 10mm-chambered revolver with a 4-inch ported barrel and Ribber grips, as well as a 6-inch vent-ribbed barreled option with finger-groove rubber grips. Both models have adjustable sights and Taurus now provides a plastic snap-on sight protector for the rear sight of all of their revolvers. Taurus also offers the Tracker in a five-shot 44 Magnum; the 44 Magnum chambering is also found in the 444 UltraLite with an alloy frame and titanium cylinder with either 2 1/4- or 4-inch barrel lengths.

One of Taurus's most popular offering is the Raging Bull, offered in 44 and 41 Magnum with six-shot cylinders, 454 with a five-shot cylinder and both the 460 and 500 S&W Magnums (*mentioned above*) with a longer five-shot cylinder and a longer frame.

Thompson/Center

For more than three decades, Thompson/Center has dominated the single-shot market for both silhouette shooters and handguns hunters. The original Contender was chambered in 38 Special and 22RF; however, it did not take long to discover the real potential of the Contender pistol. Basically stated, the Contender is a single-shot, break-open action pistol built to accept interchangeable barrels in a wide variety of chamberings, including both rimfire and centerfire cartridges, made possible by a rotating firing pin in the frame.

The original Contender has been replaced by the G2, which opens much easier and is available in blue with walnut grips and forearm, weighs approximately 3-3/4 pounds, and is offered in both 12- and 14-inch versions. Current factory chamberings include 17 HMR, 17 Mach II, 22 Long Rifle Match, 22 Hornet, 204 Ruger, 223 Remington, 6.8 Remington, 7-30 Waters, 30-30 Winchester, 357 Magnum, 375 JDJ, 44 Magnum and 45-70.

As strong as it is, the Contender is basically limited to those same cartridges found in lever-action rifles; the answer for higher pressure bolt-action rifle cartridges is the Thompson/Center Encore. The Encore is the same basic break-open, single-action pistol as the Contender, but is built for greater strength and weighs nearly one pound more. The Encore is offered in both 12- and 15-inch models, blued with walnut grip and forearm or stainless steel with rubber grip and forearm. Both the Contender and Encore are equipped

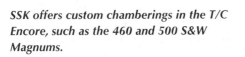

SSK offers custom chamberings in the T/C Encore, such as the 460 and 500 S&W Magnums.

with an adjustable rear sight and ramp front sight, triggers adjustable for over-travel, and drilled and tapped for scope mount bases. The Encore is factory chambered in 204 Ruger, 22-250, 223, 243 Winchester, 6.8 Remington, 7-08, 25-06, .270 Winchester, 30-06, 308 Winchester, 375 JDJ, 44 Magnum, 45-70, and 460 and 500 S&W Magnums. My favorite chamberings are the 22-250, 7-08, 308, and 500 Magnum. With these cartridges I can handle anything in any hunting situation.

United States Firearms (USFA)

"They don't make them like they used to!" Those of us who have been around long enough have said this many times when talking about cars, firearms —just about anything factory-produced. Times have changed, and production methods have changed However, there is one company still making them like they used to and that company is United State Firearms. USFA specializes in single-action six-guns ... and not just any single actions, but those built like they were from the 1870s up to the eve of World War II. In fact, USFA even started building revolvers

under the old Blue Dome in Hartford, Connecticut. They have now moved into a thoroughly modern factory and the Blue Dome serves as office space.

The standard offering from USFA is the Single Action which is available in the same chamberings as in the "good old days" —the 45 Colt, 44-40, 44 Special, 44 Russian, 41 Long Colt, 38-40 and 32-20.

The first thing one notices about the USFA Single Action is the beautiful finish. The main frame and hammer are beautifully case-colored in what is described as Armory Bone Case, while the balance of the six-gun is finished in a deep, dark Dome

Blue. Grips furnished as standard are checkered hard rubber with a "US" molded into the top part of the grip. Normally, I prefer to fit favored single-action six-guns with custom grips made of ivory, stag or some exotic wood. However, in the case of USFA Single Action Army six-guns, the grips are so perfectly fitted to the frame and feel so good that I am very hesitant to change them. If one looks at the grips on most single-action six-guns the fitting leaves a lot to be desired; not so here. These grips have been fitted to the grip frame on a factory-built revolver as carefully as custom grips by a master gripmaker.

The Single Action is available with barrel lengths of 4-3/4, 5-1/2, and 7-1/2 inches, and is joined by several other models such as the matte-blue finish Rodeo, the high-polish Dome Blued Cowboy and the antique patina-finished Gunslinger. Just as in the 1890s, one can also have a Flat-Top Target Single Action or a Bisley Model. Special versions include the Omnipotent with a grip frame reminiscent of the 1878 Double Action, the Snub Nose having the same grip frame but with a 2-, 3- or 4-inch barrel, and the Sheriff's Model offered in several barrel lengths without an ejector rod assembly. The Sheriff's Model is now up and running, and our version is a 2 1/2-inch nickel-plated 45 Colt.

United States Firearms Single Actions are not what you would call inexpensive. These revolvers are not assembly

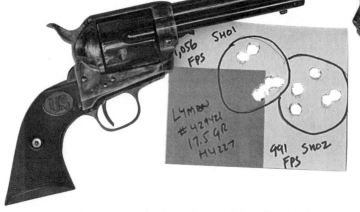

USFA's Single Action is a high-quality, traditionally-styled six-gun which shoots very well.

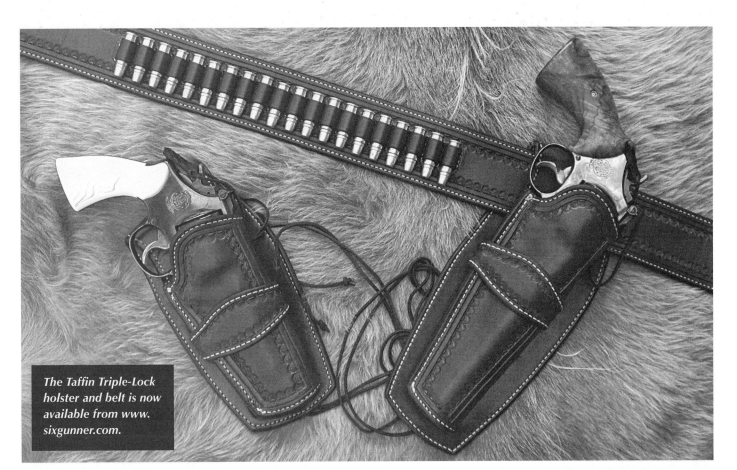

line mass-produced, and it is obvious the gunsmiths at United States Firearms are a whole lot more than parts assemblers. It takes a lot of expensive hand-fitting to produce a single-action six-gun of this quality. This six-gunner, and a lot of others think they are worth it.

In addition to their standard line of single-action six-guns, USFA also has a complete custom shop offering many features found more than a century ago. For example, there is the famous 1902 Sears Gun duplicated in 45 Colt with a 4 3/4-inch barrel, full coverage engraving and full blue with gold accents and pearl grips. Then, the equally famous —if not more so —Theodore Roosevelt's 7 1/2-inch 44-40 Frontier Six Shooter with full engraving, silver- and gold-plated and ivory grips carved with TR's initials. Next, the Frontier Six-Shooter: another 7 1/2-inch 44-40 with full "C" engraving and scrimshawed pearl grips.

On any of their single-action six-guns, USFA offers a choice of A, B, C, or D engraving as well as a complete line of custom grips in ivory, stag, pearl, and fancy walnut.

When I was recently contacted by Joel Cosby of www.six-gunner.com to design a holster for marketing at his website, I pulled out my cardboard patterns from the 1960s and sent them off. The result is the Taffin Triple-Lock holster and matching 2 1/2-inch cartridge belt, fully lined with suede leather to help keep it from slipping while being worn, and the holsters are also fully lined with smooth leather. Both belt and holster are crafted of premium leather with decorative border stamping; and the holster gets its name from the fact the body proper is locked to the back flap in three places, a wraparound loop in the middle, tie-down thong at the bottom and —most importantly —two Chicago screws that allow the holster to be tightly fitted to the belt. Each holster is fitted with a hammer thong with an easy-to-grasp release. By the way, any money I might make from the sale of this rig goes directly to the NRA. Check the web site for more details on availability for different revolvers.

Thanks to the efforts of Cimarron, EMF, Navy Arms and Taylor's & Co. it is now possible to shoot and enjoy

quality replicas of almost every single-action six-gun available during the last three decades of the 19th century, including the Colt Richards Mason, Open-Top, Single Action Army and Bisley Model; the Remington 1875 and 1890 and the S&W Schofield and Model #3 Russian. This year the newest offerings from these importers are rifles —the 1876 Winchester and 1892 Takedown, as well as replicas of the Colt Lightning pump-action rifle. Colt is still producing only one revolver, the Single Action Army in 45 Colt, 44-40, 38-40, 357 Magnum, and 32-20. Rumors continue about their future; we will just have to wait and see what transpires.

I expect to spend another great six-gunning year shooting the 50th Anniversary 44 Magnum Models from Ruger and Smith & Wesson, a pair of 44 Specials from USFA, several custom 44s on Ruger Old Models, and a pair of AWA's octagon-barreled Ultimates set up with two cylinders for both 44 Special and 44 Magnum. All of this will just work in fine with my latest project —a book titled *44 Six-guns, Leverguns, Cartridges, and Loads*. May you have as much fun as I do.

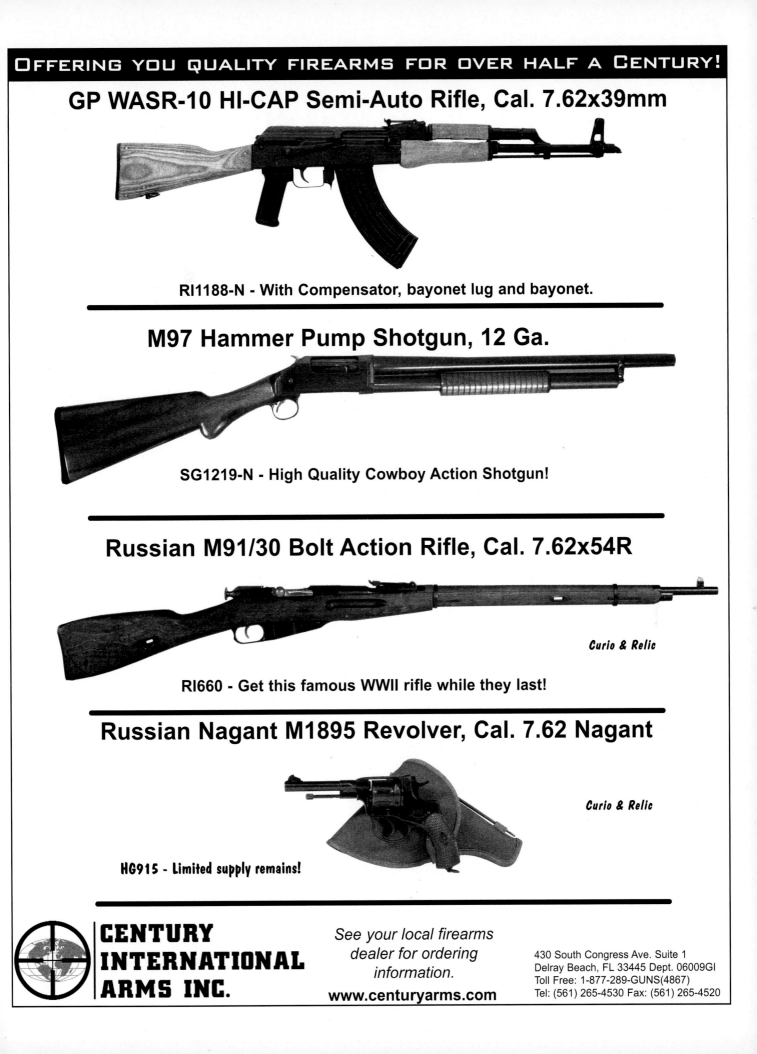

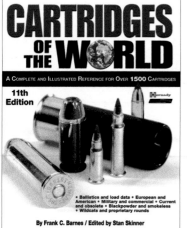
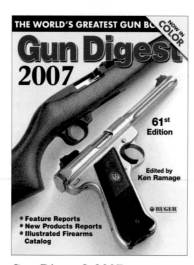

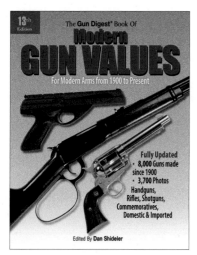
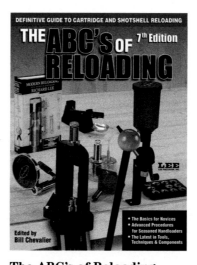

RIFLES TODAY:

RIFLE REVIEW

by Layne Simpson

Gun Digest Tidbits From The Past

How far back does your collection of Gun Digest go? I have all the years back to 1963 (17th Edition) but I am missing several before that. I have edition numbers 2, 5, 7, 8, 12, 13, 14, and 15 but am missing the eight remaining editions.

Gun Digest has long had a reputation for accuracy but a glitch or two has managed to escape the editor's red pen through the years. Page 15 of the 2nd Edition is always worth a chuckle. The story on big-game rifles was written by Elmer Keith but the lead photo has Jack O'Connor sitting on a rock with his trusty 270 resting across his lap. Considering how those two felt about each other, you can bet that mix-up went over like a foreign object in the Governor's punch bowl.

Firearms manufacturers were still gearing down from war production so there were no prices in that issue but a few years later the Model 94 Winchester was $62.45 and a box of 30-30s went for $2.50. Price of the standard-grade Model 94 had increased to about $450 when it was dropped from production during early 2006 and a box of cartridges was just over 12 bucks. An automobile that sold in the neighborhood of $1000 back then will set you back at least 30 times that today. A gallon of gas now costs about 30 times what it did back then. Who

says today's rifles are not bargains?

Under the "so what's new?" category, turn to page 172 of the 1992 edition and read what I had to say under the Precision Imports heading about the Mauser Model 210 rifle chambered for a prototype cartridge under development at Federal. It was the 22 WMR case necked down to 17-caliber and they called it the 17 FMR. Sound familiar?

Now let us take a look at what actually is new and exciting for 2006.

Anschutz

In 1856 Julius Gottfried Anschutz founded the company to manufacture shotguns and pocket pistols and five generations later Jochen Anschutz is running the company that builds what many consider to be the most consistently accurate 22 rimfire rifles in the world. Other chambering options include 17 Mach 2, 17 HMR and 22 Hornet. New additions to the rifle lineup are Classic Beavertail variants of the Model 1416 in 22 Long Rifle, Model 1502 in 17 Mach 2 and Model 1517 in 17 HMR. As you might expect, the shape of the stock makes this one ideal for shooting over a sandbag. The heavy barrel is 23 inches long and the rifle weighs just over six pounds.

Benelli USA

These days, Benelli is about much more than shotguns. Possibilities for the R1 autoloading centerfire

rifle keep growing in number with a ComforTech recoil-dampening stock being the latest addition. Made of a black synthetic material (as is the forearm) the buttstock is easily adjusted for lengths of pull ranging from 13-1/2 inches to 14-3/8 inches by choosing among interchangeable, quick-switch recoil pad of three different thicknesses. Three gel-pad style inserts allow comb height to be varied and protect the cheek from recoil as well. Also available with its original wood stock, the R1 is offered in 270 WSM, 308 Winchester, 300 Winchester Magnum, 30-06 and 300 WSM.

Benelli USA is also the importer of Uberti-manufactured reproductions of various famous American firearms, including the Model 1860 Henry in 44-40 and 45 Colt; the Winchester 1886 Yellowboy in those two chamberings plus 38 Special; the Winchester 1873 in 357 Magnum, 44-40 and 45 Colt; the 1874 Sharps and Trapdoor Springfield in 45-70 Government; the Winchester 1885 High Wall in 45-70, 45-90 and 45-120 and the Colt Lightning in 357 Magnum and 45 Colt. From what I have seen, quality is at least as good as in the originals.

Beretta USA

Everybody who is anybody (and a few who are not) is now offering a reproduction of the Colt Lightning pump gun and one of the best I have examined is imported by Beretta USA.

Called the Gold Rush, it is available in carbine and rifle versions in 38 Special and 45 Colt. Everything––including stock finish, receiver case-coloring and barrel bluing––on the rifle I examined was very nice. In fact, if I were to come down with a burning desire to trade my LeMond Crox de Fer for a four-legged mount, dress up like a cowpoke and arm myself with an affordable Colt Lightning, this is the one I would ride off into the sunset with.

Browning

One of the highlights for me during 2005 was a fabulous elk hunt in southern New Mexico and the rifle and bullet I used absolutely won my heart. I already own far more rifles than I actually need and seldom even think about adding another to my battery but the Browning A-Bolt Mountain Ti is surely tempting. As you have probably already guessed, its receiver is titanium and its stock is synthetic. Chambered to 300 WSM, the one I bumped off an elk with weighs exactly 7-1/2 pounds with three cartridges, a Zeiss 3-9X scope and a lightweight nylon carrying sling on board.

The

ammo I used was the new Supreme Elite loading with the equally new 180-grain XP3 bullet. Back home, prior to the hunt, I checked the 100-yard accuracy of that load along with Winchester's four other 180-grain loadings of the 300 WSM and not a single one exceeded two inches for three-shot averages; depending on the load, muzzle velocity averaged from 2879 to 2931 fps. Other chambering options for the A-Bolt Mountain Ti are 243 Winchester, 7mm-08, 308 Winchester, 270 Winchester, 270 WSM, 7mm WSM and 325 WSM.

Remember the Browning T-Bolt of the 1970s? Mine was the T-2 deluxe version with cut checkering on its stock and back then it sold for $97.50 or $25 more than the T-1 version. The latter actually sold for about two bucks less than the Remington Model 591 and that made it a genuine bargain in anybody's book. At the time, the T-Bolt was the most accurate rifle in 22 rimfire I had ever fired; the one I foolishly traded away would consistently average less than half an inch for five shots at 50 yards with Winchester Super Match ammo.

After several decades of absence, the T-Bolt is back and while it differs from the original in several ways, its straight-pull bolt locks up the same. The big difference is in the double helix magazine of the new rifle. It is a 10-round rotary magazine but since it has a slimmer profile than the rotary magazine designed by Ruger, it allows the midsection of the rifle to be slimmer. Very nice rifle.

Ed Brown Products

All of Ed Brown's rifles are now built around his new Model 704 action with controlled cartridge feeding; his old push-feed action is no longer being produced. Seven different rifle variations are available, five for big-game hunting and varmint shooting (Savannah, Damara, Bushveld, Express and Compact Varmint) and two (Marine and Tactical) for everything else. Chambering options range from 223 Remington to 458 Lott with (oddly enough) not a single one of the super-short magnums included in the list. On the other hand, the complete line of Remington Ultra Mags from 7mm to 375 are offered. Standard barrel length for all calibers is 24 inches with the exceptions of 26 inches for the Tactical rifle and 22 inches for the Compact Varmint. The latter rifle, by the way, is available in 17 Remington, 204 Ruger, 223 Remington, 22-250, 243 Winchester, 6mm Remington, 260 Remington and 6.5-284 Norma.

Chipmunk Rifle Company

Some little girls love to shoot as much as some little boys and this is why Chipmunk introduced a pink laminated stock last year. It obviously was not pink enough to suit plinkers who wear pretty dresses and long curls and you really should wear sunshades when looking at this year's version. It's really cute and that's important to cute little girls. For the benefit of those who don't already know I will

At the heart of Brown's new M-704 controlled-feed action is this bolt with integral spring-loaded extractor.

Ed Brown's Compact Varmint rifle packs benchrest features into a handy, accurate 8-3/4 pounds.

New for 2006 is The Express, built on Brown's new M-704 controlled-feed bolt action. Chamberings include 375 H&H, 416 Remington Magnum and 458 Lott.

mention that the Chipmunk rifle is a single-shot and to make it as safe as possible in little hands, the firing pin has to be manually cocked after a round is chambered. Other features include a rebounding firing pin and a fully adjustable aperture-style rear sight. A scope mounting base is included with rifles wearing bull barrels. The barrel is 16 inches long and nominal rifle weights are 2-1/2 pounds for the standard barrel and 3-1/2 pounds for the bull barrel. Overall length is 30 inches. The Chipmunk is available in stainless or blued steel and with several stock options.

Cimarron Firearms

Lots of interesting rifles from this company for 2006. For starters there are reproductions of the Winchester Model 1892 in both solid-frame and takedown styles. Caliber options are 357 Magnum, 44-40 and 45 Colt. Magazine capacities are 12 rounds for the 24-inch barrel and 10 rounds for the 20-inch barrel. Then we have the Model 1885 Low Wall (thick-side version) with 30-inch octagon barrel in 22 LR, 22 Hornet, 30-30, 32-20, 32-40, 357 Magnum, 44-40 or 44 Magnum. Moving on to fans of the old Colt slide-action rifle, the Lightning is available in three variations, carbine in 32-20 with 20-inch barrel, sporting rifle with 24- or 26-inch round barrel in 38-40 and the same rifle with octagon barrel in 44-40. Moving back to single-shots, there is the "Adobe Walls" reproduction of the Remington Block in 45-70, a rifle that just about anybody including Billy Dixon would probably be proud to own. Among other nice things it has a 30-inch octagon barrel, Creedmore-style sights, case-colored receiver and hand-checkered walnut stock with German silver nose cap. Equally interesting is the Spencer Repeating Rifle in 56-50.

Cooper Arms

Dan Cooper says orders for his new repeating rifle have already far exceeded his expectations and shipment should commence sometime during late 2006. From what I have seen, it will be worth the wait. Mine will be in 25-06 and I promise to tell you all about it next time we meet.

My new Cooper repeating rifle will be in 25-06 and it will look a lot like this one.

CZ-USA

Chambered to 300 Winchester Magnum, the new Model 550 bolt gun comes with a minute-of-angle accuracy guarantee. On top of that, it has a very nice walnut stock replete with cut checkering. If that's not enough, the craftsmen in CZ's new custom shop will build one your way with the list of options including a McMillan synthetic stock. As centerfire rifles go, my favorite CZ is the custom grade Safari Classic with its fancy walnut stock, express-style rear sight and barrel-mounted front carrying sling swivel post. My pick would be 404 Jeffery but it is also available in 450 Rigby and 505 Gibbs.

GAMO

I don't often include air guns in this report but the new Viper Express from GAMO is so interesting I could not resist. Of spring piston design, it is both a shotgun and a rifle. When loaded with a reusable "shotshell" containing No. 9 lead shot, it shoots a 12-inch pattern at 10 yards, making it just the ticket for ridding the barn of rats and thinning out the gophers and starlings in your vegetable garden. Slide an adaptor into its chamber and it will fire a 22-caliber lead pellet at 850 fps. Very interesting. Fastest airgun in the GAMO lineup is the 17-caliber Viper with a muzzle velocity of 1200 fps. For several years now I have been using the 17-caliber Stutezen model (1150 fps) to control the gray squirrel population around my home and it sits ready and waiting in the corner beside my desk as I write this.

Just as interesting as the airguns is the new MTS 1000 Moving Target System. Set up the six-foot target, drop in the motorized carriage and a steel deer silhouette travels back and forth nonstop until you run out of pellets and switch it off. Designed for backyard shooting, it can be set at various distances to simulate shooting an actual deer-size target at various ranges. For example, when the target is 10 yards away, it simulates shots at a real running deer at about 90 yards. What fun!

Kimber

If any company builds a more handsome big-game rifle than Kimber, I have not discovered it and the new Model 8400 Classic is more of the same. Among other nice things, it has a lightly figured walnut stock with hand-rubbed finish and cut checkering, a Pachmayr Decelerator pad, steel grip cap and matte-finished metal. The rifle also has a Model 70-type three-position safety and hinged floorplate with its release tab located inside the trigger guard. Barrel lengths and calibers are 24 inches in 25-06, 270 Winchester and 30-06 Springfield and 26 inches in 300 Winchester Magnum and 338 Winchester Magnum. Nominal weights are 7-1/4 pounds for the magnums and seven pounds for the standards.

The Kimber family of 22 rimfire rifles keeps growing as well. I recently shot a couple of Pro Varmint rifles in 22 Long Rifle and 17 Mach 2 and both would consistently keep five bullets inside half an inch at 50 yards.

Like all Kimber rimfires, those two have a three-position, Model 70-style safety, a free-floated, match-grade barrel replete with target-dimension chamber and hand-lapped bore.

Lapua

This Finnish company does not build rifles but it does make some of the world's best ammunition and I found out some of the things they do to make it that way during a recent visit to the factory. I kicked things off with a bang by heading to the woods where I took a moose with a Sako rifle in one of my favorite chamberings, 9.3x62mm Mauser. It was the second moose I have taken in Finland with that cartridge. And yes, I used Lapua ammo. It just happened to be loaded with the recently-introduced Naturalis lead-free bullet and it worked quite nicely on moose. Then it was onward to the Lapua test range where I tried unsuccessfully to shoot up ammo of various calibers faster than they could make it. Most fun of all was shooting steel targets that

had been torched from the body of an old Russian armored vehicle (or so they told me). For that I used an extremely accurate rifle in 338 Lapua. The armor-piercing load zipped right through out to 600 yards. I then switched to a match load with the Scenar match bullet (which is Lapua's answer to our Sierra MatchKing) and no paper target inside 1000 yards was safe. To cap it all off, I rode as navigator in a rally car driven by one of Europe's top drivers and just before I closed my eyes the speedometer read 120 and we had just become airborne after topping a hill. I'd love to do that again, too.

Legacy Sports International

The Howa family of rifles imported from Japan by Legacy Sports gets bigger every year. One recent addition is the Ultralight Mountain Rifle at 6-1/2 pounds in 243 Winchester, 7mm-08 and 308. Moving from one weight extreme to another we have the Thumbhole Varminter Extreme with thumbhole-style laminated stock

Regardless of the distance, no steel target was safe from me and this rifle in 338 Lapua.

and a variety of calibers ranging from 204 Ruger to 308 Winchester.

Marlin

With the Winchester Model 94 no longer in production, Marlin now owns the entire the lever-action deer rifle market among American manufacturers, rather than just most of it as has been the case during these past few years. Latest version of the unsinkable Model 336 is the XLR with stainless steel barreled action and black/gray laminated woods stock. Regardless of whether you buy one in 30-30, 444 Marlin, 45-70 or 450 Marlin, barrel length will be 24 inches, as it should be on a rifle of its style. Nominal weight is seven pounds. And while I am on the subject of American-built firearms (which seems to mean less and less as the years go by) the Marlin 39A in 22 Rimfire is still available and still made just like it was when I bought my first one during the 1950s. Also still alive and well is the Marlin 1894 in 32 H&R Magnum, 32-20, 357 Magnum/38 Special and 44 Magnum/44 Special.

Mossberg

There are two new options in the Model 100 ATR rifle lineup for 2006. One is a short-action version with wood or synthetic stock in 243 Winchester and 308 Winchester. Another is the Combo with wood or synthetic stock in 270 Winchester or 30-06; both wearing a Bushnell 3-9X scope. Also new from Mossberg is the 802 Plinkster (where do they get these names?), a bolt-action rifle in 22 Long Rifle with an 18-inch barrel and a black synthetic stock. It is available with or without a 4x scope.

Navy Arms

If you have enjoyed watching the 1960s movie "Zulu" as many times as I have you know that in 1879, 139 British soldiers armed with Martini Henry rifles successfully defended their position at Rorke's Drift from 4000 Zulu warriors. Well, the staff at Navy Arms recently discovered a cache of those rifles. After 100 years of storage, they are now for sale. Listed in the Navy Arms catalog as "British P-1871 Short Lever Martini Henry" rifles, they are

chambered to 577-450, are complete with their original parts, and are classified as "NRA Good". Having one of these laying across your lap as you watch the movie yet another time will put you a wee bit closer to the action.

New England Firearms

The absolutely affordable break-action Handi-Rifle is now available with three interchangeable barrels in six different combinations: Sportster Combo with barrels in 223 Remington, 17 HMR and 22 Long Rifle; Pardner 20-gauge in 243 Winchester, 22 Long Rifle and 20-gauge; Pardner 12-gauge No. 1 in 270 Winchester, 22 Long Rifle and 12-gauge and Pardner 12-gauge No. 2 in 30-06, 22 Long Rifle and 12-gauge. Also available are a couple of youth versions with shortened buttstocks in 243, 22 LR and 20- or 12-gauge. Nominal weights run from five to seven pounds and barrel lengths range from 20 to 28 inches. Stocks and forearms are black synthetic. New chambering options for the wood-stocked version are 7.62x39mm Russian and 35 Whelen.

NoslerCustom

If you read my report last year, you know that only 500 rifles from NoslerCustom were to be built during 2005, all chambered to 300 WSM. Production will be limited to the same number of rifles in 2006 but the chambering is 280 Ackley Improved. The rifle will wear a Vari-X-III scope from the Leupold custom shop in the magnification range of your choice, 2.5-8X, 3.5-10X or 4.5-14X. Regardless of which scope you decide on, its range-compensation style of reticle will be calibrated for dead-on holds out to 500 yards with NoslerCustom ammo loaded with the 140-grain AccuBond bullet (40 rounds are included with the rifle). The scope will bear the same serial number as the rifle, as will the airline-approved travel case it will come in.

Also new from NoslerCustom is a less expensive version of the limited-edition rifle called Model 48. About the only difference I see in their actions is the receiver of the Model 48 is drilled and tapped for a standard scope-mounting base while

the base of the limited-edition rifle is an integral part of its receiver. The new rifle also wears a synthetic stock and is rated at 5-3/4 pounds. All metal wears a gray protective coating described by Nosler as MicroSlick. The rust-resistant finish is also applied to the inside of the bolt body and on the firing pin and its spring, making this the kind of rifle you want to have hanging from your shoulder when the weather turns nasty. The rifling of the match-grade, 24-inch stainless steel barrel is hand-lapped for smoothness. Only the 270 WSM chambering will be offered during 2006 and accuracy is guaranteed at 3/4-MOA for three shots with NoslerCustom ammo loaded with the 140-grain AccuBond bullet.

Remington

Believe it or not, our oldest firearms manufacturer who builds the world's most popular centerfire rifle (the Model 700) is now importing bolt-action rifles from other countries and they are built around the 1898 Mauser action. Two versions are slated for introduction. The Model 798 in 243 Winchester, 270 Winchester, 308 Winchester 30-06, 7mm Remington Magnum, 300 Winchester Mangnum, 375 H&H Magnum and 458 Winchester Magnum has Paul Mauser's non-rotating outside extractor. The Model 799 Mini in 22 Hornet, 222 Remington, 223 Remington, 22-250 and 7.62x39mm Russian looks like a Mauser but it has a Sako-style extractor. Barrel lengths are 20 inches for the Mini, 22 inches for the Model 798 in standard chamberings and 24 inches for magnum cartridges. Plinkers and small-game hunters are not being neglected either. Another bolt-action rifle is available in 22 Long Rifle and 22 WMR. Among other things, it has a 22-inch barrel and a brown stock of laminated wood.

Remington's Model 7400 autoloader (which began life many years ago as the Model 742) has an improved gas system and is now called Model 750 Woodsmaster. The Woodsmaster moniker, by the way, has been around for a very long time and my 1940s vintage Remington Model 81 in 300 Savage goes by the same name. At any rate, the new Model 750 is slated for availability in a rifle version with 22-inch barrel and as a carbine with 18 1/2-inch barrel. Both have a Monte Carlo style walnut stock with cut checkering and R3 recoil pad. Caliber options are 243 Winchester, 308 Winchester, 270 Winchester, 30-06 and 35 Whelen.

Then we have the new Classic Deluxe version of the Model Seven. Barrel lengths are 22 inches in 300 WSM and 20 inches in 204 Ruger, 223 Remington and 350 Remington Magnum. This would also be the perfect candidate for the 338 Federal.

Rossi

The break-action, single shot rifle from Rossi is available in combo sets with a variety of interchangeable barrels and most are available with two types of buttstocks, standard for grownups and shortened for youngsters. To name but a couple of the combinations available—243 Winchester, 22 Rimfire and 20-gauge smoothbore or 12-gauge slug barrel and 50-caliber muzzleloader barrel.

Ruger

The new Compact version of the ever-popular 10/22 autoloader from Ruger has a barrel length of 16-1/4 inches and its stock is shortened to a 12 3/4-inch pull. Nominal weight is 4-1/2 pounds, making this the perfect partner for running the old trap line. Other features include full-adjustable rear and fiber-optic front sights, birch stock and Weaver-style scope mounting base. To raise support funds for the USA Shooting Team's trip to the 2008 Summer Games in Beijing, Ruger and TALO Distributors have joined forces to come up with a special edition of the 10/22. Its features include a 20-inch heavy barrel, barracuda-style stock of red, white and blue laminated wood and two magazines. The equally new Stainless Frontier version of the Model 77 with its barrel-attached scope mounting rib has a stainless steel barreled action, a gray/black laminated wood stock, weighs 6-3/4 pounds and is available in several chamberings, including 323 WSM. I won't be surprised to see Ruger add the 338 Federal chambering to

its list of options for the Model 77 rifle. If it becomes available in the Model 77RSI International I will most certainly have to have one.

Sako

The new single-set trigger now available on Sako varmint rifles works quite similar to the Canjar trigger I had years ago on a Model 70 in 220 Swift. Pull weight in its standard mode is adjustable from two to four pounds. Pushing forward on the fingerpiece reduces weight to nine ounces, or so says the owner's manual; when in its set mode, the trigger on my rifle breaks at a crisp two ounces. While using a couple of rifles in 223 Remington to thin out the prairie dog and coyote population I concluded that it is the best trigger available on a standard-production rifle. To answer another of your questions—yes it can be installed on any Model 75 rifle.

The Sako Quad with its four interchangeable barrels is the most interesting rifle I have shot in a very long time. Before using one to shoot prairie dogs for several days (the .22 Mac 2 barrel was the most fun), I spent some time shooting groups at 100 yards from a benchrest. I used a Burris Quad scope in the field, but when punching paper the little rifle wore a Bushnell Elite 4200 with a 4-16x magnification range. I shot five different loads in each of the four barrels and the one in 17 Mach 2 proved to be the most accurate with an overall average of 1.12 inches. Of the five loads fired, CCI and Remington were most accurate with respective averages of 0.79- and 0.83-inch. Virtually tied for second place in accuracy were the 17 HMR and 22 WMR barrels with averages of 1.20 and 1.26 inches. The .22 Long Rifle barrel averaged 0.88-inch with Federal Classic and 0.91-inch with Remington Eley but its overall average was dead last at 1.45 inches. The Quad is now available in two versions, the original with synthetic stock and the new Hunter with walnut stock.

The Sako rifle I used to take an elk in Colorado during 2005 had been rebarreled to 338 Federal because the factory could not get one ready in time for my hunt. That cartridge is the same as the old 33-08 wildcat and I used to

The Sako Quad I took on a Wyoming prairie dog shoot is now available with wood or synthetic stock.

own a Remington Model 600 in that caliber. I no longer have the rifle but I still have reloading dies and was prepared to put them to use in case factory ammo did not arrive in time from Federal. But it did and I used it to take a young bull at just over 300 yards. The first shot through the lungs would have done it but I've learned to take no chances with elk and quickly followed up with a second shot. The animal took about half a dozen steps and piled up. Great little cartridge! It is kind to the shoulder and yet powerful enough any game up to elk and moose.

Savage

Savage has borrowed an idea that I believe originated among benchrest shooters—a single-shot rifle with a right-hand bolt and left-hand ejection port. A rifle of this type can be fired quite rapidly since the shooter's left hand feeds cartridges while his right hand operates the bolt. This is important among benchrest shooters who try to get off five or 10 shots before range conditions change. An increase in firepower is not all that important to a varmint shooter but the fact that both hands share the loading and shooting chores is something to take note of. The new Model 12 Long Range Precision Varminter from Savage has this type of receiver and that along with an oversized knob on the bolt handle, a sandbag-friendly synthetic stock and the AccuTrigger add up to make it one serious varmint rifle. Chamberings are 204 Ruger, 223 Remington and 22-250.

Steyr Arms, Inc.

The 338 Federal chambering is a new addition to various Mannlicher rifles from Steyr. They include the Fullstock, Halfstock and Mountain versions of the Classic as well as the Pro Hunter and Ultra Light models. Weights vary from six to 7-1/2 pounds depending on model and barrel lengths range from 19 to 25-1/2 inches.

Also new is the 450 Marlin chambering in the Big Bore ProHunter with a 22-inch barrel. I examined one of these in early February and it took me back to the old days of rebarreling short-action bolt guns for Frank Barnes' 458 American. That's the 458

Winchester Magnum case shortened to two inches and, in case you haven't noticed, the 450 Marlin is the same except for a thicker headspacing belt on its case. At any rate, the Steyr rifle allows the use of pointed X-Bullets from Barnes in the Marlin cartridge and magazine length allows them to be seated out to an overall length of about three inches for an increase in useable case capacity over what is possible in a Marlin lever-action. Steyr is claiming muzzle velocities of 2450, 2300 and 2100 fps with Barnes X-Bullets weighing 300, 350 and 400 grains, respectively. This is treading quite closely on the heels of the 458 Winchester Magnum in performance.

Taylor's & Company, Inc.

This company is known for its good-quality, imported reproductions of American-designed rifles of yesteryear, including the Model 1860 Henry in 44-40 and 45 Colt; the Model 1885 Winchester single-shot in 38-55 and 45-70; the Winchester 1866 in 32-20, 38 Special, 44-40 and 45 Colt, and the Model 1873 in the same chamberings. Or if your taste in rifles leans toward the Spencer 1865 repeater, you can get one here in 44-40, 45 Schofield or 56-50. Same goes for the 1874 Sharps in 45-70 and 45-120. Latest additions are a Winchester 1892 takedown rifle with 20- or 24-inch barrel in

357 Magnum, 38-40, 44-40 and 45 Colt and a lightweight, break-action single-shot rifle in 223 Remington and 243 Winchester called (oddly enough) the Spirit Overtop. How do they come up with these names?

Thompson/Center

Two of the best whitetail bucks I have taken during close to a half century of hunting them fell victim to the same rifle. I took one of the bucks in South Carolina with a rifle in 6mm-06 and took the other in Iowa with a 50-caliber muzzleloader. I have also used that same rifle in 204 Ruger and 223 Remington to bump off a varmint or two. I managed to accomplish all of that with a single rifle because it is a T/C Encore. The new ProHunter version of that rifle has what T/C describes as a Swing Hammer; by rotating the hammer spur left for a left-handed and right for a right-handed shooter, the need for a separate offset hammer spur is eliminated when a low-mounted scope is used. When used in its middle position the hammer is like any other. Once the spur is moved to your chosen position it is locked into place with a screw. Equally new is the FlexTech stock, said to reduce perceived recoil by as much as 40 percent. Four rubber arches are incorporated into the buttstock just forward of a rather thick recoil pad and they all add up to ease

A wonderful small-game rifle, the T/C R-55 is now available in four versions and in 22 Long Rifle or in 17 Mach 2, the latter used to harvest these fox squirrels.

the pain from hard-kicking cartridges.

I have been having a ball with a Thompson/Center R-55 in 22 Mach 2. Incredibly accurate, it is one of the most fun small-game rifles I have ever carried in the woods. The R-55 is now available in four variations: Classic with walnut stock and blued steel; All Weather in synthetic and stainless steel; Benchmark with laminated wood stock and bull barrel, and a light-barrel version of that rifle called Sporter. All models are also available in 22 Long Rifle.

Tikka

Where can you find better accuracy for your money than in a Tikka T3? Every single one I've worked with shot the way some writers say all rifles shoot. Latest variations are the Deluxe with walnut stock and Camo Stainless with (I'll let you guess). Chambering options range from 223 Remington to 338 Winchester Magnum with the 6.5x55mm Swedish somewhere in between those two.

U.S. Repeating Arms Co.

By the time you read this, U.S. Repeating Arms Company will have ceased production of three Winchester firearms, the Model 70 and Model 94 rifles and the Model 1300 Shotgun. The New Haven, Connecticut factory closed its doors on March 31, 2006. Incredibly sad, but true. So, if you

have been putting off the purchase of one of those rifles in a particular caliber you'd better move quickly before they disappear from the shelves of dealers forever. I rushed out and latched onto a Model 94 in 25-35 I had been considering and am glad I did for several reasons, not the least of which it has proven to be a very nice 100-yard deer rifle and quite accurate to boot.

What it all boils down to is USRAC has ceased to be a manufacturer of firearms and has become an importer of firearms manufactured in other countries. An example of things to come is a new knockabout-quality bolt-action rifle in 22 rimfire called the Wildcat. Made is Russia, it weighs 4-1/2 pounds, has a five- or ten-shot detachable magazine and a barrel length of 21 inches. Another foreign-built rifle to be initially sold under the USRAC banner is the equally new SXR gas-operated autoloader in 270 WSM, 30-06, 300 WSM and 300 Winchester Magnum, replete with racy European styling. Last but not least in the guns-made-somewhere-else department is the "High Wall" Hunter single-shot in 223 Remington, 22-250, 270 WSM, 7mm WSM, 300 WSM and 325 WSM.

Volquartsen Custom

As sometimes happens with totally new firearms, the production of Tom Volquartsen's new match-grade autoloader in 223 Remington and

204 Ruger has been delayed a bit, but judging by the level of accuracy being produced by the prototypes, I'd say it will be well worth the wait. Tom hopes to deliver the first rifles during late 2006 and if he does I will let you know how mine shoots next year. A Volquartsen rifle I have been shooting a lot is a little autoloader in 17 Mach 2. The more I shoot that rifle and its cartridge the more fond I become of both. Last spring I took it to a ranch in California and no ground squirrel or crow within 150 yards was safe. The smallest five-shot, 100-yard group I have fired on paper with that rifle measured 0.322-inch center-to-center. I used Federal ammo to shoot that group.

Weatherby

According to the 2006 Weatherby catalog, the Mark V Ultramark bridges the gap in features between the Mark V Deluxe and a budget-busting Mark V from Weatherby's custom shop. They start with a hand-selected blank of highly-figured walnut and give it a high-gloss finish replete with 20-line cut checkering. Add maple spacers between the solid recoil pad at the rear and a rosewood forearm tip up front, along with Monte Carlo styling and highly polished metal that would make Roy Weatherby proud and you have a Weatherby rifle that looks the way a Weatherby rifle is supposed to look. I don't care what they say about the advantages of stainless steel and plastic stocks––I still love blued steel and a good piece of walnut. Fact of the matter is, not long ago I started itching all over for another Weatherby Mark V and I chose the Deluxe grade in 240 Weatherby Magnum. Built around the standard-size Mark V receiver rather than the original magnum version, it is a wonderful little deer rifle. Back to the Ultramark, it is available in Roy's two favorite magnum cartridges, the 257 and the 300.

While I am on the subject of Deluxe rifles, you can also choose one from the Vanguard rifle lineup. From a distance you might mistake it for a Mark V Deluxe but upon closer examination you will discover about $1200 difference in its price. This is,

The smallest five-shot group I have fired at 100 yards with this Volquartsen auto-loader in 17 Mach 2 measured well under half an inch.

The Winchester Model 94 in 25-35 I used to take this Texas whitetail was one of the last built before U. S. Repeating Arms ceased production.

without doubt, the most handsome Vanguard ever offered by Weatherby. It's got the right chamberings too—270 Winchester, 30-06, 300 Weatherby Magnum and my favorite, the 257 Weatherby Magnum. I have a Vanguard Custom in that caliber and it just might be the best pronghorn antelope rifle I have ever owned. When zeroed three inches high with Weatherby ammo loaded with the 115-grain Ballistic Tip, the bullet is dead on point of aim at 300 yards and only half an antelope low at 400 yards.

Off and on through the years Weatherby has built a few pistols on the small Mark V action and the latest version is called Short Firing Platform or CFP for short (where do they get these names?). Of rear-grip design (as opposed to the center-grip design of the original Remington XP-100), it has a synthetic stock, a 16-inch barrel and is rated at 5-1/4 pounds. Chambering options are 223 Remington, 22-250, 243 Winchester and 7mm-08 Remington. The grip is ambidextrous so nobody can complain about being not being invited to the party.

So What's New?

A few months back I hunted chamois in the Austrian Alps. The rifle I used was a Mannlicher-Schoenauer built during the late 1940s and wearing a Kahles scope of the same vintage. While visiting the Kahles factory in Vienna I compared that scope with those being made today and was surprised to see very little difference in their optical quality. The fact that Kahles builds some of the clearest and brightest scopes in the world is not something that only recently happened—they have been doing it for a very long time. The Mannlicher-Schoenauer I used to bump off a chamois was chambered to 7x64mm Brenneke. Introduced in 1917, it duplicates the performance of the 280 Remington, which did not come along until 40 years later. So what's new?

At first glance you'll think the new Weatherby Vanguard Deluxe with its handsome Mark V style stock actually is a Mark V rifle.

Tes Salb with her buck taken with a Remington BuckHammer 20-gauge slug fired from a Remington Sportsman 11-87 20-gauge slug gun.

SHOTGUN REVIEW

by John Haviland

More and more shotguns are being imported into America. Marlin firearms justified having their new L.C. Smith guns made in Italy because: "Manufacturing costs prevent them from being American-made." Several American companies still haven't admitted defeat. Ruger makes all its guns in America and its Gold Label side-by-side sells very well. Remington, for the most part, fills its green boxes with American-made shotguns. Time will tell whether its new Model 105 Cti autoloader will put a dent in the popularity of Italian-made autoloaders.

Let's see what's new in shotguns, both imported and those made in America:

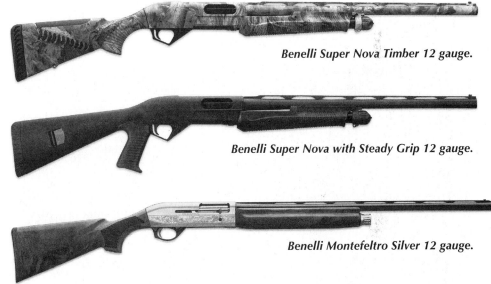

Benelli Super Nova Timber 12 gauge.

Benelli Super Nova with Steady Grip 12 gauge.

Benelli Montefeltro Silver 12 gauge.

Benelli

The Nova pump is the gun many hunters carry when the mud's deep and the geese fly high. This year the Nova's one-piece buttstock and receiver separate at the head of the grip and the new gun is called the SuperNova. This allows the choice of several different buttstocks: the SteadyGrip vertical grip; camo and black ComforTech with gel inserts to reduce recoil and the ComforTech with an extra high comb for using a scope and a collapsible stock.

The Ultra Light 12 gauge is the M2 autoloader slimmed down to six pounds. The Ultra Light loses a pound of weight with a shorter forearm,

a 24-inch barrel and rib made of carbon fiber. The gun's walnut stock is coated with a "WeatherCoat" finish that Benelli states is impervious to any kind of weather. The gun comes with a set of shims to adjust cast and comb height, and five screw-in chokes. Everything fits in a hard case.

The M2 Field 20 gauge now has the ComforTech system in its buttstock. The gel buttpad spreads recoil over a wide area to reduce felt recoil. The gel inserts in the stock also flex during recoil to absorb some of the recoil's bite, and the soft comb insert is gentle to the cheek.

A dressed up Montefeltro is now called the Montefeltro Silver. The 12- or 20-gauge guns wear fancy walnut. The nickel-plated receiver

is engraved with a pair of quail and a pointing setter in gold.

Beretta

There are four new Beretta shotguns: the 682 LTD, AL391 Teknys Gold Target featuring two interchangeable vent ribs, the 3901 Rifled Slug Shotgun for the American big-game hunter, and the 3901 Target RL created especially for new shooters, women and youth.

The Target RL 12-gauge shotgun is for smaller-stature shooters with an adjustable length of pull from 12 to 13 inches. The stock is also adjustable for cast on/off and comes equipped with Beretta's Memory System II to adjust the parallel comb. Magazine plugs can limit the gun to a single shot. This semiautomatic comes with either 26- or 28-inch barrels, a flat rib and a white mid and front bead. The stock and forearm are walnut finished in satin matte.

The 682 LTD is limited to 400 guns and has oil-finished expensive walnut stocks and hand checkering. Gold-filled engraving accents the sides and bottom of the matte-silver receiver. The gun is available in Sporting and Trap models.

The AL391 Teknys Gold Target has a 30-inch barrel with two interchangeable ribs. One is a flat rib for sporting, Skeet and the field that shoots flat patterns. A second is a stepped rib for trap shooting that shoots 70 percent of patterns above the point of aim. An 8.5-ounce recoil reducer in the stock cuts kick. A weighted magazine cap is also available to move balance forward.

The 3901 Rifled Slug Shotgun is a 12-gauge, gas-operated semiautomatic

gun with a three-inch chamber. Its rifled 24-inch barrel has a cantilever rail to mount either sights or a scope. The stock is black synthetic, with pressed-in checkering.

Blaser

Because of Blaser's new F3 over/under, I cannot go back to South Dakota. During a pheasant hunt there last season I missed only three shots with the F3 the whole trip. While I stood on top of a dirt bank a rooster flushed behind me and I turned and killed it. Another rooster flew far to my left and I killed it with the second barrel. A third cock jumped up 35 yards out as I closed the gun on two new shells. I knocked it out of the air. That went on the whole trip.

I was shooting way over my head. But I'm not going to tell that to Scott Mathews and his guides at Bad River Bucks & Birds (www.

The Blaser F3 12 gauge.

badriverhunts.com), in order to keep my reputation intact.

The new F3 had a lot to do with my above-average shooting. The gun weighed about eight pounds and its 28-inch barrels kept the gun's balance about in the middle of the gun. That worked well for point-and-shoot-shots and swinging the gun on crossing pheasants.

The F3 is made in Germany by Blaser Jagdwaffen and imported by Sigarms. The 12-gauge gun comes in Game and Competition Sporting and Trap models and guns with extensive engraving and high dollar wood.

The F3's steel receiver measures slightly less than 2.5 inches tall to make a very low profile gun. An underlug engages a recess in the bottom of the receiver to lock up the gun. The front of this lock is adjustable

The inner workings of the Blaser F3.

The Blaser F3's steel receiver measurers slightly less than 2.5 inches tall to make a very low profile gun.

and can be replaced, if it wears over time. The hinge pins on both sides of the receiver that the barrels pivot on, the face of the breech and the firing pins can also be easily replaced.

The trigger assembly has what Blaser calls the Inertia Block System to prevent the hammers from striking forward unless the trigger is pulled and to prevent double firing. The trigger blade is also adjustable for length and angle. A barrel selection button is located inside the trigger guard ahead of the trigger and the safety on the tang is not automatic. All barrel sets weigh the same, no matter if they are 27 to 32 inches, because contours are changed slightly.

The Game model I shot in South Dakota had a full forearm and both barrels fit in my forward hand. The right side of the grip had a slight swell. My hands and my eyes worked together and the pheasants never had a chance.

Kevin Wistner, Sigarms national manager, said the German engineers listened to what Americans wanted in an over/under shotgun. "I think they got it right," Wistner said.

Browning

The Gold Superlite Micro shotgun promises to be a favorite among smaller-stature shooters. Weighing 6 pounds, 6 ounces, this little 20 gauge has a back-bored barrel, speed loading and soft shooting gas-operated system. Add to that a three-inch chamber in its 26-inch barrel and the Superlite can handle everything from dove to waterfowl.

The limited edition Browning NRA Gold Sporting shotgun represents the latest collaboration between Browning and the National Rifle Association. This model features a gold-filled NRA Heritage mark and motto on the left side of the receiver. With every gun sold, Browning will make a donation to the NRA Basic Firearms Training Program to help folks learn to enjoy firearms safely. The gun is available in 12-gauge with a 2 3/4-inch chamber and a 28 or 30-inch barrel.

The Gold Evolve has taken on a new configuration in the Gold Evolve Sporting. This sleek version of the Gold has an alloy receiver, ported and back-bored barrel and 2 3/4-inch

chamber. Five Invector-Plus choke tubes and a Hi Viz Tri-comp fiber-optic front sight round out the gun.

Evidently more than one shooter likes the Browning Cynergy over/under shotguns, but not its lines and strange-looking recoil pad. For those, Browning has made the Cynergy Classic Field and Sporting. These guns have traditional shotgun lines and a conventional butt stock configuration and silver nitride receiver.

The Browning Silver autoloading shotgun comes in three styles with a slight hump at the back of its receiver reminiscent of the old Browning A-5. The gas-operated gun is being promoted as a slightly less expensive gun than the Gold.

The Silver Hunter has a silver finish on the receiver and a checkered walnut stock and forearm. The gun comes in 3 or 3 1/2-inch 12 gauge with a 26-, 28- or 30-inch barrel. The Silver Stalker has a matte black finish and a composite stock and forearm. The Silver Camo is covered with either Mossy Oak Break-Up or Shadow Grass.

Ithaca

For the last 20-some years Ithaca has gone through financial difficulties. When the company closed its doors in 2005 nearly everyone thought that would be the end of the Ithaca. But Floyd and Craig Marshall had other ideas and bought the company in late 2005 and moved it to their MoldCraft mold and tool manufacturing plant in Upper Sandusky, Ohio.

In early 2006 the new Ithaca company concentrated on assembling guns from Model 37 parts on hand. In March of this year the Marshalls produced their first batch of Model 37 receivers and barrels. "First we're making a Turkey Slayer gun and then a police gun," Craig Marshall said. "A lot of people got stiffed by the old company on the 125th anniversary (Model 37) guns, so we'll also be making what I call the 125th-plus one anniversary gun."

In the near future Marshall hopes to introduce more Model 37 guns. One is a small-bore gun for skeet shooters and young hunters. "There's a lot of interest," Marshall said. "The phone has been just ringing off the hook."

Remington

Remington has gone all out with its completely new CTi autoloader. The most notable feature is its skeleton receiver of titanium with a carbon-fiber housing. The gun feeds and ejects from the bottom of the receiver. A speed-loader system feeds the first shell into the chamber. The shell in the chamber and in the magazine can be quickly unloaded. The 12-gauge gun with a three-inch chamber weighs seven pounds.

Other features include a rotating, locking bolt head, Remington's TriNyte coating to protect the receiver, a trigger with a pull of 3-1/2 to 4 pounds and a cross-bolt safety that can be switched for a left-hand shooter.

Remington states four features in the CTi reduces felt recoil by half:
* An oil-filled cylinder in the stock regulates bolt speed.
* An R3 recoil pad absorbs recoil.
* A gas system spreads recoil over a longer time.
* An overbored barrel and a lengthened forcing cone provide less resistance to the shot column.

The Model 1100 G3 is said to have an enhanced gas-operating system that will handle 2-3/4 and 3-inch shells, keep the gun cleaner and reduce wear. The G3 comes in 12 and 20 gauge and the receiver wears Remington's Titanium PVD coating to guard against handling and the weather. All internal operating parts are nickel-plated and Teflon coated.

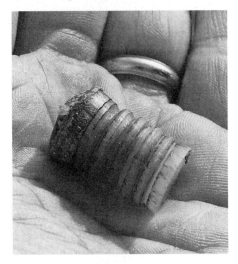

This Remington BuckHammer 20-gauge slug was retrieved from a dead Alabama buck.

The Model 1100 Competition 12-gauge has an extended carrier release and a 30-inch barrel with a wide ten millimeter rib. The barrel bore is overbored and its forcing cone is lengthened. Five ProBore choke tubes are standard. A trap version has an adjustable comb. All internal operating parts are nickel-plated and Teflon-coated.

The Special Purpose shotguns have received some enhancements. The 11-87 and 870 SPS-Turkey Super Magnum Camos are covered with Mossy Oak Obsession and their receivers are drilled and tapped for scope mounts. The 11-87 Turkey and Slug guns also have the option of a thumbhole stock.

The 11-87 Sportsman line now includes a 20-gauge slug gun. This synthetic stocked gun has a matching black matte finish on its metal. A cantilever scope base is mounted on its 21-inch rifled barrel. With a scope locked onto the barrel, instead of the receiver, a slug gun seems to shoot much more precisely. That is certainly the case with one of these 20-gauge 11-87s I used deer hunting last fall. The gun punched out groups from two to three inches at 100 yards time after time with Remington's 2-3/4 and 3-inch BuckHammer slugs. I shot one whitetail doe with the 2 3/4-inch BuckHammer slug at about 80 yards. The slug went through both shoulders

and the deer was dead right there.

The whole idea of the 11-87 20-gauge is a light-recoiling slug gun. The Sportsman 11-87 does that with a gas system that spreads recoil over a longer period and a R3 recoil pad thick as a pillow. The new Managed-Recoil BuckHammer slugs make the gun even gentler on the shoulder.

The Model 870 pump continues to add models and features:

* This is the last year for the Dale Earnhardt Tribute shotguns. This year's gun is an 870 Wingmaster 20 gauge. Earnhardt's likeness and signature are engraved on the left side of the receiver.

* The 870 Express line has the option of a brown laminate stock and forearm.

* The 870 Express synthetic versions are offered in Mossy Oak Break-Up and Shadow Grass camo patterns.

* A Super Magnum Turkey barrel is available for 870s. The barrel comes with TruGlo fiber optic sights and a super-Full Hevi-Shot Choke Tube.

* The well-worn term "Tactical" has been applied to 870. The Tactical Speedfeed and SpecOps 870s have 18-inch barrels, olive drab finishes and pistol grip stocks.

* The NRA Edition Wingmaster is a 12 gauge with the NRA logo engraved on the right side of the receiver and the NRA Heritage logo on the left side.

Remington has given up on making an over/under shotgun and instead put its name on an Italian gun, the Premier Over & Under. Models available include the Competition in 12-gauge and the Field and Upland in 12, 20 and 28 gauge.

The Competition has 28 or 30-inch barrels with a wide rib and white mid and front beads. The walnut stock has a slight swell on the right of the grip. The forearm has a Schnabel tip. The barrel selector is located on the tang safety and the receiver has a titanium coating.

The Field and Upland share most of the same features. But the Field has 26 or 28-inch barrels and a nickel-finished receiver. The Upland has a case-colored receiver with game scene engraving accented with gold.

Remington's Spartan line of imported guns continues to grow. The SPR453 autoloader handles all 12-gauge shells up to 3-1/2 inches. The gun's bolt face has dual extractors and its gas system is adjustable for smooth cycling.

Dave Henderson with his buck taken with a Remington BuckHammer 20-gauge slug fired from a Remington Sportsman 11-87 20-gauge slug gun.

Barrel lengths are 24, 26 or 28 inches and include four screw-in choke tubes.

Marlin

Back in 1945, Marlin bought The Hunter Arms Company, of Fulton, New York, maker of the L.C. Smith side-by-side shotgun. Nicknamed the "Elsie", this sidelock double gun was made for a few years in the Marlin plant before being phased out.

To bring back the name, Marlin is importing an Italian gun and calling it the L.C. Smith. The new side-by-side wears side plates to echo the look of the original Smith guns. Although there was no over-and-under L.C. Smith, Marlin is offering 12 and 20-gauge over-and-under models.

The LC12-DB 12-gauge double barrel has three-inch chambers, a single trigger and selective automatic ejectors. The 28-inch barrels have a solid rib, and come with three screw-in choke tubes. Its walnut stock is checkered and the forearm has a beavertail shape. The 20-gauge version is similar, with 26-inch barrels.

The LC12-OU over/under wears 28-inch barrels with a ventilated rib, three-inch chambers and comes with three screw-in choke tubes. The 20 gauge has 26-inch barrels.

Mossberg

The Tactical Turkey Hunting Series features a polymer stock with a length of pull that is easily adjusted with a push of a button from 10-3/4 to 14-5/8 inches. The forend strap provides a stable resting position for the shooter's hand. These features are on the 835 Ulti-Mag, 535 ATS and 500 pumps. The guns include 20-inch ventilated rib barrels with adjustable fiber-optic sights and the new X-Factor ported Turkey choke tubes. The same setup is on the Special Purpose 500 Tactical, although in all black or Marinecote metal finish and black stock and forearm.

Savage

Savage is also importing Italian over/under shotguns. The Milano guns come in 12, 20, 28 gauges and .410-bore. Savage states the

receivers of the guns are scaled to fit each gauge. However, the 12 gauge weighs 7-1/4 pounds, the 20 and 28 6 pounds and the .410 6-1/4 pounds. The guns have walnut stocks and firearms with modest point checkering patterns. The guns have automatic ejectors, a single selective trigger and a manual safety on the tang.

Winchester

Winchester has upgraded its Super X2 autoloader to the Super X3. The new gun's stock, grip and forearm are slimmer. An alloy magazine tube and a lightweight barrel with a narrow profile further reduce weight. The barrel bore is backbored to .742-inch and the new gunmetal gray Perma-Cote is more durable than traditional bluing. The X3's self-adjusting Active Valve ensures recoil reduction and durability in all conditions with all 12-gauge shells.

The SX3 comes in four models. The SX3 Field weighs only 6-1/2 pounds. A Pachmayr Decelerator recoil pad takes the sting out of three-inch magnum shells. A hard heel insert provides a slick surface on the pad that won't grab clothing when shouldering the gun. Spacers between the pad and stock are easily added or removed to adjust length of pull. The composite synthetic stock wears a Dura-Touch Armor Coating ensuring a sure grip on the gun. Its metal wears a Perma-Cote finish on its metal. The Cantilever Deer is similar to the Composite, but wears a 22-inch rifled barrel. The barrel has a TRUGLO fiber optic front sight and a cantilever base to accept sights and scopes. The Waterfowl and Camo Field chambers 12-gauge 3-1/2 shells and wears Mossy Oak camo from muzzle to butt.

Winchester has added three models to its Select over/unders. The Midnight has high gloss bluing on its metal, and engraving of game birds accented with gold on both sides of the receiver. The White Field Extreme has an engraved silver nitrate receiver with oval pattern checkering on its grip and forearm. The White Field Traditional has more customary point pattern checkering.

Here's a wrap-up of new guns—

* The CZ Ringneck and Bobwhite side-by-sides are now chambered in 16 gauge. The Ringneck has a

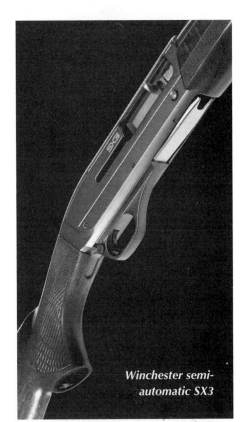

Winchester semi-automatic SX3

round knob grip and semi-beavertail forearm. It has a single trigger and 28-inch barrels choked Improved Cylinder and Modified. The Bobwhite has 26-inch barrels with the same chokes, double triggers and a straight grip and splinter forearm.

* New England Firearms' Partner pump line has been expanded to include walnut stocks in 12 and 20 gauge. A 12 gauge with a 3 1/2-inch chamber has also been added as well as a slug gun in 12 and 20, with rifled barrels and adjustable sights.

* SKB has an adjustable rib for its 85TSS trap over/unders. Patterns can be adjusted from flat-shooting to placing 90 percent of the pattern above the point of aim.

* Weatherby's Athena D'Italia Deluxe Shotgun is available in 12, 20 and 28 gauge. The side-by-side has extensive engraving, a single trigger and a wide choice of screw-in chokes. The Turkish walnut stock has a straight grip and a splinter forearm. Checkering is 24 lines per inch.

* Zoli of Italy Columbus target and game guns are aimed at the American market. The guns have titanium choke tubes, easy trigger assembly removal and extensive engraving on the receiver.

TODAY'S MUZZLELOADING:

BLACKPOWDER REVIEW

by Doc Carlson

There is no doubt the modern inline has taken over as the foremost rifle for muzzleloading hunters. Since its introduction in the mid-1980s this style of muzzleloader has taken the hunting market by storm. Many of the older muzzleloading manufacturers have dropped the majority of their traditional models in favor of the faster-selling inline rifle. There are still some, however, that like the style, beauty and nostalgia of a traditional muzzleloading rifle. These guns are still a large part of the hunting scene and prized family heirlooms, in many cases. And while there are still a wide range of models and styles available, many are turning to custom, hand-built guns that combine artistry with practical function in a gun to be used for hunting, target shooting, display as an art object—or all three.

Jim Chambers is a well-known contemporary gunmaker who made his reputation building fine Kentucky-style rifles. A few years back, he began assembling kits that could be sold to amateur gunmakers. The kit is a way for those who don't feel they can afford the services of a custom maker to acquire a top quality rifle. They also appeal to those who get a lot of satisfaction creating a finished rifle from the various parts. Many of the well-known custom makers often start with one of the Chambers kits also, as they take a lot of the drudgery and sweat out of the building process, leaving more time for the artistry of carving, engraving and inlay work.

Chambers' kits start with top quality parts, using components that represent the epitome of 18th century rifle-making technology. He starts with locks that he produces himself. These are patterned after period locks

and made from high carbon steel. The lock is carefully assembled and fitted, with all parts hardened and tempered where required. These locks would be right at home on the bench of the finest English or American gunbuilders of yesteryear. All that is required of the home builder is to polish and finish the outside of the lock, which is ready to go as furnished with the kit.

Stocks supplied as standard with the kits are nicely-figured hard maple. More highly figured wood can be ordered if one wishes, or cherry or walnut can be specified. The hard grunt work has been done on the stock wood. The stock, as supplied, is 95 percent shaped to the style of the rifle ordered, and inletting for the lock and barrel are 95 percent complete. Buttplate (always an inletting challenge), trigger guard, patch box and side plate are all 95 percent inletted. The machining of the stock is held to a

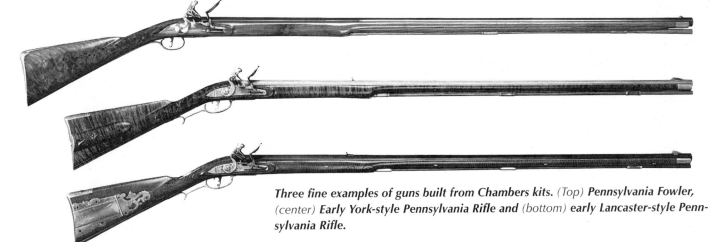

Three fine examples of guns built from Chambers kits. (Top) **Pennsylvania Fowler,** (center) **Early York-style Pennsylvania Rifle** and (bottom) **early Lancaster-style Pennsylvania Rifle.**

few thousands of an inch tolerance, and the final fitting of parts is well within the capabilities of anyone with even marginal tool savvy. The ramrod hole is drilled and the groove in the forend is machined. Stocks can be ordered with either a sliding wood patch box or a brass one—whichever catches your fancy. There is enough wood left on the stock so that any carving or individual decoration that the builder wishes can be done.

Barrels are top quality and supplied by Getz Barrel Company, Rice Barrel Company, Long Hammock Barrels and W.E. Rayl, Inc.—all well-known for fine-shooting barrels. You can specify which barrel company you want, if you have a preference. Barrels come with the barrel tennons installed, the front sight dovetail cut and the breech plug fitted. The breech plug carries a long tang that allows the builder to shape it, or cut it back to his preference. All screws and pins required for installation of the barrel and other parts are included with the kit.

The brass fittings—the buttplate, trigger guard, ramrod thimbles, end cap, etc.—are all easily worked soft yellow brass. This material finishes and polishes well and doesn't have any of the off-red color of the more common bronze.

The kits can be ordered in several styles including Early Lancaster, Early York, Isaac Haines, Edward Marshall or Virginia-style Kentucky rifles. An early smooth-bored "rifle," New England colonial fowler and English fowler styles are also offered. Recently added is a nicely designed English

Gentleman's Sporting Rifle in English walnut. There is also a Kentucky-style American pistol, if you are so inclined.

While these kits have most of the difficult fitting and shaping done, they still require some familiarity with working wood and metal. The components are of the best quality but, of course, the look and quality of the finished gun will depend upon your skills in finishing etc. If, on receiving the kit, it appears to be beyond what you can handle, Jim Chambers will either set you up with a professional gun builder who can put it together for you—or he'll take it back for a full refund, no questions asked, if the kit parts are unaltered.

The Chambers kits are an excellent starting place for the creation of a top-quality functional firearm that can become a family heirloom. They allow the part-time hobby gun builder to produce a rifle of which he can be justly proud. The parts supplied are of the best quality and prices are well within the reach of the Average Joe. As stated before, many well-known custom rifle builders start with a Chambers kit. That tells you something about the quality that is in the box you receive.

If you are just getting your feet wet in gun-building, there are several good books that will lead you through the process. A couple that come to mind are *The Art of Building the Pennsylvania Longrifle* by Dixon and *The Gunsmith of Greenville* by Peter Alexander; either or both will give step-by-step building directions and get you into carving and engraving.

Both books are readily available from various muzzleloading suppliers.

American Pioneer Powder

American Pioneer Powder has added a premium-grade powder called Jim Shockey's Gold to their blackpowder substitute line of products. This new powder has one extra step added to the production process to give gilt-edged accuracy to the hunter. Available in either 50-grain premeasured compressed charge sticks for 45- or 50-caliber, or as loose powder in 2Fg or 3Fg granulations, the new powder is said to be even cleaner-burning and to give higher velocities with less variance shot-to-shot. As with other American Pioneer products, the powder contains no sulfur and is recommended for sidelock guns in flint or percussion, inlines or cartridges for hunting or cowboy action shooting. It is easily ignited with a standard #11 percussion cap.

The Gun Works Muzzleloading Emporium

If building your own rifle isn't your cup of tea, there are many folks out there building top-quality traditional firearms. There is a wide variety of period correct, custom and semi-custom-made guns available to delight the heart of the shooter, hunter or collector who appreciates the guns of our forefathers.

During the time when the sun never set on the British Empire, English gunmakers were making beautiful hunting guns of large caliber for use in India and Africa. These guns were designed to take the largest and most dangerous animals on the face of the earth, and reliably served the hunter and explorer of the day. There are a few folks still producing these fine firearms today.

One of these is The Gun Works Muzzleloading Emporium, owned and operated by Joe and Suzi Williams. It is located in the Willamette Valley of Oregon, the destination of the Oregon Trail in days gone by. While the Williams offer all kinds of parts, etc., in their catalog, they also offer custom traditional muzzleloading arms: the Hawken, Pennsylvania and American Fowler-type guns (the Fowler available in both smoothbore and rifled versions). The Northwest Trade Gun is also available.

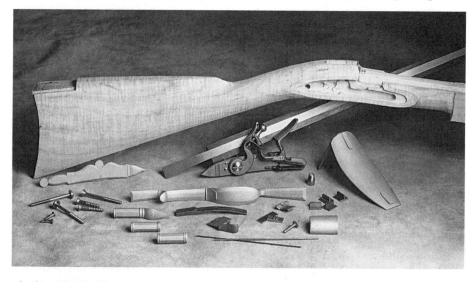

The kit comes with everything required to build a fine firearm except tools, finish and elbow grease.

The Gun Works English 4-bore rifle is one massive gun!

The gun that really caught my eye, however, was their English Sporting Rifle. The English gunmakers brought the muzzleloading hunting rifle to the peak of its development as a fast-handling well-fitting rifle that handled the recoil of big bores and heavy charges. Most English rifles that one handles are truly fine examples of the gunmakers' art; they literally ask to be taken hunting.

The English sporting rifles offered by The Gun Works are available in calibers from .45 to .69 as a normal thing. However, part of The Gun Works is the Oregon Barrel Company, and they make the barrels for the guns that they offer. The Oregon Barrel Company makes barrels from 32-caliber up to 2-bore. For those who are not up on the British designation of bore size, it is based upon the number of bore-sized lead round balls in a pound. Our modern shotgun gauges are based upon that same measure. Therefore, a 12-bore gun ran 12 balls to the pound—about a 72-caliber. The 2-bore would run two balls to the pound (an 8-ounce lead ball); about 1 1/4-inch bore diameter. There are very few barrel makers that make anything near that size. The fact that Oregon Barrel Co. does allows them to offer a real, honest-to-gosh large-bore elephant gun of the type used by Baker, Selous and the other famous ivory hunters of the mid-1800s.

The rifle in question is a 4-bore, English Sporting Rifle, typical of the highest development of the very large bore muzzle-loading African rifle. The pistol grip half-stock is walnut, with ebony grip cap and nose cap. The grip and forend are nicely checkered, as was typical on these guns. The Davis percussion lock is patterned after Alexander Henry locks. Alexander Henry was one of the better known makers of this type of rifle in the 1800s. The lock is a massive bar type that fits well on a gun of this size. The Oregon Barrel Company rifled barrel is octagon and tapers from 1-3/4 inches at the breech to 1-1/2 inches at the muzzle. It is 31-1/2 inches long and features a snail-type breech. Sights are the adjustable California type.

This massive gun weighs 18 pounds. The standard load is 250 grains of 1Fg or 2 Fg blackpowder behind a round ball that weighs around 1700 grains—about 1/4 of a pound! Suffice to say that this is not a rifle you shoot off a bench all day. Surprisingly, the big heavy rifles with English-styled stocks handle the heavy recoil very well. While they are not comparable to a 32-caliber squirrel rifle, the big guns are not seriously uncomfortable to shoot. The Brits definitely knew what they were about when they built guns.

In addition to the massive English sporting rifle, The Gun Works also offers custom rifles and smoothbores in about any style that one could wish for. So, if you are looking for a gun for any type of hunting or target shooting, or a serious rifle for dangerous game—or just want to have something that your hunting buddies will be impressed by—this is the outfit to contact.

Pacific Rifle Company

It appears Oregon is the place for the big-bore aficionado. Pacific Rifle Company, also based in Oregon, makes a large-bore rifle they call the 1837 Zephyr. This rifle is a little different than the average traditional gun. The rifle is based on the proven under-hammer action. This action has been around for well over a hundred years and offers several advantages. It is very simple, utilizing two moving parts: the trigger and the hammer. The mainspring is also the trigger guard. The geometry of the trigger/hammer system delivers a very good trigger pull, one reason that many of this type action are seen on target rifles. The nipple is threaded directly into the bottom of the barrel, delivering the cap flame directly to the powder charge, similar to the modern in-line guns. The cap is protected from weather by being under the barrel, and the shooter is protected from flying cap parts upon firing. As the hammer is on the bottom of the gun, there is nothing to clutter the sight picture. The top of the barrel is clean, with no distractions. The barrel is seated into the steel receiver and the buttstock is held to the back side of the receiver with a through-bolt, a very stiff and solid setup. Hammer and trigger pivot on hardened steel pins. All-in-all, the under-hammer system is solid and relatively problem-free.

Pacific Rifle Company utilizes the Forsyth style of rifling with narrow lands and shallow grooves and very slow twist. This type of rifling was developed by a British officer in the mid-1800s for use with large-caliber round balls. It works very well and allows the ubiquitous round ball to be launched at higher velocities for flatter trajectories.

Pacific offers three major models of the Zephyr. All use musket caps for sure ignition of large powder charges. They all can be had with an integral recoil reduction system. Sights are buckhorn rear with German silver front blade, with other sight options available. The guns are supplied with browned barrels and receivers but engraving and optional finishes are available. Stocks are fancy American walnut finished with an oil and beeswax, hand rubbed finish. The buttplate is a wide, modified crescent style that handles recoil well. Hardware and fittings are browned steel.

The standard 1837 Zephyr is offered in a 62-caliber (20-bore) 30-inch tapered octagon barrel. It is intended for charges in the 175-grain range giving pretty much a flat trajectory out to 125 yards or so. It is recommended for any Western game, up to and including smaller bears.

The Alaskan Zephyr is the same as the standard except the 28-inch tapered octagon barrel is 72-caliber (12-bore) and the ignition system utilizes two musket caps on side-by-side nipples that are fired simultaneously to ignite the 300-grain charges this big-game rifle is capable of digesting. At the 250-grain charge level, the gun shoots reasonably flat to 100 yards, and the blow from the 72-caliber round ball is sufficient to handle anything on the American continents, and most African game.

The largest-caliber Zephyr is called the African. The 26-inch barrel on this one is made in a 84-caliber (8-bore).

The receiver on this gun is color-case hardened and the caliber designation and legend on the barrel are gold-filled. The receiver is tastefully engraved, the barrel sports English-type sights, and the stock utilizes a shotgun-type buttplate. This one is intended to be adequate for the largest game on the planet.

North Star West

One of the most popular guns among reenactors—at least the pre-1840 crowd, the buck skinners—is the Northwest Trade Gun. These smooth-bore flintlock firearms were a fixture of the fur trade in America from the mid-1600s to the 1860s. They were somewhat standardized, varying slightly depending upon the company that ordered them and the gunsmiths who made them. They all shared basically the same look and style.

In the 1970s, when the buckskinning hobby was really taking off, Curly Gostomski, a Dayton, Ohio tool and die maker, began to reproduce both French and British trade guns. He used guns in his collection for patterns, and refined the reproductions during correspondence with Charles Hanson, curator of The Museum of the Fur Trade in Chadron, Nebraska. What he put on the market was a reproduction of the original Fur Trade guns that would fool experts.

Curly sold the business, called North Star Enterprises, in the early 1990s and, after another sale, it is now owned by Matt and Mary Denison as North Star West based in Montana. They are continuing to produce exact copies of the Northwest Trade Gun.

North Star West produces five different long guns and a pistol; all flintlock and smoothbore, as were the originals. The models offered cover the various styles offered by fur-trading outfits—French, English and American—over a span of a couple of hundred years. The guns were in general use clear up to the early 1900s. No wonder they are so popular with the reenactment folks.

North Star West make their own locks, utilizing patterns by Barnett, Ketland and Whately—all well-known English makers of trade guns. All the iron hardware used on the guns is from molds designed and owned by the company. The guns are supplied in three ways—as a kit with a 95 percent inletted stock, completed lock, all hardware,

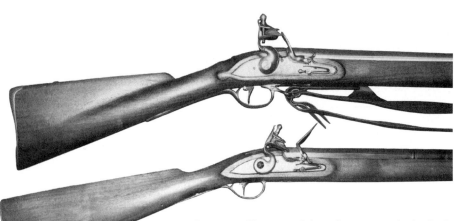

Top: *North Star's Officer's Model Musket uses a Whatley lock and a 16-gauge barrel finished in-the-white.*
Bottom: *The Chief's Trade Gun is a higher-grade model featuring a Ketland lock, blued finish and a walnut stock.*

and a set of instructions; as a completed gun "in the white," that is, completely assembled and shootable but with no finish on either barrel or stock, and as a complete, finished gun. This allows the buyer to tailor the order to match his pocketbook and gunsmithing ability.

The five long guns include, first, the Northwest Trade gun which is typical of the guns handled by Hudson Bay Company, the Northwest Company, and the American Fur Company, John Jacob Astor's outfit. They were in common use and trade from around 1770 until 1860 or so when percussion guns came into common use. It has the brass serpent sideplate and the proper sitting fox logo that the Indians looked for to ensure they were getting a good quality gun.

Next is an Early English-style gun, typical of those sold by English traders prior to the French and Indian War. It follows the typical trade gun style etc...but is an earlier style, typical of what the Hudson Bay Company traded before the French and Indian War. There were never a lot of these made and they are quite rare today.

The third type is a Chief's Grade Gun. These guns were a bit fancier than the standard trade gun. They were produced during a 20-year span, from 1790 to 1810. They were used by the British military as gifts to prominent Indian leaders to induce them to join the British against the Americans during the War of 1812.

The fourth type is an Officers Model Musket of the type that would have been typically carried by Rogers Rangers or high-ranking British officers during the French and Indian War. The gun would be quite correct for the period of the American Revolution, for that

matter. It is copied from an original gun in the collection of the Smithsonian Institution in Washington, D.C. While this one is not technically a trade gun, it fits into the period quite nicely. A wide range of accoutrements are available for this gun: a bayonet & tomahawk, leather belt with cartridge box for paper cartridges, leather sling, leather frog scabbard for the bayonet and tomahawk, worm for the ramrod and instructions for making paper cartridges. The French and Indian War reenactors will be very interested in this one.

The fifth long gun is a Blanket Gun; basically a Northwest Trade Gun that has had the barrel cut back to 18 inches and the buttstock shortened 6 inches or so. This is to reproduce a common modification that Indians performed on their guns to make them shorter and easier to handle while hunting, especially on horseback. It also made the gun easy to carry under a blanket—an early "concealed carry option."

The Trade Pistol offered by North Star West is a copy of the flintlock smoothbore pistol that was typically used by traders, trappers and factors of trading posts. These were imported in large numbers during the entire period of the North American fur trade.

All the guns are offered in a choice of 24- or 20-gauge, and in a variety of barrel lengths—with the exception of the Officer's Model Musket which is 66-caliber with a 37 1/2-inch barrel, like the original.

An interesting sidelight, the price of a typical trade gun during the heyday of the trade was 20 or so beaver pelts. With the price of beaver today, prices of the North Star West guns are pretty close to an equivalent with the fur trade prices. These guns are very nicely made and very period-correct. They fit perfectly in the hands of a reenactor, a primitive season hunter—or on the wall over the fireplace.

Remington

A couple of years ago Remington dropped their Model 700 ML bolt-action muzzleloading rifle, and many thought Remington was out of the muzzleloading business. Not so. They are back with a new muzzleloading rifle called the Genesis.

This new rifle uses a side-rotating block that pivots to the left, exposing the breech of the barrel which takes the popular 209 shotgun primer. When rotated back in position, the block, called the Torch Cam action, seals the 209 into a weather-resistant package. The primer is fired by an external center-hung hammer that strikes a firing pin that extends through the block. There is no blow-back of fouling to bother the shooter, or get into the trigger group. After firing, the Torch Cam breech block is pivoted to the side, exposing the fired primer which can then be removed easily without the use of tools, something that is important in the hunting field. The 28-inch barrel utilizes a 1:28-inch twist and is capable of handling loads of 150 grains of black powder or black powder equivalent. Sights are fiber optic and the ramrod is aluminum for durability. The stock sports swivel studs, of course, and the barrel is drilled and tapped for scope mounting.

The gun features a dual safety, consisting of a traditional cross-bolt safety at the rear of the trigger guard and a rebounding hammer that locks in the cocked position, holding it away from the firing pin. Bumping the hammer accidentally will not fire the rifle. The breechplug is easily removed for cleaning,

and the gun can be torn completely down in a few minutes for a thorough cleaning.

The new rifle is available in a variety of configurations and finishes. The metal can be had in blued steel, stainless or camouflage and the stock is available in either synthetic or laminated wood, in either thumb-hole or standard styles. Stocks can be had in a camo design also.

It's good to see Remington back in the muzzleloading market. After all, the company had its origin some 190 years ago as a maker of muzzleloading firearms and barrels. This new, very affordable rifle should be a good addition to the Remington line.

There are a couple of new items in the muzzleloading ammunition department that will be available to hunters and shooters.

Traditions Performance Firearms

A problem often facing muzzleloading hunters is a fast second shot. There are many different things on the market to facilitate a relatively quick reload, but even the most efficient and fast reloading accessory can take too long to accomplish its purpose if an animal is bent on leaving the vicinity.

Traditions Performance Firearms has the answer. They are marketing their Express Double Shot double-barrel muzzleloader. This over-under rifle offers two shots as quick as you can pull the trigger. Looking very much like a 20-gauge O/U shotgun, the Express utilizes two 50-caliber 24-inch barrels with a 1:28 twist for the popular sabot, or slug-type bullets. The barrels are factory set to shoot to point of aim at 75 yards. The barrels have a screw-adjusted "barrel jack" system for fine-tuning the shot placement for different loads and bullets.

The gun features a top-break lever, similar to a shotgun, which allows access to the breech end of the barrels for the installation of 209 primers. The gun is rated for loads up to 150 grains; its four locking lugs give a great deal of strength. Double triggers allow for a quick second shot by merely pulling the other trigger.

Other features include fiber optic sights, sling swivels, rubber recoil pad, top tang safety and an aluminum ramrod. The top barrel is drilled and tapped for scope mounting, if you are so inclined.

The gun points and handles well, given its rather heavy 12 1/2-pound weight. The overall length is 41-1/2 inches. It features a walnut stock and forend, and blued steel receiver and barrels. In states where "two-shoot" guns are legal, this one should be very popular.

Winchester/ Hodgdon Powder Company

Winchester has partnered with Hodgdon Powder Company to produce a new 209 primer called the Winchester Triple 7. This primer is specifically designed for Hodgdon's Triple 7, and Pyrodex powders and pellets. The primer is formulated to give clean-burning of the propellant, and eliminate the ring that often forms just ahead of the chamber portion of the barrel. This has been a recurring problem with the 209 shotgun primer in in-lines for some time.

Muzzleloading hunters and shooters truly live in the best possible time, it would appear. There is a virtual cornucopia of powders, bullets, primers, accessories and guns available to delight the heart of any shooter—whether his interest is in hunting with the latest modern inline, or target-shooting with accurate reproductions of the guns of our forefathers. Something for everybody. ✹

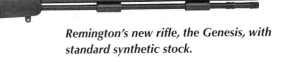

Remington's new rifle, the Genesis, with standard synthetic stock.

The Remington Genesis with the thumb-hole-style stock and the camo option.

HANDLOADING UPDATE

by Larry S. Sterett

Handloading for handgun, rifle, and shotgun cartridges is alive and doing well. In fact, with the retail price of loaded ammunition increasing, more shooters seem to be getting into handloading for their favorite calibers and gauges. This results in new equipment and components being introduced.

Remington introduced the 6.8mm SPC cartridge for the military back in 2004, but sporting rifles and ammunition were slow in getting into the hands of civilians. However, reloading dies, unprimed brass and reloading data are now available. Hornady, Silver State and Barrett (and possibly others) have brass, and Remington should have bullets. Reloading dies are available from Hornady, Lee Precision, Huntington

Ballistic Products Inc. carries just about everything a handloading shotgunner needs—equipment, components and data.

and Redding, and Hodgdon's has reloading data in their *2006 Annual* (page 83) and so does IMR in their basic manual; others will no doubt feature such data in their updated manuals. Suitable primers, powders, and bullets are available for most dealers handling handloading supplies.

Ballistic Products Inc.

Ballistic Products Inc. advertises it has everything for shotgunners, and there's not much the firm does not carry, at least for shotshell handloaders. Hulls, primers, powder, wads, presses, buffer, manuals, 'load log systems,' measures, loading blocks, shell boxes, roll-crimp tools and much more. Currently there are at least sixteen special loading manuals by Ballistic Products, and a baker's dozen 'Technical Guides.' Loading 16-gauge shells, and need more data? Try *The Sixteen Gauge Manual*. Thinking about loading Hevi-Shot? Check out *Handloading Hevi-Shot*. For those whose favorite shotgun is a fine double, maybe chambered for 2-inch shells, there's *Care and Feeding of Fine Doubles*' with loads for 2, 2-1/4 and 2-1/2 inch, plus regular shells, and lots of useful information. BP has roll crimpers in seven sizes: 8, 10, 12, 16, 20, 28 gauges, plus .410-bore. For neatly packaging those reloads, the firm has 25-round boxes to fit most shotshells except the 8-gauge, 3-inch .410 and the 12-gauge hulls measuring

3-1/2 inches. They have 5- and 10-round boxes to fit the 12 gauge in 2-3/4, 3 and 3-1/2 inches length, the 10 gauge, and the 3-inch .410-bore. Other hard-to-find items include Mica Wad-Slick to dust plastic wad column, hull Shape-Up tools, and a Shot & Powder Separator capable of separating size 6 through 9 shot from the powder charge for those times when you forgot to put in the wad column. (You've never done that? Never? Well ... hardly ever.)

Berry's Manufacturing

Berry's Manufacturing produces a wide variety of copper-plated swaged bullets and plastic cartridge boxes in a wide variety of sizes for handloaders. New is an improved formula case lube, a 10-round slip-top box to handle 50 BMG cartridges, a 20-round slip-top box for 416 Rigby and 338 Lapua cartridges, and 50-round hinged-top boxes to handle 45-70 Gov't., Remington Ultra and Winchester WSM cartridges. Their 350-grain 50-caliber Blue Diamond Ballistic Tipped bullets are intended for muzzleloaders, but they might be a surprise in some of the handgun cartridges, such as the 500 Smith & Wesson, 50 Action Express, and even rifles, such as the 502 Thunder Sabre.

Brooks' Tru-Bore Moulds

Another source of moulds for cast bullet users is Brooks' Tru-Bore

Moulds. The cast-iron blocks are lathe-bored in calibers from .320 to .600, and the blocks will fit Saeco handles. Almost any bullet nose design and groove layout can be produced, in a bullet length up to 1-1/2 inches.

Caldwell Shooting Supplies

Reloaders need to check out the end product, especially if it's a new load, prior to loading several hundred rounds. Caldwell Shooting Supplies has just what's needed, a Lead Sled DFT and ZeroMax shooting rest, both for rifles. The ZeroMax is a no-frills full-length rest of steel construction. It permits adjustment for windage and elevation, and comes with an unfilled medium-size varmint bag front rest. The Lead Sled DFT is five inches longer than the original Lead Sled, permitting 22 inches of adjustment, and features a dual frame to help absorb recoil, has 2.5 inches of elevation adjustment on the front rest and two inches of elevation adjustment on the rear rest. The baffled forward tray will hold up to 100 pounds of lead shot, and rubber-tipped feet reduce any tendency of the sled to slide. For handgunners, Caldwell has a new HAMMR rest with built-in windage and elevation adjustments and a hydraulic cylinder that absorbs recoil and resets the handgun. Inserts are available to fit M-1911s, Ruger single actions and S&W K-Frame square-butt handguns, and a universal handgun grip casting kit is available. It's also compatible with Ransom Rest grip inserts.

Colorado Shooter's Supply

Colorado Shooter's Supply has been turning out Hoch custom bullet moulds for a number of years. The moulds are custom-made, lathe-bored, in from one to four cavities. (No moulds are carried in stock.) They are made to the customer's design, are nose-pour, with plain or gascheck base, and can be produced in single cavity up to 75-caliber, and up to 45-caliber in the four-cavity version. (Minimum size is 25-caliber for rifle moulds, and 35 for base-pour handgun moulds. Moulds for handgun bullets contain two, three, or four cavities.) Weights of the cast bullets depend on

the alloy used and the design of the mould, but an 875-grain gas-check bullet for the 50 Sharps or one of the modern firearms with a 1/2-inch bore is possible, and even larger for the really big bores. You design the bullet and Colorado Shooter's Supply will produce the mould for it.

In the 2006 GUN DIGEST, mention was made of the 510 DTC EUROP cartridge as an answer to those states, such as California, where shooting 50 BMG cartridges was nixed. Now there's another new cartridge, the 416 Barrett, which is even better, with a flatter trajectory. Based on a necked-down and shortened 50 BMG case, the 416 Barrett is capable of sending a 400-grain grain bullet downrange at 3250 fps; the bullet is still supersonic at 2500 yards. Currently the only rifle so chambered is the single-

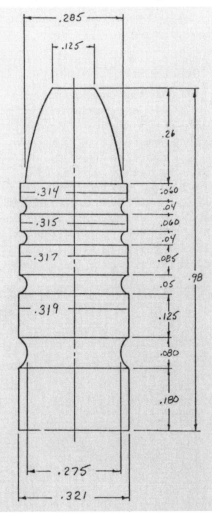

This drawing illustrates the type of bullet design for which Colorado Shooter's Supply can produce bullet moulds.

shot Barrett Model 99 from Barrett Firearms Manufacturing, but Lee Precision has loading dies for the cartridge. Regular 416 bullets should function in the new cartridge, but the two-inch long solid brass 416-size bullets with a ballistic coefficient of 0.943 will be necessary to achieve the desired downrange trajectory. They should be available by the time you read this, along with suggested loading data. (The 1000-yard shooters may enjoy shooting this new gem even more than the 50 BMG.)

Dillon Precision Products

Dillon Precision Products introduced an electric case feeder for the Dillon RL 550 press. It can be retrofitted to all RL 550 presses, and features technology used in the Dillon Super 1050 press. (Use of the case feeder increases productivity by at least 25 percent by reducing hand movements.) It comes with all necessary hardware and step-by-step instructions to make the conversion, and separate conversion kits can be purchased separately for most popular handgun calibers.

Forster

Forster Precision Products has new benchrest dies sets for the 6mm Dasher (BRImp), 6mm XC, 6.8mm SPC, and 325 Winchester Short Magnum (SWM) cartridges. All are available with full-length sizing dies, and the 6.8 SPC may be obtained with a neck-sizing die. Seating dies are available in original Bench Rest Ultra-Micrometer versions. Owners of a Forster Co-Ax reloading press who may have found the standard handle provides more leverage than they require can now order a new shorter handle with a comfortable ball fitting on the end. Another handy item is the stuck case remover for those times you forgot to lube the case prior to resizing and it became stuck in the die. Forster does not produce dies for the 50 BMG cartridge, but the firm does produce a case trimmer especially for this cartridge. The trimmer comes with a .510 pilot and a rim holder; no collet is required as the trimmer is for use only on the 50 BMG case. (An optional .505 pilot is available, if needed.)

Frankford Arsenal

Frankford Arsenal has a new electronic Micro Reloading Scale with a capacity of 750 grains ± .1 grain. (It can weigh in grains, grams and ounces.) Complete with battery, powder tray, cover, case, and calibration weight, the scale is small enough to fit in a shirt pocket. Other handy Frankford products for handloaders include corncob and walnut hull polishing media in treated and untreated grades, overall cartridge length gages, a Vibra-Prime Primer Tube Filler and, for bullet casters, Bullet Mould Cleaner, CleanCast Fluxing Compound and Drop Out, a way to "smoke" your bullet moulds.

GSI International

GSI has a new rotary bullet feeder and feed system to fit the Dillon RL 1050 progressive reloaders. The GSI toolhead features an integrated feed system that delivers bullets to the seating station. Every cycle of the handle feeds and seats a bullet in true progressive fashion.

Bob Hayley

Another source of loading tools, dies, and loaded ammunition and components for obsolete and odd-ball cartridges is Bob Hayley in Seymour, Texas. Need 8.15x46R bullets with central driving band, six-sided Metford bullets, pinfire cartridges, 577 Snider brass, or cartridges or brass for the 401 Winchester Self-Loader? Hayley may have them, and the necessary reloading dies.

Hodgdon

Handloaders can never have enough reloading data, and every new manual is worth having for reference. Hodgdon's *2006 Annual Manual* contains 202 pages of useful information, including ten interesting articles. There are 140 pages of loading data covering nearly 140 rifle cartridges from the 17 Ackley Hornet to the 50 BMG, and including the 6.8mm SPC and 325 WSM; 80 handgun cartridges from the 17 Bumble Bee to the 500 Smith & Wesson, and shotshells from the 10 gauge down to the .410-bore. Data for 17 of the rifle and handgun cartridges has been updated from previous manuals, and five new cartridges have been included, although the 5.7x28mm and 460 Smith & Wesson cartridges are not among them. (All told, this manual features more than 5000 loads.)

Hornady Mfg. Company

Hornady Mfg. Company has gone all out for handloaders in recent years. The Case Activated Powder Drop has been improved for smoother operation, quick change-overs, and to drop powder only when a case is present. The Quick Change Powder Die can now be preset to permit rapid caliber conversions, and to work with the new Powder Through Expanders. (The new expanders (PTX), available in seven sizes: .355, .357, .400, .430, .451/452, .475, and .500––eliminate the need for a separate case mouth expander die.) The Shell Holders have been improved by widening the mouth and rounding the edges, and five new sizes––455 Webley, 460 S&W, 8x56R H-M, 7.5mm Swiss Ordnance and 8x50R––have been introduced. The Shell Plates have also been improved with bevels and a radius at the mouth to provide smooth functioning.

Hornady has improved the Handheld Priming Tool with a new one-piece primer tray and improved lid retaining system. The body has been modified to permit shellholders and primer trays to be changed without removing the spring and punch.

A Pistol Rotor with standard metering insert is now available for use in the L-N-L Powder Measures, and a micrometer metering insert

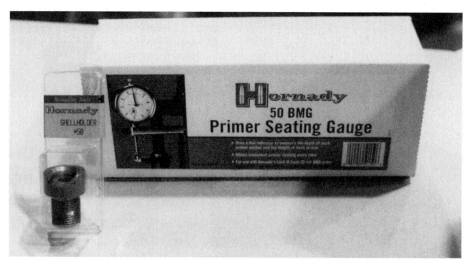

Hornady's new Primer Seating Gauge for the 50 BMG cartridge uses a dial indicator. The 50 BMG cartridge needs a #50 shellholder, shown on the left.

The Hornady Case Activated Powder Drop has been improved for smoother operation, and quick changeovers. One of the new Hornady power-through expander dies can be seen below the Powder Measure.

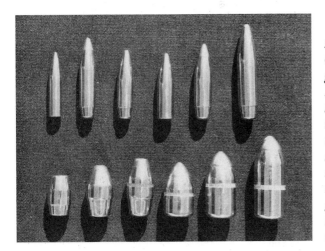

Some specialty rifle and handgun bullets for handloading by Northwest Custom Projectiles. Upper row (L/R): 90-grain bonded core .224, 160-grain .284 with rebated boattail base and work-hardened tip, 140-grain .284 with open tip and rebated boattail base, 140-grain .284 with flat base and open tip, 177-grain .308 with rebated base and work-hardened tip, 300 grain .338 with open tip and rebated boattail base. Lower row (L/R): 180-grain 10mm with rebated boattail base and truncated open nose, 260-grain .452 with rebated boattail base and truncated flat-tip nose, 300-grain .452 with rebated boattail base and truncated flat-tip nose, 350 grain .500 with flat base and flat base and pointed nose, 450-grain .500 with flat base and pointed nose, and 600-grain .510 with flat base and pointed tip for varmint hunting using the 50 BMG or similar cartridge. Other weights are possible.

can be obtained. Hornady has a 50 BMG Powder Measure, and a high-capacity metering kit is an option. (The 50 BMG measure can drop up to 265 grains of powder at a time, and the kit, which comes with a large hopper and a clear drop lube, and two metering units, will allow dropping 80 to 180 grains or 165 to 265 grains.)

Handloaders turning out a lot of 50 BMG, 50 Spotter, 510 DTC EUROP or 416 Barrett ammunition, may find the Hornady 50 BMG Primer Seating Gauge useful. It uses a dial indicator to measure the depth of each primer pocket and the height of each primer to permit the anvil to just touch the bottom of the primer pocket every single time. Thousand-yard shooters may find the bit of added effort pays off in small group sizes.

Hornady now features new and improved zip spindles on their die sets, and has added an even dozen new calibers to the die sets available. These include the 25 WSSM, 6.8mm Rem. SPC, 20 VT, 5.7x28mm FN, 22/250 Ackley Improved, 22x6mm, 280 Ackley Improved, 30-30 Ackley Improved 325 WSM, 7.92x33mm Kurz and the 8x50Rmm. The Ackley Improved cartridges are becoming popular again after more than four decades of seeming decline. (Maybe the 228 Ackley will even gain a new following.)

Another new Hornady die is one for loading blank cartridges for cowboy action shooting. Fitting any standard press that will accept 7/8x14 TPI dies, the 'blank dies' will handle cartridges from the 32-20 Winchester to the 45-70 Government.

Huntington Reloading Products

If a handloader ever needs a piece of equipment; dies, scales, presses, trimmers powder measures, empty brass, bullets, moulds, etc., Huntington in Oroville, California, either has it in stock or can supply it in short order. In 2006 the firm added more than 125 new products for handloaders, including new Norma-produced brass cases for the 303 Savage cartridge. (The 303 Savage seems to be enjoying an increase in popularity and good brass for handloading has been difficult to find. The case can be formed from other calibers, with a bit of work, but Huntington had Norma produce new brass in this caliber.) The firm stocks the RCBS line, including the new Universal Hand Priming Tool, which features an ergonomic grip comfortable for use by right or left-hand users, and it will accept cases from the 32 ACP to the 45-70 Gov't. Two other new RCBS items are the Quick Change Powder Funnel and the Pan Scale Powder Funnel. Constructed of anti-static polymers, the QC funnel comes with five adapters and one drop tube, while the QC Pan Funnel will accommodate cases from 22 to 50-caliber. Huntington has more reloading and case-forming dies than any firm in the U. S., and probably worldwide. (The smallest forming dies are the 17s, and the largest are for the 585 Nyati.) Case brands available include Bertram, Magtech, Jamison, Norma, Starline, Winchester, Weatherby, HDS, Remington, Graf, Hornady, Horneber, Bell, Buffalo Bore, Federal, Lapua, Hirtenberger, Howell, RWS and Walter Gehmann brands. (Single cases can be purchased for many of the calibers, at prices ranging

J & J Products has a couple of new plastic cases for ammunition. This one will accept almost all cases from the 45-70 Gov't. to the 600 Nitro Express. It will not accept the 50 BMG or the 50-140 Express, but the cartridges shown are the 50-110, 338 Lapua, 416 Rigby, 408 CheyTac (This particular bullet is just a bit too long for the lid to fit properly.), 500 Jeffery, 400 A-Square and 500 Phantom.

from sixteen cents each (Starline 9mm Makarov) to thirty-five dollars each (700 NE and 4-Bore).

Lee Precision

Lee Precision has new Bottleneck Crimp Dies for the 30 (7.65mm) Luger, 30 Tokarev (7.62mm), 30 Mauser (7.63mm), 357 SIG, and 400 Cor-Bon cartridges, and EasyX reloading dies from the 17 Remington to the 458 Winchester Magnum, including the 6.8mm Remington SPC. Lee also produces dies for the 50 BMG cartridge, and has a case length gauge for the 50 BMG cartridge. The Lee Turret Press (3 die), and the Lee Classic Turret Press (4 die), which is large enough to handle the 50 BMG case––with the Auto-Index disconnected––are fitted with the Lever Prime System.

Load Data

More and more loading data is available through computer programs and via the net. Purchasing the programs or subscribing to the service is the only requirement (read, *get out your credit card.*) One such service, Load Data, at www.loaddata.com, allows access to over 35 years of information from the pages of *Rifle* and *Handloader* magazines for one year.

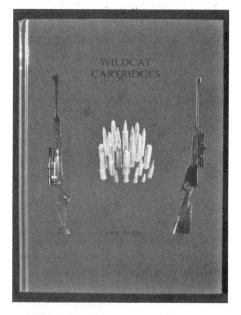

Wildcat Cartridges contains handloading data on many of the newer wildcat cartridges, and a number of the older designs.

LR Books

I have always had a fondness for wildcat cartridges, both for handguns and rifles. Finding loading data for such cartridges is not always easy, as many manuals do not provide such data. One of the newest sources for wildcat loading data can be found in *Wildcat Cartridges* by Fred Zeglin and published by LR Books. This 292-page hardbound volume doesn't cover every wildcat cartridge ever produced, but it covers many of both the older and newer designs, plus contains some good information on cartridges such as the 400 Whelen. (Chamber dimensions for the Whelen are included, along with a number of loads featuring modern bullet designs.) Chapter 18 is devoted to today's popular wildcats, from the 10 Eichelberger Squirrel, which can push a 7.2 grain bullet past 4000 fps, to the 50 BMD Short which is capable of sending a 750-grain A-MAX downrange at 1250 fps. (The 458 SOCOM is covered, but not the 500 Phantom, a design capable of pushing a 900-grain bullet out the muzzle at over 1100 fps. Loading data accompanies most of the wildcats discussed, along with a dimensioned case drawing, and background text. Data for the Rocky Gibbs cartridges is provided in a separate chapter, as are the designs of Charles Newton and other earlier experimenters. Anyone handloading for a wildcat cartridge will find this a useful reference volume.

Lyman Products Corporation

Lyman Products Corporation has new die sets for the 6.8mm SPC and the 405 Winchester cartridges, and new bullet moulds for the 405 and for 50-caliber shooters. The 405 Winchester mould will cast a 288-grain round-nose bullet, while the 50 mould will cast a 515-grain flat nose design. Both designs are originals from the heyday of these cartridges, and have been returned to production status.

The 48th edition of the *Lyman Reloading Handbook* and the third edition of the *Pistol & Revolver Handbook* need to be on every handloader's reference shelf. The *Reloading Handbook* features pressure-tested reloading data for all but the very latest rifle cartridges, plus

Norma's Reloading Manual *is the first in the history of the century-old firm, and it is excellent.*

an expanded handgun section. It includes some smokeless powder loads for modern blackpowder guns. Most powders, from Alliant to VihtaVuori and Winchester, are covered, along with most modern jacketed bullet brands, and many cast bullets. (No loading data for the 6.8mm SPC, 5.7x28mm, etc. cartridges in this edition.) The *Pistol & Revolver Handbook* covers the majority of current production handgun cartridges, with the exception on the 460 Smith & Wesson cartridge. Loading data is provided for the 45 GAP, 480 Ruger and 500 Smith & Wesson cartridges, with updating on the 'Cowboy' cartridges such as the 38-40, 44-40, 44 Russian, 45 Schofield and 45 Colt.

Magma Engineering Company

Magma Engineering Company, manufacturer of the Mark 7 Bullet Master, the Master Caster, Masterpot and other equipment for turning out cast bullets in quantity, has several new items. The firm has more than 200 styles of bullet moulds available, which can be machine-ready or fitted with RCBS or Lyman handles. A new Multi-Impact System is available for the Bullet Master, and so is a Bullet Separator System. The Multi-Impact provides multiple taps to the bullet mould to aid in releasing large and/or sticking bullets, and the Bullet Separator separates the bullets into trays for easy inspection. (Both systems can be retrofitted to earlier Bullet Masters.) New conversions to handle longer rifle bullets are standard on current production Lube Master machines, and they can be retrofitted to earlier models.

Montana Vintage Arms

MVA has a new visible powder measure with a micrometer-adjustable scale. Intended for use when loading blackpowder cartridges, the measure comes with a brass hopper of choice, holding 1/4, 1/2 or a full pound of powder. (The scale holds approximately 125 grains of FFg powder.) Extra hopper and scale are available.

NECO

NECO is distributing a new German-manufactured chronograph––the PVN-21. Based on a quarter-century of experimental engineering ballistic velocity measurement systems, the PVN-21 can handle calibers from the 17 to 50 and velocities from 280 to 6500 fps. It features a daylight-independent infrared light-screen for indoor or outdoor use with a 4 x 8-inch sensor, and an accuracy of ±1 percent. It has a 250-shot memory, and a power consumption of 2.1 watts.

NECO is a source of computer-based handloading data. The firm will even provide a free demo disk for their QuickDesign and QuickLoad programs. These computer-aided cartridge design and viewer software, and interior and exterior ballistics programs require MS-Windows versions 98SE, ME, 2000 SP3 and XP SP1 systems to operate. Such programs may not provide all the answers, but it's another method of obtaining desired data.

Norma Precision

Over a century ago in Amotfors, Sweden, the firm of Norma Precision AB (www.norma.cc) got its start. Set up to produce 6.5x55mm bullets for Swedish Mauser rifle cartridges, the firm gained a reputation for

producing top quality ammunition and reloading components, including powders for reloading. Yet, during that time the firm never published a loading manual––until now.

The Norma manual includes loading data for over six dozen cartridges, from the 222 Remington to the 505 Gibbs. Norma cases, powders and bullets are featured, coupled with Winchester primers. (Data is provided for some other bullet brands, including Hornady, Sierra, Nosier, Swift A-Frame and Woodleigh.) For each cartridge, a dimensioned drawing is provided, along with specs of the test barrel, the case brand and primer used. A short history of the cartridge is presented, and an illustration of each bullet for which loading data is listed precedes the actual data, along with the ballistic coefficient, overall cartridge length and bullet number. Minimum and maximum powder charges are listed for each bullet weight, along with the muzzle velocity in feet/second (fps) and meters/second (m/s).

No data is provided for handgun cartridges such as the 44 AutoMag and 44 Remington Magnum, both of which Norma produced, or for the 7x61mm Sharpe & Hart rifle cartridge. Data is included for the 308 and 358 Norma Magnum cartridges, plus a number of the military cartridges for which Norma produces brass.

Other material in this manual include the history of the Norma firm, descriptions of the Norma bullets,

A 'demo' QuickDesign and QuickLoad CD available from Nostalgia Enterprises Co.

powder production, how to make a cartridge, a discussion of primers, step-by-step reloading, and much more. Loading data for cartridges such as the 6.8mm SPC and 50 BMG is missing.

Nosler

Nosler, a leading name in bullet manufacturing, has been in business since 1948, and now builds bolt-action rifles––the Model 48 Sporter and the 2006 NoslerCustom––loads ammunition, and features a line of premium brass cartridge cases for handloaders in thirteen calibers, in addition to the regular bullet line. (The unprimed cases range from the 204 Ruger to the 300 Weatherby Magnum, and include the 6.5-284 Norma. The loaded ammunition

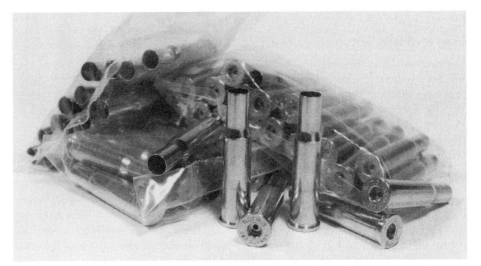

Unprimed Norma brass available from Huntington for the 303 Savage cartridge. Huntington also has loading dies for the 303 Savage, an early cartridge equal to the 30-30 Winchester and claimed by some riflemen to be even better.

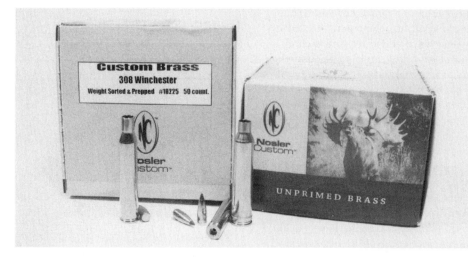

Nosler's unprimed brass for handloaders is available for cartridges ranging from the 204 Ruger to the 300 Weatherby Magnum.

covers more than forty different cartridges from the 204 Ruger to the 416 Weatherby Magnum, and the *Nosler Reloading Guide No. 5* provides the data for reloading the empties after you've fired the ammunition.

Oehler Research

Every handloader should have access to a chronograph and Ken Oehler's are among the best available. However, production of the excellent Model 35 was suspended on January 1, 2006, although tech support and spare parts are still available. The Model 43 chronograph with SS3 and Windows Software is available. Acoustic targets, strain gages, pressure starter kit and other accessories are also available from Oehler Research in Austin, Texas.

Power Aisle, Inc.

Power Aisle, Inc. has several items handloaders can use, including the Precision Sighting Rest, Back Pack Varmint Bench, Pivoting Pistol Rest, Pivoting Varmint Rest, and the new Danger Game Machine Rest. This latter item, which should be available by the time you read this, rigidly holds a rifle or shotgun in firing position, is fully adjustable for leveling, windage and elevation, and is hydraulically fired. It eliminates the human error, and provides a look at exactly what the cartridge (handload or factory) will do in that particular firearm. It's a worthwhile investment for anyone doing much handloading.

RCE Co.

RCE Co. produces a full line of swaging gear for bullet production, plus a couple of special bullet jacket drawing presses. Swaged bullets can be turned out in sizes from 12-caliber to 37mm. RCE presses include the heavy-duty Walnut Hill hand press, a small MultiSwage hydraulic press for home or light commercial use and the larger Benchmaster and HydraSwage presses intended for continuous commercial use. With a background of more than thirty years in the business, RCE swaging equipment is time-tested.

A few of the big-bore cartridges for which reloading dies are available from various die manufacturers, such as Hornady, Lee Precision, and RCBS, or dealers handling their products. (Huntington and The Old Western Scrounger are also good sources for such dies.) (L/R): 50 BMG, 510 DTC EUROP, 50 Spotter, 416 Rigby, 408 CheyTac and the 416 Barrett.

Not everything new for handloaders has been covered. No doubt something has been missed, but a good majority has been touched on. What's been missed will hopefully be covered in the next edition, along with more new products.

RCBS

RCBS has a new 284-page *Handbook of Shotshell Reloading*, featuring over 2000 loads. It also contains a color identification photo of plastic wad columns, a tear-out safety wall chart, 56 separate reference notes on shotshell hulls, color identification photos of external and sectioned views of various hulls currently available, a section showing parts and drawings of RCBS shotshell presses, and much more.

For shooters reloading for handgun and rifle cartridges, there's a new 325 SWM Precision Mic for headspace measurement, two new deburring tools: one to handle deburring and outside chamfering of cases from 17 to 60 caliber, and a second for use when loading VLD-style bullets, a Hand Case Neck Turner, a Universal Hand Priming Tool with a shellholder that will accept cases from the 32 ACP to the 45-70 Government, and several new reloading die calibers. (New dies are available for the 5.7x28mm FN, 325 WSM, 338 Federal, and 460 Smith & Wesson cartridges, with the 460 S&W available in the 3-Die Carbide Roll Crimp set and the 325 WSM available in full length and X-Die sets.) For bullet casters, RCBS has over forty mould designs for handgun bullets, including one for a 400-grain SWC intended for use in the 500 Smith & Wesson.

RCBS has two new quick-change powder measures, one regular and one high capacity. This latter one can drop up to 240 grains of smokeless powder at a time, and will accommodate two pounds of powder in the hopper. Each measure comes with drop tubes, metering assembly, and quick-drain attachment. (These qc attachments are also available separately to permit upgrading existing Uniflow power measures.)

Redding

Redding Reloading Equipment celebrated its 60th anniversary in 2006 with the introduction of a considerable number of new products for handloaders. The Model 2400 Match Precision Case Trimming Lathe features micrometer adjustment to 0.001-inch, and will handle cases up to 3-1/4 inches in length. The cutter is titanium nitride-coated, and is replaceable, if necessary. The frame is cast iron with storage holes for extra pilots. (Primer pocket cleaners and neck-cleaning brushes can be mounted on the frame, if desired.) A universal collet, with push-button chuck lock, will handle most cases, and an optional power adapter with 1/4-inch hex is available to permit powering with a cordless screwdriver.

Other new Redding products include the "E-Z Feed" shellholders to permit easier case head entry, and a shellholder set containing six of the most popular shellholders—#1, #6, #10, #12, #18, and #19. These six shellholders will accommodate the most common (popular) rifle and handgun cartridges; examples include 30-06 Springfield, 7mm Remington Magnum, 223 Remington, 7.62x39mm, 45-70 Gov't. and 44 Magnum, plus those cartridges with similar rim sizes. Shellholders are available to fit most other cartridges, except the 50 BMG.

New Redding Competition Handgun Seating Dies and Competition Pro Series Die Sets are now available for the 460 and 500 Smith & Wesson Magnum cartridges. Other new die sets are available for the 338 Federal and 5.7x28mm FN cartridges in Type S, Match Die, and Competition Seating Dies. In addition, Bushing Style dies are available for the 20 Vartarg, 20 PPC, 20 BR, 6mm XC, and 30 BR Remington cartridges, plus in the regular die sets. Special small base, full length sizing dies are available to size 22 PPC, 6mm PPC, and 6mm BR Remington cases. Universal Decapping Die in small and large sizes can be obtained to deprime cases prior to resizing for those reloaders desiring to do so. The small die will handle cases from 22 through 50 caliber up to 2.625 inches in length, while the large die will do those cases from 25 through 50 caliber up to 3.00 inches in length. An optional 17-caliber decapping rod is available.

Imperial Sizing Die Wax has been available for a number of years, but Redding is now producing it, along with an Action Wax for use on autoloading pistol slides, bolt ways, etc. The paraffin-based Imperial Wax is excellent for sizing cases; it does the job without the mess and sticking of some lubricants used for sizing.

The Shiloh Sharps Rifle Mfg. Co.

Shiloh has an inline seater press that fits into the top of a regular press. Coupled with a Shiloh inline-seating die it seats bullets without distortion. Made specifically for 40- and 45-caliber Sharps cartridges, such as the 40-60, 40-90, 45-70, 45-100 and 45-120; nose punches are available for specific designs. Shiloh also has 20- and 50-hole loading blocks available to fit the large 40- and 45-caliber cartridges, and a 24-hole version for the rimmed 50-calibers (not the 50 BMG). For those handloaders with a preference for long drop tubes, Shiloh has one mounted on an oak base. Useful for a single case or with cases in a loading block, the tube and funnel are of polished brass.

VihtaVuori

Lapua ammunition, primers, bullets and VihtaVuori powders from Finland have been available for more than seven decades, and the excellent VihtaVuori Reloading Manual has gone through three editions. The loading data section includes loads for some cartridges not always found in other manuals. Among such cartridges are the 5.6x35R Vierling, 220 Russian, 5.6x50 and 5.6x50R Magnum, 5.7x57, 6.5x53R Finnish, 7x33 SAKO, and 8.2x53R Finnish. Loading data for handgun cartridges ranges from the 25 ACP to the 50 Action Express, including a few of the lesser known designs, such as the 7x49 GJW. (The 7x49 GJW is based on the 5.6x50 Magnum case with expanded neck to use in silhouette shooting.) Lapua has introduced a new 6.5x47 cartridge with a head diameter and overall length similar to that of the 308 Winchester (7.62 NATO). Loading data was not available as this is being written,

A video Reloading With the Master is available through dealers handling VihtaVuori smokeless powder and Lapua bullets and/or ammunition.

but should be in the new, expanded fourth edition of the VihtaVuori Manual, available at your local dealer about the time you read this.

Not everything new for handloaders has been covered. No doubt something has been missed, but a good majority has been touched on. What's been missed will hopefully be covered in the next edition, along with more new products. ✸

AMMUNITION, BALLISTICS & COMPONENTS

by Holt Bodinson

Just when you begin to feel there's just not room for another commercially viable cartridge, the manufacturers surprise us again and again with some great new offerings.

Who would have thought the venerable 308 Winchester case that has been around since 1952 would be morphed into yet another successful cartridge? This year Federal did it and names the case after the company-- the 338 Federal. A-Square unleashes the 400 Dual Purpose Magnum. Freedom Arms comes roaring in with their belted 500 Wyoming Express. Hornady pumps new power into the 30-30, 35 Rem., 444 Rem., 45-70 and 450 Marlin lever-gun cartridges under the catchy banner of "LeverEvolution."

And new high-tech game bullets! Winchester engineers the XP3 and Barnes comes across with the MRX.

And high-tech shot! Remington stops loading Hevi-Shot and launches Wingmaster HD across the line while Winchester ramps up their Xtended Range Hi-Density shot offerings for waterfowl and turkey.

Industry shifts go on. Hodgdon seems to have a magic touch. Two years ago it acquired IMR Powder. This year Winchester Ammunition licenses Hodgdon to take over all their canister sales of the Winchester powder line. Meanwhile, Hodgdon even has time to come to the table with a new magnum powder of their own—US869.

The ammunition, ballistic and components markets just get more interesting with every passing year.

A-Square Company

A-Square's founder, Arthur Alphin, has resumed management of the company. Well known for its unique cartridge offerings, A-Square hasn't disappointed us for 2007. The new member of the lineup is the 400 A-Square Dual Purpose Magnum. Dual purpose? Based on the belted H&H case, the new 400 is loaded with either the company's "Triad" of 400-grain big game bullets or lighter .410-inch pistol bullets for medium-size game and varmints. Velocity of the 400- and 210-grain pills is 2400 fps while the 170-grain pistol bullet steps out at 2980 fps. Intriguing, to say the least. www.a-squarecompany.com

Alliant Powder

Alliant has a new target shotgun powder. It's Clay Dot and appears to have a loading equivalence and burning rate similar to Hodgdon's Clays. Look for it, and its loading data, at your dealer. www.alliantpowder.com

Ballistic Products

Here's the one-stop store for all your shotgun shell reloading and component needs bound in one of the most entertaining and informative catalogs ever fielded.

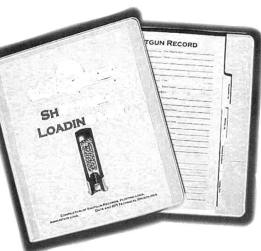

Ballistic Products' "Shotshell Reloaders Log" provides a permanent record of personal handloads and their performance.

The best of their new products this year are their new publications. The shotshell reloader's bible is their "Advantages IV," that chronicles everything you need to know to build a better shell. "Dove & Pigeon Magic" serves up some natural history and the most effective recipes for bagging and eating our most common avian fauna.

There's a brand-new *Shotshell Reloading Log*, and don't pass up their informative "Ballistic Products Technical Brochures." Need a deadly 20-gauge load for late-season pheasants, or a light load for directing the mighty 10-gauge toward crows and clays? Ballistic Products is the mother lode. www.ballisticproducts.com

Barnes Bullets

The highly successful Triple-Shock bullet has been morphed into the MRX bullet, standing for "Maximum-Range X-Bullet." As a cooperative venture with Federal, that will be loading the new bullet in its Premium line, the MRX bullet features a tungsten-alloy core and a polymer tip in the familiar Triple-Shock platform. Field reports indicate the MRX performs well on light game as well as heavy game—and at both close and distant ranges. Available as a reloading component from Barnes, the MRX will initially be offered in 20-bullet packs in 270, 7mm, 30 and 338 calibers in a variety of bullet weights. Also new to the line this year is a new solid copper, 50-caliber muzzleloading bullet featuring a boattail base and polymer tip for exceptional ballistic

Black Hills offers a full ammunition line spiked with Barnes Triple-Shock bullets.

performance. Labeled the "Spit-Fire TMZ," it is available in 250- and 290-grain weights in 15- and 24-bullet packs. www.barnesbullets.com

Berger Bullets

Designed for long-range varminting, hot 22-caliber cf rifles, and fast twist barrels, Berger is now offering a 90-grain VLD hunting bullet with a BC of .517 and a 77-grain boattail with a BC of .387. Both new bullets are available with either conventional or moly-coated jackets. www.bergerbullets.com

Black Hills Ammunition

When our armed services go shopping for match- and sniper-grade ammunition, where do they go? They go to Black Hills, which now holds the 5.56mm contracts for the USMC rifle team, the Army's Marksmanship Unit, and the Navy's Surface Warfare Center. In fact, Black Hills offers more loads for the 223 Rem. than any other manufacturer, ranging from a 40-grain V-MAX at 3600 fps to a 77-grain Sierra MatchKing at 2750 fps. Lots of new hunting loads this year feature Barnes Triple-Shock and Hornady A-MAX and V-MAX bullets. See them at www.black-hills.com

Brenneke USA

Wilhelm Brenneke invented the composite

shotgun slug in 1898. The classic Brenneke was just redesigned, or tweaked a bit, with supporting plastic disks on both ends of the attached wad and a new H-wad between the powder and the slug. Brenneke USA indicates the new "Classic" 12-gauge, 2 3/4-inch slug is delivering groups under two inches at 50 yards and is suitable for either smooth or rifled bores. www.brennekeusa.com

CCI

CCI's Green Tag 22 LR match cartridge has an enviable record on the target range. Well, Green Tag has now been joined by a new match load specifically tuned to target-grade semi-auto rifles. The new "22 LR Select" features a 40-grain bullet at 1200 fps to keep those semi-autos functioning reliably in a competitive environment. The 22 Win. Mag. has been given a 21st century face lift

Barnes' technologically crafted MRX and Spit-Fire TMZs are among the most advanced bullets ever produced.

The classic Brenneke slug has been updated and is proving more accurate than ever.

CCI and Federal both offer a new 22 LR match cartridge for semi-autos.

with a new load featuring a 40-grain GamePoint controlled expansion softpoint at 1875 fps. The bullet is designed to hold together and mushroom, not fragment. It is proving effective on larger varmints like coyotes, while not destroying meat and hides on small species. Speaking of limiting tissue destruction in game, CCI is also fielding a new 20-grain FMJ loading for the 17 HMR at 2375 fps. www.cci-ammunition.com

CheyTac

Designed to fill the gap between the 338 Lapua and the 50 BMG, while outperforming the 50 BMG downrange, the 408 CheyTac cartridge features a 419-grain, lathe-turned, copper nickel alloy bullet manufactured by Lost River Ballistic Technologies. The long, pointy bullet has an average BC of .945 with a muzzle velocity of 2900 fps.

The CheyTac sniping system—which consists of a rifle, sound moderator, ballistics calculator linked to a weather sensor and a variety of sighting devices—is designed to neutralize soft targets to a distance of 2500 yards. www.cheytac.com

Cor-Bon

It's taken Cor-Bon many years to offer a premium line of rifle ammunition, but 2007 changes that. Their new DPX line of hunting ammunition is based on loading the Barnes Triple-Shock bullet in calibers from 223 Rem. through 45-70. The company continues to offer their original high performance handgun

ammunition line as well as their Glaser Safety Slug, Pow'R Ball, Cowboy Action and DPX pistol lines. www.corbon.com

Federal

Do you know that Federal has never launched a cartridge that carries its name? Now they have! The new 338 Federal is based on a necked-up 308 Win. case and the ballistic performance it offers is impressive, especially when chambered in the short, light, handy rifles of today. The factory loads consist of a 180-grain Nosler AccuBond at 2830 fps; a 185-grain Barnes Triple-Shock at 2750 fps and a 210-grain Nosler Partition at 2630 fps. Excellent game loads all!

The big news in the Premium rifle ammunition line is the addition of the new Barnes MRX bullet as a 180-grain loading for the 308 Win., 30-06, 300 WSM and 300 Win. Mag. Look for the addition of Barnes Triple-Shock bullets to the 375 H&H, 416 Rem. Mag and Rigby and 458 Win. Mag. loadings that are now appropriately labeled "Cape. Shok." Federal's "Fusion" line, which features hunting bullets with the jacket plated to the core, has been expanded to include handgun calibers, specifically the 357 Mag., 41 Mag., 44 Mag. and 454 Casull, as well as a number of new rifle calibers. Federal's tight patterning "Flitecontrol" wad that first appeared in their turkey loads is now being employed in their 12-gauge 00 buckshot loads to improve pattern density at all ranges.

Recognizing that shooters are increasingly using computer-based ballistics programs, Federal now offers its own version, either online or as a download. See it at www.federalpremium.com

Federal finally has a cartridge that carries its name—the 338 Federal.

Fiocchi

Fiocchi introduced some interesting new ammunition lines being produced at their Ozark, Missouri plant. Loaded with Sierra MatchKing bullets, there's an Exacta Rifle Match line composed of the 223 Rem., 30-06 and 308 Win. cartridges as well as an Exacta Pistol IPSC Match line covering the 38 Super, 40 S&W, 45 Auto and 9mm Luger. Then there's an Extrema Rifle Hunting line featuring Hornady SST and Sierra GameKing bullets, and also an Extrema Pistol line based around the Hornady XTPHP bullets. www.fiocchiusa.com

Freedom Arms

Searching for a way to chamber a 50-caliber cartridge in their Model 83 series revolvers, Bob Baker, president of Freedom Arms, created an entirely new case that headspaces on a belt rather than a conventional rim. Named the Freedom Arms 500 Wyoming express (500WE), the 1.37-inch case is designed for .500-inch diameter bullets in the 350-450-grain range. Baker writes that "the cartridge was designed to not only get outstanding and predictable ballistic performance but to minimize forcing cone erosion, thereby extending the useful life of your Freedom Arms revolver. This is done by matching powder column length, powder volume, and bullet diameter to an expected range of bullet weights, velocity ranges and pressure levels." Brass and handloading data are available at the web site. Factory loaded ammunition should be available later in the year. There's something new at www.freedomarms.com

Hevi-Shot

Look out pheasants! Hevi-Shot has come up with two pheasant loads packing #5 Hevi-Shot. There's a 2-3/4-inch/12-ga. loading consisting of 1-1/8 oz. at 1350 fps and a 2 3/4-inch/20-ga. load with 1 oz. at 1250 fps. Speaking about the 20 gauge, there are three, exciting, new 3-inch/20-ga. waterfowl loads consisting of 1-1/4 oz. of #2, 4, and 6 Hevi-Shot at 1250 fps. The licensing agreement with Remington has expired so Hevi-Shot has launched its own independent ammunition company using the trademarks Hevi-Steel, Hevi-13, and Dead Coyote.

Look for their new ammo on your dealer's shelves. www.hevishot.com

Hodgdon

Here's an interesting development. Hodgdon will now handle all of Winchester Ammunition's canister powder sales and distribution. Under their own labels, Hodgdon is introducing a super magnum spherical rifle powder, US869, designed for the 50 BMG—but equally useful in cartridges like the 300 Rem. Ultra-Mag. and the 30-378 Weatherby. New in the IMR powder line is "Trail Boss," a light, fluffy, high-bulk powder designed for the reduced loads commonly used in cowboy action events. Offering excellent ballistic uniformity, it occupies so much case volume that it is difficult to double-charge a case. The new Hodgdon manual is out, and it's a dilly, covering over 5000 loads and new cartridges like the 325 WSM and the 204 Ruger. www.hodgdon.com

Hornady

Who would have thought that lever-action ammunition would get a major work over in the 21st century? It did. Hornady's "LeverEvolution" ammo for the 30-30, 35 Rem., 444 Marlin, 45-70 and 450 Marlin has set new performance benchmarks for trajectory, energy and expansion. The secret is a newly-

50 BMG shooters will find Hodgdon's new US 869 the perfect companion.

Hornady's "LeverEvolution" loads put some snap into our woods rifles.

designed series of sleek spitzer boattail bullets that are safe when stacked in a tubular magazine—thanks to their soft elastomer tips. The new loads are fast, too. The 30-30 ammunition carries a 160-grain bullet with a velocity of 2400 fps. Sighted in 3 inches high at 100 yards, the new 30-30 round is on at 200 yards and 12 inches low at 300. That's flat. Other new ammunition offerings include the 416 Rigby, 338 Lapua, spitzer loads for the 460 S&W and 500 S&W, a 250-grain/20-gauge SST shotgun slug at 1800 fps and a 45-grain loading for the 204 Ruger at 3625 fps. New components? There's a 25-grain/17-caliber V-MAX, an 80-grain/224-caliber A-MAX and a 250-grain/338 BTHP. Big Red has been busy. www.hornady.com

Huntington

Buzz Huntington scours the globe for hard-to-find reloading components. If it's not catalogued, he can usually find it. Looking for a 500-grain bullet

for your 50-110 Win. or 50 Alaskan? Huntington's has it under the excellent Woodleigh "Weldcore" label. In fact, Huntington's is the U.S. importer for the complete Woodleigh bullet line. Look for a wide selection of Jamison-made brass this year, including the 404 Jeffrey, 500 Jeffrey, 577-450 MH, 45-110/2 7/8-inch SS, 50-140/3 1/4-inch, 256 Win., and 351 WSL. Huntington's is also the place to shop for RCBS tooling and parts, both old and new. Try www.huntingtons.com. You'll be amazed what's there.

Lapua

The Finns have cooked up a new 6.5mm match cartridge, the 6.5x47 Lapua. The 6.5x47 case has been optimized for powder efficiency and match bullets. It has the same base diameter and a slightly shorter case than the 308 Win. so that it will function in 308 Win.-length actions. With a working pressure of 63,090 psi, it's a high-intensity cartridge offering 3084 fps with the 108-grain Scenar bullet, 2887 fps with the 123-grain Scenar and 2288 fps with the 139-grain Scenar. www.lapua.com

Magkor

Makers of that blackpowder substitute, Black Mag'3, Magkor is introducing the "Thundercharge." Thundercharge is a 45- or 50-caliber bullet wedded to a rigid column of Black Mag'3. They're calling it a "caseless cartridge for in-line muzzleloaders" and they're right. See it at www.magkor.com

Magtech Ammunition

When I went looking for a basic brass case to form into a 577 Snider, Magtech came to the rescue with their imported 24-gauge, brass shotshells. In fact, they offer brass shells designed to accept Large Pistol primers for the 9.1, 36, 32, 28, 24, 20, 16 and 12 gauges. In their popular handgun cartridge lines, they've added solid copper hollowpoint (SCHP) bullets across the board, to include the 454 Casull and 500 S&W. www.magtechammunition.com

Midway

Check out Midway's new on-line "GunTec Dictionary." It contains 5,300 firearm terms and definitions. If you want a short, concise definition for a complex term like "ballistic coefficient," visit www.midwayusa.com/dictionary for an answer.

NobelSport

Look for NobelSpeed Sporting Clays 12-gauge shotshells this year. Speedy they are. With 1 or 1-1/8 oz. of # 7.5 or 8, the new NobelSpeed shells are ripping out there at 1300 fps. www.nobelsportammo.com

Norma

Here's one for that special shooter who has everything. It's the "Norma Special Edition" set. Norma will engrave his or her name on thirty handloaded cartridges in either 9.3x74R or 300 Win. Mag. The cartridges feature gold-plated bullets and black ruthenium-plated cases, and are neatly displayed in a deluxe locking case. There's even a personalized certificate of authenticity included with the set. www.norma.cc

Nosler

Interesting line extensions. New this year in the AccuBond line are a 165-grain/308-caliber and a 200-grain/338-caliber bullet. The increasingly popular 204 Ruger got some attention with the introduction of the 40-grain/204-caliber Ballistic Tip Varmint pill, while in Nosler's Custom Competition line, there's a new 52-grain/.224-inch HPBT. www.nosler.com

Polywad

Hold on to those beautiful, vintage shotguns. Ever-innovative Polywad has designed two shotshells that keep pressures low, recoil mild while delivering great patterns. The "Vintager" comes as a 2-inch/12-gauge shell loaded with 24 grams of #6, 7.5 or 8 shot or as a 2 1/2-inch/20-gauge shell with a 3/4-oz. shot load. The companion shell is called the "DoubleWide," which carries the shot charge in Polywad's famous "Spred-R" wad. www.polywad.com

Prvi Partizan

Located in Serbia, Prvi Partizan has become a significant force in the international ammunition market, supplying not only loaded ammunition but component brass and bullets. One of its specialties is making runs of difficult-to-find and obsolete ammunition and brass which this year includes the 22 Rem. Jet Magnum, 7.92x33 Kurz, 8x50R Lebel, 7.5x55 Swiss, 6.5 Grendel and 7.62 Nagant. See www.prvipartizan.com and www.grafs.com

Puff-Lon

Puff-Lon is a new lubricating granulated filler that eliminates air space inside cartridge cases, isolates the base of the bullet from hot gases, and lubricates the barrel when fired. It's made from 100% pure cellulose blended with a mix of dry, synthetic lubricants. Those who've tried it, like it. www.pufflon.com

Remington

The big news at Big Green is Wingmaster HD, a proprietary shot composed of tungsten, bronze and iron with a density of 12 grams/cc

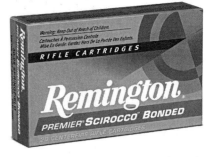

Remington continues to upgrade its big-game loads with bullets like the Swift Scirocco.

that will replace the company's use of Hevi-Shot. The new shot is round, smooth and consistent in size—which translates into equal energy in every pellet and dense, efficient patterns without troublesome flyers. Having a hardness rating similar to steel, Wingmaster HD responds well to similar choke settings. Approved for waterfowling, Wingmaster HD will be loaded across-the-board from the 3 1/2-inch /10-gauge to the 3-inch /20-gauge. The new loads are fast, too, ranging from 1300-1450 fps. The company slogan for Wingmaster HD is "Drop-Dead-Better." In the rifle ammunition lines, the 7mm Rem. Ultra Mag and the 300 WSM are being upgraded with Swift Scirocco Bonded bullets; the 270 WSM, 7mm Rem. Mag., 30-06, and 300 WSM are now offered with the AccuTip bullets; and the 7mm Rem. Ultra Mag and 300 Rem. Ultra Mag are being topped off with Swift's stout A-Frame projectiles. Managed recoil is still in, with two new STS target loads for the 2-3/4-inch/12 and 20 gauges consisting of 7/8-oz. of #8-1/2s at 1100 fps as well as a 7/8-oz. "Buckhammer" slug in the 20 gauge at 1275 fps. www.remington.com

Schroeder Bullets

Steve Schroeder is known for his 5mm conversion kits for the 5mm Remington Models 591/592, as well as for one of the most comprehensive offerings of difficult-to-find bullets and formed cases. Here's the place to find 130-grain/8mm bullets for the 7.92x33, or 10 bullet designs for the 8mm Nambu, or .351-

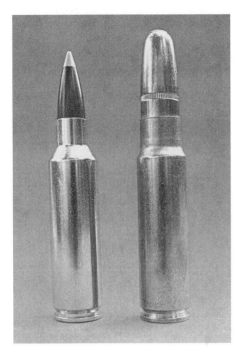

Sisk Rifles took the 325 WSM, necked it up to 416, and created a short magnum that equals the 404 Jeffrey.

inch diameter bullets for the 351 Win., or cases for Herter's 401 Powermag. You can reach him in San Diego at (619) 423-3523.

Sierra

The Bulletsmiths have been busy. Imagine a 90-grain/.224-inch HPBT match bullet requiring a 1x6.5" twist or faster for the 223 Rem/5.56x45 cartridge. The BC of this long, snaky, new pill is .504 at 2200 fps or faster! Then there's a 115-grain/.277-inch HPBT MatchKing aimed at the 6.8mm SPC market but equally useful in any 270-caliber gun. For those 1000-yard matches, there's a new 210-grain/.308-inch MatchKing that has been optimized with a longer ogive, smaller meplat, and improved boattail for downrange efficiency. www.sierrabullets.com

SinterFire

The leading industry supplier of lead-free, powdered copper/tin bullets, SinterFire has now developed its own lines of loaded ammunition. Its "Reduced Hazard Ammunition" offers two bullet weights in each

of the following calibers: 9mm, 40 S&W, and 45 ACP. It's designed for reduced "splash-back" range training. The "GreenLine" adds a lead-free primer to the load. "Special Duty" law enforcement ammunition features a hollowpoint bullet that will fragment upon any object harder than the bullet itself, making it ideal for urban environments. SinterFire also offers a full line of its frangible bullets as components. www.sinterfire.com

Sisk Rifles

Sisk has taken the 325 WSM case, necked it up to 416-caliber and produced a proprietary 416-caliber cartridge that offers full 404 Jeffery ballistic performance in a short-action rifle. www.siskguns.com

Speer

Look for a whole lot of component Trophy Bonded Sledgehammer Solids in 375, 416, 458 and 474-calibers ... plus a new 350-grain/500-caliber Uni-Cor soft point for the 500 S&W and 500 WE. www.speer-bullets.com

SSK

JD Jones' newest creation is the 6.5 MPC (Multi-Purpose Cartridge). Based on a shortened 223 case, the cartridge is designed for close combat and designed to function in a 12-inch-barreled AR. The 6.5 is super-efficient, producing 2600 fps with a 95-grain solid in a 12-inch barrel and 2803 fps in a 20-inch barrel. SSK has also gone into the "machine-turned" bullet business, using both copper and brass alloys.

SSK offers a line of its own bullets, ranging in caliber from 6.5mm to 14.5mm, and will custom-turn small lots of bullets for experimenters for a nominal fee. www.sskindustries.com

Winchester

Winchester Ammunition has licensed Hodgdon its Winchester-branded reloading powders. Under the agreement, Hodgdon will be responsible for all orders, shipments, customer and technical service, and reloading data. On another

Look for a lot more component bullets from Speer.

cooperative front, Winchester has developed a new in-line primer designed specifically for Hodgdon's Triple Se7en and Pyrodex powders. The Winchester Triple Se7en primer reduces the classic fouling ring build-up that has plagued in-line muzzleloaders when using standard 209 shotgun primers. Searching for the perfect hunting bullet that would be suitable for all sizes of big game, Winchester has developed the XP3. The XP3 combines a solid copper HP bullet with a bonded lead core and a polycarbonate tip. Available in 270, 7mm and 30-calibers, the new bullet retains 100 percent of its weight upon impact and will be incorporated into the Supreme Elite ammunition line. I shot Winchester's Xtended Range Hi-Density turkey loads for the 2005 Spring season and can attest to their lethality at ranges out to 50 yards. Now the new High-Density shot (55 percent more dense than steel) has been approved for waterfowl and will be introduced in the 3-inch/20 gauge, and the 3- and 3 1/2-inch/12 gauge. Twenty-gauge shotgun slug shooters will be pleased to see a new 260-grain Partition Gold 3-inch sabot load being offered with a muzzle velocity of 2000 fps as well as a 3/4 oz. Foster slug moving out at 1800 fps for the smooth bores. Pheasants watch out! The Super-Pheasant has been expanded to include a 2-3/4-inch /12-gauge loading of 1-3/8 oz. of # 4, 5, and 6 plated lead shot sizzling out at 1450 fps. And for fields where non-toxic shot must be used, there's a new 3-inch/12-gauge load using 1-1/4 oz. of #4 steel shot at 1400 fps. Big Red's been busy! www.winchester.com

AVERAGE CENTERFIRE RIFLE CARTRIDGE BALLISTICS AND PRICES

Many manufacturers do not supply suggested retail prices. Others did not get their pricing to us before press time. All pricing can vary dependent on the exact brand and style of ammo selected and/or the retail outlet from which you make your purchase. Pricing has been rounded to the nearest dollar and represents our best estimate of average pricing.
An * after the cartridge means these loads are available with Nosler Partition or Swift A-Frame bullets. Listed pricing may or may not reflect this bullet type.
** = these are packed 50 to box, all others are 20 to box. Wea. Mag.= Weatherby Magnum. Spfd. = Springfield. A-A-Sq. = A-Square. N.E.=Nitro Express.

Cartridge	Bullet Wgt. Grs.	VELOCITY (fps)					ENERGY (ft. lbs.)					TRAJ. (in.)				Est. Price/ box
		Muzzle	100 yds.	200 yds.	300 yds.	400 yds.	Muzzle	100 yds.	200 yds.	300 yds.	400 yds.	100 yds.	200 yds.	300 yds.	400 yds.	
17, 22																
17 Remington	25	4040	3284	2644	2086	1606	906	599	388	242	143	+2.0	+1.7	-4.0	-17.0	$17
204 Ruger	32	4225	3632	3114	2652	2234	1268	937	689	500	355	.6	0.0	-4.2	-13.4	NA
204 Ruger	40	3900	3451	3046	2677	2336	1351	1058	824	636	485	.7	0.0	-4.5	-13.9	NA
204 Ruger	45	3625	3188	2792	2428	2093	1313	1015	778	589	438	1.00	0.0	-5.5	-16.9	NA
221 Fireball	50	2800	2137	1580	1180	988	870	507	277	155	109	+0.0	-7.0	-28.0	0.0	$14
22 Hornet	34	3050	2132	1415	1017	852	700	343	151	78	55	+0.0	-6.6	-15.5	-29.9	NA
22 Hornet	35	3100	2278	1601	1135	929	747	403	199	100	67	+2.75	0.0	-16.9	-60.4	NA
22 Hornet	45	2690	2042	1502	1128	948	723	417	225	127	90	+0.0	-7.7	-31.0	0.0	$27**
218 Bee	46	2760	2102	1550	1155	961	788	451	245	136	94	+0.0	-7.2	-29.0	0.0	$46**
222 Remington	40	3600	3117	2673	2269	1911	1151	863	634	457	324	+1.07	0.0	-6.13	-18.9	NA
222 Remington	50	3140	2602	2123	1700	1350	1094	752	500	321	202	+2.0	-0.4	-11.0	-33.0	$11
222 Remington	55	3020	2562	2147	1773	1451	1114	801	563	384	257	+2.0	-0.4	-11.0	-33.0	$12
22 PPC	52	3400	2930	2510	2130	NA	1335	990	730	525	NA	+2.0	1.4	-5.0	0.0	NA
223 Remington	40	3650	3010	2450	1950	1530	1185	805	535	340	265	+2.0	+1.0	-6.0	-22.0	$14
223 Remington	40	3800	3305	2845	2424	2044	1282	970	719	522	371	0.84	0.0	-5.34	-16.6	NA
223 Remington	50	3300	2874	2484	2130	1809	1209	917	685	504	363	1.37	0.0	-7.05	-21.8	NA
223 Remington	52/53	3330	2882	2477	2106	1770	1305	978	722	522	369	+2.0	+0.6	-6.5	-21.5	$14
223 Remington	55	3240	2748	2305	1906	1556	1282	922	649	444	296	+2.0	-0.2	-9.0	-27.0	$12
223 Remington	60	3100	2712	2355	2026	1726	1280	979	739	547	397	+2.0	+0.2	-8.0	-24.7	$16
223 Remington	64	3020	2621	2256	1920	1619	1296	977	723	524	373	+2.0	-0.2	-9.3	-23.0	$14
223 Remington	69	3000	2720	2460	2210	1980	1380	1135	925	750	600	+2.0	+0.8	-5.8	-17.5	$15
223 Remington	75	2790	2554	2330	2119	1926	1296	1086	904	747	617	2.37	0.0	-8.75	-25.1	NA
223 Remington	77	2750	2584	2354	2169	1992	1293	1110	948	804	679	1.93	0.0	-8.2	-23.8	NA
223 WSSM	55	3850	3438	3064	2721	2402	1810	1444	1147	904	704	0.7	0.0	-4.4	-13.6	NA
223 WSSM	64	3600	3144	2732	2356	2011	1841	1404	1061	789	574	1.0	0.0	-5.7	-17.7	NA
222 Rem. Mag.	55	3240	2748	2305	1906	1556	1282	922	649	444	296	+2.0	-0.2	-9.0	-27.0	$14
225 Winchester	55	3570	3066	2616	2208	1838	1556	1148	836	595	412	+2.0	+1.0	-5.0	-20.0	$19
224 Wea. Mag.	55	3650	3192	2780	2403	2057	1627	1244	943	705	516	+2.0	+1.2	-4.0	-17.0	$32
22-250 Rem.	40	4000	3320	2720	2200	1740	1420	980	660	430	265	+2.0	+1.8	-3.0	-16.0	$14
22-250 Rem.	50	3725	3264	2641	2455	2103	1540	1183	896	669	491	0.89	0.0	-5.23	-16.3	NA
22-250 Rem.	52/55	3680	3137	2656	2222	1832	1654	1201	861	603	410	+2.0	+1.3	-4.0	-17.0	$13
22-250 Rem.	60	3600	3195	2826	2485	2169	1727	1360	1064	823	627	+2.0	+2.0	-2.4	-12.3	$19
220 Swift	40	4200	3678	3190	2739	2329	1566	1201	904	666	482	+0.51	0.0	-4.0	-12.9	NA
220 Swift	50	3780	3158	2617	2135	1710	1586	1107	760	506	325	+2.0	+1.4	-4.4	-17.9	$20
220 Swift	50	3850	3396	2970	2576	2215	1645	1280	979	736	545	0.74	0.0	-4.84	-15.1	NA
220 Swift	55	3800	3370	2990	2630	2310	1765	1390	1090	850	650	0.8	0.0	-4.7	-14.4	NA
220 Swift	55	3650	3194	2772	2384	2035	1627	1246	939	694	506	+2.0	+2.0	-2.6	-13.4	$19
220 Swift	60	3600	3199	2824	2475	2156	1727	1364	1063	816	619	+2.0	+1.6	-4.1	-13.1	$19
22 Savage H.P.	71	2790	2340	1930	1570	1280	1225	860	585	390	190	+2.0	-1.0	-10.4	-35.7	NA
6mm (24)																
6mm BR Rem.	100	2550	2310	2083	1870	1671	1444	1185	963	776	620	+2.5	-0.6	-11.8	0.0	$22
6mm Norma BR	107	2822	2667	2517	2372	2229	1893	1690	1506	1337	1181	+1.73	0.0	-7.24	-20.6	NA
6mm PPC	70	3140	2750	2400	2070	NA	1535	1175	895	665	NA	+2.0	+1.4	-5.0	0.0	NA
243 Winchester	55	4025	3597	3209	2853	2525	1978	1579	1257	994	779	+0.6	0.0	-4.0	-12.2	NA
243 Winchester	60	3600	3110	2660	2260	1890	1725	1285	945	680	475	+2.0	+1.8	-3.3	-15.5	$17
243 Winchester	70	3400	3040	2700	2390	2100	1795	1435	1135	890	685	1.1	0.0	-5.9	-18.0	NA
243 Winchester	75/80	3350	2955	2593	2259	1951	1993	1551	1194	906	676	+2.0	+0.9	-5.0	-19.0	$16
243 Winchester	85	3320	3070	2830	2600	2380	2080	1770	1510	1280	1070	+2.0	+1.2	-4.0	-14.0	$18
243 Winchester	90	3120	2871	2635	2411	2199	1946	1647	1388	1162	966	1.4	0.0	-6.4	-18.8	NA
243 Winchester*	100	2960	2697	2449	2215	1993	1945	1615	1332	1089	882	+2.5	+1.2	-6.0	-20.0	$16
243 Winchester	105	2920	2689	2470	2261	2062	1988	1686	1422	1192	992	+2.5	+1.6	-5.0	-18.4	$21
243 Light Mag.	100	3100	2839	2592	2358	2138	2133	1790	1491	1235	1014	+1.5	0.0	-6.8	-19.8	NA
243 WSSM	55	4060	3628	3237	2880	2550	2013	1607	1280	1013	794	0.6	0.0	-3.9	-12.0	NA
243 WSSM	95	3250	3000	2763	2538	2325	2258	1898	1610	1359	1140	1.2	0.0	-5.7	-16.9	NA
243 WSSM	100	3110	2838	2583	2341	2112	2147	1789	1481	1217	991	1.4	0.0	-6.6	-19.7	NA
6mm Remington	80	3470	3064	2694	2352	2036	2139	1667	1289	982	736	+2.0	+1.1	-5.0	-17.0	$16
6mm Remington	100	3100	2829	2573	2332	2104	2133	1777	1470	1207	983	+2.5	+1.6	-5.0	-17.0	$16
6mm Remington	105	3060	2822	2596	2381	2177	2105	1788	1512	1270	1059	+2.5	+1.1	-3.3	-15.0	$21
6mm Rem. Light Mag.	100	3250	2997	2756	2528	2311	2345	1995	1687	1418	1186	1.59	0.0	-6.33	-18.3	NA
6.17(.243) Spitfire	100	3350	3122	2905	2698	2501	2493	2164	1874	1617	1389	2.4	3.20	0.0	-8.0	NA
240 Wea. Mag.	87	3500	3202	2924	2663	2416	2366	1980	1651	1370	1127	+2.0	+2.0	-2.0	-12.0	$32
240 Wea. Mag.	100	3395	3106	2835	2581	2339	2559	2142	1785	1478	1215	+2.5	+2.8	-2.0	-11.0	$43
25																
25-20 Win.	86	1460	1194	1030	931	858	407	272	203	165	141	0.0	-23.5	0.0	0.0	$32**
25-35 Win.	117	2230	1866	1545	1282	1097	1292	904	620	427	313	+2.5	-4.2	-26.0	0.0	$24
250 Savage	100	2820	2504	2210	1936	1684	1765	1392	1084	832	630	+2.5	+0.4	-9.0	-28.0	$17
257 Roberts	100	2980	2661	2363	2085	1827	1972	1572	1240	965	741	+2.5	-0.8	-5.2	-21.6	$20

Many manufacturers do not supply suggested retail prices. Others did not get their pricing to us before press time. All pricing can vary dependent on the exact brand and style of ammo selected and/or the retail outlet from which you make your purchase. Pricing has been rounded to the nearest dollar and represents our best estimate of average pricing.
An * after the cartridge means these loads are available with Nosler Partition or Swift A-Frame bullets. Listed pricing may or may not reflect this bullet type.
** = these are packed 50 to box, all others are 20 to box. Wea. Mag.= Weatherby Magnum. Spfd. = Springfield. A-A-Sq.= A-Square. N.E.=Nitro Express.

Cartridge	Bullet Wgt. Grs.	VELOCITY (fps)					ENERGY (ft. lbs.)					TRAJ. (in.)				Est. Price/ box
		Muzzle	100 yds.	200 yds.	300 yds.	400 yds.	Muzzle	100 yds.	200 yds.	300 yds.	400 yds.	100 yds.	200 yds.	300 yds.	400 yds.	
257 Roberts+P	117	2780	2411	2071	1761	1488	2009	1511	1115	806	576	+2.5	-0.2	-10.2	-32.6	$18
257 Roberts+P	120	2780	2560	2360	2160	1970	2060	1750	1480	1240	1030	+2.5	+1.2	-6.4	-23.6	$22
257 Roberts	122	2600	2331	2078	1842	1625	1831	1472	1169	919	715	+2.5	0.0	-10.6	-31.4	$21
257 Light Mag.	117	2940	2694	2460	2240	2031	2245	1885	1572	1303	1071	+1.7	0.0	-7.6	-21.8	NA
25-06 Rem.	87	3440	2995	2591	2222	1884	2286	1733	1297	954	686	+2.0	+1.1	-2.5	-14.4	$17
25-06 Rem.	90	3440	3043	2680	2344	2034	2364	1850	1435	1098	827	+2.0	+1.8	-3.3	-15.6	$17
25-06 Rem.	100	3230	2893	2580	2287	2014	2316	1858	1478	1161	901	+2.0	+0.8	-5.7	-18.9	$17
25-06 Rem.	117	2990	2770	2570	2370	2190	2320	2000	1715	1465	1246	+2.5	+1.0	-7.9	-26.6	$19
25-06 Rem.*	120	2990	2730	2484	2252	2032	2382	1985	1644	1351	1100	+2.5	+1.2	-5.3	-19.6	$17
25-06 Rem.	122	2930	2706	2492	2289	2095	2325	1983	1683	1419	1189	+2.5	+1.8	-4.5	-17.5	$23
25 WSSM	85	3470	3156	2863	2589	2331	2273	1880	1548	1266	1026	1.0	0.0	-5.2	-15.7	NA
25 WSSM	115	3060	284	2639	2442	2254	2392	2066	1778	1523	1398	1.4	0.0	-6.4	-18.6	NA
25 WSSM	120	2990	2717	2459	2216	1987	2383	1967	1612	1309	1053	1.6	0.0	-7.4	-21.8	NA
257 Wea. Mag.	87	3825	3456	3118	2805	2513	2826	2308	1870	1520	1220	+2.0	+2.7	-0.3	-7.6	$32
257 Wea. Mag.	100	3555	3237	2941	2665	2404	2806	2326	1920	1576	1283	+2.5	+3.2	0.0	-8.0	$32
257 Scramjet	100	3745	3450	3173	2912	2666	3114	2643	2235	1883	1578	+2.1	+2.77	0.0	-6.93	NA

6.5

Cartridge	Bullet Wgt. Grs.	Muzzle	100 yds.	200 yds.	300 yds.	400 yds.	Muzzle	100 yds.	200 yds.	300 yds.	400 yds.	100 yds.	200 yds.	300 yds.	400 yds.	Est. Price/ box
6.5x47 Lapua	123	2887	NA	2554	NA	2244	2285	NA	1788	NA	1380	NA	4.53	0.00	-10.7	NA
6.5x50mm Jap.	139	2360	2160	1970	1790	1620	1720	1440	1195	985	810	+2.5	-1.0	-13.5	0.0	NA
6.5x50mm Jap.	156	2070	1830	1610	1430	1260	1475	1155	900	695	550	+2.5	-4.0	-23.8	0.0	NA
6.5x52mm Car.	139	2580	2360	2160	1970	1790	2045	1725	1440	1195	985	+2.5	0.0	-9.9	-29.0	NA
6.5x52mm Car.	156	2430	2170	1930	1700	1500	2045	1630	1285	1005	780	+2.5	-1.0	-13.9	0.0	NA
6.5x52mm Carcano	160	2250	1963	1700	1467	1271	1798	1369	1027	764	574	+3.8	0.0	-15.9	-48.1	NA
6.5x55mm Light Mag.	129	2750	2549	2355	2171	1994	2166	1860	1589	1350	1139	+2.0	0.0	-8.2	-23.9	NA
6.5x55mm Swe.	140	2550	NA	NA	NA	NA	2020	NA	NA	NA	NA	0.0	0.0	0.0	0.0	$18
6.5x55mm Swe.*	139/140	2850	2640	2440	2250	2070	2525	2170	1855	1575	1330	+2.5	+1.6	-5.4	-18.9	$18
6.5x55mm Swe.	156	2650	2370	2110	1870	1650	2425	1950	1550	1215	945	+2.5	0.0	-10.3	-30.6	NA
260 Remington	125	2875	2669	2473	2285	2105	2294	1977	1697	1449	1230	1.71	0.0	-7.4	-21.4	NA
260 Remington	140	2750	2544	2347	2158	1979	2351	2011	1712	1448	1217	+2.2	0.0	-8.6	-24.6	NA
6.5-284 Norma	142	3025	2890	2758	2631	2507	2886	2634	2400	2183	1982	1.13	0.0	-5.7	-16.4	NA
6.71 (264) Phantom	120	3150	2929	2718	2517	2325	2645	2286	1969	1698	1440	+1.3	0.0	-6.0	-17.5	NA
6.5 Rem. Mag.	120	3210	2905	2621	2353	2102	2745	2248	1830	1475	1177	+2.5	+1.7	-4.1	-16.3	Disc.
264 Win. Mag.	140	3030	2782	2548	2326	2114	2854	2406	2018	1682	1389	+2.5	+1.4	-5.1	-18.0	$24
6.71 (264) Blackbird	140	3480	3261	3053	2855	2665	3766	3307	2899	2534	2208	+2.4	+3.1	0.0	-7.4	NA
6.8mm Rem.	115	2775	2472	2190	1926	1683	1966	1561	1224	947	723	+2.1	0.0	-3.7	-9.4	NA

27

Cartridge	Bullet Wgt. Grs.	Muzzle	100 yds.	200 yds.	300 yds.	400 yds.	Muzzle	100 yds.	200 yds.	300 yds.	400 yds.	100 yds.	200 yds.	300 yds.	400 yds.	Est. Price/ box
270 Winchester	100	3430	3021	2649	2305	1988	2612	2027	1557	1179	877	+2.0	+1.0	-4.9	-17.5	$17
270 Win. (Rem.)	115	2710	2482	2265	2059	NA	1875	1485	1161	896	NA	0.0	4.8	-17.3	0.0	NA
270 Winchester	130	3060	2776	2510	2259	2022	2702	2225	1818	1472	1180	+2.5	+1.4	-5.3	-18.2	$17
270 Win. Supreme	130	3150	2881	2628	2388	2161	2865	2396	1993	1646	1348	1.3	0.0	-6.4	-18.9	NA
270 Winchester	135	3000	2780	2570	2369	2178	2697	2315	1979	1682	1421	+2.5	+1.4	-6.0	-17.6	$23
270 Winchester*	140	2940	2700	2480	2260	2060	2685	2270	1905	1590	1315	+2.5	+1.8	-4.6	-17.9	$20
270 Win. Light Magnum	130	3215	2998	2790	2590	2400	2983	2594	2246	1936	1662	1.21	0.0	-5.83	-17.0	NA
270 Winchester*	150	2850	2585	2336	2100	1879	2705	2226	1817	1468	1175	+2.5	+1.2	-6.5	-22.0	$17
270 Win. Supreme	150	2930	2693	2468	2254	2051	2860	2416	2030	1693	1402	1.7	0.0	-7.4	-21.6	NA
270 WSM	130	3275	3041	2820	2609	2408	3096	2669	2295	1564	1673	1.1	0.0	-5.5	-16.1	NA
270 WSM	140	3125	2865	2619	2386	2165	3035	2559	2132	1769	1457	1.4	0.0	-6.5	-19.0	NA
270 WSM	150	3120	2923	2734	2554	2380	3242	2845	2490	2172	1886	1.3	0.0	-5.9	-17.2	NA
270 Wea. Mag.	100	3760	3380	3033	2712	2412	3139	2537	2042	1633	1292	+2.0	+2.4	-1.2	-10.1	$32
270 Wea. Mag.	130	3375	3119	2878	2649	2432	3287	2808	2390	2026	1707	+2.5	-2.9	-0.9	-9.9	$32
270 Wea. Mag.*	150	3245	3036	2837	2647	2465	3507	3070	2681	2334	2023	+2.5	+2.6	-1.8	-11.4	$47

7mm

Cartridge	Bullet Wgt. Grs.	Muzzle	100 yds.	200 yds.	300 yds.	400 yds.	Muzzle	100 yds.	200 yds.	300 yds.	400 yds.	100 yds.	200 yds.	300 yds.	400 yds.	Est. Price/ box
7mm BR	140	2216	2012	1821	1643	1481	1525	1259	1031	839	681	+2.0	-3.7	-20.0	0.0	$23
7mm Mauser*	139/140	2660	2435	2221	2018	1827	2199	1843	1533	1266	1037	+2.5	0.0	-9.6	-27.7	$17
7mm Mauser	145	2690	2442	2206	1985	1777	2334	1920	1568	1268	1017	+2.5	+0.1	-9.6	-28.3	$18
7mm Mauser	154	2690	2490	2300	2120	1940	2475	2120	1810	1530	1285	+2.5	+0.8	-7.5	-23.5	$17
7mm Mauser	175	2440	2137	1857	1603	1382	2313	1774	1340	998	742	+2.5	-1.7	-16.1	0.0	$17
7x57 Light Mag.	139	2970	2730	2503	2287	2082	2722	2301	1933	1614	1337	+1.6	0.0	-7.2	-21.0	NA
7x30 Waters	120	2700	2300	1930	1600	1330	1940	1405	990	685	470	-0.2	-12.3	0.0		$18
7mm-08 Rem.	120	3000	2725	2467	2223	1992	2398	1979	1621	1316	1058	+2.0	0.0	-7.6	-22.3	$18
7mm-08 Rem.*	140	2860	2625	2402	2189	1988	2542	2142	1793	1490	1228	+2.5	+0.8	-6.9	-21.9	$18
7mm-08 Rem.	154	2715	2510	2315	2128	1950	2520	2155	1832	1548	1300	+2.5	+1.0	-7.0	-22.7	$23
7mm-08 Light Mag.	139	3000	2790	2590	2399	2216	2777	2403	2071	1776	1515	+1.5	0.0	-6.7	-19.4	NA
7x64mm Bren.	140				Not Yet Announced											$17
7x64mm Bren.	154	2820	2610	2420	2230	2050	2720	2335	1995	1695	1430	+2.5	+1.4	-5.7	-19.9	NA
7x64mm Bren.*	160	2850	2669	2495	2327	2166	2885	2530	2211	1924	1667	+2.5	+1.6	-4.8	-17.8	$24
7x64mm Bren.	175				Not Yet Announced											$17
284 Winchester	150	2860	2595	2344	2108	1886	2724	2243	1830	1480	1185	+2.5	+0.8	-7.3	-23.2	$24

Many manufacturers do not supply suggested retail prices. Others did not get their pricing to us before press time. All pricing can vary dependent on the exact brand and style of ammo selected and/or the retail outlet from which you make your purchase. Pricing has been rounded to the nearest dollar and represents our best estimate of average pricing.

An * after the cartridge means these loads are available with Nosler Partition or Swift A-Frame bullets. Listed pricing may or may not reflect this bullet type.

** = these are packed 50 to box, all others are 20 to box. Wea. Mag.= Weatherby Magnum. Spfd. = Springfield. A-A-Sq.= A-Square. N.E.=Nitro Express.

Cartridge	Bullet Wgt. Grs.	VELOCITY (fps)					ENERGY (ft. lbs.)					TRAJ. (in.)				Est. Price/ box
		Muzzle	100 yds.	200 yds.	300 yds.	400 yds.	Muzzle	100 yds.	200 yds.	300 yds.	400 yds.	100 yds.	200 yds.	300 yds.	400 yds.	
280 Remington	120	3150	2866	2599	2348	2110	2643	2188	1800	1468	1186	+2.0	+0.6	-6.0	-17.9	$17
280 Remington	140	3000	2758	2528	2309	2102	2797	2363	1986	1657	1373	+2.5	+1.4	-5.2	-18.3	$17
280 Remington*	150	2890	2624	2373	2135	1912	2781	2293	1875	1518	1217	+2.5	+0.8	-7.1	-22.6	$17
280 Remington	160	2840	2637	2442	2556	2078	2866	2471	2120	1809	1535	+2.5	+0.8	-6.7	-21.0	$20
280 Remington	165	2820	2510	2220	1950	1701	2913	2308	1805	1393	1060	+2.5	+0.4	-8.8	-26.5	$17
7x61mm S&H Sup.	154	3060	2720	2400	2100	1820	3200	2520	1965	1505	1135	+2.5	+1.8	-5.0	-19.8	NA
7mm Dakota	160	3200	3001	2811	2630	2455	3637	3200	2808	2456	2140	+2.1	+1.9	-2.8	-12.5	NA
7mm Rem. Mag. (Rem.)	140	2710	2482	2265	2059	NA	2283	1915	1595	1318	NA	0.0	-4.5	-1.57	0.0	NA
7mm Rem. Mag.*	139/140	3150	2930	2710	2510	2320	3085	2660	2290	1960	1670	+2.5	+2.4	-2.4	-12.7	$21
7mm Rem. Hvy Mag	139	3250	3044	2847	2657	2475	3259	2860	2501	2178	1890	1.1	0.0	-5.5	-16.2	NA
7mm Rem. Mag.	150/154	3110	2830	2568	2320	2085	3221	2667	2196	1792	1448	+2.5	+1.6	-4.6	-16.5	$21
7mm Rem. Mag.*	160/162	2950	2730	2520	2320	2120	3090	2650	2250	1910	1600	+2.5	+1.8	-4.4	-17.8	$34
7mm Rem. Mag.	165	2900	2699	2507	2324	2147	3081	2669	2303	1978	1689	+2.5	+1.2	-5.9	-19.0	$28
7mm Rem Mag.	175	2860	2645	2440	2244	2057	3178	2718	2313	1956	1644	+2.5	+1.0	-6.5	-20.7	$21
7mm Rem. SA ULTRA MAG	140	3175	2934	2707	2490	2283	3033	2676	2277	1927	1620	1.3	0.0	-6	-17.7	NA
7mm Rem. SA ULTRA MAG	150	3110	2828	2563	2313	2077	3221	2663	2188	1782	1437	2.5	2.1	-3.6	-15.8	NA
7mm Rem. SA ULTRA MAG	160	2960	2762	2572	2390	2215	3112	2709	2350	2029	1743	2.6	2.2	-3.6	-15.4	NA
7mm Rem. WSM	140	3225	3008	2801	2603	2414	3233	2812	2438	2106	1812	1.2	0.0	-5.6	-16.4	NA
7mm Rem. WSM	160	2990	2744	2512	2081	1883	3176	2675	2241	1864	1538	1.6	0.0	-7.1	-20.8	NA
7mm Wea. Mag.	140	3225	2970	2729	2501	2283	3233	2741	2315	1943	1621	+2.5	+2.0	-3.2	-14.0	$35
7mm Wea. Mag.	154	3260	3023	2799	2586	2382	3539	3044	2609	2227	1890	+2.5	+2.8	-1.5	-10.8	$32
7mm Wea. Mag.*	160	3200	3004	2816	2637	2464	3637	3205	2817	2469	2156	+2.5	+2.7	-1.5	-10.6	$47
7mm Wea. Mag.	165	2950	2747	2553	2367	2189	3188	2765	2388	2053	1756	+2.5	+1.8	-4.2	-16.4	$43
7mm Wea. Mag.	175	2910	2693	2486	2288	2098	3293	2818	2401	2033	1711	+2.5	+1.2	-5.9	-19.4	$35
7.21(.284) Tomahawk	140	3300	3118	2943	2774	2612	3386	3022	2693	2393	2122	2.3	3.20	0.0	-7.7	NA
7mm STW	140	3325	3064	2818	2585	2364	3436	2918	2468	2077	1737	+2.3	+1.8	-3.0	-13.1	NA
7mm STW Supreme	160	3150	2894	2652	2422	2204	3526	2976	2499	2085	1727	1.3	0.0	-6.3	-18.5	NA
7mm Rem. Ultra Mag.	140	3425	3184	2956	2740	2534	3646	3151	2715	2333	1995	1.7	1.60	-2.6	-11.4	NA
7mm Firehawk	140	3625	3373	3135	2909	2695	4084	3536	3054	2631	2258	+2.2	+2.9	0.0	-7.03	NA
30																
7.21 (.284) Firebird	140	3750	3522	3306	3101	2905	4372	3857	3399	2990	2625	1.6	2.4	0.0	-6.0	NA
30 Carbine	110	1990	1567	1236	1035	923	977	600	373	262	208	0.0	-13.5	0.0	0.0	$28**
303 Savage	190	1890	1612	1327	1183	1055	1507	1096	794	591	469	+2.5	-7.6	0.0	0.0	$24
30 Remington	170	2120	1822	1555	1328	1153	1696	1253	913	666	502	+2.5	-4.7	-26.3	0.0	$20
7.62x39mm Rus.	123/125	2300	2030	1780	1550	1350	1445	1125	860	655	500	+2.5	-2.0	-17.5	0.0	$13
30-30 Win.	55	3400	2693	2085	1570	1187	1412	886	521	301	172	+2.0	0.0	-10.2	-35.0	$18
30-30 Win.	125	2570	2090	1660	1320	1080	1830	1210	770	480	320	-2.0	-2.6	-19.9	0.0	$13
30-30 Win.	150	2390	1973	1605	1303	1095	1902	1296	858	565	399	+2.5	-3.2	-22.5	0.0	$13
30-30 Win. Supreme	150	2480	2095	1747	1446	1209	2049	1462	1017	697	487	0.0	-6.5	-24.5	0.0	NA
30-30 Win.	160	2300	1997	1719	1473	1268	1879	1416	1050	771	571	+2.5	-2.9	-20.2	0.0	$18
30-30 Win. Lever Evolution	160	2400	2150	1916	1699	NA	2046	1643	1304	1025	NA	3.00	0.20	-12.1	NA	NA
30-30 PMC Cowboy	170	1300	1198	1121			638	474				0.0	-27.0	0.0	0.0	NA
30-30 Win.*	170	2200	1895	1619	1381	1191	1827	1355	989	720	535	+2.5	-5.8	-23.6	0.0	$13
300 Savage	150	2630	2354	2094	1853	1631	2303	1845	1462	1143	886	+2.5	-0.4	-10.1	-30.7	$17
300 Savage	180	2350	2137	1935	1754	1570	2207	1825	1496	1217	985	+2.5	-1.6	-15.2	0.0	$17
30-40 Krag	180	2430	2213	2007	1813	1632	2360	1957	1610	1314	1064	+2.5	-1.4	-13.8	0.0	Est
7.65x53mm Arg.	180	2590	2390	2200	2010	1830	2685	2280	1925	1615	1345	+2.5	0.0	-27.6	0.0	NA
7.5x53mm Argentine	150	2785	2519	2269	2032	1814	2583	2113	1714	1376	1096	+2.0	0.0	-8.8	-25.5	NA
307 Winchester	150	2760	2321	1924	1575	1289	2530	1795	1233	826	554	+2.5	-1.5	-13.6	0.0	Disc.
307 Winchester	180	2510	2179	1874	1599	1362	2519	1898	1404	1022	742	+2.5	-1.6	-15.6	0.0	$20
7.5x55 Swiss	180	2650	2450	2250	2060	1880	2805	2390	2020	1700	1415	+2.5	+0.6	-8.1	-24.9	NA
7.5x55mm Swiss	165	2720	2515	2319	2132	1954	2710	2317	1970	1665	1398	+2.0	0.0	-8.5	-24.6	NA
308 Winchester	55	3770	3215	2726	2286	1888	1735	1262	907	638	435	-2.0	+1.4	-3.8	-15.8	$22
308 Winchester	150	2820	2533	2263	2009	1774	2648	2137	1705	1344	1048	+2.5	+0.4	-8.5	-26.1	$17
308 Winchester	165	2700	2440	2194	1963	1748	2670	2180	1763	1411	1199	+2.5	0.0	-9.7	-28.5	$20
308 Winchester	168	2680	2493	2314	2143	1979	2678	2318	1998	1713	1460	+2.5	0.0	-8.9	-25.3	$18
308 Win. (Fed.)	170	2000	1740	1510	NA	NA	1510	1145	860	NA	NA	0.0	0.0	0.0	0.0	NA
308 Winchester	178	2620	2415	2220	2034	1857	2713	2306	1948	1635	1363	+2.5	0.0	-9.6	-27.6	$23
308 Winchester*	180	2620	2393	2178	1974	1782	2743	2288	1896	1557	1269	+2.5	-0.2	-10.2	-28.5	$17
308 Light Mag.*	150	2980	2703	2442	2195	1964	2959	2433	1986	1606	1285	+1.6	0.0	-7.5	-22.2	NA
308 Light Mag.	165	2870	2658	2456	2263	2078	3019	2589	2211	1877	1583	+1.7	0.0	-7.5	-21.8	NA
308 High Energy	165	2870	2600	2350	2120	1890	3020	2485	2030	1640	1310	+1.8	0.0	-8.2	-24.0	NA
308 Light Mag.	168	2870	2658	2456	2263	2078	3019	2589	2211	1877	1583	+1.7	0.0	-7.5	-21.8	NA
308 High Energy	180	2740	2550	2370	2200	2030	3000	2600	2245	1925	1645	+1.9	0.0	-8.2	-23.5	NA
30-06 Spfd.	55	4080	3485	2965	2502	2083	2033	1483	1074	764	530	+2.0	+1.9	-2.1	-11.7	$22
30-06 Spfd. (Rem.)	125	2660	2335	2034	1757	NA	1964	1513	1148	856	NA	0.0	-5.2	-18.9	0.0	NA
30-06 Spfd.	125	3140	2780	2447	2138	1853	2736	2145	1662	1279	953	+2.0	+1.0	-6.2	-21.0	$17
30-06 Spfd.	150	2910	2617	2342	2083	1853	2820	2281	1827	1445	1135	+2.5	+0.8	-7.2	-23.4	$17

Many manufacturers do not supply suggested retail prices. Others did not get their pricing to us before press time. All pricing can vary dependent on the exact brand and style of ammo selected and/or the retail outlet from which you make your purchase. Pricing has been rounded to the nearest dollar and represents our best estimate of average pricing.

An * after the cartridge means these loads are available with Nosler Partition or Swift A-Frame bullets. Listed pricing may or may not reflect this bullet type.

** = these are packed 50 to box, all others are 20 to box. Wea. Mag.= Weatherby Magnum. Spfd. = Springfield. A-A-Sq. = A-Square. N.E.=Nitro Express.

Cartridge	Bullet Wgt. Grs.	VELOCITY (fps)					ENERGY (ft. lbs.)					TRAJ. (in.)				Est. Price/ box
		Muzzle	100 yds.	200 yds.	300 yds.	400 yds.	Muzzle	100 yds.	200 yds.	300 yds.	400 yds.	100 yds.	200 yds.	300 yds.	400 yds.	
30-06 Spfd.	152	2910	2654	2413	2184	1968	2858	2378	1965	1610	1307	+2.5	+1.0	-6.6	-21.3	$23
30-06 Spfd. *	165	2800	2534	2283	2047	1825	2872	2352	1909	1534	1220	+2.5	+0.4	-8.4	-25.5	$17
30-06 Spfd.	168	2710	2522	2346	2169	2003	2739	2372	2045	1754	1497	+2.5	+0.4	-8.0	-23.5	$18
30-06 Spfd. (Fed.)	170	2000	1740	1510	NA	NA	1510	1145	860	NA	NA	0.0	0.0	0.0	0.0	NA
30-06 Spfd.	178	2720	2511	2311	2121	1939	2924	2491	2111	1777	1486	+2.5	+0.4	-8.2	-24.6	$23
30-06 Spfd. *	180	2700	2469	2250	2042	1846	2913	2436	2023	1666	1362	-2.5	0.0	-9.3	-27.0	$17
30-06 Spfd.	220	2410	2130	1870	1632	1422	2837	2216	1708	1301	988	+2.5	-1.7	-18.0	0.0	$17
30 Mag.																
30-06 Light Mag.	150	3100	2815	2548	2295	2058	3200	2639	2161	1755	1410	+1.4	0.0	-6.8	-20.3	NA
30-06 Light Mag.	180	2880	2676	2480	2293	2114	3316	2862	2459	2102	1786	+1.7	0.0	-7.3	-21.3	NA
30-06 High Energy	180	2880	2690	2500	2320	2150	3315	2880	2495	2150	1845	+1.7	0.0	-7.2	-21.0	NA
300 REM SA ULTRA MAG	150	3200	2901	2622	2359	2112	3410	2803	2290	1854	1485	1.3	0.0	-6.4	-19.1	NA
300 REM SA ULTRA MAG	165	3075	2792	2527	2276	2040	3464	2856	2339	1898	1525	1.5	0.0	-7	-20.7	NA
300 REM SA ULTRA MAG	180	2960	2761	2571	2389	2214	3501	3047	2642	2280	1959	2.6	2.2	-3.6	-15.4	NA
7.82 (308) Patriot	150	3250	2999	2762	2537	2323	3519	2997	2542	2145	1798	+1.2	0.0	-5.8	-16.9	NA
300 WSM	150	3300	3061	2834	2619	2414	3628	3121	2676	2285	1941	1.1	0.0	-5.4	-15.9	NA
300 WSM	180	2970	2741	2524	2317	2120	3526	3005	2547	2147	1797	1.6	0.0	-7.0	-20.5	NA
300 WSM	180	3010	2923	2734	2554	2380	3242	2845	2490	2172	1886	1.3	0	-5.9	-17.2	NA
308 Norma Mag.	180	3020	2820	2630	2440	2270	3645	3175	2755	2385	2050	+2.5	+2.0	-3.5	-14.8	NA
300 Dakota	200	3000	2824	2656	2493	2336	3996	3542	3131	2760	2423	+2.2	+1.5	-4.0	-15.2	NA
300 H&H Magnum*	180	2880	2640	2412	2196	1990	3315	2785	2325	1927	1583	+2.5	+0.8	-6.8	-21.7	$24
300 H&H Magnum	220	2550	2267	2002	1757	NA	3167	2510	1958	1508	NA	-2.5	-0.4	-12.0	0.0	NA
300 Win. Mag.	150	3290	2951	2636	2342	2068	3605	2900	2314	1827	1424	+2.5	+1.9	-3.8	-15.8	$22
300 Win. Mag.	165	3100	2877	2665	2462	2269	3522	3033	2603	2221	1897	+2.5	+2.4	-3.0	-16.9	$24
300 Win. Mag.	178	2900	2760	2568	2375	2191	3509	3030	2606	2230	1897	+2.5	+1.4	-5.0	-17.6	$29
300 Win. Mag.*	180	2960	2745	2540	2344	2157	3501	3011	2578	2196	1859	+2.5	+1.2	-5.5	-18.5	$22
300 W.M. High Energy	180	3100	2830	2580	2340	2110	3840	3205	2660	2190	1790	+1.4	0.0	-6.6	-19.7	NA
300 W.M. Light Mag.	180	3100	2879	2668	2467	2275	3840	3313	2845	2431	2068	+1.39	0.0	-6.45	-18.7	NA
300 Win. Mag.	190	2885	1691	2506	2327	2156	3511	3055	2648	2285	1961	+2.5	+1.2	-5.7	-19.0	$26
300 W.M. High Energy	200	2930	2740	2550	2370	2200	3810	3325	2885	2495	2145	+1.6	0.0	-6.9	-20.1	NA
300 Win. Mag.*	200	2825	2595	2376	2167	1970	3545	2991	2508	2086	1742	-2.5	+1.6	-4.7	-17.2	$36
300 Win. Mag.	220	2680	2448	2228	2020	1823	3508	2927	2424	1993	1623	+2.5	0.0	-9.5	-27.5	$23
300 Rem. Ultra Mag.	150	3450	3208	2980	2762	2556	3964	3427	2956	2541	2175	1.7	1.5	-2.6	-11.2	NA
300 Rem. Ultra Mag.	180	3250	3037	2834	2640	2454	4221	3686	3201	2786	2407	2.4	0.0	-3.0	-12.7	NA
300 Wea. Mag.	100	3900	3441	3038	2652	2305	3714	2891	2239	1717	1297	+2.0	+2.6	-0.6	-8.7	$32
300 Wea. Mag.	150	3600	3307	3033	2776	2533	4316	3642	3064	2566	2137	+2.5	+3.2	0.0	-8.1	$32
300 Wea. Mag.	165	3450	3210	3000	2792	2593	4360	3796	3297	2855	2464	+2.5	+3.2	0.0	-7.8	NA
300 Wea. Mag.	178	3120	2902	2695	2497	2308	3847	3329	2870	2464	2104	+2.5	-1.7	-3.6	-14.7	$43
300 Wea. Mag.	180	3330	3110	2910	2710	2520	4430	3875	3375	2935	2540	+1.0	0.0	-5.2	-15.1	NA
300 Wea. Mag.	190	3030	2830	2638	2455	2279	3873	3378	2936	2542	2190	+2.5	+1.6	-4.3	-16.0	$38
300 Wea. Mag.	220	2850	2541	2283	1964	1736	3967	3155	2480	1922	1471	+2.5	+0.4	-8.5	-26.4	$35
300 Warbird	180	3400	3180	2971	2772	2582	4620	4042	3528	3071	2664	+2.59	+3.25	0.0	-7.95	NA
300 Pegasus	180	3500	3319	3145	2978	2817	4896	4401	3953	3544	3172	+2.28	+2.89	0.0	-6.79	NA
31																
32-20 Win.	100	1210	1021	913	834	769	325	231	185	154	131	0.0	-32.3	0.0	0.0	$23**
303 British	150	2685	2441	2210	1992	1787	2401	1984	1627	1321	1064	+2.5	+0.6	-8.4	-26.2	$18
303 British	180	2460	2124	1817	1542	1311	2418	1803	1319	950	687	+2.5	-1.8	-16.8	0.0	$18
303 Light Mag.	150	2830	2570	2325	2094	1884	2667	2199	1800	1461	1185	+2.0	0.0	-8.4	-24.6	NA
7.62x54mm Rus.	146	2950	2730	2520	2320	NA	2820	2415	2055	1740	NA	+2.5	+2.0	-4.4	-17.7	NA
7.62x54mm Rus.	180	2580	2370	2180	2000	1820	2650	2250	1900	1590	1100	+2.5	0.0	-9.8	-28.5	NA
7.7x58mm Jap.	150	2640	2399	2170	1954	1752	2321	1916	1568	1271	1022	+2.3	0.0	-9.7	-28.5	NA
7.7x58mm Jap.	180	2500	2300	2100	1920	1750	2490	2105	1770	1475	1225	+2.5	0.0	-10.4	-30.2	NA
8x56 R	205	2400	2188	1987	1797	1621	2621	2178	1796	1470	1196	+2.9	0.0	-11.7	-34.3	NA
8mm																
8x57mm JS Mau.	165	2850	2520	2210	1930	1670	2965	2330	1795	1360	1015	+2.5	+1.0	-7.7	0.0	NA
32 Win. Special	170	2250	1921	1626	1372	1175	1911	1393	998	710	521	+2.5	-3.5	-22.9	0.0	$14
8mm Mauser	170	2360	1969	1622	1333	1123	2102	1464	993	671	476	+2.5	-3.1	-22.2	0.0	$18
325 WSM	180	3060	2841	2632	2432	2242	3743	3226	2769	2365	2009	+1.4	0.0	-6.4	-18.7	NA
325 WSM	200	2950	2753	2565	2384	2210	3866	3367	2922	2524	2170	+1.5	0.0	-6.8	-19.8	NA
325 WSM	220	2840	2605	2382	2169	1968	3941	3316	2772	2300	1893	+1.8	0.0	-8.0	-23.3	NA
8mm Rem. Mag.	185	3080	2761	2464	2186	1927	3896	3131	2494	1963	1525	+2.5	+1.4	-5.5	-19.7	$30
8mm Rem. Mag.	220	2830	2581	2346	2123	1913	3912	3254	2688	2201	1787	+2.5	+0.6	-7.6	-23.5	Disc.
33																
338 Federal	180	2830	2590	2350	2130	1930	3200	2670	2215	1820	1480	1.80	0.00	-8.2	-23.9	NA
338 Federal	185	2750	2550	2350	2160	1980	3105	2660	2265	1920	1615	1.90	0.00	-8.3	-24.1	NA
338 Federal	210	2630	2410	2200	2010	1820	3225	2710	2265	1880	1545	2.30	0.00	-9.4	-27.3	NA
338-06	200	2750	2553	2364	2184	2011	3358	2894	2482	2118	1796	+1.9	0.0	-8.22	-23.6	NA

Many manufacturers do not supply suggested retail prices. Others did not get their pricing to us before press time. All pricing can vary dependent on the exact brand and style of ammo selected and/or the retail outlet from which you make your purchase. Pricing has been rounded to the nearest dollar and represents our best estimate of average pricing.
An * after the cartridge means these loads are available with Nosler Partition or Swift A-Frame bullets. Listed pricing may or may not reflect this bullet type.
** = these are packed 50 to box, all others are 20 to box. Wea. Mag.= Weatherby Magnum. Spfd. = Springfield. A-A-Sq. = A-Square. N.E.=Nitro Express.

Cartridge	Bullet Wgt. Grs.	VELOCITY (fps)					ENERGY (ft. lbs.)					TRAJ. (in.)				Est. Price/ box
		Muzzle	100 yds.	200 yds.	300 yds.	400 yds.	Muzzle	100 yds.	200 yds.	300 yds.	400 yds.	100 yds.	200 yds.	300 yds.	400 yds.	
330 Dakota	250	2900	2719	2545	2378	2217	4668	4103	3595	3138	2727	+2.3	+1.3	-5.0	-17.5	NA
338 Lapua	250	2963	2795	2640	2493	NA	4842	4341	3881	3458	NA	+1.9	0.0	-7.9	0.0	NA
338 Win. Mag.	200	2960	2658	2375	2110	1862	3890	3137	2505	1977	1539	+2.5	+1.0	-6.7	-22.3	$27
338 Win. Mag.*	210	2830	2590	2370	2150	1940	3735	3130	2610	2155	1760	+2.5	+1.4	-6.0	-20.9	$33
338 Win. Mag.*	225	2785	2517	2266	2029	1808	3871	3165	2565	2057	1633	+2.5	+0.4	-8.5	-25.9	$27
338 W.M. Heavy Mag.	225	2920	2678	2449	2232	2027	4259	3583	2996	2489	2053	+1.75	0.0	-7.65	-22.0	NA
338 W.M. High Energy	225	2940	2690	2450	2230	2010	4320	3610	3000	2475	2025	+1.7	0.0	-7.5	-22.0	NA
338 Win. Mag.	230	2780	2573	2375	2186	2005	3948	3382	2881	2441	2054	+1.2	0.0	-6.3	-21.0	$40
338 Win. Mag.*	250	2660	2456	2261	2075	1898	3927	3348	2837	2389	1999	+2.5	+0.2	-9.0	-26.2	$27
338 W.M. High Energy	250	2800	2610	2420	2250	2080	4350	3775	3260	2805	2395	+1.8	0.0	-7.8	-22.5	NA
338 Ultra Mag.	250	2860	2645	2440	2244	2057	4540	3882	3303	2794	2347	1.7	0.0	-7.6	-22.1	NA
8.59(.338) Galaxy	200	3100	2899	2707	2524	2347	4269	3734	3256	2829	2446	3	3.80	0.0	-9.3	NA
340 Wea. Mag.*	210	3250	2991	2746	2515	2295	4924	4170	3516	2948	2455	+2.5	+1.9	-1.8	-11.8	$56
340 Wea. Mag.*	250	3000	2806	2621	2443	2272	4995	4371	3812	3311	2864	+2.5	+2.0	-3.5	-14.8	$56
338 A-Square	250	3120	2799	2500	2220	1958	5403	4348	3469	2736	2128	+2.5	+2.7	-1.5	-10.5	NA
338-378 Wea. Mag.	225	3180	2974	2778	2591	2410	5052	4420	3856	3353	2902	3.1	3.80	0.0	-8.9	NA
338 Titan	225	3230	3010	2800	2600	2409	5211	4524	3916	3377	2898	+3.07	+3.80	0.0	-8.95	NA
338 Excalibur	200	3600	3361	3134	2920	2715	5755	5015	4363	3785	3274	+2.23	+2.87	0.0	-6.99	NA
338 Excalibur	250	3250	2922	2618	2333	2066	5863	4740	3804	3021	2370	+1.3	0.0	-6.35	-19.2	NA
34, 35																
348 Winchester	200	2520	2215	1931	1672	1443	2820	2178	1656	1241	925	+2.5	-1.4	-14.7	0.0	$42
357 Magnum	158	1830	1427	1138	980	883	1175	715	454	337	274	0.0	-16.2	-33.1	0.0	$25**
35 Remington	150	2300	1874	1506	1218	1039	1762	1169	755	494	359	+2.5	-4.1	-26.3	0.0	$16
35 Remington	200	2080	1698	1376	1140	1001	1921	1280	841	577	445	+2.5	-6.3	-17.1	-33.6	$16
35 Rem. Lever Evolution	200	2225	1963	1721	1503	NA	2198	1711	1315	1003	NA	3.00	-1.30	-17.5	NA	NA
356 Winchester	200	2460	2114	1797	1517	1284	2688	1985	1434	1022	732	+2.5	-1.8	-15.1	0.0	$31
356 Winchester	250	2160	1911	1682	1476	1299	2591	2028	1571	1210	937	+2.5	-3.7	-22.2	0.0	$31
358 Winchester	200	2490	2171	1876	1619	1379	2753	2093	1563	1151	844	+2.5	-1.6	-15.6	0.0	$31
358 STA	275	2850	2562	2292	2039	NA	4958	4009	3208	2539	NA	+1.9	0.0	-8.6	0.0	NA
350 Rem. Mag.	200	2710	2410	2130	1870	1631	3261	2579	2014	1553	1181	+2.5	-0.2	-10.0	-30.1	$33
35 Whelen	200	2675	2378	2100	1842	1606	3177	2510	1958	1506	1145	+2.5	-0.2	-10.3	-31.1	$20
35 Whelen	225	2500	2300	2110	1930	1770	3120	2650	2235	1870	1560	+2.6	0.0	-10.2	-29.9	NA
35 Whelen	250	2400	2197	2005	1823	1652	3197	2680	2230	1844	1515	+2.5	-1.2	-13.7	0.0	$20
358 Norma Mag.	250	2800	2510	2230	1970	1730	4350	3480	2750	2145	1655	+2.5	+1.0	-7.6	-25.2	NA
358 STA	275	2850	2562	229*2	2039	1764	4959	4009	3208	2539	1899	+1.9	0.0	-8.58	-26.1	NA
9.3mm																
9.3x57mm Mau.	286	2070	1810	1590	1390	1110	2710	2090	1600	1220	955	+2.5	-2.6	-22.5	0.0	NA
9.3x62mm Mau.	286	2360	2089	1844	1623	NA	3538	2771	2157	1670	1260	+2.5	-1.6	-21.0	0.0	NA
9.3x64mm	286	2700	2505	2318	2139	1968	4629	3984	3411	2906	2460	+2.5	+2.7	-4.5	-19.2	NA
9.3x74Rmm	286	2360	2089	1844	1623	NA	3538	2771	2157	1670	NA	+2.5	-2.0	-11.0	0.0	NA
375																
38-55 Win.	255	1320	1190	1091	1018	963	987	802	674	587	525	0.0	-23.4	0.0	0.0	$25
375 Winchester	200	2200	1841	1526	1268	1089	2150	1506	1034	714	527	+2.5	-4.0	-26.2	0.0	$27
375 Winchester	250	1900	1647	1424	1239	1103	2005	1506	1126	852	676	+2.5	-6.9	-33.3	0.0	$27
376 Steyr	225	2600	2331	2078	1842	1625	3377	2714	2157	1694	1319	2.5	0.0	-10.6	-31.4	NA
376 Steyr	270	2600	2372	2156	1951	1759	4052	3373	2787	2283	1855	2.3	0.0	-9.9	-28.9	NA
375 Dakota	300	2600	2316	2051	1804	1579	4502	3573	2800	2167	1661	+2.4	0.0	-11.0	-32.7	NA
375 N.E. 2-1/2"	270	2000	1740	1507	1310	NA	2398	1815	1362	1026	NA	+2.5	-6.0	-30.0	0.0	NA
375 Flanged	300	2450	2150	1886	1640	NA	3998	3102	2369	1790	NA	+2.5	-2.4	-17.0	0.0	NA
375 H&H Magnum	250	2670	2450	2240	2040	1850	3955	3335	2790	2315	1905	+2.5	-0.4	-10.2	-28.4	NA
375 H&H Magnum	270	2690	2420	2166	1928	1707	4337	3510	2812	2228	1747	+2.5	0.0	-10.0	-29.4	$28
375 H&H Magnum*	300	2530	2245	1979	1733	1512	4263	3357	2608	2001	1523	+2.5	-1.0	-10.5	-33.6	$28
375 H&H Hvy. Mag.	270	2870	2628	2399	2182	1976	4937	4141	3451	2150	1845	+1.7	0.0	-7.2	-21.0	NA
375 H&H Hvy. Mag.	300	2705	2386	2090	1816	1568	4873	3793	2908	2195	1637	+2.3	0.0	-10.4	-31.4	NA
375 Rem. Ultra Mag.	270	2900	2558	2241	1947	1678	5041	3922	3010	2272	1689	1.9	2.7	-8.9	-27	NA
375 Rem. Ultra Mag.	300	2760	2505	2263	2035	1822	5073	4178	3412	2759	2210	2.0	0.0	-8.8	-26.1	NA
375 Wea. Mag.	300	2700	2420	2157	1911	1685	4856	3901	3100	2432	1891	+2.5	-.04	-10.7	0.0	NA
378 Wea. Mag.	270	3180	2976	2781	2594	2415	6062	5308	4635	4034	3495	+2.5	+2.6	-1.8	-11.3	$71
378 Wea. Mag.	300	2929	2576	2252	1952	1680	5698	4419	3379	2538	1881	+2.5	+1.2	-7.0	-24.5	$77
375 A-Square	300	2920	2626	2351	2093	1850	5679	4594	3681	2917	2281	+2.5	+1.4	-6.0	-21.0	NA
38-40 Win.	180	1160	999	901	827	764	538	399	324	273	233	0.0	-33.9	0.0	0.0	$42**
40, 41																
400 A-Square DPM	400	2400	2146	1909	1689	NA	5116	2092	3236	2533	NA	2.98	0.00	-10.0	NA	NA
400 A-Square DPM	170	2980	2463	2001	1598	NA	3352	2289	1512	964	NA	2.16	0.00	-11.1	NA	NA
408 CheyTac	419	2850	2752	2657	2562	2470	7551	7048	6565	6108	5675	-1.02	0.00	1.9	4.2	NA
405 Win.	300	2200	1851	1545	1296		3224	2282	1589	1119		4.6	0.0	-19.5	0.0	NA
450/400-3"	400	2150	1932	1730	1545	1379	4105	3316	2659	2119	1689	+2.5	-4.0	-9.5	-30.0	NA

Many manufacturers do not supply suggested retail prices. Others did not get their pricing to us before press time. All pricing can vary dependent on the exact brand and style of ammo selected and/or the retail outlet from which you make your purchase. Pricing has been rounded to the nearest dollar and represents our best estimate of average pricing.
An * after the cartridge means these loads are available with Nosler Partition or Swift A-Frame bullets. Listed pricing may or may not reflect this bullet type.
** = these are packed 50 to box, all others are 20 to box. Wea. Mag.= Weatherby Magnum. Spfd. = Springfield. A-A-Sq. = A-Square. N.E.=Nitro Express.

Cartridge	Bullet Wgt. Grs.	VELOCITY (fps)					ENERGY (ft. lbs.)					TRAJ. (in.)				Est. Price/ box
		Muzzle	100 yds.	200 yds.	300 yds.	400 yds.	Muzzle	100 yds.	200 yds.	300 yds.	400 yds.	100 yds.	200 yds.	300 yds.	400 yds.	
416 Dakota	400	2450	2294	2143	1998	1859	5330	4671	4077	3544	3068	+2.5	-0.2	-10.5	-29.4	NA
416 Taylor	400	2350	2117	1896	1693	NA	4905	3980	3194	2547	NA	+2.5	-1.2	15.0	0.0	NA
416 Hoffman	400	2380	2145	1923	1718	1529	5031	4087	3285	2620	2077	+2.5	-1.0	-14.1	0.0	NA
416 Rigby	350	2600	2449	2303	2162	2026	5253	4661	4122	3632	3189	+2.5	-1.8	-10.2	-26.0	NA
416 Rigby	400	2370	2210	2050	1900	NA	4990	4315	3720	3185	NA	+2.5	-0.7	-12.1	0.0	NA
416 Rigby	410	2370	2110	1870	1640	NA	5115	4050	3165	2455	NA	+2.5	-2.4	-17.3	0.0	$110
416 Rem. Mag.*	350	2520	2270	2034	1814	1611	4935	4004	3216	2557	2017	+2.5	-0.8	-12.6	-35.0	$82
416 Rem. Mag.*	400	2400	2175	1962	1763	1579	5115	4201	3419	2760	2214	+2.5	-1.5	-14.6	0.0	$80
416 Wea. Mag.*	400	2700	2397	2115	1852	1613	6474	5104	3971	3047	2310	+2.5	0.0	-10.1	-30.4	$96
10.57 (416) Meteor	400	2730	2532	2342	2161	1987	6621	5695	4874	4147	3508	+1.9	0.0	-8.3	-24.0	NA
404 Jeffrey	400	2150	1924	1716	1525	NA	4105	3289	2614	2064	NA	+2.5	-4.0	-22.1	0.0	NA
425, 44																
425 Express	400	2400	2160	1934	1725	NA	5115	4145	3322	2641	NA	+2.5	-1.0	-14.0	0.0	NA
44-40 Win.	200	1190	1006	900	822	756	629	449	360	300	254	0.0	-33.3	0.0	0.0	$36**
44 Rem. Mag.	210	1920	1477	1155	982	880	1719	1017	622	450	361	0.0	-17.6	0.0	0.0	$14
44 Rem. Mag.	240	1760	1380	1114	970	878	1650	1015	661	501	411	0.0	-17.6	0.0	0.0	$13
444 Marlin	240	2350	1815	1377	1087	941	2942	1753	1001	630	472	+2.5	-15.1	-31.0	0.0	$22
444 Marlin	265	2120	1733	1405	1160	1012	2644	1768	1162	791	603	+2.5	-6.0	-32.2	0.0	Disc.
444 Marlin Light Mag	265	2335	1913	1551	1266		3208	2153	1415	943		2.0	-4.90	-26.5	0.0	NA
444 Mar. Lever Evolution	265	2325	1971	1652	1380	NA	3180	2285	1606	1120	NA	3.00	-1.40	-18.6	NA	NA
45																
45-70 Govt.	300	1810	1497	1244	1073	969	2182	1492	1031	767	625	0.0	-14.8	0.0	0.0	$21
45-70 Govt. Supreme	300	1880	1558	1292	1103	988	2355	1616	1112	811	651	0.0	-12.9	-46.0	-105.0	NA
45-70 Lever Evolution	325	2050	1729	1450	1225	NA	3032	2158	1516	1083	NA	3.00	-4.10	-27.8	NA	NA
45-70 Govt. CorBon	350	1800	1526	1296			2519	1810	1307			0.0	-14.6	0.0	0.0	NA
45-70 Govt.	405	1330	1168	1055	977	918	1590	1227	1001	858	758	0.0	-24.6	0.0	0.0	$21
45-70 Govt. PMC Cowboy	405	1550	1193				1639	1280				0.0	-23.9	0.0	0.0	NA
45-70 Govt. Garrett	415	1850					3150					3.0	-7.0	0.0	0.0	NA
45-70 Govt. Garrett	530	1550	1343	1178	1062	982	2828	2123	1633	1327	1135	0.0	-17.8	0.0	0.0	NA
450 Marlin	350	2100	1774	1488	1254	1089	3427	2446	1720	1222	922	0.0	-9.7	-35.2	0.0	NA
450 Mar. Lever Evolution	325	2225	1887	1585	1331	NA	3572	2569	1813	1278	NA	3.00	-2.20	-21.3	NA	NA
458 Win. Magnum	350	2470	1990	1570	1250	1060	4740	3065	1915	1205	870	+2.5	-2.5	-21.6	0.0	$43
458 Win. Magnum	400	2380	2170	1960	1770	NA	5030	4165	3415	2785	NA	+2.5	-0.4	-13.4	0.0	$73
458 Win. Magnum	465	2220	1999	1791	1601	NA	5088	4127	3312	2646	NA	+2.5	-2.0	-17.7	0.0	NA
458 Win. Magnum	500	2040	1823	1623	1442	1237	4620	3689	2924	2308	1839	+2.5	-3.5	-22.0	0.0	$61
458 Win. Magnum	510	2040	1770	1527	1319	1157	4712	3547	2640	1970	1516	+2.5	-4.1	-25.0	0.0	$41
450 Dakota	500	2450	2235	2030	1838	1658	6663	5544	4576	3748	3051	+2.5	-0.6	-12.0	-33.8	NA
450 N.E. 3-1/4"	465	2190	1970	1765	1577	NA	4952	4009	3216	2567	NA	+2.5	-3.0	-20.0	0.0	NA
450 N.E. 3-1/4"	500	2150	1920	1708	1514	NA	5132	4093	3238	2544	NA	+2.5	-4.0	-22.9	0.0	NA
450 No. 2	465	2190	1970	1765	1577	NA	4952	4009	3216	2567	NA	+2.5	-3.0	-20.0	0.0	NA
450 No. 2	500	2150	1920	1708	1514	NA	5132	4093	3238	2544	NA	+2.5	-4.0	-22.9	0.0	NA
458 Lott	465	2380	2150	1932	1730	NA	5848	4773	3855	3091	NA	+2.5	-1.0	-14.0	0.0	NA
458 Lott	500	2300	2062	1838	1633	NA	5873	4719	3748	2960	NA	+2.5	-1.6	-16.4	0.0	NA
450 Ackley Mag.	465	2400	2169	1950	1747	NA	5947	4857	3927	3150	NA	+2.5	-1.0	-13.7	0.0	NA
450 Ackley Mag.	500	2320	2081	1855	1649	NA	5975	4085	3820	3018	NA	+2.5	-1.2	-15.0	0.0	NA
460 Short A-Sq.	500	2420	2175	1943	1729	NA	6501	5250	4193	3319	NA	+2.5	-0.8	-12.8	0.0	NA
460 Wea. Mag.	500	2700	2404	2128	1869	1635	8092	6416	5026	3878	2969	+2.5	+0.6	-8.9	-28.0	$72
475																
500/465 N.E.	480	2150	1917	1703	1507	NA	4926	3917	3089	2419	NA	+2.5	-4.0	-22.2	0.0	NA
470 Rigby	500	2150	1940	1740	1560	NA	5130	4170	3360	2695	NA	+2.5	-2.8	-19.4	0.0	NA
470 Nitro Ex.	480	2190	1954	1735	1536	NA	5111	4070	3210	2515	NA	+2.5	-3.5	-20.8	0.0	NA
470 Nitro Ex.	500	2150	1890	1650	1440	1270	5130	3965	3040	2310	1790	+2.5	-4.3	-24.0	0.0	$177
475 No. 2	500	2200	1955	1728	1522	NA	5375	4243	3316	2573	NA	+2.5	-3.2	-20.9	0.0	NA
50, 58																
505 Gibbs	525	2300	2063	1840	1637	NA	6166	4922	3948	3122	NA	+2.5	-3.0	-18.0	0.0	NA
500 N.E.-3"	570	2150	1928	1722	1533	NA	5850	4703	3752	2975	NA	+2.5	-3.7	-22.0	0.0	NA
500 N.E.-3"	600	2150	1927	1721	1531	NA	6158	4947	3944	3124	NA	+2.5	-4.0	-22.0	0.0	NA
495 A-Square	570	2350	2117	1896	1693	NA	5850	4703	3752	2975	NA	+2.5	-1.0	-14.5	0.0	NA
495 A-Square	600	2280	2050	1833	1635	NA	6925	5598	4478	3562	NA	+2.5	-2.0	-17.0	0.0	NA
500 A-Square	600	2380	2144	1922	1766	NA	7546	6126	4920	3922	NA	+2.5	-3.0	-17.0	0.0	NA
500 A-Square	707	2250	2040	1841	1567	NA	7947	6530	5318	4311	NA	+2.5	-2.0	-17.0	0.0	NA
500 BMG PMC	660	3080	2854	2639	2444	2248	13688		500 yd. zero			+3.1	+3.9	+4.7	+2.8	NA
577 Nitro Ex.	750	2050	1793	1562	1360	NA	6990	5356	4065	3079	NA	+2.5	-5.0	-26.0	0.0	NA
577 Tyrannosaur	750	2400	2141	1898	1675	NA	9591	7633	5996	4671	NA	+3.0	0.0	-12.9	0.0	NA
600, 700																
600 N.E.	900	1950	1680	1452	NA	NA	7596	5634	4212	NA	NA	+5.6	0.0	0.0	0.0	NA

Notes: Blanks are available in 32 S&W, 38 S&W and 38 Special. "V" after barrel length indicates test barrel was vented to produce ballistics similar to a revolver with a normal barrel-to-cylinder gap. Ammo prices are per 50 rounds except when marked with an ** which signifies a 20 round box; *** signifies a 25-round box. Not all loads are available from all ammo manufacturers. Listed loads are those made by Remington, Winchester, Federal, and others. DISC. is a discontinued load. Prices are rounded to nearest whole dollar and will vary with brand and retail outlet. † = new bullet weight this year; "c" indicates a change in data.

Cartridge	Bullet Wgt. Grs.	VELOCITY (fps)			ENERGY (ft. lbs.)			Mid-Range Traj. (in.)		Bbl. Lgth. (in).	Est. Price/ box
		Muzzle	50 yds.	100 yds.	Muzzle	50 yds.	100 yds.	50 yds.	100 yds.		
22, 25											
221 Rem. Fireball	50	2650	2380	2130	780	630	505	0.2	0.8	10.5"	$15
25 Automatic	35	900	813	742	63	51	43	NA	NA	2"	$18
25 Automatic	45	815	730	655	65	55	40	1.8	7.7	2"	$21
25 Automatic	50	760	705	660	65	55	50	2.0	8.7	2"	$17
30											
7.5mm Swiss	107	1010	NA	NA	240	NA	NA	NA	NA	NA	NEW
7.62mm Tokarev	87	1390	NA	NA	365	NA	NA	0.6	NA	4.5"	NA
7.62 Nagant	97	790	NA	NA	134	NA	NA	NA	NA	NA	NEW
7.63 Mauser	88	1440	NA	NA	405	NA	NA	NA	NA	NA	NEW
30 Luger	93†	1220	1110	1040	305	255	225	0.9	3.5	4.5"	$34
30 Carbine	110	1790	1600	1430	785	625	500	0.4	1.7	10"	$28
30-357 AeT	123	1992	NA	NA	1084	NA	NA	NA	NA	10"	NA
32											
32 S&W	88	680	645	610	90	80	75	2.5	10.5	3"	$17
32 S&W Long	98	705	670	635	115	100	90	2.3	10.5	4"	$17
32 Short Colt	80	745	665	590	100	80	60	2.2	9.9	4"	$19
32 H&R Magnum	85	1100	1020	930	230	195	165	1.0	4.3	4.5"	$21
32 H&R Magnum	95	1030	940	900	225	190	170	1.1	4.7	4.5"	$19
32 Automatic	60	970	895	835	125	105	95	1.3	5.4	4"	$22
32 Automatic	60	1000	917	849	133	112	96			4"	NA
32 Automatic	65	950	890	830	130	115	100	1.3	5.6	NA	NA
32 Automatic	71	905	855	810	130	115	95	1.4	5.8	4"	$19
8mm Lebel Pistol	111	850	NA	NA	180	NA	NA	NA	NA	NA	NEW
8mm Steyr	112	1080	NA	NA	290	NA	NA	NA	NA	NA	NEW
8mm Gasser	126	850	NA	NA	200	NA	NA	NA	NA	NA	NEW
9mm, 38											
380 Automatic	60	1130	960	NA	170	120	NA	1.0	NA	NA	NA
380 Automatic	85/88	990	920	870	190	165	145	1.2	5.1	4"	$20
380 Automatic	90	1000	890	800	200	160	130	1.2	5.5	3.75"	$10
380 Automatic	95/100	955	865	785	190	160	130	1.4	5.9	4"	$20
38 Super Auto +P	115	1300	1145	1040	430	335	275	0.7	3.3	5"	$26
38 Super Auto +P	125/130	1215	1100	1015	425	350	300	0.8	3.6	5"	$26
38 Super Auto +P	147	1100	1050	1000	395	355	325	0.9	4.0	5"	NA
9x18mm Makarov	95	1000	NA	NA	NA	NA	NA	NA	NA	NA	NEW
9x18mm Ultra	100	1050	NA	NA	240	NA	NA	NA	NA	NA	NEW
9x23mm Largo	124	1190	1055	966	390	306	257	0.7	3.7	4"	NA
9x23mm Win.	125	1450	1249	1103	583	433	338	0.6	2.8	NA	NA
9mm Steyr	115	1180	NA	NA	350	NA	NA	NA	NA	NA	NEW
9mm Luger	88	1500	1190	1010	440	275	200	0.6	3.1	4"	$24
9mm Luger	90	1360	1112	978	370	247	191	NA	NA	4"	$26
9mm Luger	95	1300	1140	1010	350	275	215	0.8	3.4	4"	NA
9mm Luger	100	1180	1080	NA	305	255	NA	0.9	NA	4"	NA
9mm Luger	115	1155	1045	970	340	280	240	0.9	3.9	4"	$21
9mm Luger	123/125	1110	1030	970	340	290	260	1.0	4.0	4"	$23
9mm Luger	140	935	890	850	270	245	225	1.3	5.5	4"	$23
9mm Luger	147	990	940	900	320	290	265	1.1	4.9	4"	$26
9mm Luger +P	90	1475	NA	NA	437	NA	NA	NA	NA	NA	NA
9mm Luger +P	115	1250	1113	1019	399	316	265	0.8	3.5	4"	$27
9mm Federal	115	1280	1130	1040	420	330	280	0.7	3.3	4"V	$24
9mm Luger Vector	115	1155	1047	971	341	280	241	NA	NA	4"	NA
9mm Luger +P	124	1180	1089	1021	384	327	287	0.8	3.8	4"	NA
38											
38 S&W	146	685	650	620	150	135	125	2.4	10.0	4"	$19
38 Short Colt	125	730	685	645	150	130	115	2.2	9.4	6"	$19
39 Special	100	950	900	NA	200	180	NA	1.3	NA	4"V	NA
38 Special	110	945	895	850	220	195	175	1.3	5.4	4"V	$23
38 Special	110	945	895	850	220	195	175	1.3	5.4	4"V	$23
38 Special	130	775	745	710	175	160	120	1.9	7.9	4"V	$22

Notes: Blanks are available in 32 S&W, 38 S&W and 38 Special. "V" after barrel length indicates test barrel was vented to produce ballistics similar to a revolver with a normal barrel-to-cylinder gap. Ammo prices are per 50 rounds except when marked with an ** which signifies a 20 round box; *** signifies a 25-round box. Not all loads are available from all ammo manufacturers. Listed loads are those made by Remington, Winchester, Federal, and others. DISC. is a discontinued load. Prices are rounded to nearest whole dollar and will vary with brand and retail outlet. † = new bullet weight this year; "c" indicates a change in data.

Cartridge	Bullet Wgt. Grs.	VELOCITY (fps)			ENERGY (ft. lbs.)			Mid-Range Traj. (in.)		Bbl. Lgth. (in).	Est. Price/ box
		Muzzle	50 yds.	100 yds.	Muzzle	50 yds.	100 yds.	50 yds.	100 yds.		
38 Special Cowboy	140	800	767	735	199	183	168			7.5" V	NA
38 (Multi-Ball)	140	830	730	505	215	130	80	2.0	10.6	4"V	$10**
38 Special	148	710	635	565	165	130	105	2.4	10.6	4"V	$17
38 Special	158	755	725	690	200	185	170	2.0	8.3	4"V	$18
38 Special +P	95	1175	1045	960	290	230	195	0.9	3.9	4"V	$23
38 Special +P	110	995	925	870	240	210	185	1.2	5.1	4"V	$23
38 Special +P	125	975	929	885	264	238	218	1	5.2	4"	NA
38 Special +P	125	945	900	860	250	225	205	1.3	5.4	4"V	#23
38 Special +P	129	945	910	870	255	235	215	1.3	5.3	4"V	$11
38 Special +P	130	925	887	852	247	227	210	1.3	5.50	4"V	NA
38 Special +P	147/150(c)	884	NA	NA	264	NA	NA	NA	NA	4"V	$27
38 Special +P	158	890	855	825	280	255	240	1.4	6.0	4"V	$20
357											
357 SIG	115	1520	NA	NA	593	NA	NA	NA	NA	NA	NA
357 SIG	124	1450	NA	NA	578	NA	NA	NA	NA	NA	NA
357 SIG	125	1350	1190	1080	510	395	325	0.7	3.1	4"	NA
357 SIG	150	1130	1030	970	420	355	310	0.9	4.0	NA	NA
356 TSW	115	1520	NA	NA	593	NA	NA	NA	NA	NA	NA
356 TSW	124	1450	NA	NA	578	NA	NA	NA	NA	NA	NA
356 TSW	135	1280	1120	1010	490	375	310	0.8	3.50	NA	NA
356 TSW	147	1220	1120	1040	485	410	355	0.8	3.5	5"	NA
357 Mag., Super Clean	105	1650									NA
357 Magnum	110	1295	1095	975	410	290	230	0.8	3.5	4"V	$25
357 (Med.Vel.)	125	1220	1075	985	415	315	270	0.8	3.7	4"V	$25
357 Magnum	125	1450	1240	1090	585	425	330	0.6	2.8	4"V	$25
357 (Multi-Ball)	140	1155	830	665	420	215	135	1.2	6.4	4"V	$11**
357 Magnum	140	1360	1195	1075	575	445	360	0.7	3.0	4"V	$25
357 Magnum	145	1290	1155	1060	535	430	360	0.8	3.5	4"V	$26
357 Magnum	150/158	1235	1105	1015	535	430	360	0.8	3.5	4"V	$25
357 Mag. Cowboy	158	800	761	725	225	203	185				NA
357 Magnum	165	1290	1189	1108	610	518	450	0.7	3.1	8-3/8"	NA
357 Magnum	180	1145	1055	985	525	445	390	0.9	3.9	4"V	$25
357 Magnum	180	1180	1088	1020	557	473	416	0.8	3.6	8"V	NA
357 Mag. CorBon F.A.	180	1650	1512	1386	1088	913	767	1.66	0.0		NA
357 Mag. CorBon	200	1200	1123	1061	640	560	500	3.19	0.0		NA
357 Rem. Maximum	158	1825	1590	1380	1170	885	670	0.4	1.7	10.5"	$14**
40, 10mm											
40 S&W	135	1140	1070	NA	390	345	NA	0.9	NA	4"	NA
40 S&W	155	1140	1026	958	447	362	309	0.9	4.1	4"	$14***
40 S&W	165	1150	NA	NA	485	NA	NA	NA	NA	4"	$18***
40 S&W	180	985	936	893	388	350	319	1.4	5.0	4"	$14***
40 S&W	180	1015	960	914	412	368	334	1.3	4.5	4"	NA
400 Cor-Bon	135	1450	NA	NA	630	NA	NA	NA	NA	5"	NA
10mm Automatic	155	1125	1046	986	436	377	335	0.9	3.9	5"	$26
10mm Automatic	170	1340	1165	1145	680	510	415	0.7	3.2	5"	$31
10mm Automatic	175	1290	1140	1035	650	505	420	0.7	3.3	5.5"	$11**
10mm Auto. (FBI)	180	950	905	865	361	327	299	1.5	5.4	4"	$16**
10mm Automatic	180	1030	970	920	425	375	340	1.1	4.7	5"	$16**
10mm Auto H.V.	180†	1240	1124	1037	618	504	430	0.8	3.4	5"	$27
10mm Automatic	200	1160	1070	1010	495	510	430	0.9	3.8	5"	$14**
10.4mm Italian	177	950	NA	NA	360	NA	NA	NA	NA	NA	NEW
41 Action Exp.	180	1000	947	903	400	359	326	0.5	4.2	5"	$13**
41 Rem. Magnum	170	1420	1165	1015	760	515	390	0.7	3.2	4"V	$33
41 Rem. Magnum	175	1250	1120	1030	605	490	410	0.8	3.4	4"V	$14**
41 (Med. Vel.)	210	965	900	840	435	375	330	1.3	5.4	4"V	$30
41 Rem. Magnum	210	1300	1160	1060	790	630	535	0.7	3.2	4"V	$33
41 Rem. Magnum	240	1250	1151	1075	833	706	616	0.8	3.3	6.5V	NA

Notes: Blanks are available in 32 S&W, 38 S&W and 38 Special. "V" after barrel length indicates test barrel was vented to produce ballistics similar to a revolver with a normal barrel-to-cylinder gap. Ammo prices are per 50 rounds except when marked with an ** which signifies a 20 round box; *** signifies a 25-round box. Not all loads are available from all ammo manufacturers. Listed loads are those made by Remington, Winchester, Federal, and others. DISC. is a discontinued load. Prices are rounded to nearest whole dollar and will vary with brand and retail outlet. † = new bullet weight this year; "c" indicates a change in data.

Cartridge	Bullet Wgt. Grs.	VELOCITY (fps)			ENERGY (ft. lbs.)			Mid-Range Traj. (in.)		Bbl. Lgth. (in).	Est. Price/ box
		Muzzle	50 yds.	100 yds.	Muzzle	50 yds.	100 yds.	50 yds.	100 yds.		
44											
44 S&W Russian	247	780	NA	NA	335	NA	NA	NA	NA	NA	NA
44 S&W Special	180	980	NA	NA	383	NA	NA	NA	NA	6.5"	NA
44 S&W Special	180	1000	935	882	400	350	311	NA	NA	7.5"V	NA
44 S&W Special	200†	875	825	780	340	302	270	1.2	6.0	6"	$13**
44 S&W Special	200	1035	940	865	475	390	335	1.1	4.9	6.5"	$13**
44 S&W Special	240/246	755	725	695	310	285	265	2.0	8.3	6.5"	$26
44-40 Win. Cowboy	225	750	723	695	281	261	242				NA
44 Rem. Magnum	180	1610	1365	1175	1035	745	550	0.5	2.3	4"V	$18**
44 Rem. Magnum	200	1400	1192	1053	870	630	492	0.6	NA	6.5"	$20
44 Rem. Magnum	210	1495	1310	1165	1040	805	635	0.6	2.5	6.5"	$18**
44 (Med. Vel.)	240	1000	945	900	535	475	435	1.1	4.8	6.5"	$17
44 R.M. (Jacketed)	240	1180	1080	1010	740	625	545	0.9	3.7	4"V	$18**
44 R.M. (Lead)	240	1350	1185	1070	970	750	610	0.7	3.1	4"V	$29
44 Rem. Magnum	250	1180	1100	1040	775	670	600	0.8	3.6	6.5"V	$21
44 Rem. Magnum	250	1250	1148	1070	867	732	635	0.8	3.3	6.5"V	NA
44 Rem. Magnum	275	1235	1142	1070	931	797	699	0.8	3.3	6.5"	NA
44 Rem. Magnum	300	1200	1100	1026	959	806	702	NA	NA	7.5"	$17
44 Rem. Magnum	330	1385	1297	1220	1406	1234	1090	1.83	0.00	NA	NA
440 CorBon	260	1700	1544	1403	1669	1377	1136	1.58	NA	10"	NA
45, 50											
450 Short Colt/450 Revolver	226	830	NA	NA	350	NA	NA	NA	NA	NA	NEW
45 S&W Schofield	180	730	NA	NA	213	NA	NA	NA	NA	NA	NA
45 S&W Schofield	230	730	NA	NA	272	NA	NA	NA	NA	NA	NA
45 G.A.P.	185	1090	970	890	490	385	320	1	4.7	5	NA
45 G.A.P.	230	880	842	NA	396	363	NA	NA	NA	NA	NA
45 Automatic	165	1030	930	NA	385	315	NA	1.2	NA	5"	NA
45 Automatic	185	1000	940	890	410	360	325	1.1	4.9	5"	$28
45 Auto. (Match)	185	770	705	650	245	204	175	2.0	8.7	5"	$28
45 Auto. (Match)	200	940	890	840	392	352	312	2.0	8.6	5"	$20
45 Automatic	200	975	917	860	421	372	328	1.4	5.0	5"	$18
45 Automatic	230	830	800	675	355	325	300	1.6	6.8	5"	$27
45 Automatic	230	880	846	816	396	366	340	1.5	6.1	5"	NA
45 Automatic +P	165	1250	NA	NA	573	NA	NA	NA	NA	NA	NA
45 Automatic +P	185	1140	1040	970	535	445	385	0.9	4.0	5"	$31
45 Automatic +P	200	1055	982	925	494	428	380	NA	NA	5"	NA
45 Super	185	1300	1190	1108	694	582	504	NA	NA	5"	NA
45 Win. Magnum	230	1400	1230	1105	1000	775	635	0.6	2.8	5"	$14**
45 Win. Magnum	260	1250	1137	1053	902	746	640	0.8	3.3	5"	$16**
45 Win. Mag. CorBon	320	1150	1080	1025	940	830	747	3.47			NA
455 Webley MKII	262	850	NA	NA	420	NA	NA	NA	NA	NA	NA
45 Colt	200	1000	938	889	444	391	351	1.3	4.8	5.5"	$21
45 Colt	225	960	890	830	460	395	345	1.3	5.5	5.5"	$22
45 Colt + P CorBon	265	1350	1225	1126	1073	884	746	2.65	0.0		NA
45 Colt + P CorBon	300	1300	1197	1114	1126	956	827	2.78	0.0		NA
45 Colt	250/255	860	820	780	410	375	340	1.6	6.6	5.5"	$27
454 Casull	250	1300	1151	1047	938	735	608	0.7	3.2	7.5"V	NA
454 Casull	260	1800	1577	1381	1871	1436	1101	0.4	1.8	7.5"V	NA
454 Casull	300	1625	1451	1308	1759	1413	1141	0.5	2.0	7.5"V	NA
454 Casull CorBon	360	1500	1387	1286	1800	1640	1323	2.01	0.0		NA
460 S&W	200	2300	2042	1801	2350	1851	1441	0	-1.60	NA	NA
460 S&W	250	1900	1640	1412	2004	1494	1106	0	-2.75	NA	NA
460 S&W	395	1550	1389	1249	2108	1691	1369	0	-4.00	NA	NA
475 Linebaugh	400	1350	1217	1119	1618	1315	1112	NA	NA	NA	NA
480 Ruger	325	1350	1191	1076	1315	1023	835	2.6	0.0	7.5"	NA
50 Action Exp.	325	1400	1209	1075	1414	1055	835	0.2	2.3	6"	$24**
500 S&W	275	1665	1392	1183	1693	1184	854	1.5	NA	8.375	NA
500 S&W	400	1675	1472	1299	2493	1926	1499	1.3	NA	8.375	NA
500 S&W	440	1625	1367	1169	2581	1825	1337	1.6	NA	8.375	NA

RIMFIRE AMMUNITION — BALLISTICS & PRICES

Note: The actual ballistics obtained with your firearm can vary considerably from the advertised ballistics. Also, ballistics can vary from lot to lot with the same brand and type load.

Cartridge	Bullet Wt. Grs.	Velocity (fps) 22-1/2" Bbl.		Energy (ft. lbs.) 22-1/2" Bbl.		Mid-Range Traj. (in.)	Muzzle Velocity
		Muzzle	100 yds.	Muzzle	100 yds.	100 yds.	6" Bbl.
17 Aguila	20	1850	1267	NA	NA	NA	NA
17 Hornady Mach 2	17	2100	1530	166	88	0.7	NA
17 HMR	17	2550	1902	245	136	NA	NA
17 HMR	20	2375	1776	250	140	NA	NA
22 Short Blank	—	—	—	—	—	—	—
22 Short CB	29	727	610	33	24	NA	706
22 Short Target	29	830	695	44	31	6.8	786
22 Short HP	27	1164	920	81	50	4.3	1077
22 Colibri	20	375	183	6	1	NA	NA
22 Super Colibri	20	500 /X	441	11	9	NA	NA
22 Long CB	29	727	610	33	24	NA	706
22 Long HV	29	1180	946	90	57	4.1	1031
22 LR Pistol Match	40	1070	890	100	70	4.6	940
22 LR Sub Sonic HP	38	1050	901	93	69	4.7	NA
22 LR Standard Velocity	40	1070	890	100	70	4.6	940
22 LR AutoMatch	40	1200	990	130	85	NA	NA
22 LR HV	40	1255	1016	140	92	3.6	1060
22 LR Silhoutte	42	1220	1003	139	94	3.6	1025
22 SSS	60	950	802	120	86	NA	NA
22 LR HV HP	40	1280	1001	146	89	3.5	1085
22 Velocitor GDHP	40	1435	0	0	0	NA	NA
22 LR Hyper HP	32/33/34	1500	1075	165	85	2.8	NA
22 LR Stinger HP	32	1640	1132	191	91	2.6	1395
22 LR Hyper Vel	30	1750	1191	204	93	NA	NA
22 LR Shot #12	31	950	NA	NA	NA	NA	NA
22 WRF LFN	45	1300	1015	169	103	3	NA
22 Win. Mag.	30	2200	1373	322	127	1.4	1610
22 Win. Mag. V-Max BT	33	2000	1495	293	164	0.60	NA
22 Win. Mag. JHP	34	2120	1435	338	155	1.4	NA
22 Win. Mag. JHP	40	1910	1326	324	156	1.7	1480
22 Win. Mag. FMJ	40	1910	1326	324	156	1.7	1480
22 Win. Mag. Dyna Point	45	1550	1147	240	131	2.60	NA
22 Win. Mag. JHP	50	1650	1280	300	180	1.3	NA
22 Win. Mag. Shot #11	52	1000	—	NA	—	—	NA

X - 600 + FPS marlin micro grove barrel / 16in

SHOTSHELL LOADS & PRICES

NOTES: * = 10 rounds per box. ** = 5 rounds per box. Pricing variations and number of rounds per box can occur with type and brand of ammunition. Listed pricing is the average nominal cost for load style and box quantity shown. Not every brand is available in all shot size variations. Some manufacturers do not provide suggested list prices. All prices rounded to nearest whole dollar. The price you pay will vary dependent upon outlet of purchase. # = new load spec this year; "C" indicates a change in data.

Dram Equiv.	Shot Ozs.	Load Style	Shot Sizes	Brands	Avg. Price/box	Velocity (fps)
10 Gauge 3-1/2" Magnum						
4-1/2	2-1/4	premium	BB, 2, 4, 5, 6	Win., Fed., Rem.	$33	1205
Max	2	premium	4, 5, 6	Fed., Win.	NA	1300
4-1/4	2	high velocity	BB, 2, 4	Rem.	$22	1210
Max	18 pellets	premium	00 buck	Fed., Win.	$7**	1100
Max	1-7/8	Bismuth	BB, 2, 4	Bis.	NA	1225
Max	1-3/4	high density	BB, 2	Rem.	NA	1300
4-1/4	1-3/4	steel	TT, T, BBB, BB, 1, 2, 3	Win., Rem.	$27	1260
Mag	1-5/8	steel	T, BBB, BB, 2	Win.	$27	1285
Max	1-5/8	Bismuth	BB, 2, 4	Bismuth	NA	1375
Max	1-1/2	steel	T, BBB, BB, 1, 2, 3	Fed.	NA	1450
Max	1-3/8	steel	T, BBB, BB, 1, 2, 3	Fed., Rem.	NA	1500
Max	1-3/8	steel	T, BBB, BB, 2	Fed., Win.	NA	1450
Max	1-3/4	slug, rifled	slug	Fed.	NA	1280
Max	24 pellets	Buckshot	1 Buck	Fed.	NA	1100
Max	54 pellets	Super-X	4 Buck	Win.	NA	1150
12 Gauge 3-1/2" Magnum						
Max	2-1/4	premium	4, 5, 6	Fed., Rem., Win.	$13*	1150
Max	2	Lead	4, 5, 6	Fed.	NA	1300
Max	2	Copper plated turkey	4, 5	Rem.	NA	1300
Max	18 pellets	premium	00 buck	Fed., Win., Rem.	$7**	1100
Max	1-7/8	heavyweight	5, 6	Fed.	NA	1300
Max	1-3/4	high density	BB, 2, 4	Rem.		1300
Max	1-7/8	Bismuth	BB, 2, 4	Bis.	NA	1225
Max	1-5/8	Hevi-shot	T	Hevi-shot	NA	1350
Max	1-5/8	high density	BB, 2	Fed.	NA	1450
Max	1-3/8	steel	T, BBB, BB, 2, 4	Fed., Win., Rem.	NA	1450
Max	1-1/2	Supreme H-V	BBB, BB, 2, 3	Win.	NA	1475
Max	1-3/8	H-speed steel	BB, 2	Rem.	NA	1550
Max	24 pellets	Premium	1 Buck	Fed.	NA	1100
Max	54 pellets	Super-X	4 Buck	Win.	NA	1050
12 Gauge 3" Magnum						
4	2	premium	BB, 2, 4, 5, 6	Win., Fed., Rem.	$9*	1175
4	1-7/8	premium	BB, 2, 4, 6	Win., Fed., Rem.	$19	1210
4	1-7/8	duplex	4x6	Rem.	$9*	1210
Max	1-3/4	turkey	4, 5, 6	Fed., Fio., Win., Rem.	NA	1300
Max	1-3/4	high density	BB, 2, 4	Rem.	NA	1450
Max	1-5/8	high density	BB, 2	Fed.	NA	1450
Max	1-5/8	high velocity	4, 5, 6	Fed.	NA	1350
4	1-5/8	premium	2, 4, 5, 6	Win., Fed., Rem.	$18	1290
Max	1-1/2	Hevi-shot	T	Hevi-shot	NA	1300
Max	1-1/2	high density	BB, 2, 4	Rem.	NA	1300
Max	1-5/8	Bismuth	BB, 2, 4, 5, 6	Bis.	NA	1250
4	24 pellets	buffered	1 buck	Win., Fed., Rem.	$5**	1040
4	15 pellets	buffered	00 buck	Win., Fed., Rem.	$6**	1210
4	10 pellets	buffered	000 buck	Win., Fed., Rem.	$6**	1225
4	41 pellets	buffered	4 buck	Win., Fed., Rem.	$6**	1210
Max	1-3/8	heavyweight	5, 6	Fed.	NA	1300
Max	1-3/8	high density	B, 2, 4, 6	Rem. Win.	NA	1450
Max	1-3/8	slug	slug	Bren.	NA	1476
Max	1-1/4	slug, rifled	slug	Fed.	NA	1600
Max	1-3/16	saboted slug	copper slug	Rem.	NA	1500
Max	7/8	slug, rifled	slug	Rem.	NA	1875
12 Gauge 3" Magnum (cont.)						
Max	1-1/8	low recoil	BB	Fed.	NA	850
Max	1-1/8	steel	BB, 2, 3, 4	Fed., Win., Rem.	NA	1550
Max	1-1/16	high density	2, 4	Win.	NA	1400
Max	1	steel	4, 6	Fed.	NA	1330
Max	1-3/8	buckhammer	slug	Rem.	NA	1500
Max	1	slug, rifled	slug, magnum	Win., Rem.	$5**	1760
Max	1	saboted slug	slug	Rem., Win., Fed.	$10**	1550
Max	385 grs.	partition gold	slug	Win.	NA	2000
3-5/8	1-3/8	steel	BBB, BB, 1, 2, 3, 4	Win., Fed., Rem.	$19	1275
Max	1-1/8	steel	BB, 2, 4	Rem.	NA	1500
Max	1-1/8	steel	T, BBB, BB, 2, 4, 5, 6	Fed., Win.	NA	1450
Max	1-1/8	steel	BB, 2	Fed.	NA	1400
4	1-1/4	steel	T, BBB, BB, 1, 2, 3, 4, 6	Win., Fed., Rem.	$18	1400
12 Gauge 2-3/4"						
Max	1-5/8	magnum	4, 5, 6	Win., Fed.	$8*	1250
Max	1-3/8	lead	4, 5, 6	Fiocchi	NA	1485
Max	1-3/8	turkey	4, 5, 6	Fio.	NA	1250
Max	1-3/8	steel	4, 5, 6	Fed.	NA	1400
Max	1-3/8	Bismuth	BB, 2, 4, 5, 6	Bis.	NA	1300
3-3/4	1-1/2	magnum	BB, 2, 4, 5, 6	Win., Fed., Rem.	$16	1260
Max	1-1/4	Supreme H-V	4, 5, 6, 7-1/2	Win. Rem.	NA	1400
3-3/4	1-1/4	high velocity	BB, 2, 4, 5, 6, 7-1/2, 8, 9	Win., Fed., Rem., Fio.	$13	1330
Max	1-1/4	high density	B, 2, 4	Win.	NA	1450
Max	1-1/4	high density	4, 6	Win.	NA	1325
3-1/4	1-1/4	standard velocity	6, 7-1/2, 8, 9	Win., Fed., Rem., Fio.	$11	1220
Max	1-1/8	Hevi-shot	5	Hevi-shot	NA	1350
3-1/4	1-1/8	standard velocity	4, 6, 7-1/2, 8, 9	Win., Fed., Rem., Fio.	$9	1255
Max	1-1/8	steel	2, 4	Win.	NA	1390
Max	1	steel	BB, 2	Fed.	NA	1450
3-1/4	1	standard velocity	6, 7-1/2, 8	Rem., Fed., Fio., Win.	$6	1290
3-1/4	1-1/4	target	7-1/2, 8, 9	Win., Fed., Rem.	$10	1220
3	1-1/8	spreader	7-1/2, 8, 8-1/2, 9	Fio.	NA	1200
3	1-1/8	target	7-1/2, 8, 9, 7-1/2x8	Win., Rem., Fio.	$7	1200
2-3/4	1-1/8	target	7-1/2, 8, 8-1/2, 9, 7-1/2x8	Win., Rem., Fio.	$7	1145
2-3/4	1-1/8	low recoil	7-1/2, 8	Rem.	NA	1145
2-1/2	26 grams	low recoil	8	Win.	NA	980
2-1/4	1-1/8	target	7-1/2, 8, 8-1/2, 9	Rem., Fed.	$7	1080
Max	1-1/8	spreader	7-1/2, 8, 8-1/2, 9	Fio.	NA	1300
3-1/4	28 grams (1 oz)	target	7-1/2, 8, 9	Win., Fed., Rem., Fio.	$8	1290
3	1	target	7-1/2, 8, 8-1/2, 9	Win., Fio.	NA	1235
2-3/4	1	target	7-1/2, 8, 8-1/2, 9	Fed., Rem., Fio.	NA	1180
3-1/4	24 grams	target	7-1/2, 8, 9	Fed., Win., Fio.	NA	1325
3	7/8	light	8	Fio.	NA	1200
3-3/4	8 pellets	buffered	000 buck	Win., Fed., Rem.	$4**	1325
4	12 pellets	premium	00 buck	Win., Fed., Rem.	$5**	1290
3-3/4	9 pellets	buffered	00 buck	Win., Fed., Rem., Fio.	$19	1325
3-3/4	12 pellets	buffered	0 buck	Win., Fed., Rem.	$4**	1275

Dram Equiv.	Shot Ozs.	Load Style	Shot Sizes	Brands	Avg. Price/box	Velocity (fps)
12 Gauge 2-3/4" (cont.)						
4	20 pellets	buffered	1 buck	Win., Fed., Rem.	$4**	1075
3-3/4	16 pellets	buffered	1 buck	Win., Fed., Rem.	$4**	1250
4	34 pellets	premium	4 buck	Fed., Rem.	$5**	1250
3-3/4	27 pellets	buffered	4 buck	Win., Fed., Rem., Fio.	$4**	1325
Max	1	saboted slug	slug	Win., Fed., Rem.	$10**	1450
Max	1-1/4	slug, rifled	slug	Fed.	NA	1520
Max	1-1/4	slug	slug	Lightfield		1440
Max	1-1/4	saboted slug	attached sabot	Rem.	NA	1550
Max	1	slug, rifled	slug, magnum	Rem., Fio.	$5**	1680
Max	1	slug, rifled	slug	Win., Fed., Rem.	$4**	1610
Max	1	sabot slug	slug	Sauvestre		1640
Max	7/8	slug, rifled	slug	Rem.	NA	1800
Max	400	plat. tip	sabot slug	Win.	NA	1700
Max	385 grains	Partition Gold Slug	slug	Win.	NA	1900
Max	385 grains	Core-Lokt bonded	sabot slug	Rem.	NA	1900
Max	325 grains	Barnes Sabot	slug	Fed.	NA	1900
Max	300 grains	SST Slug	sabot slug	Hornady	NA	2050
3	1-1/8	steel target	6-1/2, 7	Rem.	NA	1200
2-3/4	1-1/8	steel target	7	Rem.	NA	1145
3	1#	steel	7	Win.	$11	1235
3-1/2	1-1/4	steel	T, BBB, BB, 1, 2, 3, 4, 5, 6	Win., Fed., Rem.	$18	1275
3-3/4	1-1/8	steel	BB, 1, 2, 3, 4, 5, 6	Win., Fed., Rem., Fio.	$16	1365
3-3/4	1	steel	2, 3, 4, 5, 6, 7	Win., Fed., Rem., Fio.	$13	1390
Max	7/8	steel	7	Fio.	NA	1440
16 Gauge 2-3/4"						
3-1/4	1-1/4	magnum	2, 4, 6	Fed., Rem.	$16	1260
3-1/4	1-1/8	high velocity	4, 6, 7-1/2	Win., Fed., Rem., Fio.	$12	1295
Max	1-1/8	Bismuth	4, 5	Bis.	NA	1200
2-3/4	1-1/8	standard velocity	6, 7-1/2, 8	Fed., Rem., Fio.	$9	1185
2-1/2	1	dove	6, 7-1/2, 8, 9	Fio., Win.	NA	1165
2-3/4	1		6, 7-1/2, 8	Fio.	NA	1200
Max	15/16	steel	2, 4	Fed., Rem.	NA	1300
Max	7/8	steel	2, 4	Win.	$16	1300
3	12 pellets	buffered	1 buck	Win., Fed., Rem.	$4**	1225
Max	4/5	slug, rifled	slug	Win., Fed., Rem.	$4**	1570
Max	.92	sabot slug	slug	Sauvestre	NA	1560
20 Gauge 3" Magnum						
3	1-1/4	premium	2, 4, 5, 6, 7-1/2	Win., Fed., Rem.	$15	1185
3	1-1/4	turkey	4, 6	Fio.	NA	1200
Max	1-1/4	Hevi-shot	2, 4, 6	Hevi-shot	NA	1250
Max	1-1/8	high density	4, 6	Rem.	NA	1300
Max	18 pellets	buck shot	2 buck	Fed.	NA	1200
Max	24 pellets	buffered	3 buck	Win.	$5**	1150
2-3/4	20 pellets	buck	3 buck	Rem.	$4**	1200
3-1/4	1	steel	1, 2, 3, 4, 5, 6	Win., Fed., Rem.	$15	1330
Max	7/8	steel	2, 4	Win.	NA	1300
Max	1-1/16	high density	2, 4	Win.	NA	1400
Max	1-1/16	Bismuth	2, 4, 5, 6	Bismuth	NA	1250
Mag	5/8	saboted slug	275 gr.	Fed.	NA	1900

Dram Equiv.	Shot Ozs.	Load Style	Shot Sizes	Brands	Avg. Price/box	Velocity (fps)
20 Gauge 2-3/4"						
2-3/4	1-1/8	magnum	4, 6, 7-1/2	Win., Fed., Rem.	$14	1175
2-3/4	1	high velocity	4, 5, 6, 7-1/2, 8, 9	Win., Fed., Rem., Fio.	$12	1220
Max	1	Bismuth	4, 6	Bis.	NA	1200
Max	1	Hevi-shot	5	Hevi-shot	NA	1250
Max	1	Supreme H-V	4, 6, 7-1/2	Win. Rem.	NA	1300
Max	7/8	Steel	2, 3, 4	Fio.	NA	1500
2-1/2	1	standard velocity	6, 7-1/2, 8	Win., Rem., Fed., Fio.	$6	1165
2-1/2	7/8	clays	8	Rem.	NA	1200
2-1/2	7/8	promotional	6, 7-1/2, 8	Win., Rem., Fio.	$6	1210
2-1/2	1	target	8, 9	Win., Rem.	$8	1165
Max	7/8	clays	7-1/2, 8	Win.	NA	1275
2-1/2	7/8	target	8, 9	Win., Fed., Rem.	$8	1200
Max	3/4	steel	2, 4	Rem.	NA	1425
2-1/2	7/8	steel - target	7	Rem.	NA	1200
Max	1	buckhammer	slug	Rem.	NA	1500
Max	5/8	Saboted Slug	Copper Slug	Rem.	NA	1500
Max	20 pellets	buffered	3 buck	Win., Fed.	$4	1200
Max	5/8	slug, saboted	slug	Win.,	$9**	1400
2-3/4	5/8	slug, rifled	slug	Rem.	$4**	1580
Max	3/4	saboted slug	copper slug	Fed., Rem.	NA	1450
Max	3/4	slug, rifled	slug	Win., Fed., Rem., Fio.	$4**	1570
Max	.9	sabot slug	slug	Sauvestre		1480
Max	260 grains	Partition Gold Slug	slug	Win.	NA	1900
Max	260 grains	Core-Lokt Ultra	slug	Rem.	NA	1900
Max	260 grains	saboted slug	platinum tip	Win.	NA	1700
Max	3/4	steel	2, 3, 4, 6	Win., Fed., Rem.	$14	1425
Max	250 grains	SST slug	slug	Hornady	NA	1800
Max	1/2	rifled, slug	slug	Rem.	NA	1800
28 Gauge 2-3/4"						
2	1	high velocity	6, 7-1/2, 8	Win.	$12	1125
2-1/4	3/4	high velocity	6, 7-1/2, 8, 9	Win., Fed., Rem., Fio.	$11	1295
2	3/4	target	8, 9	Win., Fed., Rem.	$9	1200
Max	3/4	sporting clays	7-1/2, 8-1/2	Win.	NA	1300
Max	5/8	Bismuth	4, 6	Bis.	NA	1250
410 Bore 3"						
Max	11/16	high velocity	4, 5, 6, 7-1/2, 8, 9	Win., Fed., Rem., Fio.	$10	1135
Max	9/16	Bismuth	4	Bis.	NA	1175
410 Bore 2-1/2"						
Max	1/2	high velocity	4, 6, 7-1/2	Win., Fed., Rem.	$9	1245
Max	1/5	slug, rifled	slug	Win., Fed., Rem.	$4**	1815
1-1/2	1/2	target	8, 8-1/2, 9	Win., Fed., Rem., Fio.	$8	1200
Max	1/2	sporting clays	7-1/2, 8, 8-1/2	Win.	NA	1300
Max		Buckshot	5-000 Buck	Win.	NA	1135

2007
GUNS ILLUSTRATED
Complete Compact
CATALOG

GUNDEX

GUNDEX

GUNDEX

SEMI-CUSTOM

HANDGUNS

RIFLES

SHOTGUNS

BLACKPOWDER

AIRGUNS

COMPENDIUM

MANUFACTURER'S DIRECTORY

GUNDEX

GUNDEX

GUNDEX

GUNDEX

Browning Luxus Grade B2

Browning Luxus Renaissance Argent

Ed Brown Classic Class A

Ed Brown Kobra Carry

Gary Reeder 1 Asterisk

Kimber Ultra CDP

BRILEY 1911-STYLE AUTO PISTOLS

Caliber: 9mm Para., 38 Super, 40 S&W, 10-shot magazine; 45 ACP, 8-shot magazine. **Barrel:** 3.6" or 5". **Weight:** NA. **Length:** NA. **Grips:** Rosewood or rubber. **Sights:** Bo-Mar adjustable rear, Briley dovetail blade front. **Features:** Modular or Caspian alloy, carbon steel or stainless steel frame; match barrel and trigger group; lowered and flared ejection port; front and rear serrations on slide; beavertail grip safety; hot blue, hard chrome or stainless steel finish. Introduced 2000. Made in U.S. From Briley Manufacturing Inc.

Price: Fantom (3.6" bbl., fixed low-mount rear sight, armor coated lower receiver), from **$1,900.00**

Price: Fantom with two-port compensator, from **$2,245.00**

Price: Advantage (5" bbl., adj. low-mount rear sight, checkered mainspring housing), from **$1,650.00**

Price: Versatility Plus (5" bbl., adj. low-mount rear sight, modular or Caspian frame), from **$1,850.00**

Price: Signature Series (5" bbl., adj. low-mount rear sight, 40 S&W only), from **$2,250.00**

Price: Plate Master (5" bbl. with compensator, lightened slide, Briley scope mount), from **$1,895.00**

Price: El Presidente (5" bbl. with Briley quad compensator, Briley scope mount), from **$2,550.00**

BROWNING HI-POWER LUXUS

The legendary Browning Hi-Power pistol still produced in Belgium is available in four grades in the Luxus series: Grade II, Renaissance Argent, Grade B2 and the gold-finished Renaissance OR. Other specifications NA.

Price: From **$4,391.00**

ED BROWN CLASSIC CUSTOM AND CLASS A LIMITED 1911-STYLE AUTO PISTOLS

Caliber: 45 ACP; 7-shot magazine; 40 S&W, 400 Cor-Bon, 38 Super, 9x23, 9mm Para. **Barrel:** 4.25", 5", 6". **Weight:** NA. **Length:** NA. **Grips:** Hogue exotic checkered wood. **Sights:** Bo-Mar or Novak rear, blade front. **Features:** Blued or stainless steel frame; ambidextrous safety; beavertail grip safety; checkered forestrap and mainspring housing; match-grade barrel; slotted hammer; long lightweight or Videki short steel trigger. Many options offered. Made in U.S. by Ed Brown Products, Inc.

Price: Classic Custom (45 ACP, 5" barrel), from **$2,895.00**

Price: Executive Elite (45 ACP, 5" barrel), from **$2,195.00**

Price: Executive Carry (4.25" bbl., has "bobtail™" modification to reduce overall length), from **$2,295.00**

Price: Kobra (45 ACP only, 5" bbl., completely hand-fitted with heavy dehorning), from **$1,995.00**

Price: Kobra Carry (45 ACP only, 4.25" bbl., has exclusive snakeskin pattern on frame, top portion of mainspring housing and slide), from . . . **$2,195.00**

NEW! Price: Executive Target, (45 ACP, 5" government model, features exclusive 25 lpi checkering and Bo-Mar adjustable sights), from **$2,370.00**

GARY REEDER 1 ASTERISK

Caliber: Full custom M1911. **Barrel:** Varies by model. **Weight:** Varies by model. **Length:** Varies by model. **Grips:** NA. **Sights:** NA. **Features:** Full combat features including see-thru Lexan grip panel. Jeweled hammer and trigger, tuned action, model name engraved on barrel, additional engraving on frame and cylinder, integral muzzle brake, finish available in blue or stainless steel. Made in U.S. by Gary Reeder Custom Guns.

Price: From **$995.00**

KIMBER CUSTOM II 1911-STYLE AUTO PISTOLS

Caliber: 9mm Para., 38 Super, 9-shot magazines; 40 S&W, 8-shot magazine; 45 ACP, 7-shot magazine. **Barrel:** 5". **Weight:** 38 oz. **Length:** 8.7" overall. **Grips:** Black synthetic, smooth or double-diamond checkered rosewood, or double-diamond checkered walnut. **Sights:** McCormick low profile or Kimber adjustable rear, blade front. **Features:** Machined steel slide, frame and barrel; front and rear beveled slide serrations; cut and button-rifled, match-grade barrel; adjustable aluminum trigger; full-length guide rod; Commander-style hammer; high-ride beavertail safety; beveled magazine well. Other models available. Made in U.S. by Kimber Mfg. Inc.

Price: Custom II (black matte finish) **$730.00**

Price: Custom Royal II (polished blue finish, checkered rosewood grips) **$886.00**

Price: Custom Stainless II (satin-finished stainless steel frame and slide) **$832.00**

Price: Custom Target II (matte black or stainless finish, Kimber adj. sight) **$945.00**

Price: Custom Compact CDP II (4" bbl., alum. frame, tritium three-dot sights, 28 oz.) **$1,141.00**

Price: Custom Pro CDP II (4" bbl., alum. frame, tritium sights, full-length grip, 28 oz.) **$1,141.00**

Price: Ultra CDP II (3" bbl., aluminum frame, tritium sights, 25 oz.) **$1,141.00**

Price: Gold Match II (polished blue finish, hand-fitted barrel, ambid. safety), from **$1,168.00**

Price: Stainless Gold Match II (stainless steel frame and slide, hand-fitted bbl., amb. safety) . . . . **$1,315.00 to $1,345.00**

Kimber Custom Target II

Les Baer Thunder Ranch Special

Rock River Arms Limited Match

Volquartsen Stingray

LES BAER CUSTOM 1911-STYLE AUTO PISTOLS

Caliber: 9mm Para., 38 Super, 40 S&W, 45 ACP, 400 Cor-Bon; 7- or 8-shot magazine. **Barrel:** 4-1/4", 5", 6". **Weight:** 28 to 40 oz. **Length:** NA. **Grips:** Checkered cocobolo. **Sights:** Low-mount combat fixed, combat fixed with tritium inserts or low-mount adjustable rear, dovetail front. **Features:** Forged steel or aluminum frame; slide serrated front and rear; lowered and flared ejection port; beveled magazine well; speed trigger with 4-pound pull; beavertail grip safety; ambidextrous safety. Other models available. Made in U.S. by Les Baer Custom.

Price: Baer 1911 Premier II 5" Model (5" bbl., optional stainless steel frame and slide), from **$1,498.00**
Price: Premier II 6" Model (6" barrel), from **$1,675.00**
Price: Premier II LW1 (forged aluminum frame, steel slide and barrel), from **$1,835.00**
Price: Custom Carry (4" or 5" barrel, steel frame), from **$1,728.00**
Price: Custom Carry (4" barrel, aluminum frame), from **$2,039.00**
Price: Swift Response Pistol (fixed tritium sights, Bear Coat finish), from **$2,339.00**
Price: Monolith (5" barrel and slide with extra-long dust cover), from **$1,660.00**
Price: Stinger (4-1/4" barrel, steel or aluminum frame), from . . . **$1,552.00**
Price: Thunder Ranch Special (tritium fixed combat sight, Thunder Ranch logo) **$1,685.00**
Price: National Match Hardball (low-mount adj. sight; meets DCM rules), from **$1,425.00**
Price: Bullseye Wadcutter Pistol (Bo-Mar rib w/ adj. sight, guar. 2-1/2" groups), from **$1,560.00**
Price: Ultimate Master Combat (5" or 6" bbl., adj. sights, checkered front strap), from **$2,530.00**
Price: Ultimate Master Combat Compensated (four-port compensator, adj. sights), from **$2,558.00**

ROCK RIVER ARMS 1911-STYLE AUTO PISTOLS

Caliber: 9mm Para., 38 Super, 40 S&W, 45 ACP. **Barrel:** 4" or 5". **Weight:** NA. **Length:** NA. **Grips:** Double-diamond, checkered cocobolo or black synthetic. **Sights:** Bo-Mar low-mount adjustable, Novak fixed with tritium inserts, Heine fixed or Rock River scope mount; dovetail front blade. **Features:** Chrome-moly, machined steel frame and slide; slide serrated front and rear; aluminum speed trigger with 3.5-4 lb. pull; national match KART barrel; lowered and flared ejection port; tuned and polished extractor; beavertail grip safety; beveled mag. well. Other frames offered. Made in U.S. by Rock River Arms Inc.

Price: Elite Commando (4" barrel, Novak tritium sights) **$1,395.00**
Price: Standard Match (5" barrel, Heine fixed sights) **$1,150.00**
Price: National Match Hardball (5" barrel, Bo-Mar adj. sights), from **$1,275.00**
Price: Bullseye Wadcutter (5" barrel, Rock River slide scope mount), from **$1,380.00**
Price: Basic Limited Match (5" barrel, Bo-Mar adj. sights), from . **$1,395.00**
Price: Limited Match (5" barrel, guaranteed 1-1/2" groups at 50 yards), from **$1,795.00**
Price: Hi-Cap Basic Limited (5" barrel, four frame choices), from **$1,895.00**

Price: Ultimate Match Achiever (5" bbl. with compensator, mount and Aimpoint), from **$2,255.00**
Price: Match Master Steel (5" bbl. with compensator, mount and Aimpoint) **$5,000.00**

STI COMPACT AUTO PISTOLS

Caliber: 9mm, 40 S&W. **Barrel:** 3.4". **Weight:** 28 oz. **Length:** 7" overall. **Grips:** Checkered double-diamond rosewood. **Sights:** Heine Low Mount fixed rear, slide integral front. **Features:** Similar to STI 2011 models except has compact frame, 7-shot magazine in 9mm (6-shot in 40 cal.), single-sided thumb safety, linkless barrel lockup system, matte blue finish. From STI International.

Price: (9mm or 40 S&W), from **$746.50**

VOLQUARTSEN CUSTOM 22 CALIBER AUTO PISTOLS

Caliber: 22 LR; 10-shot magazine. **Barrel:** 3.5" to 10"; stainless steel air gauge. **Weight:** 2-1/2 to 3 lbs. 10 oz. **Length:** NA. **Grips:** Finger-grooved plastic or walnut. **Sights:** Adjustable rear and blade front or Weaver-style scope mount. **Features:** Conversions of Ruger Mk. II Auto pistol. Variety of configurations featuring compensators, underlug barrels, etc. Stainless steel finish; black Teflon finish available for additional $85; target hammer, trigger. Made in U.S. by Volquartsen Custom.

Price: 3.5 Compact (3.5" barrel, T/L adjustable rear sight, scope base optional) **$640.00**
Price: Deluxe (barrel to 10", T/L adjustable rear sight) **$675.00**
Price: Deluxe with compensator **$745.00**
Price: Masters (6.5" barrel, finned underlug, T/L adjustable rear sight, compensator) **$950.00**
Price: Olympic (7" barrel, recoil-reducing gas chamber, T/L adjustable rear sight) **$870.00**
Price: Stingray (7.5" ribbed, ported barrel; red-dot sight) **$995.00**
Price: Terminator (7.5" ported barrel, grooved receiver, scope rings) **$730.00**
Price: Ultra-Light Match (6" tensioned barrel, Weaver mount, weighs 2-1/2 lbs.) **$885.00**
Price: V-6 (6", triangular, ventilated barrel with underlug, T/L adj. sight) **$1,030.00**
Price: V-2000 (6" barrel with finned underlug, T/L adj. sight) **$1,095.00**
Price: V-Magic II (7.5" barrel, red-dot sight) **$1,055.00**

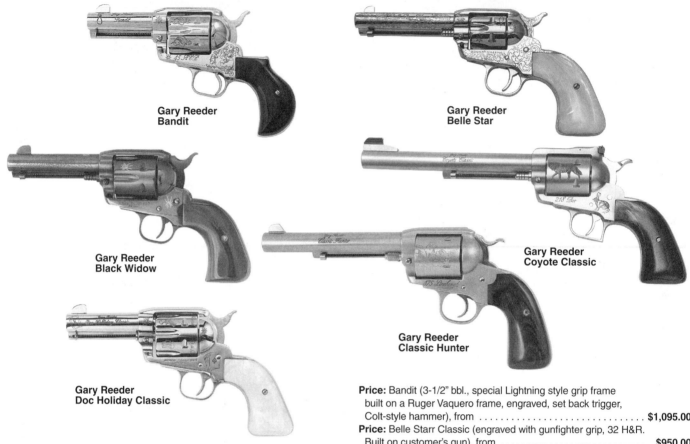

Gary Reeder Bandit

Gary Reeder Belle Star

Gary Reeder Black Widow

Gary Reeder Coyote Classic

Gary Reeder Classic Hunter

Gary Reeder Doc Holiday Classic

GARY REEDER CUSTOM GUNS REVOLVERS

Caliber: 22 WMR, 22 Hornet, 218 Bee, 356 GMR, 41 GNR, 410 GNR, 510 GNR, 357 Magnum, 45 Colt, 44-40, 41 Magnum, 44 Magnum, 454 Casull, 475 Linebaugh, 500 Linebaugh. **Barrel:** 2-1/2" to 12". **Weight:** Varies by model. **Length:** Varies by model. **Grips:** Black Cape buffalo horn, laminated walnut, simulated pearl, black and ivory micarta, others. **Sights:** Notch fixed or adjustable rear, blade or ramp front. **Features:** Custom conversions of Ruger Vaquero, Blackhawk Bisley and Super Blackhawk frames. Jeweled hammer and trigger, tuned action, model name engraved on barrel, additional engraving on frame and cylinder, integral muzzle brake, finish available in high-polish or satin stainless steel or black Chromex. Also available on customer's gun at reduced cost. Other models available. Made in U.S. by Gary Reeder Custom Guns.

Price: 45 Backpacker (weighs 28 oz., comes in 45 Long Colt, all stainless except for lightweight aircraft aluminum gripframe, black Micarta grips, not recommended for Plus P ammo), from **$995.00**

Price: 510 Hunter (octagonal bbl., set back trigger, adjustable sights, 510 GNR 5-shot, built on customer-furnished Ruger frame), from . . **$1,295.00**

Price: African Hunter (6" bbl., with or without muzzle brake, 475 or 500 Linebaugh. Built on customer's gun), from **$1,295.00**

Price: Alaskan Hunter (4-1/2" bbl., 5-shot unfluted freewheeling cylinder, black Micarta grips, soft satin vapor honed finish. Built on customer's gun), from **$1,295.00**

Price: Alaskan Survivalist (3" bbl., Redhawk frame, engraved bear, 45 Colt or 44 Magnum. Built on customer's gun), from **$995.00**

Price: American Hunter (475 Linebaugh or 500 Linebaugh, built to customers specs on furnished Ruger frame), from **$1,395.00**

Price: Arizona Ranger (choice of calibers and barrel lengths, stainless or Black Chromex finish, engraved with original Arizona Ranger badge), from **$850.00**

Price: Badlands Classic (all stainless, 4-1/2" bbl., high polished, fully engraved, Gunfighter grip and cowboy pearl grips), from . . . **$950.00**

Price: Bandit (3-1/2" bbl., special Lightning style grip frame built on a Ruger Vaquero frame, engraved, set back trigger, Colt-style hammer), from **$1,095.00**

Price: Belle Starr Classic (engraved with gunfighter grip, 32 H&R. Built on customer's gun), from **$950.00**

Price: Black Widow (4-5/8" bbl., black Chromex finish, black widow spider engraving), from **$950.00**

Price: BMF (500 Maximum or 500 Linebaugh, 4" barrel, round butt), from **$2,395.00**

Price: Border Classic (Built on customer furnished Schofield; 3" bbl., full scroll engraving, solid silver Mexican coin front sight, custom grips), from **$1,095.00**

Price: Classic 475 (Built on customer furnished base gun, 475 Linebaugh, 5 shot; satin black finish, gunfighter grip, set-back trigger, from **$1,295.00**

Price: Cowtown Classic (stainless finish, engraved with imaged symbolizing the old west, from **$950.00**

Price: Coyote Classic (chambered in 22 Hornet, 22 K-Hornet, 218 Bee, 218 Mashburn Bee, 17 Ackley Bee, 17 Ackley Hornet, 256 Winchester, 25-20, 6-shot unfluted cylinder, heavy 8" barrel, Super Blackhawk gripframe, finish of satin stainless, satin Black Chromex or high polished, comes with laminated cherry grips and Gunfighter grip. Built on customer's gun), from **$1,295.00**

Price: Doc Holliday Classic (3-1/2" bbl., engraved cards and dice, white pearl grips), from **$950.00**

Price: Double Deuce (8" heavy bbl., adjustable sights, laminated grips, 22 WMR 8-shot), from **$995.00**

Price: Gamblers Classic (2-1/2" bbl., engraved cards and dice, no ejector rod housing), from **$950.00**

Price: Improved #5 (field grade or deluxe grade, many options to choose from. **$1,495.00**

Price: Kodiak Magnum (heavy 8-1/2" bbl. with deep crown and tight barrel/cylinder gap, satin vapor honed finish), from **$1,095.00**

Price: Lawman Classic (Full custom Vaquero, two-tone finish, Lawman-style engraving, special Lawman gripframe with lanyard ring), from **$950.00**

SEMI-CUSTOM HANDGUNS — Revolvers

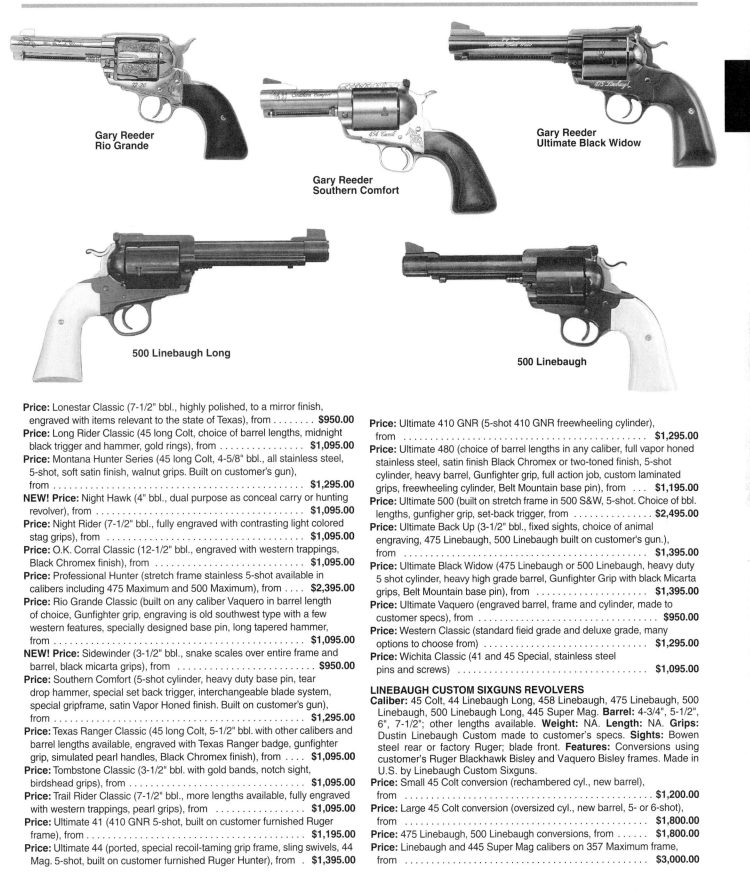

Gary Reeder
Rio Grande

Gary Reeder
Southern Comfort

Gary Reeder
Ultimate Black Widow

500 Linebaugh Long

500 Linebaugh

Price: Lonestar Classic (7-1/2" bbl., highly polished, to a mirror finish, engraved with items relevant to the state of Texas), from **$950.00**

Price: Long Rider Classic (45 long Colt, choice of barrel lengths, midnight black trigger and hammer, gold rings), from **$1,095.00**

Price: Montana Hunter Series (45 long Colt, 4-5/8" bbl., all stainless steel, 5-shot, soft satin finish, walnut grips. Built on customer's gun), from **$1,295.00**

NEW! Price: Night Hawk (4" bbl., dual purpose as conceal carry or hunting revolver), from **$1,095.00**

Price: Night Rider (7-1/2" bbl., fully engraved with contrasting light colored stag grips), from **$1,095.00**

Price: O.K. Corral Classic (12-1/2" bbl., engraved with western trappings, Black Chromex finish), from **$1,095.00**

Price: Professional Hunter (stretch frame stainless 5-shot available in calibers including 475 Maximum and 500 Maximum), from **$2,395.00**

Price: Rio Grande Classic (built on any caliber Vaquero in barrel length of choice, Gunfighter grip, engraving is old southwest type with a few western features, specially designed base pin, long tapered hammer, from **$1,095.00**

NEW! Price: Sidewinder (3-1/2" bbl., snake scales over entire frame and barrel, black micarta grips, from **$950.00**

Price: Southern Comfort (5-shot cylinder, heavy duty base pin, tear drop hammer, special set back trigger, interchangeable blade system, special gripframe, satin Vapor Honed finish. Built on customer's gun), from **$1,295.00**

Price: Texas Ranger Classic (45 long Colt, 5-1/2" bbl. with other calibers and barrel lengths available, engraved with Texas Ranger badge, gunfighter grip, simulated pearl handles, Black Chromex finish), from **$1,095.00**

Price: Tombstone Classic (3-1/2" bbl. with gold bands, notch sight, birdshead grips), from **$1,095.00**

Price: Trail Rider Classic (7-1/2" bbl., more lengths available, fully engraved with western trappings, pearl grips), from **$1,095.00**

Price: Ultimate 41 (410 GNR 5-shot, built on customer furnished Ruger frame), from **$1,195.00**

Price: Ultimate 44 (ported, special recoil-taming grip frame, sling swivels, 44 Mag. 5-shot, built on customer furnished Ruger Hunter), from . **$1,395.00**

Price: Ultimate 410 GNR (5-shot 410 GNR freewheeling cylinder), from **$1,295.00**

Price: Ultimate 480 (choice of barrel lengths in any caliber, full vapor honed stainless steel, satin finish Black Chromex or two-toned finish, 5-shot cylinder, heavy barrel, Gunfighter grip, full action job, custom laminated grips, freewheeling cylinder, Belt Mountain base pin), from . . . **$1,195.00**

Price: Ultimate 500 (built on stretch frame in 500 S&W, 5-shot. Choice of bbl. lengths, gunfigher grip, set-back trigger, from **$2,495.00**

Price: Ultimate Back Up (3-1/2" bbl., fixed sights, choice of animal engraving, 475 Linebaugh, 500 Linebaugh built on customer's gun.), from **$1,395.00**

Price: Ultimate Black Widow (475 Linebaugh or 500 Linebaugh, heavy duty 5 shot cylinder, heavy high grade barrel, Gunfighter Grip with black Micarta grips, Belt Mountain base pin), from **$1,395.00**

Price: Ultimate Vaquero (engraved barrel, frame and cylinder, made to customer specs), from **$950.00**

Price: Western Classic (standard fied grade and deluxe grade, many options to choose from) **$1,295.00**

Price: Wichita Classic (41 and 45 Special, stainless steel pins and screws) **$1,095.00**

LINEBAUGH CUSTOM SIXGUNS REVOLVERS
Caliber: 45 Colt, 44 Linebaugh Long, 458 Linebaugh, 475 Linebaugh, 500 Linebaugh, 500 Linebaugh Long, 445 Super Mag. **Barrel:** 4-3/4", 5-1/2", 6", 7-1/2"; other lengths available. **Weight:** NA. **Length:** NA. **Grips:** Dustin Linebaugh Custom made to customer's specs. **Sights:** Bowen steel rear or factory Ruger; blade front. **Features:** Conversions using customer's Ruger Blackhawk Bisley and Vaquero Bisley frames. Made in U.S. by Linebaugh Custom Sixguns.

Price: Small 45 Colt conversion (rechambered cyl., new barrel), from **$1,200.00**

Price: Large 45 Colt conversion (oversized cyl., new barrel, 5- or 6-shot), from **$1,800.00**

Price: 475 Linebaugh, 500 Linebaugh conversions, from **$1,800.00**

Price: Linebaugh and 445 Super Mag calibers on 357 Maximum frame, from **$3,000.00**

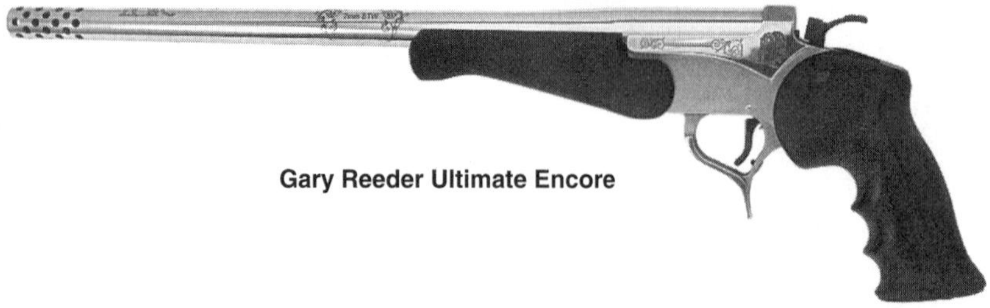

Gary Reeder Ultimate Encore

Gary Reeder Kodiak
Hunter Dall Sheep

SSK Industries Contender

GARY REEDER CUSTOM GUNS G-2 AND ENCORE PISTOLS
Caliber: 22 Cheetah, 218 Bee, 22 K-Hornet, 22 Hornet, 218 Mashburn Bee, 22-250 Improved, 6mm/284, 7mm STW, 7mm GNR, 30 GNR, 338 GNR, 300 Win. Magnum, 338 Win. Magnum, 350 Rem. Magnum, 358 STA, 375 H&H, 378 GNR, 416 Remington, 416 GNR, 450 GNR, 475 Linebaugh, 500 Linebaugh, 50 Alaskan, 50 AE, 454 Casull; others available. **Barrel:** 8" to 15" (others available). **Weight:** NA. **Length:** Varies with barrel length. **Grips:** Walnut fingergroove. **Sights:** Express-style adjustable rear and barrel band front (Kodiak Hunter); none furnished most models. **Features:** Offers complete guns and barrels in the T/C Contender and Encore. Integral muzzle brake, engraved animals and model name, tuned action, high-polish or satin stainless steel or black Chromex finish. Made in U.S. by Gary Reeder Custom Guns.
Price: Kodiak Hunter (50 AE, 475 Linebaugh, 500 Linebaugh,
510 GNR, or 454 Casull, from **$1,195.00**
Price: Ultimate Encore (15" bbl. with muzzle brake, custom
engraving), from **$1,195.00**

SSK INDUSTRIES CONTENDER AND ENCORE PISTOLS
Caliber: More than 400, including most standard pistol and rifle calibers, as well as 226 JDJ, 6mm JDJ, 257 JDJ, 6.5mm JDJ, 7mm JDJ, 6.5mm Mini-Dreadnaught, 30-06 JDJ, 280 JDJ, 375 JDJ, 6mm Whisper, 300 Whisper and 338 Whisper. **Barrel:** 10" to 26"; blued or stainless; variety of configurations. **Weight:** Varies with barrel length and features. **Length:** Varies with barrel length. **Grips:** Pachmayr, wood models available. **Features:** Offers frames, barrels and complete guns in the T/C Contender and Encore. Fluted, diamond, octagon and round barrels; chrome-plating; muzzle brakes; trigger jobs; variety of stocks and forends; sights and optics. Made in U.S. by SSK Industries.
Price: Blued Contender frame, from **$390.00**
Price: Stainless Contender frame, from **$390.00**
Price: Blued Encore frame, from **$290.00**
Price: Stainless Encore frame, from **$318.00**
Price: Contender barrels, from **$315.00**
Price: Encore barrels, from **$340.00**

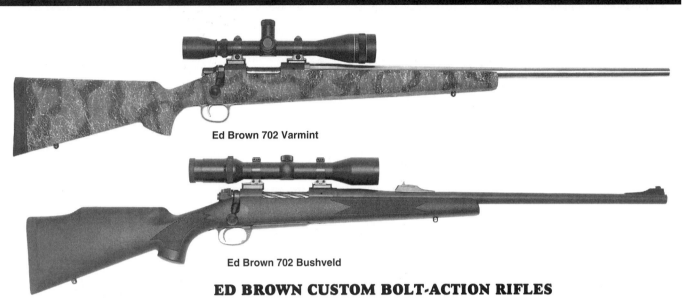

Ed Brown 702 Varmint

Ed Brown 702 Bushveld

ED BROWN CUSTOM BOLT-ACTION RIFLES

Caliber: 222, 223, 22-250, 220 Swift, 243, 243 Ackley Imp., 25-06, 270 Win., 280 Rem., 280 Ackley Imp., 6mm, 6.5/284, 7mm/08, 7mm Rem. Mag., 7STW, 30/06, 308, 300 Win. Mag., 338 Win. Mag., 375 H&H, 404 Jeffery, 416 Rem. Mag., 416 Rigby, 458 Win. Mag. **Barrel:** 21", 24", 26". **Weight:** NA. **Length:** NA. **Stock:** Fiberglass syn-thetic; swivel studs; recoil pad. **Sights:** Optional; Talley scope rings and base furnished; scope mounting included in price (scope extra). **Features:** Machined receiver; hand-fitted bolt with welded handle; M16-type extractor; three-position safety; trigger adjustable for pull and overtravel; match-quality, hand-lapped barrel with deep countersunk crowning. Made in U.S. by Ed Brown Custom, Inc.

Price: Model 702 Savanna short- or long-action repeater (lightweight 24" or medium-weight 26" barrel), from . **$2,800.00**
Price: Model 702 Tactical long-action repeater (heavy contour 26" barrel), from **$2,900.00**
Price: Model 702 Ozark short-action repeater (lightweight 21" barrel), from **$2,800.00**
Price: Model 702 Varmint short-action single shot (med. 26" or hvy. 24"), from **$2,800.00**
Price: Model 702 Light Tactical short-action repeater (med. 21" barrel), from **$2,800.00**
Price: Model 702 Bushveld dangerous game rifle (24" med. or heavy barrel), from **$2,900.00**
Price: Model 702 Denali mountain hunting rifle (22" super light weight bbl. or 23" light weight bbl.), from **$2,800.00**
Price: Model 702 Tactical sniper rifle (26" heavy bbl.), from **$2,900.00**
Price: Model 702 Marine Sniper (24" heavy bbl.), from **$2,900.00**

Dakota 76 Classic

Dakota 97 Hunter

DAKOTA 76 RIFLE

Caliber: All calibers from 22-250 through 458 Win. Mag. **Barrel:** 23". **Weight:** 6-1/2 lbs. **Length:** NA. **Stock:** Choice of X-grade oil-finished English, Bastogne or Claro walnut. **Features:** Short, standard short magnum or long magnum actions, hand checkered stock with 1" black recoil pad, steel grip cap and single screw stud sling swivels. Many options and upgrades available.

Price: Dakota 76 Classic, from **$4,995.00**
Price: Dakota 76 Safari (23" bbl., calibers from 257 Roberts through 458 Win. Mag. drop belly magazine
with straddle floorplate) **$5,995.00**
Price: Dakota 76 African (24" bbl., 450 Dakota, 416 Dakota, 416 Rigby, 404 Jeffrey, four-round magazine),
from **$6,795.00**
Price: Dakota 97 Hunter (24" bbl., calibers from 25-06 to 375 Dakota, synthetic stock), from **$2,195.00**
Price: Longbow Tactical Engagement Rifle (28" bbl., 338 Lapua Mag., 330 Dakota, 300 Dakota, McMillan fiberglass stock with
full-length action bedding), from **$4,500.00**

SEMI-CUSTOM RIFLES — Bolt-Action

Remington Model ABG

REMINGTON MODEL 700 CUSTOM SHOP RIFLES

Caliber: 270 Win., 280 Rem., 30-06, 7mm Rem. Mag., 7mm STW, 300 Win. Mag., 300 Wea. Mag., 338 Win. Mag., 8mm Rem. Mag., 35 Whelen, 375 H&H Mag., 416 Rem. Mag., 458 Win. Mag., 7mm RUM, 300 RUM, 338 RUM, 375 RUM. **Barrel:** 22", 24", 26". **Weight:** 6 lbs. 6 oz. to 9 lbs. **Length:** 44-1/4" to 46-1/2" overall. **Stock:** Laminated hardwood, walnut or Kevlar-reinforced fiberglass. **Sights:** Adjustable rear (Safari models); all receivers drilled and tapped for scope mounts. **Features:** Black matte, satin blue or uncolored stainless steel finish; hand-fitted action is epoxy-bedded to stock; tuned trigger; bolt-supported extractor for sure extraction; fancy wood and other options available. Made in U.S. by Remington Arms Co.

    Price: Custom KS Mountain Rifle (24" barrel, synthetic stock, 6-3/4 lbs. in mag. cals.), from $1,314.00
    Price: Custom KS Safari Stainless (22" barrel, synthetic stock, 9 lbs.), from $1,697.00
    Price: Model ABG (African Big Game: 26" bbl., laminated stock, satin blue finish), from $1,726.00
    Price: APR (African Plains Rifle: 26" barrel, laminated stock, satin blue finish), from $1,716.00
    Price: AWR (Alaskan Wilderness Rifle: 24" barrel, syn. stock, black matte finish), from $1,593.00
    Price: Model 700 Custom C Grade, from $1,733.00; Custom High Grade, from $3,297.00

Remington 40-XB with thumbhole stock

REMINGTON MODEL 40-X CUSTOM SHOP TARGET RIFLES

Caliber: 22 LR, 22 WMR, 22 BR Rem., 222 Rem., 223 Rem., 22-250, 220 Swift, 6mm BR Rem., 6mm Rem., 243 Win., 25-06, 260 Rem., 7.62mm NATO, 7mm BR Rem., 7mm Rem. Mag., 7mm STW, 308 Win., 30-06, 300 Win. Mag. **Barrel:** 24", 27-1/4"; various twist rates offered. **Weight:** 9-3/4 to 11 lbs. **Length:** 40" to 47" overall. **Stock:** Walnut, laminated wood or Kevlar-reinforced fiberglass. **Sights:** None; receiver drilled and tapped for scope mounts. **Features:** Single shot or 5-shot repeater; carbon steel or stainless steel receiver; externally adjustable trigger (1-1/2 to 3-1/2 lbs.); rubber butt pad. From Remington Arms Co.

    Price: 40-XB Rangemaster (27-1/4" bbl., walnut stock, forend rail with hand stop), from $1,636.00
    Price: 40-XB (with thumbhole stock), from $1,848.00
    Price: 40-XB KS (27-1/4" bbl., black synthetic stock), from $1,876.00
    Price: 40-XRBR KS (24" bbl., Remington green synthetic stock with straight comb), from $1,894.00
    Price: 40-XC KS (24" bbl., gray synthetic stock with adj. comb), from $1,821.00
    Price: 40-XB Tactical (27-1/4" bbl., synthetic stock, matte finish), from $2,108.00

Remington Model Seven Custom MS

REMINGTON MODEL SEVEN CUSTOM SHOP RIFLES

Caliber: 222 Rem., 223 Rem., 22-250 Rem., 243 Win., 6mm Rem., 250 Savage, 257 Roberts, 260 Rem., 308 Win., 7mm-08 Rem., 35 Rem., 350 Rem. Mag. **Barrel:** 20". **Weight:** 5-3/4 to 6-1/2 lbs. **Length:** 39-1/2" overall. **Stock:** Laminated hardwood or Kevlar-reinforced fiberglass. **Sights:** Adjustable ramp rear, hooded blade front. **Features:** Hand-fitted action; epoxy bedded; deep blue or non-reflective black matte finish; drilled and tapped for scope mounts. From Remington Arms Co.

    Price: Model Seven Custom MS (20" bbl., Mannlicher stock, deep blue finish), from $1,332.00
    Price: Model Seven Custom KS (20" bbl., synthetic stock, matte finish), from $1,314.00
    Price: Model Seven AWR Alaskan Wilderness Rifle (22" bbl., synthetic stock, 7mm Rem. SAUM,
    300 Rem. SAUM), from $1,546.00

John Rigby African Express Rifle

JOHN RIGBY CUSTOM AFRICAN EXPRESS RIFLE

Caliber: 375 H&H Magnum, 416 Rigby, 458 Winchester. **Barrel:** To customer specs. **Weight:** NA. **Length:** To customer specs. **Stock:** Customer's choice. **Sights:** Express-type rear, hooded ramp front; scope mounts offered. **Features:** Handcrafted bolt-action rifle built to customer specifications. Variety of engraving and stock wood options available.
 Price: African Express Rifle,
   from **$23,500.00**

John Rigby African Express Rifle engraving

JOHN RIGBY BOLT-ACTION RIFLES

Caliber: 300 H&H, 375 H&H, 416 Rigby, 458 Win., 500 Jeffrey (other calibers upon request) **Barrel:** NA. **Weight:** NA. **Length:** NA. **Stock:** Exhibition grade English walnut. **Sights:** Quarter rib with Express sights containing flip up night sight. **Features:** Stock custom-fitted to buyer specifications, detachable scope mounts included, Pac Nor Match Grade barrel.
 Price: John Rigby Bolt Action Rifle, from **$23,500.00**

TIME PRECISION BOLT-ACTION RIFLES

Caliber: 22 LR, 222, 223, 308, 378, 300 Win. Mag., 416 Rigby, others. **Barrel:** NA. **Weight:** 10 lbs. and up. **Length:** NA. **Stock:** Fiberglass. **Sights:** None; receiver drilled and tapped for scope mount. **Features:** Thirty different action types offered, including single shots and repeaters for bench rest, varmint and big-game hunting. Machined chrome-moly action; three-position safety; Shilen match trigger (other triggers available); twin cocking cams; dual firing pin. Built to customer specifications. From Time Precision.
 Price: 22 LR Bench Rest Rifle (Shilen match-grade stainless steel bbl., fiberglass stock), from **$2,202.00**
 Price: 22 LR Target Rifle, from **$2,220.00**
 Price: 22 LR Sporter, from **$1,980.00**
 Price: 22 LR Benchrest Rifle, from **$2,202.00**
 Price: Hunting Rifle (calibers to 30-06), from **$2,202.00**
 Price: Benchrest Rifle (most calibers), from **$2,202.00**
 Price: Hunting Rifle (7mm Rem. Mag., 300 Win. Mag., 338 Win. Mag.), from **$2,322.00**

SEMI-CUSTOM RIFLES — Bolt-Action

Weatherby Safari Grade

Weatherby Crown Custom

Weatherby Custom close-up

WEATHERBY CUSTOM SHOP BOLT-ACTION RIFLES

Caliber: 257 Wby. Mag., 270 Wby. Mag., 7mm Wby. Mag., 300 Wby. Mag., 340 Wby. Mag., 375 H&H Mag., 378 Wby. Mag., 416 Wby. Mag., 460 Wby. Mag. **Barrel:** 24", 26", 28". **Weight:** NA. **Length:** NA. **Stock:** Monte Carlo, modified Monte Carlo or Classic design in Exhibition- or Exhibition Special Select grades of claro or French wal-nut; injection-molded synthetic in Snow Camo, Alpine Camo or Dark Timber colors. **Sights:** Quarter-rib rear with one standing and one folding leaf, hooded ramp front (Safari Grade); drilled and tapped for scope mount. Features: Rosewood or ebony pistol-grip caps with inlaid diamonds in rosewood, walnut or maple; three grades of engraving patterns for receiver, bolt and handle; gold inlays; wooden inlaid buttstock, forearm and magazine box; three grades of engraved and gold inlaid rings and bases; canvas/leather, solid leather or leather with oak trim case. From the Weatherby Custom Shop.

Price: Safari Grade (engr. floorplate, oil-finished French wal. stock w/fleur-de-lis checkering.) $6,050.00
Price: Crown (engr., inlaid floorplate, engr. bbl. and receiver, hand-carved walnut stock) $7,757.00
Price: Crown Custom (engraved barrel, receiver and triggerguard, hand-carved walnut stock,
    damascened bolt and follower with checkered knob), from $7,757.00
Price: Outfitter Krieger (Krieger stainless steel bbl.) $3,639.00
Price: Outfitter Custom (standard barrel, Bell and Carlson syn. camo stock), from $2,583.00
Price: Dangerous Game Rifle (chrome moly Criterion barrel by Krieger Monte Carlo-style
    composite stock, Mark V action), from $3,095.00

Winchester African Express

WINCHESTER MODEL 70 CLASSIC CUSTOM RIFLES

Caliber: 375 H&H Mag., 416 Rem. Mag., 458 Win. Mag., 458 Lott, 470 Capstick, 257 Roberts, 260 Rem., 7mm- 08 Rem., 300 WSM, 270 WSM, 7mm WSM, 308 Win., 358 Win., 450 Marlin, 270 Win., 7mm Win., 30-06 Spfld., 25-06 Rem., 6.5x55 Swe., 264 Win. Mag., 280 Rem., 35 Whelen, 7mm Rem. Mag., 7mm Ultra Mag., 7mm STW, 300 Win. Mag., 300 Wea. Mag., 300 Ultra. Mag., 338 Ultra Mag., 375 H&H (Lwt). **Barrel:** 22", 24", 26". **Weight:** 6.5 to 9.5 lbs. **Length:** NA. **Stock:** Various grades of walnut and synthetic stocks available. **Sights:** Three-leaf express rear, adjustable front, (Express models); none furnished on other models. **Features:** Match-grade cut rifled barrels with squared, hand-honed actions. Most are available in stainless or blued, and right- or left-handed, hand-fitted actions. All utilize the pre-'64 type action with controlled round feed, receiver-mounted blade ejector and specially-tuned trigger systems. All are shipped in a hard case. Made in U.S.A. by Winchester/U.S. Repeating Arms Co.

Price: Model 70 Classic Custom African Express (22" or 24" barrel, 9.25 to 9.5 lbs), from $4,572.00
Price: Safari Express (24" barrel, 9 to 9.25 lbs.), from $3,043.00
Price: Short Action (24" barrel, 7.5 to 8.25 lbs.), from $2,708.00
Price: Featherweight (22" barrel, 7.25 lbs., 270 Win., 7mm Win., 30-06 Spfld.), from $2,708.00
Price: Carbon (24" or 26" barrel, 6.5 to 7 lbs.), from $3,233.00
Price: Ultimate Classic (24" or 26" barrel, 7.5 to 7.75 lbs.), from $2,941.00
Price: Extreme Weather (22", 24" or 26" barrel, 7.25 to 7.5 lbs.), from $2,525.00

Bushmaster DCM Competition Rifle

Volquartsen Grey Ghost

BROWNING SEMI-AUTO 22 LUXE

Caliber: 22 LR. **Barrel:** 19-1/4". **Weight:** 5 lbs. 3 oz. **Length:** 37". **Stock:** Polished walnut. **Sights:** Adjustable folding leaf rear, gold bead front. **Features:** The traditional John Browning-designed .22 takedown autoloader with bottom eject. Grooved receiver will accept most groove or tip-off type mounts or receiver sights. Custom shop ver-sions are available in two grades: SA 22 Grade II and SA 22 Grade III.
   Price: From **$2,920.00**

BROWNING BAR MARK I

The original Browning BAR Mark I from the Browning Custom Shop in Belgium available in Grade IV and Grade D.
   Price: From **$7,216.00**

BUSHMASTER SEMI-AUTO RIFLES

Caliber: 223. **Barrel:** 16" regular or fluted, 20" regular, heavy or fluted, 24" heavy or fluted. **Weight:** 6.9 to 8.37 lbs. **Length:** 34.5" to 38.25" overall. **Stock:** Polymer. **Sights:** Fully adjustable dual flip-up aperture rear, blade front or Picatinny rail for scope mount. **Features:** Versions of the AR-15 style rifle. Aircraft-quality aluminum receiver; chrome-lined barrel and chamber; chrome-moly-vanadium steel barrel with 1:9" twist; manganese phosphate matte finish; forged front sight; receiver takes down without tools; serrated, finger groove pistol grip. Made in U.S.A. by Bushmaster Firearms/Quality Parts Co.
   Price: DCM Competition Rifle **$1,495.00**

LES BAER AR 223 AUTO RIFLES

Caliber: 223. **Barrel:** 16-1/4", 20", 22" or 24"; cryo-treated, stainless steel bench-rest grade. **Weight:** NA. **Length:** NA. **Stock:** Polymer. **Sights:** None; Picatinny rail for scope mount. **Features:** Forged and machined upper and lower receiver; single- or double-stage adjustable trigger; free-float handguard; Bear Coat protective finish. Made in U.S.A. by Les Baer Custom.
   Price: Ultimate Super Varmint (Jewell two-stage trigger, guar. to shoot 1/2 MOA groups), from **$1,989.00**
   Price: Ultimate M4 Flattop (16-1/4" bbl., Ultra single-stage trigger), from **$2,195.00**
   Price: Ultimate IPSC Action (20" bbl., Jewell two-stage trigger), from **$2,230.00**

SSK INDUSTRIES AR-15 RIFLES

Caliber: 223, 6mm PPC, 6.5mm PPC, 6.5 Grendel, 300 Whisper and other wildcats. **Barrel:** 16-1/2" and longer (to order). **Weight:** NA. **Length:** NA. **Stock:** Black plastic. **Sights:** Blade front, adjustable rear (scopes and red-dot sights available). **Features:** Variety of designs to full match-grade guns offered. Customer's gun can be rebarreled or accurized. From SSK Industries.
   Price: Complete AR-15, from **$1,800.00**
   Price: A2 upper unit (front sight, short handguard) **$1,100.00**
   Price: Match Grade upper unit (bull barrel, tubular handguard, scope mount) **$1,100.00**

VOLQUARTSEN CUSTOM 22 CALIBER AUTO RIFLES

Caliber: 22 LR, 22 Magnum. **Barrel:** 16-1/2" to 20"; stainless steel air gauge. **Weight:** 4-3/4 to 5-3/4 lbs. **Length:** NA. **Stock:** Synthetic or laminated. **Sights:** Not furnished; Weaver base provided. **Features:** Conversions of the Ruger 10/22 rifle. Tuned trigger with 2-1/2 to 3-1/2 lb. pull. Variety of configurations and features. From Volquartsen Custom.
   Price: Ultra-Light (22 LR, 16-1/2" tensioned barrel, synthetic stock, from **$670.00**
   Price: Grey Ghost (22 LR, 18-1/2" barrel, laminated wood stock), from **$690.00**
   Price: Deluxe (22 LR, 20" barrel, laminated wood or fiberglass stock), from **$850.00**
   Price: Mossad (22 LR, 20" fluted and ported barrel, fiberglass thumbhole stock), from **$970.00**
   Price: VX-2500 (22 LR, 20" fluted and ported barrel, aluminum/fiberglass stock), from **$1,044.00**
   Price: Volquartsen 22 LR (stainless steel receiver), from **$920.00**
   Price: Volquartsen 22 Mag (22 WMR, stainless steel receiver), from **$950.00**

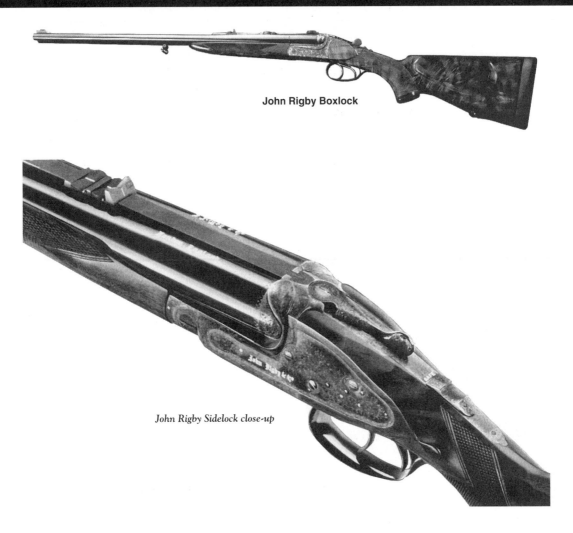

John Rigby Boxlock

John Rigby Sidelock close-up

BERETTA EXPRESS DOUBLE RIFLES

Caliber: 9.3x74R, 375 H&H Mag., 416 Rigby, 458 Win. Mag., 470 Nitro Express, 500 Nitro Express. **Barrel:** 23" to 25". **Weight:** 11 lbs. **Length:** NA. **Stock:** Hand-finished, hand-checkered walnut with cheek rest. **Sights:** Folding-leaf, Express-type rear, blade front. **Features:** High-strength steel action with reinforced receiver sides; top tang extends to stock comb for strength; double triggers (articulated front trigger and automatic blocking device eliminate chance of simultaneous discharge); hand-cut, stepped rib; engraved receiver; trapdoor compartment in stock for extra cartridges; spare front sights stored in pistol-grip cap. Imported from Italy by Beretta USA.

    Price: SSO6 o/u (optional claw mounts for scope), from **$21,000.00**
    Price: SSO6 EELL o/u (engraved game scenes or color case-hardened with gold inlays), from **$23,500.00**
    Price: 455 s/s (color case-hardened action), from **$36,000.00**
    Price: 455 EELL s/s (receiver engraved with big-game animals), from **$47,000.00**

BROWNING EXPRESS RIFLES

Still made in Belgium in the traditional manner, two models are available, Herstal and CCS 375. Produced in five different grades of embellishment. Other specifications NA.

    Price: From **$11,733.00**

JOHN RIGBY DOUBLE RIFLES

Caliber: 375 H&H, 500/416, 450 Nitro Express, 470 Nitro Express, 500 Nitro Express, 577 Nitro Express. **Barrel:** To customer specs. **Weight:** NA. **Length:** To customer specs. **Stock:** To customer specs. **Sights:** Dovetail, express-type sights; claw-foot scope mount available. **Features:** Handcrafted to customer specifications. Boxlock or sidelock action, hand-fitted; variety of engraving and other options offered.

    Price: Rigby Boxlock, from **$22,500.00**
    Price: Rigby Sidelock, from **$45,700.00**

Ballard No. 5 Pacific

BALLARD RIFLE, LLC

Caliber: 22 LR, 32-40, 38-55, 40-65 Win., 40-70 SS, 40-90, 45-70 Gov't., 45-90, 45-110, 50-70 Gov't., 50-90. **Barrel:** 24", 26", 30", 32", 34". **Weight:** 7-1/2 to 11-1/2 lbs. **Stock:** American black walnut. **Sights:** Blade front, Rocky Mountain rear, others. **Features:** Authentic reproductions faithful to the original patent. Receivers and internal parts machined from solid 8620 steel stock, not castings. Hand finished. Many options.

Price: No. 1-1/2 Hunter's Rifle (30" round bbl., single trigger, S lever), from	**$2,050.00**
Price: No. 1-3/4 Far West (30" round regular or heavyweight bbl., S lever), from	**$2,250.00**
Price: No. 3 Gallery Rifle (24", 26" or 30" lightweight octagon bbl., rifle bottsrock with steel crescent buttplate, S lever), from	**$2,050.00**
Price: No. 3F Fine Gallery Rifle (26", 28" or 30" octagon bbl., pistol grip, single or double set triggers), from	**$2,500.00**
Price: No. 4 Perfection (30" or 32" octagon bbl. single or double set trigger), from	**$2,250.00**
Price: No. 4-1/2 Mid Range (30" or 32" standard or heavyweight half octagon bbl., single or double set triggers, pistol grip shotgun buttstock), from	**$2,250.00**
Price: No. 5 Pacific (30" or 32" standard or heavyweight octagon bbl., standard stocks in rifle or shotgun configuration), from	**$2,575.00**
Price: No. 5-1/2 Montana Model (30" or 32" heavyweight octagon bbl., under-barrel wiping rod, set triggers, ring lever), from	**$2,725.00**
Price: No. 6 Off Hand Rifle (30", 32" or 34" half octagon bbl., blade front sight, pistol grip receiver, double set triggers), from	**$2,550.00**
Price: No. 7 Long Range (32" or 34" standard or heavyweight half octagon bbl., pistol grip shotgun buttstock, single or double set trigger), from	**$2,250.00**
Price: No. 8 Union Hill Model (30" half octagon standard or heavyweight bbl., double set triggers, pistol grip stock with cheekpiece, full loop lever) from	**$2,500.00**
Price: Standard Sporting Model 1885 High Wall (30" or 32" octagonal bbl., single trigger, small S lever), from	**$2,050.00**
Price: Special Sporting Model 1885 High Wall (32" bbl., shotgun buttstock with cheekpiece, shotgun buttplate, double set triggers), from	**$2,200.00**

C. Sharps Model 1885 Highwall Classic Sporting

C. Sharps Model 1877 Custom LR Target

C. SHARPS ARMS RIFLES

Caliber: 22 RF to 50-140-3 1/4 Sharps. **Barrel:** Octagon 18" to 34". **Weight:** 9-18 lbs. **Stock:** American English walnut (premium straight grain to presentation). **Sights:** Short range to long range target. **Features:** Authentic replicas of Sharps rifles. Models 1874, 1877 & 1885 machined from solid steel. Made in U.S. by C. Sharps Arms Co. Inc.

Price: Model 1874 Hartford, from	**$1,775.00**
Price: Model 1874 Bridgeport, from	**$1,495.00**
Price: Model 1875 Sporting, from	**$1,095.00**
Price: Model 1875 Classic, from	**$1,385.00**
Price: Model 1875 Target, from	**$1,136.63**
Price: Model 1877 Custom LR Target, from	**$5,500.00**
Price: Model 1885 Highwall Sporting, from	**$1,350.00**
Price: Model 1885 Highwall Classic Sporting, from	**$1,550.00**

SEMI-CUSTOM RIFLES — Single Shot

Dakota Model 10

DAKOTA MODEL 10

Caliber: Most from 22 LR through 404 Dakota. **Barrel:** 23". **Length:** NA. **Weight:** 5-1/2 lbs. **Stock:** Walnut. **Sights:** NA. **Features:** Falling block action machined from prehardened 4140 bar stock. Many options.
Price: Dakota Model 10, from $3,795.00

Lone Star Silhouette

LONE STAR ROLLING BLOCK RIFLES

Caliber: 30-40 Krag, 30-30, 32-40, 38-55, 40-50 SS, 40-50 BN, 40-65, 40-70 SS, 40-70 BN, 40-82, 40-90 SBN, 40-90 SS, 44-90 Rem. Sp., 45 Colt, 45-110 (3-1/4"), 45-110 (2-7/8"), 45-100, 45-90, 45- 70, 50-70, 50-90. **Barrel:** 26" to 34". **Weight:** 6 to 11 lbs. **Length:** NA. **Stock:** American walnut. **Sights:** Buckhorn rear, blade or Beech front. **Features:** Authentic replicas of Remington rolling block rifles. Octagon barrel; bone-pack, color case-hardened action; drilled and tapped for Vernier sight; single, single-set or double-set trigger; variety of sight, finish and engraving options. Fires blackpowder or factory ammo. Made in U.S. by Lone Star Rifle Co. Inc.
Price: No. 5 Sporting Rifle (30-30 or 30-40 Krag, 26" barrel, buckhorn rear sight) $1,995.00
Price: Cowboy Action Rifle (28" octagonal barrel, buckhorn rear sight) $1,995.00
Price: Silhouette Rifle (32" or 34" octagonal barrel, drilled and tapped for Vernier sight) $1,995.00
Price: Sporting Rifle (straight grip, semi-crescent butt, octagonal bbl.), from $1,995.00
Price: Creedmoor (34" bbl. identical to original rifle) $1,995.00
Price: Buffalo Rifle (12 or 16 lbs., octagonal bbl.) $3,200.00
Price: Custer Commemorative (50-70 only, octagonal bbl.) exact replica of General George Armstrong
Custer's Remington Sporting Rifle $3,500.00

Meacham Low-Wall

MEACHAM HIGH-WALL SILHOUETTE RIFLE

Caliber: Any rimmed cartridge. **Barrel:** 30", 34" octagon. **Weight:** 11-1/2 to 11.9 lbs. **Length:** NA. **Stock:** Fancy eastern black walnut with cheekpiece and shadow line. **Sights:** Tang drilled for Win. base, 3/8" front dovetail. **Features:** Parts interchangeable copy of '85 Winchester. Numerous options include single trigger, single set trigger, or Schuetzen double set triggers, thick side or thin side bone charcoal color case-hardened action.
Price: Meacham High-Wall Silhouette, from $3,299.00
Price: Meacham Low-Wall Rifle (Calibers: 22 RF Match or 17 HMR, rimfire and centerfire pistol cartridges,
.22 Hornet or Bee), from $3,299.00

Remington No. 1 Mid-Range Sporter

REMINGTON CUSTOM SHOP ROLLING BLOCK RIFLES

Caliber: 45-70. **Barrel:** 30". **Weight:** NA. **Length:** NA. **Stock:** American walnut. **Sights:** Buckhorn rear and blade front (optional tang-mounted Vernier rear, globe with spirit level front). **Features:** Satin blue finish with case-colored receiver; single set trigger; steel Schnabel fore end tip; steel buttplate. From Remington Arms Co. Custom Gun Shop.
Price: No. 1 Mid-Range Sporter (round or half-octagon barrel) $1,450.00
Price: No. 1 Silhouette (heavy barrel with 1:18" twist; no sights) $1,560.00

SEMI-CUSTOM SHOTGUNS

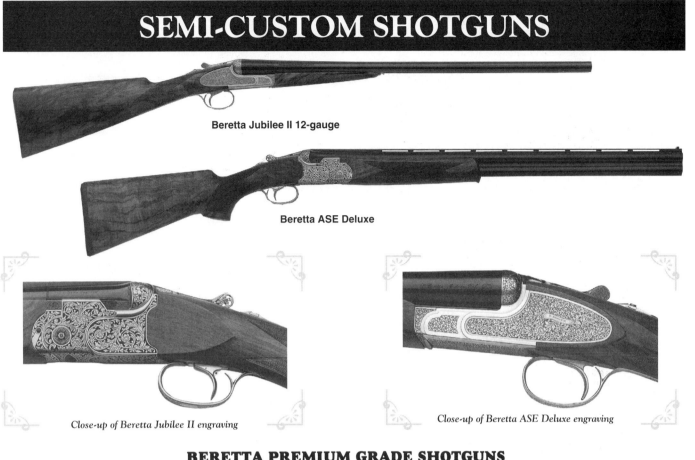

Beretta Jubilee II 12-gauge

Beretta ASE Deluxe

Close-up of Beretta Jubilee II engraving

Close-up of Beretta ASE Deluxe engraving

BERETTA PREMIUM GRADE SHOTGUNS

Gauge: 12, 20, 410, 3" chamber; 28, 2-3/4" chamber. **Barrel:** 26", 28", 30", 32". **Weight:** 5 to 7-1/2 lbs. **Length:** NA. **Stock:** Highly figured English or American walnut; straight or pistol grip; hand-checkered. **Features:** Machined nickel-chrome-moly action, hand-fitted; cross-bolt breech lock; Boehler Antinit steel barrels with fixed chokes or Mobilchoke tubes; single selective or non-selective or double trigger; numerous stock and engraving options. From Beretta USA.

Price: Giubileo (Jubilee) o/u (engraved sideplates, trigger guard, safety and top lever), from $12,900.00
Price: Giubileo II (Jubilee II) s/s (English-style stock, engraved sideplates and fixtures), from $12,900.00
Price: ASE Deluxe o/u (engraved receiver and forend cap), from $24,000.00
Price: SO5 Trap (single, non-selective trigger, heavy beavertail forend, fixed chokes), from $17,490.00
Price: SO5 Skeet (26" or 28" bbl., heavy beavertail forend, fixed chokes), from $17,490.00
Price: SO5 Sporting (single, selective trigger, Mobilchoke tubes), from $17,490.00
Price: SO6 EELL o/u (engraved receiver with gold inlays, custom-fit stock), from $34,900.00
Price: SO6 EL o/u (light English scroll engravings on receiver), from $23,900.00
Price: SO6 EESS o/u (enamel-colored receiver in green, red or blue, arabesque engravings), from $34,900.00
Price: SO9 o/u (single, non-selective trigger, engraved receiver and fixtures), from $44,500.00

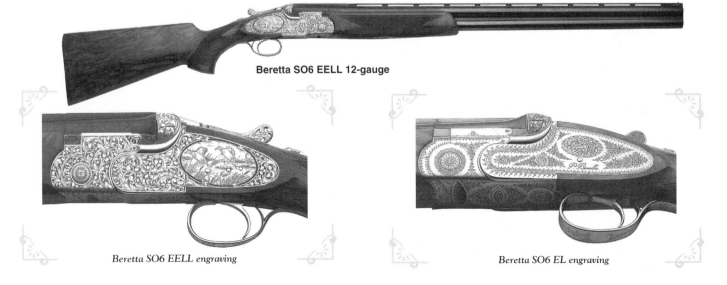

Beretta SO6 EELL 12-gauge

Beretta SO6 EELL engraving

Beretta SO6 EL engraving

SEMI-CUSTOM SHOTGUNS

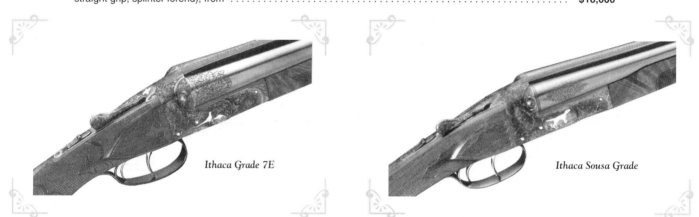

Browning LC1

Browning LC2

BROWNING SUPERPOSED & BSL SHOTGUNS

Gauge: 20, Both the BSL side-by-side and the Superposed over-and under are still made in Belgium in the traditional, time-honored manner. The BSL is available in two grades, LC1 (blued receiver) and LC2 (silver-colored receiver). The Superposed is available in 18 grades. Custom options include: engraving of name or initials, second set of barrels, special finish or checkering, special stock dimensions, personalized engraving scenes and upgraded wood. Other specifications NA.
Price: From **$18,566.00**

DAKOTA LEGEND/PREMIER SHOTGUNS

Available in all standard gauges, features include exhibition English walnut stock, French grey finish, 50% coverage engraving, straight grip, splinter forend, double trigger, 27" barrels, game rib with gold bead, selective ejectors, choice of chokes. Various options available.
Price: Dakota Premier Grade, from **$13,950.00**
Price: Dakota Legend Shotgun (27" bbls., special selection English walnut stock,
straight grip, splinter forend), from **$18,000**

Ithaca Grade 7E

Ithaca Sousa Grade

ITHACA CLASSIC DOUBLES SIDE-BY-SIDE SHOTGUNS

Gauge: 20, 28, 2-3/4" chamber; 410, 3" chamber. **Barrel:** 26", 28", 30". **Weight:** 5 lbs. 5 oz. (410 bore) to 5 lbs. 14 oz. (20 ga.). **Length:** NA. **Stock:** Exhibition-grade American black walnut, hand-checkered with hand-rubbed oil finish. **Features:** Updated duplicates of original New Ithaca Double double-barrel shotguns. Hand-fitted box-lock action; splinter or beavertail forend; bone-charcoal color case-hardened receiver; chrome-moly steel rust- blued barrels; ejectors; gold double triggers; fixed chokes; hand-engraved game scenes. Made in U.S. by Ithaca Classic Doubles.
Price: Special Skeet Grade (plain color case-hardened receiver, feather crotch walnut stock) **$3,465.00**
Price: Grade 4E (gold-plated triggers, jeweled barrel flats, engraved game-bird scene) **$4,625.00**
Price: Grade 7E (gold-inlaid ducks, pheasants and bald eagle on scroll engraving) **$9,200.00**
Price: Sousa Grade (gold-inlaid setter, pointer, flying ducks and Sousa mermaid) **$11,550.00**

JOHN RIGBY SHOTGUNS

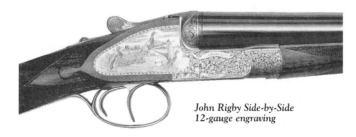

*John Rigby Side-by-Side
12-gauge engraving*

Gauge: 12, 16, 20, 28 and 410 bore. **Barrel:** To customer specs. **Weight:** NA. **Length:** To customer specs. **Stock:** Customer's choice. **Features:** True sidelock side-by-side and over-under shotguns made to customer's specifications. Hand-fitted actions and stocks; engraved receivers embellished with game scenes; over-under includes removable choke tubes.
Price: Sidelock over-under (single selective, non-selective or
double triggers), from **$47,500.00**
Price: Sidelock side-by-side (engraved receiver,
choice of stock wood), from **$39,950.00**
Price: Hammer shotguns (manual-cocking hammers,
rebounding firing pins and hammers;
extractors only), from **$30,000.00**

SEMI-CUSTOM SHOTGUNS

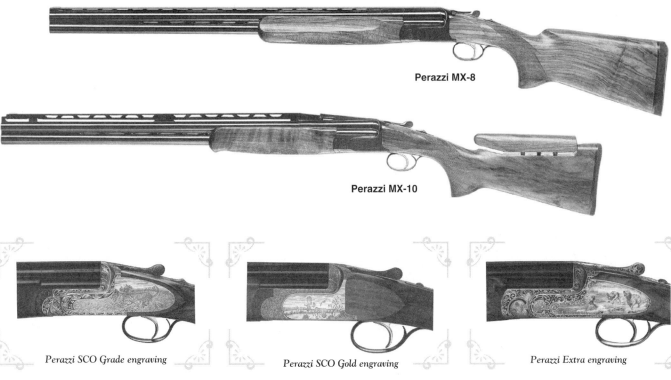

Merkel 47E

Merkel 47SL

Merkel 280EL

Merkel 303EL

Merkel 2001EL

MERKEL EXHIBITION, VINTAGERS EXPO AND CUSTOM ENGRAVED SHOTGUNS

Gauge: 12, 16, 20, 28, 410. **Barrel:** 26-3/4", 28"; others optional. **Weight:** NA. **Length:** NA. **Stock:** Highly figured walnut; En-glish (straight) or pistol grip. **Features:** Highly engraved versions of Merkel over-under and side-by-side shotguns. Imported from Germany by GSI Inc.
Price: . . . . **Call**

PERAZZI SCO, SCO GOLD, EXTRA AND EXTRA GOLD SHOTGUNS

Gauge: 12, 20, 28, 410. **Barrel:** 23-5/8" to 34". **Weight:** 6 lbs. 3 oz. to 8 lb. 13 oz. **Length:** NA. **Stock:** To customer specs. **Features:** Enhanced, engraved models of game and competition over-under shotguns. Customer may choose from many engraved hunting and wildlife scenes. Imported from Italy by Perazzi USA Inc.
Price: SCO Grade in competition and game o/u guns (fully engraved receiver), from **$31,275.00**
Price: SCO Gold Grade in comp. and game o/u guns (engraved w/gold inlays), from **$35,336.00**
Price: Extra Grade in competition and game o/u guns (highly detailed engraving), from **$85,140.00**
Price: Extra Gold Grade in comp. and game o/u guns (detailed engraving w/gold inlays), from **$91,684.00**
Price: SCO Grade with engraved sideplates (extends engraved area), from **$47,968.00**
Price: SCO Gold Grade with engraved sideplates, from **$54,137.00**

Perazzi MX-8

Perazzi MX-10

Perazzi SCO Grade engraving

Perazzi SCO Gold engraving

Perazzi Extra engraving

SEMI-CUSTOM SHOTGUNS

Remington 11-87 "F" Grade

REMINGTON CUSTOM SHOP AUTO SHOTGUNS

Gauge: 10, 12, 20, 28. **Barrel:** 21" to 30". **Weight:** NA. **Length:** NA. **Stock:** Two grades of American walnut. **Features:** Engraved versions of the Model 11-87 and Model 1100 shotgun. "D" or "F" grade fancy walnut, hand-checkered stock; choice of ebony, rosewood, skeleton steel or solid steel grip cap; choice of solid steel, standard, Old English or ventilated recoil pad; optional inletted gold oval with three initials on bottom of stock. From Remington Arms. Co. Custom Gun Shop.
> **Price:** 11-87 and 1100 "D" Grade (English scroll engraving on receiver, breech and trig. guard) **$3,723.00**
> **Price:** 11-87 and 1100 "F" Grade (engraved game scene, "F" Grade walnut stock) **$7,245.00**
> **Price:** 11-87 and 1100 "F" Grade with gold inlay (inlaid three-panel engraved game scene) **$10,663.00**

REMINGTON CUSTOM SHOP PUMP SHOTGUNS

Gauge: 10, 12, 20, 28, 410. **Barrel:** 20" to 30". **Weight:** NA. **Length:** NA. **Stock:** Two grades of American walnut. **Features:** Engraved versions of the Model 870 shotgun. "D" or "F" grade fancy walnut hand-checkered stock; choice of ebony, rosewood, skeleton steel or solid steel grip cap; choice of solid steel, standard, Old English or ventilated recoil pad; optional inletted gold oval with three initials on bottom of stock. From Remington Arms Co. Custom Gun Shop.
> **Price:** 870 "D" Grade (English scroll engraving on receiver, breech and trig. guard) **$3,723.00**
> **Price:** 870 "F" Grade (engraved game scene, "F" grade walnut stock) **$7,245.00**
> **Price:** 870 "F" Grade with gold inlay (inlaid three-panel engraved game scene) **$10,663.00**

REMINGTON CUSTOM SHOP OVER/UNDER SHOTGUNS

Gauge: 12. **Barrel:** 26", 28", 30". **Weight:** 7-1/2 to 8 lbs. **Length:** 42-1/2" to 47-1/4". **Stock:** American walnut. **Features:** Barrels made of chrome-moly steel with 3" chambers, finger grooved forend, fully brazed barrel side ribs, hardened trunions, automatic ejectors. Made in U.S. by Remington Arms Co. Custom Gun Shop.
> **Price:** Remington Model 332 D Grade, from **$4,184.00**
> **Price:** Model 332 F Grade, from **$7,706.00**
> **Price:** Model 332 F Grade w/gold inlay, from **$11,122.00**

Tar-Hunt DSG

TAR-HUNT DSG (DESIGNATED SLUG GUN)

Gauge: 12, 16. **Barrel:** 23". **Weight:** NA. **Length:** NA. **Stock:** NA. **Features:** Tar-Hunt converts the basic Remington 870 shotgun into a configuration for shooting slugs only by installation of a non-removable custom fit Shaw rifled slug barrel with muzzle brake. The 870 Wingmaster is fitted with a barrel with 2-3/4" chamber, the 870 Express Mag. and Wingmaster Mag. have a 3-inch chamber and the 870 Express Super Mag. will have a 3-1/2" chamber. Included are Leupold two-piece windage bases which will accept any standard type turn in rings.
> **Price:** Tar-Hunt DSG . . . . **$450.00** (with customer furnished Remington 870)
> **Price:** Tar-Hunt Express . . . . **$695.00** (complete gun with black synthetic stock)
> **Price:** Tar-Hunt Wingmaster **$950.00**

Includes models suitable for several forms of competition and other sporting purposes.

Accu-Tek AT-380 II 380 ACP

Auto-Ordnance 1911A1 Standard

Baer Custom Carry

Auto-Ordnance Deluxe

Baer Premium II

ACCU-TEK AT-380 II 380 ACP PISTOL
Caliber: 380 ACP, 6-shot magazine. **Barrel:** 2.8". **Weight:** 23.5 oz. **Length:** 6.125" overall. **Grips:** Textured black composition. **Sights:** Blade front, rear adjustable for windage. **Features:** Made from 17-4 stainless steel, has an exposed hammer, manual firing-pin safety block and trigger disconnect. Magazine release located on the bottom of the grip. American made, lifetime warranty. Comes with two 6-round stainless steel magazines and a California-approved cable lock. Introduced 2006. Made in U.S.A. by Accu-Tek.
Price: Satin stainless $249.00

AMERICAN DERRINGER LM5 AUTOMATIC PISTOL
Caliber: 25 ACP, 5-shot magazine; 32 Mag., 4-shot magazine. **Barrel:** 2". **Weight:** 15 oz. **Length:** 4". **Grips:** Wood. **Sights:** Fixed. **Features:** Compact, stainless, semi-auto, double-action hammerless design.
Price: $2,660.00

AMERICAN DERRINGER LM SIMMERLING AUTOMATIC PISTOL
Caliber: 45 ACP, 5-shot magazine. **Barrel:** 2". **Weight:** 24 oz. **Length:** 5". **Grips:** Polymer. **Sights:** Fixed. **Features:** Compact, stainless, semi-auto, double-action hammerless design.
Price: $358.00

AUTO-ORDNANCE 1911A1 AUTOMATIC PISTOL
Caliber: 45 ACP, 7-shot magazine. **Barrel:** 5". **Weight:** 39 oz. **Length:** 8.5" overall. **Grips:** Brown checkered plastic with medallion. **Sights:** Blade front, rear drift-adjustable for windage. **Features:** Same specs as 1911A1 military guns-parts interchangeable. Frame and slide blued; each radius has non-glare finish. Made in U.S.A. by Kahr Arms.
Price: 1911SE Standard, blued $609.00
Price: 1911WGSE Deluxe, black textured wraparound grips $615.00
Price: 1911PKZ Parkerized, lanyard loop, military rollstamp $598.00

BAER 1911 CUSTOM CARRY AUTO PISTOL
Caliber: 45 ACP, 7- or 10-shot magazine. **Barrel:** 5". **Weight:** 37 oz. **Length:** 8.5" overall. **Grips:** Checkered walnut. **Sights:** Baer improved ramp-style dovetailed front, Novak low-mount rear. **Features:** Baer forged NM frame, slide and barrel with stainless bushing. Baer speed trigger with 4-lb. pull. Partial listing shown. Made in U.S.A. by Les Baer Custom, Inc.
Price: Standard size, blued $1,640.00
Price: Standard size, stainless $1,690.00
Price: Comanche size, blued $1,640.00
Price: Comanche size, stainless $1,690.00
Price: Comanche size, aluminum frame, blued slide $1,923.00
Price: Comanche size, aluminum frame, stainless slide $1,995.00

BAER 1911 ULTIMATE RECON PISTOL
Caliber: 45 ACP, 7- or 10-shot magazine. **Barrel:** 5". **Weight:** 37 oz. **Length:** 8.5" overall. **Grips:** Checkered cocobolo. **Sights:** Baer improved ramp-style dovetailed front, Novak low-mount rear. **Features:** NM Caspian frame, slide and barrel with stainless bushing. Baer speed trigger with 4-lb. pull. Includes integral Picatinny rail and Sure-Fire X-200 light. Made in U.S.A. by Les Baer Custom, Inc. Introduced 2006.
Price: Bead blast blued $2,988.00
Price: Bead blast chrome $3,230.00

BAER 1911 PREMIER II AUTO PISTOL
Caliber: 38 Super, 400 Cor-Bon, 45 ACP, 7- or 10-shot magazine. **Barrel:** 5". **Weight:** 37 oz. **Length:** 8.5" overall. **Grips:** Checkered rosewood, double diamond pattern. **Sights:** Baer dovetailed front, low-mount Bo-Mar rear with hidden leaf. **Features:** Baer NM forged steel frame and barrel with stainless bushing, deluxe Commander hammer and sear, beavertail grip safety with pad, extended ambidextrous safety; flat mainspring housing; 30 lpi checkered front strap. Made in U.S.A. by Les Baer Custom, Inc.
Price: 5" 45 ACP $1,598.00
Price: 5" 400 Cor-Bon $1,645.00
Price: 5" 38 Super $1,789.00
Price: 6" 45 ACP (400 Cor-Bon and 38 Super available) $1,755.00
Price: Super-Tac 45 ACP (400 Cor-Bon and 38 Super available) . $2,098.00

Baer 1911 Stinger

Beretta 92FS

Beretta Model 80 Cheetah

Beretta Bobcat

Beretta Tomcat

Beretta U22 Neos

Beretta PX4 Storm

BAER 1911 S.R.P. PISTOL

Caliber: 45 ACP. **Barrel:** 5". **Weight:** 37 oz. **Length:** 8.5" overall. **Grips:** Checkered walnut. **Sights:** Trijicon night sights. **Features:** Similar to the F.B.I. contract gun except uses Baer forged steel frame. Has Baer match barrel with supported chamber, Complete tactical action. Has Baer Ultra Coat finish. Introduced 1996. Made in U.S.A. by Les Baer Custom, Inc.
Price: Government or Comanche length **$2,339.00**

BAER 1911 STINGER PISTOL

Caliber: 45 ACP, 7-round magazine. **Barrel:** 5". **Weight:** 34 oz. **Length:** 8.5" overall. **Grips:** Checkered cocobolo. **Sights:** Baer dovetailed front, low-mount Bo-Mar rear with hidden leaf. **Features:** Baer NM frame. Baer Commanche slide, Officer's style grip frame, beveled mag well. Made in U.S.A. by Les Baer Custom, Inc.
Price: Blued **$1,666.00**
Price: Stainless **$1,675.00**

BAER 1911 PROWLER III PISTOL

Caliber: 45 ACP, 8-round magazine. **Barrel:** 5". **Weight:** 34 oz. **Length:** 8.5" overall. **Grips:** Checkered cocobolo. **Sights:** Baer dovetailed front, low-mount Bo-Mar rear with hidden leaf. **Features:** Similar to Premier II with tapered cone stub weight, rounded corners. Made in U.S.A. by Les Baer Custom, Inc.
Price: Blued **$2,215.00**

BERETTA MODEL 92FS PISTOL

Caliber: 9mm Para., 10-shot magazine. **Barrel:** 4.9". **Weight:** 34 oz. **Length:** 8.5" overall. **Grips:** Checkered black plastic. **Sights:** Blade front, rear adjustable for windage. Tritium night sights available. **Features:** Double action. Extractor acts as chamber loaded indicator, squared trigger guard, grooved front and backstraps, inertia firing pin. Matte or blued finish. Introduced 1977. Made in U.S.A.
Price: With plastic grips **$650.00**

BERETTA MODEL 80 CHEETAH SERIES DA PISTOLS

Caliber: 380 ACP, 10-shot magazine (M84); 8-shot (M85); 22 LR, 7-shot (M87). **Barrel:** 3.82". **Weight:** About 23 oz. (M84/85); 20.8 oz. (M87). **Length:** 6.8" overall. **Grips:** Glossy black plastic (wood optional at extra cost). **Sights:** Fixed front, drift-adjustable rear. **Features:** Double action, quick takedown, convenient magazine release. Introduced 1977. Made in U.S.A.
Price: Model 84 Cheetah, plastic grips **$625.00**
Price: Model 85 Cheetah, plastic grips, 8-shot **$575.00**
Price: Model 87 Cheetah, wood, 22 LR, 7-shot **$625.00**
Price: Model 87 Target, plastic grips **$698.00**

BERETTA MODEL 21 BOBCAT PISTOL

Caliber: 22 LR or 25 ACP. Both double action. **Barrel:** 2.4". **Weight:** 11.5 oz.; 11.8 oz. **Length:** 4.9" overall. **Grips:** Plastic. **Features:** Available in nickel, matte, engraved or blue finish. Introduced in 1985.

Price: Bobcat, 22 or 25, blue **$275.00**
Price: Bobcat, 22, stainless **$325.00**
Price: Bobcat, 22 or 25, matte **$250.00**

BERETTA MODEL 3032 TOMCAT PISTOL

Caliber: 32 ACP, 7-shot magazine. **Barrel:** 2.45". **Weight:** 14.5 oz. **Length:** 5" overall. **Grips:** Checkered black plastic. **Sights:** Blade front, drift-adjustable rear. **Features:** Double action with exposed hammer; tip-up barrel for direct loading/unloading; thumb safety; polished or matte blue finish. Made in U.S.A. Introduced 1996.
Price: Blue **$375.00**
Price: Matte **$350.00**
Price: Stainless **$450.00**
Price: With Tritium sights **$425.00**

BERETTA MODEL U22 NEOS

Caliber: 22 LR, 10-shot magazine. **Barrel:** 4.5"; 6". **Weight:** 32 oz.; 36 oz. **Length:** 8.8"; 10.3". **Sights:** Target. **Features:** Integral rail for standard scope mounts, light, perfectly weighted, 100% American made by Beretta.
Price: **$250.00**
Price: Inox **$325.00**
Price: DLX **$350.00**
Price: Inox **$375.00**

BERETTA MODEL PX4 STORM

Caliber: 9mm, 40 S&W. **Capacity:** 17 (9mm); 14 (40 S&W). **Barrel:** 4". **Weight:** 27.5 oz. **Grips:** Black checkered w/3 interchangeable backstraps. **Sights:** 3-dot ystems coated in Superluminova; removable front and rear sights. **Features:** DA/SA, manual safety/hammer decocking lever (ambi) and automatic firing pin block safety. Picatinny rail. Comes with two magazines (17/10 in 9mm and 14/10 in 40 S&W). Removable hammer unit. American made by Beretta. Introduced 2005.
Price: **$598.00**

Beretta Model M9

Beretta Model M9A1

Bersa Thunder 380

Browning Hi-Power 9mm

BERETTA MODEL M9
Caliber: 9mm. **Capacity:** 15. **Barrel:** 4.9". **Weight:** 32.2-35.3 oz. **Grips:** Plastic. **Sights:** Dot and post, low profile, windage adjustable rear. **Features:** DA/SA, forged aluminum alloy frame, delayed locking-bolt system, manual safety doubles as decocking lever, combat-style trigger guard, loaded chamber indicator. Comes with two magazines (15/10). American made by Beretta. Introduced 2005.
Price: **$650.00**

BERETTA MODEL M9A1
Caliber: 9mm. **Capacity:** 15. **Barrel:** 4.9". **Weight:** 32.2-35.3 oz. **Grips:** Plastic. **Sights:** Dot and post, low profile, windage adjustable rear. **Features:** Same as M9, but also includes integral Mil-Std-1913 Picatinny rail, has checkered frontstrap and backstrap. Comes with two magazines (15/10). American made by Beretta. Introduced 2005.
Price: **$650.00**

BERSA THUNDER 45 ULTRA COMPACT PISTOL
Caliber: 45 ACP. **Barrel:** 3.6". **Weight:** 27 oz. **Length:** 6.7" overall. **Grips:** Anatomicaly designed polymer. **Sights:** White outline rear. **Features:** Double action; firing pin safeties, integral locking system. Available in matte, satin nickel, gold, or duo-tone. Introduced 2003. Imported from Argentina by Eagle Imports, Inc.
Price: Thunder 45, matte blue **$424.95**
Price: Thunder 45, duo-tone **$449.95**
Price: Thunder 45, Satin nickel **$466.95**

BERSA THUNDER 380 SERIES PISTOLS
Caliber: 380 Auto, 7 rounds **Barrel:** 3.5". **Weight:** 23 oz. **Length:** 6.6" overall. **Features:** Otherwise similar to Thunder 45 Ultra Compact. 380 DLX has 9-round capacity. 380 Concealed Carry has 8 round capacity. Imported from Argentina by Eagle Imports, Inc.
Price: Thunder 380 Matte **$274.95**
Price: Thunder 380 Satin Nickle **$299.95**
Price: Thunder 380 Blue DLX **$308.95**
Price: Thunder 380 Matte CC (2006) **$291.95**

Bersa Thunder 9 Ultra Compact/40 Series Pistols
Caliber: 9mm, 40 S&W. **Barrel:** 3.5". **Weight:** 24.5 oz. **Length:** 6.6" overall. **Features:** Otherwise similar to Thunder 45 Ultra Compact. 9mm High Capacity model has 17-round capacity. 40 High Capacity model has 13-round capacity. Imported from Argentina by Eagle Imports, Inc.
Price: Thunder 9mm Matte **$424.95**
Price: Thunder 9mm High Capacity Satin Nickel **$466.95**
Price: Thunder 40 High Capacity Satin Nickel **$466.95**

BROWNING HI-POWER 9mm AUTOMATIC PISTOL
Caliber: 9mm Para., 13-round magazine; 40 S&W, 10-round magazine. **Barrel:** 4-5/8". **Weight:** 32 to 39 oz. **Overall length:** 7-3/4". **Metal Finishes:** Blued (Standard); black-epoxy/silver-chrome (Practical); black-epoxy (Mark III). **Grips:** Molded (Mark III); wraparound Pachmayr (Practical); or walnut grips (Standard). **Sights:** Fixed (Practical, Mark III, Standard); low-mount adjustable rear (Standard). Cable lock supplied. **Features:** External hammer with half-cock and thumb safeties. Fixed rear sight model available. Commander-style (Practical) or spur-type hammer, single action. Includes gun lock. Imported from Belgium by Browning.
Price: Practical **$846.00**
Price: Mark III. **$781.00**
Price: Standard, fixed sights **$804.00**
Price: Standard, adjustable sights. **$861.00**

BROWNING BUCK MARK PISTOLS
Common Features: **Caliber:** 22 LR, 10-shot magazine. **Action:** Blowback semi-auto. **Trigger:** Wide grooved style. **Sights:** Ramp front, Browning Pro-Target rear adjustable for windage and elevation. **Features:** Machined aluminum frame. Includes gun lock. Introduced 1985. Hunter, Camper Stainless, STD Stainless, 5.5 Target, 5.5 Field all introduced 2005. 18 variations, as noted below. **Grips:** Cocobolo, target-style (Hunter, 5.5 Target, 5.5 Field); polymer (Camper, Camper Stainless, Micro Nickel, Standard, STD Stainless); checkered walnut (Challenge); laminated (Plus and Plus Nickel); laminated rosewood (Bullseye Target, FLD Plus); rubber (Bullseye Standard). **Metal finishes:** Matte blue (Hunter, Camper, Challenge, Plus, Bullseye Target, Bullseye Standard, 5.5 Target, 5.5 Field, FLD Plus); matte stainless (Camper Stainless, STD Stainless, Micro Standard); nickel-plated (Micro Nickel, Plus Nickel, and Nickel). Made in U.S.A. From Browning.
Price: Hunter, 7.25" heavy barrel, 38 oz., Truglo sight **$360.00**
Price: Camper, 5.5" heavy barrel, 34 oz. **$287.00**
Price: Camper Stainless, 5.5" tapered bull barrel, 34 oz **$310.00**
Price: Camper Nickel, 5.5" tapered bull barrel, 34 oz. **$320.00**
Price: Micro Nickel, 4" bull barrel, 32 oz **$377.00**
Price: Nickel, 5.5" bull barrel, 34 oz **$377.00**
Price: Standard, 5.5" flat-side bull barrel, 34 oz **$319.00**
Price: Standard Stainless, 5.5" flat-side bull barrel, 34 oz **$345.00**
Price: Micro Standard, 4" flat-side bull barrel, 32 oz **$319.00**
Price: Micro Standard Stainless, 4" flat-side bull barrel, 32 oz. **$345.00**
Price: Plus Nickel, 5.5" flat-side bull barrel, 34 oz **$427.00**
Price: Plus, 5.5" flat-side bull barrel, 34 oz. **$390.00**
Price: Challenge, 5.5" lightweight taper barrel, 25 oz. **$356.00**
Price: Bullseye Standard, 7.25" fluted bull barrel, 36 oz **$468.00**
Price: Bullseye Target, 7.25" fluted bull barrel, 36 oz **$604.00**
Price: 5.5 Target, 5.5" round bull barrel, target sights, 35.5 oz. **$511.00**
Price: 5.5 Field, 5.5" round bull barrel, 35 oz **$511.00**
Price: FLD Plus, 5.5" flat-side bull barrel, 34 oz, Truglo sights **$390.00**

BROWNING PRO-9, PRO-40 PISTOLS
Caliber: 9mm Luger, 16-round magazine; 40 S&W, 14-round magazine. **Barrel:** 4". **Weight:** 30-33 oz. **Overall length:** 7.25". **Features:** Polymer frame, stainless-steel frames and barrels, double-action, ambidextrous decocker and safety. Fixed, 3-dot-style sights, 6" sight radius. Molded composite grips with interchangeable backstrap inserts. Cable lock supplied.
Price: **$628.00**

Browning Buck Mark Hunter

Browning Buck Mark Camper

Browning Buck Mark 5.5 Field

Browning Buck Mark 5.5 Target

Browning Buck Mark Standard

Browning Pro-9

Charles Daly M-1911-A1P

CHARLES DALY ENHANCED 1911 PISTOLS

Caliber: 45 ACP. **Barrel:** 5". **Weight:** 38 oz. **Length:** 8-3/4" overall. **Grips:** Checkered double diamond hardwood. **Sights:** Dovetailed front and dovetailed snag-free low profile rear sights, 3-dot system. **Features:** Extended high-rise beavertail grip safety, combat trigger, combat hammer, beveled magazine well, flared and lowered ejection port. Field Grade models are satin-finished blued steel. EMS series includes an ambidextrous safety, 4" barrel, 8-shot magazine. ECS series has a contoured left hand safety, 3.5" barrel , 6-shot magazine Two magazines, lockable carrying case. Introduced 1998. Empire series are stainless versions. Imported from the Philippines by K.B.I., Inc.

Price: EFS, blued, 39.5 oz., 5" barrel **$529.00**
Price: EMS, blued, 37 oz., 4" barrel **$529.00**
Price: ECS, blued, 34.5 oz., 3.5" barrel. **$529.00**
Price: EFS Empire, stainless, 38.5 oz., 5" barrel **$629.00**
Price: EMS Empire, matte stainless, 36.5 oz., 4" barrel **$619.00**
Price: ECS Empire, matte stainless, 33.5 oz., 3.5" barrel. **$619.00**

CHARLES DALY ENHANCED TARGET 1911 PISTOLS

Caliber: 45 ACP. **Barrel:** 5". **Weight:** 38.5 oz. **Length:** 8-3/4" overall. **Features:** Similar to Daly Field and Empire models but with dovetailed front and fully adjustable rear target sights. Imported from the Philippines by K.B.I., Inc.

Price: EFS Target, stainless, 38.5 oz., 5" barrel **$724.00**
Price: EFS Custom Match Target, high-polish stainless **$799.00**

CHARLES DALY HP 9MM SINGLE-ACTION PISTOL

Caliber: 9mm, 10 round magazine. **Barrel:** 4.6". **Weight:** 34.5 oz. **Length:** 7-3/8" overall. **Grips:** Uncle Mike's padded rubber grip panels. **Sights:** XS Express Sight system set into front and rear dovetails. **Features:** John Browning design. Matte-blued steel frame and slide, thumb safety. Made in the U.S. by K.B.I., Inc.
Price: Hi-Power w/XS Sights. **$549.00**

CHARLES DALY M-5 POLYMER-FRAMED HI-CAP 1911 PISTOL

Caliber: 9mm, 12-round magazine; 40 S&W 17-round magazine; 45 ACP, 13-round magazine. **Barrel:** 5". **Weight:** 33.5 oz. **Length:** 8.5" overall. **Grips:** Checkered polymer. **Sights:** Blade front, adjustable low-profile rear. **Features:** Stainless steel beaver-tail grip safety, rounded trigger-guard, tapered bull barrel, full-length guide rod, matte blue finish on frame and slide. 40 S&W models in M-5 Govt. 1911, M-5 Commander, and M-5 IPSC introduced 2006; M-5 Ultra X Compact in 9mm and 45 ACP introduced 2006; M-5 IPSC .45 ACP introduced 2006. Made in Israel by BUL, imported by K.B.I., Inc.

Price: M-5 Govt. 1911, 40 S&W/45 ACP, matte blue **$719.00**
Price: M-5 Commander, 40 S&W/45 ACP, matte blue **$719.00**
Price: M-5 Ultra X Compact, 9mm, 3.1" barrel, 7" OAL, 28 oz. **$719.00**
Price: M-5 Ultra X Compact, 45 ACP, 3.1" barrel, 7" OAL, 28 oz. . . **$719.00**
Price: M-5 IPSC, 40 S&W/45 ACP, 5" barrel, 8.5" OAL, 33.5 oz.. . **$1,499.00**

Cobra FS380

Cobra CA32

Colt Model 1991 Model O

Colt XSE Lightweight Commander

Colt XSE Government

Colt 38 Super

Colt Defender

COBRA ENTERPRISES FS380 AUTO PISTOL

Caliber: 380 ACP, 7-shot magazine. **Barrel:** 3.5". **Weight:** 2.1 lbs. **Length:** 6-3/8" overall. **Grips:** Black composition. **Sights:** Fixed. **Features:** Choice of bright chrome, satin nickel or black finish. Introduced 2002. Made in U.S.A. by Cobra Enterprises, Inc.
Price: $130.00

COBRA ENTERPRISES FS32 AUTO PISTOL

Caliber: 32 ACP, 8-shot magazine. **Barrel:** 3.5". **Weight:** 2.1 lbs. **Length:** 6-3/8" overall. **Grips:** Black composition. **Sights:** Fixed. **Features:** Choice of black, satin nickel or bright chrome finish. Introduced 2002. Made in U.S.A. by Cobra Enterprises, Inc.
Price: $130.00

COBRA INDUSTRIES PATRIOT PISTOL

Caliber: 380 ACP, 9mm Luger, 10-shot magazine. **Barrel:** 3.3". **Weight:** 20 oz. **Length:** 6" overall. **Grips:** Checkered polymer. **Sights:** Fixed. **Features:** Stainless steel slide with load indicator; double-action-only trigger system. Introduced 2002. Made in U.S.A. by Cobra Enterprises, Inc.
Price: $279.00

COBRA INDUSTRIES CA32, CA380

Caliber: 32 ACP, 380 ACP. **Barrel:** 2.8" **Weight:** 22 oz. **Length:** 5.4". **Grips:** Laminated wood (CA32); Black molded synthetic (CA380). **Sights:** Fixed. **Features:** True pocket pistol size. Made in U.S.A. by Cobra Enterprises, Inc.
Price: $110.00

COLT MODEL 1991 MODEL O AUTO PISTOL

Caliber: 45 ACP, 7-shot magazine. **Barrel:** 5". **Weight:** 38 oz. **Length:** 8.5" overall. **Grips:** Checkered black composition. **Sights:** Ramped blade front, fixed square notch rear, high profile. **Features:** Matte finish. Continuation of serial number range used on original G.I. 1911A1 guns. Comes with one magazine and molded carrying case. Introduced 1991.
Price: Blue $764.00
Price: Stainless $814.00

COLT XSE SERIES MODEL O AUTO PISTOLS

Caliber: 45 ACP, 8-shot magazine. **Barrel:** 4.25", 5". **Grips:** Checkered, double diamond rosewood. **Sights:** Drift-adjustable 3-dot combat. **Features:** Brushed stainless finish; adjustable, two-cut aluminum trigger; extended ambidextrous thumb safety; upswept beavertail with palm swell; elongated slot hammer. Introduced 1999. From Colt's Mfg. Co., Inc.
Price: XSE Government (5" bbl.) $917.00
Price: XSE Government (4.25" bbl.) $917.00

COLT XSE LIGHTWEIGHT COMMANDER AUTO PISTOL

Caliber: 45 ACP, 8-shot. **Barrel:** 4-1/4". **Weight:** 26 oz. **Length:** 7-3/4" overall. **Grips:** Double diamond checkered rosewood. **Sights:** Fixed, glare-proofed blade front, square notch rear; 3-dot system. **Features:** Brushed stainless slide, nickeled aluminum frame; McCormick elongated slot enhanced hammer, McCormick two-cut adjustable aluminum hammer. Made in U.S.A. by Colt's Mfg. Co., Inc.
Price: Stainless $917.00

COLT DEFENDER

Caliber: 45 ACP, 7-shot magazine. **Barrel:** 3". **Weight:** 22-1/2 oz. **Length:** 6-3/4" overall. **Grips:** Pebble-finish rubber wraparound with finger grooves. **Sights:** White dot front, snag-free Colt competition rear. **Features:** Stainless finish; aluminum frame; combat-style hammer; Hi Ride grip safety, extended manual safety, disconnect safety. Introduced 1998. Made in U.S.A. by Colt's Mfg. Co., Inc.
Price: $860.00

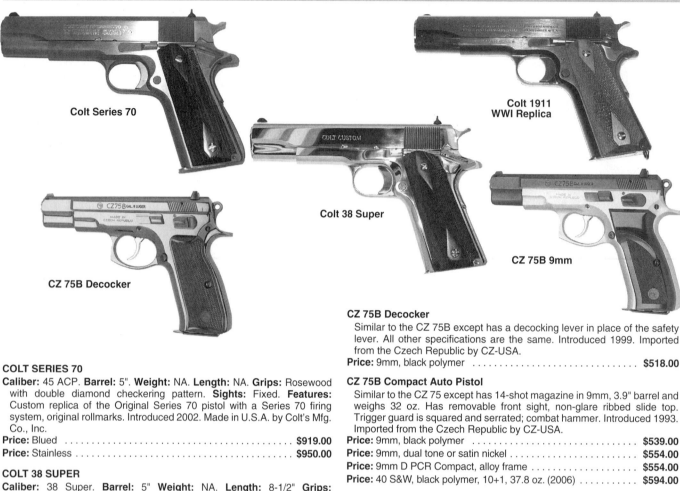

Colt Series 70

Colt 1911 WWI Replica

Colt 38 Super

CZ 75B 9mm

CZ 75B Decocker

COLT SERIES 70

Caliber: 45 ACP. **Barrel:** 5". **Weight:** NA. **Length:** NA. **Grips:** Rosewood with double diamond checkering pattern. **Sights:** Fixed. **Features:** Custom replica of the Original Series 70 pistol with a Series 70 firing system, original rollmarks. Introduced 2002. Made in U.S.A. by Colt's Mfg. Co., Inc.
Price: Blued **$919.00**
Price: Stainless **$950.00**

COLT 38 SUPER

Caliber: 38 Super. **Barrel:** 5" **Weight:** NA. **Length:** 8-1/2" **Grips:** Checkered rubber (stainless and blue models); wood with double diamond checkering pattern (bright stainless model). **Sights:** 3-dot. **Features:** Beveled magazine well, standard thumb safety and service-style grip safety. Introduced 2003. Made in U.S.A. by Colt's Mfg. Co., Inc.
Price: Blued **$837.00**
Price: Stainless **$866.00**
Price: Bright Stainless **$1,058.00**

COLT 1911 WWI REPLICA

Caliber: 45 ACP, 2 7-round magazines. **Barrel:** 5" **Weight:** 38 oz. **Length:** 8.5". **Grips:** Checkered walnut with double diamond checkering pattern. **Sights:** Tapered blade front sight, U-shaped rear notch. **Features:** Reproduction based on original 1911 blueprints. Original rollmarks and inspector marks. Smooth mainspring housing with lanyard loop, WWI-style manual thumb and grip safety, Carbonia blued finish. Introduced 2005. Made in U.S.A. by Colt's Mfg. Co., Inc.
Price: Blued **$990.00**

CZ 75B AUTO PISTOL

Caliber: 9mm Para., 40 S&W, 10-shot magazine. **Barrel:** 4.7". **Weight:** 34.3 oz. **Length:** 8.1" overall. **Grips:** High impact checkered plastic. **Sights:** Square post front, rear adjustable for windage; 3-dot system. **Features:** Single action/double action design; firing pin block safety; choice of black polymer, matte or high-polish blue finishes. All-steel frame. B-SA is a single action with a drop-free magazine. Imported from the Czech Republic by CZ-USA.
Price: 75B, black polymer, 16-shot magazine **$509.00**
Price: 75B, glossy blue, dual-tone or satin nickel **$525.00**
Price: 40 S&W, black polymer, 12-shot magazine, ... **$525.00**
Price: 75B SA, 9mm/40 S&W, single action . . . . **$518.00/$535.00**
Price: 75 Stainless 9mm (2006), 16-shot magazine **$565.00**

CZ 75B Decocker

Similar to the CZ 75B except has a decocking lever in place of the safety lever. All other specifications are the same. Introduced 1999. Imported from the Czech Republic by CZ-USA.
Price: 9mm, black polymer **$518.00**

CZ 75B Compact Auto Pistol

Similar to the CZ 75 except has 14-shot magazine in 9mm, 3.9" barrel and weighs 32 oz. Has removable front sight, non-glare ribbed slide top. Trigger guard is squared and serrated; combat hammer. Introduced 1993. Imported from the Czech Republic by CZ-USA.
Price: 9mm, black polymer **$539.00**
Price: 9mm, dual tone or satin nickel **$554.00**
Price: 9mm D PCR Compact, alloy frame **$554.00**
Price: 40 S&W, black polymer, 10+1, 37.8 oz. (2006) **$594.00**

CZ 75 Champion Pistol

Similar to the CZ 75B except has a longer frame and slide, rubber grip to accommodate new heavy-duty magazine. Ambidextrous thumb safety, extended magazine release; three-port compensator. Blued slide and stain nickel frame finish. Introduced 2005. Imported from the Czech Republic by CZ USA.
Price: 9mm, 16-shot mag. **$1,646.00**

CZ 75 Tactical Sport

Similar to the CZ 75B except the CZ 75 TS is a competition ready pistol designed for IPSC standard division (USPSA limited division). Fixed target sights, tuned single-action operation, lightweight polymer match trigger with adjustments for take-up and overtravel, competition hammer, extended magazine catch, ambidextrous manual safety, checkered walnut grips, polymer magazine well, two tone finish. Introduced 2005. Imported from the Czech Republic by CZ USA.
Price: 9mm, 20-shot mag. **$1,152.00**
Price: 40 S&W, 16-shot mag. **$1,152.00**

CZ 75 SP-01 Pistol

Similar to NATO-approved CZ 75 Compact P-01 model. Features an integral 1913 accessory rail on the dust cover, rubber grip panels, black polycoat finish, extended beavertail, new grip geometry with checkering on front and back straps, and double or single action operation. Introduced 2005. The Shadow variant designed as an IPSC "production" division competition firearm. Includes competition hammer, competition rear sight and fiber-optic front sight, modified slide release, lighter recoil and main spring for use with "minor power factor" competition ammunition. Includes polycoat finish and slim walnut grips. Finished by CZ Custom Shop. Imported from the Czech Republic by CZ-USA.
Price: SP-01 9mm, black polymer, 19+1 . . . . **$595.00**
Price: SP-01 Shadow **$615.00**

CZ 85

CZ 97B

CZ 75/85 Kadet

CZ 100

CZ 85B/85 Combat Auto Pistol

Same gun as the CZ 75 except has ambidextrous slide release and safety levers; non-glare, ribbed slide top; squared, serrated trigger guard; trigger stop to prevent overtravel. Introduced 1986. The CZ 85 Combat features a fully adjustable rear sight, extended magazine release, ambidextrous slide stop and safety catch, drop free magazine and overtravel adjustment. Imported from the Czech Republic by CZ-USA.

Price: 9mm, Black polymer $536.00
Price: Combat, black polymer $599.00
Price: Combat, dual-tone, glossy blue, satin nickel. $623.00

CZ 83B DOUBLE-ACTION PISTOL

Caliber: 32 ACP, 380 ACP, 12-shot magazine. Barrel: 3.8". Weight: 26.2 oz. Length: 6.8" overall. Grips: High impact checkered plastic. Sights: Removable square post front, rear adjustable for windage; 3-dot system. Features: Single action/double action; ambidextrous magazine release and safety. Blue finish; non-glare ribbed slide top. Imported from the Czech Republic by CZ-USA.

Price: Glossy blue, 32 ACP or 380 ACP $420.00
Price: Satin Nickel $420.00

CZ 97B AUTO PISTOL

Caliber: 45 ACP, 10-shot magazine. Barrel: 4.85". Weight: 40 oz. Length: 8.34" overall. Grips: Checkered walnut. Sights: Fixed. Features: Single action/double action; full-length slide rails; screw-in barrel bushing; linkless barrel; all-steel construction; chamber loaded indicator; dual transfer bars. Introduced 1999. Imported from the Czech Republic by CZ-USA.

Price: Black polymer $663.00
Price: Glossy blue $680.00

CZ 75 KADET AUTO PISTOL

Caliber: 22 LR, 10-shot magazine. Barrel: 4.88". Weight: 36 oz. Grips: High impact checkered plastic. Sights: Blade front, fully adjustable rear. Features: Single action/double action mechanism; all-steel construction. Introduced 1999. Kadet conversion kit consists of barrel, slide, adjustable sights, and magazine to convert the centerfire 75 to rimfire. Imported from the Czech Republic by CZ-USA.

Price: Black polymer $510.00
Price: Kadet conversion kit $299.00

CZ 100 B AUTO PISTOL

Caliber: 9mm Para., 40 S&W. Barrel: 3.7". Weight: 24 oz. Length: 6.9" overall. Grips: Grooved polymer. Sights: Blade front with dot, white outline rear drift adjustable for windage. Features: Double action only with firing pin block; polymer frame, steel slide; has laser sight mount. Introduced 1996. Imported from the Czech Republic by CZ-USA.

Price: 9mm Para, 12-shot magazine $449.00
Price: 40 S&W, 10-shot magazine $449.00

CZ 2075 RAMI AUTO PISTOL

Caliber: 9mm Para., 40 S&W. Barrel: 3". Weight: 25 oz. Length: 6.5" overall. Grips: Rubber. Sights: Blade front with dot, white outline rear drift adjustable for windage. Features: Single-action/double-action; alloy or polymer frame, steel slide; has laser sight mount. Imported from the Czech Republic by CZ-USA.

Price: 9mm Para, alloy frame, 10 and 14-shot magazines $576.00
Price: 40 S&W, alloy frame, 8-shot magazine $576.00
Price: 9mm Para, polymer frame, 10 and 14-shot magazines $510.00
Price: 40 S&W, alloy frame, 8-shot magazine $510.00

CZ P-01 AUTO PISTOL

Caliber: 9mm Para. Barrel: 3.85". Weight: 27 oz. Length: 7.2" overall. Grips: Checkered rubber. Sights: Blade front with dot, white outline drift adjustable for windage. Features: Based on the CZ 75, except with forged aircraft-grade aluminum alloy frame. Hammer forged barrel, de-cocker, firing-pin block, M3 rail, dual slide serrations, squared triggerguard, re-contoured trigger, lanyard loop on butt. Serrated front-and back strap. Introduced 2006. Imported from the Czech Republic by CZ-USA.

Price: 9mm Para,14-shot magazines $586.00

DAN WESSON FIREARMS POINTMAN SEVEN AUTO PISTOL

Caliber: 10mm, 45 ACP. Barrel: 5". Grips: Diamond checkered cocobolo. Sights: Bo-Mar style adjustable target sight. Weight: 38 oz. Features: Stainless-steel frame and serrated slide. Series 70-style 1911, stainless-steel frame, forged stainless-steel slide. One-piece match-grade barrel and bushing. 20-LPI checkered mainspring housing, front and rear slide cocking serrations, beveled magwell, dehorned by hand. Lowered and flared ejection port, Ed Brown slide stop and memory groove grip safety, tactical extended thumb safety. Commander-style match hammer, match grade sear, aluminum trigger with stainless bow, Wolff springs. Introduced 2000. Made in U.S.A. by Dan Wesson Firearms, distributed by CZ-USA.

Price: 45 ACP, 7+1 .... $1,079.00
Price: 10mm, 8+1 .... $1,079.00

Dan Wesson Commander Classic Bobtail Auto Pistols

Similar to Pointman Seven, a Commander-sized frame with 4.25" barrel. Available with stainless finish, fixed night sights. Introduced 2005. Made in U.S.A. by Dan Wesson Firearms, distributed by CZ-USA.

Price: 45 ACP, 7+1, 34 oz. $1,169.00
Price: 10mm, 8+1, 34 oz. $1,179.00

DAN WESSON DW RZ-10 AUTO PISTOL

Caliber: 10mm. Barrel: 5". Grips: Diamond checkered cocobolo. Sights: Bo-Mar style adjustable target sight. Weight: 38.3 oz. Features: Stainless-steel frame and serrated slide. Series 70-style 1911, stainless-steel frame, forged stainless-steel slide. Commander-style match hammer. Reintroduced 2005. Made in U.S.A. by Dan Wesson Firearms, distributed by CZ-USA.

Price: 10mm, 8+1 .... $1,089.00

Desert Eagle Mark XIX

Desert Baby Eagle

EAA Witness

Ed Brown Commander Bobtail

Ed Brown Classic Custom

Ed Brown Kobra Executive Carry

DESERT EAGLE MARK XIX PISTOL

Caliber: 357 Mag., 9-shot; 44 Mag., 8-shot; 50 AE, 7-shot. **Barrel:** 6", 10", interchangeable. **Weight:** 357 Mag.-62 oz.; 44 Mag.-69 oz.; 50 AE-72 oz. **Length:** 10-1/4" overall (6" bbl.). **Grips:** Polymer; rubber available. **Sights:** Blade on ramp front, combat-style rear. Adjustable available. **Features:** Interchangeable barrels; rotating three-lug bolt; ambidextrous safety; adjustable trigger. Military epoxy finish. Satin, bright nickel, chrome, brushed, matte or black finishes available. 10" barrel extra. Imported from Israel by Magnum Research, Inc.
Price: 357, 6" bbl., standard pistol **$1,299.00**
Price: 44 Mag., 6", standard pistol **$1,299.00**
Price: 50 Magnum, 6" bbl., standard pistol **$1,299.00**

DESERT BABY EAGLE PISTOLS

Caliber: 9mm Para., 40 S&W, 45 ACP, 10-round magazine. **Barrel:** 3.5", 3.7", 4.72". **Weight:** 26.8-39.8 oz. **Length:** 7.25" to 8.25" overall. **Grips:** Polymer. **Sights:** Drift-adjustable rear, blade front. **Features:** Steel frame and slide; slide safety; decocker. Reintroduced in 1999. Imported from Israel by Magnum Research, Inc.
Price: Standard (9mm or 40 cal.; 4.72" barrel, 8.25" overall) **$549.00**
Price: Semi-Compact (9mm, 40 or 45 cal.; 3.7" barrel,
7.75" overall) **$549.00**
Price: Compact (9mm or 40 cal.; 3.5" barrel, 7.25" overall) **$549.00**
Price: Polymer (9mm or 40 cal; polymer frame; 3.25" barrel,
7.25" overall) **$549.00**

EAA WITNESS FULL SIZE AUTO PISTOL

Caliber: 9mm Para., 38 Super, 18-shot magazine; 40 S&W, 10mm, 15-shot magazine; 45 ACP, 10-shot magazine. **Barrel:** 4.50". **Weight:** 35.33 oz. **Length:** 8.10" overall. **Grips:** Checkered rubber. **Sights:** Undercut blade front, open rear adjustable for windage. **Features:** Double-action/single-action trigger system; round trigger guard; frame-mounted safety. Introduced 1991. Polymer frame introduced 2005. Imported from Italy by European American Armory.
Price: 9mm, 38 Super, 10mm, 40 S&W, 45 ACP, full-size steel frame,
Wonder finish **$459.00**
Price: 45/22 22 LR, full-size steel frame, blued **$429.00**
Price: 9mm, 40 S&W, 45 ACP, full-size polymer frame **$429.00**

EAA WITNESS COMPACT AUTO PISTOL

Caliber: 9mm Para., 40 S&W, 10mm, 12-shot magazine; 45 ACP, 8-shot magazine. **Barrel:** 3.6". **Weight:** 30 oz. **Length:** 7.3" overall. Otherwise similar to Full Size Witness. Polymer frame introduced 2005. Imported from Italy by European American Armory.
Price: 9mm, 10mm, 40 S&W, 45 ACP, steel frame, Wonder finish . **$459.00**
Price: 9mm, 40 S&W, 45 ACP, polymer frame **$429.00**

EAA WITNESS-P CARRY AUTO PISTOL

Caliber: 10mm, 15-shot magazine; 45 ACP, 10-shot magazine. **Barrel:** 3.6". **Weight:** 27 oz. **Length:** 7.5" overall. Otherwise similar to Full Size Witness. Polymer frame introduced 2005. Imported from Italy by European American Armory.
Price: 10mm, 45 ACP, polymer frame. . . . . from **$469.00**

ED BROWN CLASSIC CUSTOM

Caliber: 45 ACP, 7 shot. **Barrel:** 5". **Weight:** 39 oz. **Stocks:** Cocobolo wood. **Sights:** Bo-Mar adjustable rear, dovetail front. **Features:** Single-action, M1911 style, custom made to order, stainless frame and slide available.
Price: Model CC-BB, blued. **$2,895.00**
Price: Model CC-SB, blued and stainless. **$2,995.00**
Price: Model CC-SS, stainless **$3,095.00**

ED BROWN KOBRA CARRY BOBTAIL

Caliber: 45 ACP, 400 Cor-Bon, 40 S&W, 357 SIG, 38 Super, 9mm Luger, 7-shot magazine. **Barrel:** 4.25". **Weight:** 34 oz. **Grips:** Hogue exotic wood. **Sights:** Customer preference front; fixed Novak low mount rear. Optional night inserts available. **Features:** Checkered forestrap and bobtailed mainspring housing.
Price: Executive Carry . . . . **$2,195.00 to $2,370.00**

ED BROWN KOBRA AND KOBRA CARRY

Caliber: 45 ACP, 7-shot magazine. **Barrel:** 5" (Kobra); 4.25" (Kobra Carry). **Weight:** 39 oz. (Kobra); 34 oz. (Kobra Carry). **Grips:** Hogue exotic wood. **Sights:** Ramp, front; fixed Novak low-mount night sights, rear. **Features:** Has snakeskin pattern serrations on forestrap and mainspring housing, dehorned edges, beavertail grip safety.
Price: Kobra K-BB, blued **$1,995.00**
Price: Kobra K-SB, stainless and blued **$2,095.00**
Price: Kobra K-SS, stainless. **$2,195.00**
Price: Kobra Carry KC-BB, blued **$2,095.00**

Ed Brown Kobra Carry

Ed Brown Kobra Carry K-SB

Ed Brown Executive Elite

Ed Brown Special Forces

Entréprise Boxer P500

Entréprise Tactical 500

Entréprise Elite P500

Excel Arms Accelerator MP-22

Ed Brown Executive Pistols

Similar to other Ed Brown products, but with 25-lpi checkered frame and mainspring housing.

Price: Elite blued, blued/stainless, or stainless, from **$2,195.00**
Price: Carry blued, blued/stainless, or stainless, from **$2,295.00**
Price: Target blued, blued/stainless, or stainless, intr. 2006, from **$2,470.00**

Ed Brown Special Forces Pistol

Similar to other Ed Brown products, but with ChainLink treatment on forestrap and mainspring housing. Slide coated with Gen III finish. "Square cut" serrations on rear of slide only. Dehorned. Introduced 2006.
Price: SF-BB blued **$1,995.00**

ENTRÉPRISE ELITE P500 AUTO PISTOL

Caliber: 45 ACP, 10-shot magazine. **Barrel:** 3.25", 4.25", 5". **Weight:** 36-40 oz. **Length:** 7.25-8.5" overall. **Grips:** Black ultra-slim, double diamond, checkered synthetic. **Sights:** Dovetailed blade front, rear adjustable for windage; 3-dot system. **Features:** Reinforced dust cover; lowered and flared ejection port; squared trigger guard; adjustable match trigger; bolstered front strap; high grip cut; high ride beavertail grip safety; steel flat mainspring housing; extended thumb lock; skeletonized hammer, match grade sear, disconnector; Wolff springs. Introduced 1998. Made in U.S.A. by Entréprise Arms.
Price: P500, P425, P325 models **$699.90**

Entréprise Medalist P500 Auto Pistol

Similar to the Elite model except has adjustable rear sight with dovetailed Patridge front; machined slide parallel rails; front and rear slide serrations; lowered and flared ejection port; full-length one-piece guide rod with plug; National Match barrel and bushing; stainless firing pin; tuned match extractor; oversize firing pin stop; slide lapped to frame. Introduced 1998. Made in U.S.A. by Entréprise Arms.
Price: 45 ACP **$979.00**
Price: 40 S&W **$1,099.00**

Entréprise Boxer P500 Auto Pistol

Similar to the Medalist model except has adjustable Competizione "melted" rear sight with dovetailed Patridge front; high mass chiseled slide with sweep cut; machined slide parallel rails; polished breech face and barrel channel. Introduced 1998. Made in U.S.A. by Entréprise Arms.
Price: 45 ACP **$1,399.00**
Price: 40 S&W intr. 2005. . . . . **$1,499.00**

Entréprise Tactical P500 Auto Pistol

Similar to the Elite model except has Tactical2 Ghost Ring sight or Novak low-mount sight; ambidextrous thumb safety; front and rear slide serrations; full-length guide rod; throated barrel; tuned match extractor; fitted barrel and bushing; stainless firing pin; slide lapped to frame. Introduced 1998. Made in U.S.A. by Entréprise Arms.
Price: **$979.90**

EXCEL ARMS ACCELERATOR MP-17/MP-22 PISTOLS

Caliber: 17HMR, 22WMR, 9-shot magazine. **Barrel:** 8.5" bull barrel. **Weight:** 54 oz. **Length:** 12.875" overall. **Grips:** Textured black composition. **Sights:** Fully adjustable target sights. **Features:** Made from 17-4 stainless steel, comes with aluminum rib, integral Weaver base, internal hammer, firing-pin block. American made, lifetime warranty. Comes with two 9-round stainless steel magazines and a California-approved cable lock. 22 WMR Introduced 2006. Made in U.S.A. by Excel Arms.
Price: **$412.00**
Price: SP-17 17 Mach 2 . . . . **$412.00**
Price: SP-22 22LR **$412.00**

Firestorm Mini

Firestorm 45 Gov't

Glock 17C

Glock 26

Glock 22

FIRESTORM AUTO PISTOLS

Caliber: 22LR, 32 ACP, 10-shot magazine; 380 ACP, 7-shot magazine; 9mm, 40 S&W, 10-shot magazine; 45 ACP, 7-shot magazine. **Barrel:** 3.5". **Weight:** from 23 oz. **Length:** from 6.6" overall. **Grips:** Rubber. **Sights:** 3-dot. **Features:** Double action. Distributed by SGS Importers International.

Price: 22LR, matte or duotone, from $241.95
Price: 380, matte or duotone, from $241.95
Price: Mini Firestorm 32 ACP, intr. 2006 .... $358.95
Price: Mini Firestorm 9mm, matte, duotone, nickel, from $358.95
Price: Mini Firestorm 40 S&W, matte, duotone, nickel, from $358.95
Price: Mini Firestorm 45 ACP, matte, duotone, chrome, from $308.95

GLOCK 17/17C AUTO PISTOL

Caliber: 9mm Para., 17/19/33-shot magazines. **Barrel:** 4.49". **Weight:** 22.04 oz. (without magazine). **Length:** 7.32" overall. **Grips:** Black polymer. **Sights:** Dot on front blade, white outline rear adjustable for windage. **Features:** Polymer frame, steel slide; double-action trigger with "Safe Action" system; mechanical firing pin safety, drop safety; simple takedown without tools; locked breech, recoil operated action. ILS designation refers to Internal Locking System. Adopted by Austrian armed forces 1983. NATO approved 1984. Imported from Austria by Glock, Inc.

Price: Fixed sight $599.00
Price: Fixed sight w/ILS................................. $624.00
Price: Adjustable sight $617.00
Price: Adjustable sight w/ILS........................... $642.00
Price: Night sight $646.00
Price: Night sight w/ILS................................ $671.00
Price: 17C Compensated (fixed sight) $621.00
Price: 17C Compensated (fixed sight) w/ILS $646.00

GLOCK 19/19C AUTO PISTOL

Caliber: 9mm Para., 15/17/19/33-shot magazines. **Barrel:** 4.02". **Weight:** 20.99 oz. (without magazine). **Length:** 6.85" overall. Compact version of Glock 17. Pricing the same as Model 17. Imported from Austria by Glock, Inc.

Price: Fixed sight $599.00
Price: 19C Compensated (fixed sight) $621.00

GLOCK 26 AUTO PISTOL

Caliber: 9mm Para. 10/12/15/17/19/33-shot magazines. **Barrel:** 3.46". **Weight:** 19.75 oz. **Length:** 6.29" overall. Subcompact version of Glock 17. Pricing the same as Model 17. Imported from Austria by Glock, Inc.

Price: Fixed sight $599.00

GLOCK 34 AUTO PISTOL

Caliber: 9mm Para. 17/19/33-shot magazines. **Barrel:** 5.32". **Weight:** 22.9 oz. **Length:** 8.15" overall. Competition version of Glock 17 with extended barrel, slide, and sight radius dimensions. Imported from Austria by Glock, Inc.

Price: Adjustable sight $679.00
Price: Adjustable sight w/ILS $704.00

GLOCK 22/22C AUTO PISTOL

Caliber: 40 S&W, 15/17-shot magazines. **Barrel:** 4.49". **Weight:** 22.92 oz. (without magazine). **Length:** 7.32" overall. **Features:** Otherwise similar to Model 17, including pricing. Imported from Austria by Glock, Inc. Introduced 1990.

Price: Fixed sight $599.00
Price: Fixed sight w/ILS $624.00
Price: Adjustable sight $617.00
Price: Adjustable sight w/ILS $642.00
Price: Night sight $646.00
Price: Night sight w/ILS................................ $671.00
Price: 22C Compensated (fixed sight) $621.00
Price: 22C Compensated (fixed sight) w/ILS $646.00

GLOCK 23/23C AUTO PISTOL

Caliber: 40 S&W, 13/15/17-shot magazines. **Barrel:** 4.02". **Weight:** 21.16 oz. (without magazine). **Length:** 6.85" overall. **Features:** Otherwise similar to Model 22, including pricing. Compact version of Glock 22. Imported from Austria by Glock, Inc. Introduced 1990.

Price: Fixed sight $599.00
Price: 23C Compensated (fixed sight) $621.00

GLOCK 27 AUTO PISTOL

Caliber: 40 S&W, 9/11/13/15/17-shot magazines. **Barrel:** 3.46". **Weight:** 19.75 oz. (without magazine). **Length:** 6.29" overall. **Features:** Otherwise similar to Model 22, including pricing. Subcompact version of Glock 22. Imported from Austria by Glock, Inc. Introduced 1996.

Price: Fixed sight $599.00

GLOCK 35 AUTO PISTOL

Caliber: 40 S&W, 15/17-shot magazines. **Barrel:** 5.32". **Weight:** 24.52 oz. (without magazine). **Length:** 8.15" overall. **Features:** Otherwise similar to Model 22. Competition version of Glock 22 with extended barrel, slide, and sight radius dimensions. Imported from Austria by Glock, Inc. Introduced 1996.

Price: Fixed sight $679.00
Price: Adjustable sight w/ILS $704.00

Glock 35

Glock 30

Glock 31

GLOCK 20/20C 10MM AUTO PISTOL

Caliber: 10mm, 15-shot magazines. **Barrel:** 4.6". **Weight:** 27.68 oz. (without magazine). **Length:** 7.59" overall. **Features:** Otherwise similar to Model 17. Imported from Austria by Glock, Inc. Introduced 1990.

Price: Fixed sight $637.00
Price: Fixed sight w/ILS $662.00
Price: Adjustable sight $655.00
Price: Adjustable sight w/ILS $680.00
Price: Night sight $684.00
Price: Night sight w/ILS $709.00
Price: 20C Compensated (fixed sight) $676.00
Price: 20C Compensated (fixed sight) w/ILS $701.00

GLOCK 29 AUTO PISTOL

Caliber: 10mm, 10/15-shot magazines. **Barrel:** 3.78". **Weight:** 24.69 oz. (without magazine). **Length:** 6.77" overall. **Features:** Otherwise similar to Model 20, including pricing. Subcompact version of Glock 20. Imported from Austria by Glock, Inc. Introduced 1997.

Price: Fixed sight $637.00

GLOCK 21/21C AUTO PISTOL

Caliber: 45 ACP, 13-shot magazines. **Barrel:** 4.6". **Weight:** 26.28 oz. (without magazine). **Length:** 7.59" overall. **Features:** Otherwise similar to Model 17. Imported from Austria by Glock, Inc. Introduced 1991.

Price: Fixed sight $637.00
Price: Fixed sight w/ILS $662.00
Price: Adjustable sight $655.00
Price: Adjustable sight w/ILS $680.00
Price: Night sight $684.00
Price: Night sight w/ILS $709.00
Price: 21C Compensated (fixed sight) $676.00
Price: 21C Compensated (fixed sight) w/ILS $701.00

GLOCK 30 AUTO PISTOL

Caliber: 45 ACP, 9/10/13-shot magazines. **Barrel:** 3.78". **Weight:** 23.99 oz. (without magazine). **Length:** 6.77" overall. **Features:** Otherwise similar to Model 21, including pricing. Subcompact version of Glock 21. Imported from Austria by Glock, Inc. Introduced 1997.

Price: Fixed sight $637.00

GLOCK 36 AUTO PISTOL

Caliber: 45 ACP, 6-shot magazines. **Barrel:** 3.78". **Weight:** 20.11 oz. (without magazine). **Length:** 6.77" overall. **Features:** Single-stack magazine, slimmer grip than Glock 21/30. Subcompact. Imported from Austria by Glock, Inc. Introduced 1997.

Price: Fixed sight $637.00

GLOCK 37 AUTO PISTOL

Caliber: 45 GAP, 10-shot magazines. **Barrel:** 4.49". **Weight:** 25.95 oz. (without magazine). **Length:** 7.32" overall. **Features:** Otherwise similar to Model 17. Imported from Austria by Glock, Inc. Introduced 2005.

Price: Fixed sight $614.00
Price: Fixed sight w/ILS $639.00
Price: Adjustable sight $632.00
Price: Adjustable sight w/ILS $657.00
Price: Night sight $661.00
Price: Night sight w/ILS $686.00

GLOCK 38 AUTO PISTOL

Caliber: 45 GAP, 8/10-shot magazines. **Barrel:** 4.02". **Weight:** 24.16 oz. (without magazine). **Length:** 6.85" overall. **Features:** Otherwise similar to Model 37. Compact. Imported from Austria by Glock, Inc.

Price: Fixed sight $614.00

GLOCK 39 AUTO PISTOL

Caliber: 45 GAP, 6/8/10-shot magazines. **Barrel:** 3.46". **Weight:** 19.33 oz. (without magazine). **Length:** 6.3" overall. **Features:** Otherwise similar to Model 37. Subcompact. Imported from Austria by Glock, Inc.

Price: Fixed sight $614.00

GLOCK 25 AUTO PISTOL

Caliber: 380 ACP, 15/17/19-shot magazines. **Barrel:** 4.02". **Weight:** 20.11 oz. (without magazine). **Length:** 6.85" overall. **Features:** Otherwise similar to Model 17. Compact. Made in Austria by Glock, Inc. Not imported to U.S.

Price: . . . . NA

GLOCK 28 AUTO PISTOL

Caliber: 380 ACP, 10/12/15/17/19-shot magazines. **Barrel:** 3.46". **Weight:** 18.66 oz. (without magazine). **Length:** 6.29" overall. **Features:** Otherwise similar to Model 25. Subcompact. Made in Austria by Glock, Inc. Not imported to U.S.

Price: . . . . NA

GLOCK 31/31C AUTO PISTOL

Caliber: 357 Auto, 15/17-shot magazines. **Barrel:** 4.49". **Weight:** 23.28 oz. (without magazine). **Length:** 7.32" overall. **Features:** Otherwise similar to Model 17. Imported from Austria by Glock, Inc.

Price: Fixed sight $599.00
Price: Fixed sight w/ILS $624.00
Price: Adjustable sight $617.00
Price: Adjustable sight w/ILS $642.00
Price: Night sight $646.00
Price: Night sight w/ILS $671.00
Price: 31C Compensated (fixed sight) $621.00
Price: 31C Compensated (fixed sight) w/ILS $646.00

GLOCK 32/32C AUTO PISTOL

Caliber: 357 Auto, 13/15/17-shot magazines. **Barrel:** 4.02". **Weight:** 21.52 oz. (without magazine). **Length:** 6.85" overall. **Features:** Otherwise similar to Model 31. Compact. Imported from Austria by Glock, Inc.

Price: Fixed sight $599.00
Price: 32C Compensated (fixed sight) $621.00

GLOCK 33 AUTO PISTOL

Caliber: 357 Auto, 9/11/13/15/17-shot magazines. **Barrel:** 3.46". **Weight:** 19.75 oz. (without magazine). **Length:** 6.29" overall. **Features:** Otherwise similar to Model 31. Subcompact. Imported from Austria by Glock, Inc.

Price: Fixed sight $599.00

HAMMERLI "TRAILSIDE" TARGET PISTOL

Caliber: 22 LR. **Barrel:** 4.5", 6". **Weight:** 28 oz. **Grips:** Synthetic. **Sights:** Fixed. **Features:** 10-shot magazine. Imported from by Larry's Guns of Maine.

Price: $579.00

Hammerli Trailside

Heckler & Koch USP45

Heckler & Koch USP Compact

Heckler & Koch USP45 Tactical

Heckler & Koch USP45 Compact

Heckler & Koch Mark 23 Special Operations

HECKLER & KOCH USP AUTO PISTOL

Caliber: 9mm Para., 15-shot magazine; 40 S&W, 13-shot magazine; 45 ACP, 12-shot magazine. **Barrel:** 4.25-4.41". **Weight:** 1.65 lbs. **Length:** 7.64-7.87" overall. **Grips:** Non-slip stippled black polymer. **Sights:** Blade front, rear adjustable for windage. **Features:** New HK design with polymer frame, modified Browning action with recoil reduction system, single control lever. Special "hostile environment" finish on all metal parts. Available in SA/ DA, DAO, left- and right-hand versions. Introduced 1993. 45 ACP Introduced 1995. Imported from Germany by Heckler & Koch, Inc.
Price: USP 45 . . . . **$839.00**
Price: USP 40 and USP 9mm **$769.00**

Heckler & Koch USP Compact Auto Pistol

Caliber: 9mm Para., 13-shot magazine; 40 S&W and .357 SIG, 12-shot magazine; 45 ACP, 8-shot magazine. Similar to the USP except the 9mm Para., 357 SIG, and 40 S&W have 3.58" barrels, measure 6.81" overall, and weigh 1.47 lbs. (9mm). Introduced 1996. 45 ACP measures 7.09" overall. Introduced 1998. Imported from Germany by Heckler & Koch, Inc.
Price: USP Compact 45 . . . . **$874.00**
Price: USP Compact 9mm Para., 357 SIG, and 40 S&W **$799.00**

HECKLER & KOCH USP45 TACTICAL PISTOL

Caliber: 40 S&W, 13-shot magazine; 45 ACP, 12-shot magazine. **Barrel:** 4.90-5.09". **Weight:** 1.9 lbs. **Length:** 8.64" overall. **Grips:** Non-slip stippled polymer. **Sights:** Blade front, fully adjustable target rear. **Features:** Has extended threaded barrel with rubber O-ring; adjustable trigger; extended magazine floorplate; adjustable trigger stop; polymer frame. Introduced 1998. Imported from Germany by Heckler & Koch, Inc.
Price: USP Tactical 45 . . . . **$1,115.00**
Price: USP Tactical 40 . . . . **$1,019.00**

Heckler & Koch USP Compact Tactical Pistol

Caliber: 45 ACP, 8-shot magazine. Similar to the USP Tactical except measures 7.72" overall, weighs 1.72 lbs. Introduced 2006. Imported from Germany by Heckler & Koch, Inc.
Price: USP Compact Tactical **$1,115.00**

HECKLER & KOCH MARK 23 SPECIAL OPERATIONS PISTOL

Caliber: 45 ACP, 12-shot magazine. **Barrel:** 5.87". **Weight:** 2.42 lbs. **Length:** 9.65" overall. **Grips:** Integral with frame; black polymer. **Sights:** Blade front, rear drift adjustable for windage; 3-dot. **Features:** Civilian version of the SOCOM pistol. Polymer frame; double action; exposed hammer; short recoil, modified Browning action. Introduced 1996. Imported from Germany by Heckler & Koch, Inc.
Price: **$2,412.00**

HECKLER & KOCH P2000 AUTO PISTOL

Caliber: 9mm Para., 13-shot magazine; 40 S&W and .357 SIG, 12-shot magazine. **Barrel:** 3.62". **Weight:** 1.5 lbs. **Length:** 7" overall. **Grips:** Interchangeable panels. **Sights:** Fixed Patridge style, drift adjustable for windage, standard 3-dot. Incorporates features of HK USP Compact pistol, including Law Enforcement Modification (LEM) trigger, double-action hammer system, ambidextrous magazine release, dual slide-release levers, accessory mounting rails, recurved, hook trigger guard, fiber-reinforced polymer frame, modular grip with exchangeable back straps, nitro-carburized finish, lock-out safety device. Introduced 2003. Imported from Germany by Heckler & Koch, Inc.
Price: **$887.00**
Price: P2000 LEM DAO, 357 SIG, intr. 2006 . . . . **$887.00**
Price: P2000 SA/DA, , 357 SIG, intr. 2006 . . . . **$887.00**

HECKLER & KOCH P2000 SK AUTO PISTOL

Caliber: 9mm Para., 10-shot magazine; 40 S&W and .357 SIG, 9-shot magazine. **Barrel:** 3.27". **Weight:** 1.3 lbs. **Length:** 6.42" overall. **Sights:** Fixed Patridge style, drift adjustable. **Features:** Standard accessory rails, ambidextrous slide release, polymer frame, polygonal bore profile. Smaller version of P2000. Introduced 2005. Imported from Germany by Heckler & Koch, Inc.
Price: **$929.00**

Hi-Point 9MM Comp   Hi-Point C-9   Kahr K9

HI-POINT FIREARMS MODEL 9MM COMPACT PISTOL

Caliber: 9mm Para., 8-shot magazine. **Barrel:** 3.5". **Weight:** 25 oz.
Length: 6.75" overall. **Grips:** Textured plastic. **Sights:** Combat-style
adjustable 3-dot system; low profile. **Features:** Single-action design;
frame-mounted magazine release; polymer frame. Scratch-resistant
matte finish. Introduced 1993. Comps are similar except they have a 4"
barrel with muzzle brake/compensator. Compensator is slotted for laser or
flashlight mounting. Introduced 1998. Made in U.S.A. by MKS Supply, Inc.
Price: C-9 9mm **$140.00**
Price: C-9 Comp **$169.00**
Price: C-9 Comp-L w/laser sight **$219.00**

Hi-Point Firearms Model 380 Polymer Pistol

Similar to the 9mm Compact model except chambered for 380 ACP, 8-
shot magazine, adjustable 3-dot sights. Weighs 25 oz. Polymer frame.
Action locks open after last shot. Includes 10-shot and 8-shot magazine;
trigger lock. Introduced 1998. Comps are similar except they have a 4"
barrel with muzzle compensator. Introduced 2001. Made in U.S.A. by
MKS Supply, Inc.
Price: CF-380 . . . . **$120.00**
Price: 380 Comp **$120.00**
Price: 380 Comp-L w/laser sight **$190.00**

HI-POINT FIREARMS 40SW/POLY AND 45 AUTO PISTOLS

Caliber: 40 S&W, 8-shot magazine; 45 ACP (9-shot). **Barrel:** 4.5". **Weight:**
32 oz. **Length:** 7.72" overall. **Sights:** Adjustable 3-dot. **Features:**
Polymer frames, last round lock-open, grip mounted magazine release,
magazine disconnect safety, integrated accessory rail, trigger lock.
Introduced 2002. Made in U.S.A. by MKS Supply, Inc.
Price: 40SW Poly **$179.00**
Price: 40SW Poly w/laser **$239.00**
Price: 45 ACP **$179.00**
Price: 45 ACP w/laser **$239.00**

KAHR K SERIES AUTO PISTOLS

Caliber: K9: 9mm Para., 7-shot; K40: 40 S&W, 6-shot magazine. **Barrel:**
3.5". **Weight:** 25 oz. **Length:** 6" overall. **Grips:** Wraparound textured soft
polymer. **Sights:** Blade front, rear drift adjustable for windage; bar-dot
combat style. **Features:** Trigger-cocking double-action mechanism with
passive firing pin block. Made of 4140 ordnance steel with matte black
finish. Contact maker for complete price list. Introduced 1994. Made in
U.S.A. by Kahr Arms.
Price: K9093C K9, matte stainless steel **$741.00**
Price: K9093NC K9, matte stainless steel w/tritium night sights . . . **$853.00**
Price: K9094C K9 matte blackened stainless steel **$772.00**
Price: K9098 K9 Elite 2003, stainless steel. **$806.00**
Price: K4043 K40, matte stainless steel **$741.00**
Price: K4043N K40, matte stainless steel w/tritium night sights. . . . **$853.00**
Price: K4044 K40, matte blackened stainless steel **$772.00**
Price: K4048 K40 Elite 2003, stainless steel **$806.00**

Kahr MK Series Micro Pistols

Similar to the K9/K40 except is 5.35" overall, 4" high, with a 3.08" barrel.
Weighs 23.1 oz. Has snag-free bar-dot sights, polished feed ramp, dual
recoil spring system, DA-only trigger. Comes with 5-round flush baseplate
and 6-shot grip extension magazine. Introduced 1998. Made in U.S.A. by
Kahr Arms.
Price: M9093 MK9, matte stainless steel **$741.00**
Price: M9093N MK9, matte stainless steel, tritium night sights **$853.00**
Price: M9093-BOX MK9, matte stainless steel frame,
matte black slide **$475.00**
Price: M9098 MK9 Elite 2003, stainless steel **$806.00**
Price: M4043 MK40, matte stainless steel **$741.00**
Price: M4043N MK40, matte stainless steel, tritium night sights . . . **$853.00**
Price: M4048 MK40 Elite 2003, stainless steel **$806.00**

Kahr P Series Pistols

Caliber: 9x19, 40 S&W. Similar to K9/K40 steel frame pistol except has
polymer frame, matte stainless steel slide. Barrel length 3.5"; overall
length 5.8"; weighs 17 oz. Includes two 7-shot magazines, hard polymer
case, trigger lock. Introduced 2000. Made in U.S.A. by Kahr Arms.
Price: KP9093 P9 . . . . **$697.00**
Price: KP9093N P9, tritium night sight **$808.00**
Price: KPS9093 P9 Covert, shortened grip, 15 oz., 6+1 . . . . **$697.00**
Price: KP4043 P40 . . . . **$697.00**
Price: KPS4043N P40 Covert, shortened grip, tritium night sights . **$697.00**

Kahr PM Series Pistols

Caliber: 9x19, 40 S&W. Similar to P-Series pistols except has smaller
polymer frame (Polymer Micro). Barrel length 3.08"; overall length 5.35";
weighs 17 oz. Includes two 7-shot magazines, hard polymer case, trigger
lock. Introduced 2000. Made in U.S.A. by Kahr Arms.
Price: PM9093 PM9 . . . . **$728.00**
Price: PM9093N PM9, tritium night sight **$839.00**
Price: PM4043 PM40 . . . . **$728.00**
Price: PM4044N PM40, Tungsten DLC finish, tritium night sights . . **$870.00**

KAHR T SERIES PISTOLS

Caliber: T9: 9mm Para., 8-shot magazine; T40: 40 S&W, 7-shot magazine.
Barrel: 4". **Weight:** 28.1-29.1 oz. **Length:** 6.5" overall. **Grips:** Checkered
Hogue Pau Ferro wood grips. **Sights:** Rear: Novak low profile 2-dot tritium
night sight, front tritium night sight. **Features:** Similar to other Kahr makes,
but with longer slide and barrel upper, longer butt. Trigger cocking DAO;
lock breech; "Browning-type" recoil lug; passive striker block; no
magazine disconnect. Comes with two magazines. Introduced 2004.
Made in U.S.A. by Kahr Arms.
Price: KT9093 T9 matte stainless steel **$741.00**
Price: KT9093-NOVAK T9, "Tactical 9," Novak night sight **$860.00**
Price: KT4093 T40 matte stainless steel **$741.00**

KAHR TP SERIES PISTOLS

Caliber: TP9: 9mm Para., 7-shot magazine; TP40: 40 S&W, 6-shot
magazine. **Barrel:** 4". **Weight:** 19.1-20.1 oz. **Length:** 6.5-6.7" overall.
Grips: Textured polymer. Similar to T-series guns, but with polymer
frame, matte stainless slide. Comes with two magazines. TP40s
introduced 2006. Made in U.S.A. by Kahr Arms.
Price: TP9093 TP9 . . . . **$697.00**
Price: TP9093-Novak TP9 . . . . **$839.00**
Price: TP4043 TP40 . . . . **$697.00**
Price: TP4043-Novak TP40, Novak night sights **$839.00**

Kel-Tec P-32   **Kel-Tec P-3AT**   **Kimber Pro Carry II**   **Kimber Ultra Carry II**

Kimber Ten II High Capacity Polymer

KAHR CW SERIES PISTOL

Caliber: 9mm Para., 7-shot magazine; 40 S&W, 6-shot magazine. **Barrel:** 3.5-3.6". **Weight:** 17.7-18.7 oz. **Length:** 5.9-6.36" overall. **Grips:** Textured polymer. Similar to P-Series, but CW Series have conventional rifling, metal-injection-molded slide stop lever, no front dovetail cut, one magazine. CW40 introduced 2006. Made in U.S.A. by Kahr Arms.
Price: CW9093 CW9 .... **$533.00**
Price: CW4043 CW40 .... **$533.00**

KEL-TEC P-11 AUTO PISTOL

Caliber: 9mm Para., 10-shot magazine. **Barrel:** 3.1". **Weight:** 14 oz. **Length:** 5.6" overall. **Grips:** Checkered black polymer. **Sights:** Blade front, rear adjustable for windage. **Features:** Ordnance steel slide, aluminum frame. Double-action-only trigger mechanism. Introduced 1995. Made in U.S.A. by Kel-Tec CNC Industries, Inc.
Price: Blue/Hard Chrome/Parkerized .... **$320 /$375 / $362**

KEL-TEC PF-9 PISTOL

Caliber: 9mm Luger; 7 rounds. **Weight:** 12.7 oz. **Sights:** Rear sight adjustable for windage and elevation. **Barrel Length:** 3.1". **Length:** 5.85". **Features:** Barrel, locking system, slide stop, assembly pin, front sight, recoil springs and guide rod adapted from P-11. Trigger system with integral hammer block and the extraction system adapted from P-3AT. MIL-STD-1913 Picatinny rail. Made in U.S.A. by Kel-Tec CNC Industries, Inc.
Price: Blue/ Parkerized/Hard Chrome .... **$314/ $355 / $368**

KEL-TEC P-32 AUTO PISTOL

Caliber: 32 ACP, 7-shot magazine. **Barrel:** 2.68". **Weight:** 6.6 oz. **Length:** 5.07" overall. **Grips:** Checkered composite. **Sights:** Fixed. **Features:** Double-action-only mechanism with 6-lb. pull; internal slide stop. Textured composite grip/frame. Now available in 380 ACP. Made in U.S.A. by Kel-Tec CNC Industries, Inc.
Price: Blue/Hard Chrome/Parkerized .... **$300 / $355 / $340**

KEL-TEC P-3AT PISTOL

Caliber: 380 Auto; 7-rounds. **Weight:** 7.2 oz. **Length:** 5.2". **Features:** Lightest 380 auto made; aluminum frame, steel barrel.
Price: Blue/Hard Chrome/Parkerized .... **$300 / $355 / $340**

KEL-TEC PLR-16 PISTOL

Caliber: 5.56mm NATO; 10-round magazine. **Weight:** 51 oz. **Sights:** Rear sight adjustable for windage, front sight is M-16 blade. **Barrel Length:** 9.2". **Length:** 18.5". **Features:** Muzzle is threaded 1/2"-28 to accept standard attachments such as a muzzle brake. Except for the barrel, bolt, sights, and mechanism, the PLR-16 pistol is made of high-impact glass fiber reinforced polymer. Gas-operated semi-auto. Conventional gas-piston operation with M-16 breech locking system. MIL-STD-1913 Picatinny rail. Made in U.S.A. by Kel-Tec CNC Industries, Inc.
Price: Blued **$640.00**

KIMBER CUSTOM II AUTO PISTOL

Caliber: 45 ACP, 40 S&W, 38 Super, 9mm, 10mm. **Barrel:** 5", match grade; 9mm, 10mm, 40 S&W, 38 Super barrels ramped. **Weight:** 38 oz. **Length:** 8.7" overall. **Grips:** Checkered black rubber, walnut, rosewood. **Sights:** Dovetailed front and rear, Kimber low profile adj. or fixed sights. **Features:** Slide, frame and barrel machined from steel or stainless steel. Match grade barrel, chamber and trigger group. Extended thumb safety, beveled magazine well, beveled front and rear slide serrations, high ride beavertail grip safety, checkered flat mainspring housing, kidney cut under trigger

guard, high cut grip, match grade stainless steel barrel bushing, polished breech face, Commander-style hammer, lowered and flared ejection port, Wolff springs, bead blasted black oxide or matte stainless finish. Introduced in 1996. Made in U.S.A. by Kimber Mfg., Inc.
Price: Custom II **$768.00**
Price: Custom II Walnut (double-diamond walnut grips) **$775.00**
Price: Stainless II **$865.00**
Price: Stainless II 40 S&W **$884.00**
Price: Stainless II Target 45 ACP (stainless, adj. sight) **$983.00**
Price: Stainless II Target 38 Super **$1,014.00**

Kimber Compact Stainless II Auto Pistol

Similar to Pro Carry II except has stainless steel frame, 4-inch bbl., grip is .400" shorter than standard, no front serrations. Weighs 34 oz. 45 ACP only. Introduced in 1998. Made in U.S.A. by Kimber Mfg., Inc.
Price: **$907.00**

Kimber Pro Carry II Auto Pistol

Similar to Custom II, has aluminum frame, 4" bull barrel fitted directly to the slide without bushing. HD with stainless steel frame. Introduced 1998. Made in U.S.A. by Kimber Mfg., Inc.
Price: Pro Carry II **$779.00**
Price: Pro Carry II w/night sights **$902.00**
Price: Pro Carry II Stainless w/night sights **$985.00**
Price: Pro Carry HD II **$906.00**

Kimber Ultra Carry II Auto Pistol

Lightweight aluminum frame, 3" match grade bull barrel fitted to slide without bushing. Grips .4" shorter. Low effort recoil. Weighs 25 oz. Introduced in 1999. Made in U.S.A. by Kimber Mfg., Inc.
Price: **$791.00**
Price: Ultra Carry II Stainless **$875.00**
Price: Ultra Carry II Stainless 40 S&W **$921.00**

Kimber Ten II High Capacity Polymer Pistol

Similar to Custom II, Pro Carry II and Ultra Carry II depending on barrel length. Thirteen-round magazine capacity (double stack and flush fitting). Polymer grip frame molded over stainless steel or aluminum (BP Ten pistols only) frame insert. Checkered front strap and belly of trigger guard. All models have fixed sights except Gold Match Ten II, which has adjustable sight. Frame grip dimensions approximately that of the standard 1911. **Weight:** 24 to 34 oz. Improved version of the Kimber Polymer series. Made in U.S.A. by Kimber Mfg., Inc.
Price: Pro Carry Ten II **$794.00**
Price: Stainless Ten II **$786.00**

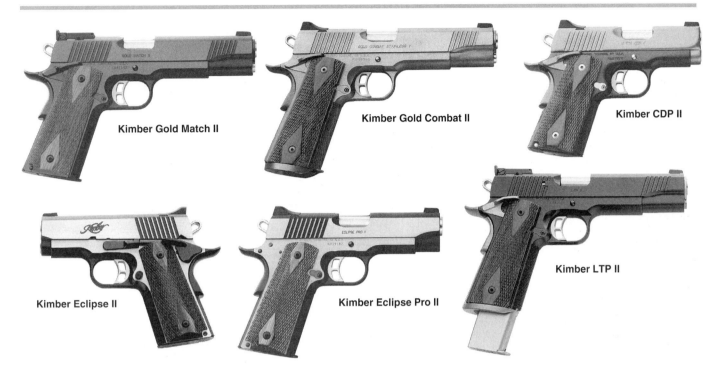

Kimber Gold Match II

Kimber Gold Combat II

Kimber CDP II

Kimber Eclipse II

Kimber Eclipse Pro II

Kimber LTP II

Kimber Gold Match II Auto Pistol

Similar to Custom II models. Includes stainless steel barrel with match grade chamber and barrel bushing, ambidextrous thumb safety, adjustable sight, premium aluminum trigger, hand-checkered double diamond rosewood grips. Barrel hand-fitted for target accuracy. Made in U.S.A. by Kimber Mfg., Inc.

Price: Gold Match II **$1,204.00**
Price: Gold Match Stainless II 45 ACP **$1,369.00**
Price: Gold Match Stainless II 40 S&W **$1,400.00**

Kimber Gold Match Ten II Polymer Auto Pistol

Similar to Stainless Gold Match II. High capacity polymer frame with 13-round magazine. Thumb safety. Introduced 1999. Made in U.S.A. by Kimber Mfg., Inc.

Price: **$1,072.00**

Kimber Gold Combat II Auto Pistol

Similar to Gold Match II except designed for concealed carry. Extended and beveled magazine well, Meprolight Tritium night sights; premium aluminum trigger; 30 lpi front strap checkering; extended magazine well. Introduced 1999. Made in U.S.A. by Kimber Mfg., Inc.

Price: Gold Combat II **$1,733.00**
Price: Gold Combat Stainless II **$1,674.00**

Kimber CDP II Series Auto Pistol

Similar to Custom II, but designed for concealed carry. Aluminum frame. Standard features include stainless steel slide, fixed Meprolight tritium 3-dot (green) dovetail-mounted night sights, match grade barrel and chamber, 30 LPI front strap checkering, two-tone finish, ambidextrous thumb safety, hand-checkered double diamond rosewood grips. Introduced in 2000. Made in U.S.A. by Kimber Mfg., Inc.

Price: Ultra CDP II 40 S&W **$1,215.00**
Price: Ultra CDP II (3" barrel, short grip) **$1,177.00**
Price: Compact CDP II (4" barrel, short grip) **$1,177.00**
Price: Pro CDP II (4" barrel, full length grip) **$1,177.00**
Price: Custom CDP II (5" barrel, full length grip) **$1,177.00**

Kimber Eclipse II Series Auto Pistol

Similar to Custom II and other stainless Kimber pistols. Stainless slide and frame, black oxide, two-tone finish. Gray/black laminated grips. 30 lpi front strap checkering. All models have night sights; Target versions have Meprolight adjustable Bar/Dot version. Made in U.S.A. by Kimber Mfg., Inc.

Price: Eclipse Ultra II (3" barrel, short grip) **$1,085.00**
Price: Eclipse Pro II (4" barrel, full length grip) **$1,085.00**
Price: Eclipse Pro Target II (4" barrel, full length grip,
adjustable sight) **$1,189.00**
Price: Eclipse Custom II (5" barrel, full length grip) **$1,105.00**
Price: Eclipse Target II (5" barrel, full length grip,
adjustable sight) **$1,189.00**
Price: Eclipse Custom II (10mm) **$1,220.00**

Kimber LTP II Auto Pistol

Similar to Gold Match II. Built for Limited Ten competition. First Kimber pistol with new, innovative Kimber external extractor. KimPro premium finish. Stainless steel match grade barrel. Extended and beveled magazine well. Checkered front strap and trigger guard belly. Tungsten full length guide rod. Premium aluminum trigger. Ten-round single stack magazine. Wide ambidextrous thumb safety. Made in U.S.A. by Kimber Mfg., Inc.

Price: **$2,099.00**

Kimber Super Match II Auto Pistol

Similar to Gold Match II. Built for target and action shooting competition. Tested for accuracy, target included. Stainless steel barrel and chamber. KimPro finish on stainless steel slide. Stainless steel frame. 30 lpi checkered front strap, premium aluminum trigger, Kimber adjustable sight. Introduced in 1999.

Price: **$1,986.00**

KORTH PISTOL

Caliber: 40 S&W, 357 SIG (9-shot); 9mm Para, 9x21 (10-shot). **Barrel:** 4" (standard), 5" (optional). **Weight:** 3.3 lbs. (single action), 11 lbs. (double action). **Sights:** Fully adjustable. **Features:** Recoil-operated action, mechanically-locked via large pivoting bolt block. Accessories include sound suppressor for qualified buyers. Imported by Korth U.S.A.

Price: **$7,578.00**

NORTH AMERICAN ARMS GUARDIAN DAO PISTOL

Caliber: 25 NAA, 32 ACP, 380 ACP, 32NAA, 6-shot magazine. **Barrel:** 2.49". **Weight:** 20.8 oz. **Length:** 4.75" overall. **Grips:** Black polymer. **Sights:** Low profile fixed. **Features:** Double-action only mechanism. All stainless steel construction. Introduced 1998. Made in U.S.A. by North American Arms.

Price: . . . . **$402.00 to $479.00**

North American Arms Guardian

Olympic Arms Matchmaster 5 1911

Olympic Arms Matchmaster 6 1911

Olympic Arms Enforcer 1911

Olympic Arms Cohort

Olympic Arms Big Deuce

Olympic Arms Westerner

OLYMPIC ARMS MATCHMASTER 5 1911 PISTOL

Caliber: 45 ACP, 7-shot magazine. **Barrel:** 5" stainless steel. **Weight:** 40 oz. **Length:** overall. **Grips:** Smooth walnut with laser etched scorpion logo. **Sights:** Ramped blade, LPA adjustable rear. **Features:** Matched frame and slide, fitted and head-spaced barrel, complete ramp and throat jobs, lowered and widened ejection port, beveled mag well, hand-stoned-to-match hammer and sear, lightweight long-shoe over-travel adjusted trigger, shaped and tensioned extractor, extended thumb safety, wide beavertail grip safety and full length guide rod. Made in U.S.A. by Olympic Arms, Inc.
Price: **$714.00**

OLYMPIC ARMS MATCHMASTER 6 1911 PISTOL

Caliber: 45 ACP, 7-shot. **Barrel:** 6" stainless steel. **Weight:** 44 oz. **Length:** 9.75" overall. **Grips:** Smooth walnut. **Sights:** Ramped blade, LPA adjustable rear. **Features:** Matched frame and slide, fitted and head-spaced barrel, complete ramp and throat jobs, lowered and widened ejection port, beveled mag well, hand-stoned-to-match hammer and sear, lightweight long-shoe over-travel adjusted trigger, shaped and tensioned extractor, extended thumb safety, wide beavertail grip safety and full length guide rod. Made in U.S.A. by Olympic Arms, Inc.
Price: **$774.00**

OLYMPIC ARMS ENFORCER 1911 PISTOL

Caliber: 45 ACP, 6-shot magazine. **Barrel:** 4" bull barrel stainless steel. **Weight:** 35 oz. **Length:** 7.75" overall. **Grips:** Smooth walnut with etched black widow spider logo. **Sights:** Ramped blade front, LPA adjustable rear. **Features:** Similar to Matchmaster, but adds a bushingless bull barrel and a triplex counter-wound self-contained spring recoil system. Matched frame and slide, fitted and head-spaced barrel, complete ramp and throat jobs, lowered and widened ejection port, beveled mag well, hand-stoned-to-match hammer and sear, lightweight longshoe over-travel adjusted trigger, shaped and tensioned extractor, extended thumb safety, wide beavertail grip safety and full length guide rod. Made in U.S.A. by Olympic Arms.
Price: **$750.00**

OLYMPIC ARMS COHORT PISTOL

Caliber: 45 ACP, 7-shot magazine. **Barrel:** 4", bull barrel stainless steel. **Weight:** 36 oz. **Length:** 7.75" overall. **Grips:** Smooth walnut with laser-etched black widow logo. **Sights:** Ramped blade front, LPA adjustable rear. **Features:** Combines short Enforcer top end and recoil system with full-sized Matchmaster round-trigger-guard M-3 frame. Matched frame

and slide, fitted and head-spaced barrel, complete ramp and throat jobs, lowered and widened ejection port, beveled mag well, hand-stoned-to-match hammer and sear, lightweight long-shoe over-travel adjusted trigger, shaped and tensioned extractor, extended thumb safety, wide beavertail grip safety and full length guide rod. Made in U.S.A. by Olympic Arms.
Price: **$779.00**

OLYMPIC ARMS BIG DEUCE PISTOL

Caliber: 45 ACP, 7-shot magazine. **Barrel:** 6", 416 stainless steel. **Weight:** 40.3 oz. **Length:** 9.5" overall. **Grips:** Smooth walnut. **Sights:** Ramped blade front, LPA adjustable rear. **Features:** Beavertail grip safety; extended thumb safety and slide release; Commander-style hammer. Throated, polished and tuned. Parkerized matte black slide with satin stainless steel frame. Introduced 1995. Made in U.S.A. by Safari Arms, Inc.
Price: **$834.00**

OLYMPIC ARMS WESTERNER SERIES PISTOLS

Caliber: 45 ACP, 7-round magazine. **Barrel:** 4", 5", 6". **Grips:** Smooth ivory style. **Weight:** 35-43 oz. **Length:** 7.75". **Sights:** Adjustable rear, fixed front blade. **Features:** Similar to Matchmaster, parts numbered to the frame, color case hardening finish. Made in U.S.A. by Olympic Arms, Inc.
Price: Westerner, 5" barrel, 39 oz. **$834.00**
Price: Trail Boss, 6" barrel, 43 oz. **$959.00**
Price: Constable, 4" barrel, 35 oz. **$935.00**

Olympic Arms Constable

Olympic Arms Trail Boss

Olympic Arms OA-93

Olympic Arms OA-98

Para-Ordnance SSP-SE1

Para-Ordnance Todd Jarrett

Para-Ordnance P12-45

OLYMPIC ARMS BLACK-TAC PISTOL

Caliber: 45 ACP, 7-round magazine. **Barrel:** 5". **Weight:** 40 oz. **Length:** 8.75". **Sights:** Low-profile adjustable rear, fixed front blade. **Features:** Blak-Tac finish process also used on AR/M-16 bolt carriers. Made in U.S.A. by Olympic Arms, Inc.
Price: **$834.00**

OLYMPIC ARMS OA-93 AR PISTOL

Caliber: 5.56 NATO. **Barrel:** 6.5", chrome-moly steel. **Weight:** 4.46 lbs. **Length:** 26.5". **Sights:** None. **Features:** Black matte finish; flash suppressor; flat-top upper, tubular handguard. Introduced 2005. Made in U.S.A. by Olympic Arms, Inc.
Price: **$1,020.00**

Olympic Arms OA-98 AR Pistol

Similar to the OA-93. **Weight:** 49 oz. Skeletonized version of OA-93, conforms to the AWB, uses standard AR15 magazines. Introduced 1998. Made in U.S.A. by Olympic Arms, Inc.
Price: **$1,020.00**

PARA-ORDNANCE PXT 1911 SINGLE-ACTION SINGLE-STACK AUTO PISTOLS

Caliber: 38 Super, 45 ACP. **Barrel:** 3.5", 4.25", 5". **Weight:** 28-40 oz. **Length:** 7.1-8.5" overall. **Grips:** Checkered cocobolo, textured composition, Mother of Pearl synthetic. **Sights:** Blade front, low-profile Novak Extreme Duty adjustable rear. High visibility 3-dot system. **Features:** Available with alloy, steel or stainless steel frames. Skeletonized trigger, spurred hammer. Manual thumb, grip and firing pin lock safeties. Full-length guide rod. PXT designates new Para Power

Extractor throughout the line. Introduced 2004. Made in Canada by Para-Ordnance.
Price: SSP-SE1 (2006), midnight blue, 7+1, 5" barrel **$1,094.00**
Price: OPS, stainless, Griptor grooves front strap (2006) **$1,043.00**
Price: LTC, blued or stainless, 7+1, 4.25" barrel . . . . . **$884.00 to 1,043.00**
Price: SSP, blued or stainless, 7+1, 4.25" barrel . . . . . **$884.00 to 1,043.00**

PARA-ORDNANCE PXT 1911 SINGLE-ACTION HIGH-CAPACITY AUTO PISTOLS

Caliber: 9mm, 45 ACP, 10//14/18-shot magazines. **Barrel:** 3", 5". **Weight:** 34-40 oz. **Length:** 7.1-8.5" overall. **Grips:** Textured composition. **Sights:** Blade front, low-profile Novak Extreme Duty adjustable rear or fixed sights. High visibility 3-dot system. **Features:** Available with alloy, steel or stainless steel frames. Skeletonized match trigger, spurred hammer, flared ejection port. Manual thumb, grip and firing pin lock safeties. Full-length guide rod. Introduced 2004. Made in Canada by Para-Ordnance.
Price: P14-45MB (2006), midnight blue, 14+1, 5" barrel **$899.00**
Price: P14-45 stainless, 14+1, 5" barrel **$998.00**
Price: P18-9 stainless,18+1 9mm, 5" barrel **$1,049.00**

Para-Ordnance PXT Limited Pistols

Similar to the PXT-Series pistols except with full-length recoil guide system; fully adjustable rear sight; tuned trigger with over-travel stop; beavertail grip safety; competition hammer; front and rear slide serrations; ambidextrous safety; lowered ejection port; ramped match-grade barrel; dove-tailed front sight. Introduced 2004. Made in Canada by Para-Ordnance.
Price: S12-45 LTD, 45 ACP, 12+1, stainless, Novak sights **$1,163.00**
Price: Todd Jarrett 40 S&W, 16+1, stainless **$1,163.00**

Para-Ordnance LDA

Para-Ordnance Carry

Para-Ordnance CCO

Para-Ordnance Tac-Four

Para-Ordnance Tac-S

Para-Ordnance Limited

Para-Ordnance Colonel

Para-Ordnance Nite-Trac

Para-Ordnance Slim Hawg

Para-Ordnance LDA Single-Stack Carry Auto Pistols

Similar to PXT-series except has double-action trigger mechanism, flush hammers, brushed stainless finish, checkered composition grips. Available in 45 ACP. Introduced 1999. Made in Canada by Para-Ordnance.

Price: Carry, 6+1, 3" barrel, stainless **$1,049.00**
Price: Carry, 6+1, 3" barrel, covert black **$1,133.00**
Price: CCO, 7+1, 3.5" barrel **$1, 049.00**
Price: CCW, 7+1, 4.5" barrel **$1, 049.00**

Para-Ordnance LDA High-Cap Carry Auto Pistols

Similar to LDA-series with double-action trigger mechanism. Also, bobbed beavertail, high-cap mags. Available in 9mm Para., 45 ACP. Introduced 1999. Made in Canada by Para-Ordnance.

Price: Carry 12, 12+1, 3.5" barrel, stainless **$1,133.00**
Price: Tac-Four, 13+1, 4.5" barrel, stainless **$1,028.00**
Price: C TX189B, 18+1, 5" barrel, covert black, Novak sights . . . **$1,163.00**

Para-Ordnance LDA Single-Stack Auto Pistols

Similar to LDA-series with double-action trigger mechanism. Cocobolo and polymer grips. Available in 45 ACP. Introduced 1999. Made in Canada by Para-Ordnance.

Price: Black Watch Companion, 7+1, 3.5" barrel **$1,133.00**
Price: Tac-S, 7+1, 4.5" barrel, Spec Ops matte finish **$944.00**
Price: Tac-S, 7+1, 4.5" barrel, stainless. **$1,028.00**
Price: Limited, 7+1, 5" barrel, stainless. **$1,193.00**

Para-Ordnance LDA Hi-Capacity Auto Pistols

Similar to LDA-series with double-action trigger mechanism. Polymer grips. Available in 9mm, 40 S&W, 45 ACP. Introduced 1999. Made in Canada by Para-Ordnance.

Price: Colonel, 14+1, 4.25" barrel. **$944.00**
Price: Hi-Cap 45, 14+1, 5" barrel, stainless **$1,028.00**
Price: Hi-Cap 9, 18+1, 5" barrel, covert black finish. **$944.00**
Price: Hi-Cap LTD 45 45 ACP, 14+1, 5" barrel, stainless. **$1,193.00**
Price: Hi-Cap LTD 40 40 S&W, 15+1, 5" barrel, stainless **$1,193.00**
Price: Hi-Cap LTD 9 9mm, 18+1, 5" barrel, stainless. **$1,193.00**

Para-Ordnance LDA Light Rail Pistols

Similar to PXT and LDA-series above, with built-in light rail. Polymer grips. Available in 9mm, 40 S&W, 45 ACP. Made in Canada by Para-Ordnance.

Price: Nite-Tac 45, 14+1 45 ACP, 5" barrel, covert black **$1,034.00**
Price: Nite-Tac 40, 16+1 40 S&W, 5" barrel, stainless (2006) **$1,103.00**
Price: Nite-Tac 9, 16+1 9mm, 5" barrel, stainless (2006). **$1,103.00**

PARA-ORDNANCE WARTHOG

Caliber: 9mm, 45 ACP, 6, 10, or 12-shot magazines. **Barrel:** 3". **Weight:** 24 to 31.5 oz. **Length:** 6.5". **Grips:** Varies by model. **Features:** Single action. Made in Canada by Para-Ordnance.

Price: Slim Hawg (2006) single stack .45 ACP, stainless, 6+1 . . . . **$1,043.00**
Price: Nite Hawg .45 ACP, black finish, 10+1 . . . . **$1,013.00**
Price: Warthog .45 ACP, Regal finish, 10+1 . . . . **$884.00**
Price: Stainless Warthog .45 ACP (2006), brushed finish, 10+1 . . . **$989.00**
Price: Hawg 9 9mm Regal finish, alloy frame, 12+1. . . . . **$884.00**
Price: Lite Hawg 9 9mm (2006) black finish, alloy frame, 12+1 . . . **$1,049.00**

Para-Ordnance Nite Hawg

Para-Ordnance Warthog

Para-Ordnance Lite Hawg

Phoenix Arms HP22

Ruger P89

Ruger P90

Ruger KP944D

PHOENIX ARMS HP22, HP25 AUTO PISTOLS
Caliber: 22 LR, 10-shot (HP22), 25 ACP, 10-shot (HP25). **Barrel:** 3".
Weight: 20 oz. **Length:** 5-1/2" overall. **Grips:** Checkered composition.
Sights: Blade front, adjustable rear. **Features:** Single action, exposed hammer; manual hold-open; button magazine release. Available in satin nickel, matte blue finish. Introduced 1993. Made in U.S.A. by Phoenix Arms.
Price: With gun lock **$130.00**
Price: HP Range kit with 5" bbl.,
locking case and assessories (1 Mag) **$171.00**
Price: HP Deluxe Range kit with 3" and 5" bbls.,
2 mags., case **$210.00**

ROCK RIVER ARMS BASIC CARRY AUTO PISTOL
Caliber: 45 ACP. **Barrel:** NA. **Weight:** NA. **Length:** NA. **Grips:** Rosewood, checkered. **Sights:** dovetail front sight, Heinie rear sight. **Features:** NM frame with 20-, 25- or 30-LPI checkered front strap, 5-inch slide with double serrations, lowered and flared ejection port, throated NM Kart barrel with NM bushing, match Commander hammer and match sear , aluminum speed trigger, dehorned, Parkerized finish, one magazine, accuracy guarantee. 3.5 lb. Trigger pull. Introduced 2006. Made in U.S.A. From Rock River Arms.
Price: PS2700 .... **$1,540.00**

RUGER P89 AUTOLOADING PISTOL
Caliber: 9mm Para., 15-shot magazine. **Barrel:** 4.50". **Weight:** 32 oz.
Length: 7.84" overall. **Grips:** Grooved black synthetic composition.
Sights: Square post front, square notch rear adjustable for windage, both with white dot inserts. **Features:** Double action, ambidextrous slide-mounted safety-levers. Slide 4140 chrome-moly steel or 400-series stainless steel, frame lightweight aluminum alloy. Ambidextrous magazine release. Blue, stainless steel. Introduced 1986; stainless 1990.
Price: P89, blue, extra mag and mag loader, plastic case locks ... **$475.00**
Price: KP89, stainless, extra mag and mag loader,
plastic case locks **$525.00**

Ruger P89D Decocker Autoloading Pistol
Similar to standard P89 except has ambidextrous decocking levers in place of regular slide-mounted safety. Decocking levers move firing pin inside slide where hammer cannot reach. Blue, stainless steel. Introduced 1990.
Price: P89D, blue, extra mag and mag loader, plastic case locks .. **$475.00**
Price: KP89D, stainless, extra mag and mag loader,
plastic case locks **$525.00**

RUGER P90 MANUAL SAFETY MODEL AUTOLOADING PISTOL
Caliber: 45 ACP, 8-shot magazine. **Barrel:** 4.50". **Weight:** 33.5 oz.
Length: 7.75" overall. **Grips:** Grooved black synthetic composition.
Sights: Square post front, square notch rear adjustable for windage, both with white dot. **Features:** Double action; ambidextrous slide-mounted safety-levers. Stainless steel only. Introduced 1991.
Price: P90 with extra mag, loader, case and gunlock **$565.00**
Price: P90 (blue) **$525.00**

Ruger KP90 Decocker Autoloading Pistol
Similar to the P90 except has a manual decocking system. Ambidextrous decocking levers move the firing pin inside the slide where the hammer cannot reach it. Available only in stainless steel. Overall length 7.75", weighs 33.5 oz. Introduced 1991.
Price: KP90D with case, extra mag and mag loading tool **$565.00**

Ruger KP94 Autoloading Pistol
Sized midway between full-size P-Series and compact KP94. 4.25" barrel, 7.5" overall length, weighs about 33 oz. KP94 manual safety model; KP94D is decocker-only in 40-caliber with 10-shot magazine. Slide gripping grooves roll over top of slide. KP94 has ambidextrous safety-levers; KP944D has ambidextrous decocking levers. Matte finish stainless slide, barrel, alloy frame. Also blue. Includes hard case and lock. Introduced 1994. Made in U.S.A. by Sturm, Ruger & Co.
Price: P944, blue (manual safety) **$495.00**
Price: KP944 (40-caliber) (manual safety-stainless) **$575.00**
Price: KP944D (40-caliber)-decocker only **$575.00**

Ruger KP512 MKIII

Ruger Mark III Hunter

Ruger KP9515

SIGARMS Revolution

RUGER P95 AUTOLOADING PISTOL

Caliber: 9mm Para., 15-shot magazine. **Barrel:** 3.9". **Weight:** 27 oz. **Length:** 7.25" overall. **Grips:** Grooved; integral with frame. **Sights:** Blade front, rear drift adjustable for windage; 3-dot system. **Features:** Molded polymer grip frame, stainless steel or chrome-moly slide. Suitable for +P+ ammunition. Safety model, decocker. Introduced 1996. Made in U.S.A. by Sturm, Ruger & Co. Comes with lockable plastic case, spare magazine, loader and lock, Picatinny rails.
Price: P95D15 decocker only **$425.00**
Price: P9515 stainless steel decocker only **$475.00**
Price: KP9515 safety model, stainless steel **$475.00**
Price: P9515 safety model, blued finish **$425.00**

RUGER MARK III STANDARD AUTOLOADING PISTOL

Caliber: 22 LR, 10-shot magazine. **Barrel:** 4-3/4", 5-1/2", 6", or 6-7/8". **Weight:** 35 oz. (4-3/4" bbl.). **Length:** 9" (4-3/4" bbl.). **Grips:** Checkered composition grip panels. **Sights:** Fixed, wide blade front, fixed rear. **Features:** Updated design of original Standard Auto and Mark II series. Standard models have lighter barrels. Target models have cocobolo grips; bull, target, competition, and hunter barrels; and adjustable sights. Introduced 2005.
Price: MKIII4, MKIII6 (blued) **$322.00**
Price: MKIII512 (blued) **$382.00**
Price: KMKIII512 (stainless) **$483.00**
Price: MKIII678 (blued) **$382.00**
Price: KMKIII678GC (stainless slabside barrel) **$555.00**
Price: KMKIII678GH (stainless fluted barrel) **$567.00**

Ruger 22/45 Mark III Pistol

Similar to other 22 Mark III autos except has Zytel grip frame that matches angle and magazine latch of Model 1911 45 ACP pistol. Available in 4" standard, 4-1/2" and 5-1/2" bull barrels. Comes with extra magazine, plastic case, lock. Introduced 1992. Hunter introduced 2006.
Price: P4MKIII, 4" bull barrel, adjustable sights **$307.00**
Price: P45GCMKIII, 4.5" bull barrel, fixed sights **$305.00**
Price: P512MKIII (5-1/2" bull blued barrel, adj. Sights) **$307.00**
Price: KP512MKIII (5-1/2" stainless bull barrel, adj. sights **$398.00**
Price: Hunter KP678HMKIII, 6-7/8" stainless fluted bull barrel,
adj. sights **$487.00**

SEECAMP LWS 32 STAINLESS DA AUTO

Caliber: 32 ACP Win. Silvertip, 6-shot magazine. **Barrel:** 2", integral with frame. **Weight:** 10.5 oz. **Length:** 4-1/8" overall. **Grips:** Glass-filled nylon. **Sights:** Smooth, no-snag, contoured slide and barrel top. **Features:** Aircraft quality 17-4 PH stainless steel. Inertia-operated firing pin.

Hammer fired double-action-only. Hammer automatically follows slide down to safety rest position after each shot, no manual safety needed. Magazine safety disconnector. Polished stainless. Introduced 1985. From L.W. Seecamp.
Price: **$425.00**

SEMMERLING LM-4 SLIDE-ACTION PISTOL

Caliber: 45 ACP, 4-shot magazine. **Barrel:** 2". **Weight:** 24 oz. **Length:** NA. **Grips:** NA. **Sights:** NA. **Features:** The Semmerling LM-4 is a super compact pistol employing a thumb activated slide mechanism (the slide is manually retracted between shots). From American Derringer Corp.
Price: **$2,635.00**

SIGARMS REVOLUTION PISTOLS

Caliber: 45 ACP, 8-shot magazine. **Barrel:** 5". **Weight:** 40.3 oz. **Length:** 8.65" overall. **Grips:** Checkered wood grips. **Sights:** Novak night sights. Blade front, drift adjustable rear for windage. **Features:** Single-action 1911. Hand-fitted dehorned stainless-steel frame and slide; match-grade barrel, hammer/sear set and trigger; 25-lpi front strap checkering, 20-lpi mainspring housing checkering. Beavertail grip safety with speed bump, extended thumb safety, firing pin safety and hammer intercept notch. Introduced 2005. XO series has contrast sights, Ergo Grip XT textured polymer grips. Target line features adjustable target night sights, match barrel, custom wood grips, non-railed frame in stainless or Nitron finishes. TTT series is two-tone 1911 with Nitron slide and black controls on stainless frame. Includes burled maple grips, adjustable combat night sights. STX line available from SIGARMS Custom Shop; two-tone 1911, non-railed, Nitron slide, stainless frame, burled maple grips. Polished cocking serrations, flat-top slide, magwell. Carry line has Novak night sights, lanyard attachment point, gray diamondwood or rosewood grips, 8+1 capacity. Compact series has 6+1 capacity, 7.7" OAL, 4.25" barrel, slim-profile wood grips, weighs 30.3 oz. RCS line (Revolution Compact SAS) is Customs Shop version with anti-snag dehorning. Stainless or Nitron finish, Novak night sights, slim-profile gray diamondwood or rosewood grips. 6+1 capacity. Imported from Germany by SIGARMS, Inc.
Price: Revolution Nitron finish, w/ or w/o Picatinny rail **$1,069.00**
Price: Revolution Stainless, w/ or w/o Picatinny rail **$1,050.00**
Price: Revolution XO Black **$890.00**
Price: Revolution XO Stainless, intr. 2006 . . . . **$860.00**
Price: Revolution Target Nitron, intr. 2006 . . . . **$1,100.00**
Price: Revolution TTT, intr. 2006 . . . . **$1,070.00**
Price: Revolution STX, intr. 2006 . . . . **$1,300.00**
Price: Revolution Carry Nitron, 4.25" barrel, intr. 2006 . . . . **$1,070.00**
Price: Revolution Compact, Nitron finish **$1,080.00**
Price: Revolution RCS, Nitron finish **$1,150.00**

SIG-Sauer P220

SIG-Sauer P245 Compact

SIG-Sauer Pro 2009

SIG-Sauer P229 Sport

SIG-Sauer P232

SIGARMS P220 AUTO PISTOLS

Caliber: 45 ACP, (7- or 8-shot magazine). **Barrel:** 4.4". **Weight:** 27.8 oz. **Length:** 7.8" overall. **Grips:** Checkered black plastic. **Sights:** Blade front, drift adjustable rear for windage. Optional Siglite night sights. **Features:** Double action. Stainless-steel slide, Nitron finish, alloy frame, M1913 Picatinny rail; safety system of decocking lever, automatic firing pin safety block, safety intercept notch, and trigger bar disconnector. Squared combat-type trigger guard. Slide stays open after last shot. Introduced 1976. P220 SAS Anti-Snag has dehorned stainless steel slide, front Siglite Night Sight, rounded trigger guard, dust cover, Custom Shop wood grips. Equinox line is Custom Shop product with Nitron stainless-steel slide with a black hard-anodized alloy frame, brush-polished flats and nickel accents. Truglo tritium fiber-optic front sight, rear Siglite night sight, gray laminated wood grips with checkering and stippling.
Imported from Germany by SIGARMS, Inc.

Price: P220R **$840.00**
Price: P220R Two-Tone, matte-stainless slide, black alloy frame . . . **$840.00**
Price: P220 Stainless **$935.00**
Price: P220 Crimson Trace, w/lasergrips **$1,150.00**
Price: P220 SAS Anti-Snag **$1,000.00**
Price: P220 Two-Tone SAO, single action, , intr. 2006, from **$929.00**
Price: P220R DAK (intr. 2006) **$840.00**
Price: P220R Equinox (intr. 2006) **$1,070.00**

SIGARMS P220 CARRY AUTO PISTOLS

Caliber: 45 ACP, 8-shot magazine. **Barrel:** 3.9". **Weight:** NA. **Length:** 7.1" overall. **Grips:** Checkered black plastic. **Sights:** Blade front, drift adjustable rear for windage. Optional Siglite night sights. **Features:** Similar to full-size P220, except is "Commander" size. Single stack, DA/SA operation, Nitron finish, Picatinny rail, and either post and dot contrast or 3-dot Siglite night sights. Introduced 2005. Imported from Germany by SIGARMS, Inc.

Price: P220 Carry, from **$840.00**
Price: P220 Carry Two-Tone, from **$915.00**
Price: P220 Carry Equinox, wood grips, two tone, from **$1,070.00**

SIG-Sauer P229 DA Auto Pistol

Similar to the P228 except chambered for 9mm Para. (10- or 15-round magazines), 40 S&W, 357 SIG (10- or 12-round magazines). Has 3.86" barrel, 7.1" overall length and 3.35" height. Weight is 32.4 oz. Introduced 1991. Frame made in Germany, stainless steel slide assembly made in U.S.; pistol assembled in U.S. From SIGARMS, Inc.

Price: P229R, from **$840.00**
Price: P229R Crimson Trace, w/lasergrips, from **$1,150.00**

SIG-SAUER SP2022 PISTOLS

Caliber: 9mm Para., 357 SIG, 40 S&W, 10-, 12-, or 15-shot magazines. **Barrel:** 3.9". **Weight:** 30.2 oz. **Length:** 7.4" overall. **Grips:** Composite and rubberized one-piece. **Sights:** Blade front, rear adjustable for windage. Optional Siglite night sights. **Features:** Polymer frame, stainless steel slide; integral frame accessory rail; replaceable steel frame rails; left- or right-handed magazine release, two interchangeable grips . From SIGARMS, Inc.

Price: SP2009, Nitron finish, from **$640.00**

SIG-Sauer P226 Pistols

Similar to the P220 pistol except has 4.4" barrel, measures 7.7" overall, weighs 34 oz. Chambered in 9mm, 357 SIG, or 40 S&W. X-Five series has factory tuned single-action trigger, 5" slide and barrel, ergonomic wood Nill grips with beavertail, ambidextrous thumb safety and stainless slide and frame with magwell, low-profile adjustable target sights, front cocking serrations and a 25-meter factory test target. Imported from Germany by SIGARMS, Inc.

Price: P226R, Nitron finish, night sights **$915.00**
Price: P226R Two Tone, Nitron/stainless finish **$969.00**
Price: P226 Stainless, from **$935.00**
Price: P226 X-Five **$2,500.00**
Price: P226 X-Five Tactical, Ilaflon finish, high cap, from **$1,500.00**

SIG-SAUER P232 PERSONAL SIZE PISTOL

Caliber: 380 ACP, 7-shot. **Barrel:** 3.6". **Weight:** 17.6-22.4 oz. **Length:** 6.6" overall. **Grips:** Checkered black composite. **Sights:** Blade front, rear adjustable for windage. **Features:** Double action/single action or DAO. Blowback operation, stationary barrel. Introduced 1997. Imported from Germany by SIGARMS, Inc.

Price: P232, blued **$519.00**
Price: P232 Stainless **$709.00**
Price: P232 Two-Tone **$539.00**

SIG-SAUER P239 PISTOL

Caliber: 9mm Para., 8-shot, 357 SIG 40 S&W, 7-shot magazine. **Barrel:** 3.6". **Weight:** 25.2 oz. **Length:** 6.6" overall. **Grips:** Checkered black composite. **Sights:** Blade front, rear adjustable for windage. Optional Siglite night sights. **Features:** SA/DA or DAO; blackened stainless steel slide, aluminum alloy frame. Introduced 1996. Made in U.S.A. by SIGARMS, Inc.

Price: P239 . . . . **$739.00**
Price: P239 Two-Tone, w/night sights, ... **$895.00**
Price: P239 DAK, double action **$739.00**

SIG-Sauer Mosquito

Smith & Wesson M&P

Smith & Wesson 457 TDA

Smith & Wesson 908

Smith & Wesson 4013 TSW

Smith & Wesson 410 DA

Smith & Wesson 910 DA

SIG-SAUER MOSQUITO PISTOL

Caliber: 22LR, 10-shot magazine. **Barrel:** 3.9". **Weight:** 24.6 oz. **Length:** 7.2" overall. **Grips:** Checkered black composite. **Sights:** Blade front, rear adjustable for windage. **Features:** Blowback operated, fixed barrel, polymer frame, slide-mounted ambidextrous safety. Introduced 2005. Made in U.S.A. by SIGARMS, Inc.

Price: Mosquito, blued **$390.00**
Price: Mosquito w/threaded barrel, intr. 2006 . . . . **$500.00**
Price: Mosquito Combat Green. **$460.00**

SMITH & WESSON M&P AUTO PISTOLS

Caliber: 9mm, 40 S&W, 357 SIG. **Barrel:** 4.25". **Weight:** 24.25 oz. **Length:** 7.5" overall. **Grips:** One-piece Xenoy, wraparound with straight backstrap. **Sights:** Ramp dovetail mount front; tritium sights optional; Novak Lo-mount Carry rear. **Features:** Zytel polymer frame, embedded stainless steel chassis; stainless steel slide and barrel, stainless steel structural components, black Melonite finish, reversible magazine catch, 3 interchangeable palmswell grip sizes, universal rail, sear deactivation lever, internal lock system, magazine disconnect. Ships with 2 magazines. Internal lock models available. Overall height: 5.5"; width: 1.2"; sight radius: 6.4". Introduced 2006. Made in U.S.A. by Smith & Wesson.

Price: M&P 40 S&W, 15+1 . . . . **$695.00**
Price: M&P 9mm, 17+1 . . . . **NA**
Price: M&P 357 SIG, 15+1 . . . . **NA**

SMITH & WESSON MODEL 457 TDA AUTO PISTOL

Caliber: 45 ACP, 7-shot magazine. **Barrel:** 3-3/4". **Weight:** 29 oz. **Length:** 7-1/4" overall. **Grips:** One-piece Xenoy, wraparound with straight backstrap. **Sights:** Post front, fixed rear, 3-dot system. **Features:** Aluminum alloy frame, matte blue carbon steel slide; bobbed hammer; smooth trigger. Introduced 1996. Made in U.S.A. by Smith & Wesson.

Price: Model 457, black matte finish **$681.00**
Price: Model 457S, matte finish stainless **$710.00**

SMITH & WESSON MODEL 908 AUTO PISTOL

Caliber: 9mm Para., 8-shot magazine. **Barrel:** 3-1/2". **Weight:** 24 oz. **Length:** 6-13/16". **Grips:** One-piece Xenoy, wraparound with straight backstrap. **Sights:** Post front, fixed rear, 3-dot system. **Features:** Aluminum alloy frame, matte blue carbon steel slide; bobbed hammer; smooth trigger. Introduced 1996. Made in U.S.A. by Smith & Wesson.

Price: Model 908, black matte finish **$617.00**
Price: Model 908S, stainless matte finish **$642.00**
Price: Model 908S Carry Combo, with holster **$656.00**

SMITH & WESSON MODEL 4013 TSW AUTO

Caliber: 40 S&W, 9-shot magazine. **Barrel:** 3-1/2". **Weight:** 26.8 oz. **Length:** 6 3/4" overall. **Grips:** Xenoy one-piece wraparound. **Sights:** Novak 3-dot system. **Features:** Traditional double-action system; stainless slide, alloy frame; fixed barrel bushing; ambidextrous decocker; reversible magazine catch, equipment rail. Introduced 1997. Made in U.S.A. by Smith & Wesson.

Price: Model 4013 TSW **$1,021.00**

SMITH & WESSON MODEL 410 DA AUTO PISTOL

Caliber: 40 S&W, 10-shot magazine. **Barrel:** 4". **Weight:** 28.5 oz. **Length:** 7.5". **Grips:** One-piece Xenoy, wraparound with straight backstrap. **Sights:** Post front, fixed rear; 3-dot system. **Features:** Aluminum alloy frame; blued carbon steel slide; traditional double action with left-side slide-mounted decocking lever. Introduced 1996. Made in U.S.A. by Smith & Wesson.

Price: Model 410, blued/black matte finish **$681.00**
Price: Model 410, blued/black matte finish **$681.00**
Price: Model 410S, stainless matte finish **$702.00**
Price: Model 410S, w/Crimson Trace lasergrips **$938.00**

SMITH & WESSON MODEL 910 DA AUTO PISTOL

Caliber: 9mm Para., 10-shot magazine. **Barrel:** 4". **Weight:** 28 oz. **Length:** 7-3/8" overall. **Grips:** One-piece Xenoy, wraparound with straight backstrap. **Sights:** Post front with white dot, fixed 2-dot rear. **Features:** Alloy frame, blue carbon steel slide. Slide-mounted decocking lever. Introduced 1995.

Price: Model 910, black matte frame **$617.00**
Price: Model 910S, stainless matte frame **$632.00**

Smith & Wesson 3913 LadySmith

Springfield Armory XD

Springfield Armory XD

SMITH & WESSON MODEL 3913 TRADITIONAL DOUBLE ACTIONS
Caliber: 9mm Para., 8-shot magazine. **Barrel:** 3-1/2". **Weight:** 24.8 oz. **Length:** 6-3/4" overall. **Grips:** One-piece Delrin wraparound, textured surface. **Sights:** Post front with white dot, Novak LoMount Carry with two dots. **Features:** TSW has aluminum alloy frame, stainless slide. Bobbed hammer with no half-cock notch; smooth .304" trigger with rounded edges. Straight backstrap. Equipment rail. Extra magazine included. Introduced 1989. The 3913-LS Ladysmith has frame that is upswept at the front, rounded trigger guard. Comes in frosted stainless steel with matching gray grips. Grips are ergonomically correct for a woman's hand. Novak LoMount Carry rear sight adjustable for windage. Extra magazine included. Introduced 1990.
Price: 3913TSW $876.00
Price: 3913-LS $901.00

SMITH & WESSON MODEL SW1911 PISTOLS
Caliber: 45 ACP, 8 rounds. **Barrel:** 5". **Weight:** 39 oz. **Length:** 8.7". **Grips:** Wood or rubber. **Sights:** Novak Lo-Mount Carry, white dot front. **Features:** Large stainless frame and slide with matte finish, single-side external safety. **No. 108284** has adjustable target rear sight, ambidextrous safety levers, 20-lpi checkered front strap, comes with two 8-round magazines. **DK model** (Doug Koenig) also has oversized magazine well, Doug Koenig speed hammer, flat competition speed trigger with overtravel stop, rosewood grips with Smith & Wesson silver medallions, oversized magazine well, special serial number run. **No. 108295** has olive drab Crimson Trace lasergrips. **No. 108299** has carbon-steel frame and slide with polished flats on slide, standard GI recoil guide, laminated double-diamond walnut grips with silver Smith & Wesson medallions, adjustable target sights. **Tactical Rail No. 108293** has a Picatinny rail, black Melonite finish, Novak Lo-Mount Carry Sights, scandium alloy frame. **Tactical Rail Stainless** introduced 2006. **SW1911PD** gun is Commander size, scandium-alloy frame, 4.25" barrel, 8" OAL, 28.0 oz., non-reflective black matte finish. **Gunsite** edition has scandium alloy frame, beveled edges, solid match aluminum trigger, Herrett's logoed tactical oval walnut stocks, special serial number run, brass bead Novak front sight. **SC** model has 4.25" barrel, scandium alloy frame, stainless-steel slide, non-reflective matte finish.
Price: SW1911 No. 108282 .... $1,008.00
Price: SW1911 No. 108284 .... $1,101.00
Price: SW1911 DK $1,274.00
Price: SW1911 No. 108295 .... $1,248.00
Price: SW1911 No. 108299 .... $1,047.00
Price: SW1911PD Tactical Rail No. 108293, scandium frame ... $1,120.00
Price: SW1911PD Tactical Rail No. 108303, stainless frame $1,057.00
Price: SW1911PD, scandium frame $1,080.00
Price: SW1911PD Gunsite, intr. 2006 .... $1,204.00
Price: SW1911SC $1,080.00

SMITH & WESSON MODEL 4040PD
Caliber: 40 S&W, 7 rounds. **Barrel:** 3.5". **Weight:** 25.6 oz. **Length:** 6.9". **Grips:** Rubber. **Sights:** Novak Lo-Mount Carry, white dot front.
Price: Scandium alloy frame $840.00

SMITH & WESSON ENHANCED SIGMA SERIES DAO PISTOLS
Caliber: 9mm Para., 40 S&W; 10-, 16-shot magazine. **Barrel:** 4". **Weight:** 24.7 oz. **Length:** 7-1/4" overall. **Grips:** Integral. **Sights:** White dot front, fixed rear; 3-dot system. Tritium night sights available. **Features:** Ergonomic polymer frame; low barrel centerline; internal striker firing system; corrosion-resistant slide; Teflon-filled, electroless-nickel coated magazine, equipment rail. Introduced 1994. Made in U.S.A. by Smith & Wesson.
Price: $409.00

SMITH & WESSON MODEL CS9 CHIEF'S SPECIAL AUTO
Caliber: 9mm Para., 7-shot magazine. **Barrel:** 3". **Weight:** 20.8 oz. **Length:** 6-1/4" overall. **Grips:** Hogue wraparound rubber. **Sights:** White dot front, fixed 2-dot rear. **Features:** Traditional double-action trigger mechanism. Alloy frame, stainless slide. Ambidextrous safety. Introduced 1999. Made in U.S.A. by Smith & Wesson.
Price: Stainless $777.00

SMITH & WESSON MODEL CS45 CHIEF'S SPECIAL AUTO
Caliber: 45 ACP, 6-shot magazine. **Weight:** 23.9 oz. **Features:** Introduced 1999. Made in U.S.A. by Smith & Wesson.
Price: Stainless $825.00

SMITH & WESSON MODEL SW990L
Caliber: 9mm Para. 4" barrel, (10 rounds); 40 S&W 4-1/8" barrel; 45 ACP 4.25" barrel; adj. sights. **Features:** Traditional double action satin stainless, black polymer frame, equipment rail, Saf-T-Trigger, interchangeable backstrap.
Price: 9mm, 40 S&W $729.00
Price: 45 ACP $773.00
Price: Compact: 9mm, 40 S&W, 3.5" barrel, 23 oz. $729.00

SPRINGFIELD ARMORY XD POLYMER AUTO PISTOLS
Caliber: 9mm Para., 357 SIG, 40 S&W, 45 ACP, 45 GAP. **Barrel:** 3", 4", 5". **Weight:** 20.5-31 oz. **Length:** 6.26-8" overall. **Grips:** Textured polymer. **Sights:** Varies by model; Fixed sights are dovetail front and rear steel 3-dot units. **Features:** Three sizes in X-Treme Duty (XD) line: Sub-Compact (3" barrel), Service (4" barrel), Tactical (5" barrel). Three ported models available. Ergonomic polymer frame, hammer-forged barrel, no-tool disassembly, ambidextrous magazine release, visual/tactile loaded chamber indicator, visual/tactile striker status indicator, grip safety, XD gear system included. Introduced 2004. XD 45 introduced 2006. From Springfield Armory.
Price: Sub-Compact Black 9mm, fixed sights $536.00
Price: Sub-Compact Black 9mm/40 S&W, Neinie night sights..... $626.00
Price: Sub-Compact Bi-Tone 9mm/40 S&W, fixed sights......... $566.00
Price: Sub-Compact OD Green 9mm/40 S&W, fixed sights $536.00
Price: Service Black 9mm/40 S&W/357 SIG, fixed sights $536.00
Price: Service Black 45 ACP, fixed sights................. $559.00
Price: Service Black 45 GAP, fixed sights.................. $536.00
Price: Service Black 9mm/40 S&W, Neinie night sights......... $626.00
Price: Service Bi-Tone 9mm/40 S&W/357 SIG/45 GAP, fixed sights $566.00
Price: Service Bi-Tone 45 ACP, fixed sights $595.00
Price: Service OD Green 9mm/40 S&W/357 SIG/45 GAP,
fixed sights. $536.00
Price: V-10 Ported Black 9mm/40 S&W/357 SIG $566.00
Price: Tactical Black 45 ACP, fixed sights $595.00
Price: Tactical Black 9mm/40 S&W/357 SIG, fixed sights $566.00
Price: Tactical Bi-Tone 45 ACP/45 GAP, fixed sights $626.00/ $595.00
Price: Tactical OD Green 9mm/40 S&W/357 SIG/45 GAP,
fixed sights. $566.00
Price: Tactical OD Green 45 ACP, fixed sights $595.00

**Springfield Armory
1911A1 Standard**

**Springfield Armory
Full-Size 1911A1**

**Springfield Armory
Micro-Compact**

Springfield Armory TRP

SPRINGFIELD ARMORY CUSTOM LOADED FULL-SIZE 1911A1 AUTO PISTOL

Caliber: 9mm Para., 9-shot; 45 ACP, 7-shot. **Barrel:** 5". **Weight:** 30-42 oz. **Length:** 8.5" overall. **Grips:** Cocobolo, polymer. **Sights:** Fixed 3-dot system or adjustable. **Features:** Beveled magazine well; lowered and flared ejection port. All forged parts, including frame, barrel, slide. All new production. Introduced 1990. From Springfield Armory.
Price: Tactical Combat Black Stainless Steel, fixed sights **$904.00**
Price: Stainless Steel, fixed sights **$902.00**
Price: Service Model 5" Lightweight, bi-tone finish. **$934.00**
Price: Stainless Steel, adjustable target sights **$966.00**
Price: Black Stainless, adjustable Bo-Mar rear, 3-dot tritium **$1,124.00**
Price: Stainless Steel 9mm, fixed combat sights **$976.00**

SPRINGFIELD ARMORY GI .45 1911-A1 AUTO PISTOLS

Caliber: 45 ACP; 6-, 7-, 13-shot magazines. **Barrel:** 3", 4", 5". **Weight:** 28-36 oz. **Length:** 5.5-8.5" overall. **Grips:** Checkered double-diamond walnut, "U.S" logo. **Sights:** Fixed GI style. **Features:** Similar to WWII GI-issue 45s at hammer, beavertail, mainspring housing. From Springfield Armory.
Price: GI .45 4" Lightweight Champion, 7+1, 28 oz. **$564.00**
Price: GI .45 5" High Capacity, 13+1, 36 oz. **$617.00**
Price: GI .45 5" OD Green, 7+1, 36 oz. **$564.00**
Price: GI .45 3" Micro Compact, 6+1, 32 oz. **$608.00**

SPRINGFIELD ARMORY MIL-SPEC 1911-A1 AUTO PISTOLS

Caliber: 38 Super, 9-shot magazines; 45 ACP, 7-shot magazines. **Barrel:** 5". **Weight:** 35.6-39 oz. **Length:** 8.5-8.625" overall. **Features:** Similar to GI 45s. From Springfield Armory.
Price: Mil-Spec Parkerized, 7+1, 35.6 oz. **$660.00**
Price: Mil-Spec Stainless Steel, 7+1, 36 oz. **$724.00**
Price: Mil-Spec 38 Super, Nickel finish, 9+1, 39 oz. **$1,254.00**

Springfield Armory Custom Loaded Champion 1911-A1 Pistol

Similar to standard 1911A1, slide and barrel are 4". 7.5" OAL. Available in 45 ACP only. Novak Night Sights. Delta hammer and cocobolo grips. Parkerized or stainless. Introduced 1989.
Price: Stainless, 34 oz. **$952.00**
Price: Lightweight, 28 oz **$913.00**

Springfield Armory Custom Loaded Ultra Compact Pistol

Similar to 1911A1 Compact, shorter slide, 3.5" barrel, 6+1, 7" OAL. Beavertail grip safety, beveled magazine well, fixed sights. Videki speed trigger, flared ejection port, stainless steel frame, blued slide, match grade barrel, rubber grips. Introduced 1996. From Springfield Armory.
Price: Stainless Steel **$952.00**

SPRINGFIELD ARMORY CUSTOM LOADED MICRO-COMPACT 1911A1 PISTOL

Caliber: 45 ACP, 6+1 capacity. **Barrel:** 3" 1:16 LH. **Weight:** 24-32 oz. **Length:** 4.7". **Grips:** Slimline cocobolo. **Sights:** Novak LoMount tritium. Dovetail front. **Features:** Aluminum hard-coat anodized alloy frame, forged steel slide, forged barrel, ambi-thumb safety, Extreme Carry Bevel dehorning. Lockable plastic case, 2 magazines.
Price: Bi-Tone Operator w/light rail **$1,284.00**
Price: Lightweight Bi-Tone **$1,220.00**

SPRINGFIELD ARMORY CUSTOM LOADED LONG SLIDE 1911A1 PISTOL

Caliber: 45 ACP, 7+1 capacity. **Barrel:** 6" 1:16 LH. **Weight:** 41 oz. **Length:** 9.5". **Grips:** Slimline cocobolo. **Sights:** Dovetail front; fully adjustable target rear. **Features:** Longer sight radius, 7.9".
Price: Bi-Tone Operator w/light rail **$1,097.00**

Springfield Armory TRP Pistols

Similar to 1911A1 except 45 ACP only, checkered front strap and main-spring housing, Novak Night Sight combat rear sight and matching dove-tailed front sight, tuned, polished extractor, oversize barrel link; lightweight speed trigger and combat action job, match barrel and bushing, extended ambidextrous thumb safety and fitted beavertail grip safety. Checkered cocobolo wood grips, comes with two Wilson 7-shot magazines. Frame is engraved "Tactical," both sides of frame with "TRP." Introduced 1998. TRP-Pro Model meets FBI specifications for SWAT Hostage Rescue Team. From Springfield Armory.
Price: Standard with Armory Kote finish **$1,606.00**
Price: Standard, stainless steel **$1,606.00**
Price: Standard with Operator Light Rail Armory Kote **$1,689.00**
Price: TRP-Pro, Armory Kote finish **$2,395.00**

Springfield Armory Loaded Operator 1911-A1Pistol

Similar to Full-Size 1911A1, except light-mounting rail is forged into frame. From Springfield Armory.
Price: Loaded Full-Size MC Operator, 42 oz., 8.5" OAL **$1,254.00**
Price: TRP Light Rail Armory Kote, 42 oz. **$1,689.00**
Price: Micro Compact LW, w/XML Mini Light , 32 oz., 6.7 OAL . . **$1,284.00**

Springfield Armory Trophy Match 1911A1 Pistol

Similar to Full Size model, 5" match barrel and slide, fully adjustable sights. From Springfield Armory.
Price: Trophy Match 45 ACP, stainless **$1,452.00**

Taurus PT-22

Taurus PT-24

Taurus PT-92

Taurus PT-100

Taurus PT-132 Millennium Pro

Taurus PT-138 Millennium Pro

TAURUS MODEL PT1911 PISTOLS
Caliber: 45 ACP. **Barrel:** 5". **Weight:** 32 oz. **Length:** 8.75". **Grips:** Checkered wood. **Sights:** Adjustable Heinie rear, blade front. **Features:** SA/DA; Steel slide, alloy frame, ventilated trigger. Bumper pads on magazines. Introduced 2005. Imported from Brazil by Taurus International.
Price: Blued, 8+1 . . . . **$599.00**
Price: Stainless **$619.00**

TAURUS MODEL PT-22/PT-25 AUTO PISTOLS
Caliber: 22 LR, 8-shot (PT 22); 25 ACP, 9-shot (PT 25). **Barrel:** 2.75". **Weight:** 12.3 oz. **Length:** 5.25" overall. **Grips:** Smooth rosewood or mother-of-pearl. **Sights:** Fixed. **Features:** Double action. Tip-up barrel for loading, cleaning. Blue, nickel, duo-tone or blue with gold accents. Introduced 1992. Made in U.S.A. by Taurus International.
Price: 22 LR, 25 ACP, blue, nickel or with duo-tone finish with
rosewood grips **$227.00**
Price: 22 LR, 25 ACP, blue with gold trim, rosewood grips **$242.00**
Price: 22 LR, 25 ACP, blue, nickel or duo-tone finish with checkered
wood grips **$227.00**
Price: 22 LR, 25 ACP, blue with gold trim, mother-of-pearl grips . . . **$258.00**

TAURUS MODEL PT-24/7
Caliber: 9mm, 40 S&W, 45 ACP. **Barrel:** 4". **Weight:** 27.2 oz. **Length:** 7-1/8". **Grips:** "Ribber" rubber-finned overlay on polymer. **Sights:** Adjustable. **Features:** SA/DA; accessory rail, four safeties, blue or stainless finish. One-piece guide rod, flush-fit magazine, flared bushingless barrel, Picatinny accessory rail, manual safety, user changeable sights, loaded chamber indicator, tuned ejector and lowered port, one piece guide rod and flat wound captive spring. Introduced 2003. Long Slide models have 5" barrels, measure 8-1/8" overall, weigh 27.2 oz. Imported from Brazil by Taurus International.
Price: 9BP, 9mm, blued, 10+1 or 17+1 . . . . **$485.00**
Price: 40BP, 40 S&W, blued, 10+1 or 15+1. . . . . **$485.00**
Price: 40SSP, 40 S&W, stainless slide, 10+1 or 15+1 . . . . **$499.00**
Price: 45BP, 45 ACP, blued, 10+1 or 12+1 . . . . **$485.00**
Price: Long Slide 40B, 40 S&W, blued, 10+1 or 15+1 . . . . **$485.00**
Price: Long Slide 45B, 45 ACP, blued, 10+1 or 12+1 . . . . **$485.00**
Price: Long Slide 9SS, 9mm, stainless, 10+1 or 17+1 . . . . **$499.00**

TAURUS MODEL PT-92 AUTO PISTOL
Caliber: 9mm Para., 10- or 17-shot mags. **Barrel:** 5". **Weight:** 34 oz. **Length:** 8.5" overall. **Grips:** Checkered rubber, rosewood, mother-of-pearl. **Sights:** Fixed notch rear. 3-dot sight system. Also offered with micrometer-click adjustable night sights. **Features:** Double action,

ambidextrous 3-way hammer drop safety, allows cocked & locked carry. Blue, stainless steel, blue with gold highlights, stainless steel with gold highlights, forged aluminum frame, integral key-lock. .22 LR conversion kit available. Imported from Brazil by Taurus International.
Price: Blued or Stainless. . . . . **$602.00 to $664.00**

Taurus Model PT-99 Auto Pistol
Similar to PT-92, fully adjustable rear sight.
Price: Blue . . . . **$617.00 to $633.00**
Price: 22 Conversion kit for PT 92 and PT99
(includes barrel and slide) **$266.00**

TAURUS MODEL PT-100/101 AUTO PISTOL
Caliber: 40 S&W, 10- or 11-shot mags. **Barrel:** 5". **Weight:** 34 oz. **Length:** 8-1/2". **Grips:** Checkered rubber, rosewood, mother-of-pearl. **Sights:** 3-dot fixed or adjustable; night sights available. **Features:** Single/double action with three-position safety/decocker. Reintroduced in 2001. Imported by Taurus International.
Price: PT100 . . . . **$602.00 to $664.00**
Price: PT101, adjustable rear sight . . . . **$617.00 to $633.00**

TAURUS MODEL PT-111 MILLENNIUM PRO AUTO PISTOL
Caliber: 9mm Para., 10- or 12-shot mags. **Barrel:** 3.25". **Weight:** 18.7 oz. **Length:** 6-1/8" overall. **Grips:** Checkered polymer. **Sights:** 3-dot fixed; night sights available. Low profile, 3-dot combat. **Features:** Double action only, polymer frame, matte stainless or blue steel slide, manual safety, integral key-lock. Deluxe models with wood grip inserts.
Price: . . . . **$395.00 to $410.00**
Price: Titanium Slide **$499.00**

TAURUS PT-132 MILLENNIUM PRO AUTO PISTOL
Caliber: 32 ACP, 10-shot mag. **Barrel:** 3.25". **Weight:** 18.7 oz. **Grips:** Polymer. **Sights:** 3-dot fixed; night sights available. **Features:** Double-action-only, polymer frame, matte stainless or blue steel slide, manual safety, integral key-lock action. Introduced 2001.
Price: . . . . **$395.00 to $410.00**

TAURUS PT-138 MILLENNIUM PRO SERIES
Caliber: 380 ACP, 10- or 12-shot mags. **Barrel:** 3.25". **Weight:** 18.7 oz. **Grips:** Polymer. **Sights:** Fixed 3-dot fixed. **Features:** Double-action-only, polymer frame, matte stainless or blue steel slide, manual safety, integral key-lock.
Price: . . . . **$395.00 to $410.00**

Taurus PT-140 Millennium Pro

Taurus PT-145 Millennium Pro

Taurus PT-911

Taurus PT-940

Taurus PT-945

U.S. Fire Arms 1911 Commercial

U.S. Fire Arms 1911 Military

TAURUS PT-140 MILLENNIUM PRO AUTO PISTOL

Caliber: 40 S&W, 10-shot mag. **Barrel:** 3.25". **Weight:** 18.7 oz. **Grips:** Checkered polymer. **Sights:** 3-dot fixed; night sights available. **Features:** Double action only; matte stainless or blue steel slide, black polymer frame, manual safety, integral key-lock action. From Taurus International.
Price: . . . . **$410.00 to $425.00**

TAURUS PT-145 MILLENNIUM AUTO PISTOL

Caliber: 45 ACP, 10-shot mag. **Barrel:** 3.27". **Weight:** 23 oz. **Stock:** Checkered polymer. **Sights:** 3-dot fixed; night sights available. **Features:** Double-action only, matte stainless or blue steel slide, black polymer frame, manual safety, integral key-lock. Compact model is 6+1 with a 3.25" barrel, weighs 20.8 oz. From Taurus International.
Price: PT-145, blued or stainless. . . . . **$410.00 to $425.00**
Price: PT-745 Compact, blued or stainless, intr. 2005 . **$410.00 to $425.00**

TAURUS MODEL PT-911 AUTO PISTOL

Caliber: 9mm Para., 10-shot mag. **Barrel:** 4". **Weight:** 28.2 oz. **Length:** 7" overall. **Grips:** Checkered rubber, rosewood, mother-of-pearl. **Sights:** Fixed, 3-dot blue or stainless; night sights optional. **Features:** Double action, semi-auto ambidextrous 3-way hammer drop safety, allows cocked & locked carry. Blue, stainless steel, blue with gold highlights, or stainless steel with gold highlights, forged aluminum frame, integral key-lock.
Price: . . . . **$547.00 to $625.00**

TAURUS MODEL PT-940 AUTO PISTOL

Caliber: 40 S&W, 10-shot mag. **Barrel:** 3-5/8". **Weight:** 28.2 oz. **Length:** 7" overall. **Grips:** Checkered rubber, rosewood or mother-of-pearl. **Sights:** Fixed, 3-dot blue or stainless; night sights optional. **Features:** Double action, semi-auto ambidextrous 3-way hammer drop safety, allows cocked & locked carry. Blue, stainless steel, blue with gold highlights, or stainless steel with gold hightlights, forged aluminum frame, integral key-lock.
Price: . . . . **$547.00 to $609.00**

TAURUS MODEL PT-945/PT38S SERIES

Caliber: 45 ACP, 8-shot mag. **Barrel:** 4.25". **Weight:** 28.2/29.5 oz. **Length:** 7.48" overall. **Grips:** Checkered rubber, rosewood or mother-of-pearl. **Sights:** Fixed, 3-dot; night sights optional. **Features:** Double-action with ambidextrous 3-way hammer drop safety allows cocked & locked carry. Forged aluminum frame, PT-945C has ported barrel/slide. Blue, stainless, blue with gold highlights, stainless with gold highlights, integral key-lock. Introduced 1995. 38 Super line based on PT-945 frame introduced 2005. PT38S series is 10+1, 30 oz., 7.5" overall. Imported by Taurus International.
Price: PT-945. . . . . **$586.00 to $648.00**
Price: PT-38S. . . . . **$586.00 to $664.00**

THOMPSON CUSTOM 1911A1 AUTOMATIC PISTOL

Caliber: 45 ACP, 7-shot magazine. **Barrel:** 4.3". **Weight:** 34 oz. **Length:** 8" overall. **Grips:** Checkered laminate grips with a Thompson bullet logo inlay. **Sights:** Front and rear sights are black with serrations and are dovetailed into the slide. **Features:** Machined from 420 stainless steel, matte finish. Thompson bullet logo on slide. Flared ejection port, angled front and rear serrations on slide, 20-lpi checkered mainspring housing and frontstrap. Adjustable trigger, combat hammer, stainless steel full-length recoil guide rod, extended beavertail grip safety; extended magazine release; checkered slide-stop lever. Made in U.S.A. by Kahr Arms.
Price: 1911CC (2006), stainless frame. **$775.00**
Price: 1911TC, 5", 39 oz., 8.5" overall, stainless frame **$775.00**
Price: 1911CCF (2006), 27 oz., aluminum frame. **$775.00**
Price: 1911CAF, 5", 31.5 oz., 8.5" overall, aluminum frame. **$775.00**

U.S. FIRE ARMS 1910 COMMERCIAL MODEL AUTOMATIC PISTOL

Caliber: 45 ACP, 7-shot magazine. **Barrel:** 5". **Weight:** NA. **Length:** NA. **Grips:** Browning original wide design, full checkered diamond walnut grips. **Sights:** Fixed. **Features:** High polish Armory Blue, fire blue appointments, 1905 patent dates, grip safety, small contoured checkered thumb safety and round 1905 fire blue hammer with hand cut checkering. Introduced 2006. Made in U.S.A. by United States Fire Arms Mfg. Co.
Price: **$1,895.00**

U.S. FIRE ARMS 1911 MILITARY MODEL AUTOMATIC PISTOL

Caliber: 45 ACP, 7-shot magazine. **Barrel:** 5". **Weight:** NA. **Length:** NA. **Grips:** Browning original wide design, full checkered diamond walnut grips. **Sights:** Fixed. **Features:** Military polish Armory Blue, fire blue appointments, 1905 patent dates, grip safety, small contoured checkered thumb safety and round 1905 fire blue hammer with hand cut checkering. Introduced 2006. Made in U.S.A. by United States Fire Arms Mfg. Co.
Price: **$1,895.00**

U.S. Fire Arms Super 38

U.S. Fire Arms Ace 22 LR

Walther PPK/S

Walther PPK

Walther P99

Walther P22

Wilkinson Sherry

U.S. FIRE ARMS SUPER 38 AUTOMATIC PISTOL
Caliber: 38 Auto, 9-shot magazine. **Barrel:** 5". **Weight:** NA. **Length:** NA. **Grips:** Browning original wide design, full checkered diamond walnut grips. **Sights:** Fixed. **Features:** Armory blue, fire blue appointments, 1913 patent date, grip safety, small contoured checkered thumb safety and spur 1911 hammer with hand cut checkering. Supplied with two Super 38 Auto. mags. Super .38 roll mark on base. Introduced 2006. Made in U.S.A. by United States Fire Arms Mfg. Co.
Price: **$1,995.00**

U.S. FIRE ARMS ACE .22 LONG RIFLE AUTOMATIC PISTOL
Caliber: 22 LR, 10-shot magazine. **Barrel:** 5". **Weight:** NA. **Length:** NA. **Grips:** Browning original wide design, full checkered diamond walnut grips. **Sights:** Fixed. **Features:** Armory blue commercial finish, fire blue appointments, 1913 patent date, grip safety, small contoured checkered thumb safety and spur 1911 hammer with hand cut checkering. Supplied with two magazines. Ace roll mark on base. Introduced 2006. Made in U.S.A. by United States Fire Arms Mfg. Co.
Price: **$1,995.00**

WALTHER PPK/S AMERICAN AUTO PISTOL
Caliber: 380 ACP, 7-shot magazine. **Barrel:** 3.27". **Weight:** 23-1/2 oz. **Length:** 6.1" overall. **Stocks:** Checkered plastic. **Sights:** Fixed, white markings. **Features:** Double action; manual safety blocks firing pin and drops hammer; chamber loaded indicator on 32 and 380; extra finger rest magazine provided. Made in the United States. Introduced 1980.
Price: 380 ACP only, blue **$563.00**
Price: As above, 32 ACP or 380 ACP, stainless **$543.00**

Walther PPK American Auto Pistol
Similar to Walther PPK/S except weighs 21 oz., has 6-shot capacity. Made in the U.S. Introduced 1986.
Price: Stainless, 32 ACP or 380 ACP **$543.00**
Price: Blue, 380 ACP only **$543.00**

WALTHER P99 AUTO PISTOL
Caliber: 9mm Para., 9x21, 40 S&W,10-shot magazine. **Barrel:** 4". **Weight:** 25 oz. **Length:** 7" overall. **Grips:** Textured polymer. **Sights:** Blade front (comes with three interchangeable blades for elevation adjustment), micrometer rear adjustable for windage. **Features:** Double-action mechanism with trigger safety, decock safety, internal striker safety; chamber loaded indicator; ambidextrous magazine release levers; polymer frame with interchangeable backstrap inserts. Comes with two

magazines. Introduced 1997. Imported from Germany by Smith & Wesson U.S.A.
Price: **$665.00**

WALTHER P22 PISTOL
Caliber: 22 LR. **Barrel:** 3.4", 5". **Weight:** 19.6 oz. (3.4"), 20.3 oz. (5"). **Length:** 6.26", 7.83". **Grips:** NA. **Sights:** Interchangeable white dot, front, 2-dot adjustable, rear. **Features:** A rimfire version of the Walther P99 pistol, available in nickel slide with black frame, or green frame with black slide versions. Made in Germany and distributed in the U.S. by Smith & Wesson.
Price: From **$295.00**

WILKINSON SHERRY AUTO PISTOL
Caliber: 22 LR, 8-shot magazine. **Barrel:** 2-1/8". **Weight:** 9-1/4 oz. **Length:** 4-3/8" overall. **Grips:** Checkered black plastic. **Sights:** Fixed, groove. **Features:** Crossbolt safety locks the sear into the hammer. Available in all-blue finish or blue slide and trigger with gold frame. Introduced 1985.
Price: **$280.00**

WILKINSON LINDA AUTO PISTOL
Caliber: 9mm Para. **Barrel:** 8-5/16". **Weight:** 4 lbs., 13 oz. **Length:** 12-1/4" overall. **Grips:** Checkered black plastic pistol grip, walnut forend. **Sights:** Protected blade front, aperture rear. **Features:** Semi-auto only. Straight blowback action. Crossbolt safety. Removable barrel. From Wilkinson Arms.
Price: **$675.00**

Includes models suitable for several forms of competition and other sporting purposes.

Baer 1911 Ultimate Master

Baer 1911 Bullseye Wadcutter

Colt Gold Cup Trophy

Colt Special Combat Government

BAER 1911 ULTIMATE MASTER COMBAT PISTOL

Caliber: 38 Super, 400 Cor-Bon 45 ACP (others available), 10-shot magazine. **Barrel:** 5", 6"; Baer NM. **Weight:** 37 oz. **Length:** 8.5" overall. **Grips:** Checkered cocobolo. **Sights:** Baer dovetail front, low-mount Bo-Mar rear with hidden leaf. **Features:** Full-house competition gun. Baer forged NM blued steel frame and double serrated slide; Baer triple port, tapered cone compensator; fitted slide to frame; lowered, flared ejection port; Baer reverse recoil plug; full-length guide rod; recoil buff; beveled magazine well; Baer Commander hammer, sear; Baer extended ambidextrous safety, extended ejector, checkered slide stop, beavertail grip safety with pad, extended magazine release button; Baer speed trigger. Made in U.S.A. by Les Baer Custom, Inc.

Price: 45 ACP Compensated	$2,599.00
Price: 38 Super Compensated	$2,789.00
Price: 6" 45 ACP	$2,586.00
Price: 6" 38 Super	$2,780.00
Price: 6" 400 Cor-Bon	$2,668.00
Price: 5" 45 ACP	$2,540.00
Price: 5" 38 Super	$2,699.00
Price: 5" 400 Cor-Bon	$2,589.00

BAER 1911 NATIONAL MATCH HARDBALL PISTOL

Caliber: 45 ACP, 7-shot magazine. **Barrel:** 5". **Weight:** 37 oz. **Length:** 8.5" overall. **Grips:** Checkered walnut. **Sights:** Baer dovetail front with under-cut post, low-mount Bo-Mar rear with hidden leaf. **Features:** Baer NM forged steel frame, double serrated slide and barrel with stainless bushing; slide fitted to frame; Baer match trigger with 4-lb. pull; polished feed ramp, throated barrel; checkered front strap, arched mainspring housing; Baer beveled magazine well; lowered, flared ejection port; tuned extractor; Baer extended ejector, checkered slide stop; recoil buff. Made in U.S.A. by Les Baer Custom, Inc.
Price: $1,689.00

Baer 1911 Bullseye Wadcutter Pistol

Similar to National Match Hardball except designed for wadcutter loads only. Polished feed ramp and barrel throat; Bo-Mar rib on slide; full length recoil rod; Baer speed trigger with 3-1/2-lb. pull; Baer deluxe hammer and sear; Baer beavertail grip safety with pad; flat mainspring housing checkered 20 lpi. Blue finish; checkered walnut grips. Made in U.S.A. by Les Baer Custom, Inc.
Price: From $1,710.00
Price: With 6" barrel, from $1,865.00

BF CLASSIC PISTOL

Caliber: Customer orders chamberings. **Barrel:** 8-15" Heavy Match Grade with 11-degree target crown. **Weight:** Approx 3.9 lbs. **Length:** from 16" overall. **Grips:** Thumbrest target style. **Sights:** Bo-Mar/Bond ScopeRib I Combo with hooded post front adjustable for height and width, rear notch available in .032", .062", .080" and .100" widths; 1/2-MOA clicks. **Features:** Hand fitted and headspaced, drilled and tapped for scope mount. Etched receiver; gold-colored trigger. Introduced 1988. Made in U.S.A. by E. Arthur Brown Co. Inc.
Price: $789.00

COLT GOLD CUP

Caliber: 45 ACP. **Barrel:** 5". **Weight:** 39 oz. **Sights:** Dovetail front, BoMar-style rear; or Colt adjustable staked front. **Features:** Stainless or blue finish; adjustable trigger; furnished with 7- and 8-round magazines.
Price: Blued $1,300.00
Price: Stainless $1,400.00

COLT MODEL 1991/2991

Caliber: 45 ACP, 38 Super. **Barrel:** 5". **Weight:** 39 oz. **Sight:** Fixed white dot style. **Features:** Stainless or blue finish; furnished with 7-round magazines.
Price: .... $764.00 to $866.00

COLT GOLD CUP MODEL O PISTOL

Caliber: 45 ACP, 8-shot magazine. **Barrel:** 5", with new design bushing. **Weight:** 39 oz. **Length:** 8-1/2". **Grips:** Checkered rubber composite with silver-plated medallion. **Sights:** Patridge-style front, Bo-Mar-style rear adjustable for windage and elevation, sight radius 6-3/4". **Features:** Arched or flat housing; wide, grooved trigger with adjustable stop; ribbed-top slide, hand fitted, with improved ejection port.
Price: Blue $992.00
Price: Stainless $1,039.00

COLT SPECIAL COMBAT GOVERNMENT

Caliber: 45 ACP, 38 Super. **Barrel:** 5". **Weight:** 39 oz. **Length:** 8-1/2". **Grips:** Rosewood w/double diamond checkering pattern. **Sights:** Clark dovetail, front; Bo-Mar adjustable, rear. **Features:** A competition-ready pistol with enhancements such as skeletonized trigger, upswept grip safety, custom tuned action, polished feed ramp. Blue or satin nickel finish. Introduced 2003. Made in U.S.A. by Colt's Mfg. Co.
Price: $1,498.00

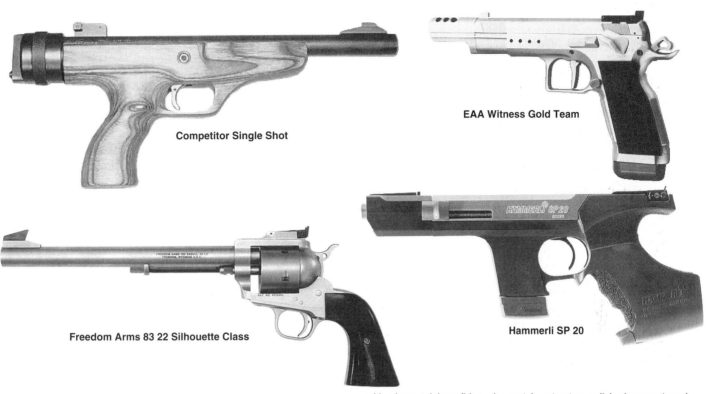

Competitor Single Shot

EAA Witness Gold Team

Freedom Arms 83 22 Silhouette Class

Hammerli SP 20

COMPETITOR SINGLE SHOT PISTOL

Caliber: 22 LR through 50 Action Express, including belted magnums. **Barrel:** 14" standard; 10.5" silhouette; 16" optional. **Weight:** About 59 oz. (14" bbl.). **Length:** 15.12" overall. **Grips:** Ambidextrous; synthetic (standard) or laminated or natural wood. **Sights:** Ramp front, adjustable rear. **Features:** Rotary canon-type action cocks on opening; cammed ejector; interchangeable barrels, ejectors. Adjustable single stage trigger, sliding thumb safety and trigger safety. Matte blue finish. Introduced 1988. From Competitor Corp., Inc.
Price: 14", standard calibers, synthetic grip **$480.00**

CZ 75 CHAMPION COMPETITION PISTOL

Caliber: 9mm Para., 40 S&W, 16-shot mag. **Barrel:** 4.4". **Weight:** 2.5 lbs. **Length:** 9.4" overall. **Grips:** Black rubber. **Sights:** Blade front, fully adjustable rear. **Features:** Single-action trigger mechanism; three-port compensator (40 S&W, 9mm have two port) full-length guide rod; extended magazine release; ambidextrous safety; flared magazine well; fully adjustable match trigger. Introduced 1999. Imported from the Czech Republic by CZ-USA.
Price: Dual-tone finish **$1,646.00**

EAA WITNESS GOLD TEAM AUTO

Caliber: 9mm Para., 9x21, 38 Super, 40 S&W, 45 ACP. **Barrel:** 5.1". **Weight:** 44 oz. **Length:** 10.5" overall. **Grips:** Checkered walnut, competition-style. **Sights:** Square post front, fully adjustable rear. **Features:** Triple-chamber cone compensator; competition SA trigger; extended safety and magazine release; competition hammer; beveled magazine well; beavertail grip. Hand-fitted major components. Hard chrome finish. Match-grade barrel. From E.A.A. Custom Shop. Introduced 1992. From European American Armory.
Price: **$1,699.00**

ENTRÉPRISE TOURNAMENT SHOOTER MODEL I

Caliber: 45 ACP, 10-shot mag. **Barrel:** 6". **Weight:** 40 oz. **Length:** 8.5" overall. **Grips:** Black ultra-slim double diamond checkered synthetic. **Sights:** Dovetailed Patridge front, adjustable rear. **Features:** Oversized magazine release button; flared magazine well; fully machined parallel slide rails; front and rear slide serrations; serrated top of slide; stainless ramped bull barrel with fully supported chamber; full-length guide rod with plug; stainless firing pin; match extractor; polished ramp; tuned match extractor; black oxide. Introduced 1998. Made in U.S.A. by Entréprise Arms.
Price: **$2,300.00**
Price: TSMIII (Satin chrome finish, two-piece guide rod) **$2,700.00**

FREEDOM ARMS MODEL 83 22 FIELD GRADE SILHOUETTE CLASS

Caliber: 22 LR, 5-shot cylinder. **Barrel:** 10". **Weight:** 63 oz. **Length:** 15.5" overall. **Grips:** Black Micarta. **Sights:** Removable Patridge front blade; Iron Sight Gun Works silhouette rear, click adjustable for windage and elevation (optional adj. front sight and hood). **Features:** Stainless steel, matte finish, manual sliding-bar safety system; dual firing pins, lightened hammer for fast lock time, pre-set trigger stop. Introduced 1991. Made in U.S.A. by Freedom Arms.
Price: Silhouette Class **$1,913.95**

FREEDOM ARMS MODEL 83 CENTERFIRE SILHOUETTE MODELS

Caliber: 357 Mag., 41 Mag., 44 Mag.; 5-shot cylinder. **Barrel:** 10", 9" (357 Mag. only). **Weight:** 63 oz. (41 Mag.). **Length:** 15.5", 14-1/2" (357 only). **Grips:** Pachmayr Presentation. **Sights:** Iron Sight Gun Works silhouette rear sight, replaceable adjustable front sight blade with hood. **Features:** Stainless steel, matte finish, manual sliding-bar safety system. Made in U.S.A. by Freedom Arms.
Price: Silhouette Models **$1,683.95**

HAMMERLI SP 20 TARGET PISTOL

Caliber: 22 LR, 32 S&W. **Barrel:** 4.6". **Weight:** 34.6-41.8 oz. **Length:** 11.8" overall. **Grips:** Anatomically shaped synthetic Hi-Grip available in five sizes. **Sights:** Integral front in three widths, adjustable rear with changeable notch widths. **Features:** Extremely low-level sight line; anatomically shaped trigger; adjustable JPS buffer system for different recoil characteristics. Receiver available in red, blue, gold, violet or black. Introduced 1998. Imported from Switzerland by Larry's Guns of Maine.
Price: Hammerli 22 LR **$1,450.00**
Price: Hammerli 32 S&W **$1,560.00**

HAMMERLI X-ESSE SPORT PISTOL

An all-steel .22 LR target pistol with a Hi-Grip in a new anatomical shape and an adjustable hand rest. Made in Switzerland. Introduced 2003.
Price: **$750.00**

High Standard Trophy

High Standard Victor

Kimber Super Match II

Smith & Wesson Model 41

HIGH STANDARD SUPERMATIC TROPHY TARGET PISTOL

Caliber: 22 LR, 9-shot mag. **Barrel:** 5.5" bull or 7.25" fluted. **Weight:** 44-46 oz. **Length:** 9.5-11.25" overall. **Stock:** Checkered hardwood with thumbrest. **Sights:** Undercut ramp front, frame-mounted micro-click rear adjustable for windage and elevation; drilled and tapped for scope mounting. **Features:** Gold-plated trigger, slide lock, safety-lever and magazine release; stippled front grip and backstrap; adjustable trigger and sear. Barrel weights optional. From High Standard Manufacturing Co., Inc.

Price: 5.5" barrel, adjustable sights **$795.00**
Price: 7.25", adjustable sights **$845.00**

HIGH STANDARD VICTOR TARGET PISTOL

Caliber: 22 LR, 10-shot magazine. **Barrel:** 4-1/2" or 5-1/2"; push-button takedown. **Weight:** 46 oz. **Length:** 9.5" overall. **Stock:** Checkered hardwood with thumbrest. **Sights:** Undercut ramp front, micro-click rear adjustable for windage and elevation. Also available with scope mount, rings, no sights. **Features:** Stainless steel construction. Full-length vent rib. Gold-plated trigger, slide lock, safety-lever and magazine release; stippled front grip and backstrap; polished slide; adjustable trigger and sear. Comes with barrel weight. From High Standard Manufacturing Co., Inc.

Price: 4.5" or 5.5" barrel, universal scope base **$745.00**

KIMBER SUPER MATCH II

Caliber: 45 ACP, 8-shot magazine. **Barrel:** 5". **Weight:** 38 oz. **Length:** 8.7" overall. **Grips:** Rosewood double diamond. **Sights:** Blade front, Kimber fully adjustable rear. **Features:** Guaranteed shoot 1" group at 25 yards. Stainless steel frame, black KimPro slide; two-piece magazine well; premium aluminum match-grade trigger; 30 lpi front strap checkering; stainless match-grade barrel; ambidextrous safety; special Custom Shop markings. Introduced 1999. Made in U.S.A. by Kimber Mfg., Inc.

Price: **$1,994.00**

KORTH MATCH REVOLVER

Caliber: 357 Mag., 38 Special, 32 S&W Long, 9mm Para., 22 WMR, 22 LR. **Barrel:** 5-1/4", 6". **Grips:** Adjustable match of oiled walnut with matte finish. **Sights:** Fully adjustable rear sight leaves (width of sight notch): 3.4mm, 3.5mm, 3.6mm); undercut Patridge, front. **Trigger:** Equipped with machined trigger shoe. Interchangeable caliber cylinders available as well as a variety of finishes. Made in Germany.

Price: From **$7,650.00**

RUGER MARK III STANDARD AUTOLOADING PISTOL

Caliber: 22 LR, 10-shot magazine. **Barrel:** 4-3/4", 5-1/2", 6", or 6-7/8". **Weight:** 35 oz. (4-3/4" bbl.). **Length:** 9" (4-3/4" bbl.). **Grips:** Checkered composition grip panels. **Sights:** Fixed, wide blade front, fixed rear. **Features:** Updated design of original Standard Auto and Mark II series. Standard models have lighter barrels. Target models have cocobolo grips; bull, target, competition, and hunter barrels; and adjustable sights. Introduced 2005.

Price: MKIII4, MKIII6 (blued) **$322.00**
Price: MKIII512 (blued) **$382.00**
Price: KMKIII512 (stainless) **$483.00**
Price: MKIII678 (blued) **$382.00**
Price: KMKIII678GC (stainless slabside barrel) **$555.00**
Price: KMKIII678GH (stainless fluted barrel) **$567.00**

RUGER MARK III TARGET MODEL AUTOLOADING PISTOL

Caliber: 22 LR, 10-shot magazine. **Barrel:** 5-1/2" to 6-7/8". **Weight:** 41 to 45 oz. **Length:** 9.75" to 11-1/8" overall. **Grips:** Checkered cocobolo. **Sights:** .125" blade front, micro-click rear, adjustable for windage and elevation, loaded chamber indicator; integral lock, magazine disconnect. Plastic case with lock included. Mark II series introduced 1982, discontinued 2004. Mark III introduced 2005.

Price: MKIII512 (bull barrel, blued) **$382.00**
Price: KMKIII512 (bull barrel, stainless) **$483.00**
Price: MKIII678 (blued Target barrel, 6-7/8") **$382.00**
Price: KMKIII678GC (stainless slabside barrel) **$555.00**
Price: KMKIII678GH (stainless fluted barrel) **$567.00**

SMITH & WESSON MODEL 41 TARGET

Caliber: 22 LR, 10-shot clip. **Barrel:** 5.5", 7". **Weight:** 41 oz. (5-1/2" barrel). **Length:** 10-1/2" overall (5-1/2" barrel). **Grips:** Checkered walnut with modified thumbrest, usable with either hand. **Sights:** 1/8" Patridge on ramp base; micro-click rear adjustable for windage and elevation. **Features:** 3/8" wide, grooved trigger; adjustable trigger stop drilled and tapped.

Price: S&W Bright Blue, either barrel **$1,115.00**

Smith & Wesson Model 22A

Smith & Wesson Model 22S

Springfield Armory 1911A1 Trophy Match

STI Executive

STI Eagle 5.0

STI Trojan 6-inch

SMITH & WESSON MODEL 22A PISTOLS

Caliber: 22 LR, 10-shot magazine. **Barrel:** 4", 5.5" bull. **Weight:** 28-39 oz. **Length:** 9-1/2" overall. **Grips:** Dymondwood® with ambidextrous thumbrests and flared bottom or rubber soft touch with thumbrest. **Sights:** Patridge front, fully adjustable rear. **Features:** Sight bridge with Weaver-style integral optics mount; alloy frame, stainless barrel and slide; blue/black finish. Introduced 1997. The **22S** is similar to the Model 22A except has stainless steel frame. Introduced 1997. Made in U.S.A. by Smith & Wesson.

Price: No. 107400, 4" light barrel, 28 oz.. . . . . $308.00
Price: No. 107410, 5.5" bull barrel, 32 oz.. $340.00
Price: No. 107412, 5.5" bull barrel, 32 oz., rubber grips $249.00
Price: No. 107426, 5.5" barrel, HiViz front sight, 39 oz. $429.00
Price: No. 107430, 7" light barrel, HiViz front sight, 39 oz. $386.00
Price: No. 107431, 5.5" bull barrel, target wood grip, 39 oz.. . . . . . . $407.00
Price: No. 107435, 5.5" barrel, camo finish. $386.00
Price: 22S No. 107300, 5.5" light barrel $416.00

SPRINGFIELD ARMORY LEATHAM LEGEND TGO SERIES PISTOLS

Three models of 5" barrel, 45 ACP 1911 pistols built for serious competition. TGO 1 has deluxe low mount Bo-Mar rear sight, Dawson fiber optics front sight, 3.5 lb. trigger pull.

Price: TGO 1 . . . . $2,999.00

Springfield Armory Trophy Match Pistol

Similar to Springfield Armory's Full Size model, but designed for bullseye and action shooting competition. Available with a Service Model 5" frame with matching slide and barrel in 5" and 6" lengths. Fully adjustable sights, checkered frame front strap, match barrel and bushing. In 45 ACP only. From Springfield Inc.

Price: $1,248.00

STI EAGLE 5.0, 6.0 PISTOL

Caliber: 9mm, 9x21, 38 & 40 Super, 40 S&W, 10mm, 45 ACP, 10-shot magazine. **Barrel:** 5", 6" bull. **Weight:** 34.5 oz. **Length:** 8.62" overall. **Grips:** Checkered polymer. **Sights:** STI front, Novak or Heine rear. **Features:** Standard frames plus 7 others; adjustable match trigger; skeletonized hammer; extended grip safety with locator pad. Introduced 1994. Made in U.S.A. by STI International.

Price: . . . . (5.0 Eagle) $1,794.00, (6.0 Eagle) $1,894.00

STI EXECUTIVE PISTOL

Caliber: 40 S&W. **Barrel:** 5" bull. **Weight:** 39 oz. **Length:** 8-5/8". **Grips:** Gray polymer. **Sights:** Dawson fiber optic, front; STI adjustable rear. **Features:** Stainless mag. well, front and rear serrations on slide. Made in U.S.A. by STI.

Price: $2,389.00

STI TROJAN

Caliber: 9mm, 38 Super, 40S&W, 45 ACP. **Barrel:** 5", 6". **Weight:** 36 oz. **Length:** 8.5". **Grips:** Rosewood. **Sights:** STI front with STI adjustable rear. **Features:** Stippled front strap, flat top slide, one-piece steel guide rod.

Price: (Trojan 5") $1,024.00
Price: (Trojan 6", not available in 38 Super) $1,344.00

*Includes models suitable for hunting and
competitive courses of fire, both police and international.*

Charter Arms Bulldog

Charter Arms Off Duty

Charter Arms Undercover

Charter Arms Mag Pug

Comanche III

**Dan Wesson Firearms
Alaskan Guide Special**

ARMSPORT MODEL 4540 REVOLVER
Caliber: 38 Special. **Barrel:** 4". **Weight:** 32 oz. **Length:** 9" overall. **Sights:** Fixed rear, blade front. **Features:** Ventilated rib; blued finish. Imported from Argentina by Armsport Inc.
Price: **$140.00**

CHARTER ARMS BULLDOG REVOLVER
Caliber: 44 Special. **Barrel:** 2.5". **Weight:** NA. **Sights:** Blade front, notch rear. **Features:** 6-round cylinder, soft-rubber pancake-style grips, shrouded ejector rod, wide trigger and hammer spur. American made by Charter Arms, distributed by MKS Supply.
Price: Blued **$324.00**
Price: Stainless **$347.00**
Price: Police Bulldog, .38 Special, 4" barrel, 24 oz. **$299.00**

CHARTER ARMS OFF DUTY REVOLVER
Caliber: 38 Special. **Barrel:** 2". **Weight:** 12.5 oz. **Sights:** Blade front, notch rear. **Features:** 5-round cylinder, aluminum casting, DAO. American made by Charter Arms, distributed by MKS Supply.
Price: Aluminum **$353.00**

CHARTER ARMS UNDERCOVER REVOLVER
Caliber: 38 Special. **Barrel:** 2". **Weight:** 16 oz. **Sights:** Blade front, notch rear. **Features:** 6-round cylinder. American made by Charter Arms, distributed by MKS Supply.
Price: Blued **$279.00**
Price: Blued DAO **$279.00**
Price: Stainless **$299.00**
Price: Stainless DAO **$299.00**

CHARTER ARMS MAG PUG REVOLVER
Caliber: 357 Magnum. **Barrel:** 2.2". **Weight:** 23 oz. **Sights:** Blade front, notch rear. **Features:** 5-round cylinder. American made by Charter Arms, distributed by MKS Supply.
Price: Blued **$325.00**
Price: Stainless **$335.00**

COLT SINGLE-ACTION ARMY
Caliber: 32-20, 38 Special, 357 Magnum, 38-40, 44-4-, 44 Special, 45 Long Colt. **Barrel:** 4.7 5", 5.5", 7.5". **Weight:** 40-44 oz. **Sights:** Blade front, notch rear. **Features:** Available in black powder and sheriff's models; nickel, blued or case-hardened frame; 6-round cylinder.
Price: .... (Blued) **$1,380.00**; (Stainless) **$1,530.00**

COMANCHE I, II, III DA REVOLVERS
Features: Adjustable sights. Blue or stainless finish. Distributed by SGS Importers.
Price: I 22 LR, 6" bbl., 9-shot, blue **$249.95**
Price: I 22LR, 6" bbl., 9-shot, stainless **$274.95**
Price: II 38 Special, 2" bbl., 6-shot, blue, intr. 2006 .... **$258.95**
Price: II 38 Special, 4" bbl., 6-shot, stainless **$249.95**
Price: III 357 Mag, 3" bbl., 6-shot, blue **$266.95**
Price: III 357 Mag. 2" bbl., 6-shot, blue **$274.95**
Price: II 38 Special, 3" bbl., 6-shot, stainless steel **$266.95**

DAN WESSON FIREARMS ALASKAN GUIDE SPECIAL
Caliber: 445 SuperMag; also chambers and fires 44 Magnum, 44 Special, 6 shots. **Sights:** Blade front, adjustable rear. **Barrel:** Compensated 4" vent heavy barrel assembly. **Weight:** 54.4 oz. **Length:** 11.7". **Features:** Stainless steel with baked on, non-glare, matte black coating, special laser engraving. Made in U.S.A. by Dan Wesson Firearms, distributed by CZ-USA.
Price: **$1,295.00**

DAN WESSON FIREARMS VH8 445 SUPERMAG
Caliber: 445 SuperMag; also chambers and fires 44 Magnum, 44 Special, 6 shots. **Sights:** Blade front, adjustable rear. **Barrel:** 8" full-length underlug. **Weight:** 54.4 oz. **Length:** 14.6". **Features:** Stainless-steel frame and barrel. Interchangeable barrels. Made in U.S.A. by Dan Wesson Firearms, distributed by CZ-USA.
Price: **$1,070.00**

EAA Windicator

Rossi Model 971

Rossi Model 972

Rossi Model 851

Ruger GP-100

Ruger KGP-141

Ruger GP-161

EAA WINDICATOR REVOLVERS

Caliber: 38 Spec., 6-shot; 357 magnum, 6-shot. **Barrel:** 2", 4". **Weight:** 30 oz. (4"). **Length:** 8.5" overall (4" bbl.). **Grips:** Rubber with finger grooves. **Sights:** Blade front, fixed or adjustable on rimfires; fixed only on 32, 38. **Features:** Swing-out cylinder; hammer block safety; blue finish. Introduced 1991. Imported from Germany by European American Armory.
Price: 38 Special 2" barrel, alloy frame **$249.00**
Price: 38 Special 4" barrel, alloy frame **$259.00**
Price: 357 Mag, 2" barrel, steel frame **$259.00**
Price: 357 Mag, 4" barrel, steel frame **$279.00**

KORTH COMBAT REVOLVER

Caliber: 357 Mag., 32 S&W Long, 9mm Para., 22 WMR, 22 LR. **Barrel:** 3", 4", 5-1/4", 6". **Sights:** Fully adjustable, rear; Baughman ramp, front. **Grips:** Walnut (checkered or smooth). Also available as a Target model in 22 LR, 38 Spl., 32 S&W Long, 357 Mag. with undercut Patridge front sight; fully adjustable rear. Made in Germany. Imported by Korth USA.
Price: From **$7,203.00**

KORTH TROJA REVOLVER

Caliber: .357 Mag. **Barrel:** 6". **Finish:** Matte blue. **Grips:** Smooth, oversized finger contoured walnut. Introduced 2003. Imported from Germany by Korth USA.
Price: From **$5,593.00**

ROSSI MODEL 351/352 REVOLVERS

Caliber: 38 Special +P, 5-shot. **Barrel:** 2". **Weight:** 24 oz. **Length:** 6-1/2" overall. **Grips:** Rubber. **Sights:** Blade front, notch rear. **Features:** Patented key-lock Taurus Security System; forged steel frame. Introduced 2001. Made in Brazil by Amadeo Rossi. Imported by BrazTech/Taurus.
Price: Model 351 (blued finish) **$313.00**
Price: Model 352 (stainless finish)......................... **$362.00**

ROSSI MODEL 461/462 REVOLVERS

Caliber: 357 Magnum +P, 6-shot. **Barrel:** 2". **Weight:** 26 oz. **Length:** 6.5" overall. **Grips:** Rubber. **Sights:** Fixed. **Features:** Single/ double action. Patented key-lock Taurus Security System; forged steel frame. Introduced 2001. Made in Brazil by Amadeo Rossi. Imported by BrazTech/Taurus.
Price: Model 461 (blued finish) **$313.00**
Price: Model 462 (stainless finish)......................... **$362.00**

ROSSI MODEL 971/972 REVOLVERS

Caliber: 357 Magnum +P, 6-shot. **Barrel:** 4", 6". **Weight:** 32 oz. **Length:** 8.5" or 10.5" overall. **Grips:** Rubber. **Sights:** Blade front, adjustable rear.

Features: Single/double action. Patented key-lock Taurus Security System; forged steel frame. Introduced 2001. Made in Brazil by Amadeo Rossi. Imported by BrazTech/Taurus.
Price: Model 971 (blued finish, 4" bbl.) **$362.00**
Price: Model 972 (stainless steel finish, 6" bbl.).............. **$410.00**

Rossi Model 851

Similar to Model 971/972, chambered for 38 Special +P. Blued finish, 4" barrel. Introduced 2001. Made in Brazil by Amadeo Rossi. From BrazTech/Taurus.
Price: **$313.00**

RUGER GP-100 REVOLVERS

Caliber: 38 Spec. +P, 357 Mag., 6-shot. **Barrel:** 3", 3" full shroud, 4", 4" full shroud, 6", 6" full shroud. **Weight:** 3" barrel-35 oz., 3" full shroud-36 oz., 4" barrel-37 oz., 4" full shroud-38 oz. **Sights:** Fixed; adjustable on 4" full shroud, all 6" barrels. **Grips:** Ruger Santoprene Cushioned Grip with Goncalo Alves inserts. **Features:** Uses action, frame features of both the Security-Six and Redhawk revolvers. Full length, short ejector shroud. Satin blue and stainless steel.
Price: GPF-141 (357, 4" full shroud, adj. sights, blue) **$557.00**
Price: GPF-161 (357, 6" full shroud, adj. sights, blue), 46 oz. **$557.00**
Price: GPF-840 (38 Special, 4" half shroud, blued) **$552.00**
Price: GPF-841 38 Special, 4" full shroud) **$552.00**
Price: KGP-141 (357, 4" full shroud, adj. sights, stainless) **$615.00**
Price: KGP-161 (357, 6" full shroud, adj. sights, stainless) 46 oz. . **$615.00**
Price: KGPF-331 (357, 3" full shroud, stainless) **$597.00**

Ruger SP101

Ruger Redhawk

Ruger Super Redhawk

Smith & Wesson Model 36LS

Smith & Wesson Model 442

Smith & Wesson Model 638

RUGER SP101 REVOLVERS

Caliber: 22 LR, 32 H&R Mag., 6-shot; 38 Spec. +P, 357 Mag., 5-shot. **Barrel:** 2-1/4", 3-1/16", 4". **Weight:** (38 & 357 mag models) 2-1/4"-25 oz.; 3-1/16"-27 oz. **Sights:** Adjustable on 22, 32, fixed on others. **Grips:** Ruger Cushioned Grip with inserts. **Features:** Compact, small frame, double-action revolver. Full-length ejector shroud. Stainless steel only. Introduced 1988.
Price: KSP-241X (4" heavy bbl., 22 LR), 34 oz. **$505.00**
Price: KSP-321X (2-1/4", 357 Mag.) **$530.00**
Price: KSP-3231X (3-1/16", 32 H&R), 30 oz. **$530.00**
Price: KSP-3241X (32 Mag., 4" bbl.) **$530.00**
Price: KSP-331X (3-1/16", 357 Mag.) **$495.00**
Price: KSP-821X (2-1/4", 38 Spec.) **$530.00**
Price: KSP-831X (3-1/16", 38 Spec.) **$530.00**

Ruger SP101 Double-Action-Only Revolver

Similar to standard SP101 except double-action-only with no single-action sear notch. Spurless hammer, floating firing pin and transfer bar safety system. Available with 2-1/4" barrel in 357 Magnum. Weighs 25 oz., overall length 7.06". Natural brushed satin, high-polish stainless steel. Introduced 1993.
Price: KSP321XL (357 Mag.) **$495.00**

RUGER REDHAWK

Caliber: 44 Rem. Mag., 6-shot. **Barrel:** 5-1/2", 7-1/2". **Weight:** About 54 oz. (7-1/2" bbl.). **Length:** 13" overall (7-1/2" barrel). **Grips:** Square butt cushioned grip panels. **Sights:** Interchangeable Patridge-type front, rear adjustable for windage and elevation. **Features:** Stainless steel, brushed satin finish, blued ordnance steel. 9-1/2" sight radius. Introduced 1979.
Price: KRH-44, stainless, 7-1/2" barrel **$730.00**
Price: KRH-44R, stainless, 7-1/2" barrel w/scope mount **$779.00**
Price: KRH-445, stainless, 5-1/2" barrel **$730.00**
Price: RH-445, blued, 5-1/2" barrel **$730.00**

RUGER SUPER REDHAWK REVOLVER

Caliber: 44 Rem. Mag., 45 Colt, 454 Casull, 480 Ruger 6-shot. **Barrel:** 2.5", 5.5", 7.5", 9.5". **Weight:** About 54 oz. (7.5" bbl.). **Length:** 13" overall (7.5" barrel). **Grips:** Square butt cushioned grip panels, Hogue Tamer Monogrip. **Features:** Similar to standard Redhawk except has heavy extended frame with Ruger Integral Scope Mounting System on wide topstrap. Wide hammer spur lowered for better scope clearance. Incorporates mechanical design features and improvements of GP-100. Ramp front sight base has Redhawk-style Interchangeable Insert sight blades, adjustable rear sight. Satin stainless steel and low-glare stainless finishes. Introduced 1987.

Price: KSRH-2454 , 2.5" 44 Mag, Hogue Tamer Monogrip **$860.00**
Price: KSRH-2480 , 2.5" 480 Ruger, Hogue Tamer Monogrip **$860.00**
Price: KSRH-7 , 7.5" 44 Mag, Ruger grip **$779.00**
Price: KSRH-7454 , 7.5" 45 Colt/454 Casull, low glare stainless. . . **$860.00**
Price: KSRH-7480 , 7.5" 480 Ruger, low glare stainless **$860.00**
Price: KSRH-9 , 9" 44 Mag, Ruger grip **$779.00**
Price: KSRH-9454 , 9.5" 45 Colt/454 Casull, low glare stainless. . . **$860.00**
Price: KSRH-9480 , 9.5" 480 Ruger, low glare stainless **$860.00**

SMITH & WESSON J-FRAME REVOLVERS

The smallest S&W wheelguns come in a variety of chamberings, barrel lengths, and materials, as noted in the individual model listings below.

SMITH & WESSON 36LS/60LS/642LS LADYSMITH REVOLVERS

Caliber: .38 Special +P, 357 Mag., 5-shot. **Barrel:** 1-7/8" (36LS, 642LS); 2-1/8" (60LS) **Weight:** 14.5 oz. (642LS); 20 oz. (36LS); 21.5 oz. (60LS); **Length:** 6.25" overall (36LS); 6.6" overall (60LS); . **Grips:** Wood. **Sights:** Black blade, serrated ramp front, fixed notch rear. **Features:** 36/60LS models have a Chiefs Special-style frame. 642LS has Centennial-style frame, frosted matte finish, smooth combat wood grips. Introduced 1996. Comes in a fitted carry/storage case. Introduced 1989. Made in U.S.A. by Smith & Wesson.
Price: Model 36LS, 38+P, carbon steel frame **$596.00**
Price: Model 60LS, 357 Mag, matte stainless frame **$652.00**
Price: Model 642LS, 38+P, alloy frame, titanium cylinder. **$664.00**

SMITH & WESSON MODEL 37/442/637/638/642 AIRWEIGHT REVOLVERS

Caliber: 38 Special +P, 5-shot. **Barrel:** 1-7/8". **Weight:** 15 oz. (37, 442); 20 oz. (3); 21.5 oz. (); **Length:** 6-3/8" overall. **Grips:** Soft rubber. **Sights:** Fixed, serrated ramp front, square notch rear. **Features:** Aluminum-alloy frames. Models 37, 637; Chiefs Special-style frame with exposed hammer. Introduced 1996. Models 442, 642; Centennial-style frame, enclosed hammer. Model 638, Bodyguard style, shrouded hammer. Comes in a fitted carry/storage case. Introduced 1989. Made in U.S.A. by Smith & Wesson.
Price: Model 37, glass-beaded black finish **$573.00**
Price: Model 442, blue/black finish, enclosed hammer, DA only . . . **$480.00**
Price: Model 637, matte silver finish. **$457.00**
Price: Model 637 Carry Combo, with holster **$470.00**
Price: Model 637 w/Crimson Trace Lasergrip. **$706.00**
Price: Model 638, matte silver finish, shrouded hammer **$480.00**
Price: Model 642, matte silver finish, DA only, introduced 1996 . . . **$476.00**
Price: Model 642 w/Crimson Trace Lasergrip. **$706.00**

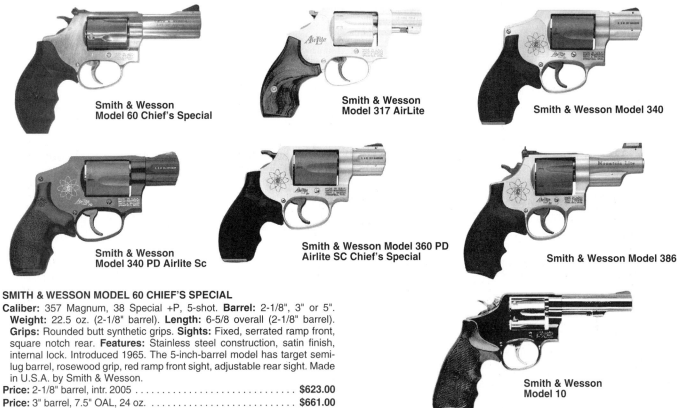

Smith & Wesson Model 60 Chief's Special

Smith & Wesson Model 317 AirLite

Smith & Wesson Model 340

Smith & Wesson Model 340 PD Airlite Sc

Smith & Wesson Model 360 PD Airlite SC Chief's Special

Smith & Wesson Model 386

Smith & Wesson Model 10

SMITH & WESSON MODEL 60 CHIEF'S SPECIAL

Caliber: 357 Magnum, 38 Special +P, 5-shot. **Barrel:** 2-1/8", 3" or 5". **Weight:** 22.5 oz. (2-1/8" barrel). **Length:** 6-5/8 overall (2-1/8" barrel). **Grips:** Rounded butt synthetic grips. **Sights:** Fixed, serrated ramp front, square notch rear. **Features:** Stainless steel construction, satin finish, internal lock. Introduced 1965. The 5-inch-barrel model has target semi-lug barrel, rosewood grip, red ramp front sight, adjustable rear sight. Made in U.S.A. by Smith & Wesson.
Price: 2-1/8" barrel, intr. 2005 . . . . $623.00
Price: 3" barrel, 7.5" OAL, 24 oz. $661.00
Price: 5" semi-lug barrel, 9-3/8" OAL, 30.5 oz. $704.00

SMITH & WESSON MODEL 317 AIRLITE REVOLVERS

Caliber: 22 LR, 8-shot. **Barrel:** 1-7/8", 3". **Weight:** 10.5 oz. **Length:** 6.25" overall (1-7/8" barrel). **Grips:** Rubber. **Sights:** Serrated ramp front, fixed notch rear. **Features:** Aluminum alloy, carbon and stainless steels, Chiefs Special-style frame with exposed hammer. Smooth combat trigger. Clear Cote finish. Introduced 1997. Made in U.S.A. by Smith & Wesson.
Price: Model 317, 1-7/8" barrel $633.00
Price: Model 317 w/HiViz front sight, 3" barrel, 7.25 OAL $691.00

SMITH & WESSON MODEL 340/340PD AIRLITE SC CENTENNIAL

Caliber: 357 Magnum, 38 Spec. +P, 5-shot. **Barrel:** 1-7/8". **Weight:** 12 oz. **Length:** 6-3/8" overall (1-7/8" barrel). **Grips:** Rounded butt. **Sights:** Black blade front, rear notch **Features:** Centennial-style frame, enclosed hammer. Internal lock. Matte silver finish. Scandium alloy frame, titanium cylinder, stainless steel barrel liner. Made in U.S.A. by Smith & Wesson.
Price: Model 340 . . . . $879.00
Price: Model 340PD, red ramp front $905.00
Price: Model 340PD, HiViz front $921.00

SMITH & WESSON MODEL 351PD REVOLVER

Caliber: 22 Mag., 7-shot. **Barrel:** 1-7/8". **Weight:** 10.6 oz. **Length:** 6.25" overall (1-7/8" barrel). **Sights:** HiViz front sight, rear notch. **Grips:** Wood. **Features:** Seven-shot, aluminum-alloy frame. Chiefs Special-style frame with exposed hammer. Nonreflective matte-black finish. Internal lock. Made in U.S.A. by Smith & Wesson.
Price: $679.00

SMITH & WESSON MODEL 360/360PD AIRLITE CHIEF'S SPECIAL

Caliber: 357 Magnum, 38 Spec. +P, 5-shot. **Barrel:** 1-7/8". **Weight:** 12 oz. **Length:** 6-3/8" overall (1-7/8" barrel). **Grips:** Rounded butt rubber. **Sights:** Black blade front, fixed rear notch. **Features:** Chiefs Special-style frame with exposed hammer. Internal lock. Scandium alloy frame, titanium cylinder, stainless steel barrel. Made in U.S.A. by Smith & Wesson.
Price: Model 360 . . . . $858.00
Price: Model 360PD, red ramp front sight $885.00
Price: Model 360PD w/HiViz front sight $901.00

SMITH & WESSON MODEL 640 CENTENNIAL DA ONLY

Caliber: 357 Mag., 38 Spec. +P, 5-shot. **Barrel:** 2-1/8". **Weight:** 23 oz. **Length:** 6-3/4" overall. **Grips:** Uncle Mike's Boot grip. **Sights:** Serrated ramp front, fixed notch rear. **Features:** Stainless steel. Fully concealed hammer, snag-proof smooth edges. Internal lock. Introduced 1995 in 357 Magnum.
Price: $690.00

SMITH & WESSON MODEL 649 BODYGUARD REVOLVER

Caliber: 357 Mag., 38 Spec. +P, 5-shot. **Barrel:** 2-1/8". **Weight:** 23 oz. **Length:** 6-5/8" overall. **Grips:** Uncle Mike's Combat. **Sights:** Black pinned ramp front, fixed notch rear. **Features:** Stainless steel construction, satin finish. Internal lock. Bodyguard style, shrouded hammer. Made in U.S.A. by Smith & Wesson.
Price: $684.00

SMITH & WESSON K-FRAME/L-FRAME REVOLVERS

These mid-size S&W wheelguns come in a variety of chamberings, barrel lengths, and materials, as noted in the individual model listings below. 17 variations for 2006.

SMITH & WESSON MODEL 10 REVOLVER

Caliber: 38 Spec.+P, 6-shot. **Barrel:** 4". **Weight:** 36 oz. **Length:** 8-7/8" overall. **Grips:** Soft rubber; square butt. **Sights:** Fixed; black blade front, square notch rear. Blued carbon steel frame.
Price: Blue $572.00

SMITH & WESSON MODEL 64/67 REVOLVERS

Caliber: 38 Spec. +P, 6-shot. **Barrel:** 3". **Weight:** 33 oz. **Length:** 8-7/8" overall. **Grips:** Soft rubber. **Sights:** Fixed, 1/8" serrated ramp front, square notch rear. Model 67 (**Weight:** 36 oz. **Length:** 8-7/8") similar to Model 64 except for adjustable sights. **Features:** Satin finished stainless steel, square butt.
Price: Model 64, 3" barrel $612.00
Price: Model 64, 4" barrel, Uncle Mike's rubber grip, 36 oz. $583.00
Price: Model 67, 4" barrel, adjustable rear sight, red ramp front . . . $674.00

Smith & Wesson Model 21

Smith & Wesson Model 625

SMITH & WESSON MODEL 386
Caliber: 357 Magnum, 38 Spec. +P, 7-shot. **Barrel:** 3-1/8". **Weight:** 18.5 oz. **Length:** 8-1/8" overall. **Grips:** Rubber. **Sights:** Adjustable, HiViz front. **Features:** Scandium alloy frame, titanium cylinder, stainless steel barrel liner. Internal lock. Made in U.S.A. by Smith & Wesson.
Price: Matte silver finish **$920.00**

SMITH & WESSON MODEL 520
Caliber: 357 Magnum, 38 Spec. +P, 7-shot. **Barrel:** 4". **Weight:** 37.9 oz. **Length:** 8-7/8". **Grips:** Wood. **Sights:** Adjustable target rear, HiViz front. **Features:** Carbon steel frame, titanium cylinder. Updated L-frame replacement for discontinued K-frame Model 19. Internal lock. Introduced 2005. Made in U.S.A. by Smith & Wesson.
Price: Blue/black finish **$731.00**

SMITH & WESSON MODEL 617 REVOLVERS
Caliber: 22 LR, 6- or 10-shot. **Barrel:** 4". **Weight:** 41 oz. (4" barrel). **Length:** 9-1/8" (4" barrel). **Grips:** Soft rubber. **Sights:** Patridge front, adjustable rear. Drilled and tapped for scope mount. **Features:** Stainless steel with satin finish; 4" has .312" smooth trigger, .375" semi-target hammer; 6" has either .312" combat or .400" serrated trigger, .375" semi-target or .500" target hammer; 8-3/8" with .400" serrated trigger, .500" target hammer. Introduced 1990.
Price: 4" barrel, ... **$742.00**
Price: 6" barrel, 11-1/8" overall length, 45 oz. . . . . **$751.00 to $770.00**

SMITH & WESSON MODELS 619/620 REVOLVERS
Caliber: 38 Special +P; 357 Mag., 7 rounds. **Barrel:** 4". **Weight:** 37.5 oz. **Length:** 9-1/2". **Grips:** Rubber. **Sights:** Integral front blade, fixed rear notch on the 619; adjustable white-outline target style rear, red ramp front on 620. **Features:** Replaces Models 65 and 66. Two-piece semi-lug barrel. Satin stainless frame and cylinder. Made in U.S.A. by Smith & Wesson.
Price: **$646.00**
Price: **$703.00**

SMITH & WESSON MODEL 686/686 PLUS REVOLVERS
Caliber: 357 Mag., 38 S&W Special; 6 rounds. **Barrel:** 2.5", 4", 6". **Weight:** 35 oz. (2.5" barrel). **Length:** 7-1/2", (2.5" barrel). **Grips:** Rubber. **Sights:** White outline adjustable rear, red ramp front. **Features:** Satin stainless frame and cylinder. Plus series guns have 7-shot cylinders. Introduced 1996. Powerport (PP) has Patridge front, adjustable rear sight. Introduced early 1980s. Made in U.S.A. by Smith & Wesson.
Price: 2.5" barrel, 6 rounds **$700.00**
Price: 4" barrel, 40 oz., 9-5/8" OAL **$728.00**
Price: 6" barrel, 44 oz., 12" OAL **$735.00**
Price: Plus, 2.5" barrel, 7 rounds **$727.00**
Price: Plus, 4" barrel, 7 rounds, 9-5/8" OAL **$752.00**
Price: Plus, 6" barrel, 7 rounds, 12" OAL **$764.00**
Price: PP, 6" barrel, 6 rounds, 11-3/8" OAL **$784.00**

SMITH & WESSON N-FRAME REVOLVERS
These large-frame S&W wheelguns come in a variety of chamberings, barrel lengths, and materials, as noted in the individual model listings below. 18 major variations for 2006.

SMITH & WESSON MODEL 21
Caliber: 44 Special, 6-round. **Barrel:** 4" tapered. **Weight:** NA. **Length:** NA. **Grips:** Smooth wood. **Sights:** Pinned half-moon service front; service rear. **Features:** Carbon steel frame, blued finish.
Price: **$855**

SMITH & WESSON MODEL 29 50TH ANNIVERSARY REVOLVER
Caliber: 44 Mag., 6-round. **Barrel:** 6.5". **Weight:** 48.5 oz. **Length:** 12". **Grips:** Cocobolo. **Sights:** Adjustable white-outline rear, red ramp front. **Features:** Carbon steel frame, polished-blued finish. Introduced 2005. Includes 24 carat gold-plated anniversary logo on frame, cleaning kit with screwdriver, mahogany presentation case, square-butt frame, serrated trigger. Original Model 29 made famous by "Dirty Harry" character created in 1971 by Clint Eastwood.
Price: Dealer pricing, no MSRP . . . . **NA**

SMITH & WESSON MODEL 325PD/329PD/357PD AIRLITE REVOLVERS
Caliber: 41 Mag. (357PD); 44 Spec., 44 Mag. (329PD); 45 ACP (325PD); 6-round. **Barrel:** 2-3/4" (325PD). **Weight:** 21.5 oz. (325PD, 2-3/4" barrel). **Length:** 7-1/4" (325PD, 2-3/4" barrel). **Grips:** Wood. **Sights:** Adj. rear, HiViz orange-dot front. **Features:** Scandium alloy frame, titanium cylinder. 4" model has HiViz green front sight and Ahrends finger-groove wood grips. Weighs 26.5 oz.
Price: 325PD, 2-3/4" barrel **$986.00**
Price: 325PD , 4" barrel, Ahrends wood grips **$1,008.00**
Price: 329PD, 4" barrel, 9.5" OAL, 26 oz. **$1,008.00**
Price: 357PD, 4" barrel, 9.5" OAL, 27.5 oz. **$1,008.00**

SMITH & WESSON MODEL 625 REVOLVERS
Caliber: 45 ACP, 6-shot. **Barrel:** 4", 5". **Weight:** 43 oz. (4" barrel). **Length:** 9-3/8" overall (4" barrel). **Grips:** Soft rubber; wood optional. **Sights:** Patridge front on ramp, S&W micrometer click rear adjustable for windage and elevation. **Features:** Stainless steel construction with .400" semi-target hammer, .312" smooth combat trigger; full lug barrel. Glass beaded finish. Introduced 1989. "Jerry Miculek" Professional (JMP) Series has .265"-wide grooved trigger, special wooden Miculek Grip, five full moon clips, gold bead Patridge front sight on interchangeable front sight base, bead blast finish. Unique serial number run. Mountain Gun has 4" tapered barrel, drilled and tapped, Hogue Rubber Monogrip, pinned black ramp front sight, micrometer click-adjustable rear sight, satin stainless frame and barrel, weighs 39.5 oz.
Price: 625, 4" or 5" barrel **$858.00**
Price: 625 JMP, 4" barrel, 9-3/9" OAL, 43 oz. **$887.00**
Price: 625 Mountain Gun, dealer pricing, no MSRP . . . . **NA**

SMITH & WESSON MODEL 629 REVOLVERS
Caliber: 44 Magnum, 44 S&W Special, 6-shot. **Barrel:** 4", 5", 6-1/2". **Weight:** 41.5 oz. (4" bbl.). **Length:** 9-5/8" overall (4" bbl.). **Grips:** Soft rubber; wood optional. **Sights:** 1/8" red ramp front, white outline rear, internal lock, adjustable for windage and elevation. Classic similar to standard Model 629, except Classic has full-lug 5" barrel, chamfered front of cylinder, interchangeable red ramp front sight with adjustable white outline rear, Hogue grips with S&W monogram, drilled and tapped for scope mounting. Factory accurizing and endurance packages. Introduced 1990. Classic Power Port has Patridge front sight and adjustable rear sight. Model 629CT has 5" barrel, Crimson Trace Hoghunter Lasergrips, 10.5" OAL, 45.5 oz. weight. Introduced 2006.
Price: 629, 4" **$826.00**
Price: 629, 6" barrel, 11-5/8" OAL, 45 oz. **$851.00**
Price: 629 Classic, 5" full lug barrel, 45.5 oz. **$885.00**
Price: 629 Classic, 6-1/2" full lug barrel, 49.5 oz. **$912.00**
Price: 629 Classic, 6-1/2" full lug barrel, HiViz front sight **$939.00**
Price: 629 Classic Power Port, 6-1/2" full lug barrel **$885.00**
Price: 629 Classic, 8-3/8" full lug barrel, 53.5 oz **$914.00**
Price: 629CT . . . . **NA**

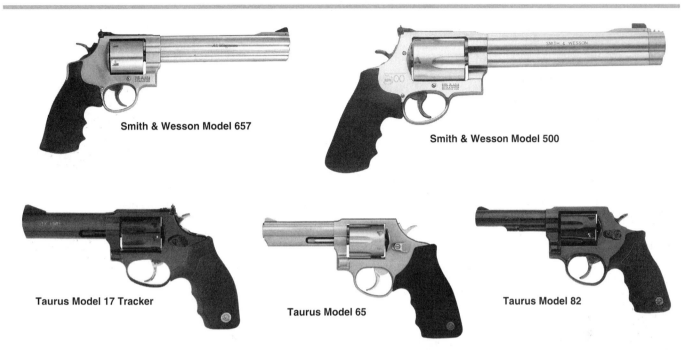

Smith & Wesson Model 657

Smith & Wesson Model 500

Taurus Model 17 Tracker

Taurus Model 65

Taurus Model 82

SMITH & WESSON MODEL 657 REVOLVER

Caliber: 41 Mag., 6-shot. **Barrel:** 7-1/2" full lug. **Weight:** 52 oz. **Grips:** Soft rubber. **Sights:** Pinned 1/8" red ramp front, micro-click rear adjustable for windage and elevation. Target hammer, drilled and tapped, unfluted cylinder. **Features:** Stainless steel construction.
Price: **$813.00**

SMITH & WESSON X-FRAME REVOLVERS

These extra-large X-frame S&W wheelguns come in a variety of chamberings, barrel lengths, and materials, as noted in the individual model listings below. 7 variations for 2006.

SMITH & WESSON MODEL 460V REVOLVERS

Caliber: 460 S&W Mag., 5-shot. Also chambers 454 Casull, 45 Colt. **Barrel:** 8-3/8" gain-twist rifling. **Weight:** 62.5 oz. **Length:** 11.25". **Grips:** Rubber. **Sights:** Adj. rear, red ramp front. **Features:** Satin stainless steel frame and cylinder, interchangeable compensator. 460XVR (X-treme Velocity Revolver) has black blade front sight with interchangeable green Hi-Viz tubes, adjustable rear sight. 7.5"-barrel version has Lothar-Walther barrel, 360-degree recoil compensator, tuned Performance Center action, pinned sear, integral Weaver base, non-glare surfaces, scope mount accessory kit for mounting full-size scopes, flashed-chromed hammer and trigger, Performance Center gun rug and shoulder sling. Interchangeable Hi-Viz green dot front sight, adjustable black rear sight, Hogue Dual Density Monogrip, matte-black frame and shroud finish with glass-bead cylinder finish, 72 oz. Compensated Hunter has tear drop chrome hammer, .312 chrome trigger, Hogue Dual Density Monogrip, satin/matte stainless finish, HiViz interchangeable front sight, adjustable black rear sight. XVR introduced 2006.
Price: 460V . . . . **NA**
Price: 460XVR, 8-3/8" barrel, 15" OAL, 72.5 oz.. . . . . **$1,313.00**
Price: 460XVR, 7.5" barrel **$1,401.00**
Price: 460XVR, 3.5" barrel, 11" OAL, 59.5 oz. . . . . **NA**
Price: 460XVR Comp. Hunter, 10.5" barrel, 18" OAL, 82.5 oz. **$1,472**

SMITH & WESSON MODEL 500 REVOLVERS

Caliber: 500 S&W Mag., 5 rounds. **Barrel:** 4", 8-3/8". **Weight:** 72.5 oz. **Length:** 15" (8-3/8" barrel). **Grips:** Hogue Sorbothane Rubber. **Sights:** Interchangeable blade, front, adjustable rear. **Features:** Recoil compensator, ball detent cylinder latch, internal lock. 6 1/2"-barrel model has orange-ramp dovetail Millett front sight, adjustable black rear sight, Hogue Dual Density Monogrip, .312" chrome trigger with over-travel stop, chrome tear-drop hammer, glassbead finish. 10-1/2"-barrel model has red ramp front front sight, adjustable rear sight, .312 chrome trigger with overtravel stop, chrome tear drop hammer with pinned sear, hunting sling. Compensated Hunter has .400 orange ramp dovetail front sight, adjustable black blade rear sight, Hogue Dual Density Monogrip, glassbead finish w/black passivate clear coat. Made in U.S.A. by Smith & Wesson.
Price: 4" barrel, 10.25" OAL, 56 oz. **$1,256.00**
Price: 8-3/8" barrel **$1,186.00**
Price: 6.5" barrel, 14" OAL, 70 oz. **$1,460.00**
Price: 8-3/8" barrel w/HiViz front sight **$1,296.00**
Price: 10.5" barrel, 82 oz., with sling **$1,460.00**
Price: Compensated Hunter, 7.5" barrel, 71 oz.. . . . . **NA**

TAURUS MODEL 17 "TRACKER"

Caliber: 17 HMR, 7-shot. **Barrel:** 6-1/2". **Weight:** 45.8 oz. **Grips:** Rubber. **Sights:** Adjustable. **Features:** Double action, matte stainless, integral key-lock.
Price: . . . . **$430.00 to $438.00**

Taurus Model 17-C Series

Similar to the Model 17 Tracker series but 8-shot cylinder, 2", 4" or 5" barrel, blue or stainless finish and regular (24 oz.) or UltraLite (18.5 oz.) versions available.
Price: . . . . **$359.00 to $391.00**

TAURUS MODEL 65 REVOLVER

Caliber: 357 Mag., 6-shot. **Barrel:** 4". **Weight:** 38 oz. **Length:** 10-1/2" overall. **Grips:** Soft rubber. **Sights:** Fixed. **Features:** Double action, integral key-lock. Seven models for 2006 Imported by Taurus International.
Price: Blue or matte stainless . . . . **$383.00 to $484.00**

Taurus Model 66 Revolver

Similar to Model 65, 4" or 6" barrel, 7-shot cylinder, adjustable rear sight. Integral key-lock action. Imported by Taurus International.
Price: Blue or matte stainless . . . . **$438.00 to $484.00**

TAURUS MODEL 82 HEAVY BARREL REVOLVER

Caliber: 38 Spec., 6-shot. **Barrel:** 4", heavy. **Weight:** 36.5 oz. **Length:** 9-1/4" overall (4" bbl.). **Grips:** Soft black rubber. **Sights:** Serrated ramp front, square notch rear. **Features:** Double action, solid rib, integral key-lock. Imported by Taurus International.
Price: Blue or matte stainless . . . . **$375.00 to $422.00**

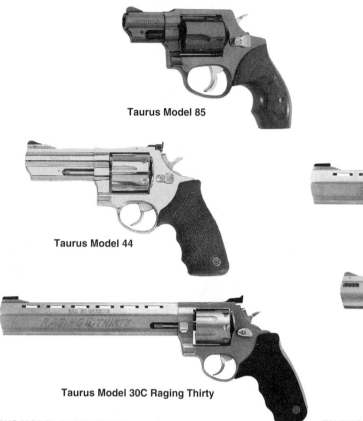

Taurus Model 85

Taurus Model 22H Raging Hornet

Taurus Model 44

Taurus Model 218 Raging Bee

Taurus Model 30C Raging Thirty

**Taurus Model 425
Total Titanium**

TAURUS MODEL 85 REVOLVER

Caliber: 38 Spec., 5-shot. **Barrel:** 2". **Weight:** 17-24.5 oz., titanium 13.5-15.4 oz. **Grips:** Rubber, rosewood or mother-of-pearl. **Sights:** Ramp front, square notch rear. **Features:** Blue, matte stainless, blue with gold accents, stainless with gold accents; rated for +P ammo. Integral keylock. Some models have titantium frame. Introduced 1980. Imported by Taurus International.
Price: . . . . **$383.00 to $548.00**

TAURUS IB INSTANT BACKUP REVOLVER

Caliber: 17 HMR, 8 shot. Barrel: 2". Weight: 17-24.5 oz., titanium 13.5-15.4 oz. Grips: Rubber, rosewood or mother-of-pearl. Sights: Notched rear sight with fixed front blade. Features: Miniaturized Model 85 design with concealed hammer. Dual lock cylinder latch. Blue or stainless. Introduced 2005. Imported by Taurus International.
Price: . . . . **$359.00 to $406.00**

TAURUS MODEL 94 REVOLVER

Caliber: 22 LR, 9-shot cylinder; 22 Mag, 8-shot cylinder **Barrel:** 2", 4", 5". **Weight:** 18.5-27.5 oz. **Grips:** Soft black rubber. **Sights:** Serrated ramp front, click-adjustable rear. **Features:** Double action, integral key-lock. Introduced 1989. Imported by Taurus International.
Price: . . . . **$359.00 to $406.00**

TAURUS MODEL 22H RAGING HORNET REVOLVER

Caliber: 22 Hornet, 8-shot. **Barrel:** 10". **Weight:** 50 oz. **Length:** 6.5" overall. **Grips:** Soft black rubber. **Sights:** Fully adjustable, scope mount base included. **Features:** Ventilated rib, stainless steel construction with matte finish. Double-action, integral key-lock. Introduced 1999. Imported by Taurus International.
Price: **$898.00**

TAURUS MODEL 30C RAGING THIRTY

Caliber: 30 Carbine, 8-shot. **Barrel:** 10". **Weight:** 72.3 oz. **Grips:** Soft black rubber. **Sights:** Adjustable. **Features:** Double-action, ventilated rib, matte stainless, comes with five "Stellar" full-moon clips, integral key-lock.
Price: **$898.00**

TAURUS MODEL 44 REVOLVER

Caliber: 44 Mag., 6-shot. **Barrel:** 4", 6-1/2", 8-3/8". **Weight:** 44-3/4 oz. **Grips:** Rubber. **Sights:** Adjustable. **Features:** Double-action. Integral key-lock. Introduced 1994. New Model 44S12 has 12" vent rib barrel. Imported from Brazil by Taurus International Manufacturing, Inc.
Price: Blue or stainless steel . . . . **$445.00 to $602.00**

TAURUS MODEL 217 TARGET "SILHOUETTE"

Caliber: 218 Bee, 8-shot. **Barrel:** 12". **Weight:** 52.3 oz. **Grips:** Rubber. **Sights:** Adjustable. **Features:** Double-action, ventilated rib, adjustable mainspring and trigger stop, matte stainless, integral key-lock.
Price: **$461.00**

TAURUS MODEL 218 RAGING BEE

Caliber: 218 Bee, 7-shot. **Barrel:** 10". **Weight:** 74.9 oz. **Grips:** Rubber. **Sights:** Adjustable rear. **Features:** Ventilated rib, adjustable action, matte stainless, integral key-lock. Also available as Model 218SS6 Tracker with 6-1/2" vent rib barrel.
Price: (Raging Bee) **$898.00**

TAURUS MODEL 425/627 TRACKER REVOLVERS

Caliber: 357 Mag., 7-shot; 41 Mag., 5-shot. **Barrel:** 4" and 6". **Weight:** 28.8-40 oz. (titanium) 24.3-28. (6"). **Grips:** Rubber. **Sights:** Fixed front, adjustable rear. **Features:** Double-action stainless steel, Shadow Gray or Total Titanium; vent rib (steel models only); integral key-lock action. Imported by Taurus International.
Price: . . . . **$531.00 to $766.00**
Price: Total Titanium **$766.00**

TAURUS MODEL 444 ULTRALIGHT

Caliber: 44 Mag, 5-shot. **Barrel:** 4". **Weight:** 28.3 oz. **Length:** 9.8" overall. **Grips:** Cushioned inset rubber. **Sights:** Fixed red-fiber optic front, adjustable rear. **Features:** UltraLite titanium blue finish, titanium/alloy frame built on Raging Bull design. Smooth trigger shoe, 1.760" wide, 6.280" tall. Barrel rate of twist 1:16", 6 grooves. Introduced 2005. Imported by Taurus International.
Price: **$650.00**

Taurus Model 445

Taurus Model 605

Taurus Model 731

Taurus Model 608

Taurus Model 450

Taurus Model 454 Raging Bull

Taurus Raging Bull Model 416

Taurus Model 617

TAURUS MODEL 445
Caliber: 44 Special, 5-shot. **Barrel:** 2". **Weight:** 20.3-28.25 oz. **Length:** 6-3/4" overall. **Grips:** Rubber. **Sights:** Ramp front, notch rear. **Features:** Blue or stainless steel. Standard or DAO concealed hammer, optional porting. Introduced 1997. Imported by Taurus International.
Price: . . . . $345.00 to $500.00
Price: Total Titanium 19.8 oz. $600.00

TAURUS MODEL 605 REVOLVER
Caliber: 357 Mag., 5-shot. **Barrel:** 2". **Weight:** 24 oz. **Grips:** Rubber. **Sights:** Fixed. **Features:** Double-action, blue or stainless or titanium, concealed hammer models DAO, porting optional, integral key-lock. Introduced 1995. Imported by Taurus International.
Price: $625.00

Taurus Model 731 Revolver
Similar to the Taurus Model 605, except in .32 Magnum.
Price: . . . . $438.00 to $531.00

TAURUS MODEL 608 REVOLVER
Caliber: 357 Mag. 38 Spec., 8-shot. **Barrel:** 4", 6-1/2", 8-3/8". **Weight:** 44-57 oz. **Length:** 9-3/8" overall. **Grips:** Soft black rubber. **Sights:** Adjustable. **Features:** Double-action, integral key-lock action. Available in blue or stainless. Introduced 1995. Imported by Taurus International.
Price: . . . . $547.00 to $570.00

Taurus Model 44 Series Revolver
Similar to Taurus Model 60 series, but in .44 Rem. Mag. With six-shot cylinder, blue and matte stainless finishes.
Price: . . . . $500.00 to $578.00

TAURUS MODEL 650CIA REVOLVER
Caliber: 357 Magnum, 5-shot. **Barrel:** 2". **Weight:** 24.5 oz. **Grips:** Rubber. **Sights:** Ramp front, square notch rear. **Features:** Double-action only, blue or matte stainless steel, integral key-lock, internal hammer. Introduced 2001. From Taurus International.
Price: . . . . $383.00 to $430.00

TAURUS MODEL 651 PROTECTOR REVOLVER
Caliber: 357 Magnum, 5-shot. **Barrel:** 2". **Weight:** 17-24.5 oz. **Grips:** Rubber. **Sights:** Fixed. **Features:** Concealed single-action/ double-action design. Shrouded cockable hammer, blue, matte stainless, Shadow Gray, Total Titanium, integral key-lock. Made in Brazil. Imported by Taurus International Manufacturing, Inc.
Price: . . . . $383.00 to $430.00

TAURUS MODEL 450 REVOLVER
Caliber: 45 Colt, 5-shot. **Barrel:** 2". **Weight:** 21.2-22.3 oz. **Length:** 6-5/8" overall. **Grips:** Rubber. **Sights:** Ramp front, notch rear. **Features:** Double-action, blue or stainless, ported, integral key-lock. Introduced 1999. Imported from Brazil by Taurus International.
Price: . . . . $523.00 to $600.00

TAURUS MODEL 444/454/480 RAGING BULL REVOLVERS
Caliber: 44 Mag., 45 LC, 454 Casull, 480 Ruger, 5-shot. **Barrel:** 5", 6-1/2", 8-3/8". **Weight:** 53-63 oz. **Length:** 12" overall (6-1/2" barrel). **Grips:** Soft black rubber. **Sights:** Patridge front, adjustable rear. **Features:** Double-action, ventilated rib, ported, integral key-lock. Introduced 1997. Imported by Taurus International.
Price: Blue . . . . $602.00 to $797.00

TAURUS RAGING BULL MODEL 416
Caliber: 41 Magnum, 6-shot. **Barrel:** 6-1/2". **Weight:** 61.9 oz. **Grips:** Rubber. **Sights:** Adjustable. **Features:** Double-action, ported, ventilated rib, matte stainless, integral key-lock.
Price: $664.00

TAURUS MODEL 617 REVOLVER
Caliber: 357 Magnum, 7-shot. **Barrel:** 2". **Weight:** 28.3 oz. **Length:** 6-3/4" overall. **Grips:** Soft black rubber. **Sights:** Fixed. **Features:** Double-action, blue, Shadow Gray, bright spectrum blue or matte stainless steel, integral key-lock. Available with porting, concealed hammer. Introduced 1998. Imported by Taurus International.
Price: . . . . $391.00 to $453.00
Price: Total Titanium, 19.9 oz. $602.00

Taurus Model 817 Taurus Model 970 Tracker Taurus Model 905

TAURUS MODEL 817 ULTRA-LITE REVOLVER

Caliber: 38 Spec., 7-shot. **Barrel:** 2". **Weight:** 21 oz. **Length:** 6-1/2" overall. **Grips:** Soft rubber. **Sights:** Fixed. **Features:** Double-action, integral key-lock. Rated for +P ammo. Introduced 1999. Imported from Brazil by Taurus International.
Price: Blue $406.00

TAURUS MODEL 850CIA REVOLVER

Caliber: 38 Special, 5-shot. **Barrel:** 2". **Weight:** 17-24.5 oz. **Grips:** Rubber, mother-of-pearl. **Sights:** Ramp front, square notch rear. **Features:** Double-action only, blue or matte stainless steel, rated for +P ammo, integral key-lock, internal hammer. Introduced 2001. From Taurus International.
Price: . . . . $383.00 to $672.00
Price: Total Titanium $578.00

TAURUS MODEL 94, 941 REVOLVER

Caliber: 22 LR (Mod. 94), 22 WMR (Mod. 941), 8-shot. **Barrel:** 2", 4", 5". **Weight:** 27.5 oz. (4" barrel). **Grips:** Soft black rubber. **Sights:** Serrated ramp front, rear adjustable. **Features:** Double-action, integral key-lock. Introduced 1992. Imported by Taurus International.
Price: . . . . $344.00 to $406.00

TAURUS MODEL 970/971 TRACKER REVOLVERS

Caliber: 22 LR (Model 970), 22 Magnum (Model 971); 7-shot. **Barrel:** 6". **Weight:** 53.6 oz. **Grips:** Rubber. **Sights:** Adjustable. **Features:** Double barrel, heavy barrel with ventilated rib; matte stainless finish, integral key-lock. Introduced 2001. From Taurus International.
Price: $422.00

TAURUS MODEL 905, 405, 455 PISTOL CALIBER REVOLVERS

Caliber: 9mm, .40, .45 ACP, 5-shot. **Barrel:** 2", 4", 6-1/2". **Weight:** 21 oz. to 40.8 oz. **Grips:** Rubber. **Sights:** Fixed, adjustable on Model 455SS6 in .45 ACP. **Features:** Produced as a backup gun for law enforcement officers. Introduced 2003. Imported from Brazil by Taurus International.
Price: . . . . $383.00 to $523.00

Both classic six-shooters and modern adaptations for hunting and sport.

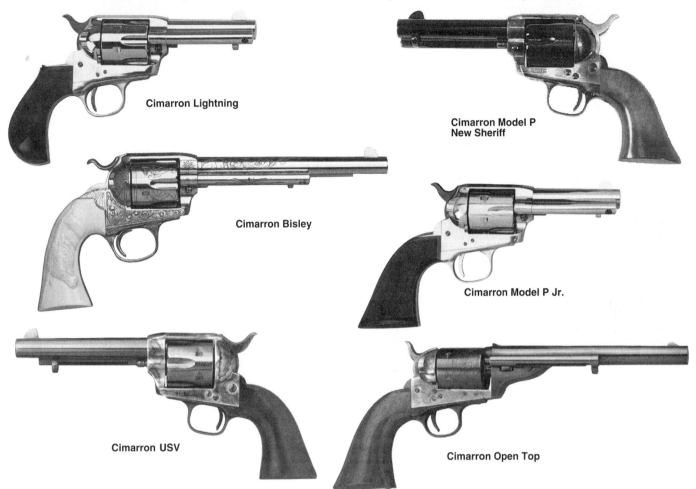

Cimarron Lightning

Cimarron Model P New Sheriff

Cimarron Bisley

Cimarron Model P Jr.

Cimarron USV

Cimarron Open Top

CHARLES DALY 1873 SINGLE-ACTION REVOLVER
Caliber: 357 Mag., 45 Colt, 6-shot. **Barrel:** 4.75", 5.5", 7.5". **Weight:** 36 oz. (4.75" barrel). **Length:** 10" overall (4.75" barrel). **Grips:** Hardwood with company logo near tang. **Sights:** Blade front, notch rear. **Features:** Stainless steel and color case hardened finishes. From K.B.I., Inc.
Price: 1873 Steel, 45 Colt, 4.75", 5.5", 7.5" barrel, brass frame **$449.00**
Price: 1873 Steel, 357 Mag, 4.75", 5.5", 7.5" barrel, brass frame . . **$479.00**
Price: 1873 Steel, 45 Colt, 4.75", 5.5", 7.5" barrel, steel frame **$449.00**
Price: 1873 Stainless Steel, 357 Mag, 4.75", 5.5", 7.5" barrel **$659.00**
Price: 1873 Stainless Steel, 45 Colt, 4.75", 5.5", 7.5" barrel **$659.00**

CIMARRON LIGHTNING SA
Caliber: 32-20, 32 H&R, 38 Colt, 38 Special. **Barrel:** 3-1/2", 4-3/4", 5-1/2". **Grips:** Smooth or checkered walnut. **Sights:** Blade front. **Features:** Replica of the Colt 1877 Lightning DA. Similar to Cimarron Thunderer™, except smaller grip frame to fit smaller hands. Standard blue, charcoal blue or nickel finish with forged, old model, or color case hardened frame. Introduced 2001. From Cimarron F.A. Co.
Price: . . . . **$499.00 to $559.00**

CIMARRON MODEL P
Caliber: 32 WCF, 38 WCF, 357 Mag., 44 WCF, 44 Spec., 45 Colt, 45 LC and 45 ACP. **Barrel:** 4-3/4", 5-1/2", 7-1/2". **Weight:** 39 oz. **Length:** 10" overall (4" barrel). **Grips:** Walnut. **Sights:** Blade front, fixed or adjustable rear. **Features:** Uses "old model" black powder frame with "Bullseye" ejector or New Model frame. Imported by Cimarron F.A. Co.
Price: . . . . **$499.00 to $559.00**
Price: New Sheriff . . . . **$499.00 to $559.00**

Cimarron Bisley Model Single-Action Revolvers
Similar to 1873 Model P, special grip frame and trigger guard, knurled wide-spur hammer, curved trigger. Available in 357 Mag., 44 WCF, 44 Spl., 45 Colt. Introduced 1999. Imported by Cimarron F.A. Co.
Price: **$525.00**

CIMARRON MODEL "P" JR.
Caliber: 32-20, 32 H&R, 38 Special. **Barrel:** 3-1/2", 4-3/4", 5-1/2". **Grips:** Checkered walnut. **Sights:** Blade front. **Features:** Styled after 1873 Colt Peacemaker, except 20 percent smaller. Blue finish with color case-hardened frame; Cowboy Comp® action. Introduced 2001. From Cimarron F.A. Co.
Price: . . . . **$489.00 to $529.00**

CIMARRON U. S. VOLUNTEER ARTILLERY MODEL SINGLE-ACTION
Caliber: 45 Colt. **Barrel:** 5-1/2". **Weight:** 39 oz. **Length:** 11-1/2" overall. **Grips:** Walnut. **Sights:** Fixed. **Features:** U.S. markings and cartouche, case-hardened frame and hammer; 45 Colt only. Imported by Cimarron F.A. Co.
Price: . . . . **$549.00 to $599.00**

CIMARRON 1872 OPEN TOP REVOLVER
Caliber: 38, 44 Special, 44 Colt, 44 Russian, 45LC, 45 S&W Schofield. **Barrel:** 5-1/2" and 7-1/2". **Grips:** Walnut. **Sights:** Blade front, fixed rear. **Features:** Replica of first cartridge-firing revolver. Blue, charcoal blue, nickel or Original® finish; Navy-style brass or steel Army-style frame. Introduced 2001 by Cimarron F.A. Co.
Price: . . . . **$529.00 to $599.00**

HANDGUNS — Single-Action Revolvers

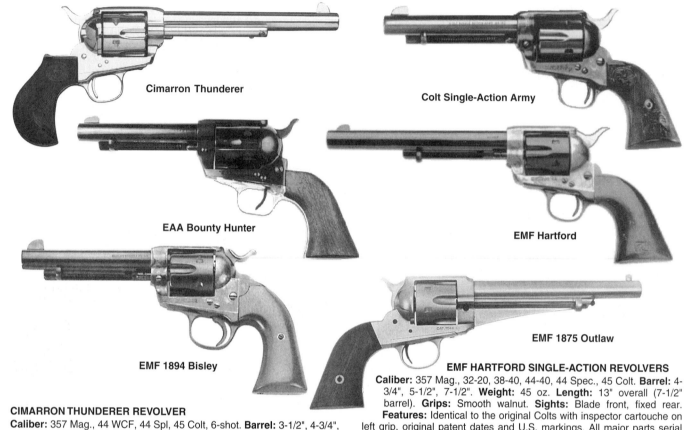

Cimarron Thunderer

Colt Single-Action Army

EAA Bounty Hunter

EMF Hartford

EMF 1894 Bisley

EMF 1875 Outlaw

CIMARRON THUNDERER REVOLVER

Caliber: 357 Mag., 44 WCF, 44 Spl, 45 Colt, 6-shot. **Barrel:** 3-1/2", 4-3/4", 5-1/2", 7-1/2", with ejector. **Weight:** 38 oz. (3-1/2" barrel). **Grips:** Smooth or checkered walnut. **Sights:** Blade front, notch rear. **Features:** Thunderer grip; color case-hardened frame with balance blued. Introduced 1993. Imported by Cimarron F.A. Co.

Price: 3-1/2", 4-3/4", smooth grips . . . . $519.00 to $549.00
Price: As above, checkered grips . . . . $564.00 to $584.00
Price: 5-1/2", 7-1/2", smooth grips . . . . $519.00 to $549.00
Price: As above, checkered grips . . . . $564.00 to $584.00

COLT SINGLE-ACTION ARMY REVOLVER

Caliber: 357 Mag., 38 Special, .32/20, 44-40, 45 Colt, 6-shot. **Barrel:** 4-3/4", 5-1/2", 7-1/2". **Weight:** 40 oz. (4-3/4" barrel). **Length:** 10-1/4" overall (4-3/4" barrel). **Grips:** Black Eagle composite. **Sights:** Blade front, notch rear. **Features:** Available in full nickel finish with nickel grip medallions, or Royal Blue with color case-hardened frame. Reintroduced 1992.

Price: . . . . $1,380.00 to $1,500.00

EAA BOUNTY HUNTER SA REVOLVERS

Caliber: 22 LR/22 WMR, 357 Mag., 44 Mag., 45 Colt, 6-shot. **Barrel:** 4-1/2", 7-1/2". **Weight:** 2.5 lbs. **Length:** 11" overall (4-5/8" barrel). **Grips:** Smooth walnut. **Sights:** Blade front, grooved topstrap rear. **Features:** Transfer bar safety; 3-position hammer; hammer forged barrel. Introduced 1992. Imported by European American Armory.

Price: Blue or case-hardened $369.00
Price: Nickel $399.00
Price: 22LR/22WMR, blue $269.00
Price: As above, nickel $299.00

EMF MODEL 1873 FRONTIER MARSHAL

Caliber: 357 Mag., 45 Colt. **Barrel:** 4-3/4", 5-1/2, 7-1/2". **Weight:** 39 oz. **Length:** 10-1/2" overall. **Grips:** One-piece walnut. **Sights:** Blade front, notch rear. **Features:** Bright brass trigger guard and backstrap, color case-hardened frame, blued barrel and cylinder. Introduced 1998. Imported from Italy by IAR, Inc.

Price: $395.00

EMF HARTFORD SINGLE-ACTION REVOLVERS

Caliber: 357 Mag., 32-20, 38-40, 44-40, 44 Spec., 45 Colt. **Barrel:** 4-3/4", 5-1/2", 7-1/2". **Weight:** 45 oz. **Length:** 13" overall (7-1/2" barrel). **Grips:** Smooth walnut. **Sights:** Blade front, fixed rear. **Features:** Identical to the original Colts with inspector cartouche on left grip, original patent dates and U.S. markings. All major parts serial numbered using original Colt-style lettering, numbering. Bullseye ejector head and color case-hardening on frame and hammer. Introduced 1990. From E.M.F.

Price: $500.00
Price: Cavalry or Artillery $390.00
Price: Nickel plated, add $125.00
Price: Case-hardened New Model frame $365.00

EMF 1894 Bisley Revolver

Similar to the Hartford single-action revolver except has special grip frame and trigger guard, wide spur hammer; available in 38-40 or 45 Colt, 4-3/4", 5-1/2" or 7-1/2" barrel. Introduced 1995. Imported by E.M.F.

Price: Case-hardened/blue $400.00
Price: Nickel $525.00

EMF Hartford Pinkerton Single-Action Revolver

Same as the regular Hartford except has 4" barrel with ejector tube and bird's-head grip. Calibers: 357 Mag., 45 Colt. Introduced 1997. Imported by E.M.F.

Price: $375.00

EMF Hartford Express Single-Action Revolver

Same as the regular Hartford model except uses grip of the Colt Lightning revolver. Barrel lengths of 4", 4-3/4", 5-1/2". Introduced 1997. Imported by E.M.F.

Price: $375.00

EMF 1875 OUTLAW REVOLVER

Caliber: 357 Mag., 44-40, 45 Colt. **Barrel:** 7-1/2". **Weight:** 46 oz. **Length:** 13-1/2" overall. **Grips:** Smooth walnut. **Sights:** Blade front, fixed groove rear. **Features:** Authentic copy of 1875 Remington with firing pin in hammer; color case-hardened frame, blue cylinder, barrel, steel backstrap and brass trigger guard. Also available in nickel, factory engraved. Imported by E.M.F.

Price: All calibers $575.00
Price: Nickel $735.00

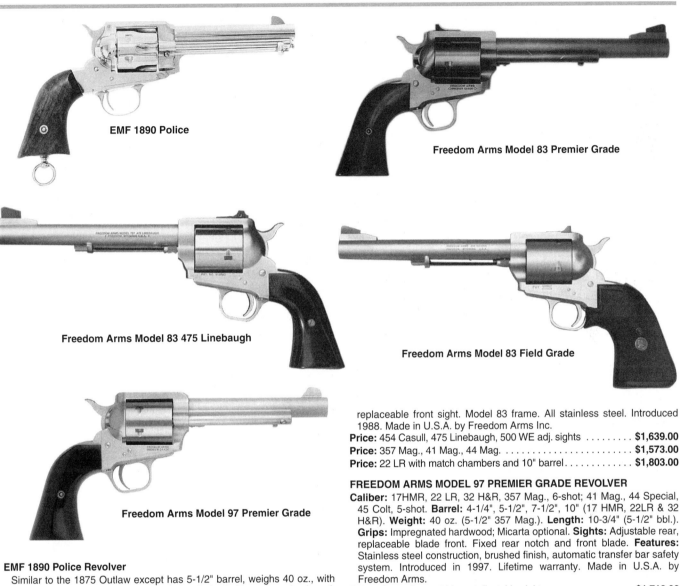

EMF 1890 Police

Freedom Arms Model 83 Premier Grade

Freedom Arms Model 83 475 Linebaugh

Freedom Arms Model 83 Field Grade

Freedom Arms Model 97 Premier Grade

replaceable front sight. Model 83 frame. All stainless steel. Introduced 1988. Made in U.S.A. by Freedom Arms Inc.

Price: 454 Casull, 475 Linebaugh, 500 WE adj. sights **$1,639.00**
Price: 357 Mag., 41 Mag., 44 Mag. **$1,573.00**
Price: 22 LR with match chambers and 10" barrel............ **$1,803.00**

FREEDOM ARMS MODEL 97 PREMIER GRADE REVOLVER

Caliber: 17HMR, 22 LR, 32 H&R, 357 Mag., 6-shot; 41 Mag., 44 Special, 45 Colt, 5-shot. **Barrel:** 4-1/4", 5-1/2", 7-1/2", 10" (17 HMR, 22LR & 32 H&R). **Weight:** 40 oz. (5-1/2" 357 Mag.). **Length:** 10-3/4" (5-1/2" bbl.). **Grips:** Impregnated hardwood; Micarta optional. **Sights:** Adjustable rear, replaceable blade front. Fixed rear notch and front blade. **Features:** Stainless steel construction, brushed finish, automatic transfer bar safety system. Introduced in 1997. Lifetime warranty. Made in U.S.A. by Freedom Arms.

Price: Centerfire cartridges, adjustable sights **$1,718.00**
Price: Rimfire cartridges **$1,784.00**
Price: 32 H&R, 357 Mag., 6-shot; 45 Colt, fixed sights **$1,624.00**
Price: Extra fitted cylinders, centerfire, 22 WMR, 17 Mach II..... **$272.00**
Price: Extra fitted 22 LR match grade cylinder............... **$404.00**
Price: 22 LR match cylinder in place of 22 LR sporting cylinder ... **$132.00**
Price: 357 Mag., 45 Colt, fixed sight **$1,576.00**
Price: Extra fitted cylinders 38 Special, 45 ACP **$264.00**
Price: 22 LR with sporting chambers **$1,732.00**
Price: Extra fitted 22 WMR cylinder **$264.00**
Price: Extra fitted 22 LR match grade cylinder **$476.00**
Price: 22 match grade chamber instead of 22 LR sport chamber . **$214.00**

HERITAGE ROUGH RIDER REVOLVER

Caliber: 17HMR, 17LR, 32 H&R, 32 S&W, 32 S&W Long, 357 Mag, 44-40, 45 LC, 22 LR, 22 LR/22 WMR combo, 6-shot. **Barrel:** 2-3/4", 3-1/2", 4-3/4", 6-1/2", 9". **Weight:** 31 to 38 oz. **Length:** NA. **Grips:** Exotic cocobolo laminated wood or mother-of-pearl; bird's-head models offered. **Sights:** Blade front, fixed rear. Adjustable sight on 4", 6" and 9" models. **Features:** Hammer block safety. High polish blue, black satin, silver satin, case-hardened and stainless finish. Introduced 1993. Made in U.S.A. by Heritage Mfg., Inc.

Price: .... **$159.95 to $499.95**

EMF 1890 Police Revolver

Similar to the 1875 Outlaw except has 5-1/2" barrel, weighs 40 oz., with 12-1/2" overall length. Has lanyard ring in butt. No web under barrel. Calibers 357, 44-40, 45 Colt. Imported by E.M.F.

Price: All calibers **$590.00**
Price: Nickel **$750.00**

FREEDOM ARMS MODEL 83 PREMIER GRADE REVOLVER

Caliber: 357 Mag., 41 Mag., 44 Mag., 454 Casull, 475 Linebaugh, 500 Wyo. Exp., 5-shot. **Barrel:** 4-3/4", 6", 7-1/2", 9" (357 Mag. only), 10" (except 357 Mag. and 500 Wyo. Exp. **Weight:** 53 oz. (7-1/2" bbl. In 454 Casull). **Length:** 13" (7-1/2" bbl.). **Grips:** Impregnated hardwood. **Sights:** Adjustable rear with replaceable front sight. Fixed rear notch and front blade. **Features:** Stainless steel construction with brushed finish; manual sliding safety bar. Micarta grips optional. 500 Wyo. Exp. Introduced 2006. Lifetime warranty. Made in U.S.A. by Freedom Arms, Inc.

Price: 500 WE, 454 Casull, 475 Linebaugh, 454 Casull **$2,120.00**
Price: 454 Casull, fixed sight........................... **$2,038.00**
Price: 357 Mag., 41 Mag., 44 Mag. **$2,035.00**

FREEDOM ARMS MODEL 83 FIELD GRADE REVOLVER

Caliber: 22 LR, 357 Mag., 41 Mag., 44 Mag., 454 Casull, 475 Linebaugh, 500 Wyo. Exp., 5-shot. **Barrel:** 4-3/4", 6", 7-1/2", 9" (357 Mag. only), 10" (except 357 Mag. and 500 Wyo. Exp.) **Weight:** 56 oz. (7-1/2" bbl. In 454 Casull). **Length:** 13.1" (7-1/2" bbl.). **Grips:** Pachmayr standard, impregnated hardwood or Micarta optional. **Sights:** Adjustable rear with

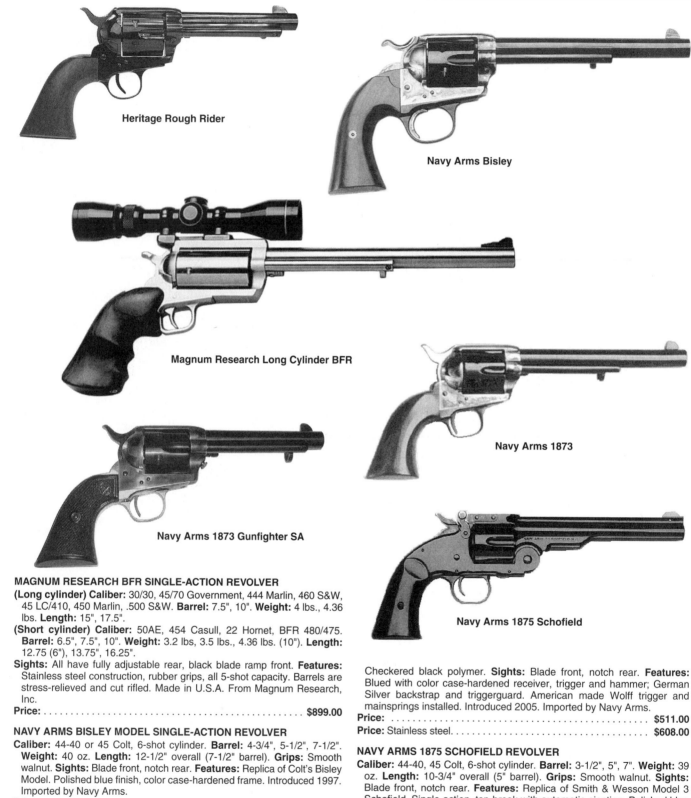

Heritage Rough Rider

Navy Arms Bisley

Magnum Research Long Cylinder BFR

Navy Arms 1873

Navy Arms 1873 Gunfighter SA

Navy Arms 1875 Schofield

MAGNUM RESEARCH BFR SINGLE-ACTION REVOLVER
(Long cylinder) Caliber: 30/30, 45/70 Government, 444 Marlin, 460 S&W, 45 LC/410, 450 Marlin, .500 S&W. **Barrel:** 7.5", 10". **Weight:** 4 lbs., 4.36 lbs. **Length:** 15", 17.5".
(Short cylinder) Caliber: 50AE, 454 Casull, 22 Hornet, BFR 480/475. **Barrel:** 6.5", 7.5", 10". **Weight:** 3.2 lbs, 3.5 lbs., 4.36 lbs. (10"). **Length:** 12.75 (6"), 13.75", 16.25".
Sights: All have fully adjustable rear, black blade ramp front. **Features:** Stainless steel construction, rubber grips, all 5-shot capacity. Barrels are stress-relieved and cut rifled. Made in U.S.A. From Magnum Research, Inc.
Price: **$899.00**

NAVY ARMS BISLEY MODEL SINGLE-ACTION REVOLVER
Caliber: 44-40 or 45 Colt, 6-shot cylinder. **Barrel:** 4-3/4", 5-1/2", 7-1/2". **Weight:** 40 oz. **Length:** 12-1/2" overall (7-1/2" barrel). **Grips:** Smooth walnut. **Sights:** Blade front, notch rear. **Features:** Replica of Colt's Bisley Model. Polished blue finish, color case-hardened frame. Introduced 1997. Imported by Navy Arms.
Price: **$511.00**

NAVY ARMS 1873 GUNFIGHTER SINGLE-ACTION REVOLVER
Caliber: 357 Mag., 44-40, 45 Colt, 6-shot cylinder. **Barrel:** 4-3/4", 5-1/2", 7-1/2". **Weight:** 37 oz. **Length:** 10-1/4" overall (4-3/4" barrel). **Grips:**

Checkered black polymer. **Sights:** Blade front, notch rear. **Features:** Blued with color case-hardened receiver, trigger and hammer; German Silver backstrap and triggerguard. American made Wolff trigger and mainsprings installed. Introduced 2005. Imported by Navy Arms.
Price: **$511.00**
Price: Stainless steel. **$608.00**

NAVY ARMS 1875 SCHOFIELD REVOLVER
Caliber: 44-40, 45 Colt, 6-shot cylinder. **Barrel:** 3-1/2", 5", 7". **Weight:** 39 oz. **Length:** 10-3/4" overall (5" barrel). **Grips:** Smooth walnut. **Sights:** Blade front, notch rear. **Features:** Replica of Smith & Wesson Model 3 Schofield. Single-action, top-break with automatic ejection. Polished blue finish. Introduced 1994. Imported by Navy Arms.
Price: Hideout Model, 3-1/2" barrel **$849.00**
Price: Wells Fargo, 5" barrel **$849.00**
Price: U.S. Cavalry model, 7" barrel, military markings **$849.00**

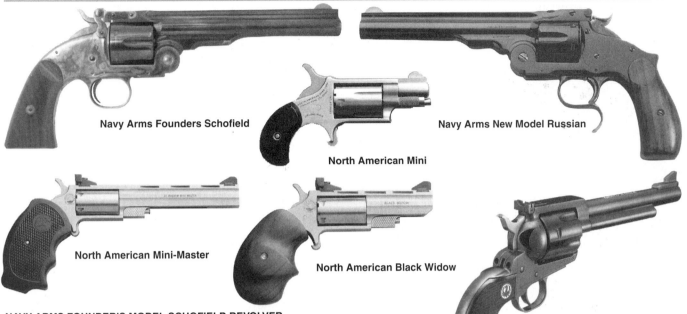

Navy Arms Founders Schofield

North American Mini

Navy Arms New Model Russian

North American Mini-Master

North American Black Widow

Ruger New Model Blackhawk 50th Anniversary

NAVY ARMS FOUNDER'S MODEL SCHOFIELD REVOLVER

Caliber: .45 Colt, .38 Spl., 6-shot cylinder. **Barrel:** 7-1/2". **Weight:** 41 oz. **Length:** 13-3/4". **Grips:** Deluxe hand-rubbed walnut with cartouching. **Sights:** Blade front, notch rear. **Features:** Charcoal blued with bone color case-hardened receiver, trigger, hammer and backstrap. Limited production "VF" serial number prefex. Introduced 2005. Imported by Navy Arms.
Price: **$946.00**

NAVY ARMS NEW MODEL RUSSIAN REVOLVER

Caliber: 44 Russian, 6-shot cylinder. **Barrel:** 6-1/2". **Weight:** 40 oz. **Length:** 12" overall. **Grips:** Smooth walnut. **Sights:** Blade front, notch rear. **Features:** Replica of the S&W Model 3 Russian Third Model revolver. Spur trigger guard, polished blue finish. Introduced 1999. Imported by Navy Arms.
Price: **$908.00**

NAVY ARMS SCOUT SMALL FRAME SINGLE-ACTION REVOLVER

Caliber: .38 Spl., 6-shot cylinder. **Barrel:** 4-3/4", 5-1/2". **Weight:** 37 oz. **Length:** 10-3/4" overall (5-1/2" barrel). **Grips:** Checkered black polymer. **Sights:** Blade front, notch rear. **Features:** Blued with color case-hardened receiver, trigger and hammer; German Silver backstrap and triggerguard. Introduced 2005. Imported by Navy Arms.
Price: **$511.00**

NORTH AMERICAN MINI REVOLVERS

Caliber: 22 Short, 22 LR, 22 WMR, 5-shot. **Barrel:** 1-1/8", 1-5/8". **Weight:** 4 to 6.6 oz. **Length:** 3-5/8" to 6-1/8" overall. **Grips:** Laminated wood. **Sights:** Blade front, notch fixed rear. **Features:** All stainless steel construction. Polished satin and matte finish. Engraved models available. From North American Arms.
Price: 22 Short, 22 LR **$193.00**
Price: 22 WMR, 1-1/8" or 1-5/8" bbl. **$193.00**
Price: 22 WMR, 1-1/8" or 1-5/8" bbl. with extra 22 LR cylinder **$193.00**

NORTH AMERICAN MINI-MASTER

Caliber: 22 LR, 22 WMR, 17 HMR, 5-shot cylinder. **Barrel:** 4". **Weight:** 10.7 oz. **Length:** 7.75" overall. **Grips:** Checkered hard black rubber. **Sights:** Blade front, white outline rear adjustable for elevation, or fixed. **Features:** Heavy vented barrel; full-size grips. Non-fluted cylinder. Introduced 1989.
Price: Adjustable sight, 22 WMR, 17 HMR or 22 LR **$301.00**
Price: As above with extra WMR/LR cylinder **$330.00**
Price: Fixed sight, 22 WMR, 17 HMR or 22 LR **$272.00**
Price: As above with extra WMR/LR cylinder **$330.00**

North American Black Widow Revolver

Similar to Mini-Master, 2" heavy vent barrel. Built on 22 WMR frame. Non-fluted cylinder, black rubber grips. Available with Millett Low Profile fixed sights or Millett sight adjustable for elevation only. Overall length 5-7/8", weighs 8.8 oz. From North American Arms.
Price: Adjustable sight, 22 LR, 17 HMR or 22 WMR **$287.00**
Price: As above with extra WMR/LR cylinder **$316.00**
Price: Fixed sight, 22 LR, 17 HMR or 22 WMR **$287.00**
Price: As above with extra WMR/LR cylinder **$287.00**

REPLICA ARMS 1873 SINGLE ACTION REVOLVER

Caliber: .357 Magnum, 6-shot cylinder. **Barrel:** 4-3/4". **Weight:** 32 oz. **Length:** 10-1/4" overall. **Grips:** Walnut finished. **Sights:** Blade front, notch rear. **Features:** bead blue matte finish, matte brass trigger guard and backstrap. Introduced 2005. Imported by Navy Arms.
Price: **$334.95**

RUGER NEW MODEL SINGLE SIX & NEW MODEL .32 H&R SINGLE SIX REVOLVERS

Caliber: 17HMR, 17 Mach 2, 22LR, 22 Mag, 32 H&R. **Barrel:** 4-5/8", 5-1/2", 6-1/2", 7-1/2", 9-1/2". 6-shot. **Grips:** Rosewood, black laminate, simulated ivory. **Sights:** Adjustable or fixed. **Features:** Blued or stainless metalwork, short grips available, convertible models available. Introduced 2003 in 17HMR .
Price: 17 HMR/17 Mach 2 (blued and satin stainless) . . **$411.00 to $695.00**
Price: 22 LR /22 Mag. (blued and satin stainless) . . . . . **$399.00 to $650.00**
Price: 32 H&R (blued and gloss stainless) . . . . **$535.00 to $576.00**

RUGER NEW MODEL BLACKHAWK/BLACKHAWK CONVERTIBLE

Caliber: 30 Carbine, 357 Mag./38 Spec., 41 Mag., 45 Colt, 6-shot. **Barrel:** 4-5/8", 5-1/2", 6-1/2", 7-1/2" (30 carbine and 45 Colt). **Weight:** 38 to 45 oz. **Lengths:** 10-3/8" to 13-3/8". **Grips:** American walnut. **Sights:** 1/8" ramp front, micro-click rear adjustable for windage and elevation. **Features:** Rosewood grips, Ruger transfer bar safety system, independent firing pin, hardened chrome-moly steel frame, music wire springs through-out. Case and lock included. Convertibles come with extra cylinder.
Price: 30 Carbine, 7-1/2" (BN31, blued) **$482.00**
Price: 357 Mag. (blued or satin stainless). . . . . **$482.00 to $589.00**
Price: 41 Mag. (blued) **$482.00**
Price: 45 Colt (blued or satin stainless) . . . . **$482.00 to $589.00**
Price: 357 Mag./9mm Convertible (BN34X, BN36X) **$546.00**
Price: 45 Colt/45 ACP Convertible (BN44X, BN455X). **$546.00**
Price: 50th Anniversary 44 Mag (S465N-50) **$605.00**

Ruger Bisley Single-Action

Ruger Blackhawk

Ruger Super Blackhawk Hunter

Ruger New Vaquero

Ruger New Bearcat

Taurus Gaucho

Ruger Bisley Single-Action Revolver

Similar to standard Blackhawk, hammer is lower with smoothly curved, deeply checkered wide spur. The trigger is strongly curved with wide smooth surface. Longer grip frame. Adjustable rear sight, ramp-style front. Unfluted cylinder and roll engraving, adjustable sights. Chambered for 22 LR, 357 Mag, 44 Mag. and 45 Colt; 6-1/2" to 7-1/2" barrel; overall length of 11-1/2" to 13-1/2"; weighs 43-51 oz. Plastic lockable case. Orig. fluted cylinder introduced 1985; discontinued 1991. Unfluted cylinder introduced 1986.
Price: RB35W (357Mag) RB-44W (44 Mag), RB45W (45 Colt) **$597.00**
Price: RB22AW (22LR) **$475.00**

RUGER NEW MODEL SUPER BLACKHAWK

Caliber: 44 Mag., 6-shot. Also fires 44 Spec. **Barrel:** 4-5/8", 5-1/2", 7-1/2", 10-1/2" bull. **Weight:** 45-55 oz. **Length:** 10.5" to 16.5" overall. **Grips:** Rosewood or black laminate. **Sights:** 1/8" ramp front, micro-click rear adjustable for windage and elevation. **Features:** Ruger transfer bar safety system, fluted or unfluted cylinder, steel grip and cylinder frame, round or square back trigger guard, wide serrated trigger, wide spur hammer. With case and lock.
Price: Blue, 4-5/8", 5-1/2", 7-1/2" (S458N, S45N, S47N) **$579.00**
Price: Blue, 10-1/2" bull barrel (S411N) **$589.00**
Price: Stainless, 4-5/8", 5-1/2", 7-1/2" (KS458N, KS45N, KS47N) . **$594.00**
Price: Stainless, 10-1/2" bull barrel (KS411N) **$617.00**
Price: Hunter model, satin stainless, 7-1/2" (KS47NHNN) **$696.00**
Price: Hunter model, Bisley frame, satin stainless 7-1/2"
(KS47NHB) **$696.00**

RUGER NEW MODEL SUPER BLACKHAWK HUNTER

Caliber: 44 Mag., 6-shot. **Barrel:** 7-1/2", full-length solid rib, unfluted cylinder. **Weight:** 52 oz. **Length:** 13-5/8". **Grips:** Black laminated wood. **Sights:** Adjustable rear, replaceable front blade. **Features:** Reintroduced Ultimate SA revolver. Includes instruction manual, high-impact case, set 1" medium scope rings, gun lock, ejector rod as standard.
Price: **$639.00**

RUGER NEW VAQUERO SINGLE-ACTION REVOLVER

Caliber: 357 Mag., 45 Colt, 6-shot. **Barrel:** 4-5/8", 5-1/2", 7-1/2". **Weight:** 39-45 oz. **Length:** 10-1/2" overall (4-5/8" barrel). **Grips:** Rubber with Ruger medallion. **Sights:** Blade front, fixed notch rear. **Features:** Transfer bar safety system and loading gate interlock. Blued model color case-hardened finish on frame, rest polished and blued. Engraved model available. Gloss stainless. Introduced 2005.
Price: 357 Mag., blued or stainless **$590.00**
Price: 45 Colt, blued or stainless **$590.00**

RUGER NEW BEARCAT SINGLE-ACTION

Caliber: 22 LR, 6-shot. **Barrel:** 4". **Weight:** 24 oz. **Length:** 9" overall. **Grips:** Smooth rosewood with Ruger medallion. **Sights:** Blade front, fixed notch rear. **Features:** Reintroduction of the Ruger Bearcat with slightly lengthened frame, Ruger transfer bar safety system. Available in blue only. Rosewood grips. Introduced 1996 (blued), 2003 (stainless). With case and lock.
Price: SBC4, blued **$410.00**
Price: KSBC-4, satin stainless **$464.00**

TAURUS SINGLE-ACTION GAUCHO REVOLVERS

Caliber: 38 Spl, 357 Mag, 44-40, 45 Colt, 6-shot. **Barrel:** 4.75", 5.5", 7.5", 12". **Weight:** 36.7-37.7 oz. **Length:** 13". **Grips:** Checkered black polymer. **Sights:** Blade front, fixed notch rear. Integral transfer bar; blue, blue with case hardened frame, matte stainless and the hand polished "Sundance" stainless finish. Removable cylinder, half-cock notch. Introduced 2005. Imported from Brazil by Taurus International.
Price: S/A-357-B, 357 Mag., Sundance blue finish, 5.5" barrel **$499.00**
Price: S/A-357-S/S7, 357 Mag., polished stainless, 7.5" barrel **$510.00**
Price: S/A-4440-CHSA4, 44-40, case-hardened, 4.75" barrel..... **$510.00**
Price: S/A-45B12, 45 Colt, Buntline, 12" barrel **$525.00**

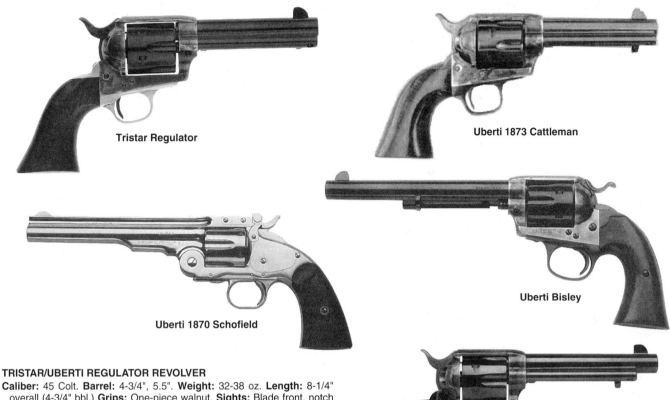

Tristar Regulator

Uberti 1873 Cattleman

Uberti 1870 Schofield

Uberti Bisley

U.S. Fire Arms Single Action Army Revolver

TRISTAR/UBERTI REGULATOR REVOLVER

Caliber: 45 Colt. **Barrel:** 4-3/4", 5.5". **Weight:** 32-38 oz. **Length:** 8-1/4" overall (4-3/4" bbl.) **Grips:** One-piece walnut. **Sights:** Blade front, notch rear. **Features:** Uberti replica of 1873 Colt Model "P" revolver. Color-case hardened steel frame, brass backstrap and trigger guard, hammer-block safety. Imported from Italy by Tristar Sporting Arms.
Price: Regulator **$455.00**
Price: Regulator Deluxe (blued backstrap, trigger guard) **$489.00**
Price: Stallion (.17 HMR and .17 M2 Cylinders) **$459.00**

UBERTI 1873 CATTLEMAN SINGLE-ACTION

Caliber: 45 Colt; 6-shot fluted cylinder **Barrel:** 4-3/4", 5-1/2", 7-1/2". **Weight:** 2.3 lbs. (5-1/2" bbl.). **Length:** 11" overall (5-1/2" bbl.). **Grips:** Styles: Frisco (pearl styled); Desperado (buffalo horn styled); Chisholm (checkered walnut); Gunfighter (black checkered), Cody (ivory styled), one-piece walnut. **Sights:** Blade front, groove rear. **Features:** Steel or brass backstrap, trigger guard; color case-hardened frame, blued barrel, cylinder. NM designates New Model plunger style frame; OM designates Old Model screw cylinder pin retainer. Imported from Italy by Uberti U.S.A.
Price: 1873 Cattleman Frisco **$635.00**
Price: 1873 Cattleman Desperado (2006) **$635.00**
Price: 1873 Cattleman Chisholm (2006) **$385.00**
Price: 1873 Cattleman NM, blued 4-3/4" barrel **$385.00**
Price: 1873 Cattleman NM, stainless steel 7-1/2" barrel **$530.00**
Price: 1873 Cattleman OM, Old West finish, 5-1/2" barrel **$525.00**
Price: 1873 Cattleman NM, Nickel finish, 7-1/2" barrel **$545.00**

UBERTI 1873 CATTLEMAN BIRD'S HEAD SINGLE ACTION

Caliber: 357 Mag., 45 Colt; 6-shot fluted cylinder **Barrel:** 3-1/2", 4", 4-3/4", 5-1/2". **Weight:** 2.3 lbs. (5-1/2" bbl.). **Length:** 10.9" overall (5-1/2" bbl.). **Grips:** One-piece walnut. **Sights:** Blade front, groove rear. **Features:** Steel or brass backstrap, trigger guard; color case-hardened frame, blued barrel, cylinder. Imported from Italy by Uberti U.S.A.
Price: 1873 Cattleman Bird's Head OM 3-1/2" barrel **$500.00**

UBERTI 1873 BUNTLINE AND REVOLVER CARBINE SINGLE ACTION

Caliber: 357 Mag., 44-40, 45 Colt; 6-shot fluted cylinder **Barrel:** 18". **Length:** 22.9" to 34". **Grips:** Walnut pistol grip or rifle stock. **Sights:** Fixed or adjustable. **Features:** Imported from Italy by Uberti U.S.A.
Price: 1873 Revolver Carbine, 18" barrel, 34" OAL **$585.00**
Price: 1873 Cattleman Buntline Target, 18" barrel, 22.9" OAL **$520.00**

UBERTI OUTLAW, FRONTIER, AND POLICE REVOLVERS

Caliber: 45 Colt, 6-shot fluted cylinder. **Barrel:** 5-1/2", 7-1/2". **Weight:** 2.5 to 2.8 lbs. **Length:** 10.8" to 13.6" overall. **Grips:** Two-piece smooth walnut. **Sights:** Blade front, notch rear. **Features:** Cartridge version of 1858 Remington percussion revolver. Nickel and blued finishes. Imported by Uberti U.S.A.
Price: 1875 Outlaw nickel finish **$515.00**
Price: 1875 Frontier, blued finish **$435.00**
Price: 1890 Police, blued finish **$440.00**

UBERTI 1870 SCHOFIELD-STYLE BREAK-TOP REVOLVER

Caliber: 38, 44 Russian, 44-40, 45 Colt, 6-shot cylinder. **Barrel:** 3-1/2", 5", 7". **Weight:** 2.4 lbs. (5" barrel) **Length:** 10.8" overall (5" barrel). **Grips:** Two-piece smooth walnut or pearl. **Sights:** Blade front, notch rear. **Features:** Replica of Smith & Wesson Model 3 Schofield. Single-action, top-break with automatic ejection. Polished blue finish (first model). Introduced 1994. Imported by Uberti U.S.A.
Price: No. 3-2nd Model, nickel finish. **$925.00**

UBERTI BISLEY AND STALLION MODELS SINGLE-ACTION REVOLVERS

Caliber: 357 Mag., 45 Colt (Bisley); 22LR and 38 Special (Stallion), both with 6-shot fluted cylinder. **Barrel:** 4-3/4", 5-1/2", 7-1/2". **Weight:** 2 to 2.5 lbs. **Length:** 12.7" overall (7-1/2" barrel). **Grips:** Two-piece walnut. **Sights:** Blade front, notch rear. **Features:** Replica of Colt's Bisley Model. Polished blue finish, color case-hardened frame. Introduced 1997. Imported by Uberti U.S.A.
Price: 1873 Stallion, 5-1/2" barrel **$425.00**
Price: 1873 Bisley, 7-1/2" barrel **$500.00**

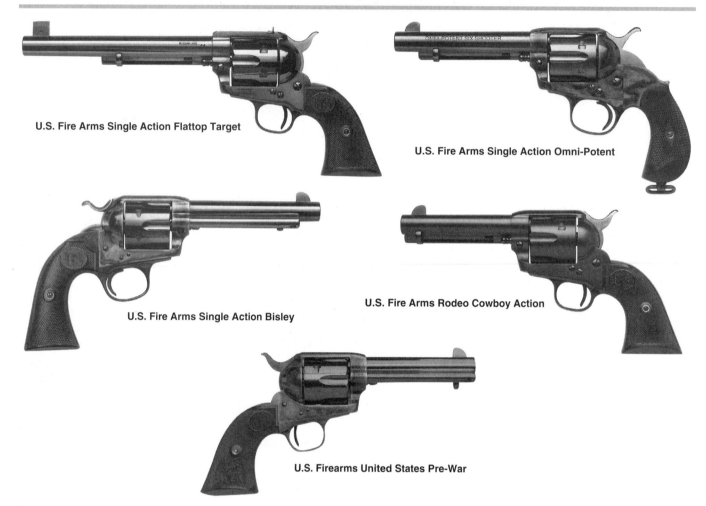

U.S. Fire Arms Single Action Flattop Target

U.S. Fire Arms Single Action Omni-Potent

U.S. Fire Arms Single Action Bisley

U.S. Fire Arms Rodeo Cowboy Action

U.S. Firearms United States Pre-War

U.S. FIRE ARMS SINGLE-ACTION REVOLVER
Caliber: 45 Colt (standard); 32 WCF, 38 WCF, 38 Special, 44 WCF, 44 Special, 6-shot cylinder. **Barrel:** 4-3/4", 5-1/2", 7-1/2". **Weight:** 37 oz. **Length:** NA. **Grips:** Hard rubber. **Sights:** Blade front, notch rear. **Features:** Recreation of original guns; 3" and 4" have no ejector. Available with all-blue, blue with color case-hardening, or full nickel-plate finish. Other models include Government Inspector Series ($1,485, walnut grips), Custer Battlefield Gun ($1,485, 7-1/2" barrel), Patriot Series ($1,280, lanyard loop in 30 Carbine), Flattop Target ($1,495), Sheriff's Model ($1,085, with barrel lengths starting at 2"), Snubnose ($1,295, barrel lengths 2", 3", 4"), Omni-Potent Six-Shooter and Omni-Target Six-Shooter (from $1,485), Bisley and Bisley Target (from $1,485, introduced 2006). Made in U.S.A. by United States Fire Arms Mfg. Co.
Price: Blue/cased-colors $1,085.00
Price: Nickel $1,485.00

U.S. FIRE ARMS RODEO COWBOY ACTION REVOLVER
Caliber: 45 Colt, 38 Special. **Barrel:** 4-3/4", 5-1/2". **Grips:** Rubber. **Features:** Historically correct Armory bone case hammer, blue satin finish, transfer bar safety system, correct solid firing pin. Entry level basic cowboy SASS gun. Other models include Cowboy ($945) and Gunslinger ($1,045). 2006 version includes brown-rubber stocks.
Price: $649.00

U.S. FIRE ARMS U.S. PRE-WAR
Caliber: 45 Colt (standard); 32 WCF, 38 WCF, 38 Special, 44 WCF, 44 Special. **Barrel:** 4-3/4", 5-1/2", 7-1/2". **Grips:** Hard rubber. **Features:** Armory bone case/Armory blue finish standard, cross-pin or black powder frame. Introduced 2002. Made in U.S.A. by United States Firearms Mfg. Co.
Price: $1,345.00

Specially adapted single-shot and multi-barrel arms.

American Derringer Model 1

American Derringer Model 4

American Derringer Model 6

American Derringer Model 7

American Derringer Lady Derringer

American Derringer DA 38

AMERICAN DERRINGER MODEL 1
Caliber: 22 LR, 22 WMR, 30 Carbine, 30 Luger, 30-30 Win., 32 H&R Mag., 32-20, 380 ACP, 38 Super, 38 Spec., 38 Spec. shotshell, 38 Spec. +P, 9mm Para., 357 Mag., 357 Mag./45/410, 357 Maximum, 10mm, 40 S&W, 41 Mag., 38-40, 44-40 Win., 44 Spec., 44 Mag., 45 Colt, 45 Win. Mag., 45 ACP, 45 Colt/410, 45-70 single shot. **Barrel:** 3". **Weight:** 15-1/2 oz. (38 Spec.). **Length:** 4.82" overall. **Grips:** Rosewood, Zebra wood. **Sights:** Blade front. **Features:** Made of stainless steel with high-polish or satin finish. Two-shot capacity. Manual hammer block safety. Introduced 1980. Available in most pistol calibers. From American Derringer Corp.

Price: 22 LR . . . . **CALL**
Price: 38 Spec. . . . . **CALL**
Price: 357 Maximum . . . . **CALL**
Price: 357 Mag. . . . . **CALL**
Price: 9mm, 380 . . . . **CALL**
Price: 40 S&W . . . . **CALL**
Price: 44 Spec. . . . . **CALL**
Price: 44-40 Win. . . . . **CALL**
Price: 45 Colt . . . . **CALL**
Price: 30-30, 45 Win. Mag. . . . . **CALL**
Price: 41, 44 Mags. . . . . **CALL**
Price: 45-70, single shot . . . . **CALL**
Price: 45 Colt, 410, 2-1/2" . . . . **CALL**
Price: 45 ACP, 10mm Auto . . . . **CALL**

American Derringer Model 4
Similar to the Model 1 except has 4.1" barrel, overall length of 6", and weighs 16-1/2 oz.; chambered for 357 Mag., 357 Maximum, 45-70, 3" 410-bore shotshells or 45 Colt or 44 Mag. Made of stainless steel. Manual hammer block safety. Introduced 1980.

Price: 3" 410/45 Colt **$425.00**
Price: 45-70 . . . . **$560.00**
Price: 44 Mag. with oversize grips **$515.00**
Price: Alaskan Survival model
(45-70 upper barrel, 410 or 45 Colt lower) **$475.00**

American Derringer Model 6
Similar to the Model 1 except has 6" barrel chambered for 3" 410 shotshells or 22 WMR, 357 Mag., 45 ACP, 45 Colt; rosewood stocks; 8.2" o.a.l. and weighs 21 oz. Manual hammer block safety. Introduced 1980.

Price: 22 WMR **$440.00**
Price: 357 Mag. **$440.00**
Price: 45 Colt/410 . . . . **$450.00**
Price: 45 ACP **$440.00**

American Derringer Model 7 Ultra Lightweight
Similar to Model 1 except made of high strength aircraft aluminum. Weighs 7-1/2 oz., 4.82" o.a.l., rosewood stocks. Available in 22 LR, 22 WMR, 32 H&R Mag., 380 ACP, 38 Spec., 44 Spec. Introduced 1980.

Price: 22 LR, WMR **$325.00**
Price: 38 Spec. **$325.00**
Price: 380 ACP **$325.00**
Price: 32 H&R Mag/32 S&W Long **$325.00**
Price: 44 Spec. **$565.00**

American Derringer Model 10 Ultra Lightweight
Similar to the Model 1 except frame is aluminum, giving weight of 10 oz. Stainless barrels. Available in 38 Spec., 45 Colt or 45 ACP only. Matte gray finish. Introduced 1980.

Price: 45 Colt **$385.00**
Price: 45 ACP **$330.00**
Price: 38 Spec. **$305.00**

American Derringer Lady Derringer
Same as the Model 1 except has tuned action, is fitted with scrimshawed synthetic ivory grips; chambered for 32 H&R Mag. and 38 Spec.; 357 Mag., 45 Colt, 45/410. Deluxe Grade is highly polished; Deluxe Engraved is engraved in a pattern similar to that used on 1880s derringers. All models come in a French-fitted jewelry box. Introduced 1989.

Price: 32 H&R Mag. **$375.00**
Price: 357 Mag. **$405.00**
Price: 38 Spec. **$360.00**
Price: 45 Colt, 45/410 . . . . **$435.00**

American Derringer Texas Commemorative
Model 1 Derringer with solid brass frame, stainless steel barrel and rosewood grips. Available in 38 Spec., 44-40 Win., or 45 Colt. Introduced 1980.

Price: 38 Spec. **$365.00**
Price: 44-40 . . . . **$420.00**
Price: Brass frame, 45 Colt **$450.00**

AMERICAN DERRINGER DA 38 MODEL
Caliber: 22 LR, 9mm Para., 38 Spec., 357 Mag., 40 S&W. **Barrel:** 3". **Weight:** 14.5 oz. **Length:** 4.8" overall. **Grips:** Rosewood, walnut or other hardwoods. **Sights:** Fixed. **Features:** Double-action only; two shots. Manual safety. Made of satin-finished stainless steel and aluminum. Introduced 1989. From American Derringer Corp.

Price: 22 LR **$435.00**
Price: 38 Spec. **$460.00**
Price: 9mm Para. **$445.00**
Price: 357 Mag. **$450.00**
Price: 40 S&W **$475.00**

ANSCHUTZ MODEL 64P SPORT/TARGET PISTOL
Caliber: 22 LR, 22 WMR, 5-shot magazine. **Barrel:** 10". **Weight:** 3 lbs. 8 oz. **Length:** 18-1/2" overall. **Stock:** Choate Rynite. **Sights:** None furnished; grooved for scope mounting. **Features:** Right-hand bolt; polished blue finish. Introduced 1998. Imported from Germany by AcuSport.

Price: 22 LR **$455.95**
Price: 22 WMR **$479.95**

Bond Arms Texas Defender

Bond Arms Century 2000 Defender

Cobra Big Bore

Cobra D-Series

Comanche Super Single Shot

Downsizer WSP Single Shot

BOND ARMS TEXAS DEFENDER DERRINGER

Caliber: From 22 LR to 45 LC/410 shotshells. **Barrel:** 3". **Weight:** 20 oz. **Length:** 5". **Grips:** Rosewood. **Sights:** Blade front, fixed rear. **Features:** Interchangeable barrels, stainless steel firing pins, cross-bolt safety, automatic extractor for rimmed calibers. Stainless steel construction, brushed finish. Right or left hand.
Price: $389.00
Price: Interchangeable barrels, 22 LR thru 45 LC, 3" $139.00
Price: Interchangeable barrels, 45 LC, 3.5" $159.00

BOND ARMS CENTURY 2000 DEFENDER

Caliber: 45LC/410 shotshells. **Barrel:** 3.5". **Weight:** 21 oz. **Length:** 5.5". **Features:** Similar to Defender series.
Price: $404.00

BOND ARMS COWBOY DEFENDER

Caliber: From 22 LR to 45 LC/410 shotshells. **Barrel:** 3". **Weight:** 19 oz. **Length:** 5.5". **Features:** Similar to Defender series. No trigger guard.
Price: $389.00

BOND ARMS SNAKE SLAYER

Caliber: 45 LC/410 shotshell (2-1/2" or 3"). **Barrel:** 3.5". **Weight:** 21 oz. **Length:** 5.5". **Grips:** Extended rosewood. **Sights:** Blade front, fixed rear. **Features:** Single-action; interchangeable barrels; stainless steel firing pin. Introduced 2005.
Price: $455.00

BOND ARMS SNAKE SLAYER IV

Caliber: 45 LC/410 shotshell (2-1/2" or 3"). **Barrel:** 4.25". **Weight:** 22 oz. **Length:** 6.25". **Grips:** Extended rosewood. **Sights:** Blade front, fixed rear. **Features:** Single-action; interchangeable barrels; stainless steel firing pin. Introduced 2006.
Price: $475.00

BROWN CLASSIC SINGLE-SHOT PISTOL

Caliber: 17 Ackley Hornet through 375x444. **Barrel:** 15" air-gauged match grade. **Weight:** About 3 lbs. 7 oz. **Grips:** Walnut; thumb rest target-style. **Sights:** None furnished; drilled and tapped for scope mounting. **Features:** Falling block action gives rigid barrel-receiver mating; hand fitted and headspaced. Introduced 1998. Made in U.S.A. by E.A. Brown Mfg.
Price: $589.00

CHARTER ARMS DIXIE DERRINGERS

Caliber: 22 LR, 22 WMR. **Barrel:** 1.125". **Weight:** 5-6 oz. **Length:** 4" overall. **Grips:** Black polymer **Sights:** Blade front, fixed notch rear. **Features:** Stainless finish. Introduced 2006. Made in U.S.A. by Charter Arms, distributed by MKS Supply.
Price: $112.00

COBRA BIG BORE DERRINGERS

Caliber: 22 WMR, 32 H&R Mag., 38 Spec., 9mm Para. **Barrel:** 2.75". **Weight:** 11.5 oz. **Length:** 4.65" overall. **Grips:** Textured black synthetic.

Sights: Blade front, fixed notch rear. **Features:** Alloy frame, steel-lined barrels, steel breech block. Plunger-type safety with integral hammer block. Chrome or black Teflon finish. Introduced 2002. Made in U.S.A. by Cobra Enterprises.
Price: $98.00
Price: 9mm Para $136.00

COBRA LONG-BORE DERRINGERS

Caliber: 22 WMR, 38 Spec., 9mm Para. **Barrel:** 3.5". **Weight:** 13 oz. **Length:** 5.65" overall. **Grips:** Textured black synthetic. **Sights:** Fixed. **Features:** Chrome or black Teflon finish. Larger than Davis D-Series models. Introduced 2002. Made in U.S.A. by Cobra Enterprises.
Price: $136.00
Price: 9mm Para. $136.00
Price: Big-Bore models (same calibers, 3/4" shorter barrels) $136.00

COBRA STARBIRD-SERIES DERRINGERS

Caliber: 22 LR, 22 WMR, 25 ACP, 32 ACP. **Barrel:** 2.4". **Weight:** 9.5 oz. **Length:** 4" overall. **Grips:** Laminated wood or pearl. **Sights:** Blade front, fixed notch rear. **Features:** Choice of black powder coat, satin nickel or chrome finish; spur trigger. Introduced 2002. Made in U.S.A. by Cobra Enterprises.
Price: $112.00

COMANCHE SUPER SINGLE-SHOT PISTOL

Caliber: 45 LC, 410 ga. **Barrel:** 10". **Sights:** Adjustable. **Features:** Blue finish, not available for sale in CA, MA. Distributed by SGS Importers International, Inc.
Price: $183.95
Price: Satin nickel $199.95
Price: Camo, intr. 2006 .... $216.95

DOWNSIZER WSP SINGLE-SHOT PISTOL

Caliber: 357 Magnum, 45 ACP, 38 Special. **Barrel:** 2.10". **Weight:** 11 oz. **Length:** 3.25" overall. **Grips:** Black polymer. **Sights:** None. **Features:** Single shot, tip-up barrel. Double action only. Stainless steel construction. Measures .900" thick. Introduced 1997. From Downsizer Corp.
Price: $499.00

GAUCHER GN1 SILHOUETTE PISTOL

Caliber: 22 LR, single shot. **Barrel:** 10". **Weight:** 2.4 lbs. **Length:** 15.5" overall. **Grips:** European hardwood. **Sights:** Blade front, open adjustable rear. **Features:** Bolt action, adjustable trigger. Introduced 1990. Imported from France by Mandall Shooting Supplies.
Price: About $525.00
Price: Model GP Silhouette $425.00

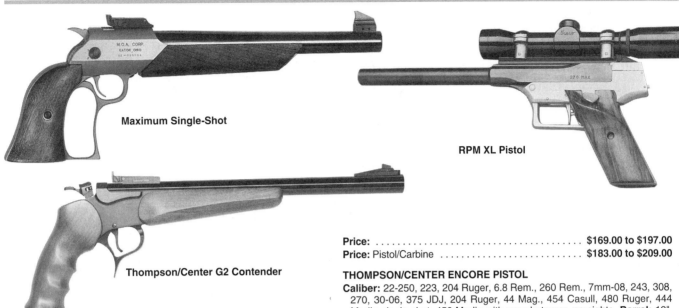

Maximum Single-Shot

RPM XL Pistol

Thompson/Center G2 Contender

MAXIMUM SINGLE-SHOT PISTOL

Caliber: 22 LR, 22 Hornet, 22 BR, 22 PPC, 223 Rem., 22-250, 6mm BR, 6mm PPC, 243, 250 Savage, 6.5mm-35M, 270 MAX, 270 Win., 7mm TCU, 7mm BR, 7mm-35, 7mm INT-R, 7mm-08, 7mm Rocket, 7mm Super-Mag., 30 Herrett, 30 Carbine, 30-30, 308 Win., 30x39, 32-20, 350 Rem. Mag., 357 Mag., 357 Maximum, 358 Win., 375 H&H, 44 Mag., 454 Casull. **Barrel:** 8-3/4", 10-1/2", 14". **Weight:** 61 oz. (10-1/2" bbl.); 78 oz. (14" bbl.). **Length:** 15", 18-1/2" overall (with 10-1/2" and 14" bbl., respectively). **Grips:** Smooth walnut stocks and forend. Also available with 17" finger groove grip. **Sights:** Ramp front, fully adjustable open rear. **Features:** Falling block action; drilled and tapped for M.O.A. scope mounts; integral grip frame/receiver; adjustable trigger; Douglas barrel (interchangeable). Introduced 1983. Made in U.S.A. by M.O.A. Corp.
Price: Stainless receiver, blue barrel $799.00
Price: Stainless receiver, stainless barrel $883.00
Price: Extra blued barrel $254.00
Price: Extra stainless barrel $317.00
Price: Scope mount $60.00

RPM XL SINGLE SHOT PISTOL

Caliber: 22 LR through 45-70. **Barrel:** 8", 10-3/4", 12", 14". **Weight:** About 60 oz. **Grips:** Smooth Goncalo Alves with thumb and heel rests. **Features:** Barrel drilled and tapped for scope mount. Visible cocking indicator. Spring-loaded barrel lock, positive hammer-block safety. Trigger adjustable for weight of pull and over-travel. Contact maker for complete price list. Made in U.S.A. by RPM.
Price: XL Hunter model (action only) $1,045.00
Price: Extra barrel . . . . $250.00 to $300.00

SPRINGFIELD M6 SCOUT PISTOL

Caliber: 22 LR/45 LC/410, 22 Hornet, 45 LC/410. **Barrel:** 10". **Weight:** NA. **Length:** NA. **Grips:** NA. **Sights:** NA. **Features:** Adapted from the U.S. Air Force M6 Survival Rifle, also available as a carbine with 16" barrel.

Price: . . . . $169.00 to $197.00
Price: Pistol/Carbine . . . . $183.00 to $209.00

THOMPSON/CENTER ENCORE PISTOL

Caliber: 22-250, 223, 204 Ruger, 6.8 Rem., 260 Rem., 7mm-08, 243, 308, 270, 30-06, 375 JDJ, 204 Ruger, 44 Mag., 454 Casull, 480 Ruger, 444 Marlin single shot, 450 Marlin with muzzle tamer, no sights. **Barrel:** 12", 15", tapered round. **Weight:** NA. **Length:** 21" overall with 12" barrel. **Grips:** American walnut with finger grooves, walnut forend. **Sights:** Blade on ramp front, adjustable rear, or none. **Features:** Interchangeable barrels; action opens by squeezing the trigger guard; drilled and tapped for scope mounting; blue finish. Announced 1996. Made in U.S.A. by Thompson/Center Arms.
Price: . . . . $589.00 to $592.00
Price: Extra 12" barrels $262.00
Price: Extra 15" barrels $270.00
Price: 45 Colt/410 barrel, 12" $292.00
Price: 45 Colt/410 barrel, 15" $299.00

Thompson/Center Stainless Encore Pistol

Similar to blued Encore, made of stainless steel, available with 15" barrel in 223, 22-250, 243 Win., 7mm-08, 308, 30/06 Sprgfld., 45/70 Gov't., 45/410 VR. With black rubber grip and forend. Made in U.S.A. by Thompson/Center Arms.
Price: . . . . $636.00 to $644.00

Thompson/Center G2 Contender Pistol

A second generation Contender pistol maintaining the same barrel interchangeability with older Contender barrels and their corresponding forends (except Herrett forend). The G2 frame will not accept old-style grips due to the change in grip angle. Incorporates an automatic hammer block safety with built-in interlock. Features include trigger adjustable for overtravel; adjustable rear sight; ramp front sight blade, blued steel finish.
Price: $570.00

UBERTI ROLLING BLOCK TARGET PISTOL

Caliber: 22LR, 22 Mag., single shot. **Barrel:** 9.5". **Weight:** 2.8 lbs. **Length:** 14". **Stocks:** Walnut grip and forend. **Sights:** Adjustable rear, blade front. **Features:** Replica of the 1871 rolling block target pistol. Case-hardened frame and backstrap, blued barrel and trigger guard. Made in Italy by Uberti, imported by Benelli USA.
Price: $480.00

Both classic arms and recent designs in American-style repeaters for sport and field shooting.

ArmaLite M15A2

ArmaLite AR-10A4

ArmaLite AR-180B

ARMALITE M15A2 CARBINE

Caliber: 223, 30-round magazine. **Barrel:** 16" heavy chrome lined; 1:9" twist. **Weight:** 7 lbs. **Length:** 35-11/16" overall. **Stock:** Green or black composition. **Sights:** Standard A2. **Features:** Upper and lower receivers have push-type pivot pin; hard coat anodized; A2-style forward assist; M16A2-type raised fence around magazine release button. Made in U.S.A. by ArmaLite, Inc.
Price: Green **$1,100.00**
Price: Black **$1,100.00**

ARMALITE AR-10A4 SPECIAL PURPOSE RIFLE

Caliber: 308 Win., 10- and 20-round magazine. **Barrel:** 20" chrome-lined, 1:11.25" twist. **Weight:** 9.6 lbs. **Length:** 41" overall. **Stock:** Green or black composition. **Sights:** Detachable handle, front sight, or scope mount available; comes with international style flattop receiver with Picatinny rail. **Features:** Forged upper receiver with case deflector. Receivers are hard-coat anodized. Introduced 1995. Made in U.S.A. by ArmaLite, Inc.
Price: Green **$1,506.00**
Price: Black **$1,506.00**

ArmaLite AR-10(T)

Similar to the ArmaLite AR-10A4 but with stainless steel, barrel, machined tool steel, two-stage National Match trigger group and other features.
Price: AR-10(T) rifle **$2,126.00**

ArmaLite AR-10A2

Utilizing the same 20" double-lapped, heavy barrel as the ArmaLite AR-10A4 Special Purpose Rifle. Offered in 308 caliber only. Made in U.S.A. by ArmaLite, Inc.
Price: AR-10A2 rifle or carbine **$1,506.00**

ARMALITE AR-180B RIFLE

Caliber: 223, 10-shot magazine. **Barrel:** 19.8". **Weight:** 6 lbs. **Length:** 38". **Stock:** Synthetic. **Sights:** Rear sight adjustable for windage, small and large apertures. **Features:** Lower receiver made of polymer, upper formed of sheet metal. Uses standard AR-15 magazines. Made in U.S.A. by ArmaLite.
Price: **$750.00**

ARSENAL USA SSR-56

Caliber: 7.62x39mm. **Barrel:** 16.25". **Weight:** 7.4 lbs. **Length:** 35.5" **Stock:** Black polymer. **Sights:** Adjustable rear. **Features:** An AK-47-style rifle built on a hardened Hungarian FEG receiver with the required six U.S.-made parts to make it legal for use with all extra-capacity magazines. From Arsenal I, LLC.
Price: **$565.00**

ARSENAL USA SSR-74-2

Caliber: 5.45x39mm **Barrel:** 16.25" **Weight:** 7 lbs. **Length:** 36.75" **Stock:** Polymer or wood. **Sights:** Adjustable. **Features:** Built with parts from an unissued Bulgarian AK-47 rifle, it has a Buffer Technologies recoil buffer, enough U.S.-made parts to allow pistol grip stock and use with all extra-capacity magazines. Assembled in U.S.A. From Arsenal I, LLC.
Price: **$499.00**

ARSENAL USA SSR-85C-2

Caliber: 7.62x39mm. **Barrel:** 16.25". **Weight:** 7.1 lbs. **Length:** 35.5". **Stock:** Polymer or wood. **Sights:** Adjustable rear calibrated to 800 meters. **Features:** Built from parts obtained from unissued Polish AK-47 rifles, the gas tube is vented and the receiver cover is plain. Rifle contains enough U.S.-sourced parts to allow pistol grip stock and use with all extra-capacity magazines. Assembled in U.S.A. by Arsenal I, LLC.
Price: **$499.00**

Auto-Ordnance 1927 A-1 Thompson

Barrett Model 82A-1

Beretta CX4 Carbine

AUTO-ORDNANCE 1927 A-1 THOMPSON
Caliber: 45 ACP. **Barrel:** 16-1/2". **Weight:** 13 lbs. **Length:** About 41" overall (Deluxe). **Stock:** Walnut stock and vertical forend. **Sights:** Blade front, open rear adjustable for windage. **Features:** Recreation of Thompson Model 1927. Semi-auto only. Deluxe model has finned barrel, adjustable rear sight and compensator; Standard model has plain barrel and military sight. From Auto-Ordnance Corp.
Price: Deluxe **$950.00**
Price: 1927A1C lightweight model (9-1/2 lbs.) **$950.00**

Auto-Ordnance Thompson M1/M1-C
Similar to the 1927 A-1 except is in the M-1 configuration with side cocking knob, horizontal forend, smooth unfinned barrel, sling swivels on butt and forend. Matte black finish. Introduced 1985.
Price: M1 semi-auto carbin **$950.00**
Price: M1-C lightweight semi-auto **$925.00**

Auto-Ordnance 1927 A-1 Commando
Similar to the 1927 A-1 except has Parkerized finish, black-finish wood butt, pistol grip, horizontal forend. Comes with black nylon sling. Introduced 1998. Made in U.S.A. by Auto-Ordnance Corp.
Price: **$950.00**

BARRETT MODEL 82A-1 SEMI-AUTOMATIC RIFLE
Caliber: 50 BMG, 10-shot detachable box magazine. **Barrel:** 29". **Weight:** 28.5 lbs. **Length:** 57" overall. **Stock:** Composition with energy-absorbing recoil pad. **Sights:** Scope optional. **Features:** Semi-automatic, recoil operated with recoiling barrel. Three-lug locking bolt; muzzle brake. Adjustable bipod. Introduced 1985. Made in U.S.A. by Barrett Firearms.
Price: From **$7,200.00**

BENELLI R1 RIFLE
Caliber: 300 Win. Mag., 300 WSM, 270 WSM (24" barrel); 30-06, 308 (22" barrel); 300 Win. Mag., 30-06, (20" barrel). **Weight:** 7.1 lbs. **Length:** 43.75" to 45.75" **Stock:** Select satin walnut or synthetic. **Sights:** None. **Features:** Auto-regulating gas-operated system, three-lug rotary bolt,

interchangeable barrels, optional recoil pads. Introduced 2003. Imported from Italy by Benelli USA.
Price: Synthetic with ComforTech gel recoil pad **$1,365.00**
Price: Satin walnut **$1,200.00**

BERETTA CX4/PX4 STORM CARBINE
Caliber: 9mm Para, 40 S&W, 45 ACP. **Weight:** 5.75 lbs. **Barrel Length:** 16.6", chrome lined, rate of twist 1:16 (40 S&W) or 1:10 (9mm). **Length:** NA. **Stock:** Black synthetic. **Sights:** NA. **Features:** Introduced 2005. Imported from Italy by Beretta USA.
Price: Cx4 Carbine, 40 S&W, 10+1 . . . . **$800.00**
Price: Cx4 Carbine, 8000 Series, 9mm, 10+1 . . . . **$775.00**
Price: Cx4 Carbine, 8045 Series, 45 ACP, 8+1 . . . . **$800.00**
Price: Cx4 Px4 Carbine, 40 S&W, 14+1 . . . . **$850.00**
Price: Cx4 Px4 Carbine, 9mm, 17+1 . . . . **$850.00**

BROWNING BAR SAFARI AND SAFARI W/BOSS SEMI-AUTO RIFLES
Caliber: Safari: 243, 25-06, 270, 7mm Rem Mag., 30-06, 308, 300 Win. Mag., 338 Win Mag. Safari w/BOSS: 270, 7mm Rem Mag., 30-06, 300 Win. Mag., 338 Win Mag., plus 270 WSM, 7mm WSM, 300 WSM. **Barrel:** 22-24" round tapered. **Weight:** 7.4-8.2 lbs. **Length:** 43-45" overall. **Stock:** French walnut pistol grip stock and forend, hand checkered. **Sights:** No sights. **Features:** Has new bolt release lever; removable trigger assembly with larger trigger guard; redesigned gas and buffer systems. Detachable 4-round box magazine. Scroll-engraved receiver is tapped for scope mounting. BOSS barrel vibration modulator and muzzle brake system available. Mark II Safari introduced 1993. Imported from Belgium by Browning.
Price: BAR Safari, 22" barrel, standard cartridge chamberings. . . . **$889.00**
Price: BAR Safari, 24" barrel, magnum cartridge chamberings. . . . **$972.00**
Price: BAR Safari w/BOSS, standard chamberings. **$988.00**
Price: BAR Safari w/BOSS, WSM and magnum chamberings . . . **$1,071.00**

Browning Mark II Safari

Browning Lightweight Stalker

Bushmaster M17S Bullpup

Bushmaster XM15 E2S Carbine

BROWNING BAR SHORTTRAC/LONGTRAC AUTO RIFLES

Caliber: (ShortTrac models) 270 WSM, 7mm WSM, 300 WSM, 243 Win., 308 Win.; (Long Trac models) 270 Win., 30-06 Sprfld., 7mm Rem. Mag., 300 Win. Mag. **Barrel:** 23". **Weight:** 6 lbs. 10 oz. to 7 lbs. 4 oz. **Length:** 41-1/2" to 44". **Stock:** Satin-finish walnut, pistol-grip, fluted forend. **Sights:** Adj. rear, bead front standard, no sights on BOSS models (optional). **Features:** Designed to handle new WSM chamberings. Gas-operated, blued finish, rotary bolt design (Long Trac models).

Price: BAR ShortTrac, 243 Win., 308 Win. **$885.00**
Price: BAR ShortTrac WSM, 270 WSM, 7mm WSM, 300 WSM, . . . **$965.00**
Price: BAR LongTrac, 270 Win., 30-06 Sprfld. **$885.00**
Price: BAR LongTrac, 7mm Rem. Mag., 300 Win. Mag. **$965.00**

BROWNING BAR LIGHTWEIGHT STALKER AUTO RIFLE

Caliber: 243, 308, 270, 30-06, 270 WSM, 7mm WSM, 300 WSM, 300 Win. Mag., 338 Win. Mag. **Barrel:** 20-24". **Weight:** 7.1-7.75 LBS. **Length:** 41-45" overall. **Stock:** Black composite stock and forearm. **Sights:** Hooded front and adjustable rear. **Features:** Gas-operated action with seven-lug rotary bolt; dual action bars; 2-, 3- or 4-shot magazine (depending on cartridge). Introduced 2001. Imported by Browning.

Price: BAR Lightweight Stalker, 243, 308, 270, 30-06 . . . . **$883.00**
Price: BAR Lightweight Stalker, WSM and magnums. **$964.00**

BUSHMASTER M17S BULLPUP RIFLE

Caliber: 223, 10-shot magazine. **Barrel:** 21.5", chrome lined; 1:9" twist. **Weight:** 8.2 lbs. **Length:** 30" overall. **Stock:** Fiberglass-filled nylon. **Sights:** Designed for optics-carrying handle incorporates scope mount rail for Weaver-type rings; also includes 25-meter open iron sights. **Features:** Gas-operated, short-stroke piston system; ambidextrous magazine release. Introduced 1993. Made in U.S.A. by Bushmaster Firearms, Inc./Quality Parts Co.
Price: **$765.00**

BUSHMASTER SHORTY XM15 E2S CARBINE

Caliber: 223, 10-shot magazine. **Barrel:** 16", heavy; 1:9" twist. **Weight:** 7.2 lbs. **Length:** 34.75" overall. **Stock:** A2 type; fixed black composition. **Sights:** Fully adjustable M16A2 sight system. **Features:** Patterned after Colt M-16A2. Chrome-lined barrel with manganese phosphate finish. "Shorty" handguards. Has forged aluminum receivers with pushpin. Made in U.S.A. by Bushmaster Firearms, Inc.
Price: (A2) **$985.00**
Price: (A3) **$1,085.00**

Bushmaster XM15 E2S Dissipator Carbine

Similar to the XM15 E2S Shorty carbine except has full-length "Dissipator" handguards. Weighs 7.6 lbs.; 34.75" overall; forged aluminum receivers with push-pin style takedown. Made in U.S.A. by Bushmaster Firearms, Inc.
Price: (A2 type) **$995.00**
Price: (A3 type) **$1,095.00**

Bushmaster XM15 E25 AK Shorty Carbine

Similar to the XM15 E2S Shorty except has 14.5" barrel with an AK muzzle brake permanently attached giving 16" barrel length. Weighs 7.3 lbs. Introduced 1999. Made in U.S.A. by Bushmaster Firearms, Inc.
Price: (A2 type) **$1,005.00**
Price: (A3 type) **$1,105.00**

Bushmaster M4/M4A3 Post-Ban Carbine

Similar to the XM15 E2S except has 14.5" barrel with Mini Y compensator, and fixed telestock. MR configuration has fixed carry handle; M4A3 has removeable carry handle.
Price: (M4). **$1,065.00**
Price: (M4A3) **$1,165.00**

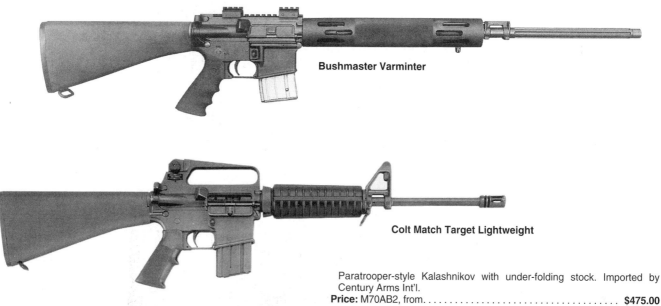

Bushmaster Varminter

Colt Match Target Lightweight

BUSHMASTER VARMINTER RIFLE
Caliber: 223 Rem., 5-shot. **Barrel:** 24", 1:9" twist, fluted, heavy, stainless. **Weight:** 8-3/4 lbs. **Length:** 42-1/4". **Stock:** Rubberized pistol grip. **Sights:** 1/2" scope risers. **Features:** Gas-operated, semi-auto, two-stage trigger, slotted free floater forend, lockable hard case.
Price: **$1,245.00**

CENTURY INTERNATIONAL AES-10 HI-CAP RIFLE
Caliber: 7.62x39mm. 30-shot magazine. **Barrel:** 23.2". **Weight:** NA. **Length:** 41.5" overall. **Stock:** Wood grip, forend. **Sights:** Fixed-notch rear, windage-adjustable post front. **Features:** RPK-style, accepts standard double-stack AK-type mags. Side-mounted scope mount, integral carry handle, bipod. Imported by Century Arms Int'l.
Price: AES-10, from **$550.00**

CENTURY INTERNATIONAL GP WASR-10 HI-CAP RIFLE
Caliber: 7.62x39mm. 30-shot magazine. **Barrel:** 16.25", 1:10 rh twist. **Weight:** 7.5 lbs. **Length:** 34.25" overall. **Stock:** Wood laminate or composite, grip, forend. **Sights:** Fixed-notch rear, windage-adjustable post front. **Features:** Two 30-rd. detachable box magazines, cleaning kit, bayonet. Version of AKM rifle; U.S.-parts added for BATFE compliance. Threaded muzzle, folding stock, bayonet lug, compensator, Dragunov stock available. Made in Romania by Cugir Arsenal. Imported by Century Arms Int'l.
Price: GP WASR-10, from **$450.00**

CENTURY INTERNATIONAL WASR-2 HI-CAP RIFLE
Caliber: 5.45x39mm. 30-shot magazine. **Barrel:** 16.25". **Weight:** 7.5 lbs. **Length:** 34.25" overall. **Stocks:** Wood laminate. **Sights:** Fixed-notch rear, windage-adjustable post front. **Features:** 1 30-rd. detachable box magazine, cleaning kit, sling. WASR-3 HI-CAP chambered in 223 Rem. Imported by Century Arms Int'l.
Price: GP WASR-2/3, from **$450.00**

CENTURY INTERNATIONAL WASR 22 RIFLE
Caliber: 22 LR. 10-shot magazine. **Barrel:** 16.25". **Weight:** 7.5 lbs. **Length:** 34.25" overall. **Stocks:** Wood laminate. **Sights:** Fixed-notch rear, windage-adjustable post front. **Features:** 2 10-rd. magazine, cleaning kit, sling. Imported by Century Arms Int'l.
Price: GP WASR 22, from **$325.00**

CENTURY INTERNATIONAL M70AB2 SPORTER RIFLE
Caliber: 7.62x39mm. 30-shot magazine. **Barrel:** 16.25". **Weight:** 7.5 lbs. **Length:** 34.25" overall. **Stocks:** Metal grip, wood forend. **Sights:** Fixed-notch rear, windage-adjustable post front. **Features:** 2 30-rd. double-stack magazine, cleaning kit, compensator, bayonet lug and bayonet.

Paratrooper-style Kalashnikov with under-folding stock. Imported by Century Arms Int'l.
Price: M70AB2, from **$475.00**

COLT MATCH TARGET MODEL RIFLE
Caliber: 223 Rem., 5-shot magazine. **Barrel:** 16.1" or 20". **Weight:** 7.1 to 8-1/2 lbs. **Length:** 34-1/2" to 39" overall. **Stock:** Composition stock, grip, forend. **Sights:** Post front, rear adjustable for windage and elevation. **Features:** 5-round detachable box magazine, flash suppressor, sling swivels. Forward bolt assist included. Introduced 1991. Made in U.S.A. by Colt's Mfg. Co., Inc.
Price: Match Target HBAR, from **$1,300.00**

DPMS PANTHER ARMS AR-15 RIFLES
Caliber: 223 Rem., 7.62x39. **Barrel:** 16" to 24". **Weight:** 7-3/4 to 11-3/4 lbs. **Length:** 34-1/2" to 42-1/4" overall. **Stock:** Black Zytel® composite. **Sights:** Square front post, adjustable A2 rear. **Features:** Steel or stainless steel heavy or bull barrel; hardcoat anodized receiver; aluminum free-float tube handguard; many options. From DPMS Panther Arms.
Price: Panther Bull A-15 (20" stainless bull bbl.) **$915.00**
Price: Panther Bull Twenty-Four (24" stainless bull bbl.) **$945.00**
Price: Bulldog (20" stainless fluted bbl., flattop receiver) **$1,219.00**
Price: Panther Bull Sweet Sixteen (16" stainless bull bbl.) **$885.00**
Price: DCM Panther (20" stainless heavy bbl., n.m. sights) **$1,099.00**
Price: Panther 7.62x39 (20" steel heavy bbl.) **$849.00**

DSA Z4 GTC CARBINE WITH C.R.O.S.
Caliber: 5.56 NATO **Barrel:** 16" 1:9 twist M4 profile fluted chrome lined heavy barrel with threaded Vortec flash hider. **Weight:** 7.6 lbs. **Stock:** 6 position collapsible M4 stock, Predator P4X free float tactical rail. **Sights:** Chrome lined Picatinny gas block w/removable front sight. **Features:** The Corrosion Resistant Operating System incorporates the new P.O.F. Gas Trap System with removable gas plug eliminates problematic features of standard AR gas system, Forged 7075T6 DSA lower receiver. Introduced 2006. Made in U.S.A. by DSA, Inc.
Price: **$1,700.00**

DSA CQB MRP, STANDARD MRP
Caliber: 5.56 NATO **Barrel:** 16" or 18" 1:7 twist chrome-lined or stainless steel barrel with A2 flash hider **Stock:** 6 position collapsible M4 stock. **Features:** LMT 1/2" MRP upper receiver with 20-1/2" Standard quad rail or 16 1/2" CQB quad rail, LMT enhanced bolt with dual extractor springs, free float barrel, quick change barrel system, forged 7075T6 DSA lower receiver. EOTech and vertical grip additional. Introduced 2006. Made in U.S.A. by DSA, Inc.
Price: CQB MRP w/16" chrome lined barrel **$2,420.00**
Price: CQB MRP w/16" stainless steel barrel **$2,540.00**
Price: Standard MRP w/16" chrome lined barrel **$2,620.00**
Price: Standard MRP w/16" or 18"stainless steel barrel **$2,720.00**

DSA SA58 Congo

DSA SA58 Para Congo

DSA SA58 Gray Wolf

DSA STD CARBINE

Caliber: 5.56 NATO. **Barrel:** 16" 1:9 twist D4 w/A2 flash hider. **Weight:** 6.25 lbs. **Length:** 31". **Stock:** A2 buttstock, D4 handguard w/heatshield. **Sights:** Forged A2 front sight with lug. **Features:** Forged 7075T6 DSA lower receiver, forged A2 or flattop upper receiver. Introduced 2006. Made in U.S.A. by DSA, Inc.
Price: A2 or Flattop STD Carbine **$1,025.00**
Price: w/LMT SOPMOD stock. **$1,267.00**

DSA 1R CARBINE

Caliber: 5.56 NATO. **Barrel:** 16" 1:9 twist D4 w/A2 flash hider. **Weight:** 6.25 lbs. **Length:** Variable. **Stock:** 6 position collapsible M4 stock, D4 handguard w/heatshield. **Sights:** Forged A2 front sight with lug. **Features:** Forged 7075T6 DSA lower receiver, forged A2 or flattop upper receiver. Introduced 2006. Made in U.S.A. by DSA, Inc.
Price: A2 or Flattop 1R Carbine **$1,055.00**
Price: w/VLTOR ModStock **$1,175.00**

DSA XM CARBINE

Caliber: 5.56 NATO. **Barrel:** 11-1/2" 1:9 twist D4 with 5-1/2" permanently attached flash hider. **Weight:** 6.25 lbs. **Length:** Variable. **Stock:** Collapsible, Handguard w/heatshield. **Sights:** Forged A2 front sight with lug. **Features:** Forged 7075T6 DSA lower receiver, forged A2 upper receiver. Introduced 2006. Made in U.S.A. by DSA, Inc.
Price: **$1,055.00**

DSA STANDARD

Caliber: 5.56 NATO. **Barrel:** 20" 1:9 twist heavy barrel w/A2 flash hider. **Weight:** 6.25 lbs. **Length:** 38-7/16". **Stock:** A2 buttstock, A2 handguard w/heatshield. **Sights:** Forged A2 front sight with lug. **Features:** Forged 7075T6 DSA lower receiver, forged A2 or flattop upper receiver. Introduced 2006. Made in U.S.A. by DSA, Inc.
Price: A2 or Flattop Standard **$1,025.00**

DSA DCM Rifle

Caliber: .223 Wylde Chamber. **Barrel:** 20" 1:8 twist chrome moly match grade Badger Barrel. **Weight:** 10 lbs. **Length:** 39.5". **Stock:** DCM freefloat handguard system, A2 buttstock. **Sights:** Forged A2 front sight with lug. **Features:** NM two stage trigger, NM rear sight, forged 7075T6 DSA lower receiver, forged A2 upper receiver. Introduced 2006. Made in U.S.A. by DSA, Inc.
Price: **$1,520.00**

DSA S1

Caliber: .223 Match Chamber. **Barrel:** 16", 20" or 24" 1:8 twist stainless steel bull barrel. **Weight:** 8.0, 9.5 and 10 lbs. **Length:** 34.25", 38.25" and 42.25". **Stock:** A2 buttstock with free float aluminum handguard. **Sights:** Picatinny gas block sight base. **Features:** Forged 7075T6 DSA lower receiver, Match two stage trigger, forged flattop upper receiver, fluted barrel optional. Introduced 2006. Made in U.S.A. by DSA, Inc.
Price: **$1,155.00**

DSA SA58 CONGO, PARA CONGO

Caliber: 308 Win. **Barrel:** 18" w/short Belgian short flash hider. **Weight:** 8.6 lbs. (Congo); 9.85 lbs. (Para Congo). **Length:** 39.75" **Stock:** Synthetic w/military grade furniture (Congo); Synthetic with non-folding steel para stock (Para Congo). **Sights:** Elevation adjustable protected post front sight, windage adjustable rear peep (Congo); Belgian type Para Flip Rear (Para Congo). **Features:** Fully-adjustable gas system, high-grade steel upper receiver with carry handle. Made in U.S.A. by DSA, Inc.
Price: Congo **$1,695.00**
Price: Para Congo. **$1,995.00**

DSA SA58 GRAY WOLF

Caliber: 308 Win. **Barrel:** 21" match-grade bull w/target crown. **Weight:** 13 lbs. **Length:** 41.75". **Stock:** Synthetic. **Sights:** Elevation-adjustable post front sight, windage-adjustable match rear peep. **Features:** Fully-adjustable gas system, high-grade steel upper receiver, Picatinny scope mount, DuraCoat finish. Made in U.S.A. by DSA, Inc.
Price: **$2,120.00**

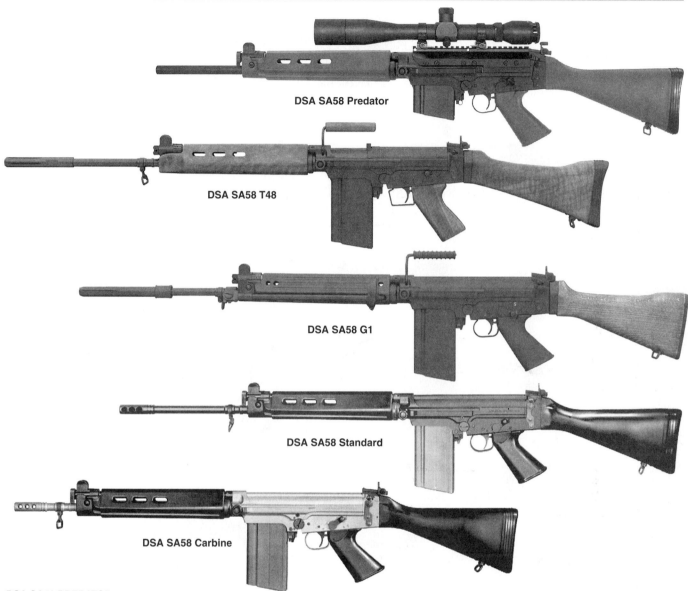

DSA SA58 Predator

DSA SA58 T48

DSA SA58 G1

DSA SA58 Standard

DSA SA58 Carbine

DSA SA58 PREDATOR

Caliber: 243 Win., 260 Rem., 308 Win. **Barrel:** 16" and 19" w/target crown. **Weight:** 9 to 9.3 lbs. **Length:** 36.25" to 39.25". **Stock:** Green synthetic. **Sights:** Elevation-adjustable post front; windage-adjustable match rear peep. **Features:** Fully-adjustable gas system, high-grade steel upper receiver, Picatinny scope mount, DuraCoat solid and camo finishes. Made in U.S.A. by DSA, Inc.

Price: 243 Win., 260 Rem. **$1,695.00**
Price: 308 Win. **$1,640.00**

DSA SA58 T48

Caliber: 308 Win. **Barrel:** 21" with Browning long flash hider. **Weight:** 9.3 lbs. **Length:** 44.5". **Stock:** European walnut. **Sights:** Elevation-adjustable post front, windage adjustable rear peep. **Features:** Gas-operated semi-auto with fully adjustable gas system, high grade steel upper receiver with carry handle. DuraCoat finishes. Made in U.S.A. by DSA, Inc.

Price: **$1,995.00**

DSA SA58 G1

Caliber: 308 Win. **Barrel:** 21" with quick-detach flash hider. **Weight:** 10.65 lbs. **Length:** 44". **Stock:** Steel bipod cut handguard with hardwood stock and synthetic pistol grip. **Sights:** Elevation-adjustable post front, windage adjustable rear peep. **Features:** Gas-operated semi-auto with fully

adjustable gas system, high grade steel upper receiver with carry handle, original GI steel lower receiver with GI bipod. DuraCoat finishes. Made in U.S.A. by DSA, Inc.

Price: **$1,850.00**

DSA SA58 STANDARD

Caliber: 308 Win. **Barrel:** 21" bipod cut w/threaded flash hider. **Weight:** 8.75 lbs. **Length:** 43". **Stock:** Synthetic, X-Series or optional folding para stock. **Sights:** Elevation-adjustable post front, windage-adjustable rear peep. **Features:** Fully adjustable short gas system, high grade steel or 416 stainless upper receiver. Made in U.S.A. by DSA, Inc.

Price: High-grade steel **$1,595.00**
Price: Folding para stock **$1,845.00**

DSA SA58 CARBINE

Caliber: 308 Win. **Barrel:** 16.25" bipod cut w/threaded flash hider. **Weight:** 8.35 lbs. **Length:** 37.5". **Stock:** Synthetic, X-Series or optional folding para stock. **Sights:** Elevation-adjustable post front, windage-adjustable rear peep. **Features:** Fully adjustable short gas system, high grade steel or 416 stainless upper receiver. Made in U.S.A. by DSA, Inc.

Price: High-grade steel **$1,595.00**
Price: Stainless steel **$1,850.00**

DSA SA58 Medium Contour Tactical

DSA SA58 Medium Contour

DSA SA58 Bull

DSA SA58 OSW

EAA/Saiga 308

DSA SA58 TACTICAL CARBINE
Caliber: 308 Win. **Barrel:** 16.25" fluted with A2 flash hider. **Weight:** 8.25 lbs. **Length:** 36.5". **Stock:** Synthetic, X-Series or optional folding para stock. **Sights:** Elevation-adjustable post front, windage-adjustable match rear peep. **Features:** Shortened fully adjustable short gas system, high grade steel or 416 stainless upper receiver. Made in U.S.A. by DSA, Inc.
Price: High-grade steel **$1,595.00**
Price: Stainless steel **$1,850.00**

DSA SA58 MEDIUM CONTOUR
Caliber: 308 Win. **Barrel:** 21" w/threaded flash hider. **Weight:** 9.75 lbs. **Length:** 43". **Stock:** Synthetic military grade. **Sights:** Elevation-adjustable post front, windage-adjustable match rear peep. **Features:** Gas-operated semi-auto with fully adjustable gas system, high grade steel receiver. Made in U.S.A. by DSA, Inc.
Price: **$1,595.00**

DSA SA58 BULL BARREL RIFLE
Caliber: 308 Win. **Barrel:** 21". **Weight:** 11.1 lbs. **Length:** 41.5". **Stock:** Synthetic, free floating handguard. **Sights:** Elevation-adjustable windage-adjustable post front, match rear peep. **Features:** Gas-operated semi-auto with fully adjustable gas system, high grade steel or stainless upper receiver. Made in U.S.A. by DSA, Inc.
Price: **$1,745.00**
Price: Stainless steel. **$1,995.00**

DSA SA58 MINI OSW
Caliber: 308 Win. **Barrel:** 11" or 13" w/A2 flash hider. **Weight:** 9 to 9.35 lbs. **Length:** 32.75" to 35". **Stock:** Fiberglass reinforced short synthetic handguard, para folding stock and synthetic pistol grip. **Sights:** Adjustable post front, para rear sight. **Features:** Semi-auto or select fire with fully adjustable short gas system, optional FAL rail handguard, SureFire Vertical Foregrip System, EOTech HOLOgraphic Sight and ITC cheekrest. Made in U.S.A. by DSA, Inc.
Price: **$1,845.00**

EAA/SAIGA SEMI-AUTO RIFLE
Caliber: 7.62x39, 308, 223. **Barrel:** 20.5", 22", 16.3". **Weight:** 7 to 8-1/2 lbs. **Length:** 43". **Stock:** Synthetic or wood. **Sights:** Adjustable, sight base. **Features:** Based on AK Combat rifle by Kalashnikov. Imported from Russia by EAA Corp.
Price: 7.62x39 (syn.). **$239.00**
Price: 308 (syn. or wood) **$429.00**
Price: 223 (syn.) **$389.00**

Excel Arms Accelerator

Heckler & Koch USC

Hi-Point Carbine

Les Baer Flattop

EXCEL ARMS ACCELERATOR RIFLES

Caliber: 17HMR, 22WMR, 17M2, 22LR, 9-shot magazine. **Barrel:** 18" fluted stainless steel bull barrel. **Weight:** 8 lbs. **Length:** 32.5" overall. **Grips:** Textured black polymer. **Sights:** Fully adjustable target sights. **Features:** Made from 17-4 stainless steel, aluminum shroud w/Weaver rail, manual safety, firing-pin block, last-round bolt-hold-open feature. Four packages with various equipment available. American made, lifetime warranty. Comes with one 9-round stainless steel magazine and a California-approved cable lock. Introduced 2006. Made in U.S.A. by Excel Arms.

Price: MR-17 17HMR $498.00
Price: MR-22 22WMR $498.00
Price: SR-17 17 Mach 2 .... $498.00
Price: SR-22 22LR $498.00

HECKLER & KOCH USC CARBINE

Caliber: 45 ACP, 10-shot magazine. **Barrel:** 16". **Weight:** 8.6 lb. **Length:** 35.4" overall. **Stock:** Skeletonized polymer thumbhole. **Sights:** Blade front with integral hood, fully adjustable diopter. **Features:** Based on German UMP submachine gun. Blowback operation; almost entirely constructed of carbon fiber-reinforced polymer. Free-floating heavy target barrel. Introduced 2000. From H&K.

Price: $1,249.00

HI-POINT 9MM CARBINE

Caliber: 9mm Para., 40 S&W, 10-shot magazine. **Barrel:** 16-1/2" (17-1/2" for 40 S&W). **Weight:** 4-1/2 lbs. **Length:** 31-1/2" overall. **Stock:** Black polymer, camouflage. **Sights:** Protected post front, aperture rear. Integral scope mount. **Features:** Grip-mounted magazine release. Black or

chrome finish. Sling swivels. Available with laser or red dot sights. Introduced 1996. Made in U.S.A. by MKS Supply, Inc.

Price: Black or chrome, 9mm $199.00
Price: 40 S&W $225.00
Price: Camo stock $210.00

IAI M-333 M1 GARAND

Caliber: 30-06, 8-shot clip. **Barrel:** 24". **Weight:** 9-1/2 lbs. **Length:** 43.6" overall. **Stock:** Hardwood. **Sights:** Blade front, aperture adjustable rear. **Features:** Parkerized finish; gas-operated semi-automatic; remanufactured to military specifications. From Intrac Arms International, Inc.

Price: $971.75

IAI M-888 M1 CARBINE SEMI-AUTOMATIC RIFLE

Caliber: 22, 30 carbine. **Barrel:** 18"-20". **Weight:** 5-1/2 lbs. **Length:** 35"-37" overall. **Stock:** Laminate, walnut or birch. **Sights:** Blade front, adjustable rear. **Features:** Gas-operated, air cooled, manufactured to military specifications. 10/15/30 rnd. mag. scope available. From Intrac Arms International, Inc.

Price: 30 cal. .... $556.00 to $604.00
Price: 22 cal. .... $567.00 to $654.00

IAI-65 Rifle

A civilian-legal version of the original HKM rifle manufactured in Hungary. Manufactured by Gordon Technologies using an original AMD-65 matching parts kit built on an AKM receiver. The original wire stock is present, but it is welded in the open position as per BATF regulations. Furnished with a 12.6" barrel with large weld-in-place muzzle brake to bring its length over the 16" federal minimum. This rifle accepts all 7.62x39mm magazines and drums. Introduced 2002. From Intrac Arms International, Inc.

Price: $799.00

LES BAER CUSTOM ULTIMATE AR 223 RIFLES

Caliber: 223. **Barrel:** 18", 20", 22", 24". **Weight:** 7-3/4 to 9-3/4 lb. **Length:** NA. **Stock:** Black synthetic. **Sights:** None furnished. Picatinny-style flattop rail for scope mounting. **Features:** Forged receiver; Ultra single-stage trigger (Jewell two-stage trigger optional); titanium firing pin; Versa-Pod bipod; chromed National Match carrier; stainless steel, hand-lapped and cryo-treated barrel; guaranteed to shoot 1/2 or 3/4 MOA, depending on model. Made in U.S.A. by Les Baer Custom Inc.

Price: Super Varmint model $1,989.00
Price: Super Match model (introduced 2006)............... $2,144.00
Price: M4 flattop model $2,195.00
Price: IPSC action model $2,310.00

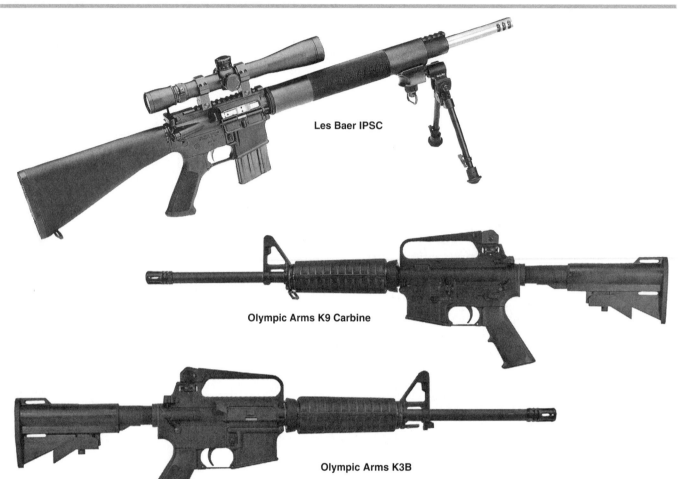

Les Baer IPSC

Olympic Arms K9 Carbine

Olympic Arms K3B

LR 300 SR LIGHT SPORT RIFLE

Caliber: 223. **Barrel:** 16-1/4"; 1:9" twist. **Weight:** 7.2 lbs. **Length:** 36" overall (extended stock), 26-1/4" (stock folded). **Stock:** Folding, tubular steel, with thumbhole-type grip. **Sights:** Trijicon post front, Trijicon rear. **Features:** Uses AR-15 type upper and lower receivers; flattop receiver with weaver base. Accepts all AR-15/M-16 magazines. Introduced 1996. Made in U.S.A. from Z-M Weapons.
Price: **$2,550.00**

OLYMPIC ARMS K9, K10, K40, K45 PISTOL CALIBER RIFLES

Caliber: 9mm, 10mm, 40 S&W, 45 ACP; 32/10 shot magazines. **Barrel:** 16", button rifled, 416 stainless steel, 1x16 twist rate. **Weight:** 6.73 lbs. **Length:** 31.625" overall. **Stock:** A2 grip, 6-point collapsible stock. **Features:** Threaded muzzle, flash suppressor, front post with bayonet lug, A2 upper, includes one appropriately modified magazine.
Price: . . . . **NA**

OLYMPIC ARMS K3B RIFLE

Caliber: 5.56 NATO, 30-shot magazines. **Barrel:** 16", button rifled, 4140 chrome-moly steel, 1x9 twist rate. **Weight:** 6.77 lbs. **Length:** 31.75" overall. **Stock:** A2 grip, 6-point collapsible buttstock. **Sights:** post front, A2 adjustable rear. **Features:** Threaded muzzles, flash suppressors, bayonet lugs, A2 uppers. Available as A3 which adds flat top upper and detachable carry handle. Available as M4 which adds M4 contoured barrel and M4 handguards. Available as CAR which adds 5.5" permanently attached A2 flash suppressor. Available as FAR, which adds feather-weight contoured barrel.
Price: K3B **$780.00**
Price: K3B-A3 . . . . **$875.00**

Price: K3B-M4 . . . . **$839.00**
Price: K3B-CAR **$810.00**
Price: K3B-FAR **$822.00**

PANTHER ARMS CLASSIC AUTO RIFLE

Caliber: 5.56x45mm. **Barrel:** Heavy 16" to 20" w/flash hider. **Weight:** 7 to 9 lbs. **Length:** 34-11/16" to 38-7/16". **Sights:** Adj. rear and front. **Stock:** Black Zytel w/trap door assembly. **Features:** Gas operated rotating bolt, mil spec or Teflon black finish.
Price: **$809.00**
Price: Stainless, match sights **$1,099.00**
Price: Southpaw **$875.00**
Price: 16" bbl. **$799.00**
Price: Panther Lite, 16" bbl. **$720.00**
Price: Panther carbine . . . . **$799.00 to $989.00**
Price: Panther bull bbl . . . . **$885.00 to $1,199.00**

REMINGTON MODEL 7400 AUTO RIFLE

Caliber: 243 Win., 270 Win., 308 Win., 30-06, 4-shot magazine. **Barrel:** 22" round tapered. **Weight:** 7-1/2 lbs. **Length:** 42-5/8" overall. **Stock:** Walnut, deluxe cut checkered pistol grip and forend. Satin or high-gloss finish. **Sights:** Gold bead front sight on ramp; step rear sight with windage adjustable. **Features:** Redesigned and improved version of the Model 742. Positive cross-bolt safety. Receiver tapped for scope mount. Introduced 1981.
Price: **$624.00**
Price: Carbine (18-1/2" bbl., 30-06 only) **$624.00**
Price: With black synthetic stock, matte black metal,
rifle or carbine **$520.00**
Price: Weathermaster, nickel-plated w/synthetic stock and forend,
270, 30-06 . . . . **$624.00**

Remington Model 7400

Ruger Deerfield 99/44 Carbine

Ruger PC4 Carbine

Ruger Ranch Mini 14/5R

ROCK RIVER ARMS STANDARD A2 RIFLE
Caliber: 45 ACP. **Barrel:** NA. **Weight:** 8.2 lbs. **Length:** NA. **Stock:** Thermoplastic. **Sights:** Standard AR-15 style sights. **Features:** Two-stage, national match trigger; optional muzzle brake. Made in U.S.A. From Rock River Arms.
Price: **$925.00**

RUGER DEERFIELD 99/44 CARBINE
Caliber: 44 Mag., 4-shot rotary magazine. **Barrel:** 18-1/2". **Weight:** 6-1/4 lbs. **Length:** 36-7/8" overall. **Stock:** Hardwood. **Sights:** Gold bead front, folding adjustable aperture rear. **Features:** Semi-automatic action; dual front-locking lugs lock directly into receiver; integral scope mount; push-button safety; includes 1" rings and gun lock. Introduced 2000. Made in U.S.A. by Sturm, Ruger & Co.
Price: **$675.00**

RUGER PC4, PC9 CARBINES
Caliber: 9mm Para., 40 cal., 10-shot magazine. **Barrel:** 16.25". **Weight:** 6 lbs., 4 oz. **Length:** 34.75" overall. **Stock:** Black high impact synthetic checkered grip and forend. **Sights:** Blade front, open adjustable rear; integral Ruger scope mounts. **Features:** Delayed blowback action; manual push-button cross bolt safety and internal firing pin block safety automatic slide lock. Introduced 1997. Made in U.S.A. by Sturm, Ruger & Co.
Price: PC9, PC4, (9mm, 40 cal.) **$623.00**
Price: PC4GR, PC9GR, (40 auto, 9mm, post sights, ghost ring) . . **$647.00**

RUGER RANCH RIFLE AUTOLOADING RIFLE
Caliber: 223 Rem., 5-shot detachable box magazine. **Barrel:** 18-1/2". Rifling twist 1:9". **Weight:** 6.4 lbs. **Length:** 37-1/4" overall. **Stock:** American hardwood, steel reinforced. **Sights:** Ramp front, fully adjustable rear. **Features:** Fixed piston gas-operated, positive primary extraction. New buffer system, redesigned ejector system. Ruger S100RM scope rings included on Ranch Rifle.
Price: Mini-14/5R, Ranch Rifle, blued, scope rings **$750.00**
Price: K-Mini-14/5R, Ranch Rifle, stainless, scope rings **$809.00**
Price: K-Mini-14/5RP, Ranch Rifle, stainless, synthetic stock **$809.00**

Ruger Mini Thirty Rifle
Similar to the Mini-14 Ranch Rifle except modified to chamber the 7.62x39 Russian service round. Weight is about 6-7/8 lbs. Has 6-groove barrel with 1:10" twist, Ruger Integral Scope Mount bases and folding peep rear sight. Detachable 5-shot staggered box magazine. Stainless w/synthetic stock. Introduced 1987.
Price: Stainless, scope rings **$809.00**

SIG 556 AUTOLOADING RIFLE
Caliber: 223 Rem., 30-shot detachable box magazine. **Barrel:** 16". Rifling twist 1:9". **Weight:** 6.8 lbs. **Length:** 36.5" overall. **Stock:** Polymer, folding style. **Sights:** Flip-up front combat sight, adjustable for windage and elevation. **Features:** Based on SG 550 series rifle. Two-position adjustable gas piston operating rod system, accepts standard AR magazines. Polymer forearm, three integrated Picatinny rails, forward mount for right- or left-side sling attachment. Aircraft-grade aluminum alloy trigger housing, hard-coat anodized finish; two-stage trigger, ambidextrous safety, 30-round polymer magazine, battery compartments, pistol-grip rubber-padded watertight adjustable butt stock with sling-attachment points. SIG 556 SWAT model has flat-top Picatinny railed receiver, tactical quad rail. Imported by Sigarms, Inc.
Price: SIG 556. . . . . **$1,300.00**

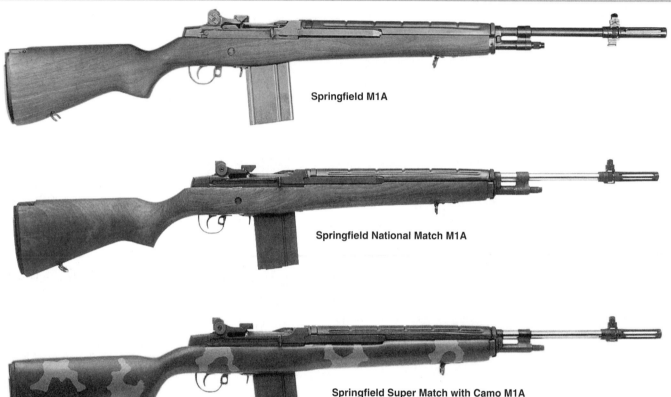

Springfield M1A

Springfield National Match M1A

Springfield Super Match with Camo M1A

SPRINGFIELD ARMORY M1A RIFLE

Caliber: 7.62mm NATO (308), 5- or 10-shot box magazine. **Barrel:** 25-1/16" with flash suppressor, 22" without suppressor. **Weight:** 9-3/4 lbs. **Length:** 44-1/4" overall. **Stock:** American walnut with walnut-colored heat-resistant fiberglass handguard. Matching walnut handguard available. Also available with fiberglass stock. **Sights:** Military, square blade front, full click-adjustable aperture rear. **Features:** Commercial equivalent of the U.S. M-14 service rifle with no provision for automatic firing. From Springfield Armory

Price: Standard M1A, black fiberglass stock. **$1,498.00**
Price: Standard M1A, black fiberglass stock, stainless **$1,727.00**
Price: Standard M1A, black stock, carbon barrel **$1,379.00**
Price: Standard M1A, Mossy Oak stock, carbon barrel **$1,507.00**
Price: Scout Squad M1A . . . . **$1,653.00 to $1,727.00**
Price: National Match . . . . **$2,049.00 to $2,098.00**
Price: Super Match (heavy premium barrel) . . . . about **$3,149.00**
Price: M1A SOCOM II rifle **$1,948.00**
Price: M25 White Feather Tactical rifle **$4,648.00**

SPRINGFIELD M1 GARAND RIFLE

Caliber: 308, 30-06. **Barrel:** 24". **Weight:** 9.5 lbs. **Length:** 43-3/5". **Stock:** Walnut. **Sights:** Military aperture with MOA adjustments for both windage and elevation, rear; military square post, front. **Features:** Original U.S. government-issue parts on a new walnut stock.
Price: . . . . **$1,348.00 to $1,378.00**

STONER SR-15 M-5 RIFLE

Caliber: 223. **Barrel:** 20". **Weight:** 7.6 lbs. **Length:** 38" overall. **Stock:** Black synthetic. **Sights:** Post front, fully adjustable rear (300-meter sight). **Features:** Modular weapon system; two-stage trigger. Black finish. Introduced 1998. Made in U.S.A. by Knight's Mfg.
Price: **$1,650.00**
Price: M-4 Carbine (16" barrel, 6.8 lbs) **$1,555.00**

STONER SR-25 CARBINE

Caliber: 7.62 NATO, 10-shot steel magazine. **Barrel:** 16" free-floating **Weight:** 7-3/4 lbs. **Length:** 35.75" overall. **Stock:** Black synthetic. **Sights:** Integral Weaver-style rail. Scope rings, iron sights optional. **Features:** Shortened, non-slip handguard; removable carrying handle. Matte black finish. Introduced 1995. Made in U.S.A. by Knight's Mfg. Co.
Price: **$3,345.00**

SMITH & WESSON M&P15 RIFLES

Caliber: 5.56mm NATO/223, 30-shot steel magazine. **Barrel:** 16", 1:9 **Weight:** 6.74 lbs., w/o magazine. **Length:** 32-35" overall. **Stock:** Black synthetic. **Sights:** Adjustable post front sight, adjustable dual aperture rear sight. **Features:** 6-position telescopic stock, thermo-set M4 handguard. 14.75" sight radius. 7-lbs. (approx.) trigger pull. 7075 T6 aluminum upper, 4140 steel barrel. Chromed barrel bore, gas key, bolt carrier. Hard-coat black-anodized receiver and barrel finish. Introduced 2006. Made in U.S.A. by Smith & Wesson.
Price: M&P15 No. 811000 . . . . **$1,200.00**
Price: M&P15T No. 811001, free float modular rail forend. **$1,700.00**
Price: M&P15A No. 811002, folding battle rear sight **$1,300.00**

WILKINSON LINDA CARBINE

Caliber: 9mm Para. **Barrel:** 16-3/16". **Weight:** 7 lbs. **Stocks:** Fixed tubular with wood pad. **Sights:** Aperture rear sight. **Features:** Aluminum receiver, pre-ban configuration (limited supplies), vent. barrel shroud, small wooden forearm, 18 or 31 shot mag. Many accessories.
Price: **$1,800.00**

Wilkinson Linda L2 Limited Edition

Manufactured from the last 600 of the original 2,200 pre-ban Linda carbines, includes many upgrades and accessories. New in 2002.
Price: **$4,800.00**

WILKINSON TERRY CARBINE

Caliber: 9mm Para. **Barrel:** 16-3/16". **Weight:** 7 lbs. **Stocks:** Black or maple. **Sights:** Adjustable. **Features:** Blowback semi-auto action, 31-shot mag., closed breech.
Price: . . . . **NA**

Both classic arms and recent designs in American-style repeaters for sport and field shooting.

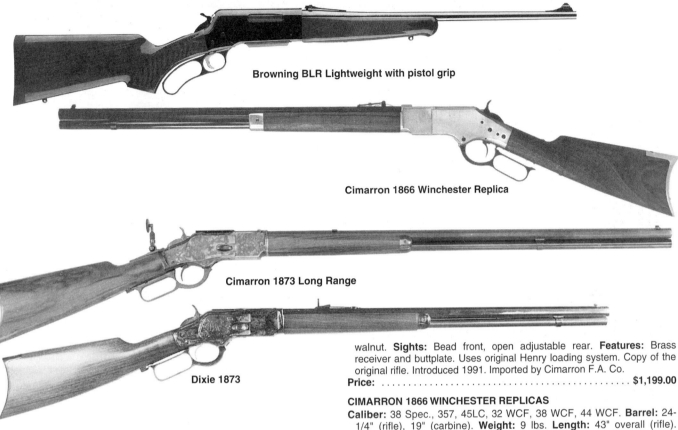

Browning BLR Lightweight with pistol grip

Cimarron 1866 Winchester Replica

Cimarron 1873 Long Range

Dixie 1873

BROWNING BLR RIFLES

Action: Lever action with rotating bolt head, multiple-lug breech bolt with recessed bolt face, side ejection. Rack-and-pinion lever. Flush-mounted detachable magazines, with 4+1 capacity for magnum cartridges, 5+1 for standard rounds. **Barrel:** Button-rifled chrome-moly steel with crowned muzzle. **Stock:** Buttstocks and forends are American walnut with grip and forend checkering. Recoil pad installed. **Trigger:** Wide-groove design, trigger travels with lever. Half-cock hammer safety; fold-down hammer. **Sights:** Gold bead on ramp front; low-profile square-notch adjustable rear. **Features:** Blued barrel and receiver, high-gloss wood finish. Receivers are drilled and tapped for scope mounts, swivel studs included. Action lock provided. Introduced 1996. Four model name variations for 2006, as noted below. Imported from Japan by Browning.

BROWNING BLR LIGHTWEIGHT W/PISTOL GRIP, SHORT AND LONG ACTION; LIGHTWEIGHT '81, SHORT AND LONG ACTION

Calibers, Short Action, 20" barrel: 22-250, 243, 7mm-08, 308, 358, 450 Marlin. **Calibers, Short Action, 22" barrel:** 270 WSM, 7mm WSM, 300 WSM, 325 WSM. **Calibers, Long Action 22" barrel:** 270, 30-06. **Calibers, Long Action 24" barrel:** 7mm Rem. Mag., 300 Win. Mag. **Weight:** 6.5-7.75 lbs. **Length:** 40-45" overall. **Stock:** New checkered pistol grip and Schnabel forearm. Lightweight '81 differs from Pistol Grip models with a Western-style straight grip stock and banded forearm. Lightweight w/Pistol Grip Short Action and Long Action introduced 2005. Model '81 Lightning Long Action introduced 1996.
Price: Lightweight w/Pistol Grip Short Action . . . . $765.00 to $836.00
Price: Lightweight w/Pistol Grip Long Action $809.00
Price: Lightweight '81 Short Action . . . . $731.00 to $802.00
Price: Lightweight '81 Long Action $775.00

CIMARRON 1860 HENRY REPLICA

Caliber: 44 WCF, 45LC; 13-shot magazine. **Barrel:** 24-1/4" (rifle), 22" (carbine). **Weight:** 9-1/2 lbs. **Length:** 43" overall (rifle). **Stock:** European

walnut. **Sights:** Bead front, open adjustable rear. **Features:** Brass receiver and buttplate. Uses original Henry loading system. Copy of the original rifle. Introduced 1991. Imported by Cimarron F.A. Co.
Price: $1,199.00

CIMARRON 1866 WINCHESTER REPLICAS

Caliber: 38 Spec., 357, 45LC, 32 WCF, 38 WCF, 44 WCF. **Barrel:** 24-1/4" (rifle), 19" (carbine). **Weight:** 9 lbs. **Length:** 43" overall (rifle). **Stock:** European walnut. **Sights:** Bead front, open adjustable rear. **Features:** Solid brass receiver, buttplate, forend cap. Octagonal barrel. Copy of the original Winchester '66 rifle. Introduced 1991. Imported by Cimarron F.A. Co.
Price: Rifle $965.00
Price: Carbine $950.00

CIMARRON 1873 SHORT RIFLE

Caliber: 357 Mag., 38 Spec., 32 WCF, 38 WCF, 44 Spec., 44 WCF, 45 Colt. **Barrel:** 20" tapered octagon. **Weight:** 7.5 lbs. **Length:** 39" overall. **Stock:** Walnut. **Sights:** Bead front, adjustable semi-buckhorn rear. **Features:** Has half "button" magazine. Original-type markings, including caliber, on barrel and elevator and "Kings" patent. From Cimarron F.A. Co.
Price: $1,149.00

Cimarron 1873 Sporting Rifle

Similar to the 1873 Short Rifle except has 24" barrel with half-magazine.
Price: $1,149.00

CIMARRON 1873 LONG RANGE RIFLE

Caliber: 44 WCF, 45 Colt. **Barrel:** 30", octagonal. **Weight:** 8-1/2 lbs. **Length:** 48" overall. **Stock:** Walnut. **Sights:** Blade front, semi-buckhorn ramp rear. Tang sight optional. **Features:** Color case-hardened frame; choice of modern blue-black or charcoal blue for other parts. Barrel marked "Kings Improvement." From Cimarron F.A. Co.
Price: $1,199.00

DIXIE ENGRAVED 1873 RIFLE

Caliber: 44-40, 11-shot magazine. **Barrel:** 20", round. **Weight:** 7-3/4 lbs. **Length:** 39" overall. **Stock:** Walnut. **Sights:** Blade front, adjustable rear. **Features:** Engraved and case-hardened frame. Replica of Winchester 1873. Made in Italy. From 21 Gun Works.
Price: $1,425.00
Price: Plain, blued carbine $1,015.00

Marlin 336C

Marlin 1894 Cowboy

E.M.F. 1860 HENRY RIFLE

Caliber: 44-40 or 45 Colt. **Barrel:** 24.25". **Weight:** About 9 lbs. **Length:** About 43.75" overall. **Stock:** Oil-stained American walnut. **Sights:** Blade front, rear adjustable for elevation. **Features:** Reproduction of the original Henry rifle with brass frame and buttplate, rest blued. From E.M.F.
Price: Brass frame $850.00
Price: Steel frame $950.00

E.M.F. 1866 YELLOWBOY LEVER ACTIONS

Caliber: 38 Spec., 44-40. **Barrel:** 19" (carbine), 24" (rifle). **Weight:** 9 lbs. **Length:** 43" overall (rifle). **Stock:** European walnut. **Sights:** Bead front, open adjustable rear. **Features:** Solid brass frame, blued barrel, lever, hammer, buttplate. Imported from Italy by E.M.F.
Price: Rifle $690.00
Price: Carbine $675.00

E.M.F. HARTFORD MODEL 1892 LEVER-ACTION RIFLE

Caliber: 45 Colt. **Barrel:** 24", octagonal. **Weight:** 7-1/2 lbs. **Length:** 43" overall. **Stock:** European walnut. **Sights:** Blade front, open adjustable rear. **Features:** Color case-hardened frame, lever, trigger and hammer with blued barrel, or overall blue finish. Introduced 1998. Imported by E.M.F.
Price: Standard $590.00

E.M.F. MODEL 1873 LEVER-ACTION RIFLE

Caliber: 32/20, 357 Mag., 38/40, 44-40, 44 Spec., 45 Colt. **Barrel:** 24". **Weight:** 8 lbs. **Length:** 43-1/4" overall. **Stock:** European walnut. **Sights:** Bead front, rear adjustable for windage and elevation. **Features:** Color case-hardened frame (blue on carbine). Imported by E.M.F.
Price: Rifle $865.00
Price: Carbine, 19" barrel $865.00

E.M.F. MODEL 1873 REVOLVER CARBINE

Caliber: 357 Mag., 45 Colt. **Barrel:** 18". **Weight:** 4 lbs., 8 oz. **Length:** 34" overall. **Stock:** One-piece walnut. **Sights:** Blade front, notch rear. **Features:** Color case-hardened frame, blue barrel, backstrap and trigger guard. Introduced 1998. Imported from Italy by IAR, Inc.
Price: Standard $490.00

MARLIN MODEL 336C LEVER-ACTION CARBINE

Caliber: 30-30 or 35 Rem., 6-shot tubular magazine. **Barrel:** 20" Micro-Groove®. **Weight:** 7 lbs. **Length:** 38-1/2" overall. **Stock:** Checkered American black walnut, capped pistol grip. Mar-Shield® finish; rubber buttpad; swivel studs. **Sights:** Ramp front with Wide-Scan hood, semi-buckhorn folding rear adjustable for windage and elevation. **Features:** Hammer-block safety. Receiver tapped for scope mount, offset hammer spur; top of receiver sandblasted to prevent glare. Includes safety lock.
Price: $570.00

Marlin Model 336A Lever-Action Carbine

Same as the Marlin 336C except has cut-checkered, walnut-finished hardwood pistol grip stock with swivel studs, 30-30 only, 6-shot. Hammer-block safety. Adjustable rear sight, brass bead front. Includes safety lock.
Price: $477.00
Price: With 4x scope and mount $527.00

Marlin Model 336SS Lever-Action Carbine

Same as the 336C except receiver, barrel and other major parts are machined from stainless steel. 30-30 only, 6-shot; receiver tapped for scope. Includes safety lock.
Price: $692.00

Marlin Model 336W Lever-Action Rifle

Similar to the Model 336C except has walnut-finished, cut-checkered Maine birch stock; blued steel barrel band has integral sling swivel; no front sight hood; comes with padded nylon sling; hard rubber buttplate. Introduced 1998. Includes safety lock. Made in U.S.A. by Marlin.
Price: $482.00
Price: With 4x scope and mount $535.00

Marlin Model 336XLR Lever-Action Rifle

Similar to Model 336C except has an 24" stainless barrel with Ballard-type cut rifling, stainless steel receiver and other parts, laminated hardwood stock with pistol grip, nickel-plated swivel studs. Chambered for 30-30 Win. with Hornady Evolution spire-pointed Flex-Tip cartridges. Includes safety lock. Introduced 2006.
Price: (Model 336XLR) $874.00

MARLIN MODEL 444 LEVER-ACTION SPORTER

Caliber: 444 Marlin, 5-shot tubular magazine. **Barrel:** 22" deep cut Ballard rifling. **Weight:** 7-1/2 lbs. **Length:** 40-1/2" overall. **Stock:** Checkered American black walnut, capped pistol grip, rubber rifle buttpad. Mar-Shield® finish; swivel studs. **Sights:** Hooded ramp front, folding semi-buckhorn rear adjustable for windage and elevation. **Features:** Hammer-block safety. Receiver tapped for scope mount; offset hammer spur. Includes safety lock.
Price: $665.00

Marlin Model 444XLR Lever-Action Rifle

Similar to Model 444 except has an 24" stainless barrel with Ballard-type cut rifling, stainless steel receiver and other parts, laminated hardwood stock with pistol grip, nickel-plated swivel studs. Chambered for 444 Marlin with Hornady Evolution spire-pointed Flex-Tip cartridges. Includes safety lock. Introduced 2006.
Price: (Model 444XLR) $874.00

MARLIN MODEL 1894 LEVER-ACTION CARBINE

Caliber: 44 Spec./44 Mag., 10-shot tubular magazine. **Barrel:** 20" Ballard-type rifling. **Weight:** 6 lbs. **Length:** 37-1/2" overall. **Stock:** Checkered American black walnut, straight grip and forend. Mar-Shield® finish. Rubber rifle buttpad; swivel studs. **Sights:** Wide-Scan hooded ramp front, semi-buckhorn folding rear adjustable for windage and elevation. **Features:** Hammer-block safety. Receiver tapped for scope mount, offset hammer spur, solid top receiver sand blasted to prevent glare. Includes safety lock.
Price: $614.00

Marlin Model 1894C Carbine

Similar to the standard Model 1894 except chambered for 38 Spec./357 Mag. with full-length 9-shot magazine, 18-1/2" barrel, hammer-block safety, hooded front sight. Introduced 1983. Includes safety lock.
Price: $614.00

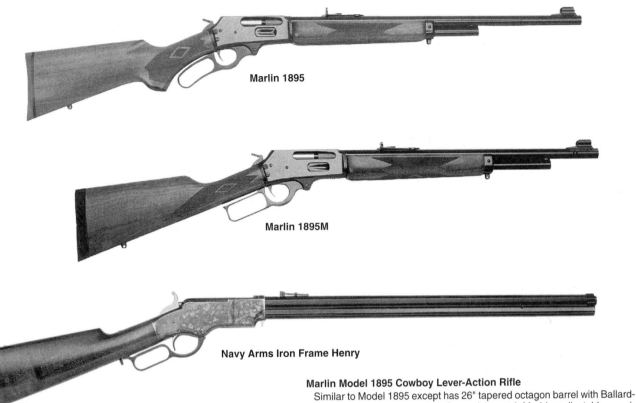

Marlin 1895

Marlin 1895M

Navy Arms Iron Frame Henry

MARLIN MODEL 1894 COWBOY

Caliber: 357 Mag., 44 Mag., 45 Colt, 10-shot magazine. **Barrel:** 20" tapered octagon, deep cut rifling. **Weight:** 7-1/2 lbs. **Length:** 41-1/2" overall. **Stock:** Straight grip American black walnut, hard rubber buttplate, Mar-Shield® finish. **Sights:** Marble carbine front, adjustable Marble semi-buckhorn rear. **Features:** Squared finger lever; straight grip stock; blued steel forend tip. Designed for Cowboy Shooting events. Introduced 1996. Includes safety lock. Made in U.S.A. by Marlin.
Price: **$889.00**

Marlin Model 1894SS

Similar to Model 1894 except has stainless steel barrel, receiver, lever, guard plate, magazine tube and loading plate. Nickel-plated swivel studs.
Price: **$752.00**

MARLIN MODEL 1895 LEVER-ACTION RIFLE

Caliber: 45-70, 4-shot tubular magazine. **Barrel:** 22" round. **Weight:** 7-1/2 lbs. **Length:** 40-1/2" overall. **Stock:** Checkered American black walnut, full pistol grip. Mar-Shield® finish; rubber buttpad; quick detachable swivel studs. **Sights:** Bead front with Wide-Scan hood, semi-buckhorn folding rear adjustable for windage and elevation. **Features:** Hammer-block safety. Solid receiver tapped for scope mounts or receiver sights; offset hammer spur. Includes safety lock.
Price: **$665.00**

Marlin Model 1895G Guide Gun Lever-Action Rifle

Similar to Model 1895 with deep-cut Ballard-type rifling; straight-grip walnut stock. Overall length is 37", weighs 7 lbs. Introduced 1998. Includes safety lock. Made in U.S.A. by Marlin.
Price: **$681.00**

Marlin Model 1895GS Guide Gun

Similar to Model 1895G except receiver, barrel and most metal parts are machined from stainless steel. Chambered for 45-70, 4-shot, 18-1/2" barrel. Overall length is 37", weighs 7 lbs. Introduced 2001. Includes safety lock. Made in U.S.A. by Marlin.
Price: **$805.00**

Marlin Model 1895 Cowboy Lever-Action Rifle

Similar to Model 1895 except has 26" tapered octagon barrel with Ballard-type rifling, Marble carbine front sight and Marble adjustable semi-buckhorn rear sight. Receiver tapped for scope or receiver sight. Overall length is 44-1/2", weighs about 8 lbs. Introduced 2001. Includes safety lock. Made in U.S.A. by Marlin.
Price: **$849.00**

Marlin Model 1895XLR Lever-Action Rifle

Similar to Model 1895 except has an 24" stainless barrel with Ballard-type cut rifling, stainless steel receiver and other parts, laminated hardwood stock with pistol grip, nickel-plated swivel studs. Chambered for 45-70 Government with Hornady Evolution spire-pointed Flex-Tip cartridges. Includes safety lock. Introduced 2006.
Price: (Model 1895MXLR) **$874.00**

Marlin Model 1895M Lever-Action Rifle

Similar to Model 1895G except has an 18-1/2" barrel with Ballard-type cut rifling. Chambered for 450 Marlin. Includes safety lock.
Price: (Model 1895M) **$733.00**

Marlin Model 1895MXLR Lever-Action Rifle

Similar to Model 1895M except has an 24" stainless barrel with Ballard-type cut rifling, stainless steel receiver and other parts, laminated hardwood stock with pistol grip, nickel-plated swivel studs. Chambered for 450 Marlin with Hornady Evolution spire-pointed Flex-Tip cartridges. Includes safety lock. Introduced 2006.
Price: (Model 1895MXLR) **$874.00**

NAVY ARMS MILITARY HENRY RIFLE

Caliber: 44-40 or 45 Colt, 12-shot magazine. **Barrel:** 24-1/4". **Weight:** 9 lbs., 4 oz. **Stock:** European walnut. **Sights:** Blade front, adjustable ladder-type rear. **Features:** Brass frame, buttplate, rest blued. Replica of the model used by cavalry units in the Civil War. Has full-length magazine tube, sling swivels; no forend. Imported from Italy by Navy Arms.
Price: **$1,199.00**

Navy Arms Iron Frame Henry

Similar to the Military Henry Rifle except receiver is blued or color case-hardened steel. Imported by Navy Arms.
Price: . . . . **$1,258.00-$1,275.00**

CENTERFIRE RIFLES — Lever & Slide

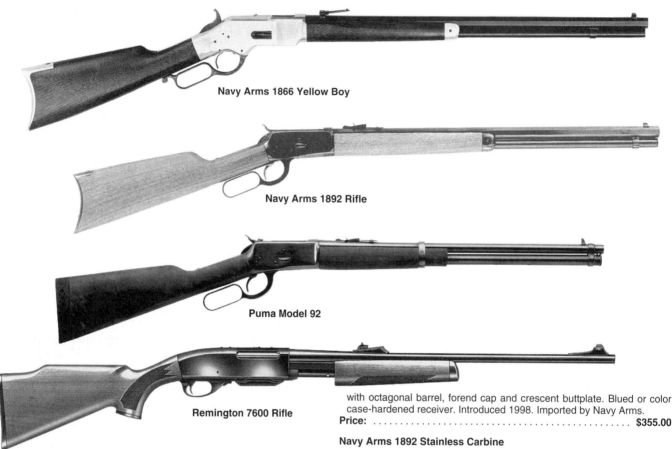

Navy Arms 1866 Yellow Boy

Navy Arms 1892 Rifle

Puma Model 92

Remington 7600 Rifle

NAVY ARMS 1866 YELLOW BOY RIFLE
Caliber: 38 Spec., 44-40, 45 Colt, 12-shot magazine. **Barrel:** 20" or 24", full octagon. **Weight:** 8-1/2 lbs. **Length:** 42-1/2" overall. **Stock:** Walnut. **Sights:** Blade front, adjustable ladder-type rear. **Features:** Brass frame, forend tip, buttplate, blued barrel, lever, hammer. Introduced 1991. Imported from Italy by Navy Arms.
Price: **$942.00**
Price: Carbine, 19" barrel **$908.00**

NAVY ARMS 1866 SPORTING YELLOW BOY RIFLES
Caliber: 45 Colt. **Barrel:** 24-1/4" octagonal; 1:16" twist. **Weight:** 8.16 lbs. **Length:** 43-3/4" overall. **Stock:** Walnut. **Sights:** Blade front, adjustable folding rear. **Features:** Brass receiver; blued or white barrel; 13-shot magazine. Introduced 2001. Imported from Uberti by Navy Arms.
Price: (blued barrel) **$942.00**

NAVY ARMS 1873 WINCHESTER-STYLE RIFLE
Caliber: 357 Mag., 44-40, 45 Colt, 12-shot magazine. **Barrel:** 24-1/4". **Weight:** 8-1/4 lbs. **Length:** 43" overall. **Stock:** European walnut. **Sights:** Blade front, buckhorn rear. **Features:** Color case-hardened frame, rest blued. Full-octagon barrel. Imported by Navy Arms.
Price: **$1,079.00**
Price: 1873 Carbine, 19" barrel **$1,054.00**
Price: 1873 Sporting Rifle (full oct. bbl., checkered walnut stock and forend) **$1,218.00**
Price: 1873 Border Model, 20" octagon barrel **$1,079.00**
Price: 1873 Deluxe Border Model **$1,218.00**

NAVY ARMS 1892 RIFLE
Caliber: 357 Mag., 44-40, 45 Colt. **Barrel:** 24-1/4" octagonal. **Weight:** 7 lbs. **Length:** 42" overall. **Stock:** American walnut. **Sights:** Blade front, semi-buckhorn rear. **Features:** Replica of Winchester's early Model 1892

with octagonal barrel, forend cap and crescent buttplate. Blued or color case-hardened receiver. Introduced 1998. Imported by Navy Arms.
Price: **$355.00**

Navy Arms 1892 Stainless Carbine
Similar to the 1892 Rifle except stainless steel, has 20" round barrel, weighs 5-3/4 lbs., and is 37-1/2" overall. Introduced 1998. Imported by Navy Arms.
Price: **$345.00**

Navy Arms 1892 Short Rifle
Similar to the 1892 Rifle except has 20" octagonal barrel, weighs 6-1/4 lbs., and is 37-3/4" overall. Replica of the rare, special order 1892 Winchester nicknamed the "Texas Special." Blued or color case-hardened receiver and furniture. Introduced 1998. Imported by Navy Arms.
Price: **$355.00**

PUMA MODEL 92 RIFLES & CARBINES
Caliber: 38 Spec./357 Mag., 44 Mag., 45 Colt, 454 Casull, 480 Ruger. **Barrel:** 16". 18", 20" round, 24" octagonal; porting and large lever loop available. **Weight:** 6.1 to 7.7 lbs. **Stock:** Walnut-stained hardwood. **Sights:** Open, buckhorn front & rear; HiViz also available. **Features:** Blue, case-hardened, stainless steel and brass receivers, matching buttplates. Blued, stainless steel barrels, full-length magazines. Thumb safety. 45 Colt and 454 Casull carbine introduced in 2002. The 480 Ruger version introduced in 2003. Imported from Brazil by Legacy Sports International.
Price: . . . . **$450.00 to $617.00**

REMINGTON MODEL 7600 PUMP ACTION
Caliber: 243, 270, 30-06, 308. **Barrel:** 22" round tapered. **Weight:** 7-1/2 lbs. **Length:** 42-5/8" overall. **Stock:** Cut-checkered walnut pistol grip and forend, Monte Carlo with full cheekpiece. Satin or high-gloss finish. **Sights:** Gold bead front sight on matted ramp, open step adjustable sporting rear. **Features:** Redesigned and improved version of the Model 760. Detachable 4-shot clip. Cross-bolt safety. Receiver tapped for scope mount. Introduced 1981.
Price: **$588.00**
Price: Carbine (18-1/2" bbl., 30-06 only) **$588.00**
Price: With black synthetic stock, matte black metal, rifle or carbine **$484.00**

CENTERFIRE RIFLES — Lever & Slide

Ruger Model 96/44

Tristar 1873 Sporting Rifle

Tristar 1866 Yellowboy Carbine

Tristar 1860 Henry

Uberti 1873 Sport

RUGER MODEL 96/44 LEVER-ACTION RIFLE
Caliber: 44 Mag., 4-shot rotary magazine. **Barrel:** 18-1/2". **Weight:** 6 lbs. **Length:** 37.75" overall. **Stock:** American hardwood. **Sights:** Gold bead front, folding leaf rear. **Features:** Solid chrome-moly steel receiver. Manual cross-bolt safety, visible cocking indicator; short-throw lever action; integral scope mount; blued finish; color case-hardened lever. Introduced 1996. Made In U.S. by Sturm, Ruger & Co.
Price: 96/44M, 44 Mag **$546.00**

TRISTAR/SHARPS 1874 SPORTING RIFLE
Caliber: 45-70. **Barrel:** 28", 32", 34" octagonal. **Weight:** 9.75 lbs. **Length:** 44.5" overall. **Stock:** Walnut. **Sights:** Dovetail front, adjustable rear. **Features:** Cut checkering, case colored frame finish.
Price: **$839.00**
Price: Bridgeport Sharps **$899.00**

TRISTAR/UBERTI 1866 SPORTING RIFLE, CARBINE
Caliber: 45 Colt. **Barrel:** 24-1/4", octagonal. **Weight:** 8.1 lbs. **Length:** 43-1/4" overall. **Stock:** Walnut. **Sights:** Blade front adjustable for windage, rear adjustable for elevation. **Features:** Frame, buttplate, forend cap of polished brass, balance charcoal blued. Imported by Tristar Sporting Arms Ltd.

Price: **$1,109.00**
Price: Yellowboy carbine (19" round bbl.) **$999.00**

TRISTAR/UBERTI 1860 HENRY RIFLE
Caliber: 45 Colt. **Barrel:** 24-1/4", half-octagon. **Weight:** 9.2 lbs. **Length:** 43-3/4" overall. **Stock:** American walnut. **Sights:** Blade front, rear adjustable for elevation. **Features:** Frame, elevator, magazine follower, buttplate are brass, balance blue. Imported by Tristar Sporting Arms Ltd. Arms, Inc.
Price: **$1,359.00**

TRISTAR/UBERTI 1873 SPORTING RIFLE
Caliber: 45 Colt. **Barrel:** 24-1/4", 30", octagonal. **Weight:** 8.1 lbs. **Length:** 43-1/4" overall. **Stock:** Walnut. **Sights:** Blade front adjustable for windage, open rear adjustable for elevation. **Features:** Color case-hardened frame, blued barrel, hammer, lever, buttplate, brass elevator. Imported from Italy by Tristar Sporting Arms Ltd.
Price: 24-1/4" barrel **$1,259.00**

UBERTI 1873 SPORTING RIFLE
Caliber: 357 Mag., 44-40, 45 Colt. **Barrel:** 19", to 24-1/4". **Weight:** Up to 8.2 lbs. **Length:** Up to 43.3" overall. **Stock:** Walnut, straight grip and pistol grip. **Sights:** Blade front adjustable for windage, open rear adjustable for elevation. **Features:** Color case-hardened frame, blued barrel, hammer, lever, buttplate, brass elevator. Imported by Benelli USA.
Price: 1873 Carbine, 19" round barrel **$945.00**
Price: 1873 Short Rifle, 20" octagonal barrel **$985.00**
Price: 1873 Special Sporting Rifle, 24.25" octagonal barrel **$1,100.00**

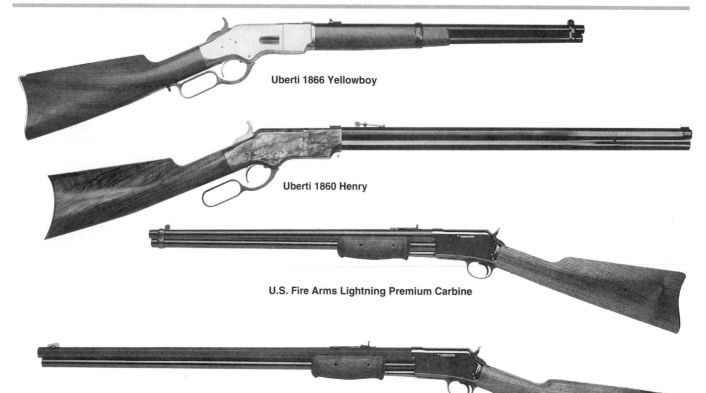

Uberti 1866 Yellowboy

Uberti 1860 Henry

U.S. Fire Arms Lightning Premium Carbine

U.S. Fire Arms Standard Lightning

UBERTI 1866 YELLOWBOY CARBINE, SHORT RIFLE, RIFLE

Caliber: 38 Spec., 44-40, 45 Colt. **Barrel:** 24-1/4", octagonal. **Weight:** 8.2 lbs. **Length:** 43-1/4" overall. **Stock:** Walnut. **Sights:** Blade front adjustable for windage, rear adjustable for elevation. **Features:** Frame, buttplate, forend cap of polished brass, balance charcoal blued. Imported by Benelli USA.
Price: 1866 Yellowboy Carbine, 19" round barrel **$885.00**
Price: 1866 Yellowboy Short Rifle, 20" octagonal barrel **$900.00**
Price: 1866 Yellowboy Rifle, 24.25" octagonal barrel **$900.00**

UBERTI 1860 HENRY RIFLE

Caliber: 44-40, 45 Colt. **Barrel:** 24-1/4", half-octagon. **Weight:** 9.2 lbs. **Length:** 43-3/4" overall. **Stock:** American walnut. **Sights:** Blade front, rear adjustable for elevation. **Features:** Imported by Benelli USA.
Price: 1860 Henry Trapper, 18.5" barrel, brass frame **$1,050.00**
Price: 1860 Henry Rifle, 24.25" barrel, brass frame **$1,050.00**
Price: 1860 Henry Rifle steel, 24.25" barrel, case-hardened
frame **$1,150.00**
Price: 1860 Henry Rifle Iron Frame, 24.25" barrel **$1,050.00**

Uberti 1860 Henry Trapper Carbine

Similar to the 1860 Henry Rifle except has 18-1/2" barrel, measures 37-3/4" overall, and weighs 8 lbs. Introduced 1999. Imported by Benelli USA.
Price: Brass frame, blued barrel **$989.00**

UBERTI LIGHTNING RIFLE

Caliber: 357 Mag., 45 Colt, 10+1. **Barrel:** 20" to 24.25". **Stock:** Walnut. **Finish:** Blue or case-hardened. Introduced 2006. Imported by Benelli USA.
Price: 1875 Lightning Rifle, 24.25" barrel **$1,199.00**
Price: 1875 Lightning Short Rifle, 20" barrel **$1,199.00**
Price: 1875 Lightning Carbine, 20" barrel **$1,049.00**

UBERTI SPRINGFIELD TRAPDOOR RIFLE

Caliber: 4-70, single shot. **Barrel:** 22" or 32.5". **Stock:** Walnut. **Finish:** Blue and case-hardened. Introduced 2006. Imported by Benelli USA.
Price: Springfield Trapdoor Carbine, 22" barrel **$1,100.00**
Price: Springfield Trapdoor Army, 32.5" barrel **$1,295.00**

U.S. FIRE ARMS STANDARD LIGHTNING MAGAZINE RIFLE

Caliber: 45 Colt, 44 WCF, 44 Spl., 38 WCF, 15-shot. **Barrel:** 26". **Stock:** Oiled walnut. **Finish:** High polish blue. Nickel finish also available. Introduced 2002. Made in U.S.A. by United States Fire-Arms Manufacturing Co.
Price: Round barrel **$1,480.00**
Price: Octagonal barrel, checkered forend **$1,750.00**
Price: Half-round barrel, checkered forend **$1,999.00**
Price: Premium Carbine, 20" round barrel **$1,480.00**
Price: Baby Carbine, 20" special taper barrel **$1,999.00**
Price: Trapper, 16" special taper barrel **$2,155.00**
Price: Cowboy Action Lightning **$1,345.00**
Price: Cowboy Action Lightning Carbine, 20" round barrel **$1,345.00**

WINCHESTER MODEL 1895 LEVER-ACTION RIFLE

Caliber: 405 Win, 4-shot magazine. **Barrel:** 24", round. **Weight:** 8 lbs. **Length:** 42" overall. **Stock:** American walnut. **Sights:** Gold bead front, buckhorn rear adjustable for elevation. **Features:** Re-creation of the original Model 1895. Polished blue finish. Two-piece cocking lever, Schnabel forend, straight-grip stock. Introduced 1995. From U.S. Repeating Arms Co., Inc.
Price: Grade I **$1,116.00**

Includes models for a wide variety of sporting and competitive purposes and uses.

Anschutz 1733D

Barrett Model 95

Blaser R93 Classic

ANSCHUTZ 1743D BOLT-ACTION RIFLE

Caliber: 222 Rem., 3-shot magazine. **Barrel:** 19.7". **Weight:** 6.4 lbs. **Length:** 39" overall. **Stock:** European walnut. **Sights:** Hooded blade front, folding leaf rear. **Features:** Receiver grooved for scope mounting; single stage trigger; claw extractor; sling safety; sling swivels. Imported from Germany by AcuSport Corp.

Price: **$1,588.95**

ANSCHUTZ 1740 MONTE CARLO RIFLE

Caliber: 22 Hornet, 5-shot clip; 222 Rem., 3-shot clip. **Barrel:** 24". **Weight:** 6-1/2 lbs. **Length:** 43.25" overall. **Stock:** Select European walnut. **Sights:** Hooded ramp front, folding leaf rear; drilled and tapped for scope mounting. **Features:** Uses Match 54 action. Adjustable single stage trigger. Stock has roll-over Monte Carlo cheekpiece, slim forend with Schnabel tip, Wundhammer palm swell on grip, rosewood gripcap with white diamond insert. Skip-line checkering on grip and forend. Introduced 1997. Imported from Germany by AcuSport Corp.

Price: From **$1,439.00**

Price: Model 1730 Monte Carlo, as above except in
22 Hornet **$1,439.00**

Anschutz 1733D Rifle

Similar to the 1740 Monte Carlo except has full-length, walnut, Mannlicher-style stock with skip-line checkering, rosewood Schnabel tip, and is chambered for 22 Hornet. Weighs 6.4 lbs., overall length 39", barrel length 19.7". Imported from Germany by AcuSport Corp.

Price: **$1,588.95**

BARRETT MODEL 95 BOLT-ACTION RIFLE

Caliber: 50 BMG, 5-shot magazine. **Barrel:** 29". **Weight:** 22 lbs. **Length:** 45" overall. **Stock:** Energy-absorbing recoil pad. **Sights:** Scope optional. **Features:** Bolt-action, bullpup design. Disassembles without tools; extendable bipod legs; match-grade barrel; muzzle brake. Introduced 1995. Made in U.S.A. by Barrett Firearms Mfg., Inc.

Price: From **$4,950.00**

BLASER R93 BOLT-ACTION RIFLE

Caliber: 22-250, 243, 6.5x55, 270, 7x57, 7mm-08, 308, 30-06, 257 Wby. Mag., 7mm Rem. Mag., 300 Win. Mag., 300 Wby. Mag., 338 Win Mag., 375 H&H, 416 Rem. Mag. **Barrel:** 22" (standard calibers), 26" (magnum). **Weight:** 7 lbs. **Length:** 40" overall (22" barrel). **Stock:** Two-piece European walnut. **Sights:** None furnished; drilled and tapped for scope mounting. **Features:** Straight pull-back bolt action with thumb-activated safety slide/cocking mechanism; interchangeable barrels and bolt heads. Introduced 1994. Imported from Germany by SIGARMS.

Price: R93 Classic **$3,680.00**
Price: R93 LX **$1,895.00**
Price: R93 Synthetic (black synthetic stock) **$1,595.00**
Price: R93 Safari Synthetic (416 Rem. Mag. only) **$1,855.00**
Price: R93 Grand Lux **$4,915.00**
Price: R93 Attaché **$5,390.00**

BRNO 98 BOLT-ACTION RIFLE

Caliber: 7x64, 243, 270, 308, 30-06, 300 Win. Mag., 9.3x62. **Barrel:** 23.6". **Weight:** 7.2 lbs. **Length:** 40.9" overall. **Stock:** European walnut. **Sights:** Blade on ramp front, open adjustable rear. **Features:** Uses Mauser 98-type action; polished blue. Announced 1998. Imported from the Czech Republic by Euro-Imports.

Price: Standard calibers **$507.00**
Price: Magnum calibers **$547.00**
Price: With set trigger, standard calibers **$615.00**
Price: As above, magnum calibers **$655.00**
Price: With full stock, set trigger, standard calibers **$703.00**
Price: As above, magnum calibers **$743.00**
Price: 300 Win. Mag., with BOSS **$933.00**

BROWNING A-BOLT RIFLES

Common Features: Short-throw (60") fluted bolt, three locking lugs, plunger-type ejector; adjustable trigger is grooved. Chrome-plated trigger sear. Hinged floorplate, detachable box magazine. Slide tang safety. Receivers are drilled and tapped for scope mounts, swivel studs included. Barrel is free-floating and glass-bedded, recessed muzzle. Safety is top-tang sliding button. Engraving available for bolt sleeve or rifle body. Introduced 1985. 30 model name variations, as noted below. Imported from Japan by Browning.

CENTERFIRE RIFLES — Bolt-Action

Browning A-Bolt Hunter

Browning A-Bolt Medallion

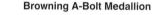

Browning A-Bolt White Gold Medallion

BROWNING A-BOLT HUNTER

Calibers, 22" barrel: 223, 22-250, 243, 270 Win., 30-06, 7mm-08, 308. **Calibers, 23" barrel:** 270 WSM, 7mm WSM, 300 WSM, 325 WSM (intr. 2005). **Calibers, 24" barrel:** 25-06. **Calibers, 26" barrel:** 7mm Rem. Mag., 300 Win. Mag., 338 Win. Mag. **Weight:** 6.25-7.2 lbs. **Length:** 41.25-46.5" overall. **Stock:** Sporter-style walnut; checkered grip and forend. **Metal Finish:** Low-luster blueing.
Price: Hunter . . . . **$705.00 to $734.00**

Browning A-Bolt Hunter Left-Hand

Calibers, 22" barrel: 223 Rem.; 223 WSSM, 243 WSSM, 25 WSSM (WSSMs intr. 2005). **Calibers, 23" barrel:** 270 WSM, 7mm WSM, 300 WSM, 325 WSM (intr. 2005). **Weight:** 6.25-6.6 lbs. **Length:** 41.25-42.75" overall. **Features:** Otherwise similar to A-Bolt Hunter.
Price: Hunter, Left-hand. . . . . **$735.00 to $785.00**

BROWNING A-BOLT HUNTER FLD

Caliber, 23" barrel: 270 WSM, 7mm WSM, 300 WSM, 325 WSM (intr. 2005). **Weight:** 6.6 lbs. **Length:** 42.75" overall. **Features:** FLD has low-luster blueing and select Monte Carlo stock with right-hand palm swell, double-border checkering. Otherwise similar to A-Bolt Hunter.
Price: FLD **$808.00**

BROWNING A-BOLT HUNTER WSSM, FLD WSSM

Calibers, 22" barrel: 223 WSSM, 243 WSSM, 25 WSSM. **Weight:** 6.3 lbs. **Length:** 41.25" overall. **Features:** WSSM has classic walnut stock. FLD has low-luster blueing and select Monte Carlo stock with right-hand palm swell, double-border checkering. Otherwise similar to A-Bolt Hunter.
Price: WSSM **$755.00**
Price: FLD WSSM **$829.00**

BROWNING A-BOLT MOUNTAIN TI

Caliber: 223 WSSM, 243 WSSM, 25 WSSM (all added 2005); 270 WSM, 7mm WSM, 300 WSM. **Barrel:** 22" or 23". **Weight:** 5.25-5.5 lbs. **Length:** 41.25-42.75" overall. **Stock:** Lightweight fiberglass Bell & Carlson model in Mossy-Oak New Break Up camo. **Metal Finish:** Stainless barrel, titanium receiver. **Features:** Pachmayr Decelerator recoil pad. Introduced 1999.
Price: . . . . **$1,669.00 to $1,690.00**

Browning A-Bolt Micro Hunter and Micro Hunter Left-Hand

Calibers, 20" barrel: 22-250, 243, 308, 7mm-08. **Calibers, 22" barrel:** 22 Hornet, 270 WSM, 7mm WSM, 300 WSM, 325 WSM (2005). **Weight:** 6.25-6.4 lbs. **Length:** 39.5-41.5" overall. **Features:** Classic walnut stock with 13.3" LOP. Otherwise similar to A-Bolt Hunter.

Price: Micro Hunter . . . . **$684.00 to $714.00**
Price: Micro Hunter Left-Hand . . . . **$714.00 to $744.00**

BROWNING A-BOLT MEDALLION

Calibers, 22" barrel: 223, 22-250, 243, 308, 270 Win., 280, 30-06. **Calibers, 23" barrel:** 270 WSM, 7mm WSM, 300 WSM, 325 WSM (intr. 2005). **Calibers, 24" barrel:** 25-06. **Calibers, 26" barrel:** 7mm Rem. Mag., 300 Win. Mag., 338 Win. Mag., 375 H&H. **Weight:** 6.25-7.1 lbs. **Length:** 41.25-46.5" overall. **Stock:** Select walnut stock, glossy finish, rosewood grip and forend caps, checkered grip and forend. **Metal Finish:** Engraved high-polish blued receiver.
Price: Medallion . . . . **$805.00 to $835.00**
Price: Medallion WSSM in 223/243/25 WSSM. **$856.00**

BROWNING A-BOLT MEDALLION W/BOSS

Calibers, 22" barrel: 223 WSSM, 243 WSSM, 25 WSSM (intr. 2005), 270, 30-06. **Calibers, 23" barrel:** 270 WSM, 7mm WSM, 300 WSM. **Calibers, 24" barrel:** 375 H&H. **Calibers, 26" barrel:** 300 Win. Mag., 338 Win. Mag. Same as the Medallion model A-Bolt except has left-hand action. Introduced 1987.
Price: Medallion Left-hand . . . . **$885.00 to $936.00**

Browning A-Bolt Medallion Left-Hand

Caliber, 22" barrel: 223 Rem., 223 WSSM, 243 WSSM, 25 WSSM (all intr. 2005), 270, 30-06. **Calibers, 23" barrel:** 270 WSM, 7mm WSM, 300 WSM, 325 WSM (intr. 2005). **Calibers, 26" barrel:** 7mm Rem. Mag., 300 Win. Mag. Same as the Medallion model A-Bolt except has left-hand action. Introduced 1987.
Price: Medallion Left-hand . . . . **$837.00 to $886.00**

Browning A-Bolt Medallion Left-Hand w/BOSS

Calibers, 22" barrel: 270, 30-06. **Calibers, 26" barrel:** 7mm Rem. Mag., 300 Win. Mag. Same as the Medallion Left-Hand except has BOSS device.
Price: Medallion Left-hand w/BOSS . . . . **$917.00 to $945.00**

BROWNING A-BOLT WHITE GOLD MEDALLION, RMEF WHITE GOLD, WHITE GOLD MEDALLION W/BOSS

Calibers, 22" barrel: 270 Win., 30-06. **Calibers, 23" barrel:** 270 WSM, 7mm WSM, 300 WSM, 325 WSM (intr. 2005). **Calibers, 26" barrel:** 7mm Rem. Mag., 300 Win. Mag. **Weight:** 6.4-7.7 lbs. **Length:** 42.75-46.5" overall. **Stock:** select walnut stock with brass spacers between rubber recoil pad and between the rosewood gripcap and forend tip; gold-filled barrel inscription; palm-swell pistol grip, Monte Carlo comb, 22 lpi checkering with double borders. **Metal Finish:** Engraved high-polish stainless receiver and barrel. BOSS version chambered in 270 Win. and 30-06 (22" barrel) and 7mm Rem. Mag. and 300 Win. Mag. (26" barrel) Introduced 1988. RMEF version has engraved gripcap, continental cheekpiece; gold engraved, stainless receiver and bbl. Introduced 2004.
Price: White Gold Medallion . . . . **$1,155.00 to $1,183.00**
Price: Rocky Mt. Elk Foundation White Gold, 7mm Rem. Mag., . . **$1,261.00**
Price: White Gold Medallion w/BOSS. . . . . **$1,235.00 to $1,263.00**

Browning A-Bolt Stainless Stalker

Browning A-Bolt Varmint Stalker

Browning A-Bolt Composite Stalker

Browning A-Bolt Eclipse Hunter

Browning A-Bolt Eclipse M-1000

Browning A-Bolt Stainless Stalker, Stainless Stalker Left-hand

Calibers, 22" barrel: 223, 243, 270, 280, 7mm-08, 30-06, 308. **Calibers, 23" barrel:** 270 WSM, 7mm WSM, 300 WSM, 325 WSM (intr. 2005). **Calibers, 24" barrel:** 25-06. **Calibers, 26" barrel:** 7mm Rem. Mag., 300 Win. Mag., 338 Win. Mag., 375 H&H. **Weight:** 6.1-7.2 lbs. **Length:** 40.9-46.5" overall. **Features:** Similar to the A-Bolt Hunter model except receiver and barrel are made of stainless steel; other exposed metal surfaces are finished silver-gray matte. Graphite-fiberglass composite textured stock. No sights are furnished, except on 375 H&H, which comes with open sights. Introduced 1987.
Price: Stainless Stalker . . . . **$897.00 to $926.00**
Price: Stainless Stalker Left-Hand. . . . . **$925.00 to $954.00**
Price: Stainless Stalker WSSM, 223/243/25 WSSM. **$808.00**

Browning A-Bolt Stainless Stalker, Stainless Stalker Left-Hand, w/BOSS

Calibers, 22" barrel: 223 WSSM, 243 WSSM, 25 WSSM, 270, 30-06. **Calibers, 23" barrel:** 270 WSM, 7mm WSM, 300 WSM, 325 WSM (intr. 2005). **Calibers, 24" barrel:** 375 H&H. **Calibers, 26" barrel:** 7mm Rem. Mag., 300 Win. Mag., 338 Win. Mag. **Features:** Similar to the A-Bolt Stainless Stalker, except includes BOSS.
Price: Stainless Stalker w/BOSS. . . . . **$977.00 to $1,027.00**
Price: Stainless Stalker Left-Hand w/BOSS . . . . . . **$1,005.00 to $1,034.00**

BROWNING A-BOLT VARMINT STALKER, VARMINT STALKER WSSM

Calibers, 24" barrel: 223 Rem., 223 WSSM, 243 WSSM, 25 WSSM. **Calibers, 26" barrel:** 22-250. **Weight:** 7.8-8.2 lbs. **Length:** 42.75-45.75"

overall. **Features:** Similar to the A-Bolt Stainless Stalker except has black graphite-fiberglass stock with textured finish and matte blue-finish on all exposed metal surfaces. Medium-heavy varmint barrel. No sights are furnished. Introduced 1987.
Price: Varmint Stalker **$860.00**
Price: Varmint Stalker WSSM **$913.00**

BROWNING A-BOLT COMPOSITE STALKER

Calibers, 22" barrel: 223, 22-250, 243, 270, 280, 7mm-08, 30-06, 308. **Calibers, 23" barrel:** 270 WSM, 7mm WSM, 300 WSM, 325 WSM (intr. 2005). **Calibers, 24" barrel:** 25-06. **Calibers, 26" barrel:** 7mm Rem. Mag., 300 Win. Mag., 338 Win. Mag. **Weight:** 6.1-7.2 lbs. **Length:** 40.75-46.5" overall. **Features:** Similar to the A-Bolt Stainless Stalker except has black composite stock with textured finish and matte-blued finish on all exposed metal surfaces except bolt sleeve. No sights are furnished.
Price: Composite Stalker . . . . **$705.00 to $735.00**

BROWNING A-BOLT ECLIPSE HUNTER W/BOSS, M-1000 ECLIPSE W/BOSS, M-1000 ECLIPSE WSM, STAINLESS M-1000 ECLIPSE WSM

Calibers, 22" barrel: 270, 30-06. **Calibers, 26" barrel:** 7mm Rem. Mag., 300 Win. Mag., 270 WSM, 7mm WSM, 300 WSM. **Weight:** 7.5-9.9 lbs. **Length:** 42.75-46.5" overall. **Features:** All models have gray/black laminated thumbhole stock. Introduced 1996. Two versions have BOSS barrel vibration modulator and muzzle brake. Hunter has sporter-weight barrel. M-1000 Eclipses have long actions and heavy target barrels, adjustable triggers, bench-style forends, 3-shot magazines. Introduced 1997.
Price: Eclipse Hunter w/BOSS . . . . **$1,134.00 to $1,162.00**
Price: M-1000 Eclipse w/BOSS, 300 Win. Mag. only **$1,168.00**
Price: M-1000 Eclipse WSM, 270 WSM, 7mm WSM, 300 WSM. . **$1,068.00**
Price: Stainless M-1000 Eclipse WSM **$1,292.00**

Charles Daly Field Mauser

Cooper Model 21 Bolt

CARBON ONE BOLT-ACTION RIFLE

Caliber: 22-250 to 375 H&H. **Barrel:** Up to 28". **Weight:** 5-1/2 to 7-1/4 lbs. **Length:** Varies. **Stock:** Synthetic or wood. **Sights:** None furnished. **Features:** Choice of Remington, Browning or Winchester action with free-floated Christensen graphite/epoxy/steel barrel, trigger pull tuned to 3 to 3-1/2 lbs. Made in U.S.A. by Christensen Arms.

Price: Carbon One Hunter Rifle, 6-1/2 to 7 lbs. **$1,499.00**
Price: Carbon One Custom, 5-1/2 to 6-1/2 lbs., Shilen trigger . . **$2,750.00**
Price: Carbon Ranger, 50 BMG, 5-shot repeater **$4,750.00**
Price: Carbon Ranger, 50 BMG, single shot **$3,950.00**

CENTURY INTERNATIONAL M70 SPORTER DOUBLE-TRIGGER BOLT-ACTION RIFLE

Caliber: 22-250, 270, 300 Win. Mag., 308 Win., 24" barrel. **Weight:** 7.95 lbs. **Length:** 44.5" **Sights:** Flip-up U-notch rear sight, hooded blade front sight. **Features:** Mauser M98-type action; 5-rd fixed box magazine. 22-250 has hinged floorplate. Monte Carlo stock, oil finish. Adjustable trigger on double-trigger models. 300 Win. Mag. Has 3-rd. fixed box magazine. 308 holds 5 rds. 300 and 308 have buttpads. Manufactured by Zastava in Yugoslavia, imported by Century International.

Price: M70 Sporter Double-Trigger **$500.00**
Price: M70 Sporter Double-Trigger 22-250 . . . . **$475.00**
Price: M70 Sporter Single-Trigger .300 Win. Mag. **$475.00**
Price: M70 Sporter Single/Double Trigger .308 Win. **$500.00**

CHARLES DALY FIELD MAUSER RIFLE

Caliber: 22-250, 243, 25-06, 270, 308, 30-06 (in 22" barrels); 7mm Rem. Mag. and 300 Win. Mag. in 24" barrels. **Weight:** NA. **Sights:** None; drilled and tapped for scope mounts. **Features:** Mauser Model 98-type action; carbon or stainless steel barrels; slide safety; polymer stock; fully adjustable trigger.

Price: Field Grade Mauser **$459.00**
Price: Mauser SS **$549.00**
Price: Magnum calibers. **$579.00**

COOPER MODEL 16 WSSM BOLT-ACTION RIFLE

Caliber: 223 WSSM, 25 WSSM, 243 WSSM. **Barrel:** 26" stainless match. **Weight:** 6.5-7.5 lbs. **Stock:** AA-AAA select Claro walnut, 22 lpi hand checkering. **Sights:** None furnished. **Features:** Three front locking-lug bolt-action.

Price: Varminter **$1,198.00**
Price: Montana Varminter **$1,459.00**
Price: Varmint Extreme **$1,895.00**

COOPER MODEL 21 BOLT-ACTION RIFLE

Caliber: 17 Rem., 17 Mach IV, 19-223, Tactical 20, 204 Ruger, 20 VarTarg, 221 Fireball, 222 Rem, 222 Rem Mag, 223 Rem, 223 Rem AI, 22 PPC, 6mm PPC, 6x45, 6x47, 6.8 SPC. **Barrel:** 22" or 24" stainless match or 4140 blued. **Weight:** 6.5-7.5 lbs. **Stock:** AA-AAA select Claro walnut, 22 lpi hand checkering. **Sights:** None furnished. **Features:** Three front locking-lug bolt-action single shot. **Action:** 6.6" long, Sako style, modified for rimmed cases. Retractable tab ejector. Fully adjustable single-stage

trigger. Options include wood upgrades, case-color metalwork, barrel fluting, custom LOP, and many others.

Price: Phoenix **$1,298.00**
Price: Varminter **$1,198.00**
Price: Montana Varminter **$1,459.00**
Price: Varmint Extreme **$1,895.00**
Price: Classic (blued barrel) **$1,398.00**
Price: Custom Classic (blued barrel) **$1,995.00**
Price: Western Classic (case color, octagonal blued barrel) **$2,698.00**

COOPER MODEL 22 BOLT-ACTION RIFLE

Caliber: 22-250 Rem., 22-250 Rem. AI, 25-06 Rem., 25-06 Rem. AI, 243 Win., 243 Win. AI, 220 Swift, 250/3000 AI, 257 Roberts, 257 Roberts AI, 7mm-08, 6mm Rem., 260 Rem., 6 x 284, 6.5 x 284, 22 BR, 6mm BR, 308 Win. **Barrel:** 24" stainless match or 4140 blued. **Weight:** 7.5 lbs. **Stock:** AA-AAA select Claro walnut, 22 lpi hand checkering. **Sights:** None furnished. **Features:** Three front locking-lug bolt-action single shot. **Action:** 8.25" long, Sako style, plunger-style ejector. Fully adjustable single-stage trigger. Options include wood upgrades, case-color metalwork, barrel fluting, custom LOP, and many others.

Price: Phoenix **$1,398.00**
Price: Varminter **$1,349.00**
Price: Montana Varminter **$1,459.00**
Price: Varmint Extreme **$1,995.00**
Price: Classic (blued barrel) **$1,398.00**
Price: Custom Classic (blued barrel) **$2,195.00**
Price: Western Classic (case color, octagonal blued barrel) **$2,896.00**

COOPER MODEL 38 BOLT-ACTION RIFLE

Caliber: 17 Squirrel, 17 Hee Bee, 17 Ackley Hornet, 19 Calhoun, 22 Hornet, 22 K Hornet, 22 Squirrel, 218 Bee, 218 Mash Bee. **Barrel:** 24" stainless match. **Weight:** 6.5-7.5 lbs. **Stock:** AA-AAA select Claro walnut, 22 lpi hand checkering. **Sights:** None furnished. **Features:** Three front locking-lug mini bolt-action single shot. **Action:** 6.6" long, Sako style, modified for rimmed cases. Retractable tab ejector. Fully adjustable single-stage trigger. Options include wood upgrades, case-color metalwork, barrel fluting, custom LOP, and many others.

Price: Varminter **$1,198.00**
Price: Montana Varminter **$1,459.00**
Price: Varmint Extreme **$1,895.00**
Price: Classic **$1,398.00**
Price: Custom Classic (blued barrel) **$1,995.00**
Price: Western Classic (case color, octagonal blued barrel) **$2,698.00**

CZ 527 LUX BOLT-ACTION RIFLE

Caliber: 22 Hornet, 222 Rem., 223 Rem., detachable 5-shot magazine. **Barrel:** 23-1/2"; standard or heavy barrel. **Weight:** 6 lbs., 1 oz. **Length:** 42-1/2" overall. **Stock:** European walnut with Monte Carlo. **Sights:** Hooded front, open adjustable rear. **Features:** Improved mini-Mauser action with non-rotating claw extractor; single set trigger; grooved receiver. Imported from the Czech Republic by CZ-USA.

Price: **$566.00**
Price: Model FS, full-length stock, cheekpiece. **$658.00**

CZ 527 Lux

CZ 527 FS

CZ 527 American

CZ 550 Lux

CZ 550 Medium Magnum

CZ 527 American Classic Bolt-Action Rifle
Similar to the CZ 527 Lux except has classic-style stock with 18 lpi checkering; free-floating barrel; recessed target crown on barrel. No sights furnished. Introduced 1999. Imported from the Czech Republic by CZ-USA.
Price: 22 Hornet, 222 Rem., 223 Rem............. **$586.00 to $609.00**

CZ 550 LUX BOLT-ACTION RIFLE
Caliber: 22-250, 243, 6.5x55, 7x57, 7x64, 308 Win., 9.3x62, 270 Win., 30-06. **Barrel:** 20.47". **Weight:** 7.5 lbs. **Length:** 44.68" overall. **Stock:** Turkish walnut in Bavarian style or FS (Mannlicher). **Sights:** Hooded front, adjustable rear. **Features:** Improved Mauser-style action with claw extractor, fixed ejector, square bridge dovetailed receiver; single set trigger. Imported from the Czech Republic by CZ-USA.
Price: Lux......................... **$566.00 to $609.00**
Price: FS (full stock) **$706.00**

CZ 550 American Classic Bolt-Action Rifle
Similar to CZ 550 Lux except has American classic-style stock with 18 lpi checkering; free-floating barrel; recessed target crown. Has 25.6" barrel; weighs 7.48 lbs. No sights furnished. Introduced 1999. Imported from the Czech Republic by CZ-USA.
Price: .... **$586.00 to $609.00**

CZ 550 Medium Magnum Bolt-Action Rifle
Similar to the CZ 550 Lux except chambered for the 300 Win. Mag. and 7mm Rem. Mag.; 5-shot magazine. Adjustable iron sights, hammer-forged barrel, single-set trigger, Turkish walnut stock. Weighs 7.5 lbs. Introduced 2001. Imported from the Czech Republic by CZ-USA.
Price: **$621.00**

CZ 550 Magnum Bolt-Action Rifle
Similar to CZ 550 Lux except has long action for 300 Win. Mag., 375 H&H, 416 Rigby, 458 Win. Mag. Overall length is 46.45"; barrel length 25"; weighs 9.24 lbs. Hooded front sight, express rear with one standing, two folding leaves. Imported from the Czech Republic by CZ-USA.
Price: 300 Win. Mag.................................... **$717.00**
Price: 375 H&H **$756.00**
Price: 416 Rigby **$809.00**
Price: 458 Win. Mag. **$744.00**

CZ 550 Magnum

Dakota 76 Traveler

Dakota 76 Classic

Dakota 76 Safari

CZ 700 M1 SNIPER RIFLE

Caliber: 308 Winchester, 10-shot magazine. **Barrel:** 25.6". **Weight:** 11.9 lbs. **Length:** 45" overall. **Stock:** Laminated wood thumbhole with adjustable buttplate and cheekpiece. **Sights:** None furnished; permanently attached Weaver rail for scope mounting. **Features:** 60-degree bolt throw; oversized trigger guard and bolt handle for use with gloves; full-length equipment rail on forend; fully adjustable trigger. Introduced 2001. Imported from the Czech Republic by CZ-USA.
Price: **$2,097.00**

DAKOTA 76 TRAVELER TAKEDOWN RIFLE

Caliber: 257 Roberts, 25-06, 7x57, 270, 280, 30-06, 338-06, 35 Whelen (standard length); 7mm Rem. Mag., 300 Win. Mag., 338 Win. Mag., 416 Taylor, 458 Win. Mag. (short magnums); 7mm, 300, 330, 375 Dakota Magnums. **Barrel:** 23". **Weight:** 7-1/2 lbs. **Length:** 43-1/2" overall. **Stock:** Medium fancy-grade walnut in classic style. Checkered grip and forend; solid buttpad. **Sights:** None furnished; drilled and tapped for scope mounts. **Features:** Threadless disassembly. Uses modified Model 76 design with many features of the Model 70 Winchester. Left-hand model also available. Introduced 1989. Made in U.S.A. by Dakota Arms, Inc.
Price: Classic. **$4,495.00**
Price: Safari **$5,495.00**
Price: Extra barrels . . . . **$1,650.00 to $1,950.00**

DAKOTA 76 CLASSIC BOLT-ACTION RIFLE

Caliber: 257 Roberts, 270, 280, 30-06, 7mm Rem. Mag., 338 Win. Mag., 300 Win. Mag., 375 H&H, 458 Win. Mag. **Barrel:** 23". **Weight:** 7-1/2 lbs. **Length:** 43-1/2" overall. **Stock:** Medium fancy grade walnut in classic style. Checkered pistol grip and forend; solid buttpad. **Sights:** None furnished; drilled and tapped for scope mounts. **Features:** Has many features of the original Winchester Model 70. One-piece rail trigger guard assembly; steel gripcap. Model 70-style trigger. Many options available. Left-hand rifle available at same price. Introduced 1988. From Dakota Arms, Inc.
Price: **$3,595.00**

DAKOTA 76 SAFARI BOLT-ACTION RIFLE

Caliber: 270 Win., 7x57, 280, 30-06, 7mm Dakota, 7mm Rem. Mag., 300 Dakota, 300 Win. Mag., 330 Dakota, 338 Win. Mag., 375 Dakota, 458 Win. Mag., 300 H&H, 375 H&H, 416 Rem. **Barrel:** 23". **Weight:** 8-1/2 lbs. **Length:** 43-1/2" overall. **Stock:** XXX fancy walnut with ebony forend tip; point-pattern with wraparound forend checkering. **Sights:** Ramp front, standing leaf rear. **Features:** Has many features of the original Winchester Model 70. Barrel band front swivel, inletted rear. Cheekpiece with shadow line. Steel gripcap. Introduced 1988. From Dakota Arms, Inc.
Price: Wood stock **$4,595.00**

Dakota African Grade

Similar to 76 Safari except chambered for 338 Lapua Mag., 404 Jeffery, 416 Rigby, 416 Dakota, 450 Dakota, 4-round magazine, select wood, two stock cross-bolts. 24" barrel, weighs 9-10 lbs. Ramp front sight, standing leaf rear. Introduced 1989.
Price: **$4,995.00**

Dakota Longbow

Dakota 97 Lightweight Hunter

Dakota Hunter

DSA DS-MP1

DAKOTA LONGBOW TACTICAL E.R. RIFLE
Caliber: 300 Dakota Magnum, 330 Dakota Magnum, 338 Lapua Magnum. **Barrel:** 28", .950" at muzzle **Weight:** 13.7 lbs. **Length:** 50" to 52" overall. **Stock:** Ambidextrous McMillan A-2 fiberglass, black or olive green color; adjustable cheekpiece and buttplate. **Sights:** None furnished. Comes with Picatinny one-piece optical rail. **Features:** Uses the Dakota 76 action with controlled-round feed; three-position firing pin block safety, claw extractor; Model 70-style trigger. Comes with bipod, case tool kit. Introduced 1997. Made in U.S.A. by Dakota Arms, Inc.
Price: **$4,250.00**

DAKOTA 97 LIGHTWEIGHT HUNTER
Caliber: 22-250 to 330. **Barrel:** 22" to 24". **Weight:** 6.1 to 6.5 lbs. **Length:** 43" overall. **Stock:** Fiberglass. **Sights:** Optional. **Features:** Matte blue finish, black stock. Right-hand action only. Introduced 1998. Made in U.S.A. by Dakota Arms, Inc.
Price: **$1,995.00**

DAKOTA LONG RANGE HUNTER RIFLE
Caliber: 25-06, 257 Roberts, 270 Win., 280 Rem., 7mm Rem. Mag., 7mm Dakota Mag., 30-06, 300 Win. Mag., 300 Dakota Mag., 338 Win. Mag., 330 Dakota Mag., 375 H&H Mag., 375 Dakota Mag. **Barrel:** 24", 26", match-quality; free-floating. **Weight:** 7.7 lbs. **Length:** 45" to 47" overall.

Stock: H-S Precision black synthetic, with one-piece bedding block system. **Sights:** None furnished. Drilled and tapped for scope mounting. **Features:** Cylindrical machined receiver controlled round feed; Mauser-style extractor; three-position striker blocking safety; fully adjustable match trigger. Right-hand action only. Introduced 1997. Made in U.S.A. by Dakota Arms, Inc.
Price: **$1,995.00**

DSA DS-MP1
Caliber: 308 Win. match chamber. **Barrel:** 22", 1:10 twist, hand-lapped stainless-steel match-grade Badger Barrel with recessed target crown. **Weight:** 11.5 lbs. **Length:** 41.75". **Stock:** Black McMillan A5 pillar bedded in Marine-Tex with 13.5" length of pull. **Sights:** Tactical Picatinny rail. **Features:** Action, action threads and action bolt locking shoulder completely trued, Badger Ordnance precision ground heavy recoil lug, machined steel Picatinny rail sight mount, trued action threads, action bolt locking shoulder, bolt face and lugs, 2.5-lb. trigger pull, barrel and action finished in Black DuraCoat, guaranteed to shoot 1/2 MOA at 100 yards with match-grade ammo. Introduced 2006. Made in U.S.A. by DSA, Inc.
Price: **$2,800.00**

ED BROWN SAVANNA RIFLE
Caliber: 30-06, 300 Win. Mag., 300 Weatherby, 338 Win. Mag. **Barrel:** 22", 23", 24". **Weight:** 8 to 8-1/2 lbs. **Stock:** Fully glass-bedded McMillan fiberglass sporter. **Sights:** None furnished. Talley scope mounts utilizing heavy duty 8-40 screws. **Features:** Custom action with machined steel trigger guard and hinged floor plate. Available in left-hand version.
Price: From . . . . **$2,795.00 to $2,895.00**

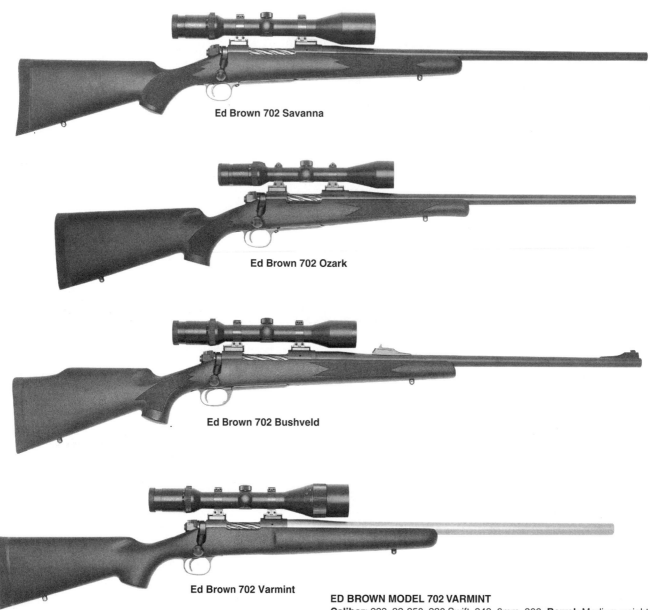

Ed Brown 702 Savanna

Ed Brown 702 Ozark

Ed Brown 702 Bushveld

Ed Brown 702 Varmint

Ed Brown Model 702 Denali, Ozark

Similar to the Ed Brown Model 702 Savanna but lighter weight, designed specifically for mountain hunting, especially suited to the 270 and 280 calibers. Right-hand only. Weighs about 7.75 lbs. The Model 702 Ozark is made on a short action with a lightweight stock. Ozark calibers are 223, 243, 6mm, 260 Rem., 7mm-08, 308. Weight 6.5 lbs.
Price: From **$2,800.00**

ED BROWN MODEL 702 BUSHVELD

Caliber: 338 Win. Mag., 375 H&H, 416 Rem. Mag., 458 Win. Mag., 458 Lott and all Ed Brown Savanna long action calibers. **Barrel:** 24" medium or heavy weight. **Weight:** 8.25 lbs. **Stock:** Fully bedded McMillan fiberglass with Monte Carlo style cheekpiece, Pachmayr Decelerator recoil pad. **Sights:** None furnished. Talley scope mounts utilizing heavy duty 8-40 screws. **Features:** Options include left-hand action, stainless steel barrel, additional calibers, iron sights.
Price: From . . . . **$2,895.00 to $3,195.00**

ED BROWN MODEL 702 VARMINT

Caliber: 223, 22-250, 220 Swift, 243, 6mm, 308. **Barrel:** Medium weight #5 contour 24"; heavyweight #17 contour 24"; 26" optional. **Weight:** 9 lbs. **Stock:** Fully glass-bedded McMillan fiberglass with recoil pad. **Sights:** None furnished. Talley scope mounts with heavy duty 8-40 screws. **Features:** Fully-adjustable trigger, steel trigger guard and floor plate, many options available.
Price: From **$2,495.00**

HOWA LIGHTNING BOLT-ACTION RIFLE

Caliber: 223, 22-250, 243, 204 Ruger, 270, 308, 30-06, 7mm Rem. Mag., 300 Win. Mag., 338 Win. Mag, 300 WSM, 7mm WSM, 270 WSM. **Barrel:** 22", 24" magnum calibers. **Weight:** 7-1/2 lbs. **Length:** 42-44" overall (22" barrel). **Stock:** Black Bell & Carlson Carbelite composite with Monte Carlo comb; checkered grip and forend; also Realtree camo available. **Sights:** None furnished. Drilled and tapped for scope mounting. **Features:** Three-position thumb safety; hinged floorplate; polished blue/black finish. Introduced 1993. From Legacy Sports International.
Price: Blue, standard calibers **$439.00**
Price: Blue, magnum calibers **$470.00**
Price: Stainless, standard calibers **$661.00**
Price: Stainless, magnum calibers **$690.00**

Howa Lightning

Howa M-1500 Hunter

Howa M-1500 Ultralight

Howa M-1500 Varmint Supreme

Howa M-1500 Hunter Bolt-Action Rifle

Similar to Lightning Model except has walnut-finished hardwood stock, three-position safety. Polished blue finish or stainless steel. Introduced 1999. From Legacy Sports International.

Price: Blue, standard calibers	**$574.00**
Price: Stainless, standard calibers	**$682.00**
Price: Blue, magnum calibers	**$595.00**
Price: Stainless, magnum calibers	**$704.00**
Price: Blued, camo stock	**$545.00**

Howa M-1500 Supreme Rifles

Similar to Howa M-1500 Lightning except stocked with JRS Classic or Thumbhole Sporter laminated wood stocks in Nutmeg (brown/black) or Pepper (gray/black) colors. Barrel: 22"; 24" magnum calibers. Weights are JRS stock 8 lbs., THS stock 8.3 lbs. Three-position safety. Introduced 2001. Imported from Japan by Legacy Sports International.

Price: Blue, standard calibers, JRS stock	**$646.00**
Price: Blue, standard calibers, THS stock	**$704.00**
Price: Blue, magnum calibers, JRS stock	**$675.00**
Price: Blue, magnum calibers, THS stock	**$733.00**
Price: Stainless, standard calibers, JRS stock	**$755.00**
Price: Stainless, standard calibers, THS stock	**$813.00**
Price: Stainless, magnum calibers, JRS stock	**$784.00**
Price: Stainless, magnum calibers, THS stock	**$842.00**

Howa M-1500 Ultralight

Similar to Howa M-1500 Lightning except receiver milled to reduce weight; three-position safety; tapered 22" barrel; 1-10" twist. Chambered for 243 Win. Stocks are black texture-finished hardwood. Weighs 6.4 lbs. Length 40" overall.

Price: Blued	**$539.00**
Price: Stainless model	**$658.00**

Howa M-1500 Varmint and Varmint Supreme Rifles

Similar to M-1500 Lightning except has heavy 24" hammer-forged barrel. Chambered for 223, 22-250, 308. Weighs 9.3 lbs.; overall length 44.5". Introduced 1999. Imported from Japan by Interarms/Howa. Varminter Supreme has heavy barrel, target crown muzzle; three-position safety. Heavy 24" barrel, laminated wood with raised comb stocks, rollover cheekpiece, vented beavertail forearm; available in 223 Rem., 22-250 Rem., 204 Ruger, 308 Win. Weighs 9.9 lbs. Carbon fiber thumbhole stock option available. Introduced 2001. Imported from Japan by Legacy Sports International.

Price: Varminter, blue, polymer stock	**$546.00**
Price: Varminter, stainless, polymer stock	**$664.00**
Price: Varminter, blue, wood stock	**$610.00**
Price: Varminter, stainless, wood stock	**$719.00**
Price: Varminter Supreme, blued	**$711.00 to $733.00**
Price: Varminter Supreme, stainless	**$820.00 to $842.00**
Price: Varminter, blued, camo stock	**$582.00**
Price: Varminter, stainless, camo stock	**$704.00**

Kimber 8400

Kimber 84M Classic

L.A.R. Grizzly

Magnum Research Tactical

KENNY JARRETT BOLT-ACTION RIFLE

Caliber: 223 Rem., 243 Improved, 243 Catbird, 7mm-08 Improved, 280 Remington, .280 Ackley Improved, 7mm Rem. Mag., 284 Jarrett, 30-06 Springfield, 300 Win. Mag., .300 Jarrett, 323 Jarrett, 338 Jarrett, 375 H&H, 416 Rem., 450 Rigby., other modern cartridges. **Barrel:** NA. **Weight:** NA. **Length:** NA. **Stock:** NA. **Features:** Tri-Lock receiver. Talley rings and bases. Accuracy guarantees and custom loaded ammunition.

Price: Signature Series	**$6,880.00**
Price: Wind Walker	**$6,650.00**
Price: Original Beanfield (customer's receiver)	**$4,850.00**
Price: Professional Hunter	**$9,390.00**

KIMBER MODEL 8400 BOLT-ACTION RIFLE

Caliber: 270, 7mm, 300 or 325 WSM, 4 shot. **Barrel:** 24". **Weight:** 6 lbs. 3 oz. to 6 lbs 10 oz. **Length:** 43.25". **Stock:** Claro walnut or Kevlar-reinforced fiberglass. **Sights:** None; drilled and tapped for bases. **Features:** Mauser claw extractor, two-position wing safety, action bedded on aluminum pillars and fiberglass, free-floated barrel, match grade adjustable trigger set at 4 lbs., matte or polished blue or matte stainless finish. Introduced 2003. Made in U.S.A. by Kimber Mfg. Inc.

Price: Classic . . . . **$1,080.00 to $2,030.00**

KIMBER MODEL 84M BOLT-ACTION RIFLE

Caliber: 22-250, 204 Ruger, 223, 243, 260 Rem., 7mm-08, 308, 5-shot. **Barrel:** 22", 24", 26". **Weight:** 5 lbs., 10 oz. to 10 lbs. **Length:** 41" to 45". **Stock:** Claro walnut, checkered with steel gripcap; synthetic or gray laminate. **Sights:** None; drilled and tapped for bases. **Features:** Mauser claw extractor, three-position wing safety, action bedded on aluminum pillars, free-floated barrel, match-grade trigger set at 4 lbs., matte blue finish. Includes cable lock. Introduced 2001. Made in U.S.A. by Kimber Mfg. Inc.

Price: Classic (243, 260, 7mm-08, 308) . . . . **$945.00 to $1,828.00**
Price: Varmint (22-250) **$1,038.00**

L.A.R. GRIZZLY 50 BIG BOAR RIFLE

Caliber: 50 BMG, single shot. **Barrel:** 36". **Weight:** 30.4 lbs. **Length:** 45.5" overall. **Stock:** Integral. Ventilated rubber recoil pad. **Sights:** None furnished; scope mount. **Features:** Bolt-action bullpup design, thumb and bolt stop safety. All-steel construction. Introduced 1994. Made in U.S.A. by L.A.R. Mfg., Inc.

Price: **$2,350.00**

MAGNUM RESEARCH MAGNUM LITE TACTICAL RIFLE

Caliber: 223 Rem., 22-250, 308 Win., 300 Win. Mag., 300 WSM. **Barrel:** 26" Magnum Lite™ graphite. **Weight:** 8.3 lbs. **Length:** NA. **Stock:** H-S Precision™ tactical black synthetic. **Sights:** None furnished; drilled and tapped for scope mount. **Features:** Accurized Remington 700 action; adjustable trigger; adjustable comb height. Tuned to shoot 1/2" MOA or better. Introduced 2001. From Magnum Research Inc.

Price: **$2,400.00**

Remington 673 Guide

Remington 700 Classic

Remington 700 ADL Synthetic

Remington 700 BDL

MOUNTAIN EAGLE MAGNUM LITE RIFLE
Caliber: 22-250, 223 Rem. (Varmint); 280, 30-06 (long action); 7mm Rem. Mag., 300 Win. Mag., (magnum action). **Barrel:** 24", 26", free floating. **Weight:** 7 lbs., 13 oz. **Length:** 44" overall (24" barrel). **Stock:** Kevlar-graphite with aluminum bedding block, high comb, recoil pad, swivel studs; made by H-S Precision. **Sights:** None furnished. **Features:** Special Sako action with one-piece forged bolt, hinged steel floorplate, lengthened receiver ring; adjustable trigger. Introduced 1996. From Magnum Research, Inc.
Price: Magnum Lite (graphite barrel) **$2,295.00**

REMINGTON MODEL 673 GUIDE RIFLE
Caliber: 65mm Rem. Mag., 308 Win., 300 Rem. SA Ultra Mag., 350 Rem. Mag. **Barrel:** 22". **Weight:** 7-1/2 lbs. **Length:** 41-3/16". **Stock:** Two-tone wide striped, laminated, weather resistant. **Features:** Magnum contour barrel with machined steel ventilated rib, iron sights.
Price: **$825.00**

REMINGTON MODEL 700 CLASSIC RIFLE
Caliber: 300 Savage. **Barrel:** 24". **Weight:** About 7-1/4 lbs. **Length:** 44-1/2" overall. **Stock:** American walnut, 20 lpi checkering on pistol grip and forend. Classic styling. Satin finish. **Sights:** None furnished. Receiver drilled and tapped for scope mounting. **Features:** A "classic" version of the BDL with straight comb stock. Fitted with rubber recoil pad. Sling swivel studs installed. Hinged floorplate. Limited production in 2003 only.
Price: **$683.00**
Price: Left-hand model . . . . **$769.00 to $796.00**

REMINGTON MODEL 700 ADL DELUXE RIFLE
Caliber: 270, 30-06. **Barrel:** 22" round tapered. **Weight:** 7-1/4 lbs. **Length:** 41-5/8" overall. **Stock:** Walnut. Satin-finished pistol grip stock with fine-line cut checkering, Monte Carlo. **Sights:** Gold bead ramp front; removable, step-adjustable rear with windage screw. **Features:** Side safety, receiver tapped for scope mounts.
Price: **$580.00**

Remington Model 700 ADL Synthetic
Similar to the 700 ADL except has a fiberglass-reinforced synthetic stock with straight comb, raised cheekpiece, positive checkering, and black rubber buttpad. Metal has matte finish. Available in 22-250, 223, 243, 270, 308, 30-06 with 22" barrel, 300 Win. Mag., 7mm Rem. Mag. with 24" barrel. Introduced 1996.
Price: From . . . . **$500.00 to $527.00**

Remington Model 700 ADL Synthetic Youth
Similar to the Model 700 ADL Synthetic except has 1" shorter stock, 20" barrel. Chambered for 243, 308. Introduced 1998.
Price: **$500.00**

Remington Model 700 BDL Custom Deluxe Rifle
Same as 700 ADL except chambered for 222, 223 (short action, 24" barrel), 7mm-08, 280, 22-250, 25-06, (short action, 22" barrel), 243, 270, 30-06, skip-line checkering, black forend tip and gripcap with white line spacers. Matted receiver top, quick-release floorplate. Hooded ramp front sight, quick detachable swivels.
Price: **$683.00**
Also available in 17 Rem., 7mm Rem. Mag., 7mm Rem. Ultra Mag., 300 Win. Mag. (long action, 24" barrel); 300 Rem. Ultra Mag. (26" barrel). Overall length 44-1/2", weight about 7-1/2 lbs.
Price: . . . . **$709.00 to $723.00**

Remington Model 700 BDL Left-Hand Custom Deluxe
Same as 700 BDL except mirror-image left-hand action, stock. Available in 270, 30-06, 7mm Rem. Mag., 300 Rem. Ultra Mag, 338 Rem. Ultra Mag., 7mm Rem. Ultra Mag.
Price: . . . . **$709.00 to $749.00**

Remington 700 BDL Left-Hand

Remington 700 BDL DM

Remington 700 BDL SS DM

Remington 700 Custom KS Mountain

Remington 700 LSS Mountain

Remington Model 700 BDL DM Rifle
Same as 700 BDL except detachable box magazine (4-shot, standard calibers, 3-shot for magnums). Glossy stock finish, open sights, recoil pad, sling swivels. Available in 270, 30-06, 7mm Rem. Mag., 300 Win. Mag. Introduced 1995.
Price: From . . . . **$749.00 to $776.00**

Remington Model 700 BDL SS Rifle
Similar to 700 BDL rifle except hinged floorplate, 24" standard weight barrel in all calibers; magnum calibers have magnum-contour barrel. No sights supplied, but comes drilled and tapped. Corrosion-resistant follower and fire control, stainless BDL-style barreled action with fine matte finish. Synthetic stock has straight comb and cheekpiece, textured finish, positive checkering, plated swivel studs. Calibers: 270, 30-06; magnums:7mm Rem. Mag., 7mm Rem. UltraMag., 300 Rem. Ultra Mag. (26" barrel) 300 Win. Mag., 338 Rem. Ultra Mag., 7mm Rem. SAUM, 300 Rem. SAUM. Weight: 7-3/8 to 7-1/2 lbs. Introduced 1993.
Price: From . . . . **$735.00 to $775.00**

Remington Model 700 BDL SS DM Rifle
Same as 700 BDL SS except detachable box magazine. Barrel, receiver and bolt made of #416 stainless steel; black synthetic stock, fine-line engraving. Available in 270, 30-06, 7mm Rem. Mag., 300 Win. Mag. Introduced 1995.
Price: From . . . . **$801.00 to $828.00**

Remington Model 700 Custom KS Mountain Rifle
Similar to 700 BDL except custom finished with aramid fiber reinforced resin synthetic stock. Available in left- and right-hand versions. Chambered 270 Win., 280 Rem., 30-06, 7mm Rem. Mag., 7mm STW, 300 Rem. Ultra Mag., 338 Rem. Ultra Mag., 300 Win. Mag., 300 Wby. Mag., 35 Whelen, 338 Win. Mag., 8mm Rem. Mag., 375 H&H, with 24" barrel (except 300 Rem. Ultra Mag., 26"), 7mm RUM, 375 RUM. Weighs 6 lbs., 6 oz. Introduced 1986.
Price: Right-hand **$1,314.00**
Price: Left-hand **$1,393.00**
Price: Stainless . . . . **$1,500.00 to $1,580.00**

Remington Model 700 LSS Mountain Rifle
Similar to Model 700 Custom KS Mountain Rifle except stainless steel 22" barrel and two-tone laminated stock. Chambered in 260 Rem., 7mm-08, 270 Winchester and 30-06. Overall length 42-1/2", weighs 6-5/8 oz. Introduced 1999.
Price: **$800.00**

Remington 700 Safari KS

Remington 700 AWR

Remington 700 APR African Plains

Remington 700 LSS

Remington 700 MTN DM

Remington Model 700 Safari Grade
Similar to 700 BDL aramid fiber reinforced fiberglass stock, blued carbon steel bbl. and action, or stainless, w/cheekpiece, custom finished and tuned. In 8mm Rem. Mag., 375 H&H, 416 Rem. Mag. or 458 Win. Mag. calibers only with heavy barrel. Right- and left-hand versions.
Price: Safari KS . . . . **$1,520.00 to $1,601.00**
Price: Safari KS (stainless right-hand only) **$1,697.00**

Remington Model 700 AWR Alaskan Wilderness Rifle
Similar to the 700 BDL except has stainless barreled action and black Teflon 24" bbl. 26" Ultra Mag raised cheekpiece, magnum-grade black rubber recoil pad. Chambered for 7mm RUM., 375 RUM, 7mm STW, 300 Rem. Ultra Mag., 300 Win. Mag., 300 Wby. Mag., 338 Rem. Ultra Mag., 338 Win. Mag., 375 H&H. Aramid fiber reinforced fiberglass stock. Introduced 1994.
Price: . . . . (right-hand) **$1,593.00**; (left-hand) **$1,673.00**

Remington Model 700 APR African Plains Rifle
Similar to Model 700 BDL except magnum receiver and specially contoured 26" Custom Shop barrel with satin blued finish, laminated wood stock with raised cheekpiece, satin finish, black buttpad, 20 lpi cut checkering. Chambered for 7mm Rem. Mag., 7mm RUM, 375 RUM, 300 Rem. Ultra Mag., 300 Win. Mag., 300 Wby. Mag., 338 Win. Mag., 338 Rem. Ultra Mag., 375 H&H. Introduced 1994.
Price: **$1,716.00**

Remington Model 700 LSS Rifle
Similar to 700 BDL except stainless steel barreled action, gray laminated wood stock with Monte Carlo comb and cheekpiece. No sights furnished. Available in (RH) 7mm Rem. Mag., 300 Win. Mag., 300 RUM, 338 RUM, 7mm Rem. Ultra Mag., 375 Rem. Ultra Mag., (LH) 7mm Rem. Ultra Mag., 300 Rem. Ultra Mag., and 338 RUM. Introduced 1996.
Price: From . . . . (right-hand) **$820.00 to $840.00**; (left-hand) **$867.00**

Remington Model 700 MTN DM Rifle
Similar to 700 BDL except weighs 6-1/2 to 6-5/8 lbs., 22" tapered barrel. Redesigned pistol grip, straight comb, contoured cheekpiece, hand-rubbed oil stock finish, deep cut checkering, hinged floorplate and magazine follower, two-position thumb safety. Chambered for 260 Rem., 270 Win., 7mm-08, 25-06, 280 Rem., 30-06, 4-shot detachable box magazine. Overall length is 41-5/8" to 42-1/2". Introduced 1995.
Price: **$728.00**

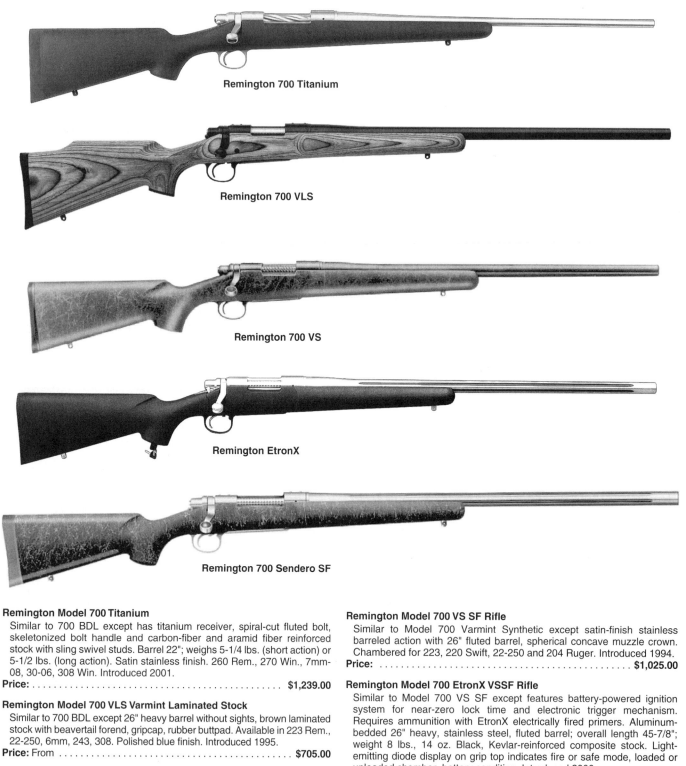

Remington 700 Titanium

Remington 700 VLS

Remington 700 VS

Remington EtronX

Remington 700 Sendero SF

Remington Model 700 Titanium

Similar to 700 BDL except has titanium receiver, spiral-cut fluted bolt, skeletonized bolt handle and carbon-fiber and aramid fiber reinforced stock with sling swivel studs. Barrel 22"; weighs 5-1/4 lbs. (short action) or 5-1/2 lbs. (long action). Satin stainless finish. 260 Rem., 270 Win., 7mm-08, 30-06, 308 Win. Introduced 2001.

Price: **$1,239.00**

Remington Model 700 VLS Varmint Laminated Stock

Similar to 700 BDL except 26" heavy barrel without sights, brown laminated stock with beavertail forend, gripcap, rubber buttpad. Available in 223 Rem., 22-250, 6mm, 243, 308. Polished blue finish. Introduced 1995.

Price: From **$705.00**

Remington Model 700 VS Varmint Synthetic Rifles

Similar to 700 BDL Varmint Laminated except composite stock reinforced with aramid fiber reinforced, fiberglass and graphite. Aluminum bedding block that runs full length of receiver. Free-floating 26" barrel. Metal has black matte finish; stock has textured black and gray finish and swivel studs. Available in 223, 22-250, 308. Right- and left-hand. Introduced 1992.

Price: .... **$811.00 to $837.00**

Remington Model 700 VS SF Rifle

Similar to Model 700 Varmint Synthetic except satin-finish stainless barreled action with 26" fluted barrel, spherical concave muzzle crown. Chambered for 223, 220 Swift, 22-250 and 204 Ruger. Introduced 1994.

Price: **$1,025.00**

Remington Model 700 EtronX VSSF Rifle

Similar to Model 700 VS SF except features battery-powered ignition system for near-zero lock time and electronic trigger mechanism. Requires ammunition with EtronX electrically fired primers. Aluminum-bedded 26" heavy, stainless steel, fluted barrel; overall length 45-7/8"; weight 8 lbs., 14 oz. Black, Kevlar-reinforced composite stock. Light-emitting diode display on grip top indicates fire or safe mode, loaded or unloaded chamber, battery condition. Introduced 2000.

Price: 220 Swift, 22-250 or 243 Win. **$1,332.00**

Remington Model 700 XCR Rifle

Similar to standard Model 700 except 24" or 26" barrel; black matte finish; stainless steel barrel and receiver; comes in standard, magnum and short/long magnum calibers.

Price: .... **$867.00 to $893.00**

Remington 710

Remington Seven LS

Remington Model Seven LS Mag

Remington Model Seven SS Mag

Remington Model Seven Custom MS

REMINGTON MODEL 700 SENDERO SF RIFLE

Caliber: 7mm Rem. SAUM, 300 Rem. SAUM, 7mm Rem. Mag., 7mm STW, 300 Rem. Ultra Mag., 338 Rem. Ultra Mag., 300 Win. Mag., 7mm Rem. Ultra Mag. **Barrel:** 26". **Weight:** 8-1/2 lbs. **Length:** 45-3/4" to 46-5/8" overall. **Stock:** Aramid fiber refinforced fiberglass. **Sights:** NA. **Features:** Stainless steel action and fluted stainless barrel. Introduced 1996.
Price: . . . . **$1,003.00 to $1,016.00**

REMINGTON MODEL 710 BOLT-ACTION RIFLE

Caliber: 270 Win., 30-06. **Barrel:** 22". **Weight:** 7-1/8 lbs. **Length:** 42-1/2" overall. **Stock:** Gray synthetic. **Sights:** Bushnell Sharpshooter 3-9x scope mounted and bore-sighted. **Features:** Unique action locks bolt directly into barrel; 60-degree bolt throw; 4-shot dual-stack magazine; key-operated Integrated Security System locks bolt open. Introduced 2001. Made in U.S.A. by Remington Arms Co.
Price: **$425.00**

REMINGTON MODEL SEVEN LS

Caliber: 223 Rem., 243 Win., 7mm-08 Rem., 308 Win. **Barrel:** 20". **Weight:** 6-1/2 lbs. **Length:** 39-1/4" overall. **Stock:** Brown laminated, satin finished. **Features:** Satin finished carbon steel barrel and action, 4-round magazine, hinged magazine floorplate. Furnished with iron sights and sling swivel studs, drilled and tapped for scope mounts.
Price: **$701.00**
Price: 7mmRSAUM, 300RSAUM, LS Magnum, 22" bbl. **$741.00**
Price: AWR model **$1,547.00**

Remington Model Seven SS

Similar to Model Seven LS except stainless steel barreled action and black synthetic stock, 20" barrel. Chambered for 243, 260 Rem., 7mm-08, 308. Introduced 1994.
Price: **$729.00**
Price: 7mmRSAUM, 300RSAUM, Model Seven SS
Magnum, 22" bbl. **$769.00**

Remington Model Seven Custom MS Rifle

Similar to Model Seven LS except full-length Mannlicher-style stock of laminated wood with straight comb, solid black recoil pad, black steel forend tip, cut checkering, gloss finish. Barrel length 20", weighs 6-3/4 lbs. Available in 222 Rem., 223, 22-250, 243, 6mm Rem., 260 Rem., 7mm-08 Rem., 308, 350 Rem. Mag., 250 Savage, 257 Roberts, 35 Rem. Polished blue finish. Introduced 1993. From Remington Custom Shop.
Price: From **$1,332.00**

Remington Model Seven Youth Rifle

Similar to Model Seven LS except hardwood stock, 1" shorter length of pull, chambered for 223, 243, 260 Rem., 7mm-08. Introduced 1993.
Price: **$547.00**

Remington Model Seven Custom KS

Similar to Model Seven LS except gray aramid fiber reinforced stock with 1" black rubber recoil pad and swivel studs. Blued satin carbon steel barreled action. No sights on 223, 260 Rem., 7mm-08, 308; 35 Rem. and 350 Rem. have iron sights.
Price: **$1,314.00**

Ruger Magnum

Ruger 77/22 Hornet Varmint

Ruger M77 Mark II

Ruger KM77RLFP MKII

Ruger KM77RFP MKII

RUGER MAGNUM RIFLE

Caliber: 338 Lapua, 375 H&H, 416 Rigby, 458 Lott. **Barrel:** 23". **Weight:** 9-1/2 to 10-1/4 lbs. **Length:** 44". **Stock:** AAA Premium Grade Circassian walnut with live-rubber recoil pad, metal gripcap, and studs for mounting sling swivels. **Sights:** Blade, front; V-notch rear express sights (one stationary, two folding) drift-adjustable for windage. **Features:** Floorplate latch secures the hinged floorplate against accidental dumping of cartridges; one-piece bolt has a non-rotating Mauser-type controlled-feed extractor; fixed-blade ejector.
Price: M77RSMMKII **$1,975.00**

RUGER 77/22 HORNET BOLT-ACTION RIFLE

Caliber: 22 Hornet, 6-shot rotary magazine. **Barrel:** 20". **Weight:** About 6 lbs. **Length:** 39-3/4" overall. **Stock:** Checkered American walnut, black rubber buttpad. **Sights:** Brass bead front, open adjustable rear; also available without sights. **Features:** Same basic features as rimfire model except slightly lengthened receiver. Uses Ruger rotary magazine. Three-position safety. Comes with 1" Ruger scope rings. Introduced 1994.
Price: 77/22RH (rings only) **$649.00**
Price: K77/22VHZ Varmint, laminated stock, no sights **$685.00**

RUGER M77 MARK II RIFLE

Caliber: 223, 220 Swift, 22-250, 204 Ruger, 243, 6mm Rem., 257 Roberts, 25-06, 6.5x55 Swedish, 270, 260 Rem., 280 Rem., 308, 30-06, 7mm Rem. Mag., 7mm WSM, 7mm/08, 300 WSM, 300 Win. Mag., 338 Win. Mag., 4-shot magazine. **Barrel:** 20", 22"; 24" (magnums). **Weight:** About 7 lbs. **Length:** 39-3/4" overall. **Stock:** Synthetic American walnut; swivel studs, rubber buttpad. **Sights:** None furnished. Receiver has Ruger integral scope mount base, Ruger 1" rings. **Features:** Short action with new trigger, 3-position safety. Steel trigger guard. Left-hand available. Introduced 1989.

Price: M77RMKII (no sights) **$716.00**
Price: M77LRMKII (left-hand, 25/06, 270, 30-06, 7mm Rem. Mag.,300 Win. Mag.) **$716.00**

Ruger M77RSI International Carbine

Same as standard Model 77 except 18" barrel, full-length International-style stock, steel forend cap, loop-type steel sling swivels. Integral base receiver, open sights, Ruger 1" steel rings. Improved front sight. Available in 243, 270, 308, 30-06. Weighs 7 lbs. Length overall is 38-3/8".
Price: M77RSIMKII **$819.00**

Ruger M77 Mark II All-Weather and Sporter Model Stainless Rifle

Similar to wood-stock M77 Mark II except all metal parts are stainless steel, has an injection-molded, glass-fiber-reinforced polymer stock. Laminated wood stock. Chambered for 223, 22/250, 25/06, 260 Rem., 7mm WSM, 7mm/08, 7mm SWM, 280 Rem., 300 WSM, 204 Ruger, 243, 270, 308, 30-06, 7mm Rem. Mag., 300 Win. Mag., 325 WSM, 338 Win. Mag. Fixed-blade-type ejector, three-position safety, new trigger guard with patented floorplate latch. Integral Scope Base Receiver, 1" Ruger scope rings, built-in sling swivel loops. Introduced 1990.
Price: K77RFPMKII **$716.00**
Price: K77RLFPMKII Ultra-Light, synthetic stock, rings, no sights . **$716.00**
Price: K77LRBBZMKII, left-hand bolt, rings, no sights, laminated stock **$773.00**
Price: K77RBZMKII, no sights, laminated wood stock, 223, 22/250, 243, 270, 280 Rem., 7mm Rem. Mag., 30-06, 308, 300 Win. Mag., 338 Win. Mag. **$773.00**
Price: KM77RFPMKII, M77RMKII **$773.00**

Ruger M77RL Ultra Light

Similar to standard M77 except weighs 6 lbs., chambered for 223, 243, 308, 270, 30-06, 257 Roberts, barrel tapped for target scope blocks, 20" Ultra Light barrel. Overall length 40". Ruger's steel 1" scope rings supplied. Introduced 1983.
Price: M77RLMKII **$729.00**

CENTERFIRE RIFLES — Bolt-Action

Ruger M77VT Target

Ruger Frontier

Sako TRG-S

Sako 85 Grey Wolf

Sako 75 Hunter

Ruger M77 Mark II Compact Rifles
Similar to standard M77 except reduced 16-1/2" barrel, weighs 5-3/4 lbs. Chambered for 223, 243, 260 Rem., 308, and 7mm-08.
Price: M77CR MKII (blued finish, walnut stock) **$675.00**
Price: KM77CRBBZ MkII (stainless finish, black laminated stock) . **$729.00**

RUGER M77VT TARGET RIFLE
Caliber: 22-250, 220 Swift, 223, 204 Ruger, 243, 25-06, 308. **Barrel:** 26" heavy stainless steel with target gray finish. **Weight:** 9-3/4 lbs. **Length:** Approx. 44" overall. **Stock:** Laminated American hardwood with beavertail forend, steel swivel studs; no checkering or gripcap. **Sights:** Integral scope mount bases in receiver. **Features:** Ruger diagonal bedding system. Ruger steel 1" scope rings supplied. Fully adjustable trigger. Steel floorplate and trigger guard. New version introduced 1992.
Price: K77VTMKII **$870.00**

RUGER FRONTIER RIFLE
Caliber: 243, 7mm/08, 308, 300WSM, 325WSM. **Barrel:** 16-1/2". **Weight:** 6-1/4 lbs. **Stock:** Black laminate. **Features:** Front scope mounting rib, blued finish; overall length 35-1/2". Introduced 2005, stainless in 2006.
Price: **$799.00**

SAKO TRG-42 BOLT-ACTION RIFLE
Caliber: 338 Lapua Mag. and 300 Win. Mag. **Barrel:** 27-1/8". **Weight:** 11-1/4 lbs. **Length:** NA. **Stock:** NA. **Sights:** NA. **Features:** 5-shot magazine,

fully adjustable stock and competition trigger. Imported from Finland by Beretta USA.
Price: **$3,525.00**

SAKO MODEL 85 BOLT-ACTION RIFLES
Caliber: 22-250, 243, 25-06, 260, 6.5x55mm, 270, 270 WSM, 7mm-08, 308, 30-06; 7mm WSM, 300 WSM, 338 Federal. **Barrel:** 22.4", 22.9", 24.4". **Weight:** 7.75 lbs. **Length:** NA. **Stock:** Polymer, laminated or high-grade walnut, straight comb, shadow-line cheekpiece. **Sights:** None furnished. **Features:** Controlled-round feeding, adjustable trigger, matte stainless or nonreflective satin blue. Quad model is polymer/stainless with four interchangeable barrels in 22LR, 22 WMR 17 HMR and 17 Mach 2; 50-degree bolt-lift, ambidextrous palm-swell, adjustable butt-pad. Introduced 2006. Imported from Finland by Beretta USA.
Price: Sako 85 Hunter, walnut/blued. **$1,595.00**
Price: Sako 85 Grey Wolf, laminated/stainless. **$1,495.00**
Price: Sako 85 Quad, polymer/stainless. **$925.00**
Price: Sako 85 Quad Combo, four barrels **$1,800.00**

SAKO 75 HUNTER BOLT-ACTION RIFLE
Caliber: 223, 22-250, 243, 25-06, 260, 270, 270 WSM, 280, 300 Win. Mag., 30-06; 7mm-08, 308 Win., 270 Wby. Mag., 7mm Rem. Mag., 7mm STW, 7mm Wby. Mag., 300 Wby. Mag., 338 Win. Mag., 340 Wby. Mag., 375 H&H. **Barrel:** 22", standard calibers; 24", 26" magnum calibers. **Weight:** About 6 lbs. **Length:** NA. **Stock:** European walnut with matte lacquer finish. **Sights:** None furnished; dovetail scope mount rails. **Features:** New design with three locking lugs and a mechanical ejector, key locks firing pin and bolt, cold hammer-forged barrel is free-floating, two-position safety, hinged floorplate or detachable magazine that can be loaded from the top, short 70-degree bolt lift. Five action lengths. Introduced 1997. Imported from Finland by Beretta USA.
Price: From **$1,375.00**

Sako 75 Stainless Hunter

Sako 75 Deluxe

Sako 75 Varmint

Savage 110GXP3

Sako 75 Stainless Synthetic Rifle

Similar to 75 Hunter except all metal is stainless steel, synthetic stock has soft composite panels molded into forend and pistol grip. Available in 22-250, 243, 308 Win., 25-06, 270, 30-06 with 22" barrel, 7mm Rem. Mag., 7mm STW, 300 Win. Mag., 338 Win. Mag. and 375 H&H Mag. with 24" barrel and 300 Wby. Mag., 300 Rem. Ultra Mag. with 26" barrel. Introduced 1997. Imported from Finland by Beretta USA.
Price: From **$1,495.00**

Sako 75 Deluxe Rifle

Similar to 75 Hunter except select wood rosewood gripcap and forend tip. Available in 17 Rem., 222, 223, 25-06, 243, 7mm-08, 308, 25-06, 270, 280, 30-06; 270 Wby. Mag., 7mm Rem. Mag., 7mm STW, 7mm Wby. Mag., 300 Win. Mag., 300 Wby. Mag., 338 Win. Mag., 340 Wby. Mag., 375 H&H, 416 Rem. Mag. Introduced 1997. Imported from Finland by Beretta USA.
Price: From **$2,050.00**

Sako 75 Varmint Stainless Laminated Rifle

Similar to Sako 75 Hunter except chambered only for 222, 223, 22-250, 22 PPC USA, 6mm PPC, heavy 24" barrel with recessed crown; set trigger; all metal is stainless steel, laminated wood stock with beavertail forend. Introduced 1999. Imported from Finland by Beretta USA.
Price: **$1,959.00**

Sako 75 Varmint Rifle

Similar to Model 75 Hunter except chambered only for 17 Rem., 222 Rem., 223 Rem., 22-250 Rem., 22 PPC and 6mm PPC, 24" heavy barrel with recessed crown; set trigger; beavertail forend. Introduced 1998. Imported from Finland by Beretta USA.
Price: **$1,850.00**

SAUER 202 BOLT-ACTION RIFLE

Caliber: Standard 243, 6.5x55, 270 Win., 308 Win., 30-06; magnum 7mm Rem. Mag., 300 Win. Mag., 300 Wby. Mag., 375 H&H. **Barrel:** 23.6" (standard), 26" (magnum). **Weight:** 7.7 lbs. (standard). **Length:** 44.3" overall (23.6" barrel). **Stock:** Select American Claro walnut with high-gloss epoxy finish, rosewood grip and forend caps; 22 lpi checkering. Synthetic also available. **Sights:** None furnished; drilled and tapped for scope mounting. **Features:** Short 60° bolt throw; detachable box magazine; six-lug bolt; quick-change barrel; tapered bore; adjustable two-stage trigger; firing pin cocking indicator. Introduced 1994. Imported from Germany by SIGARMS, Inc.
Price: Standard calibers, right-hand **$1,035.00**
Price: Magnum calibers, right-hand **$1,106.00**
Price: Standard calibers, synthetic stock **$985.00**
Price: Magnum calibers, synthetic stock **$1,056.00**

SAVAGE MODEL 10GXP3, 110GXP3 PACKAGE GUNS

Caliber: 223 Rem., 22-250 Rem., 243 Win., 7mm-08 Rem., 308 Win., 300 WSM (10GXP3). 25-06 Rem., 270 Win., 30-06 Spfld., 7mm Rem. Mag., 300 Win. Mag., 300 Rem. Ultra Mag. (110GXP3). **Barrel:** 22" 24", 26". **Weight:** 7.5 lbs. average. **Length:** 43" to 47". **Stock:** Walnut Monte Carlo with checkering. **Sights:** 3-9x40mm scope, mounted & bore sighted. **Features:** Blued, free floating and button rifled, internal box magazines, swivel studs, leather sling. Left-hand available.
Price: Accu-trigger **$539.00**

SAVAGE MODEL 11FXP3, 111FXP3, 111FCXP3, 11FYXP3 (Youth) PACKAGE GUNS

Caliber: 223 Rem., 22-250 Rem., 243 Win., 308 Win., 300 WSM (11FXP3). 270 Win., 30-06 Spfld., 25-06 Rem., 7mm Rem. Mag., 300 Win. Mag., 338 Win. Mag., 300 Rem. Ultra Mag. (11FCXPE & 111FXP3). **Barrel:** 22" to 26". **Weight:** 6.5 lbs. **Length:** 41" to 47". **Stock:** Synthetic checkering, dual pillar bed. **Sights:** 3-9X40mm scope, mounted & bore sighted. **Features:** Blued, free floating and button rifled, Top loading internal box mag (except 11FXCP3 has detachable box mag.). Nylon sling and swivel studs. Some left-hand available.
Price: Model 11FXP3 . . . . **$516.00**
Price: Model 111FCXP3 . . . . **$411.00**
Price: Model 11FYXP3, 243 Win., 12.5" pull (youth) **$501.00**

Savage Model 10FP

Savage Model 10FPLE1

Savage Model 10FPXP-LE

Savage Model 111F

SAVAGE MODEL 16FXP3, 116FXP3 SS ACTION PACKAGE GUNS

Caliber: 223 Rem., 243 Win., 308 Win., 300 WSM, 270 Win., 30-06 Spfld., 7mm Rem. Mag., 300 Win. Mag., 338 Win. Mag., 375 H&H, 7mm S&W, 7mm Rem. Ultra Mag., 300 Rem. Ultra Mag. **Barrel:** 22", 24", 26". **Weight:** 6.75 lbs. average. **Length:** 41" to 46". **Stock:** Synthetic checkering, dual pillar bed. **Sights:** 3-9X40mm scope, mounted & bore sighted. **Features:** Free floating and button rifled. Internal box mag., nylon sling and swivel studs.
Price: **$601.00**

SAVAGE MODEL 10FM SIERRA ULTRA LIGHT RIFLE

Caliber: 223, 243, 308. **Barrel:** 20". **Weight:** 6 lbs. **Length:** 41-1/2". **Stock:** "Dual Pillar" bedding in black synthetic stock with silver medallion in gripcap. **Sights:** None furnished; drilled and tapped for scope mounting. **Features:** True short action. Model 10FCM has detachable box magazine. Comes with sling and quick-detachable swivels. Introduced 1998. Made in U.S.A. by Savage Arms, Inc.
Price: **$552.00**

SAVAGE MODEL 10/110FP LONG RANGE RIFLE

Caliber: 223, 25-06, 308, 30-06, 300 Win. Mag., 7mm Rem. Mag., 4-shot magazine. **Barrel:** 24", heavy; recessed target muzzle. **Weight:** 8-1/2 lbs. **Length:** 45.5" overall. **Stock:** Black graphite/fiberglass composition; positive checkering. **Sights:** None furnished. Receiver drilled and tapped for scope mounting. **Features:** Pillar-bedded stock. Black matte finish on all metal parts. Double swivel studs on the forend for sling and/or bipod mount. Right- or left-hand. Introduced 1990. From Savage Arms, Inc.
Price: Right- or left-hand **$601.00**

Savage Model 10FP Tactical Rifle

Similar to the Model 110FP except has true short action, chambered for 223, 308; black synthetic stock with "Dual Pillar" bedding. Introduced 1998. Made in U.S.A. by Savage Arms, Inc.
Price: **$601.00**
Price: Model 10FLP (left-hand) **$601.00**
Price: Model 10FP-LE1 (20"), 10FPLE2 (26") **$601.00**
Price: Model 10FPXP-LE w/Burris 3.5-10x50 scope,
Harris bipod package **$1,805.00**

Savage Model 10FP-LE1A Tactical Rifle

Similar to the Model 110FP except weighs 10.75 lbs. and has overall length of 39.75". Chambered for 223 Rem., 308 Win. Black synthetic Choate™ adjustable stock with accessory rail and swivel studs.
Price: **$729.00**

SAVAGE MODEL 111 CLASSIC HUNTER RIFLES

Caliber: 25-06 Rem., 270 Win., 30-06 Spfld., 7mm Rem. Mag, 300 Win. Mag., 7mm RUM, 300 RUM. **Barrel:** 22", 24", 26" (magnum calibers). **Weight:** 6.5 to 7.5 lbs. **Length:** 42.75" to 47.25". **Stock:** Walnut-finished hardwood (M111G, GC); graphite/fiberglass filled composite. **Sights:** Ramp front, open fully adjustable rear; drilled and tapped for scope mounting. **Features:** Three-position top tang safety, double front locking lugs, free-floated button-rifled barrel. Comes with trigger lock, target, ear puffs. Introduced 1994. Made in U.S.A. by Savage Arms, Inc.
Price: Model 111F (270 Win., 30-06 Spfld., 7mm Rem. Mag., 300 Win. Mag.) **$486.00**
Price: Model 111F (25-06 Rem., 338 Win. Mag., 7mm Rem. Ultra Mag, 300 Rem. Ultra Mag.) **$486.00**
Price: Model 111G
(wood stock, top-loading magazine, right- or left-hand) **$436.00**
Price: Model 111GNS (wood stock, detachable box magazine, no sights, right-hand only) **$518.00**

CENTERFIRE RIFLES — Bolt-Action

Savage Model 111F

Savage Model 11FCNS

Savage Model 11G

Savage Model 10GY

Savage Model 12FV

Savage Model 12VSS

Savage Model 11 Classic Hunter Rifles, Short Action

Similar to the Model 111F except has true short action, chambered for 22-250, Rem., 243 Win., 7mm-08 Rem., 308 Win.; black synthetic stock with "Dual Pillar" bedding, positive checkering. Introduced 1998. Made in U.S.A. by Savage Arms, Inc.

Price: Model 11F **$486.00**
Price: Model 11FL (left-hand) **$486.00**
Price: Model 11FCNS (right-hand, no sights) **$507.00**
Price: Model 11G (wood stock) **$496.00**
Price: Model 11GL (as above, left-hand) **$496.00**

Savage Model 10GY

Similar to the Model 111G except weighs 6.3 lbs., is 42-1/2" overall, and the stock is scaled for ladies, small-framed adults and youths. Chambered for 223, 243, 308. Ramp front sight, open adjustable rear; drilled and tapped for scope mounts. Made in U.S.A. by Savage Arms, Inc.

Price: Model 10GY (short action, calibers 223, 243, 308) **$496.00**

SAVAGE MODEL 112 LONG RANGE RIFLES

Caliber: 5-shot magazine. **Barrel:** 26" heavy. **Weight:** 8.8 lbs. **Length:** 47.5" overall. **Stock:** Black graphite/fiberglass filled composite with positive checkering. **Sights:** None furnished; drilled and tapped for scope mounting. **Features:** Pillar-bedded stock. Blued barrel with recessed target-style muzzle. Double front swivel studs for attaching bipod. Introduced 1991. Made in U.S.A. by Savage Arms, Inc.

Price: Model 112BVSS (heavy-prone laminated stock with high comb, Wundhammer swell, fluted stainless barrel, bolt handle, trigger guard) **$675.00**

Savage Model 12 Long Range Rifles

Similar to the Model 112 Long Range except with true short action, chambered for 223, 22-250, 308. Models 12FV, 12FVSS have black synthetic stocks with "Dual Pillar" bedding, positive checkering, swivel studs; Model 12BVSS has brown laminated stock with beavertail forend, fluted stainless barrel. Introduced 1998. Made in U.S.A. by Savage Arms, Inc.

Price: Model 12FV (223, 22-250, 243 Win., 308 Win., blue) **$549.00**
Price: Model 12FVSS (blue action, fluted stainless barrel) **$667.00**
Price: Model 12FLV (as above, left-hand) **$549.00**
Price: Model 12FVS (blue action, fluted stainless barrel, single shot) **$667.00**
Price: Model 12BVSS (laminated stock) **$721.00**
Price: Model 12BVSS-S (as above, single shot) **$721.00**

Savage Model 16FCSS

Savage Model 116FSAK

SIGARMS SHR 970

Steyr Mannlicher SBS

Steyr SBS Forester

Savage Model 12VSS Varminter Rifle

Similar to other Model 12s except blue/stainless steel action, fluted stainless barrel, Choate full pistol grip, adjustable synthetic stock, Sharp Shooter trigger. Overall length 47-1/2", weighs appx. 15 lbs. No sights; drilled and tapped for scope mounts. Chambered in 223, 22-250, 308 Win. Made in U.S.A. by Savage Arms, Inc.

Price: **$934.00**

SAVAGE MODEL 116 WEATHER WARRIORS

Caliber: 375 H&H, 300 Rem. Ultra Mag., 308 Win., 300 Rem. Ultra Mag., 300 WSM, 7mm Rem. Ultra Mag., 7mm Rem. Short Ultra Mag., 7mm S&W, 7mm-08 Rem. **Barrel:** 22", 24" for 7mm Rem. Mag., 300 Win. Mag., 338 Win. Mag. (M116FSS only). **Weight:** 6.25 to 6.5 lbs. **Length:** 41" to 47". **Stock:** Graphite/fiberglass filled composite. **Sights:** None furnished; drilled and tapped for scope mounting. **Features:** Stainless steel with matte finish; free-floated barrel; quick-detachable swivel studs; laser-etched bolt; scope bases and rings. Left-hand models available in all models, calibers at same price. Model 116FSS introduced 1991; 116FSAK introduced 1994. Made in U.S.A. by Savage Arms, Inc.

Price: Model 116FSS (top-loading magazine) **$520.00**
Price: Model 116FSAK (top-loading magazine,
Savage adjustable muzzle brake system) **$601.00**
Price: Model 16BSS (brown laminate, 24") **$668.00**
Price: Model 116BSS (brown laminate, 26") **$668.00**

Savage Model 16FCSS Rifle

Similar to Model 116FSS except true short action, chambered for 223, 243, 22" free-floated barrel; black graphite/fiberglass stock, "Dual Pillar" bedding. Also left-hand version available. Introduced 1998. Made in U.S.A. by Savage Arms, Inc.

Price: **$552.00**

SIGARMS SHR 970 SYNTHETIC RIFLE

Caliber: 270, 30-06. **Barrel:** 22". **Weight:** 7.2 lbs. **Length:** 41.9" overall. **Stock:** Textured black fiberglass or walnut. **Sights:** None furnished; drilled and tapped for scope mounting. **Features:** Quick takedown; interchangeable barrels; removable box magazine; cocking indicator; three-position safety. Introduced 1998. Imported by SIGARMS, Inc.

Price: Synthetic stock **$499.00**
Price: Walnut stock **$550.00**

STEYR CLASSIC MANNLICHER SBS RIFLE

Caliber: 243, 25-06, 308, 6.5x55, 6.5x57, 270, 7x64 Brenneke, 7mm-08, 7.5x55, 30-06, 9.3x62, 6.5x68, 7mm Rem. Mag., 300 Win. Mag., 8x68S, 4-shot magazine. **Barrel:** 23.6" standard; 26" magnum; 20" full stock standard calibers. **Weight:** 7 lbs. **Length:** 40.1" overall. **Stock:** Hand-checkered fancy European oiled walnut with standard forend. **Sights:** Ramp front adjustable for elevation, V-notch rear adjustable for windage. **Features:** Single adjustable trigger; 3-position roller safety with "safe-bolt" setting; drilled and tapped for Steyr factory scope mounts. Introduced 1997. Imported from Austria by GSI, Inc.

Price: Full-stock, standard calibers. **$1,749.00**

STEYR SBS FORESTER RIFLE

Caliber: 243, 25-06, 270, 7mm-08, 308 Win., 30-06, 7mm Rem. Mag., 300 Win. Mag. Detachable 4-shot magazine. **Barrel:** 23.6", standard calibers; 25.6", magnum calibers. **Weight:** 7.5 lbs. **Length:** 44.5" overall (23.6" barrel). **Stock:** Oil-finished American walnut with Monte Carlo cheekpiece. Pachmayr 1" swivels. **Sights:** None furnished. Drilled and tapped for Browning A-Bolt mounts. **Features:** Three-position ambidextrous roller tang safety. Matte finish on barrel and receiver; adjustable trigger. Rotary cold-hammer forged barrel. Introduced 1997. Imported by GSI, Inc.

Price: Standard calibers **$799.00**
Price: Magnum calibers **$829.00**

Steyr SBS Prohunter

Steyr Scout Rifle

Tikka T-3 Hunter

Weatherby Mark V Lazermark

Steyr SBS Prohunter Rifle

Similar to the SBS Forester except has ABS synthetic stock with adjustable butt spacers, straight comb without cheekpiece, palm swell, Pachmayr 1" swivels. Special 10-round magazine conversion kit available. Introduced 1997. Imported by GSI.

Price: Standard calibers **$769.00**
Price: Magnum calibers **$799.00**

STEYR SCOUT BOLT-ACTION RIFLE

Caliber: 308 Win., 5-shot magazine. **Barrel:** 19", fluted. **Weight:** NA. **Length:** NA. **Stock:** Gray Zytel. **Sights:** Pop-up front & rear, Leupold M8 2.5x28 IER scope on Picatinny optic rail with Steyr mounts. **Features:** luggage case, scout sling, two stock spacers, two magazines. Introduced 1998. From GSI.

Price: From **$1,969.00**

STEYR SSG BOLT-ACTION RIFLE

Caliber: 308 Win., detachable 5-shot rotary magazine. **Barrel:** 26". **Weight:** 8.5 lbs. **Length:** 44.5" overall. **Stock:** Black ABS Cycolac with spacers for length of pull adjustment. **Sights:** Hooded ramp front adjustable for elevation, V-notch rear adjustable for windage. **Features:** Sliding safety; NATO rail for bipod; 1" swivels; Parkerized finish; single or double-set triggers. Imported from Austria by GSI, Inc.

Price: SSG-PI, iron sights **$1,699.00**
Price: SSG-PII, heavy barrel, no sights **$1,699.00**
Price: SSG-PIIK, 20" heavy barrel, no sights **$1,699.00**
Price: SSG-PIV, 16.75" threaded heavy barrel with flash hider .. **$2,659.00**

TIKKA T-3 BIG BOAR SYNTHETIC BOLT-ACTION RIFLE

Caliber: 308, 30-06, 300 WSM. **Barrel:** 19". **Weight:** 6 lbs. **Length:** 39.5" overall. **Stock:** Laminated. **Sights:** None furnished. **Features:**

Detachable, 3-round. Receiver dove-tailed for scope mounting. Reintroduced 1996. Imported from Finland by Beretta USA.

Price: Left-hand **$695.00**

Tikka T-3 Super Varmint Rifle

Similar to the standard T-3 rifle except has 23-3/8" heavy stainless barrel. Chambered for 22-250, 223, 308. Reintroduced 2005. Made in Finland by Sako. Imported by Beretta USA.

Price: **$1,425.00**

TIKKA T-3 HUNTER

Caliber: 223, 22-250, 243, 308, 25-06, 270, 30-06, 300 Win. Mag., 338 Win. Mag., 270 WSM, 300 WSM, 6.5x55 Swedish Mauser, 7mm Rem. Mag. **Stock:** Walnut. **Sight:** None furnished. **Barrel:** 22-7/16", 24-3/8". **Features:** Detachable magazine, aluminum scope rings. Introduced 2005. Imported from Finland by Beretta USA.

Price: **$695.00**

Tikka T-3 Stainless Synthetic

Similar to the T-3 Hunter except stainless steel, synthetic stock. Available in 243, 25-06, 270, 308, 30-06, 270 WSM, 300 WSM, 7mm Rem. Mag., 300 Win. Mag., 338 Win. Mag. Introduced 2005. Imported from Finland by Beretta USA.

Price: **$895.00**

ULTRA LIGHT ARMS BOLT-ACTION RIFLES

Caliber: 17 Rem. to 416 Rigby. **Barrel:** Douglas, length to order. **Weight:** 4-3/4 to 7-1/2 lbs. **Length:** Varies. **Stock:** Kevlar® graphite composite, variety of finishes. **Sights:** None furnished; drilled and tapped for scope mounts. **Features:** Timney trigger, hand-lapped action, button-rifled barrel, hand-bedded action, recoil pad, sling-swivel studs, optional Jewell trigger. Made in U.S.A. by New Ultra Light Arms.

Price: Model 20 (short action) **$2,800.00**
Price: Model 24 (long action) **$2,900.00**
Price: Model 28 (magnum action) **$3,200.00**
Price: Model 40 (300 Wby. Mag., 416 Rigby) **$3,200.00**
Price: Left-hand models, add **$100.00**

Weatherby Mark V Sporter

Weatherby Mark V Stainless

Weatherby Mark V Synthetic

Weatherby Mark V Accumark

WEATHERBY MARK V DELUXE BOLT-ACTION RIFLE

Caliber: All Weatherby calibers plus 22-250, 243, 25-06, 270 Win., 280 Rem., 7mm-08, 30-06, 308 Win. **Barrel:** 24" barrel on standard calibers. **Weight:** 8-1/2 to 10-1/2 lbs. **Length:** 46-5/8" to 46-3/4" overall. **Stock:** Walnut, Monte Carlo with cheekpiece; high luster finish; checkered pistol grip and forend; recoil pad. **Sights:** None furnished. **Features:** Cocking indicator; adjustable trigger; hinged floorplate, thumb safety; quick detachable sling swivels. Made in U.S.A. From Weatherby.

Price: 257, 270, 7mm. 300, 340 Wby. Mags., 26" barrel **$1,767.00**
Price: 416 Wby. Mag. with Accubrake, 28" barrel **$2,079.00**
Price: 460 Wby. Mag. with Accubrake, 28" barrel **$2,443.00**
Price: 24" barrel **$1,715.00**

Weatherby Mark V Lazermark Rifle

Same as Mark V Deluxe except stock has extensive oak leaf pattern laser carving on pistol grip and forend. Introduced 1981.

Price: 257, 270, 7mm Wby. Mag., 300, 340, 26" **$1,923.00**
Price: 378 Wby. Mag., 28" **$2,266.00**
Price: 416 Wby. Mag., 28", Accubrake **$2,266.00**
Price: 460 Wby. Mag., 28", Accubrake **$2,661.00**

Weatherby Mark V Sporter Rifle

Same as the Mark V Deluxe without the embellishments. Metal has low-luster blue, stock is Claro walnut with matte finish, Monte Carlo comb, recoil pad. Introduced 1993. From Weatherby.

Price: 22-250, 243, 240 Wby. Mag., 25-06, 7mm-08,
270 WCF, 280, 30-06, 308; 24" **$1,091.00**
Price: 257 Wby., 270, 7 mm Wby., 7mm Rem., 300 Wby.,
300 Win., 340 Wby., 338 Win. Mag., 26" barrel for Wby. calibers;
24" for non-Wby. calibers **$1,143.00**

Weatherby Mark V Stainless Rifle

Similar to the Mark V Deluxe except made of 410-series stainless steel. Also available in 30-378 Wby. Mag. Has lightweight injection-molded synthetic stock with raised Monte Carlo comb, checkered grip and forend, custom floorplate release. Right-hand only. Introduced 1995. Made in U.S.A. From Weatherby.

Price: 22-250 Rem., 243 Win., 240 Wby. Mag., 25-06 Rem.,
270 Win., 280 Rem., 7mm-08 Rem., 30-06 Spfld., 308 Win.,
24" barrel **$1,018.00**
Price: 257, 270, 7mm, 300, 340 Wby. Mag., 26" barrel **$1,070.00**
Price: 7mm Rem. Mag., 300 Win. Mag., 338 Win. Mag.,
375 H&H Mag., 24" barrel **$1,070.00**

Weatherby Mark V Synthetic

Similar to the Mark V Stainless except made of matte finished blued steel. Injection molded synthetic stock. Weighs 6-1/2 lbs., 24" barrel. Available in 22-250, 240 Wby. Mag., 243, 25-06, 270, 7mm-08, 280, 30-06, 308. Introduced 1997. Made in U.S.A. From Weatherby.

Price: **$923.00**
Price: 257, 270, 7mm, 300, 340 Wby. Mags., 26" barrel **$975.00**
Price: 7mm STW, 7mm Rem. Mag., 300, 338 Win. Mags **$975.00**
Price: 375 H&H, 24" barrel **$975.00**
Price: 30-378 Wby. Mag., 338-378 Wby. 28" barrel **$1,151.00**

WEATHERBY MARK V ACCUMARK RIFLE

Caliber: 257, 270, 7mm, 300, 340 Wby. Mags., 338-378 Wby. Mag., 30-378 Wby. Mag., 7mm STW, 7mm Rem. Mag., 300 Win. Mag. **Barrel:** 26", 28". **Weight:** 8-1/2 lbs. **Length:** 46-5/8" overall. **Stock:** Bell & Carlson with full length aluminum bedding block. **Sights:** None furnished. Drilled and tapped for scope mounting. **Features:** Uses Mark V action with heavy-contour stainless barrel with black oxidized flutes, muzzle diameter of .705". Introduced 1996. Made in U.S.A. From Weatherby.

Price: 26". **$1,507.00**
Price: 30-378 Wby. Mag., 338-378 Wby. Mag., 28",
Accubrake **$1,724.00**
Price: 223, 22-250, 243, 240 Wby. Mag., 25-06, 270,
280 Rem., 7mm-08, 30-06, 308; 24" **$1,455.00**
Price: Accumark left-hand 257, 270, 7mm, 300, 340 Wby.
Mag., 7mm Rem. Mag., 7mm STW, 300 Win. Mag. **$1,559.00**
Price: Accumark left-hand 30-378, 333-378 Wby. Mags. **$1,788.00**

Weatherby Mark V SVR

Weatherby Mark V Dangerous Game Rifle

Wilderness Explorer

Weatherby Mark V Accumark Ultra Lightweight Rifles

Similar to the Mark V Accumark except weighs 5-3/4 lbs., 6-3/4 lbs. in Mag. calibers.; 24", 26" fluted barrel with recessed target crown; hand-laminated stock with CNC-machined aluminum bedding plate and faint gray "spider web" finish. Available in 257, 270, 7mm, 300 Wby. Mags., (26"); 243, 240 Wby. Mag., 25-06, 270 Win., 280 Rem., 7mm-08, 7mm Rem. Mag., 30-06, 338-06 A-Square, 308, 300 Win. Mag. (24"). Introduced 1998. Made in U.S.A. by Weatherby.
Price: . . . . **$1,459.00 to $1,517.00**
Price: Left-hand models **$1,559.00**

Weatherby Mark V SVM/SPM Rifles

Similar to the Mark V Accumark except has 26" fluted (SVM) or 24" fluted Krieger barrel, spiderweb-pattern tan laminated synthetic stock. SVM has a fully adjustable trigger. Chambered for 223, 22-250, 220 Swift (SVM only), 243, 7mm-08 and 308. Made in U.S.A. by Weatherby.
Price: SVM (Super VarmintMaster), repeater or single-shot. **$1,517.00**
Price: SPM (Super Predator Master) **$1,459.00**

Weatherby Mark V Special Varmint Rifle (SVR)

Similar to the Super VarmintMaster and Accumark with 22", #3 contour chrome-moly 4140 steel Krieger Criterion button-rifled barrel with one-degree target crown and hand-laminated composite stock. Available in .223 Rem. (5+1 magazine capacity) and .22-250 Rem. (4+1 magazine capacity) in right-hand models only.
Price: **$999.00**

Weatherby Mark V Fibermark Rifles

Similar to other Mark V models except has black Kevlar® and fiberglass composite stock and bead-blast blue or stainless finish. Chambered for 19 standard and magnum calibers. Introduced 1983; reintroduced 2001. Made in U.S.A. by Weatherby.
Price: Fibermark . . . . **$1,070.00 to $1,347.00**
Price: Fibermark stainless . . . . **$1,165.00 to $1,390.00**

WEATHERBY MARK V DANGEROUS GAME RIFLE

Caliber: 375 H&H, 375 Wby. Mag., 378 Wby. Mag., 416 Rem. Mag., 416 Wby. Mag., 458 Win. Mag., .458 Lott, 460 Wby. Mag. 300 Win. Mag., 300 Wby., Mag., 338 Win. Mag., 340 Wby. Mag., 24" only **Barrel:** 24" or 26". **Weight:** 8-3/4 to 9-1/2 lbs. **Length:** 44-5/8" to 46-5/8" overall. **Stock:** Kevlar® and fiberglass composite. **Sights:** Barrel-band hooded front with large gold bead, adjustable ramp/shallow "V" rear. **Features:** Designed for dangerous game hunting. Black oxide matte finish on all metalwork; Pachmayr Decelerator™ recoil pad, short-throw Mark V action. Introduced 2001. Made in U.S.A. by Weatherby.
Price: . . . . **$2,703.00 to $2,935.00**

WEATHERBY MARK V SUPER BIG GAMEMASTER DEER RIFLE

Caliber: 240 Wby. Mag., 25-06 Rem., 270 Win., 280 Rem., 30-06 Spfld., 257 Wby. Mag., 270 Wby. Mag., 7mm Rem., Mag., 7mm Wby. Mag., 338-06 A-Square, 300 Win. Mag., 300 Wby. Mag. **Barrel:** 26", target crown. **Weight:** 5-3/4 lbs., (6-3/4 lbs. Magnum). **Stock:** Raised comb Monte Carlo composite. **Features:** Fluted barrel, aluminum bedding block, Pachmayr decelerator, 54-degree bolt lift, adj. trigger.
Price: **$1,459.00**
Price: Magnum **$1,517.00**

WEATHERBY MARK V ROYAL CUSTOM RIFLE

Caliber: 257, 270, 7mm, 300, 340 all Wby. Mags. Other calibers available upon request. **Barrel:** 26". **Stock:** Monte Carlo hand-checkered Claro walnut with high gloss finish. **Features:** Bolt and follower are damascened with checkered knob. Engraved receiver, bolt sleeve and floorplate sport scroll pattern. Animal images on floorplate optional. High gloss blue, 24-karat gold and nickel-plating. Made in U.S.A. From Weatherby.
Price: **$5,831.00**

WEATHERBY THREAT RESPONSE RIFLES (TRR) SERIES

Caliber: TRR 223 Rem., 300 Win. TRR Magnum and Magnum Custom 300 Win. Mag., 300 Wby. Mag., 30-378 Wby. Mag., 328-378 Wby. Mag. **Barrel:** 22", 26", target crown. **Stock:** Hand-laminated composite. TTR & TRR Magnum have raised comb Monte Carlo style. TRR Magnum Custom adjustable ergonomic stock. **Features:** Adjustable trigger, aluminum bedding block, beavertail forearms dual tapered, flat-bottomed. "Rocker Arm" lockdown scope mounting. 54 degree bolt. Pachmayr decelerator pad. Made in U.S.A.
Price: TRR Magnum Custom 300. . . . . **$2,699.00**
Price: 30-378, 338-378 with accubrake **$2,861.00**

WILDERNESS EXPLORER MULTI-CALIBER CARBINE

Caliber: 22 Hornet, 218 Bee, 44 Magnum, 50 A.E. (interchangeable). **Barrel:** 18", match grade. **Weight:** 5.5 lbs **Length:** 38-1/2" overall. **Stock:** Synthetic or wood. **Sights:** None furnished; comes with Weaver-style mount on barrel. **Features:** Quick-change barrel and bolt face for caliber switch. Removable box magazine; adjustable trigger with side safety; detachable swivel studs. Introduced 1997. Made in U.S.A. by Phillips & Rogers, Inc.
Price: **$995.00**

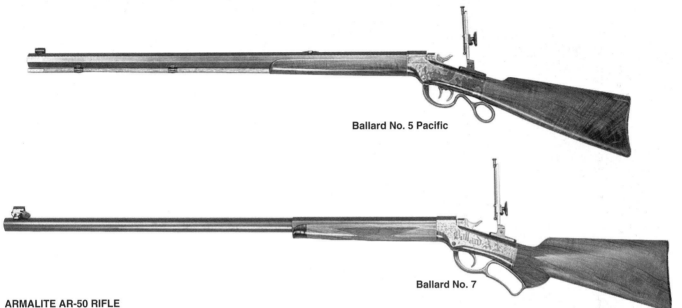

Ballard No. 5 Pacific

Ballard No. 7

ARMALITE AR-50 RIFLE
Caliber: 50 BMG **Barrel:** 31". **Weight:** 33.2 lbs. **Length:** 59.5" **Stock:** Synthetic. **Sights:** None furnished. **Features:** A single-shot bolt action rifle designed for long range shooting. Available in left-hand model. Made in U.S.A. by ArmaLite.
Price: **$2,999.00**

ARMSPORT 1866 SHARPS RIFLE, CARBINE
Caliber: 45-70. **Barrel:** 28", round or octagonal. **Weight:** 8.10 lbs. **Length:** 46" overall. **Stock:** Walnut. **Sights:** Blade front, folding adjustable rear. Tang sight set optionally available. **Features:** Replica of the 1866 Sharps. Color case-hardened frame, rest blued. Imported by Armsport.
Price: **$865.00**
Price: With octagonal barrel **$900.00**
Price: Carbine, 22" round barrel **$850.00**

BALLARD NO. 1 3/4 FAR WEST RIFLE
Caliber: 22 LR, 32-40, 38-55, 40-65, 40-70, 45-70, 45-110, 50-70, 50-90. **Barrel:** 30" std. or heavyweight. **Weight:** 10-1/2 lbs. (std.) or 11-3/4 lbs. (heavyweight bbl.) **Length:** NA. **Stock:** Walnut. **Sights:** Blade front, Rocky Mountain rear. **Features:** Single- or double-set triggers, S-lever or ring-style lever; color case-hardened finish; hand polished and lapped Badger barrel. Made in U.S.A. by Ballard Rifle & Cartridge Co.
Price: **$2,250.00**

BALLARD NO. 4 PERFECTION RIFLE
Caliber: 22 LR, 32-40, 38-55, 40-65, 40-70, 45-70, 45-90, 45-110, 50-70, 50-90. **Barrel:** 30" or 32" octagon, standard or heavyweight. **Weight:** 10-1/2 lbs. (standard) or 11-3/4 lbs. (heavyweight bbl.). **Length:** NA. **Stock:** Smooth walnut. **Sights:** Blade front, Rocky Mountain rear. **Features:** Rifle or shotgun-style buttstock, straight grip action, single or double-set trigger, "S" or right lever, hand polished and lapped Badger barrel. Made in U.S.A. by Ballard Rifle & Cartridge Co.
Price: **$2,250.00**

BALLARD NO. 5 PACIFIC SINGLE-SHOT RIFLE
Caliber: 32-40, 38-55, 40-65, 40-90, 40-70 SS, 45-70 Govt., 45-110 SS, 50-70 Govt., 50-90 SS. **Barrel:** 30", or 32" octagonal. **Weight:** 10-1/2 lbs. **Length:** NA. **Stock:** High-grade walnut; rifle or shotgun style. **Sights:** Blade front, Rocky Mountain rear. **Features:** Standard or heavy barrel; double-set triggers; under-barrel wiping rod; ring lever. Introduced 1999. Made in U.S.A. by Ballard Rifle & Cartridge Co.
Price: **$2,575.00**

BALLARD NO. 7 LONG RANGE RIFLE
Caliber: 32-40, 38-55, 40-65, 40-70 SS, 45-70 Govt., 45-90, 45-110. **Barrel:** 32", 34" half-octagon. **Weight:** 11-3/4 lbs. **Length:** NA. **Stock:**

Walnut; checkered pistol grip shotgun butt, ebony forend cap. **Sights:** Globe front. **Features:** Designed for shooting up to 1000 yards. Standard or heavy barrel; single or double-set trigger; hard rubber or steel buttplate. Introduced 1999. Made in U.S.A. by Ballard Rifle & Cartridge Co.
Price: From **$2,475.00**

BALLARD NO. 8 UNION HILL RIFLE
Caliber: 22 LR, 32-40, 38-55, 40-65, 40-70 SS. **Barrel:** 30" half-octagon. **Weight:** About 10-1/2 lbs. **Length:** NA. **Stock:** Walnut; pistol grip butt with cheekpiece. **Sights:** Globe front. **Features:** Designed for 200-yard offhand shooting. Standard or heavy barrel; double-set triggers; full loop lever; hook Schuetzen buttplate. Introduced 1999. Made in U.S.A. by Ballard Rifle & Cartridge Co.
Price: From **$2,500.00**

BALLARD MODEL 1885 HIGH WALL SINGLE SHOT RIFLE
Caliber: 17 Bee, 22 Hornet, 218 Bee, 219 Don Wasp, 219 Zipper, 22 Hi-Power, 225 Win., 25-20 WCF, 25-35 WCF, 25 Krag, 7mmx57R, 30-30, 30-40 Krag, 303 British, 33 WCF, 348 WCF, 35 WCF, 35-30/30, 9.3x74R, 405 WCF, 50-110 WCF, 500 Express, 577 Express. **Barrel:** Lengths to 34". **Weight:** NA. **Length:** NA. **Stock:** Straight-grain American walnut. **Sights:** buckhorn or flattop rear, blade front. **Features:** Faithful copy of original Model 1885 High Wall; parts interchange with original rifles; variety of options available. Introduced 2000. Made in U.S.A. by Ballard Rifle & Cartridge LLC.
Price: From **$2,313.00**
Price: With single set trigger from **$2,355.00**

BARRETT MODEL 99 SINGLE SHOT RIFLE
Caliber: 50 BMG. **Barrel:** 33". **Weight:** 25 lbs. **Length:** 50.4" overall. **Stock:** Anodized aluminum with energy-absorbing recoil pad. **Sights:** None furnished; integral M1913 scope rail. **Features:** Bolt action; detachable bipod; match-grade barrel with high-efficiency muzzle brake. Introduced 1999. Made in U.S.A. by Barrett Firearms.
Price: From **$3,000.00**

BROWN MODEL 97D SINGLE-SHOT RIFLE
Caliber: 17 Ackley Hornet through 45-70 Govt. **Barrel:** Up to 26", air gauged match grade. **Weight:** About 5 lbs., 11 oz. **Stock:** Sporter style with pistol grip, cheekpiece and Schnabel forend. **Sights:** None furnished; drilled and tapped for scope mounting. **Features:** Falling block action gives rigid barrel-receiver matting; polished blue/black finish. Hand-fitted action. Many options. Made in U.S.A. by E. Arthur Brown Co., Inc.
Price: From **$699.00**

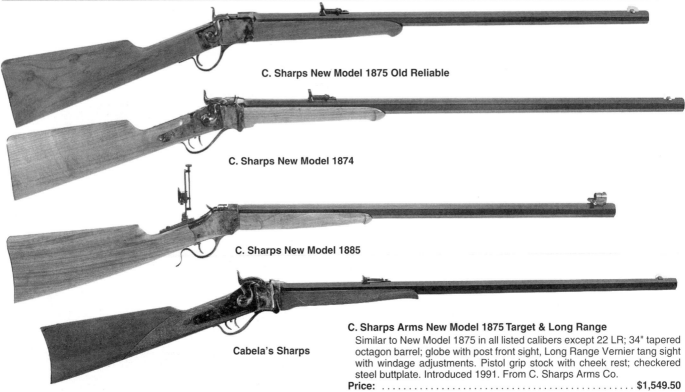

C. Sharps New Model 1875 Old Reliable

C. Sharps New Model 1874

C. Sharps New Model 1885

Cabela's Sharps

BROWNING MODEL 1885 HIGH WALL SINGLE-SHOT RIFLE

Caliber: 22-250, 30-06, 270, 7mm Rem. Mag., 454 Casull, 45-70. **Barrel:** 28". **Weight:** 8 lbs., 12 oz. **Length:** 43-1/2" overall. **Stock:** Walnut with straight grip, Schnabel forend. **Sights:** None furnished; drilled and tapped for scope mounting. **Features:** Replica of J.M. Browning's high-wall falling block rifle. Octagon barrel with recessed muzzle. Imported from Japan by Browning. Introduced 1985.
Price: **$1,027.00**

BRNO ZBK 110 SINGLE-SHOT RIFLE

Caliber: 222 Rem., 5.6x52R, 22 Hornet, 5.6x50 Mag., 6.5x57R, 7x57R, 8x57JRS. **Barrel:** 23.6". **Weight:** 5.9 lbs. **Length:** 40.1" overall. **Stock:** European walnut. **Sights:** None furnished; drilled and tapped for scope mounting. **Features:** Top tang opening lever; cross-bolt safety; polished blue finish. Announced 1998. Imported from The Czech Republic by Euro-Imports.
Price: Standard calibers **$223.00**
Price: 7x57R, 8x57JRS **$245.00**
Price: Lux model, standard calibers **$311.00**
Price: Lux model, 7x57R, 8x57JRS **$333.00**

C. SHARPS ARMS NEW MODEL 1875 OLD RELIABLE RIFLE

Caliber: 22LR, 32-40 & 38-55 Ballard, 38-56 WCF, 40-65 WCF, 40-90 3-1/4", 40-90 2-5/8", 40-70 2-1/10", 40-70 2-1/4", 40-70 2-1/2", 40-50 1-11/16", 40-50 1-7/8", 45-90, 45-70, 45-100, 45-110, 45-120. Also available on special order only in 50-70, 50-90, 50-140. **Barrel:** 24", 26", 30" (standard), 32", 34" optional. **Weight:** 8-12 lbs. **Stock:** Walnut, straight grip, shotgun butt with checkered steel buttplate. **Sights:** Silver blade front, Rocky Mountain buckhorn rear. **Features:** Recreation of the 1875 Sharps rifle. Production guns will have case-colored receiver. Available in Custom Sporting and Target versions upon request. Announced 1986. From C. Sharps Arms Co.
Price: 1875 Sporting Rifle (30" tapered oct. bbl.) **$1,185.00**

C. Sharps Arms 1875 Classic Sharps

Similar to New Model 1875 Sporting Rifle except 26", 28" or 30" full octagon barrel, crescent buttplate with toe plate, Hartford-style forend with cast German silver nose cap. Blade front sight, Rocky Mountain buckhorn rear. Weighs 10 lbs. Introduced 1987. From C. Sharps Arms Co.
Price: **$1,470.00**

C. Sharps Arms New Model 1875 Target & Long Range

Similar to New Model 1875 in all listed calibers except 22 LR; 34" tapered octagon barrel; globe with post front sight, Long Range Vernier tang sight with windage adjustments. Pistol grip stock with cheek rest; checkered steel buttplate. Introduced 1991. From C. Sharps Arms Co.
Price: **$1,549.50**

C. SHARPS ARMS NEW MODEL 1874 OLD RELIABLE

Caliber: 40-50, 40-70, 40-90, 45-70, 45-90, 45-100, 45-110, 45-120, 50-70, 50-90, 50-140. **Barrel:** 26", 28", 30" tapered octagon. **Weight:** About 10 lbs. **Length:** NA. **Stock:** American black walnut; shotgun butt with checkered steel buttplate; straight grip, heavy forend with Schnabel tip. **Sights:** Blade front, buckhorn rear. Drilled and tapped for tang sight. **Features:** Recreation of the Model 1874 Old Reliable Sharps Sporting Rifle. Double-set triggers. Reintroduced 1991. Made in U.S.A. by C. Sharps Arms.
Price: **$1,584.00**

C. SHARPS ARMS NEW MODEL 1885 HIGHWALL RIFLE

Caliber: 22 LR, 22 Hornet, 219 Zipper, 25-35 WCF, 32-40 WCF, 38-55 WCF, 40-65, 30-40 Krag, 40-50 ST or BN, 40-70 ST or BN, 40-90 ST or BN, 45-70 2-1/10" ST, 45-90 2-4/10" ST, 45-100 2-6/10" ST, 45-110 2-7/8" ST, 45-120 3-1/4" ST. **Barrel:** 26", 28", 30", tapered full octagon. **Weight:** About 9 lbs., 4 oz. **Length:** 47" overall. **Stock:** Oil-finished American walnut; Schnabel-style forend. **Sights:** Blade front, buckhorn rear. Drilled and tapped for optional tang sight. **Features:** Single trigger; octagonal receiver top; checkered steel buttplate; color case-hardened receiver and buttplate, blued barrel. Many options available. Made in U.S.A. by C. Sharps Arms Co
Price: From **$1,439.00**

C. SHARPS ARMS CUSTOM NEW MODEL 1877 LONG RANGE TARGET RIFLE

Caliber: 44-90 Sharps/Rem., 45-70, 45-90, 45-100 Sharps. **Barrel:** 32", 34" tapered round with Rigby flat. **Weight:** Appx. 10 lbs. **Stock:** Walnut checkered. Pistol grip/forend. **Sights:** Classic long range with windage. **Features:** Custom production only.
Price: . . . . **$5,550.00 and up**

CABELA'S SHARPS SPORTING RIFLE

Caliber: 45-70, 45-120, 45-110. **Barrel:** 32", tapered octagon. **Weight:** 9 lbs. **Length:** 47-1/4" overall. **Stock:** Checkered walnut. **Sights:** Blade front, open adjustable rear. **Features:** Color case-hardened receiver and hammer, rest blued. Introduced 1995. Imported by Cabela's.
Price: **$1199.99**
Price: (Heavy target Sharps, 45-70, 45-120, 50-70) **$1,399.99**
Price: (Quigley Sharps, 45-70, 45-120, 45-110) **$1,699.99**

CENTERFIRE RIFLES — Single Shot

Cimarron Billy Dixon

Cimarron Quigley

Cimarron 1885 High Wall

Cumberland Mountain Plateau

Dakota Single Shot

CIMARRON BILLY DIXON 1874 SHARPS SPORTING RIFLE
Caliber: 40-40, 50-90, 50-70, 45-70. **Barrel:** 32" tapered octagonal. **Weight:** NA. **Length:** NA. **Stock:** European walnut. **Sights:** Blade front, Creedmoor rear. **Features:** Color case-hardened frame, blued barrel. Hand-checkered grip and forend; hand-rubbed oil finish. Introduced 1999. Imported by Cimarron F.A. Co.
Price: **$1,670.00**

CIMARRON QUIGLEY MODEL 1874 SHARPS SPORTING RIFLE
Caliber: 45-110, 50-70, 50-40, 45-70, 45-90, 45-120. **Barrel:** 34" octagonal. **Weight:** NA. **Length:** NA. **Stock:** Checkered walnut. **Sights:** Blade front, adjustable rear. **Features:** Blued finish; double-set triggers. From Cimarron F.A. Co.
Price: **$1,805.00**

CIMARRON SILHOUETTE MODEL 1874 SHARPS SPORTING RIFLE
Caliber: 45-70, 50-70. **Barrel:** 32" octagonal. **Weight:** NA. **Length:** NA. **Stock:** Walnut. **Sights:** Blade front, adjustable rear. **Features:** Pistol-grip stock with shotgun-style buttplate; cut-rifled barrel. From Cimarron F.A. Co.
Price: **$1,620.00**

CIMARRON MODEL 1885 HIGH WALL RIFLE
Caliber: 38-55, 40-65, 45-70, 45-90, 45-120, 30-40 Krag, 348 Winchester. **Barrel:** 30" octagonal. **Weight:** NA. **Length:** NA. **Stock:** European walnut. **Sights:** Bead front, semi-buckhorn rear. **Features:** Replica of the

Winchester 1885 High Wall rifle. Color case-hardened receiver and lever, blued barrel. Curved buttplate. Optional double-set triggers. Introduced 1999. Imported by Cimarron F.A. Co.
Price: **$995.00**
Price: With pistol grip **$1,175.00**

CUMBERLAND MOUNTAIN PLATEAU RIFLE
Caliber: 40-65, 45-70. **Barrel:** Up to 32"; round. **Weight:** About 10-1/2 lbs. (32" barrel). **Length:** 48" overall (32" barrel). **Stock:** American walnut. **Sights:** Marble's bead front, Marble's open rear. **Features:** Falling block action with underlever. Blued barrel and receiver. Stock has lacquer finish, crescent buttplate. Introduced 1995. Made in U.S.A. by Cumberland Mountain Arms, Inc.
Price: **$1,085.00**

DAKOTA MODEL 10 SINGLE-SHOT RIFLE
Caliber: Most rimmed and rimless commercial calibers. **Barrel:** 23". **Weight:** 6 lbs. **Length:** 39-1/2" overall. **Stock:** Medium fancy grade walnut in classic style. Checkered grip and forend. **Sights:** None furnished. Drilled and tapped for scope mounting. **Features:** Falling block action with underlever. Top tang safety. Removable trigger plate for conversion to single set trigger. Introduced 1990. Made in U.S.A. by Dakota Arms.
Price: **$3,595.00**
Price: Barreled action **$2,095.00**
Price: Action only **$1,850.00**
Price: Magnum calibers **$3,595.00**
Price: Magnum barreled action **$2,050.00**
Price: Magnum action only **$1,675.00**

Dixie 1874 Sharps Silhouette

H&R Ultra Varmint

H&R Ultra Hunter

H&R Buffalo

DIXIE 1874 SHARPS BLACK POWDER SILHOUETTE RIFLE

Caliber: 45-70. **Barrel:** 30"; tapered octagon; blued; 1:18" twist. **Weight:** 10 lbs., 3 oz. **Length:** 47-1/2" overall. **Stock:** Oiled walnut. **Sights:** Blade front, ladder-type hunting rear. **Features:** Replica of the Sharps #1 Sporter. Shotgun-style butt with checkered metal buttplate; color case-hardened receiver, hammer, lever and buttplate. Tang is drilled and tapped for tang sight. Double-set triggers. Meets standards for NRA blackpowder cartridge matches. Introduced 1995. Imported from Italy by Dixie Gun Works.

Price: **$1,075.00**

Dixie 1874 Sharps Lightweight Hunter/Target Rifle

Same as the Dixie 1874 Sharps Black Powder Silhouette model except has a straight-grip buttstock with military-style buttplate. Based on the 1874 military model. Introduced 1995. Imported from Italy by Dixie Gun Works.

Price: **$1,025.00**

E.M.F. 1874 METALLIC CARTRIDGE SHARPS RIFLE

Caliber: 45-70, 45/120. **Barrel:** 28", octagon. **Weight:** 10-3/4 lbs. **Length:** NA. **Stock:** Oiled walnut. **Sights:** Blade front, flip-up open rear. **Features:** Replica of the 1874 Sharps Sporting rifle. Color case-hardened lock; double-set trigger; blue finish. Imported by E.M.F.

Price: From **$700.00**
Price: With browned finish **$1,000.00**
Price: Military Carbine **$650.00**

HARRINGTON & RICHARDSON ULTRA VARMINT/ULTRA HUNTER RIFLES

Caliber: 204 Ruger, 22 WMR, 22-250, 223, 243, 25-06, 30-06. **Barrel:** 22" to 26" heavy taper. **Weight:** About 7.5 lbs. **Stock:** Laminated birch with Monte Carlo comb or skeletonized polymer. **Sights:** None furnished. Drilled and tapped for scope mounting. **Features:** Break-open action with side-lever release, positive ejection. Scope mount. Blued receiver and barrel. Swivel studs. Introduced 1993. Ultra Hunter introduced 1995. From H&R 1871, Inc.

Price: Ultra Varmint Fluted, 24" bull barrel, polymer stock **$406.00**
Price: Ultra Hunter Rifle, 26" bull barrel in 25-06, laminated stock . **$357.00**
Price: Ultra Varmint Rifle, 22" bull barrel in 223, laminated stock . . **$357.00**

HARRINGTON & RICHARDSON BUFFALO CLASSIC & TARGET RIFLES

Caliber: 45-70. **Barrel:** 32" heavy. **Weight:** 8 lbs. **Length:** 46" overall. **Stock:** Cut-checkered American black walnut. **Sights:** Williams receiver sight; Lyman target front sight with 8 aperture inserts. **Features:** Color case-hardened Handi-Rifle action with exposed hammer; color case-hardened crescent buttplate; 19th century checkering pattern. Introduced 1995. Target model (introduced 1998) is similar to the Buffalo Classic rifle except chambered for 38-55 Win., has 28" barrel. The barrel, steel trigger guard and forend spacer, are highly polished and blued. Color case-hardened receiver and buttplate. Made in U.S.A. by H&R 1871, LLC.

Price: Buffalo Classic Rifle **$449.00**
Price: Target Model Rifle **$449.00**

HARRIS GUNWORKS ANTIETAM SHARPS RIFLE

Caliber: 40-65, 45-75. **Barrel:** 30", 32", octagon or round, hand-lapped stainless or chrome-moly. **Weight:** 11.25 lbs. **Length:** 47" overall. **Stock:** Choice of straight grip, pistol grip or Creedmoor with Schnabel forend; pewter tip optional. Standard wood is A Fancy; higher grades available. **Sights:** Montana Vintage Arms #111 Low Profile Spirit Level front, #108 mid-range tang rear with windage adjustments. **Features:** Recreation of the 1874 Sharps sidehammer. Action is color case-hardened, barrel satin black. Chrome-moly barrel optionally blued. Optional sights include #112 Spirit Level Globe front with windage, #107 Long Range rear with windage. Introduced 1994. Made in U.S.A. by Harris Gunworks.

Price: **$2,400.00**

Lone Star Silhouette

Model 1885 High Wall

Mossberg SSi-One Sporter

Mossberg SSi-One Varminter

KRIEGHOFF HUBERTUS SINGLE-SHOT RIFLE
Caliber: 222, 243, 270, 308, 30-06, 5.6x50R Mag., 5.6x52R, 6x62R Freres, 6.5x57R, 6.5x65R, 7x57R, 7x65R, 8x57JRS, 8x75RS, 9.3x74R, 7mm Rem. Mag., 300 Win. Mag. **Barrel:** 23-1/2". **Weight:** 6-1/2 lbs. **Length:** 40.5. **Stock:** High-grade walnut. **Sights:** Blade front, open rear. **Features:** Break-open loading with manual cocking lever on top tang; takedown; extractor; Schnabel forearm; many options. Imported from Germany by Krieghoff International Inc.
Price: Hubertus single shot, from **$5,995.00**
Price: Hubertus, magnum calibers **$6,995.00**

LONE STAR NO. 5 REMINGTON PATTERN ROLLING BLOCK RIFLE
Caliber: 25-35, 30-30, 30-40 Krag. **Barrel:** 26" to 34". **Weight:** NA. **Length:** NA. **Stock:** American walnut. **Sights:** Beech style, Marble bead, Rocky Mountain-style, front; Buckhorn, early or late combination, rear. **Features:** Round, tapered round, octagon, tapered octagon, half octagon-half round barrels; bone-pack color case-hardened actions; single, single set, or double-set triggers. Made in U.S.A. by Lone Star Rifle Co., Inc.
Price: **$1,995.00**

Lone Star Cowboy Action Rifle
Similar to the Lone Star No. 5 rifle, but designed for cowboy action shooting with 28-33" barrel, buckhorn rear sight.
Price: **$1,595.00**

Lone Star Custom Silhouette Rifle
Similar to the Lone Star No. 5 rifle but custom made in any caliber or barrel length.
Price: **$1,995.00**

MEACHAM HIGHWALL SILHOUETTE or SCHUETZEN RIFLE
Caliber: any rimmed cartridge. **Barrel:** 26-34". **Weight:** 7-15 lbs. **Sights:** none. Tang drilled for Win. base, 3/8 dovetail slot front. **Stock:** Fancy eastern walnut with cheekpiece; ebony insert in forearm tip. **Features:** Exact copy of 1885 Winchester. With most Winchester factory options

available including double set triggers. Introduced 1994. Made in U.S.A. by Meacham T&H Inc.
Price: . . . . from **$3,899.00**

MERKEL K-1 MODEL LIGHTWEIGHT STALKING RIFLE
Caliber: 243 Win., 270 Win., 7x57R, 308 Win., 30-06, 7mm Rem. Mag., 300 Win. Mag., 9.3x74R. **Barrel:** 23.6". **Weight:** 5.6 lbs. unscoped. **Stock:** Satin-finished walnut, fluted and checkered; sling-swivel studs. **Sights:** None (scope base furnished). **Features:** Franz Jager single-shot break-open action, cocking/uncocking slide-type safety, matte silver receiver, selectable trigger pull weights, integrated, quick detach 1" or 30mm optic mounts (optic not included). Imported from Germany by GSI.
Price: Standard, simple border engraving **$3,795.00**
Price: Premium, light arabesque scroll **$3,795.00**
Price: Jagd, fine engraved hunting scenes. **$4,395.00**

MODEL 1885 HIGH WALL RIFLE
Caliber: 30-40 Krag, 32-40, 38-55, 40-65 WCF, 45-70. **Barrel:** 26" (30-40), 28" to 30" all others. Douglas Premium #3 tapered octagon. **Weight:** 9 lbs, 4 oz. **Length:** 47" overall. **Stock:** Premium American black walnut. **Sights:** Marble's standard ivory bead front, #66 long blade top rear with reversible notch and elevator. **Features:** Receiver with octagon top, thick-wall High Wall with coil spring action. Tang drilled, tapped for High Wall tang sight. Receiver, lever, hammer and breechblock color case-hardened. Available from Montana Armory, Inc.
Price: **$1,350.00**

MOSSBERG SSi-ONE SINGLE-SHOT RIFLE
Caliber: 223 Rem., 22-250 Rem., 243 Win., 270 Win., 308 Rem., 30-06. **Barrel:** 24". **Weight:** 8 lbs. **Length:** 40". **Stock:** Satin-finished walnut, fluted and checkered; sling-swivel studs. **Sights:** None (scope base furnished). **Features:** Frame accepts interchangeable barrels including 12 gauge, fully rifled slug barrel and 12 ga., 3-1/2" chambered barrel with Ulti-Full Turkey choke tube. Lever-opening, break-action design; single-stage trigger; ambidextrous, top-tang safety; internal eject/extract selector. Introduced 2000. From Mossberg.
Price: SSi-One Sporter (standard barrel) or 12 ga., 3-1/2" chamber **$459.00**
Price: SSi-One Varmint (bull barrel, 22-250 Rem. only;
weighs 10 lbs.) **$480.00**
Price: SSi-One 12 gauge Slug (fully rifled barrel, no sights,
scope base) **$480.00**

Navy Arms #2 Creedmoor

Navy Arms 1874 Sharps Cavalry Carbine

Navy Arms 1874 Sharps Plains

Navy Arms 1874 Sharps Sporting

Navy Arms Sharps #2 Sporting

Navy Arms Sharps #2 Silhouette

NAVY ARMS 1873 SHARPS "QUIGLEY" RIFLE
Caliber: 45/70. **Barrel:** 34" heavy octagonal. **Stock:** Walnut. **Features:** Case-hardened receiver and military patchbox. Exact reproduction from "Quigley Down Under."
Price: $1,826.00

NAVY ARMS 1873 SHARPS NO. 2 CREEDMOOR RIFLE
Caliber: 45/70. **Barrel:** 30" tapered round. **Stock:** Walnut. **Sights:** Front globe, "soule" tang rear. **Features:** Nickel receiver and action. Lightweight sporting rifle.
Price: $1,739.00

NAVY ARMS 1874 SHARPS CAVALRY CARBINE
Caliber: 45-70. **Barrel:** 22". **Weight:** 7 lbs., 12 oz. **Length:** 39" overall. **Stock:** Walnut. **Sights:** Blade front, military ladder-type rear. **Features:**

Replica of the 1874 Sharps miltary carbine. Color case-hardened receiver and furniture. Imported by Navy Arms.
Price: $1,245.00

Navy Arms Sharps Sporting Rifle
Same as the Navy Arms Sharps Plains Rifle except has pistol grip stock. Introduced 1997. Imported by Navy Arms.
Price: 45-70 only $1,739.00
Price: #2 Sporting with case-hardened receiver $1,739.00
Price: #2 Silhouette with full octagonal barrel $1,739.00

NAVY ARMS 1885 HIGH WALL RIFLE
Caliber: 45-70; others available on special order. **Barrel:** 28" round, 30" octagonal. **Weight:** 9.5 lbs. **Length:** 45-1/2" overall (30" barrel). **Stock:** Walnut. **Sights:** Blade front, vernier tang-mounted peep rear. **Features:** Replica of Winchester's High Wall designed by Browning. Color case-hardened receiver, blued barrel. Introduced 1998. Imported by Navy Arms.
Price: 28", round barrel, target sights $1,169.00
Price: 30" octagonal barrel, target sights $1,169.00

Navy Arms 1873 Springfield

Navy Arms Rolling Block Buffalo

New England Firearms Handi-Rifle

New England Firearms Super Light

NAVY ARMS 1873 SPRINGFIELD CAVALRY CARBINE
Caliber: 45-70. **Barrel:** 22". **Weight:** 7 lbs. **Length:** 40-1/2" overall. **Stock:** Walnut. **Sights:** Blade front, military ladder rear. **Features:** Blued lockplate and barrel; color case-hardened breechblock; saddle ring with bar. Replica of 7th Cavalry gun. Imported by Navy Arms.
Price: **$1,195.00**

NAVY ARMS "JOHN BODINE" ROLLING BLOCK RIFLE
Caliber: 45-70. **Barrel:** 30" heavy octagonal. **Stock:** Walnut. **Sights:** Globe front, "soule" tang rear. **Features:** Double-set triggers.
Price: **$1,856.00**
Price: (#2 with deluxe nickel finished receiver) **$1,856.00**

NAVY ARMS SHARPS NO. 3 LONG RANGE RIFLE
Caliber: 45-70, 45-90. **Barrel:** 34" octagon. **Weight:** 10 lbs., 12 oz. **Length:** 51-1/2". **Stock:** Deluxe walnut. **Sights:** Globe target front and match grade rear tang. **Features:** Shotgun buttplate, German silver forend cap, color case hardenend receiver. Imported by Navy Arms.
Price: **$2,194.00**

NEW ENGLAND FIREARMS HANDI-RIFLE
Caliber: 204 Ruger, 22 Hornet, 223, 243, 30-30, 270, 280 Rem., 7mm-08, 308, 7.62x39 Russian, 30-06, 357 Mag., 35 Whelen, 44 Mag., 45-70, 500 S&W. **Barrel:** from 20" to 26", blued or stainless. **Weight:** 5.5 to 7 lbs. **Stock:** Walnut-finished hardwood or synthetic. **Sights:** Vary by model, but most have ramp front, folding rear, or are drilled and tapped for scope mount. **Features:** Break-open action with side-lever release. Swivel studs on all models. Blue finish. Introduced 1989. From New England Firearms.
Price: Various cartridges **$292.00**
Price: 7.62x39 Russian, 35 Whelen, intr. 2006 .... **$292.00**
Price: Youth, 37" OAL, 11.75" LOP, 6.75 lbs. **$292.00**
Price: Handi-Rifle/Pardner combo, 20 ga. synthetic, intr. 2006 .... **$325.00**
Price: Handi-Rifle/Pardner Superlight, 20 ga., 5.5 lbs. , intr. 2006 .. **$325.00**
Price: Synthetic **$302.00**
Price: Stainless **$364.00**
Price: Superlight, 20" barrel, 35.25" OAL, 5.5 lbs. **$302.00**

NEW ENGLAND FIREARMS SURVIVOR RIFLE
Caliber: 223, 308 Win., .410 shotgun, 45 Colt, single shot. **Barrel:** 20" to 22". **Weight:** 6 lbs. **Length:** 34.5" to 36" overall. **Stock:** Black polymer, thumbhole design. **Sights:** None furnished; scope mount provided. **Features:** Receiver drilled and tapped for scope mounting. Stock and forend have storage compartments for ammo, etc.; comes with integral swivels and black nylon sling. Introduced 1996. Made in U.S.A. by New England Firearms.
Price: Blue or nickel finish **$304.00**

New England Firearms Survivor

Remington No. 1 Mid-Range

Replica Arms Sharps "Quigley"

Ruger No. 1B

NEW ENGLAND FIREARMS SPORTSTER/VERSA PACK RIFLE

Caliber: 17M2, 17HMR, 22LR, 22 WMR, .410 bore single shot. **Barrel:** 20" to 22". **Weight:** 5.4 to 7 lbs. **Length:** 33" to 38.25" overall. **Stock:** Black polymer. **Sights:** Adjustable rear, ramp front. **Features:** Receiver drilled and tapped for scope mounting. Made in U.S.A. by New England Firearms.

Price: Sportster 17M2, 17HMR $193.00
Price: Sportster $161.00
Price: Sportster Youth $161.00
Price: Sportster 22/410 Versa Pack $176.00

REMINGTON NO. 1 ROLLING BLOCK MID-RANGE SPORTER

Caliber: 45-70. **Barrel:** 30" round. **Weight:** 8-3/4 lbs. **Length:** 46-1/2" overall. **Stock:** American walnut with checkered pistol grip and forend. **Sights:** Beaded blade front, adjustable center-notch buckhorn rear. **Features:** Recreation of the original. Polished blue metal finish. Many options available. Introduced 1998. Made in U.S.A. by Remington.

Price: $1,450.00
Price: Silhouette model with single-set trigger, heavy barrel $1,560.00

REPLICA ARMS SHARPS "QUIGLEY" RIFLE

Caliber: .45-70. **Barrel:** 28" octagon. **Weight:** 10 lbs. **Length:** 47-1/4" overall. **Grips:** Walnut checkered at wrist and forend. **Sights:** High blade front, full buckhorn rear. **Features:** Color case-hardened receiver, trigger, patchbox, hammer and lever. Double-set triggers, German silver gripcap.

Price: $1,241.95

REPLICA ARMS SHARPS "BIG GAME" RIFLE

Caliber: .45-70. **Barrel:** 28" Deluxe Heavy Round. **Weight:** 8.8 lbs. **Length:** 44.8" overall. **Grips:** Walnut. **Sights:** Gold bead front, full buckhorn rear. **Features:** Color case-hardened receiver, trigger, hammer and lever. Double-set triggers.

Price: $1,014.00

ROSSI SINGLE-SHOT CENTERFIRE RIFLE

Caliber: 308 Win., 270 Win., 30-06 Spfld., 223 Rem., 243 Win. **Barrel:** 23". **Weight:** 6 to 6.5 lbs. **Stock:** Monte Carlo, exotic woods, walnut finish & swivels with white line space and recoil pad. **Sights:** None, scope rails and hammer extension included. **Features:** Break-open, positive ejection, internal transfer bar mechanism and manual external safety. Trigger block system included.

Price: $179.95

ROSSI CENTERFIRE/SHOTGUN "MATCHED PAIRS"

Caliber: 12 ga./223 Rem., full size, 20 ga./223 Rem. full & youth, 12 ga./342 Win. full, 20 ga./243 Win., full & youth, 12 ga./308 Win. full, 20 ga./308 Win. full & youth, 12 ga./30-06 Spfld. full, 20 ga./30-06 Spfld. full, 12 ga./270 Win. full, 20 ga./270 Win. full. **Barrel:** 28"/23" full, 22"/22" youth. **Weight:** 5 to 7 lbs. **Stock:** Straight, exotic woods, walnut finish and swivels with white line spacer and recoil pad. **Sights:** Bead front shotgun, fully adjustable rifle, drilled and tapped. **Features:** Break-open, positive ejection, internal transfer bar mechanism and manual external safety. Trigger block system included.

Price: $350.00

RUGER NO. 1B SINGLE SHOT

Caliber: 218 Bee, 22 Hornet, 220 Swift, 22-250, 223, 204 Ruger, 243, 25-06, 270, 30-06, 7mm Rem. Mag., 300 Win. Mag., 308 Win., 338 Win. Mag., 270 Wby., 300 Wby. **Barrel:** 26" round tapered with quarter-rib; with Ruger 1" rings. **Weight:** 8 lbs. **Length:** 42-1/4" overall. **Stock:** Walnut, two-piece, checkered pistol grip and semi-beavertail forend. **Sights:** None, 1" scope rings supplied for integral mounts. **Features:** Under-lever, hammerless falling block design has auto ejector, top tang safety.

Price: 1B $1,000.00
Price: K1-B-BBZ stainless steel, laminated stock 25-06, 7MM mag, 7MM STW, 300 Win Mag., 243 Win., 30-06, 308 Win. $1,032.00

CENTERFIRE RIFLES — Single Shot

Ruger K1-B-BBZ

Ruger No. 1A Light Sporter

Ruger No. 1V Varminter

Ruger No. 1 RSI

Ruger No. 1H Tropical

Ruger No. 1S Medium Sporter

RUGER NO. 1A LIGHT SPORTER
Caliber: 204 Ruger, 243, 30-06, 270 and 7x57. **Weight**: About 7-1/4 lbs. Similar to the No. 1B Standard Rifle except has lightweight 22" barrel, Alexander Henry-style forend, adjustable folding leaf rear sight on quarter-rib, dovetailed ramp front with gold bead.
Price: No. 1A **$1,000.00**

Ruger No. 1V Varminter
Similar to the No. 1B Standard Rifle except has 24" heavy barrel. Semi-beavertail forend, barrel ribbed for target scope block, with 1" Ruger scope rings. Calibers 22-250, 220 Swift (w/26" bbl.), 223, 25-06, 6mm Rem. Weight about 9 lbs.
Price: No. 1V **$1,000.00**
Price: K1-V-BBZ stainless steel, laminated stock 22-250 . . . . . . **$1,032.00**

Ruger No. 1 RSI International
Similar to the No. 1B Standard Rifle except has lightweight 20" barrel, full-length International-style forend with loop sling swivel, adjustable folding leaf rear sight on quarter-rib, ramp front with gold bead. Calibers 243, 30-06, 270 and 7x57. Weight is about 7-1/4 lbs.
Price: No. 1 RSI **$1,032.00**

Ruger No. 1H Tropical Rifle
Similar to the No. 1B Standard Rifle except has Alexander Henry forend, adjustable folding leaf rear sight on quarter-rib, ramp front with dovetail gold bead, 24" heavy barrel. Calibers 375 H&H, 416 Rigby, 458 Lott, 405 Win. and 458 Win. Mag. (weighs about 9 lbs.).
Price: No. 1H **$1,000.00**
Price: K1-H-BBZ, S/S, 375 H&H, 416 Rigby **$1,032.00**

Ruger No. 1S Medium Sporter
Similar to the No. 1B Standard Rifle except has Alexander Henry-style forend, adjustable folding leaf rear sight on quarter-rib, ramp front sight base and dovetail-type gold bead front sight. Calibers: 9.3x74R, 45-70 with 22" barrel. Weighs about 7-1/2 lbs. In 45-70.
Price: No. 1S **$1,000.00**
Price: K1-S-BBZ, S/S, 45-70 . . . . **$1032.00**

CENTERFIRE RIFLES — Single Shot

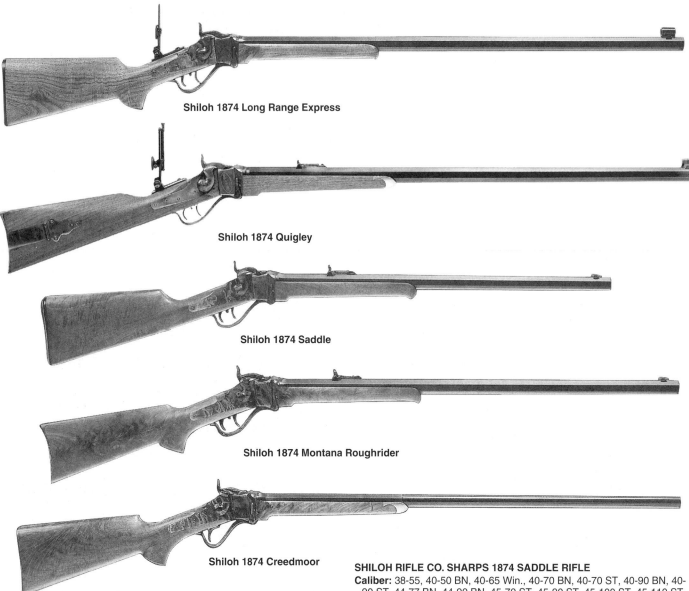

Shiloh 1874 Long Range Express

Shiloh 1874 Quigley

Shiloh 1874 Saddle

Shiloh 1874 Montana Roughrider

Shiloh 1874 Creedmoor

SHILOH RIFLE CO. SHARPS 1874 LONG RANGE EXPRESS
Caliber: 40-50 BN, 40-70 BN, 40-90 BN, 45-70 ST, 45-90 ST, 45-110 ST, 50-70 ST, 50-90 ST, 38-55, 40-70 ST, 40-90 ST. **Barrel:** 34" tapered octagon. **Weight:** 10-1/2 lbs. **Length:** 51" overall. **Stock:** Oil-finished walnut (upgrades available) with pistol grip, shotgun-style butt, traditional cheek rest, Schnabel forend. **Sights:** Customer's choice. **Features:** Re-creation of the Model 1874 Sharps rifle. Double-set triggers. Made in U.S.A. by Shiloh Rifle Mfg. Co.
Price: $1,638.00
Price: Sporting Rifle No. 1 (similar to above except with 30" bbl., blade front, buckhorn rear sight) $1,638.00
Price: Sporting Rifle No. 3 (similar to No. 1 except straight-grip stock, standard wood) $1,547.00

SHILOH RIFLE CO. SHARPS 1874 QUIGLEY
Caliber: 45-70, 45-110. **Barrel:** 34" heavy octagon. **Stock:** Military-style with patch box, standard grade American walnut. **Sights:** Semi buckhorn, interchangeable front and midrange vernier tang sight with windage. **Features:** Gold inlay initials, pewter tip, Hartford collar, case color or antique finish. Double-set triggers.
Price: $2,903.00

SHILOH RIFLE CO. SHARPS 1874 SADDLE RIFLE
Caliber: 38-55, 40-50 BN, 40-65 Win., 40-70 BN, 40-70 ST, 40-90 BN, 40-90 ST, 44-77 BN, 44-90 BN, 45-70 ST, 45-90 ST, 45-100 ST, 45-110 ST, 45-120 ST, 50-70 ST, 50-90 ST. **Barrel:** 26" full or half octagon. **Stock:** Semi fancy American walnut. Shotgun style with cheekrest. **Sights:** Buckhorn and blade. **Features:** Double-set trigger, numerous custom features can be added.
Price: $1,594.00

SHILOH RIFLE CO. SHARPS 1874 MONTANA ROUGHRIDER
Caliber: 38-55, 40-50 BN, 40-65 Win., 40-70 BN, 40-70 ST, 40-90 BN, 40-90 ST, 44-77 BN, 44-90 BN, 45-70 ST, 45-90 ST, 45-100 ST, 45-110 ST, 45-120 ST, 50-70 ST, 50-90 ST. **Barrel:** 30" full or half octagon. **Stock:** American walnut in shotgun or military style. **Sights:** Buckhorn and blade. **Features:** Double-set triggers, numerous custom features can be added.
Price: $1,638.00

SHILOH RIFLE CO. SHARPS CREEDMOOR TARGET
Caliber: 38-55, 40-50 BN, 40-65 Win., 40-70 BN, 40-70 ST, 40-90 BN, 40-90 ST, 44-77 BN, 44-90 BN, 45-70 ST, 45-90 ST, 45-100 ST, 45-110 ST, 45-120 ST, 50-70 ST, 50-90 ST. **Barrel:** 32", half round-half octagon. **Stock:** Extra fancy American walnut. Shotgun style with pistol grip. **Sights:** Customer's choice. **Features:** Single trigger, AA finish on stock, polished barrel and screws, pewter tip.
Price: $2,485.00

Thompson/Center Encore

Thompson/Center Encore "Katahdin"

Thompson/Center Contender

Traditions 1874 Sharps Deluxe

Traditions 1874 Sharps Sporting Deluxe

THOMPSON/CENTER ENCORE RIFLE

Caliber: 22-250, 223, 243, 204 Ruger, 6.8 Rem. Spec., 25-06, 270, 7mm-08, 308, 30-06, 7mm Rem. Mag., 300 Win. Mag. **Barrel:** 24", 26". **Weight:** 6 lbs., 12 oz. (24" barrel). **Length:** 38-1/2" (24" barrel). **Stock:** American walnut. Monte Carlo style; Schnabel forend or black composite. **Sights:** Ramp-style white bead front, fully adjustable leaf-type rear. **Features:** Interchangeable barrels; action opens by squeezing trigger guard; drilled and tapped for T/C scope mounts; polished blue finish. Introduced 1996. Made in U.S.A. by Thompson/Center Arms.
Price: . . . . **$604.00 to $663.00**
Price: Extra barrels **$277.00**

Thompson/Center Stainless Encore Rifle
Similar to blued Encore except stainless steel with blued sights, black composite stock and forend. Available in 22-250, 223, 7mm-08, 30-06, 308. Introduced 1999. Made in U.S.A. by Thompson/Center Arms.
Price: . . . . **$680.00 to $738.00**

THOMPSON/CENTER ENCORE "KATAHDIN" CARBINE
Caliber: 45-70 Gov't., 450 Marlin. **Barrel:** 18" with muzzle tamer. **Stock:** Composite.
Price: **$619.00**

Thompson/Center G2 Contender Rifle
Similar to the G2 Contender pistol, but in a compact rifle format. Weighs 5-1/2 lbs. Features interchangeable 23" barrels, chambered for 17 HMR, 22LR, 223 Rem., 30/30 Win. and 45/70 Gov't; plus a 45 Cal. Muzzleloading barrel. All of the 16-1/4" and 21" barrels made for the old-style Contender will fit. Introduced 2003. Made in U.S.A. by Thompson/Center Arms.
Price: . . . . **$622.00 to $637.00**

TRADITIONS 1874 SHARPS DELUXE RIFLE
Caliber: 45-70. **Barrel:** 32" octagonal; 1:18" twist. **Weight:** 11.67 lbs. **Length:** 48.8" overall. **Stock:** Checkered walnut with German silver nose cap and steel buttplate. **Sights:** Globe front, adjustable Creedmore rear with 12 inserts. **Features:** Color case-hardened receiver; double-set triggers. Introduced 2001. Imported from Pedersoli by Traditions.
Price: **$999.00**

Traditions 1874 Sharps Sporting Deluxe Rifle
Similar to Sharps Deluxe but custom silver engraved receiver, European walnut stock and forend, satin finish, set trigger, fully adjustable.
Price: **$1,999.00**

Traditions 1874 Sharps Standard Rifle
Similar to 1874 Sharps Deluxe except has blade front and adjustable buckhorn-style rear sight. Weighs 10.67 pounds. Introduced 2001. Imported from Pedersoli by Traditions.
Price: **$769.00**

**Tristar/Uberti
1885 Single Shot**

Winchester 1885 High Wall Hunter

Winchester 1885 Centennial

TRADITIONS ROLLING BLOCK SPORTING RIFLE

Caliber: 45-70. **Barrel:** 30" octagonal; 1:18" twist. **Weight:** 11.67 lbs. **Length:** 46.7" overall. **Stock:** Walnut. **Sights:** Blade front, adjustable rear. **Features:** Antique silver, color case-hardened receiver, drilled and tapped for tang/globe sights; brass buttplate and trigger guard. Introduced 2001. Imported from Pedersoli by Traditions.
Price: $769.00

TRADITIONS ROLLING BLOCK SPORTING RIFLE IN 30-30 WINCHESTER

Caliber: 30-30. **Barrel:** 28" round, blued. **Weight:** 8.25 lbs. **Stock:** Walnut. **Sights:** Fixed front, adjustable rear. **Features:** Steel buttplate, trigger guard, barrel band.
Price: $769.00

UBERTI 1874 SHARPS SPORTING RIFLE

Caliber: 45-70. **Barrel:** 30", 32", 34" octagonal. **Weight:** 10.57 lbs. with 32" barrel. **Length:** 48.9" with 32" barrel. **Stock:** Walnut. **Sights:** Dovetail front, Vernier tang rear. **Features:** Cut checkering, case-colored finish on frame, buttplate, and lever.
Price: Standard Sharps (2006), 30" barrel $1,195.00
Price: Special Sharps (2006) 32" barrel $1,450.00
Price: Deluxe Sharps (2006) 34" barrel. $2,200.00
Price: Down Under Sharps (2006) 34" barrel $1,799.00
Price: Adobe Walls Sharps (2006) 32" barrel $1,750.00
Price: Longe Range Sharps (2006) 34" barrel $1,799.00

UBERTI ROLLING BLOCK CARBINE AND RIFLE

Caliber: 22 LR, 22 WMR, 22 Hornet, 357 Mag., single shot. **Barrel:** 22" to 26". **Weight:** 4.9 lbs. (Carbine) **Length:** 35.5" overall. **Stock:** Walnut stock and forend. **Sights:** Blade front, fully adjustable open rear. **Features:** Resembles Remington New Model No. 4 carbine. Brass trigger guard and buttplate; color case-hardened frame, blued barrel. Imported by Uberti USA Inc.
Price: Carbine, 22" barrel $535.00
Price: Rifle, 26" barrel $600.00

UBERTI HIGH-WALL RIFLE

Caliber: 45-70, 45-90, 45-120 single shot. **Barrel:** 28" to 23". **Weight:** 9.3 to 9.9 lbs. **Length:** 44.5" to 47" overall. **Stock:** Walnut stock and forend. **Sights:** Blade front, fully adjustable open rear. **Features:** Based on Winchester High-Wall design by John Browning. Color case-hardened frame and lever, blued barrel and buttplate. Imported by Uberti USA Inc.
Price: 1885 High-Wall, 28" round barrel $850.00
Price: 1885 High-Wall Sporting, 30" octagonal barrel $850.00
Price: 1885 High-Wall Special Sporting, 32" octagonal barrel. . . . $1,035.00

WINCHESTER MODEL 1885 HIGH WALL HUNTER

Caliber: 22-250 Rem., 223 Rem., 270 WSM, 300 WSM, 7mm WSM, 325 WSM. **Barrel:** 28". **Weight:** 8.5 lbs. **Length:** 44". **Stock:** Walnut. **Features:** Single-shot, Pachmayr recoil pad.
Price: $1,085.00

Winchester Model 1885 30-06 Centennial High Wall Hunter

Similar to the Model 1885 High Wall Hunter except chambered 30-06 Springfield with satin finished checkered walnut stock.
Price: $1,617.00

Designs for sporting and utility purposes worldwide.

Beretta Express SSO

Beretta Model 455 SxS

Charles Daly Superior

Charles Daly Empire Combo

BERETTA EXPRESS SSO O/U DOUBLE RIFLES

Caliber: 375 H&H, 458 Win. Mag., 9.3x74R. **Barrel:** 25.5". **Weight:** 11 lbs. **Stock:** European walnut with hand-checkered grip and forend. **Sights:** Blade front on ramp, open V-notch rear. **Features:** Sidelock action with color case-hardened receiver (gold inlays on SSO6 Gold). Ejectors, double triggers, recoil pad. Introduced 1990. Imported from Italy by Beretta U.S.A.

Price: SSO6 . . . . **$21,000.00**
Price: SSO6 Gold **$23,500.00**

BERETTA MODEL 455 SxS EXPRESS RIFLE

Caliber: 375 H&H, 458 Win. Mag., 470 NE, 500 NE 3", 416 Rigby. **Barrel:** 23-1/2" or 25-1/2". **Weight:** 11 lbs. **Stock:** European walnut with hand-checkered grip and forend. **Sights:** Blade front, folding leaf V-notch rear. **Features:** Sidelock action with easily removable sideplates; color case-hardened finish (455), custom big game or floral motif engraving (455EELL). Double triggers, recoil pad. Introduced 1990. Imported from Italy by Beretta U.S.A.

Price: Model 455 . . . . **$36,000.00**
Price: Model 455EELL **$47,000.00**

BRNO 500 COMBINATION GUNS

Caliber/Gauge: 12 (2-3/4" chamber) over 5.6x52R, 5.6x50R, 222 Rem., 243, 6.x55, 308, 7x57R, 7x65R, 30-06. **Barrel:** 23.6". **Weight:** 7.6 lbs. **Length:** 40.5" overall. **Stock:** European walnut. **Sights:** Bead front, V-notch rear; grooved for scope mounting. **Features:** Boxlock action; double-set trigger; blue finish with etched engraving. Announced 1998. Imported from The Czech Republic by Euro-Imports.

Price: **$1,023.00**
Price: O/U double rifle, 7x57R, 7x65R, 8x57JRS **$1,125.00**

BRNO ZH 300 COMBINATION GUN

Caliber/Gauge: 22 Hornet, 5.6x50R Mag., 5.6x52R, 7x57R, 7x65R, 8x57JRS over 12, 16 (2-3/4" chamber). **Barrel:** 23.6". **Weight:** 7.9 lbs. **Length:** 40.5" overall. **Stock:** European walnut. **Sights:** Blade front, open adjustable rear. **Features:** Boxlock action; double triggers; automatic safety. Announced 1998. Imported from The Czech Republic by Euro-Imports.

Price: **$724.00**

BRNO ZH Double Rifles

Similar to ZH 300 Combination guns except double rifle barrels. Available in 7x65R, 7x57R and 8x57JRS. Announced 1998. Imported from The Czech Republic by Euro-Imports.

Price: **$1,125.00**

CHARLES DALY SUPERIOR COMBINATION GUN

Caliber/Gauge: 12 ga. over 22 Hornet, 223 Rem., 22-250, 243 Win., 270 Win., 308 Win., 30-06. **Barrel:** 23.5", shotgun choked Imp. Cyl. **Weight:** About 7.5 lbs. **Stock:** Checkered walnut pistol grip buttstock and semi-beavertail forend. **Features:** Silvered, engraved receiver; chrome-moly steel barrels; double triggers; extractors; sling swivels; gold bead front sight. Introduced 1997. Imported from Italy by K.B.I. Inc.

Price: **$1,479.00**

Charles Daly Empire Combination Gun

Same as the Superior grade except has deluxe wood with European-style comb and cheekpiece; slim forend. Introduced 1997. Imported from Italy by K.B.I., Inc.

Price: **$2,189.00**

CZ 584 SOLO COMBINATION GUN

Caliber/Gauge: 7x57R; 12, 2-3/4" chamber. **Barrel:** 24.4". **Weight:** 7.37 lbs. **Length:** 45.25" overall. **Stock:** Circassian walnut. **Sights:** Blade front, open rear adjustable for windage. **Features:** Kersten-style double lump locking system; double-trigger Blitz-type mechanism with drop safety and adjustable set trigger for the rifle barrel; auto safety, dual extractors; receiver dovetailed for scope mounting. Imported from the Czech Republic by CZ-USA.

Price: **$851.00**

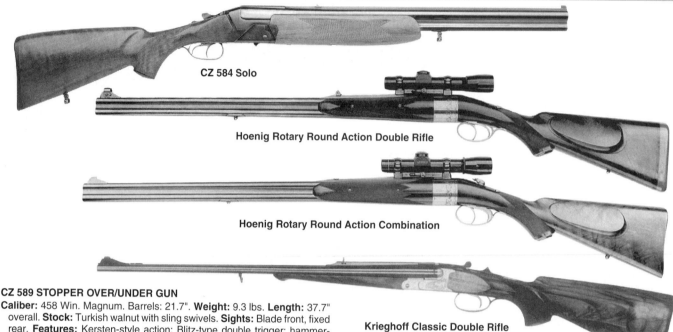

CZ 584 Solo

Hoenig Rotary Round Action Double Rifle

Hoenig Rotary Round Action Combination

Krieghoff Classic Double Rifle

CZ 589 STOPPER OVER/UNDER GUN

Caliber: 458 Win. Magnum. **Barrels:** 21.7". **Weight:** 9.3 lbs. **Length:** 37.7" overall. **Stock:** Turkish walnut with sling swivels. **Sights:** Blade front, fixed rear. **Features:** Kersten-style action; Blitz-type double trigger; hammer-forged, blued barrels; satin-nickel, engraved receiver. Introduced 2001. Imported from the Czech Republic by CZ USA.

Price: **$2,999.00**
Price: Fully engraved model **$3,999.00**

DAKOTA DOUBLE RIFLE

Caliber: 470 Nitro Express, 500 Nitro Express. **Barrel:** 25". **Stock:** Exhibition-grade walnut. **Sights:** Express-style. **Features:** Round action; selective ejectors; recoil pad; Americase. From Dakota Arms Inc.

Price: **$25,000.00**

EAA/BAIKAL IZH-94 COMBINATION GUN

Caliber/Gauge: 12, 3" chamber; 222 Rem., 223, 5.6x50R, 5.6x55E, 7x57R, 7x65R, 7.62x39, 7.62x51, 308, 7.62x53R, 7.62x54R, 30-06. **Barrel:** 24", 26"; imp., mod. and full choke tubes. **Weight:** 7.28 lbs. **Stock:** Walnut; rubber buttpad. **Sights:** Express-style. **Features:** Hammer-forged barrels with chrome-lined bores; machined receiver; single-selective or double triggers. Imported by European American Armory.

Price: Blued finish **$549.00**
Price: 20 ga./22 LR, 20/22 Mag, 3" **$629.00**

GARBI EXPRESS DOUBLE RIFLE

Caliber: 7x65R, 9.3x74R, 375 H&H. **Barrel:** 24-3/4". **Weight:** 7-3/4 to 8-1/2 lbs. **Length:** 41-1/2" overall. **Stock:** Turkish walnut. **Sights:** Quarter-rib with express sight. **Features:** Side-by-side double; H&H-pattern sidelock ejector with reinforced action; chopper lump barrels of Boehler steel; double triggers; fine scroll and rosette engraving, or full coverage ornamental; coin-finished action. Introduced 1997. Imported from Spain by Wm. Larkin Moore.

Price: **$19,900.00**

HOENIG ROTARY ROUND ACTION DOUBLE RIFLE

Caliber: Most popular calibers from 225 Win. to 9.3x74R. **Barrel:** 22" to 26". **Stock:** English Walnut; to customer specs. **Sights:** Swivel hood front with button release (extra bead stored in trap door gripcap), express-style rear on quarter-rib adjustable for windage and elevation; scope mount. **Features:** Round action opens by rotating barrels, pulling forward. Inertia extractor system, rotary safety blocks strikers. Single lever quick-detachable scope mount. Simple takedown without removing forend. Introduced 1997. Made in U.S.A. by George Hoenig.

Price: **$25,000.00**

HOENIG ROTARY ROUND ACTION COMBINATION

Caliber: 28 ga. **Barrel:** 26". **Weight:** 7 lbs. **Stock:** English Walnut to customer specs. **Sights:** Front ramp with button release blades. Foldable aperture tang sight windage and elevation adjustable. Quarter-rib with scope mount. **Features:** Round action opens by rotating barrels, pulling forward. Inertia extractor; rotary safety blocks strikers. Simple takedown without removing forend. Made in U.S.A. by George Hoenig.

Price: **$25,000.00**

KRIEGHOFF CLASSIC DOUBLE RIFLE

Caliber: 7x57R, 7x65R, 308 Win., 30-06, 8x57 JRS, 8x75RS, 9.3x74R, 375NE, 500/416NE, 470NE, 500NE. **Barrel:** 23.5". **Weight:** 7.3 to 8 lbs; 10-11 lbs. Big 5. **Stock:** High grade European walnut. Standard model has conventional rounded cheekpiece, Bavaria model has Bavarian-style cheekpiece. **Sights:** Bead front with removable, adjustable wedge (375 H&H and below), standing leaf rear on quarter-rib. **Features:** Boxlock action; double triggers; short opening angle for fast loading; quiet extractors; sliding, self-adjusting wedge for secure bolting; Purdey-style barrel extension; horizontal firing pin placement. Many options available. Introduced 1997. Imported from Germany by Krieghoff International.

Price: With small Arabesque engraving **$8,950.00**
Price: With engraved sideplates **$12,300.00**
Price: For extra barrels **$5,450.00**
Price: Extra 20-ga., 28" shotshell barrels **$3,950.00**

Krieghoff Classic Big Five Double Rifle

Similar to the standard Classic except available in 375 Flanged Mag. N.E., 500/416 N.E., 470 N.E., 500 N.E. Has hinged front trigger, non-removable muzzle wedge (models larger than 375 caliber), Universal Trigger System, Combi Cocking Device, steel trigger guard, specially weighted stock bolt for weight and balance. Many options available. Introduced 1997. Imported from Germany by Krieghoff International. Imperial Model introduced 2006.

Price: **$11,450.00**
Price: With engraved sideplates **$14,800.00**

LEBEAU-COURALLY EXPRESS RIFLE SxS

Caliber: 7x65R, 8x57JRS, 9.3x74R, 375 H&H, 470 N.E. **Barrel:** 24" to 26". **Weight:** 7-3/4 to 10-1/2 lbs. **Stock:** Fancy French walnut with cheekpiece. **Sights:** Bead on ramp front, standing left express rear on quarter-rib. **Features:** Holland & Holland-type sidelock with automatic ejectors; double triggers. Built to order only. Imported from Belgium by Wm. Larkin Moore.

Price: **$41,000.00**

Merkel 96K Engraved

Merkel 140-1

Rizzini Express

Savage 24F Combination

Springfield M6 Scout

MERKEL DRILLINGS

Caliber/Gauge: 12, 20, 3" chambers, 16, 2-3/4" chambers; 22 Hornet, 5.6x50R Mag., 5.6x52R, 222 Rem., 243 Win., 6.5x55, 6.5x57R, 7x57R, 7x65R, 308, 30-06, 8x57JRS, 9.3x74R, 375 H&H. **Barrel:** 25.6". **Weight:** 7.9 to 8.4 lbs. depending upon caliber. **Stock:** Oil-finished walnut with pistol grip; cheekpiece on 12-, 16-gauge. **Sights:** Blade front, fixed rear. **Features:** Double barrel locking lug with Greener cross bolt; scroll-engraved, case-hardened receiver; automatic trigger safety; Blitz action; double triggers. Imported from Germany by GSI.
Price: Model 96K (manually cocked rifle system), from **$7,495.00**
Price: Model 96K Engraved (hunting series on receiver) **$8,595.00**

MERKEL BOXLOCK DOUBLE RIFLES

Caliber: 5.6x52R, 243 Winchester, 6.5x55, 6.5x57R, 7x57R, 7x65R, 308 Winchester, 30-06 Springfield, 8x57 IRS, 9.3x74R. **Barrel:** 23.6". **Weight:** 7.7 oz. **Length:** NA. **Stock:** Walnut, oil finished, pistol grip. **Sights:** Fixed 100 meter. **Features:** Anson & Deely boxlock action with cocking indicators, double triggers, engraved color case-hardened receiver. Introduced 1995. Imported from Germany by GSI.
Price: Model 140-1, from **$6,695.00**
Price: Model 140-1.1 (engraved silver-gray receiver), from **$7,795.00**

RIZZINI EXPRESS 90L DOUBLE RIFLE

Caliber: 30-06, 7x65R, 9.3x74R. **Barrel:** 24". **Weight:** 7-1/2 lbs. **Length:** 40" overall. **Stock:** Select European walnut with satin oil finish; English-style cheekpiece. **Sights:** Ramp front, quarter-rib with express sight. **Features:** Color case-hardened boxlock action; automatic ejectors; single selective trigger; polished blue barrels. Extra 20 gauge shotgun barrels available. Imported for Italy by Wm. Larkin Moore.
Price: With case **$3,850.00**

SAVAGE 24F PREDATOR O/U COMBINATION GUN

Caliber/Gauge: 22 Hornet, 223, 30-30 over 12 (24F-12) or 22 LR, 22 Hornet, 223, 30-30 over 20 ga. (24F-20); 3" chambers. **Action:** Takedown, low rebounding visible hammer. Single trigger, barrel selector spur on hammer. **Barrel:** 24" separated barrels; 12 ga. has mod. choke tubes, 20 ga. has fixed Mod. choke. **Weight:** 8 lbs. **Length:** 40-1/2" overall. **Stock:** Black Rynite composition. **Sights:** Blade front, rear open adjustable for elevation. **Features:** Introduced 1989.
Price: 24F-12 .... **$661.00**
Price: 24F-20 .... **$628.00**

SPRINGFIELD ARMORY M6 SCOUT RIFLE/SHOTGUN

Caliber/Gauge: 22 LR or 22 Hornet over 410 bore. **Barrel:** 18.25". **Weight:** 4 lbs. **Length:** 32" overall. **Stock:** Folding detachable with storage for 15 22 LR, four 410 shells. **Sights:** Blade front, military aperture for 22; V-notch for 410. **Features:** All metal construction. Designed for quick disassembly and minimum maintenance. Folds for compact storage. Introduced 1982; reintroduced 1996. Imported from the Czech Republic by Springfield Armory.
Price: Parkerized **$185.00**
Price: Stainless steel **$219.00**

Designs for hunting, utility and sporting purposes, including training for competition.

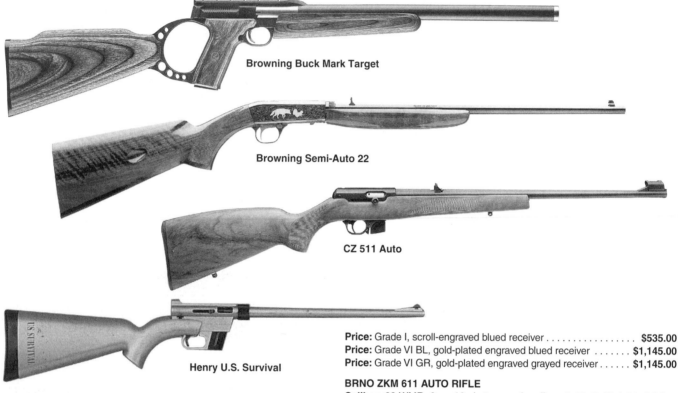

Browning Buck Mark Target

Browning Semi-Auto 22

CZ 511 Auto

Henry U.S. Survival

AR-7 EXPLORER CARBINE

Caliber: 22 LR, 8-shot magazine. **Barrel:** 16". **Weight:** 2-1/2 lbs. **Length:** 34-1/2", 16-1/2" stowed. **Stock:** Molded Cycolac; snap-on rubber buttpad. **Sights:** Square blade front, aperture rear. **Features:** Takedown design stores barrel and action in hollow stock. Light enough to float. Reintroduced 1999. From AR-7 Industries, LLC.

Price: Black matte finish **$150.00**
Price: AR-20 Sporter (tubular stock, barrel shroud) **$200.00**
Price: AR-7 camo- or walnut-finish stock **$164.95**

BROWNING BUCK MARK SEMI-AUTO RIFLES

Caliber: 22 LR, 10+1. **Action:** A rifle version of the Buck Mark Pistol; straight blowback action; machined aluminum receiver with integral rail scope mount; manual thumb safety. **Barrel:** Recessed crowns. **Stock:** Stock and forearm with full pistol grip. **Features:** Action lock provided. Introduced 2001. Four model name variations for 2006, as noted below. **Sights:** FLD Target, FLD Carbon, and Target models have integrated scope rails. Sporter has Truglo/Marble fiber optic sights. Imported from Japan by Browning.

Price: FLD Target, 5.5 lbs., bull barrel, laminated stock **$589.00**
Price: FLD Carbon, 3.6 lbs., carbon composite barrel **$652.00**
Price: Target, 5.4 lbs., blued bull barrel, wood stock **$572.00**
Price: Sporter, 4.4 lbs., blued sporter barrel w/sights **$572.00**

BROWNING SEMI-AUTO 22 RIFLE

Caliber: 22 LR, 11+1. **Barrel:** 16.25". **Weight:** 5.2 lbs. **Length:** 37" overall. **Stock:** Checkered select walnut with pistol grip and semi-beavertail forend. **Sights:** Gold bead front, folding leaf rear. **Features:** Engraved receiver with polished blue finish; cross-bolt safety; tubular magazine in buttstock; easy takedown for carrying or storage. The Grade VI is available with either grayed or blued receiver with extensive engraving with gold-plated animals: right side pictures a fox and squirrel in a woodland scene; left side shows a beagle chasing a rabbit. On top is a portrait of the beagle. Stock and forend are of high-grade walnut with a double-bordered cut checkering design. Introduced 1987. Imported from Japan by Browning.

Price: Grade I, scroll-engraved blued receiver **$535.00**
Price: Grade VI BL, gold-plated engraved blued receiver **$1,145.00**
Price: Grade VI GR, gold-plated engraved grayed receiver **$1,145.00**

BRNO ZKM 611 AUTO RIFLE

Caliber: 22 WMR, 6- or 10-shot magazine. **Barrel:** 20.4". **Weight:** 5.9 lbs. **Length:** 38.9" overall. **Stock:** European walnut. **Sights:** Hooded blade front, open adjustable rear. **Features:** Removable box magazine; polished blue finish; cross-bolt safety; grooved receiver for scope mounting; easy takedown for storage. Imported from The Czech Republic by Euro-Imports.

Price: **$475.00**

CZ 511 AUTO RIFLE

Caliber: 22 LR, 8-shot magazine. **Barrel:** 22.2". **Weight:** 5.39 lbs. **Length:** 38.6" overall. **Stock:** Walnut with checkered pistol grip. **Sights:** Hooded front, adjustable rear. **Features:** Polished blue finish; detachable magazine; sling swivel studs. Imported from the Czech Republic by CZ-USA.

Price: **$351.00**

HENRY U.S. SURVIVAL RIFLE .22

Caliber: 22 LR, 8-shot magazine. **Barrel:** 16" steel lined. **Weight:** 2.5 lbs. **Stock:** ABS plastic. **Sights:** Blade front on ramp, aperture rear. **Features:** Takedown design stores barrel and action in hollow stock. Light enough to float. Silver, black or camo finish. Comes with two magazines. Introduced 1998. From Henry Repeating Arms Co.

Price: **$205.00**

MARLIN MODEL 60 AUTO RIFLE

Caliber: 22 LR, 14-shot tubular magazine. **Barrel:** 19" round tapered. **Weight:** About 5-1/2 lbs. **Length:** 37-1/2" overall. **Stock:** Press-checkered, walnut-finished Maine birch with Monte Carlo, full pistol grip; Mar-Shield® finish. **Sights:** Ramp front, open adjustable rear. **Features:** Matted receiver is grooved for scope mount. Manual bolt hold-open; automatic last-shot bolt hold-open. Model 60C is similar except has hardwood Monte Carlo stock with Mossy Oak Break-Up camouflage pattern. From Marlin.

Price: **$200.00**
Price: With 4x scope **$208.00**
Price: (Model 60C camo) **$236.00**
Price: (Model 60DL walnut tone finish) **$236.00**

Marlin Model 60

Marlin Model 70PSS Papoose

Marlin 795

Remington 552 BDL Speedmaster

Marlin Model 60SS Self-Loading Rifle

Same as the Model 60 except breech bolt, barrel and outer magazine tube are made of stainless steel; most other parts are either nickel-plated or coated to match the stainless finish. Monte Carlo stock is of black/gray Maine birch laminate, and has nickel-plated swivel studs, rubber buttpad. Introduced 1993. From Marlin.

Price: $318.00
Price: Model 60SSK (black fiberglass-filled stock) $269.00
Price: Model 60SB (walnut-finished birch stock) $235.00
Price: Model 60SB with 4x scope $270.00

MARLIN 70PSS PAPOOSE STAINLESS RIFLE

Caliber: 22 LR, 7-shot magazine. **Barrel:** 16-1/4" stainless steel, Micro-Groove® rifling. **Weight:** 3-1/4 lbs. **Length:** 35-1/4" overall. **Stock:** Black fiberglass-filled synthetic with abbreviated forend, nickel-plated swivel studs, molded-in checkering. **Sights:** Ramp front with orange post, cut-away Wide Scan™ hood; adjustable open rear. Receiver grooved for scope mounting. **Features:** Takedown barrel; cross-bolt safety; manual bolt hold-open; last shot bolt hold-open; comes with padded carrying case. Introduced 1986. Made in U.S.A. by Marlin.

Price: $318.00

MARLIN MODEL 717M2 17 MACH 2 RIFLE

Caliber: 17 Mach 2, 7-shot. **Barrel:** 22" sporter. **Weight:** 5.5 lbs. **Length:** 37". **Stock:** Walnut-finished hardwood stock. **Sights:** Adjustable open rear, ramp front, grooved for scope mount. **Features:** Swivel studs, cross-bolt safety. Similar in design to 917 series bolt guns.

Price: 717M2 .... $264.00

MARLIN MODEL 7000 AUTO RIFLE

Caliber: 22 LR, 10-shot magazine **Barrel:** 18" heavy target with 12-groove Micro-Groove® rifling, recessed muzzle. **Weight:** 5-1/2 lbs. **Length:** 37" overall. **Stock:** Black fiberglass-filled synthetic with Monte Carlo combo, swivel studs, molded-in checkering. **Sights:** None furnished; comes with

ring mounts. **Features:** Automatic last-shot bolt hold-open, manual bolt hold-open; cross-bolt safety; steel charging handle; blue finish, nickel-plated magazine. Introduced 1997. Made in U.S.A. by Marlin Firearms Co.

Price: $263.00

MARLIN MODEL 795 AUTO RIFLE

Caliber: 22. **Barrel:** 18" with 16-groove Micro-Groove® rifling. Ramp front sight, adjustable rear. Receiver grooved for scope mount. **Stock:** Black synthetic. **Features:** 10-round magazine, last shot hold-open feature. Introduced 1997. SS is similar to Model 795 except stainless steel barrel. Most other parts nickel-plated. Adjustable folding semi-buckhorn rear sights, ramp front high-visibility post and removeable cutaway wide scan hood. Made in U.S.A. by Marlin Firearms Co.

Price: 795 .... $172.00
Price: 795SS $255.00

REMINGTON MODEL 552 BDL DELUXE SPEEDMASTER RIFLE

Caliber: 22 S (20), L (17) or LR (15) tubular mag. **Barrel:** 21" round tapered. **Weight:** 5-3/4 lbs. **Length:** 40" overall. **Stock:** Walnut. Checkered grip and forend. **Sights:** Big game. **Features:** Positive cross-bolt safety, receiver grooved for tip-off mount.

Price: $393.00

REMINGTON 597 AUTO RIFLE

Caliber: 22 LR, 10-shot clip. **Barrel:** 20". **Weight:** 5-1/2 lbs. **Length:** 40" overall. **Stock:** Black synthetic. **Sights:** Big game. **Features:** Matte black finish, nickel-plated bolt. Receiver is grooved and drilled and tapped for scope mounts. Introduced 1997. Made in U.S.A. by Remington.

Price: $169.00
Price: Model 597 Magnum, 22 WMR, 8-shot clip $335.00
Price: Model 597 LSS (laminated stock, stainless) $279.00
Price: Model 597 SS
(22 LR, stainless steel, black synthetic stock) $224.00
Price: Model 597 LS heavy barrel (22 LR, laminated stock) $265.00
Price: Model 597 Magnum LS heavy barrel
(22 WMR, lam. stock) $399.00
Price: Model 597 Magnum 17 HMR, 8-shot clip $361.00

Remington 597

Ruger 10/22 Deluxe Sporter

Ruger 10/22 Target

Savage Model 64FV

RUGER 10/22 AUTOLOADING CARBINE

Caliber: 22 LR, 10-shot rotary magazine. **Barrel:** 18-1/2" round tapered. **Weight:** 5 lbs. **Length:** 37-1/4" overall. **Stock:** American hardwood with pistol grip and barrel band or synthetic. **Sights:** Brass bead front, folding leaf rear adjustable for elevation. **Features:** Detachable rotary magazine fits flush into stock, cross-bolt safety, receiver tapped and grooved for scope blocks or tip-off mount. Scope base adaptor furnished with each rifle.
Price: Model 10/22 RB (blue) $250.00
Price: Model K10/22RB (bright finish stainless barrel) $295.00
Price: Model 10/22RPF (blue, synthetic stock) $250.00
Price: Model 10/22CRR Compact RB (blued), intr. 2006 . . . . $275.00

Ruger 10/22 Deluxe Sporter

Same as 10/22 Carbine except walnut stock with hand checkered pistol grip and forend; straight buttplate, no barrel band, has sling swivels.
Price: Model 10/22 DSP $314.00

Ruger 10/22T Target Rifle

Similar to the 10/22 except has 20" heavy, hammer-forged barrel with tight chamber dimensions, improved trigger pull, laminated hardwood stock dimensioned for optical sights. No iron sights supplied. Introduced 1996. Made in U.S.A. by Sturm, Ruger & Co.
Price: 10/22T $432.00
Price: K10/22T, stainless steel $480.00
Price: K10/22RR, 20" bbl. $275.00

Ruger K10/22RPF All-Weather Rifle

Similar to the stainless K10/22/RB except has black composite stock of thermoplastic polyester resin reinforced with fiberglass; checkered grip and forend. Brushed satin, natural metal finish with clear hardcoat finish. Weighs 5 lbs., measures 36-3/4" overall. Introduced 1997. From Sturm, Ruger & Co.
Price: $295.00

RUGER 10/22 MAGNUM AUTOLOADING CARBINE

Caliber: 22 WMR, 9-shot rotary magazine. **Barrel:** 18-1/2". **Weight:** 6 lbs. **Length:** 37-1/4" overall. **Stock:** Birch. **Sights:** Gold bead front, folding rear. **Features:** All-steel receiver has integral Ruger scope bases for the included 1" rings. Introduced 1999. Made in U.S.A. by Sturm, Ruger & Co.
Price: 10/22RBM $536.00

SAVAGE MODEL 64G AUTO RIFLE

Caliber: 22 LR, 10-shot magazine. **Barrel:** 20", 21". **Weight:** 5-1/2 lbs. **Length:** 40", 41". **Stock:** Walnut-finished hardwood with Monte Carlo-type comb, checkered grip and forend. **Sights:** Bead front, open adjustable rear. Receiver grooved for scope mounting. **Features:** Thumb-operated rotating safety. Blue finish. Side ejection, bolt hold-open device. Introduced 1990. Made in Canada, from Savage Arms.
Price: $162.00
Price: Model 64FSS, stainless $202.00
Price: Model 64F, black synthetic stock $135.00
Price: Model 64GXP package gun includes
4x15 scope and mounts $171.00
Price: Model 64FXP (black stock, 4x15 scope) $142.00
Price: Model 64F Camo $135.00

Savage Model 64FV Auto Rifle

Similar to the Model 64F except has heavy 21" barrel with recessed crown; no sights provided, comes with Weaver-style bases. Introduced 1998. Imported from Canada by Savage Arms, Inc.
Price: $135.00
Price: Model 64FSS, stainless $202.00

TAURUS MODEL 63 RIFLE

Caliber: 22 LR, 10-shot tube-fed magazine. **Barrel:** 23". **Weight:** 72 oz. **Length:** 32-1/2". **Stock:** Hand-fitted walnut-finished hardwood. **Sights:** Adjustable rear, fixed front. **Features:** Manual safety, metal buttplate, can accept Taurus tang sight. Charged and cocked with operating plunger at front of forend. Available in blue or polished stainless steel.
Price: 63 . . . . $295.00
Price: 63SS $311.00

THOMPSON/CENTER 22 LR CLASSIC RIFLE

Caliber: 22 LR, 8-shot magazine. **Barrel:** 22" match-grade. **Weight:** 5-1/2 pounds. **Length:** 39-1/2". **Stock:** Satin-finished American walnut with Monte Carlo-type comb and pistol gripcap, swivel studs. **Sights:** Ramp-style front and fully adjustable rear, both with fiber optics. **Features:** All-steel receiver drilled and tapped for scope mounting; barrel threaded to receiver; thumb-operated safety; trigger guard safety lock included. New .22 Classic Benchmark TGT target rifle variant has 18" heavy barrel, brown laminated target stock, blued with matte finish, 10-shot magazine and no sights; drilled and tapped.
Price: T/C 22 LR Classic (blue) $396.00
Price: T/C 22 LR Classic Benchmark $505.00

Classic and modern models for sport and utility, including training.

Browning BL-22

Henry Lever-Action 22

Henry Golden Boy 22

Henry Pump-Action 22

Marlin Model 39A

BROWNING BL-22 and BL-17 RIFLES

Action: Short-throw lever action, side ejection. Rack-and-pinion lever. Tubular magazines, with 15+1 capacity for 22LR or 17M2. **Barrel:** Recessed muzzle. **Stock:** Walnut, two-piece straight grip Western style. **Trigger:** Half-cock hammer safety; fold-down hammer. **Sights:** Bead post front, folding-leaf rear. Steel receiver grooved for scope mount. **Weight:** 5-5.4 lbs. **Length:** 36.75-40.75" overall. **Features:** Action lock provided. Introduced 1996. FLD Grade II Octagon has octagonal 24" barrel, silver nitride receiver with scroll engraving, gold-colored trigger; 17M2 introduced 2005. FLD Grade I has satin-nickel receiver, blued trigger, no stock checkering. FLD Grade II has satin-nickel receivers with scroll engraving; gold-colored trigger, cut checkering. Both introduced 2005. Grade I has blued receiver and trigger, no stock checkering. Grade II has gold-colored trigger, cut checkering, blued receiver with scroll engraving. 17M2 models introduced 2005. Imported from Japan by Browning.

Price: BL-22 Grade I/II . . . . $462.00 /$524.00
Price: BL-22 FLD Grade I/II . . . . $494.00 /$555.00
Price: BL-22 FLD, Grade II Octagon $726.00
Price: BL-17 Grade I/II . . . . $484.00 /$546.00
Price: BL-17 FLD Grade I/II . . . . $516.00 /$577.00
Price: BL-17 FLD, Grade II Octagon $748.00

HENRY LEVER-ACTION 22

Caliber: 22 Long Rifle (15-shot). **Barrel:** 18-1/4" round. **Weight:** 5-1/2 lbs. **Length:** 34" overall. **Stock:** Walnut. **Sights:** Hooded blade front, open adjustable rear. **Features:** Polished blue finish; full-length tubular magazine; side ejection; receiver grooved for scope mounting. Introduced 1997. Made in U.S.A. by Henry Repeating Arms Co.

Price: $279.95
Price: Youth model (33" overall, 11-round 22 LR) $279.95

HENRY GOLDEN BOY 22 LEVER-ACTION RIFLE

Caliber: 22 LR, 22 Magnum, 16-shot. **Barrel:** 20" octagonal. **Weight:** 6.25 lbs. **Length:** 38" overall. **Stock:** American walnut. **Sights:** Blade front, open rear. **Features:** Brasslite receiver, brass buttplate, blued barrel and lever. Introduced 1998. Made in U.S.A. from Henry Repeating Arms Co.

Price: $409.95
Price: Magnum $485.00

HENRY PUMP-ACTION 22 PUMP RIFLE

Caliber: 22 LR, 15-shot. **Barrel:** 18.25". **Weight:** 5.5 lbs. **Length:** NA. **Stock:** American walnut. **Sights:** Bead on ramp front, open adjustable rear. **Features:** Polished blue finish; receiver groved for scope mount; grooved slide handle; two barrel bands. Introduced 1998. Made in U.S.A. from Henry Repeating Arms Co.

Price: $309.95

MARLIN MODEL 39A GOLDEN LEVER-ACTION RIFLE

Caliber: 22, S (26), L (21), LR (19), tubular mag. **Barrel:** 24" Micro-Groove®. **Weight:** 6-1/2 lbs. **Length:** 40" overall. **Stock:** Checkered American black walnut; Mar-Shield® finish. Swivel studs; rubber buttpad. **Sights:** Bead ramp front with detachable Wide-Scan™ hood, folding rear semi-buckhorn adjustable for windage and elevation. **Features:** Hammer block safety; rebounding hammer. Takedown action, receiver tapped for scope mount (supplied), offset hammer spur, gold-colored steel trigger. From Marlin Firearms.

Price: $552.00

Remington Model 572 BDL Deluxe Fieldmaster

Ruger Model 96/22

Ruger Model 96/17

Taurus 62R

Taurus 72C-SS

REMINGTON 572 BDL DELUXE FIELDMASTER PUMP RIFLE

Caliber: 22 S (20), L (17) or LR (15), tubular mag. **Barrel:** 21" round tapered. **Weight:** 5-1/2 lbs. **Length:** 40" overall. **Stock:** Walnut with checkered pistol grip and slide handle. **Sights:** Big game. **Features:** Cross-bolt safety; removing inner magazine tube converts rifle to single shot; receiver grooved for tip-off scope mount.
Price: **$407.00**

RUGER MODEL 96 LEVER-ACTION RIFLE

Caliber: 22 WMR, 9 rounds; 44 Magnum, 4 rounds; 17 HMR 9 rounds. **Barrel:** 18-1/2". **Weight:** 5-1/4 lbs. **Length:** 37-1/4" overall. **Stock:** Hardwood. **Sights:** Gold bead front, folding leaf rear. **Features:** Sliding cross button safety, visible cocking indicator; short-throw lever action. Introduced 1996. Made in U.S.A. by Sturm, Ruger & Co.
Price: 96/22M (22 WMR) **$390.00**
Price: 96/22M (44 Mag.) **$546.00**
Price: 96/17M (17 HMR) **$390.00**

TAURUS MODEL 62 PUMP RIFLE

Caliber: 22 LR, 12- or 13-shot. **Barrel:** 16-1/2" or 23" round. **Weight:** 72 oz. to 80 oz. **Length:** 39" overall. **Stock:** Premium hardwood. **Sights:** Adjustable rear, bead blade front, optional tang. **Features:** Blue, case hardened or stainless, bolt-mounted safety, pump action, manual firing pin block, integral security lock system. Imported from Brazil by Taurus International.
Price: M62C (blue) **$280.00**
Price: M62C-CH (case-hardened, blue) **$280.00**
Price: M62CCH-T (case-hardened, blue) **$358.00**
Price: M62C-SS (stainless steel) **$295.00**
Price: M62CSS-T (stainless steel) **$373.00**
Price: M62C-SS-Y (stainless steel) **$327.00**

Price: M62C-T (blue) **$358.00**
Price: M62C-Y (blue) **$311.00**
Price: M62R (blue) **$280.00**
Price: M62R-CH (case-hardened, blue) **$280.00**
Price: M62RCH-T (case-hardened, blue) **$358.00**
Price: M62R-SS (stainless steel) **$295.00**
Price: M62RSS-T (stainless steel) **$373.00**
Price: M62R-T (blue). **$358.00**

Taurus Model 72 Pump Rifle

Same as Model 62 except chambered in 22 Magnum or .17 HMR; 16-1/2" bbl. holds 10-12 shots, 23" bbl. holds 11-13 shots. Weighs 72 oz. to 80 oz. Introduced 2001. Imported from Brazil by Taurus International.
Price: M72C (blue) **$295.00**
Price: M72C-CH (case-hardened, blue) **$295.00**
Price: M72CCH-T (case-hardened, blue) **$373.00**
Price: M72C-SS (stainless steel) **$311.00**
Price: M72CSS-T (stainless steel) **$389.00**
Price: M72C-T (blue) **$373.00**
Price: M72R (blue) **$295.00**
Price: M72R-CH (case-hardened, blue) **$295.00**
Price: M72RCH-T (case-hardened, blue) **$373.00**
Price: M72R-SS (stainless steel) **$311.00**
Price: M72RSS-T (stainless steel) **$389.00**
Price: M72R-T (blue) **$373.00**

Includes models for a variety of sports, utility and competitive shooting.

Anschutz 1710D

Chipmunk Standard

Chipmunk Deluxe

ANSCHUTZ 1416D/1516D CLASSIC RIFLES
Caliber: 22 LR (1416D), 5-shot clip; 22 WMR (1516D), 4-shot clip. **Barrel:** 22-1/2". **Weight:** 6 lbs. **Length:** 41" overall. **Stock:** European hardwood with walnut finish; classic style with straight comb, checkered pistol grip and forend. **Sights:** Hooded ramp front, folding leaf rear. **Features:** Uses Match 64 action. Adjustable single stage trigger. Receiver grooved for scope mounting. Imported from Germany by AcuSport Corp.
Price: 1416D, 22 LR $755.95
Price: 1516D, 22 WMR $779.95
Price: 1416D Classic left-hand $679.95

Anschutz 1416D/1516D Walnut Luxus Rifles
Similar to the Classic models except have European walnut stocks with Monte Carlo cheekpiece, slim forend with Schnabel tip, cut checkering on grip and forend. Introduced 1997. Imported from Germany by AcuSport Corp.
Price: 1416D (22 LR) $755.95
Price: 1516D (22 WMR) $779.95

ANSCHUTZ 1518D LUXUS BOLT-ACTION RIFLE
Caliber: 22 WMR, 4-shot magazine. **Barrel:** 19-3/4". **Weight:** 5-1/2 lbs. **Length:** 37-1/2" overall. **Stock:** European walnut. **Sights:** Blade on ramp front, folding leaf rear. **Features:** Receiver grooved for scope mounting; single stage trigger; skip-line checkering; rosewood forend tip; sling swivels. Imported from Germany by AcuSport Corp.
Price: $1,186.95

ANSCHUTZ 1710D CUSTOM RIFLE
Caliber: 22 LR, 5-shot clip. **Barrel:** 24-1/4". **Weight:** 7-3/8 lbs. **Length:** 42-1/2" overall. **Stock:** Select European walnut. **Sights:** Hooded ramp front, folding leaf rear; drilled and tapped for scope mounting. **Features:** Match 54 action with adjustable single-stage trigger; roll-over Monte Carlo cheekpiece, slim forend with Schnabel tip, Wundhammer palm swell on pistol grip, rosewood gripcap with white diamond insert; skip-line checkering on grip and forend. Introduced 1988. Imported from Germany by AcuSport Corp.
Price: $1,289.95

CHARLES DALY SUPERIOR II RIMFIRE RIFLE
Caliber: 22LR, 22MRF, 17HRM. **Barrel:** 22". **Weight:** 6 pounds. **Sights:** None. Drilled and tapped for scope mounts. **Features:** Manufactured by Zastava. Walnut stock, two-position safety; 5-round magazine capacity. Introduced 2005.

Price: 22LR $259.00
Price: 22WMR $299.00
Price: 17HMR $334.00

CHIPMUNK SINGLE-SHOT RIFLE
Caliber: 22 LR, 22 WMR, single shot. **Barrel:** 16-1/8". **Weight:** About 2-1/2 lbs. **Length:** 30" overall. **Stocks:** American walnut. **Sights:** Post on ramp front, peep rear adjustable for windage and elevation. **Features:** Drilled and tapped for scope mounting using special Chipmunk base ($13.95). Engraved model also available. Made in U.S.A. Introduced 1982. From Rogue Rifle Co., Inc.
Price: Standard $194.25
Price: Standard 22 WMR $209.95
Price: Deluxe (better wood, checkering) $246.95
Price: Deluxe 22 WMR $262.95
Price: Laminated stock $209.95
Price: Laminated stock, 22 WMR $225.95
Price: Bull barrel models of above, add $16.00

CHIPMUNK TM (TARGET MODEL)
Caliber: 22 S, L, or LR. **Barrel:** 18" blue. **Weight:** 5 lbs. **Length:** 33". **Stocks:** Walnut with accessory rail. **Sights:** 1/4 minute micrometer adjustable. **Features:** Manually cocking single shot bolt action, blue receiver, adjustable buttplate and buttpad.
Price: $329.95

COOPER MODEL 57-M BOLT-ACTION RIFLE
Caliber: 22 LR, 22 WMR, 17 HMR, 17 Mach 2. **Barrel:** 22" or 24" stainless steel or 4140 match grade. **Weight:** 6.5-7.5 lbs. **Stock:** AA-AAA select Claro walnut, 22 lpi hand checkering. **Sights:** None furnished. **Features:** Three rear locking lug, repeating bolt-action with 5-shot mag. for 22 LR and 17M2; 4-shot mag for 22 WMR and 17 HMR. Fully adjustable trigger. Left-hand models add $150 to base rifle price. 1/4"-group rimfire accuracy guarantee at 50 yds.; 1/2"-group centerfire accuracy guarantee at 100 yds. Options include wood upgrades, case-color metalwork, barrel fluting, custom LOP, and many others.
Price: Classic $1,349.00
Price: LVT $1,459.00
Price: Custom Classic $1,995.00
Price: Western Classic $2,698.00
Price: TRP-3 (22 LR only, benchrest style) $1,295.00
Price: Jackson Squirrel Rifle $1,498.00
Price: Jackson Hunter (synthetic) $1,298.00

Cooper Model 57 Classic

Cooper Custom Classic

CZ 452 Lux

CZ 452 Varmint

CZ 452 American Classic

Henry "Mini" Bolt 22

CZ 452 LUX BOLT-ACTION RIFLE
Caliber: 22 LR, 22 WMR, 5-shot detachable magazine. **Barrel:** 24.8". **Weight:** 6.6 lbs. **Length:** 42.63" overall. **Stock:** Walnut with checkered pistol grip. **Sights:** Hooded front, fully adjustable tangent rear. **Features:** All-steel construction, adjustable trigger, polished blue finish. Imported from the Czech Republic by CZ-USA.
Price: 22 LR, 22 WMR **$378.00**

CZ 452 Varmint Rifle
Similar to the Lux model except has heavy 20.8" barrel; stock has beavertail forend; weighs 7 lbs.; no sights furnished. Available only in 22 LR. Imported from the Czech Republic by CZ-USA.
Price: **$407.00**

CZ 452 American Classic Bolt-Action Rifle
Similar to the CZ 452 M 2E Lux except has classic-style stock of Circassian walnut; 22.5" free-floating barrel with recessed target crown;

receiver dovetail for scope mounting. No open sights furnished. Introduced 1999. Imported from the Czech Republic by CZ-USA.
Price: 22 LR, 22 WMR **$420.00**

HARRINGTON & RICHARDSON
ULTRA HEAVY BARREL 22 MAG RIFLE
Caliber: 22 WMR, single shot. **Barrel:** 22" bull. **Stock:** Cinnamon laminated wood with Monte Carlo cheekpiece. **Sights:** None furnished; scope mount rail included. **Features:** Hand-checkered stock and forend; deep-crown rifling; tuned trigger; trigger locking system; hammer extension. Introduced 2001. From H&R 1871 LLC.
Price: **$193.00**

HENRY ACU-BOLT RIFLE
Caliber: 22, 22 Mag., 17HMR; single shot. **Barrel:** 20". **Weight:** 4.15 lbs. **Length:** 36". **Stock:** One-piece fiberglass synthetic. **Sights:** Scope mount and 4x scope included. **Features:** Stainless barrel and receiver, bolt-action.
Price: **$325.00**

HENRY "MINI" BOLT ACTION 22 RIFLE
Caliber: 22 LR, single shot youth gun. **Barrel:** 16" stainless, 8-groove rifling. **Weight:** 3.25 lbs. **Length:** 30", LOP 11-1/2". **Stock:** Synthetic, pistol grip, wraparound checkering and beavertail forearm. **Sights:** William Fire sights. **Features:** One-piece bolt configuration manually operated safety.
Price: **$169.95**

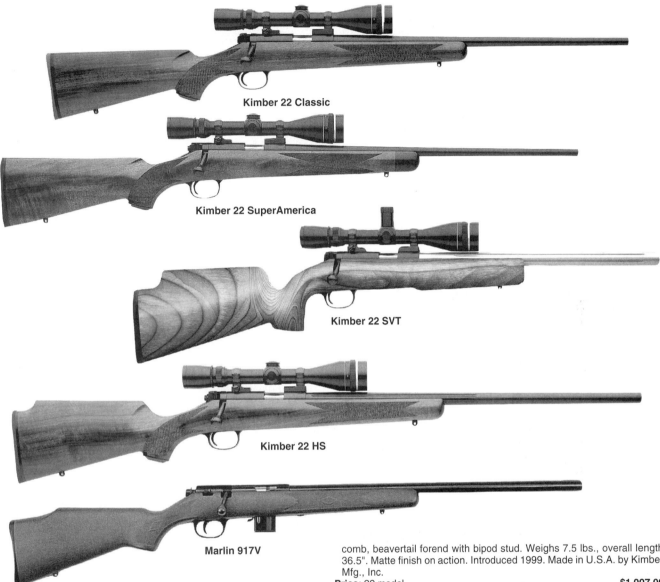

Kimber 22 Classic

Kimber 22 SuperAmerica

Kimber 22 SVT

Kimber 22 HS

Marlin 917V

KIMBER 22 CLASSIC BOLT-ACTION RIFLE

Caliber: 22 LR and 17 Mach 2, 5-shot magazine. **Barrel:** 18", 22", 24" match grade; 11-degree target crown. **Weight:** 5 to 8 lbs. **Length:** 35" to 43". **Stock:** Classic Claro walnut, hand-cut checkering, steel gripcap, swivel studs. **Sights:** None, drilled and tapped. **Features:** All-new action with Mauser-style full-length claw extractor, two-position wing safety, match trigger, pillar-bedded action with recoil lug. Introduced 1999. Made in U.S.A. by Kimber Mfg., Inc.

Price: Classic 22 . . . . **$1,147.00**
Price: Classic Varmint (22 or 17M2) **$1,055.00**
Price: Hunter (22) **$809.00**
Price: Hunter (17M2) **$846.00**

Kimber 22 SuperAmerica Bolt-Action Rifle

Similar to 22 Classic except has AAA Claro walnut stock with wraparound 22 lpi hand-cut checkering, ebony forend tip, beaded cheekpiece. Introduced 1999. Made in U.S.A. by Kimber Mfg., Inc.

Price: **$1,865.00**

Kimber 22 SVT Bolt-Action Rifle

Similar to 22 Classic except has 18" stainless steel, fluted bull barrel, gray laminated, high-comb target-style stock with deep pistol grip, high comb, beavertail forend with bipod stud. Weighs 7.5 lbs., overall length 36.5". Matte finish on action. Introduced 1999. Made in U.S.A. by Kimber Mfg., Inc.

Price: 22 model **$1,007.00**
Price: 17M2 model **$1,055.00**

Kimber 22 HS (Hunter Silhouette) Bolt-Action Rifle

Similar to 22 Classic except 24" medium sporter match-grade barrel with half-fluting; high comb, walnut, Monte Carlo target stock with 18 lpi checkering; matte blue metal finish. Introduced 1999. Made in U.S.A. by Kimber Mfg., Inc.

Price: **$915.00**

MARLIN MODEL 917/717 17 HMR/17 MACH 2 BOLT-ACTION RIFLES

Caliber: 17 HMR, 17 Mach 2, 7-shot. **Barrel:** 22". **Weight:** 6 lbs., stainless 7 lbs. **Length:** 41". **Stock:** Checkered walnut Monte Carlo SS, laminated black/grey. **Sights:** No sights but receiver grooved. **Features:** Swivel studs, positive thumb safety, red cocking indicator, safety lock, SS 1" brushed aluminum scope rings.

Price: 917 (new version 17 HMR intr. 2006, black synthetic stock) . **$269.00**
Price: 917V (17 HMR, walnut-finished hardwood stock) **$292.00**
Price: 917VS (17 HMR, heavy stainless barrel) **$433.00**
Price: 917VR (17 HMR, intr. 2006, heavy barrel) **$282.00**
Price: 917VR (17 HMR, heavy stainless fluted barrel) **$459.00**
Price: 917M2 (17 Mach 2, walnut-finished hardwood stock) **$274.00**
Price: 917M2S (17 Mach 2, 22" heavy stainless barrel) **$410.00**

Marlin Model 15YN "Little Buckaroo"

Marlin Model 980S

Marlin 880V

Marlin 925

Marlin 925C

MARLIN MODEL 915YN "LITTLE BUCKAROO"

Caliber: 22 S, L, LR, single shot. **Barrel:** 16-1/4" Micro-Groove®. **Weight:** 4-1/4 lbs. **Length:** 33-1/4" overall. **Stock:** One-piece walnut-finished, press-checkered Maine birch with Monte Carlo; Mar-Shield® finish. **Sights:** Ramp front, adjustable open rear. **Features:** Beginner's rifle with thumb safety, easy-load feed throat, red cocking indicator. Receiver grooved for scope mounting. Introduced 1989.

Price: **$225.00**
Price: 915YS (stainless steel with fire sights) **$255.00**

MARLIN MODEL 980S BOLT-ACTION RIFLE

Caliber: 22 LR, 7-shot clip magazine. **Barrel:** 22" Micro-Groove®. **Weight:** 6 lbs. **Length:** 41" overall. **Stock:** Black fiberglass-filled synthetic with nickel-plated swivel studs and molded-in checkering. **Sights:** Ramp front with orange post and cutaway Wide-Scan™ hood, adjustable semi-buckhorn folding rear. **Features:** Stainless steel barrel, receiver, front breech bolt and striker; receiver grooved for scope mounting. Introduced 1994. Model 880SQ (Squirrel Rifle) is similar but has heavy 22" barrel. Made in U.S.A. by Marlin.

Price: 980S **$349.00**
Price: 980V, heavy target barrel, 7 lbs., no sights. **$349.00**

Marlin Model 981T Bolt-Action Rifle

Same as Marlin 980S except blued steel, tubular magazine, holds 17 Long Rifle cartridges. Weighs 6 lbs.

Price: **$229.00**

Marlin Model 925 Bolt-Action Repeater

Similar to Marlin 980S, except walnut-finished hardwood stock, adjustable open rear sight, ramp front. Weighs 5.5 lbs.

Price: **$229.00**
Price: With 4x scope and mount **$239.00**

Marlin Model 925R Bolt-Action Repeater

Similar to Marlin 925, except Monte Carlo black-fiberglass synthetic stock. Weighs 5.5 lbs. OAL: 41". Introduced 2006.

Price: **$229.00**
Price: With 4x scope and mount **$239.00**

Marlin Model 925C Bolt-Action Repeater

Same as Model 980S except Mossy Oak® Break-Up camouflage stock. Made in U.S.A. by Marlin. Weighs 5.5 lbs.

Price: **$268.00**

Marlin 983T

Ruger K77/22 Varmint

Ruger 77/22R

MARLIN MODEL 982 BOLT-ACTION RIFLE

Caliber: 22 WMR. **Barrel:** 22" Micro-Groove®. **Weight:** 6 lbs. **Length:** 41" overall. **Stock:** Walnut Monte Carlo genuine American black walnut with swivel studs; full pistol grip; classic cut checkering; rubber rifle butt pad; tough Mar-Shield® finish. **Sights:** Adjustable semi-buckhorn folding rear, ramp front sight with brass bead and Wide-Scan™ front sight hood. **Features:** 7-shot clip, thumb safety, red cocking indicator, receiver grooved for scope mount. 982S has stainless steel front breech bolt, barrel, receiver and bolt knob. All other parts are either stainless steel or nickel-plated. Has black Monte Carlo stock of fiberglass-filled polycarbonate with molded-in checkering, nickel-plated swivel studs. Introduced 2005. Model 982S has selected heavy 22" stainless steel barrel with recessed muzzle, and comes without sights; receiver is grooved for scope mount and 1" ring mounts are included. Weighs 7 lbs. Introduced 1997. Made in U.S.A. by Marlin Firearms Co.

Price: 982. . . . . **$341.00**
Price: 982L (laminated hardwood stock, 6.25 lbs). **$361.00**
Price: 982S (stainless parts, 6.25 lbs). **$377.00**
Price: 982VS (heavy stainless barrel, 7 lbs). **$357.00**

Marlin Model 925M/925MC Bolt-Action Rifles

Similar to the Model 982 except chambered for 22 WMR. Has 7-shot clip magazine, 22" Micro-Groove® barrel, checkered walnut-finished Maine birch stock. Introduced 1989.

Price: 925M **$260.00**
Price: 925MC (Mossy Oak Break-Up camouflage stock) **$300.00**

MARLIN MODEL 983 BOLT-ACTION RIFLE

Caliber: 22 WMR. **Barrel:** 22"; 1:16" twist. **Weight:** 6 lbs. **Length:** 41" overall. **Stock:** Walnut Monte Carlo with sling swivel studs, rubber buttpad. **Sights:** Ramp front with brass bead, removable hood; adjustable semi-buckhorn folding rear. **Features:** Thumb safety, red cocking indicator, receiver grooved for scope mount. 983S is same as the Model 983 except front breech bolt, striker knob, trigger stud, cartridge lifter stud and outer magazine tube are of stainless steel; other parts are nickel-plated. Introduced 1993. 983T has a black Monte Carlo fiberglass-filled synthetic stock with sling swivel studs. Introduced 2001.Made in U.S.A. by Marlin Firearms Co.

Price: 983. . . . . **$356.00**
Price: 983S (stainless barrel) **$377.00**
Price: 983T (fiberglass stock) **$273.00**

MEACHAM LOW-WALL RIFLE

Caliber: any rimfire cartridge. **Barrel:** 26-34". **Weight:** 7-15 lbs. **Sights**: none. Tang drilled for Win. base, 3/8 dovetail slot front. **Stock:** Fancy eastern walnut with cheekpiece; ebony insert in forearm tip. **Features**: Exact copy of 1885 Winchester. With most Winchester factory options available including double set triggers. Introduced 1994. Made in U.S.A. by Meacham T&H Inc.

Price: From **$3,899.00**

NEW ENGLAND FIREARMS SPORTSTER™ SINGLE-SHOT RIFLES

Caliber: 22 LR, 22 WMR, 17 HMR, single-shot. **Barrel:** 20". **Weight:** 5-1/2 lbs. **Length:** 36-1/4" overall. **Stock:** Black polymer. **Sights:** None furnished; scope mount included. **Features:** Break open, side-lever release; automatic ejection; recoil pad; sling swivel studs; trigger locking system. Introduced 2001. Made in U.S.A. by New England Firearms.

Price: **$149.00**
Price: Youth model (20" bbl., 33" overall, weighs 5-1/3 lbs.) **$149.00**
Price: Sportster 17 HMR **$180.00**

NEW ULTRA LIGHT ARMS 20RF BOLT-ACTION RIFLE

Caliber: 22 LR, single shot or repeater. **Barrel:** Douglas, length to order. **Weight:** 5-1/4 lbs. **Length:** Varies. **Stock:** Kevlar®/graphite composite, variety of finishes. **Sights:** None furnished; drilled and tapped for scope mount. **Features:** Timney trigger, hand-lapped action, button-rifled barrel, hand-bedded action, recoil pad, sling-swivel studs, optional Jewell trigger. Made in U.S.A. by New Ultra Light Arms.

Price: 20 RF single shot **$800.00**
Price: 20 RF repeater **$850.00**

ROSSI MATCHED PAIR SINGLE-SHOT RIFLE/SHOTGUN

Caliber: 22 LR or 22 Mag. **Barrel:** 18-1/2" or 23". **Weight:** 6 lbs. **Stock:** Hardwood (brown or black finish). **Sights:** Fully adjustable front and rear. **Features:** Break-open breech, transfer-bar manual safety, includes matched 410-, 20 or 12 gauge shotgun barrel with bead front sight. Introduced 2001. Imported by BrazTech/Taurus.

Price: Blue. **$139.95**
Price: Stainless steel **$169.95**

RUGER K77/22 VARMINT RIFLE

Caliber: 22 LR, 10-shot, 22 WMR, 9-shot detachable rotary magazine. **Barrel:** 24", heavy. **Weight:** 6-7/8 lbs. **Length:** 43.25" overall. **Stock:** Laminated hardwood with rubber buttpad, quick-detachable swivel studs. **Sights:** None furnished. Comes with Ruger 1" scope rings. **Features:** Stainless steel or blued finish. Three-position safety, dual extractors. Stock has wide, flat forend. Introduced 1993.

Price: K77/22VBZ, 22 LR **$746.00**
Price: K77/22VMBZ, 22 WMR **$746.00**

RUGER 77/22 RIMFIRE BOLT-ACTION RIFLE

Caliber: 22 LR, 10-shot rotary magazine; 22 WMR, 9-shot rotary magazine. **Barrel:** 20". **Weight:** About 6 lbs. **Length:** 39-3/4" overall. **Stock:** Checkered American walnut, laminated hardwood, or synthetic stocks, stainless sling swivels. **Sights:** Plain barrel with 1" Ruger rings. **Features:** Mauser-type action uses Ruger's rotary magazine. Three-position safety, simplified bolt stop, patented bolt locking system. Uses the dual-screw barrel attachment system of the 10/22 rifle. Integral scope mounting system with 1" Ruger rings. Blued model introduced 1983. Stainless steel and blued with synthetic stock introduced 1989.

Price: 77/22R (no sights, rings, walnut stock) **$674.00**
Price: K77/22RP (stainless, no sights, rings, synthetic stock) **$674.00**
Price: 77/22RM (22 WMR, blue, walnut stock) **$674.00**
Price: K77/22RMP (22 WMR, stainless, synthetic stock) **$674.00**

Savage Mark I-G

Savage Mark II-BV

Savage Mark II-FXP

Savage Mark II-FSS

Savage Model 93G

RUGER 77/17 RIMFIRE BOLT-ACTION RIFLE

Caliber: 17HMR (9-shot rotary magazine); 17 Mach 2 (10-shot rotary magazine). **Barrel:** 20" to 24". **Weight:** 6-7.5 lbs. **Length:** 39"-to 41.75" overall. **Stock:** Checkered American walnut, laminated hardwood, or synthetic stocks, stainless sling swivels. **Sights:** Plain barrel with 1" Ruger rings. **Features:** Mauser-type action uses Ruger's rotary magazine. Three-position safety, simplified bolt stop, patented bolt locking system. Uses the dual-screw barrel attachment system of the 10/22 rifle. Integral scope mounting system with 1" Ruger rings. Introduced 2002.

Price: 77/17RM (no sights, rings, walnut stock) **$674.00**
Price: 77/17RMP (stainless, no sights, rings, synthetic stock) **$674.00**
Price: K77/17VMBBZ (Target grey bbl, black laminate stock) **$746.00**
Price: 77/17RMP (blued, walnut stock) **$674.00**
Price: K77/17VM2BBZ (Target grey bbl, black laminate stock) **$746.00**

SAVAGE MARK I-G BOLT-ACTION RIFLE

Caliber: 22 LR, single shot. **Barrel:** 20-3/4". **Weight:** 5-1/2 lbs. **Length:** 39-1/2" overall. **Stock:** Walnut-finished hardwood with Monte Carlo-type comb, checkered grip and forend. **Sights:** Bead front, open adjustable rear. Receiver grooved for scope mounting. **Features:** Thumb-operated rotating safety. Blue finish. Rifled or smooth bore. Introduced 1990. Made in Canada, from Savage Arms Inc.

Price: Mark IG, rifled or smooth bore, right- or left-handed **$152.00**
Price: Mark I-GY (Youth), 19" bbl., 37" overall, 5 lbs. **$152.00**
Price: Mark I-LY (Youth), 19" bbl., color laminate **$187.00**
Price: Mark I-GSB (22 LR shot cartridge) **$152.00**

SAVAGE MARK II BOLT-ACTION RIFLE

Caliber: 22 LR, 10-shot magazine. **Barrel:** 20-1/2". **Weight:** 5-1/2 lbs. **Length:** 39-1/2" overall. **Stock:** Walnut-finished hardwood with Monte Carlo-type comb, checkered grip and forend. **Sights:** Bead front, open adjustable rear. Receiver grooved for scope mounting. **Features:** Thumb-operated rotating safety. Blue finish. Introduced 1990. Made in Canada, from Savage Arms, Inc.

Price: Mark II-BV **$264.00**
Price: Mark II Camo **$184.00**
Price: Mark II-GY (youth), 19" barrel, 37" overall, 5 lbs. **$169.00**
Price: Mark II-GL, left-hand **$169.00**
Price: Mark II-GLY (youth) left-hand **$169.00**
Price: Mark II-FXP (as above with black synthetic stock) **$158.00**
Price: Mark II-F (as above, no scope) **$151.00**

Savage Mark II-FSS Stainless Rifle

Similar to the Mark II except has stainless steel barreled action and black synthetic stock with positive checkering, swivel studs, and 20.75" free-floating and button-rifled barrel with detacheable magazine. Weighs 5.5 lbs. Introduced 1997. Imported from Canada by Savage Arms, Inc.
Price: **$213.00**

SAVAGE MODEL 93G MAGNUM BOLT-ACTION RIFLE

Caliber: 22 WMR, 5-shot magazine. **Barrel:** 20-3/4". **Weight:** 5-3/4 lbs. **Length:** 39-1/2" overall. **Stock:** Walnut-finished hardwood with Monte Carlo-type comb, checkered grip and forend. **Sights:** Bead front, adjustable open rear. Receiver grooved for scope mount. **Features:** Thumb-operated rotary safety. Blue finish. Introduced 1994. Made in Canada, from Savage Arms.
Price: **$195.00**
Price: Model 93F (as above with black graphite/fiberglass stock) . . **$187.00**

Savage Model 93FSS

Savage Model 93FVSS

Savage Model 30G Stevens "Favorite"

Savage Cub G Youth

Winchester Model 1885 Low Wall

Savage Model 93FSS Magnum Rifle
Similar to Model 93G except stainless steel barreled action and black synthetic stock with positive checkering. Weighs 5-1/2 lbs. Introduced 1997. Imported from Canada by Savage Arms, Inc.
Price: $236.00

Savage Model 93FVSS Magnum Rifle
Similar to Model 93FSS Magnum except 21" heavy barrel with recessed target-style crown, satin-finished stainless barreled action, black graphite/fiberglass stock. Drilled and tapped for scope mounting; comes with Weaver-style bases. Introduced 1998. Imported from Canada by Savage Arms, Inc.
Price: $267.00
Price: With scope $305.00

SAVAGE MODEL 30G STEVENS "FAVORITE"
Caliber: 22 LR, 22WMR Model 30GM, 17 HMR Model 30R17. **Barrel:** 21".
Weight: 4.25 lbs. **Length:** 36.75". **Stock:** Walnut, straight grip, Schnabel forend. **Sights:** Adjustable rear, bead post front. **Features:** Lever action falling block, inertia firing pin system, Model 30G half octagonal bbl. Model 30GM full octagonal bbl.
Price: Model 30G $228.00
Price: Model 30GM $266.00
Price: Model 30R17 . . . . $292.00

SAVAGE CUB G YOUTH
Caliber: 22 S, L, LR; 17 Mach 2. **Barrel:** 16.125" **Weight:** 3.3 lbs. **Length:** 33" **Stock:** Walnut finished hardwood. **Sights:** Bead post, front; peep, rear. **Features:** Mini single shot bolt action, free-floating button-rifled barrel, blued finish. From Savage Arms.
Price: 22 S, L, LR $156.00
Price: 17 Mach 2 . . . . $165.00

WINCHESTER MODEL 1885 LOW WALL RIMFIRE
Caliber: 17 Mach 2. **Barrel:** 24". **Weight:** 8 lbs. **Length:** 41" overall. **Stock:** Walnut. **Features:** Drilled and tapped for scope mount or tang sight. Case-colored receiver, buttplate and lever, fine-line checkering.
Price: Grade I $1,014.00

*Includes models for classic American and ISU target competition
and other sporting and competitive shooting.*

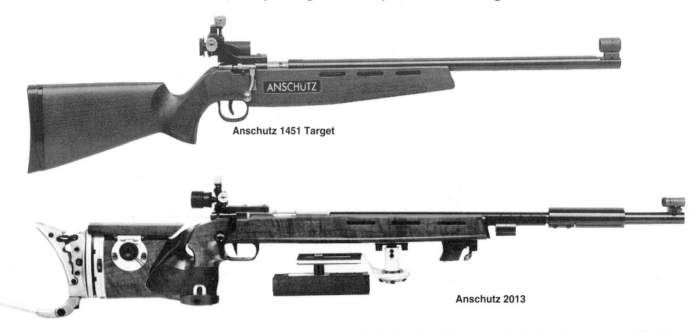

Anschutz 1451 Target

Anschutz 2013

ANSCHUTZ 1451R SPORTER TARGET RIFLE

Caliber: 22 LR, 5-shot magazine. **Barrel:** 22" heavy match. **Weight:** 6.4 lbs. **Length:** 39.75" overall. **Stock:** European hardwood with walnut finish. **Sights:** None furnished. Grooved receiver for scope mounting or Anschutz micrometer rear sight. **Features:** Sliding safety, two-stage trigger. Adjustable buttplate; forend slide rail to accept Anschutz accessories. Imported from Germany by GSI.
Price: **$549.00**

ANSCHUTZ 1451 TARGET RIFLE

Caliber: 22 LR. **Barrel:** 22". **Weight:** About 6.5 lbs. **Length:** 40". **Sights:** Optional. Receiver grooved for scope mounting. **Features:** Designed for the beginning junior shooter with adjustable length of pull from 13.25" to 14.25" via removable butt spacers. Two-stage trigger factory set at 2.6 lbs. Introduced 1999. Imported from Germany by Gunsmithing, Inc.
Price: **$347.00**
Price: #6834 Match Sight Set **$227.10**

ANSCHUTZ 1808D-RT SUPER RUNNING TARGET RIFLE

Caliber: 22 LR, single shot. **Barrel:** 32-1/2". **Weight:** 9 lbs. **Length:** 50" overall. **Stock:** European walnut. Heavy beavertail forend; adjustable cheekpiece and buttplate. Stippled grip and forend. **Sights:** None furnished. Grooved for scope mounting. **Features:** Designed for Running Target competition. Nine-way adjustable single-stage trigger, slide safety. Introduced 1991. Imported from Germany by Gunsmithing, Inc.
Price: Right-hand. **$1,364.10**

ANSCHUTZ 1903 MATCH RIFLE

Caliber: 22 LR, single shot. **Barrel:** 25.5", .75" diameter. **Weight:** 10.1 lbs. **Length:** 43.75" overall. **Stock:** Walnut-finished hardwood with adjustable cheekpiece; stippled grip and forend. **Sights:** None furnished. **Features:** Uses Anschutz Match 64 action and #5098 two-stage trigger. A medium weight rifle for intermediate and advanced Junior Match competition. Introduced 1987. Imported from Germany by Gunsmithing, Inc.
Price: Right-hand. **$720.40**
Price: Left-hand **$757.90**

ANSCHUTZ 64-MS R SILHOUETTE RIFLE

Caliber: 22 LR, 5-shot magazine. **Barrel:** 21-1/2", medium heavy; 7/8" diameter. **Weight:** 8 lbs. **Length:** 39.5" overall. **Stock:** Walnut-finished hardwood, silhouette-type. **Sights:** None furnished. **Features:** Uses

Match 64 action. Designed for metallic silhouette competition. Stock has stippled checkering, contoured thumb groove with Wundhammer swell. Two-stage #5098 trigger. Slide safety locks sear and bolt. Introduced 1980. Imported from Germany by AcuSport Corp., Gunsmithing, Inc.
Price: 64-MS R **$704.30**

ANSCHUTZ 2013 BENCHREST RIFLE

Caliber: 22 LR, single shot. **Barrel:** 19.6". **Weight:** About 10.3 lbs. **Length:** 37.75" to 42.5" overall. **Stock:** Benchrest style of European hardwood. Stock length adjustable via spacers and buttplate. **Sights:** None furnished. Receiver grooved for mounts. **Features:** Uses the Anschutz 2013 target action; two-stage adjustable target trigger factory set at 3.9 oz. Introduced 1994. Imported from Germany by Gunsmithing, Inc.
Price: **$1,757.20**

Anschutz 2007 Match Rifle

Uses same action as the Model 2013, but has a lighter barrel. European walnut stock in right-hand, true left-hand or extra-short models. Sights optional. Available with 19.6" barrel with extension tube, or 26", both in stainless or blue. Introduced 1998. Imported from Germany by Gunsmithing, Inc.
Price: Right-hand, blue, no sights. **$1,766.60**
Price: Right-hand, blue, no sights, extra-short stock **$1,756.60**
Price: Left-hand, blue, no sights **$1,856.80**

ANSCHUTZ 1827 BIATHLON RIFLE

Caliber: 22 LR, 5-shot magazine. **Barrel:** 21-1/2". **Weight:** 8-1/2 lbs. with sights. **Length:** 42-1/2" overall. **Stock:** European walnut with cheekpiece, stippled pistol grip and forend. **Sights:** Optional globe front specially designed for Biathlon shooting, micrometer rear with hinged snow cap. **Features:** Uses Super Match 54 action and nine-way adjustable trigger; adjustable wooden buttplate, biathlon butthook, adjustable hand-stop rail. Introduced 1982. Imported from Germany by Gunsmithing, Inc.
Price: Right-hand, with sights, about .... **$1,500.50 to $1,555.00**

Anschutz 1827BT Fortner Biathlon Rifle

Similar to the Anschutz 1827 Biathlon rifle except uses Anschutz/Fortner system straight-pull bolt action, blued or stainless steel barrel. Introduced 1982. Imported from Germany by Gunsmithing, Inc.
Price: Right-hand, with sights .... **$1,908.00 to $2,210.00**
Price: Left-hand, with sights .... **$2,099.20 to $2,395.00**
Price: Right-hand, sights, stainless barrel **$2,045.20**

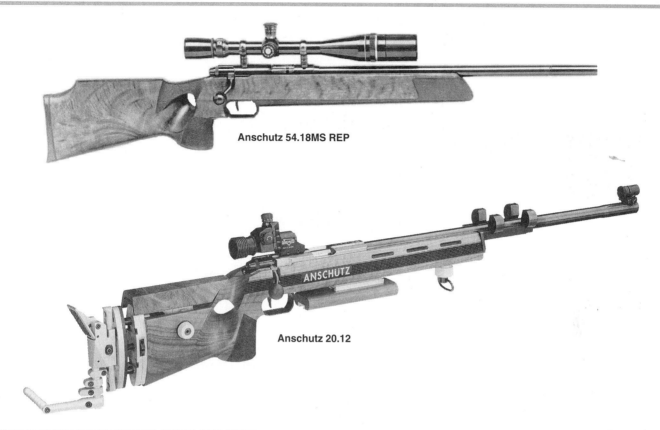

Anschutz 54.18MS REP

Anschutz 20.12

ANSCHUTZ SUPER MATCH SPECIAL MODEL 2013 RIFLE

Caliber: 22 LR, single shot. **Barrel:** 25.9". **Weight:** 13 lbs. **Length:** 41.7" to 42.9". **Stock:** A thumbhole version made of European walnut, both the cheekpiece and buttplate are highly adjustable. **Sights:** None furnished. **Features:** Developed by Anschütz for women to shoot in the sport rifle category. Stainless or blue. Introduced in 1997.
Price: Right-hand, blue, no sights, walnut **$2,219.30**
Price: Right-hand, stainless, no sights, walnut **$2,345.30**
Price: Left-hand, blue, no sights, walnut **$2,319.50**

ANSCHUTZ 2012 SPORT RIFLE

Caliber: 22 LR, 5-shot magazine. **Barrel:** 22.4" match; detachable muzzle tube. **Weight:** 7.9 lbs. **Length:** 40.9" overall. **Stock:** European walnut, thumbhole design. **Sights:** None furnished. **Features:** Uses Anschutz 54.18 barreled action with two-stage match trigger. Introduced 1997. Imported from Germany by AcuSport Corp.
Price: . . . . **$1,425.00 to $2,219.95**

ANSCHUTZ 1911 PRONE MATCH RIFLE

Caliber: 22 LR, single shot. **Barrel:** 27-1/4". **Weight:** 11 lbs. **Length:** 46" overall. **Stock:** Walnut-finished European hardwood; American prone-style with adjustable cheekpiece, textured pistol grip, forend with swivel rail and adjustable rubber buttplate. **Sights:** None furnished. Receiver grooved for Anschutz sights (extra). **Features:** Two-stage trigger adjustable from 2.1 to 8.6 oz. Extremely fast lock time. Stainless or blue barrel. Imported from Germany by Gunsmithing, Inc.
Price: Right-hand, no sights **$1,714.20**

ANSCHUTZ 1912 SPORT RIFLE

Caliber: 22 LR, single shot. **Barrel:** 25.9". **Weight:** About 11.4 lbs. **Length:** 41.7 to 42.9". **Stock:** European walnut or aluminum. **Sights:** None furnished. **Features:** Lightweight sport rifle version of the 1913 but weighs 1.5 pounds less. Stainless or blue barrel. Introduced 1997.
Price: Right-hand, blue, no sights, walnut **$1,789.50**
Price: Right-hand, blue, no sights, aluminum **$2,129.80**
Price: Right-hand, stainless, no sights, walnut **$1,910.30**
Price: Left-hand, blue, no sights, walnut **$1,879.00**

Anschutz 1913 Super Match Rifle

Same as the Model 1911 except European walnut International-type stock with adjustable cheekpiece, or color laminate, both available with straight or lowered forend, adjustable aluminum hook buttplate, adjustable hand stop, weighs 15.5 lbs., 46" overall. Stainless or blue barrel. Imported from Germany by Gunsmithing, Inc.
Price: Right-hand, blue, no sights, walnut stock . . . . **$2,139.00 to $2,175.00**
Price: Right-hand, blue, no sights, color laminate stock **$2,199.40**
Price: Right-hand, blue, no sights, walnut, lowered forend **$2,181.80**
Price: Right-hand, blue, no sights, color laminate,
lowered forend **$2,242.20**
Price: Left-hand, blue, no sights, walnut stock . . . . **$2,233.10 to $2,275.00**

Anschutz 54.18MS REP Deluxe Silhouette Rifle

Same basic action and trigger specifications as the Anschutz 1913 Super Match but with removable 5-shot clip magazine, 22.4" barrel extendable to 30" using optional extension and weight set. Weight is 8.1 lbs. Receiver drilled and tapped for scope mounting. Stock is thumbhole silhouette version or standard silhouette version, both are European walnut. Introduced 1990. Imported from Germany by Gunsmithing, Inc.
Price: Thumbhole stock **$1,461.40**
Price: Standard stock **$1,212.10**

Anschutz 1907 Standard Match Rifle

Same action as Model 1913 but with 7/8" diameter 26" barrel (stainless or blue). Length is 44.5" overall, weighs 10.5 lbs. Choice of stock configurations. Vented forend. Designed for prone and position shooting ISU requirements; suitable for NRA matches. Also available with walnut flat-forend stock for benchrest shooting. Imported from Germany by Gunsmithing, Inc.
Price: Right-hand, blue, no sights,
hardwood stock . . . . **$1,253.40 to $1,299.00**
Price: Right-hand, blue, no sights, colored laminated
stock . . . . **$1,316.10 to $1,375.00**
Price: Right-hand, blue, no sights, walnut stock **$1,521.10**
Price: Left-hand, blue barrel, no sights, walnut stock **$1,584.60**

Anschutz 1907

ArmaLite AR-10(T)

Bushmaster A2

Bushmaster DCM

ARMALITE AR-10(T) RIFLE

Caliber: 308, 10-shot magazine. **Barrel:** 24" target-weight Rock 5R custom. **Weight:** 10.4 lbs. **Length:** 43.5" overall. **Stock:** Green or black compostion; N.M. fiberglass handguard tube. **Sights:** Detachable handle, front sight, or scope mount available. Comes with international-style flattop receiver with Picatinny rail. **Features:** National Match two-stage trigger. Forged upper receiver. Receivers hard-coat anodized. Introduced 1995. Made in U.S.A. by ArmaLite, Inc.
Price: Green. **$2,126.00**
Price: Black **$2,126.00**

ARMALITE M15A4(T) EAGLE EYE RIFLE

Caliber: 223, 10-round magazine. **Barrel:** 24" heavy stainless; 1:8" twist. **Weight:** 9.2 lbs. **Length:** 42-3/8" overall. **Stock:** Green or black butt, N.M. fiberglass handguard tube. **Sights:** One-piece international-style flattop receiver with Weaver-type rail, including case deflector. **Features:** Detachable carry handle, front sight and scope mount (30mm or 1") available. Upper and lower receivers have push-type pivot pin, hard coat anodized. Made in U.S.A. by ArmaLite, Inc.
Price: Green. **$1,378.00**
Price: Black **$1,504.00**

BLASER R93 LONG RANGE RIFLE

Caliber: 308 Win., 10-shot detachable box magazine. **Barrel:** 24". **Weight:** 10.4 lbs. **Length:** 44" overall. **Stock:** Aluminum with synthetic lining. **Sights:** None furnished; accepts detachable scope mount. **Features:** Straight-pull bolt action with adjustable trigger; fully adjustable stock; quick takedown; corrosion resistant finish. Introduced 1998. Imported from Germany by SIGARMS.
Price: **$2,360.00**

BUSHMASTER A2 RIFLE

Caliber: 308, 5.56mm. **Barrel:** 16", 20". **Weight:** 8.3 lbs. **Length:** 38.25" overall (20" barrel). **Stock:** Black composition; A2 type. **Sights:** Adjustable post front, adjustable aperture rear. **Features:** Patterned after Colt M-16A2. Chrome-lined barrel with manganese phosphate exterior. Forged aluminum receivers with push-pin takedown. Available in stainless barrel and camo stock versions. Made in U.S.A. by Bushmaster Firearms Co.
Price: 20" match heavy barrel (A2 type). . . . . **$1,025.00 to $1,185.00**
Price: (A3 type) **$1,135.00**

BUSHMASTER DCM COMPETITION RIFLE

Caliber: 223. **Barrel:** 20" extra-heavy (1" diameter) barrel with 1.8" twist for heavier competition bullets. **Weight:** Appx. 12 lbs. with balance weights. **Length:** NA. **Stock:** NA. **Sights:** A2 rear sight. **Features:** Has special competition rear sight with interchangeable apertures, extra-fine 1/2- or 1/4-MOA windage and elevation adjustments; specially ground front sight post in choice of three widths. Full-length handguards over free-floater barrel tube. Introduced 1998. Made in U.S.A. by Bushmaster Firearms, Inc.
Price: **$1,395.00**

Colt Accurized

Colt Match Target HBAR

Colt Match Target HBAR II

EAA/Izhmash URAL 5.1

BUSHMASTER VARMINTER RIFLE

Caliber: 5.56mm. **Barrel:** 24", fluted. **Weight:** 8.4 lbs. **Length:** 42.25" overall. **Stock:** Black composition, A2 type. **Sights:** None furnished; upper receiver has integral scope mount base. **Features:** Chrome-lined .950" extra heavy barrel with counter-bored crown, manganese phosphate finish, free-floating aluminum handguard, forged aluminum receivers with push-pin takedown, hard anodized mil-spec finish. Competition trigger optional. Made in U.S.A. by Bushmaster Firearms, Inc.
Price: 20" Match heavy barrel **$1,265.00**
Price: Stainless barrel **$1,265.00**

COLT MATCH TARGET MODEL RIFLE

Caliber: 223 Rem., 8-shot magazine. **Barrel:** 20". **Weight:** 7.5 lbs. **Length:** 39" overall. **Stock:** Composition stock, grip, forend. **Sights:** Post front, aperture rear adjustable for windage and elevation. **Features:** Five-round detachable box magazine, standard-weight barrel, sling swivels. Has forward bolt assist. Military matte black finish. Introduced 1991.
Price: **$1,144.00**
Price: With compensator **$1,150.00**

Colt Accurized Rifle

Similar to the Match Target Model except has 24" barrel. Features flat-top receiver for scope mounting, stainless steel heavy barrel, tubular handguard, and free-floating barrel. Matte black finish. Weighs 9.25 lbs. Made in U.S.A. by Colt's Mfg. Co., Inc.
Price: Model CR6724 . . . . **$1,290.00 to $1,470.00**

Colt Match Target HBAR Rifle

Similar to the Target Model except has heavy barrel, 800-meter rear sight adjustable for windage and elevation, 9-round capacity. Weighs 8 lbs. Introduced 1991.
Price: Model MT6601, MT6601C **$1,300.00**

Colt Match Target Competition HBAR Rifle

Similar to the Match Target except has removeable carry handle for scope mounting, 1:9" rifling twist, 9-round magazine. Weighs 8.5 lbs. Introduced 1991.
Price: Model MT6700, MT6700C **$1,315.00**

Colt Match Target Competition HBAR II Rifle

Similar to the Match Target Competition HBAR except has 16:1" barrel, overall length 34.5", and weighs 7.1 lbs. Introduced 1995.
Price: Model MT6731 . . . . **$1,290.00**

EAA/HW 660 MATCH RIFLE

Caliber: 22 LR. **Barrel:** 26". **Weight:** 10.7 lbs. **Length:** 45.3" overall. **Stock:** Match-type walnut with adjustable cheekpiece and buttplate. **Sights:** Globe front, match aperture rear. **Features:** Adjustable match trigger; stippled pistol grip and forend; forend accessory rail. Introduced 1991. Imported from Germany by European American Armory.
Price: About. **$999.00**
Price: With laminate stock **$1,159.00**

EAA/IZHMASH URAL 5.1 TARGET RIFLE

Caliber: 22 LR. **Barrel:** 26.5". **Weight:** 11.3 lbs. **Length:** 44.5". **Stock:** Wood, international style. **Sights:** Adjustable click rear, hooded front with inserts. **Features:** Forged barrel with rifling, adjustable trigger, aluminum rail for accessories, hooked adjustable buttplate. Adjustable comb, adjustable large palm rest. Hand stippling on grip area.
Price: . . . . **NA**

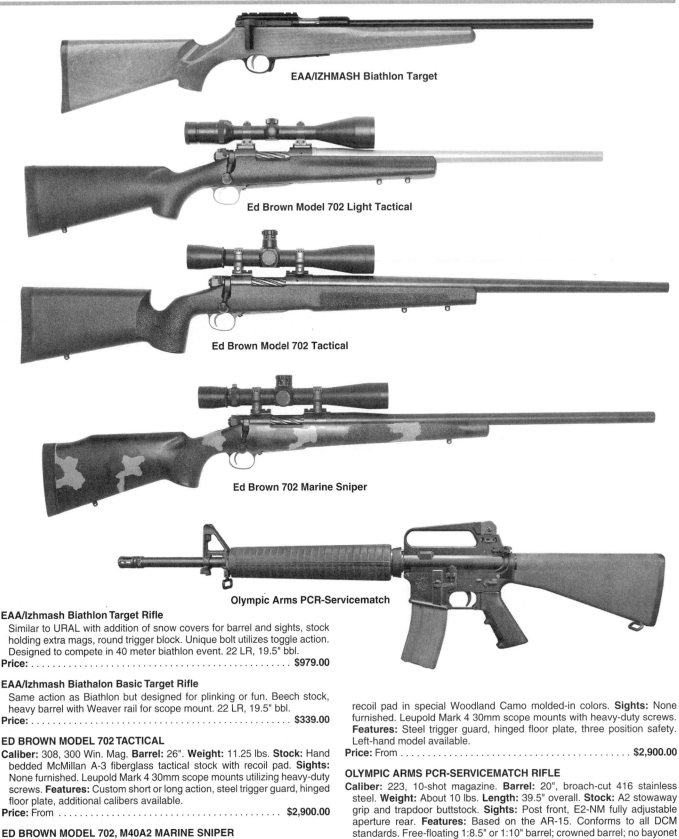

EAA/IZHMASH Biathlon Target

Ed Brown Model 702 Light Tactical

Ed Brown Model 702 Tactical

Ed Brown 702 Marine Sniper

Olympic Arms PCR-Servicematch

EAA/Izhmash Biathlon Target Rifle
Similar to URAL with addition of snow covers for barrel and sights, stock holding extra mags, round trigger block. Unique bolt utilizes toggle action. Designed to compete in 40 meter biathlon event. 22 LR, 19.5" bbl.
Price: **$979.00**

EAA/Izhmash Biathalon Basic Target Rifle
Same action as Biathlon but designed for plinking or fun. Beech stock, heavy barrel with Weaver rail for scope mount. 22 LR, 19.5" bbl.
Price: **$339.00**

ED BROWN MODEL 702 TACTICAL
Caliber: 308, 300 Win. Mag. **Barrel:** 26". **Weight:** 11.25 lbs. **Stock:** Hand bedded McMillan A-3 fiberglass tactical stock with recoil pad. **Sights:** None furnished. Leupold Mark 4 30mm scope mounts utilizing heavy-duty screws. **Features:** Custom short or long action, steel trigger guard, hinged floor plate, additional calibers available.
Price: From **$2,900.00**

ED BROWN MODEL 702, M40A2 MARINE SNIPER
Caliber: 308 Win., 30-06 Springfield. **Barrel:** Match-grade 24". **Weight:** 9.25 lbs. **Stock:** Hand bedded McMillan GP fiberglass tactical stock with

recoil pad in special Woodland Camo molded-in colors. **Sights:** None furnished. Leupold Mark 4 30mm scope mounts with heavy-duty screws. **Features:** Steel trigger guard, hinged floor plate, three position safety. Left-hand model available.
Price: From **$2,900.00**

OLYMPIC ARMS PCR-SERVICEMATCH RIFLE
Caliber: 223, 10-shot magazine. **Barrel:** 20", broach-cut 416 stainless steel. **Weight:** About 10 lbs. **Length:** 39.5" overall. **Stock:** A2 stowaway grip and trapdoor buttstock. **Sights:** Post front, E2-NM fully adjustable aperture rear. **Features:** Based on the AR-15. Conforms to all DCM standards. Free-floating 1:8.5" or 1:10" barrel; crowned barrel; no bayonet lug. Introduced 1996. Made in U.S.A. by Olympic Arms, Inc.
Price: **$1,062.00**

Remington 40-XB Rangemaster

Remington 40-XC KS

Sako TRG-22

OLYMPIC ARMS PCR-1 RIFLE

Caliber: 223, 10-shot magazine. **Barrel:** 20", 24"; 416 stainless steel. **Weight:** 10 lbs., 3 oz. **Length:** 38.25" overall with 20" barrel. **Stock:** A2 stowaway grip and trapdoor butt. **Sights:** None supplied; flattop upper receiver, cut-down front sight base. **Features:** Based on the AR-15 rifle. Broach-cut, free-floating barrel with 1:8.5" or 1:10" twist. No bayonet lug. Crowned barrel; fluting available. Introduced 1994. Made in U.S.A. by Olympic Arms, Inc.
Price: **$1,038.00**

Olympic Arms PCR-2, PCR-3 Rifles

Similar to the PCR-1 except has 16" barrel, weighs 8 lbs., 2 oz.; has post front sight, fully adjustable aperture rear. Model PCR-3 has flattop upper receiver, cut-down front sight base. Introduced 1994. Made in U.S.A. by Olympic Arms, Inc.
Price: **$958.00**

REMINGTON 40-XB RANGEMASTER TARGET CENTERFIRE

Caliber: 15 calibers from 220 Swift to 300 Win. Mag. **Barrel:** 27-1/4". **Weight:** 11-1/4 lbs. **Length:** 47" overall. **Stock:** American walnut, laminated thumbhole or Kevlar with high comb and beavertail forend stop. Rubber non-slip buttplate. **Sights:** None. Scope blocks installed. **Features:** Adjustable trigger. Stainless barrel and action. Receiver drilled and tapped for sights.
Price: Standard single shot . (right-hand) **$1,636.00**; (left-hand) **$1,761.00**
Price: Repeater **$1,734.00**

REMINGTON 40-XBBR KS

Caliber: Five calibers from 22 BR to 308 Win. **Barrel:** 20" (light varmint class), 24" (heavy varmint class). **Weight:** 7-1/4 lbs. (light varmint class); 12 lbs. (heavy varmint class). **Length:** 38" (20" bbl.), 42" (24" bbl.). **Stock:** Aramid fiber. **Sights:** None. Supplied with scope blocks. **Features:** Unblued benchrest with stainless steel barrel, trigger adjustable from 1-1/2 lbs. to 3-1/2 lbs. Special two-oz. trigger extra cost. Scope and mounts extra.
Price: Single shot. **$1,876.00**

REMINGTON 40-XC KS TARGET RIFLE

Caliber: 7.62 NATO, 5-shot. **Barrel:** 24", stainless steel. **Weight:** 11 lbs. without sights. **Length:** 43-1/2" overall. **Stock:** Aramid fiber. **Sights:** None furnished. **Features:** Designed to meet the needs of competitive shooters. Stainless steel barrel and action.
Price: **$1,821.00**

REMINGTON 40-XR CUSTOM SPORTER

Caliber: 22 LR, 22 WM. **Features:** Model XR-40 Target rifle action. Many options available.
Price: Single shot **$3,383.00**

SAKO TRG-22/TRG-42 BOLT-ACTION RIFLE

Caliber: 308 Win., 10-shot magazine. **Barrel:** 26". **Weight:** 10-1/4 lbs. **Length:** 45-1/4" overall. **Stock:** Reinforced polyurethane with fully adjustable cheekpiece and buttplate. **Sights:** None furnished. Optional quick-detachable, one-piece scope mount base, 1" or 30mm rings. **Features:** Resistance-free bolt, free-floating heavy stainless barrel, 60-degree bolt lift. Two-stage trigger is adjustable for length, pull, horizontal or vertical pitch. Introduced 2000. Imported from Finland by Beretta USA.
Price: TRG-22 Green Folding Stock. **$4,525.00**
Price: TRG-22 Green or black stock. **$2,825.00**
Price: TRG-42 300 Win Mag., green stock . . . . **$2,825.00 to $3,525.00**
Price: TRG-42 338 Lapua Mag., green stock . . . . . **$2,825.00 to $3,525.00**

SPRINGFIELD ARMORY M1A SUPER MATCH

Caliber: 308 Win. **Barrel:** 22", heavy Douglas Premium. **Weight:** About 11 lbs. **Length:** 44.31" overall. **Stock:** Heavy walnut competition stock with longer pistol grip, contoured area behind the rear sight, thicker butt and forend, glass bedded. **Sights:** National Match front and rear. **Features:** Has figure-eight-style operating rod guide. Introduced 1987. From Springfield Armory.
Price: About. **$2,479.00**

Springfield Armory M1A Super Match

Springfield Armory M1A/M-21

Springfield Armory M-1 Garand

Stoner SR-25

Springfield Armory M1A/M-21 Tactical Model Rifle
Similar to M1A Super Match except special sniper stock with adjustable cheekpiece and rubber recoil pad. Weighs 11.6 lbs. From Springfield Armory.
Price: **$2,975.00**

SPRINGFIELD ARMORY M-1 GARAND
Caliber: 30-06, 308 Win., 8-shot. **Barrel:** 24". **Weight:** 9.5 lbs. **Length:** 43.6". **Stock:** American walnut. **Sights:** Military square post front, military aperture, MOA adjustable rear. **Features:** Limited production, certificate of authenticity, all new receiver, barrel and stock with remaining parts USGI mil-spec. Two-stage military trigger.
Price: About **$2,479.00**

STONER SR-15 MATCH RIFLE
Caliber: 223. **Barrel:** 20". **Weight:** 7.9 lbs. **Length:** 38" overall. **Stock:** Black synthetic. **Sights:** None furnished; flattop upper receiver for scope mounting. **Features:** Short Picatinny rail, two-stage match trigger. Introduced 1998. Made in U.S.A. by Knight's Mfg.Co.
Price: **$1,650.00**

STONER SR-25 MATCH RIFLE
Caliber: 7.62 NATO, 10-shot steel magazine, 5-shot optional. **Barrel:** 24" heavy match; 1:11.25" twist. **Weight:** 10.75 lbs. **Length:** 44" overall. **Stock:** Black synthetic AR-15A2 design. Full floating forend of mil-spec synthetic attaches to upper receiver at a single point. **Sights:** None furnished. Has integral Weaver-style rail. Rings and iron sights optional. **Features:** Improved AR-15 trigger, AR-15-style seven-lug rotating bolt. Introduced 1993. Made in U.S.A. by Knight's Mfg. Co.
Price: **$3,345.00**
Price: SR-25 Lightweight Match (20" medium match target contour barrel, 9.5 lbs., 40" overall) **$3,345.00**

Includes a wide variety of sporting guns and guns suitable for various competitions.

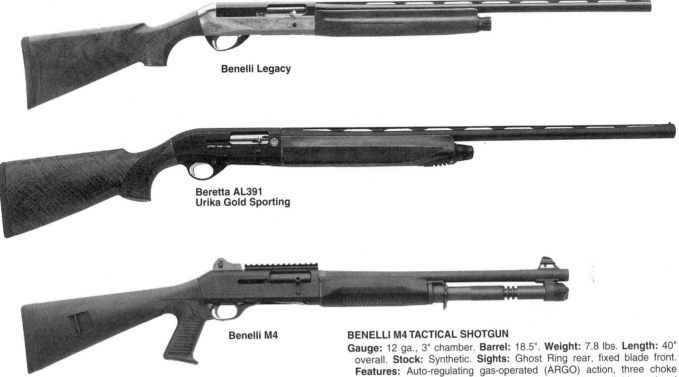

Benelli Legacy

Beretta AL391 Urika Gold Sporting

Benelli M4

AYA MODEL 4/53 SHOTGUNS
Gauge: 12, 16, 20, 28, 410. **Barrel:** 27" (28 and 410) or 28". **Weight:** To customer specifications. **Length:** To customer specifications. **Features:** Hammerless boxlock action; double triggers; light scroll engraving; automatic safety; straight grip oil finish walnut stock; checkered butt.
Price: **$2,850.00**

BENELLI LEGACY SHOTGUN
Gauge: 12, 20, 2-3/4" and 3" chamber. **Barrel:** 24", 26", 28" (Full, Mod., Imp. Cyl., Imp. Mod., cylinder choke tubes). Mid-bead sight. **Weight:** 5.8 to 7.4 lbs. **Length:** 49-5/8" overall (28" barrel). **Stock:** Select European walnut with satin finish. **Features:** Uses the rotating bolt inertia recoil operating system with a two-piece steel/aluminum etched receiver (bright on lower, blue upper). Drop adjustment kit allows the stock to be custom fitted without modifying the stock. Introduced 1998. Imported from Italy by Benelli USA, Corp.
Price: **$1,435.00**

Benelli Sport II Shotgun
Similar to the Legacy model except has dual tone blue/silver receiver, two carbon fiber interchangeable vent ribs, adjustable butt pad, adjustable buttstock, and functions with ultra-light target loads. Walnut stock with satin finish. Introduced 1997. Imported from Italy by Benelli USA.
Price: **$1,470.00**

BENELLI M2 FIELD SHOTGUNS
Gauge: 12 ga., 3" chamber. **Barrel:** 21", 24", 26", 28". **Weight:** 6.9 to 7.2 lbs. **Length:** 42.5 to 49.5" overall. **Stock:** Synthetic, Advantage® Max-4 HD™, Advantage® Timber HD™. **Sights:** Red bar. **Features:** Uses the Inertia Driven™ bolt mechanism. Vent rib. Comes with set of five choke tubes. Imported from Italy by Benelli USA.
Price: Synthetic ComforTech gel recoil pad **$1,175.00**
Price: Camo ComforTech gel recoil pad **$1,295.00**
Price: Satin walnut **$1,110.00**
Price: Rifled slug synthetic **$1,240.00**
Price: Timber HD turkey model w/SteadyGrip stock.......... **$1,335.00**

BENELLI M4 TACTICAL SHOTGUN
Gauge: 12 ga., 3" chamber. **Barrel:** 18.5". **Weight:** 7.8 lbs. **Length:** 40" overall. **Stock:** Synthetic. **Sights:** Ghost Ring rear, fixed blade front. **Features:** Auto-regulating gas-operated (ARGO) action, three choke tubes, Picatinny rail, standard and collapsible stocks available, optional tactical gun case. Introduced 2006. Imported from Italy by Benelli USA.
Price: Pistol grip stock.................................. **$1,535.00**

BENELLI MONTEFELTRO SHOTGUNS
Gauge: 12 and 20 ga. Full, Imp. Mod, Mod., Imp. Cyl. choke tubes. **Barrel:** 24", 26", 28". **Weight:** 5.3 to 7.1 lbs. **Stock:** Checkered walnut with satin finish. **Length of Pull:** 12-1/2 to 14-3/8" overall. **Length:** 43.6 to 49.5" overall. **Features:** Uses the Montefeltro rotating bolt system with a simple inertia recoil design. Finish is blue. Introduced 1987.
Price: 24", 26", 28" **$1,070.00**
Price: Grade II **$1,220.00**
Price: 20 ga. **$1,070.00**
Price: 20 ga. short stock (LOP: 12.5") **$1,080.00**

BENELLI SUPER BLACK EAGLE II SHOTGUNS
Gauge: 12, 3-1/2" chamber. **Barrel:** 24", 26", 28" (Cyl. Imp. Cyl., Mod., Imp. Mod., Full choke tubes). **Weight:** 7.1 to 7.3 lbs. **Length:** 45.6 to 49.6" overall. **Stock:** European walnut with satin finish, polymer, or camo. Adjustable for drop. **Sights:** Red bar front. **Features:** Uses Montefeltro inertia recoil bolt system. Vent rib. Advantage® Max-4 HD™, Advantage® Timber HD™ camo patterns. Minimum recommend load in all Benelli semi-autos: 3 dram, 1-1/8 oz. Introduced 1991. Left-hand models available. Imported from Italy by Benelli USA.
Price: Synthetic stock, ComforTech gel recoil pad **$1,515.00**
Price: Camo stock, ComforTech gel recoil pad............... **$1,635.00**
Price: Satin walnut stock................................. **$1,450.00**
Price: Synthetic stock **$1,380.00**
Price: Camo stock.. **$1,500.00**
Price: Rifled slug synthetic **$1,580.00**
Price: Timber HD turkey model w/SteadyGrip stock **$1,535.00**

Benelli Ultra Light
Uses the inertia recoil bolt system. Gloss-blued finish receiver. Weight is 6.0 lbs., 24" barrel, 45.5 overall length. WeatherCoat walnut stock. Introduced 2006. Imported from Italy by Benelli USA.
Price: **$1,335.00**

Benelli Ultralight

Beretta 3901 Ambassador

Beretta 3901 Citizen

Beretta AL391 Urika Sporting

BENELLI CORDOBA HIGH-VOLUME SHOTGUN

Gauge: 12; 3" chamber. **Barrel:** 28" and 30", ported, 10mm sporting rib. **Weight:** 7.2 to 7.3 lbs. **Length:** 49.6 to 51.6". **Features:** Designed for high-volume sporting clays and Argentina dove shooting. Inertia-driven action, Extended Sport CrioChokes, 4+1 capacity. Imported from Italy by Benelli USA.
Price: $1,665.00

BERETTA 3901 SHOTGUNS

Gauge: 12, 20 gauge; 3" chamber, semi-auto. **Barrel:** 26", 28". **Weight:** 6.55 lbs. (20 ga.), 7.2 lbs. (12 ga.). **Length:** NA. **Stock:** Wood, X-tra wood (special process wood enhancement), and polymer. **Features:** Based on A390 shotgun introduced in 1996. Mobilchokes, removable trigger group. 3901 Target RL uses gas operating system; Sporting style flat rib with steel front bead and mid-bead, walnut stock and forearm, satin matte finish, adjustable LOP from 12-13", adjustable for cast on/off, Beretta's Memory System II to adjust the parallel comb. Weighs 7.2 lbs. 3901 Citizen has polymer stock. 3901 Statesman has basic wood and checkering treatment. 3901 Ambassador has X-tra wood stock and fore end; high-polished receiver with engraving, Gel-Tek recoil pad, optional TruGlo fiber-optic front sight. 3901 Rifled Slug Shotgun has black high-impact synthetic stock and fore end, 24" barrel, 1:28 twist, Picatinny cantilever rail. Introduced 2006. Made in U.S. by Beretta USA.
Price: $1,295.00
Price: 3901 Target RL $898.00
Price: 3901 Citizen. $750.00
Price: 3901 Citizen. $898.00
Price: 3901 Ambassador. $998.00
Price: 3901 Rifled Slug Shotgun $799.00

BERETTA UGB25 XCEL

Gauge: 12, 2-3/4" chambers. **Barrel:** 28", 30", 32"; competition-style interchangeable vent rib; Optima choke tubes. **Weight:** 7.7-9 lbs. **Stock:** High-grade walnut with oil finish; hand-checkered grip and forend, adjustable. **Features:** Break-open semiautomatic. High-resistance fiberglass-reinforced technopolymer trigger plate, self-lubricating firing mechanism. Rounded alloy receiver, polished sides, external cartridge carrier and feeding port, bottom eject. two technopolymer recoil dampers on breech bolt, double recoil dampers located in the receiver, Beretta Recoil Reduction System, recoil-absorbing Beretta Gel Tek recoil pad. Optima-Bore barrel with a lengthened forcing cone, Optimachoke and Extended Optimachoke tubes. Steel-shot capable, interchangeable aluminum alloy top rib. Introduced 2006. Imported from Italy by Beretta USA.
Price: $3,275.00

BERETTA AL391 TEKNYS SHOTGUNS

Gauge: 12, 20 gauge; 3" chamber, semi-auto. **Barrel:** 26", 28". **Weight:** 5.9 lbs. (20 ga.), 7.3 lbs. (12 ga.). **Length:** NA. **Stock:** X-tra wood (special process wood enhancement). **Features:** Flat 1/4 rib, TruGlo Tru-Bead sight, recoil reducer, stock spacers, overbored bbls., flush choke tubes. Comes with fitted, lined case.
Price: From $1,425.00

BERETTA AL391 URIKA AND URIKA OPTIMA AUTO SHOTGUNS

Gauge: 12, 20 gauge; 3" chamber. **Barrel:** 22", 24", 26", 28", 30"; five Mobilchoke choke tubes. **Weight:** 5.95 to 7.28 lbs. **Length:** Varies by model. **Stock:** Walnut, black or camo synthetic; shims, spacers and interchangeable recoil pads allow custom fit. **Features:** Self-compensating gas operation handles full range of loads; recoil reducer in receiver; enlarged trigger guard; reduced-weight receiver, barrel and forend; hard-chromed bore. Introduced 2000. Urika Gold and Gold Sporting models are similar to AL391 Urika except features deluxe wood, jewelled bolt and carrier, gold-inlaid receiver with black or silver finish. Introduced 2000. Urika Sporting models are similar to AL391 Urika except has competition sporting stock with rounded rubber recoil pad, wide vent rib with white front and mid-rib beads, satin-black receiver with silver markings. Available in 12 and 20 gauge. Introduced 2000. Urika Trap has wide vent rib with white front and mid-rib beads, Monte Carlo stock and special trap recoil pad. Gold Trap features highly figured walnut stock and forend, gold-filled Beretta logo and signature on receiver. Optima bore and Optima choke tubes. Introduced 2000. Urika Parallel Target RL and SL models have parallel comb, Monte Carlo stock with tighter grip radius and stepped vent rib. SL model has same features but with 13.5" length of pull stock. Introduced 2000. Urika Youth has a 24" or 26" barrel with 13.5" stock for youths and smaller shooters. Introduced 2000. Imported from Italy by Beretta USA.
Price: . . . . $998.00 to $1,500.00

SHOTGUNS — Autoloaders

Beretta A391 Xtrema2 3.5

Browning Gold Deer Hunter

Browning Gold Fusion

Browning Gold Superlite Micro

Browning NWTF Mossy Oak® Break-Up

BERETTA A391 XTREMA2 3.5 AUTO SHOTGUNS
Gauge: 12 ga. 3.5" chamber. **Barrel:** 24", 26", 28". **Weight:** 7.8 lbs. **Stock:** Synthetic. **Features:** Semi-auto goes with two-lug rotating bolt and self-compensating gas valve, extended tang, cross bolt safety, self-cleaning, with case.
Price: From **$1,098.00**

BROWNING GOLD AUTO SHOTGUNS
Gauge: 12, 3" or 3-1/2" chamber; 20, 3" chamber. **Barrel:** 12 ga.-26", 28", 30", Invector choke tubes; 20 ga.-26", 30", Invector choke tubes. **Weight:** 7 lbs., 9 oz. (12 ga.), 6 lbs., 12 oz. (20 ga.). **Length:** 46-1/4" overall (20 ga., 26" barrel). **Stock:** 14"x1-1/2"x2-1/3"; select walnut with gloss finish; palm swell grip. **Features:** Self-regulating, self-cleaning gas system shoots all loads; lightweight receiver with special non-glare deep black finish; large reversible safety button; large rounded trigger guard, gold trigger. The 20 gauge has slightly smaller dimensions; 12 gauge have back-bored barrels, Invector Plus tube system. Introduced 1994. Gold Evolve shotguns have new rib design, HiViz sights. Gold Micro has a 26" barrel, 13-7/8" pull length and smaller pistol grip for youths and other small shooters. Introduced 2001. Gold Fusion has front HiViz Pro-Comp and center bead on tapered vent rib; ported and back-bored Invector Plus barrel; 2-3/4" chamber; satin-finished stock with solid, radiused recoil pad with hard heel insert; non-glare black alloy receiver, shim-adj. stock. Imported by Browning.
Price: Gold Evolve, 12 or 20 ga., 3" chamber **$1,196.00**
Price: Gold Hunter, 12 or 20 ga., 3" or 3-1/2" chamber, from **$1,025.00**

Price: Gold FLD, 12 or 20 ga., semi-humpback receiver **$1,025.00**
Price: Gold Rifled Deer Hunter, 12 or 20 ga., scope mount **$1,131.00**
Price: Gold Upland Special, 12 or 20 ga., 24" or 26" barrel **$1,025.00**
Price: Gold Superlite Micro, 20 ga., 24" or 26" barrel, 6.6 lbs. . . . **$1,025.00**
Price: Gold Fusion, 12 or 20 ga., 6.4 to 7 lbs. **$1,129.00**
Price: Gold Fusion High Grade, 12 or 20 ga., intr. 2005 . . . . **$2,095.00**

Browning Gold Stalker Auto Shotgun
Similar to the Gold Hunter except has black composite stock and forend. Chambered in 12 gauge, 3" or 3-1/2" chamber. Gold Deer Stalker has fully rifled barrel, cantilever scope mount. Introduced 1999. Imported by Browning.
Price: Gold Stalker, 3" or 3-1/2" chamber, 26" or 28" barrel, from . . **$981.00**
Price: Gold FLD Stalker, 3" chamber, semi-humpback receiver . . . **$981.00**
Price: Gold Rifled Deer Stalker, 12 ga. 3" chamber, 22" barrel **$981.00**

Browning Gold NWTF Turkey Series and Mossy Oak Shotguns
Similar to the Gold Hunter except has specialized camouflage patterns, including National Wild Turkey Federation design. Includes extra-full choke tube and HiViz fiber-optic sights on some models and Dura-Touch coating. Camouflage patterns include Mossy Oak New Break-Up (NBU) or Mossy Oak New Shadow Grass (NSG). NWTF models include NWTF logo on stock. Introduced 2001. From Browning.
Price: NWFT Gold Ultimate Turkey, 24" barrel, 3-1/2" chamber . . . **$1,440.00**
Price: NWFT Gold Turkey, 24" barrel, 3" chamber **$1,202.00**
Price: Gold NSG, 26" or 28" barrel, 3" or 3-1/2" chamber, from . . . **$1,127.00**
Price: Gold NBU, 26" barrel, 3" or 3-1/2" chamber, from **$1,127.00**
Price: Gold Rifle Deer NBU, 22" barrel, 3" chamber, from **$1,218.00**

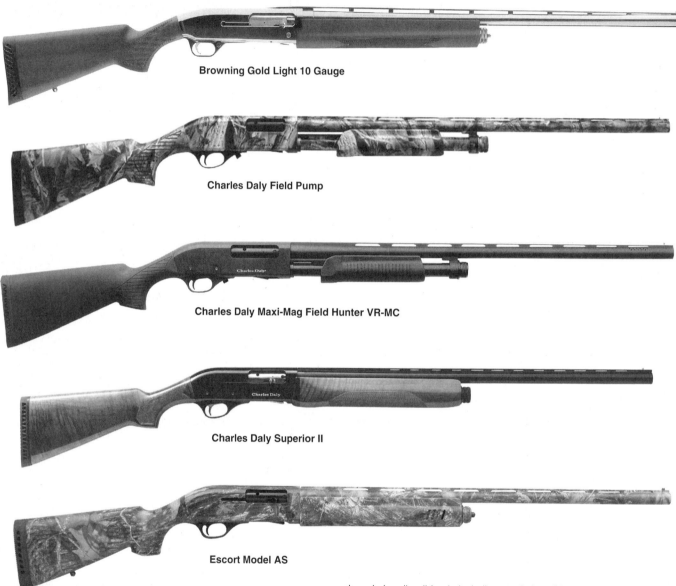

Browning Gold Light 10 Gauge

Charles Daly Field Pump

Charles Daly Maxi-Mag Field Hunter VR-MC

Charles Daly Superior II

Escort Model AS

BROWNING GOLD "CLAYS" AUTO SHOTGUNS

Gauge: 12, 2-3/4" chamber. **Barrel:** 28", 30", Invector Plus choke tubes. **Weight:** about 7.75 lbs. **Length:** From 47.75 to 50.5". **Stock:** Select walnut with gloss finish; palm swell grip, shim adjustable. **Features:** Ported barrels, "Golden Clays" models feature gold inlays and engraving. Otherwise similar to Gold series guns. Imported by Browning.

Price: Gold "Golden Clays" Sporting Clays, intr. 2005. . . . . **$1,812.00**
Price: Gold Sporting Clays **$1,105.00**
Price: Gold "Golden Clays" Ladies Sporting Clays, intr. 2005. . . . **$1,812.00**
Price: Gold Ladies Sporting Clays **$1,105.00**

Browning Gold Light 10 Gauge Auto Shotgun

Similar to the Gold Hunter except has an alloy receiver that is 1 lb. lighter than standard model. Offered in 26" or 28" bbls. With Mossy Oak® Break-Up™ or Shadow Grass coverage; 5-shot magazine. Weighs 9 lbs., 10 oz. (28" bbl.). Introduced 2001. Imported by Browning.

Price: Camo model only **$1,336.00**

CHARLES DALY FIELD SEMI-AUTO SHOTGUNS

Gauge: 12, 20, 28. **Barrel:** 22", 24", 26", 28" or 30". **Stock:** Synthetic black, Realtree Hardwoods or Advantage Timber. **Features:** Interchangeable barrels handle all loads including steel shot. Slug model has adjustable sights. Maxi-Mag is 3.5" chamber.

Price: Field Hunter **$389.00**

CHARLES DALY SUPERIOR II SEMI-AUTO SHOTGUNS

Gauge: 12, 20, 28. **Barrel:** 26", 28" or 30". **Stock:** Select Turkish walnut. **Features:** Factory ported interchangeable barrels; wide vent rib on Trap and Sport models; fluorescent red sights.

Price: Superior Hunter VR-MC **$539.00**
Price: Superior Sport **$569.00**

ESCORT SEMI-AUTO SHOTGUNS

Gauge: 12, 20. **Barrel:** 22", 24", 26", 18" (AimGuard model); 3" chambers. **Weight:** 6 lbs, 4 0. to 7 lbs., 6 oz. **Stock:** Polymer, black, or camo finish; also Turkish walnut. **Features:** Black chrome finish; top of receiver dovetailed for sight mounting. Gold-plated trigger, trigger guard safety, magazine cut-off. Three choke tubes (IC, M, F — except AimGuard); 24" bbl. model comes with turkey choke tube. **Sights:** Optional HiViz Spark and TriViz fiber-optic sights. Introduced 2002. Camo model introduced 2003. Youth, Slug, Obsession Camo models introduced 2005. Three-barrel pumpset introduced 2006. Imported from Turkey by Legacy Sports International.

Price: From **$392.00**

Remington Model 105 CTI

Remington Model 1100 G3

Remington Model 11-87 Premier

FRANCHI INERTIA I-12 SHOTGUN

Gauge: 12, 3" chamber. **Barrel:** 24", 26", 28" (Cyl., IC, Mod., IM, F choke tubes). **Weight:** 7.5 to 7.7. lbs. **Length:** 45" to 49". **Stock:** 14-3.8" LOP, satin walnut with checkered grip and forend, synthetic, Advantage Timber HD or Max-4 camo patterns. **Features:** Inertia-Driven action. AA walnut stock. Red bar front sight, metal mid sight. Imported from Italy by Benelli USA.

Price: Synthetic **$679.00**
Price: Camo **$749.00**
Price: Satin walnut **$779.00**
Price: White Gold engraved receiver, hard case **$1,399.00**

FRANCHI MODEL 712/720 RAPTOR SHOTGUNS

Gauge: 12, 20 3" chamber. **Barrel:** 28", 30". **Weight:** 6.2 to 7.1 lbs. **Length:** 50" to 52". **Stock:** Satin walnut, WeatherCoat finish. **Sights:** Front and mid metal beads. **Features:** Comes with custom-fitted hard case and cleaning kit, extended choke tubes. Made in Italy and imported by Benelli USA.

Price: Walnut **$899.00**

FRANCHI MODEL 720 SHOTGUNS

Gauge: 20, 3" chamber. **Barrel:** 24", 26", 28" w/(IC, Mod., F) choke tubes. **Weight:** 5.9 to 6.1 lbs. **Length:** 43.25" to 49". **Stock:** WeatherCoat finish walnut, Max-4 and Timber HD camo. **Sights:** Front bead. **Features:** Made in Italy and imported by Benelli USA.

Price: Walnut **$749.00**
Price: Camo **$799.00**
Price: Walnut, 12.5" LOP, 43.25" OAL **$739.00**

FRANCHI 48AL FIELD AND DELUXE SHOTGUNS

Gauge: 20 or 28, 2-3/4" chamber. **Barrel:** 24", 26", 28" (Full, Cyl., Mod., choke tubes). **Weight:** 5.4 to 5.7 lbs. **Length:** 42.25" to 48". **Stock:** Walnut with checkered grip and forend. **Features:** Long recoil-operated action. Chrome-lined bore; cross-bolt safety. Imported from Italy by Benelli USA.

Price: 20 ga. **$749.00**
Price: 20 ga. Deluxe A grade walnut **$970.00**
Price: 28 ga. **$850.00**

FRANCHI RAPTOR SPORTING CLAYS SHOTGUN

Gauge: 12 and 20; 6-round capacity. **Barrel:** 30" (12 ga.) or 28" (20 ga.); ported; tapered target rib and bead front sight. **Weight:** 7.1 lbs. (Model 712) or 6.2 lbs. (Model 720). **Stock:** Walnut with WeatherCoat (impervious to weather). **Features:** Gas-operated, satin nickel receiver.

Price: **$850.00**

HARRINGTON & RICHARDSON EXCELL AUTO 5 SHOTGUNS

Gauge: 12, 3" chamber. **Barrel:** 22", 24", 28", four screw-in choke tubes (IC, M, IM, F). **Weight:** About 7 lbs. **Length:** 42.5" to 48.5" overall, depending on barrel length. **Stock:** American walnut with satin finish; cut checkering; ventilated buttpad. Synthetic stock or camo-finish. **Sights:** Metal bead front or fiber-optic front and rear. **Features:** Ventilated rib on all models except slug gun. Imported by H&R 1871, Inc.

Price: Synthetic, black, 28" barrel, 48.5" OAL **$415.00**
Price: Walnut, checkered grip/forend, 28" barrel, 48.5" OAL **$461.00**
Price: Waterfowl, camo finish **$521.00**
Price: Turkey, camo finish, 22" barrel, fiber optic sights **$521.00**
Price: Combo, synthetic black stock, with slug barrel. **$583.00**

REMINGTON MODEL 105 CTI SHOTGUN

Gauge: 12, 3" chamber, 2-shot magazine. **Barrel:** 26", 28" (IC, Mod., Full ProBore chokes). **Weight:** 7 lbs. **Length:** 46.25" overall (26" barrel). **Stock:** Walnut with satin finish. Checkered grip and forend. **Sights:** Front bead. **Features:** Aircraft-grade titanium receiver body, skeletonized receiver with carbon fiber shell. Bottom feed and eject, target grade trigger, R3 recoil pad, FAA-approved lockable hard case, .735" overbored barrel with lengthened forcing cones. TriNyte coating; carbon/aramid barrel rib. Introduced 2006.

Price: **$1,332.00**

REMINGTON MODEL 1100 G3 SHOTGUN

Gauge: 20, 12; 3" chamber **Barrel:** 26", 28". **Weight:** 6.75-7.6 lbs. **Stock:** Realwood semi-Fancy carbon fiber laminate stock, high gloss finish, machine cut checkering. **Features:** Gas operating system, pressure compensated barrel, solid carbon-steel engraved receiver, titanium coating. Action bars, trigger and extended carrier release, action bar sleeve, action spring, locking block, hammer, sear and magazine tube have nickel-plated, Teflon coating. R3 recoil pad, overbored (.735" dia.) vent rib barrels, ProBore choke tubes. 20-gauges have Rem Chokes. Comes with lockable hard case. Introduced 2006. Competition model has overbored 30" barrel, 10mm target-style rib with twin beads. Optimized for 2 3/4" target and light field loads. Introduced 2006.

Price: 12 or 20 gauge **$1,065.00**

REMINGTON MODEL 11-87 PREMIER SHOTGUNS

Gauge: 12, 20, 3" chamber. **Barrel:** 26", 28", 30" RemChoke tubes. Light Contour barrel. **Weight:** About 7-3/4 lbs. **Length:** 46" overall (26" bbl.). **Stock:** Walnut with satin or high-gloss finish; cut checkering; solid brown buttpad; no white spacers. **Sights:** Bradley-type white-faced front, metal bead middle. **Features:** Pressure compensating gas system allows shooting 2-3/4" or 3" loads interchangeably with no adjustments. Stainless magazine tube; redesigned feed latch, barrel support ring on operating bars; pinned forend. Introduced 1987.

Price: From **$860.00**

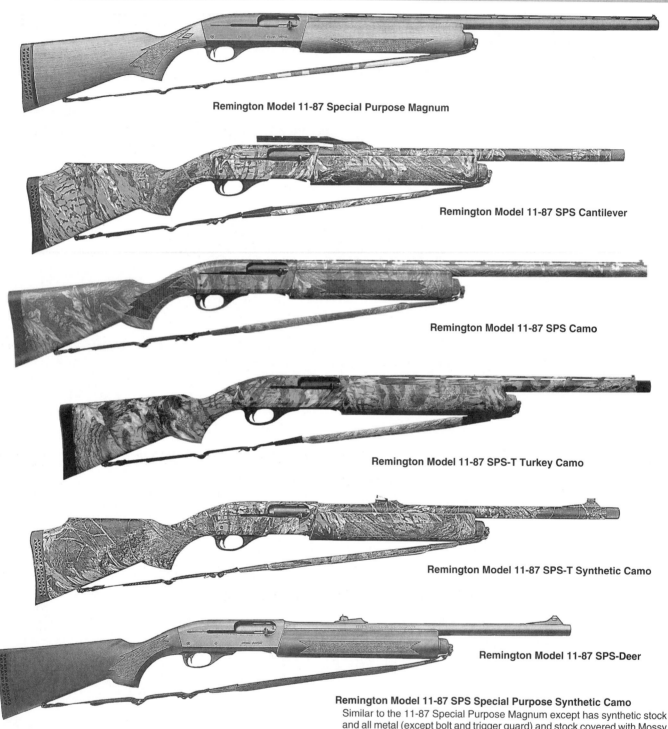

Remington Model 11-87 Special Purpose Magnum

Remington Model 11-87 SPS Cantilever

Remington Model 11-87 SPS Camo

Remington Model 11-87 SPS-T Turkey Camo

Remington Model 11-87 SPS-T Synthetic Camo

Remington Model 11-87 SPS-Deer

Remington Model 11-87 Special Purpose Magnum

Similar to the 11-87 Premier except has dull stock finish, Parkerized exposed metal surfaces. Bolt and carrier have dull blackened coloring. Comes with 26" or 28" barrel with RemChokes, padded Cordura nylon sling and quick detachable swivels. Introduced 1987. Thumbhole model available. Cantilever model has fully rifled barrel; synthetic stock with Monte Carlo comb; cantilever scope mount deer barrel. Comes with sling and swivels. Introduced 1994.

Price: With synthetic stock and forend (SPS) **$791.00**

Remington Model 11-87 SPS Special Purpose Synthetic Camo

Similar to the 11-87 Special Purpose Magnum except has synthetic stock and all metal (except bolt and trigger guard) and stock covered with Mossy Oak® Break-Up™ camo finish. In 12 gauge only, 26", RemChoke. Comes with camo sling, swivels. Introduced 1992. Turkey Camo model has 21" vent rib barrel with RemChoke tube. Completely covered with Mossy Oak® Break-Up™ Brown camouflage. Bolt body, trigger guard and recoil pad are non-reflective black. Super Magnum Synthetic Camo has 23" vent rib barrel with Turkey Super full choke tube, chambered for 12 ga., 3-1/2", TruGlo rifle sights. Version available without TruGlo sights. Introduced 2001. Special Purpose-Deer Shotgun has fully-rifled 21" barrel with rifle sights, black non-reflective, synthetic stock and forend, black carrying sling. Introduced 1993.

Price: From **$963.00**

Remington Model 11-87 SP

Remington Model 1100 Youth Turkey Camo

Remington 1100 LT-20 Deer

Remington Model 1100 Sporting 28

Remington Model 1100 Classic Trap

Remington Model 1100 Sporting 12

Remington Model 11-87 SP and SPS Super Magnum Shotguns

Similar to Model 11-87 Special Purpose Magnum except has 3-1/2" chamber. Available in flat finish American walnut or black synthetic stock, 26" or 28" black matte finished barrel and receiver; Imp. Cyl., Modified and Full RemChoke tubes. Overall length 45-3/4", weighs 8 lbs., 2 oz. Introduced 2000. From Remington Arms Co.

Price: From **$948.00**

Remington Model 11-87 Upland Special Shotgun

Similar to 11-87 Premier except has 23" vent rib barrel with straight grip, English-style walnut stock. Available in 12 or 20 gauge. Overall length 43-1/2", weighs 7-1/4 lbs. (6-1/2 lbs. in 20 ga.). Comes with Imp. Cyl., Modified and Full choke tubes. Introduced 2000.

Price: 12 or 20 gauge **$860.00**

REMINGTON MODEL 1100 CLASSIC FIELD SHOTGUN

Gauge: 12, 16, 20, 28 ga., 2-3/4" chamber; 410 bore; 3" chamber. **Barrel:** 25", 26", 28". **Weight:** 6.5-7.9 lbs. **Stock:** Semi-gloss American walnut stock and fore-end with cut checkering. **Features:** Gas operating system, pressure compensated barrel, machined steel receiver and barrel, high-polish blued finish.White diamond grip cap, white line spacers, butt plate, and Classic Field roll mark. Rem Chokes. Classic Trap model carries a 30" low-profile, light-target contoured vent rib barrel with standard .727" dimensions. Included are three specialized Rem Choke trap tubes: Singles (.027"), Mid Handicap (.034"), and Long Handicap (.041"). The fore-end and Monte Carlo stock are semi-fancy American walnut with deep-cut checkering and a high-gloss finish. Sporting line comes in 12, 20, and 28 gauges and .410 bore. Sporting models include semi-fancy American walnut stock and fore-end, cut checkering, high-gloss finish, 28-inch vent rib, Rem Choke barrel.

Price: Classic Field **$833.00**
Price: Classic Trap **$972.00**
Price: Sporting 12, 20, 28, .410 . . . . **$932.00 to $972.00**

Remington Model SP-10

Remington Model SP-10 Camo

Stoeger Model 2000

Traditions ALS 2100

REMINGTON MODEL SP-10 MAGNUM SHOTGUN
Gauge: 10, 3-1/2" chamber, 2-shot magazine. **Barrel:** 26", 30" (full and mod. RemChokes). **Weight:** 10-3/4 to 11 lbs. **Length:** 47-1/ 2" overall (26" barrel). **Stock:** Walnut with satin finish or black synthetic with 26" barrel. Checkered grip and forend. **Sights:** Twin bead. **Features:** Stainless steel gas system with moving cylinder; 3/8" vent rib. Receiver and barrel have matte finish. Brown recoil pad. Comes with padded Cordura nylon sling. Introduced 1989. SP-10 Magnum Camo has buttstock, forend, receiver, barrel and magazine cap covered with Mossy Oak® Break-Up™ camo finish; bolt body and trigger guard have matte black finish. RemChoke tube, 26" vent rib barrel with mid-rib bead and Bradley-style front sight, swivel studs and quick-detachable swivels, non-slip Cordura carrying sling in same camo pattern. Introduced 1993.
Price: . . . . **$1,484.00 to $1,627.00**

SARSILMAZ SEMI-AUTOMATIC SHOTGUN
Gauge: 12, 3" chamber. **Barrel:** 26" or 28"; fixed chokes. **Stock:** Walnut or synthetic. **Features:** Handles 2-3/4" or 3" magnum loads. Introduced 2000. Imported from Turkey by Armsport Inc.
Price: With walnut stock $969.95
Price: With synthetic stock $919.95

STOEGER MODEL 2000 SHOTGUNS
Gauge: 12, 3" chamber, set of five choke tubes (C, IC, M, F, XFT). **Barrel:** 24", 26", 28", 30". **Stock:** Walnut, synthetic, Timber HD, Max-4. **Sights:** Red bar front. **Features:** Inertia-recoil. Minimum recommended load: 3 dram, 1-1/8 oz. Imported by Benelli USA.
Price: Walnut $435.00
Price: Synthetic $425.00
Price: Max-4, Timber HD $485.00
Price: Field and slug barrel combo . . . . $635.00 to $715.00

TRADITIONS ALS 2100 SERIES SEMI-AUTOMATIC SHOTGUNS
Gauge: 12, 3" chamber; 20, 3" chamber. **Barrel:** 24", 26", 28" (Imp. Cyl., Mod. and Full choke tubes). **Weight:** 5 lbs., 10 oz. to 6 lbs., 5 oz. **Length:** 44" to 48" overall. **Stock:** Walnut or black composite. **Features:** Gas-operated; vent rib barrel with Beretta-style threaded muzzle. Introduced 2001 by Traditions.
Price: Field Model (12 or 20 ga., 26" or 28" bbl., walnut stock) **$479.00**
Price: Youth Model (12 or 20 ga., 24" bbl., walnut stock) **$479.00**
Price: (12 or 20 ga., 26" or 28" barrel, composite stock) **$459.00**

Traditions ALS 2100 Turkey Semi-Automatic Shotgun
Similar to ALS 2100 Field Model except chambered in 12 gauge, 3" only with 26" barrel and Mossy Oak® Break Up™ camo finish. Weighs 6 !bs.; 46" overall.
Price: **$519.00**

Traditions ALS 2100 Waterfowl Semi-Automatic Shotgun
Similar to ALS 2100 Field Model except chambered in 12 gauge, 3" only with 28" barrel and Advantage® Wetlands™ camo finish. Weighs 6.25 lbs.; 48" overall. Multi chokes.
Price: **$529.00**

Traditions ALS 2100 Hunter Combo
Similar to ALS 2100 Field Model except 2 barrels, 28" vent rib and 24" fully rifled deer. Weighs 6 to 6.5 lbs.; 48" overall. Choice TruGlo adj. sights or fixed cantilever mount on rifled barrel. Multi chokes.
Price: Walnut, rifle barrel **$609.00**
Price: Walnut, cantilever **$629.00**
Price: Synthetic **$579.00**

Traditions ALS 2100 Slug Hunter Shotgun
Similar to ALS 2100 Field Model, 12 ga., 24" barrel, overall length 44"; weighs 6.25 lbs. Designed specifically for the deer hunter. Rifled barrel has 1 in 36" twist. Fully adjustable fiber-optic sights.
Price: Walnut, rifle barrel **$529.00**
Price: Synthetic, rifle barrel **$499.00**
Price: Walnut, cantilever **$549.00**
Price: Synthetic, cantilever **$529.00**

Traditions ALS 2100 Home Security Shotgun
Similar to ALS 2100 Field Model, 12 ga., 20" barrel, overall length 40", weighs 6 lbs. Can be reloaded with one hand while shouldered and on-target. Swivel studs installed in stock.
Price: **$399.00**

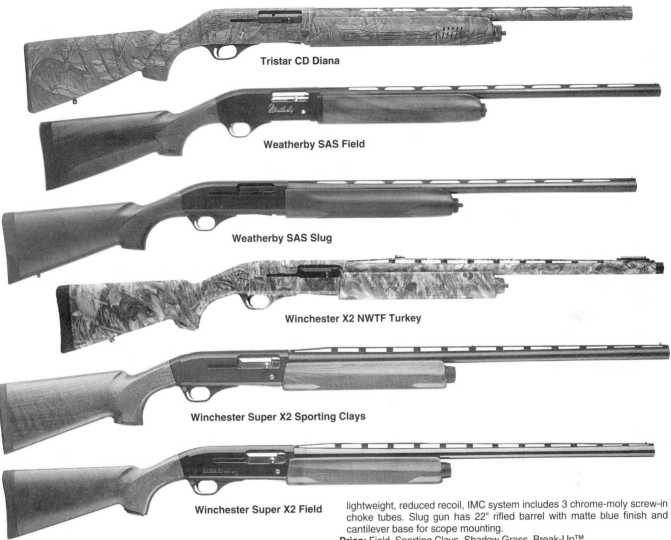

Tristar CD Diana

Weatherby SAS Field

Weatherby SAS Slug

Winchester X2 NWTF Turkey

Winchester Super X2 Sporting Clays

Winchester Super X2 Field

TRISTAR CD DIANA AUTO SHOTGUNS

Gauge: 12, shoots 2-3/4" or 3" interchangeably. **Barrel:** 24", 26", 28" (Imp. Cyl., Mod., Full choke tubes). **Stock:** European walnut or black synthetic. **Features:** Gas-operated action; blued barrel; checkered pistol grip and forend; vent rib barrel. Available with synthetic and camo stock and in slug model. First introduced 1999 under the name "Tristar Phantom." Imported by Tristar Sporting Arms Ltd.
Price: .... **$399.00 to $535.00**

VERONA MODEL SX400 SEMI AUTO SHOTGUNS

Gauge: 12. **Barrel:** 26", 30". **Weight:** 6-1/2 lbs. **Stock:** Walnut, black composite. **Sights:** Red dot. **Features:** Aluminum receivers, gas-operated, 2-3/4" or 3" Magnum shells without adj. or Mod., 4 screw-in chokes and wrench included. Sling swivels, gold trigger. Blued barrel. Imported from Italy by B.C. Outdoors.
Price: 401S, 12 ga. **$398.40**
Price: 405SDS, 12 ga. **$610.00**
Price: 405L, 12 ga. **$331.20**

WEATHERBY SAS (SEMI-AUTOMATIC SHOTGUNS)

Gauge: 12 ga. **Barrel:** Vent ribbed, 24" to 30". **Weight:** 7 lbs. to 7-3/4 lbs. **Stock:** SAS field and sporting clays, walnut. SAS Shadow Grass, Break-Up™, Synthetic, composite. **Sights:** SAS sporting clays, brass front and mid-point rear. SAS Shadow Grass and Break-Up™, HiViz front and brass mid. Synthetic has brass front. **Features:** Easy to shoot, load, clean; lightweight, reduced recoil, IMC system includes 3 chrome-moly screw-in choke tubes. Slug gun has 22" rifled barrel with matte blue finish and cantilever base for scope mounting.
Price: Field, Sporting Clays, Shadow Grass, Break-Up™,
Synthetic, Slug Gun .... **$879.00 to $969.00**

WINCHESTER SUPER X2 AUTO SHOTGUNS

Gauge: 12, 3", 3-1/2" chamber. **Barrel:** Belgian, 24", 26", 28"; Invector Plus choke tubes. **Weight:** 7-1/4 to 7-1/2 lbs. **Stock:** 14-1/4"x1-3/4"x2". Walnut or black synthetic. **Features:** Gas-operated action shoots all loads without adjustment; vent rib barrels; 4-shot magazine. Introduced 1999. Assembled in Portugal by U.S. Repeating Arms Co.
Price: Magnum, 3-1/2", synthetic stock, 26" or 28" bbl. **$1,185.00**
Price: Camo Waterfowl, 3-1/2", Mossy Oak® Shadow Grass **$1,185.00**
Price: NWTF Turkey, 3-1/2", Mossy Oak® Break-Up™ camo **$1,236.00**
Price: Universal Hunter Model **$1,252.00**

Winchester Super X2 Sporting Clays Auto Shotguns

Similar to the Super X2 except has two gas pistons (one for target loads, one for heavy 3" loads), adjustable comb system and high-post rib. Back-bored barrel with Invector Plus choke tubes. Offered in 28" and 30" barrels. Introduced 2001. From U.S. Repeating Arms Co.
Price: Super X2 sporting clays **$1,015.00**
Price: Signature red stock **$976.00**

Winchester Super X2 Field 3" Auto Shotgun

Similar to the Super X2 except 3" chamber, walnut stock and forearm and high-profile rib. Back-bored barrel and Invector Plus choke tubes. Introduced 2001. From U.S. Repeating Arms Co.
Price: Super X2 Field 3", 26" or 28" bbl. **$1,015.00**

Benelli Nova Pump

Benelli Nova Pump Slug

Browning BPS 10 gauge

Browning BPS 10 gauge Mossy Oak® Shadow Grass

BENELLI NOVA PUMP SHOTGUNS
Gauge: 12, 20. **Barrel:** 24", 26", 28". **Stock:** Synthetic, Max-4 and Timber H-D (12 ga. and 20 ga). **Sights:** Red bar. **Features:** 2-3/4", 3" chamber (3-1/2" 12 ga. only). Montefeltro rotating bolt design with dual action bars, magazine cut-off, synthetic trigger assembly, 4-shot magazine. Introduced 1999. Imported from Italy by Benelli USA.

Price: Synthetic	**$360.00**
Price: Timber HD	**$440.00**
Price: Max-4	**$440.00**

Benelli Nova Pump Tactical Shotgun
Similar to the Nova except has 18.5" barrel with adjustable rifle-type or ghost ring sights; weighs 7.2 lbs.; black synthetic stock. Introduced 1999. Imported from Italy by Benelli USA.

Price: With rifle sights	**$325.00**
Price: With ghost-ring sights	**$360.00**

Benelli Nova Pump Rifled Slug Gun
Similar to Nova Pump Slug Gun except has 24" barrel and rifled bore; open rifle sights; synthetic stock; weighs 8.1 lbs.

Price: Synthetic	**$535.00**
Price: Timber HD	**$625.00**
Price: Field/Slug combo, synthetic	**$560.00**

BROWNING BPS PUMP SHOTGUNS
Gauge: 10, 12, 3-1/2" chamber; 12 or 20, 3" chamber (2-3/4" in target guns), 28, 2-3/4" chamber, 5-shot magazine, .410, 3" chamber. **Barrel:** 10 ga.-24" Buck Special, 28", 30", 32" Invector; 12, 20 ga.-22", 24", 26", 28", 30", 32" (Imp. Cyl., Mod. or Full), .410-26" barrel. (Imp. Cyl., Mod. and Full choke tubes.) Also available with Invector choke tubes, 12 or 20 ga.; Upland Special has 22" barrel with Invector tubes. BPS 3" and 3-1/2" have back-bored barrel. **Weight:** 7 lbs., 8 oz. (28" barrel). **Length:** 48-3/4" overall (28" barrel). **Stock:** 14-1/4"x1-1/2"x2-1/2". Select walnut, semi-beavertail forend, full pistol grip stock. **Features:** All 12 gauge 3" guns except Buck Special and game guns have back-bored barrels with Invector Plus choke tubes. Bottom feeding and ejection, receiver top safety, high post vent rib. Double action bars eliminate binding. Vent rib barrels only. All 12 and 20 gauge guns with 3" chamber available with fully engraved receiver flats at no extra cost. Each gauge has its own unique game scene. Introduced 1977. Imported from Japan by Browning.

Price: 12 ga., 3-1/2" Stalker (black syn. stock)	**$596.00**
Price: 12, 20 ga., Hunter, Invector Plus	**$509.00**
Price: 12 ga. Deer Hunter (22" rifled bbl., cantilever mount)	**$624.00**
Price: 28 ga., Hunter, Invector	**$544.00**
Price: .410, Hunter, Invector	**$544.00**

Browning BPS 10 Gauge Camo Pump Shotgun
Similar to the standard BPS except completely covered with Mossy Oak® Shadow Grass camouflage. Available with 24", 26", 28" barrel. Introduced 1999. Imported by Browning.

Price:	**$709.00**

Browning BPS Game Gun Deer Hunter
Similar to the standard BPS except has newly designed receiver/magazine tube/barrel mounting system to eliminate play, heavy 20.5" barrel with rifle-type sights with adjustable rear, solid receiver scope mount, "rifle" stock dimensions for scope or open sights, sling swivel studs. Gloss or matte finished wood with checkering, polished blue metal. Introduced 1992.

Price:	**$624.00**

Charles Daly Maxi-Mag Turkey

Escort AimGuard

Escort Field Hunter

Browning BPS Stalker Pump Shotgun

Same gun as the standard BPS except all exposed metal parts have a matte blued finish and the stock has a durable black finish with a black recoil pad. Available in 10 ga. (3-1/2") and 12 ga. with 3" or 3-1/2" chamber, 22", 28", 30" barrel with Invector choke system. Introduced 1987.

Price: 12 ga., 3" chamber, Invector Plus **$492.00**
Price: 10, 12 ga., 3-1/2" chamber **$596.00**

Browning BPS NWTF Turkey Series Pump Shotgun

Similar to the BPS Stalker except has full coverage Mossy Oak® Break-Up™ camo finish on synthetic stock, forearm and exposed metal parts. Offered in 10 and 12 gauge, 3" or 3-1/2" chamber; 24" bbl. has extra-full choke tube and HiViz fiber-optic sights. Introduced 2001. From Browning.

Price: 10 ga., 3-1/2" chamber **$760.00**
Price: 12 ga., 3-1/2" chamber **$760.00**
Price: 12 ga., 3" chamber **$636.00**

Browning BPS Micro Pump Shotgun

Similar to the BPS Stalker except 20 ga. only, 22" Invector barrel, stock has pistol grip with recoil pad. Length of pull is 13-1/4"; weighs 6 lbs., 12 oz. Introduced 1986.

Price: **$509.00**

CHARLES DALY FIELD PUMP SHOTGUNS

Gauge: 12, 20. **Barrel:** Interchangeable 18-1/2", 24", 26", 28", 30" multi-choked. **Weight:** NA. **Stock:** Synthetic, various finishes, recoil pad. **Receiver:** Machined aluminum. **Features:** Field Tactical and Slug models come with adustable sights; Youth models may be upgraded to full size. Imported from Akkar, Turkey.

Price: Field Tactical **$199.00**
Price: Field Hunter **$219.00**
Price: Field Hunter, Realtree Hardwood **$219.00**
Price: Field Hunter Advantage **$219.00**

CHARLES DALY MAXI-MAG PUMP SHOTGUNS

Gauge: 12 gauge, 3-1/2". **Barrel:** 24", 26", 28"; multi-choke system. **Weight:** NA. **Stock:** Synthetic black, Realtree Hardwoods, or Advantage Timber receiver, aluminum alloy. **Features:** Handles 2-3/4", 3" and 3-1/2" loads. Interchangeable ported barrels; Turkey package includes sling, HiViz sights, XX Full choke. Imported from Akkar, Turkey.

Price: Field Hunter **$259.00**
Price: Field Hunter Advantage **$319.00**
Price: Field Hunter Hardwoods. **$319.00**
Price: Field Hunter Turkey. **$389.00**

DIAMOND 12 GA. PUMP SHOTGUNS

Gauge: 12, 2-3/4" and 3" chambers. **Barrel:** 18"-30". **Weight:** 7 lbs. **Stock:** Walnut, synthetic. **Features:** Aluminum one-piece receiver sculpted for lighter weight. Double locking on fixed bolt. Gold, Elite and Panther series with vented barrels and 3 chokes. All series slug guns available (Gold and Elite with sights). Imported from Istanbul by ADCO Sales.

Price: Gold, 28" vent rib w/3 chokes, walnut **$359.00**
Price: Gold, 28", synthetic **$329.00**
Price: Gold Slug, 24" w/sights, walnut or synthetic . . . . **$329.00 to $359.00**
Price: Silver Mariner 18.5" Slug, synthetic **$399.00**
Price: Silver Mariner 22" vent rib w/3 chokes **$419.00**
Price: Elite, 22" slug w/sights; 24", 28" vent rib w/3 chokes, walnut . . . . **$329.00 to $349.00**
Price: Panther, 28", 30" vent rib w/3 chokes, synthetic **$279.00**
Price: Panther,18.5", 22" Slug, synthetic . . . . **$209.00 to $265.00**
Price: Imperial 12 ga., 28" vent rib w/3 chokes, 3.5" chamber, walnut **$399.00**

ESCORT PUMP SHOTGUNS

Gauge: 12, 20; 3" chamber. **Barrel:** 18" (AimGuard model); 22" (FH Slug model), 24", 26" and 28" (Field Hunter models), choke tubes (M, IC, F); turkey choke w/24" bbl. **Weight:** 6.4 to 7 lbs. **Stock:** Polymer, black chrome or camo finish. **Features:** Alloy receiver w/ dovetail for sight mounting. Two stock adjusting spacers included. Introduced 2003. From Legacy Sports International.

Price: Field Hunter, black stock **$247.00**
Price: Camo, 24" bbl. **$363.00**
Price: AimGuard, 20" bbl., black stock **$211.00**
Price: MarineGuard, nickel finish **$254.00**
Price: Combo (2 bbls.) **$270.00**

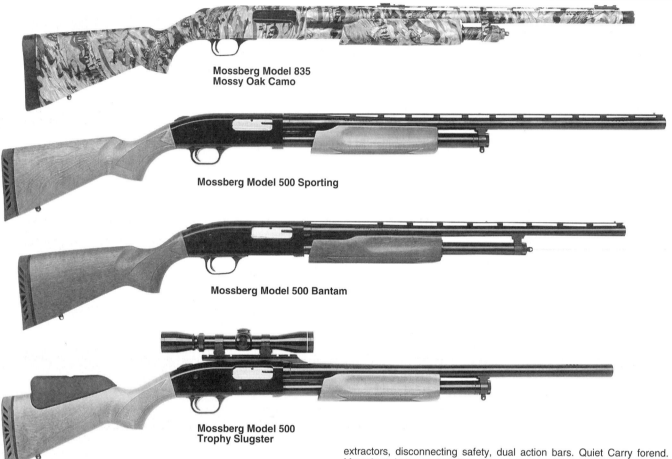

**Mossberg Model 835
Mossy Oak Camo**

Mossberg Model 500 Sporting

Mossberg Model 500 Bantam

**Mossberg Model 500
Trophy Slugster**

MOSSBERG MODEL 835 ULTI-MAG PUMP SHOTGUNS

Gauge: 12, 3-1/2" chamber. **Barrel:** Ported 24" rifled bore, 24", 28", Accu-Mag choke tubes for steel or lead shot. **Weight:** 7-3/4 lbs. **Length:** 48-1/2" overall. **Stock:** 14"x1-1/2"x2-1/2". Dual Comb. Cut-checkered hardwood or camo synthetic; both have recoil pad. **Sights:** White bead front, brass mid-bead; fiber-optic rear. **Features:** Shoots 2-3/4", 3" or 3-1/2" shells. Back-bored and ported barrel to reduce recoil, improve patterns. Ambidextrous thumb safety, twin extractors, dual slide bars. Mossberg Cablelock included. Introduced 1988.
Price: 28" vent rib, hardwood stock **$394.00**
Price: Combos, 24" rifled or smooth bore, rifle sights, 24" vent rib
Accu-Mag Ulti-Full choke tube, Mossy Oak® camo finish **$556.00**
Price: RealTree Camo Turkey, 24" vent rib, Accu-Mag extra-full
tube, synthetic stock **$574.00**
Price: Mossy Oak® Camo, 28" vent rib, Accu-Mag tubes,
synthetic stock **$574.00**
Price: OFM Camo, 28" vent rib, Accu-Mag Mod. tube,
synthetic stock **$438.00**

Mossberg Model 835 Synthetic Stock Shotgun

Similar to the Model 835, except with 28" ported barrel with Accu-Mag Mod. choke tube, Parkerized finish, black synthetic stock and forend. Introduced 1998. Made in U.S. by Mossberg.
Price: **$394.00**

MOSSBERG MODEL 500 SPORTING PUMP SHOTGUNS

Gauge: 12, 20, .410, 3" chamber. **Barrel:** 18-1/2" to 28" with fixed or Accu-Choke, plain or vent rib. **Weight:** 6-1/4 lbs. (.410), 7-1/4 lbs. (12). **Length:** 48" overall (28" barrel). **Stock:** 14"x1-1/2"x2-1/2". Walnut-stained hardwood. Cut-checkered grip and forend. **Sights:** White bead front, brass mid-bead; fiber-optic. **Features:** Ambidextrous thumb safety, twin

extractors, disconnecting safety, dual action bars. Quiet Carry forend. Many barrels are ported. From Mossberg.
Price: From about **$316.00**
Price: Sporting Combos (field barrel and Slugster barrel). From . . **$381.00**

Mossberg Model 500 Bantam Pump Shotgun

Same as the Model 500 Sporting Pump except 12 or 20 gauge, 22" vent rib Accu-Choke barrel with choke tube set; has 1" shorter stock, reduced length from pistol grip to trigger, reduced forend reach. Introduced 1992.
Price: **$316.00**
Price: With Realtree Hardwoods camouflage finish (20 ga. only) . . **$364.00**

Mossberg Model 500 Camo Pump Shotgun

Same as the Model 500 Sporting Pump except 12 gauge only and entire gun is covered with Mossy Oak® Advantage camouflage finish. Receiver drilled and tapped for scope mounting. Comes with quick detachable swivel studs, swivels, camouflage sling, Mossberg Cablelock.
Price: From about **$364.00**

Mossberg Model 500 Persuader/Cruiser Shotguns

Similar to Mossberg Model 500 except has 18-1/2" or 20" barrel with cylinder bore choke, synthetic stock and blue or Parkerized finish. Available in 12, 20 and .410 with bead or ghost ring sights, 6- or 8-shot magazines. From Mossberg.
Price: 12 gauge, 20" barrel, 8-shot, bead sight. **$357.00**
Price: 20 gauge or .410, 18-1/2" barrel, 6-shot, bead sight **$357.00**
Price: Home Security 410 (.410, 18-1/2" barrel
with spreader choke) **$360.00**

Mossberg Model 590 Special Purpose Shotgun

Similar to Model 500 except has Parkerized or Marinecote finish, 9-shot magazine and black synthetic stock (some models feature Speed Feed). Available in 12 gauge only with 20", cylinder bore barrel. Weighs 7-1/4 lbs. From Mossberg.
Price: Bead sight, heat shield over barrel **$525.00**

Remington 870 Wingmaster

Remington Model 870 50th Anniversary Classic Trap

Remington Model 870 Marine Magnum

Remington Model 870 Wingmaster LW

NEW ENGLAND PARDNER PUMP SHOTGUN

Gauge: 12 ga., 3". **Barrel:** 28" vent rib, screw-in Modified choke tube. **Weight:** 7-1/2 lbs. **Length:** 48-1/2". **Stock:** American walnut, grooved forend, ventilated recoil pad. **Sights:** Bead front. **Features:** Machined steel receiver, double action bars, five-shot magazine.
Price: $200.00

REMINGTON MODEL 870 WINGMASTER SHOTGUNS

Gauge: 12 ga., 16 ga., 3" chamber. **Barrel:** 26", 28", 30" (RemChokes). **Weight:** 7-1/4 lbs. **Length:** 46", 48". **Stock:** Walnut, hardwood, synthetic. **Sights:** Single bead (Twin bead Wingmaster). **Features:** Light contour barrel. Double action bars, cross-bolt safety, blue finish.
Price: Wingmaster, walnut, blued, 26", 28", 30" $665.00
Price: 870 Wingmaster Super Magnum, 3-1/2" chamber, 28" $732.00

Remington Model 870 Classic Trap Shotgun

Similar to Model 870 Wingmaster except has 30" vent rib, light contour barrel, singles, mid- and long-handicap choke tubes, semi-fancy American walnut stock, high-polish blued receiver with engraving. Chamber 2-1/2". From Remington Arms Co.
Price: $872.00

Remington Model 870 Marine Magnum Shotgun

Similar to 870 Wingmaster except all metal plated with electroless nickel, black synthetic stock and forend. Has 18" plain barrel (cyl.), bead front sight, 7-shot magazine. Introduced 1992.
Price: $647.00

Remington Model 870 Wingmaster LW Shotgun

Similar to Model 870 Wingmaster except in 28 gauge and .410-bore only, 25" vent rib barrel with RemChoke tubes, high-gloss wood finish.
Price: .410-bore $695.00
Price: 28 gauge $749.00

Remington Model 870 Express Shotguns

Similar to Model 870 Wingmaster except walnut-toned hardwood stock with solid, black recoil pad and pressed checkering on grip and forend. Outside metal surfaces have black oxide finish. Comes with 26" or 28" vent rib barrel with mod. RemChoke tube.
Price: 12 ga., 20 ga., 16 ga. (28") $345.00
Price: Express Combo, 12 ga., 26" vent rib with mod. RemChoke and 20" fully rifled barrel with rifle sights, or RemChoke .. **$469.00 to $503.00**
Price: Express synthetic, 12-ga., 26" or 28" $345.00
Price: Express combo (20 ga.) with extra deer rifled barrel, fully rifled or RemChoke .... **$469.00 to $503.00**

Remington Model 870 Express Super Magnum Shotgun

Similar to Model 870 Express except 28" vent rib barrel with 3-1/2" chamber, vented recoil pad. Introduced 1998.
Price: $389.00
Price: Super Magnum synthetic, 26" $389.00
Price: Super Magnum turkey camo (full-coverage RealTree Advantage camo), 23" $513.00
Price: Super Magnum combo (26" with Mod. RemChoke and 20" fully rifled deer barrel with 3" chamber and rifle sights; wood stock) .. **$536.00**
Price: Super Magnum synthetic turkey, 23" (black) $403.00

Remington Model 870 Wingmaster Super Magnum Shotgun

Similar to Model 870 Express Super Magnum except high-polish blued finish, 28" ventilated barrel with Imp. Cyl., Modified and Full choke tubes, checkered high-gloss walnut stock. Overall length 48", weighs 7-1/2 lbs. Introduced 2000.
Price: 3-1/2" chamber $732.00

Remington Model 870 Sps Super Slug Deer Gun Shotgun

Similar to the Model 870 Express synthetic except has 23" rifled, modified contour barrel with cantilever scope mount. Comes with black synthetic stock and forend with swivel studs, black Cordura nylon sling. Fully rifled centilever barrel. Introduced 1999.
Price: $580.00

Remington Model 870 Express Super Magnum

Remington Model 870 Express Deer Gun

Remington Model 870 Express Turkey

Remington Model 870 SPS Super Slug Deer Gun

Remington Model 870 SPS-T Camo

Remington Model 870 SPS-T Super Magnum Camo Shotguns

Similar to the Model 870 Express synthetic, chambered for 12 ga., 3" shells, has Mossy Oak® Break-Up™ synthetic stock and metal treatment, TruGlo fiber-optic sights. Introduced 2001.
Price: 20" RS, Rem. choke $653.00

Remington Model 870 Express Deer Shotguns

Same as Model 870 Express except 20" barrel with fixed imp. cyl. choke, open iron sights, Monte Carlo stock. Introduced 1991.
Price: $345.00
Price: With fully rifled barrel $385.00

Remington Model 870 Express Turkey Shotguns

Same as Model 870 Express except 3" chamber, 21" vent rib turkey barrel and extra-full Rem. choke turkey tube; 12 ga. only. Introduced 1991.
Price: $359.00
Price: Express Turkey Camo stock has Skyline Excel camo, matte black metal $412.00

Remington Model 870 Express Synthetic 18" Shotgun

Similar to Model 870 Express with 18" barrel except synthetic stock and forend; 7-shot. Introduced 1994.
Price: $332.00

REMINGTON MODEL 870 SPS SUPER MAGNUM CAMO SHOTGUN

Gauge: 12, 3-1/2" chamber. **Barrel:** 26", 28", vent rib, with Full, Mod., Imp. Cyl. RemChoke. **Weight:** 7-1/4 lbs. to 7-1/2 lbs. **Length:** 46" to 481/2" overall. **Stock:** Mossy Oak® Break-Up™ camo finish. **Sights:** Metal bead front. **Features:** Synthetic stock and all metal (except bolt and trigger guard) and stock covered with Mossy Oak® Break-Up™ camo finish. Comes with camo sling, swivels.
Price: $653.00

WINCHESTER MODEL 9410 LEVER-ACTION SHOTGUN

Gauge: .410, 2-1/2" chamber. **Barrel:** 24" cyl. bore, also Invector choke system. **Weight:** 6-3/4 lbs. **Length:** 42-1/8" overall. **Stock:** Checkered walnut straight-grip; checkered walnut forearm. **Sights:** Adjustable "V" rear, TruGlo® front. **Features:** Model 94 rifle action (smoothbore) chambered for .410 shotgun. Angle Controlled Eject extractor/ejector; choke tubes; 9-shot tubular magazine; 13-1/2" length of pull. Introduced 2001. From U.S. Repeating Arms Co.
Price: 9410 fixed choke................................... $626.00
Price: 9410 Packer w/chokes $647.00
Price: 9410 w/Invector, traditional model $626.00
Price: 9410 w/Invector, Packer model $647.00
Price: 9410 w/Invector, semi-fancy traditional $626.00

Includes a variety of game guns and guns for competitive shooting.

Beretta DT Trident Skeet

Beretta Series 682 Gold E Sporting

Beretta Series 682 Gold E Trap Combo

Beretta S687 EELL Combo

Beretta 686 Onyx

BERETTA DT10 TRIDENT SHOTGUNS

Gauge: 12, 2-3/4", 3" chambers. **Barrel:** 28", 30", 32", 34"; competition-style vent rib; fixed or Optima choke tubes. **Weight:** 7.9 to 9 lbs. **Stock:** High-grade walnut stock with oil finish; hand-checkered grip and forend, adjustable stocks available. **Features:** Detachable, adjustable trigger group, raised and thickened receiver, forend iron has adjustment nut to guarantee wood-to-metal fit. Introduced 2000. Imported from Italy by Beretta USA.

Price: DT10 Trident Trap (selective, lockable single trigger, adjustable stock. .... **$,8500.00**

Price: DT10 Trident Top Single **$10,790.00**

Price: DT10 Trident X Trap Combo (single and o/u barrels) **$11,040.00**

Price: DT10 Trident Skeet (skeet stock with rounded recoil pad, tapered rib). **$8,030.00**

Price: DT10 Trident Sporting (sporting clays stock with rounded recoil pad) **$7,850.00**

Price: DT10L Sporting **$8,475.00**

BERETTA SERIES 682 GOLD E SKEET, TRAP, SPORTING O/U SHOTGUNS

Gauge: 12, 2-3/4" chambers. **Barrel:** skeet-28"; trap-30" and 32", Imp. Mod. & Full and Mobilchoke; trap mono shotguns-32" and 34" Mobilchoke; trap top single guns-32" and 34" Full and Mobilchoke; trap combo sets-from 30" O/U, to 32" O/U, 34" top single. **Stock:** Close-grained walnut, hand checkered. **Sights:** White Bradley bead front sight and center bead. **Features:** Receiver has Greystone gunmetal gray finish with gold accents. Trap Monte Carlo stock has deluxe trap recoil pad. Various grades available. Imported from Italy by Beretta USA.

Price: 682 Gold E Trap with adjustable stock **$4,325.00**

Price: 682 Gold E Trap Top Combo **$5,475.00**

Price: 682 Gold E Sporting **$3,550.00**

Price: 682 Gold E skeet, adjustable stock **$4,325.00**

BERETTA 686 ONYX O/U SHOTGUNS

Gauge: 12, 20, 28; 3", 3.5" chambers. **Barrel:** 26", 28" (Mobilchoke tubes). **Weight:** 6.8-6.9 lbs. **Stock:** Checkered American walnut. **Features:** Intended for the beginning sporting clays shooter. Has wide, vented target rib, radiused recoil pad. Polished black finish on receiver and barrels. Introduced 1993. Imported from Italy by Beretta U.S.A.

Price: White Onyx **$1,875.00**

Price: Onyx Pro **$1,875.00**

Price: Onyx Pro 3.5 .... **$1,975.00**

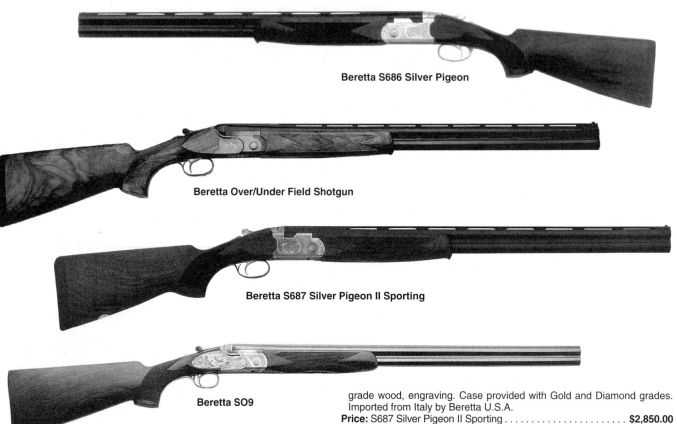

Beretta S686 Silver Pigeon

Beretta Over/Under Field Shotgun

Beretta S687 Silver Pigeon II Sporting

Beretta SO9

BERETTA SILVER PIGEON O/U SHOTGUNS

Gauge: 12, 20, 28, 3" chambers (2-3/4" 28 ga.). .410 bore, 3" chamber. **Barrel:** 26", 28". **Weight:** 6.8 lbs. **Stock:** Checkered walnut. **Features:** Interchangeable barrels (20 and 28 ga.), single selective gold-plated trigger, boxlock action, auto safety, Schnabel forend.

Price: Silver Pigeon S	$2,150.00
Price: Silver Pigeon S Combo	$2,975.00
Price: Silver Pigeon II	$2,525.00
Price: Silver Pigeon II, 28 ga.	$3,475.00
Price: Silver Pigeon III	$2,650.00
Price: Silver Pigeon IV	$2,955.00
Price: Silver Pigeon V	$3,495.00

BERETTA ULTRALIGHT O/U SHOTGUNS

Gauge: 12, 2-3/4" chambers. **Barrel:** 26", 28", Mobilchoke tubes. **Weight:** About 5 lbs., 13 oz. **Stock:** Select American walnut with checkered grip and forend. **Features:** Low-profile aluminum alloy receiver with titanium breech face insert. Electroless nickel receiver with game scene engraving. Single selective trigger; automatic safety. Introduced 1992. Ultralight Deluxe except has matte electroless nickel finish receiver with gold game scene engraving; matte oil-finished, select walnut stock and forend. Imported from Italy by Beretta U.S.A.

Price:	$1,975.00
Price: Ultralight Deluxe	$2,350.00

BERETTA COMPETITION SHOTGUNS

Gauge: 12, 20, 28, and .410 bore, 2-3/4", 3" and 3-1/2" chambers. **Barrel:** 26" and 28" (Mobilchoke tubes). **Stock:** Close-grained walnut. **Features:** Highly-figured, American walnut stocks and forends, and a unique, weather-resistant finish on barrels. Silver designates standard 686, 687 models with silver receivers; 686 Silver Pigeon has enhanced engraving pattern, Schnabel forend; Gold indicates higher grade 686EL, 687EL models with full sideplates; Diamond is for 687EELL models with highest grade wood, engraving. Case provided with Gold and Diamond grades. Imported from Italy by Beretta U.S.A.

Price: S687 Silver Pigeon II Sporting	$2,850.00
Price: S687 EL Gold Pigeon II (deep relief engraving)	$5,095.00
Price: S687 EL Gold Pigeon II combo, 20/28 or 28/.410	$6,195.00
Price: S687 EELL Gold Pigeon Sporting (D.R. engraving)	$6,495.00
Price: Gold Sporting Pigeon	$4,971.00
Price: 28 and 410 combo	NA

BERETTA MODEL SO5, SO6, SO9 SHOTGUNS

Gauge: 12, 2-3/4" chambers. **Barrel:** To customer specs. **Stock:** To customer specs. **Features:** SO5-trap, skeet and sporting clays models SO5; SO6-SO6 and SO6 EELL are field models. SO6 has a case-hardened or silver receiver with contour hand engraving. SO6 EELL has hand-engraved receiver in a fine floral or "fine English" pattern or game scene, with bas-relief chisel work and gold inlays. SO6 and SO6 EELL are available with sidelocks removable by hand. Imported from Italy by Beretta U.S.A.

Price: SO5 Trap, skeet, Sporting	$13,000.00
Price: SO6 Trap, skeet, Sporting	$17,500.00
Price: SO6 EELL Field, custom specs	$28,000.00
Price: SO9 (12, 20, 28, .410, 26", 28", 30", any choke)	$31,000.00

BRNO ZH 300 O/U SHOTGUNS

Gauge: 12, 2-3/4" chambers. **Barrel:** 26", 27-1/2", 29" (skeet, Imp. Cyl., Mod., Full). **Weight:** 7 lbs. **Length:** 44.4" overall. **Stock:** European walnut. **Features:** Double triggers; automatic safety; polished blue finish, engraved receiver. Announced 1998. Imported from the Czech Republic by Euro-Imports.

Price: ZH 301, field	$594.00
Price: ZH 302, skeet	$608.00
Price: ZH 303, 12 ga. trap	$608.00
Price: ZH 321, 16 ga.	$595.00

BRNO 501.2 O/U SHOTGUN

Gauge: 12, 2-3/4" chambers. **Barrel:** 27.5" (Full & Mod.). **Weight:** 7 lbs. **Length:** 44" overall. **Stock:** European walnut. **Features:** Boxlock action with double triggers; ejectors; automatic safety; hand-cut checkering. Announced 1998. Imported from the Czech Republic by Euro-Imports.

Price:	$850.00

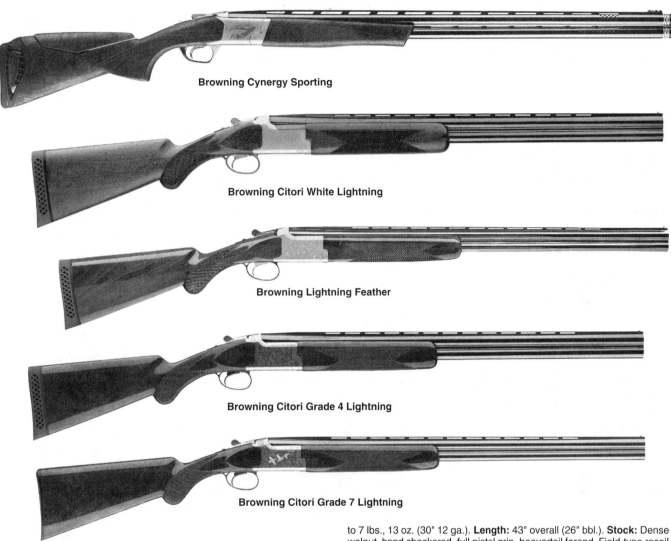

Browning Cynergy Sporting

Browning Citori White Lightning

Browning Lightning Feather

Browning Citori Grade 4 Lightning

Browning Citori Grade 7 Lightning

BROWNING CYNERGY O/U SHOTGUNS

Gauge: 12, 20, 28. **Barrel:** 26", 28", 30", 32". **Stock:** Walnut or composite. **Sights:** White bead front most models; HiViz Pro-Comp sight on some models; mid bead. **Features:** Mono-Lock hinge, recoil-reducing interchangeable Inflex recoil pad, silver nitride receiver; striker-based trigger, ported barrel option. 12 models cataloged for 2006. Nine new models introduced 2006: Cynergy Sporting, Adjustable Comb; Cynergy Sporting Composite with TopCote; Cynergy Sporting Composite CF; Cynergy Field, Composite; Cynergy Classic Sporting; Cynergy Classic Field; Cynergy Camo Mossy Oak New Shadow Grass; Cynergy Camo Mossy Oak New Break-Up; and Cynergy Camo Mossy Oak Brush. Imported from Japan by Browning.

Price: Cynergy Field, 12 ga., Grade 1 walnut, ... **$2,048.00**
Price: Cynergy Field Small Gauge, 20 /28 ga., intr. 2005 . . . . . . **$2,062.00**
Price: Cynergy Sporting Small Gauge, 20 /28 ga., intr. 2005 . . . **$3,080.00**
Price: Cynergy Field Composite, 12 ga., ... **$1,890.00**
Price: Cynergy Sporting, 12 ga.; 28", 30", or 32" barrels **$3,046.00**
Price: Cynergy Sporting Composite 12 ga.. . . . . **$2,846.00**
Price: Cynergy Sporting, adjustable comb, intr. 2006 . . . . **$3,351.00**
Price: Cynergy Sporting Composite w/TopCote, intr. 2006. . . . . . **$2,979.00**

BROWNING CITORI O/U SHOTGUNS

Gauge: 12, 20, 28 and .410. **Barrel:** 26", 28" in 28 and .410. Offered with Invector choke tubes. All 12 and 20 gauge models have back-bored barrels and Invector Plus choke system. **Weight:** 6 lbs., 8 oz. (26" .410)

to 7 lbs., 13 oz. (30" 12 ga.). **Length:** 43" overall (26" bbl.). **Stock:** Dense walnut, hand checkered, full pistol grip, beavertail forend. Field-type recoil pad on 12 ga. field guns and trap and skeet models. **Sights:** Medium raised beads, German nickel silver. **Features:** Barrel selector integral with safety, automatic ejectors, three-piece takedown. 25 models cataloged for 2006. Two limited-run models reintroduced 2006: Citori 4-Barrel Skeet Set, Grade I; Citori 4-Barrel Skeet Set, Grade VII. Imported from Japan by Browning.

Price: Lightning, 12 and 20 ga. **$1,645.00**
Price: Lightning, 28 ga. and .410 bore **$1,709.00**
Price: White Lightning, 12 and 20 ga.. . . . . **$1,714.00**
Price: White Lightning, 28 ga. and .410 bore **$1,790.00**
Price: 525 Field, 12 and 20 ga.. . . . . **$1,981.00**
Price: 525 Field, 28 ga. and .410 bore. **$2,010.00**
Price: Superlight Feather, 12 and 20 ga. (2-3/4"), 6.25/5.7 lbs.. . . . **$1,938.00**
Price: Lightning Feather, 12 and 20 ga.,. **$1,869.00**
Price: Citori 4-Barrel Skeet Set, Grade I, intr. 2006 . . . . **$8,412.00**

Browning Citori High Grade Shotguns

Similar to standard Citori except has engraved hunting scenes and gold inlays, high-grade, hand-oiled walnut stock and forearm. Introduced 2000. From Browning.

Price: Gran Lightning, engraved receiver, from **$2,429.00**
Price: Grade IV Lightning, engraved gray receiver,
introduced 2005, from. **$2,608.00**
Price: Grade VII Lightning, engraved gray or blue receiver,
introduced 2005, from **$4,146.00**

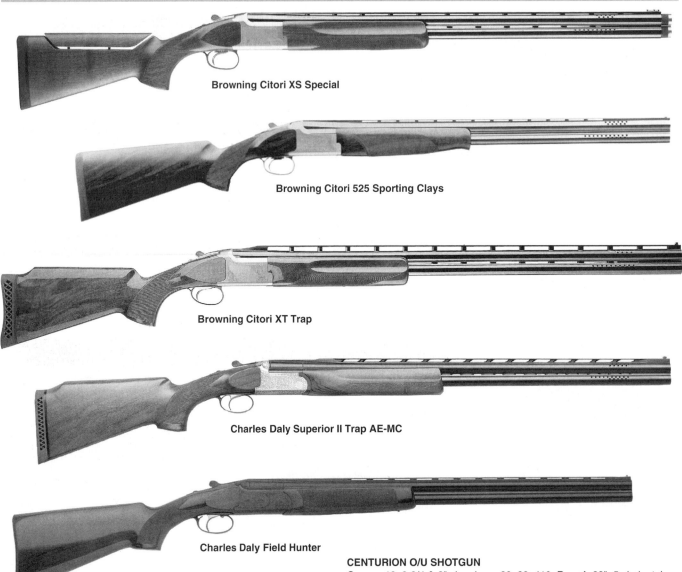

Browning Citori XS Special

Browning Citori 525 Sporting Clays

Browning Citori XT Trap

Charles Daly Superior II Trap AE-MC

Charles Daly Field Hunter

Browning Citori XS Sporting O/U Shotguns

Similar to the standard Citori except available in 12, 20, 28 or .410 with 28", 30", 32" ported barrels with various screw-in choke combinations: S (Skeet), C (Cylinder), IC (Improved Cylinder), M (Modified), and IM (Improved Modified). Has pistol grip stock, rounded or Schnabel forend. Weighs 7.1 lbs. to 8.75 lbs. Introduced 2004.

Price: XS Special, 12 ga.; 30", 32" barrels $2,727.00
Price: XS Sporting, 12 or 20 ga. $2,472.00
Price: XS Skeet, 12 or 20 ga. $2,434.00
Price: 525 Sporting Grade I, 12 ga. intr. 2005 . . . . $2,319.00
Price: 525 Golden Clays, 12 or 20 gauge $3,058.00
Price: 525 Golden Clays, 28 or .410 . . . . $4,653.00

Browning Citori XT Trap O/U Shotgun

Similar to the Citori XS Special except has engraved silver nitride receiver with gold highlights, vented side barrel rib. Available in 12 gauge with 30" or 32" barrels, Invector-Plus choke tubes, adjustable comb and buttplate. Introduced 1999. Imported by Browning.

Price: XT Trap $2,275.00
Price: XT Trap w/adjustable comb $2,549.00
Price: XT Trap Gold w/adjustable comb, introduced 2005 . . . . . . $4,221.00

CENTURION O/U SHOTGUN

Gauge: 12, 2-3/4 & 3" chambers, 20, 28, 410. **Barrel:** 28", 5 choke tubes. **Weight:** 7.35 lbs. (12); 6.14 lbs. (20); 5.8 lbs. (28); 5.3 lbs. (410). **Length:** 45". **Stock:** Glossy Turkish walnut. **Features:** Single selective trigger, automatic safety, extractors, ventilated recoil pad, front bead sight. Manufactured by CFS in Turkey. Imported by Century International.
Price: $470.00

CHARLES DALY SUPERIOR II TRAP AE-MC O/U SHOTGUN

Gauge: 12, 2-3/4" chambers. **Barrel:** 30" choke tubes. **Weight:** About 7 lbs. **Length:** 47-3/8". **Stock:** Checkered walnut; pistol grip, semi-beavertail forend. **Features:** Silver engraved receiver, chrome-moly steel barrels; gold single selective trigger; automatic safety, automatic ejectors; red bead front sight, metal bead center; recoil pad. Introduced 1997. Imported from Italy by K.B.I., Inc.
Price: $1,699.00

CHARLES DALY FIELD II HUNTER O/U SHOTGUN

Gauge: 12, 20, 28 and .410 bore (3" chambers, 28 ga. has 2-3/4"). **Barrel:** 28" Mod & Full, 26" Imp. Cyl. & Mod (.410 is Full & Full). **Weight:** About 7 lbs. **Length:** 42-3/4" to 44-3/4". **Stock:** Checkered walnut pistol grip and forend. **Features:** Blued engraved receiver, chrome-moly steel barrels; gold single selective trigger; automatic safety; extractors; gold bead front sight. Introduced 1997. Imported from Italy by K.B.I., Inc.
Price: 12 or 20 ga. $1,029.00
Price: 28 ga., .410 bore $1,129.00

Charles Daly Superior Hunter

Charles Daly Empire II Mono Trap

Charles Daly Empire II EDL Hunter

Charles Daly Empire Sporting O/U

Charles Daly Superior II Hunter AE O/U Shotgun
Similar to the Field Hunter AE except has silvered, engraved receiver. Introduced 1997. Imported from Italy by F.B.I., Inc.
Price: 28 ga., .410 bore **$1,519.00**

Charles Daly Field Hunter AE-MC O/U Shotgun
Similar to the Field Hunter except in 12 or 20 only, 26" or 28" barrels with five multi-choke tubes; automatic ejectors. Introduced 1997. Imported from Italy by K.B.I., Inc.
Price: 12 or 20 ga. **$1,279.00**

Charles Daly Superior II Sporting O/U Shotgun
Similar to the Field Hunter AE-MC except 28" or 30" barrels; silvered, engraved receiver; five choke tubes; ported barrels; red bead front sight. Introduced 1997. Imported from Italy by K.B.I., Inc.
Price: **$1,659.00**

CHARLES DALY EMPIRE II EDL HUNTER AE, AE-MC O/U SHOTGUNS
Gauge: 12, 20, .410, 3" chambers, 28 ga., 2-3/4". **Barrel:** 26", 28" (12, 20, choke tubes), 26" (Imp. Cyl. & Mod., 28 ga.), 26" (Full & Full, .410). **Weight:** About 7 lbs. **Stocks:** Checkered walnut pistol grip buttstock, semi-beavertail forend; recoil pad. **Features:** Silvered, engraved receiver; chrome-moly barrels; gold single selective trigger; automatic safety; automatic ejectors; red bead front sight, metal bead middle sight. Introduced 1997. Imported from Italy by K.B.I., Inc.
Price: Empire II EDL AE-MC (dummy sideplates) 12 or 20 . . . . . **$2,029.00**
Price: Empire II EDL AE, 28 . . . . **$2,019.00**
Price: Empire II EDL AE, .410 . . . . **$2,019.00**

Charles Daly Empire II Sporting AE-MC O/U Shotgun
Similar to the Empire II EDL Hunter except 12 or 20 gauge only, 28", 30" barrels with choke tubes; ported barrels; special stock dimensions. Introduced 1997. Imported from Italy by K.B.I., Inc.
Price: **$2,049.00**

CHARLES DALY EMPIRE II TRAP AE-MC O/U SHOTGUNS
Gauge: 12, 2-3/4" chambers. **Barrel:** 30" choke tubes. **Weight:** About 7 lbs. **Stock:** Checkered walnut; pistol grip, semi-beavertail forend. **Features:** Silvered, engraved, reinforced receiver; chrome-moly steel barrels; gold single selective trigger; automatic safety, automatic ejector; red bead front sight, metal bead center; recoil pad. Imported from Italy by K.B.I., Inc.
Price: **$2,099.00**
Price: Mono AE-MC, adj. comb **$2,999.00**
Price: AE-MC combo set, adj. comb **$3,919.00**

CHARLES DALY DIAMOND REGENT GTX DL HUNTER O/U SHOTGUNS
Gauge: 12, 20, .410, 3" chambers, 28, 2-3/4" chambers. **Barrel:** 26", 28", 30" (choke tubes), 26" (Imp. Cyl. & Mod. in 28, 26" (Full & Full) in .410. **Weight:** About 7 lbs. **Stock:** Extra select fancy European walnut with 24" hand checkering, hand rubbed oil finish. **Features:** Boss-type action with internal side lumps. Deep cut hand-engraved scrollwork and game scene set in full sideplates. GTX detachable single selective trigger system with coil springs; chrome-moly steel barrels; automatic safety; automatic ejectors; white bead front sight, metal bead center sight. Introduced 1997. Imported from Italy by K.B.I., Inc.
Price: 12 or 20. . . . . **Special order only**
Price: 28 . . . . **Special order only**
Price: .410 bore . . . . **Special order only**
Price: Diamond Regent GTX EDL Hunter (as above with engraved scroll and birds, 10 gold inlays), 12 or 20 . . . . **Special order only**
Price: As above, 28 . . . . **Special order only**
Price: As above, .410 . . . . **Special order only**

CHARLES DALY DIAMOND GTX SPORTING O/U SHOTGUN
Gauge: 12, 20, 3" chambers. **Barrel:** 28", 30" with choke tubes. **Weight:** About 8.5 lbs. **Stock:** Checkered deluxe walnut; sporting clays dimensions. Pistol grip; semi-beavertail forend; hand rubbed oil finish. **Features:** Chromed, hand-engraved receiver; chrome-moly steel barrels; GTX detachable single selective trigger system with coil springs, automatic safety; automatic ejectors; red bead front sight; ported barrels. Introduced 1997. Imported from Italy by K.B.I., Inc.
Price: . . . . **Price on request**

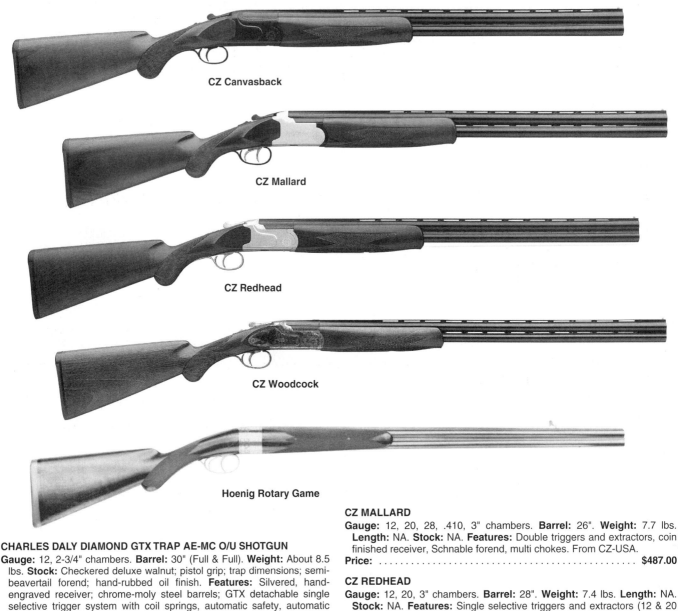

CZ Canvasback

CZ Mallard

CZ Redhead

CZ Woodcock

Hoenig Rotary Game

CHARLES DALY DIAMOND GTX TRAP AE-MC O/U SHOTGUN

Gauge: 12, 2-3/4" chambers. **Barrel:** 30" (Full & Full). **Weight:** About 8.5 lbs. **Stock:** Checkered deluxe walnut; pistol grip; trap dimensions; semi-beavertail forend; hand-rubbed oil finish. **Features:** Silvered, hand-engraved receiver; chrome-moly steel barrels; GTX detachable single selective trigger system with coil springs, automatic safety, automatic ejectors, red bead front sight, metal bead middle; recoil pad. Imported from Italy by K.B.I., Inc.
Price: . . . . **Price on request**

CHARLES DALY DIAMOND GTX DL HUNTER O/U SHOTGUN

Gauge: 12, 20, .410, 3" chambers, 28, 2-3/4" chambers. **Barrel:** 26", 28", choke tubes in 12 and 20 ga., 26" (Imp. Cyl. & Mod.), 26" (Full & Full) in .410-bore. **Weight:** About 8.5 lbs. **Stock:** Select fancy European walnut stock, with 24 lpi hand checkering; hand-rubbed oil finish. **Features:** Boss-type action with internal side lugs, hand-engraved scrollwork and game scene. GTX detachable single selective trigger system with coil springs; chrome-moly steel barrels, automatic safety, automatic ejectors, red bead front sight, recoil pad. Introduced 1997. Imported from Italy by K.B.I., Inc.
Price: . . . . **Special order only**

CZ CANVASBACK

Gauge: 12, 20, 3" chambers. **Barrel:** 26", 28". **Weight:** 7.3 lbs. **Length:** NA. **Stock:** NA. **Features:** Single selective trigger, set of 5 screw-in chokes, black chrome finished receiver, Schnable forend. From CZ-USA.
Price: **$708.00**

CZ MALLARD

Gauge: 12, 20, 28, .410, 3" chambers. **Barrel:** 26". **Weight:** 7.7 lbs. **Length:** NA. **Stock:** NA. **Features:** Double triggers and extractors, coin finished receiver, Schnable forend, multi chokes. From CZ-USA.
Price: **$487.00**

CZ REDHEAD

Gauge: 12, 20, 3" chambers. **Barrel:** 28". **Weight:** 7.4 lbs. **Length:** NA. **Stock:** NA. **Features:** Single selective triggers and extractors (12 & 20 ga.), screw-in chokes (12, 20, 28 ga.) choked IC and Mod (.410), coin finished receiver, Schnable forend, multi chokes. From CZ-USA.
Price: **$836.00**

CZ WOODCOCK

Gauge: 12, 20, 28, .410, 3" chambers. **Barrel:** 26". **Weight:** 7.7 lbs. **Length:** NA. **Stock:** NA. **Features:** Single selective triggers and extractors (auto ejectors on 12 & 20 ga.), screw-in chokes (12, 20, 28 ga.) choked IC and Mod (.410), coin finished receiver, Schnable forend, multi chokes. The sculptured frame incorporates a side plate, resembling a true side lock, embellished with hand engraving and finished wtih color casehardening. From CZ-USA.
Price: **$1,078.00**

HOENIG ROTARY ROUND ACTION GAME GUN O/U SHOTGUN

Gauge: 20, 28. **Barrel:** 26", 28", solid tapered rib. **Weight:** 6 lbs. and 6-1/4 lbs. **Stock:** English walnut to customer specifications. **Features:** Round action opens by rotating barrels, pulling forward. Inertia extraction system, rotary wing safety blocks strikers. Simple takedown without removing forend. Introduced 1997. Made in U.S.A. by George Hoenig.
Price: **$20,000.00**

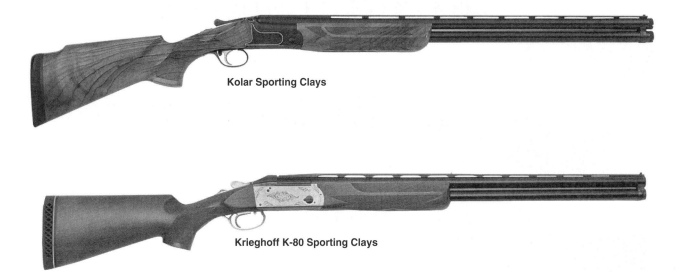

Kolar Sporting Clays

Krieghoff K-80 Sporting Clays

KIMBER MARIAS O/U SHOTGUNS

Gauge: 12, 20; 3". **Barrel:** 26", 28", 30". **Weight:** 7.4 lbs. **Length:** NA. **Stock:** Turkish walnut stocks, 24-lpi checkering, oil finish. LOP: 14.75 inches. **Features:** Hand-detachable back-action sidelock, bone-charcoal case coloring. Hand-engraving on receiver and locks, Belgian rust blue barrels, chrome lined. Five thinwall choke tubes, automatic ejectors, ventilated rib. Gold line cocking indicators on locks. Grade I has 28-inch barrels, Prince of Wales stock in grade three Turkish walnut in either 12 or 20 gauge. Grade II shas grade four Turkish walnut stocks, 12 gauge in Prince of Wales and 20 with either Prince of Wales or English profiles. Imported from Italy by Kimber Mfg., Inc.

Price: Grade I . . . . **NA**
Price: Grade II . . . . **NA**

KOLAR SPORTING CLAYS O/U SHOTGUNS

Gauge: 12, 2-3/4" chambers. **Barrel:** 30", 32", 34"; extended choke tubes. **Stock:** 14-5/8"x2-1/2"x1-7/8"x1-3/8". French walnut. Four stock versions available. **Features:** Single selective trigger, detachable, adjustable for length; overbored barrels with long forcing cones; flat tramline rib; matte blue finish. Made in U.S. by Kolar.

Price: Standard **$8,995.00**
Price: Elite **$12,495.00**
Price: Elite Gold **$15,295.00**
Price: Legend **$15,995.00**
Price: Select **$18,995.00**
Price: Custom . . . . **Price on request**

Kolar AAA Competition Trap O/U Shotgun

Similar to the Sporting Clays gun except has 32" O/U /34" Unsingle or 30" O/U /34" Unsingle barrels as an over/under, unsingle, or combination set. Stock dimensions are 14-1/2"x2-1/2"x1-1/2"; American or French walnut; step parallel rib standard. Contact maker for full listings. Made in U.S.A. by Kolar.

Price: Over/under, choke tubes, standard **$9,595.00**
Price: Unsingle, choke tubes, standard **$10,195.00**
Price: Combo (30"/34", 32"/34"), standard **$12,595.00**

Kolar AAA Competition Skeet O/U Shotgun

Similar to the Sporting Clays gun except has 28" or 30" barrels with Kolarite AAA sub gauge tubes; stock of American or French walnut with matte finish; flat tramline rib; under barrel adjustable for point of impact. Many options available. Contact maker for complete listing. Made in U.S.A. by Kolar.

Price: Standard, choke tubes **$10,495.00**
Price: Standard, choke tubes, two-barrel set **$12,995.00**

KRIEGHOFF K-80 SPORTING CLAYS O/U SHOTGUN

Gauge: 12. **Barrel:** 28", 30", 32", 34" with choke tubes. **Weight:** About 8 lbs. **Stock:** #3 Sporting stock designed for gun-down shooting. **Features:** Standard receiver with satin nickel finish and classic scroll engraving. Selective mechanical trigger adjustable for position. Choice of tapered flat or 8mm parallel flat barrel rib. Free-floating barrels. Aluminum case. Imported from Germany by Krieghoff International, Inc.

Price: Standard grade with five choke tubes, from **$9,395.00**

KRIEGHOFF K-80 SKEET O/U SHOTGUNS

Gauge: 12, 2-3/4" chambers. **Barrel:** 28", 30", 32", (skeet & skeet), optional choke tubes). **Weight:** About 7-3/4 lbs. **Stock:** American skeet or straight skeet stocks, with palm-swell grips. Walnut. **Features:** Satin gray receiver finish. Selective mechanical trigger adjustable for position. Choice of ventilated 8mm parallel flat rib or ventilated 8-12mm tapered flat rib. Introduced 1980. Imported from Germany by Krieghoff International, Inc.

Price: Standard, skeet chokes **$8,375.00**
Price: Skeet Special (28", 30", 32" tapered flat rib,
skeet & skeet choke tubes) **$9,100.00**

KRIEGHOFF K-80 TRAP O/U SHOTGUNS

Gauge: 12, 2-3/4" chambers. **Barrel:** 30", 32" (Imp. Mod. & Full or choke tubes). **Weight:** About 8-1/2 lbs. **Stock:** Four stock dimensions or adjustable stock available; all have palm-swell grips. Checkered European walnut. **Features:** Satin nickel receiver. Selective mechanical trigger, adjustable for position. Ventilated step rib. Introduced 1980. Imported from Germany by Krieghoff International, Inc.

Price: K-80 O/U (30", 32", Imp. Mod. & Full), from **$8,850.00**
Price: K-80 Unsingle (32", 34", Full), standard, from **$10,080.00**
Price: K-80 Combo (two-barrel set), standard, from **$13,275.00**

Krieghoff K-20 O/U Shotgun

Similar to the K-80 except built on a 20-gauge frame. Designed for skeet, sporting clays and field use. Offered in 20, 28 and .410; 28"; 30" and 32" barrels. Imported from Germany by Krieghoff International Inc.

Price: K-20, 20 gauge, from **$9,575.00**
Price: K-20, 28 gauge, from **$9,725.00**
Price: K-20, .410, from **$9,725.00**

LEBEAU-COURALLY BOSS-VEREES O/U SHOTGUN

Gauge: 12, 20, 2-3/4" chambers. **Barrel:** 25" to 32". **Weight:** To customer specifications. **Stock:** Exhibition-quality French walnut. **Features:** Boss-type sidelock with automatic ejectors; single or double triggers; chopper lump barrels. A custom gun built to customer specifications. Imported from Belgium by Wm. Larkin Moore.

Price: From **$96,000.00**

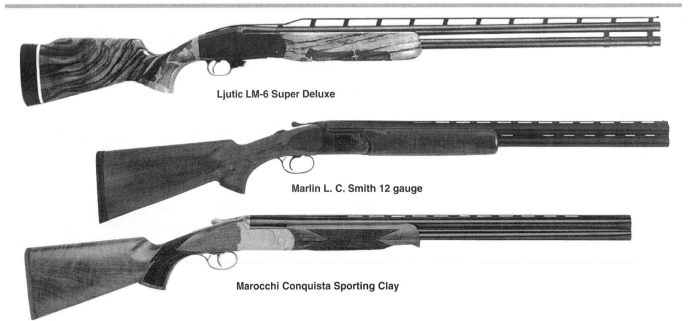

Ljutic LM-6 Super Deluxe

Marlin L. C. Smith 12 gauge

Marocchi Conquista Sporting Clay

LJUTIC LM-6 SUPER DELUXE O/U SHOTGUNS

Gauge: 12. **Barrel:** 28" to 34", choked to customer specs for live birds, trap, international trap. **Weight:** To customer specs. **Stock:** To customer specs. Oil finish, hand checkered. **Features:** Custom-made gun. Hollow-milled rib, pull or release trigger, push-button opener in front of trigger guard. From Ljutic Industries.
Price: Super Deluxe LM-6 O/U **$19,995.00**
Price: Over/Under combo (interchangeable single barrel,
two trigger guards, one for single trigger, one for doubles) . . . **$27,995.00**
Price: Extra over/under barrel sets, 29"-32" **$6,995.00**

LUGER CLASSIC O/U SHOTGUNS

Gauge: 12, 3" and 3-1/2" chambers. **Barrel:** 26", 28", 30"; Imp. Cyl. Mod. and Full choke tubes. **Weight:** 7-1/2 lbs. **Length:** 45" overall (28" barrel) **Stock:** Select-grade European walnut, hand-checkered grip and forend. **Features:** Gold, single selective trigger; automatic ejectors. Introduced 2000.
Price: Classic (26", 28" or 30" barrel; 3-1/2" chambers) **$919.00**
Price: Classic Sporting (30" barrel; 3" chambers) **$964.00**

MARLIN L. C. SMITH O/U SHOTGUNS

Gauge: 12, 20. **Barrel:** 26", 28". **Stock:** Checkered walnut w/recoil pad. **Length:** 45". **Weight:** 7.25 lbs. **Features:** 3" chambers; 3 choke tubes (IC, Mod., Full), single selective trigger, selective automatic ejectors; vent rib; bead front sight. Imported from Italy by Marlin. Introduced 2005.
Price: LC12-OU (12 ga., 28" barrel) **$1,416.00**
Price: LC20-OU (20 ga., 26" barrel, 6.25 lbs., OAL 43"). **$1,416.00**

MAROCCHI CONQUISTA SPORTING CLAYS O/U SHOTGUNS

Gauge: 12, 2-3/4" chambers. **Barrel:** 28", 30", 32" (ContreChoke tubes); 10mm concave vent rib. **Weight:** About 8 lbs. **Stock:** 14-1/ 2"-14-7/8" x2-3/16"x1-7/16"; American walnut with checkered grip and forend; sporting clays butt pad. **Sights:** 16mm luminescent front. **Features:** Lower mono-block and frame profile. Fast lock time. Ergonomically-shaped trigger adjustable for pull length. Automatic selective ejectors. Coin-finished receiver, blued barrels. Five choke tubes, hard case. Available as true left-hand model, opening lever operates from left to right; stock has left-hand cast. Introduced 1994. Imported from Italy by Precision Sales International.
Price: Grade I, right-hand **$1,490.00**
Price: Grade I, left-hand **$1,615.00**
Price: Grade II, right-hand **$1,828.00**
Price: Grade II, left-hand **$2,180.00**
Price: Grade III, right-hand, from **$3,093.00**
Price: Grade III, left-hand, from **$3,093.00**

Marocchi Conquista Trap O/U Shotguns

Similar to Conquista Sporting Clays model except 30" or 32" barrels choked Full & Full, stock dimensions of 14-1/2"-14-7/8"x1-11/ 16"x1-9/32"; weighs about 8-1/4 lbs. Introduced 1994. Imported from Italy by Precision Sales International.
Price: Grade I, right-hand **$1,490.00**
Price: Grade II, right-hand **$1,828.00**
Price: Grade III, right-hand, from **$3,093.00**

Marocchi Conquista Skeet O/U Shotguns

Similar to Conquista Sporting Clays model except 28" (skeet & skeet) barrels, stock dimensions of 14-3/8"-14-3/4"x2-3/16"x1-1/2". Weighs about 7-3/4 lbs. Introduced 1994. Imported from Italy by Precision Sales International.
Price: Grade I, right-hand **$1,490.00**
Price: Grade II, right-hand **$1,828.00**
Price: Grade III, right-hand, from **$3,093.00**

MAROCCHI MODEL 99 SPORTING TRAP AND SKEET O/U SHOTGUNS

Gauge: 12, 2-3/4", 3" chambers. **Barrel:** 28", 30", 32". **Stock:** French walnut. **Features:** Boss Locking system, screw-in chokes, low recoil, lightweight Monoblock barrels and ribs. Imported from Italy by Precision Sales International.
Price: Grade I **$2,350.00**
Price: Grade II **$2,870.00**
Price: Grade II Gold **$3,025.00**
Price: Grade III **$3,275.00**
Price: Grade III Gold **$3,450.00**
Price: Blackgold **$4,150.00**
Price: Lodestar **$5,125.00**
Price: Brittania. **$5,125.00**
Price: Diana **$6,350.00**

MAROCCHI CONQUISTA USA MODEL 92 SPORTING CLAYS O/U SHOTGUN

Gauge: 12, 3" chambers. **Barrel:** 30"; back-bored, ported (ContreChoke Plus tubes); 10 mm concave ventilated top rib, ventilated middle rib. **Weight:** 8 lbs. 2 oz. **Stock:** 14-1/4"-14-5/8"x 2-1/8"x1-3/8"; American walnut with checkered grip and forend; sporting clays butt pad. **Features:** Low profile frame; fast lock time; automatic selective ejectors; blued receiver and barrels. Comes with three choke tubes. Ergonomically shaped trigger adjustable for pull length without tools. Barrels are back-bored and ported. Introduced 1996. Imported from Italy by Precision Sales International.
Price:. **$1,490.00**

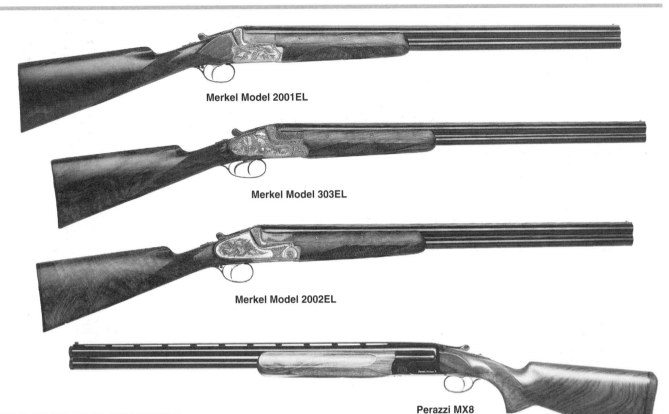

Merkel Model 2001EL

Merkel Model 303EL

Merkel Model 2002EL

Perazzi MX8

MERKEL MODEL 2001EL O/U SHOTGUN

Gauge: 12, 20, 3" chambers, 28, 2-3/4" chambers. **Barrel:** 12-28"; 20, 28 ga.-26-3/4". **Weight:** About 7 lbs. (12 ga.). **Stock:** Oil-finished walnut; English or pistol grip. **Features:** Self-cocking Blitz boxlock action with cocking indicators; Kersten double cross-bolt lock; silver-grayed receiver with engraved hunting scenes; coil spring ejectors; single selective or double triggers. Imported from Germany by GSI, Inc.

Price: 12, 20. . . . . **$7,295.00**
Price: 28 ga. **$7,295.00**
Price: Model 2000EL (scroll engraving, 12, 20 or 28) **$5,795.00**

Merkel Model 303EL O/U Shotgun

Similar to Model 2001EL except Holland & Holland-style sidelock action with cocking indicators; English-style arabesque engraving. Available in 12, 20, 28 gauge. Imported from Germany by GSI, Inc.

Price: **$19,995.00**

Merkel Model 2002EL O/U Shotgun

Similar to Model 2001EL except dummy sideplates, arabesque engraving with hunting scenes; 12, 20, 28 gauge. Imported from Germany by GSI, Inc.

Price: **$10,995.00**

PERAZZI MX8/MX8 SPECIAL TRAP, SKEET O/U SHOTGUNS

Gauge: 12, 2-3/4" chambers. **Barrel:** Trap: 29-1/2" (Imp. Mod. & Extra Full), 31-1/2" (Full & Extra Full). Choke tubes optional. Skeet: 27-5/8" (skeet & skeet). **Weight:** About 8-1/2 lbs. (trap); 7 lbs., 15 oz. (skeet). **Stock:** Interchangeable and custom made to customer specs. **Features:** Has detachable and interchangeable trigger group with flat V springs. Flat 7/16" vent rib. Many options available. Imported from Italy by Perazzi U.S.A., Inc.

Price: From **$12,756.00**
Price: MX8 Special (adj. four-position trigger). From **$11,476.00**
Price: MX8 Special combo (o/u and single barrel sets). From . . **$15,127.00**

Perazzi MX8 Special Skeet O/U Shotgun

Similar to the MX8 Skeet except has adjustable four-position trigger, skeet stock dimensions. Imported from Italy by Perazzi U.S.A., Inc.

Price: From **$11,166.00**

PERAZZI MX8 O/U SHOTGUNS

Gauge: 12, 2-3/4" chambers. **Barrel:** 28-3/8" (Imp. Mod. & Extra Full), 29-1/2" (choke tubes). **Weight:** 7 lbs., 12 oz. **Stock:** Special specifications. **Features:** Has single selective trigger; flat 7/16" x 5/16" vent rib. Many options available. Imported from Italy by Perazzi U.S.A., Inc.

Price: Standard **$12,532.00**
Price: Sporting **$11,166.00**
Price: Trap Double Trap (removable trigger group) **$15,581.00**
Price: Skeet **$12,756.00**
Price: SC3 grade (variety of engraving patterns) . . . . **$23,000.00+**
Price: SCO grade (more intricate engraving, gold inlays) . . . . . **$39,199.00+**

Perazzi MX8/20 O/U Shotgun

Similar to the MX8 except has smaller frame and has a removable trigger mechanism. Available in trap, skeet, sporting or game models with fixed chokes or choke tubes. Stock is made to customer specifications. Introduced 1993. Imported from Italy by Perazzi U.S.A., Inc.

Price: From **$11,166.00**

PERAZZI MX12 HUNTING O/U SHOTGUNS

Gauge: 12, 2-3/4" chambers. **Barrel:** 26-3/4", 27-1/2", 28-3/8", 29-1/2" (Mod. & Full); choke tubes available in 27-5/8", 29-1/2" only (MX12C). **Weight:** 7 lbs., 4 oz. **Stock:** To customer specs; interchangeable. **Features:** Single selective trigger; coil springs used in action; Schnabel forend tip. Imported from Italy by Perazzi U.S.A., Inc.

Price: From **$11,166.00**
Price: MX12C (with choke tubes). From **$11,960.00**

Perazzi MX20 Hunting O/U Shotguns

Similar to the MX12 except 20 ga. frame size. Non-removable trigger group. Available in 20, 28, .410 with 2-3/4" or 3" chambers. 26" standard, and choked Mod. & Full. Weight is 6 lbs., 6 oz. Imported from Italy by Perazzi U.S.A., Inc.

Price: From **$11,166.00**
Price: MX20C (as above, 20 ga. only, choke tubes). From **$11,960.00**

Perazzi MX28

Piotti Boss

Remington Premier Field Grade

Remington Premier Upland Grade

Rizzini S790 Emel

PERAZZI MX10 O/U SHOTGUN

Gauge: 12, 2-3/4" chambers. **Barrel:** 29.5", 31.5" (fixed chokes). **Weight:** NA. **Stock:** Walnut; cheekpiece adjustable for elevation and cast. **Features:** Adjustable rib; vent side rib. Externally selective trigger. Available in single barrel, combo, over/under trap, skeet, pigeon and sporting models. Introduced 1993. Imported from Italy by Perazzi U.S.A., Inc.
Price: MX200410 . . . . **$18,007.00**

PERAZZI MX28, MX410 GAME O/U SHOTGUN

Gauge: 28, 2-3/4" chambers, .410, 3" chambers. **Barrel:** 26" (Imp. Cyl. & Full). **Weight:** NA. **Stock:** To customer specifications. **Features:** Made on scaled-down frames proportioned to the gauge. Introduced 1993. Imported from Italy by Perazzi U.S.A., Inc.
Price: From **$22,332.00**

PIOTTI BOSS O/U SHOTGUN

Gauge: 12, 20. **Barrel:** 26" to 32", chokes as specified. **Weight:** 6.5 to 8 lbs. **Stock:** Dimensions to customer specs. Best quality figured walnut. **Features:** Essentially a custom-made gun with many options. Introduced 1993. Imported from Italy by Wm. Larkin Moore.
Price: From **$48,000.00**

POINTER O/U SHOTGUN

Gauge: 12. **Barrel:** 28". **Stock:** Walnut. **Features:** Kickeez buttpad, Tru-Glo sight, extractors, barrel selector, engraved receiver, gold trigger and 5 choke tubes. Introduced 2006. Imported by Legacy Sports Int.
Price: **$599.00**

REMINGTON PREMIER O/U SHOTGUN

Gauge: 12, 20, 28; 3" chambers. **Barrel:** 26", 28", 30". **Weight:** 6.5-7.5 lbs. **Length:** 45.25" to 47.25". **Stock:** Satin-finished walnut, cut checkering, Schnabel forends. **Sights:** 10mm target-style rib, ivory front bead and steel midpost. **Features:** Competition STS has Titanium PVD-finished receiver, right-hand palm swell, gold-colored trigger, engraved receiver, 12-gauge overbored barrel (0.735") with lengthened forcing cones. Includes five ProBore choke tubes w/knurled extensions. Field Grade has nickel-finished receiver with game scene engraving, 5 flush-mount ProBore choke tubes; 28-gauge equipped with 3 tubes. Upland Grade has oil-finished walnut stock and forend, case-colored receiver with gold-accent game-scene engraving. Hard case included for all models. Introduced 2006. Imported from Italy by Remington.
Price: Field Grade, from **$1,840.00**
Price: Upland Grade, from **$1,920.00**
Price: Competition STS **$2,240.00**
Price: Field Grade, from **$1,840.00**

RIZZINI S790 EMEL O/U SHOTGUN

Gauge: 20, 28, .410. **Barrel:** 26", 27.5" (Imp. Cyl. & Imp. Mod.). **Weight:** About 6 lbs. **Stock:** 14"x1-1/2"x2-1/8". Extra fancy select walnut. **Features:** Boxlock action with profuse engraving; automatic ejectors; single selective trigger; silvered receiver. Comes with Nizzoli leather case. Introduced 1996. Imported from Italy by Wm. Larkin Moore & Co.
Price: From **$9,725.00**

RIZZINI S792 EMEL O/U Shotgun

Similar to S790 EMEL except dummy sideplates with extensive engraving coverage. Nizzoli leather case. Introduced 1996. Imported from Italy by Wm. Larkin Moore & Co.
Price: From **$9,075.00**

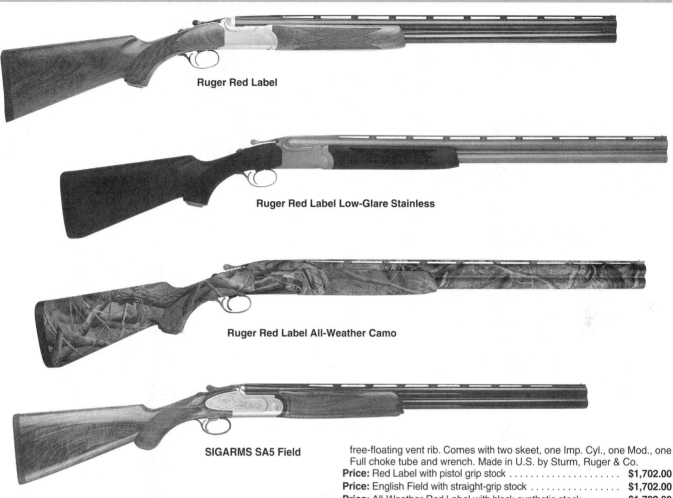

Ruger Red Label

Ruger Red Label Low-Glare Stainless

Ruger Red Label All-Weather Camo

SIGARMS SA5 Field

RIZZINI UPLAND EL O/U SHOTGUN
Gauge: 12, 16, 20, 28, .410. **Barrel:** 26", 27-1/2", Mod. & Full, Imp. Cyl. & Imp. Mod. choke tubes. **Weight:** About 6.6 lbs. **Stock:** 14-1/ 2"x1-1/2"x2-1/4". **Features:** Boxlock action; single selective trigger; ejectors; profuse engraving on silvered receiver. Comes with fitted case. Introduced 1996. Imported from Italy by Wm. Larkin Moore & Co.
Price: From **$3,350.00**

Rizzini Artemis O/U Shotgun
Same as Upland EL model except dummy sideplates with extensive game scene engraving. Fancy European walnut stock. Fitted case. Introduced 1996. Imported from Italy by Wm. Larkin Moore & Co.
Price: From **$2,100.00**

RIZZINI S782 EMEL O/U SHOTGUN
Gauge: 12, 2-3/4" chambers. **Barrel:** 26", 27.5" (Imp. Cyl. & Imp. Mod.). **Weight:** About 6.75 lbs. **Stock:** 14-1/2"x1-1/2"x2-1/4". Extra fancy select walnut. **Features:** Boxlock action with dummy sideplates, extensive engraving with gold inlaid game birds, silvered receiver, automatic ejectors, single selective trigger. Nizzoli leather case. Introduced 1996. Imported from Italy by Wm. Larkin Moore & Co.
Price: From **$11,450.00**

RUGER RED LABEL O/U SHOTGUNS
Gauge: 12, 20, 3" chambers; 28 2-3/4" chambers. **Barrel:** 26", 28", 30" in 12 and 20 gauge (skeet [two], Imp. Cyl., Full, Mod. screw-in choke tubes). Proved for steel shot. **Weight:** About 7 lbs. (20 ga.); 7-1/2 lbs. (12 ga.). **Length:** 43" overall (26" barrels). **Stock:** 14"x1-1/2"x2-1/2". Straight grain American walnut or black synthetic. Checkered pistol grip or straight grip, checkered forend, rubber butt pad. **Features:** Stainless steel receiver. Single selective mechanical trigger, selective automatic ejectors; serrated free-floating vent rib. Comes with two skeet, one Imp. Cyl., one Mod., one Full choke tube and wrench. Made in U.S. by Sturm, Ruger & Co.
Price: Red Label with pistol grip stock **$1,702.00**
Price: English Field with straight-grip stock **$1,702.00**
Price: All-Weather Red Label with black synthetic stock **$1,702.00**
Price: Sporting clays (30" bbl.) **$1,702.00**

Ruger Engraved Red Label O/U Shotgun
Similar to Red Label except scroll engraved receiver with 24-carat gold game bird (pheasant in 12 gauge, grouse in 20 gauge, woodcock in 28 gauge). Introduced 2000.
Price: Engraved Red Label
(12, 20 and 28 gauge in 26" and 28" barrels) **$1,902.00**

SARSILMAZ O/U SHOTGUNS
Gauge: 12, 3" chambers. **Barrel:** 26", 28"; fixed chokes or choke tubes. **Weight:** NA. **Length:** NA. **Stock:** Oil-finished hardwood. **Features:** Double or single selective trigger, wide vent rib, chrome-plated parts, blued finish. Introduced 2000. Imported from Turkey by Armsport Inc.
Price: Double triggers; mod. and full or imp. cyl.
and mod. fixed chokes **$499.95**
Price: Single selective trigger; imp. cyl. and mod. or mod.
and full fixed chokes **$575.00**
Price: Single selective trigger; five choke tubes and wrench **$695.00**

SIGARMS SA5 O/U SHOTGUNS
Gauge: 12, 20, 3" chamber. **Barrel:** 26-1/2", 27" (Full, Imp. Mod., Mod., Imp. Cyl., Cyl. choke tubes). **Weight:** 6.9 lbs. (12 gauge), 5.9 lbs. (20 gauge). **Stock:** 14-1/2" x 1-1/2" x 2-1/2". Select grade walnut; checkered 20 lpi at grip and forend. **Features:** Single selective trigger, automatic ejectors; hand engraved detachable side plate; matte nickel receiver, rest blued; tapered bolt lock-up. Introduced 1997. Imported by SIGARMS, Inc.
Price: Field, 12 gauge **$2,670.00**
Price: Sporting clays **$2,800.00**
Price: Field 20 gauge **$2,670.00**

SHOTGUNS — Over/Unders

Stoeger Condor

Traditions Classic Field Hunter

Traditions Classic Field III

Traditions Classic Upland II

SKB MODEL 85TSS O/U SHOTGUNS
Gauge: 12, 20, .410: 3"; 28, 2-3/4". **Barrel:** Chrome lined 26", 28", 30", 32" (w/choke tubes). **Weight:** 7 lbs., 7 oz. to 8 lbs., 14 oz. **Stock:** Hand-checkered American walnut with matte finish, Schnabel or grooved forend. Target stocks available in various styles. **Sights:** Metal bead front or HiViz competition sights. **Features:** Low profile boxlock action with Greener-style cross bolt; single selective trigger; manual safety. Back-bored barrels with lengthened forcing cones. Introduced 2004. Imported from Japan by G.U. Inc.

Price: Sporting clays, 12 or 20	**$1,949.00**
Price: Sporting clays, 28	**$1,949.00**
Price: Sporting clays set, 12 and 20	**$3,149.00**
Price: Skeet, 12 or 20	**$1,949.00**
Price: Skeet, 28 or .410	**$2,129.00 to $2,179.00**
Price: Skeet, three-barrel set, 20, 28, .410	**$4,679.00**
Price: Trap, standard or Monte Carlo	**$1,499.00**
Price: Trap adjustable comb	**$2,129.00**

SKB MODEL 585 O/U SHOTGUNS
Gauge: 12 or 20, 3"; 28, 2-3/4"; .410, 3". **Barrel:** 12 ga.-26", 28", 30", 32", 34" (InterChoke tubes); 20 ga.-26", 28" (InterChoke tubes); 28-26", 28" (InterChoke tubes); .410-26", 28" (InterChoke tubes). Ventilated side ribs. **Weight:** 6.6 to 8.5 lbs. **Length:** 43" to 51-3/8" overall. **Stock:** 14-1/8"x1-1/2"x2-3/16". Hand checkered walnut with high-gloss finish. Target stocks available in standard and Monte Carlo. **Sights:** Metal bead front (field), target style on skeet, trap, sporting clays. **Features:** Boxlock action; silver nitride finish with field or target pattern engraving; manual safety, automatic ejectors, single selective trigger. All 12 gauge barrels are back-bored, have lengthened forcing cones and longer choke tube system. Sporting clays models in 12 gauge with 28" or 30" barrels available with optional 3/8" step-up target-style rib, matte finish, nickel center bead, white front bead. Introduced 1992. Imported from Japan by G.U., Inc.

Price: Field	**$1,499.00**
Price: Two-barrel field set, 12 & 20	**$2,399.00**
Price: Two-barrel field set, 20 & 28 or 28 & .410	**$2,469.00**

SKB Model 585 Gold Package
Similar to Model 585 Field except gold-plated trigger, two gold-plated game inlays, Schnabel forend. Silver or blue receiver. Introduced 1998. Imported from Japan by G.U. Inc.

Price: 12, 20 ga.	**$1,689.00**
Price: 28, .410	**$1,749.00**

SKB Model 505 O/U Shotgun
Similar to Model 585 except blued receiver, standard bore diameter, standard InterChoke system on 12, 20, 28, different receiver engraving. Imported from Japan by G.U. Inc.

Price: Field, 12 (26", 28"), 20 (26", 28") **$1,229.00**

STOEGER CONDOR SPECIAL O/U SHOTGUNS
Gauge: 12, 20, 2-3/4" 3" chambers; 16, .410. **Barrel:** 22", 24", 26", 28", 30" **Weight:** 5.5 to 7.8 lbs. **Sights:** Brass bead. **Features:** IC, M, or F screw-in choke tubes with each gun. Oil finished hardwood with pistol grip and forend. Auto safety, single trigger, automatic extractors.

Price: Condor, 12, 20, 16 ga. or .410	**$350.00**
Price: Condor Supreme (w/mid bead), 12 or 20 ga.	**$539.00**
Price: Condor Combo, 12 and 20 ga. barrels	**$550.00 to $650.00**
Price: Condor Youth, 20 ga. or .410	**$350.00**
Price: Condor Competition, 12 or 20 ga.	**$599.00**

TRADITIONS CLASSIC SERIES O/U SHOTGUNS
Gauge: 12, 3"; 20, 3"; 16, 2-3/4"; 28, 2-3/4"; .410, 3". **Barrel:** 26" and 28". **Weight:** 6 lbs., 5 oz. to 7 lbs., 6 oz. **Length:** 43" to 45" overall. **Stock:** Walnut. **Features:** Single-selective trigger; chrome-lined barrels with screw-in choke tubes; extractors (Field Hunter and Field I models) or automatic ejectors (Field II and Field III models); rubber butt pad; top tang safety. Imported from Fausti of Italy by Traditions.

Price: Field Hunter: Blued receiver; 12 or 20 ga.; 26" bbl. has IC and Mod. tubes, 28" has mod. and full tubes	**$669.00**
Price: Field I: Blued receiver; 12, 20, 28 ga. or .410; fixed chokes (26" has I.C. and mod., 28" has mod. and full)	**$619.00**
Price: Field II: Coin-finish receiver; 12, 16, 20, 28 ga. or .410; gold trigger; choke tubes	**$789.00**
Price: Field III: Coin-finish receiver; gold engraving and trigger; 12 ga.; 26" or 28" bbl.; choke tubes	**$999.00**
Price: Upland II: Blued receiver; 12 or 20 ga.; English-style straight walnut stock; choke tubes	**$839.00**
Price: Upland III: Blued receiver, gold engraving; 20 ga.; high-grade pistol grip walnut stock; choke tubes	**$1,059.00**
Price: Upland III: Blued, gold engraved receiver, 12 ga. Round pistol grip stock, choke tubes	**$1,059.00**
Price: Sporting Clay II: Silver receiver; 12 ga.; ported barrels with skeet, i.c., mod. and full extended tubes	**$959.00**
Price: Sporting Clay III: Engraved receivers, 12 and 20 ga., walnut stock, vent rib, extended choke tubes	**$1,189.00**

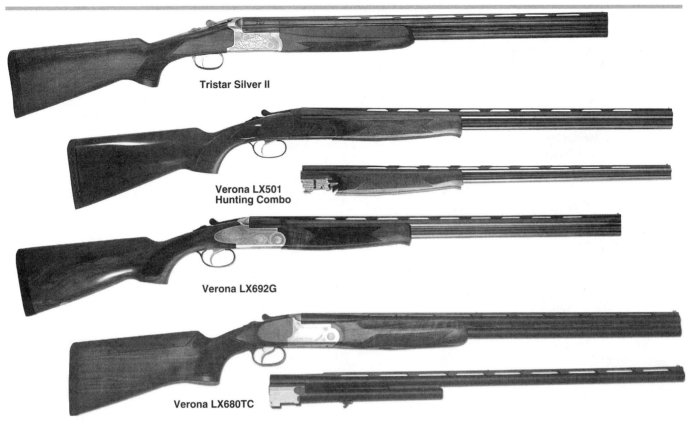

Tristar Silver II

Verona LX501 Hunting Combo

Verona LX692G

Verona LX680TC

TRADITIONS MAG 350 SERIES O/U SHOTGUNS

Gauge: 12, 3-1/2". **Barrel:** 24", 26" and 28". **Weight:** 7 lbs. to 7 lbs., 4 oz. **Length:** 41" to 45" overall. **Stock:** Walnut or composite with Mossy Oak® Break-Up™ or Advantage® Wetlands ™ camouflage. **Features:** Black matte, engraved receiver; vent rib; automatic ejectors; single-selective trigger; three screw-in choke tubes; rubber recoil pad; top tang safety. Imported from Fausti of Italy by Traditions.

Price: (Mag Hunter II: 28" black matte barrels, walnut stock, includes I.C., Mod. and Full tubes) **$799.00**

Price: (Turkey II: 24" or 26" camo barrels, Break-Up™ camo stock, includes Mod., Full and X-Full tubes) **$889.00**

Price: (Waterfowl II: 28" camo barrels, Advantage Wetlands camo stock, includes IC, Mod. and Full tubes) **$899.00**

TRISTAR SILVER II O/U SHOTGUN

Gauge: 12, 20, .410. **Barrel:** 26" barrel (Imp. Cyl., Mod., Full choke tubes, 12 and 20 ga.), 28" (Imp. Cyl., Mod., Full choke tubes, 12 ga. only), 26" (Imp. Cyl. & Mod. fixed chokes, 28 and .410) automatic selective ejectors. **Weight:** 6 lbs., 15 oz. (12 ga., 26"). **Length:** 45-1/2" overall. **Stock:** 14-3/8"x1-1/2"x2-3/8". Figured walnut, cut checkering; sporting clays quick-mount buttpad. **Sights:** Target bead front. **Features:** Boxlock action with single selective trigger, automatic selective ejectors; special broadway channeled rib; vented barrel rib; chrome bores. Chrome-nickel finish on frame, with engraving. Imported from Italy by Tristar Sporting Arms Ltd.

Price: **$669.00**

VERONA LX501 HUNTING O/U SHOTGUNS

Gauge: 12, 20, 28, .410 (2-3/4", 3" chambers). **Barrel:** 28"; 12, 20 ga. have Interchoke tubes, 28 ga. and .410 have fixed Full & Mod. **Weight:** 6-7 lbs. **Stock:** Matte-finished walnut with machine-cut checkering. **Features:** Gold-plated single-selective trigger; ejectors; engraved, blued receiver, non-automatic safety; coil spring-operated firing pins. Introduced 1999. Imported from Italy by B.C. Outdoors.

Price: 12 and 20 ga. **$878.08**
Price: 28 ga. and .410 . . . . **$926.72**
Price: .410 . . . . **$907.01**
Price: Combos 20/28, 28/.410 . . . . **$1,459.20**

Verona LX692 Gold Hunting O/U Shotguns

Similar to Verona LX501 except engraved, silvered receiver with false sideplates showing gold inlaid bird hunting scenes on three sides; Schnabel forend tip; hand-cut checkering; black rubber butt pad. Available in 12 and 20 gauge only, five Interchoke tubes. Introduced 1999. Imported from Italy by B.C. Outdoors.

Price: **$1,295.00**
Price: LX692G Combo 28/.410 . . . . **$2,192.40**

Verona LX680 Sporting O/U Shotgun

Similar to Verona LX501 except engraved, silvered receiver; ventilated middle rib; beavertail forend; hand-cut checkering; available in 12 or 20 gauge only with 2-3/4" chambers. Introduced 1999. Imported from Italy by B.C. Outdoors.

Price: **$1,159.68**

Verona LX680 Skeet/Sporting/Trap O/U Shotgun

Similar to Verona LX501 except skeet or trap stock dimensions; beavertail forend, palm swell on pistol grip; ventilated center barrel rib. Introduced 1999. Imported from Italy by B.C. Outdoors.

Price: **$1,736.96**

Verona LX692 Gold Sporting O/U Shotgun

Similar to Verona LX680 except false sideplates have gold-inlaid bird hunting scenes on three sides; red high-visibility front sight. Introduced 1999. Imported from Italy by B.C. Outdoors.

Price: Skeet/sporting **$1,765.12**
Price: Trap (32" barrel, 7-7/8 lbs.) **$1,594.80**

VERONA LX680 COMPETITION TRAP O/U SHOTGUNS

Gauge: 12. **Barrel:** 30" O/U, 32" single bbl. **Weight:** 8-3/8 lbs. combo, 7 lbs. single. **Stock:** Walnut. **Sights:** White front, mid-rib bead. **Features:** Interchangeable barrels switch from o/u to single configurations. 5 Briley chokes in combo, 4 in single bbl. extended forcing cones, ported barrels 32" with raised rib. By B.C. Outdoors.

Price: Trap Single (LX680TGTSB) **$1,736.96**
Price: Trap Combo (LX680TC) **$2,553.60**

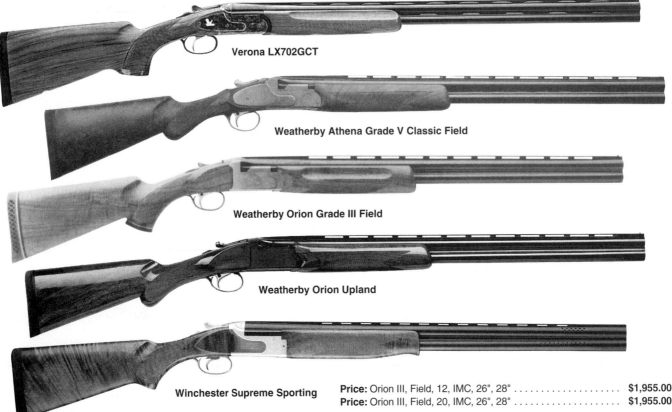

Verona LX702GCT

Weatherby Athena Grade V Classic Field

Weatherby Orion Grade III Field

Weatherby Orion Upland

Winchester Supreme Sporting

VERONA LX702 GOLD TRAP COMBO O/U SHOTGUNS

Gauge: 20/28, 2-3/4" chamber. **Barrel:** 30". **Weight:** 7 lbs. **Stock:** Turkish walnut with beavertail forearm. **Sights:** White front bead. **Features:** 2-barrel competition gun. Color case-hardened side plates and receiver with gold inlaid pheasant. Vent rib between barrels. 5 Interchokes. Imported from Italy by B.C. Outdoors.
Price: Combo **$2,467.84**
Price: 20 ga. **$1,829.12**

Verona LX702 Skeet/Trap O/U Shotguns

Similar to Verona LX702. Both are 12 gauge and 2-3/4" chamber. Skeet has 28" barrel and weighs 7-3/4 lbs. Trap has 32" barrel and weighs 7-7/8 lbs. By B.C. Outdoors.
Price: Skeet **$1,829.12**
Price: Trap **$1,829.12**

WEATHERBY ATHENA GRADE V CLASSIC FIELD O/U SHOTGUN

Gauge: 12, 20, 3" chambers. **Barrel:** 26", 28", IMC multi-choke tubes. **Weight:** 12 ga., 7-1/4 to 8 lbs.; 20 ga. 6-1/2 to 7-1/4 lbs. **Stock:** Oil-finished American Claro walnut with fine-line checkering, rounded pistol grip and slender forend. **Features:** Old English recoil pad. Sideplate receiver has rose and scroll engraving.
Price: **$3,037.00**

Weatherby Athena Grade III Classic Field O/U Shotgun

Similar to Athena Grade V, has Grade III Claro walnut with oil finish, rounded pistol grip, slender forend; silver nitride/gray receiver has rose and scroll engraving with gold-overlay upland game scenes. Introduced 1999. Imported from Japan by Weatherby.
Price: 12, 20, 28 ga. **$2,173.00**

WEATHERBY ORION GRADE III FIELD O/U SHOTGUNS

Gauge: 12, 20, 3" chambers. **Barrel:** 26", 28", IMC multi-choke tubes. **Weight:** 6-1/2 to 8 lbs. **Stock:** 14-1/4"x1-1/2"x2-1/2". American walnut, checkered grip and forend. Rubber recoil pad. **Features:** Selective automatic ejectors, single selective inertia trigger. Top tang safety, Greener cross bolt. Has silver-gray receiver with engraving and gold duck/pheasant. Imported from Japan by Weatherby.

Price: Orion III, Field, 12, IMC, 26", 28" **$1,955.00**
Price: Orion III, Field, 20, IMC, 26", 28" **$1,955.00**

Weatherby Orion Grade II Classic Field O/U Shotgun

Similar to Orion Grade III Field except stock has high-gloss finish, and bird on receiver is not gold. Available in 12 gauge, 26", 28", 30" barrels, 20 gauge, 26" 28", both with 3" chambers, 28 gauge, 26", 2-3/4" chambers. All have IMC choke tubes. Imported from Japan by Weatherby.
Price: **$1,622.00**

Weatherby Orion Upland O/U Shotgun

Similar to Orion Grade III Field. Plain blued receiver, gold W on trigger guard; rounded pistol grip, slender forend of Claro walnut with high-gloss finish; black butt pad. Available in 12 and 20 gauge with 26" and 28" barrels. Introduced 1999. Imported from Japan by Weatherby.
Price: **$1,299.00**

WEATHERBY ORION SSC O/U SHOTGUN

Gauge: 12, 3" chambers. **Barrel:** 28", 30", 32" (skeet, SC1, Imp. Cyl., SC2, Mod. IMC choke tubes). **Weight:** About 8 lbs. **Stock:** 14-3/ 4"x2-1/4"x1-1/2". Claro walnut with satin oil finish; Schnabel forend tip; sporter-style pistol grip; Pachmayr Decelerator recoil pad. **Features:** Designed for sporting clays competition. Has lengthened forcing cones and back-boring; ported barrels with 12mm grooved rib with mid-bead sight; mechanical trigger is adjustable for length of pull. Introduced 1998. Imported from Japan by Weatherby.
Price: SSC (Super Sporting Clays). **$2,059.00**

WINCHESTER SELECT O/U SHOTGUNS

Gauge: 12, 2-3/4", 3" chambers. **Barrel:** 28", 30", Invector Plus choke tubes. **Weight:** 7 lbs. 6 oz. to 7 lbs. 12. oz. **Length:** 45" overall (28" barrel). **Stock:** Checkered walnut stock. **Features:** Chrome-plated chambers; back-bored barrels; tang barrel selector/safety; deep-blued finish. Introduced 2000. From U.S. Repeating Arms. Co.
Price: Select Field (26" or 28" barrel, 6mm vent rib) **$1,498.00**
Price: Select Energy **$1,950.00**
Price: Select Elegance **$2,320.00**
Price: Select Energy Trap **$1,871.00**
Price: Select Energy Trap adjustable **$2,115.00**
Price: Select Energy Sporting adjustable **$2,115.00**

Variety of models for utility and sporting use, including some competitive shooting.

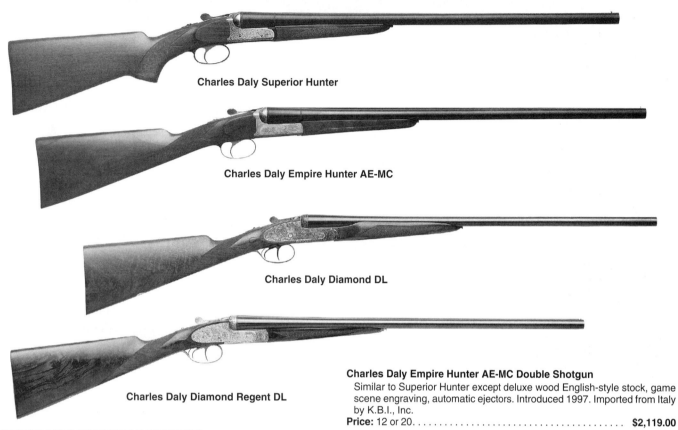

Charles Daly Superior Hunter

Charles Daly Empire Hunter AE-MC

Charles Daly Diamond DL

Charles Daly Diamond Regent DL

ARRIETA SIDELOCK DOUBLE SHOTGUNS
Gauge: 12, 16, 20, 28, .410. **Barrel:** Length and chokes to customer specs. **Weight:** To customer specs. **Stock:** To customer specs. Straight English with checkered butt (standard), or pistol grip. Select European walnut with oil finish. **Features:** Essentially custom gun with myriad options. H&H pattern hand-detachable sidelocks, selective automatic ejectors, double triggers (hinged front) standard. Some have self-opening action. Finish and engraving to customer specs. Imported from Spain by Wingshooting Adventures.

Price: Model 557, auto ejectors. From	**$3,250.00**
Price: Model 570, auto ejectors. From	**$3,950.00**
Price: Model 578, auto ejectors. From	**$4,350.00**
Price: Model 600 Imperial, self-opening. From	**$6,050.00**
Price: Model 601 Imperial Tiro, self-opening. From	**$6,950.00**
Price: Model 801. From	**$9,135.00**
Price: Model 802. From	**$9,135.00**
Price: Model 803. From	**$6,930.00**
Price: Model 871, auto ejectors. From	**$5,060.00**
Price: Model 872, self-opening. From	**$12,375.00**
Price: Model 873, self-opening. From	**$8,200.00**
Price: Model 874, self-opening. From	**$9,250.00**
Price: Model 875, self-opening. From	**$14,900.00**

CHARLES DALY SUPERIOR HUNTER AND SUPERIOR MC DOUBLE SHOTGUNS
Gauge: 12, 20, 3" chambers; 28, 2-3/4" chambers. **Barrel:** 28" (Mod. & Full) 26" (Imp. Cyl. & Mod.). **Weight:** About 7 lbs. **Stock:** Checkered walnut pistol grip buttstock, splinter forend. **Features:** Silvered, engraved receiver; chrome-lined barrels; gold single trigger; automatic safety; extractors; gold bead front sight. Introduced 1997. Imported from Italy by K.B.I., Inc.

Price: Superior Hunter, 28 gauge and .410	**$1,659.00**
Price: Superior Hunter MC 26"-28"	**$1,629.00**

Charles Daly Empire Hunter AE-MC Double Shotgun
Similar to Superior Hunter except deluxe wood English-style stock, game scene engraving, automatic ejectors. Introduced 1997. Imported from Italy by K.B.I., Inc.

Price: 12 or 20	**$2,119.00**

CHARLES DALY DIAMOND DL DOUBLE SHOTGUN
Gauge: 12, 20, .410, 3" chambers, 28, 2-3/4" chambers. **Barrel:** 28" (Mod. & Full), 26" (Imp. Cyl. & Mod.), 26" (Full & Full, .410). **Weight:** From 5 lbs. to 7 lbs. **Stock:** Select fancy European walnut, English-style butt, beavertail forend; hand-checkered, hand-rubbed oil finish. **Features:** Drop-forged action with gas escape valves; demi-block barrels with concave rib; selective automatic ejectors; hand-detachable double safety sidelocks with hand-engraved rose and scrollwork. Hinged front trigger. Color case-hardened receiver. Introduced 1997. Imported from Spain by K.B.I., Inc.

Price:	**Special order only**

CHARLES DALY DIAMOND REGENT DL DOUBLE SHOTGUN
Gauge: 12, 20, .410, 3" chambers; 28, 2-3/4" chambers. **Barrel:** 28" (Mod. & Full), 26" (Imp. Cyl. & Mod.), 26" (Full & Full, .410). **Weight:** About 5-7 lbs. **Stock:** Special select fancy European walnut, English-style butt, splinter forend; hand-checkered; hand-rubbed oil finish. **Features:** Drop-forged action with gas escape valves; demi-block barrels of chrome-nickel steel with concave rib; selective automatic-ejectors; hand-detachable, double-safety H&H sidelocks with demi-relief hand engraving; H&H pattern easy-opening feature; hinged trigger; coin finished action. Introduced 1997. Imported from Spain by K.B.I., Inc.

Price: Special Custom Order	**NA**

CHARLES DALY FIELD II, AE-MC HUNTER DOUBLE SHOTGUN
Gauge: 12, 20, 28, .410 (3" chambers; 28 has 2-3/4"). **Barrel:** 32" (Mod. & Mod.), 28, 30" (Mod. & Full), 26" (Imp. Cyl. & Mod.) .410 (Full & Full). **Weight:** 6 lbs. to 11.4 lbs. **Stock:** Checkered walnut pistol grip and forend. **Features:** Silvered, engraved receiver; gold single selective trigger in 10, 12, and 20 ga.; double triggers in 28 and .410; automatic safety; extractors; gold bead front sight. Introduced 1997. Imported from Spain by K.B.I., Inc.

Price: 28 ga., .410-bore	**$1,189.00**
Price: 12 or 20 AE-MC	**$1,099.00**

SHOTGUNS — Side-by-Side

Charles Daly Field II Hunter

CZ Bobwhite

CZ Ringneck

CZ Durango

CZ Hammer Coach

CZ BOBWHITE AND RINGNECK SHOTGUNS
Gauge: 12, 20, 28, .410. (5 screw-in chokes in 12 and 20 ga. and fixed chokes in IC and Mod in .410). **Barrel:** 20". **Weight:** 6.5 lbs. **Length:** NA. **Stock:** Sculptured Turkish walnut with straight English-style grip and double triggers (Bobwhite) or conventional American pistol grip with a single trigger (Ringneck). Both are hand checkered 20 lpi. **Features:** Both color case-hardened shotguns are hand engraved.
Price: Bobwhite $695.00
Price: Ringneck $912.00

CZ DURANGO AND AMARILLO SHOTGUNS
Gauge: 12, 3" chambers. **Barrel:** 20". **Weight:** 6.7 lbs. **Length:** NA. **Stock:** Hand checkered walnut with old style round knob pistol grip. **Features:** The Durango comes with a single trigger, while the Amarillo is a double trigger shotgun The receiver, trigger guard, and forend metal are finished in 19th century color case-hardening.
Price: $795.00

CZ HAMMER COACH SHOTGUNS
Gauge: 12, 3" chambers. **Barrel:** 20". **Weight:** 6.7 lbs. **Length:** NA. **Stock:** NA. **Features:** Following in the tradition of the guns used by the stagecoach guards of the 1880's, this cowboy gun features double triggers, 19th century color case-hardening and fully functional external hammers.
Price: $795.00

DAKOTA PREMIER GRADE SHOTGUN
Gauge: 12, 16, 20, 28, .410. **Barrel:** 27". **Weight:** NA. **Length:** NA. **Stock:** Exhibition-grade English walnut, hand-rubbed oil finish with straight grip and splinter forend. **Features:** French grey finish; 50 percent coverage engraving; double triggers; selective ejectors. Finished to customer specifications. Made in U.S. by Dakota Arms.
Price: 12, 16, 20 gauge $13,950.00
Price: 28 gauge and .410 . . . . $15,345.00

Dakota Legend Shotgun
Similar to Premier Grade except has special selection English walnut, full-coverage scroll engraving, oak and leather case. Made in U.S. by Dakota Arms.
Price: 12, 16, 20 gauge $18,000.00
Price: 28 gauge and .410 . . . . $19,800.00

E.M.F. HARTFORD MODEL COWBOY SHOTGUN
Gauge: 12. **Barrel:** 20". **Weight:** NA. **Length:** NA. **Stock:** Checkered walnut. **Sights:** Center bead. **Features:** Exposed hammers; color case-hardened receiver; blued barrel. Introduced 2001. Imported from Spain by E.M.F. Co. Inc.
Price: $625.00

A.H. Fox DE Grade

Garbi Model 100

Bill Hanus Birdgun

FOX, A.H., SIDE-BY-SIDE SHOTGUNS

Gauge: 16, 20, 28, .410. **Barrel:** Length and chokes to customer specifications. Rust-blued Chromox or Krupp steel. **Weight:** 5-1/2 to 6-3/4 lbs. **Stock:** Dimensions to customer specifications. Hand-checkered Turkish Circassian walnut with hand-rubbed oil finish. Straight, semi or full pistol grip; splinter, Schnabel or beavertail forend; traditional pad, hard rubber buttplate or skeleton butt. **Features:** Boxlock action with automatic ejectors; double or Fox single selective trigger. Scalloped, rebated and color case-hardened receiver; hand finished and hand-engraved. Grades differ in engraving, inlays, grade of wood, amount of hand finishing. Introduced 1993. Made in U.S. by Connecticut Shotgun Mfg.

Price: CE Grade	$11,000.00
Price: XE Grade	$12,500.00
Price: DE Grade	$15,000.00
Price: FE Grade	$20,000.00
Price: Exhibition Grade	$30,000.00
Price: 28/.410 CE Grade	$12,500.00
Price: 28/.410 XE Grade	$14,000.00
Price: 28/.410 DE Grade	$16,500.00
Price: 28/.410 FE Grade	$21,500.00
Price: 28/.410 Exhibition Grade	$30,000.00
Price: 28 or .410-bore	$1,500.00

GARBI MODEL 100 DOUBLE SHOTGUN

Gauge: 12, 16, 20, 28. **Barrel:** 26", 28", choked to customer specs. **Weight:** 5-1/2 to 7-1/2 lbs. **Stock:** 14-1/2"x2-1/4"x1-1/2". European walnut. Straight grip, checkered butt, classic forend. **Features:** Sidelock action, automatic ejectors, double triggers standard. Color case-hardened action, coin finish optional. Single trigger; beavertail forend, etc. optional. Five additional models available. Imported from Spain by Wm. Larkin Moore.

Price: From **$4,850.00**

Garbi Model 101 Side-by-Side Shotgun

Similar to the Garbi Model 100 except hand engraved with scroll engraving; select walnut stock; better overall quality than the Model 100. Imported from Spain by Wm. Larkin Moore.

Price: From **$6,250.00**

Garbi Model 103 A & B Side-by-Side Shotguns

Similar to the Garbi Model 100 except has Purdey-type fine scroll and rosette engraving. Better overall quality than the Model 101. Model 103B has nickel-chrome steel barrels, H&H-type easy opening mechanism; other mechanical details remain the same. Imported from Spain by Wm. Larkin Moore.

Price: Model 103A. From **$8,000.00**
Price: Model 103B. From **$11,800.00**

Garbi Model 200 Side-by-Side Shotgun

Similar to the Garbi Model 100 except has heavy-duty locks, magnum proofed. Very fine Continental-style floral and scroll engraving, well figured walnut stock. Other mechanical features remain the same. Imported from Spain by Wm. Larkin Moore.

Price: **$11,200.00**

HANUS BIRDGUN SHOTGUN

Gauge: 16, 20, 28. **Barrel:** 27", 20 and 28 ga.; 28", 16 ga. (skeet 1 & skeet 2). **Weight:** 5 lbs., 4 oz. to 6 lbs., 4 oz. **Stock:** 14-3/8"x1-1/2"x2-3/8", with 1/4" cast-off. Select walnut. **Features:** Boxlock action with ejectors; splinter forend, straight English grip; checkered butt; English leather-covered handguard and AyA snap caps included. Made by AyA. Introduced 1998. Imported from Spain by Bill Hanus Birdguns.

Price: **$2,995.00**

KIMBER VALIER GRADE I and II SHOTGUN

Gauge: 20, 3" chambers. **Barrels:** 26" or 28", IC and M. **Weight:** 6 lbs. 8 oz. **Stock:** Turkish walnut, English style. **Features:** Sidelock design, double triggers, 50-percent engraving; 24 lpi checkering; auto-ejectors (extractors only on Grade I). Color case-hardened sidelocks, rust blue barrels. Imported from Turkey by Kimber Mfg., Inc.

Price: Grade I **$3,879.00**
Price: Grade II **$4,480.00**

LEBEAU — COURALLY BOXLOCK SIDE-BY-SIDE SHOTGUN

Gauge: 12, 16, 20, 28, .410-bore. **Barrel:** 25" to 32". **Weight:** To customer specifications. **Stock:** French walnut. **Features:** Anson & Deely-type action with automatic ejectors; single or double triggers. Custom gun built to customer specifications. Imported from Belgium by Wm. Larkin Moore.

Price: From **$25,500.00**

LEBEAU-COURALLY SIDELOCK SIDE-BY-SIDE SHOTGUN

Gauge: 12, 16, 20, 28, .410-bore. **Barrel:** 25" to 32". **Weight:** To customer specifications. **Stock:** Fancy French walnut. **Features:** Holland & Holland-type action with automatic ejectors; single or double triggers. Custom gun built to customer specifications. Imported from Belgium by Wm. Larkin Moore.

Price: From **$56,000.00**

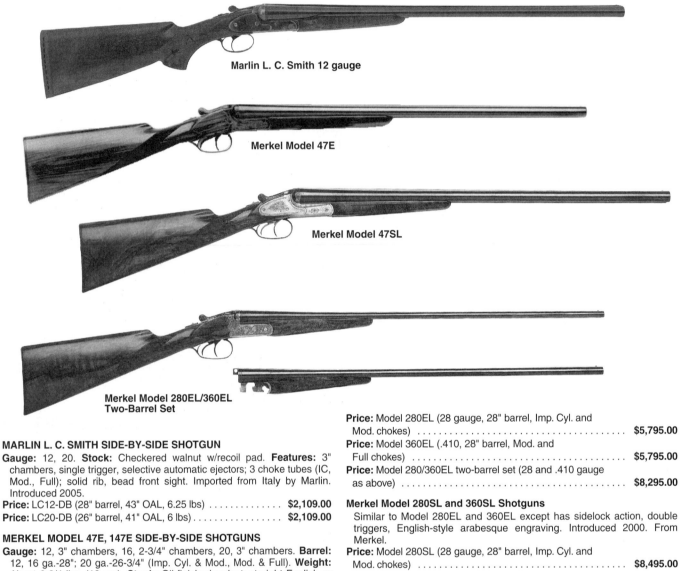

Marlin L. C. Smith 12 gauge

Merkel Model 47E

Merkel Model 47SL

Merkel Model 280EL/360EL Two-Barrel Set

MARLIN L. C. SMITH SIDE-BY-SIDE SHOTGUN

Gauge: 12, 20. **Stock:** Checkered walnut w/recoil pad. **Features:** 3" chambers, single trigger, selective automatic ejectors; 3 choke tubes (IC, Mod., Full); solid rib, bead front sight. Imported from Italy by Marlin. Introduced 2005.
Price: LC12-DB (28" barrel, 43" OAL, 6.25 lbs) **$2,109.00**
Price: LC20-DB (26" barrel, 41" OAL, 6 lbs) **$2,109.00**

MERKEL MODEL 47E, 147E SIDE-BY-SIDE SHOTGUNS

Gauge: 12, 3" chambers, 16, 2-3/4" chambers, 20, 3" chambers. **Barrel:** 12, 16 ga.-28"; 20 ga.-26-3/4" (Imp. Cyl. & Mod., Mod. & Full). **Weight:** About 6-3/4 lbs. (12 ga.). **Stock:** Oil-finished walnut; straight English or pistol grip. **Features:** Anson & Deeley-type boxlock action with single selective or double triggers, automatic safety, cocking indicators. Color case-hardened receiver with standard arabesque engraving. Imported from Germany by GSI.
Price: Model 47E (H&H ejectors) **$3,295.00**
Price: Model 147E (as above with ejectors) **$3,995.00**

Merkel Model 47SL, 147SL Side-by-Side Shotguns

Similar to Model 47E except H&H style sidelock action with cocking indicators, ejectors. Silver-grayed receiver and sideplates have arabesque engraving, engraved border and screws (Model 47S), or fine hunting scene engraving (Model 147S). Imported from Germany by GSI.
Price: Model 47SL **$5,995.00**
Price: Model 147SL **$7,995.00**
Price: Model 247SL (English-style engraving, large scrolls) **$7,995.00**
Price: Model 447SL (English-style engraving, small scrolls) **$9,995.00**

Merkel Model 280EL, 360EL Shotguns

Similar to Model 47E except smaller frame. Greener cross bolt with double under-barrel locking lugs, fine engraved hunting scenes on silver-grayed receiver, luxury-grade wood, Anson and Deely box-lock action. H&H ejectors, single-selective or double triggers. Introduced 2000. From Merkel.

Price: Model 280EL (28 gauge, 28" barrel, Imp. Cyl. and Mod. chokes) **$5,795.00**
Price: Model 360EL (.410, 28" barrel, Mod. and Full chokes) **$5,795.00**
Price: Model 280/360EL two-barrel set (28 and .410 gauge as above) **$8,295.00**

Merkel Model 280SL and 360SL Shotguns

Similar to Model 280EL and 360EL except has sidelock action, double triggers, English-style arabesque engraving. Introduced 2000. From Merkel.
Price: Model 280SL (28 gauge, 28" barrel, Imp. Cyl. and Mod. chokes) **$8,495.00**
Price: Model 360SL (.410, 28" barrel, Mod. and Full chokes) **$8,495.00**
Price: Model 280/360SL two-barrel set **$11,995.00**

PIOTTI KING NO. 1 SIDE-BY-SIDE SHOTGUN

Gauge: 12, 16, 20, 28, .410. **Barrel:** 25" to 30" (12 ga.), 25" to 28" (16, 20, 28, .410). To customer specs. Chokes as specified. **Weight:** 6-1/2 lbs. to 8 lbs. (12 ga. to customer specs.). **Stock:** Dimensions to customer specs. Finely figured walnut; straight grip with checkered butt with classic splinter forend and hand-rubbed oil finish standard. Pistol grip, beavertail forend. **Features:** Holland & Holland pattern sidelock action, automatic ejectors. Double trigger; non-selective single trigger optional. Coin finish standard; color case-hardened optional. Top rib; level, file-cut; concave, ventilated optional. Very fine, full coverage scroll engraving with small floral bouquets. Imported from Italy by Wm. Larkin Moore.
Price: From **$29,600.00**

Piotti King Extra Side-by-Side Shotgun

Similar to the Piotti King No. 1 except with upgraded engraving. Choice of any type of engraving, including bulino game scene engraving and game scene engraving with gold inlays. Engraved and signed by a master engraver. Other mechanical specifications remain the same. Imported from Italy by Wm. Larkin Moore.
Price: From **$35,000.00**

Piotti Lunik

Rizzini Sidelock

Ruger Gold Label

Stoeger Uplander

Stoeger Silverado Coach

Piotti Lunik Side-by-Side Shotgun

Similar to the Piotti King No. 1 in overall quality. Has Renaissance-style large scroll engraving in relief. Best quality Holland & Holland-pattern sidelock ejector double with chopper lump (demi-bloc) barrels. Other mechanical specifications remain the same. Imported from Italy by Wm. Larkin Moore.
Price: From **$30,900.00**

PIOTTI PIUMA SIDE-BY-SIDE SHOTGUN

Gauge: 12, 16, 20, 28, .410. **Barrel:** 25" to 30" (12 ga.), 25" to 28" (16, 20, 28, .410). **Weight:** 5-1/2 to 6-1/4 lbs. (20 ga.). **Stock:** Dimensions to customer specs. Straight grip stock with walnut checkered butt, classic splinter forend, hand-rubbed oil finish are standard; pistol grip, beavertail forend, satin luster finish optional. **Features:** Anson & Deeley boxlock ejector double with chopper lump barrels. Level, file-cut rib, light scroll and rosette engraving, scalloped frame. Double triggers; single non-selective optional. Coin finish standard, color case-hardened optional. Imported from Italy by Wm. Larkin Moore.
Price: From **$14,800.00**

RIZZINI SIDELOCK SIDE-BY-SIDE SHOTGUN

Gauge: 12, 16, 20, 28, .410. **Barrel:** 25" to 30" (12, 16, 20 ga.), 25" to 28" (28, .410). Chokes as specified. **Weight:** 6-1/2 lbs. to 8 lbs. (12 ga. to customer specs). **Stock:** Dimensions to customer specs. Finely figured walnut; straight grip with checkered butt with classic splinter forend and hand-rubbed oil finish standard. Pistol grip, beavertail forend. **Features:** Sidelock action, auto ejectors. Double triggers or non-selective single trigger standard. Coin finish standard. Imported from Italy by Wm. Larkin Moore.

Price: 12, 20 ga. From **$66,900.00**
Price: 28, .410 bore. From **$75,500.00**

RUGER GOLD LABEL SIDE-BY-SIDE SHOTGUN

Gauge: 12, 3" chambers. **Barrel:** 28" with skeet tubes. **Weight:** 6-1/2 lbs. **Length:** 45". **Stock:** American walnut straight or pistol grip. **Sights:** Gold bead front, full length rib, serrated top. **Features:** Spring-assisted break-open, SS trigger, auto eject. Five interchangeable screw-in choke tubes, combination safety/barrel selector with auto safety reset.
Price: **$2,050.00**

STOEGER UPLANDER SIDE-BY-SIDE SHOTGUNS

Gauge: 16, 28, 2-3/4 chambers. 12, 20, .410, 3" chambers. **Barrel:** 22", 24", 26", 28". **Weight:** 7.3 lbs. **Sights:** Brass bead. **Features:** Double trigger, IC & M fixed choke tubes with gun.
Price: With fixed or screw-in chokes **$350.00**
Price: Supreme, screw-in chokes, 12 or 20 ga. **$475.00**
Price: Youth, 20 ga. or .410, 22" barrel, double trigger **$350.00**
Price: Combo, 20/28 ga. or 12/20 ga. **$629.00**

STOEGER COACH GUN SIDE-BY-SIDE SHOTGUNS

Gauge: 12, 20, 2-3/4", 3" chambers. **Barrel:** 20". **Weight:** 6-1/2 lbs. **Stock:** Brown hardwood, classic beavertail forend. **Sights:** Brass bead. **Features:** IC & M fixed chokes, tang auto safety, auto extractors, black plastic buttplate. Imported by Benelli USA.
Price: Supreme blued finish **$410.00**
Price: Supreme blued barrel, stainless receiver. **$420.00**
Price: Supreme polished nickel receiver. **$440.00**
Price: Coach Gun synthetic stock, stainless receiver/barrel **$340.00**
Price: Nickel Coach Gun synthetic stock, stainless **$400.00**
Price: Silverado Coach Gun with English synthetic stock **$400.00**

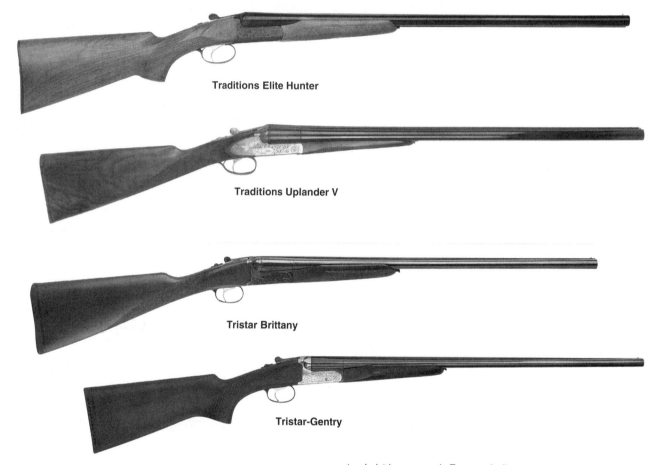

Traditions Elite Hunter

Traditions Uplander V

Tristar Brittany

Tristar-Gentry

TRADITIONS ELITE SERIES SIDE-BY-SIDE SHOTGUNS

Gauge: 12, 3"; 20, 3"; 28, 2-3/4"; .410, 3". **Barrel:** 26". **Weight:** 5 lbs., 12 oz. to 6-1/2 lbs. **Length:** 43" overall. **Stock:** Walnut. **Features:** Chrome-lined barrels; fixed chokes (Elite Field III ST, Field I DT and Field I ST) or choke tubes (Elite Hunter ST); extractors (Hunter ST and Field I models) or automatic ejectors (Field III ST); top tang safety. Imported from Fausti of Italy by Traditions.

Price: Elite Field I DT — 12, 20, 28 ga. or .410; IC and Mod. fixed chokes (F and F on .410); double triggers ..... **$789.00 to $969.00**

Price: Elite Field I ST — 12, 20, 28 ga. or .410; same as DT but with single trigger .... **$969.00 to $1,169.00**

Price: Elite Field III ST — 28 ga. or .410; gold-engraved receiver; high-grade walnut stock **$2,099.00**

Price: Elite Hunter ST — 12 or 20 ga.; blued receiver; IC and Mod. choke tubes **$999.00**

TRADITIONS UPLANDER SERIES SIDE-BY-SIDE SHOTGUNS

Gauge: 12, 3"; 20, 3". **Barrel:** 26", 28". **Weight:** 6-1/4 lbs. to 6-1/2 lbs. **Length:** 43" to 45" overall. **Stock:** Walnut. **Features:** Barrels threaded for choke tubes (Improved Cylinder, Modified and Full); top tang safety, extended trigger guard. Engraved silver receiver with side plates and lavish gold inlays. Imported from Fausti of Italy by Traditions.

Price: Uplander III Silver 12, 20 ga. **$2,699.00**
Price: Uplander V Silver 12, 20 ga. **$3,199.00**

TRISTAR BRITTANY SIDE-BY-SIDE SHOTGUN

Gauge: 12, 16, 20, 28, .410, 3" chambers. **Barrel:** 12 ga., 20 ga., 26", 28"; 16 ga., 27", 28 ga., 27", 410 ga., 27". All have CT-3 Chokes. **Weight:** 6.2 to 7.2 lbs. **Stock:** Walnut English-style, semi-beavertail forearm with cut checkering, standard semi-gloss finish. **Features:** Boxlock action, engraved case colored frame, auto selective ejectors, single selective trigger.

Price: .... **$1,050.00 to $1,069.00**

TRISTAR GENTRY SIDE-BY-SIDE SHOTGUN

Gauge: 12, 16, 20, 28, .410, 3" chambers (16 and 28-ga. @ 2 3/4"). **Barrel:** 12 ga., 27", 20 ga., 28"; 28 ga., 26", 410 ga., 26". All have CT-3 Chokes. **Weight:** 6.2 to 6.8 lbs. **Stock:** Walnut pistol grip stock, semi-beavertail forearm with cut checkering, standard semi-gloss finish. **Features:** Boxlock action, engraved antique silver frame, extractors, single selective trigger with top tang selector.

Price: .... **$929.00 to $945.00**

Variety of designs for utility and sporting purposes, as well as for competitive shooting.

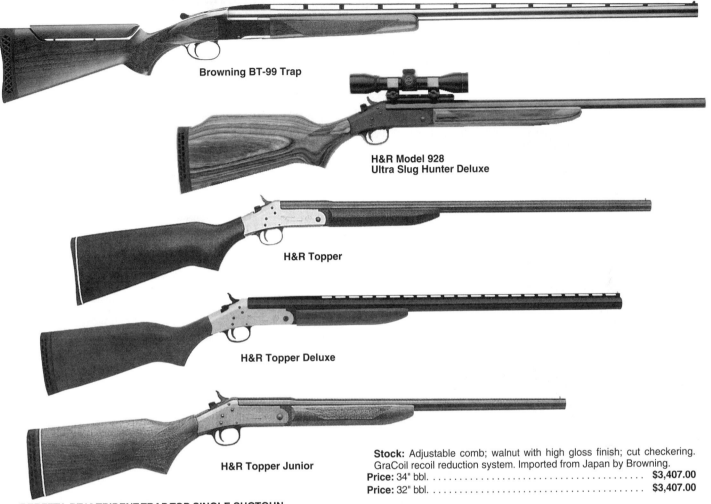

Browning BT-99 Trap

**H&R Model 928
Ultra Slug Hunter Deluxe**

H&R Topper

H&R Topper Deluxe

H&R Topper Junior

BERETTA DT10 TRIDENT TRAP TOP SINGLE SHOTGUN

Gauge: 12, 3" chamber. **Barrel:** 34"; five Optima Choke tubes (Full, Full, Imp. Modified, Mod. and Imp. Cyl.). **Weight:** 8.8 lbs. **Stock:** High-grade walnut; adjustable. **Features:** Detachable, adjustable trigger group; Optima Bore for improved shot pattern and reduced recoil; slim Optima Choke tubes; raised and thickened receiver for long life. Introduced 2000. Imported from Italy by Beretta USA.
Price: **$6,995.00**

BRNO ZBK 100 SINGLE BARREL SHOTGUN

Gauge: 12 or 20. **Barrel:** 27.5". **Weight:** 5.5 lbs. **Length:** 44" overall. **Stock:** Beech. **Features:** Polished blue finish; sling swivels. Announced 1998. Imported from the Czech Republic by Euro-Imports.
Price: **$185.00**

BROWNING BT-99 TRAP O/U SHOTGUNS

Gauge: 12. **Barrel:** 30", 32", 34". **Stock:** Walnut; standard or adjustable. **Weight:** 7 lbs. 11 oz. to 9 lbs. **Features:** Back-bored single barrel; interchangeable chokes; beavertail forearm; extractor only; high rib.
Price: BT-99 w/conventional comb, 32" or 34" barrels **$1,329.00**
Price: BT-99 w/adjustable comb, 32" or 34" barrels **$1,584.00**
Price: BT-99 Golden Clays w/adjustable comb,
32" or 34" barrels **$3,509.00**
Price: BT-99 Micro w/conventional comb, 30" or 32" barrels **$1,329.00**

BROWNING GOLDEN CLAYS SHOTGUN

Gauge: 12, 3" chamber. **Barrel:** 32", 34" with Full, Improved Modified, Modified tubes. **Weight:** 8 lbs. 14 oz. to 9 lbs. **Length:** 49" to 51" overall.

Stock: Adjustable comb; walnut with high gloss finish; cut checkering. GraCoil recoil reduction system. Imported from Japan by Browning.
Price: 34" bbl. **$3,407.00**
Price: 32" bbl. **$3,407.00**

CHIPMUNK 410 YOUTH SHOTGUN

Gauge: .410. **Barrel:** 18-1/4" tapered, blue. **Weight:** 3.25 lbs. **Length:** 33". **Stock:** Walnut. **Features:** Manually cocking single shot bolt, blued receiver.
Price: **$225.95**

HARRINGTON & RICHARDSON ULTRA SLUG HUNTER/TAMER SHOTGUNS

Gauge: 12, 20 ga., 3" chamber, .410. **Barrel:** 20" to 24" rifled. **Weight:** 6 to 9 lbs. **Length:** 34-1/2" to 40". **Stock:** Hardwood, laminate, or polymer with full pistol grip; semi-beavertail forend. **Sights:** Gold bead front. **Features:** Break-open action with side-lever release, automatic ejector. Introduced 1994. From H&R 1871, LLC.
Price: Ultra Slug Hunter, blued, hardwood **$273.00**
Price: Ultra Slug Hunter Youth, blued, hardwood, 13-1/8" LOP **$273.00**
Price: Ultra Slug Hunter Deluxe, blued, laminated **$273.00**
Price: Tamer .410 bore, stainless barrel, black polymer stock **$173.00**

HARRINGTON & RICHARDSON TOPPER MODEL S

Gauge: 12, 16, 20, .410, up to 3.5" chamber. **Barrel:** 22 to 28". **Weight:** 5-7 lbs. **Stock:** Polymer, hardwood, or black walnut. **Features:** Satin nickel frame, blued barrel. Reintroduced 1992. From H&R 1871, LLC.
Price: Deluxe Classic, 12/20 ga., 28" barrel w/vent rib **$225.00**
Price: Topper Deluxe 12 ga., 28" barrel, black hardwood **$179.00**
Price: Topper 12, 16, 20 ga., .410, 26" to 28", black hardwood **$153.00**
Price: Topper Junior 20 ga., .410, 22" barrel, hardwood **$160.00**
Price: Topper Junior Classic, 20 ga., .410, checkered hardwood . . **$160.00**

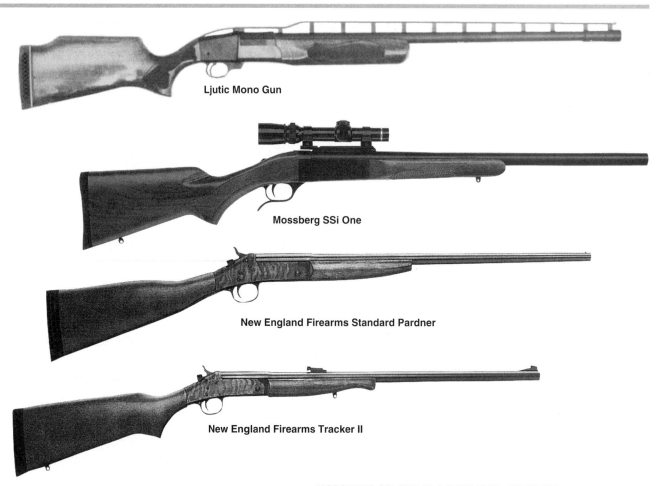

Ljutic Mono Gun

Mossberg SSi One

New England Firearms Standard Pardner

New England Firearms Tracker II

KRIEGHOFF K-80 SINGLE BARREL TRAP GUN
Gauge: 12, 2-3/4" chamber. **Barrel:** 32" or 34" Unsingle. Fixed Full or choke tubes. **Weight:** About 8-3/4 lbs. **Stock:** Four stock dimensions or adjustable stock available. All hand-checkered European walnut. **Features:** Satin nickel finish. Selective mechanical trigger adjustable for finger position. Tapered step vent rib. Adjustable point of impact.
Price: Standard grade Full Unsingle, from **$10,080.00**

KRIEGHOFF KX-5 TRAP GUN
Gauge: 12, 2-3/4" chamber. **Barrel:** 32", 34"; choke tubes. **Weight:** About 8-1/2 lbs. **Stock:** Factory adjustable stock. European walnut. **Features:** Ventilated tapered step rib. Adjustable position trigger, optional release trigger. Fully adjustable rib. Satin gray electroless nickel receiver. Fitted aluminum case. Imported from Germany by Krieghoff International, Inc.
Price: **$5,395.00**

LJUTIC MONO GUN SINGLE BARREL SHOTGUN
Gauge: 12 only. **Barrel:** 34", choked to customer specs; hollow-milled rib, 35-1/2" sight plane. **Weight:** Approx. 9 lbs. **Stock:** To customer specs. Oil finish, hand checkered. **Features:** Custom gun. Pull or release trigger; removable trigger guard contains trigger and hammer mechanism; Ljutic pushbutton opener on front of trigger guard. From Ljutic Industries.
Price: Std., med. or Olympic rib, custom bbls., fixed choke..... **$6,995.00**
Price: As above with screw-in choke barrel **$7,395.00**
Price: Stainless steel mono gun **$7,995.00**

Ljutic LTX Pro 3 Deluxe Mono Gun
Deluxe, lightweight version of the Mono gun with high quality wood, upgrade checkering, special rib height, screw-in chokes, ported and cased.
Price: **$8,995.00**
Price: Stainless steel model **$9,995.00**

MOSSBERG SSi-ONE 12 GAUGE SLUG SHOTGUN
Gauge: 12, 3" chamber. **Barrel:** 24", fully rifled. **Weight:** 8 lbs. **Length:** 40" overall. **Stock:** Walnut, fluted and cut checkered; sling-swivel studs; drilled and tapped for scope base. **Sights:** None (scope base supplied). **Features:** Frame accepts interchangeable rifle barrels (see Mossberg SSi-One rifle listing); lever-opening, break-action design; ambidextrous, top-tang safety; internal eject/extract selector. Introduced 2000. From Mossberg.
Price: **$480.00**

Mossberg SSi-One Turkey Shotgun
Similar to SSi-One 12 gauge slug shotgun, but chambered for 12 ga., 3-1/2" loads. Includes Accu-Mag Turkey Tube. Introduced 2001. From Mossberg.
Price: **$459.00**

NEW ENGLAND FIREARMS PARDNER AND TRACKER II SHOTGUNS
Gauge: 10, 12, 16, 20, 28, .410, up to 3.5" chamber for 10 and 12 ga. 16, 28, 2-3/4" chamber. **Barrel:** 24" to 30". **Weight:** Varies from 5 to 9.5 lbs. **Length:** Varies from 36" to 48". **Stock:** Walnut-finished hardwood with full pistol grip, synthetic, or camo finish. **Sights:** Bead front on most. **Features:** Transfer bar ignition; break-open action with side-lever release. Introduced 1987. From New England Firearms.
Price: Pardner, all gauges, hardwood stock, 26" to 32" blued barrel, Mod. or Full choke, ... **$140.00**
Price: Pardner Youth, hardwood stock, straight grip, 22" blued barrel **$149.00**
Price: Pardner Screw-In Choke model, intr. 2006............ **$164.00**
Price: Turkey model, 10/12 ga., camo finish or black .. **$192.00 to $259.00**
Price: Youth Turkey, 20 ga., camo finish or black **$192.00**
Price: Waterfowl, 10 ga., camo finish or hardwood **$227.00**
Price: Tracker II slug gun, 12/20 ga., hardwood **$196.00**

Rossi Single-Shot

Rossi Matched Pair

Savage 210F Slug Warrior

Stoeger Single-Shot

Tar-Hunt RSG-20 Mountaineer

STOEGER SINGLE-SHOT SHOTGUN
Gauge: 12, 20, .410, 2-3/4", 3" chambers. **Barrel:** 26", 28". **Weight:** 5.4 lbs. **Length:** 40-1/2" to 42-1/2" overall. **Sights:** Brass bead. **Features:** .410, Full fixed choke tubes, screw-in. .410 12 ga. hardwood pistol-grip stock and forend. 20 ga. 26" bbl., hardwood forend.
Price: Blue; Youth **$109.00**
Price: Youth with English stock **$119.00**

TAR-HUNT RSG-12 PROFESSIONAL RIFLED SLUG GUN
Gauge: 12, 2-3/4" or 3" chamber, 1-shot magazine. **Barrel:** 23", fully rifled with muzzle brake. **Weight:** 7-3/4 lbs. **Length:** 41-1/2" overall. **Stock:** Matte black McMillan fiberglass with Pachmayr Decelerator pad. **Sights:** None furnished; comes with Leupold windage or Weaver bases. **Features:** Uses rifle-style action with two locking lugs; two-position safety; Shaw barrel; single-stage, trigger; muzzle brake. Many options available. Right- and left-hand models at same prices. Introduced 1991. Made in U.S. by Tar-Hunt Custom Rifles, Inc.
Price: 12 ga. Professional model, right- or left-hand; **$2,585.00**

Tar-Hunt RSG-16 Elite Shotgun
Similar to RSG-12 Professional except 16 gauge; right- or left-hand versions.
Price: **$2,585.00**

Tar-Hunt RSG-20 Mountaineer Slug Gun
Similar to the RSG-12 Professional except chambered for 20 gauge (2-3/4" and 3" shells); 23" Shaw rifled barrel, with muzzle brake; two-lug bolt; one-shot blind magazine; matte black finish; McMillan fiberglass stock with Pachmayr Decelerator pad; receiver drilled and tapped for Rem. 700 bases. Right- or left-hand versions. Weighs 6-1/2 lbs. Introduced 1997. Made in U.S. by Tar-Hunt Custom Rifles, Inc.
Price: **$2,585.00**

ROSSI SINGLE-SHOT SHOTGUN
Gauge: 12, 20, 2-3/4" chamber; .410, 3" chamber. **Barrel:** 28" full, 22" Youth. **Weight:** 5 lbs. **Stock:** Stained hardwood. **Sights:** Bead. **Features:** Break-open, positive ejection, internal transfer bar, trigger block.
Price: **$101.00**

ROSSI MATCHED PAIR SINGLE-SHOT SHOTGUN/RIFLE
Gauge: .410, 20 or 12. **Barrel:** 22" (18.5" Youth), 28" (23" full). **Weight:** 4-6 lbs. **Stock:** Hardwood (brown or black finish). **Sights:** Bead front. **Features:** Break-open internal transfer bar manual external safety; blued or stainless steel finish; sling-swivel studs; includes matched 22 LR or 22 mag. barrel with fully adjustable front and rear sight. Trigger block system. Introduced 2001. Imported by BrazTech/Taurus.
Price: Blue **$139.95**
Price: Stainless steel **$169.95**

SAVAGE MODEL 210F SLUG WARRIOR SHOTGUN
Gauge: 12, 3" chamber; 2-shot magazine. **Barrel:** 24" 1:35" rifling twist. **Weight:** 7-1/2 lbs. **Length:** 43.5" overall. **Stock:** Glass-filled polymer with positive checkering. **Features:** Based on the Savage Model 110 action; 60-degree bolt lift; controlled round feed; comes with scope mount. Introduced 1996. Made in U.S. by Savage Arms.
Price: **$475.00**
Price: (Camo) **$513.00**

Thompson/Center Encore Rifled Slug

Thompson/Center Encore Turkey

THOMPSON/CENTER ENCORE RIFLED SLUG GUN
Gauge: 20, 3" chamber. **Barrel:** 26", fully rifled. **Weight:** About 7 lbs. **Length:** 40-1/2" overall. **Stock:** Walnut with walnut forearm. **Sights:** Steel; click-adjustable rear and ramp-style front, both with fiber optics. **Features:** Encore system features a variety of rifle, shotgun and muzzle-loading rifle barrels interchangeable with the same frame. Break-open design operates by pulling up and back on trigger guard spur. Composite stock and forearm available. Introduced 2000.
Price: **$684.00**

THOMPSON/CENTER ENCORE TURKEY GUN
Gauge: 12 ga. **Barrel:** 24". **Features:** All-camo finish, high definition Realtree Hardwoods HD camo.
Price: **$763.00**

Designs for utility, suitable for and adaptable to competitions and other sporting purposes.

Benelli M3 Convertible

Mossberg Model 500 Persuader

Mossberg Ghost Ring

BENELLI M3 CONVERTIBLE SHOTGUN

Gauge: 12, 2-3/4", 3" chambers, 5-shot magazine. **Barrel:** 19-3/4" (Cyl.). **Weight:** 7 lbs., 4oz. **Length:** 41" overall. **Stock:** High-impact polymer with sling loop in side of butt; rubberized pistol grip on stock. **Sights:** Open rifle, fully adjustable. Ghost ring and rifle type. **Features:** Combination pump/auto action. Alloy receiver with inertia recoil rotating locking lug bolt; matte finish; automatic shell release lever. Introduced 1989. Imported by Benelli USA. Price with pistol grip, open rifle sights.

Price: With standard stock, open rifle sights	**$1,235.00**
Price: With ghost ring sight system, standard stock	**$1,185.00**
Price: With ghost ring sights, pistol grip stock	**$1,165.00**

BENELLI M2 TACTICAL SHOTGUN

Gauge: 12, 2-3/4", 3" chambers, 5-shot magazine. **Barrel:** 18.5" IC, M, F choke tubes. **Weight:** 6.7 lbs. **Length:** 39.75" overall. **Stock:** Black polymer. **Sights:** Rifle type with ghost ring system, tritium night sights optional. **Features:** Semi-auto intertia recoil action. Cross-bolt safety; bolt release button; matte-finish metal. Introduced 1993. Imported from Italy by Benelli USA.

Price: With rifle sights, standard stock.	**$1,000.00**
Price: With ghost ring rifle sights, standard stock	**$1,065.00**
Price: With ghost ring sights, pistol grip stock	**$1,065.00**
Price: With rifle sights, pistol grip stock	**$1,000.00**
Price: ComforTech stock, rifle sights	**$1,135.00**
Price: Comfortech Stock, Ghost-Ring	**$1,185.00**

Benelli M2 Practical Shotgun

Similar to M2 Tactical shotgun, Picatinny receiver rail for scope mounting, nine-round magazine, 26" compensated barrel and ghost ring sights. Designed for IPSC competition.

Price:	**$1,335.00**

CROSSFIRE SHOTGUN/RIFLE

Gauge/Caliber: 12, 2-3/4" Chamber: 4-shot/223 Rem. (5-shot). **Barrel:** 20" (shotgun), 18" (rifle). **Weight:** About 8.6 lbs. **Length:** 40" overall. **Stock:** Composite. **Sights:** Meprolight night sights. Integral Weaver-style scope rail. **Features:** Combination pump-action shotgun, rifle; single selector, single trigger; dual action bars for both upper and lower actions; ambidextrous selector and safety. Introduced 1997. Made in U.S. From Hesco.

Price: About	**$1,895.00**
Price: With camo finish	**$1,995.00**

FABARM TACTICAL SEMI-AUTOMATIC SHOTGUN

Gauge: 12, 3" chamber. **Barrel:** 20". **Weight:** 6.6 lbs. **Length:** 41.2" overall. **Stock:** Polymer or folding. **Sights:** Ghost ring (tritium night sights optional). **Features:** Gas operated; matte receiver; twin forged action bars; over-sized bolt handle and safety button; Picatinny rail; includes cylinder bore choke tube. New features include polymer pistol grip stock. Introduced 2001. Imported from Italy by Heckler & Koch Inc.

Price:	**$999.00**

FABARM FP6 PUMP SHOTGUN

Gauge: 12, 3" chamber. **Barrel:** 20" (Cyl.); accepts choke tubes. **Weight:** 6.6 lbs. **Length:** 41.25" overall. **Stock:** Black polymer with textured grip, grooved slide handle. **Sights:** Blade front. **Features:** Twin action bars; anodized finish; free carrier for smooth reloading. Introduced 1998. New features include ghost-ring sighting system, low profile Picatinny rail, and pistol grip stock. Imported from Italy by Heckler & Koch, Inc.

Price: (Carbon fiber finish)	**$499.00**
Price: With flip-up front sight, Picatinny rail with rear sight, oversize safety button	**$499.00**

MOSSBERG MODEL 500 PERSUADER SECURITY SHOTGUNS

Gauge: 12, 20, .410, 3" chamber. **Barrel:** 18-1/2", 20" (Cyl.). **Weight:** 7 lbs. **Stock:** Walnut-finished hardwood or black synthetic. **Sights:** Metal bead front. **Features:** Available in 6- or 8-shot models. Top-mounted safety, double action slide bars, swivel studs, rubber recoil pad. Blue, Parkerized, Marinecote finishes. Mossberg Cablelock included. From Mossberg.

Price: 12 ga., 18-1/2", blue, wood or synthetic stock, 6-shot.	**$353.00**
Price: Cruiser, 12 ga., 18-1/2", blue, pistol grip, heat shield	**$357.00**
Price: As above, 20 ga. or .410 bore	**$345.00**

Mossberg Model 500, 590 Mariner Pump Shotgun

Similar to the Model 500 or 590 Persuader except all metal parts finished with Marinecote metal finish to resist rust and corrosion. Synthetic field stock; pistol grip kit included. Mossberg Cablelock included.

Price: 6-shot, 18-1/2" barrel	**$497.00**
Price: 9-shot, 20" barrel	**$513.00**

Mossberg Model 500, 590 Ghost-Ring Shotgun

Similar to the Model 500 Persuader except has adjustable blade front, adjustable Ghost-Ring rear sight with protective "ears." Model 500 has 18.5" (Cyl.) barrel, 6-shot capacity; Model 590 has 20" (Cyl.) barrel, 9-shot capacity. Both have synthetic field stock. Mossberg Cablelock included. Introduced 1990. From Mossberg.

Price: 500 Parkerized	**$468.00**
Price: 590 Parkerized	**$543.00**
Price: 590 Parkerized Speedfeed stock	**$586.00**

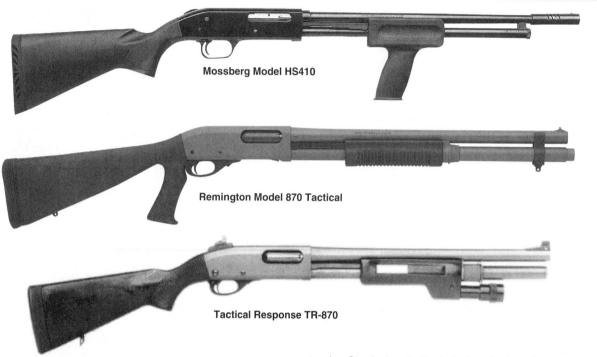

Mossberg Model HS410

Remington Model 870 Tactical

Tactical Response TR-870

Mossberg Model HS410 Shotgun

Similar to the Model 500 Persuader pump except chambered for 20 gauge or .410 with 3" chamber; has pistol grip forend, thick recoil pad, muzzle brake and has special spreader choke on the 18.5" barrel. Overall length is 37.5", weight is 6.25 lbs. Blue finish; synthetic field stock. Mossberg Cablelock and video included. Introduced 1990.
Price: HS 410. . . . . **$355.00**

MOSSBERG MODEL 590 SHOTGUN

Gauge: 12, 3" chamber. **Barrel:** 20" (Cyl). **Weight:** 7-1/4 lbs. **Stock:** Synthetic field or Speedfeed. **Sights:** Metal bead front. **Features:** Top-mounted safety, double slide action bars. Comes with heat shield, bayonet lug, swivel studs, rubber recoil pad. Blue, Parkerized or Marinecote finish. Mossberg Cablelock included. From Mossberg.
Price: Blue, synthetic stock **$417.00**
Price: Parkerized, synthetic stock **$476.00**
Price: Parkerized, Speedfeed stock **$519.00**

REMINGTON MODEL 870 AND MODEL 1100 TACTICAL SHOTGUNS

Gauge: 12, 2-3/4 or 3" chamber, 7-shot magazine. **Barrel:** 18", 20", 22" (Cyl or IC). **Weight:** 7.5-7.75 lbs. **Length:** 38.5-42.5" overall. **Stock:** Black synthetic, synthetic Speedfeed IV full pistol-grip stock, or Knoxx Industries SpecOps stock w/recoil-absorbing spring-loaded cam and adjustable length of pull (12" to 16", 870 only). **Sights:** Front post w/dot only on 870; rib and front dot on 1100. **Features:** R3 recoil pads, LimbSaver technology to reduce felt recoil, 2-, 3- or 4-shot extensions based on barrel length; matte-olive-drab barrels and receivers. Model 1100 Tactical is available with Speedfeed IV pistol grip stock or standard black synthetic stock and forend. Speedfeed IV model has an 18" barrel with two-shot

extension. Standard synthetic-stocked version is equipped with 22" barrel and four-shot extension. Introduced 2006. From Remington Arms Co.
Price: 870, Speedfeed IV stock, 3" chamber, 38.5" overall **$599.00**
Price: 870, SpecOps stock, 3" chamber, 38.5" overall **$625.00**
Price: 1100, synthetic stock, 2-3/4" chamber, 42.5" overall **$759.00**

TACTICAL RESPONSE TR-870 STANDARD MODEL SHOTGUNS

Gauge: 12, 3" chamber, 7-shot magazine. **Barrel:** 18" (Cyl). **Weight:** 9 lbs. **Length:** 38" overall. **Stock:** Fiberglass-filled polypropolene with non-snag recoil absorbing butt pad. Nylon tactical forend houses flashlight. **Sights:** Trak-Lock ghost ring sight system. Front sight has Tritium insert. **Features:** Highly modified Remington 870P with Parkerized finish. Comes with nylon three-way adjustable sling, high visibility non-binding follower, high performance magazine spring, Jumbo Head safety, and Side Saddle extended 6-shot shell carrier on left side of receiver. Introduced 1991. From Scattergun Technologies, Inc.
Price: Standard model **$815.00**
Price: FBI model **$770.00**
Price: Patrol model **$595.00**
Price: Border Patrol model **$605.00**
Price: K-9 model (Rem. 11-87 action) **$995.00**
Price: Urban Sniper, Rem. 11-87 action **$1,290.00**
Price: Louis Awerbuck model **$705.00**
Price: Practical Turkey model **$725.00**
Price: Expert model **$1,350.00**
Price: Professional model **$815.00**
Price: Entry model **$840.00**
Price: Compact model **$635.00**
Price: SWAT model **$1,195.00**

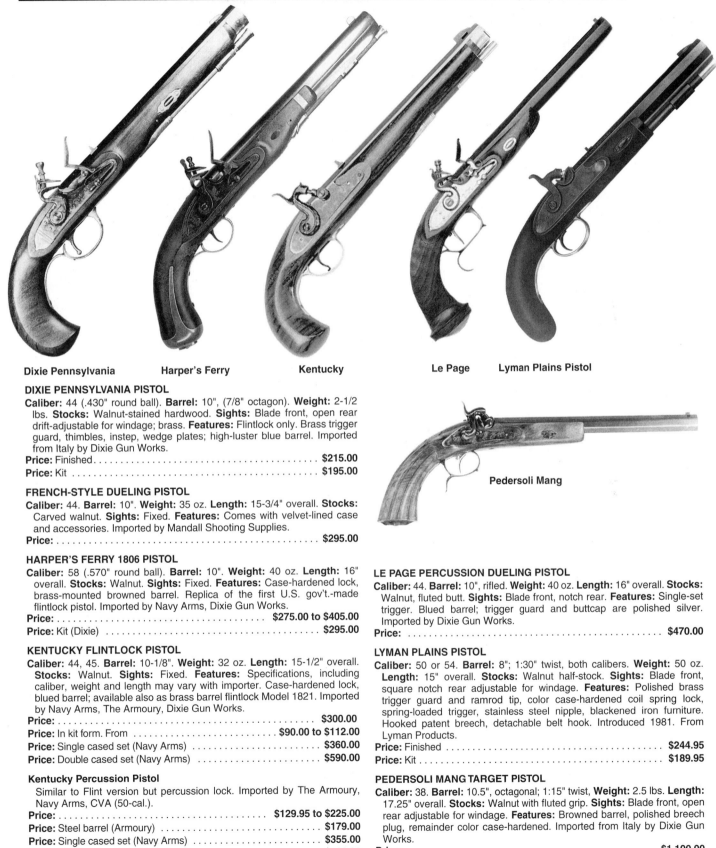

Dixie Pennsylvania   Harper's Ferry   Kentucky   Le Page   Lyman Plains Pistol

Pedersoli Mang

DIXIE PENNSYLVANIA PISTOL
Caliber: 44 (.430" round ball). **Barrel:** 10", (7/8" octagon). **Weight:** 2-1/2 lbs. **Stocks:** Walnut-stained hardwood. **Sights:** Blade front, open rear drift-adjustable for windage; brass. **Features:** Flintlock only. Brass trigger guard, thimbles, instep, wedge plates; high-luster blue barrel. Imported from Italy by Dixie Gun Works.
Price: Finished **$215.00**
Price: Kit **$195.00**

FRENCH-STYLE DUELING PISTOL
Caliber: 44. **Barrel:** 10". **Weight:** 35 oz. **Length:** 15-3/4" overall. **Stocks:** Carved walnut. **Sights:** Fixed. **Features:** Comes with velvet-lined case and accessories. Imported by Mandall Shooting Supplies.
Price: **$295.00**

HARPER'S FERRY 1806 PISTOL
Caliber: 58 (.570" round ball). **Barrel:** 10". **Weight:** 40 oz. **Length:** 16" overall. **Stocks:** Walnut. **Sights:** Fixed. **Features:** Case-hardened lock, brass-mounted browned barrel. Replica of the first U.S. gov't.-made flintlock pistol. Imported by Navy Arms, Dixie Gun Works.
Price: . . . . **$275.00 to $405.00**
Price: Kit (Dixie) **$295.00**

KENTUCKY FLINTLOCK PISTOL
Caliber: 44, 45. **Barrel:** 10-1/8". **Weight:** 32 oz. **Length:** 15-1/2" overall. **Stocks:** Walnut. **Sights:** Fixed. **Features:** Specifications, including caliber, weight and length may vary with importer. Case-hardened lock, blued barrel; available also as brass barrel flintlock Model 1821. Imported by Navy Arms, The Armoury, Dixie Gun Works.
Price: **$300.00**
Price: In kit form. From . . . . **$90.00 to $112.00**
Price: Single cased set (Navy Arms) **$360.00**
Price: Double cased set (Navy Arms) **$590.00**

Kentucky Percussion Pistol
Similar to Flint version but percussion lock. Imported by The Armoury, Navy Arms, CVA (50-cal.).
Price: . . . . **$129.95 to $225.00**
Price: Steel barrel (Armoury) **$179.00**
Price: Single cased set (Navy Arms) **$355.00**
Price: Double cased set (Navy Arms) **$600.00**

LE PAGE PERCUSSION DUELING PISTOL
Caliber: 44. **Barrel:** 10", rifled. **Weight:** 40 oz. **Length:** 16" overall. **Stocks:** Walnut, fluted butt. **Sights:** Blade front, notch rear. **Features:** Single-set trigger. Blued barrel; trigger guard and buttcap are polished silver. Imported by Dixie Gun Works.
Price: **$470.00**

LYMAN PLAINS PISTOL
Caliber: 50 or 54. **Barrel:** 8"; 1:30" twist, both calibers. **Weight:** 50 oz. **Length:** 15" overall. **Stocks:** Walnut half-stock. **Sights:** Blade front, square notch rear adjustable for windage. **Features:** Polished brass trigger guard and ramrod tip, color case-hardened coil spring lock, spring-loaded trigger, stainless steel nipple, blackened iron furniture. Hooked patent breech, detachable belt hook. Introduced 1981. From Lyman Products.
Price: Finished **$244.95**
Price: Kit **$189.95**

PEDERSOLI MANG TARGET PISTOL
Caliber: 38. **Barrel:** 10.5", octagonal; 1:15" twist. **Weight:** 2.5 lbs. **Length:** 17.25" overall. **Stocks:** Walnut with fluted grip. **Sights:** Blade front, open adjustable for windage. **Features:** Browned barrel, polished breech plug, remainder color case-hardened. Imported from Italy by Dixie Gun Works.
Price: **$1,100.00**

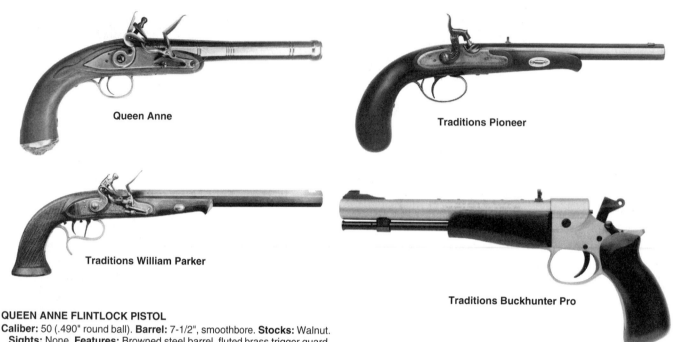

Queen Anne

Traditions Pioneer

Traditions William Parker

Traditions Buckhunter Pro

QUEEN ANNE FLINTLOCK PISTOL
Caliber: 50 (.490" round ball). **Barrel:** 7-1/2", smoothbore. **Stocks:** Walnut. **Sights:** None. **Features:** Browned steel barrel, fluted brass trigger guard, brass mask on butt. Lockplate left in the white. Made by Pedersoli in Italy. Introduced 1983. Imported by Dixie Gun Works.
Price: $290.00
Price: Kit $195.00

REPLICA ARMS "SEVEN SEAS" DERRINGER
Caliber: 36 cal., smoothbore percussion. **Barrel:** 4-5/8". **Weight:** 21 oz. **Length:** 11" overall. **Grips:** Walnut finished. **Features:** All steel barrel with brass accents. Introduced 2005. Imported by Navy Arms.
Price: $99.95

TRADITIONS BUCKHUNTER PRO IN-LINE PISTOL
Caliber: 50. **Barrel:** 9-1/2", round. **Weight:** 48 oz. **Length:** 14" overall. **Stocks:** Smooth walnut or black epoxy-coated hardwood grip and forend. **Sights:** Beaded blade front, folding adjustable rear. **Features:** Thumb safety; removable stainless steel breech plug; adjustable trigger, barrel drilled and tapped for scope mounting. From Traditions.
Price: With walnut grip...................................... $229.00
Price: Nickel with black grip $239.00
Price: With walnut grip and 12-1/2" barrel $239.00
Price: Nickel with black grip, muzzle brake and 14-3/4"
fluted barrel $289.00
Price: 45 cal. nickel w/bl. grip,
muzzle brake and 14-3/4" fluted bbl....................... $289.00

TRADITIONS KENTUCKY PISTOL
Caliber: 50. **Barrel:** 10"; octagon with 7/8" flats; 1:20" twist. **Weight:** 40 oz. **Length:** 15" overall. **Stocks:** Stained beech. **Sights:** Blade front, fixed rear. **Features:** Bird's-head grip; brass thimbles; color case-hardened lock. Percussion only. Introduced 1995. From Traditions.
Price: Finished... $139.00
Price: Kit $109.00

TRADITIONS PIONEER PISTOL
Caliber: 45. **Barrel:** 9-5/8"; 13/16" flats, 1:16" twist. **Weight:** 31 oz. **Length:** 15" overall. **Stocks:** Beech. **Sights:** Blade front, fixed rear. **Features:** V-type mainspring. Single trigger. German silver furniture, blackened hardware. From Traditions.
Price: $139.00
Price: Kit $119.00

TRADITIONS TRAPPER PISTOL
Caliber: 50. **Barrel:** 9-3/4"; 7/8" flats; 1:20" twist. **Weight:** 2-3/4 lbs. **Length:** 16" overall. **Stocks:** Beech. **Sights:** Blade front, adjustable rear. **Features:** Double-set triggers; brass buttcap, trigger guard, wedge plate, forend tip, thimble. From Traditions.
Price: Percussion $189.00
Price: Flintlock $209.00
Price: Kit $149.00

TRADITIONS VEST-POCKET DERRINGER
Caliber: 31. **Barrel:** 2-1/4"; brass. **Weight:** 8 oz. **Length:** 4-3/4" overall. **Stocks:** Simulated ivory. **Sights:** Bead front. **Features:** Replica of riverboat gamblers' derringer; authentic spur trigger. From Traditions.
Price: $109.00

TRADITIONS WILLIAM PARKER PISTOL
Caliber: 50. **Barrel:** 10-3/8"; 15/16" flats; polished steel. **Weight:** 37 oz. **Length:** 17-1/2" overall. **Stocks:** Walnut with checkered grip. **Sights:** Brass blade front, fixed rear. **Features:** Replica dueling pistol with 1:20" twist, hooked breech. Brass wedge plate, trigger guard, cap guard; separate ramrod. Double-set triggers. Polished steel barrel, lock. Imported by Traditions.
Price:... $269.00

BLACKPOWDER REVOLVERS

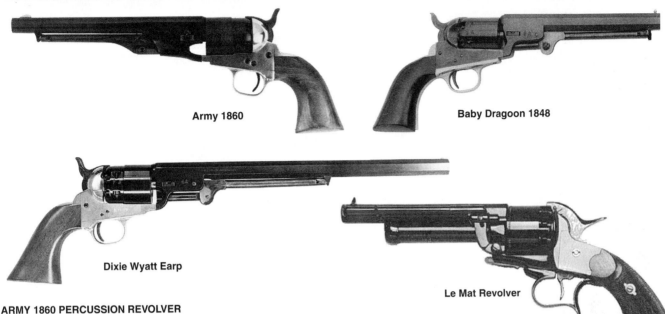

Army 1860

Baby Dragoon 1848

Dixie Wyatt Earp

Le Mat Revolver

ARMY 1860 PERCUSSION REVOLVER
Caliber: 44, 6-shot. **Barrel:** 8". **Weight:** 40 oz. **Length:** 13-5/8" overall. **Stocks:** Walnut. **Sights:** Fixed. **Features:** Engraved Navy scene on cylinder; brass trigger guard; case-hardened frame, loading lever and hammer. Some importers supply pistol cut for detachable shoulder stock, have accessory stock available. Imported by Cabela's (1860 Lawman), E.M.F., Navy Arms, The Armoury, Cimarron, Dixie Gun Works (half-fluted cylinder, not roll engraved), Euroarms of America (brass or steel model), Armsport, Traditions (brass or steel), Uberti U.S.A. Inc., United States Patent Fire-Arms.
Price: About **$232.00**
Price: Hartford model, steel frame, German silver trim, cartouches (E.M.F.) **$215.00**
Price: Single cased set (Navy Arms) **$300.00**
Price: Double cased set (Navy Arms) **$490.00**
Price: 1861 Navy: Same as Army except 36-cal., 7-1/2" bbl., weighs 41 oz., cut for shoulder stock; round cylinder (fluted available), from Cabela's, CVA (brass frame, 44 cal.), United States Patent Fire-Arms . . . . **$99.95 to $385.00**
Price: Steel frame kit (E.M.F., Euroarms) . . . . **$125.00 to $216.25**
Price: Colt Army Police, fluted cyl., 5-1/2", 36-cal. (Cabela's) **$124.95**
Price: With nickeled frame, barrel and backstrap, gold-tone fluted cylinder, trigger and hammer, simulated ivory grips (Traditions) **$199.00**

BABY DRAGOON 1848, 1849 POCKET, WELLS FARGO
Caliber: 31. **Barrel:** 3", 4", 5", 6"; seven-groove; RH twist. **Weight:** About 21 oz. **Stocks:** Varnished walnut. **Sights:** Brass pin front, hammer notch rear. **Features:** No loading lever on Baby Dragoon or Wells Fargo models. Unfluted cylinder with stagecoach holdup scene; cupped cylinder pin; no grease grooves; one safety pin on cylinder and slot in hammer face; straight (flat) mainspring. From Armsport, Cimarron F.A. Co., Dixie Gun Works, Uberti U.S.A. Inc.
Price: 6" barrel, with loading lever (Dixie Gun Works) **$232.00**
Price: 4" (Uberti USA Inc.) **$275.00**

DIXIE WYATT EARP REVOLVER
Caliber: 44. **Barrel:** 12", octagon. **Weight:** 46 oz. **Length:** 18" overall. **Stocks:** Two-piece walnut. **Sights:** Fixed. **Features:** Highly polished brass frame, backstrap and trigger guard; blued barrel and cylinder; case-hardened hammer, trigger and loading lever. Navy-size shoulder stock ($45) requires minor fitting. From Dixie Gun Works.
Price: **$180.00**

LE MAT REVOLVER
Caliber: 44/65. **Barrel:** 6-3/4" (revolver); 4-7/8" (single shot). **Weight:** 3 lbs., 7 oz. **Stocks:** Hand-checkered walnut. **Sights:** Post front, hammer notch rear. **Features:** Exact reproduction with all-steel construction; 44-cal. 9-shot cylinder, 65-cal. single barrel; color case-hardened hammer with selector; spur trigger guard; ring at butt; lever-type barrel release. From Navy Arms and Dixie Gun Works.
Price: Cavalry model (lanyard ring, spur trigger guard) **$645.00**
Price: Army model (round trigger guard, pin-type barrel release) . . **$645.00**
Price: Naval-style (thumb selector on hammer) **$645.00**

NEW MODEL 1858 ARMY PERCUSSION REVOLVER
Caliber: 36 or 44, 6-shot. **Barrel:** 6-1/2" or 8". **Weight:** 38 oz. **Length:** 13-1/2" overall. **Stocks:** Walnut. **Sights:** Blade front, groove-in-frame rear. **Features:** Replica of Remington Model 1858. Also available from some importers as Army Model Belt Revolver in 36-cal., a shortened and lightened version of the 44. Target Model (Uberti U.S.A. Inc., Navy Arms) has fully adjustable target rear sight, target front, 36 or 44. Imported by Cabela's, Cimarron F.A. Co., CVA (as 1858 Army, brass frame, 44 only), Dixie Gun Works, Navy Arms, The Armoury, E.M.F., Euroarms of America (engraved, stainless and plain), Armsport, Traditions (44 only), Uberti U.S.A. Inc.
Price: Steel frame, about . . . . **$99.95 to $280.00**
Price: Steel frame kit (Euroarms, Navy Arms) . . . . **$115.95 to $150.00**
Price: Stainless steel Model 1858 (Euroarms, Uberti U.S.A. Inc., Cabela's, Navy Arms, Armsport, Traditions) . . . . **$169.95 to $380.00**
Price: Target Model, adjustable rear sight (Cabela's, Euroarms, Uberti U.S.A. Inc., Stone Mountain Arms) . . . . **$95.95 to $399.00**
Price: Brass frame (CVA, Cabela's, Traditions, Navy Arms) . . . . **$79.95 to $187.000**
Price: As above, kit (Dixie Gun Works) . . . . **$145.00 to $188.95**
Price: Buffalo model, 44-cal. (Cabela's) **$119.99**
Price: Hartford model, steel frame, German silver trim, cartouche (E.M.F.) **$215.00**

NAVY ARMS NEW MODEL POCKET REVOLVER
Caliber: 31, 5-shot. **Barrel:** 3-1/2", octagon. **Weight:** 15 oz. **Length:** 7-3/4". **Stocks:** Two-piece walnut. **Sights:** Fixed. **Features:** Replica of the Remington New Model Pocket. Available with polished brass frame or nickel-plated finish. Introduced 2000. Imported by Navy Arms.
Price: **$300.00**

BLACKPOWDER REVOLVERS

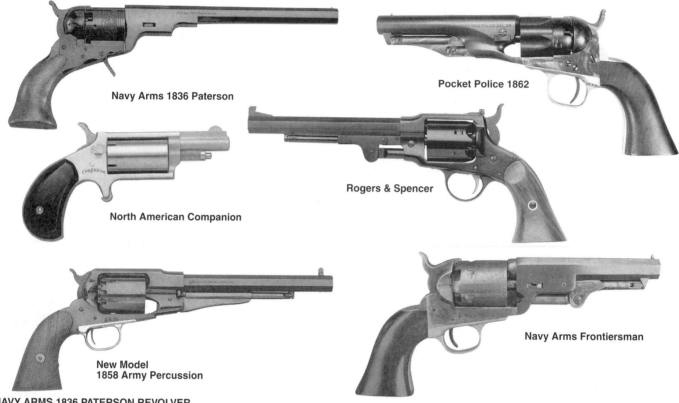

Navy Arms 1836 Paterson

Pocket Police 1862

North American Companion

Rogers & Spencer

New Model 1858 Army Percussion

Navy Arms Frontiersman

NAVY ARMS 1836 PATERSON REVOLVER

Caliber: 36. **Barrel:** 9". **Weight:** 2 lbs., 11 oz. **Length:** NA. **Stocks:** Walnut. **Sights:** NA. **Features:** Hidden trigger, blued barrel, replica of 5-shooter, roll-engraved with stagecoach holdup scene.
Price: . . . . **$425.00 to $461.00**

NAVY ARMS 1851 NAVY "FRONTIERSMAN" REVOLVER

Caliber: .36, 6-shot cylinder. **Barrel:** 5". **Weight:** 32 oz. **Length:** 10-1/2" overall . **Grips:** One piece walnut. **Sights:** Post front, notch rear. **Features:** Blued with color case-hardened receiver, trigger and hammer; German Silver backstrap and triggerguard. Introduced 2005. Imported by Navy Arms.
Price: **$315.00**

NAVY MODEL 1851 PERCUSSION REVOLVER

Caliber: 36, 44, 6-shot. **Barrel:** 7-1/2". **Weight:** 44 oz. **Length:** 13" overall. **Stocks:** Walnut finish. **Sights:** Post front, hammer notch rear. **Features:** Brass backstrap and trigger guard; some have 1st Model squareback trigger guard, engraved cylinder with navy battle scene; case-hardened frame, hammer, loading lever. Imported by The Armoury, Cabela's, Cimarron F.A. Co., Navy Arms, E.M.F., Dixie Gun Works, Euroarms of America, Armsport, CVA (44-cal. only), Traditions (44 only), Uberti U.S.A. Inc., United States Patent Fire-Arms.

Price: Brass frame	**$99.95 to $385.00**
Price: Steel frame	**$130.00 to $285.00**
Price: Kit form	**$110.00 to $142.50**
Price: Engraved model (Dixie Gun Works)	**$190.00**
Price: Single cased set, steel frame (Navy Arms)	**$280.00**
Price: Double cased set, steel frame (Navy Arms)	**$455.00**
Price: Confederate Navy (Cabela's)	**$89.99**
Price: Hartford model, steel frame, German silver trim, cartouche (E.M.F.)	**$190.00**

NORTH AMERICAN COMPANION PERCUSSION REVOLVER

Caliber: 22. **Barrel:** 1-1/8". **Weight:** 5.1 oz. **Length:** 4-1/2" overall. **Stocks:** Laminated wood. **Sights:** Blade front, notch fixed rear. **Features:** All stainless steel construction. Uses standard #11 percussion caps. Comes with bullets, powder measure, bullet seater, leather clip holster, gun rag.

Long Rifle or Magnum frame size. Introduced 1996. Made in U.S. by North American Arms.
Price: Long Rifle frame **$156.00**

North American Magnum Companion Percussion Revolver

Similar to the Companion except has larger frame. Weighs 7.2 oz., has 1-5/8" barrel, measures 5-7/16" overall. Comes with bullets, powder measure, bullet seater, leather clip holster, gun rag. Introduced 1996. Made in U.S. by North American Arms.
Price: **$215.00**

POCKET POLICE 1862 PERCUSSION REVOLVER

Caliber: 36, 5-shot. **Barrel:** 4-1/2", 5-1/2", 6-1/2", 7-1/2". **Weight:** 26 oz. **Length:** 12" overall (6-1/2" bbl.). **Stocks:** Walnut. **Sights:** Fixed. **Features:** Round tapered barrel; half-fluted and rebated cylinder; case-hardened frame, loading lever and hammer; silver or brass trigger guard and backstrap. Imported by Dixie Gun Works, Navy Arms (5-1/2" only), Uberti U.S.A. Inc. (5-1/2", 6-1/2" only), United States Patent Fire-Arms and Cimarron F.A. Co.
Price: About. . . . . **$139.95 to $335.00**
Price: Single cased set with accessories (Navy Arms) **$365.00**
Price: Hartford model, steel frame, German silver trim, cartouche (E.M.F.) **$215.00**

ROGERS & SPENCER PERCUSSION REVOLVER

Caliber: 44. **Barrel:** 7-1/2". **Weight:** 47 oz. **Length:** 13-3/4" overall. **Stocks:** Walnut. **Sights:** Cone front, integral groove in frame for rear. **Features:** Accurate reproduction of a Civil War design. Solid frame; extra large nipple cut-out on rear of cylinder; loading lever and cylinder easily removed for cleaning. From Dixie Gun Works, Euroarms of America (standard blue, engraved, burnished, target models), Navy Arms.
Price: . . . . **$160.00 to $299.95**
Price: Nickel-plated **$215.00**
Price: Engraved (Euroarms) **$287.00**
Price: Kit version . . . . **$245.00 to $252.00**
Price: Target version (Euroarms) . . . . **$239.00 to $270.00**
Price: Burnished London Gray (Euroarms) . . . . **$245.00 to $270.00**

BLACKPOWDER REVOLVERS

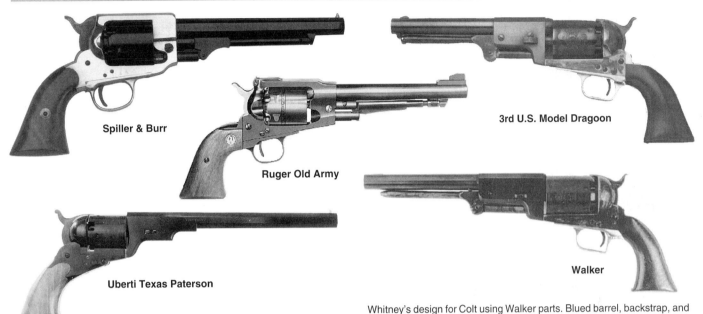

Spiller & Burr

Ruger Old Army

3rd U.S. Model Dragoon

Uberti Texas Paterson

Walker

RUGER OLD ARMY PERCUSSION REVOLVER

Caliber: 45, 6-shot. Uses .457" dia. lead bullets or 454 conical. **Barrel:** 5-1/2", 7-1/2" (6-groove; 1:16" twist). **Weight:** 2-7/8 lbs. **Length:** 11-1/2" and 13-1/2" overall. **Stocks:** Rosewood, simulated ivory. **Sights:** Ramp front, rear adjustable for windage and elevation; or fixed (groove). **Features:** Stainless steel; standard size nipples, chrome-moly steel cylinder and frame, same lockwork as original Super Blackhawk. Also stainless steel. Includes hard case and lock. Introduced 1972.
Price: Blued steel, fixed sight (Model BP-5F) **$568.00**
Price: Stainless steel, fixed sight (Model KBP-5F-I) **$654.00**
Price: Stainless steel (Model KBP-7) **$606.00**
Price: Stainless steel, fixed sight (KBP-7F) **$606.00**

SHERIFF MODEL 1851 PERCUSSION REVOLVER

Caliber: 36, 44, 6-shot. **Barrel:** 5". **Weight:** 40 oz. **Length:** 10-1/2" overall. **Stocks:** Walnut. **Sights:** Fixed. **Features:** Brass backstrap and trigger guard; engraved navy scene; case-hardened frame, hammer, loading lever. Imported by E.M.F.
Price: Steel frame **$169.95**
Price: Brass frame **$140.00**

SPILLER & BURR REVOLVER

Caliber: 36 (.375" round ball). **Barrel:** 7", octagon. **Weight:** 2-1/2 lbs. **Length:** 12-1/2" overall. **Stocks:** Two-piece walnut. **Sights:** Fixed. **Features:** Reproduction of the C.S.A. revolver. Brass frame and trigger guard. Also available as a kit. From Dixie Gun Works, Navy Arms.
Price: **$205.00**
Price: Kit form (Dixie) **$155.00**
Price: Single cased set (Navy Arms) **$270.00**
Price: Double cased set (Navy Arms) **$430.00**

UBERTI TEXAS PATERSON 1836 AND 1847 WALKER REVOLVERS

Caliber: 36 (.375" round ball), 5-shot engraved cylinder. **Barrel:** 7-1/2" 11 grooves. **Weight:** 2.6 lbs. **Stocks:** One-piece walnut. **Sights:** Fixed. **Features:** Copy of Sam Colt's first commercially-made revolving pistol, loading lever available, no trigger guard, Made in Italy by Uberti, imported by Benelli USA.
Price: Paterson with loading lever, 7-1/2" barrel **$425.00**
Price: Paterson w/o loading lever, 7-1/2" barrel **$400.00**
Price: Walker with loading lever, 9" barrel, 6 shot **$350.00**

UBERTI 1848 DRAGOON AND POCKET REVOLVERS

Caliber: 44 6-shot engraved cylinder. **Barrel:** 7-1/2" 7 grooves. **Weight:** 4.1 lbs. **Stocks:** One-piece walnut. **Sights:** Fixed. **Features:** Copy of Eli Whitney's design for Colt using Walker parts. Blued barrel, backstrap, and trigger guard. Made in Italy by Uberti, imported by Benelli USA.
Price: 1848 Whitneyville Dragoon, 7-1/2" barrel **$380.00**
Price: 1848 Dragoon, 1st thru 3rd models, 7-1/2" barrel **$325.00**
Price: 1848 Baby Dragoon, 4" barrel **$285.00**

UBERTI 1858 NEW ARMY REVOLVERS

Caliber: 44 6-shot engraved cylinder. **Barrel:** 8" 7 grooves. **Weight:** 2.7 lbs. **Length:** 13.6". **Stocks:** Two-piece walnut. **Sights:** Fixed. **Features:** Blued or stainless barrel, backstrap; brass trigger guard. Made in Italy by Uberti, imported by Benelli USA.
Price: 1858 New Army Stainless 8" barrel **$355.00**
Price: 1858 New Army 8" barrel **$285.00**
Price: 1858 Target Carbine 18" barrel **$455.00**
Price: 1862 Pocket Navy 5.5" barrel, 36 caliber, ... **$285.00**
Price: 1862 Police 5.5" barrel, 36 caliber, ... **$285.00**

UBERTI 1861 NAVY PERCUSSION REVOLVER

Caliber: 36, 6-shot. **Barrel:** 7-1/2", 7-groove, round. **Weight:** 2 lbs., 6 oz. **Length:** 13". **Stocks:** One-piece walnut. **Sights:** German silver blade front sight. **Features:** Rounded trigger guard, "creeping" loading lever, fluted or round cylinder, steel backstrap, trigger guard, cut for stock. Imported by Cimarron F.A. Co., Uberti U.S.A. Inc., Dixie Gunworks.
Price: . . . . **$255.00 to $300.00**

1862 POCKET NAVY PERCUSSION REVOLVER

Caliber: 36, 5-shot. **Barrel:** 5-1/2", 6-1/2", octagonal, 7-groove, LH twist. **Weight:** 27 oz. (5-1/2" barrel). **Length:** 10-1/2" overall (5-1/2" bbl.). **Stocks:** One-piece varnished walnut. **Sights:** Brass pin front, hammer notch rear. **Features:** Rebated cylinder, hinged loading lever, brass or silver-plated backstrap and trigger guard, color-cased frame, hammer, loading lever, plunger and latch, rest blued. Has original-type markings. From Cimarron F.A. Co., Uberti U.S.A. Inc., Dixie Gunworks.
Price: With brass backstrap, trigger guard . . . . **$240.00 to $310.00**

WALKER 1847 PERCUSSION REVOLVER

Caliber: 44, 6-shot. **Barrel:** 9". **Weight:** 84 oz. **Length:** 15-1/2" overall. **Stocks:** Walnut. **Sights:** Fixed. **Features:** Case-hardened frame, loading lever and hammer; iron backstrap; brass trigger guard; engraved cylinder. Imported by Cabela's, Cimarron F.A. Co., Navy Arms, Dixie Gun Works, Uberti U.S.A. Inc., E.M.F., Cimarron, Traditions, United States Patent Fire-Arms.
Price: About. . . . . **$225.00 to $445.00**
Price: Single cased set (Navy Arms) **$405.00**
Price: Deluxe Walker with French fitted case (Navy Arms) **$540.00**
Price: Hartford model, steel frame, German silver trim,
cartouche (E.M.F.) **$295.00**

Austin & Halleck 420 LR In-Line

Cabela's Traditional Hawken

ARMOURY R140 HAWKEN RIFLE
Caliber: 45, 50 or 54.**Barrel:** 29". **Weight:** 8-3/4 to 9 lbs. **Length:** 45-3/4" overall. **Stock:** Walnut, with cheekpiece. **Sights:** Dovetailed front, fully adjustable rear. **Features:** Octagon barrel, removable breech plug; double set triggers; blued barrel, brass stock fittings, color case-hardened percussion lock. From Armsport, The Armoury.
Price: .... **$225.00 to $245.00**

AUSTIN & HALLECK MODEL 420 LR IN-LINE RIFLE
Caliber: 45 and 50. **Barrel:** 26", 1" octagon to 3/4" round; 1:28" twist. **Weight:** 7-7/8 lbs. **Length:** 47-1/2" overall. **Stock:** Lightly figured maple in Classic or Monte Carlo style. **Sights:** Ramp front, fully adjustable rear. **Features:** Blue or electroless nickel finish; in-line percussion action with removable weather shroud; Timney adjustable target trigger with sear block safety. Introduced 1998.
Price: Blue **$549.00**
Price: Stainless steel **$579.00**
Price: Blue, hand-select highly figured stock **$709.00**
Price: Stainless steel, select stock **$739.00**

Austin & Halleck Model 320 LR In-Line Rifle
Similar to the Model 420 LR (45 and 50 calibers) except has black resin synthetic stock with checkered grip and forend. Introduced 1998.
Price: Blue **$419.00**
Price: Stainless steel **$449.00**

AUSTIN & HALLECK MOUNTAIN RIFLE
Caliber: 50. **Barrel:** 32"; 1:28" or 1:66" twist; 1" flats. **Weight:** 7-1/2 lbs. **Length:** 49" overall. **Stock:** Curly maple. **Sights:** Silver blade front, buckhorn rear. **Features:** Available in percussion or flintlock; double throw adjustable set triggers; rust brown finish.
Price: Flintlock, fancy wood **$589.00**
Price: Flintlock, select wood **$769.00**
Price: Percussion, fancy wood **$539.00**
Price: Percussion, select wood **$719.00**

AUSTIN & HALLECK MODEL 649 AMERICAN CLASSIC LEVER ACTION
Caliber: 45 or 50. **Barrel:** 22" Krieger, 1:24". **Weight:** 6.7 lbs. **Length:** 39.5" overall. **Stock:** Boyd's walnut or curly maple. **Sights:** Adjustable rear, Tru-Glo front blade. **Features:** A&H Brush Country trigger; blued finish. Introduced 2006.
Price: **$599.00**

BOSTONIAN PERCUSSION RIFLE
Caliber: 45. **Barrel:** 30", octagonal. **Weight:** 7-1/4 lbs. **Length:** 46" overall. **Stock:** Walnut. **Sights:** Blade front, fixed notch rear. **Features:** Color case-hardened lock, brass trigger guard, buttplate, patchbox. Imported from Italy by E.M.F.
Price: **$285.00**

CABELA'S BLUE RIDGE RIFLE
Caliber: 32, 36, 45, 50, .54. **Barrel:** 39", octagonal. **Weight:** About 7-3/4 lbs. **Length:** 55" overall. **Stock:** American black walnut. **Sights:** Blade front, rear drift adjustable for windage. **Features:** Color case-hardened lockplate and cock/hammer, brass trigger guard and buttplate, double set, double-phased triggers. From Cabela's.
Price: Percussion **$459.99**
Price: Flintlock **$489.99**

CABELA'S TRADITIONAL HAWKEN
Caliber: 50, 54. **Barrel:** 29". **Weight:** About 9 lbs. **Stock:** Walnut. **Sights:** Blade front, open adjustable rear. **Features:** Flintlock or percussion. Adjustable double-set triggers. Polished brass furniture, color case-hardened lock. Imported by Cabela's.
Price: Percussion, right-hand **$299.99**
Price: Percussion, left-hand **$299.99**
Price: Flintlock, right-hand **$339.99**

Cabela's Sporterized Hawken Hunter Rifle
Similar to the Traditional Hawken except has more modern stock style with rubber recoil pad, blued furniture, sling swivels. Percussion only, in 50- or 54-caliber.
Price: Carbine or rifle, right-hand **$369.99**

CABELA'S KODIAK EXPRESS DOUBLE RIFLE
Caliber: 50, 54, 58, 72. **Barrel:** Length NA; 1:48" twist. **Weight:** 9.3 lbs. **Length:** 45-1/4" overall. **Stock:** European walnut, oil finish. **Sights:** Fully adjustable double folding-leaf rear, ramp front. **Features:** Percussion. Barrels regulated to point of aim at 75 yards; polished and engraved lock, top tang and trigger guard. From Cabela's.
Price: 50, 54, 58 calibers **$829.99**
Price: 72 caliber **$859.99**

COOK & BROTHER CONFEDERATE CARBINE
Caliber: 58. **Barrel:** 24". **Weight:** 7-1/2 lbs. **Length:** 40-1/2" overall. **Stock:** Select walnut. **Features:** Re-creation of the 1861 New Orleans-made artillery carbine. Color case-hardened lock, browned barrel. Buttplate, trigger guard, barrel bands, sling swivels and nosecap of polished brass. From Euroarms of America.
Price: **$513.00**
Price: Cook & Brother rifle (33" barrel) **$552.00**

CVA OPTIMA PRO 209 BREAK-ACTION RIFLE
Caliber: 45, 50. **Barrel:** 29" fluted, blue or nickel. **Weight:** 8.8 lbs. **Stock:** Ambidextrous Mossy Oak® Camo or black FiberGrip. **Sights:** Adj. fiber-optic. **Features:** Break-action, stainless No. 209 breech plug, aluminum loading rod, cocking spur, lifetime warranty.
Price: Mossy Oak® Camo **$399.95**
Price: Camo, nickel bbl. **$379.95**
Price: Mossy Oak® Camo/blued **$349.95**
Price: Black/nickel **$329.95**
Price: Black/blued **$299.95**
Price: Blued fluted bbl. **$99.95**
Price: Nickel fluted bbl. **$115.95**

CVA Optima 209 Magnum Break-Action Rifle
Similar to Optima Pro but with 26" bbl., nickel or blue finish, 50 cal.
Price: Mossy Oak® Camo/nickel **$310.00**
Price: Mossy Oak® Camo/blue **$290.00**
Price: Black/blued **$235.00**

BLACKPOWDER MUSKETS & RIFLES

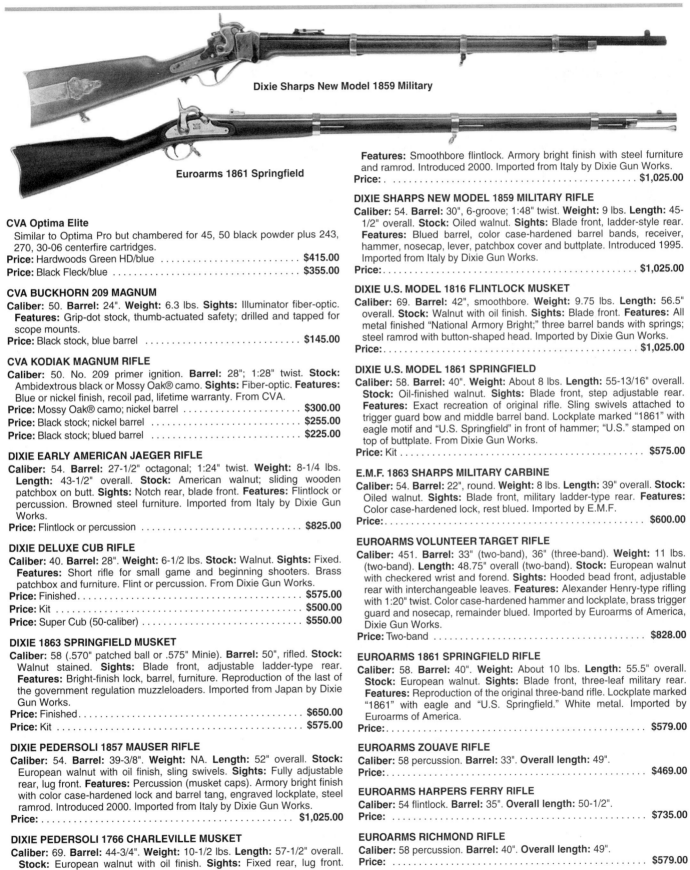

Dixie Sharps New Model 1859 Military

Euroarms 1861 Springfield

CVA Optima Elite
Similar to Optima Pro but chambered for 45, 50 black powder plus 243, 270, 30-06 centerfire cartridges.
Price: Hardwoods Green HD/blue **$415.00**
Price: Black Fleck/blue **$355.00**

CVA BUCKHORN 209 MAGNUM
Caliber: 50. **Barrel:** 24". **Weight:** 6.3 lbs. **Sights:** Illuminator fiber-optic. **Features:** Grip-dot stock, thumb-actuated safety; drilled and tapped for scope mounts.
Price: Black stock, blue barrel **$145.00**

CVA KODIAK MAGNUM RIFLE
Caliber: 50. No. 209 primer ignition. **Barrel:** 28"; 1:28" twist. **Stock:** Ambidextrous black or Mossy Oak® camo. **Sights:** Fiber-optic. **Features:** Blue or nickel finish, recoil pad, lifetime warranty. From CVA.
Price: Mossy Oak® camo; nickel barrel **$300.00**
Price: Black stock; nickel barrel **$255.00**
Price: Black stock; blued barrel **$225.00**

DIXIE EARLY AMERICAN JAEGER RIFLE
Caliber: 54. **Barrel:** 27-1/2" octagonal; 1:24" twist. **Weight:** 8-1/4 lbs. **Length:** 43-1/2" overall. **Stock:** American walnut; sliding wooden patchbox on butt. **Sights:** Notch rear, blade front. **Features:** Flintlock or percussion. Browned steel furniture. Imported from Italy by Dixie Gun Works.
Price: Flintlock or percussion **$825.00**

DIXIE DELUXE CUB RIFLE
Caliber: 40. **Barrel:** 28". **Weight:** 6-1/2 lbs. **Stock:** Walnut. **Sights:** Fixed. **Features:** Short rifle for small game and beginning shooters. Brass patchbox and furniture. Flint or percussion. From Dixie Gun Works.
Price: Finished. **$575.00**
Price: Kit **$500.00**
Price: Super Cub (50-caliber) **$550.00**

DIXIE 1863 SPRINGFIELD MUSKET
Caliber: 58 (.570" patched ball or .575" Minie). **Barrel:** 50", rifled. **Stock:** Walnut stained. **Sights:** Blade front, adjustable ladder-type rear. **Features:** Bright-finish lock, barrel, furniture. Reproduction of the last of the government regulation muzzleloaders. Imported from Japan by Dixie Gun Works.
Price: Finished. **$650.00**
Price: Kit **$575.00**

DIXIE PEDERSOLI 1857 MAUSER RIFLE
Caliber: 54. **Barrel:** 39-3/8". **Weight:** NA. **Length:** 52" overall. **Stock:** European walnut with oil finish, sling swivels. **Sights:** Fully adjustable rear, lug front. **Features:** Percussion (musket caps). Armory bright finish with color case-hardened lock and barrel tang, engraved lockplate, steel ramrod. Introduced 2000. Imported from Italy by Dixie Gun Works.
Price: **$1,025.00**

DIXIE PEDERSOLI 1766 CHARLEVILLE MUSKET
Caliber: 69. **Barrel:** 44-3/4". **Weight:** 10-1/2 lbs. **Length:** 57-1/2" overall. **Stock:** European walnut with oil finish. **Sights:** Fixed rear, lug front.

Features: Smoothbore flintlock. Armory bright finish with steel furniture and ramrod. Introduced 2000. Imported from Italy by Dixie Gun Works.
Price: **$1,025.00**

DIXIE SHARPS NEW MODEL 1859 MILITARY RIFLE
Caliber: 54. **Barrel:** 30", 6-groove; 1:48" twist. **Weight:** 9 lbs. **Length:** 45-1/2" overall. **Stock:** Oiled walnut. **Sights:** Blade front, ladder-style rear. **Features:** Blued barrel, color case-hardened barrel bands, receiver, hammer, nosecap, lever, patchbox cover and buttplate. Introduced 1995. Imported from Italy by Dixie Gun Works.
Price: **$1,025.00**

DIXIE U.S. MODEL 1816 FLINTLOCK MUSKET
Caliber: 69. **Barrel:** 42", smoothbore. **Weight:** 9.75 lbs. **Length:** 56.5" overall. **Stock:** Walnut with oil finish. **Sights:** Blade front. **Features:** All metal finished "National Armory Bright;" three barrel bands with springs; steel ramrod with button-shaped head. Imported by Dixie Gun Works.
Price: **$1,025.00**

DIXIE U.S. MODEL 1861 SPRINGFIELD
Caliber: 58. **Barrel:** 40". **Weight:** About 8 lbs. **Length:** 55-13/16" overall. **Stock:** Oil-finished walnut. **Sights:** Blade front, step adjustable rear. **Features:** Exact recreation of original rifle. Sling swivels attached to trigger guard bow and middle barrel band. Lockplate marked "1861" with eagle motif and "U.S. Springfield" in front of hammer; "U.S." stamped on top of buttplate. From Dixie Gun Works.
Price: Kit **$575.00**

E.M.F. 1863 SHARPS MILITARY CARBINE
Caliber: 54. **Barrel:** 22", round. **Weight:** 8 lbs. **Length:** 39" overall. **Stock:** Oiled walnut. **Sights:** Blade front, military ladder-type rear. **Features:** Color case-hardened lock, rest blued. Imported by E.M.F.
Price: **$600.00**

EUROARMS VOLUNTEER TARGET RIFLE
Caliber: 451. **Barrel:** 33" (two-band), 36" (three-band). **Weight:** 11 lbs. (two-band). **Length:** 48.75" overall (two-band). **Stock:** European walnut with checkered wrist and forend. **Sights:** Hooded bead front, adjustable rear with interchangeable leaves. **Features:** Alexander Henry-type rifling with 1:20" twist. Color case-hardened hammer and lockplate, brass trigger guard and nosecap, remainder blued. Imported by Euroarms of America, Dixie Gun Works.
Price: Two-band **$828.00**

EUROARMS 1861 SPRINGFIELD RIFLE
Caliber: 58. **Barrel:** 40". **Weight:** About 10 lbs. **Length:** 55.5" overall. **Stock:** European walnut. **Sights:** Blade front, three-leaf military rear. **Features:** Reproduction of the original three-band rifle. Lockplate marked "1861" with eagle and "U.S. Springfield." White metal. Imported by Euroarms of America.
Price: **$579.00**

EUROARMS ZOUAVE RIFLE
Caliber: 58 percussion. **Barrel:** 33". **Overall length:** 49".
Price: **$469.00**

EUROARMS HARPERS FERRY RIFLE
Caliber: 54 flintlock. **Barrel:** 35". **Overall length:** 50-1/2".
Price: **$735.00**

EUROARMS RICHMOND RIFLE
Caliber: 58 percussion. **Barrel:** 40". **Overall length:** 49".
Price: **$579.00**

Gonic Model 93 Thumbhole

Harper's Ferry 1803

J.P. Murray

Kentucky Flintlock

GONIC MODEL 93 M/L RIFLE
Caliber: 45, 50. **Barrel:** 26"; 1:24" twist. **Weight:** 6-1/2 to 7 lbs. **Length:** 43" overall. **Stock:** American hardwood with black finish. **Sights:** Adjustable or aperture rear, hooded post front. **Features:** Adjustable trigger with side safety; unbreakable ramrod; comes with A. Z. scope bases installed. Introduced 1993. Made in U.S. by Gonic Arms, Inc.
Price: Model 93 Standard (blued barrel) **$720.00**
Price: Model 93 Standard (stainless brl., 50 cal. only) **$782.00**

Gonic Model 93 Deluxe M/L Rifle
Similar to the Model 93 except has classic-style walnut or gray laminated wood stock. Introduced 1998. Made in U.S. by Gonic Arms, Inc.
Price: Blue barrel, sights, scope base, choice of stock **$902.00**
Price: Stainless barrel, sights, scope base, choice of stock
(50 cal. only) **$964.00**

Gonic Model 93 Mountain Thumbhole M/L Rifles
Similar to the Model 93 except has high-grade walnut or gray laminate stock with extensive hand-checkered panels, Monte Carlo cheekpiece and beavertail forend; integral muzzle brake. Introduced 1998. Made in U.S. by Gonic Arms, Inc.
Price: Blued or stainless **$2,700.00**

HARPER'S FERRY 1803 FLINTLOCK RIFLE
Caliber: 54 or 58. **Barrel:** 35". **Weight:** 9 lbs. **Length:** 59-1/2" overall. **Stock:** Walnut with cheekpiece. **Sights:** Brass blade front, fixed steel rear. **Features:** Brass trigger guard, sideplate, buttplate; steel patchbox. Imported by Euroarms of America, Navy Arms (54-cal. only), Cabela's, and Dixie Gun Works.
Price: . . . . **$495.95 to $995.00**
Price: 54-cal. (Navy Arms) **$625.00**
Price: 54-cal. (Cabela's) **$599.99**
Price: 54-cal. (Dixie Gun Works) **$995.00**
Price: 54-cal. (Euroarms) **$575.00**

HAWKEN RIFLE
Caliber: 45, 50, 54 or 58. **Barrel:** 28", blued, 6-groove rifling. **Weight:** 8-3/4 lbs. **Length:** 44" overall. **Stock:** Walnut with cheekpiece. **Sights:** Blade front, fully adjustable rear. **Features:** Coil mainspring, double-set triggers, polished brass furniture. From Armsport and E.M.F.
Price: . . . . **$220.00 to $345.00**

J.P. HENRY TRADE RIFLE
Caliber: 54. **Barrel:** 34"; 1" flats. **Weight:** 8-1/2 lbs. **Length:** 45" overall. **Stock:** Premium curly maple. **Sights:** Silver blade front, fixed buckhorn rear. **Features:** Brass buttplate, side plate, trigger guard and nosecap; browned barrel and lock; L&R Large English percussion lock; single trigger. Made in U.S. by J.P. Gunstocks, Inc.
Price: **$965.50**

J.P. MURRAY 1862-1864 CAVALRY CARBINE
Caliber: 58 (.577" Minie). **Barrel:** 23". **Weight:** 7 lbs., 9 oz. **Length:** 39" overall. **Stock:** Walnut. **Sights:** Blade front, rear drift adjustable for windage. **Features:** Browned barrel, color case-hardened lock, blued swivel and band springs, polished brass buttplate, trigger guard, barrel bands. From Euroarms of America.
Price: **$521.00**

KENTUCKY FLINTLOCK RIFLE
Caliber: 44, 45, or 50. **Barrel:** 35". **Weight:** 7 lbs. **Length:** 50" overall. **Stock:** Walnut stained, brass fittings. **Sights:** Fixed. **Features:** Available in carbine model also, 28" bbl. Some variations in detail, finish. Kits also available from some importers. Imported by The Armoury.
Price: About. . . . . **$217.95 to $345.00**

Kentucky Percussion Rifle
Similar to Flintlock except percussion lock. Finish and features vary with importer. Imported by The Armoury and CVA.
Price: About. **$259.95**
Price: 45 or 50 cal. (Navy Arms) **$425.00**
Price: Kit, 50 cal. (CVA) **$189.95**

KNIGHT 50 CALIBER DISC IN-LINE RIFLE
Caliber: 50. **Barrel:** 24", 26". **Weight:** 7 lbs., 14 oz. **Length:** 43" overall (24" barrel). **Stock:** Checkered synthetic with palm swell grip, rubber recoil pad, swivel studs; black, Advantage or Mossy Oak® Break-Up camouflage. **Sights:** Bead on ramp front, fully adjustable open rear. **Features:** Bolt-action in-line system uses #209 shotshell primer for ignition; primer is held in plastic drop-in Primer Disc. Available in blued or stainless steel. Made in U.S. by Knight Rifles (Modern Muzzleloading).
Price: . . . . **$439.95 to $632.45**

Knight 50 Caliber DISC In-Line

Knight Master Hunter DISC Extreme

London Armory 1861

Knight Master Hunter II DISC In-Line Rifle

Similar to Knight 50 caliber DISC rifle except features premium, wood laminated two-tone stock, gold-plated trigger and engraved trigger guard, jeweled bolt and fluted, air-gauged Green Mountain 26" barrel. Length 45" overall, weighs 7 lbs., 7 oz. Includes black composite thumbhole stock. Introduced 2000. Made in U.S. by Knight Rifles (Modern Muzzleloading).
Price: **$1,099.95**

KNIGHT MUZZLELOADER DISC EXTREME

Caliber: 45 fluted, 50. **Barrel:** 26". **Stock:** Stainless steel laminate, blued walnut, black composite thumbhole with blued or SS. **Sights:** Fully adjustable metallic. **Features:** New full plastic jacket ignition system.
Price: 50 SS laminate **$703.95**
Price: 45 SS laminate **$769.95**
Price: 50 blue walnut **$626.95**
Price: 45 blue walnut **$703.95**
Price: 50 blue composite **$549.95**
Price: 45 blue composite **$632.45**
Price: 50 SS composite **$632.45**
Price: 45 SS composite **$703.95**

Knight Master Hunter DISC Extreme

Similar to DISC Extreme except fluted barrel, two-tone laminated thumbhole Monte Carlo-style stock, black composite thumbhole field stock included. Jeweled bolt, adjustable premium trigger.
Price: 50 .... **$1,044.95**

KNIGHT AMERICAN KNIGHT M/L RIFLE

Caliber: 50. **Barrel:** 22"; 1:28" twist. **Weight:** 6 lbs. **Length:** 41" overall. **Stock:** Black composite. **Sights:** Bead on ramp front, open fully adjustable rear. **Features:** Double safety system; one-piece removable hammer assembly; drilled and tapped for scope mounting. Introduced 1998. Made in U.S. by Knight Rifles.
Price: Blued, black comp **$197.95**
Price: Blued, black comp VP **$225.45**

KNIGHT WOLVERINE 209

Caliber: 50. **Barrel:** 22". **Stock:** HD stock with SS barrel, break-up stock blued, black composite thumbhole with stainless steel, standard black composite with blued or SS. **Sights:** Metallic with fiber-optic. **Features:** Double safety system, adjustable match grade trigger, left-hand model available. Full plastic jacket ignition system.
Price: Starting at **$302.45**

KNIGHT REVOLUTION

Caliber: 50, 209 primer ignition. **Barrel:** Stainless, 27". **Weight:** 7 lbs., 14 oz. **Stock:** Walnut, laminated, black composite, Mossy Oak® Break-Up™ or Hardwoods Green finish. **Features:** Blued or stainless finish, adjustable trigger and sights.
Price: .... **NA**

LONDON ARMORY 1861 ENFIELD MUSKETOON

Caliber: 58, Minie ball. **Barrel:** 24", round. **Weight:** 7 to 7-1/2 lbs. **Length:** 40-1/2" overall. **Stock:** Walnut, with sling swivels. **Sights:** Blade front, graduated military-leaf rear. **Features:** Brass trigger guard, nosecap, buttplate; blued barrel, bands, lockplate, swivels. Imported by Euroarms of America, Navy Arms.
Price: .... **$300.00 to $475.00**
Price: Kit .... **$365.00 to $367.00**

LONDON ARMORY 2-BAND 1858 ENFIELD

Caliber: .577" Minie, .575" round ball. **Barrel:** 33". **Weight:** 10 lbs. **Length:** 49" overall. **Stock:** Walnut. **Sights:** Folding leaf rear adjustable for elevation. **Features:** Blued barrel, color case-hardened lock and hammer, polished brass buttplate, trigger guard, nosecap. From Navy Arms, Euroarms of America, Dixie Gun Works.
Price: .... **$385.00 to $513.00**

LONDON ARMORY 3-BAND 1853 ENFIELD

Caliber: 58 (.577" Minie, .575" round ball, .580" maxi ball). **Barrel:** 39". **Weight:** 9-1/2 lbs. **Length:** 54" overall. **Stock:** European walnut. **Sights:** Inverted "V" front, traditional Enfield folding ladder rear. **Features:** Re-creation of the famed London Armory Company Pattern 1853 Enfield Musket. One-piece walnut stock, brass buttplate, trigger guard and nosecap. Lockplate marked "London Armoury Co." and with a British crown. Blued Baddeley barrel bands. From Dixie Gun Works, Euroarms of America, Navy Arms.
Price: About .... **$350.00 to $528.00**
Price: Assembled kit (Dixie, Euroarms of America) **$469.00**

LYMAN TRADE RIFLE

Caliber: 50, 54. **Barrel:** 28" octagon; 1:48" twist. **Weight:** 8-3/4 lbs. **Length:** 45" overall. **Stock:** European walnut. **Sights:** Blade front, open rear adjustable for windage or optional fixed sights. **Features:** Fast twist rifling for conical bullets. Polished brass furniture with blue steel parts, stainless steel nipple. Hook breech, single trigger, coil spring percussion lock. Steel barrel rib and ramrod ferrules. Introduced 1980. From Lyman.
Price: 50 cal. percussion **$581.80**
Price: 50 cal. flintlock **$652.80**
Price: 54 cal. percussion **$581.80**
Price: 54 cal. flintlock **$652.80**

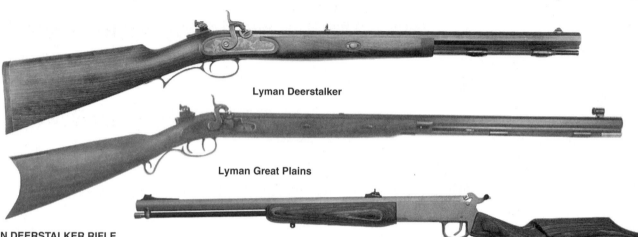

Lyman Deerstalker

Lyman Great Plains

Markesbery KM Colorado

LYMAN DEERSTALKER RIFLE
Caliber: 50, 54. **Barrel:** 24", octagonal; 1:48" rifling. **Weight:** 7-1/2 lbs. **Stock:** Walnut with black rubber buttpad. **Sights:** Lyman #37MA beaded front, fully adjustable fold-down Lyman #16A rear. **Features:** Stock has less drop for quick sighting. All metal parts are blackened, with color case-hardened lock; single trigger. Comes with sling and swivels. Available in flint or percussion. Introduced 1990. From Lyman.

Price: 50 cal. flintlock	$652.80
Price: 50 or 54 cal., percussion, left-hand, carbine	$695.40
Price: 50 or 54 cal., flintlock, left-hand	$645.00
Price: 54 cal. flintlock	$780.50
Price: 54 cal. percussion	$821.80
Price: Stainless steel	$959.80

LYMAN GREAT PLAINS RIFLE
Caliber: 50, 54. **Barrel:** 32"; 1:60" twist. **Weight:** 9 lbs. **Stock:** Walnut. **Sights:** Steel blade front, buckhorn rear adjustable for windage and elevation and fixed notch primitive sight included. **Features:** Blued steel furniture. Stainless steel nipple. Coil spring lock, Hawken-style trigger guard and double-set triggers. Round thimbles recessed and sweated into rib. Steel wedge plates and toe plate. Introduced 1979. From Lyman.

Price: Percussion	$469.95
Price: Flintlock	$494.95
Price: Percussion kit	$359.95
Price: Flintlock kit	$384.95
Price: Left-hand percussion	$474.95
Price: Left-hand flintlock	$499.95

Lyman Great Plains Hunter Model
Similar to Great Plains model except 1:32" twist shallow-groove barrel and comes drilled and tapped for Lyman 57GPR peep sight.

Price:	$959.80

MARKESBERY KM BLACK BEAR M/L RIFLE
Caliber: 36, 45, 50, 54. **Barrel:** 24"; 1:26" twist. **Weight:** 6-1/2 lbs. **Length:** 38-1/2" overall. **Stock:** Two-piece American hardwood, walnut, black laminate, green laminate, black composition, X-Tra or Mossy Oak® Break-Up™ camouflage. **Sights:** Bead front, open fully adjustable rear. **Features:** Interchangeable barrels; exposed hammer; Outer-Line Magnum ignition system uses small rifle primer or standard No. 11 cap and nipple. Blue, black matte, or stainless. Made in U.S. by Markesbery Muzzle Loaders.

Price: American hardwood walnut, blue finish	$536.63
Price: American hardwood walnut, stainless	$553.09
Price: Black laminate, blue finish	$539.67
Price: Black laminate, stainless	$556.27
Price: Camouflage stock, blue finish	$556.46
Price: Camouflage stock, stainless	$573.73
Price: Black composite, blue finish	$532.65
Price: Black composite, stainless	$549.93
Price: Green laminate, blue finish	$539.00
Price: Green laminate, stainless	$556.27

Markesbery KM Brown Bear Rifle
Similar to KM Black Bear except one-piece thumbhole stock with Monte Carlo comb. Stock in Crotch Walnut composite, green or black laminate, black composite or X-Tra or Mossy Oak® Break-Up™ camouflage. Made in U.S. by Markesbery Muzzle Loaders, Inc.

Price: Black composite, blue finish	$658.83
Price: Crotch Walnut, blue finish	$658.83
Price: Camo composite, blue finish	$682.64
Price: Walnut wood	$662.81
Price: Black wood	$662.81
Price: Black laminated wood	$662.81
Price: Green laminated wood	$662.81
Price: Camo wood	$684.69
Price: Black composite, stainless	$676.11
Price: Crotch Walnut composite, stainless	$676.11
Price: Camo composite, stainless	$697.69
Price: Walnut wood, stainless	$680.07
Price: Black wood, stainless	$680.07
Price: Black laminated wood, stainless	$680.07
Price: Green laminate, stainless	$680.07
Price: Camo wood, stainless	$702.76

Markesbery KM Grizzly Bear Rifle
Similar to KM Black Bear except thumbhole buttstock with Monte Carlo comb. Stock in Crotch Walnut composite, green or black laminate, black composite or X-Tra or Mossy Oak® Break-Up camouflage. Made in U.S. by Markesbery Muzzle Loaders, Inc.

Price: Black composite, blue finish	$642.96
Price: Crotch Walnut, blue finish	$642.96
Price: Camo composite, blue finish	$666.67
Price: Walnut wood	$646.93
Price: Black wood	$646.93
Price: Black laminate wood	$646.93
Price: Green laminate wood	$646.93
Price: Camo wood	$670.74
Price: Black composite, stainless	$660.98
Price: Crotch Walnut composite, stainless	$660.98
Price: Black laminate wood, stainless	$664.20
Price: Green laminate, stainless	$664.20
Price: Camo wood, stainless	$685.74
Price: Camo composite, stainless	$684.04
Price: Walnut wood, stainless	$664.20
Price: Black wood, stainless	$664.20

BLACKPOWDER MUSKETS & RIFLES

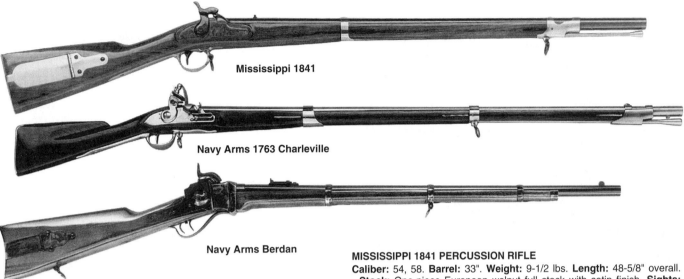

Mississippi 1841

Navy Arms 1763 Charleville

Navy Arms Berdan

Markesbery KM Polar Bear Rifle

Similar to KM Black Bear except one-piece stock with Monte Carlo comb. Stock in American Hardwood walnut, green or black laminate, black composite, or X-Tra or Mossy Oak® Break-Up™ camouflage. Interchangeable barrel system, Outer-Line ignition system, cross-bolt double safety. Available in 36, 45, 50, 54 caliber. Made in U.S. by Markesbery Muzzle Loaders, Inc.

Price: American Hardwood walnut, blue finish **$539.01**
Price: Black composite, blue finish **$536.63**
Price: Black laminate, blue finish **$541.17**
Price: Green laminate, blue finish **$541.17**
Price: Camo, blue finish. **$560.43**
Price: American Hardwood walnut, stainless **$556.27**
Price: Black composite, stainless **$556.04**
Price: Black laminate, stainless. **$570.56**
Price: Green laminate, stainless **$570.56**
Price: Camo, stainless. **$573.94**

MARKESBERY KM COLORADO ROCKY MOUNTAIN RIFLE

Caliber: 36, 45, 50, 54. **Barrel:** 24"; 1:26" twist. **Weight:** 6-1/2 lbs. **Length:** 38-1/2" overall. **Stock:** American hardwood walnut, green or black laminate. **Sights:** Firesight bead on ramp front, fully adjustable open rear. **Features:** Replicates Reed/Watson rifle of 1851. Straight grip stock with or without two barrel bands, rubber recoil pad, large-spur hammer. Made in U.S. by Markesbery Muzzle Loaders, Inc.

Price: American hardwood walnut, blue finish **$545.92**
Price: Black or green laminate, blue finish **$548.30**
Price: American hardwood walnut, stainless. **$563.17**
Price: Black or green laminate, stainless **$566.34**

MDM BUCKWACKA IN-LINE RIFLES

Caliber: 45, 50. **Barrel:** 23", 25". **Weight:** 7 to 7-3/4 lbs. **Stock:** Black, walnut, laminated and camouflage finishes. **Sights:** Williams Fire Sight blade front, Williams fully adjustable rear with ghost-ring peep aperture. **Features:** Break-open action; Incinerating Ignition System incorporates 209 shotshell primer directly into breech plug; 50-caliber models handle up to 150 grains of Pyrodex; synthetic ramrod; transfer bar safety; stainless or blued finish. Made in U.S. by Millennium Designed Muzzleloaders Ltd.

Price: 50 cal., blued finish **$309.95**
Price: 50 cal., stainless **$339.95**
Price: Camouflage stock . . . . **$359.95 to $389.95**

MDM M2K In-Line Rifle

Similar to Buckwacka except adjustable trigger and double-safety mechanism designed to prevent misfires. Made in U.S. by Millennium Designed Muzzleloaders Ltd.

Price: . . . . **$529.00 to $549.00**

MISSISSIPPI 1841 PERCUSSION RIFLE

Caliber: 54, 58. **Barrel:** 33". **Weight:** 9-1/2 lbs. **Length:** 48-5/8" overall. **Stock:** One-piece European walnut full stock with satin finish. **Sights:** Brass blade front, fixed steel rear. **Features:** Case-hardened lockplate marked "U.S." surmounted by American eagle. Two barrel bands, sling swivels. Steel ramrod with brass end, browned barrel. From Navy Arms, Dixie Gun Works, E.M.F., Cabela's, Euroarms of America.

Price: About. **$575.00**

NAVY ARMS 1763 CHARLEVILLE

Caliber: 69. **Barrel:** 44-5/8". **Weight:** 8 lbs., 12 oz. **Length:** 59-3/8" overall. **Stock:** Walnut. **Sights:** Brass blade front. **Features:** Replica of French musket used by American troops during the American Revolution. Imported by Navy Arms.

Price: **$1,020.00**

NAVY ARMS BERDAN 1859 SHARPS RIFLE

Caliber: 54. **Barrel:** 30". **Weight:** 8 lbs., 8 oz. **Length:** 46-3/4" overall. **Stock:** Walnut. **Sights:** Blade front, folding military ladder-type rear. **Features:** Replica of the Union sniper rifle used by Berdan's 1st and 2nd Sharpshooter regiments. Color case-hardened receiver, patchbox, furniture. Double-set triggers. Imported by Navy Arms.

Price: **$1,165.00**
Price: 1859 Sharps Infantry Rifle (three-band). **$1,100.00**

NAVY ARMS 1859 SHARPS CAVALRY CARBINE

Caliber: 54. **Barrel:** 22". **Weight:** 7-3/4 lbs. **Length:** 39" overall. **Stock:** Walnut. **Sights:** Blade front, military ladder-type rear. **Features:** Color case-hardened action, blued barrel. Has saddle ring. Introduced 1991. Imported from Navy Arms.

Price: **$1,000.00**

NAVY ARMS 1861 SPRINGFIELD RIFLE

Caliber: 58. **Barrel:** 40". **Weight:** 10 lbs., 4 oz. **Length:** 56" overall. **Stock:** Walnut. **Sights:** Blade front, military leaf rear. **Features:** Steel barrel, lock and all furniture have polished bright finish. Has 1855-style hammer. Imported by Navy Arms.

Price: **$590.00**

NAVY ARMS 1863 C.S. RICHMOND RIFLE

Caliber: 58. **Barrel:** 40". **Weight:** 10 lbs. **Length:** NA. **Stocks:** Walnut. **Sights:** Blade front, adjustable rear. **Features:** Copy of three-band rifle musket made at Richmond Armory for the Confederacy. All steel polished bright. Imported by Navy Arms.

Price: **$590.00**

NAVY ARMS 1863 SPRINGFIELD

Caliber: 58, uses .575 Minie. **Barrel:** 40", rifled. **Weight:** 9-1/2 lbs. **Length:** 56" overall. **Stock:** Walnut. **Sights:** Open rear adjustable for elevation. **Features:** Full-size, three-band musket. Polished bright metal, including lock. From Navy Arms.

Price: Finished rifle **$590.00**

BLACKPOWDER MUSKETS & RIFLES

Navy Arms Whitworth

New England Firearms Huntsman

Peifer TS-93

NAVY ARMS PARKER-HALE VOLUNTEER RIFLE
Caliber: .451. **Barrel:** 32". **Weight:** 9-1/2 lbs. **Length:** 49" overall. **Stock:** Walnut, checkered wrist and forend. **Sights:** Globe front, adjustable ladder-type rear. **Features:** Recreation of the type of gun issued to volunteer regiments during the 1860s. Rigby-pattern rifling, patent breech, detented lock. Stock is glass bedded for accuracy. Imported by Navy Arms.
Price: **$905.00**

NAVY ARMS PARKER-HALE WHITWORTH MILITARY TARGET RIFLE
Caliber: 45. **Barrel:** 36". **Weight:** 9-1/4 lbs. **Length:** 52-1/2" overall. **Stock:** Walnut. Checkered at wrist and forend. **Sights:** Hooded post front, open step-adjustable rear. **Features:** Faithful reproduction of Whitworth rifle. Trigger has detented lock, capable of fine adjustments without risk of the sear nose catching on the half-cock notch and damaging both parts. Introduced 1978. Imported by Navy Arms.
Price: **$930.00**

NAVY ARMS SMITH CARBINE
Caliber: 50. **Barrel:** 21-1/2". **Weight:** 7-3/4 lbs. **Length:** 39" overall. **Stock:** American walnut. **Sights:** Brass blade front, folding ladder-type rear. **Features:** Replica of breech-loading Civil War carbine. Color case-hardened receiver, rest blued. Cavalry model has saddle ring and bar, Artillery model has sling swivels. Imported by Navy Arms.
Price: Cavalry model **$645.00**
Price: Artillery model **$645.00**

NEW ENGLAND FIREARMS SIDEKICK
Caliber: 50, 209 primer ignition. **Barrel:** 26" (magnum). **Weight:** 6.5 lbs. **Length:** 41.25". **Stock:** Black matte polymer or hardwood. **Sights:** Adjustable fiber-optic open, tapped for scope mounts. **Features:** Single-shot based on H&R break-open action. Uses No. 209 shotgun primer held in place by special primer carrier. Telescoping brass ramrod. Introduced 2004.
Price: Wood stock, blued frame, black-oxide barrel) **$216.00**
Price: Stainless barrel and frame, synthetic stock) **$310.00**

NEW ENGLAND FIREARMS HUNTSMAN
Caliber: 50, 209 primer ignition. **Barrel:** 22" to 26". **Weight:** 5.25 to 6.5 lbs. **Length:** 40" to 43". **Stock:** Black matte polymer or hardwood. **Sights:** Fiber-optic open sights, tapped for scope mounts. **Features:** Break-open action, transfer-bar safety system, breech plug removable for cleaning. Introduced 2004.
Price: Stainless Huntsman **$306.00**
Price: Huntsman **$212.00**
Price: Pardner Combo 12 ga./50 cal muzzleloader **$259.00**
Price: Tracker II Combo 12 ga. rifled slug barrel /50 cal. **$288.00**
Price: Handi-Rifle Combo 243/50 cal. **$405.00**

New England Firearms Stainless Huntsman
Similar to Huntsman, but with matte nickel finish receiver and stainless bbl. Introduced 2003. From New England Firearms.
Price: **$81.00**

PACIFIC RIFLE MODEL 1837 ZEPHYR
Caliber: 62. **Barrel:** 30", tapered octagon. **Weight:** 7-3/4 lbs. **Length:** NA. **Stock:** Oil-finished fancy walnut. **Sights:** German silver blade front, semi-buckhorn rear. Options available. **Features:** Improved underhammer action. First production rifle to offer Forsyth rifle, with narrow lands and shallow rifling with 1:14" pitch for high-velocity round balls. Metal finish is slow rust brown with nitre blue accents. Optional sights, finishes and integral muzzle brake available. Introduced 1995. Made in U.S. by Pacific Rifle Co.
Price: From **$995.00**

Pacific Rifle Big Bore African Rifles
Similar to the 1837 Zephyr except in 72-caliber and 8-bore. The 72-caliber is available in standard form with 28" barrel, or as the African with flat buttplate, checkered upgraded wood; weight is 9 lbs. The 8-bore African has dual-cap ignition, 24" barrel, weighs 12 lbs., checkered English walnut, engraving, gold inlays. Introduced 1998. Made in U.S. by Pacific Rifle Co.
Price: 72-caliber, from **$1,150.00**
Price: 8-bore, from **$2,500.00**

PEIFER MODEL TS-93 RIFLE
Caliber: 45, 50. **Barrel:** 24" Douglas premium; 1:20" twist in 45; 1:28" in 50. **Weight:** 7 lbs. **Length:** 43-1/4" overall. **Stock:** Bell & Carlson solid composite, with recoil pad, swivel studs. **Sights:** Williams bead front on ramp, fully adjustable open rear. Drilled and tapped for Weaver scope mounts with dovetail for rear peep. **Features:** In-line ignition uses #209 shotshell primer; fast lock time; fully enclosed breech; adjustable trigger; automatic safety; removable primer holder. Blue or stainless. Made in U.S. by Peifer Rifle Co. Introduced 1996.
Price: Blue, black stock **$730.00**
Price: Blue, wood or camouflage composite stock, or stainless with black composite stock **$803.00**
Price: Stainless, wood or camouflage composite stock **$876.00**

PRAIRIE RIVER ARMS PRA BULLPUP RIFLE
Caliber: 50. **Barrel:** 28"; 1:28" twist. **Weight:** 7-1/2 lbs. **Length:** 31-1/2" overall. **Stock:** Hardwood or black all-weather. **Sights:** Blade front, open adjustable rear. **Features:** Bullpup design thumbhole stock. Patented internal percussion ignition system. Left-hand model available. Dovetailed for scope mount. Introduced 1995. Made in U.S. by Prairie River Arms, Ltd.
Price: 4140 alloy barrel, hardwood stock **$199.00**
Price: All Weather stock, alloy barrel **$205.00**

REPLICA ARMS 1863 SHARPS SPORTING RIFLE
Caliber: .54 cal percussion. **Barrel:** 28" Octagonal. **Weight:** 8.82 lbs. **Length:** 45" overall. **Grips:** Walnut checkered at wrist and forend. **Sights:** Blade front, full buckhorn rear. **Features:** Color case-hardened receiver, trigger, hammer and lever. Double-set triggers.
Price: **$939.00**

BLACKPOWDER MUSKETS & RIFLES

C.S. Richmond 1863

Savage 10MLSS-IIXP

Second Model Brown Bess

Thompson/Center Hawken

RICHMOND, C.S., 1863 MUSKET
Caliber: 58. **Barrel:** 40". **Weight:** 11 lbs. **Length:** 56-1/4" overall. **Stock:** European walnut with oil finish. **Sights:** Blade front, adjustable folding leaf rear. **Features:** Reproduction of the three-band Civil War musket. Sling swivels attached to trigger guard and middle barrel band. Lockplate marked "1863" and "C.S. Richmond." All white metal. Brass buttplate and forend cap. Imported by Euroarms of America, Navy Arms, and Dixie Gun Works.
Price: Euroarms $530.00
Price: Dixie Gun Works $1,025.00

SAVAGE MODEL 10ML MUZZLELOADER RIFLE SERIES
Caliber: 50. **Barrel:** 24", 1:24 twist, blue or stainless. **Weight:** 7.75 lbs. **Stock:** Black synthetic, Realtree Hardwood JD Camo, brown laminate. **Sights:** Green adjustable rear, Red FiberOptic front. **Features:** XP Models scoped, no sights, designed for smokeless powder, #209 primer ignition. Removeable breech plug and vent liner.
Price: Model 10ML-II $531.00
Price: Model 10ML-II Camo $569.00
Price: Model 10MLSS-II Camo $628.00
Price: Model 10MLBSS-II $667.00
Price: Model 10ML-IIXP $569.00
Price: Model 10MLSS-IIXP $628.00

SECOND MODEL BROWN BESS MUSKET
Caliber: 75, uses .735" round ball. **Barrel:** 42", smoothbore. **Weight:** 9-1/2 lbs. **Length:** 59" overall. **Stock:** Walnut (Navy); walnut-stained hardwood (Dixie). **Sights:** Fixed. **Features:** Polished barrel and lock with brass trigger guard and buttplate. Bayonet and scabbard available. From Navy Arms, Dixie Gun Works, Cabela's.
Price: Finished . . . . $475.00 to $950.00
Price: Kit (Dixie Gun Works, Navy Arms) . . . . $575.00 to $775.00
Price: Carbine (Navy Arms) $835.00
Price: Dixie Gun Works $950.00

THOMPSON/CENTER BLACK DIAMOND RIFLE XR
Caliber: 50. **Barrel:** 26" with QLA; 1:28" twist. **Weight:** 6 lbs., 9 oz. **Length:** 41-1/2" overall. **Stock:** Black Rynite with molded-in checkering and gripcap, or walnut. **Sights:** TruGlo fiber-optic ramp-style front, TruGlo fiber-optic open rear. **Features:** In-line ignition system for musket cap, No.

11 cap, or 209 shotshell primer; removable universal breech plug; stainless steel construction. Selected models available in .45 cal. Made in U.S. by Thompson/Center Arms.
Price: With composite stock, blued $337.00
Price: With walnut stock $412.00

THOMPSON/CENTER ENCORE 209x50 MAGNUM
Caliber: 50. **Barrel:** 26"; interchangeable with centerfire calibers. **Weight:** 7 lbs. **Length:** 40-1/2" overall. **Stock:** American walnut butt and forend, or black composite. **Sights:** TruGlo fiber-optic front and rear. **Features:** Blue or stainless steel. Uses the stock, frame and forend of the Encore centerfire pistol; break-open design using trigger guard spur; stainless steel universal breech plug; uses #209 shotshell primers. Introduced 1998. Made in U.S. by Thompson/Center Arms.
Price: Stainless wtih camo stock $772.00
Price: Blue, walnut stock and forend $678.00
Price: Blue, composite stock and forend $637.00
Price: Stainless, composite stock and forend $713.00
Price: All camo Realtree Hardwoods $729.00

THOMPSON/CENTER FIRE STORM RIFLE
Caliber: 50. **Barrel:** 26"; 1:28" twist. **Weight:** 7 lbs. **Length:** 41-3/4" overall. **Stock:** Black synthetic with rubber recoil pad, swivel studs. **Sights:** Click-adjustable steel rear and ramp-style front, both with fiber-optic inserts. **Features:** Side hammer lock is the first designed for up to three 50-grain Pyrodex pellets; patented Pyrodex Pyramid breech directs ignition fire 360 degrees around base of pellet. Quick Load Accurizor Muzzle System; aluminum ramrod. Flintlock only. Introduced 2000. Made in U.S. by Thompson/Center Arms.
Price: Blue finish, flintlock model with 1:48" twist for round balls, conicals $436.00
Price: SST, flintlock $488.00

THOMPSON/CENTER HAWKEN RIFLE
Caliber: 50. **Barrel:** 28" octagon, hooked breech. **Stock:** American walnut. **Sights:** Blade front, rear adjustable for windage and elevation. **Features:** Solid brass furniture, double-set triggers, button rifled barrel, coil-type mainspring. From Thompson/Center Arms.
Price: Percussion model $590.00
Price: Flintlock model $615.00

BLACKPOWDER MUSKETS & RIFLES

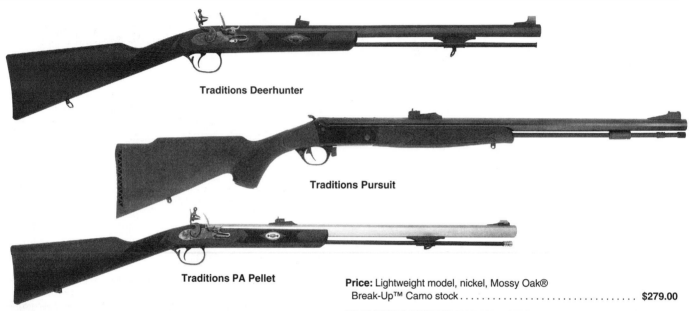

Traditions Deerhunter

Traditions Pursuit

Traditions PA Pellet

TRADITIONS BUCKSKINNER CARBINE

Caliber: 50. **Barrel:** 21"; 15/16" flats, half octagon, half round; 1:20" or 1:66" twist. **Weight:** 6 lbs. **Length:** 37" overall. **Stock:** Beech or black laminated. **Sights:** Beaded blade front, fiber-optic open rear click adjustable for windage and elevation or fiber-optics. **Features:** Uses V-type mainspring, single trigger. Non-glare hardware; sling swivels. From Traditions.
Price: Flintlock **$249.00**
Price: Flintlock, laminated stock **$303.00**

TRADITIONS DEERHUNTER RIFLE SERIES

Caliber: 32, 50 or 54. **Barrel:** 24", octagonal; 15/16" flats; 1:48" or 1:66" twist. **Weight:** 6 lbs. **Length:** 40" overall. **Stock:** Stained hardwood or All-Weather composite with rubber buttpad, sling swivels. **Sights:** Lite Optic blade front, adjustable rear fiber-optics. **Features:** Flint or percussion with color case-hardened lock. Hooked breech, oversized trigger guard, blackened furniture, PVC ramrod. All-Weather has composite stock and C-nickel barrel. Drilled and tapped for scope mounting. Imported by Traditions, Inc.
Price: Percussion, 50; blued barrel; 1:48" twist **$189.00**
Price: Percussion, 54 . . . . **$169.00**
Price: Flintlock, 50 caliber only; 1:48" twist **$179.00**
Price: Flintlock, All-Weather, 50-cal. **$239.00**
Price: Redi-Pak, 50 cal. flintlock **$219.00**
Price: Flintlock, left-handed hardwood, 50 cal. **$209.00**
Price: Percussion, All-Weather, 50 or 54 cal. **$179.00**
Price: Percussion, 32 cal. **$199.00**

Traditions Panther Sidelock Rifle

Similar to Deerhunter rifle, but has blade front and windage-adjustable-only rear sights, black composite stock.
Price: **$129.00**

TRADITIONS PURSUIT BREAK-OPEN MUZZLELOADER

Caliber: 45, 54 and 12 gauge. **Barrel:** 28", tapered, fluted; blued, stainless or Hardwoods Green camo. **Weight:** 8-1/4 lbs. **Length:** 44" overall. **Stock:** Synthetic black or Hardwoods Green. **Sights:** Steel fiber-optic rear, bead front. Introduced 2004 by Traditions, Inc.
Price: Steel, blued, 45 or 50 cal., synthetic stock **$279.00**
Price: Steel, nickel, 45 or 50 cal., synthetic stock **$309.00**
Price: Steel, nickel w/Hardwoods Green stock **$359.00**
Price: Matte blued; 12 ga., synthetic stock **$369.00**
Price: Matte blued; 12 ga. w/Hardwoods Green stock **$439.00**
Price: Lightweight model, blued, synthetic stock. **$199.00**
Price: Lightweight model, blued, Mossy Oak®
Break-Up™ Camo stock **$239.00**

Price: Lightweight model, nickel, Mossy Oak®
Break-Up™ Camo stock **$279.00**

TRADITIONS EVOLUTION BOLT-ACTION BLACKPOWDER RIFLE

Caliber: 50 percussion. **Barrel:** 26", fluted with porting. **Sights:** Steel fiber-optic. **Weight:** 7 to 7-1/4 lbs. **Length:** 45" overall. **Features:** Bolt-action, cocking indicator, thumb safety, aluminum ramrod, sling studs. Wide variety of stocks and metal finishes. Introduced 2004 by Traditions, Inc.
Price: Synthetic stock **$279.00**
Price: Walnut X-wood **$349.00**
Price: Brown laminated. **$469.00**
Price: Advantage Timber **$369.00**
Price: Synthetic, TruGlo sights **$249.00**
Price: Mossy Oak® Break-up™ **$279.00**
Price: Nickel finish. **$309.00**
Price: Beech/nickel, Advantage/nickel, Advantage 54 cal. **$289.00**

TRADITIONS PA PELLET FLINTLOCK

Caliber: 50. **Barrel:** 26", blued, nickel. **Weight:** 7 lbs. **Stock:** Hardwood, synthetic and synthetic break-up. **Sights:** Fiber-optic. **Features:** Removeable breech plug, left-hand model with hardwood stock. 1:48" twist.
Price: Hardwood, blued. **$259.00**
Price: Hardwood left, blued. **$269.00**

TRADITIONS HAWKEN WOODSMAN RIFLE

Caliber: 50 and 54. **Barrel:** 28"; 15/16" flats. **Weight:** 7 lbs., 11 oz. **Length:** 44-1/2" overall. **Stock:** Walnut-stained hardwood. **Sights:** Beaded blade front, hunting-style open rear adjustable for windage and elevation. **Features:** Percussion only. Brass patchbox and furniture. Double triggers. From Traditions.
Price: 50 or 54. . . . . **$299.00**
Price: 50-cal., left-hand **$279.00**
Price: 50-cal., flintlock **$299.00**

TRADITIONS KENTUCKY RIFLE

Caliber: 50. **Barrel:** 33-1/2"; 7/8" flats; 1:66" twist. **Weight:** 7 lbs. **Length:** 49" overall. **Stock:** Beech; inletted toe plate. **Sights:** Blade front, fixed rear. **Features:** Full-length, two-piece stock; brass furniture; color case-hardened lock. From Traditions.
Price: **$279.00**

TRADITIONS PENNSYLVANIA RIFLE

Caliber: 50. **Barrel:** 40-1/4"; 7/8" flats; 1:66" twist, octagon. **Weight:** 9 lbs. **Length:** 57-1/2" overall. **Stock:** Walnut. **Sights:** Blade front, adjustable rear. **Features:** Brass patchbox and ornamentation. Double-set triggers. From Traditions.
Price: Flintlock. **$529.00**
Price: Percussion **$519.00**

BLACKPOWDER MUSKETS & RIFLES

Zouave Percussion

TRADITIONS SHENANDOAH RIFLE
Caliber: 36, 50. **Barrel:** 33-1/2" octagon; 1:66" twist. **Weight:** 7 lbs., 3 oz. **Length:** 49-1/2" overall. **Stock:** Walnut. **Sights:** Blade front, buckhorn rear. **Features:** V-type mainspring; double-set trigger; solid brass buttplate, patchbox, nosecap, thimbles, trigger guard. Introduced 1996. From Traditions.
Price: Flintloc **$419.00**
Price: Percussion **$399.00**
Price: 36 cal. flintlock, 1:48" twist **$419.00**
Price: 36 cal. percussion, 1:48" twist **$449.00**

TRADITIONS TENNESSEE RIFLE
Caliber: 50. **Barrel:** 24", octagon; 15/16" flats; 1:66" twist. **Weight:** 6 lbs. **Length:** 40-1/2" overall. **Stock:** Stained beech. **Sights:** Blade front, fixed rear. **Features:** One-piece stock has inletted brass furniture, cheekpiece; double-set trigger; V-type mainspring. Flint or percussion. From Traditions.
Price: Flintlock **$339.00**
Price: Percussion **$329.00**

TRADITIONS TRACKER 209 IN-LINE RIFLES
Caliber: 45, 50. **Barrel:** 22" blued or C-nickel finish; 1:28" twist, 50 cal. 1:20" 45 cal. **Weight:** 6 lbs., 4 oz. **Length:** 41" overall. **Stock:** Black, Advantage Timber® composite, synthetic. **Sights:** Lite Optic blade front, adjustable rear. **Features:** Thumb safety; adjustable trigger; rubber butt pad and sling swivel studs; takes 150 grains of Pyrodex pellets; one-piece breech system takes 209 shotshell primers. Drilled and tapped for scope. From Traditions.
Price: (Black composite or synthetic stock, 22" blued barrel) **$129.00**
Price: (Black composite or synthetic stock, 22" C-nickel barrel) . . . **$139.00**
Price: (Advantage Timber® stock, 22" C-nickel barrel) **$189.00**
Price: (Redi-Pak, black stock and blued barrel, powder flask,
capper, ball starter, other accessories) **$179.00**
Price: (Redi-Pak, synthetic stock and blued barrel, with scope) **$229.00**

ULTRA LIGHT ARMS MODEL 209 MUZZLELOADER
Caliber: 45 or 50. **Barrel:** 24" button rifled; 1:32 twist. **Weight:** Under 5 lbs. **Stock:** Kevlar/Graphite. **Features:** Recoil pad, sling swivels included. Some color options available. Adj. Timney trigger, positive primer extraction.
Price: **$1,100.00**

WHITE MODEL 97 WHITETAIL HUNTER RIFLE
Caliber: 45, 50. **Barrel:** 22", 1:20 twist (45 cal.); 1:24 twist (50 cal.). **Weight:** 7.7 lbs. **Length:** 40" overall. **Stock:** Black laminated or black composite. **Sights:** Marble TruGlo fully adjustable, steel rear with white diamond, red bead front with high-visibility inserts. **Features:** In-line ignition with FlashFire one-piece nipple and breech plug that uses standard or magnum No. 11 caps, fully adjustable trigger, double safety system, aluminum ramrod; drilled and tapped for scope. Hard case. Made in U.S.A. by Split Fire Sporting Goods.
Price: Whitetail w/laminated or composite stock **$499.95**
Price: Adventurer w/26" stainless barrel & thumbhole stock) **$699.95**
Price: Odyssey w/24" carbon fiber wrapped
barrel & thumbhole stock **$1,299.95**

WHITE MODEL 98 ELITE HUNTER RIFLE
Caliber: 45, 50. **Barrel:** 24", 1:24" twist (50 cal). **Weight:** 8.6 lbs. **Length:** 43-1/2" overall. **Stock:** Black laminate wtih swivel studs. **Sights:** TruGlo fully adjustable, steel rear with white diamond, red bead front with high-visibility inserts. **Features:** In-line ignition with FlashFire one-piece nipple and breech plug that uses standard or magnum No. 11 caps, fully adjustable trigger, double safety system, aluminum ramrod, drilled and tapped for scope, hard gun case. Made in U.S.A. by Split Fire Sporting Goods.
Price: Composite or laminate wood stock **$499.95**

White Thunderbolt Rifle
Similar to the Elite Hunter but is designed to handle 209 shotgun primers only. Has 26" stainless steel barrel, weighs 9.3 lbs. and is 45-1/2" long. Composite or laminate stock. Made in U.S.A. by Split Fire Sporting Goods.
Price: **$599.95**

WHITE MODEL 2000 BLACKTAIL HUNTER RIFLE
Caliber: 50. **Barrel:** 22", 1:24" twist (50 cal.). **Weight:** 7.6 lbs. **Length:** 39-7/8" overall. **Stock:** Black laminated with swivel studs with laser engraved deer or elk scene. **Sights:** TruGlo fully adjustable, steel rear with white diamond, red bead front with high-visibility inserts. **Features:** Teflon finished barrel, in-line ignition with FlashFire one-piece nipple and breech plug that uses standard or magnum No. 11 caps, fully adjustable trigger, double safety system, aluminum ramrod, drilled and tapped for scope. Hard gun case. Made in U.S.A. by Split Fire Sporting Goods.
Price: Laminate wood stock, w/laser engraved game scene **$599.95**

WHITE LIGHTNING II RIFLE
Caliber: 45 and 50 percussion. **Barrel:** 24", 1:32 twist. **Sights:** Adj. rear. **Stock:** Black polymer. **Weight:** 6 lbs. **Features:** In-line, 209 primer ignition system, blued or nickel-plated bbl., adj. trigger, Delrin ramrod, sling studs, recoil pad. Made in U.S.A. by Split Fire Sporting Goods.
Price: **$299.95**

WHITE ALPHA RIFLE
Caliber: 45, 50 percussion. **Barrel:** 27" tapered, stainless. **Sights:** Marble TruGlo rear, fiber-optic front. **Stock:** Laminated. **Features:** Lever action rotating block, hammerless; adj. trigger, positive safety. All stainless metal, including trigger. Made in U.S.A. by Split Fire Sporting Goods.
Price: **$449.95**

WINCHESTER APEX SWING-ACTION MAGNUM RIFLE
Caliber: 45, 50. **Barrel:** 28". **Stock:** Mossy Oak® Camo, Black Fleck. **Sights:** Adj. fiber-optic. **Weight:** 7 lbs., 12 oz. **Overall length:** 42". **Features:** Monte Carlo cheekpiece, swing-action design, external hammer.
Price: Mossy Oak®/stainless **$489.95**
Price: Black Fleck/stainless **$449.95**
Price: Full Mossy Oak® **$469.95**
Price: Black Fleck/blued **$364.95**

WINCHESTER X-150 BOLT-ACTION MAGNUM RIFLE
Caliber: 45, 50. **Barrel:** 26". **Stock:** Hardwoods or Timber HD, Black Fleck, Break-Up™. **Weight:** 8 lbs., 3 oz. **Sights:** Adj. fiber-optic. **Features:** No. 209 shotgun primer ignition, stainless steel bolt, stainless fluted bbl.
Price: Mossy Oak®, Timber, Hardwoods/stainless **$349.95**
Price: Black Fleck/stainless **$299.95**
Price: Mossy Oak®, Timber, Hardwoods/blued **$279.95**
Price: Black Fleck/blued **$229.95**

ZOUAVE PERCUSSION RIFLE
Caliber: 58, 59. **Barrel:** 32-1/2". **Weight:** 9-1/2 lbs. **Length:** 48-1/2" overall. **Stock:** Walnut finish, brass patchbox and buttplate. **Sights:** Fixed front, rear adjustable for elevation. **Features:** Color case-hardened lockplate, blued barrel. From Navy Arms, Dixie Gun Works, E.M.F., Cabela's, Euroarms of America.
Price: . . . . **$415.00 to $625.00**

Knight TK2000

AUSTIN & HALLECK MODEL 520 LR MUZZLELOADING SHOTGUN

Caliber: 12. **Barrel:** 26" w/screw-in chokes. **Weight:** 6.5 lbs. **Length:** 47-1/2" overall. **Stock:** Lightly figured maple in Classic or Monte Carlo style. **Sights:** Rib with Tru-Glo front dot. **Features:** In-line percussion action with removable weather shroud; Timney adjustable target trigger with sear block safety. Introduced 2006.
Price: Blue $549.00

CABELA'S BLACKPOWDER SHOTGUNS

Gauge: 10, 12, 20. **Barrel:** 10-ga., 30"; 12-ga., 28-1/2" (Extra-Full, Mod., Imp. Cyl. choke tubes); 20-ga., 27-1/2" (Imp. Cyl. & Mod. fixed chokes). **Weight:** 6-1/2 to 7 lbs. **Length:** 45" overall. **Stock:** American walnut with checkered grip; 12- and 20-gauge have straight stock, 10-gauge has pistol grip. **Features:** Blued barrels, engraved, color case-hardened locks and hammers, brass ramrod tip. From Cabela's.
Price: 10-gauge $759.99
Price: 12-gauge $649.99
Price: 20-gauge $599.99

DIXIE MAGNUM PERCUSSION SHOTGUN

Gauge: 10, 12, 20. **Barrel:** 30" (Imp. Cyl. & Mod.) in 10-gauge; 28" in 12-gauge. **Weight:** 6-1/4 lbs. **Length:** 45" overall. **Stock:** Hand-checkered walnut, 14" pull. **Features:** Double triggers; light hand engraving; case-hardened locks in 12-gauge, polished steel in 10-gauge; sling swivels. From Dixie Gun Works.
Price: 12 ga. $685.00
Price: 12-ga. kit $500.00
Price: 20-ga. $685.00
Price: 10-ga. $685.00
Price: 10-ga. kit $500.00
Price: Coach Gun, 12 ga. 20" bbl $625.00

KNIGHT TK2000 MUZZLELOADING SHOTGUN (209)

Gauge: 12. **Barrel:** 26", extra-full choke tube. **Weight:** 7 lbs., 9 oz. **Length:** 45" overall. **Stock:** Synthetic black or Advantage Timber HD; recoil pad; swivel studs. **Sights:** Fully adjustable rear, blade front with fiber-optics. **Features:** Receiver drilled and tapped for scope mount; in-line ignition; adjustable trigger; removable breech plug; double safety system; Imp. Cyl. choke tube available. Made in U.S. by Knight Rifles.
Price: . . . . $349.95 to $399.95

KNIGHT VERSATILE TK2002

Gauge: 12. **Stock:** Black composite, blued, Advantage Timber HD finish. Both with sling swivel studs installed. **Sights:** Adjustable metallic TruGlo fiber-optic. **Features:** Full plastic jacket ignition system, screw-on choke tubes, load without removing choke tubes, jug-choked barrel design. Improved cylinder and modified choke tubes available.
Price: . . . . $349.95 to $399.95

NAVY ARMS STEEL SHOT MAGNUM SHOTGUN

Gauge: 10. **Barrel:** 28" (Cyl. & Cyl.). **Weight:** 7 lbs., 9 oz. **Length:** 45-1/2" overall. **Stock:** Walnut, with cheekpiece. **Features:** Designed specifically for steel shot. Engraved, polished locks; sling swivels; blued barrels. Imported by Navy Arms.
Price: $605.00

NAVY ARMS T&T SHOTGUN

Gauge: 12. **Barrel:** 28" (Full & Full). **Weight:** 7-1/2 lbs. **Stock:** Walnut. **Sights:** Bead front. **Features:** Color case-hardened locks, double triggers, blued steel furniture. From Navy Arms.
Price: $580.00

WHITE TOMINATOR SHOTGUN

Caliber: 12. **Barrel:** 25" blue, straight, tapered stainless steel. **Weight:** NA. **Length:** NA. **Stock:** Black laminated or black wood. **Sights:** Drilled and tapped for easy scope mounting. **Features:** Internchangeable choke tubes. Custom vent rib with high visibility front bead. Double safeties. Fully adjustable custom trigger. Recoil pad and sling swivel studs. Made in U.S.A. by Split Fire Sporting Goods.
Price: $349.95

ARS HUNTING MASTER AR6 AIR PISTOL
Caliber: 22 (177 +20 special order). **Barrel:** 12" rifled. **Weight:** 3 lbs. **Length:** 18.25 overall. **Power:** NA. **Grips:** Indonesian walnut with checkered grip. **Sights:** Adjustable rear, blade front. **Features:** 6 shot repeater with rotary magazine, single or double action, receiver grooved for scope, hammer block and trigger block safeties.
Price: .... **NA**

BEEMAN P1 MAGNUM AIR PISTOL
Caliber: 177, 20. **Barrel:** 8.4". **Weight:** 2.5 lbs. **Length:** 11" overall. **Power:** Top lever cocking; spring-piston. **Grips:** Checkered walnut. **Sights:** Blade front, square notch rear with click micrometer adjustments for windage and elevation. Grooved for scope mounting. **Features:** Dual power for 177 and 20 cal.: low setting gives 350-400 fps; high setting 500-600 fps. All Colt 45 auto grips fit gun. Dry-firing feature for practice. Optional wood shoulder stock. Imported by Beeman.
Price: **$430.00**

BEEMAN P3 PNEUMATIC AIR PISTOL
Caliber: 177. **Barrel:** NA. **Weight:** 1.7 lbs. **Length:** 9.6" overall. **Power:** Single-stroke pneumatic; overlever barrel cocking. **Grips:** Reinforced polymer. **Sights:** Adjustable rear, blade front. **Features:** Velocity 410 fps. Polymer frame; automatic safety; two-stage trigger; built-in muzzle brake.
Price: **$200.00**
Price: Combo **$315.00**

BEEMAN/FWB 103 AIR PISTOL
Caliber: 177. **Barrel:** 10.1", 12-groove rifling. **Weight:** 2.5 lbs. **Length:** 16.5" overall. **Power:** Single-stroke pneumatic, underlever cocking. **Grips:** Stippled walnut with adjustable palm shelf. **Sights:** Blade front, open rear adjustable for windage and elevation. Notch size adjustable for width. Interchangeable front blades. **Features:** Velocity 510 fps. Fully adjustable trigger. Cocking effort 2 lbs. Imported by Beeman.
Price: Right-hand **$1,750.00**
Price: Left-hand **$1,865.00**

BEEMAN HW70A AIR PISTOL
Caliber: 177. **Barrel:** 6-1/4", rifled. **Weight:** 38 oz. **Length:** 12-3/4" overall. **Power:** Spring, barrel cocking. **Grips:** Plastic, with thumbrest. **Sights:** Hooded post front, square notch rear adjustable for windage and elevation. Comes with scope base. **Features:** Adjustable trigger, 31-lb. cocking effort, 440 fps MV; automatic barrel safety. Imported by Beeman.
Price: **$220.00**

BEEMAN/WEBLEY TEMPEST AIR PISTOL
Caliber: 177. **Barrel:** 6-7/8". **Weight:** 32 oz. **Length:** 8.9" overall. **Power:** Spring-piston, break barrel. **Grips:** Checkered black plastic with thumbrest. **Sights:** Blade front, adjustable rear. **Features:** Velocity to 500 fps (177), 400 fps (22). Aluminum frame; black epoxy finish; manual safety. Imported from England by Beeman.
Price: **$235.00**

Beeman/Webley Hurricane Air Pistol
Similar to the Tempest except has extended frame in the rear for a click-adjustable rear sight; hooded front sight; comes with scope mount. Imported from England by Beeman.
Price: **$275.00**

BENJAMIN & SHERIDAN CO2 PISTOLS
Caliber: 177, 22, single shot. **Barrel:** 6-3/8", brass. **Weight:** 1 lb. 12 oz. **Length:** 9" overall. **Power:** 12-gram CO2 cylinder. **Grips:** American Hardwood. **Sights:** High ramp front, fully adjustable notched rear. **Features:** Velocity to 500 fps. Turnbolt action with cross-bolt safety. Gives about 40 shots per CO2 cylinder. Black or nickel finish. Made in U.S. by Crosman Corp.
Price: EB17 (177), EB22 (22) **$185.00**

BENJAMIN & SHERIDAN PNEUMATIC PELLET PISTOLS
Caliber: 177, 22, single shot. **Barrel:** 9-3/8", rifled brass. **Weight:** 2 lbs., 8 oz. **Length:** 12.25" overall. **Power:** Underlever pneumatic, hand pumped. **Grips:** American Hardwood. **Sights:** High ramp front, fully adjustable notch rear. **Features:** Velocity to 525 fps (variable). Bolt action with cross-bolt safety. Choice of black or nickel finish. Made in U.S. by Crosman Corp.
Price: Black finish, HB17 (177), HB22 (22) **$115.00**

BRNO TAU-7 CO2 MATCH AIR PISTOL
Caliber: 177. **Barrel:** 10.25". **Weight:** 2.31 lbs. **Length:** 15.75" overall. **Power:** 12-gram CO2 cartridge. **Grips:** Stippled hardwood with adjustable palm rest. **Sights:** Blade front, open fully adjustable rear. **Features:** Comes with extra seals and counterweight. Blue finish.
Price: **$500.00**

CROSMAN AUTO AIR II RED DOT PISTOLS
Caliber: BB, 17-shot magazine; 177 pellet, single shot. **Barrel:** 8-5/8" steel, smooth-bore. **Weight:** 13 oz. **Length:** 10-3/4" overall. **Power:** CO2 Powerlet. **Grips:** NA. **Sights:** Blade front, adjustable rear; highlighted system. **Features:** Velocity to 480 fps (BBs), 430 fps (pellets). Semi-automatic action with BBs, single shot with pellets. Black. From Crosman.
Price: AAIIB **$38.00**

CROSMAN MODEL 1008 REPEAT AIR PISTOL
Caliber: 177, 8-shot pellet clip. **Barrel:** 4.25", rifled steel. **Weight:** 17 oz. **Length:** 8.625" overall. **Power:** CO2 Powerlet. **Grips:** Checkered black plastic. **Sights:** Post front, adjustable rear. **Features:** Velocity about 430 fps. Break-open barrel for easy loading; single or double semi-automatic action; two 8-shot clips included. Optional carrying case available. From Crosman.
Price: **$60.00**

CROSMAN MAGNUM AIR PISTOLS
Caliber: 177, pellets. **Barrel:** Rifled steel. **Weight:** 2 lbs. **Length:** 9.38". **Power:** CO2. **Grips:** NA. **Sights:** Blade front, rear adjustable. **Features:** Single/double action accepts sights and scopes with standard 3/8" dovetail mount. Model 3576W features 6" barrel for increased accuracy. From Crosman.
Price: 3576W **$50.00**

DAISY/POWERLINE MODEL 15XT AIR PISTOL
Caliber: 177 BB, 15-shot built-in magazine. **Barrel:** NA. **Weight:** NA. **Length:** 7.21". **Power:** CO2. **Grips:** NA. **Sights:** NA. **Features:** Velocity 425 fps. Made in the U.S.A. by Daisy Mfg. Co.
Price: **$47.99**
Price: With electronic point sight **$57.99**

DAISY MODEL 717 AIR PISTOL
Caliber: 177, single shot. **Weight:** 2.25 lbs. **Length:** 13-1/2" overall. **Grips:** Molded checkered woodgrain with contoured thumbrest. **Sights:** Blade and ramp front, open rear with windage and elevation adjustments. **Features:** Single pump pneumatic pistol. Rifled steel barrel. Crossbolt trigger block. Muzzle velocity 360 fps. From Daisy Mfg. Co.
Price: **$152.99**

DAISY MODEL 747 TRIUMPH AIR PISTOL
Caliber: 177, single shot. **Weight:** 2.35 lbs. **Length:** 13-1/2" overall. **Grips:** Molded checkered woodgrain with contoured thumbrest. **Sights:** Blade and ramp front, open rear with windage and elevation adjustments. **Features:** Single pump pneumatic pistol. Lothar Walther rifled high-grade steel barrel; crowned 12 lands and grooves, right-hand twist. Precision bore sized for match pellets. Muzzle veocity 360 fps. From Daisy Mfg. Co.
Price: **$203.99**

DAISY/POWERLINE 693 AIR PISTOL
Caliber: 177, single shot. **Weight:** 1.10 lbs. **Length:** 7.9" overall. **Grips:** Molded brown checkered. **Sights:** Blade and ramp front, fixed open rear. **Features:** Semi-automoatic BB pistol with a nickel finish and smooth bore steel barrel. Muzzle veocity 400 fps. From Daisy Mfg. Co.
Price: **$66.99**

EAA/BAIKAL IZH-M46 TARGET AIR PISTOL
Caliber: 177, single shot. **Barrel:** 10". **Weight:** 2.4 lbs. **Length:** 16.8" overall. **Power:** Underlever single-stroke pneumatic. **Grips:** Adjustable wooden target. **Sights:** Micrometer fully adjustable rear, blade front. **Features:** Velocity about 440 fps. Hammer-forged, rifled barrel. Imported from Russia by European American Armory.
Price: **$349.00**

EAA MP651K

Gamo PT-80

GAMO P-23, P-23 LASER PISTOL
Caliber: 177, 12-shot. **Barrel:** 4.25". **Weight:** 1 lb. **Length:** 7.5". **Power:** CO2 cartridge, semi-automatic, 410 fps. **Grips:** Plastic. **Sights:** NA. **Features:** Walther PPK cartridge pistol copy, optional laser sight. Imported from Spain by Gamo.
Price: . . . . **$89.95**, (with laser) **$129.95**

GAMO PT-80, PT-80 LASER PISTOL
Caliber: 177, 8-shot. **Barrel:** 4.25". **Weight:** 1.2 lbs. **Length:** 7.2". **Power:** CO2 cartridge, semi-automatic, 410 fps. **Grips:** Plastic. **Sights:** 3-dot. **Features:** Optional laser sight and walnut grips available. Imported from Spain by Gamo.
Price: . . . . **$108.95**, (with laser) **$129.95**
Price: . . . . (with walnut grip) **$119.95**

HAMMERLI AP-40 AIR PISTOL
Caliber: 177. **Barrel:** 10". **Weight:** 2.2 lbs. **Length:** 15.5". **Power:** NA. **Grips:** Adjustable orthopedic. **Sights:** Fully adjustable micrometer. **Features:** Sleek, light, well balanced and accurate.
Price: **$1,400.00**

MORINI CM 162 EL MATCH AIR PISTOLS
Caliber: 177, single shot. **Barrel:** 9.4". **Weight:** 32 oz. **Length:** 16.1" overall. **Power:** Scuba air. **Grips:** Adjustable match type. **Sights:** Interchangeable blade front, fully adjustable match-type rear. **Features:** Power mechanism shuts down when pressure drops to a preset level. Adjustable electronic trigger.
Price: **$1,075.00**

PARDINI K58 MATCH AIR PISTOLS
Caliber: 177, single shot. **Barrel:** 9". **Weight:** 37.7 oz. **Length:** 15.5" overall. **Power:** Precharged compressed air; single-stroke cocking. **Grips:** Adjustable match type; stippled walnut. **Sights:** Interchangeable post front, fully adjustable match rear. **Features:** Fully adjustable trigger. Short version K-2 available. Imported from Italy by Larry's Guns.
Price: **$819.00**

RWS 9B/9N AIR PISTOLS
Caliber: 177, single shot. **Barrel:** 8". **Weight:** 2.38 lbs. **Length:** 10.4". **Power:** 550 fps. **Grips:** Right hand with thumbrest. **Sights:** Adjustable. **Features:** Spring-piston powered. Black or nickel finish.
Price: 9B/9N **$150.00**

STEYR LP10P MATCH AIR PISTOL
Caliber: 177, single shot. **Barrel:** 9". **Weight:** 38.7 oz. **Length:** 15.3" overall. **Power:** Scuba air. **Grips:** Adjustable Morini match, palm shelf, stippled walnut. **Sights:** Interchangeable blade in 4mm, 4.5mm or 5mm widths, adjustable open rear, interchangeable 3.5mm or 4mm leaves. **Features:** Velocity about 500 fps. Adjustable trigger, adjustable sight radius from 12.4" to 13.2". With compensator. Recoil elimination.
Price: **$1,400.00**

TECH FORCE SS2 OLYMPIC COMPETITION AIR PISTOL
Caliber: 177 pellet, single shot. **Barrel:** 7.4". **Weight:** 2.8 lbs. **Length:** 16.5" overall. **Power:** Spring piston, sidelever. **Grips:** Hardwood. **Sights:** Extended adjustable rear, blade front accepts inserts. **Features:** Velocity 520 fps. Recoilless design; adjustments allow duplication of a firearm's feel. Match-grade, adjustable trigger; includes carrying case. Imported from China by Compasseco, Inc.
Price: **$295.00**

TECH FORCE 35 AIR PISTOL
Caliber: 177 pellet, single shot. **Weight:** 2.86 lbs. **Length:** 14.9" overall. **Power:** Spring-piston, underlever. **Grips:** Hardwood. **Sights:** Micrometer adjustable rear, blade front. **Features:** Velocity 400 fps. Grooved for scope mount; trigger safety. Imported from China by Compasseco, Inc.
Price: **$39.95**

Tech Force S2-1 Air Pistol
Similar to Tech Force 8 except basic grips and sights for plinking.
Price: **$29.95**

WALTHER LP300 MATCH PISTOL
Caliber: 177. **Barrel:** 236mm. **Weight:** 1.018g. **Length:** NA. **Power:** NA. **Grips:** NA. **Sights:** Integrated front with three different widths, adjustable rear. **Features:** Adjustable grip and trigger.
Price: **$1,800.00**

AIRFORCE CONDOR RIFLE

Caliber: 177, 22. **Barrel:** 24" rifled. **Weight:** 6.5 lbs. **Length:** 38.75" overall. **Power:** NA. **Grips:** NA. **Sights:** None, integral mount supplied. **Features:** 600-1,300 fps. 3,000 psi fill pressure. Automatic safety. Air tank volume: 490cc.

Price: Gun only (22 or 177) **$569.95**

AIRFORCE TALON AIR RIFLE

Caliber: 177, 22, single shot. **Barrel:** 18". **Weight:** 5.5 lbs. **Length:** 32.6". **Power:** Precharged pneumatic. **Stock:** NA. **Sights:** Intended for scope use, fiber-optic open sights optional. **Features:** Lothar Walther match barrel, adjustable power levels from 400-1000 FPS, operates on high pressure air from scuba tank or hand pump. Accessories attach to multiple dovetailed mounting rails. Manufactured in the U.S.A. by AirForce Airguns.

Price: **$459.95**

AIRFORCE TALON SS AIR RIFLE

Caliber: 177, 22, single shot. **Barrel:** 12". **Weight:** 5.25 lbs. **Length:** 32.75". **Power:** Precharged pneumatic. **Stock:** NA. **Sights:** Intended for scope use, fiber-optic open sights optional. **Features:** Lothar Walther match barrel, adjustable power levels from 400-1000 FPS. Chamber in front of barrel strips away air turbulence, protects muzzle and reduces firing report. Operates on high pressure air from scuba tank or hand pump. Accessories attach to multiple dovetailed mounting rails. Manufactured in the U.S.A. by AirForce Airguns.

Price: **$459.95**

AIRROW MODEL A-8SRB STEALTH AIR RIFLE

Caliber: 177, 22, 25, 9-shot. **Barrel:** 20"; rifled. **Weight:** 6 lbs. **Length:** 34" overall. **Power:** CO_2 or compressed air; variable power. **Stock:** Telescoping CAR-15-type. **Sights:** Variable 3.5-10x scope. **Features:** Velocity 1100 fps in all calibers. Pneumatic air trigger. All aircraft aluminum and stainless steel construction. Mil-spec materials and finishes. From Swivel Machine Works, Inc.

Price: About **$2,299.00**

AIRROW MODEL A-8S1P STEALTH AIR RIFLE

Caliber: #2512 16" arrow. **Barrel:** 16". **Weight:** 4.4 lbs. **Length:** 30.1" overall. **Power:** CO_2 or compressed air; variable power. **Stock:** Telescoping CAR-15-type. **Sights:** Scope rings only. 7 oz. rechargeable cylinder and valve. **Features:** Velocity to 650 fps with 260-grain arrow. Pneumatic air trigger. Broadhead guard. All aircraft aluminum and stainless steel construction. Mil-spec materials and finishes. A-8S Models perform to 2,000 PSIG above or below water levels. Waterproof case. From Swivel Machine Works, Inc.

Price: **$1,699.00**

ANSCHUTZ 2002 MATCH AIR RIFLES

Caliber: 177, single shot. **Barrel:** 25.2". **Weight:** 10.8 lbs. **Length:** 42.5" overall. **Stock:** European walnut, blonde hardwood or colored laminated hardwood; stippled grip and forend. Also available with flat-forend walnut stock for benchrest shooting and aluminum. **Sights:** Optional sight set #6834. **Features:** Muzzle velocity 575 fps. Balance, weight match the 1907 ISU smallbore rifle. Uses #5021 match trigger. Recoil and vibration free. Fully adjustable cheekpiece and buttplate; accessory rail under forend. Available in pneumatic and compressed air versions. Imported from Germany by Gunsmithing, Inc., Accuracy International, Champion's Choice.

Price: Right-hand, blonde hardwood stock, with sights **$1,275.00**
Price: Right-hand, walnut stock **$1,275.00**
Price: Right-hand, color laminate stock **$1,300.00**
Price: Right-hand, aluminum stock, butt plate **$1,495.00**
Price: Left-hand, color laminate stock **$1,595.00**
Price: Model 2002D-RT Running Target, right-hand, no sights . . **$1,248.90**
Price: #6834 Sight Set **$227.10**

ARS HUNTING MASTER AR6 AIR RIFLE

Caliber: 22, 6-shot repeater. **Barrel:** 25-1/2". **Weight:** 7 lbs. **Length:** 41-1/4" overall. **Power:** Precompressed air from 3000 psi diving tank. **Stock:** Indonesian walnut with checkered grip; rubber buttpad. **Sights:** Blade front, adjustable peep rear. **Features:** Velocity over 1000 fps with 32-grain pellet. Receiver grooved for scope mounting. Has 6-shot rotary magazine. Imported by Air Rifle Specialists.

Price: **$580.00**

BEEMAN KODIAK AIR RIFLE

Caliber: 25, single shot. **Barrel:** 17.6". **Weight:** 9 lbs. **Length:** 45.6" overall. **Power:** Spring-piston, barrel cocking. **Stock:** Stained hardwood. **Sights:** Blade front, open fully adjustable rear. **Features:** Velocity to 820 fps. Up to 30 foot pounds muzzle energy. Imported by Beeman.

Price: **$725.00**

BEEMAN R1 AIR RIFLE

Caliber: 177, 20 or 22, single shot. **Barrel:** 19.6", 12-groove rifling. **Weight:** 8.5 lbs. **Length:** 45.2" overall. **Power:** Spring-piston, barrel cocking. **Stock:** Walnut-stained beech; cut-checkered pistol grip; Monte Carlo comb and cheekpiece; rubber buttpad. **Sights:** Tunnel front with interchangeable inserts, open rear click-adjustable for windage and elevation. Grooved for scope mounting. **Features:** Velocity 940-1000 fps (177), 860 fps (20), 800 fps (22). Non-drying nylon piston and breech seals. Adjustable metal trigger. Milled steel safety. Right- or left-hand stock. Adjustable cheekpiece and buttplate at extra cost. Custom and Super Laser versions available. Imported by Beeman.

Price: Right-hand **$665.00**
Price: Left-hand **$720.00**

BEEMAN R7 AIR RIFLE

Caliber: 177, 20, single shot. **Barrel:** 17". **Weight:** 6.1 lbs. **Length:** 40.2" overall. **Power:** Spring-piston. **Stock:** Stained beech. **Sights:** Hooded front, fully adjustable micrometer click open rear. **Features:** Velocity to 700 fps (177), 620 fps (20). Receiver grooved for scope mounting; double-jointed cocking lever; fully adjustable trigger; checkered grip. Imported by Beeman.

Price: **$350.00**

BEEMAN R9 AIR RIFLE

Caliber: 177, 20, single shot. **Barrel:** NA. **Weight:** 7.3 lbs. **Length:** 43" overall. **Power:** Spring-piston, barrel cocking. **Stock:** Stained hardwood. **Sights:** Tunnel post front, fully adjustable open rear. **Features:** Velocity to 1000 fps (177), 800 fps (20). Adjustable Rekord trigger; automatic safety; receiver dovetailed for scope mounting. Imported from Germany by Beeman Precision Airguns.

Price: **$420.00**

BEEMAN R11 MKII AIR RIFLE

Caliber: 177, single shot. **Barrel:** 19.6". **Weight:** 8.6 lbs. **Length:** 43.5" overall. **Power:** Spring-piston, barrel cocking. **Stock:** Walnut-stained beech; adjustable buttplate and cheekpiece. **Sights:** None furnished. Has dovetail for scope mounting. **Features:** Velocity 910-940 fps. All-steel barrel sleeve. Imported by Beeman.

Price: **$650.00**

BEEMAN RX-2 GAS-SPRING MAGNUM AIR RIFLE

Caliber: 177, 20, 22, 25, single shot. **Barrel:** 19.6", 12-groove rifling. **Weight:** 8.8 lbs. **Power:** Gas-spring piston air; single stroke barrel cocking. **Stock:** Walnut-finished hardwood, hand checkered, with cheekpiece. Adjustable cheekpiece and buttplate. **Sights:** Tunnel front, click-adjustable rear. **Features:** Velocity adjustable to about 1200 fps. Imported by Beeman.

Price: 177, 20, 22 or 25 regular, right-hand **$750.00**

BEEMAN R1 CARBINE

Caliber: 177, 20, 22, 25, single shot. **Barrel:** 16.1". **Weight:** 8.6 lbs. **Length:** 41.7" overall. **Power:** Spring-piston, barrel cocking. **Stock:** Stained beech; Monte Carlo comb and checkpiece; cut checkered pistol grip; rubber buttpad. **Sights:** Tunnel front with interchangeable inserts, open adjustable rear; receiver grooved for scope mounting. **Features:** Velocity up to 1000 fps (177). Non-drying nylon piston and breech seals. Adjustable metal trigger. Machined steel receiver end cap and safety. Right- or left-hand stock. Imported by Beeman.

Price: 177, 20, 22, 25, right-hand . . . . **$665.00;** left-hand **$720.00**

Crosman 2289G

BEEMAN/FEINWERKBAU 603 AIR RIFLE

Caliber: 177, single shot. **Barrel:** 16.6". **Weight:** 10.8 lbs. **Length:** 43" overall. **Power:** Single stroke pneumatic. **Stock:** Special laminated hardwoods and hard rubber for stability. Multi-colored stock also available. **Sights:** Tunnel front with interchangeable inserts, click micrometer match aperture rear. **Features:** Velocity to 570 fps. Recoilless action; double supported barrel; special, short rifled area frees pellet from barrel faster. Fully adjustable match trigger with separately adjustable trigger and trigger slack weight. Trigger and sights blocked when loading latch is open. Imported by Beeman.
Price: Right-hand............................... **$2,395.00**
Price: Left-hand **$2,495.00**
Price: Junior **$2,095.00**

BEEMAN/FEINWERKBAU P70 AND P70 JUNIOR AIR RIFLE

Caliber: 177, single shot. **Barrel:** 16.6". **Weight:** 10.6 lbs. **Length:** 42.6" overall. **Power:** Precharged pneumatic. **Stock:** Laminated hardwoods and hard rubber for stability. Multi-colored stock also available. **Sights:** Tunnel front with interchangeable inserts, click micrometer match aperture rear. **Features:** Velocity to 570 fps. Recoilless action; double supported barrel; special short rifled area frees pellet from barrel faster. Fully adjustable match trigger with separately adjustable trigger and trigger slack weight. Trigger and sights blocked when loading latch is open. Imported by Beeman.
Price: P70, precharged, right-hand **$2,825.00**
Price: P70, precharged, left-hand **$2,925.00**
Price: P70, precharged, Junior **$2,150.00**

BEEMAN/HW 97 AIR RIFLE

Caliber: 177, 20, single shot. **Barrel:** 17.75". **Weight:** 9.2 lbs. **Length:** 44.1" overall. **Power:** Spring-piston, underlever cocking. **Stock:** Walnut-stained beech; rubber buttpad. **Sights:** None. Receiver grooved for scope mounting. **Features:** Velocity 830 fps (177). Fixed barrel with fully opening, direct loading breech. Adjustable trigger. Imported by Beeman Precision Airguns.
Price: Right-hand only................................ **$595.00**

BENJAMIN & SHERIDAN PNEUMATIC (PUMP-UP) AIR RIFLE

Caliber: 177 or 22, single shot. **Barrel:** 19-3/8", rifled brass. **Weight:** 5-1/2 lbs. **Length:** 36-1/4" overall. **Power:** Underlever pneumatic, hand pumped. **Stock:** American walnut stock and forend. **Sights:** High ramp front, fully adjustable notched rear. **Features:** Variable velocity to 800 fps. Bolt action with ambidextrous push-pull safety. Black or nickel finish. Made in the U.S. by Benjamin Sheridan Co.
Price: **$140.95**

BRNO TAU-200 AIR RIFLES

Caliber: 177, single shot. **Barrel:** 19", rifled. **Weight:** 7-1/2 lbs. **Length:** 42" overall. **Power:** 6-oz. CO2 cartridge. **Stock:** Wood match style with adjustable comb and buttplate. **Sights:** Globe front with interchangeable inserts, fully adjustable open rear. **Features:** Adjustable trigger. Comes with extra seals, large CO2 bottle, counterweight. Imported by Pyramyd Air.
Price: **$495.00**

BSA SUPERTEN MK3 AIR RIFLE

Caliber: 177, 22 10-shot repeater. **Barrel:** 17-1/2". **Weight:** 7 lbs., 8 oz. **Length:** 37" overall. **Power:** Precharged pneumatic via buddy bottle. **Stock:** Oil-finished hardwood; Monte Carlo with cheekpiece, cut checkered grip; adjustable recoil pad. **Sights:** No sights; intended for scope use. **Features:** Velocity 1000+ fps (177), 1000+ fps (22). Patented 10-shot indexing magazine, bolt-action loading. Left-hand version also available. Imported from U.K.
Price: **$599.95**

BSA SUPERTEN MK3 BULLBARREL

Caliber: 177, 22, 25, single shot. **Barrel:** 18-1/2". **Weight:** 8 lbs., 8 oz. **Length:** 43" overall. **Power:** Spring-air, underlever cocking. **Stock:** Oil-finished hardwood; Monte Carlo with cheekpiece, checkered at grip; recoil pad. **Sights:** Ramp front, micrometer adjustable rear. Maxi-Grip scope rail. **Features:** Velocity 950 fps (177), 750 fps (22), 600 fps (25). Patented rotating breech design. Maxi-Grip scope rail protects optics from recoil; automatic anti-beartrap plus manual safety. Imported from U.K.
Price: Rifle, MKII Carbine (14" barrel, 39-1/2" overall) **$349.95**

BSA MAGNUM SUPERSPORT™ AIR RIFLE, CARBINE

Caliber: 177, 22, 25, single shot. **Barrel:** 18-1/2". **Weight:** 6 lbs., 8 oz. **Length:** 41" overall. **Power:** Spring-air, barrel cocking. **Stock:** Oil-finished hardwood; Monte Carlo with cheekpiece, recoil pad. **Sights:** Ramp front, micrometer adjustable rear. Maxi-Grip scope rail. **Features:** Velocity 950 fps (177), 750 fps (22), 600 fps (25). Patented Maxi-Grip scope rail protects optics from recoil; automatic anti-beartrap plus manual tang safety. Muzzle brake standard. Imported for U.K.
Price: **$194.95**
Price: Carbine, 14" barrel, muzzle brake **$214.95**

BSA METEOR AIR RIFLE

Caliber: 177, 22, single shot. **Barrel:** 18-1/2". **Weight:** 6 lbs. **Length:** 41" overall. **Power:** Spring-air, barrel cocking. **Stock:** Oil-finished hardwood. **Sights:** Ramp front, micrometer adjustable rear. **Features:** Velocity 650 fps (177), 500 fps (22). Automatic anti-beartrap; manual tang safety. Receiver grooved for scope mounting. Imported from U.K.
Price: Rifle **$144.95**
Price: Carbine **$164.95**

CROSMAN MODEL POWERMASTER 664SBAIR RIFLES

Caliber: 177 (single shot pellet) or BB, 200-shot reservoir. **Barrel:** 20", rifled steel. **Weight:** 2 lbs. 15 oz. **Length:** 38-1/2" overall. **Power:** Pneumatic; hand-pumped. **Stock:** Wood-grained ABS plastic; checkered pistol grip and forend. **Sights:** Fiber-optic front, fully adjustable open rear. **Features:** Velocity about 645 fps. Bolt action, cross-bolt safety. From Crosman.
Price: **$65.00**

CROSMAN MODEL PUMPMASTER 760AIR RIFLES

Caliber: 177 pellets (single shot) or BB (200-shot reservoir). **Barrel:** 19-1/2", rifled steel. **Weight:** 2 lbs., 12 oz. **Length:** 33.5" overall. **Power:** Pneumatic, hand-pump. **Stock:** Walnut-finished ABS plastic stock and forend. **Features:** Velocity to 590 fps (BBs, 10 pumps). Short stroke, power determined by number of strokes. Fiber-optic front sight and adjustable rear sight. Cross-bolt safety. From Crosman.
Price: Model 760 .... **$40.00**

CROSMAN MODEL REPEATAIR 1077 RIFLES

Caliber: 177 pellets, 12-shot clip. **Barrel:** 20.3", rifled steel. **Weight:** 3 lbs., 11 oz. **Length:** 38.8" overall. **Power:** CO2 Powerlet. **Stock:** Textured synthetic or hardwood. **Sights:** Blade front, fully adjustable rear. **Features:** Velocity 590 fps. Removable 12-shot clip. True semi-automatic action. From Crosman.
Price: **$68.00**
Price: 1077W (walnut stock) **$100.00**

CROSMAN 2260 AIR RIFLE

Caliber: 22, single shot. **Barrel:** 24". **Weight:** 4 lbs., 12 oz. **Length:** 39.75" overall. **Power:** CO2 Powerlet. **Stock:** Hardwood. **Sights:** Blade front, adjustable rear open or peep. **Features:** About 600 fps. Made in U.S. by Crosman Corp.
Price: **$80.00**

CROSMAN MODEL CLASSIC 2100 AIR RIFLE

Caliber: 177 pellets (single shot), or BB (200-shot BB reservoir). **Barrel:** 21", rifled. **Weight:** 4 lbs., 13 oz. **Length:** 39-3/4" overall. **Power:** Pump-up, pneumatic. **Stock:** Wood-grained checkered ABS plastic. **Features:** Three pumps give about 450 fps, 10 pumps about 755 fps (BBs). Cross-bolt safety; concealed reservoir holds over 200 BBs. From Crosman.
Price: Model 2100B **$55.00**

AIRGUNS — Long Guns

CROSMAN MODEL 2260 AIR RIFLE
Caliber: 22, single shot. **Barrel:** 19", rifled steel. **Weight:** 4 lbs., 12 oz. **Length:** 39.75" overall. **Stock:** Full-size, American hardwood. **Features:** Variable pump power; three pumps give 395 fps, six pumps 530 fps, 10 pumps 600 fps (average). Full-size adult air rifle. From Crosman.
Price: **$80.00**

DAISY 1938 RED RYDER AIR RIFLE
Caliber: BB, 650-shot repeating action. **Barrel:** Smoothbore steel with shroud. **Weight:** 2.2 lbs. **Length:** 35.4" overall. **Stock:** Walnut stock burned with Red Ryder lariat signature. **Sights:** Post front, adjustable V-slot rear. **Features:** Walnut forend. Saddle ring with leather thong. Lever cocking. Gravity feed. Controlled velocity. From Daisy Mfg. Co.
Price: **$44.95**

DAISY MODEL 840B GRIZZLY AIR RIFLE
Caliber: 177 pellet single shot; or BB 350-shot. **Barrel:** 19", smoothbore, steel. **Weight:** 2.25 lbs. **Length:** 36.8" overall. **Power:** Single pump pneumatic. **Stock:** Molded wood-grain stock and forend. **Sights:** Ramp front, open, adjustable rear. **Features:** Muzzle velocity 320 fps (BB), 300 fps (pellet). Steel buttplate; straight pull bolt action; cross-bolt safety. Forend forms pump lever. From Daisy Mfg. Co.
Price: **$47.99**
Price: (840C in Mossy Oak Breakup Camo) **$54.99**

DAISY MODEL 105 BUCK AIR RIFLE
Caliber: 177 or BB. **Barrel:** Smoothbore steel. **Weight:** 1.6 lbs. **Length:** 29.8" overall. **Power:** Lever cocking, spring air. **Stock:** Stained solid wood. **Sights:** TruGlo fiber-optic, open fixed rear. **Features:** Velocity to 275. Cross-bolt trigger block safety. From Daisy Mfg. Co.
Price: **$35.99**

DAISY/POWERLINE TARGET PRO 953 AIR RIFLE
Caliber: 177 pellets, single shot. **Weight:** 6.40 lbs. **Length:** 39.75" overall. **Power:** Pneumatic single-pump cocking lever; straight-pull bolt. **Stock:** Full-length, match-style black composite. **Sights:** Front and rear fiber optic. **Features:** Rifled high-grade steel barrel with 1:15 twist. Max. Muzzle Velocity of 560 fps. From Daisy Mfg. Co
Price: **$89.99**

DAISY/POWERLINE 880 AIR RIFLE
Caliber: 177 pellet or BB, 50-shot BB magazine, single shot for pellets. **Barrel:** Rifled steel. **Weight:** 3.7 lbs. **Length:** 37.6" overall. **Power:** Multi-pump pneumatic. **Stock:** Molded wood grain; Monte Carlo comb. **Sights:** Hooded front, adjustable rear. **Features:** Velocity to 685 fps. (BB). Variable power (velocity, range) increase with pump strokes; resin receiver with dovetailed scope mount. Made in U.S.A. by Daisy Mfg. Co.
Price: **$60.99**

DAISY/POWERLINE 901 AIR RIFLE
Caliber: 177. **Barrel:** Rifled steel. **Weight:** 3.7 lbs. **Length:** 37.5" overall. **Power:** Multi-pump pneumatic. **Stock:** Advanced composite. **Sights:** Fiber-optic front, adjustable rear. **Features:** Velocity to 750 fps. (BB); advanced composite receiver with dovetailed mounts for optics. Made in U.S.A. by Daisy Mfg. Co.
Price: **$66.99**

EAA/BAIKAL MP-512 AIR RIFLE
Caliber: 177, single shot. **Barrel:** 17.7". **Weight:** 6.2 lbs. **Length:** 41.3" overall. **Power:** Spring-piston, single stroke. **Stock:** Black synthetic. **Sights:** Adjustable rear, hooded front. **Features:** Velocity 490 fps. Hammer-forged, rifled barrel; automatic safety; scope mount rail. Imported from Russia by European American Armory.
Price: 177 caliber **$49.00**

EAA/BAIKAL IZH-61 AIR RIFLE
Caliber: 177 pellet, 5-shot magazine. **Barrel:** 17.8". **Weight:** 6.4 lbs. **Length:** 31" overall. **Power:** Spring-piston, side-cocking lever. **Stock:** Black plastic. **Sights:** Adjustable rear, fully hooded front. **Features:** Velocity 490 fps. Futuristic design with adjustable stock. Imported from Russia by European American Armory.
Price: **$99.00**

EAA/BAIKAL IZHMP-532 AIR RIFLE
Caliber: 177 pellet, single shot. **Barrel:** 15.8". **Weight:** 9.3 lbs. **Length:** 46.1" overall. **Power:** Single-stroke pneumatic. **Stock:** One- or two-piece competition-style stock with adjustable buttpad, pistol grip. **Sights:** Fully adjustable rear, hooded front. **Features:** Velocity 460 fps. Five-way adjustable trigger. Imported from Russia by European American Armory.
Price: **$599.00**

GAMO DELTA AIR RIFLE
Caliber: 177. **Barrel:** 15.7". **Weight:** 4.2 lbs. **Length:** 37.8". **Power:** Single-stroke pneumatic, 525 fps. **Stock:** Synthetic. **Sights:** TruGlo fiber-optic.
Price: **$89.95**

GAMO SPORTER AIR RIFLE
Caliber: 177. **Barrel:** NA. **Weight:** 5.5 lbs. **Length:** 42.5". **Power:** Single-stroke pneumatic, 760 fps. **Stock:** Wood. **Sights:** Adjustable TruGlo fiber-optic. **Features:** Intended to bridge the gap between Gamo's Young Hunter model and the adult-sized Hunter 440. Imported from Spain by Gamo.
Price: **$159.95**

GAMO HUNTER 440 AIR RIFLES
Caliber: 177, 22. **Barrel:** NA. **Weight:** 6.6 lbs. **Length:** 43.3". **Power:** Single-stroke pneumatifc, 1,000 fps (177), 750 fps (22). **Stock:** Wood. **Sights:** Adjustable TruGlo fiber-optic. **Features:** Adjustable two-stage trigger, rifled barrel, raised scope ramp on receiver. Realtree camo model available.
Price: **$229.95**
Price: Hunter 440 Combo with BSA 4x32mm scope **$259.95**

HAMMERLI AR 50 AIR RIFLE
Caliber: 177. **Barrel:** 19.8". **Weight:** 10 lbs. **Length:** 43.2" overall. **Power:** Compressed-air. **Stock:** Anatomically-shaped universal and right-hand; match style; multi-colored laminated wood. **Sights:** Interchangeable element tunnel front, adjustable Hammerli peep rear. **Features:** Vibration-free firing release; adjustable match trigger and trigger stop; stainless air tank, built-in pressure gauge. Gives 270 shots per filling. Imported from Switzerland by SIGARMS, Inc.
Price: **$1,653.00**

HAMMERLI MODEL 450 MATCH AIR RIFLE
Caliber: 177, single shot. **Barrel:** 19.5". **Weight:** 9.8 lbs. **Length:** 43.3" overall. **Power:** Pneumatic. **Stock:** Match style with stippled grip, rubber buttpad. Beech or walnut. **Sights:** Match tunnel front, Hammerli diopter rear. **Features:** Velocity about 560 fps. Removable sights; forend sling rail; adjustable trigger; adjustable comb. Imported from Switzerland by SIGARMS, Inc.
Price: Beech stock **$1,355.00**
Price: Walnut stock **$1,395.00**

RWS/DIANA MODEL 24 AIR RIFLES
Caliber: 177, 22, single shot. **Barrel:** 17", rifled. **Weight:** 6 lbs. **Length:** 42" overall. **Power:** Spring-air, barrel cocking. **Stock:** Beech. **Sights:** Hooded front, adjustable rear. **Features:** Velocity of 700 fps (177). Easy cocking effort; blue finish. Imported from Germany by Dynamit Nobel-RWS, Inc.
Price: 24, 24C **$215.00**

RWS/Diana Model 34 Air Rifles
Similar to the Model 24 except has 19" barrel, weighs 7.5 lbs. Gives velocity of 1000 fps (177), 800 fps (22). Adjustable trigger, synthetic seals. Comes with scope rail.
Price: 177 or 22 . . . . **$290.00**
Price: Model 34N (nickel-plated metal, black epoxy-coated wood stock) **$350.00**
Price: Model 34BC (matte black metal, black stock, 4x32 scope, mounts) **$510.00**

RWS/DIANA MODEL 36 AIR RIFLES
Caliber: 177, 22, single shot. **Barrel:** 19", rifled. **Weight:** 8 lbs. **Length:** 45" overall. **Power:** Spring-air, barrel cocking. **Stock:** Beech. **Sights:** Hooded front (interchangeable inserts available), adjustable rear. **Features:** Velocity of 1000 fps (177-cal.). Comes with scope mount; two-stage adjustable trigger. Imported from Germany by Dynamit Nobel-RWS, Inc.
Price: 36, 36C **$435.00**

Daisy 7840 Buckmaster

RWS/DIANA MODEL 52 AIR RIFLES

Caliber: 177, 22, 25, single shot. **Barrel:** 17", rifled. **Weight:** 8-1/2 lbs. **Length:** 43" overall. **Power:** Spring-air, sidelever cocking. **Stock:** Beech, with Monte Carlo, cheekpiece, checkered grip and forend. **Sights:** Ramp front, adjustable rear. **Features:** Velocity of 1100 fps (177). Blue finish. Solid rubber buttpad. Imported from Germany by Dynamit Nobel-RWS, Inc.
Price: 177, 22 . . . . **$565.00**
Price: 25 . . . . **$605.00**
Price: Model 52 Deluxe (177) **$810.00**

RWS/DIANA MODEL 45 AIR RIFLE

Caliber: 177, single shot. **Weight:** 8 lbs. **Length:** 45" overall. **Power:** Spring-air, barrel cocking. **Stock:** Walnut-finished hardwood with rubber recoil pad. **Sights:** Globe front with interchangeable inserts, micro. click open rear with four-way blade. **Features:** Velocity of 820 fps. Dovetailed base for either micrometer peep sight or scope mounting. Automatic safety. Imported from Germany by Dynamit Nobel-RWS, Inc.
Price: **$350.00**

RWS/DIANA MODEL 46 AIR RIFLES

Caliber: 177, 22, single shot. **Barrel:** 18". **Weight:** 8.2 lbs. **Length:** 45" overall. **Stock:** Hardwood; Monte Carlo. **Sights:** Blade front, adjustable rear. **Features:** Underlever cocking spring-air (950 fps in 177, 780 fps in 22); extended scope rail, automatic safety, rubber buttpad, adjustable trigger. Imported from Germany by Dynamit Nobel-RWS, Inc.
Price: **$470.00**
Price: Model 46E (as above except matte black metal, black stock)
. . . . **$430.00**

RWS/DIANA MODEL 54 AIR RIFLE

Caliber: 177, 22, single shot. **Barrel:** 17". **Weight:** 9 lbs. **Length:** 43" overall. **Power:** Spring-air, sidelever cocking. **Stock:** Walnut with Monte Carlo cheekpiece, checkered grip and forend. **Sights:** Ramp front, fully adjustable rear. **Features:** Velocity to 1000 fps (177), 900 fps (22). Totally recoilless system; floating action absorbs recoil. Imported from Germany by Dynamit Nobel-RWS, Inc.
Price: **$785.00**

RWS/DIANA MODEL 350 MAGNUM AIR RIFLE

Caliber: 177, 22, single shot. **Barrel:** 19-1/2". **Weight:** 8 lbs. **Length:** 48". **Stock:** Beechwood; Monte Carlo. **Sights:** Hooded front, fully adjustable rear. **Features:** Break-barrel, spring-air; 1,250 fps. Imported from Germany by Dynamit Nobel-RWS, Inc.
Price: . . . . **NA**

TECH FORCE 6 AIR RIFLE

Caliber: 177 pellet, single shot. **Barrel:** 14". **Weight:** 6 lbs. **Length:** 35.5" overall. **Power:** Spring-piston, sidelever action. **Stock:** Paratrooper-style folding, full pistol grip. **Sights:** Adjustable rear, hooded front. **Features:** Velocity 800 fps. All-metal construction; grooved for scope mounting. Imported from China by Compasseco, Inc.
Price: **$69.95**

TECH FORCE 25 AIR RIFLE

Caliber: 177, 22 pellet; single shot. **Barrel:** NA. **Weight:** 7.5 lbs. **Length:** 46.2" overall. **Power:** Spring piston, break-action barrel. **Stock:** Oil-finished wood; Monte Carlo stock with recoil pad. **Sights:** Adjustable rear, hooded front with insert. **Features:** Velocity 1,000 fps (177); grooved receiver and scope stop for scope mounting; adjustable trigger; trigger safety. Imported from China by Compasseco, Inc.
Price: 177 or 22 caliber **$125.00**
Price: Includes rifle and Tech Force 96 red dot point sight **$164.95**

COMPENDIUM OF STATE LAWS GOVERNING FIREARMS

The following chart lists the main provisions of state firearms laws as of the date of publication. In addition to the state provisions, the purchase, sale, and, in certain circumstances, the possession and interstate transportation of firearms are regulated by the Federal Gun Control Act of 1968 as amended by the Firearms Owners' Protection Act of 1986. Also, cities and localities may have their own gun ordinances in addition to federal and state restrictions. Details may be obtained by contacting local law enforcement authorities or by consulting your state's firearms law digest compiled by the NRA Institute for Legislative Action.

STATE	GUN BAN	EXEMPTIONS TO NICS$_{2}$	STATE WAITING PERIOD - NUMBER OF DAYS		LICENSE OR PERMIT TO PURCHASE or other prerequesite		REGISTRATION		RECORD OF SALE REPORTED TO STATE OR LOCAL GOVT.
			HANDGUNS	LONG GUNS	HANDGUNS	LONG GUNS	HANDGUNS	LONG GUNS	
Alabama	—	—	—	—	—	—	—	—	—
Alaska	—	RTC	—	—	—	—	—	—	—
Arizona	—	RTC	—	—	—	—	—	—	—
Arkansas	—	RTC$_{3}$	—	—	—	—	—	—	—
California	X_{1}	—	10_{5}	$10_{5,6}$	$X_{10,11}$	—	X_{12}	X_{13}	X
Colorado	—	—	—	—	—	—	—	—	—
Connecticut	X_{1}	—	$14_{5,6}$	$14_{5,6}$	$X_{9,11}$	—	—	X_{13}	X
Delaware	—	—	—	—	—	—	—	—	—
Florida	—	—	3_{6}	—	—	—	—	—	—
Georgia	—	—	—	—	—	—	—	—	—
Hawaii	X_{1}	L, RTC	—	—	$X_{9,11}$	X_{9}	X_{12}	X_{12}	X
Idaho	—	RTC	—	—	—	—	—	—	—
Illinois	$_{1,7}$	—	3	2	X_{9}	X_{9}	X_{14}	X_{14}	X
Indiana	—	—	—	—	—	—	—	—	—
Iowa	—	L, RTC	—	—	X_{9}	—	—	—	—
Kansas	—	—	—	—	—	—	—	—	—
Kentucky	—	—	—	—	—	—	—	—	—
Louisiana	—	—	—	—	—	—	—	—	—
Maine	—	—	—	—	—	—	—	—	—
Maryland	X_{1}	—	7_{5}	$7_{4,5}$	$X_{10,11}$	—	—	—	X
Massachusetts	X_{1}	—	—	—	X_{9}	X_{9}	—	—	X
Michigan	—	L	—	—	$X_{9, 11}$	—	X	—	X
Minnesota	—	—	7_{9}	X_{9}	X_{9}	X_{9}	—	—	—
Mississippi	—	RTC$_{3}$	—	—	—	—	—	—	—
Missouri	—	—	—	—	X_{9}	—	—	—	X
Montana	—	RTC	—	—	—	—	—	—	—
Nebraska	—	L	—	—	X	—	—	—	—
Nevada	—	RTC	$_{7}$	—	—	—	X_{7}	X_{7}	—
New Hampshire	—	—	—	—	—	—	—	—	—
New Jersey	X_{1}	—	—	—	X_{9}	X_{9}	—	X_{13}	X
New Mexico	—	—	—	—	—	—	—	—	—
New York	X_{1}	L, RTC	—	—	$X_{9,11}$	X_{9}	X	X_{15}	X
North Carolina	—	L, RTC	—	—	X_{9}	—	—	—	X
North Dakota	—	RTC	—	—	—	—	—	—	—
Ohio	$_{7}$	—	$_{7}$	—	X_{7}	—	X_{7}	—	$_{7}$
Oklahoma	—	—	—	—	—	—	—	—	—
Oregon	—	—	—	—	—	—	—	—	X
Pennsylvania	—	—	—	—	—	—	—	—	X
Rhode Island	—	—	7_{5}	7_{5}	X_{11}	—	—	—	X
South Carolina	—	RTC	—	—	—	—	—	—	X
South Dakota	—	—	2_{6}	—	—	—	—	—	X_{16}
Tennessee	—	—	—	—	—	—	—	—	—
Texas	—	RTC	—	—	—	—	—	—	—
Utah	—	RTC	—	—	—	—	—	—	—
Vermont	—	—	—	—	—	—	—	—	—
Virginia	X_{1}	—	—	—	X_{10}	—	—	—	—
Washington	—	—	5_{8}	—	—	—	—	—	X
West Virginia	—	—	—	—	—	—	—	—	—
Wisconsin	—	—	2	—	—	—	—	—	—
Wyoming	—	RTC	—	—	—	—	—	—	—
District of Columbia	X_{1}	—	—	—	X_{9}	X_{9}	X_{9}	X	X

COMPENDIUM OF STATE LAWS GOVERNING FIREARMS

Since state laws are subject to frequent change, this chart is
not to be considered legal advice or a restatement of the law.

All fifty states have sportsmen's protections laws to halt harassment.

STATE	STATE PROVISION FOR RIGHT-TO-CARRY CONCEALED	CARRYING OPENLY PROHIBITED	OWNER ID CARDS OR LICENSING	FIREARM RIGHTS CONSTITUTIONAL PROVISION	STATE FIREARMS PREEMPTION LAWS	RANGE PROTECTION LAW
Alabama	M	X[19]	—	X	X	X
Alaska	R[17]	—	—	X	X	X
Arizona	R	—	—	X	X	X
Arkansas	R	X[20]	—	X	X	X
California	L	X[21]	—	—	X	X
Colorado	R	X[22]	—	X	X[22]	X
Connecticut	M	X	—	X	X[25]	X
Delaware	L	—	—	X	X	X
Florida	R	X	—	X	X	X
Georgia	R	X	—	X	X	X
Hawaii	L	X	X	X	—	—
Idaho	R	—	—	X	X	X
Illinois	D	X	X	X	—	X
Indiana	R	X	—	X	X[25]	X
Iowa	M	X	—	—	X	X
Kansas	D	—	—	X	X	X
Kentucky	R	—	—	X	X	X
Louisiana	R	—	—	X	X	X
Maine	R	—	—	X	X	X
Maryland	L	X	—	—	X	X
Massachusetts	L	X	X	X	X[24]	X
Michigan	R	X[19]	—	X	X	X
Minnesota	R	X	—	—	X	X
Mississippi	R	—	—	X	X	X
Missouri	R	—	—	X	X	X
Montana	R	—	—	X	X	X
Nebraska	D	—	—	X	—	—
Nevada	R	—	—	X	X	X
New Hampshire	R	—	—	X	X	X
New Jersey	L	X	X	—	X[25]	X
New Mexico	R	—	—	X	X	X
New York	L	X	X	—	X[26]	X
North Carolina	R	—	—	X	X	X
North Dakota	R	X[21]	—	X	X	X
Ohio	R	X[7,18]	[7]	X	—	X
Oklahoma	R	X[21]	—	X	X	X
Oregon	R	—	—	X	X	X
Pennsylvania	R	X[19]	—	X	X	X
Rhode Island	L	X	—	X	X	X
South Carolina	R	X	—	X	X	X
South Dakota	R	—	—	X	X	X
Tennessee	R	X[20]	—	X	X	X
Texas	R	X	—	X	X	X
Utah	R	X[21]	—	X	X	X
Vermont	R[17]	X[20]	—	X	X	X
Virginia	R	—	—	X	X	X
Washington	R	X[23]	—	X	X	—
West Virginia	R	—	—	X	X	X
Wisconsin	D	—	—	X	X	X
Wyoming	R	—	—	X	X	X
District of Columbia	D	X	X	NA	—	—

COMPENDIUM OF STATE LAWS GOVERNING FIREARMS

> With over 20,000 "gun control" laws on the books in America, there are two challenges facing every gun owner. First, you owe it to yourself to become familiar with the federal laws on gun ownership. Only by knowing the laws can you avoid innocently breaking one.
>
> Second, while federal legislation receives much more media attention, state legislatures and city councils make many more decisions regarding your right to own and carry firearms. NRA members and all gun owners must take extra care to be aware of anti-gun laws and ordinances at the state and local levels.

Notes:
1. "Assault weapons" are prohibited in **Connecticut, New Jersey** and **New York**. Some local jurisdictions in **Ohio** also ban "assault weapons." **Hawaii** prohibits "assault pistols." **California** bans "assault weapons", .50BMG caliber firearms, some .50 caliber ammunition and "unsafe handguns." **Illinois:** Chicago, Evanston, Oak Park, Morton Grove, Winnetka, Wilmette, and Highland Park prohibit handguns; some cities prohibit other kinds of firearms. **Maryland** prohibits "assault pistols"; the sale or manufacture of any handgun manufactured after Jan. 1, 1985, that does not appear on the Handgun Roster; and the sale of any handgun manufactured after January 1, 2003 that is not equipped with an "integrated mechanical safety device." **Massachusetts:** It is unlawful to sell, transfer or possess "any assault weapon or large capacity feeding device" [more than 10 rounds] that was not legally possessed on September 13, 1994 and the sale of handguns not on the Firearms Roster. The City of Boston has a separate "assault weapons" law. The **District of Columbia** prohibits new acquisition of handguns and any semi-automatic firearm capable of using a detachable ammunition magazine of more than 12 rounds capacity and any handgun not registered after February 5, 1977. **Virginia** prohibits "Street Sweeper" shotguns. (With respect to some of these laws and ordinances, individuals may retain prohibited firearms owned previously, with certain restrictions.) *The sunset of the federal assault weapons ban does not affect the validity of state and local "assault weapons" bans.*

2. **National Instant Check System (NICS) exemption codes:**
   RTC-Carry Permit Holders Exempt From NICS
   L-Holders of state licenses to possess or purchase or firearms ID cards exempt from NICS.

3. **NICS exemption notes**: **Arkansas**: Those issued on and after 4/1/99 qualify. **Mississippi**: Permits issued to security guards do not qualify. **North Dakota**: Those issued on or after 12/1/1999 qualify.

4. **Maryland** subjects purchases of "assault weapons" to a 7-day waiting period.

5. Waiting period for all sales. **California**: 10 days; sales, transfers and loans of handguns must be made through a dealer or through a sheriff's office. **Maryland**: 7 days; purchasers of regulated firearms must undergo background checks performed by the State Police, either through a dealer or directly through the State Police. **Rhode Island**: 7 days; private sales can be made through a dealer or the seller must follow the same guidelines as a sale from a dealer.

6. The waiting period does not apply to a person holding a valid permit or license to carry a firearm. In **Connecticut**, a certificate of eligibility exempts the holder from the waiting period for handgun purchases; a hunting license exempts the holder for long gun purchasers. **California**: transfers of a long gun to a person's parent, child or grandparent are exempt from the waiting period.

7. In certain cities or counties.

8. May be extended by police to 30 days in some circumstances. An individual not holding a driver's license must wait 60 days.

9. **Connecticut:** A certificate of eligibility or a carry permit is required to obtain a handgun and a carry permit is required to transport a handgun outside your home. **District of Columbia:** No handgun may be possessed unless it was registered prior to Sept. 23, 1976 and re-registered by Feb. 5, 1977. A permit to purchase is required for a rifle or shotgun. **Hawaii:** Purchase permits are required for all firearms **Illinois:** A Firearm Owner's Identification Card (FOI) is required to possess or purchase a firearm, must be issued to qualified applicants within 30 days, and is valid for 5 years. **Iowa:** A purchase permit is required for handguns, and is valid for one year. **Massachusetts:** Firearms and feeding devices for firearms are divided into classes. Depending on the class, a firearm identification card (FID) or class A license or class B license is required to possess, purchase, or carry a firearm, ammunition thereof, or firearm feeding device, or "large capacity feeding device." **Michigan:** A handgun purchaser must obtain a license to purchase from local law enforcement, and within 10 days present the license and handgun to obtain a certificate of inspection. **Minnesota:** A handgun transfer or carrying permit, or a 7-day waiting period and handgun transfer report, is required to purchase handguns or "assault weapons" from a dealer. A permit is valid for one year, a transfer report for 30 days. **Missouri:** A purchase permit is required for a handgun, must be issued to qualified applicants within 7 days, and is valid for 30 days. **New Jersey:** Firearm owners must possess a FID, which must be issued to qualified applicants within 30 days. To purchase a handgun, a purchase permit, which must be issued within 30 days to qualified applicants and is valid for 90 days, is required. An FID is required to purchase long guns. **New York:** Purchase, possession and/or carrying of a handgun require a single license, which includes any restrictions made upon the bearer. New York City also requires a license for long guns. **North Carolina:** To purchase a handgun, a license or permit is required, which must be issued to qualified applicants within 30 days. Persons with a Right-to-Carry license are exempt.

10. A permit is required to acquire another handgun before 30 days have elapsed following the acquisition of a handgun. In **Virginia**, those with a permit to carry a concealed weapon are exempt from this prohibition.

11. Requires proof of safety training for purchase. **California**: Must have Handgun Safety Certificate receipt, which is valid for five years. **Connecticut:** To receive certificate of eligibility, must complete a handgun safety course approved by the Commissioner of Public Safety. **Hawaii:** Must have completed an approved handgun safety course. **Maryland:** Must complete an approved handgun safety course. **Michigan:** A person must correctly answer 70% of the questions on a basic safety review questionnaire in order to obtain a license to purchase. **New York:** Some counties require a handgun safety training course to receive a license. **Rhode Island**: Must receive a state-issued handgun safety card.

12. Every person arriving in **Hawaii** is required to register any firearm(s) brought into the State within 3 days of arrival of the person or firearm(s), whichever occurs later. Handguns purchased from licensed dealers must be registered within 5 days. California is sixty days.

13. "Assault weapon" registration. **California** had two dates by which assault weapons had to be registered or possession after such date would be considered a felony: March 31, 1992 for the named make and model firearms banned in the 1989 legislation and December 31, 2000 for the firearms meeting the definition of the "assault weapons in the 1999 legislation. In **Connecticut**, those firearms banned by specific make and model in the 1993 law had to be registered by October 1, 1994 or possession would be considered a felony. A recent law requires registration of additional guns by October 1, 2003. In **New Jersey**, any "assault weapon" not registered, licensed, or rendered inoperable pursuant to a state police certificate by May 1, 1991, is considered contraband.

14. Chicago only. No handgun not already registered may be possessed. Must get FOID card after receiving drivers' license.

15. New York City only.

16. Purchasers of handguns who do not possess a permit to carry a pistol must file an application for purchase, which will be retained by the chief of police or sheriff for one year. However state law prohibits the establishment of a centralized registry of gun owners.

17. **Vermont and Alaska** law respect your right to carry without a permit. Alaska also has a permit to carry system to establish reciprocity with other states.

18. A person with a concealed handgun license may transport a loaded handgun in a vehicle if it is in a holster.

19. Carrying a handgun openly in a motor vehicle requires a license.

20. **Arkansas** prohibits carrying a firearm "with a purpose to employ it as a weapon against a person." **Tennessee** prohibits carrying "with the intent to go armed." **Vermont** prohibits carrying a firearm "with the intent or purpose of injuring another."

21. Loaded.

22. Municipalities may prohibit open carry in government buildings if such prohibition is clearly posted.

23. Local jurisdictions may opt of the prohibition.

24. Preemption through judicial ruling. Local regulation may be instituted in **Massachusetts** if ratified by the legislature.

25. Except Gary and East Chicago and local laws enacted before January 1994.

26. Preemption only applies to handguns.

Concealed carry codes:

R: Right-to-Carry "Shall issue" or less restrictive discretionary permit system (Ala., Conn.) (See also note #21.)
M: Reasonable May Issue; the state has a permissive may issue law, but the authorities recognize the right to keep and bear arms.
L: Right-to-Carry Limited by local authority's discretion over permit issuance.
D: Right-to-Carry Denied, no permit system exists; concealed carry is prohibited.

NL 00930

Rev. 4/2006 10m

A

A Zone Bullets, 2039 Walter Rd., Billings, MT 59105 / 800-252-3111; FAX: 406-248-1961

A&W Repair, 2930 Schneider Dr., Arnold, MO 63010 / 617-287-3725

A.A. Arms, Inc., 4811 Persimmont Ct., Monroe, NC 28110 / 704-289-5356 or 800-935-1119; FAX: 704-289-5859

A.B.S. III, 9238 St. Morritz Dr., Fern Creek, KY 40291

A.G. Russell Knives, Inc., 2900 S. 26th St., Rogers, AR 72758 / 800-255-9034; FAX: 479-636-8493 ag@agrussell.com agrussell.com

A.R.M.S., Inc., 230 W. Center St., West Bridgewater, MA 02379-1620 / 508-584-7816; FAX: 508-588-8045

A.W. Peterson Gun Shop, Inc., The, 4255 West Old U.S. 441, Mount Dora, FL 32757-3299 / 352-383-4258; FAX: 352-735-1001

AC Dyna-tite Corp., 155 Kelly St., P.O. Box 0984, Elk Grove Village, IL 60007 / 847-593-5566; FAX: 847-593-1304

Acadian Ballistic Specialties, P.O. Box 787, Folsom, LA 70437 / 504-796-0078 gunsmith@neasolft.com

Accuracy Den, The, 25 Bitterbrush Rd., Reno, NV 89523 / 702-345-0225

Accuracy International, Foster, P.O. Box 111, Wilsall, MT 59086 / 406-587-7922; FAX: 406-585-9434

Accuracy Internationl Precision Rifles (See U.S.)

Accuracy Int'l. North America, Inc., P.O. Box 5267, Oak Ridge, TN 37831 / 423-482-0330; FAX: 423-482-0336

Accuracy Unlimited, 7479 S. DePew St., Littleton, CO 80123

Accuracy Unlimited, 16036 N. 49 Ave., Glendale, AZ 85306 / 602-978-9089; FAX: 602-978-9089 fglenn@cox.net www.glenncustom.com

Accura-Site (See All's, The Jim Tembelis Co., Inc.)

Accurate Arms Co., Inc., 5891 Hwy. 230 West, McEwen, TN 37101 / 931-729-4207; FAX: 931-729-4211 burrensburg@aac-ca.com www.accuratepowder.com

Accu-Tek, 4510 Carter Ct., Chino, CA 91710

Ackerman & Co., Box 133 U.S. Highway Rt. 7, Pownal, VT 05261 / 802-823-9874 muskets@togsther.net

Ackerman, Bill (See Optical Services Co.)

Acra-Bond Laminates, 134 Zimmerman Rd., Kalispell, MT 59901 / 406-257-9003; FAX: 406-257-9003 merlins@digisys.net www.acrabondlaminates.com

Action Bullets & Alloy Inc., RR 1, P.O. Box 189, Quinter, KS 67752 / 785-754-3609; FAX: 785-754-3629 bullets@ruraltel.net

Action Direct, Inc., 14285 SW 142nd St., Miami, FL 33186-6720 / 800-472-2388; FAX: 305-256-3541 info@action-direct.com www.action-direct.com

Action Products, Inc., 22 N. Mulberry St., Hagerstown, MD 21740 / 301-797-1414; FAX: 301-733-2073

Action Target, Inc., P.O. Box 636, Provo, UT 84603 / 801-377-8033; FAX: 801-377-8096 www.actiontarget.com

Actions by "T" Teddy Jacobson, 16315 Redwood Forest Ct., Sugar Land, TX 77478 / 281-565-6977 or 281-277-4008 tjacobson@houston.rr.com www.actionsbyt.blogspot.com

AcuSport Corporation, William L. Fraim, One Hunter Place, Bellefontaine, OH 43311-3001 / 937-593-7010; FAX: 937-592-5625 www.acusport.com

Ad Hominem, 3130 Gun Club Lane, RR #3, Orillia, ON L3V 6H3 CANADA / 705-689-5303; FAX: 705-689-5303

Adair Custom Shop, Bill, 2886 Westridge, Carrollton, TX 75006

ADCO Sales, Inc., 4 Draper St. #A, Woburn, MA 01801 / 781-935-1799; FAX: 781-935-1011

Advance Car Mover Co., Rowell Div., P.O. Box 1, 240 N. Depot St., Juneau, WI 53039 / 414-386-4464; FAX: 414-386-4416

Advantage Arms, Inc., 25163 W. Ave. Stanford, Valencia, CA 91355 / 661-257-2290

Adventure 16, Inc., 4620 Alvarado Canyon Rd., San Diego, CA 92120 / 619-283-6314

Aero Peltor, 90 Mechanic St., Southbridge, MA 01550 / 508-764-5500; FAX: 508-764-0188

African Import Co., 22 Goodwin Rd., Plymouth, MA 02360 / 508-746-8552; FAX: 508-746-0404 africanimport@aol.com

AFSCO Ammunition, 731 W. Third St., P.O. Box L, Owen, WI 54460 / 715-229-2516 sailers@webtv.net

Ahlman Guns, 9525 W. 230th St., Morristown, MN 55052 / 507-685-4243; FAX: 507-685-4280 www.ahlmans.com

Ahrends Grips, Box 203, Clarion, IA 50525 / 515-532-3449; FAX: 515-532-3926 ahrends@goldfieldaccess.net www.ahrendsgripsusa.com

Aimpoint, Inc., 14103 Mariah Ct., Chantilly, VA 20151-2113 / 877-246-7668; FAX: 703-263-9463 info@aimpoint.com www.aimpoint.com

Aimtech Mount Systems, P.O. Box 223, Thomasville, GA 31799 / 229-226-4313; FAX: 229-227-0222 mail@aimtech-mounts.com www.aimtech-mounts.com

Air Arms, Hailsham Industrial Park, Diplocks Way, Hailsham, E. Sussex, BN27 3JF ENGLAND / 011-0323-845853; FAX: 1323 440573 general.air-arms.co.uk. www.air-arms.co.uk.

Air Venture Airguns, 9752 E. Flower St., Bellflower, CA 90706 / 562-867-6355

AirForce Airguns, P.O. Box 2478, Fort Worth, TX 76113 / 817-451-8966; FAX: 817-451-1613 www.airforceairguns.com

Airrow, 11 Monitor Hill Rd., Newtown, CT 06470 / 203-270-6343

Aitor-Berrizargo S.L., Eitua 15 P.O. Box 26, 48240, Berriz (Viscaya), SPAIN / 43-17-08-50 info@aitor.com www.ailor.com

Ajax Custom Grips, Inc., 9130 Viscount Row, Dallas, TX 75247 / 214-630-8893; FAX: 214-630-4942

Aker International, Inc., 2248 Main St., Suite 6, Chula Vista, CA 91911 / 619-423-5182; FAX: 619-423-1363 aker@akerleather.com www.akerleather.com

AKJ Concealco, P.O. Box 871596, Vancouver, WA 98687-1596 / 360-891-8222; FAX: 360-891-8221 Concealco@aol.com www.greatholsters.com

Alana Cupp Custom Engraver, P.O. Box 207, Annabella, UT 84711 / 801-896-4834

Alaska Bullet Works, Inc., 9978 Crazy Horse Drive, Juneau, AK 99801 / 907-789-3834; FAX: 907-789-3433

Alaskan Silversmith, The, 2145 Wagner Hollow Rd., Fort Plain, NY 13339 / 518-993-3983 sidbell@capital.net www.sidbell.cizland.com

Aldis Gunsmithing & Shooting Supply, 502 S. Montezuma St., Prescott, AZ 86303 / 602-445-6723; FAX: 602-445-6763

Alessi Holsters, Inc., 2465 Niagara Falls Blvd., Amherst, NY 14228-3527 / 716-691-5615

Alex, Inc., 3420 Cameron Bridge Rd., Manhattan, MT 59741-8523 / 406-282-7396; FAX: 406-282-7396

All American Lead Shot Corp., P.O. Box 224566, Dallas, TX 75062

All Rite Products, Inc., 9554 Wells Circle, Suite D, West Jordan, UT 84088-6226 / 800-771-8471; FAX: 801-280-8302 info@allriteproducts.com www.allriteproducts.com

Allard, Gary/Creek Side Metal & Woodcrafters, Fishers Hill, VA 22626 / 540-465-3903

Allen Co., Inc., 525 Burbank St., Broomfield, CO 80020 / 303-469-1857 or 800-876-8600; FAX: 303-466-7437

Allen Firearm Engraving, P.O. Box 155, Camp Verde, AZ 86322 / 928-567-6711 rosebudmulgco@netzero.com rosebudmulgco@netzero.com

Allen Mfg., 6449 Hodgson Rd., Circle Pines, MN 55014 / 612-429-8231

Alley Supply Co., P.O. Box 848, Gardnerville, NV 89410 / 775-782-3800; FAX: 775-782-3827 jetalley@aol.com www.alleysupplyco.com

Alliant Techsystems, Smokeless Powder Group, P.O. Box 6, Rt. 114, Bldg. 229, Radford, VA 24141-0096 www.alliantpowder.com

Allred Bullet Co., 932 Evergreen Drive, Logan, UT 84321 / 435-752-6983; FAX: 435-752-6983

Alpec Team, Inc., 201 Rickenbacker Cir., Livermore, CA 94550 / 510-606-8245; FAX: 510-606-4279

Alpha 1 Drop Zone, 2121 N. Tyler, Wichita, KS 67212 / 316-729-0800; FAX: 316-729-4262 www.alpha1dropzone.com

Alpha LaFranck Enterprises, P.O. Box 81072, Lincoln, NE 68501 / 402-466-3193

Alpha Precision, Inc., 3238 Della Slaton Rd., Comer, GA 30629-2212 / 706-783-2131 jim@alphaprecisioninc.com www.alphaprecisioninc.com

Alpine Indoor Shooting Range, 2401 Government Way, Coeur d'Alene, ID 83814 / 208-676-8824; FAX: 208-676-8824

Altamont Co., 901 N. Church St., P.O. Box 309, Thomasboro, IL 61878 / 217-643-3125 or 800-626-5774; FAX: 217-643-7973

Alumna Sport by Dee Zee, 1572 NE 58th Ave., P.O. Box 3090, Des Moines, IA 50316 / 800-798-9899

Amadeo Rossi S.A., Rua: Amadeo Rossi, 143, Sao Leopoldo, RS 93030-220 BRAZIL / 051-592-5566 rossi.firearms@pnet.com.br

Amato, Jeff. See: J&M PRECISION MACHINING

AmBr Software Group Ltd., P.O. Box 301, Reisterstown, MD 21136-0301 / 800-888-1917; FAX: 410-526-7212

American Ammunition, 3545 NW 71st St., Miami, FL 33147 / 305-835-7400; FAX: 305-694-0037

American Derringer Corp., 127 N. Lacy Dr., Waco, TX 76705 / 800-642-7817 or 254-799-9111; FAX: 254-799-7935

American Display Co., 55 Cromwell St., Providence, RI 02907 / 401-331-2464; FAX: 401-421-1264

American Gas & Chemical Co., Ltd.,, 220 Pegasus Ave., Northvale, NJ 07647 / 201-767-7300

American Gunsmithing Institute, 1325 Imola Ave. #504, Napa, CA 94559 / 707-253-0462; FAX: 707-253-7149 www.americangunsmith.com

American Handgunner Magazine, 12345 World Trade Dr., San Diego, CA 92128 / 800-537-3006; FAX: 858-605-0204 www.americanhandgunner.com

American Pioneer Video, P.O. Box 50049, Bowling Green, KY 42102-2649 / 800-743-4675

American Products, Inc., 14729 Spring Valley Road, Morrison, IL 61270 / 815-772-3336; FAX: 815-772-8046

American Safe Arms, Inc., 1240 Riverview Dr., Garland, UT 84312 / 801-257-7472; FAX: 801-785-8156

American Security Products Co., 11925 Pacific Ave., Fontana, CA 92337 / 909-685-9680 or 800-421-6142; FAX: 909-685-9685

American Small Arms Academy, P.O. Box 12111, Prescott, AZ 86304 / 602-778-5623

American Target, 1328 S. Jason St., Denver, CO 80223 / 303-733-0433; FAX: 303-777-0311

American Target Knives, 1030 Brownwood NW, Grand Rapids, MI 49504 / 616-453-1998

Americase, P.O. Box 271, 1610 E. Main, Waxahachie, TX 75165 / 800-880-3629; FAX: 214-937-8373

Ames Metal Products Co., 4323 S. Western Blvd., Chicago, IL 60609 / 773-523-3230 or 800-255-6937; FAX: 773-523-3854 amesmetal@webtv.net

Amherst Arms, P.O. Box 1457, Englewood, FL 34295 / 941-475-2020; FAX: 941-473-1212

Ammo Load Worldwide, Inc., 815 D St., Lewiston, ID 83501 / 800-528-5610; FAX: 208-746-1730 info@ammoload.com www.ammoload.com

Amrine's Gun Shop, 937 La Luna, Ojai, CA 93023 / 805-646-2376

Amsec, 11925 Pacific Ave., Fontana, CA 92337

Analog Devices, Box 9106, Norwood, MA 02062

Andela Tool & Machine, Inc., RD3, Box 246, Richfield Springs, NY 13439

Anderson Manufacturing Co., Inc., 22602 53rd Ave. SE, Bothell, WA 98021 / 206-481-1858; FAX: 206-481-7839

Andres & Dworsky KG, Bergstrasse 18, A-3822 Karlstein, Thaya, AUSTRIA / 0 28 44-285; FAX: 0 28 44-28619 andres.dnorsky@wvnet.as

Angelo & Little Custom Gun Stock Blanks, P.O. Box 240046, Dell, MT 59724-0046

Answer Products Co., 1519 Westbury Drive, Davison, MI 48423 / 810-653-2911

Antique American Firearms, P.O. Box 71035, Dept. GD, Des Moines, IA 50325 / 515-224-6552

Antique Arms Co., 1110 Cleveland Ave., Monett, MO 65708 / 417-235-6501

AO Sight Systems, 2401 Ludelle St., Fort Worth, TX 76105 / 888-744-4880; or 817-536-0136; FAX: 817-536-3517

Apel GmbH, Ernst, Am Kirschberg 3, D-97218, Gerbrunn, GERMANY / 0 (931) 707192 info@eaw.de www.eaw.de

Aplan Antiques & Art, James O., HC 80, Box 793-25, Piedmont, SD 57769 / 605-347-5016

AR-7 Industries, LLC, 998 N. Colony Rd., Meriden, CT 06450 / 203-630-3536; FAX: 203-630-3637

Arizona Ammunition, Inc., 21421 No. 14th Ave., Suite E, Phoenix, AZ 85027 / 623-516-9004; FAX: 623-516-9012 www.azammo.com

ArmaLite, Inc., P.O. Box 299, Geneseo, IL 61254 / 800-336-0184 or 309-944-6939; FAX: 309-944-6949

Armament Gunsmithing Co., Inc., 525 Rt. 22, Hillside, NJ 07205 / 908-686-0960; FAX: 718-738-5019 armamentgunsmithing@worldnet.att.net

Armas Garbi, S.A., 12-14 20.600 Urki, 12, Eibar (Guipuzcoa), SPAIN / 943 20 3873; FAX: 943 20 3873 armosgarbi@euskalnet.n

Armas Kemen S. A. (See U.S. Importers)

Armfield Custom Bullets, 10584 County Road 100, Carthage, MO 64836 / 417-359-8480; FAX: 417-359-8497

Armi Perazzi S.P.A., Via Fontanelle 1/3, 1-25080, Botticino Mattina, ITALY / 030-2692591; FAX: 030-2692594

Armi San Marco (See Taylor's & Co.)

Armi San Paolo, 172-A, I-25062, via Europa, ITALY / 030-2751725

Armi Sport (See Cape Outfitters)

Armite Laboratories Inc., 1560 Superior Ave., Costa Mesa, CA 92627 / 949-646-9035; FAX: 949-646-8319 armite@pacbell.net www.armitelahs.com

Armoloy Co. of Ft. Worth, 204 E. Daggett St., Fort Worth, TX 76104 / 817-332-5604; FAX: 817-335-6517 info@armoloyftworth.com www.armoloyftworth.com

Armor (See Buck Stop Lure Co., Inc.)

Armor Metal Products, P.O. Box 4609, Helena, MT 59604 / 406-442-5560; FAX: 406-442-5650

Armory Publications, 2120 S. Reserve St., PMB 253, Missoula, MT 59801 / 406-549-7670; FAX: 406-728-0597 armorypub@aol.com www.armorypub.com

Arms & Armour Press, Wellington House, 125 Strand, London, WC2R 0BB ENGLAND / 0171-420-5555; FAX: 0171-240-7265

Arms Corporation of the Philippines, Armscor Ave. Brgy. Fortune, Marikina City, PHILIPPINES / 632-941-6243 or 632-941-6244; FAX: 632-942-0682 info@armscor.com.ph www.armscor.com.ph

Arms Craft Gunsmithing, 1106 Linda Dr., Arroyo Grande, CA 93420 / 805-481-2830

Arms, Programming Solutions (See Arms Software)

Armscor Precision, 5740 S. Arville St. #219, Las Vegas, NV 89118 / 702-362-7750

Armscorp USA, Inc., 4424 John Ave., Baltimore, MD 21227 / 301-775-8134 info@armscorpusa.com www.armscorpusa.com

Arratoonian, Andy (See Horseshoe Leather Products)

Arrieta S.L., Morkaiko 5, 20870, Elgoibar, SPAIN / 34-43-743150; FAX: 34-43-743154

Art Jewel Enterprises Ltd., Eagle Business Ctr., 460 Randy Rd., Carol Stream, IL 60188 / 708-260-0400

Artistry in Wood, 134 Zimmerman Rd., Kalispell, MT 59901 / 406-257-9003; FAX: 406-257-9167 merlins@digisys.net www.acrabondlaminates.com

Art's Gun & Sport Shop, Inc., 6008 Hwy. Y, Hillsboro, MO 63050

Aspen Outfitting Co., Jon Hollinger, 9 Dean St., Aspen, CO 81611 / 970-925-3406

A-Square Co., 205 Fairfield Ave., Jeffersonville, IN 47130 / 812-283-0577; FAX: 812-283-0375

Astra Sport, S.A., Apartado 3, 48300 Guernica, Espagne, SPAIN / 34-4-6250100; FAX: 34-4-6255186

Atamec-Bretton, 19 rue Victor Grignard, F-42026, St.-Etienne (Cedex 1, FRANCE / 33-77-93-54-69; FAX: 33-77-93-57-98

Atlanta Cutlery Corp., 2143 Gees Mill Rd., Box 839 CIS, Conyers, GA 30207 / 800-883-0300; FAX: 404-388-0246

Atlantic Mills, Inc., 1295 Towbin Ave., Lakewood, NJ 08701-5934 / 800-242-7374

Atsko/Sno-Seal, Inc., 2664 Russell St., Orangeburg, SC 29115 / 803-531-1820; FAX: 803-531-2139 info@atsko.com www.atsko.com

Austin & Halleck, Inc., 2150 South 950 East, Provo, UT 84606-6285 / 877-543-3256 or 801-374-9990; FAX: 801-374-9998 www.austinhallek.com

Austin Sheridan USA, Inc., 490 Main St., Middlefield, CT 06455 / 860-349-1772; FAX: 860-349-1771 asusa@sbcglobal.net

Auto Arms, 738 Clearview, San Antonio, TX 78228 / 512-434-5450

Auto-Ordnance Corp., P.O. Box 220, Blauvelt, NY 10913 / 914-353-7770

Autumn Sales, Inc. (Blaser), 1320 Lake St., Fort Worth, TX 76102 / 817-335-1634; FAX: 817-338-0119

Avnda Otaola Norica, 16 Apartado 68, 20600, Eibar, SPAIN

AWC Systems Technology, P.O. Box 41938, Phoenix, AZ 85080-1938 / 623-780-1050; FAX: 623-780-2967 awc@awcsystech.com www.awcsystech.com

Axtell Rifle Co., 353 Mill Creek Road, Sheridan, MT 59749 / 406-842-5814

AYA (See U.S. Importer-New England Custom Gun Serv

B

B&D Trading Co., Inc., 3935 Fair Hill Rd., Fair Oaks, CA 95628 / 800-334-3790 or 916-967-9366; FAX: 916-967-4873

B&P America, 12321 Brittany Cir., Dallas, TX 75230 / 972-726-9069

B.A.C., 17101 Los Modelos St., Fountain Valley, CA 92708 / 435-586-3286

B.C. Outdoors, Larry McGhee, PO Box 61497, Boulder City, NV 89006 / 702-294-3056; FAX: 702-294-0413 jdalton@pmccammo.com www.pmccammo.com

B.M.F. Activator, Inc., 12145 Mill Creek Run, Plantersville, TX 77363 / 936-894-2397; FAX: 936-894-2397 bmf25years@aol.com

Baelder, Harry, Alte Goennebeker Strasse 5, 24635, Rickling, GERMANY / 04328-722732; FAX: 04328-722733

Baer's Hollows, P.O. Box 603, Taft, CA 93268 / 719-438-5718

Bagmaster Mfg., Inc., 2731 Sutton Ave., St. Louis, MO 63143 / 314-781-8002; FAX: 314-781-3363 sales@bagmaster.com www.bagmaster.com

Bain & Davis, Inc., 307 E. Valley Blvd., San Gabriel, CA 91776-3522 / 626-573-4241; FAX: 323-283-7449 baindavis@aol.com

Baker, Stan. See: STAN BAKER SPORTS

Bald Eagle Precision Machine Co., 101-A Allison St., Lock Haven, PA 17745 / 570-748-6772; FAX: 570-748-4443 bepmachine@aol.com baldeaglemachine.com

Balickie, Joe, 408 Trelawney Lane, Apex, NC 27502 / 919-362-5185

Ballard, Donald. See: BALLARD INDUSTRIES

Ballard Industries, Donald Ballard Sr., P.O. Box 2035, Arnold, CA 95223 / 408-996-0957; FAX: 408-257-6828

Ballard Rifle & Cartridge Co., LLC, 113 W. Yellowstone Ave., Cody, WY 82414 / 307-587-4914; FAX: 307-527-6097 ballard@wyoming.com www.ballardrifles.com

Ballistic Products, Inc., 20015 75th Ave. North, Corcoran, MN 55340-9456 / 763-494-9237; FAX: 763-494-9236 info@ballisticproducts.com www.ballisticproducts.com

Ballistic Program Co., Inc., The, 2417 N. Patterson St., Thomasville, GA 31792 / 912-228-5739 or 800-368-0835

Ballistic Research, 1108 W. May Ave., McHenry, IL 60050 / 815-385-0037

Ballisti-Cast, Inc., P.O. Box 1057, Minot, ND 58702-1057 / 701-497-3333; FAX: 701-497-3335

Bandcor Industries, Div. of Man-Sew Corp., 6108 Sherwin Dr., Port Richey, FL 34668 / 813-848-0432

Bang-Bang Boutique (See Holster Shop, The)

Bansner's Ultimate Rifles, LLC, P.O. Box 839, 261 E. Main St., Adamstown, PA 19501 / 717-484-2370; FAX: 717-484-0523 bansner@aol.com www.bansnersrifle.com

Barbour, Inc., 55 Meadowbrook Dr., Milford, NH 03055 / 603-673-1313; FAX: 603-673-6510

Barnes, 4347 Tweed Dr., Eau Claire, WI 54703-6302

Barnes Bullets, Inc., P.O. Box 215, American Fork, UT 84003 / 801-756-4222 or 800-574-9200; FAX: 801-756-2465 email@barnesbullets.com www.barnesbullets.com

Baron Technology, 62 Spring Hill Rd., Trumbull, CT 06611 / 203-452-0515; FAX: 203-452-0663 dbaron@baronengraving.com www.baronengraving.com

Barraclough, John K., 55 Merit Park Dr., Gardena, CA 90247 / 310-324-2574 jbarraclough@sbcglobal.net

Barramundi Corp., P.O. Drawer 4259, Homosassa Springs, FL 32687 / 904-628-0200

Barrel & Gunworks, 2601 Lake Valley Rd., Prescott Valley, AZ 86314 / 928-772-4060 www.cutrifle.com

Barrett Firearms Manufacturer, Inc., P.O. Box 1077, Murfreesboro, TN 37133 / 615-896-2938; FAX: 615-896-7313

Bar-Sto Precision Machine, 73377 Sullivan Rd., P.O. Box 1838, Twentynine Palms, CA 92277 / 760-367-2747; FAX: 760-367-2407 barsto@eee.org www.barsto.com

Barta's Gunsmithing, 10231 U.S. Hwy. 10, Cato, WI 54230 / 920-732-4472

Barteaux Machete, 1916 SE 50th Ave., Portland, OR 97215-3238 / 503-233-5880

Bartlett Engineering, 40 South 200 East, Smithfield, UT 84335-1645 / 801-563-5910

Bates Engraving, Billy, 2302 Winthrop Dr. SW, Decatur, AL 35603 / 256-355-3690 bbrn@aol.com www.angelfire.com/al/billybates

Battenfeld Technologies, Inc., 5885 W. Van Horn Tavern Rd., Columbia, MO 65203 / 573-445-9200; FAX: 573-447-4158 battenfeldtechnologies.com

Bauer, Eddie, 15010 NE 36th St., Redmond, WA 98052

Baumgartner Bullets, 3011 S. Alane St., W. Valley City, UT 84120

Bauska Barrels, 105 9th Ave. W., Kalispell, MT 59901 / 406-752-7706

BC-Handmade Bullets, 482 Comerwood Court, S. San Francisco, CA 94080 / 650-583-1550; FAX: 650-583-1550

Bear Archery, RR 4, 4600 Southwest 41st Blvd., Gainesville, FL 32601 / 904-376-2327

Bear Arms, 374-A Carson Rd., St. Mathews, SC 29135

Bear Mountain Gun & Tool, 120 N. Plymouth, New Plymouth, ID 83655 / 208-278-5221; FAX: 208-278-5221

Beartooth Bullets, P.O. Box 491, Dept. HLD, Dover, ID 83825-0491 / 208-448-1865 bullets@beartoothbullets.com www.beartoothbullets.com

Beaver Park Product, Inc., 840 J St., Penrose, CO 81240 / 719-372-6744

BEC, Inc., 1227 W. Valley Blvd., Suite 204, Alhambra, CA 91803 / 626-281-5751; FAX: 626-293-7073

Beeks, Mike. See: GRAYBACK WILDCATS

Beeman Precision Airguns, 5454 Argosy Dr., Huntington Beach, CA 92649 / 714-890-4808; FAX: 714-890-4808

Behlert Precision, Inc., P.O. Box 288, 7067 Easton Rd., Pipersville, PA 18947 / 215-766-8681 or 215-766-7301; FAX: 215-766-8681

Beitzinger, George, 116-20 Atlantic Ave., Richmond Hill, NY 11419 / 718-847-7661

Belding's Custom Gun Shop, 10691 Sayers Rd., Munith, MI 49259 / 517-596-2388

Bell & Carlson, Inc., Dodge City Industrial Park, 101 Allen Rd., Dodge City, KS 67801 / 800-634-8586 or 620-225-6688; FAX: 620-225-6688 email@bellandcarlson.com www.bellandcarlson.com

Bell Reloading, Inc., 1725 Harlin Lane Rd., Villa Rica, GA 30180

Bell's Gun & Sport Shop, 3309-19 Mannheim Rd., Franklin Park, IL 60131

Bell's Legendary Country Wear, 22 Circle Dr., Bellmore, NY 11710 / 516-679-1158

MANUFACTURER'S DIRECTORY

Benchmark Knives (See Gerber Legendary Blades)

Benelli Armi S.P.A., Via della Stazione, 61029, Urbino, ITALY / 39-722-307-1; FAX: 39-722-327427

Benelli USA Corp., 17603 Indian Head Hwy., Accokeek, MD 20607 / 301-283-6981; FAX: 301-283-6988 benelliusa.com

Bengtson Arms Co., L., 6345-B E. Akron St., Mesa, AZ 85205 / 602-981-6375

Benjamin/Sheridan Co., Crosman, Rts. 5 and 20, E. Bloomfield, NY 14443 / 716-657-6161; FAX: 716-657-5405 www.crosman.com

Bentley, John, 128-D Watson Dr., Turtle Creek, PA 15145

Beretta Pietro S.P.A., Via Beretta, 18, 25063, Gardone Valtrompia, ITALY / 39-30-8341-1 info@beretta.com www.beretta.com

Beretta U.S.A. Corp., 17601 Beretta Dr., Accokeek, MD 20607 / 301-283-2191; FAX: 301-283-0435

Berger Bullets Ltd., 5443 W. Westwind Dr., Glendale, AZ 85310 / 602-842-4001; FAX: 602-934-9083

Bernadelli, Vincenzo, P.O. Box 460243, Houston, TX 77056-8243 www.bernardelli.com

Bernardelli, Vincenzo, Via Grande, 10, Sede Legale Torbole Casaglia, Brescia, ITALY / 39-30-8912851-2-3; FAX: 39-030-2150963 bernardelli@bernardelli.com www.bernardelli.com

Berry's Mfg., Inc., 401 North 3050 East St., St. George, UT 84770 / 435-634-1682; FAX: 435-634-1683 sales@berrysmfg.com www.berrysmfg.com

Bersa S.A., Benso Bonadimani, Magallanes 775 B1704 FLC, Ramos Mejia, ARGENTINA / 011-4656-2377; FAX: 011-4656-2093+ info@bersa-sa.com.dr www.bersa-sa.com.ar

Bert Johanssons Vapentillbehor, S-430 20 Veddige, SWEDEN

Bertuzzi (See U.S. Importer-New England Arms Co.)

Better Concepts Co., 663 New Castle Rd., Butler, PA 16001 / 412-285-9000

Beverly, Mary, 3201 Horseshoe Trail, Tallahassee, FL 32312

Bianchi International, Inc., 100 Calle Cortez, Temecula, CA 92590 / 909-676-5621; FAX: 909-676-6777

Big Bore Bullets of Alaska, P.O. Box 521455, Big Lake, AK 99652 / 907-373-2673; FAX: 907-373-2673 doug@mtaonline.net ww.awloo.com/bbb/index.

Big Bore Express, 2316 E. Railroad St., Nampa, ID 83651 / 800-376-4010 FAX: 208-466-6927 info@powerbeltbullets.com bigbore.com

Big Spring Enterprises "Bore Stores", P.O. Box 1115, Big Spring Rd., Yellville, AR 72687 / 870-449-5297; FAX: 870-449-4446

Bilal, Mustafa. See: TURK'S HEAD PRODUCTIONS

Bilinski, Bryan. See: FIELDSPORT LTD.

Bill Adair Custom Shop, 2886 Westridge, Carrollton, TX 75006 / 972-418-0950

Bill Austin's Calls, Box 284, Kaycee, WY 82639 / 307-738-2552

Bill Hanus Birdguns, LLC, P.O. Box 533, Newport, OR 97365 / 541-265-7433; FAX: 541-265-7400 www.billhanusbirdguns.com

Bill Russ Trading Post, William A. Russ, 25 William St., Addison, NY 14801-1326 / 607-359-3896

Bill Wiseman and Co., P.O. Box 3427, Bryan, TX 77805 / 409-690-3456; FAX: 409-690-0156

Billeb, Stephen. See: QUALITY CUSTOM FIREARMS

Billings Gunsmiths, 1841 Grand Ave., Billings, MT 59102 / 406-256-8390; FAX: 406-256-6530 blgsgunsmiths@msn.com www.billingsgunsmiths.net

Billingsley & Brownell, P.O. Box 25, Dayton, WY 82836 / 307-655-9344

Bill's Gun Repair, 1007 Burlington St., Mendota, IL 61342 / 815-539-5786

Billy Bates Engraving, 2302 Winthrop Dr. SW, Decatur, AL 35603 / 256-355-3690 bbrn@aol.com www.angelfire.com/al/billybates

Birchwood Casey, 7900 Fuller Rd., Eden Prairie, MN 55344 / 800-328-6156 or 612-937-7933; FAX: 612-937-7979

Birdsong & Assoc., W. E., 1435 Monterey Rd., Florence, MS 39073-9748 / 601-366-8270

Bismuth Cartridge Co., 3500 Maple Ave., Suite 1650, Dallas, TX 75219 / 214-521-5880; FAX: 214-521-9035

Bison Studios, 1409 South Commerce St., Las Vegas, NV 89102 / 702-388-2891; FAX: 702-383-9967

Bitterroot Bullet Co., 2001 Cedar Ave., Lewiston, ID 83501-0412 / 208-743-5635 brootbil@lewiston.com

BKL Technologies, P.O. Box 5237, Brownsville, TX 78523

Black Belt Bullets (See Big Bore Express)

Black Hills Ammunition, Inc., P.O. Box 3090, Rapid City, SD 57709-3090 / 605-348-5150; FAX: 605-348-9827

Black Hills Shooters Supply, P.O. Box 4220, Rapid City, SD 57709 / 800-289-2506

Black Powder Products, 67 Township Rd. 1411, Chesapeake, OH 45619 / 614-867-8047

Black Sheep Brand, 3220 W. Gentry Pkwy., Tyler, TX 75702 / 903-592-3853; FAX: 903-592-0527

Blacksmith Corp., P.O. Box 280, North Hampton, OH 45349 / 937-969-8389; FAX: 937-969-8399 sales@blacksmithcorp.com www.blacksmithcorp.com

BlackStar AccuMax Barrels, 11501 Brittmoore Park Drive, Houston, TX 77041 / 281-721-6040; FAX: 281-721-6041

BlackStar Barrel Accurizing (See BlackStar AccuMax)

Blacktail Mountain Books, 42 First Ave. W., Kalispell, MT 59901 / 406-257-5573

Blammo Ammo, P.O. Box 1677, Seneca, SC 29679 / 803-882-1768

Blaser Jagdwaffen GmbH, D-88316, Isny Im Allgau, GERMANY

Blount, Inc., Sporting Equipment Div., 2299 Snake River Ave., P.O. Box 856, Lewiston, ID 83501 / 800-627-3640 or 208-746-2351; FAX: 208-799-3904

Blount/Outers ATK, P.O. Box 39, Onalaska, WI 54650 / 608-781-5800; FAX: 608-781-0368

Blue and Gray Products Inc. (See Ox-Yoke Originals)

Blue Book Publications, Inc., 8009 34th Ave. S., Ste. 175, Minneapolis, MN 55425 / 952-854-5229; FAX: 952-853-1486 bluebook@bluebookinc.com www.bluebookinc.com

Blue Mountain Bullets, 64146 Quail Ln., Box 231, John Day, OR 97845 / 541-820-4594; FAX: 541-820-4594

Blue Ridge Machinery & Tools, Inc., P.O. Box 536-GD, Hurricane, WV 25526 / 800-872-6500; FAX: 304-562-5311 blueridgemachine@worldnet.att.net www.blueridgemachinery.com

BMC Supply, Inc., 26051 - 179th Ave. SE, Kent, WA 98042

Bob Allen Co., P.O. Box 477, 214 SW Jackson, Des Moines, IA 50315 / 800-685-7020; FAX: 515-283-0779

Bob Allen Sportswear, 220 S. Main St., Osceola, IA 50213 / 210-344-8531; FAX: 210-342-2703 sales@bob-allen.com www.bob-allen.com

Bob Rogers Gunsmithing, P.O. Box 305, 344 S. Walnut St., Franklin Grove, IL 61031 / 815-456-2685; FAX: 815-456-2685 3006bud@netscape.comm

Bob's Gun Shop, P.O. Box 200, Royal, AR 71968 / 501-767-1970; FAX: 501-767-1970 gunparts@hsnp.com www.gun-parts.com

Bob's Tactical Indoor Shooting Range & Gun Shop, 90 Lafayette Rd., Salisbury, MA 01952 / 508-465-5561

Boessler, Erich, Am Vogeltal 3, 97702, Munnerstadt, GERMANY

Boker USA, Inc., 1550 Balsam Street, Lakewood, CO 80214 / 303-462-0662; FAX: 303-462-0668 sales@bokerusa.com bokerusa.com

Boltin, John M., P.O. Box 644, Estill, SC 29918 / 803-625-2185

Bo-Mar Tool & Mfg. Co., 6136 State Hwy. 300, Longview, TX 75604 / 903-759-4784; FAX: 903-759-9141 marykor@earthlink.net bo-mar.com

Bonadimani, Benso. See: BERSA S.A.

Bonanza (See Forster Products), 310 E. Lanark Ave., Lanark, IL 61046 / 815-493-6360; FAX: 815-493-2371

Bond Arms, Inc., P.O. Box 1296, Granbury, TX 76048 / 817-573-4445; FAX: 817-573-5636 www.bondarms.com

Bond Custom Firearms, 8954 N. Lewis Ln., Bloomington, IN 47408 / 812-332-4519

Bonham's & Butterfields, 220 San Bruno Ave., San Francisco, CA 94103 / 415-861-7500; FAX: 415-861-0183 arms@butterfields.com www.butterfields.com

Boone Trading Co., Inc., P.O. Box 669, Brinnon, WA 98320 / 800-423-1945 or 360-796-4330; FAX: 360-796-4511 sales@boonetrading.com boonetrading.com

Boone's Custom Ivory Grips, Inc., 562 Coyote Rd., Brinnon, WA 98320 / 206-796-4330

Boonie Packer Products, P.O. Box 12517, Salem, OR 97309-0517 / 800-477-3244 or 503-581-3244; FAX: 503-581-3191 customerservice@booniepacker.com www.booniepacker.com

Borden Ridges Rimrock Stocks, RR 1 Box 250 BC, Springville, PA 18844 / 570-965-2505; FAX: 570-965-2328

Borden Rifles Inc., RD 1, Box 250 #BC, Springville, PA 18844 / 717-965-2505; FAX: 717-965-2328

Border Barrels Ltd., Riccarton Farm, Newcastleton, SCOTLAND UK

Borovnik K.G., Ludwig, 9170 Ferlach, Bahnhofstrasse 7, AUSTRIA / 042 27 24 42; FAX: 042 26 43 49

Bosis (See U.S. Importer-New England Arms Co.)

Boss Manufacturing Co., 221 W. First St., Kewanee, IL 61443 / 309-852-2131 or 800-447-4581; FAX: 309-852-0848

Bostick Wildlife Calls, Inc., P.O. Box 728, Estill, SC 29918 / 803-625-2210; or 803-625-4512

Bowen Classic Arms Corp., P.O. Box 67, Louisville, TN 37777 / 865-984-3583 www.bowenclassicarms.com

Bowen Knife Co., Inc., P.O. Box 802, Magnolia, AR 71754 / 800-397-4794; FAX: 870-234-9005 info@bowen.com www.bowenknife.com

Bowerly, Kent, 710 Golden Pheasant Dr., Redmond, OR 97756 / 541-923-3501 bowerly@bendbroadband.com

Boyds' Gunstock Industries, Inc., 25376 403 Rd. Ave., Mitchell, SD 57301 / 605-996-5011; FAX: 605-996-9878 www.boydsgunstocks.com

Brace, Larry D., 771 Blackfoot Ave., Eugene, OR 97404 / 541-688-1278; FAX: 541-607-5833

Brauer Bros., 345 Industrial Blvd., Ste. B, McKinney, TX 75069 / 976-548-8881; FAX: 972-548-8886 www.brauerbros.com

Break-Free, Inc., 13386 International Pkwy., Jacksonville, FL 32218 / 800-428-0588; FAX: 904-741-5407 contactus@armorholdings.com www.break-free.com

Brenneke GmbH, P.O. Box 1646, 30837, Langenhagen, GERMANY / +49-511-97262-0; FAX: +49-511-97262-62 info@brenneke.de brenneke.com

Bridgeman Products, Harry Jaffin, 153 B Cross Slope Ct., Englishtown, NJ 07726 / 732-536-3604; FAX: 732-972-1004

Briese Bullet Co., Inc., 3442 42nd Ave. SE, Tappen, ND 58487 / 701-327-4578; FAX: 701-327-4579

Brigade Quartermasters, 1025 Cobb International Blvd., Dept. VH, Kennesaw, GA 30144-4300 / 404-428-1248 or 800-241-3125; FAX: 404-426-7726

Briganti, A.J. See: BRIGANTI CUSTOM GUNSMITH

Briganti Custom Gunsmith, A.J. Briganti, 512 Rt. 32, Highland Mills, NY 10930 / 845-928-9573

Briley Mfg. Inc., 1230 Lumpkin, Houston, TX 77043 / 800-331-5718 or 713-932-6995; FAX: 713-932-1043

Brill, R. See: ROYAL ARMS INTERNATIONAL

British Sporting Arms, RR 1, Box 193A, Millbrook, NY 12545 / 845-677-8303; FAX: 845-677-5756 info@bsaltd.com www.bsaltd.com

Broad Creek Rifle Works, Ltd., 120 Horsey Ave., Laurel, DE 19956 / 302-875-5446; FAX: 302-875-1448 bcrw4guns@aol.com

Brockman's Custom Gunsmithing, P.O. Box 357, Gooding, ID 83330 / 208-934-5050

Broken Gun Ranch, 10739 126 Rd., Spearville, KS 67876 / 316-385-2587; FAX: 316-385-2597 nbowlin@ucom.net www.brokengunranch

Brooker, Dennis, Rt. 1, Box 12A, Derby, IA 50068 / 515-533-2103

Brooks Tactical Systems-Agrip, 279-C Shorewood Ct., Fox Island, WA 98333 / 253-549-2866 FAX: 253-549-2703 brooks@brookstactical.com www.brookstactical.com

Brown Precision, Inc., 7786 Molinos Ave., Los Molinos, CA 96055 / 530-384-2506; FAX: 916-384-1638 www.brownprecision.com

Brownells, Inc., 200 S. Front St., Montezuma, IA 50171 / 800-741-0015; FAX: 800-264-3068 orderdesk@brownells.com www.brownells.com

Browning Arms Co., One Browning Place, Morgan, UT 84050 / 801-876-2711; FAX: 801-876-3331 www.browning.com

Browning Arms Co. (Parts & Service), 3005 Arnold Tenbrook Rd., Arnold, MO 63010 / 617-287-6800; FAX: 617-287-9751

BRP, Inc. High Performance Cast Bullets, 1210 Alexander Rd., Colorado Springs, CO 80909 / 719-633-0658

Brunton U.S.A., 620 E. Monroe Ave., Riverton, WY 82501 / 307-856-6559; FAX: 307-857-4702 info@brunton.com www.brunton.com

Bryan & Assoc., R. D. Sauls, P.O. Box 5772, Anderson, SC 29623-5772 / 864-261-6810 bryanandac@aol.com www.huntersweb.com/bryanandac

Brynin, Milton, P.O. Box 383, Yonkers, NY 10710 / 914-779-4333

BSA Guns Ltd., Armoury Rd. Small Heath, Birmingham B11 2PP, ENGLAND / 011-021-772-8543; FAX: 011-021-773-0845 sales@bsagun.com www.bsagun.com

BSA Optics, 3911 SW 47th Ave., Ste. 914, Ft. Lauderdale, FL 33314 / 954-581-2144; FAX: 954-581-3165 4info@basaoptics.com www.bsaoptics.com

B-Square Company, Inc., 8909 Forum Way, Ft. Worth, TX 76140 / 800-433-2909; FAX: 817-926-7012 bsquare@b-square.com www.b-square.com

Buchsenmachermeister, Peter Hofer Jagdwaffen, A-9170 Ferlach, Kirchgasse 24, Kirchgasse, AUSTRIA / 43 4227 3683; or 43 664 3200216; FAX: 43 4227 368330 peterhofer@hoferwaffen.com www.hoferwaffen.com

Buck Knives, Inc., 1900 Weld Blvd., P.O. Box 1267, El Cajon, CA 92020 / 619-449-1100 or 800-326-2825; FAX: 619-562-5774

Buck Stix-SOS Products Co., Box 3, Neenah, WI 54956

Buck Stop Lure Co., Inc., 3600 Grow Rd. NW, P.O. Box 636, Stanton, MI 48888 / 989-762-5091; FAX: 989-762-5124 buckstop@nethawk.com www.buckstopscents.com

Buckeye Custom Bullets, 6490 Stewart Rd., Elida, OH 45807 / 419-641-4463

Buckhorn Gun Works, 8109 Woodland Dr., Black Hawk, SD 57718 / 605-787-6472

Buckskin Bullet Co., P.O. Box 1893, Cedar City, UT 84721 / 435-586-3286

Budin, Dave, 817 Main St., P.O. Box 685, Margaretville, NY 12455 / 914-568-4103; FAX: 914-586-4105

Budin, Dave. See: DEL-SPORTS, INC.

Buehler Custom Sporting Arms, P.O. Box 4096, Medford, OR 97501 / 541-664-9109 rbrifle@earthlink.net

Buenger Enterprises/Goldenrod Dehumidifier, 3600 S. Harbor Blvd., Oxnard, CA 93035 / 800-451-6797 or 805-985-5828; FAX: 805-985-1534

Buffalo Arms Co., 660 Vermeer Ct., Ponderay, ID 83852 / 208-263-6953; FAX: 208-265-2096 www.buffaloarms.com

Buffalo Bullet Co., Inc., 12637 Los Nietos Rd., Unit A, Santa Fe Springs, CA 90670 / 800-423-8069; FAX: 562-944-5054 rdanlitz@verizon.net

Buffalo Gun Center, 3385 Harlem Rd., Buffalo, NY 14225 / 716-833-2581; FAX: 716-833-2265 www.buffaloguncenter.com

Buffalo Rock Shooters Supply, R.R. 1, Ottawa, IL 61350 / 815-433-2471

Buffer Technologies, P.O. Box 105047, Jefferson City, MO 65110 / 573-634-8529; FAX: 573-634-8522 sales@buffertech.com www.buffertech.com

Bull Mountain Rifle Co., 6327 Golden West Terrace, Billings, MT 59106 / 406-656-0778

Bullberry Barrel Works, Ltd., 2430 W. Bullberry Ln., Hurricane, UT 84737 / 435-635-9866; FAX: 435-635-0348 fred@bullberry.com www.bullberry.com

Bullet Metals, Bill Ferguson, P.O. Box 1238, Sierra Vista, AZ 85636 / 520-458-5321; FAX: 520-458-1421 info@theantimonyman.com www.bullet-metals.com

Bullet N Press, 1210 Jones St., Gastonia, NC 28052 / 704-853-0265 bnpress@quik.com www.oldwestgunsmith.com

Bullet Swaging Supply, Inc., P.O. Box 1056, 303 McMillan Rd., West Monroe, LA 71291 / 318-387-3266; FAX: 318-387-7779 leblackmon@colla.com

Bull-X, Inc., 411 E. Water St., Farmer City, IL 61842-1556 / 309-928-2574 or 800-248-3845; FAX: 309-928-2130

Burkhart Gunsmithing, Don, P.O. Box 852, Rawlins, WY 82301 / 307-324-6007

Burnham Bros., P.O. Box 1148, Menard, TX 78659 / 915-396-4572; FAX: 915-396-4574

Burris Co., Inc., P.O. Box 1747, 331 E. 8th St., Greeley, CO 80631 / 970-356-1670; FAX: 970-356-8702

Bushmaster Firearms, Inc., 999 Roosevelt Trail, Windham, ME 04062 / 800-998-7928; FAX: 207-892-8068 info@bushmaster.com www.bushmaster.com

Bushmaster Hunting & Fishing, 451 Alliance Ave., Toronto, ON M6N 2J1 CANADA / 416-763-4040; FAX: 416-763-0623

Bushnell Outdoor Products, 9200 Cody, Overland Park, KS 66214 / 913-752-3400 or 800-423-3537; FAX: 913-752-3550

Buster's Custom Knives, P.O. Box 214, Richfield, UT 84701 / 435-896-5319; FAX: 435-896-8333 www.warenskiknives.com

Butler Creek Corp., 9200 Cody St., Overland Park, KS 66214 / 800-845-2444 or 406-388-1356; FAX: 406-388-7204

Butler Enterprises, 834 Oberting Rd., Lawrenceburg, IN 47025 / 812-537-3584

Buzz Fletcher Custom Stockmaker, 117 Silver Road, P.O. Box 189, Taos, NM 87571 / 505-758-3486

C

C&D Special Products (See Claybuster Wads & Harvester Bullets)

C&H Research, 115 Sunnyside Dr., Box 351, Lewis, KS 67552 / 316-324-5445 or 888-324-5445; FAX: 620-324-5984 info@mercuryrecoil.com www.mercuryrecoil.com

C. Sharps Arms Co. Inc./Montana Armory, 100 Centennial Dr., P.O. Box 885, Big Timber, MT 59011 / 406-932-4353; FAX: 406-932-4443

C.S. Van Gorden & Son, Inc., 1815 Main St., Bloomer, WI 54724 / 715-568-2612 vangorden@bloomer.net

C.W. Erickson's Mfg., L.L.C., P.O. Box 522, Buffalo, MN 55313 / 763-682-3665; FAX: 763-682-4328 cwerickson@archerhunter.com www.archerhunter.com

Cabanas (See U.S. Importer-Mandall Shooting Supply

Cabela's, One Cabela Drive, Sidney, NE 69160 / 308-254-5505; FAX: 308-254-8420

Cabinet Mtn. Outfitters Scents & Lures, P.O. Box 766, Plains, MT 59859 / 406-826-3970

Cache La Poudre Rifleworks, 140 N. College, Ft. Collins, CO 80524 / 920-482-6913

Caesar Guerini USA, Inc., 700 Lake St., Cambridge, MD 21613 / 410-901-1131; FAX: 410-901-1137 info@gueriniusa.com www.gueriniusa.com

Cain's Outdoors, Inc., 1832 Williams Hwy., Williamstown, WV 26187 / 304-375-7842; FAX: 304-375-7842 muzzleloading@cainsoutdoor.com www.cainsoutdoor.com

Cali'co Hardwoods, Inc., 3580 Westwind Blvd., Santa Rosa, CA 95403 / 707-546-4045; FAX: 707-546-4027 calicohardwoods@msn.com

California Sights (See Fautheree, Andy)

Cambos Outdoorsman, 532 E. Idaho Ave., Ontario, OR 97914 / 541-889-3135; FAX: 541-889-2633

Cambos Outdoorsman, Fritz Hallberg, 532 E. Idaho Ave., Ontario, OR 97914 / 541-889-3135; FAX: 541-889-2633

Camdex, Inc., 2330 Alger, Troy, MI 48083 / 810-528-2300; FAX: 810-528-0989

Cameron's, 16690 W. 11th Ave., Golden, CO 80401 / 303-279-7365; FAX: 303-568-1009 ncnoremac@aol.com

Camillus Cutlery Co., 54 Main St., Camillus, NY 13031 / 315-672-8111; FAX: 315-672-8832

Campbell, Dick, 196 Garden Homes Dr., Colville, WA 99114 / 509-684-6080; FAX: 509-684-6080 dicksknives@aol.com

Camp-Cap Products, P.O. Box 3805, Chesterfield, MO 63006 / 866-212-4639; FAX: 636-536-6320 mandrytrc@sbcglobal.net www.langenberghats.com

Cannon Safe, Inc., 216 S. 2nd Ave. #BLD-932, San Bernardino, CA 92400 / 310-692-0636 or 800-242-1055; FAX: 310-692-7252

Canyon Cartridge Corp., P.O. Box 152, Albertson, NY 11507 FAX: 516-294-8946

Cape Outfitters, 599 County Rd. 206, Cape Girardeau, MO 63701 / 573-335-4103; FAX: 573-335-1555

Caraville Manufacturing, P.O. Box 4545, Thousand Oaks, CA 91359 / 805-499-1234

Carbide Checkering Tools (See J&R Engineering)

Carhartt, Inc., 5750 Mercury Dr., Dearborn, MI 48126 / 800-833-3118 www.carhartt.com

Carl Walther GmbH, B.P. 4325, D-89033, Ulm, GERMANY

Carl Zeiss Inc., 13005 N. Kingston Ave., Chester, VA 23836 / 800-441-3005; FAX: 804-530-8481

Carolina Precision Rifles, 1200 Old Jackson Hwy., Jackson, SC 29831 / 803-827-2069

Carrell, William. See: CARRELL'S PRECISION FIREARMS

Carrell's Precision Firearms, William Carrell, 1952 W.Silver Falls Ct., Meridian, ID 83642-3837

Carry-Lite, Inc., P.O. Box 1587, Fort Smith, AR 72902 / 479-782-8971; FAX: 479-783-0234

Carter's Gun Shop, 225 G St., Penrose, CO 81240 / 719-372-6240 rlewiscarter@msn.com

Case & Sons Cutlery Co., W R, Owens Way, Bradford, PA 16701 / 814-368-4123 or 800-523-6350; FAX: 814-768-5369

Case Sorting System, 12695 Cobblestone Creek Rd., Poway, CA 92064 / 619-486-9340

Cash Mfg. Co./ TDC, P.O. Box 130, 201 S. Klein Dr., Waunakee, WI 53597-0130 / 608-849-5664; FAX: 608-849-5664 office@tdcmfg.com www.tdcmfg.com

Caspian Arms, Ltd., 14 North Main St., Hardwick, VT 05843 / 802-472-6454; FAX: 802-472-6709

Cast Bullet Association, The, 12857 S. Road, Hoyt, KS 66440-9116 cbamemdir@castbulletassoc.org www.castbulletassoc.org

Cast Performance Bullet Company, P.O. Box 153, Riverton, WY 82501 / 307-857-2940; FAX: 307-857-3132 castperform@wyoming.com castperformance.com

Casull Arms Corp., P.O. Box 1629, Afton, WY 83110 / 307-886-0200

Caswell International, 720 Industrial Dr. No. 112, Cary, IL 60013 / 847-639-7666; FAX: 847-639-7694 www.caswellintl.com

Cathey Enterprises, Inc., P.O. Box 2202, Brownwood, TX 76804 / 915-643-2553; FAX: 915-643-3653

Cation, 2341 Alger St., Troy, MI 48083 / 810-689-0658; FAX: 810-689-7558

Caywood, Shane J., P.O. Box 321, Minocqua, WI 54548 / 715-277-3866

Caywood Gunmakers, 18 Kings Hill Estates, Berryville, AR 72616 / 870-423-4741 www.caywoodguns.com

CBC, Avenida Humberto de Campos 3220, 09400-000, Ribeirao Pires, SP, BRAZIL / 55 11 4822 8378; FAX: 55 11 4822 8323 export@cbc.com.bc www.cbc.com.bc

CBC-BRAZIL, 3 Cuckoo Lane, Honley, Yorkshire HD7 2BR, ENGLAND / 44-1484-661062; FAX: 44-1484-663709

CCG Enterprises, 5217 E. Belknap St., Halton City, TX 76117 / 800-819-7464

CCI/Speer Div of ATK, P.O. Box 856, 2299 Snake River Ave., Lewiston, ID 83501 / 800-627-3640 or 208-746-2351

CCL Security Products, 199 Whiting St., New Britain, CT 06051 / 800-733-8588

Cedar Hill Game Calls, LLC, 238 Vic Allen Rd., Downsville, LA 71234 / 318-982-5632; FAX: 318-982-2031

Centaur Systems, Inc., 1602 Foothill Rd., Kalispell, MT 59901 / 406-755-8609; FAX: 406-755-8609

Center Lock Scope Rings, 9901 France Ct., Lakeville, MN 55044 / 952-461-2114; FAX: 952-461-2194 marklee55044@usfamily.net

Central Specialties Ltd. (See Trigger Lock Division)

MANUFACTURER'S DIRECTORY

Century International Arms, Inc., 430 S. Congress Ave. Ste. 1, Delray Beach, FL 33445-4701 / 800-527-1252; FAX: 561-998-1993 support@centuryarms.com www.centuryarms.com

CFVentures, 509 Harvey Dr., Bloomington, IN 47403-1715 paladinwilltravel@yahoo.com www.caversam16.freeserve.co.uk

CH Tool & Die Co. (See 4-D Custom Die Co.), 711 N Sandusky St., P.O. Box 889, Mt. Vernon, OH 43050-0889 / 740-397-7214; FAX: 740-397-6600

Chace Leather Products, 507 Alden St., Fall River, MA 02722 / 508-678-7556; FAX: 508-675-9666 chacelea@aol.com www.chaceleather.com

Chadick's Ltd., P.O. Box 100, Terrell, TX 75160 / 214-563-7577

Chambers Flintlocks Ltd., Jim, 116 Sams Branch Rd., Candler, NC 28715 / 828-667-8361; FAX: 828-665-0852 www.flintlocks.com

Champion Shooters' Supply, P.O. Box 303, New Albany, OH 43054 / 614-855-1603; FAX: 614-855-1209

Champion Target Co., 232 Industrial Parkway, Richmond, IN 47374 / 800-441-4971

Champion's Choice, Inc., 201 International Blvd., LaVergne, TN 37086 / 615-793-4066; FAX: 615-793-4070 champ.choice@earthlink.net www.champchoice.com

Champlin Firearms, Inc., P.O. Box 3191, Woodring Airport, Enid, OK 73701 / 580-237-7388; FAX: 580-242-6922 info@champlinarms.com www.champlinarms.com

Chapman Academy of Practical Shooting, 4350 Academy Rd., Hallsville, MO 65255 / 573-696-5544; FAX: 573-696-2266 hq@chapmanacademy.com chapmanacademy.com

Chapman, J. Ken. See: OLD WEST BULLET MOULDS

Chapman Manufacturing Co., 471 New Haven Rd., P.O. Box 250, Durham, CT 06422 / 860-349-9228; FAX: 860-349-0084 sales@chapmanmfg.com www.chapmanmfg.com

Chapuis Armes, Z1 La Gravoux, BP15, 42380 P.O. Box 15, St. Bonnet-le-Chatea, FRANCE / (33)477.50.06.96; FAX: (33)477 50 10 70 info@chapuis.armes.com www.chapuis-armes.com

Charter 2000, 273 Canal St., Shelton, CT 06484 / 203-922-1652

Checkmate Refinishing, 370 Champion Dr., Brooksville, FL 34601 / 352-799-5774; FAX: 352-799-2986 checkmatecustom.com

Cheddite, France S.A., 99 Route de Lyon, F-26501, Bourg-les-Valence, FRANCE / 33-75-56-4545; FAX: 33-75-56-3587 export@cheddite.com

Chelsea Gun Club of New York City Inc., 237 Ovington Ave., Apt. D53, Brooklyn, NY 11209 / 718-836-9422; or 718-833-2704

CheVron Bullets, RR1, Ottawa, IL 61350 / 815-433-2471

Cheyenne Pioneer Products, P.O. Box 28425, Kansas City, MO 64188 / 816-413-9196; FAX: 816-455-2859 cheyennepp@aol.com www.cartridgeboxes.com

Chicago Cutlery Co., 5500 N. Pearl St., Ste. 400, Rosemont, IL 60018 / 847-678-8600 www.chicagocutlery.com

Chicasaw Gun Works, 4 Mi. Mkr., Pluto Rd., Box 2024, Shady Spring, WV 25918-0868 / 304-763-2848; FAX: 304-763-3725

Chip McCormick Corp., P.O. Box 694, Spicewood, TX 78669 / 800-328-2447; FAX: 830-693-4975 www.chipmccormickcorp.com

Chipmunk (See Oregon Arms, Inc.)

Choate Machine & Tool Co., Inc., P.O. Box 218, 116 Lovers Ln., Bald Knob, AR 72010 / 501-724-6193; or 800-972-6390; FAX: 501-724-5873

Christensen Arms, 192 East 100 North, Fayette, UT 84630 / 435-528-7999; FAX: 435-528-7494 www.christensenarms.com

Christie's East, 20 Rockefeller Plz., New York, NY 10020-1902 / 212-606-0406 christics.com

Chu Tani Ind., Inc., P.O. Box 2064, Cody, WY 82414-2064

Chuck's Gun Shop, P.O. Box 597, Waldo, FL 32694 / 904-468-2264

Churchill (See U.S. Importer-Ellett Bros.)

Churchill, Winston G., 2838 20 Mile Stream Rd., Proctorville, VT 05153 / 802-226-7772

Churchill Glove Co., James, P.O. Box 298, Centralia, WA 98531 / 360-736-2816; FAX: 360-330-0151

CIDCO, 21480 Pacific Blvd., Sterling, VA 22170 / 703-444-5353

Cimarron F.A. Co., P.O. Box 906, Fredericksburg, TX 78624-0906 / 830-997-9090; FAX: 830-997-0802 cimgraph@koc.com www.cimarron-firearms.com

Cincinnati Swaging, 2605 Marlington Ave., Cincinnati, OH 45208

Clark Custom Guns, Inc., 336 Shootout Lane, Princeton, LA 71067 / 318-949-9884; FAX: 318-949-9829

Clark Firearms Engraving, 6347 Avon Ave., San Gabriel, CA 91775-1801 / 818-287-1652

Clarkfield Enterprises, Inc., 1032 10th Ave., Clarkfield, MN 56223 / 612-669-7140

Claro Walnut Gunstock Co., 1235 Stanley Ave., Chico, CA 95928 / 530-342-5188; FAX: 530-342-5199 wally@clarowalnutgunstocks.com www.clarowalnutgunstocks.com

Classic Arms Company, Rt 1 Box 120F, Burnet, TX 78611 / 512-756-4001

Classic Arms Corp., P.O. Box 106, Dunsmuir, CA 96025-0106 / 530-235-2000

Classic Old West Styles, 1060 Doniphan Park Circle C, El Paso, TX 79936 / 915-587-0684

Claybuster Wads & Harvester Bullets, 309 Sequoya Dr., Hopkinsville, KY 42240 / 800-922-6287; or 800-284-1746; FAX: 502-885-8088

Clean Shot Technologies, 21218 St. Andrews Blvd. Ste 504, Boca Raton, FL 33433 / 888-866-2532

Clearview Mfg. Co., Inc., 413 S. Oakley St., Fordyce, AR 71742 / 870-352-8557; FAX: 870-352-7120

Clearview Products, 3021 N. Portland, Oklahoma City, OK 73107

Cleland's Outdoor World, Inc., 10306 Airport Hwy., Swanton, OH 43558 / 419-865-4713; FAX: 419-865-5865 hasresa@cieiancs.com www.clelands.com

Clements' Custom Leathercraft, Chas, 1741 Dallas St., Aurora, CO 80010-2018 / 303-364-0403; FAX: 303-739-9824 gryphons@home.com kuntaoslcat.com

Clenzoil Worldwide Corp., Jack Fitzgerald, 25670 1st St., Westlake, OH 44145-1430 / 440-899-0482; FAX: 440-899-0483

Clift Mfg., L. R., 3821 Hammonton Rd., Marysville, CA 95901 / 916-755-3390; FAX: 916-755-3393

Clymer Mfg. Co., 1645 W. Hamlin Rd., Rochester Hills, MI 48309-3312 / 248-853-5555; FAX: 248-853-1530

C-More Systems, P.O. Box 1750, 7553 Gary Rd., Manassas, VA 20108 / 703-361-2663; FAX: 703-361-5881

Cobra Enterprises, Inc., 1960 S. Milestone Drive, Suite F, Salt Lake City, UT 84104 FAX: 801-908-8301 www.cobrapistols@networld.com

Cobra Sport S.R.I., Via Caduti Nei Lager No. 1, 56020 San Romano, Montopoli v/Arno Pi, ITALY / 0039-571-450490; FAX: 0039-571-450492

Coffin, Charles H., 3719 Scarlet Ave., Odessa, TX 79762 / 915-366-4729; FAX: 915-366-4729

Cogar's Gunsmithing, 206 Redwine Dr., Houghton Lake, MI 48629 / 517-422-4591 ecogar@peoplepc.com

Coghlan's Ltd., 121 Irene St., Winnipeg, MB R3T 4C7 CANADA / 204-284-9550; FAX: 204-475-4127

Cold Steel Inc., 3036 Seaborg Ave. Ste. A, Ventura, CA 93003 / 800-255-4716; or 800-624-2363; FAX: 805-642-9727

Cole-Grip, 16135 Cohasset St., Van Nuys, CA 91406 / 818-782-4424

Coleman Co., Inc., 3600 N. Hydraulic, Wichita, KS 67219 / 800-835-3278 www.coleman.com

Cole's Gun Works, Old Bank Building, Rt. 4 Box 250, Moyock, NC 27958 / 919-435-2345

Collector's Armoury, Ltd., Tom Nelson, 9404 Gunston Cove Rd., Lorton, VA 22079 / 703-493-9120; FAX: 703-493-9424 www.collectorsarmoury.com

Collings, Ronald, 1006 Cielta Linda, Vista, CA 92083

Colonial Arms, Inc., P.O. Box 636, Selma, AL 36702-0636 / 334-872-9455; FAX: 334-872-9540 colonialarms@mindspring.com www.colonialarms.com

Colonial Repair, 47 Navarre St., Roslindale, MA 02131-4725 / 617-469-4951

Colorado Gunsmithing Academy, RR 3 Box 79B, El Campo, TX 77437 / 719-336-4099 or 800-754-2046; FAX: 719-336-9642

Colorado School of Trades, 1575 Hoyt St., Lakewood, CO 80215 / 800-234-4594; FAX: 303-233-4723

Colt Blackpowder Arms Co., 110 8th Street, Brooklyn, NY 11215 / 718-499-4678; FAX: 718-768-8056

Colt's Mfg. Co., Inc., P.O. Box 1868, Hartford, CT 06144-1868 / 800-962-COLT or 860-236-6311; FAX: 860-244-1449

Compass Industries, Inc., 104 East 25th St., New York, NY 10010 / 212-473-2614 or 800-221-9904; FAX: 212-353-0826

Compasseco, Ltd., 151 Atkinson Hill Ave., Bardstown, KY 40004 / 502-349-0910

Competition Electronics, Inc., 3469 Precision Dr., Rockford, IL 61109 / 815-874-8001; FAX: 815-874-8181

Competitive Pistol Shop, The, 5233 Palmer Dr., Fort Worth, TX 76117-2433 / 817-834-8479

Competitor Corp., Inc., 26 Knight St. Unit 3, P.O. Box 352, Jaffrey, NH 03452 / 603-532-9483; FAX: 603-532-8209 competitorcorp@aol.com competitor-pistol.com

Component Concepts, Inc., 530 S. Springbrook Road, Newberg, OR 97132 / 503-554-8095; FAX: 503-554-9370 cci@cybcon.com www.phantomonline.com

Concealment Shop, Inc., The, 3550 E. Hwy. 80, Mesquite, TX 75149 / 972-289-8997 or 800-444-7090; FAX: 972-289-4410 info@theconcealmentshop.com www.theconcealmentshop.com

Concept Development Corp., 16610 E. Laser Drive, Suite 5, Fountain Hills, AZ 85268-6644

Conetrol Scope Mounts, 10225 Hwy. 123 S., Seguin, TX 78155 / 830-379-3030 or 800-CONETROL; FAX: 830-379-3030 email@conetrol.com www.conetrol.com

Connecticut Shotgun Mfg. Co., P.O. Box 1692, 35 Woodland St., New Britain, CT 06051 / 860-225-6581; FAX: 860-832-8707

Connecticut Valley Classics (See CVC, BPI)

Conrad, C. A., 3964 Ebert St., Winston-Salem, NC 27127 / 919-788-5469

Cook Engineering Service, 891 Highbury Rd., Vict 3133, 3133 AUSTRALIA

Cooper Arms, P.O. Box 114, Stevensville, MT 59870 / 406-777-0373; FAX: 406-777-5228

Cooper-Woodward Perfect Lube, 4120 Oesterle Rd., Helena, MT 59602 / 406-459-2287 cwperfectlube@mt.net cwperfectlube.com

Corbin Mfg. & Supply, Inc., 600 Industrial Circle, P.O. Box 2659, White City, OR 97503 / 541-826-5211; FAX: 541-826-8669 sales@corbins.com www.corbins.com

Cor-Bon Inc./Glaser LLC, P.O. Box 173, 1311 Industry Rd., Sturgis, SD 57785 / 605-347-4544 or 800-221-3489; FAX: 605-347-5055 email@corbon.com www.corbon.com

Corkys Gun Clinic, 4401 Hot Springs Dr., Greeley, CO 80634-9226 / 970-330-0516

Corry, John, 861 Princeton Ct., Neshanic Station, NJ 08853 / 908-369-8019

Cosmi Americo & Figlio S.N.C., Via Flaminia 307, Ancona, ITALY / 071-888208; FAX: 39-071-887008

Coulston Products, Inc., P.O. Box 30, 201 Ferry St. Suite 212, Easton, PA 18044-0030 / 215-253-0167 or 800-445-9927; FAX: 215-252-1511

Counter Assault, 120 Industrial Court, Kalispell, MT 59901 / 406-257-4740; FAX: 406-257-6674

Country Armourer, The, P.O. Box 308, Ashby, MA 01431-0308 / 508-827-6797; FAX: 508-827-4845

Cousin Bob's Mountain Products, 7119 Ohio River Blvd., Ben Avon, PA 15202 / 412-766-5114; FAX: 412-766-9354

MANUFACTURER'S DIRECTORY

CP Bullets, 1310 Industrial Hwy #5-6, Southhampton, PA 18966 / 215-953-7264; FAX: 215-953-7275

CQB Training, P.O. Box 1739, Manchester, MO 63011

Craftguard, 3624 Logan Ave., Waterloo, IA 50703 / 319-232-2959; FAX: 319-234-0804

Crandall Tool & Machine Co., 19163 21 Mile Rd., Tustin, MI 49688 / 616-829-4430

Creative Craftsman, Inc., The, 95 Highway 29 N., P.O. Box 331, Lawrenceville, GA 30246 / 404-963-2112; FAX: 404-513-9488

Creedmoor Sports, Inc., 3052 Industry St. #103, Oceanside, CA 92054 / 767-757-5529; FAX: 760-757-5558 shoot@creedmoorsports.com www.creedmoorsports.com

Creek Side Metal & Woodcrafters, Fishers Hill, VA 22626 / 703-465-3903

Creighton Audette, 19 Highland Circle, Springfield, VT 05156 / 802-885-2331

Crimson Trace Lasers, 8090 S.W. Cirrus Dr., Beverton, OR 97008 / 800-442-2406; FAX: 503-627-0166 travis@crimsontrace.com www.crimsontrace.com

Crit' R Calls, P.O. Box 999, La Porte, CO 80535 / 970-484-2768; FAX: 970-484-0807 critrcall@larinet.net www.critrcall.com

Crit'R Call (See Rocky Mountain Wildlife Products)

Crosman Airguns, Rts. 5 and 20, E. Bloomfield, NY 14443 / 716-657-6161; FAX: 716-657-5405

Crosman Blades (See Coleman Co., Inc.)

CRR, Inc./Marble's Inc., 420 Industrial Park, P.O. Box 111, Gladstone, MI 49837 / 906-428-3710; FAX: 906-428-3711

Crucelegui, Hermanos (See U.S. Importer-Mandall)

Cubic Shot Shell Co., Inc., 98 Fatima Dr., Campbell, OH 44405 / 330-755-0349

Cullity Restoration, 209 Old Country Rd., East Sandwich, MA 02537 / 508-888-1147

Cumberland Arms, 514 Shafer Road, Manchester, TN 37355 / 800-797-8414

Cummings Bullets, 1417 Esperanza Way, Escondido, CA 92027

Cupp, Alana, Custom Engraver, P.O. Box 207, Annabella, UT 84711 / 801-896-4834

Curly Maple Stock Blanks (See Tiger-Hunt)

Curtis Cast Bullets, 527 W. Babcock St., Bozeman, MT 59715 / 406-587-8117; FAX: 406-587-8117

Curtis Gun Shop (See Curtis Cast Bullets)

Custom Bullets by Hoffman, 2604 Peconic Ave., Seaford, NY 11783

Custom Calls, 607 N. 5th St., Burlington, IA 52601 / 319-752-4465

Custom Checkering Service, Kathy Forster, 2124 S.E. Yamhill St., Portland, OR 97214 / 503-236-5874

Custom Products (See Jones Custom Products)

Custom Shop, The, 890 Cochrane Crescent, Peterborough, ON K9H 5N3 CANADA / 705-742-6693

Custom Single Shot Rifles, 9651 Meadows Lane, Guthrie, OK 73044 / 405-282-3634

Custom Tackle and Ammo, P.O. Box 1886, Farmington, NM 87499 / 505-632-3539

Cutco Cutlery, P.O. Box 810, Olean, NY 14760 / 716-372-3111

CVA, 5988 Peachtree Corners East, Norcross, GA 30071 / 770-449-4687; FAX: 770-242-8546 info@cva.com www.cva.com

Cylinder & Slide, Inc., William R. Laughridge, 245 E. 4th St., Fremont, NE 68025 / 402-721-4277; FAX: 402-721-0263 bill@cylinder-slide.com www.clinder-slide.com

CZ USA, P.O. Box 171073, Kansas City, KS 66117 / 913-321-1811; FAX: 913-321-4901

D

D&D Gunsmiths, Ltd., 363 E. Elmwood, Troy, MI 48083 / 248-583-1512; FAX: 248-583-1524

D&G Precision Duplicators (See Greenwood Precision)

D&L Industries (See D.J. Marketing)

D&L Sports, P.O. Box 651, Gillette, WY 82717 / 307-686-4008

D.C. Engineering, Inc., 8633 Southfield Fwy., Detroit, MI 48228-1975 / 248-634-0941 guns@rifletech.com www.rifletech.com

D.C.C. Enterprises, 259 Wynburn Ave., Athens, GA 30601

D.J. Marketing, 10602 Horton Ave., Downey, CA 90241 / 310-806-0891; FAX: 310-806-6231

D.L. Unmussig Bullets, 7862 Brentford Dr., Richmond, VA 23225 / 804-320-1165; FAX: 804-320-4587

Dade Screw Machine Products, 2319 N.W. 7th Ave., Miami, FL 33127 / 305-573-5050

Daisy Outdoor Products, P.O. Box 220, Rogers, AR 72757 / 479-636-1200; FAX: 479-636-0573 www.daisy.com

Dakota (See U.S. Importer-EMF Co., Inc.)

Dakota Arms, Inc., 130 Industry Road, Sturgis, SD 57785 / 605-347-4686; FAX: 605-347-4459 info@dakotaarms.com www.dakotaarms.com

Dakota Corp., 77 Wales St., P.O. Box 543, Rutland, VT 05701 / 802-775-6062 or 800-451-4167; FAX: 802-773-3919

Daly, Charles/KBI, P.O. Box 6625, Harrisburg, PA 17112 / 866-DALY GUN

Da-Mar Gunsmith's, Inc., 102 1st St., Solvay, NY 13209 damascususa@inteliport.com, 149 Deans Farm Rd., Tyner, NC 27980 / 252-221-2010; FAX: 252-221-2010 damascususa@inteliport.com www.damascususa.com

Dan Wesson Firearms, 5169 Rt. 12 South, Norwich, NY 13815 / 607-336-1174; FAX: 607-336-2730 dwservice@cz-usa.com dz-usa.com

Dangler, Homer L., 2870 Lee Marie Dr., Adrian, MI 49221 / 517-266-1997

Danner Shoe Mfg. Co., 12722 N.E. Airport Way, Portland, OR 97230 / 503-251-1100 or 800-345-0430; FAX: 503-251-1119

Dan's Whetstone Co., Inc., 418 Hilltop Rd., Pearcy, AR 71964 / 501-767-1616; FAX: 501-767-9598 questions@danswhetstone.com www.danswhetstone.com

Danuser Machine Co., 550 E. Third St., P.O. Box 368, Fulton, MO 65251 / 573-642-2246; FAX: 573-642-2240 sales@danuser.com www.danuser.com

Dara-Nes, Inc. (See Nesci Enterprises, Inc.)

D'Arcy Echols & Co., P.O. Box 421, Millville, UT 84326 / 435-755-6842

Darlington Gun Works, Inc., P.O. Box 698, 516 S. 52 Bypass, Darlington, SC 29532 / 803-393-3931

Darwin Hensley Gunmaker, P.O. Box 329, Brightwood, OR 97011 / 503-622-5411

Data Tech Software Systems, 19312 East Eldorado Drive, Aurora, CO 80013

Dave Norin Schrank's Smoke & Gun, 2010 Washington St., Waukegan, IL 60085 / 708-662-4034

Dave's Gun Shop, P.O. Box 2824, Casper, WY 82602-2824 / 307-754-9724

David Clark Co., Inc., P.O. Box 15054, Worcester, MA 01615 / 508-756-6216; FAX: 508-753-5827 sales@davidclark.com www.davidclark.com

David Condon, Inc., 109 E. Washington St., Middleburg, VA 22117 / 703-687-5642

David Miller Co., 3131 E. Greenlee Rd., Tucson, AZ 85716 / 520-326-3117

David R. Chicoine, 1210 Jones Street, Gastonia, NC 28052 / 704-853-0265 bnpress@quik.com www.oldwestgunsmith.com

David W. Schwartz Custom Guns, 2505 Waller St., Eau Claire, WI 54703 / 715-832-1735

Davide Pedersoli and Co., Via Artigiani 57, Gardone VT, Brescia 25063, ITALY / 030-8915000; FAX: 030-8911019 info@davidepedersoli.com www.davide_pedersoli.com

Davis, Don, 1619 Heights, Katy, TX 77493 / 713-391-3090

Davis Industries (See Cobra Enterprises, Inc.)

Davis Products, Mike, 643 Loop Dr., Moses Lake, WA 98837 / 509-765-6178 or 509-766-7281

Daystate Ltd., Birch House Lanee, Cotes Heath Staffs, ST15.022, ENGLAND / 01782-791755; FAX: 01782-791617

Dayton Traister, 4778 N. Monkey Hill Rd., P.O. Box 593, Oak Harbor, WA 98277 / 360-679-4657; FAX: 360-675-1114

D-Boone Ent., Inc., 5900 Colwyn Dr., Harrisburg, PA 17109

Dead Eye's Sport Center, 76 Baer Rd., Shickshinny, PA 18655 / 570-256-7432 deadeyeprizz@aol.com

Deepeeka Exports Pvt. Ltd., D-78, Saket, Meerut-250-006, INDIA / 011-91-121-640363 or ; FAX: 011-91-121-640988 deepeeka@poboxes.com www.deepeeka.com

Defense Training International, Inc., 749 S. Lemay, Ste. A3-337, Ft. Collins, CO 80524 / 303-482-2520; FAX: 303-482-0548

deHaas Barrels, 20049 W. State Hwy. Z, Ridgeway, MO 64481 / 660-872-6308

Del Rey Products, P.O. Box 5134, Playa Del Rey, CA 90296-5134 / 213-823-0494

Delhi Gun House, 1374 Kashmere Gate, New Delhi 110 006, INDIA / 2940974; or 394-0974; FAX: 2917344 dgh@vsnl.com

Delorge, Ed, 6734 W. Main, Houma, LA 70360 / 985-223-0206 delorge@triparish.net www.eddelorge.com

Del-Sports, Inc., Dave Budin, P.O. Box 685, 817 Main St., Margaretville, NY 12455 / 845-586-4103; FAX: 845-586-4105

Delta Arms Ltd., P.O. Box 1000, Delta, VT 84624-1000

Delta Enterprises, 284 Hagemann Drive, Livermore, CA 94550

Delta Frangible Ammunition LLC, P.O. Box 2350, Stafford, VA 22555-2350 / 540-720-5778 or 800-339-1933; FAX: 540-720-5667 dfa@dfanet.com www.dfanet.com

Dem-Bart Checkering Tools, Inc., 1825 Bickford Ave., Snohomish, WA 98290 / 360-568-7356 walt@dembartco.com www.dembartco.com

Denver Instrument Co., 6542 Fig St., Arvada, CO 80004 / 800-321-1135; or 303-431-7255; FAX: 303-423-4831

DeSantis Holster & Leather Goods, Inc., 431 Bayview Ave., Amityville, NY 11701 / 631-841-6300; FAX: 631-841-6320 www.desantisholster.com

Desert Mountain Mfg., P.O. Box 130184, Coram, MT 59913 / 800-477-0762 or 406-387-5361; FAX: 406-387-5361

Detonics USA, 53 Perimeter Center East #200, Atlanta, GA 30346 / 866-759-1169

DGR Custom Rifles, 4191 37th Ave. SE, Tappen, ND 58487 / 701-327-8135

DGS, Inc., Dale A. Storey, 1117 E. 12th, Casper, WY 82601 / 307-237-2414; FAX: 307-237-2414 dalest@trib.com www.dgsrifle.com

DHB Products, 336 River View Dr., Verona, VA 24482-2547 / 703-836-2648

Diamond Machining Technology Inc. (See DMT)

Diamond Mfg. Co., P.O. Box 174, Wyoming, PA 18644 / 800-233-9601

Dibble, Derek A., 555 John Downey Dr., New Britain, CT 06051 / 203-224-2630

Dietz Gun Shop & Range, Inc., 421 Range Rd., New Braunfels, TX 78132 / 830-885-4662

Dilliott Gunsmithing, Inc., 657 Scarlett Rd., Dandridge, TN 37725 / 865-397-9204 gunsmithd@aol.com dilliottgunsmithing.com

Dillon Precision Products, Inc., 8009 East Dillon's Way, Scottsdale, AZ 85260 / 480-948-8009 or 800-762-3845; FAX: 480-998-2786 sales@dillonprecision.com www.dillonprecision.com

Dina Arms Corporation, P.O. Box 46, Royersford, PA 19468 / 610-287-0266; FAX: 610-287-0266 dinaarms@erols.com www.users.erds.com/dinarms

Dixie Gun Works, P.O. Box 130, Union City, TN 38281 / 731-885-0700; FAX: 731-885-0440 info@dixiegunworks.com www.dixiegunworks.com

Dixon Muzzleloading Shop, Inc., 9952 Kunkels Mill Rd., Kempton, PA 19529 / 610-756-6271 dixonmuzzleloading.com

DJ Illinois River Valley Calls, Inc., P.O. Box 370, S. Pekin, IL 61564-0370 / 866-352-2557; FAX: 309-348-3987 djcalls@grics.net www.djcalls.com

DKT, Inc., 14623 Vera Dr., Union, MI 49130-9744 / 800-741-7083 orders; FAX: 616-641-2015

DLO Mfg., 10807 SE Foster Ave., Arcadia, FL 33821-7304

DMT-Diamond Machining Technology, Inc., 85 Hayes Memorial Dr., Marlborough, MA 01752 FAX: 508-485-3924

Dohring Bullets, 100 W. 8 Mile Rd., Ferndale, MI 48220

MANUFACTURER'S DIRECTORY

Dolbare, Elizabeth, P.O. Box 502, Dubois, WY 82513-0502 / 307-450-7500 edolbare@hotmail.com www.scrimshaw-engraving.com

Domino, P.O. Box 108, 20019 Settimo Milanese, Milano, ITALY / 1-39-2-33512040; FAX: 1-39-2-33511587

Don Klein Custom Guns, 433 Murray Park Dr., Ripon, WI 54971 / 920-748-2931 daklein@charter.net www.donkleincustomguns.com

Donnelly, C. P., 405 Kubli Rd., Grants Pass, OR 97527 / 541-846-6604

Doskocil Mfg. Co., Inc., P.O. Box 1246, 4209 Barnett, Arlington, TX 76017 / 817-467-5116; FAX: 817-472-9810

Douglas Barrels, Inc., 5504 Big Tyler Rd., Charleston, WV 25313-1398 / 304-776-1341; FAX: 304-776-8560 www.benchrest.com/douglas

Downsizer Corp., P.O. Box 710316, Santee, CA 92072-0316 / 619-448-5510 www.downsizer.com

DPMS (Defense Procurement Manufacturing Services, Inc.), 13983 Industry Ave., Becker, MN 55308 / 800-578-DPMS or 763-261-5600; FAX: 763-261-5599

Dr. O's Products Ltd., P.O. Box 111, Niverville, NY 12130 / 518-784-3333; FAX: 518-784-2800

Dremel Mfg. Co., 4915-21st St., Racine, WI 53406

Dri-Slide, Inc., 411 N. Darling, Fremont, MI 49412 / 616-924-3950

Dropkick, 1460 Washington Blvd., Williamsport, PA 17701 / 717-326-6561; FAX: 717-326-4950

DS Arms, Inc., P.O. Box 370, 27 West 990 Industrial Ave., Barrington, IL 60010 / 847-277-7258; FAX: 847-277-7259 www.dsarms.com

DTM International, Inc., 40 Joslyn Rd., P.O. Box 5, Lake Orion, MI 48362 / 313-693-6670

Duane A. Hobbie Gunsmithing, 2412 Pattie Ave., Wichita, KS 67216 / 316-264-8266

Duane's Gun Repair (See DGR Custom Rifles)

Dubber, Michael W., P.O. Box 312, Evansville, IN 47702 / 812-424-9000; FAX: 812-424-6551

Duffy, Charles E. (See Guns Antique & Modern DBA), 224 Williams Ln., P.O. Box 2, West Hurley, NY 12491 / 845-679-2997 ceo1923@prodigy.net

Du-Lite Corp., 171 River Rd., Middletown, CT 06457 / 203-347-2505; FAX: 203-347-9404

Dumoulin, Ernest, Rue Florent Boclinville 8-10, 13-4041, Votten, BELGIUM / 41 27 78 92

Duncan's Gun Works, Inc., 1619 Grand Ave., San Marcos, CA 92078 / 760-727-0515

DunLyon R&D, Inc., 52151 E. U.S. Hwy. 60, Miami, AZ 85539 / 928-473-9027

Duofold, Inc., RD 3 Rt. 309, Valley Square Mall, Tamaqua, PA 18252 / 717-386-2666; FAX: 717-386-3652

Dybala Gun Shop, P.O. Box 1024, FM 3156, Bay City, TX 77414 / 409-245-0866

Dykstra, Doug, 411 N. Darling, Fremont, MI 49412 / 616-924-3950

Dynalite Products, Inc., 215 S. Washington St., Greenfield, OH 45123 / 513-981-2124

Dynamit Nobel-RWS, Inc., 81 Ruckman Rd., Closter, NJ 07624 / 201-767-7971; FAX: 201-767-1589

E

E&L Mfg., Inc., 4177 Riddle Bypass Rd., Riddle, OR 97469 / 541-874-2137; FAX: 541-874-3107

E. Arthur Brown Co. Inc., 4353 Hwy. 27 E., Alexandria, MN 56308 / 320-762-8847; FAX: 320-763-4310 www.eabco.com

E.A.A. Corp., P.O. Box 1299, Sharpes, FL 32959 / 407-639-4842 or 800-536-4442; FAX: 407-639-7006

Eagan, Donald. See: EAGAN GUNSMITHS

Eagan Gunsmiths, Donald V. Eagan, P.O. Box 196, Benton, PA 17814 / 570-925-6134

Eagle Arms, Inc. (See ArmaLite, Inc.)

Eagle Grips, Eagle Business Center, 460 Randy Rd., Carol Stream, IL 60188 / 800-323-6144 or 708-260-0400; FAX: 708-260-0486

Eagle Imports, Inc., 1750 Brielle Ave., Unit B1, Wanamassa, NJ 07712 / 732-493-0333; FAX: 732-493-0301 gsodini@aol.com www.bersafirearmsusa.com

E-A-R, Inc., Div. of Cabot Safety Corp., 5457 W. 79th St., Indianapolis, IN 46268 / 800-327-3431; FAX: 800-488-8007

EAW (See U.S. Importer-New England Custom Gun Serv

Eckelman Gunshop, CR 215, Brainerd, MN 56401 / 218-829-3176

Ed Brown Products, Inc., P.O. Box 492, Perry, MO 63462 / 573-565-3261; FAX: 573-565-2791 edbrown@edbrown.com www.edbrown.com

Ed Brown Products, Inc., 43825 Muldrow Trl., P.O. Box 492, Perry, MO 63462 / 573-565-3261; FAX: 573-565-2791 edbrown@edbrown.com www.edbrown.com

Edenpine, Inc. c/o Six Enterprises, Inc., 320 D Turtle Creek Ct., San Jose, CA 95125 / 408-999-0201; FAX: 408-999-0216

EdgeCraft Corp., S. Weiner, 825 Southwood Rd., Avondale, PA 19311 / 610-268-0500 or 800-342-3255; FAX: 610-268-3545 www.edgecraft.com

Edmisten Co., P.O. Box 1293, Boone, NC 28607

Edmund Scientific Co., 101 E. Gloucester Pike, Barrington, NJ 08033 / 609-543-6250

Ed's Gun House, Ed Kukowski, P.O. Box 62, Minnesota City, MN 55959 / 507-689-2925

Effebi SNC-Dr. Franco Beretta, via Rossa, 4, 25062, ITALY / 030-2751955; FAX: 030-2180414

Eggleston, Jere D., 400 Saluda Ave., Columbia, SC 29205 / 803-799-3402

Eichelberger Bullets, Wm., 158 Crossfield Rd., King Of Prussia, PA 19406

El Paso Saddlery Co., P.O. Box 27194, El Paso, TX 79926 / 915-544-2233; FAX: 915-544-2535 info@epsaddlery.com www.epsaddlery.com

Electro Prismatic Collimators, Inc., 1441 Manatt St., Lincoln, NE 68521

Electronic Shooters Protection, Inc., 15290 Gadsden Ct., Brighton, CO 80603 / 800-797-7791; FAX: 303-659-8668 esp@usa.net espamerican.com

Eley Ltd., Selco Way Minworth Industrial Estate, Minworth Sutton Coldfield, West Midlands, B76 1BA ENGLAND / 44 0 121-313-4567; FAX: 44 0 121-313-4568 www.eley.co.uk

Ellett Bros., 267 Columbia Ave., P.O. Box 128, Chapin, SC 29036 / 803-345-3751 or 800-845-3711; FAX: 803-345-1820 www.ellettbrothers.com

Ellicott Arms, Inc. / Woods Pistolsmithing, 8390 Sunset Dr., Ellicott City, MD 21043 / 410-465-7979

EMAP USA, 6420 Wilshire Blvd., Los Angeles, CA 90048 / 213-782-2000; FAX: 213-782-2867

Emerging Technologies, Inc. (See Laseraim Technologies, Inc.)

EMF Co. Inc., 1900 E. Warner Ave., Suite 1-D, Santa Ana, CA 92705 / 949-261-6611; FAX: 949-756-0133

Empire Cutlery Corp., 12 Kruger Ct., Clifton, NJ 07013 / 201-472-5155; FAX: 201-779-0759

Empire Rifles, P.O. Box 406, Meriden, NH 03770 info@empirerifles.com www.empirerifles.com

English, Inc., A.G., 708 S. 12th St., Broken Arrow, OK 74012 / 918-251-3399 info@agenglish.com www.agenglish.com

Engraving Artistry, 36 Alto Rd., Burlington, CT 06013 / 860-673-6837 bobburt44@hotmail.com

Enguix Import-Export, Alpujarras 58, Alzira, Valencia, SPAIN / (96) 241 43 95; FAX: (96) 241 43 95

Enhanced Presentations, Inc., 5929 Market St., Wilmington, NC 28405 / 910-799-1622; FAX: 910-799-5004

Ensign-Bickford Co., The, 660 Hopmeadow St., Simsbury, CT 06070

Entreprise Arms, Inc., 5321 Irwindale Ave., Irwindale, CA 91706-2025 / 626-962-8712; FAX: 626-962-4692 www.entreprise.com

EPC, 1441 Manatt St., Lincoln, NE 68521 / 402-476-3946

Erhardt, Dennis, 4508 N. Montana Ave., Helena, MT 59602 / 406-442-4533

Essex Arms, P.O. Box 363, Island Pond, VT 05846 / 802-723-6203; FAX: 802-723-6203

Estate Cartridge, Inc., 900 Bob Ehlen Dr., Anoka, MN 55303-7502 / 409-856-7277; FAX: 409-856-5486

Euber Bullets, No. Orwell Rd., Orwell, VT 05760 / 802-948-2621

Euroarms of America, Inc., P.O. Box 3277, Winchester, VA 22604 / 540-662-1863; FAX: 540-662-4464 tell-us@euroarms.net www.euroarms.net

Euro-Imports, George Tripes, 412 Slayden St., Yoakum, TX 77995 / 361-293-9353; FAX: 361-293-9353 mrbrno@yahoo.com

European American Armory Corp. (See E.A.A. Corp.)

Eversull Co., Inc., 1 Tracemont, Boyce, LA 71409 / 318-793-8728; FAX: 318-793-5483 bestguns@aol.com

Evolution Gun Works, Inc., 48 Belmont Ave., Quakertown, PA 18951-1347 www.egw-guns.com

Excalibur Electro Optics, Inc., P.O. Box 400, Fogelsville, PA 18051-0400 / 610-391-9105; FAX: 610-391-9220

Excalibur Publications, P.O. Box 89667, Tucson, AZ 85752 / 520-575-9057 excalibureditor@earthlink.net

Excel Industries, Inc., 4510 Carter Ct., Chino, CA 91710 / 909-627-2404; FAX: 909-627-7817

Executive Protection Institute, P.O. Box 802, Berryville, VA 22611 / 540-554-2540; FAX: 540-554-2558 ruk@crosslink.net www.personalprotecion.com

Eze-Lap Diamond Prods., P.O. Box 2229, 15164 W. State St., Westminster, CA 92683 / 714-847-1555; FAX: 714-897-0280

E-Z-Way Systems, P.O. Box 4310, Newark, OH 43058-4310 / 614-345-6645 or 800-848-2072; FAX: 614-345-6600

F

F.A.I.R., Via Gitti, 41, 25060 Marcheno (BS), 25060 Marcheno Bresc, ITALY / 030 861162-8610344; FAX: 030 8610179 info@fair.it www.fair.it

F+W Publications, Inc., 700 E. State St., Iola, WI 54990 / 715-445-2214; FAX: 715-445-4087

Fabarm S.p.A., Via Averolda 31, 25039 Travagliato, Brescia, ITALY / 030-6863629; FAX: 030-6863684 info@fabarm.com www.fabarm.com

Fagan Arms, 22952 15 Mile Rd., Clinton Township, MI 48035 / 810-465-4637; FAX: 810-792-6996

Faith Associates, P.O. Box 549, Flat Rock, NC 28731-0549 FAX: 828-697-6827

Falcon Industries, Inc., P.O. Box 1690, Edgewood, NM 87015 / 505-281-3783; FAX: 505-281-3991 shines@ergogrips.net www.ergogrips.net

Far North Outfitters, Box 1252, Bethel, AK 99559

Farm Form Decoys, Inc., 1602 Biovu, P.O. Box 748, Galveston, TX 77553 / 409-744-0762 or 409-765-6361; FAX: 409-765-8513

Farr Studio, Inc., 17149 Bournbrook Ln., Jeffersonton, VA 22724-1796 / 615-638-8825

Farrar Tool Co., Inc., 11855 Cog Hill Dr., Whittier, CA 90601-1902 / 310-863-4367; FAX: 310-863-5123

Faulhaber Wildlocker, Dipl.-Ing. Norbert Wittasek, Seilergasse 2, A-1010 Wien, AUSTRIA / 43-1-5137001; FAX: 43-1-5137001 faulhaber1@utanet.at

Faulk's Game Call Co., Inc., 616 18th St., Lake Charles, LA 70601 / 337-436-9726; FAX: 337-494-7205

Faust Inc., T. G., 544 Minor St., Reading, PA 19602 / 610-375-8549; FAX: 610-375-4488

Fautheree, Andy, P.O. Box 4607, Pagosa Springs, CO 81157 / 970-731-5003; FAX: 970-731-5009

Feather, Flex Decoys, 4500 Doniphan Dr., Neosho, MO 64850 / 318-746-8596; FAX: 318-742-4815

Federal Cartridge Co., 900 Ehlen Dr., Anoka, MN 55303 / 612-323-2300; FAX: 612-323-2506

Federal Champion Target Co., 232 Industrial Pkwy., Richmond, IN 47374 / 800-441-4971; FAX: 317-966-7747

Federated-Fry (See Fry Metals)

FEG, Budapest, Soroksariut 158, H-1095, HUNGARY

Feinwerkbau Westinger & Altenburger, Neckarstrasse 43, 78727, Oberndorf a. N., GERMANY / 07423-814-0; FAX: 07423-814-200 info@feinwerkbau.de www.feinwerkbau.de

Ferguson, Bill, P.O. Box 1238, Sierra Vista, AZ 85636 / 520-458-5321; FAX: 520-458-9125

Ferguson, Bill. See: BULLET METALS

FERLIB, Via Parte 33 Marcheno/BS, Marcheno/BS, ITALY / 00390308610191; FAX: 00390308966882 info@ferlib.com www.ferlib.com

Ferris Firearms, 7110 F.M. 1863, Bulverde, TX 78163 / 210-980-4424

Fieldsport Ltd., Bryan Bilinski, 3313 W. South Airport Rd., Traverse City, MI 49684 / 616-933-0767

Fiocchi Munizioni S.A. (See U.S. Importer-Fiocch

Fiocchi of America, Inc., 5030 Fremont Rd., Ozark, MO 65721 / 417-725-4118 or 800-721-2666; FAX: 417-725-1039

Firearm Brokers, 4143 Taylor Blvd., Louisville, KY 40215 / 502-366-0555 firearmbrokers@aol.com www.firearmbrokers.com

Firearms Co. Ltd. / Alpine (See U.S. Importer-Mandall

Firearms Engraver's Guild of America, 3011 E. Pine Dr., Flagstaff, AZ 86004 / 928-527-8427 fegainfo@fega.com

Fisher, Jerry A., 631 Crane Mt. Rd., Big Fork, MT 59911 / 406-837-2722

Fisher Custom Firearms, 2199 S. Kittredge Way, Aurora, CO 80013 / 303-755-3710

Fitzgerald, Jack. See: CLENZOIL WORLDWIDE CORP.

Flambeau, Inc., 15981 Valplast Rd., Middlefield, OH 44062 / 216-632-1631; FAX: 216-632-1581 www.flambeau.com

Flayderman & Co., Inc., P.O. Box 2446, Fort Lauderdale, FL 33303 / 954-761-8855 www.flayderman.com

Fleming Firearms, 7720 E. 126th St. N., Collinsville, OK 74021-7016 / 918-665-3624

Fletcher-Bidwell, LLC, 305 E. Terhune St., Viroqua, WI 54665-1631 / 866-637-1860 fbguns@netscape.net

Flintlocks, Etc., 160 Rossiter Rd., P.O. Box 181, Richmond, MA 01254 / 413-698-3822; FAX: 413-698-3866 flintetc@berkshire.rr.com

Flitz International Ltd., 821 Mohr Ave., Waterford, WI 53185 / 414-534-5898; FAX: 414-534-2991

Fluoramics, Inc., 18 Industrial Ave., Mahwah, NJ 07430 / 800-922-0075; FAX: 201-825-7035 pdouglas@fluoramics.com www.tufoil.com

Flynn's Custom Guns, P.O. Box 7461, Alexandria, LA 71306 / 318-455-7130

FN Manufacturing, P.O. Box 24257, Columbia, SC 29224 / 803-736-0522

Folks, Donald E., 205 W. Lincoln St., Pontiac, IL 61764 / 815-844-7901

Foredom Electric Co., Rt. 6, 16 Stony Hill Rd., Bethel, CT 06801 / 203-792-8622

Forgreens Tool & Mfg., Inc., P.O. Box 955, Robert Lee, TX 76945 / 915-453-2800; FAX: 915-453-2460

Forkin Custom Classics, 205 10th Ave. S.W., White Sulphur Spring, MT 59645 / 406-547-2344

Forrest Tool Co., P.O. Box 768, 44380 Gordon Ln., Mendocino, CA 95460 / 707-937-2141; FAX: 717-937-1817

Forster, Kathy (See Custom Checkering)

Forster, Larry L., Box 212, 216 Hwy. 13 E., Gwinner, ND 58040-0212 / 701-678-2475

Forster Products, Inc., 310 E. Lanark Ave., Lanark, IL 61046 / 815-493-6360; FAX: 815-493-2371 info@forsterproducts.com www.forsterproductscom

Fort Hill Gunstocks, 12807 Fort Hill Rd., Hillsboro, OH 45133 / 513-466-2763

Fort Knox Security Products, 1051 N. Industrial Park Rd., Orem, UT 84057 / 801-224-7233 or 800-821-5216; FAX: 801-226-5493

Forthofer's Gunsmithing & Knifemaking, 5535 U.S. Hwy. 93S, Whitefish, MT 59937-8411 / 406-862-2674

Fortune Products, Inc., 205 Hickory Creek Rd., Marble Falls, TX 78654 / 210-693-6111; FAX: 210-693-6394 randy@accusharp.com

Forty-Five Ranch Enterprises, Box 1080, Miami, OK 74355-1080 / 918-542-5875

Foster, . See: ACCURACY INTERNATIONAL

Fountain Products, 492 Prospect Ave., West Springfield, MA 01089 / 413-781-4651; FAX: 413-733-8217

Fowler, Bob (See Black Powder Products)

Fox River Mills, Inc., P.O. Box 298, 227 Poplar St., Osage, IA 50461 / 515-732-3798; FAX: 515-732-5128

Fraim, William. See: ACUSPORT CORPORATION

Frank Knives, 1147 SW Bryson Str. 1, Dallas, OR 97338 / 503-831-1489; FAX: 541-563-3041

Frank Mittermeier, Inc., P.O. Box 1, Bronx, NY 10465

Franzen International, Inc. (See U.S. Importer-Importer Co.)

Fred F. Wells/Wells Sport Store, 110 N. Summit St., Prescott, AZ 86301 / 928-445-3655 www.wellssportstore@cableone.net

Freedom Arms, Inc., P.O. Box 150, Freedom, WY 83120 / 307-883-2468; FAX: 307-883-2005

Fremont Tool Works, 1214 Prairie, Ford, KS 67842 / 316-369-2327

Front Sight Firearms Training Institute, P.O. Box 2619, Aptos, CA 95001 / 800-987-7719; FAX: 408-684-2137

Frontier, 2910 San Bernardo, Laredo, TX 78040 / 956-723-5409; FAX: 956-723-1774

Frontier Arms Co., Inc., 401 W. Rio Santa Cruz, Green Valley, AZ 85614-3932

Frontier Products Co., 2401 Walker Rd., Roswell, NM 88201-8950 / 505-627-0763

Frost Cutlery Co., P.O. Box 22636, Chattanooga, TN 37422 / 615-894-6079; FAX: 615-894-9576

Fry Metals, 4100 6th Ave., Altoona, PA 16602 / 814-946-1611

Fujinon, Inc., 10 High Point Dr., Wayne, NJ 07470 / 201-633-5600; FAX: 201-633-5216

Fullmer, Geo. M., 2499 Mavis St., Oakland, CA 94601 / 510-533-4193

Fulton Armory, 8725 Bollman Place No. 1, Savage, MD 20763 / 301-490-9485; FAX: 301-490-9547 www.fulton.armory.com

Furr Arms, 91 N. 970 West, Orem, UT 84057 / 801-226-3877; FAX: 801-226-3877

G

G&H Decoys, Inc., P.O. Box 1208, Hwy. 75 North, Henryetta, OK 74437 / 918-652-3314; FAX: 918-652-3400

G.C. Bullet Co., Inc., 40 Mokelumne River Dr., Lodi, CA 95240

G.G. & G., 3602 E. 42nd Stravenue, Tucson, AZ 85713 / 520-748-7167; FAX: 520-748-7583 ggg&3@aol.com www.ggg&3.com

G.H. Enterprises Ltd., Bag 10, Okotoks, AB T0L 1T0 CANADA / 403-938-6070

G.U., Inc. (See U.S. Importer-New SKB Arms Co.)

G96 Products Co., Inc., 85 5th Ave., Bldg. #6, Paterson, NJ 07544 / 973-684-4050; FAX: 973-684-3848 g96prod@aol

Gage Manufacturing, 663 W. 7th St., A, San Pedro, CA 90731 / 310-832-3546

Gaillard Barrels, Box 68, St. Brieux, SK S0K 3V0 CANADA / 306-752-3769; FAX: 306-752-5969

Galati International, P.O. Box 10, 616 Burley Ridge Rd., Wesco, MO 65586 / 636-584-0785; FAX: 573-775-4308 support@galatiinternational.com www.galatiinternational.com

Galaxy Imports Ltd., Inc., P.O. Box 3361, Victoria, TX 77903 / 361-573-4867; FAX: 361-576-9622 galaxy@cox-internet.com

GALCO International Ltd., 2019 W. Quail Ave., Phoenix, AZ 85027 / 623-474-7070; FAX: 623-582-6854 customerservice@usgalco.com www.usgalco.com

Galena Industries AMT, 5463 Diaz St., Irwindale, CA 91706 / 626-856-8883; FAX: 626-856-8878

Gamba Renato Bremec Srl, Via Artigiani 93, 25063 Gardone V.T. BS, ITALY / 30-8910264-5; FAX: 30-8912180 infocomm@renatogamba.it www.renatogamba.it

Gamba, USA, P.O. Box 60452, Colorado Springs, CO 80960 / 719-578-1145; FAX: 719-444-0731

Game Haven Gunstocks, 13750 Shire Rd., Wolverine, MI 49799 / 616-525-8257

Gamebore Division, Polywad, Inc., P.O. Box 7916, Macon, GA 31209 / 478-477-0669; or 800-998-0669

Gamo (See U.S. Importers-Arms United Corp., Daisy M

Gamo USA, Inc., 3911 SW 47th Ave., Suite 914, Fort Lauderdale, FL 33314 / 954-581-5822; FAX: 954-581-3165 gamousa@gate.net www.gamo.com

Gander Mountain, Inc., 12400 Fox River Rd., Wilmont, WI 53192 / 414-862-6848

GAR, 590 McBride Ave., West Paterson, NJ 07424 / 973-754-1114; FAX: 973-754-1114 garreloading@aol.com www.garreloading.com

Garcia National Gun Traders, Inc., 225 SW 22nd Ave., Miami, FL 33135 / 305-642-2355

Garrett Cartridges, Inc., P.O. Box 178, Chehalis, WA 98532 / 360-736-0702 www.garrettcartridges.com

Garthwaite Pistolsmith, Inc., Jim, 12130 State Route 405, Watsontown, PA 17777 / 570-538-1566 www.garthwaite.com

Gary Goudy Classic Stocks, 1512 S. 5th St., Dayton, WA 99328 / 509-382-2726 goudy@icehouse.net

Gary Reeder Custom Guns, 2601 7th Ave. E., Flagstaff, AZ 86004 / 928-526-3313; FAX: 928-527-0840 gary@reedercustomguns.com www.reedercustomguns.com

Gator Guns & Repair, 7952 Kenai Spur Hwy., Kenai, AK 99611-8311

Gaucher Armes, S.A., 46 rue Desjoyaux, 42000, Saint-Etienne, FRANCE / 04-77-33-38-92; FAX: 04-77-61-95-72

GDL Enterprises, 409 Le Gardeur, Slidell, LA 70460 / 504-649-0693

Gehmann, Walter (See Huntington Die Specialties)

Genco, P.O. Box 5704, Asheville, NC 28803

Genecco Gun Works, 10512 Lower Sacramento Rd., Stockton, CA 95210 / 209-951-0706; FAX: 209-931-3872

Gene's Custom Guns, P.O. Box 10534, White Bear Lake, MN 55110 / 651-429-5105; FAX: 651-429-7365

Gentex Corp., 5 Tinkham Ave., Derry, NH 03038 / 603-434-0311; FAX: 603-434-3002 sales@derry.gentexcorp.com www.derry.gentexcorp.com

Gentner Bullets, 109 Woodlawn Ave., Upper Darby, PA 19082 / 610-352-9396 dongentner@rcn.com www.gentnerbullets.com

Gentry Custom LLC, 314 N. Hoffman, Belgrade, MT 59714 / 406-388-GUNS gentryshop@earthlink.net www.gentrycustom.com

George & Roy's, P.O. Box 2125, Sisters, OR 97759-2125 / 503-228-5424 or 800-553-3022; FAX: 503-225-9409

George Hoenig, Inc., 6521 Morton Dr., Boise, ID 83704 / 208-375-1116; FAX: 208-375-1116

George Ibberson (Sheffield) Ltd., 25-31 Allen St., Sheffield, S3 7AW ENGLAND / 0114-2766123; FAX: 0114-2738465 sales@eggintongroup.co.uk www.eggintongroup.com

Gerber Legendary Blades, 14200 SW 72nd Ave., Portland, OR 97223 / 503-639-6161 or 800-950-6161; FAX: 503-684-7008

Gervais, Mike, 3804 S. Cruise Dr., Salt Lake City, UT 84109 / 801-277-7729

Getz Barrel Company, P.O. Box 88, 426 E. Market St., Beavertown, PA 17813 / 570-658-7263; FAX: 570-658-4110 www.getzbrl.com

Giacomo Sporting USA, 6234 Stokes Lee Center Rd., Lee Center, NY 13363

Gibbs Rifle Co., Inc., 219 Lawn St., Martinsburg, WV 25401 / 304-262-1651; FAX: 304-262-1658 support@gibbsrifle.com www.gibbsrifle.com

Gil Hebard Guns, Inc., 125 Public Square, Knoxville, IL 61448 / 309-289-2700; FAX: 309-289-2233

Gilbert Equipment Co., Inc., 960 Downtowner Rd., Mobile, AL 36609 / 205-344-3322

Gillmann, Edwin, 33 Valley View Dr., Hanover, PA 17331 / 717-632-1662 gillmaned@superpa.net

Gilmore Sports Concepts, Inc., 5949 S. Garnett Rd., Tulsa, OK 74146 / 918-250-3810; FAX: 918-250-3845 info@gilmoresports.com www.gilmoresports.com

Glacier Glove, 4890 Aircenter Circle, Suite 210, Reno, NV 89502 / 702-825-8225; FAX: 702-825-6544

Glaser LLC, P.O. Box 173, Sturgis, SD 57785 / 605-347-4544 or 800-221-3489; FAX: 605-347-5055 email@corbon.com www.safetyslug.com

Glaser Safety Slug, Inc. (see CorBon/Glaser safetyslug.com

Glass, Herb, P.O. Box 25, Bullville, NY 10915 / 914-361-3021

Glimm, Jerome. See: GLIMM'S CUSTOM GUN ENGRAVING

Glimm's Custom Gun Engraving, Jerome C. Glimm, 19 S. Maryland, Conrad, MT 59425 / 406-278-3574 lag@mcn.net www.gunengraver.biz

Glock GmbH, P.O. Box 50, A-2232, Deutsch, Wagram, AUSTRIA

Glock, Inc., P.O. Box 369, Smyrna, GA 30081 / 770-432-1202; FAX: 770-433-8719

Glynn Scobey Duck & Goose Calls, Rt. 3, Box 37, Newbern, TN 38059 / 731-643-6128

GML Products, Inc., 394 Laredo Dr., Birmingham, AL 35226 / 205-979-4867

Goens, Dale W., P.O. Box 224, Cedar Crest, NM 87008 / 505-281-5419

Goergen's Gun Shop, Inc., 17985 538th Ave., Austin, MN 55912 / 507-433-9280

GOEX, Inc., P.O. Box 659, Doyline, LA 71023-0659 / 318-382-9300; FAX: 318-382-9303 mfahringer@goexpowder.com www.goexpowder.com

Golden Age Arms Co., 115 E. High St., Ashley, OH 43003 / 614-747-2488

Golden Bear Bullets, 3065 Fairfax Ave., San Jose, CA 95148 / 408-238-9515

Goodling's Gunsmithing, 1950 Stoverstown Rd., Spring Grove, PA 17362 / 717-225-3350

Goodwin, Fred. See: GOODWIN'S GUNS

Goodwin's Guns, Fred Goodwin, Silver Ridge, ME 04776 / 207-365-4451

Gotz Bullets, 11426 Edgemere Ter., Roscoe, IL 61073-8232

Gould & Goodrich Leather, Inc., 709 E. McNeil St., Lillington, NC 27546 / 910-893-2071; FAX: 910-893-4742 info@gouldusa.com www.gouldusa.com

Gourmet Artistic Engraving, Geoffroy Gournet, 820 Paxinosa Ave., Easton, PA 18042 / 610-559-0710 www.geoffroygournet.com

Gournet, Geoffroy. See: GOURNET ARTISTIC ENGRAVING

Grace, Charles E., 718 E. 2nd, Trinidad, CO 81082 / 719-846-9435 chuckgrace@sensonics.org

Grace Metal Products, P.O. Box 67, Elk Rapids, MI 49629 / 616-264-8133

Graf & Sons, 4050 S. Clark St., Mexico, MO 65265 / 573-581-2266; FAX: 573-581-2875 customerservice@grafs.com www.grafs.com

Grand Slam Hunting Products, Box 121, 25454 Military Rd., Cascade, MD 21719 / 301-241-4900; FAX: 301-241-4900 rlj6call@aol.com

Granite Mountain Arms, Inc., 3145 W. Hidden Acres Trail, Prescott, AZ 86305 / 520-541-9758; FAX: 520-445-6826

Grant, Howard V., Hiawatha 15, Woodruff, WI 54568 / 715-356-7146

Graphics Direct, P.O. Box 372421, Reseda, CA 91337-2421 / 818-344-9002

Graves Co., 1800 Andrews Ave., Pompano Beach, FL 33069 / 800-327-9103; FAX: 305-960-0301

Grayback Wildcats, Mike Beeks, 5306 Bryant Ave., Klamath Falls, OR 97603 / 541-884-1072; FAX: 541-884-1072 graybackwildcats@aol.com

Graybill's Gun Shop, 1035 Ironville Pike, Columbia, PA 17512 / 717-684-2739

Great American Gunstock Co., 3420 Industrial Drive, Yuba City, CA 95993 / 800-784-4867; FAX: 530-671-3906 gunstox@hotmail.com www.gunstocks.com

Green, Arthur S., 485 S. Robertson Blvd., Beverly Hills, CA 90211 / 310-274-1283

Green Head Game Call Co., RR 1, Box 33, Lacon, IL 61540 / 309-246-2155

Green Mountain Rifle Barrel Co., Inc., P.O. Box 2670, 153 W. Main St., Conway, NH 03818 / 603-447-1095; FAX: 603-447-1099 info@gmriflebarrel.com www.gmriflebarrel.com

Greenwood Precision, P.O. Box 407, Rogersville, MO 65742 / 417-725-2330

Greg Gunsmithing Repair, 3732 26th Ave. N., Robbinsdale, MN 55422 / 612-529-8103

Greg's Superior Products, P.O. Box 46219, Seattle, WA 98146

Greider Precision, 431 Santa Marina Ct., Escondido, CA 92029 / 760-480-8892; FAX: 760-480-9800 greider@msn.com

Gre-Tan Rifles, 29742 W.C.R. 50, Kersey, CO 80644 / 970-353-6176; FAX: 970-356-5940 www.gtrtooling.com

Griffin & Howe, Inc., 340 W. Putnam Ave., Greenwich, CT 06830 / 203-618-0270 info@griffinhowe.com www.griffinhowe.com

Griffin & Howe, Inc., 33 Claremont Rd., Bernardsville, NJ 07924 / 908-766-2287; FAX: 908-766-1068 info@griffinhowe.com www.griffinhowe.com

Grifon, Inc., 58 Guinam St., Waltham, MS 02154

Groenewold, John. See: JG AIRGUNS, LLC

GRS/Glendo Corp., P.O. Box 1153, 900 Overlander St., Emporia, KS 66801 / 620-343-1084 or 800-836-3519; FAX: 620-343-9640 glendo@glendo.com www.glendo.com

Grulla Armes, Apartado 453, Avda Otaloa 12, Eiber, SPAIN

Gruning Precision, Inc., 7101 Jurupa Ave., No. 12, Riverside, CA 92504 / 909-289-4371; FAX: 909-689-7791 gruningprecision@earthlink.net www.gruningprecision.com

GSI, Inc., 7661 Commerce Ln., Trussville, AL 35173 / 205-655-8299

Guarasi, Robert. See: WILCOX INDUSTRIES CORP.

Guardsman Products, 411 N. Darling, Fremont, MI 49412 / 616-924-3950

Gun City, 212 W. Main Ave., Bismarck, ND 58501 / 701-223-2304

Gun Doc, Inc., 5405 NW 82nd Ave., Miami, FL 33166 / 305-477-2777; FAX: 305-477-2778 www.gundoc.com

Gun Doctor, The, P.O. Box 72817, Roselle, IL 60172 / 708-894-0668

Gun Hunter Books (See Gun Hunter Trading Co.), 5075 Heisig St., Beaumont, TX 77705 / 409-835-3006; FAX: 409-838-2266 gunhuntertrading@hotmail.com

Gun Hunter Trading Co., 5075 Heisig St., Beaumont, TX 77705 / 409-835-3006; FAX: 409-838-2266 gunhuntertrading@hotmail.com

Gun Leather Limited, 116 Lipscomb, Fort Worth, TX 76104 / 817-334-0225; FAX: 800-247-0609

Gun List (See F+W Publications), 700 E. State St., Iola, WI 54990 / 715-445-2214; FAX: 715-445-4087

Gun Room Press, The, 127 Raritan Ave., Highland Park, NJ 08904 / 732-545-4344; FAX: 732-545-6686 gunbooks@rutgersgunbooks.com www.rutgersgunbooks.com

Gun Room, The, 1121 Burlington, Muncie, IN 47302 / 765-282-9073; FAX: 765-282-5270 bshstleguns@aol.com

Gun Shop, The, 62778 Spring Creek Rd., Montrose, CO 81401

Gun Shop, The, 5550 S. 900 East, Salt Lake City, UT 84117 / 801-263-3633

Gun South, Inc. (See GSI, Inc.)

Gun Vault, 7339 E. Acoma Dr., Ste. 7, Scottsdale, AZ 85260 / 602-951-6855

Gun Works, The, 247 S. 2nd St., Springfield, OR 97477 / 541-741-4118; FAX: 541-988-1097 info@thegunworks.com www.thegunworks.com

Gun-Alert, 1010 N. Maclay Ave., San Fernando, CA 91340 / 818-365-0864; FAX: 818-365-1308

Guncraft Books (See Guncraft Sports, Inc.), 10737 Dutchtown Rd., Knoxville, TN 37932 / 865-966-4545; FAX: 865-966-4500 findit@guncraft.com www.guncraft.com

Guncraft Sports, Inc., 10737 Dutchtown Rd., Knoxville, TN 37932 / 865-966-4545; FAX: 865-966-4500 findit@guncraft.com www.usit.net/guncraft

Guncraft Sports, Inc., Marie C. Wiest, 10737 Dutchtown Rd., Knoxville, TN 37932 / 865-966-4545; FAX: 865-966-4500 findit@guncraft.com www.guncraft.com

Guncrafter Industries, 171 Madison 1510, Huntsville, AR 72740 / 479-665-2466 www.guncrafterindustries.com

Gun-Ho Sports Cases, 110 E. 10th St., St. Paul, MN 55101 / 612-224-9491

Gunline Tools, 2950 Saturn St., "O", Brea, CA 92821 / 714-993-5100; FAX: 714-572-4128

Gunnerman Books, P.O. Box 81697, Rochester Hills, MI 48308 / 248-608-2856 gunnermanbks@att.net

Guns Antique & Modern DBA / Charles E. Duffy, 224 Williams Lane, P.O. Box 2, West Hurley, NY 12491 / 845-679-2997 ceo1923@prodigy.net

GUNS Magazine, 12345 World Trade Dr., San Diego, CA 92128-3743 / 619-297-5350; FAX: 619-297-5353

Gunsight, The, 1712 N. Placentia Ave., Fullerton, CA 92631

Gunsite Training Center, P.O. Box 700, Paulden, AZ 86334 / 520-636-4565; FAX: 520-636-1236

Gunsmithing Ltd., 57 Unquowa Rd., Fairfield, CT 06824 / 203-254-0436; FAX: 203-254-1535

Gunsmithing, Inc., 30 W. Buchanan St., Colorado Springs, CO 80907 / 719-632-3795; FAX: 719-632-3493 www.nealsguns.com

Gurney, F. R., Box 13, Sooke, BC V0S 1N0 CANADA / 604-642-5282; FAX: 604-642-7859

H

H&B Forge Co., Rt. 2, Geisinger Rd., Shiloh, OH 44878 / 419-895-1856

H&P Publishing, 7174 Hoffman Rd., San Angelo, TX 76905 / 915-655-5953

H&R 1871.LLC, 60 Industrial Rowe, Gardner, MA 01440 / 508-632-9393; FAX: 508-632-2300 hr1871@hr1871.com www.hr1871.com

H. Krieghoff Gun Co., Boschstrasse 22, D-89079, Ulm, GERMANY / 731-401820; FAX: 731-4018270

H.K.S. Products, 7841 Founion Dr., Florence, KY 41042 / 606-342-7841 or 800-354-9814; FAX: 606-342-5865

H.P. White Laboratory, Inc., 3114 Scarboro Rd., Street, MD 21154 / 410-838-6550; FAX: 410-838-2802 info@hpwhite.com www.hpwhite.com

Hafner World Wide, Inc., P.O. Box 1987, Lake City, FL 32055 / 904-755-6481; FAX: 904-755-6595 hafner@isgroupe.net

Hakko Co. Ltd., 1-13-12, Narimasu, Itabashiku Tokyo, JAPAN / 03-5997-7870/2; FAX: 81-3-5997-7840

Half Moon Rifle Shop, 490 Halfmoon Rd., Columbia Falls, MT 59912 / 406-892-4409 halfmoonrs@centurytel.net

Hall Manufacturing, 142 CR 406, Clanton, AL 35045 / 205-755-4094

Hall Plastics, Inc., John, P.O. Box 1526, Alvin, TX 77512 / 713-489-8709

Hallberg, Fritz. See: CAMBOS OUTDOORSMAN

Hallowell & Co., P.O. Box 1445, Livingston, MT 59047 / 406-222-4770; FAX: 406-222-4792 morris@hallowellco.com www.hallowellco.com

Hally Caller, 443 Wells Rd., Doylestown, PA 18901 / 215-345-6354; FAX: 215-345-6354 info@hallycaller.com www.hallycaller.com

Hamilton, Alex B. (See Ten-Ring Precision, Inc.)

Hammans, Charles E., P.O. Box 788, 2022 McCracken, Stuttgart, AR 72160-0788 / 870-673-1388

Hammerli AG, Industrieplaz, a/Rheinpall, CH-8212 Neuhausen, SWITZERLAND info@hammerli.com www.haemmerliich.com

Hammerli Service-Precision Mac, Rudolf Marent, 9711 Tiltree St., Houston, TX 77075 / 713-946-7028 rmarent@webtv.net

Hammerli USA, 19296 Oak Grove Circle, Groveland, CA 95321 FAX: 209-962-5311

Hammond Custom Guns Ltd., 619 S. Pandora, Gilbert, AZ 85234 / 602-892-3437

HandCrafts Unltd. (See Clements' Custom Leathercraft), 1741 Dallas St., Aurora, CO 80010-2018 / 303-364-0403; FAX: 303-739-9824 gryphons@home.com kuntaoslcat.com

Handgun Press, P.O. Box 406, Glenview, IL 60025 / 847-657-6500; FAX: 847-724-8831 handgunpress@comcast.net

Hank's Gun Shop, Box 370, 50 W. 100 South, Monroe, UT 84754 / 435-527-4456 hanksgs@altazip.com

Hanned Line, The, 4463 Madoc Way, San Jose, CA 95130 smith@hanned.com

Hanned Precision (See The Hanned Line)

Hansen & Co., 244-246 Old Post Rd., Southport, CT 06490 / 203-259-6222; FAX: 203-254-3832

Hanson's Gun Center, Dick, 233 Everett Dr., Colorado Springs, CO 80911

Harford (See U.S. Importer-EMF Co., Inc.)

Harper's Custom Stocks, 928 Lombrano St., San Antonio, TX 78207 / 210-732-7174

Harrell's Precision, 5756 Hickory Dr., Salem, VA 24153 / 540-380-2683

Harrington & Richardson (See H&R 1871, Inc.)

Harris Engineering Inc., Dept. GD54, 999 Broadway, Barlow, KY 42024 / 270-334-3633; FAX: 270-334-3000

Harris Enterprises, P.O. Box 105, Bly, OR 97622 / 503-353-2625

Harris Hand Engraving, Paul A., 113 Rusty Ln., Boerne, TX 78006-5746 / 512-391-5121

Harris Publications, 1115 Broadway, New York, NY 10010 / 212-807-7100; FAX: 212-627-4678

Harrison Bullets, 6437 E. Hobart St., Mesa, AZ 85205

Harry Lawson Co., 3328 N. Richey Blvd., Tucson, AZ 85716 / 520-326-1117; FAX: 520-326-1117

Hart & Son, Inc., Robert W., 401 Montgomery St., Nescopeck, PA 18635 / 717-752-3655; FAX: 717-752-1088

Hart Rifle Barrels, Inc., P.O. Box 182, 1690 Apulia Rd., Lafayette, NY 13084 / 315-677-9841; FAX: 315-677-9610 hartrb@aol.com hartbarrels.com

Hartford (See U.S. Importer-EMF Co. Inc.)

Hartmann & Weiss GmbH, Rahlstedter Bahnhofstr. 47, 22143, Hamburg, GERMANY / (40) 677 55 85; FAX: (40) 677 55 92 hartmannundweiss@t-online.de

Harvey, Frank, 218 Nightfall, Terrace, NV 89015 / 702-558-6998

Hastings, P.O. Box 135, Clay Center, KS 67432 / 785-632-3169; FAX: 785-632-6554

Hatfield Gun, 224 N. 4th St., St. Joseph, MO 64501

Hawk Laboratories, Inc. (See Hawk, Inc.), 849 Hawks Bridge Rd., Salem, NJ 08079 / 609-299-2700; FAX: 609-299-2800

Hawk, Inc., 849 Hawks Bridge Rd., Salem, NJ 08079 / 609-299-2700; FAX: 609-299-2800 info@hawkbullets.com www.hawkbullets.com

Hawken Shop, The, P.O. Box 593, Oak Harbor, WA 98277 / 206-679-4657; FAX: 206-675-1114

Hawken Shop, The (See Dayton Traister)

Haydel's Game Calls, Inc., 5018 Hazel Jones Rd., Bossier City, LA 71111 / 318-746-3586; FAX: 318-746-3711 www.haydels.com

Hecht, Hubert J., Waffen-Hecht, P.O. Box 2635, Fair Oaks, CA 95628 / 916-966-1020

Heckler & Koch GmbH, P.O. Box 1329, 78722 Oberndorf, Neckar, GERMANY / 49-7423179-0; FAX: 49-7423179-2406

Heckler & Koch, Inc., 21480 Pacific Blvd., Sterling, VA 20166-8900 / 703-450-1900; FAX: 703-450-8160 www.hecklerkoch-usa.com

Hege Jagd-u. Sporthandels GmbH, P.O. Box 101461, W-7770, Ueberlingen a. Boden, GERMANY

Heidenstrom Bullets, Dalghte 86-3660 Rjukan, 35091818, NORWAY, olau.joh@online.tuo

Heilmann, Stephen, P.O. Box 657, Grass Valley, CA 95945 / 530-272-8758; FAX: 530-274-0285 sheilmann@jps.net www.metalwood.com

Heinie Specialty Products, 301 Oak St., Quincy, IL 62301-2500 / 217-228-9500; FAX: 217-228-9502 rheinie@heinie.com www.heinie.com

Helwan (See U.S. Importer-Interarms)

Henigson & Associates, Steve, P.O. Box 2726, Culver City, CA 90231 / 310-305-8288; FAX: 310-305-1905

Henriksen Tool Co., Inc., 8515 Wagner Creek Rd., Talent, OR 97540 / 541-535-2309; FAX: 541-535-2309

Henry Repeating Arms Co., 110 8th St., Brooklyn, NY 11215 / 718-499-5600; FAX: 718-768-8056 info@henryrepeating.com www.henryrepeating.com

Hensley, Gunmaker, Darwin, P.O. Box 329, Brightwood, OR 97011 / 503-622-5411

Heppler, Keith. See: KEITH'S CUSTOM GUNSTOCKS

Hercules, Inc. (See Alliant Techsystems Smokeless Powder Group)

Heritage Firearms (See Heritage Mfg., Inc.)

Heritage Manufacturing, Inc., 4600 NW 135th St., Opa Locka, FL 33054 / 305-685-5966; FAX: 305-687-6721 infohmi@heritagemfg.com www.heritagemfg.com

Heritage/VSP Gun Books, P.O. Box 887, McCall, ID 83638 / 208-634-4104; FAX: 208-634-3101 heritage@gunbooks.com www.gunbooks.com

Herrett's Stocks, Inc., P.O. Box 741, Twin Falls, ID 83303 / 208-733-1498

Hesco-Meprolight, 2139 Greenville Rd., LaGrange, GA 30241 / 706-884-7967; FAX: 706-882-4683

Hesse Arms, Robert Hesse, 1126 70th St. E., Inver Grove Heights, MN 55077-2416 / 651-455-5760; FAX: 612-455-5760

Hesse, Robert. See: HESSE ARMS

Heydenberk, Warren R., 1059 W. Sawmill Rd., Quakertown, PA 18951 / 215-538-2682

Hickman, Jaclyn, Box 1900, Glenrock, WY 82637

Hidalgo, Tony, 12701 SW 9th Pl., Davie, FL 33325 / 954-476-7645

High Bridge Arms, Inc., 3185 Mission St., San Francisco, CA 94110 / 415-282-8358

High North Products, Inc., P.O. Box 2, Antigo, WI 54409 / 715-627-2331; FAX: 715-623-5451

High Performance International, 5734 W. Florist Ave., Milwaukee, WI 53218 / 414-466-9040; FAX: 414-466-7050 mike@hpirifles.com hpirifles.com

High Precision, Bud Welsh, 80 New Road, E. Amherst, NY 14051 / 716-688-6344; FAX: 716-688-0425 welsh5168@aol.com www.high-precision.com

High Standard Mfg. Co./F.I., Inc., 5200 Mitchelldale St., Ste. E17, Houston, TX 77092-7222 / 713-462-4200 or 800-272-7816; FAX: 713-681-5665 info@highstandard.com www.highstandard.com

High Tech Specialties, Inc., P.O. Box 839, 293 E Main St., Rear, Adamstown, PA 19501 / 717-484-0405; FAX: 717-484-0523 bansner@aol.com www.bansmersrifle.com/hightech

Highline Machine Co., Randall Thompson, Randall Thompson, 654 Lela Place, Grand Junction, CO 81504 / 970-434-4971

Highwood Special Products, 1531 E. Highwood, Pontiac, MI 48340

Hill, Loring F., 304 Cedar Rd., Elkins Park, PA 19027

Hill Speed Leather, Ernie, 4507 N 195th Ave., Litchfield Park, AZ 85340 / 602-853-9222; FAX: 602-853-9235

Hinman Outfitters, Bob, 107 N Sanderson Ave., Bartonville, IL 61607-1839 / 309-691-8132

Hi-Performance Ammunition Company, 484 State Route 366, Apollo, PA 15613 / 304-674-9000; FAX: 304-675-6700

HIP-GRIP Barami Corp., P.O. Box 252224, West Bloomfield, MI 48325-2224 / 248-738-0462; FAX: 248-738-2542 hipgripja@aol.com www.hipgrip.com

Hi-Point Firearms/MKS Supply, 8611-A North Dixie Dr., Dayton, OH 45414 / 877-425-4867; FAX: 937-454-0503 www.hi-pointfirearms.com

Hiptmayer, Armurier, RR 112 750, P.O. Box 136, Eastman, PQ J0E 1P0 CANADA / 514-297-2492

Hiptmayer, Heidemarie, RR 112 750, P.O. Box 136, Eastman, PQ J0E 1P0 CANADA / 514-297-2492

Hiptmayer, Klaus, RR 112 750, P.O. Box 136, Eastman, PQ J0E 1P0 CANADA / 514-297-2492

Hirtenberger AG, Leobersdorferstrasse 31, A-2552, Hirtenberg, AUSTRIA / 43(0)2256 81184; FAX: 43(0)2256 81808 www.hirtenberger.ot

HJS Arms, Inc., P.O. Box 3711, Brownsville, TX 78523-3711 / 956-542-2767; FAX: 956-542-2767

Hoag, James W., 8523 Canoga Ave., Suite C, Canoga Park, CA 91304 / 818-998-1510

Hobson Precision Mfg. Co., 210 Big Oak Ln., Brent, AL 35034 / 205-926-4662; FAX: 205-926-3193 cahobbob@dbtech.net

Hodgdon Powder Co., 6231 Robinson, Shawnee Mission, KS 66202 / 913-362-9455; FAX: 913-362-1307

Hodgman, Inc., 1750 Orchard Rd., Montgomery, IL 60538 / 708-897-7555; FAX: 708-897-7558

Hodgson, Richard, 9081 Tahoe Lane, Boulder, CO 80301

Hoehn Sales, Inc., 2045 Kohn Road, Wright City, MO 63390 / 636-745-8144; FAX: 636-745-7868 hoehnsales@direcway.com

Hofer Jagdwaffen, P., A9170 Ferlach, Kirchgasse 24, Kirchgasse, AUSTRIA / 43 4227 3683; FAX: 43 4227 368330 peterhofer@hoferwaffen.com www.hoferwaffen.com

Hoffman New Ideas, 821 Northmoor Rd., Lake Forest, IL 60045 / 312-234-4075

Hogue Grips, P.O. Box 1138, Paso Robles, CA 93447 / 800-438-4747 or 805-239-1440; FAX: 805-239-2553

Holland & Holland Ltd., 33 Bruton St., London, ENGLAND / 44-171-499-4411; FAX: 44-171-408-7962

Holland's Gunsmithing, P.O. Box 69, Powers, OR 97466 / 541-439-5155; FAX: 541-439-5155

Hollinger, Jon. See: ASPEN OUTFITTING CO.

Hollywood Engineering, 10642 Arminta St., Sun Valley, CA 91352 / 818-842-8376; FAX: 818-504-4168 cadqueenel1@aol.com

Homak, 350 N. La Salle Dr. Ste. 1100, Chicago, IL 60610-4731 / 312-523-3100; FAX: 312-523-9455

Hoppe's Div. Penguin Industries, Inc., 9200 Cody St., Overland Park, KS 66214 / 800-845-2444

Horizons Unlimited, P.O. Box 426, Warm Springs, GA 31830 / 706-655-3603; FAX: 706-655-3603

Hornady Mfg. Co., P.O. Box 1848, Grand Island, NE 68802 / 800-338-3220 or 308-382-1390; FAX: 308-382-5761

Horseshoe Leather Products, Andy Arratoonian, The Cottage Sharow, Ripon, ENGLAND U.K. / 44-1765-605858 andy@horseshoe.co.uk www.holsters.org

House of Muskets, Inc., The, PO Box 4640, Pagosa Springs, CO 81157 / 970-731-2295

Houtz & Barwick, P.O. Box 435, W. Church St., Elizabeth City, NC 27909 / 800-775-0337 or 919-335-4191; FAX: 919-335-1152

Howa Machinery, Ltd., 1900-1 Sukaguchi Kiyosu, Aichi 452-8601, JAPAN / 81-52-408-1231; FAX: 81-52-401-4999 howa@howa.co.jp http://www.howa.cojpl

Howell Machine, Inc., 815 D St., Lewiston, ID 83501 / 208-743-7418; FAX: 208-746-1703 ammoload@microwavedsl.com www.ammoload.com

H-S Precision, Inc., 1301 Turbine Dr., Rapid City, SD 57701 / 605-341-3006; FAX: 605-342-8964

HT Bullets, 244 Belleville Rd., New Bedford, MA 02745 / 508-999-3338

Hubert J. Hecht Waffen-Hecht, P.O. Box 2635, Fair Oaks, CA 95628 / 916-966-1020

Huebner, Corey O., P.O. Box 564, Frenchtown, MT 59834 / 406-721-7168 bugsboys@hotmail.com

Huey Gun Cases, 820 Indiana St., Lawrence, KS 66044-2645 / 785-842-0062; FAX: 785-842-0062 hueycases@aol.com www.hueycases.com

Hume, Don, P.O. Box 351, Miami, OK 74355 / 800-331-2686; FAX: 918-542-4340 info@donhume.com www.donhume.com

Hunkeler, A. (See Buckskin Machine Works), 3235 S 358th St., Auburn, WA 98001 / 206-927-5412

Hunter Co., Inc., 3300 W. 71st Ave., Westminster, CO 80030 / 303-427-4626; FAX: 303-428-3980 debbiet@huntercompany.com www.huntercompany.com

Hunterjohn, P.O. Box 771457, St. Louis, MO 63177 / 314-531-7250 www.hunterjohn.com

Hunter's Specialties Inc., 6000 Huntington Ct. NE, Cedar Rapids, IA 52402-1268 / 319-395-0321; FAX: 319-395-0326

Hunters Supply, Inc., P.O. Box 313, Tioga, TX 76271 / 940-437-2458; FAX: 940-437-2228 hunterssupply@hotmail.com www.hunterssupply.net

Huntington Die Specialties, 601 Oro Dam Blvd., Oroville, CA 95965 / 530-534-1210 or 866-735-6237; FAX: 530-534-1212 buy@huntingtons.com www.huntingtons.com

Hutton Rifle Ranch, P.O. Box 170317, Boise, ID 83717 / 208-345-8781 www.martinbrevik@aol.com

Hydra-Tone Chemicals, Inc., 7785 Foundation Dr., Suite 6, Florence, KY 41042 / 859-342-5553; FAX: 859-342-2380 www.hydra-tone.com

Hydrosorbent Products, P.O. Box 437, Ashley Falls, MA 01222 / 800-448-7903; FAX: 413-229-8743 orders@dehumidify.com www.dehumidify.com

I

I.A.B. (See U.S. Importer-Taylor's & Co., Inc.)

I.D.S.A. Books, 1324 Stratford Drive, Piqua, OH 45356 / 937-773-4203; FAX: 937-778-1922

MANUFACTURER'S DIRECTORY

I.N.C. Inc. (See Kickeez I.N.C., Inc.)

I.S.W., 106 E. Cairo Dr., Tempe, AZ 85282

IAR Inc., 33171 Camino Capistrano, San Juan Capistrano, CA 92675 / 949-443-3642; FAX: 949-443-3647 sales@iar-arms.com iar-arms.com

Ide, Ken. See: STURGEON VALLEY SPORTERS

IGA (See U.S. Importer-Stoeger Industries)

Image Ind. Inc., 11220 E. Main St., Huntley, IL 60142-7369 / 630-766-2402; FAX: 630-766-7373

Impact Case & Container, Inc., P.O. Box 1129, Rathdrum, ID 83858 / 877-687-2452; FAX: 208-687-0632 bradk@icc-case.com www.icc-case.com

Imperial (See E-Z-Way Systems), P.O. Box 4310, Newark, OH 43058-4310 / 614-345-6645; FAX: 614-345-6600 ezway@infinet.com www.jcunald.com

Imperial Magnum Corp., P.O. Box 249, Oroville, WA 98844 / 604-495-3131; FAX: 604-495-2816

Imperial Miniature Armory, 1115 FM 359, Houston, TX 77035-3305 / 800-646-4288; FAX: 832-595-8787 miniguns@houston.rr.com www.1800miniature.com

IMR Powder Co., 1080 Military Turnpike, Suite 2, Plattsburgh, NY 12901 / 518-563-2253; FAX: 518-563-6916

Info-Arm, P.O. Box 1262, Champlain, NY 12919 / 514-955-0355; FAX: 514-955-0357 infoarm@qc.aira.com

Innovative Weaponry Inc., 2513 E. Loop 820 N., Fort Worth, TX 76118 / 817-284-0099 or 800-334-3573

INTEC International, Inc., P.O. Box 5708, Scottsdale, AZ 85261 / 602-483-1708

Inter Ordnance of America LP, 3305 Westwood Industrial Dr., Monroe, NC 28110-5204 / 704-821-8337; FAX: 704-821-8523

Intercontinental Distributors, Ltd., P.O. Box 815, Beulah, ND 58523

International Shooters Service, P.O. Box 185234, Ft. Worth, TX 76181 / 817-595-2090; FAX: 817-595-2090 is_s_@sbcglobal.net www.iss-internationalshootersservice.com

Intrac Arms International, 5005 Chapman Hwy., Knoxville, TN 37920

Ion Industries, Inc., 3508 E Allerton Ave., Cudahy, WI 53110 / 414-486-2007; FAX: 414-486-2017

Iosso Products, 1485 Lively Blvd., Elk Grove Village, IL 60007 / 847-437-8400; FAX: 847-437-8478

Iron Bench, 12619 Bailey Rd., Redding, CA 96003 / 916-241-4623

Ironside International Publishers, Inc., P.O. Box 1050, Lorton, VA 22199

Ironsighter Co., P.O. Box 85070, Westland, MI 48185 / 734-326-8731; FAX: 734-326-3378 www.ironsighter.com

Irwin, Campbell H., 140 Hartland Blvd., East Hartland, CT 06027 / 203-653-3901

Israel Arms Inc., 5625 Star Ln. #B, Houston, TX 77057 / 713-789-0745; FAX: 713-914-9515 www.israelarms.com

Ithaca Classic Doubles, Stephen Lamboy, No. 5 Railroad St., Victor, NY 14564 / 716-924-2710; FAX: 716-924-2737 ithacadoubles.com

Ithaca Gun Company LLC, 901 Rt. 34 B, King Ferry, NY 13081 / 315-364-7171; FAX: 315-364-5134 info@ithacagun.com

Ithaca Guns USA, LLC, 420 N. Walpole St., Upper Sandusky, OH 43351 / 419-294-4113; FAX: 419-294-9433 service@ithacaguns.com www.ithacagunusa.com

Ivanoff, Thomas G. (See Tom's Gun Repair)

J

J J Roberts Firearm Engraver, 7808 Lake Dr., Manassas, VA 20111 / 703-330-0448; FAX: 703-264-8600 james.roberts@angelfire.com www.angelfire.com/va2/engraver

J&D Components, 75 East 350 North, Orem, UT 84057-4719 / 801-225-7007 www.jdcomponents.com

J&J Products, Inc., 9240 Whitmore, El Monte, CA 91731 / 818-571-5228; FAX: 800-927-8361

J&J Sales, 1501 21st Ave. S., Great Falls, MT 59405 / 406-727-9789 mtshootingbench@yahoo.com www.j&jsales.us

J&L Superior Bullets (See Huntington Die Specialties)

J&M Precision Machining, Jeff Amato, RR 1 Box 91, Bloomfield, IN 47424

J&R Engineering, P.O. Box 77, 200 Lyons Hill Rd., Athol, MA 01331 / 508-249-9241

J&R Enterprises, 4550 Scotts Valley Rd., Lakeport, CA 95453

J&S Heat Treat, 803 S. 16th St., Blue Springs, MO 64015 / 816-229-2149; FAX: 816-228-1135

J. Dewey Mfg. Co., Inc., P.O. Box 2014, Southbury, CT 06488 / 203-264-3064; FAX: 203-262-6907 deweyrods@worldnet.att.net www.deweyrods.com

J. Korzinek Riflesmith, RD 2, Box 73D, Canton, PA 17724 / 717-673-8512

J.A. Blades, Inc. (See Christopher Firearms Co.)

J.A. Henckels Zwillingswerk Inc., 9 Skyline Dr., Hawthorne, NY 10532 / 914-592-7370

J.G. Anschutz GmbH & Co. KG, Daimlerstr. 12, D-89079 Ulm, Ulm, GERMANY / 49 731 40120; FAX: 49 731 4012700 JGA-info@anschuetz-sport.com www.anschuetz-sport.com

J.G. Dapkus Co., Inc., Commerce Circle, P.O. Box 293, Durham, CT 06422 www.explodingtargets.com

J.I.T. Ltd., P.O. Box 230, Freedom, WY 83120 / 708-494-0937

J.J. Roberts / Engraver, 7808 Lake Dr., Manassas, VA 20111 / 703-330-0448 jjrengraver@aol.com www.angelfire.com/va2/engraver

J.R. Williams Bullet Co., 2008 Tucker Rd., Perry, GA 31069 / 912-987-0274

J.W. Morrison Custom Rifles, 4015 W. Sharon, Phoenix, AZ 85029 / 602-978-3754

J.W. Wasmundt-Gunsmith, Jim Wasmundt, P.O. Box 130, 140 Alder St., Powers, OR 97466-0130 / 541-439-2044 jwasm@juno.com

Jack A. Rosenberg & Sons, 12229 Cox Ln., Dallas, TX 75234 / 214-241-6302

Jack Dever Co., 8520 NW 90th St., Oklahoma City, OK 73132 / 405-721-6393 jbdever1@home.com

Jack First, Inc., 1201 Turbine Dr., Rapid City, SD 57703 / 605-343-9544; FAX: 605-343-9420

Jack Jonas Appraisals & Taki, 13952 E. Marina Dr., #604, Aurora, CO 80014

Jackalope Gun Shop, 1048 S. 5th St., Douglas, WY 82633 / 307-358-3441 wildcatoutfitters@msn.com www.jackalopegunshop.com

Jaffin, Harry. See: BRIDGEMAN PRODUCTS

Jagdwaffen, Peter. See: BUCHSENMACHERMEISTER

James Calhoon Mfg., 4343 U.S. Highway 87, Havre, MT 59501 / 406-395-4079 www.jamescalhoon.com

James Churchill Glove Co., PO Box 298, Centralia, WA 98531 / 360-736-2816; FAX: 360-330-0151 churchillglove@localaccess.com

James Wayne Firearms for Collectors and Investors, 2608 N. Laurent, Victoria, TX 77901 / 361-578-1258; FAX: 361-578-3559

Jamison International, Marc Jamison, 3551 Mayer Ave., Sturgis, SD 57785 / 605-347-5090; FAX: 605-347-4704 jbell2@masttechnology.com

Jamison, Marc. See: JAMISON INTERNATIONAL

Jamison's Forge Works, 4527 Rd. 6.5 NE, Moses Lake, WA 98837 / 509-762-2659

Jantz Supply, Inc., 309 West Main Dept HD, Davis, OK 73030-0584 / 580-369-2316; FAX: 580-369-3082 jantz@brightok.net www.knifemaking.com

Jarrett Rifles, Inc., 383 Brown Rd., Jackson, SC 29831 / 803-471-3616 www.jarrettrifles.com

Jarvis, Inc., 1123 Cherry Orchard Lane, Hamilton, MT 59840 / 406-961-4392

Javelina Lube Products, P.O. Box 337, San Bernardino, CA 92402 / 909-350-9556; FAX: 909-429-1211

Jay McCament Custom Gunmaker, Jay McCament, 1730-134th St. Ct. S., Tacoma, WA 98444 / 253-531-8832

JB Custom, P.O. Box 6912, Leawood, KS 66206 / 913-381-2329

Jeff Flannery Engraving, 11034 Riddles Run Rd., Union, KY 41091 / 859-384-3127; FAX: 859-384-2222 engraving@fuse.net http://home.fuse.net/engraving/

Jeff's Outfitters, 63F Sena Fawn, Cape Girardeau, MO 63701 / 573-651-3200; FAX: 573-651-3207 info@jeffsoutfitters.com www.jeffsoutfitters.com

Jena Eur, P.O. Box 319, Dunmore, PA 18512

Jenco Sales, Inc., P.O. Box 1000, Manchaca, TX 78652 / 800-531-5301; FAX: 800-266-2373 jencosales@sbcglobal.net

Jenkins Recoil Pads, 5438 E. Frontage Ln., Olney, IL 62450 / 618-395-3416

Jensen Bullets, RR 1 Box 187, Arco, ID 83213 / 208-785-5590

Jensen's Custom Ammunition, 5146 E. Pima, Tucson, AZ 85712 / 602-325-3346; FAX: 602-322-5704

Jensen's Firearms Academy, 1280 W. Prince, Tucson, AZ 85705 / 602-293-8516

Jericho Tool & Die Co., Inc., 121 W. Keech Rd., Bainbridge, NY 13733-3248 / 607-563-8222; FAX: 607-563-8560 jerichotool.com www.jerichotool.com

Jerry Phillips Optics, P.O. Box L632, Langhorne, PA 19047 / 215-757-5037; FAX: 215-757-7097

Jesse W. Smith Saddlery, 0499 County Road J, Pritchett, CO 81064 / 509-325-0622

Jester Bullets, Rt. 1 Box 27, Orienta, OK 73737

Jewell Triggers, Inc., 3620 Hwy. 123, San Marcos, TX 78666 / 512-353-2999; FAX: 512-392-0543

JG Airguns, LLC, John Groenewold, P.O. Box 830, Mundelein, IL 60060 / 847-566-2365; FAX: 847-566-4065 info@jgairguns.biz www.jgairguns.biz

JGS Precision Tool Mfg., LLC, 60819 Selander Rd., Coos Bay, OR 97420 / 541-267-4331; FAX: 541-267-5996 jgstools@harborside.com www.jgstools.com

Jim Blair Engraving, P.O. Box 64, Glenrock, WY 82637 / 307-436-8115 jblairengrav@msn.com

Jim Noble Co., 204 W. 5th St., Vancouver, WA 98660 / 360-695-1309; FAX: 360-695-6835 jnobleco@aol.com

Jim Norman Custom Gunstocks, 14281 Cane Rd., Valley Center, CA 92082 / 619-749-6252

Jim's Precision, Jim Ketchum, 1725 Moclips Dr., Petaluma, CA 94952 / 707-762-3014

JLK Bullets, 414 Turner Rd., Dover, AR 72837 / 501-331-4194

Johanssons Vapentillbehor, Bert, S-430 20, Veddige, SWEDEN

John Hall Plastics, Inc., P.O. Box 1526, Alvin, TX 77512 / 713-489-8709

John J. Adams & Son Engravers, 7040 VT Rt 113, Vershire, VT 05079 / 802-685-0019

John Masen Co. Inc., 1305 Jelmak, Grand Prairie, TX 75050 / 817-430-8732; FAX: 817-430-1715

John Partridge Sales Ltd., Trent Meadows Rugeley, Staffordshire, WS15 2HS ENGLAND

John Rigby & Co., 500 Linne Rd. Ste. D, Paso Robles, CA 93446 / 805-227-4236; FAX: 805-227-4723 jrigby@calinet www.johnrigbyandco.com

John's Custom Leather, 523 S. Liberty St., Blairsville, PA 15717 / 724-459-6802; FAX: 724-459-5996

Johnson Wood Products, 34897 Crystal Road, Strawberry Point, IA 52076 / 563-933-6504 johnsonwoodproducts@yahoo.com

Jonad Corp., 2091 Lakeland Ave., Lakewood, OH 44107 / 216-226-3161

Jonathan Arthur Ciener, Inc., 8700 Commerce St., Cape Canaveral, FL 32920 / 321-868-2200; FAX: 321-868-2201 www.22lrconversions.com

Jones Custom Products, Neil A., 17217 Brookhouser Rd., Saegertown, PA 16433 / 814-763-2769; FAX: 814-763-4228 njones@mdvl.net neiljones.com

Jones, J. See: SSK INDUSTRIES

Jones Moulds, Paul, 4901 Telegraph Rd., Los Angeles, CA 90022 / 213-262-1510

JP Enterprises, Inc., P.O. Box 378, Hugo, MN 55038 / 651-426-9196; FAX: 651-426-2472 www.jprifles.com

JP Sales, Box 307, Anderson, TX 77830

JRP Custom Bullets, RR2 2233 Carlton Rd., Whitehall, NY 12887 / 518-282-0084 or 802-438-5548

JSL Ltd. (See U.S. Importer-Specialty Shooters Supply)

Juenke, Vern, 25 Bitterbush Rd., Reno, NV 89523 / 702-345-0225

Jungkind, Reeves C., 509 E. Granite St., Llano, TX 78643-3055 / 325-247-1151

Jurras, L. See: L. E. JURRAS & ASSOC.

Justin Phillippi Custom Bullets, P.O. Box 773, Ligonier, PA 15658 / 412-238-9671

K

K&M Industries, Inc., Box 66, 510 S. Main, Troy, ID 83871 / 208-835-2281; FAX: 208-835-5211

K&M Services, 5430 Salmon Run Rd., Dover, PA 17315 / 717-292-3175; FAX: 717-292-3175

K. Eversull Co., Inc., 1 Tracemont, Boyce, LA 71409 / 318-793-8728; FAX: 318-793-5483 bestguns@aol.com

K.B.I. Inc., P.O. Box 6625, Harrisburg, PA 17112 / 717-540-8518; FAX: 717-540-8567

KA-BAR Knives, 200 Homer St., Olean, NY 14760 / 800-282-0130; FAX: 716-790-7188 info@ka-bar.com www.ka-bar.com

Kahles A. Swarovski Company, 2 Slater Rd., Cranston, RI 02920 / 401-946-2220; FAX: 401-946-2587

Kahr Arms, P.O. Box 220, 630 Route 303, Blauvelt, NY 10913 / 845-353-7770; FAX: 845-353-7833 www.kahr.com

Kailua Custom Guns Inc., 51 N. Dean Street, Coquille, OR 97423 / 541-396-5413 kailuacustom@aol.com www.kailuacustom.com

Kalispel Case Line, P.O. Box 267, Cusick, WA 99119 / 509-445-1121

Kamik Outdoor Footwear, 554 Montee de Liesse, Montreal, PQ H4T 1P1 CANADA / 514-341-3950; FAX: 514-341-1861

Kane, Edward, P.O. Box 385, Ukiah, CA 95482 / 707-462-2937

Kapro Mfg. Co. Inc. (See R.E.I.)

Kasenit Co., Inc., 39 Park Ave., Highland Mills, NY 10930 / 845-928-9595; FAX: 845-986-8038

Kaswer Custom, Inc., 13 Surrey Drive, Brookfield, CT 06804 / 203-775-0564; FAX: 203-775-6872

KDF, Inc., 2485 Hwy. 46 N., Seguin, TX 78155 / 830-379-8141; FAX: 830-379-5420

KeeCo Impressions, Inc., 346 Wood Ave., North Brunswick, NJ 08902 / 800-468-0546

Kehr, Roger, 2131 Agate Ct. SE, Lacy, WA 98503 / 360-491-0691

Keith's Bullets, 942 Twisted Oak, Algonquin, IL 60102 / 708-658-3520

Keith's Custom Gunstocks, Keith M. Heppler, 540 Banyan Circle, Walnut Creek, CA 94598 / 925-934-3509; FAX: 925-934-3143 kmheppler@hotmail.com

Kelbly, Inc., 7222 Dalton Fox Lake Rd., North Lawrence, OH 44666 / 216-683-4674; FAX: 216-683-7349

Keller Co., The, P.O. Box 4057, Port Angeles, WA 98363-0997 / 214-770-8585

Kelley's, P.O. Box 125, Woburn, MA 01801-0125 / 800-879-7273; FAX: 781-272-7077 kels@star.net www.kelsmilitary.com

Kellogg's Professional Products, 325 Pearl St., Sandusky, OH 44870 / 419-625-6551; FAX: 419-625-6167 skwigton@aol.com

Kelly, Lance, 1723 Willow Oak Dr., Edgewater, FL 32132 / 904-423-4933

Kel-Tec CNC Industries, Inc., P.O. Box 236009, Cocoa, FL 32923 / 321-631-0068; FAX: 321-631-1169 www.kel-tec.com

Kemen America, 2550 Hwy. 23, Wrenshall, MN 55797 / 218-384-3670 patrickl@midwestshootingschool.com midwestshootingschool.com

Ken Eyster Heritage Gunsmiths, Inc., 6441 Bisop Rd., Centerburg, OH 43011 / 740-625-6131; FAX: 740-625-7811

Ken Starnes Gunmaker, 15617 NE 324th Circle, Battle Ground, WA 98604 / 360-666-5025; FAX: 360-666-5024 kstarnes@kdsa.com

Keng's Firearms Specialty, Inc./US Tactical Systems, 875 Wharton Dr., P.O. Box 44405, Atlanta, GA 30336-1405 / 404-691-7611; FAX: 404-505-8445

Kennebec Journal, 274 Western Ave., Augusta, ME 04330 / 207-622-6288

Kennedy Firearms, 10 N. Market St., Muncy, PA 17756 / 717-546-6695

Kenneth W. Warren Engraver, P.O. Box 2842, Wenatchee, WA 98807 / 509-663-6123; FAX: 509-665-6123

Ken's Kustom Kartridges, 331 Jacobs Rd., Hubbard, OH 44425 / 216-534-4595

Kent Cartridge America, Inc., P.O. Box 849, 1000 Zigor Rd., Kearneysville, WV 25430

Keowee Game Calls, 608 Hwy. 25 North, Travelers Rest, SC 29690 / 864-834-7204; FAX: 864-834-7831

Kershaw Knives, 18600 SW Teton Ave., Tualatin, OR 97062 / 503-682-1966 or 800-325-2891; FAX: 503-682-7168

Kesselring Gun Shop, 4024 Old Hwy. 99N, Burlington, WA 98233 / 360-724-3113; FAX: 360-724-7003 info@kesselrings.com www.kesselrings.com

Ketchum, Jim (See Jim's Precision)

Keystone Sporting Arms, Inc. (Crickett Rifles), 8920 State Route 405, Milton, PA 17847 / 800-742-2777; FAX: 570-742-1455

Kickeez I.N.C., Inc., 301 Industrial Dr., Carl Junction, MO 64834-8806 / 419-649-2100; FAX: 417-649-2200 kickeez@sbcglobal.net www.kickeez.net

Kilham & Co., Main St., P.O. Box 37, Lyme, NH 03768 / 603-795-4112

Kimar (See U.S. Importer-IAR, Inc.)

Kimber of America, Inc., 1 Lawton St., Yonkers, NY 10705 / 800-880-2418; FAX: 914-964-9340

King & Co., P.O. Box 1242, Bloomington, IL 61702 / 309-473-3964 or 800-914-5464; FAX: 309-473-2161

King's Gun Works, 1837 W. Glenoaks Blvd., Glendale, CA 91201 / 818-956-6010; FAX: 818-548-8606

Kirkpatrick Leather Co., P.O. Box 677, Laredo, TX 78040 / 956-723-6631; FAX: 956-725-0672 mike@kirkpatrickleather.com www.kirkpatrickleather.com

KK Air International (See Impact Case & Container Co., Inc.)

Kleen-Bore, Inc., 8909 Forum Way, Ft. Worth, TX 76140 / 413-527-0300; FAX: 817-926-7012 info@kleen-bore.com www.kleen-bore.com

Kleinendorst, K. W., RR 1, Box 1500, Hop Bottom, PA 18824 / 570-289-4687; FAX: 570-289-8673

Klinger Woodcarving, P.O. Box 141, Thistle Hill, Cabot, VT 05647 / 802-426-3811 www.vermartcrafts.com

Knifeware, Inc., P.O. Box 3, Greenville, WV 24945 / 304-832-6878

Knight Rifles, 21852 Hwy. J46, P.O. Box 130, Centerville, IA 52544 / 515-856-2626; FAX: 515-856-2628 www.knightrifles.com

Knight Rifles (See Modern Muzzleloading, Inc.)

Knight's Manufacturing Co., 701 Columbia Blvd., Titusville, FL 32780 / 321-607-9900; FAX: 321-268-1498 civiliansales@knightarmco.com www.knightarmco.com

Knock on Wood Antiques, 355 Post Rd., Darien, CT 06820 / 203-655-9031

Knoell, Doug, 9737 McCardle Way, Santee, CA 92071 / 619-449-5189

Knopp, Gary. See: SUPER 6 LLC

Koevenig's Engraving Service, Box 55 Rabbit Gulch, Hill City, SD 57745 / 605-574-2239 ekoevenig@msn.com

KOGOT, 410 College, Trinidad, CO 81082 / 719-846-9406; FAX: 719-846-9406

Kolar, 1925 Roosevelt Ave., Racine, WI 53406 / 414-554-0800; FAX: 414-554-9093

Kolpin Outdoors, Inc., P.O. Box 107, 205 Depot St., Fox Lake, WI 53933 / 414-928-3118; FAX: 414-928-3687 cdutton@kolpin.com www.kolpin.com

Korth Germany GmbH, Robert Bosch Strasse, 11, D-23909, 23909 Ratzeburg, GERMANY / 4541-840363; FAX: 4541-84 05 35 info@korthwaffen.de www.korthwaffen.com

Korth USA, 437R Chandler St., Tewksbury, MA 01876 / 978-851-8656; FAX: 978-851-9462 info@korthusa.com www.korthusa.com

Korzinek Riflesmith, J., RD 2 Box 73D, Canton, PA 17724 / 717-673-8512

Koval Knives, 5819 Zarley St., Suite A, New Albany, OH 43054 / 614-855-0777; FAX: 614-855-0945 koval@kovalknives.com www.kovalknives.com

Kowa Optimed, Inc., 20001 S. Vermont Ave., Torrance, CA 90502 / 310-327-1913; FAX: 310-327-4177 scopekowa@kowa.com www.kowascope.com

KP Books Division of F+W Publications, 700 E. State St., Iola, WI 54990-0001 / 715-445-2214

Kramer Designs, P.O. Box 129, Clancy, MT 59634 / 406-933-8658; FAX: 406-933-8658

Kramer Handgun Leather, P.O. Box 112154, Tacoma, WA 98411 / 800-510-2666; FAX: 253-564-1214 www.kramerleather.com

Krico Deutschland GmbH, Nurnbergerstrasse 6, D-90602, Pyrbaum, GERMANY / 09180-2780; FAX: 09180-2661

Krieger Barrels, Inc., 2024 Mayfield Rd, Richfield, WI 53076 / 262-628-8558; FAX: 262-628-8748

Krieghoff Gun Co., H., Boschstrasse 22, D-89079 Elm, GERMANY / 731-4018270

Krieghoff International, Inc., 7528 Easton Rd., Ottsville, PA 18942 / 610-847-5173; FAX: 610-847-8691

Kukowski, Ed. See: ED'S GUN HOUSE

Kulis Freeze Dry Taxidermy, 725 Broadway Ave., Bedford, OH 44146 / 440-232-8352; FAX: 440-232-7305 jkulis@kastaway.com kastaway.com

KVH Industries, Inc., 110 Enterprise Center, Middletown, RI 02842 / 401-847-3327; FAX: 401-849-0045

Kwik-Site Co., 5555 Treadwell St., Wayne, MI 48184 / 734-326-1500; FAX: 734-326-4120 kwiksiteco@aol.com

L

L&R Lock Co., 2328 Cains Mill Rd., Sumter, SC 29154 / 803-481-5790; FAX: 803-481-5795

L&S Technologies Inc. (See Aimtech Mount Systems)

L. Bengtson Arms Co., 6345-B E. Akron St., Mesa, AZ 85205 / 602-981-6375

L. E. Jurras & Assoc., L. E. Jurras, P.O. Box 680, Washington, IN 47501 / 812-254-6170; FAX: 812-254-6170 jurras@sbcglobal.net www.leejurras.com

L.A.R. Mfg., Inc., 4133 W. Farm Rd., West Jordan, UT 84088 / 801-280-3505; FAX: 801-280-1972

L.B.T., Judy Smith, HCR 62, Box 145, Moyie Springs, ID 83845 / 208-267-3588 lbtisaccuracy@imbris.net

L.E. Wilson, Inc., Box 324, 404 Pioneer Ave., Cashmere, WA 98815 / 509-782-1328; FAX: 509-782-7200

L.L. Bean, Inc., Freeport, ME 04032 / 207-865-4761; FAX: 207-552-2802

L.P.A. Inc., Via Alfieri 26, Gardone V.T., Brescia, ITALY / 30-891-14-81; FAX: 30-891-09-51

L.R. Clift Mfg., 3821 Hammonton Rd., Marysville, CA 95901 / 916-755-3390; FAX: 916-755-3393

La Clinique du .45, 1432 Rougemont, Chambly, PQ J3L 2L8 CANADA / 514-658-1144

Labanu Inc., 2201-F Fifth Ave., Ronkonkoma, NY 11779 / 516-467-6197; FAX: 516-981-4112

LaBoone, Pat. See: MIDWEST SHOOTING SCHOOL, THE

LaBounty Precision Reboring, Inc, 7968 Silver Lake Rd., PO Box 186, Maple Falls, WA 98266 / 360-599-2047; FAX: 360-599-3018

LaCrosse Footwear, Inc., 18550 NE Riverside Parkway, Portland, OR 97230 / 503-766-1010 or 800-323-2668; FAX: 503-766-1015 customerservice@lacrossefootwear.com www.lacrossefootwear.com

LaFrance Specialties, P.O. Box 87933, San Diego, CA 92138 / 619-293-3373; FAX: 619-293-0819 timlafrance@att.net lafrancespecialties.com

Lake Center Marina, P.O. Box 670, St. Charles, MO 63302 / 314-946-7500

Lakefield Arms Ltd. (See Savage Arms, Inc.)

Lakewood Products LLC, 275 June St., Berlin, WI 54923 / 800-872-8458; FAX: 920-361-7719 lakewood@centurytel.net www.lakewoodproducts.com

Lamboy, Stephen. See: ITHACA CLASSIC DOUBLES

Lampert, Ron, Rt. 1, 44857 Schoolcraft Trl., Guthrie, MN 56461 / 218-854-7345

Lamson & Goodnow Mfg. Co., 45 Conway St., Shelburne Falls, MA 03170 / 413-625-6564 or 800-872-6564; FAX: 413-625-9816 www.lamsonsharp.com

Lansky Levine, Arthur. See: LANSKY SHARPENERS

MANUFACTURER'S DIRECTORY

Lansky Sharpeners, Arthur Lansky Levine, P.O. Box 50830, Las Vegas, NV 89016 / 702-361-7511; FAX: 702-896-9511

LaPrade, P.O. Box 250, Ewing, VA 24248 / 423-733-2615

LaRocca Gun Works, 51 Union Place, Worcester, MA 01608 / 508-754-2887; FAX: 508-754-2887 www.laroccagunworks.com

Larry Lyons Gunworks, 110 Hamilton St., Dowagiac, MI 49047 / 616-782-9478

Laser Devices, Inc., 2 Harris Ct. A-4, Monterey, CA 93940 / 831-373-0701; FAX: 831-373-0903 sales@laserdevices.com www.laserdevices.com

Laseraim Technologies, Inc., P.O. Box 3548, Little Rock, AR 72203 / 501-375-2227

Laserlyte, 2201 Amapola Ct., Torrance, CA 90501

LaserMax, 3495 Winton Place, Rochester, NY 14623-2807 / 800-527-3703; FAX: 585-272-5427 customerservice@lasermax-inc.com www.lasermax.com

Lassen Community College, Gunsmithing Dept., P.O. Box 3000, Hwy. 139, Susanville, CA 96130 / 916-251-8800; FAX: 916-251-8838 staylor@lassencollege.edu www.lassencommunitycollege.edu

Lathrop's, Inc., 5146 E. Pima, Tucson, AZ 85712 / 520-881-0266 or 800-875-4867; FAX: 520-322-5704

Laughridge, William R. (See Cylinder & Slide, Inc.)

Laurel Mountain Forge, P.O. Box 52, Crown Point, IN 46308 / 219-548-2950; FAX: 219-548-2950

Laurona Armas Eibar, S.A.L., Avenida de Otaola 25, P.O. Box 260, Eibar 20600, SPAIN / 34-43-700600; FAX: 34-43-700616

Lawrence Brand Shot (See Precision Reloading, Inc.)

Lawrence Leather Co., P.O. Box 1479, Lillington, NC 27546 / 910-893-2071; FAX: 910-893-4742

Lawson Co., Harry, 3328 N. Richey Blvd., Tucson, AZ 85716 / 520-326-1117; FAX: 520-326-1117

Lawson, John. See: SIGHT SHOP, THE

Lawson, John G. (See Sight Shop, The)

Lazzeroni Arms Co., P.O. Box 26696, Tucson, AZ 85726 / 888-492-7247; FAX: 520-624-4250

Le Clear Industries (See E-Z-Way Systems)

Leapers, Inc., 7675 Five Mile Rd., Northville, MI 48167 / 248-486-1231; FAX: 248-486-1430

Leatherman Tool Group, Inc., 12106 NE Ainsworth Cir., P.O. Box 20595, Portland, OR 97294 / 503-253-7826; FAX: 503-253-7830

Lebeau-Courally, Rue St. Gilles, 386 4000, Liege, BELGIUM / 042-52-48-43; FAX: 32-4-252-2008 info@lebeau-courally.com www.lebeau-courally.com

Leckie Professional Gunsmithing, 546 Quarry Rd., Ottsville, PA 18942 / 215-847-8594

Ledbetter Airguns, Riley, 1804 E Sprague St., Winston Salem, NC 27107-3521 / 919-784-0676

Lee Precision, Inc., 4275 Hwy. U, Hartford, WI 53027 / 262-673-3075; FAX: 262-673-9273 info@leeprecision.com www.leeprecision.com

Lee Supplies, Mark, 9901 France Ct., Lakeville, MN 55044 / 612-461-2114

LeFever Arms Co., Inc., 6234 Stokes, Lee Center Rd., Lee Center, NY 13363 / 315-337-6722; FAX: 315-337-1543

Legacy Sports International, 206 S. Union St., Alexandria, VA 22314 / 703-548-4837 www.legacysports.com

Leica USA, Inc., 156 Ludlow Ave., Northvale, NJ 07647 / 201-767-7500; FAX: 201-767-8666

Leonard Day, 3 Kings Hwy., West Hatfield, MA 01027-9506 / 413-337-8369

Les Baer Custom, Inc., 29601 34th Ave., Hillsdale, IL 61257 / 309-658-2716; FAX: 309-658-2610 www.lesbaer.com

LesMerises, Felix. See: ROCKY MOUNTAIN ARMOURY

Lethal Force Institute (See Police Bookshelf), P.O. Box 122, Concord, NH 03301 / 603-224-6814; FAX: 603-226-3554

Lett Custom Grips, 672 Currier Rd., Hopkinton, NH 03229-2652 / 800-421-5388; FAX: 603-226-4580 info@lettgrips.com www.lettgrips.com

Leupold & Stevens, Inc., 14400 NW Greenbrier Pky., Beaverton, OR 97006 / 503-646-9171; FAX: 503-526-1455

Lever Arms Service Ltd., 2131 Burrard St., Vancouver, BC V6J 3H7 CANADA / 604-736-2711; FAX: 604-738-3503 leverarms@leverarms.com www.leverarms.com

Lew Horton Dist. Co., Inc., 15 Walkup Dr., Westboro, MA 01581 / 508-366-7400; FAX: 508-366-5332

Lewis Lead Remover, The (See Brownells, Inc.)

Liberty Mfg., Inc., 2233 East 16th St., Los Angeles, CA 90021 / 323-581-9171; FAX: 323-581-9351 libertymfginc@aol.com

Liberty Safe, 999 W. Utah Ave., Payson, UT 84651-1744 / 800-247-5625; FAX: 801-489-6409

Liberty Shooting Supplies, P.O. Box 357, Hillsboro, OR 97123 / 503-640-5518; FAX: 503-640-5518 info@libertyshootingsupplies.com www.libertyshootingsupplies.com

Lightning Performance Innovations, Inc., RD1 Box 555, Mohawk, NY 13407 / 315-866-8819; FAX: 315-867-5701

Lilja Precision Rifle Barrels, P.O. Box 372, Plains, MT 59859 / 406-826-3084; FAX: 406-826-3083 lilja@riflebarrels.com www.riflebarrels.com

Lincoln, Dean, Box 1886, Farmington, NM 87401

Linder Solingen Knives, 4401 Sentry Dr. #B, Tucker, GA 30084 / 770-939-6915; FAX: 770-939-6738

Lindsay Engraving & Tools, Steve Lindsay, 3714 W. Cedar Hills, Kearney, NE 68845 / 308-236-7885 steve@lindsayengraving.com www.handgravers.com

Lindsay, Steve. See: LINDSAY ENGRAVING & TOOLS

Lindsley Arms Cartridge Co., P.O. Box 757, 20 College Hill Rd., Henniker, NH 03242 / 603-995-1267

Linebaugh Custom Sixguns, P.O. Box 455, Cody, WY 82414 / 307-645-3332 www.sixgunner.com

Lion Country Supply, P.O. Box 480, Port Matilda, PA 16870

List Precision Engineering, Unit 1 Ingley Works, 13 River Road, Barking, ENGLAND / 011-081-594-1686

Lithi Bee Bullet Lube, 1728 Carr Rd., Muskegon, MI 49442 / 616-788-4479 lithibee@att.net

"Little John's" Antique Arms, 1740 W. Laveta, Orange, CA 92668

Littler Sales Co., 20815 W. Chicago, Detroit, MI 48228 / 313-273-6889; FAX: 313-273-1099 littlersales@aol.com

Littleton, J. F., 275 Pinedale Ave., Oroville, CA 95966 / 916-533-6084

Ljutic Industries, Inc., 732 N. 16th Ave., Suite 22, Yakima, WA 98902 / 509-248-0476; FAX: 509-576-8233 ljuticgun@earthlink.net www.ljuticgun.com

Lock's Philadelphia Gun Exchange, 6700 Rowland Ave., Philadelphia, PA 19149 / 215-332-6225; FAX: 215-332-4800 locks.gunshop@verizon.net

Lodewick, Walter H., 2816 NE Halsey St., Portland, OR 97232 / 503-284-2554 wlodewick@aol.com

Lodgewood Mfg., P.O. Box 611, Whitewater, WI 53190 / 262-473-5444; FAX: 262-473-6448 lodgewd@idcnet.com lodgewood.com

Log Cabin Sport Shop, 8010 Lafayette Rd., Lodi, OH 44254 / 330-948-1082; FAX: 330-948-4307 logcabin@logcabinshop.com www.logcabinshop.com

Logdewood Mfg., P.O. Box 611, Whitewater, WI 53190 / 262-473-5444; FAX: 262-473-6448 lodgewd@idcnet.com www.lodgewood.com

Lohman Mfg. Co., Inc., 4500 Doniphan Dr., P.O. Box 220, Neosho, MO 64850 / 417-451-4438; FAX: 417-451-2576

Lomont Precision Bullets, 278 Sandy Creek Rd., Salmon, ID 83467 / 208-756-6819; FAX: 208-756-6824 www.klomont.com

London Guns Ltd., Box 3750, Santa Barbara, CA 93130 / 805-683-4141; FAX: 805-683-1712

Lone Star Gunleather, 1301 Brushy Bend Dr., Round Rock, TX 78681 / 512-255-1805

Lone Star Rifle Company, 11231 Rose Road, Conroe, TX 77303 / 936-856-3363; FAX: 936-856-3363 dave@lonestar.com

Long, George F., 1402 Kokanee Ln., Grants Pass, OR 97527 / 541-476-0836

Lortone Inc., 2856 NW Market St., Seattle, WA 98107

Lothar Walther Precision Tool Inc., 3425 Hutchinson Rd., Cumming, GA 30040 / 770-889-9998; FAX: 770-889-4919 lotharwalther@mindspring.com www.lothar-walther.com

LPS Laboratories, Inc., 4647 Hugh Howell Rd., P.O. Box 3050, Tucker, GA 30084 / 404-934-7800

Lucas, Edward E, 32 Garfield Ave., East Brunswick, NJ 08816 / 201-251-5526

Lupton, Keith. See: PAWLING MOUNTAIN CLUB

Lyman Instant Targets, Inc. (See Lyman Products Corp.)

Lyman Products Corp., 475 Smith St., Middletown, CT 06457-1541 / 800-423-9704; FAX: 860-632-1699 lymansales@cshore.com www.lymanproducts.com

M

M.H. Canjar Co., 6510 Raleigh St., Arvada, CO 80003 / 303-295-2638; FAX: 303-295-2638

MA Systems, Inc., P.O. Box 894, Pryor, OK 74362-0894 / 918-824-3705; FAX: 918-824-3710

Mac-1 Airgun Distributors, 13974 Van Ness Ave., Gardena, CA 90249-2900 / 310-327-3581; FAX: 310-327-0238 mac1@maclairgun.com www.mac1airgun.com

Machinist's Workshop-Village Press, P.O. Box 1810, Traverse City, MI 49685 / 800-447-7367; FAX: 616-946-3289

Madis Books, 2453 West Five Mile Pkwy., Dallas, TX 75233 / 214-330-7168

Madis, George. See: WINCHESTER CONSULTANTS

MAG Instrument, Inc., 1635 S. Sacramento Ave., Ontario, CA 91761 / 909-947-1006; FAX: 909-947-3116

Magma Engineering Co., P.O. Box 161, 20955 E. Ocotillo Rd., Queen Creek, AZ 85242 / 602-987-9008; FAX: 602-987-0148

Mag-Na-Port International, Inc., 41302 Executive Dr., Harrison Twp., MI 48045-1306 / 586-469-6727; FAX: 586-469-0425 email@magnaport.com www.magnaport.com

Magnum Power Products, Inc., P.O. Box 17768, Fountain Hills, AZ 85268

Magnum Research, Inc., 7110 University Ave. NE, Minneapolis, MN 55432 / 800-772-6168 or 763-574-1868; FAX: 763-574-0109 info@magnumresearch.com

Magnus Bullets, P.O. Box 239, Toney, AL 35773 / 256-420-8359; FAX: 256-420-8360 bulletman@mchsi.com www.magnusbullets.com

Mag-Pack Corp., P.O. Box 846, Chesterland, OH 44026 / 440-285-9480 magpack@hotmail.com

MagSafe Ammo, Inc., 4700 S. US Highway 17/92, Casselberry, FL 32707-3814 / 407-834-9966; FAX: 407-834-8185 www.magsafeammo.com

Magtech Ammunition Co. Inc., 6845 20th Ave. S., Ste. 120, Centerville, MN 55038 / 651-762-8500; FAX: 651-429-9485 www.magtechammunition.com

Mahovsky's Metalife, R.D. 1, Box 149a Eureka Road, Grand Valley, PA 16420 / 814-436-7747

Makinson, Nicholas, RR 3, Komoka, ON N0L 1R0 CANADA / 519-471-5462

Mallardtone Game Calls, 10406 96th St., Court West, Taylor Ridge, IL 61284 / 309-798-2481; FAX: 309-798-2501

Marble Arms (See CRR, Inc./Marble's Inc.)

Marchmon Bullets, 6502 Riverdale Rd., Whitmore Lake, MI 48189

Marent, Rudolf. See: HAMMERLI SERVICE-PRECISION MAC

Mark Lee Supplies, 9901 France Ct., Lakeville, MN 55044 / 952-461-2114; FAX: 952-461-2194 marklee55044@usfamily.net

Markell, Inc., 422 Larkfield Center 235, Santa Rosa, CA 95403 / 707-573-0792; FAX: 707-573-9867

Markesbery Muzzle Loaders, Inc., 7065 Production Ct., Florence, KY 41042 / 859-342-5553; FAX: 859-342-2380 www.markesbery.com

Marksman Products, 5482 Argosy Dr., Huntington Beach, CA 92649 / 714-898-7535 or 800-822-8005; FAX: 714-891-0782

Marlin Firearms Co., 100 Kenna Dr., North Haven, CT 06473 / 203-239-5621; FAX: 203-234-7991 www.marlinfirearms.com

Marocchi F.lli S.p.A, Via Galileo Galilei 8, I-25068 Zanano, ITALY

Marsh, Mike, Croft Cottage, Main St., Derbyshire, DE4 2BY ENGLAND / 01629 650 669

Marshall Enterprises, 792 Canyon Rd., Redwood City, CA 94062

Marshall Fish Mfg. Gunsmith Sptg. Co., 87 Champlain Ave., Westport, NY 12993 / 518-962-4897; FAX: 518-962-4897

Martin B. Retting Inc., 11029 Washington, Culver City, CA 90232 / 213-837-2412 retting@retting.com

Martini & Hagn, Ltd., 1264 Jimsmith Lake Rd., Cranbrook, BC V1C 6V6 CANADA / 250-417-2926; FAX: 250-417-2928 martini-hagn@shaw.ca www.martiniandhagngunmakers.com

Martin's Gun Shop, 937 S. Sheridan Blvd., Lakewood, CO 80226 / 303-922-2184

Martz, John V., 8060 Lakeview Lane, Lincoln, CA 95648 FAX: 916-645-3815

Marvel, Alan, 3922 Madonna Rd., Jarretsville, MD 21084 / 301-557-6545

Marx, Harry (See U.S. Importer for FERLIB)

Maryland Paintball Supply, 8507 Harford Rd., Parkville, MD 21234 / 410-882-5607

Master Lock Co., 2600 N. 32nd St., Milwaukee, WI 53245 / 414-444-2800

Match Prep-Doyle Gracey, P.O. Box 155, Tehachapi, CA 93581 / 661-822-5383; FAX: 661-823-8680 gracenotes@csurpers.net www.matchprep.com

Mathews Gun Shop & Gunsmithing, Inc., 2791 S. Gaffey St., San Pedro, CA 90731-6515 / 562-928-2129; FAX: 562-928-8629

Matthews Cutlery, 4401 Sentry Dr. #B, Tucker, GA 30084 / 770-939-6915

Mauser Werke Oberndorf Waffensysteme GmbH, Postfach 1349, 78722, Oberndorf/N., GERMANY

Maverick Arms, Inc., 7 Grasso Ave., P.O. Box 497, North Haven, CT 06473 / 203-230-5300; FAX: 203-230-5420

Maxi-Mount Inc., P.O. Box 291, Willoughby Hills, OH 44096-0291 / 440-944-9456; FAX: 440-944-9456 maximount454@yahoo.com

Mayville Engineering Co. (See MEC, Inc.)

Mazur Restoration, Pete, 13083 Drummer Way, Grass Valley, CA 95949 / 530-268-2412

McCament, Jay. See: JAY MCCAMENT CUSTOM GUNMAKER

McCann, Tom, 14 Walton Dr., New Hope, PA 18938 / 215-862-2728

McCann Industries, P.O. Box 641, Spanaway, WA 98387 / 253-537-6919; FAX: 253-537-6919 mccann.machine@worldnet.att.net www.mccannindustries.com

McCluskey Precision Rifles, 10502 14th Ave. NW, Seattle, WA 98177 / 206-781-2776

McCombs, Leo, 1862 White Cemetery Rd., Patriot, OH 45658 / 740-256-1714

McDonald, Dennis, 8359 Brady St., Peosta, IA 52068 / 319-556-7940

McFarland, Stan, 2221 Idella Ct., Grand Junction, CO 81505 / 970-243-4704

McGhee, Larry. See: B.C. OUTDOORS

McGowen Rifle Barrels, 5961 Spruce Lane, St. Anne, IL 60964 / 815-937-9816; FAX: 815-937-4024

Mchalik, Gary. See: ROSSI FIREARMS

McKenzie, Lynton, 6940 N. Alvernon Way, Tucson, AZ 85718 / 520-299-5090

McMillan Fiberglass Stocks, Inc., 1638 W. Knudsen Dr. #102, Phoenix, AZ 85027 / 623-582-9635; FAX: 623-581-3825 mfsinc@mcmfamily.com www.mcmfamily.com

McMillan Optical Gunsight Co., 28638 N. 42nd St., Cave Creek, AZ 85331 / 602-585-7868; FAX: 602-585-7872

McMillan Rifle Barrels, P.O. Box 3427, Bryan, TX 77805 / 409-690-3456; FAX: 409-690-0156

McMurdo, Lynn, P.O. Box 404, Afton, WY 83110 / 307-886-5535

MCS, Inc., 166 Pocono Rd., Brookfield, CT 06804-2023 / 203-775-1013; FAX: 203-775-9462

McWelco Products, 6730 Santa Fe Ave., Hesperia, CA 92345 / 619-244-8876; FAX: 619-244-9398 products@mcwelco.com www.mcwelco.com

MDS, P.O. Box 1441, Brandon, FL 33509-1441 / 813-653-1180; FAX: 813-684-5953

Meacham Tool & Hardware Co., Inc., 37052 Eberhardt Rd., Peck, ID 83545 / 208-486-7171 smeacham@clearwater.net www.meachamrifles.com

Measures, Leon. See: SHOOT WHERE YOU LOOK

MEC, Inc., 715 South St., Mayville, WI 53050 reloaders@mayvl.com www.mecreloaders.com

MEC-Gar S.R.L., Via Madonnina 64, Gardone V.T. Brescia, ITALY / 39-030-3733668; FAX: 39-030-3733687 info@mec-gar.it www.mec-gar.it

MEC-Gar U.S.A., Inc., Hurley Farms Industr. Park, 115, Hurley Road 6G, Oxford, CT 06478 / 203-262-1525; FAX: 203-262-1719 mecgar@aol.com www.mec-gar.com

Mech-Tech Systems, Inc., 1602 Foothill Rd., Kalispell, MT 59901 / 406-755-8055

Meister Bullets (See Gander Mountain)

Mele, Frank, 201 S. Wellow Ave., Cookeville, TN 38501 / 615-526-4860

Menck, Gunsmith Inc., T.W., 5703 S 77th St., Ralston, NE 68127

Mendez, John A., 1309 Continental Dr., Daytona Beach, FL 32117-3807 / 407-344-2791

Men-Metallwerk Elisenhuette GmbH, P.O. Box 1263, Nassau/Lahn, D-56372 GERMANY / 2604-7819

Meopta USA, LLC, 50 Davids Dr., Hauppauge, NY 11788 / 631-436-5900 ussales@meopta.com www.meopta.com

Meprolight (See Hesco-Meprolight)

Mercer Custom Guns, 216 S. Whitewater Ave., Jefferson, WI 53549 / 920-674-3839

Merit Corp., P.O. Box 9044, Schenectady, NY 12309 / 518-346-1420 sales@meritcorporation.com www.meritcorporation.com

Merkel, Schutzenstrasse 26, D-98527 Suhl, Suhl, GERMANY FAX: 011-49-3681-854-203 www.merkel-waffen.de

Metal Merchants, P.O. Box 186, Walled Lake, MI 48390-0186

Metalife Industries (See Mahovsky's Metalife)

Michael's Antiques, Box 591, Waldoboro, ME 04572

Michaels of Oregon Co., 9200 Cody St., Overland Park, KS 66214 / 800-845-2444 www.michaels-oregon.com

Micro Sight Co., 502 May St., Arroyo Grande, CA 93420-2832

Microfusion Alfa S.A., Paseo San Andres N8, P.O. Box 271, Eibar 20600, 20600 SPAIN / 34-43-11-89-16; FAX: 34-43-11-40-38

Mid-America Recreation, Inc., 1328 5th Ave., Moline, IL 61265 / 309-764-5089; FAX: 309-764-5089 fmilcusguns@aol.com www.midamericarecreation.com

Middlebrooks Custom Shop, 7366 Colonial Trail East, Surry, VA 23883 / 757-357-0881; FAX: 757-365-0442

Midway Arms, Inc., 5875 W. Van Horn Tavern Rd., Columbia, MO 65203 / 800-243-3220; FAX: 800-992-8312 www.midwayusa.com

Midwest Gun Sport, 1108 Herbert Dr., Zebulon, NC 27597 / 919-269-5570

Midwest Shooting School, The, Pat LaBoone, 2550 Hwy. 23, Wrenshall, MN 55797 / 218-384-3670 shootingschool@starband.net

Midwest Sport Distributors, Box 129, Fayette, MO 65248

Mike Davis Products, 643 Loop Dr., Moses Lake, WA 98837 / 509-765-6178; or 509-766-7281

Mike Yee Custom Stocking, 29927 56 Pl. S., Auburn, WA 98001 / 253-839-3991 miknadyee@comcast.net

Military Armament Corp., P.O. Box 120, Mt. Zion Rd., Lingleville, TX 76461 / 817-965-3253

Millennium Designed Muzzleloaders, P.O. Box 536, Routes 11 & 25, Limington, ME 04049 / 207-637-2316

Miller Arms, Inc., 1310 Industry Rd., Sturgis, SD 57785-9129 / 605-642-5160; FAX: 605-642-5160

Miller Custom, 210 E. Julia, Clinton, IL 61727 / 217-935-9362

Miller Single Trigger Mfg. Co., 6680 Rt. 5-20, P.O. Box 471, Bloomfield, NY 14469 / 585-657-6338

Millett Sights, 7275 Murdy Circle, Adm. Office, Huntington Beach, CA 92647 / 714-842-5575 or 800-645-5388; FAX: 714-843-5707

Mills Jr., Hugh B., 3615 Canterbury Rd., New Bern, NC 28560 / 919-637-4631

Milstor Corp., 80-975 Indio Blvd. C-7, Indio, CA 92201 / 760-775-9998; FAX: 760-775-5229 milstor@webtv.net

Minute Man High Tech Industries, 10611 Canyon Rd. E., Suite 151, Puyallup, WA 98373 / 800-233-2734

Mirador Optical Corp., P.O. Box 11614, Marina Del Rey, CA 90295-7614 / 310-821-5587; FAX: 310-305-0386

Mitchell, Jack, c/o Geoff Gaebe, Addieville East Farm, 200 Pheasant Dr., Mapleville, RI 02839 / 401-568-3185

Mitchell Mfg. Corp., P.O. Box 9295, Fountain Valley, CA 92728 / 714-444-2220

Mitchell Optics, Inc., 2072 CR 1100 N, Sidney, IL 61877 / 217-688-2219 or 217-621-3018; FAX: 217-688-2505 mitchell@attglobal.net

Mitchell's Accuracy Shop, 68 Greenridge Dr., Stafford, VA 22554 / 703-659-0165

Mitchell's Mauser, P.O. Box 9295, Fountain Valley, CA 92728 / 714-979-7663; FAX: 714-899-3660

MI-TE Bullets, 1396 Ave. K, Ellsworth, KS 67439 / 785-472-4575; FAX: 785-472-5579

Mixson Corp., 7635 W. 28th Ave., Hialeah, FL 33016 / 305-821-5190 or 800-327-0078; FAX: 305-558-9318

MJK Gunsmithing, Inc., 417 N. Huber Ct., E. Wenatchee, WA 98802 / 509-884-7683

MKS Supply, Inc. (See Hi-Point Firearms)

MMC, 4430 Mitchell St., North Las Vegas, NV 89081 / 800-998-7483; FAX: 702-267-9463 info@mmcsight.com www.mmcsight.com

MOA Corporation, 285 Government Valley Rd., Sundance, WY 82729 / 307-283-3030 www.moaguns.com

Mobile Area Networks, Inc., 2772 Depot St., Sanford, FL 32773 / 407-333-2350; FAX: 407-333-9903 georgew@mobilan.com www.mobilan.com

Modern Gun Repair School, P.O. Box 846, Saint Albans, VT 05478 / 802-524-2223; FAX: 802-524-2053 jfwp@dlilearn.com www.mgsinfoadlifearn.com

Modern Muzzleloading, Inc., P.O. Box 130, Centerville, IA 52544 / 515-856-2626

Moeller, Steve, 1213 4th St., Fulton, IL 61252 / 815-589-2300

Mogul Co./Life Jacket, 500 N. Kimball Rd., Ste. 109, South Lake, TX 76092

Monell Custom Guns, 228 Red Mills Rd., Pine Bush, NY 12566 / 914-744-3021

Moneymaker Guncraft Corp., 1420 Military Ave., Omaha, NE 68131 / 402-556-0226

Montana Armory, Inc., 100 Centennial Dr., P.O. Box 885, Big Timber, MT 59011 / 406-932-4353; FAX: 406-932-4443

Montana Outfitters, Lewis E. Yearout, 308 Riverview Dr. E., Great Falls, MT 59404 / 406-761-0859; or 406-727-4560

Montana Precision Swaging, P.O. Box 4746, Butte, MT 59702 / 406-494-0600; FAX: 406-494-0600

Montana Rifleman, Inc., 2593A Hwy. 2 East, Kalispell, MT 59901 / 406-755-4867

Montana Vintage Arms, 2354 Bear Canyon Rd., Bozeman, MT 59715

Morini (See U.S. Importers-Mandall Shooting Supplies, Inc.)

Morrison Custom Rifles, J. W., 4015 W Sharon, Phoenix, AZ 85029 / 602-978-3754

Morrison Precision, 6719 Calle Mango, Hereford, AZ 85615 / 520-378-6207 morprec@c2i2.com

Morrow, Bud, 11 Hillside Lane, Sheridan, WY 82801-9729 / 307-674-8360

Morton Booth Co., P.O. Box 123, Joplin, MO 64802 / 417-673-1962; FAX: 417-673-3642

Mo's Competitor Supplies (See MCS, Inc.)

Moss Double Tone, Inc., P.O. Box 1112, 2101 S. Kentucky, Sedalia, MO 65301 / 816-827-0827

Mountain Plains Industries, 3720 Otter Place, Lynchburg, VA 24503 / 800-687-3000; FAX: 434-386-6217 MPI_targets@adelphia.net

MANUFACTURER'S DIRECTORY

Mowrey Gun Works, P.O. Box 246, Waldron, IN 46182 / 317-525-6181; FAX: 317-525-9595

Mowrey's Guns & Gunsmithing, 119 Fredericks St., Canajoharie, NY 13317 / 518-673-3483

MPC, P.O. Box 450, McMinnville, TN 37110-0450 / 615-473-5513; FAX: 615-473-5516 thebox@blomand.net www.mpc-thebox.com

MPI Stocks, P.O. Box 83266, Portland, OR 97283 / 503-226-1215; FAX: 503-226-2661

MSR Targets, P.O. Box 1042, West Covina, CA 91793 / 818-331-7840

MTM Molded Products Co., Inc., 3370 Obco Ct., Dayton, OH 45414 / 937-890-7461; FAX: 937-890-1747

Mulberry House Publishing, P.O. Box 2180, Apache Junction, AZ 85217 / 888-738-1567; FAX: 480-671-1015

Mulhern, Rick, Rt. 5, Box 152, Rayville, LA 71269 / 318-728-2688

Mullins Ammunition, Rt. 2 Box 304N, Clintwood, VA 24228 / 276-926-6772; FAX: 276-926-6092 mammo@extremeshockusa.com www.extremeshockusa.com

Mullis Guncraft, 3523 Lawyers Road E., Monroe, NC 28110 / 704-283-6683

Multiplex International, 26 S. Main St., Concord, NH 03301 FAX: 603-796-2223

Multipropulseurs, La Bertrandiere, 42580, FRANCE / 77 74 01 30; FAX: 77 93 19 34

Mundy, Thomas A., 69 Robbins Road, Somerville, NJ 08876 / 201-722-2199

Murmur Corp., 2823 N. Westmoreland Ave., Dallas, TX 75222 / 214-630-5400

Murphy, R.R. Murphy Co., Inc. See: MURPHY, R.R. CO., INC.

Murphy, R.R. Co., Inc., R.R. Murphy Co., Inc. Murphy, P.O. Box 102, Ripley, TN 38063 / 901-635-4003; FAX: 901-635-2320

Murray State College, 1 Murray Campus St., Tishomingo, OK 73460 / 508-371-2371 darnold@mscol.edu

Muscle Products Corp., 112 Fennell Dr., Butler, PA 16002 / 800-227-7049 or 724-283-0567; FAX: 724-283-8310 mpc@mpc_home.com www.mpc_home.com

Muzzleloaders Etcetera, Inc., 9901 Lyndale Ave. S., Bloomington, MN 55420 / 952-884-1161 www.muzzleloaders-etcetera.com

MWG Co., P.O. Box 971202, Miami, FL 33197 / 800-428-9394 or 305-253-8393; FAX: 305-232-1247

N

N.B.B., Inc., 24 Elliot Rd., Sterling, MA 01564 / 508-422-7538 or 800-942-9444

N.C. Ordnance Co., P.O. Box 3254, Wilson, NC 27895 / 919-237-2440; FAX: 919-243-9845 bharvey@nc.rr.com www.gungrip.com

Nagel's Custom Bullets, 100 Scott St., Baytown, TX 77520-2849

Nalpak, 1267 Vernon Way, El Cajon, CA 92020

Nammo Lapua Oy, P.O. Box 5, Lapua, FINLAND / 358-6-4310111; FAX: 358-6-4310317 info@nammo.ti www.lapua.com

Nastoff, Steve. See: NASTOFFS 45 SHOP, INC.

Nastoffs 45 Shop, Inc., Steve Nastoff, 1057 Laverne Dr., Youngstown, OH 44511

National Bullet Co., 1585 E. 361 St., Eastlake, OH 44095 / 216-951-1854; FAX: 216-951-7761

National Target Co., 3958-D Dartmouth Ct., Frederick, MD 21703 / 800-827-7060; FAX: 301-874-4764

Nationwide Airgun Repair, 2310 Windsor Forest Dr., Louisville, KY 40272 / 502-937-2614; FAX: 812-637-1463 shortshoestring@insightbb.com

Naval Ordnance Works, 467 Knott Rd., Sheperdstown, WV 25443 / 304-876-0998; FAX: 304-876-0998 nvordfdy@earthlink.net

Navy Arms Company, 219 Lawn St., Martinsburg, WV 25401 / 304-262-9870; FAX: 304-262-1658 info@navyarms.com www.navyarms.com

NCP Products, Inc., 3500 12th St. N.W., Canton, OH 44708 / 330-456-5130; FAX: 330-456-5234

Necessary Concepts, Inc., P.O. Box 571, Deer Park, NY 11729 / 516-667-8509; FAX: 516-667-8588

NEI Handtools, Inc., 10960 Gary Player Dr., El Paso, TX 79935

Neil A. Jones Custom Products, 17217 Brookhouser Road, Saegertown, PA 16433 / 814-763-2769; FAX: 814-763-4228

Nelson, Gary K., 975 Terrace Dr., Oakdale, CA 95361 / 209-847-4590

Nelson, Stephen. See: NELSON'S CUSTOM GUNS, INC.

Nelson's Custom Guns, Inc., Stephen Nelson, 7430 Valley View Dr. N.W., Corvallis, OR 97330 / 541-745-5232 nelsons-custom@attbi.com

Nesci Enterprises Inc., P.O. Box 119, Summit St., East Hampton, CT 06424 / 203-267-2588

Nesika Bay Precision, 22239 Big Valley Rd., Poulsbo, WA 98370 / 206-697-3830

Nettestad Gun Works, 38962 160th Avenue, Pelican Rapids, MN 56572 / 218-863-1338

Neumann GmbH, Am Galgenberg 6, 90575, GERMANY / 09101/8258; FAX: 09101/6356

New England Ammunition Co., 1771 Post Rd. East, Suite 223, Westport, CT 06880 / 203-254-8048

New England Arms Co., Box 278, Lawrence Lane, Kittery Point, ME 03905 / 207-439-0593; FAX: 207-439-0525 info@newenglandarms.com www.newenglandarms.com

New England Custom Gun Service, 438 Willow Brook Rd., Plainfield, NH 03781 / 603-469-3450; FAX: 603-469-3471 bestguns@adelphia.net www.newenglandcustom.com

New Orleans Jewelers Supply Co., 206 Charters St., New Orleans, LA 70130 / 504-523-3839; FAX: 504-523-3836

New SKB Arms Co., C.P.O. Box 1401, Tokyo, JAPAN / 81-3-3943-9550; FAX: 81-3-3943-0695

New Ultra Light Arms, LLC, P.O. Box 340, Granville, WV 26534

Newark Electronics, 4801 N. Ravenswood Ave., Chicago, IL 60640

Newell, Robert H., 55 Coyote, Los Alamos, NM 87544 / 505-662-7135

Newman Gunshop, 2035 Chester Ave. #411, Ottumwa, IA 52501-3715 / 515-937-5775

NgraveR Co., The, 67 Wawecus Hill Rd., Bozrah, CT 06334 / 860-823-1533; FAX: 860-887-6252 ngraver98@aol.com www.ngraver.com

Nicholson Custom, 17285 Thornlay Road, Hughesville, MO 65334 / 816-826-8746

Nickels, Paul R., 2216 Jacob Dr., Santa Clara, UT 84765-5399 / 435-652-1959

Niemi Engineering, W. B., Box 126 Center Rd., Greensboro, VT 05841 / 802-533-7180; FAX: 802-533-7141

Nighthawk Custom, 1306 W. Trimble, Berryville, AR 72616 / 877-268-GUNS; (4867) or 870-423-GUNS; FAX: 870-423-4230 www.nighthawkcustom.com

Nikon, Inc., 1300 Walt Whitman Rd., Melville, NY 11747 / 516-547-8623; FAX: 516-547-0309

Noreen, Peter H., 5075 Buena Vista Dr., Belgrade, MT 59714 / 406-586-7383

Norica, Avnda Otaola, 16 Apartado 68, Eibar, SPAIN

Norinco, 7A Yun Tan N, Beijing, CHINA

Norincoptics (See BEC, Inc.)

Norma Precision AB (See U.S. Importers-Dynamit)

Normark Corp., 10395 Yellow Circle Dr., Minnetonka, MN 55343-9101 / 612-933-7060; FAX: 612-933-0046

North American Arms, Inc., 2150 South 950 East, Provo, UT 84606-6285 / 800-821-5783 or 801-374-9990; FAX: 801-374-9998

North American Correspondence Schools, The Gun Pro, Oak & Pawney St., Scranton, PA 18515 / 717-342-7701

North American Shooting Systems, P.O. Box 306, Osoyoos, BC V0H 1V0 CANADA / 250-495-3131; FAX: 250-495-3131 rifle@cablerocket.com

North Devon Firearms Services, 3 North St., Braunton, EX33 1AJ ENGLAND / 01271 813624; FAX: 01271 813624

North Mountain Pine Training Center (See Executive Protection Institute)

North Star West, 20242 Smokey Rd., Frenchtown, MT 59834 / 406-626-4081 northstarwest.com

Northern Precision, 329 S. James St., Carthage, NY 13619 / 315-493-1711

Northside Gun Shop, 2725 NW 109th, Oklahoma City, OK 73120 / 405-840-2353

Northwest Custom Projectile, P.O. Box 127, Butte, MT 59703-0127 www.customprojectile.com

No-Sho Mfg. Co., 10727 Glenfield Ct., Houston, TX 77096 / 713-723-5332

Nosler, Inc., P.O. Box 671, Bend, OR 97709 / 800-285-3701 or 541-382-3921; FAX: 541-388-4667 www.nosler.com

Novak's, Inc., 1206 1/2 30th St., P.O. Box 4045, Parkersburg, WV 26101 / 304-485-9295; FAX: 304-428-6722 www.novaksights.com

Nowlin Mfg. Co., 20622 S 4092 Rd., Claremore, OK 74017 / 918-342-0689; FAX: 918-342-0624 nowlinguns@msn.com nowlinguns.com

NRI Gunsmith School, P.O. Box 182968, Columbus, OH 43218-2968

Nu Line Guns, 8150 CR 4055, Rhineland, MO 65069 / 573-676-5500; FAX: 314-447-5018 nlg@ktis.net

Null Holsters Ltd. K.L., 161 School St. N.W., Resaca, GA 30735 / 706-625-5643; FAX: 706-625-9392 ken@klnullholsters.com www.klnullholsters.com

Numrich Gun Parts Corporation, 226 Williams Lane, P.O. Box 299, West Hurley, NY 12491 / 866-686-7424; FAX: 877-GUNPART info@gunpartscorp.com www.@e-gunparts.com

O

O.F. Mossberg & Sons, Inc., 7 Grasso Ave., North Haven, CT 06473 / 203-230-5300; FAX: 203-230-5420

Oakman Turkey Calls, RD 1, Box 825, Harrisonville, PA 17228 / 717-485-4620

Obermeyer Rifled Barrels, 23122 60th St., Bristol, WI 53104 / 262-843-3537; FAX: 262-843-2129 www.obermeyerbarrels.com

October Country Muzzleloading, P.O. Box 969, Dept. GD, Hayden, ID 83835 / 208-772-2068; FAX: 208-772-9230 ocinfo@octobercountry.com www.octobercountry.com

Oehler Research, Inc., P.O. Box 9135, Austin, TX 78766 / 512-327-6900 or 800-531-5125; FAX: 512-327-6903 www.oehler-research.com

Oil Rod and Gun Shop, 69 Oak St., East Douglas, MA 01516 / 508-476-3687

OK Weber, Inc., P.O. Box 7485, Eugene, OR 97401 / 541-747-0458; FAX: 541-747-5927 okweber@pacinfo www.okweber.com

Oker's Engraving, P.O. Box 126, Shawnee, CO 80475 / 303-838-6042 engraver@netscape.com

Oklahoma Ammunition Co., 3701A S. Harvard Ave., No. 367, Tulsa, OK 74135-2265 / 918-396-3187; FAX: 918-396-4270

Oklahoma Leather Products, Inc., 500 26th NW, Miami, OK 74354 / 918-542-6651; FAX: 918-542-6653

Olathe Gun Shop, 716-A South Rogers Road, Olathe, KS 66062 / 913-782-6900; FAX: 913-782-6902 info@olathegunshop.com www.olathegunshop.com

Old Wagon Bullets, 32 Old Wagon Rd., Wilton, CT 06897

Old West Bullet Moulds, J. Ken Chapman, P.O. Box 519, Flora Vista, NM 87415 / 505-334-6970

Old West Reproductions, Inc. R.M. Bachman, 446 Florence S. Loop, Florence, MT 59833 / 406-273-2615; FAX: 406-273-2615 rick@oldwestreproductions.com www.oldwestreproductions.com

Old Western Scrounger LLC, 219 Lawn St., Martinsburg, NV 25401 / 304-262-9870; FAX: 304-262-1658 www.ows-ammo.com

Ole Frontier Gunsmith Shop, 2617 Hwy. 29 S., Cantonment, FL 32533 / 904-477-8074

Olson, Myron, 989 W. Kemp, Watertown, SD 57201 / 605-886-9787

Olson, Vic, 5002 Countryside Dr., Imperial, MO 63052 / 314-296-8086

Olympic Arms Inc., 620-626 Old Pacific Hwy. SE, Olympia, WA 98513 / 360-456-3471; FAX: 360-491-3447 info@olyarms.com www.olyarms.com

Olympic Optical Co., P.O. Box 752377, Memphis, TN 38175-2377 / 901-794-3890 or 800-238-7120; FAX: 901-794-0676

One Of A Kind, 15610 Purple Sage, San Antonio, TX 78255 / 512-695-3364

One Ragged Hole, P.O. Box 13624, Tallahassee, FL 32317-3624

Op-Tec, P.O. Box L632, Langhorn, PA 19047 / 215-757-5037; FAX: 215-757-7097

Optical Services Co., P.O. Box 1174, Santa Teresa, NM 88008-1174 / 505-589-3833

Orchard Park Enterprise, P.O. Box 563, Orchard Park, NY 14127 / 616-656-0356

Ordnance Works, The, 2969 Pigeon Point Rd., Eureka, CA 95501 / 707-443-3252

Oregon Arms, Inc. (See Rogue Rifle Co., Inc.)

Oregon Trail Bullet Company, P.O. Box 529, Dept. P, Baker City, OR 97814 / 800-811-0548; FAX: 514-523-1803

Original Deer Formula Co., The, P.O. Box 1705, Dickson, TN 37056 / 800-874-6965; FAX: 615-446-0646 deerformula1@aol.com www.deerformula.com

Orion Rifle Barrel Co., RR2, 137 Cobler Village, Kalispell, MT 59901 / 406-257-5649

Orvis Co., The, Rt. 7, Manchester, VT 05254 / 802-362-3622; FAX: 802-362-3525

Otis Technology, Inc., RR 1 Box 84, Boonville, NY 13309 / 315-942-3320

Ottmar, Maurice, Box 657, 113 E. Fir, Coulee City, WA 99115 / 509-632-5717

Outa-Site Gun Carriers, 219 Market St., Laredo, TX 78040 / 210-722-4678 or 800-880-9715; FAX: 210-726-4858

Outdoor Connection, Inc., The, 7901 Panther Way, Waco, TX 76712-6556 / 800-533-6076; FAX: 254-776-3553 info@outdoorconnection.com www.outdoorconnection.com

Outdoor Edge Cutlery Corp., 4699 Nautilus Ct. S. Ste. 503, Boulder, CO 80301-5310 / 303-530-7667; FAX: 303-530-7020 www.outdooredge.com

Outdoor Enthusiast, 3784 W. Woodland, Springfield, MO 65807 / 417-883-9841

Outdoor Sports Headquarters, Inc., 967 Watertower Ln., West Carrollton, OH 45449 / 513-865-5855; FAX: 513-865-5962

Outers Laboratories Div. of ATK, Route 2, P.O. Box 39, Onalaska, WI 54650 / 608-781-5800; FAX: 608-781-0368

Ox-Yoke Originals, Inc., 34 Main St., Milo, ME 04463 / 800-231-8313 or 207-943-7351; FAX: 207-943-2416

Ozark Gun Works, 11830 Cemetery Rd., Rogers, AR 72756 / 479-631-1024; FAX: 479-631-1024 ozarkgunworks@cox.net www.geocities.com

P

P&M Sales & Services, LLC, 4697 Tote Rd. Bldg. H-B, Comins, MI 48619 / 989-848-8364; FAX: 989-848-8364 info@pmsales-online.com

P.S.M.G. Gun Co., 10 Park Ave., Arlington, MA 02174 / 781-646-1699; FAX: 781-643-7212 psmg2@aol.com

Pachmayr Div. Lyman Products, 475 Smith St., Middletown, CT 06457 / 860-632-2020 or 800-225-9626; FAX: 860-632-1699 lymansales@cshore.com www.pachmayr.com

Pacific Armament Corp, 4813 Enterprise Way, Unit K, Modesto, CA 95356 / 209-545-2800 gunsparts@att.net

Pacific Rifle Co., P.O. Box 841, Carlton, OR 97111 / 503-852-6276 pacificrifle@aol.com

PAC-NOR Barreling, 99299 Overlook Rd., P.O. Box 6188, Brookings, OR 97415 / 503-469-7330; FAX: 503-469-7331 info@pac-nor.com www.pac-nor.com

PACT, Inc., P.O. Box 535025, Grand Prairie, TX 75053 / 972-641-0049; FAX: 972-641-2641

Page Custom Bullets, P.O. Box 25, Port Moresby, NEW GUINEA

Pagel Gun Works, Inc., 2 SE 1st St., Grand Rapids, MN 55744

Pager Pal, P.O. Box 54864, Hurst, TX 76054-4864 / 800-561-1603; FAX: 817-285-8769 info@pagerpal.com www.pagerpal.com

Paintball Games International Magazine Aceville, Castle House 97 High St., Essex, ENGLAND / 011-44-206-564840

Palsa Outdoor Products, P.O. Box 81336, Lincoln, NE 68501 / 402-488-5288; FAX: 402-488-2321

Pansch, Robert F, 1004 Main St. #10, Neenah, WI 54956 / 920-725-8175

Paragon Sales & Services, Inc., 2501 Theodore St., Crest Hill, IL 60435-1613 / 815-725-9212; FAX: 815-725-8974

Para-Ordnance Mfg., Inc., 980 Tapscott Rd., Scarborough, ON M1X 1E7 CANADA / 416-297-7855; FAX: 416-297-1289

Para-Ordnance, Inc., 1919 NE 45th St., Ste 215, Ft. Lauderdale, FL 33308 / 416-297-7855; FAX: 416-297-1289 info@paraord.com www.paraord.com

Pardini Armi Srl, Via Italica 154, 55043, Lido Di Camaiore Lu, ITALY / 584-90121; FAX: 584-90122

Paris, Frank J., 17417 Pershing St., Livonia, MI 48152-3822

Park Rifle Co., Ltd., The, Unit 6a Dartford Trade Park, Power Mill Lane, Dartford DA7 7NX, ENGLAND / 011-0322-222512

Parker & Sons Shooting Supply, 9337 Smoky Row Road, Strawberry Plains, TN 37871 / 865-933-3286; FAX: 865-932-8586

Parker Gun Finishes, 9337 Smokey Row Rd., Strawberry Plains, TN 37871 / 865-933-3286; FAX: 865-932-8586 parcraft7838@netzero.com

Parsons Optical Mfg. Co., PO Box 192, Ross, OH 45061 / 513-867-0820; FAX: 513-867-8380 psscopes@concentric.net

Partridge Sales Ltd., John, Trent Meadows, Rugeley, ENGLAND

Pasadena Gun Center, 206 E. Shaw, Pasadena, TX 77506 / 713-472-0417; FAX: 713-472-1322

Passive Bullet Traps, Inc. (See Savage Range Systems, Inc.)

Paterson Gunsmithing, 438 Main St., Paterson, NJ 07502 / 201-345-4100

Pathfinder Sports Leather, 2920 E. Chambers St., Phoenix, AZ 85040 / 602-276-0016

Patrick W. Price Bullets, 16520 Worthley Drive, San Lorenzo, CA 94580 / 510-278-1547

Pattern Control, 114 N. Third St., P.O. Box 462105, Garland, TX 75046 / 214-494-3551; FAX: 214-272-8447

Paul A. Harris Hand Engraving, 113 Rusty Lane, Boerne, TX 78006-5746 / 512-391-5121

Paul and Sharon Dressel, 209 N. 92nd Ave., Yakima, WA 98908 / 509-966-9233; FAX: 509-966-3365 dressels@nwinfo.net www.dressels.com

Paul Co., The, 27385 Pressonville Rd., Wellsville, KS 66092 / 785-883-4444; FAX: 785-883-2525

Paul D. Hillmer Custom Gunstocks, 7251 Hudson Heights, Hudson, IA 50643 / 319-988-3941

Paul Jones Moulds, 4901 Telegraph Rd., Los Angeles, CA 90022 / 213-262-1510

Paulsen Gunstocks, Rt. 71, Box 11, Chinook, MT 59523 / 406-357-3403

Pawling Mountain Club, Keith Lupton, P.O. Box 573, Pawling, NY 12564 / 914-855-3825

Paxton Quigley's Personal Protection Strategies, 9903 Santa Monica Blvd., 300, Beverly Hills, CA 90212 / 310-281-1762 www.defend-net.com/paxton

Payne Photography, Robert, Robert, P.O. Box 141471, Austin, TX 78714 / 512-272-4554

Peacemaker Specialists, 144 Via Fuchsia, Paso Robles, CA 93446 / 805-238-9100; FAX: 805-238-9100 www.peacemakerspecialists.com

Pearce Grip, Inc., P.O. Box 40367, Fort Worth, TX 76140 / 817-568-9704; FAX: 817-568-9707 info@pearcegrip.com www.pearcegrip.com

PECAR Herbert Schwarz GmbH, Kreuzbergstrasse 6, 10965, Berlin, GERMANY / 004930-785-7383; FAX: 004930-785-1934 michael.schwart@pecar-berlin.de www.pecar-berlin.de

Pecatonica River Longrifle, 5205 Nottingham Dr., Rockford, IL 61111 / 815-968-1995; FAX: 815-968-1996

Pedersen, C. R., 2717 S. Pere Marquette Hwy., Ludington, MI 49431 / 231-843-2061; FAX: 231-845-7695 fega@fega.com

Pedersen, Rex C., 2717 S. Pere Marquette Hwy., Ludington, MI 49431 / 231-843-2061; FAX: 231-845-7695 fega@fega.com

Peifer Rifle Co., P.O. Box 220, Nokomis, IL 62075

Pejsa Ballistics, 1314 Marquette Ave., Apt 906, Minneapolis, MN 55403 / 612-332-5073; FAX: 612-332-5204 pejsa@sprintmail.com pejsa.com

Peltor, Inc. (See Aero Peltor)

Pence Precision Barrels, 7567 E. 900 S., S. Whitley, IN 46787 / 219-839-4745

Pendleton Woolen Mills, P.O. Box 3030, 220 N.W. Broadway, Portland, OR 97208 / 503-226-4801

Penn Bullets, P.O. Box 756, Indianola, PA 15051

Pennsylvania Gun Parts Inc., RR 7 Box 150, Mount Pleasant, PA 15666

Pennsylvania Gunsmith School, 812 Ohio River Blvd., Avalon, Pittsburgh, PA 15202 / 412-766-1812; FAX: 412-766-0855 pgs@pagunsmith.com www.pagunsmith.com

Penrod, Mark. See: PENROD PRECISION

Penrod Precision, Mark Penrod, 312 College Ave., P.O. Box 307, N. Manchester, IN 46962 / 260-982-8385; FAX: 260-982-1819 markpenrod@kconline.com

Pentax U.S.A., Inc., 600 12th St. Ste. 300, Golden, CO 80401 / 303-799-8000; FAX: 303-460-1628 www.pentaxlightseeker.com

Pentheny de Pentheny, c/o H.P. Okelly, 321 S. Main St., Sebastopol, CA 95472 / 707-824-1637; FAX: 707-824-1637

Perazone-Gunsmith, Brian, Cold Spring Rd., Roxbury, NY 12474 / 607-326-4088; FAX: 607-326-3140 bpgunsmith@catskill.net www.bpgunsmith@catskill.net

Perazzi U.S.A. Inc., 1010 West Tenth, Azusa, CA 91702 / 626-334-1234; FAX: 626-334-0344 perazziusa@aol.com

Performance Specialists, 308 Eanes School Rd., Austin, TX 78746 / 512-327-0119

Perugini Visini & Co. S.r.l., Via Camprelle, 126, 25080 Nuvolera, ITALY / 30-6897535; FAX: 30-6897821 peruvisi@virgilia.it

Pete de Coux Auction House, 14940 Brenda Dr., Prescott, AZ 86305-7447 / 928-776-8285; FAX: 928-776-8276 pdbullets@commspeed.net

Pete Mazur Restoration, 13083 Drummer Way, Grass Valley, CA 95949 / 530-268-2412; FAX: 530-268-2412

Pete Rickard, Inc., 115 Roy Walsh Rd, Cobleskill, NY 12043 / 518-234-2731; FAX: 518-234-2454 rickard@telenet.net www.peterickard.com

Peter Dyson & Son Ltd., 3 Cuckoo Lane, Honley, Holmfirth, West Yorkshire, HD9 6AS ENGLAND / 44-1484-661062; FAX: 44-1484-663709 peter@peterdyson.co.uk www.peterdyson.co.uk

Peter Hale/Engraver, 997 Maple Dr., Spanish Fork, UT 84660-2524 / 801-798-8215

Peters Stahl GmbH, Stettiner Strasse 42, D-33106, Paderborn, GERMANY / 05251-750025; FAX: 05251-75611 info@peters-stahl.com www.peters-stahl.com

Peterson Gun Shop, Inc., A.W., 4255 W. Old U.S. 441, Mt. Dora, FL 32757-3299 / 352-383-4258; FAX: 352-735-1001

Petro-Explo Inc., 7650 U.S. Hwy. 287, Suite 100, Arlington, TX 76017 / 817-478-8888

Pettinger Books, Gerald, 47827 300th Ave., Russell, IA 50238 / 641-535-2239 gpettinger@lisco.com

Pflumm Mfg. Co., 10662 Widmer Rd., Lenexa, KS 66215 / 800-888-4867; FAX: 913-451-7857

PFRB Co., P.O. Box 1242, Bloomington, IL 61702 / 309-473-3964 or 800-914-5464; FAX: 309-473-2161

Phillippi Custom Bullets, Justin, P.O. Box 773, Ligonier, PA 15658 / 724-238-2962; FAX: 724-238-9671 jrp@wpa.net http://www.wpa.net~jrphil

Phoenix Arms, 4231 Brickell St., Ontario, CA 91761 / 909-937-6900; FAX: 909-937-0060

MANUFACTURER'S DIRECTORY

Piedmont Community College, P.O. Box 1197, Roxboro, NC 27573 / 336-599-1181; FAX: 336-597-3817 www.piedmont.cc.nc.us

Pietta (See U.S. Importers-Navy Arms Co, Taylor's

Pine Technical College, 1100 4th St., Pine City, MN 55063 / 800-521-7463; FAX: 612-629-6766

Pinetree Bullets, 133 Skeena St., Kitimat, BC V8C 1Z1 CANADA / 604-632-3768; FAX: 604-632-3768

Pioneer Arms Co., 355 Lawrence Rd., Broomall, PA 19008 / 215-356-5203

Piotti (See U.S. Importer-Moore & Co., Wm. Larkin)

Piquette, Paul. See: PIQUETTE'S CUSTOM ENGRAVING

Piquette's Custom Engraving, Paul R. Piquette, 511 Southwick St., Feeding Hills, MA 01030 / 413-789-4582 ppiquette@comcast.net www.pistoldynamics.com

PJL Industries/ProChemCo/ProLixr, P.O. Box 1466, West Jordan, UT 84084-1466 / 801-569-2763 or 800-248-LUBE(5823); FAX: 801-569-8225 prolix@prolixlubricant.com www.prolixlubricant.com

Plaza Cutlery, Inc., 3333 Bristol, 161 South Coast Plaza, Costa Mesa, CA 92626 / 714-549-3932

Plum City Ballistic Range, N2162 80th St., Plum City, WI 54761 / 715-647-2539

PlumFire Press, Inc., 30-A Grove Ave., Patchogue, NY 11772-4112 / 800-695-7246; FAX: 516-758-4071

PMC/Eldorado Cartridge Corp., P.O. Box 62508, 12801 U.S. Hwy. 95 S., Boulder City, NV 89005 / 702-294-0025; FAX: 702-294-0121 kbauer@pmcammo.com www.pmcammo.com

Poburka, Philip (See Bison Studios)

Pointing Dog Journal, Village Press Publications, P.O. Box 968, Dept. PGD, Traverse City, MI 49685 / 800-272-3246; FAX: 616-946-3289

Police Bookshelf, P.O. Box 122, Concord, NH 03301 / 603-224-6814; FAX: 603-226-3554

Polywad, Inc., P.O. Box 7916, Macon, GA 31209 / 478-477-0669 or 800-998-0669 FAX: 478-477-0666 polywadmpb@aol.com www.polywad.com

Ponsness, Warren, 7634 W. Ohio St., Rathdrum, ID 83858 / 800-732-0706; FAX: 208-687-2233 www.reloaders.com

Pony Express Reloaders, 608 E. Co. Rd. D, Suite 3, St. Paul, MN 55117 / 612-483-9406; FAX: 612-483-9884

Pony Express Sport Shop, 23404 Lyons Ave., PMB 448, Newhall, CA 91321-2511 / 818-895-1231

Powder Horn Ltd., P.O. Box 565, Glenview, IL 60025 / 305-565-6060

Powell & Son (Gunmakers) Ltd., William, 35-37 Carrs Lane, Birmingham, B4 7SX ENGLAND / 121-643-0689; FAX: 121-631-3504 sales@william-powell.co.uk www.william-powell.co.uk

Powell Agency, William, 22 Circle Dr., Bellmore, NY 11710 / 516-679-1158

Power Custom, Inc., 29739 Hwy. J, Gravois Mills, MO 65037 / 573-372-5684; FAX: 573-372-5799 rwpowers@laurie.net www.powercustom.com

Power Plus Enterprises, Inc., P.O. Box 38, Warm Springs, GA 31830 / 706-655-2132

Powley Computer (See Hutton Rifle Ranch)

Practical Tools, Inc., 7067 Easton Rd., P.O. Box 133, Pipersville, PA 18947 / 215-766-7301; FAX: 215-766-8681

Prairie Gun Works, 1-761 Marion St., Winnipeg, MB R2J 0K6 CANADA / 204-231-2976; FAX: 204-231-8566

Pranger, Ed G., 1414 7th St., Anacortes, WA 98221 / 206-293-3488

Precision Airgun Sales, Inc., 5247 Warrensville Ctr. Rd., Maple Hts., OH 44137 / 216-587-5005; FAX: 216-587-5005

Precision Cast Bullets, 101 Mud Creek Lane, Ronan, MT 59864 / 406-676-5135

Precision Delta Corp., P.O. Box 128, Ruleville, MS 38771 / 662-756-2810; FAX: 662-756-2590

Precision Firearm Finishing, 25 N.W. 44th Avenue, Des Moines, IA 50313 / 515-288-8680; FAX: 515-244-3925

Precision Gun Works, 104 Sierra Rd., Dept. GD, Kerrville, TX 78028 / 830-367-4587

Precision Reloading, 124 S. Main St., Mitchell, SD 57301 / 605-996-9984

Precision Reloading, Inc., P.O. Box 122, Stafford Springs, CT 06076 / 860-684-7979; FAX: 860-684-6788 info@precisionreloading.com www.precisionreloading.com

Precision Shooting, Inc., 222 McKee St., Manchester, CT 06040 / 860-645-8776; FAX: 860-643-8215 www.precisionshooting.com

Precision Small Arms Inc., 9272 Jeronimo Rd., Ste. 121, Irvine, CA 92618 / 800-554-5515 or 949-768-3530; FAX: 949-768-4808 www.tcbebe.com

Precision Specialties, 131 Hendom Dr., Feeding Hills, MA 01030 / 413-786-3365; FAX: 413-786-3365

Precision Sport Optics, 15571 Producer Lane, Unit G, Huntington Beach, CA 92649 / 714-891-1309; FAX: 714-892-6920

Premier Reticles, 920 Breckinridge Lane, Winchester, VA 22601-6707 / 540-722-0601; FAX: 540-722-3522

Prescott Projectile Co., 1808 Meadowbrook Road, Prescott, AZ 86303

Preslik's Gunstocks, 4245 Keith Ln., Chico, CA 95926 / 916-891-8236

Price Bullets, Patrick W., 16520 Worthley Dr., San Lorenzo, CA 94580 / 510-278-1547

Primedia Publishing Co., 6420 Wilshire Blvd., Los Angeles, CA 90048 / 213-782-2000; FAX: 213-782-2867

Primos Hunting Calls, 604 First St., Flora, MS 39071 / 601-879-9323; FAX: 601-879-9324 www.primos.com

PRL Bullets, c/o Blackburn Enterprises, 114 Stuart Rd., Ste. 110, Cleveland, TN 37312 / 423-559-0340

Pro Load Ammunition, Inc., 5180 E. Seltice Way, Post Falls, ID 83854 / 208-773-9444; FAX: 208-773-9441

Professional Gunsmiths of America, 1201 South 13 Hwy., Lexington, MO 64067 / 816-529-1337

Professional Hunter Supplies, P.O. Box 608, 468 Main St., Ferndale, CA 95536 / 707-786-9140; FAX: 707-786-9117 wmebride@humboldt.com

Pro-Mark Div. of Wells Lamont, 6640 W. Touhy, Chicago, IL 60648 / 312-647-8200

Proofmark Corp., P.O. Box 357, Burgess, VA 22432 / 804-453-4337; FAX: 804-453-4337 proofmark@direcway.com www.proofmarkbullets.com

Pro-Port Ltd., 41302 Executive Dr., Harrison Twp., MI 48045-1306 / 586-469-6727; FAX: 586-469-0425 e-mail@magnaport.com www.magnaport.com

Pro-Shot Products, Inc., P.O. Box 763, Taylorville, IL 62568 / 217-824-9133; FAX: 217-824-8861 www.proshotproducts.com

Protector Mfg. Co., Inc., The, 443 Ashwood Pl., Boca Raton, FL 33431 / 407-394-6011

Protektor Model, 1-11 Bridge St., Galeton, PA 16922 / 814-435-2442 mail@protektormodel.com www.protektormodel.com

Prototech Industries, Inc., 10532 E Road, Delia, KS 66418 / 785-771-3571 prototec@grapevine.net

ProWare, Inc., 15847 NE Hancock St., Portland, OR 97230 / 503-239-0159

PWL Gunleather, P.O. Box 450432, Atlanta, GA 31145 / 800-960-4072; FAX: 770-822-1704 covert@pwlusa.com www.pwlusa.com

PWM Sales Ltd., N.D.F.S., Gowdall Lane, Pollington DN14 0AU, ENGLAND / 01405862688; FAX: 01405862622 Paulwelburn9@aol.com

Pyramyd Stone Inter. Corp., 2447 Suffolk Lane, Pepper Pike, OH 44124-4540

Q

Quack Decoy & Sporting Clays, 4 Ann & Hope Way, P.O. Box 98, Cumberland, RI 02864 / 401-723-8202; FAX: 401-722-5910

Quaker Boy, Inc., 5455 Webster Rd., Orchard Parks, NY 14127 / 716-662-3979; FAX: 716-662-9426

Quality Arms, Inc., Box 19477, Dept. GD, Houston, TX 77224 / 281-870-8377 arrieta2@excite.com www.arrieta.com

Quality Cartridge, P.O. Box 445, Hollywood, MD 20636 / 301-373-3719 www.qual-cart.com

Quality Custom Firearms, Stephen Billeb, 22 Vista View Dr., Cody, WY 82414 / 307-587-4278; FAX: 307-587-4297 stevebilleb@wyoming.com

Quarton Beamshot, 4538 Centerview Dr., Ste. 149, San Antonio, TX 78228 / 800-520-8435; FAX: 210-735-1326 www.beamshot.com

Que Industries, Inc., P.O. Box 2471, Everett, WA 98203 / 425-303-9088; FAX: 206-514-3266 queinfo@queindustries.com

Queen Cutlery Co., P.O. Box 500, Franklinville, NY 14737 / 800-222-5233; FAX: 800-299-2618

R

R&C Knives & Such, 2136 Candy Cane Walk, Manteca, CA 95336-9501 / 209-239-3722; FAX: 209-825-6947

R&D Gun Repair, Kenny Howell, RR1 Box 283, Beloit, WI 53511

R&J Gun Shop, 337 S. Humbolt St., Canyon City, OR 97820 / 541-575-2130 rjgunshop@highdesertnet.com

R&S Industries Corp., 8255 Brentwood Industrial Dr., St. Louis, MO 63144 / 314-781-5169 ron@miraclepolishingcloth.com www.miraclepolishingcloth.com

R. Murphy Co., Inc., 13 Groton-Harvard Rd., P.O. Box 376, Ayer, MA 01432 / 617-772-3481 www.r.murphyknives.com

R.A. Wells Custom Gunsmith, 3452 1st Ave., Racine, WI 53402 / 414-639-5223

R.E. Seebeck Assoc., P.O. Box 59752, Dallas, TX 75229

R.E.I., P.O. Box 88, Tallevast, FL 34270 / 813-755-0085

R.E.T. Enterprises, 2608 S. Chestnut, Broken Arrow, OK 74012 / 918-251-GUNS; (4867) FAX: 918-251-0587

R.T. Eastman Products, P.O. Box 1531, Jackson, WY 83001 / 307-733-3217; or 800-624-4311

Rabeno, Martin, 530 The Eagle Pass, Durango, CO 81301 / 970-382-0353 fancygun@aol.com

Radack Photography, Lauren, 21140 Jib Court L-12, Aventura, FL 33180 / 305-931-3110

Radiator Specialty Co., 1900 Wilkinson Blvd., P.O. Box 34689, Charlotte, NC 28234 / 800-438-6947; FAX: 800-421-9525 tkrossell@gunk.com www.gunk.com

Radical Concepts, P.O. Box 1473, Lake Grove, OR 97035 / 503-538-7437

Rainier Ballistics, 4500 15th St. East, Tacoma, WA 98424 / 800-638-8722; FAX: 253-922-7854 sales@rainierballistics.com www.rainierballistics.com

Ralph Bone Engraving, 718 N. Atlanta St., Owasso, OK 74055 / 918-272-9745

Ram-Line ATK, P.O. Box 39, Onalaska, WI 54650

Ramon B. Gonzalez Guns, P.O. Box 370, Monticello, NY 12701 / 845-794-2510

Rampart International, 2781 W. MacArthur Blvd., B-283, Santa Ana, CA 92704 / 800-976-7240 or 714-557-6405

Ranch Products, P.O. Box 145, Malinta, OH 43535 / 313-277-3118; FAX: 313-565-8536 stevenacrawford@msn.com ranchproducts.com

Randall-Made Knives, P.O. Box 1988, Orlando, FL 32802 / 407-855-8075

Randco UK, 286 Gipsy Rd., Welling, DA16 1JJ ENGLAND / 44 81 303 4118

Randolph Engineering, Inc., Ranger Shooting Glasses, 26 Thomas Patten Dr., Randolph, MA 02368 / 800-541-1405; FAX: 781-986-0337 sales@randolphusa.com www.randolphusa.com

Range Brass Products Company, P.O. Box 218, Rockport, TX 78381

Ransom International Corp., P.O. Box 3845, Prescott, AZ 86302 / 928-778-7899; FAX: 928-778-7993 ransom@cableone.net www.ransomrest.com

Rapine Bullet Mould Mfg. Co., 9503 Landis Lane, East Greenville, PA 18041 / 215-679-5413; FAX: 215-679-9795

Ravell Ltd., 289 Diputacion St., 08009, Barcelona, SPAIN / 34(3) 4874486; FAX: 34(3) 4881394

Ray Riling Arms Books Co., 6844 Gorsten St., Philadelphia, PA 19119 / 215-438-2456; FAX: 215-438-5395 sales@rayrilingarmsbooks.com www.rayrilingarmsbooks.com

MANUFACTURER'S DIRECTORY

Ray's Gunsmith Shop, 3199 Elm Ave., Grand Junction, CO 81504 / 970-434-6162; FAX: 970-434-3452

Raytech Div. of Lyman Products Corp., 475 Smith Street, Middletown, CT 06457-1541 / 860-632-2020 or 800-225-9626; FAX: 860-632-1699 raysales@cshore.com www.raytech-ind.com

RCBS Operations/ATK, 605 Oro Dam Blvd., Oroville, CA 95965 / 800-533-5000; FAX: 530-533-1647 www.rcbs.com

Reardon Products, P.O. Box 126, Morrison, IL 61270 / 815-772-3155

Recoilless Technologies, Inc. (RTI), RTI/High-Low, 2141 E. Cedar #2, Tempe, AZ 85281 / 480-966-7051

Red Diamond Dist. Co., 1304 Snowdon Dr., Knoxville, TN 37912

Redding Reloading Equipment, 1089 Starr Rd., Cortland, NY 13045 / 607-753-3331; FAX: 607-756-8445 techline@redding-reloading.com www.redding-reloading.com

Redfield Media Resource Center, 4607 N.E. Cedar Creek Rd., Woodland, WA 98674 / 360-225-5000; FAX: 360-225-7616

Redman's Rifling & Reboring, 189 Nichols Rd., Omak, WA 98841 / 509-826-5512

Redwood Bullet Works, 3559 Bay Rd., Redwood City, CA 94063 / 415-367-6741

Reed, Dave, Rt. 1, Box 374, Minnesota City, MN 55959 / 507-689-2944

Reimer Johannsen, Inc., 438 Willow Brook Rd., Plainfield, NH 03781 / 603-469-3450; FAX: 603-469-3471

Reloaders Equipment Co., 4680 High St., Ecorse, MI 48229

Reloading Specialties, Inc., Box 1130, Pine Island, MN 55463 / 507-356-8500; FAX: 507-356-8800

Remington Arms Co., Inc., 870 Remington Drive, P.O. Box 700, Madison, NC 27025-0700 / 800-243-9700; FAX: 336-548-8700 info@remington.com www.remington.com

Remington Double Shotguns, 7885 Cyd Dr., Denver, CO 80221 / 303-429-6947

Renegade, P.O. Box 31546, Phoenix, AZ 85046 / 602-482-6777; FAX: 602-482-1952

Renfrew Guns & Supplies, R.R. 4, Renfrew, ON K7V 3Z7 CANADA / 613-432-7080

Reno, Wayne, 2808 Stagestop Road, Jefferson, CO 80456

Republic Arms, Inc. (See Cobra Enterprises, Inc.)

Retting, Inc., Martin B., 11029 Washington, Culver City, CA 90232 / 213-837-2412

RG-G, Inc., P.O. Box 935, Trinidad, CO 81082 / 719-845-1436

RH Machine & Consulting Inc., P.O. Box 394, Pacific, MO 63069 / 314-271-8465

Rhino, P.O. Box 787, Locust, NC 28097 / 704-753-2198

Rhodeside, Inc., 1704 Commerce Dr., Piqua, OH 45356 / 513-773-5781

Rice, Keith (See White Rock Tool & Die)

Richards MicroFit Stocks, Inc., P.O. Box 1066, Sun Valley, CA 91352 / 800-895-7420; FAX: 818-771-1242 sales@rifle-stocks.com www.rifle-stocks.com

Ridgeline, Inc., Bruce Sheldon, P.O. Box 930, Dewey, AZ 86327-0930 / 800-632-5900; FAX: 520-632-5900

Ridgetop Sporting Goods, P.O. Box 306, 42907 Hilligoss Ln. East, Eatonville, WA 98328 / 360-832-6422; FAX: 360-832-6422

Ries, Chuck, 415 Ridgecrest Dr., Grants Pass, OR 97527 / 503-476-5623

Rifles, Inc., 3580 Leal Rd., Pleasanton, TX 78064 / 830-569-2055; FAX: 830-569-2297

Riggs, Jim, 206 Azalea, Boerne, TX 78006 / 210-249-8567

Riley Ledbetter Airguns, 1804 E. Sprague St., Winston Salem, NC 27107-3521 / 919-784-0676

Rim Pac Sports, Inc., 1034 N. Soldano Ave., Azusa, CA 91702-2135

Ringler Custom Leather Co., 31 Shining Mtn. Rd., Powell, WY 82435 / 307-645-3255

Ripley Rifles, 42 Fletcher Street, Ripley, Derbyshire, DE5 3LP ENGLAND / 011-0773-748353

Rizzini F.lli (See U.S. Importers-Wm. Larkin Moore & Co., N.E. Arms Corp.)

Rizzini SNC, Via 2 Giugno, 7/7Bis-25060, Marcheno (Brescia), ITALY

RLCM Enterprises, 110 Hill Crest Drive, Burleson, TX 76028

RMS Custom Gunsmithing, 4120 N. Bitterwell, Prescott Valley, AZ 86314 / 520-772-7626 www.customstockmaker.com

Robar Co., Inc., The, 21438 N. 7th Ave., Suite B, Phoenix, AZ 85027 / 623-581-2648; FAX: 623-582-0059 info@robarguns.com www.robarguns.com

Robert Evans Engraving, 332 Vine St., Oregon City, OR 97045 / 503-656-5693

Robert Valade Engraving, 931 3rd Ave., Seaside, OR 97138 / 503-738-7672

Robinett, R. G., P.O. Box 72, Madrid, IA 50156 / 515-795-2906

Robinson, Don, Pennsylvania Hse, 36 Fairfax Crescent, W Yorkshire, ENGLAND / 0422-364458 donrobinsonuk@yahoo.co.uk www.guns4u2.co.uk

Robinson Armament Co., P.O. Box 16776, Salt Lake City, UT 84116 / 801-355-0401; FAX: 801-355-0402 zdf@robarm.com www.robarm.com

Robinson Firearms Mfg. Ltd., 1699 Blondeaux Crescent, Kelowna, BC V1Y 4J8 CANADA / 604-868-9596

Robinson H.V. Bullets, 3145 Church St., Zachary, LA 70791 / 504-654-4029

Rochester Lead Works, 76 Anderson Ave., Rochester, NY 14607 / 716-442-8500; FAX: 716-442-4712

Rock River Arms, 101 Noble St., Cleveland, IL 61241

Rockwood Corp., Speedwell Division, 136 Lincoln Blvd., Middlesex, NJ 08846 / 800-243-8274; FAX: 980-560-7475

Rocky Mountain Armoury, Mr. Felix LesMerises, 610 Main Street, P.O. Box 691, Frisco, CO 80443-0691 / 970-668-0136; FAX: 970-668-4484 felix@rockymountainarmoury.com

Rocky Mountain Target Co., 3 Aloe Way, Leesburg, FL 34788 / 352-365-9598

Rocky Shoes & Boots, 294 Harper St., Nelsonville, OH 45764 / 800-848-9452 or 614-753-1951; FAX: 614-753-4024

Rogue Rifle Co., Inc./Chipmunk Rifles, 1140 36th St. N., Ste. B, Lewiston, ID 83501 / 208-743-4355; FAX: 208-743-4163 customerservice@roguerifle.com www.roguerifle.com

Rogue River Rifleworks, 500 Linne Road #D, Paso Robles, CA 93446 / 805-227-4706; FAX: 805-227-4723 rrrifles@calinet.com

Rohner, Hans, 1148 Twin Sisters Ranch Rd., Nederland, CO 80466-9600

Rohner, John, 186 Virginia Ave., Asheville, NC 28806 / 828-281-3704

Rohrbaugh, P.O. Box 785, Bayport, NY 11705 / 631-363-2843; FAX: 631-363-2681 API380@aol.com

Romain's Custom Guns, Inc., RD 1, Whetstone Rd., Brockport, PA 15823 / 814-265-1948 romwhetstone@penn.com

Ron Frank Custom Classic, Inc., 7131 Richland Rd., Ft. Worth, TX 76118 / 817-284-9300; FAX: 817-284-9300 rfrank3974@aol.com

Rooster Laboratories, P.O. Box 414605, Kansas City, MO 64141 / 816-474-1622; FAX: 816-474-7622

Rorschach Precision Products, 417 Keats Cir., Irving, TX 75061 / 214-790-3487

Rosenberg & Son, Jack A., 12229 Cox Ln., Dallas, TX 75234 / 214-241-6302

Ross, Don, 12813 West 83 Terrace, Lenexa, KS 66215 / 913-492-6982

Rosser, Bob, 2809 Crescent Ave., Suite 20, Homewood, AL 35209 / 205-870-4422; FAX: 205-870-4421 www.hand-engravers.com

Rossi Firearms, Gary Mchalik, 16175 NW 49th Ave., Miami, FL 33014-6314 / 305-474-0401; FAX: 305-623-7506

Rottweil Compe, 1330 Glassell, Orange, CA 92667

Royal Arms Gunstocks, 919 8th Ave. NW, Great Falls, MT 59404 / 406-453-1149 royalarms@lmt.net www.lmt.net/~royalarms

Royal Arms International, R J Brill, P.O. Box 6083, Woodland Hills, CA 91365 / 818-704-5110; FAX: 818-887-2059 royalarms.com

Roy's Custom Grips, 793 Mt. Olivet Church Rd., Lynchburg, VA 24504 / 434-993-3470

RPM, 15481 N. Twin Lakes Dr., Tucson, AZ 85739 / 520-825-1233; FAX: 520-825-3333

Rubright Bullets, 1008 S. Quince Rd., Walnutport, PA 18088 / 215-767-1339

Rucker Dist. Inc., P.O. Box 479, Terrell, TX 75160 / 214-563-2094

Ruger (See Sturm Ruger & Co., Inc.)

Ruger, Chris. See: RUGER'S CUSTOM GUNS

Ruger's Custom Guns, Chris Ruger, 1050 Morton Blvd., Kingston, NY 12401 / 845-336-7106; FAX: 845-336-7106 rugerscustom@outdrs.net rugergunsmith.com

Rundell's Gun Shop, 6198 Frances Rd., Clio, MI 48420 / 313-687-0559

Rupert's Gun Shop, 2202 Dick Rd., Suite B, Fenwick, MI 48834 / 517-248-3252 17rupert@pathwaynet.com

Russ Haydon's Shooters' Supply, 15018 Goodrich Dr. NW, Gig Harbor, WA 98329 / 877-663-6249; FAX: 253-857-7884 info@shooters-supply.com www.shooters-supply.com

Russ, William. See: BILL RUSS TRADING POST

Rusteprufe Laboratories, 1319 Jefferson Ave., Sparta, WI 54656 / 608-269-4144; FAX: 608-366-1972 rusteprufe@centurytel.net www.rusteprufe.com

Rutgers Book Center, 127 Raritan Ave., Highland Park, NJ 08904 / 732-545-4344; FAX: 732-545-6686 gunbooks@rutgersgunbooks.com www.rutgersgunbooks.com

Rutten (See U.S. Importer-Labanu Inc.)

RWS (See U.S. Importer-Dynamit Nobel-RWS, Inc.), 81 Ruckman Rd., Closter, NJ 07624 / 201-767-7971; FAX: 201-767-1589

S

S&K Scope Mounts, RD 2 Box 21C, Sugar Grove, PA 16350 / 814-489-3091 or 800-578-9862; FAX: 814-489-5466 comments@scopemounts.com www.scopemounts.com

S&S Firearms, 74-11 Myrtle Ave., Glendale, NY 11385 / 718-497-1100; FAX: 718-497-1105 info@ssfirearms.com ssfirearms.com

S.A.R.L. G. Granger, 66 Cours Fauriel, 42100, Saint Etienne, FRANCE / 04 77 25 14 73; FAX: 04 77 38 66 99

S.C.R.C., P.O. Box 660, Katy, TX 77492-0660 FAX: 281-492-6332

S.D. Meacham, 1070 Angel Ridge, Peck, ID 83545

S.I.A.C.E. (See U.S. Importer-IAR Inc.)

Sabatti SPA, Via A Volta 90, 25063 Gandome V.T.(BS), Brescia, ITALY / 030-8912207-831312; FAX: 030-8912059 info@sabatti.it www.sabatti.com

SAECO (See Redding Reloading Equipment)

Safari Arms/Schuetzen Pistol Works, 620-626 Old Pacific Hwy. SE, Olympia, WA 98513 / 360-459-3471; FAX: 360-491-3447 info@olyarms.com www.olyarms.com

Safari Press, Inc., 15621 Chemical Lane B, Huntington Beach, CA 92649 / 714-894-9080; FAX: 714-894-4949 info@safaripress.com www.safaripress.com

Safariland Ltd., Inc., 3120 E. Mission Blvd., P.O. Box 51478, Ontario, CA 91761 / 909-923-7300; FAX: 909-923-7400

SAFE, P.O. Box 864, Post Falls, ID 83877 / 208-773-3624; FAX: 208-773-6819 staysafe@safe-llc.com www.safe-llc.com

Sako Ltd. (See U.S. Importer-Stoeger Industries)

Sam Welch Gun Engraving, Sam Welch, HC 64 Box 2110, Moab, UT 84532 / 435-259-8131

Samco Global Arms, Inc., 6995 NW 43rd St., Miami, FL 33166 / 305-593-9782; FAX: 305-593-1014 samco@samcoglobal.com www.samcoglobal.com

Sampson, Roger, 2316 Mahogany St., Mora, MN 55051 / 612-679-4868

San Marco (See U.S. Importers-Cape Outfitters-EMF Co., Inc.

Sandia Die & Cartridge Co., 37 Atancacio Rd. NE, Albuquerque, NM 87123 / 505-298-5729

Sarco, Inc., 323 Union St., Stirling, NJ 07980 / 908-647-3800; FAX: 908-647-9413

Sarsilmaz Shotguns-Turkey (see B.C. Outdoors)

Sauer (See U.S. Importers-Paul Co., The Sigarms Inc.)

MANUFACTURER'S DIRECTORY

Sauls, R. See: BRYAN & ASSOC.
Saunders Gun & Machine Shop, 145 Delhi Rd., Manchester, IA 52057 / 563-927-4026
Savage Arms (Canada), Inc., 248 Water St., P.O. Box 1240, Lakefield, ON K0L 2H0 CANADA / 705-652-8000; FAX: 705-652-8431 www.savagearms.com
Savage Arms, Inc., 100 Springdale Rd., Westfield, MA 01085 / 413-568-7001; FAX: 413-562-7764
Savage Range Systems, Inc., 100 Springdale Rd., Westfield, MA 01085 / 413-568-7001; FAX: 413-562-1152 snailtraps@savagearms.com www.snailtraps.com
Saville Iron Co. (See Greenwood Precision)
Scansport, Inc., P.O. Box 700, Enfield, NH 03748 / 603-632-7654
Sceery Game Calls, P.O. Box 6520, Sante Fe, NM 87502 / 505-471-9110; FAX: 505-471-3476
Schaefer Shooting Sports, P.O. Box 1515, Melville, NY 11747-0515 / 516-643-5466; FAX: 516-643-2426 robert@robertschaefer.com www.schaefershooting.com
Scharch Mfg., Inc.-Top Brass, 10325 Co. Rd. 120, Salida, CO 81201 / 800-836-4683; FAX: 719-539-3021 topbrass@scharch.com www.handgun-brass.com
Scherer, Liz. See: SCHERER SUPPLIES
Scherer Supplies, Liz Scherer, Box 250, Ewing, VA 24248 FAX: 423-733-2073
Schiffman, Mike, 8233 S. Crystal Springs, McCammon, ID 83250 / 208-254-9114
Schmidt & Bender, Inc., P.O. Box 134, Meriden, NH 03770 / 603-469-3565; FAX: 603-469-3471 scopes@adelphia.net www.schmidtbender.com
Schneider Bullets, 3655 West 214th St., Fairview Park, OH 44126
Schneider Rifle Barrels, Inc., 1403 W. Red Baron Rd., Payson, AZ 85541 / 602-948-2525
School of Gunsmithing, The, 6065 Roswell Rd., Atlanta, GA 30328 / 800-223-4542
Schroeder Bullets, 1421 Thermal Ave., San Diego, CA 92154 / 619-423-3523; FAX: 619-423-8124
Schulz Industries, 16247 Minnesota Ave., Paramount, CA 90723 / 213-439-5903
Schumakers Gun Shop, 512 Prouty Corner Lp. A, Colville, WA 99114 / 509-684-4848
Scope Control, Inc., 5775 Co. Rd. 23 SE, Alexandria, MN 56308 / 612-762-7295
Score High Gunsmithing, 9812-A, Cochiti SE, Albuquerque, NM 87123 / 800-326-5632 or 505-292-5532; FAX: 505-292-2592 scorehi@scorehi.com www.probed2000.com
Scott Fine Guns Inc., Thad, P.O. Box 412, Indianola, MS 38751 / 601-887-5929
Searcy Enterprises, P.O. Box 584, Boron, CA 93596 / 760-762-6771; FAX: 760-762-0191
Second Chance Body Armor, P.O. Box 578, Central Lake, MI 49622 / 616-544-5721; FAX: 616-544-9824
Seebeck Assoc., R.E., P.O. Box 59752, Dallas, TX 75229
Segway Industries, P.O. Box 783, Suffern, NY 10901-0783 / 914-357-5510
Seligman Shooting Products, Box 133, Seligman, AZ 86337 / 602-422-3607 shootssp@yahoo.com
Sellier & Bellot, USA, Inc., P.O. Box 27006, Shawnee Mission, KS 66225 / 913-685-0916; FAX: 913-685-0917
Selsi Co., Inc., P.O. Box 10, Midland Park, NJ 07432-0010 / 201-935-0388; FAX: 201-935-5851
Semmer, Charles (See Remington Double Shotguns), 7885 Cyd Dr., Denver, CO 80221 / 303-429-6947
Sentinel Arms, P.O. Box 57, Detroit, MI 48231 / 313-331-1951; FAX: 313-331-1456
Servus Footwear Co., 1136 2nd St., Rock Island, IL 61204 / 309-786-7741; FAX: 309-786-9808
SGS Importer's International, Inc., 1750 Brielle Ave., Unit B1, Wanamassa, NJ 07712 / 732-493-0302; FAX: 732-493-0301 gsodini@aol.com www.firestorm-sgs.com
Shappy Bullets, 76 Milldale Ave., Plantsville, CT 06479 / 203-621-3704
Sharp Shooter Supply, 4970 Lehman Road, Delphos, OH 45833 / 419-695-3179

Sharps Arms Co., Inc., C., 100 Centennial, Box 885, Big Timber, MT 59011 / 406-932-4353
Shaw, Inc., E. R. (See Small Arms Mfg. Co.)
Shay's Gunsmithing, 931 Marvin Ave., Lebanon, PA 17042
Sheffield Knifemakers Supply, Inc., P.O. Box 741107, Orange City, FL 32774-1107 / 386-775-6453; FAX: 386-774-5754
Sheldon, Bruce. See: RIDGELINE, INC.
Shepherd Enterprises, Inc., Box 189, Waterloo, NE 68069 / 402-779-2424; FAX: 402-779-4010 sshepherd@shepherdscopes.com www.shepherdscopes.com
Sherwood, George, 46 N. River Dr., Roseburg, OR 97470 / 541-672-3159
Shilen, Inc., 205 Metro Park Blvd., Ennis, TX 75119 / 972-875-5318; FAX: 972-875-5402
Shiloh Rifle Mfg., P.O. Box 279, Big Timber, MT 59011
Shoot Where You Look, Leon Measures, Dept GD, 408 Fair, Livingston, TX 77351
Shooters Arms Manufacturing, Inc., Rivergate Mall, Gen. Maxilom Ave., Cebu City 6000, PHILIPPINES / 6332-254-8478 www.shootersarms.com.ph
Shooter's Choice Gun Care, 15050 Berkshire Ind. Pkwy., Middlefield, OH 44062 / 440-834-8888; FAX: 440-834-3388 www.shooterschoice.com
Shooter's Edge Inc., 3313 Creekstone Dr., Fort Collins, CO 80525
Shooters Supply, 1120 Tieton Dr., Yakima, WA 98902 / 509-452-1181
Shooter's World, 3828 N. 28th Ave., Phoenix, AZ 85017 / 602-266-0170
Shooters, Inc., 5139 Stanart St., Norfolk, VA 23502 / 757-461-9152; FAX: 757-461-9155 gflocker@aol.com
Shootin' Shack, 357 Cypress Drive, No. 10, Tequesta, FL 33469 / 561-746-2731; FAX: 561-545-4861
Shooting Gallery, The, 8070 Southern Blvd., Boardman, OH 44512 / 216-726-7788
Shoot-N-C Targets (See Birchwood Casey)
Shotgun Sports, P.O. Box 6810, Auburn, CA 95604 / 530-889-2220; FAX: 530-889-9106 custsrv@shotgunsportsmagazine.com shotgunsportsmagazine.com
Shotgun Sports Magazine, dba Shootin' Accessories Ltd., P.O. Box 6810, Auburn, CA 95604 / 916-889-2220 custsrv@shotgunsportsmagazine.com shotgunspotsmagazine.com
Shotguns Unlimited, 2307 Fon Du Lac Rd., Richmond, VA 23229 / 804-752-7115
Siegrist Gun Shop, 8752 Turtle Road, Whittemore, MI 48770 / 989-873-3929
Sierra Bullets, 1400 W. Henry St., Sedalia, MO 65301 / 816-827-6300; FAX: 816-827-6300
Sierra Specialty Prod. Co., 1344 Oakhurst Ave., Los Altos, CA 94024 FAX: 415-965-1536
SIG, CH-8212 Neuhausen, SWITZERLAND
Sigarms Inc., 18 Industrial Dr., Exeter, NH 03833 / 603-772-2302; FAX: 603-772-9082 www.sigarms.com
Sight Shop, The, John G. Lawson, 1802 E. Columbia Ave., Tacoma, WA 98404 / 253-474-5465 parahellum9@aol.com www.thesightshop.org
Sightron, Inc., 1672B Hwy. 96, Franklinton, NC 27525 / 919-528-8783; FAX: 919-528-0995 info@sightron.com www.sightron.com
SIG-Sauer (See U.S. Importer-Sigarms, Inc.)
Silencio/Safety Direct, 56 Coney Island Dr., Sparks, NV 89431 / 800-648-1812 or 702-354-4451; FAX: 702-359-1074
Silent Hunter, 1100 Newton Ave., W. Collingswood, NJ 08107 / 609-854-3276
Silhouette Leathers, 8598 Hwy. 51 N. #4, Millington, TN 38053 silhouetteleathers@yahoo.com silhouetteleathers.com
Silver Eagle Machining, 18007 N. 69th Ave., Glendale, AZ 85308
Silver Ridge Gun Shop (See Goodwin Guns)
Simmons, Jerry, 715 Middlebury St., Goshen, IN 46528-2717 / 574-533-8546
Simmons Gun Repair, Inc., 700 S. Rogers Rd., Olathe, KS 66062 / 913-782-3131; FAX: 913-782-4189

Simmons Outdoor Corp., 6001 Oak Canyon, Irvine, CA 92618 / 949-451-1450; FAX: 949-451-1460 www.meade.com
Sinclair International, Inc., 2330 Wayne Haven St., Fort Wayne, IN 46803 / 260-493-1858 or 800-717-8211; FAX: 260-493-2530 sales@sinclairintl.com www.sinclairintl.com
Singletary, Kent, 4538 W. Carol Ave., Glendale, AZ 85302 / 602-526-6836 kent@kscustom www.kscustom.com
Siskiyou Gun Works (See Donnelly, C. P.)
Six Enterprises, 320-D Turtle Creek Ct., San Jose, CA 95125 / 408-999-0201; FAX: 408-999-0216
SKB Shotguns, 4325 S. 120th St., Omaha, NE 68137 / 800-752-2767; FAX: 402-330-8040 skb@skbshotguns.com www.skbshotguns.com
Skeoch, Brian R., P.O. Box 279, Glenrock, WY 82637 / 307-436-9655 skeochbrian@netzero.com
Skip's Machine, 364 29 Road, Grand Junction, CO 81501 / 303-245-5417
Sklany's Machine Shop, 566 Birch Grove Dr., Kalispell, MT 59901 / 406-755-4257
Slug Site, Ozark Wilds, 21300 Hwy. 5, Versailles, MO 65084 / 573-378-6430 john@ebeling.com john.ebeling.com
Small Arms Mfg. Co., 5312 Thoms Run Rd., Bridgeville, PA 15017 / 412-221-4343; FAX: 412-221-4303
Small Arms Specialists, 443 Firchburg Rd., Mason, NH 03048 / 603-878-0427; FAX: 603-878-3905 miniguns@empire.net miniguns.com
Smires, C. L., 5222 Windmill Lane, Columbia, MD 21044-1328
Smith & Wesson, 2100 Roosevelt Ave., Springfield, MA 01104 / 413-781-8300; FAX: 413-731-8980 qa@smith-wesson.com www.smith-wesson.com
Smith, Art, P.O. Box 645, Park Rapids, MN 56470 / 218-732-5333
Smith, Mark A., P.O. Box 182, Sinclair, WY 82334 / 307-324-7929
Smith, Michael, 2612 Ashmore Ave., Red Bank, TN 37415 / 615-267-8341
Smith, Ron, 5869 Straley, Fort Worth, TX 76114 / 817-732-6768
Smith, Sharmon, 4545 Speas Rd., Fruitland, ID 83619 / 208-452-6329 sharmon@fmtc.com
Smith Abrasives, Inc., 1700 Sleepy Valley Rd., Hot Springs, AR 71902-5095 / 501-321-2244; FAX: 501-321-9232 www.smithabrasives.com
Smith, Judy. See: L.B.T.
Smith Saddlery, Jesse W., 0499 County Road J, Pritchett, CO 81064 / 509-325-0622
Smokey Valley Rifles, E1976 Smokey Valley Rd., Scandinavia, WI 54977 / 715-467-2674
Snapp's Gunshop, 6911 E. Washington Rd., Clare, MI 48617 / 989-386-9226 snapp@glccomputers.com
Sno-Seal, Inc. (See Atsko/Sno-Seal, Inc.)
Societa Armi Bresciane Srl (See U.S. Importer-Cape Outfitters)
SOS Products Co. (See Buck Stix-SOS Products Co.), Box 3, Neenah, WI 54956
Sotheby's, 1334 York Ave. at 72nd St., New York, NY 10021 / 212-606-7260
Sound Tech, Box 738, Logan, NM 88426 / 205-999-0416; or 505-487-2277 silenceio@wmconnect.com www.soundtechsilencers.com
South Bend Replicas, Inc., 61650 Oak Rd., South Bend, IN 46614 / 574-289-4500
Southeastern Community College, 1015 S. Gear Ave., West Burlington, IA 52655 / 319-752-2731
Southern Ammunition Co., Inc., 4232 Meadow St., Loris, SC 29569-3124 / 803-756-3262; FAX: 803-756-3583
Southern Armory, The, 25 Millstone Rd., Woodlawn, VA 24381 / 703-238-1343; FAX: 703-238-1453
Southern Bloomer Mfg. Co., P.O. Box 1621, Bristol, TN 37620 / 615-878-6660; FAX: 615-878-8761
Southern Security, 1700 Oak Hills Dr., Kingston, TN 37763 / 423-376-6297; FAX: 800-251-9992
Sparks, Milt, 605 E. 44th St. No. 2, Boise, ID 83714-4800
Spartan-Realtree Products, Inc., 1390 Box Circle, Columbus, GA 31907 / 706-569-9101; FAX: 706-569-0042

MANUFACTURER'S DIRECTORY

Specialty Gunsmithing, Lynn McMurdo, P.O. Box 404, Afton, WY 83110 / 307-886-5535

Specialty Shooters Supply, Inc., 3325 Griffin Rd., Suite 9mm, Fort Lauderdale, FL 33317

Speer Bullets, P.O. Box 856, Lewiston, ID 83501 / 208-746-2351 www.speer-bullets.com

Spegel, Craig, P.O. Box 387, Nehalem, OR 97131 / 503-368-5653

Speiser, Fred D., 2229 Dearborn, Missoula, MT 59801 / 406-549-8133

Spencer Reblue Service, 1820 Tupelo Trail, Holt, MI 48842 / 517-694-7474

Spencer's Rifle Barrels, Inc., 4107 Jacobs Creek Dr., Scottsville, VA 24590 / 804-293-6836; FAX: 804-293-6836 www.spencersriflebarrels.com

SPG, Inc., P.O. Box 1625, Cody, WY 82414 / 307-587-7621; FAX: 307-587-7695 spg@cody.wtp.net www.blackpowderspg.com

Sphinx Systems Ltd., Gesteigtstrasse 12, CH-3800, Matten, BRNE, SWITZERLAND

Splitfire Sporting Goods, L.L.C., P.O. Box 1044, Orem, UT 84059-1044 / 801-932-7950; FAX: 801-932-7959 www.splitfireguns.com

Spolar Power Load, Inc., 17376 Filbert, Fontana, CA 92335 / 800-227-9667

Sport Flite Manufacturing Co., 637 Kingsley Trl., Bloomfield Hills, MI 48304-2320 / 248-647-3747

Sporting Clays Of America, 9257 Buckeye Rd., Sugar Grove, OH 43155-9632 / 740-746-8334 FAX: 740-746-8605

Sports Afield Magazine, 15621 Chemical Lane B, Huntington Beach, CA 92649 / 714-894-9080; FAX: 714-894-4949 info@sportsafield.com www.sportsafield.com

Sportsman Safe Mfg. Co., 6309-6311 Paramount Blvd., Long Beach, CA 90805 / 800-266-7150; or 310-984-5445

Sportsman's Communicators, 588 Radcliffe Ave., Pacific Palisades, CA 90272 / 800-538-3752

Sportsmatch U.K. Ltd., 16 Summer St. Leighton, Buzzard Beds, Bedfordshire, LU7 1HT ENGLAND / 4401525-381638; FAX: 4401525-851236 info@sportsmatch-uk.com www.sportsmatch-uk.com

Sportsmen's Exchange & Western Gun Traders, Inc., 813 Doris Ave., Oxnard, CA 93030 / 805-483-1917

Spradlin's, 457 Shannon Rd., Texas Creek Cotopaxi, CO 81223 / 719-275-7105; FAX: 719-275-3852 spradlins@prodigy.net www.spradlins.net

Springfield Armory, 420 W. Main St., Geneseo, IL 61254 / 309-944-5631; FAX: 309-944-3676 sales@springfield-armory.com www.springfieldarmory.com

Springfield Sporters, Inc., RD 1, Penn Run, PA 15765 / 412-254-2626; FAX: 412-254-9173

Springfield, Inc., 420 W. Main St., Geneseo, IL 61254 / 309-944-5631; FAX: 309-944-3676

Spyderco, Inc., 820 Spyderco Way, Golden, CO 80403 / 800-525-7770; FAX: 303-278-2229 sales@spyderco.com www.spyderco.com

SSK Industries, J. D. Jones, 590 Woodvue Lane, Wintersville, OH 43953 / 740-264-0176; FAX: 740-264-2257 www.sskindustries.com

Stackpole Books, 5067 Ritter Rd., Mechanicsburg, PA 17055-6921 / 717-796-0411 or 800-732-3669; FAX: 717-796-0412 tmanney@stackpolebooks.com www.stackpolebooks.com

Stalker, Inc., P.O. Box 21, Fishermans Wharf Rd., Malakoff, TX 75148 / 903-489-1010

Stalwart Corporation, P.O. Box 46, Evanston, WY 82931 / 307-789-7687; FAX: 307-789-7688

Stan Baker Sports, Stan Baker, 10000 Lake City Way, Seattle, WA 98125 / 206-522-4575

Stan De Treville & Co., 4129 Normal St., San Diego, CA 92103 / 619-298-3393

Stanley Bullets, 2085 Heatheridge Ln., Reno, NV 89509

Star Ammunition, Inc., 5520 Rock Hampton Ct., Indianapolis, IN 46268 / 800-221-5927; FAX: 317-872-5847

Star Custom Bullets, P.O. Box 608, 468 Main St., Ferndale, CA 95536 / 707-786-9140; FAX: 707-786-9117 wmebridge@humboldt.com

Star Machine Works, P.O. Box 1872, Pioneer, CA 95666 / 209-295-5000

Starke Bullet Company, P.O. Box 400, 605 6th St. NW, Cooperstown, ND 58425 / 888-797-3431

Starkey Labs, 6700 Washington Ave. S., Eden Prairie, MN 55344

Starkey's Gun Shop, 9430 McCombs, El Paso, TX 79924 / 915-751-3030

Starlight Training Center, Inc., Rt. 1, P.O. Box 88, Bronaugh, MO 64728 / 417-843-3555

Starline, Inc., 1300 W. Henry St., Sedalia, MO 65301 / 660-827-6640; FAX: 660-827-6650 info@starlinebrass.com http://www.starlinebrass.com

Starr Trading Co., Jedediah, P.O. Box 2007, Farmington Hills, MI 48333 / 877-857-8277; FAX: 248-683-3282 mtman1849@aol.com www.jedediah-starr.com

Starrett Co., L. S., 121 Crescent St., Athol, MA 01331 / 978-249-3551; FAX: 978-249-8495

Steelman's Gun Shop, 10465 Beers Rd., Swartz Creek, MI 48473 / 810-735-4884

Steffens, Ron, 18396 Mariposa Creek Rd., Willits, CA 95490 / 707-485-0873

Stegall, James B., 26 Forest Rd., Wallkill, NY 12589

Steve Henigson & Associates, P.O. Box 2726, Culver City, CA 90231 / 310-305-8288; FAX: 310-305-1905

Steve Kamyk Engraver, 9 Grandview Dr., Westfield, MA 01085-1810 / 413-568-0457 stevek201@comcast.net

Steven Dodd Hughes, P.O. Box 545, Livingston, MT 59047 / 406-222-9377; FAX: 406-222-9377

Steves House of Guns, Rt. 1, Minnesota City, MN 55959 / 507-689-2573

Stewart's Gunsmithing, P.O. Box 5854, Pietersburg North 0750, Transvaal, SOUTH AFRICA / 01521-89401

Steyr Arms, P.O. Box 2609, Cumming, GA 30028 / 770-888-4201 www.steyrarms.com

Steyr Mannlicher GmbH & Co. KG, Mannlicherstrasse 1, 4400 Steyr, Steyr, AUSTRIA / 0043-7252-896-0; FAX: 0043-7252-78620 office@steyr-mannlicher.com www.steyr-mannlicher.com

STI International, 114 Halmar Cove, Georgetown, TX 78628 / 800-959-8201; FAX: 512-819-0465 www.stiguns.com

Stiles Custom Guns, 76 Cherry Run Rd., Box 1605, Homer City, PA 15748 / 712-479-9945 glstiles@yourinter.net www.yourinter.net/glstiles

Stillwell, Robert, 421 Judith Ann Dr., Schertz, TX 78154

Stoeger Industries, 17603 Indian Head Hwy., Suite 200, Accokeek, MD 20607-2501 / 301-283-6300; FAX: 301-283-6986 www.stoegerindustries.com

Stoeger Publishing Co. (See Stoeger Industries)

Stone Enterprises Ltd., 426 Harveys Neck Rd., P.O. Box 335, Wicomico Church, VA 22579 / 804-580-5114; FAX: 804-580-8421

Stone Mountain Arms, 5988 Peachtree Corners E., Norcross, GA 30071 / 800-251-9412

Stoney Point Products, Inc., 9200 Cody St., Overland Park, KS 66214 / 800-845-2444; FAX: 507-354-7236 stoney@newulmtel.net www.stoneypoint.com

Storm, Gary, P.O. Box 5211, Richardson, TX 75083 / 214-340-0862

Stott's Creek Armory, Inc., 2526 S. 475W, Morgantown, IN 46160 / 317-878-5489 stottscrk@aol.com www.Sccalendar.aol.com

Stratco, Inc., P.O. Box 2270, Kalispell, MT 59901 / 406-755-1221; FAX: 406-755-1226

Strayer, Sandy. See: STRAYER-VOIGT, INC.

Strayer-Voigt, Inc., Sandy Strayer, 3435 Ray Orr Blvd., Grand Prairie, TX 75050 / 972-513-0575

Strong Holster Co., 39 Grove St., Gloucester, MA 01930 / 508-281-3300; FAX: 508-281-6321

Strutz Rifle Barrels, Inc., W. C., P.O. Box 611, Eagle River, WI 54521 / 715-479-4766

Stuart, V. Pat, Rt. 1, Box 447-S, Greenville, VA 24440 / 804-556-3845

Sturgeon Valley Sporters, Ken Ide, P.O. Box 283, Vanderbilt, MI 49795 / 989-983-4338 k.ide@mail.com

Sturm Ruger & Co. Inc., 200 Ruger Rd., Prescott, AZ 86301 / 928-541-8820; FAX: 520-541-8850 www.ruger.com

Sullivan, David S. (See Westwind Rifles, Inc.)

"Su-Press-On", Inc., P.O. Box 09161, Detroit, MI 48209 / 313-842-4222

Sun Welding Safe Co., 290 Easy St. No. 3, Simi Valley, CA 93065 / 805-584-6678; or 800-729-SAFE; (7233) FAX: 805-584-6169 sunwelding.com

Sunny Hill Enterprises, Inc., W1790 Cty. HHH, Malone, WI 53049 / 920-418-3906; FAX: 920-795-4822 triggerguard@sunny-hill.com www.sunny-hill.com

Super 6 LLC, Gary Knopp, 3806 W. Lisbon Ave., Milwaukee, WI 53208 / 414-344-3343; FAX: 414-344-0304

Surecase Co., The, 233 Wilshire Blvd., Ste. 900, Santa Monica, CA 90401 / 800-92ARMLOC

Sure-Shot Game Calls, Inc., P.O. Box 816, 6835 Capitol, Groves, TX 77619 / 409-962-1636; FAX: 409-962-5465

Svon Corp., 2107 W. Blue Heron Blvd., Riviera Beach, FL 33404 / 508-881-8852

Swampfire Shop, The (See Peterson Gun Shop, Inc., A.W.)

Swann, D. J., 5 Orsova Close, Eltham North Vic., 3095 AUSTRALIA / 03-431-0323

Swanndri New Zealand, 152 Elm Ave., Burlingame, CA 94010 / 415-347-6158

Swanson, Mark, 975 Heap Avenue, Prescott, AZ 86301 / 928-778-4423

Swarovski Optik North America Ltd., 2 Slater Rd., Cranston, RI 02920 / 401-946-2220 or 800-426-3089; FAX: 401-946-2587

Sweet Home, Inc., P.O. Box 900, Orrville, OH 44667-0900

Swenson's 45 Shop, A. D., 3839 Ladera Vista Rd., Fallbrook, CA 92028-9431

Swift Bullet Co., P.O. Box 27, 201 Main St., Quinter, KS 67752 / 913-754-3959; FAX: 913-754-2359

Swift Instruments, 2055 Gateway Place, Ste. 500, San Jose, CA 95110 / 800-523-4544; FAX: 408-292-7967 www.swiftoptics.com

Swift River Gunworks, 450 State St., Belchertown, MA 01007 / 413-323-4052

Szweda, Robert (See RMS Custom Gunsmithing)

T

T&S Industries, Inc., 1027 Skyview Dr., W. Carrollton, OH 45449 / 513-859-8414; FAX: 937-859-8404 keith.tomlinson@tandsshellcatcher.com www.tandsshellcatcher.com

T.F.C. S.p.A., Via G. Marconi 118, B, Villa Carcina 25069, ITALY / 030-881271; FAX: 030-881826

T.G. Faust, Inc., 544 Minor St., Reading, PA 19602 / 610-375-8549; FAX: 610-375-4488

T.K. Lee Co., 1282 Branchwater Ln., Birmingham, AL 35216 / 205-913-5222 odonmich@aol.com www.scopedot.com

T.W. Mench Gunsmith, Inc., 5703 S. 77th St., Ralston, NE 68127 guntools@cox.net http://llwww.members.cox.net/guntools

Tabler Marketing, 2554 Lincoln Blvd., Suite 555, Marina Del Rey, CA 90291 / 818-386-0373; FAX: 818-386-0373

Taconic Firearms Ltd., Perry Lane, P.O. Box 553, Cambridge, NY 12816 / 518-677-2704; FAX: 518-677-5974

Tactical Defense Institute, 2174 Bethany Ridges, West Union, OH 45693 / 937-544-7228; FAX: 937-544-2887 tdiohio@dragonbbs.com www.tdiohio.com

Talley, Dave, P.O. Box 369, Santee, SC 29142 / 803-854-5700 or 307-436-9315; FAX: 803-854-9315 talley@diretway www.talleyrings.com

Talon Industries Inc. (See Cobra Enterprises, Inc.)

Tanfoglio Fratelli S.r.l., via Valtrompia 39, 41, Brescia, ITALY / 011-39-030-8910361; FAX: 011-39-030-8910183 info@tanfoglio.it www.tanfoglio.it

Tanglefree Industries, 1261 Heavenly Dr., Martinez, CA 94553 / 800-982-4868; FAX: 510-825-3874

Tank's Rifle Shop, P.O. Box 474, Fremont, NE 68026-0474 / 402-727-1317 jtank@tanksrifleshop.com www.tanksrifleshop.com

Tanner (See U.S. Importer-Mandall Shooting Supplies, Inc.)

Taracorp Industries, Inc., 1200 Sixteenth St., Granite City, IL 62040 / 618-451-4400

Target Shooting, Inc., P.O. Box 773, Watertown, SD 57201 / 605-882-6955; FAX: 605-882-8840

Tar-Hunt Custom Rifles, Inc., 101 Dogtown Rd., Bloomsburg, PA 17815 / 570-784-6368; FAX: 570-389-9150 www.tar-hunt.com

Tarnhelm Supply Co., Inc., 431 High St., Boscawen, NH 03303 / 603-796-2551; FAX: 603-796-2918 info@tarnhelm.com www.tarnhelm.com

Tasco Sales, Inc., 2889 Commerce Pkwy., Miramar, FL 33025

Taurus Firearms, Inc., 16175 NW 49th Ave., Miami, FL 33014 / 305-624-1115; FAX: 305-623-7506

Taurus International Firearms (See U.S. Importer Taurus Firearms, Inc.)

Taurus S.A. Forjas, Avenida Do Forte 511, Porto Alegre, RS BRAZIL 91360 / 55-51-347-4050; FAX: 55-51-347-3065

Taylor & Robbins, P.O. Box 164, Rixford, PA 16745 / 814-966-3233

Taylor's & Co., Inc., 304 Lenoir Dr., Winchester, VA 22603 / 540-722-2017; FAX: 540-722-2018 info@taylorsfirearms.com www.taylorsfirearms.com

TCCI, P.O. Box 302, Phoenix, AZ 85001 / 602-237-3823; FAX: 602-237-3858

TCSR, 3998 Hoffman Rd., White Bear Lake, MN 55110-4626 / 800-328-5323; FAX: 612-429-0526

Techno Arms (See U.S. Importer- Auto-Ordnance Corp.)

Tecnolegno S.p.A., Via A. Locatelli, 6 10, 24019 Zogno, ITALY / 0345-55111; FAX: 0345-55155

Ted Blocker Holsters, 9438 SW Tigard St., Tigard, OR 97223 / 800-650-9742; FAX: 503-670-9692 www.tedblockerholsters.com

Tele-Optics, 630 E. Rockland Rd., P.O. Box 6313, Libertyville, IL 60048 / 847-362-7757; FAX: 847-362-7757

Tennessee Valley Mfg., 14 County Road 521, Corinth, MS 38834 / 601-286-5014 tvm@avsia.com www.avsia.com/tvm

Ten-Ring Precision, Inc., Alex B. Hamilton, 1449 Blue Crest Lane, San Antonio, TX 78232 / 210-494-3063; FAX: 210-494-3066

TEN-X Products Group, 1905 N. Main St., Suite 133, Cleburne, TX 76031-1305 / 972-243-4016 or 800-433-2225; FAX: 972-243-4112

Tepeco, P.O. Box 342, Friendswood, TX 77546 / 713-482-2702

Terry K. Kopp Professional Gunsmithing, 1201 South 13 Hwy., Lexington, MO 64067 / 816-529-1337

Terry Theis-Engraver, Terry Theis, 21452 FM 2093, Harper, TX 78631 / 830-864-4438

Testing Systems, Inc., 220 Pegasus Ave., Northvale, NJ 07647

Tetra Gun Care, 8 Vreeland Rd., Florham Park, NJ 07932 / 973-443-0004; FAX: 973-443-0263

Tex Shoemaker & Sons, Inc., 714 W. Cienega Ave., San Dimas, CA 91773 / 909-592-2071; FAX: 909-592-2378 texshoemaker@texshoemaker.com www.texshoemaker.com

Texas Armory (See Bond Arms, Inc.)

Texas Platers Supply Co., 2453 W. Five Mile Parkway, Dallas, TX 75233 / 214-330-7168

Thad Rybka Custom Leather Equipment, 2050 Canoe Creek Rd., Springvale, AL 35146-6709

Thad Scott Fine Guns, Inc., P.O. Box 412, Indianola, MS 38751 / 601-887-5929

Theis, Terry. See: TERRY THEIS-ENGRAVER

Thiewes, George W., 14329 W. Parada Dr., Sun City West, AZ 85375

Things Unlimited, 235 N. Kimbau, Casper, WY 82601 / 307-234-5277

Thirion Gun Engraving, Denise, P.O. Box 408, Graton, CA 95444 / 707-829-1876

Thomas, Charles C., 2600 S. First St., Springfield, IL 62704 / 217-789-8980; FAX: 217-789-9130 books@ccthomas.com ccthomas.com

Thompson Bullet Lube Co., P.O. Box 409, Wills Point, TX 75169 / 866-476-1500; FAX: 866-476-1500 thompsonbulletlube.com www.thompsonbulletlube.com

Thompson Precision, 110 Mary St., P.O. Box 251, Warren, IL 61087 / 815-745-3625

Thompson, Randall. See: HIGHLINE MACHINE CO.

Thompson Target Technology, 4804 Sherman Church Ave. S.W., Canton, OH 44710 / 330-484-6480; FAX: 330-491-1087 www.thompsontarget.com

Thompson Tool Mount, 1550 Solomon Rd., Santa Maria, CA 93455 / 805-934-1281 ttm@pronet.net www.thompsontoolmount.com

Thompson/Center Arms, P.O. Box 5002, Rochester, NH 03866 / 603-332-2394; FAX: 603-332-5133 tech@tcarms.com www.tcarms.com

Thunder Ranch, 96747 Hwy. 140 East, Lakeview, OR 97630 / 541-947-4104; FAX: 541-947-4105 troregon@centurytel.net www.thunderranchinc.com

Tiger-Hunt Longrifle Gunstocks, Box 379, Beaverdale, PA 15921 / 814-472-5161 tigerhunt4@aol.com www.gunstockwood.com

Tikka (See U.S. Importer-Stoeger Industries)

Time Precision, 4 Nicholas Sq., New Milford, CT 06776-3506 / 860-350-8343; FAX: 860-350-6343 timeprecision@aol.com www.benchrest.com/timeprecision

Tinks & Ben Lee Hunting Products (See Wellington Outdoors)

Tink's Safariland Hunting Corp., P.O. Box 244, 1140 Monticello Rd., Madison, GA 30650 / 706-342-4915; FAX: 706-342-7568

Tioga Engineering Co., Inc., P.O. Box 913, 13 Cone St., Wellsboro, PA 16901 / 570-724-3533; FAX: 570-724-3895 tiogaeng@epix.net

Tippman Sports, LLC, 2955 Adams Center Rd., Fort Wayne, IN 46803 / 260-749-6022; FAX: 260-441-8504 www.tippmann.com

Tirelli, Snc Di Tirelli Primo E.C., Via Matteotti No. 359, Gardone V.T. Brescia, ITALY / 0039-030-8912819; FAX: 0039-030-832240 tirelli@tirelli.it www.tirelli.it

TM Stockworks, 6355 Maplecrest Rd., Fort Wayne, IN 46835 / 219-485-5389

Tom Forrest, Inc., P.O. Box 326, Lakeside, CA 92040 / 619-561-5800; FAX: 888-GUN-CLIP info@gunmag.com www.gunmags.com

Tombstone Smoken' Deals, 4038 E. Taro Ln., Phoenix, AZ 85050

Tom's Gun Repair, Thomas G. Ivanoff, 76-6 Rt. Southfork Rd., Cody, WY 82414 / 307-587-6949

Tom's Gunshop, 3601 Central Ave., Hot Springs, AR 71913 / 501-624-3856

Tonoloway Tack Drives, HCR 81, Box 100, Needmore, PA 17238

Torel, Inc./Tandy Brands Outdoors/AA & E, 208 Industrial Loop, Yoakum, TX 77995 / 361-293-6366; FAX: 361-293-9127

TOZ (See U.S. Importer-Nygord Precision Products, Inc.)

Track of the Wolf, Inc., 18308 Joplin St. NW, Elk River, MN 55330-1773 / 763-633-2500; FAX: 763-633-2550 www.trackofthewolf.com

Traditions Performance Firearms, P.O. Box 776, 1375 Boston Post Rd., Old Saybrook, CT 06475 / 860-388-4656; FAX: 860-388-4657 info@traditionsfirearms.com www.traditionsfirearms.com

Trafalgar Square, P.O. Box 257, N. Pomfret, VT 05053 / 802-457-1911

Trail Visions, 5800 N. Ames Terrace, Glendale, WI 53209 / 414-228-1328

Treadlok Gun Safe, Inc., 1764 Granby St. NE, Roanoke, VA 24012 / 800-729-8732 or 703-982-6881; FAX: 703-982-1059

Treebone Carving, P.O. Box 551, Cimarron, NJ 87714 / 505-376-2145 treebonecarving.com

Treemaster, P.O. Box 247, Guntersville, AL 35976 / 205-878-3597

Trevallion Gunstocks, 9 Old Mountain Rd., Cape Neddick, ME 03902 / 207-361-1130

Trigger Lock Division / Central Specialties Ltd., 220-D Exchange Dr., Crystal Lake, IL 60014 / 847-639-3900; FAX: 847-639-3972

Trijicon, Inc., 49385 Shafer Ave., P.O. Box 930059, Wixom, MI 48393-0059 / 248-960-7700 or 800-338-0563

Trilby Sport Shop, 1623 Hagley Rd., Toledo, OH 43612-2024 / 419-472-6222

Trilux, Inc., P.O. Box 24608, Winston-Salem, NC 27114 / 910-659-9438; FAX: 910-768-7720

Trinidad St. Jr. Col. Gunsmith Dept., 600 Prospect St., Trinidad, CO 81082 / 719-846-5631; FAX: 719-846-5667

Tripes, George. See: EURO-IMPORTS

Triple-K Mfg. Co., Inc., 2222 Commercial St., San Diego, CA 92113 / 619-232-2066; FAX: 619-232-7675 sales@triplek.com www.triplek.com

Tristar Sporting Arms, Ltd., 1816 Linn St. #16, N. Kansas City, MO 64116-3627 / 816-421-1400; FAX: 816-421-4182 tristarsporting@sbcglobal.net www.tristarsportingarms

Trius Traps, Inc., P.O. Box 25, 221 S. Miami Ave., Cleves, OH 45002 / 513-941-5682; FAX: 513-941-7970 triustraps@fuse.net www.triustraps.com

Trooper Walsh, 2393 N. Edgewood St., Arlington, VA 22207

Trotman, Ken, P. O. Box 505, Huntingdon, PE 29 2XW ENGLAND / 01480 454292; FAX: 01480 384651 enquiries@kentrotman.com www.kentrotman.com

Tru-Balance Knife Co., P.O. Box 140555, Grand Rapids, MI 49514 / 616-647-1215

True Flight Bullet Co., 5581 Roosevelt St., Whitehall, PA 18052 / 610-262-7630; FAX: 610-262-7806

Truglo, Inc., P.O. Box 1612, McKinna, TX 75070 / 972-774-0300; FAX: 972-774-0323 www.truglosights.com

Trulock Tool, P.O. Box 530, Whigham, GA 31797 / 229-762-4678; FAX: 229-762-4050 trulockchokes@hotmail.com trulockchokes.com

Tru-Nord Compass, 1504 Erick Lane, Brainerd, MN 56401 / 218-829-2870; FAX: 218-829-2870 www.trunord.com

Tru-Square Metal Products, Inc., 640 First St. SW, P.O. Box 585, Auburn, WA 98071 / 253-833-2310 or 800-225-1017; FAX: 253-833-2349 t-tumbler@qwest.net

Tucker, James C., P.O. Box 366, Medford, OR 97501 / 541-664-9160 jctstocker@yahoo.com

Tucson Mold, Inc., 930 S. Plumer Ave., Tucson, AZ 85719 / 520-792-1075; FAX: 520-792-1075

Turk's Head Productions, Mustafa Bilal, 13545 Erickson Pl. NE, Seattle, WA 98125-3794 / 206-782-4164; FAX: 206-783-5677 info@turkshead.com www.turkshead.com

Turnbull Restoration, Doug, 6680 Rts. 5 & 20, P.O. Box 471, Bloomfield, NY 14469 / 585-657-6338; FAX: 585-657-6338 turnbullrest@mindspring.com www.turnbullrestoration.com

Tuttle, Dale, 4046 Russell Rd., Muskegon, MI 49445 / 616-766-2250

U

U.S. Importer-Wm. Larkin Moore, 8430 E. Raintree Ste. B-7, Scottsdale, AZ 85260

U.S. Optics, A Division of Zeitz Optics U.S.A., 5900 Dale St., Buena Park, CA 90621 / 714-994-4901; FAX: 714-994-4904 www.usoptics.com

U.S. Repeating Arms Co., Inc., 275 Winchester Ave., Morgan, UT 84050-9333 / 801-876-3440; FAX: 801-876-3737 www.winchester-guns.com

U.S. Tactical Systems (See Keng's Firearms Specialty, Inc.)

Ugartechea S. A., Ignacio, Chonta 26, Eibar, SPAIN / 43-121257; FAX: 43-121669

Ultra Dot Distribution, P.O. Box 362, 6304 Riverside Dr., Yankeetown, FL 34498 / 352-447-2255; FAX: 352-447-2266

Ultralux (See U.S. Importer-Keng's Firearms Specialty, Inc.)

Uncle Bud's, HCR 81, Box 100, Needmore, PA 17238 / 717-294-6000; FAX: 717-294-6005

Uncle Mike's (See Michaels of Oregon, Co.)

Unertl Optical Co., Inc., 103 Grand Avenue, P.O. Box 895, Mars, PA 16046-0895 / 724-625-3810; FAX: 724-625-3819 unertl@nauticom.net www.unertloptics.net

UniTec, 1250 Bedford SW, Canton, OH 44710 / 216-452-4017

United Binocular Co., 9043 S. Western Ave., Chicago, IL 60620

United Cutlery Corp., 1425 United Blvd., Sevierville, TN 37876 / 865-428-2532 or 800-548-0835; FAX: 865-428-2267 www.unitedcutlery.com

United States Products Co., 518 Melwood Ave., Pittsburgh, PA 15213-1136 / 412-621-2130; FAX: 412-621-8740 sales@us-products.com www.usporepaste.com

Universal Sports, P.O. Box 532, Vincennes, IN 47591 / 812-882-8680; FAX: 812-882-8680

Upper Missouri Trading Co., P.O. Box 100, 304 Harold St., Crofton, NE 68730-0100 / 402-388-4844 www.uppermotradingco.com

USAC, 4500-15th St. East, Tacoma, WA 98424 / 206-922-7589

Uselton/Arms, Inc., 842 Conference Dr., Goodlettsville, TN 37072 / 615-851-4919

Utica Cutlery Co., 820 Noyes St., Utica, NY 13503 / 315-733-4663; FAX: 315-733-6602

V

V. H. Blackinton & Co., Inc., 221 John L. Dietsch, Attleboro Falls, MA 02763-0300 / 508-699-4436; FAX: 508-695-5349

Valdada Enterprises, P.O. Box 773122, 31733 County Road 35, Steamboat Springs, CO 80477 / 970-879-2983; FAX: 970-879-0851 www.valdada.com

Valtro USA, Inc., 1281 Andersen Dr., San Rafael, CA 94901 / 415-256-2575; FAX: 415-256-2576

VAM Distribution Co. LLC, 1141-B Mechanicsburg Rd., Wooster, OH 44691 www.rex10.com

Van Gorden & Son Inc., C. S., 1815 Main St., Bloomer, WI 54724 / 715-568-2612

Van Horn, Gil, P.O. Box 207, Llano, CA 93544

Van Patten, J. W., P.O. Box 145, Foster Hill, Milford, PA 18337 / 717-296-7069

Vann Custom Bullets, 2766 N. Willowside Way, Meridian, ID 83642

Varmint Masters, LLC, Rick Vecqueray, P.O. Box 6724, Bend, OR 97708 / 541-318-7306; FAX: 541-318-7306 varmintmasters@bendcable.com www.varmintmasters.net

Vecqueray, Rick. See: VARMINT MASTERS, LLC

Vector Arms, Inc., 270 W. 500 N., North Salt Lake, UT 84054 / 801-295-1917; FAX: 801-295-9316 vectorarms@bbscmail.com www.vectorarms.com

Vega Tool Co., c/o T. R. Ross, 4865 Tanglewood Ct., Boulder, CO 80301 / 303-530-0174 clanlaird@aol.com www.vegatool.com

Venco Industries, Inc. (See Shooter's Choice Gun Care)

Venus Industries, P.O. Box 246, Sialkot-1, PAKISTAN FAX: 92 432 85579

Verney-Carron, 54 Boulevard Thiers-B.P. 72, 42002 St. Etienne Cedex 1, St. Etienne Cedex 1, FRANCE / 33-477791500; FAX: 33-477790702 email@verney-carron.com www.verney-carron.com

Vest, John, 1923 NE 7th St., Redmond, OR 97756 / 541-923-8898

VibraShine, Inc., P.O. Box 577, Taylorsville, MS 39168 / 601-785-9854; FAX: 601-785-9874 rdbeke@vibrashine.com www.vibrashine.com

Vibra-Tek Co., 1844 Arroya Rd., Colorado Springs, CO 80906 / 719-634-8611; FAX: 719-634-6886

Vic's Gun Refinishing, 6 Pineview Dr., Dover, NH 03820-6422 / 603-742-0013

Victory Ammunition, P.O. Box 1022, Milford, PA 18337 / 717-296-5768; FAX: 717-296-9298

Victory USA, P.O. Box 1021, Pine Bush, NY 12566 / 914-744-2060; FAX: 914-744-5181

Vihtavuori Oy, FIN-41330 Vihtavuori, FINLAND, / 358-41-3779211; FAX: 358-41-3771643

Vihtavuori Oy/Kaltron-Pettibone, 1241 Ellis St., Bensenville, IL 60106 / 708-350-1116; FAX: 708-350-1606

Viking Video Productions, P.O. Box 251, Roseburg, OR 97470

Village Restorations & Consulting, Inc., P.O. Box 569, Claysburg, PA 16625 / 814-239-8200; FAX: 814-239-2165 www.villagerestoration@yahoo.com

Vincent's Shop, 210 Antoinette, Fairbanks, AK 99701

Viper Bullet and Brass Works, 11 Brock St., Box 582, Norwich, ON N0J 1P0 CANADA

Viramontez Engraving, Ray Viramontez, 601 Springfield Dr., Albany, GA 31721 / 229-432-9683 sgtvira@aol.com

Viramontez, Ray. See: VIRAMONTEZ ENGRAVING

Virgin Valley Custom Guns, 450 E 800 N. #20, Hurricane, UT 84737 / 435-635-8941; FAX: 435-635-8943 vvcguns@infowest.com www.virginvalleyguns.com

Visible Impact Targets, Rts. 5 & 20, E. Bloomfield, NY 14443 / 716-657-6161; FAX: 716-657-5405

Vitt/Boos, 1195 Buck Hill Rd., Townshend, VT 05353 / 802-365-9232

Voere-KGH GmbH, Untere Sparchen 56, A-6330 Kufstein, Tirol, AUSTRIA / 0043-5372-62547; FAX: 0043-5372-65752 voere@aon.com www.voere.com

Volquartsen Custom Ltd., 24276 240th Street, P.O. Box 397, Carroll, IA 51401 / 712-792-4238; FAX: 712-792-2542 info@volquartsen.com www.volquartsen.com

Vorhes, David, 3042 Beecham St., Napa, CA 94558 / 707-226-9116; FAX: 707-253-7334

VSP Publishers (See Heritage/VSP Gun Books), P.O. Box 887, McCall, ID 83638 / 208-634-4104; FAX: 208-634-3101 heritage@gunbooks.com www.gunbooks.com

VTI Gun Parts, P.O. Box 509, Lakeville, CT 06039 / 860-435-8068; FAX: 860-435-8146 mail@vtigunparts.com www.vtigunparts.com

Vulpes Ventures, Inc., Fox Cartridge Division, P.O. Box 1363, Bolingbrook, IL 60440-7363 / 630-759-1229

W

W. Square Enterprises, 9826 Sagedale Dr., Houston, TX 77089 / 281-484-0935; FAX: 281-464-9940 lfdw@pdq.net www.loadammo.com

W. Waller & Son, Inc., 52 Coventry Dr., Sunapee, NH 03782 / 603-763-3320 or 800-874-2247 FAX: 603-763-3225; waller@wallerandson.com www.wallerandson.com

W.B. Niemi Engineering, Box 126 Center Road, Greensboro, VT 05841 / 802-533-7180 or 802-533-7141

W.C. Wolff Co., P.O. Box 458, Newtown Square, PA 19073 / 610-359-9600 or 800-545-0077 mail@gunsprings.com www.gunsprings.com

W.E. Birdsong & Assoc., 1435 Monterey Rd., Florence, MS 39073-9748 / 601-366-8270

W.E. Brownell Checkering Tools, 9390 Twin Mountain Cir., San Diego, CA 92126 / 858-695-2479; FAX: 858-695-2479

W.J. Riebe Co., 3434 Tucker Rd., Boise, ID 83703

W.R. Case & Sons Cutlery Co., Owens Way, Bradford, PA 16701 / 814-368-4123 or 800-523-6350; FAX: 814-368-1736 jsullivan@wrcase.com www.wrcase.com

Wagoner, Vernon G., 2325 E. Encanto St., Mesa, AZ 85213-5917 / 480-835-1307

Waldron, Herman, Box 475, 80 N. 17th St., Pomeroy, WA 99347 / 509-843-1404

Walker Arms Co., Inc., 499 County Rd. 820, Selma, AL 36701 / 334-872-6231; FAX: 334-872-6262

Wallace, Terry, 385 San Marino, Vallejo, CA 94589 / 707-642-7041

Walls Industries, Inc., P.O. Box 98, 1905 N. Main, Cleburne, TX 76033 / 817-645-4366; FAX: 817-645-7946 www.wallsoutdoors.com

Walters Industries, 6226 Park Lane, Dallas, TX 75225 / 214-691-6973

Walters, John. See: WALTERS WADS

Walters Wads, John Walters, 500 N. Avery Dr., Moore, OK 73160 / 405-799-0376; FAX: 405-799-7727 www.tinwadman@cs.com

Walther America, P.O. Box 22, Springfield, MA 01102 / 800-331-0852 www.waltheramerica.com

Walther GmbH, Carl, B.P. 4325, D-89033 Ulm, GERMANY

Walt's Custom Leather, Walt Whinnery, 1947 Meadow Creek Dr., Louisville, KY 40218 / 502-458-4361

WAMCO-New Mexico, P.O. Box 205, Peralta, NM 87042-0205 / 505-869-0826

Ward & Van Valkenburg, 114 32nd Ave. N., Fargo, ND 58102 / 701-232-2351

Ward Machine, 5620 Lexington Rd., Corpus Christi, TX 78412 / 512-992-1221

Wardell Precision, P.O. Box 391, Clyde, TX 79510-0391 / 325-893-3763 fwardell@valornet.com

Warenski Engraving, Julie Warenski, 590 E. 500 N., Richfield, UT 84701 / 435-896-5319; FAX: 435-896-8333 julie@warenskiknives.com

Warenski, Julie. See: WARENSKI ENGRAVING

Warne Manufacturing Co., 9560 SW Herman Rd., Tualatin, OR 97062 / 503-657-5590 or 800-683-5590; FAX: 503-657-5695 info@warnescopemounts.com www.warnescopemounts.com

Washita Mountain Whetstone Co., P.O. Box 20378, Hot Springs, AR 71903 / 501-525-3914 www.@hsnp.com

Wasmundt, Jim. See: J.W. WASMUNDT-GUNSMITH

Watson Bros., 39 Redcross Way, London Bridge SE1 1H6, London, ENGLAND FAX: 44-171-403-336

Watson Bullets, 231 Allies Pass, Frostproof, FL 33843 / 863-635-7948 cbestbullet@aol.com

Wayne Specialty Services, 260 Waterford Drive, Florissant, MO 63033 / 413-831-7083

WD-40 Co., 1061 Cudahy Pl., San Diego, CA 92110 / 619-275-1400; FAX: 619-275-5823

Weatherby, Inc., 3100 El Camino Real, Atascadero, CA 93422 / 805-466-1767; FAX: 805-466-2527 www.weatherby.com

Weaver Products ATK, P.O. Box 39, Onalaska, WI 54650 / 800-648-9624 or 608-781-5800; FAX: 608-781-0368

Weaver Scope Repair Service, 1121 Larry Mahan Dr., Suite B, El Paso, TX 79925 / 915-593-1005 frank@weaver-scope-repair.com www.weaver-scope-repair.com

Webb, Bill, 6504 North Bellefontaine, Kansas City, MO 64119 / 816-453-7431

Weber & Markin Custom Gunsmiths, 4-1691 Powick Rd., Kelowna, BC V1X 4L1 CANADA / 250-762-7575; FAX: 250-861-3655 www.weberandmarkinguns.com

Webley and Scott Ltd., Frankley Industrial Park, Tay Rd., Birmingham, B45 0PA ENGLAND / 011-021-453-1864; FAX: 0121-457-7846 guns@webley.co.uk www.webley.co.uk

Webster Scale Mfg. Co., P.O. Box 188, Sebring, FL 33870 / 813-385-6362

Weems, Cecil, 510 W. Hubbard St., Mineral Wells, TX 76067-4847 / 817-325-1462

Weigand Combat Handguns, Inc., 1057 South Main Rd., Mountain Top, PA 18707 / 570-868-8358; FAX: 570-868-5218 sales@jackweigand.com www.jackweigand.com

Weihrauch KG, Hermann, Industriestrasse 11, 8744 Mellrichstadt, Mellrichstadt, GERMANY

Welch, Sam. See: SAM WELCH GUN ENGRAVING

Wellington Outdoors, P.O. Box 244, 1140 Monticello Rd., Madison, GA 30650 / 706-342-4915; FAX: 706-342-7568

Wells, Rachel, 110 N. Summit St., Prescott, AZ 86301 / 928-445-3655 wellssportstore@cableone.net

Wells Creek Knife & Gun Works, 32956 State Hwy. 38, Scottsburg, OR 97473 / 541-587-4202; FAX: 541-587-4223

Welsh, Bud. See: HIGH PRECISION

Wenger North America/Precise Int'l., 15 Corporate Dr., Orangeburg, NY 10962 / 800-431-2996; FAX: 914-425-4700

Wenig Custom Gunstocks, 103 N. Market St., P.O. Box 249, Lincoln, MO 65338 / 660-547-3334; FAX: 660-547-2881 gustock@wenig.com www.wenig.com

Werth, T. W., 1203 Woodlawn Rd., Lincoln, IL 62656 / 217-732-1300; FAX: 217-735-5106

Wescombe, Bill (See North Star West)

Wessinger Custom Guns & Engraving, 268 Limestone Rd., Chapin, SC 29036 / 803-345-5677

West, Jack L., 1220 W. Fifth, P.O. Box 427, Arlington, OR 97812

Western Cutlery (See Camillus Cutlery Co.)

MANUFACTURER'S DIRECTORY

Western Mfg. Co., 550 Valencia School Rd., Aptos, CA 95003 / 831-688-5884 lotsabears@eathlink.net

Western Missouri Shooters Alliance, P.O. Box 11144, Kansas City, MO 64119 / 816-597-3950; FAX: 816-229-7350

Western Nevada West Coast Bullets, P.O. Box 2270, Dayton, NV 89403-2270 / 702-246-3941; FAX: 702-246-0836

Westley Richards & Co. Ltd., 40 Grange Rd., Birmingham, ENGLAND / 010-214722953; FAX: 010-214141138 sales@westleyrichards.com www.westleyrichards.com

Westley Richards Agency USA (See U.S. Importer

Westwind Rifles, Inc., David S. Sullivan, P.O. Box 261, 640 Briggs St., Erie, CO 80516 / 303-828-3823

Weyer International, 2740 Nebraska Ave., Toledo, OH 43607 / 419-534-2020; FAX: 419-534-2697

Whinnery, Walt (See Walt's Custom Leather)

White Barn Wor, 431 County Road, Broadlands, IL 61816

White Pine Photographic Services, Hwy. 60, General Delivery, Wilno, ON K0J 2N0 CANADA / 613-756-3452

White Rifles, Inc., 234 S. 1250 W., Linden, UT 84042 / 801-932-7950 www.whiterifles.com

White Rock Tool & Die, 6400 N. Brighton Ave., Kansas City, MO 64119 / 816-454-0478

Whitestone Lumber Corp., 148-02 14th Ave., Whitestone, NY 11357 / 718-746-4400; FAX: 718-767-1748 whstco@aol.com

Wichita Arms, Inc., 923 E. Gilbert, Wichita, KS 67211 / 316-265-0661; FAX: 316-265-0760 sales@wichitaarms.com www.wichitaarms.com

Wick, David E., 1504 Michigan Ave., Columbus, IN 47201 / 812-376-6960

Widener's Reloading & Shooting Supply, Inc., P.O. Box 3009 CRS, Johnson City, TN 37602 / 615-282-6786; FAX: 615-282-6651

Wideview Scope Mount Corp., 13535 S. Hwy. 16, Rapid City, SD 57702 / 605-341-3220; FAX: 605-341-9142 wvdon@rapidnet.com www.wideviewscopemount.com

Wiebe, Duane, 1111 157th St. Ct. E., Tacoma, WA 98445 / 530-344-1357; FAX: 530-344-1357 duane@directcom.net

Wiest, Marie. See: GUNCRAFT SPORTS, INC.

Wilcox All-Pro Tools & Supply, 4880 147th St., Montezuma, IA 50171 / 515-623-3138; FAX: 515-623-3104

Wilcox Industries Corp., Robert F. Guarasi, 53 Durham St., Portsmouth, NH 03801 / 603-431-1331; FAX: 603-431-1221

Wild Bill's Originals, P.O. Box 13037, Burton, WA 98013 / 206-463-5738; FAX: 206-465-5925 billcleaver@centurytel.net billcleaver@centurytel.net

Wild West Guns, 7100 Homer Dr., Anchorage, AK 99518 / 800-992-4570 or 907-344-4500; FAX: 907-344-4005 wwguns@ak.net www.wildwestguns.com

Wilderness Sound Products Ltd., 4015 Main St. A, Springfield, OR 97478

Wildey F. A., Inc., 45 Angevin Rd., Warren, CT 06754-1818 / 860-355-9000; FAX: 860-354-7759 wildeyfa@optonline.net www.wildeyguns.com

Wildlife Research Center, Inc., 1050 McKinley St., Anoka, MN 55303 / 763-427-3350 or 800-USE-LURE; (873-5873) FAX: 763-427-8354 www.wildlife.com

Will-Burt Co., 169 S. Main, Orrville, OH 44667

William E. Phillips Firearms, 38 Avondale Rd., Wigston, Leicester, ENGLAND / 0116 2886334; FAX: 0116 2810644 william.phillips2@tesco.net

William Powell Agency, 22 Circle Dr., Bellmore, NY 11710 / 516-679-1158

Williams Gun Sight Co., 7389 Lapeer Rd., Box 329, Davison, MI 48423 / 810-653-2131 or 800-530-9028; FAX: 810-658-2140 williamsgunsight.com

Williams Mfg. of Oregon, 110 East B St., Drain, OR 97435 / 503-836-7461; FAX: 503-836-7245

Williams Shootin' Iron Service, The Lynx-Line, Rt. 2 Box 223A, Mountain Grove, MO 65711 / 417-948-0902; FAX: 417-948-0902

Williamson Precision Gunsmithing, 117 W. Pipeline, Hurst, TX 76053 / 817-285-0064; FAX: 817-280-0044

Willow Bend, P.O. Box 203, Chelmsford, MA 01824 / 978-256-8508; FAX: 978-256-8508

Wilsom Combat, 2234 CR 719, Berryville, AR 72616-4573 / 800-955-4856; FAX: 870-545-3310 info@wilsoncombat.com www.wilsoncombat.com

Wilson Arms Co., The, 63 Leetes Island Rd., Branford, CT 06405 / 203-488-7297; FAX: 203-488-0135

Wilson Case, Inc., P.O. Box 1106, Hastings, NE 68902-1106 / 800-322-5493; FAX: 402-463-5276 sales@wilsoncase.com www.wilsoncase.com

Wilson Combat, 2234 CR 719, Berryville, AR 72616-4573 / 800-955-4856

Winchester Consultants, George Madis, P.O. Box 545, Brownsboro, TX 75756 / 903-852-6480; FAX: 903-852-5486 gmadis@earthlink.com www.georgemadis.com

Winchester Div. Olin Corp., 427 N. Shamrock, E. Alton, IL 62024 / 618-258-3566; FAX: 618-258-3599

Winchester Sutler, Inc., The, 270 Shadow Brook Lane, Winchester, VA 22603 / 540-888-3595; FAX: 540-888-4632

Windish, Jim, 2510 Dawn Dr., Alexandria, VA 22306 / 703-765-1994

Winfield Galleries LLC, 748 Hanley Industrial Ct., St. Louis, MO 63144 / 314-645-7636; FAX: 314-781-0224 info@winfieldgalleries.com www.winfieldgalleries.com

Wingshooting Adventures, 0-1845 W. Leonard, Grand Rapids, MI 49544 / 616-677-1980; FAX: 616-677-1986

Winter, Robert M., P.O. Box 484, 42975-287th St., Menno, SD 57045 / 605-387-5322

Wise Custom Guns, 1402 Blanco Rd., San Antonio, TX 78212-2716 / 210-828-3388

Wise Guns, Dale, 1402 Blanco Rd., San Antonio, TX 78212 / 210-734-9999

Wiseman and Co., Bill, P.O. Box 3427, Bryan, TX 77805 / 409-690-3456; FAX: 409-690-0156

Wisners, Inc., P.O. Box 58, Adna, WA 98522 / 360-748-4590; FAX: 360-748-6028 parts@wisnersinc.com www.wisnersinc.com

Wolf Performance Ammunition, 2201 E. Winston Rd., Ste. K, Anaheim, CA 92806-5537 / 702-837-8506; FAX: 702-837-9250

Wolfe Publishing Co., 2625 Stearman Rd., Ste. A, Prescott, AZ 86301 / 928-445-7810 or 800-899-7810; FAX: 928-778-5124 wolfepub@riflemag.com www.riflemagazine.com

Wolverine Footwear Group, 9341 Courtland Dr. NE, Rockford, MI 49351 / 616-866-5500; FAX: 616-866-5658

Woodleigh (See Huntington Die Specialties)

Woods Wise Products, P.O. Box 681552, Franklin, TN 37068 / 800-735-8182; FAX: 615-726-2637

Woodstream, P.O. Box 327, Lititz, PA 17543 / 717-626-2125; FAX: 717-626-1912

Woodworker's Supply, 1108 North Glenn Rd., Casper, WY 82601 / 307-237-5354

Woolrich, Inc., Mill St., Woolrich, PA 17701 / 800-995-1299; FAX: 717-769-6234/6259

World of Targets (See Birchwood Casey)

World Trek, Inc., 7170 Turkey Creek Rd., Pueblo, CO 81007-1046 / 719-546-2121; FAX: 719-543-6886

Worthy Products, Inc., RR 1, P.O. Box 213, Martville, NY 13111 / 315-324-5298

Wright's Gunstock Blanks, 8540 SE Kane Rd., Gresham, OR 97080 / 503-666-1705 doyal@wrightsguns.com www.wrightsguns.com

WTA Manufacturing, P.O. Box 164, Kit Carson, CO 80825 / 719-962-3570 or 719-962-3570 wta@rebeltec.net http://www.members.aol.com/ductman249/wta.html

Wyant Bullets, Gen. Del., Swan Lake, MT 59911

Wyoming Custom Bullets, 1626 21st St., Cody, WY 82414

Wyoming Knife Corp., 101 Commerce Dr., Fort Collins, CO 80524 / 303-224-3454

X

XS Sight Systems, 2401 Ludelle St., Fort Worth, TX 76105 / 888-744-4880; FAX: 800-734-7939

X-Spand Target Systems, 26-10th St. SE, Medicine Hat, AB T1A 1P7 CANADA / 403-526-7997; FAX: 403-528-2362

Y

Yankee Gunsmith "Just Glocks", 2901 Deer Flat Dr., Copperas Cove, TX 76522 / 817-547-8433; FAX: 254-547-8887 ed@justglocks.com www.justglocks.com

Yavapai College, 1100 E. Sheldon St., Prescott, AZ 86301 / 520-776-2353; FAX: 520-776-2355

Yavapai Firearms Academy Ltd., P.O. Box 27290, Prescott Valley, AZ 86312 / 928-772-8262; FAX: 928-772-0062 info@yfainc.com www.yfainc.com

Yearout, Lewis E. (See Montana Outfitters)

Yellowstone Wilderness Supply, P.O. Box 129, West Yellowstone, MT 59758 / 406-646-7613

Yesteryear Armory & Supply, P.O. Box 408, Carthage, TN 37030

York M-1 Conversion, 12145 Mill Creek Run, Plantersville, TX 77363 / 936-894-2397; FAX: 936-894-2397 bmf25years@aol.com

Young Country Arms, William, 1409 Kuehner Dr. #13, Simi Valley, CA 93063-4478

Z

Zabala Hermanos S.A., P.O. Box 97, Elbar Lasao, 6, Elgueta, Guipuzcoa, 20600 SPAIN / 34-943-768076; FAX: 34-943-768201 imanol@zabalahermanos.com www.zabalahermanos.com

Zander's Sporting Goods, 7525 Hwy. 154 West, Baldwin, IL 62217-9706 / 800-851-4373; FAX: 618-785-2320

Zanotti Armor, Inc., 123 W. Lone Tree Rd., Cedar Falls, IA 50613 / 319-232-9650 www.zanottiarmor.com

Zeeryp, Russ, 1601 Foard Dr., Lynn Ross Manor, Morristown, TN 37814 / 615-586-2357

Zero Ammunition Co., Inc., 1601 22nd St. SE, P.O. Box 1188, Cullman, AL 35056-1188 / 800-545-9376; FAX: 205-739-4683 zerobulletco@aoz.com www.zerobullets.com

Ziegel Engineering, 1390 E. Bunnett St. "F", Signal Hill, CA 90755 / 562-596-9481; FAX: 562-598-4734 ziegel@aol.com www.ziegeleng.com

Zim's, Inc., 4370 S. 3rd West, Salt Lake City, UT 84107 / 801-268-2505

Z-M Weapons, 203 South St., Bernardston, MA 01337 / 413-648-9501; FAX: 413-648-0219

NUMBERS

100 Straight Products, Inc., P.O. Box 6148, Omaha, NE 68106 / 402-556-1055; FAX: 402-556-1055

3-Ten Corp., P.O. Box 269, Feeding Hills, MA 01030 / 413-789-2086; FAX: 413-789-1549 www.3-ten.com

4-D Custom Die Co., 711 N. Sandusky St., P.O. Box 889, Mt. Vernon, OH 43050-0889 / 740-397-7214; FAX: 740-397-6600 info@ch4d.com ch4d.com